Advanced Microsoft® Excel® 2016

Jan Davidson | Jan Marrelli

PARADIGM
EDUCATION SOLUTIONS

St. Paul

Division President: Linda Hein
Vice President, Content Management: Christine Hurney
Managing Editor: Cheryl Drivdahl
Developmental Editor: Jennifer Gehlhar
Associate Developmental Editor: Katie Werdick
Assistant Developmental Editor: Melora Pappas
Testers and Contributing Writers: Janet Blum; Danielle Davidson;
Pat Jarvis, Truckee Meadows Community College; Jeff Johnson; Traci J.H. Post; Denise Seguin
Director of Production: Timothy W. Larson
Production Editor: Jen Weaverling
Cover and Text Designer and Senior Design and Production Specialist: Valerie King
Copy Editor: Communicáto, Ltd.
Proofreader: Joanna Groate
Indexer: Terry Casey
Vice President, Digital Solutions: Chuck Bratton
Digital Projects Manager: Tom Modl
Digital Solutions Manager: Gerry Yumul
Digital Production Manager: Aaron Esnough
Vice President, Sales and Marketing: Scott Burns
Director of Marketing: Lara Weber McLellan

ISBN 978-0-76387-773-6 (print)
ISBN 978-0-76387-778-1 (digital)

875 Montreal Way
St. Paul, MN 55102
Email: educate@emcp.com
Website: ParadigmEducation.com

Printed in the United States of America

26 25 24 23 22 21 20 19 18 17 1 2 3 4 5 6 7 8 9 10

Brief Contents

Contents

Preface

Advanced Microsoft® Excel® 2016 offers an analytical approach to exploring the full capabilities of Microsoft's popular spreadsheet program in a business context. The comprehensive content is presented in a simple, straightforward format that combines brief topic introductions, bulleted lists highlighting key information, and step-by-step exercises providing opportunities to apply new knowledge as you acquire it. This unique instructional style presents what you most need to learn in concise points that are easy to remember and apply. Related marginal features expand on those points without interrupting the flow of learning.

This course provides in-depth coverage of Excel with a focus on organizing, analyzing, and presenting data to solve real-world business problems. It provides the instruction you need to fully utilize the powerful features available in Excel and succeed in a data-intensive career, such as business or finance. Fully aligned with all the Microsoft Office Specialist Excel 2016 objectives and Microsoft Office Expert Excel 2016 objectives, this course will help you prepare to meet the challenges of today's data-rich job market.

Course Goals

After successfully completing a course using this courseware, you will be able to do the following:

- Prepare a workbook by entering data, applying formatting, checking spelling, and setting basic print options
- Create useful formulas, use common functions effectively, and identify common formula/function errors
- Enhance the readability of a workbook by applying formatting to text and data
- Enhance the appearance of worksheets and communicate additional information by adding visual elements and modifying page setup
- Manage a workbook with multiple worksheets, consolidate data, and work with templates
- Create charts that best represent different types of data visually, and add hyperlinks that open other items, such as web pages
- Create tables and modify them to effectively organize, manage, and display data
- Summarize and analyze data using PivotTables and PivotCharts
- Create formulas using advanced functions that aid in the summation and interpretation of data
- Use Financial functions to calculate and analyze data, use data validation and formula auditing tools to identify and correct errors, use Goal Seek and Scenario Manager for what-if analysis, and use sparkles, map features, and infographics to represent data visually
- Enhance the readability of a workbook by applying advanced formatting to text and data, and analyze data using grouping, summarizing, and outlining tools
- Create financial statements and enter, calculate, and analyze business data in financial statements

- Export and import data in various file formats and transform imported data
- Manage collaboration in a workbook, including editing by multiple users at the same time
- Improve productivity, accuracy, and efficiency by automating and customizing the Excel environment

Courseware Elements for Students

The following visual tour shows how you can use the engaging and robust features in this program to develop the skills you need to solve complex data analysis problems using Microsoft Excel.

Student Textbook and Ebook

Central to the courseware is the textbook, which can be purchased as a printed textbook packaged with an ebook or as an ebook on its own. Interactive textbook features are accessed from the student ebook and in SNAP. Students using SNAP should access the Precheck quizzes, tutorials, and Recheck quizzes from their SNAP assignments page.

Get off to a good start with a clear overview of the chapter content

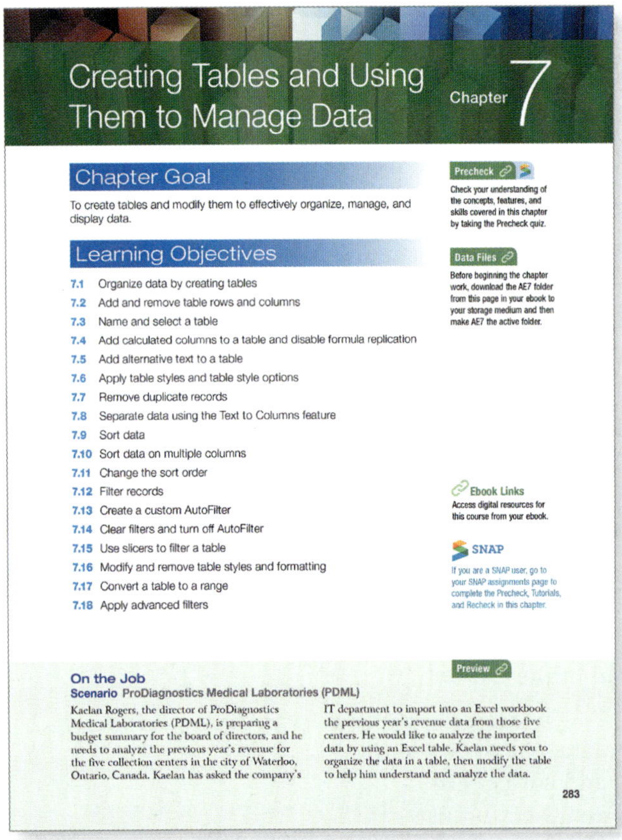
Creating Tables and Using Them to Manage Data

Chapter 7

Chapter Goal

To create tables and modify them to effectively organize, manage, and display data.

Learning Objectives

7.1 Organize data by creating tables
7.2 Add and remove table rows and columns
7.3 Name and select a table
7.4 Add calculated columns to a table and disable formula replication
7.5 Add alternative text to a table
7.6 Apply table styles and table style options
7.7 Remove duplicate records
7.8 Separate data using the Text to Columns feature
7.9 Sort data
7.10 Sort data on multiple columns
7.11 Change the sort order
7.12 Filter records
7.13 Create a custom AutoFilter
7.14 Clear filters and turn off AutoFilter
7.15 Use slicers to filter a table
7.16 Modify and remove table styles and formatting
7.17 Convert a table to a range
7.18 Apply advanced filters

Precheck

Check your understanding of the concepts, features, and skills covered in this chapter by taking the Precheck quiz.

Data Files

Before beginning the chapter work, download the AE7 folder from this page in your ebook to your storage medium and then make AE7 the active folder.

Ebook Links

Access digital resources for this course from your ebook.

SNAP

If you are a SNAP user, go to your SNAP assignments page to complete the Precheck, Tutorials, and Recheck in this chapter.

Preview

On the Job

Scenario ProDiagnostics Medical Laboratories (PDML)

Kaelan Rogers, the director of ProDiagnostics Medical Laboratories (PDML), is preparing a budget summary for the board of directors, and he needs to analyze the previous year's revenue for the five collection centers in the city of Waterloo, Ontario, Canada. Kaelan has asked the company's IT department to import into an Excel workbook the previous year's revenue data from those five centers. He would like to analyze the imported data by using an Excel table. Kaelan needs you to organize the data in a table, then modify the table to help him understand and analyze the data.

283

Chapter openers present the goal, learning objectives, and scenario for each chapter.

Chapter goals describe the overarching knowledge students will master by accomplishing the learning objectives.

Learning objectives define the concepts and skills students will demonstrate after successfully completing the chapter.

Precheck quizzes allow students to check their current skills and understanding before starting chapter work. SNAP users should access these quizzes from their SNAP assignments page.

Data files are provided for On the Job Tasks, Skills Reviews, Skills Assessments, Visual Assessments, Skills Challenges, and Capstone Challenges. A folder containing all the files needed for a chapter can be accessed from the chapter opener page in the student ebook.

Previews show students how their files should look after they complete the last assigned task in the chapter. Each Preview is provided in a locked, watermarked PDF that can be viewed and downloaded from the student ebook.

On the Job Scenarios describe a business and financial situation that is used in tasks throughout the chapter. Each scenario and its related tasks involves one of three businesses: a robotics manufacturer (WareBot), a diagnostic laboratory (ProDiagnostics Medical Laboratories, or PDML), or an auto parts company (DV Auto Parts).

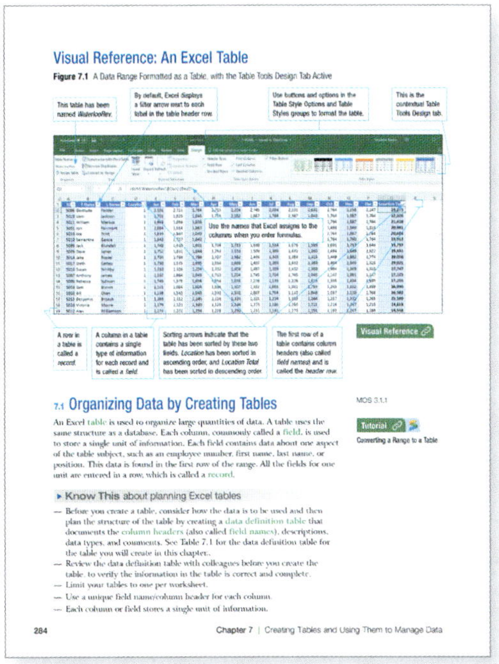

Green link icons indicate interactive resources that can be accessed from the student ebook.

SNAP icons indicate interactive resources that are available in SNAP. SNAP users should access these resources from their SNAP assignments page.

Visual references illustrate the features and tools covered in the chapter. Visual references are also provided in downloadable, printable PDFs that can be accessed from the ebook.

Explore Excel features in depth through concise text and video content

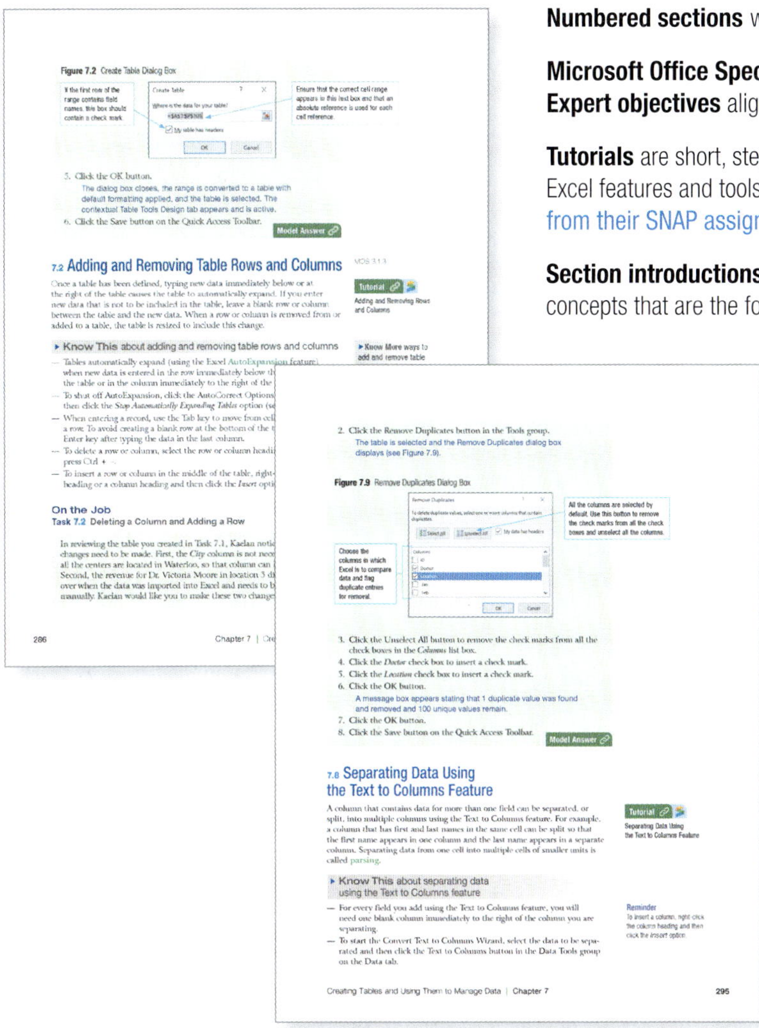

Numbered sections with the chapter learning objectives.

Microsoft Office Specialist objectives and **Microsoft Office Expert objectives** align with the learning objectives.

Tutorials are short, step-by-step videos demonstrating how to use Excel features and tools. SNAP users should access these tutorials from their SNAP assignments page.

Section introductions provide brief overviews of the features and concepts that are the focus of study.

Key terms, highlighted in a green font, are accompanied by specific definitions and examples.

Know This features communicate key information in clear, concise bullet points to facilitate easy learning and immediate recall.

Know More features provide related information to support Know This content without interrupting the flow of learning.

Reminders review relevant information presented earlier.

Build mastery through hands-on application in real-world situations

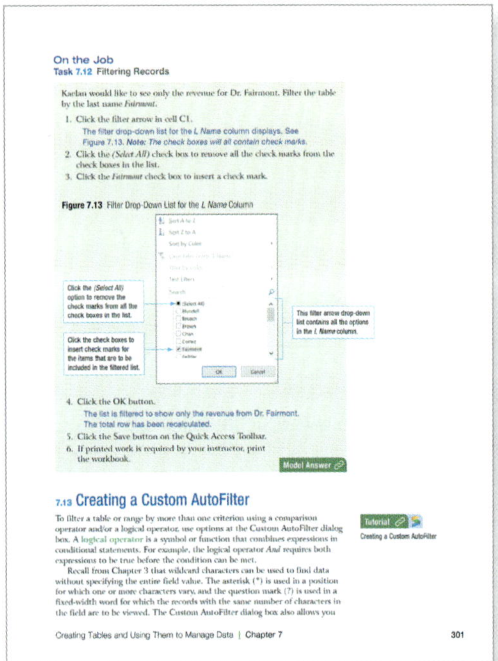

On the Job
Task 7.12 Filtering Records

Kaelan would like to see only the revenue for Dr. Fairmont. Filter the table by the last name *Fairmont*.

1. Click the filter arrow in cell C1.
   The filter drop-down list for the *L Name* column displays. See Figure 7.13. ***Note:** The check boxes will all contain check marks.*
2. Click the *(Select All)* check box to remove all the check marks from the check boxes in the list.
3. Click the *Fairmont* check box to insert a check mark.

Figure 7.13 Filter Drop-Down List for the *L Name* Column

4. Click the OK button.
   The list is filtered to show only the revenue from Dr. Fairmont. The total row has been recalculated.
5. Click the Save button on the Quick Access Toolbar.
6. If printed work is required by your instructor, print the workbook.

Model Answer

7.13 Creating a Custom AutoFilter

Tutorial
Creating a Custom AutoFilter

To filter a table or range by more than one criterion using a comparison operator and/or a logical operator, use options at the Custom AutoFilter dialog box. A logical operator is a symbol or function that combines expressions in conditional statements. For example, the logical operator *And* requires both expressions to be true before the condition can be met.

Recall from Chapter 3 that wildcard characters can be used to find data without specifying the entire field value. The asterisk (*) is used in a position for which one or more characters vary, and the question mark (?) is used in a fixed-width word for which the records with the same number of characters in the field are to be viewed. The Custom AutoFilter dialog box also allows you

Creating Tables and Using Them to Manage Data | Chapter 7 301

On the Job Tasks guide students step by step through the application of spreadsheet and data analysis skills to solve realistic problems for the business introduced in the On the Job Scenario. Students complete these tasks using data files provided in the chapter folder.

Typically, a data file remains open throughout the chapter and students save their work at the end of each task. At the end of the last task that changes a file, students are instructed to save, print, and then close the file. Students are also asked to print a file at the end of a task if a later task will overwrite changes made in the current task.

Model answers show students how their files should look after they complete the assigned tasks. Model answers are provided in locked, watermarked PDFs that can be viewed and downloaded from the student ebook.

Review and assess understanding through chapter summaries and quizzes

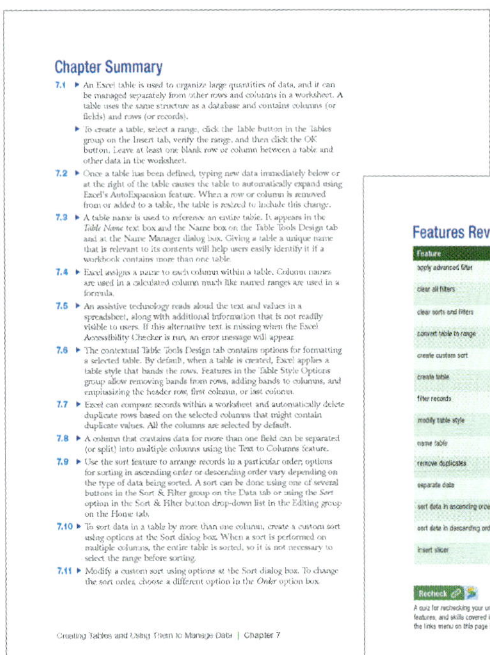

Chapter Summary

7.1 ▸ An Excel table is used to organize large quantities of data, and it can be managed separately from other rows and columns in a worksheet. A table uses the same structure as a database and contains columns (or fields) and rows (or records).
▸ To create a table, select a range, click the Table button in the Tables group on the Insert tab, verify the range, and then click the OK button. Leave at least one blank row or column between a table and other data in the worksheet.

7.2 ▸ Once a table has been defined, typing new data immediately below or at the right of the table causes the table to automatically expand using Excel's AutoExpansion feature. When a row or column is removed from or added to a table, the table is resized to include this change.

7.3 ▸ A table name is used to reference an entire table. It appears in the *Table Name* text box and the Name box on the Table Tools Design tab and at the Name Manager dialog box. Giving a table a unique name that is relevant to its contents will help users easily identify it if a workbook contains more than one table.

7.4 ▸ Excel assigns a name to each column within a table. Column names are used in a calculated column much like named ranges are used in a formula.

7.5 ▸ An assistive technology reads aloud the text and values in a spreadsheet, along with additional information that is not readily visible to users. If this alternative text is missing when the Excel Accessibility Checker is run, an error message will appear.

7.6 ▸ The contextual Table Tools Design tab contains options for formatting a selected table. By default, when a table is created, Excel applies a table style that bands the rows. Features in the Table Style Options group allow removing bands from rows, adding bands to columns, and emphasizing the header row, first column, or last column.

7.7 ▸ Excel can compare records within a worksheet and automatically delete duplicate rows based on the selected columns that might contain duplicate values. All the columns are selected by default.

7.8 ▸ A column that contains data for more than one field can be separated (or split) into multiple columns using the Text to Columns feature.

7.9 ▸ Use the sort feature to arrange records in a particular order; options for sorting in ascending order or descending order vary depending on the type of data being sorted. A sort can be done using one of several buttons in the Sort & Filter group on the Data tab or using the *Sort* option in the Sort & Filter button drop-down list in the Editing group on the Home tab.

7.10 ▸ To sort data in a table by more than one column, create a custom sort using options at the Sort dialog box. When a sort is performed on multiple columns, the entire table is sorted, so it is not necessary to select the range before sorting.

7.11 ▸ Modify a custom sort using options at the Sort dialog box. To change the sort order, choose a different option in the *Order* option box.

Creating Tables and Using Them to Manage Data | Chapter 7

Chapter Summaries highlight the key concepts and Excel features covered by the chapter learning objectives.

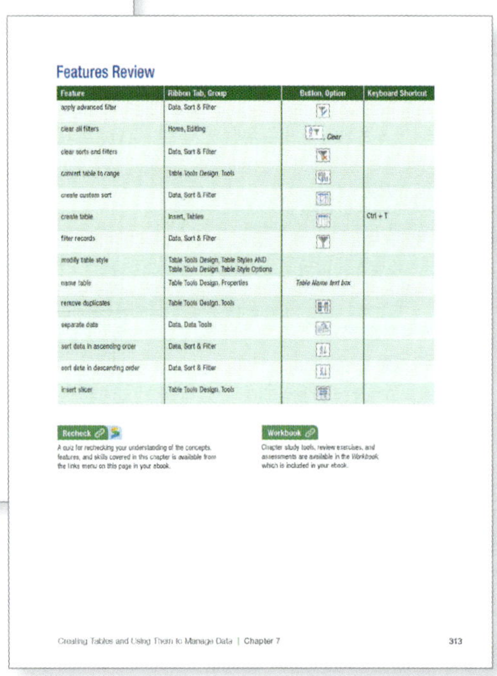

Features Review

Feature	Ribbon Tab, Group	Button, Option	Keyboard Shortcut
apply advanced filter	Data, Sort & Filter		
clear all filters	Home, Editing	, *Clear*	
clear sorts and filters	Data, Sort & Filter		
convert table to range	Table Tools Design, Tools		
create custom sort	Data, Sort & Filter		
create table	Insert, Tables		Ctrl + T
filter records	Data, Sort & Filter		
modify table style	Table Tools Design, Table Styles AND Table Tools Design, Table Style Options		
name table	Table Tools Design, Properties	*Table Name* text box	
remove duplicates	Table Tools Design, Tools		
separate data	Data, Data Tools		
sort data in ascending order	Data, Sort & Filter		
sort data in descending order	Data, Sort & Filter		
insert slicer	Table Tools Design, Tools		

Recheck

A quiz for rechecking your understanding of the concepts, features, and skills covered in this chapter is available from the links menu on this page in your ebook.

Workbook

Chapter study tools, review exercises, and assessments are available in the *Workbook* which is included in your ebook.

Creating Tables and Using Them to Manage Data | Chapter 7 313

Features Reviews provide visual references to Excel features and the methods for accessing and applying them.

Recheck quizzes enable students to determine how their understanding has improved after completing chapter work. SNAP users should access these quizzes from their SNAP assignments page.

Workbook pages deliver chapter study tools, review exercises, assessments, and challenges. The workbook pages are included in the student ebook.

Workbook

The workbook pages are included in the student ebook. Interactive workbook resources are accessed from the student ebook and, in some cases, SNAP. Students using SNAP should access the Concepts Reviews and Skills Reviews from their SNAP assignments page.

Solidify mastery of Excel features and skills through study, review, and hands-on assessment

Study Tools—including a glossary, presentations with audio support, and Quick Steps documents—reinforce understanding of the topics.

Concepts Reviews allow students to test their comprehension and recall of Excel features, terms, and functions. SNAP users should access these reviews from their SNAP assignments page.

Skills Reviews guide students through additional practice of skills covered in the chapter tasks. SNAP users should access these reviews from their SNAP assignments page.

Data files for workbook activities are delivered at point of use for easy access in the workbook ebook. They are also provided in the folder downloaded from the chapter opener page.

Skills Assessments prompt students to apply data analysis and spreadsheet skills to solve new business problems.

Visual Assessments use a combination of brief instruction and visual references to assess students' abilities to use Excel tools in solving business problems.

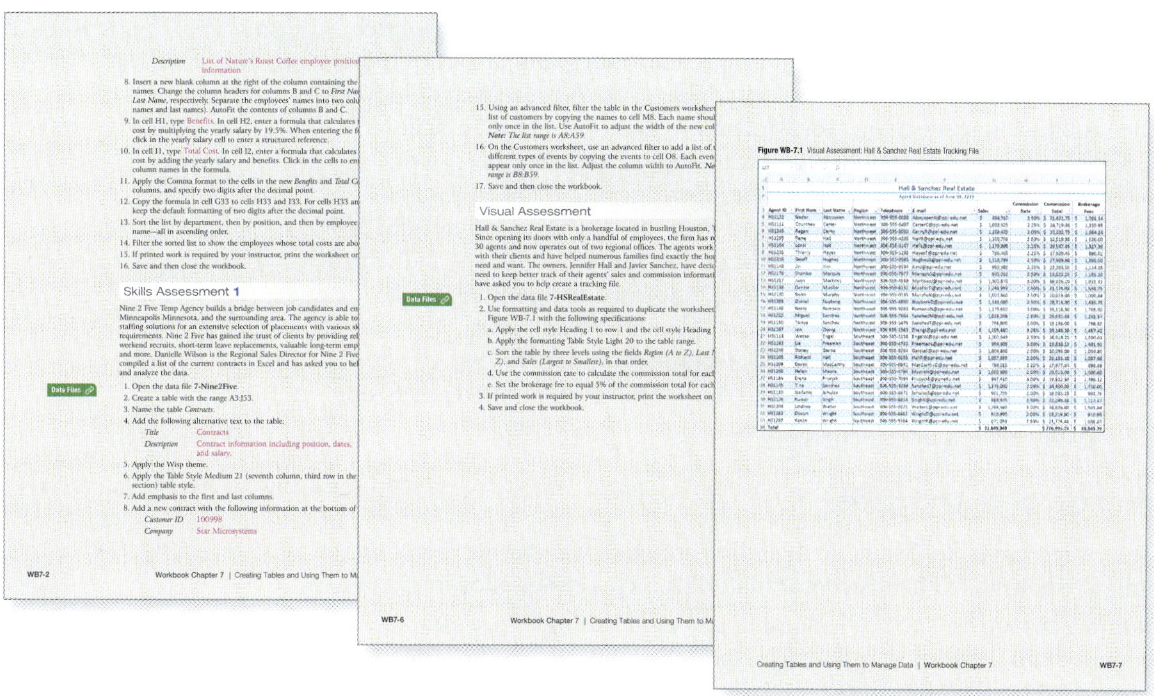

Challenge understanding with chapter-based critical-thinking and portfolio assignments

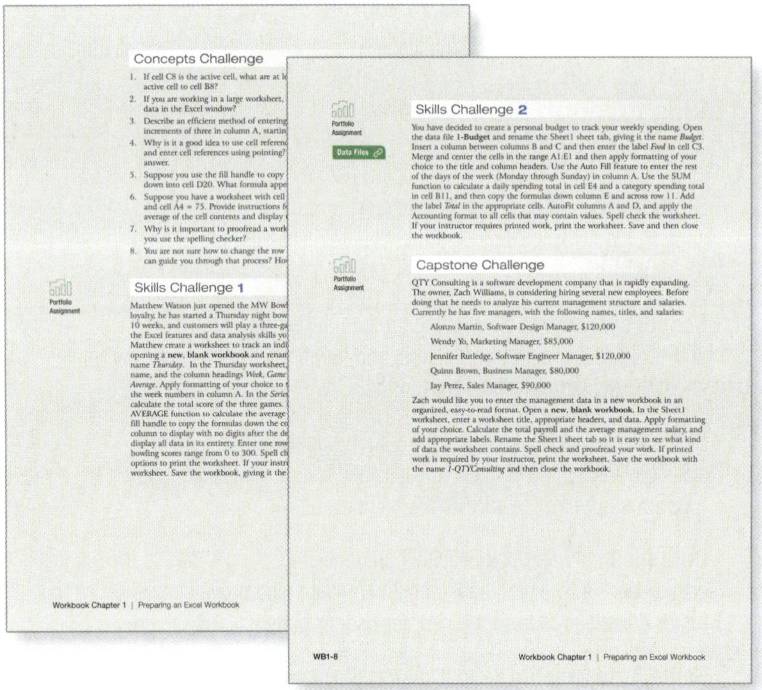

Concepts Challenges present a wide variety of problems that ask for short written descriptions of the Excel and data analysis tools needed to solve them.

Skills Challenges are brief, open-ended portfolio assignments that each describe a business problem to be solved using a set of learning objectives covered in the chapter. Students choose their own solutions and, in some cases, provide their own data files.

Capstone Challenges are comprehensive, open-ended portfolio assignments that present a single, broad business situation to test mastery of learning objectives tied to Microsoft Office Specialist and Microsoft Office Expert objectives.

An **Integrated Capstone Challenge** at the end of the last workbook chapter is a comprehensive, open-ended portfolio assignment that tests mastery of the Excel features and data analysis tools taught throughout the course.

Instructors using SNAP have access to additional assessment opportunities, including live-in-the-Office-application Projects and Skills Check items.

SNAP Training and Assessment

SNAP

SNAP is a web-based training and assessment program and learning management system (LMS) for learning Microsoft Office 2016. SNAP comprises rich content, a sophisticated grade book, and robust scheduling and analytics tools. SNAP courseware supports *Advanced Microsoft® Excel® 2016* content and delivers live-in-the-application assessments for students to demonstrate their skills mastery. Video tutorials show students how to apply Excel features in brief, step-by-step videos. SNAP provides automatic scoring and detailed feedback on the many activities, exercises, and quizzes to help identify areas where additional support is needed, evaluating student performance at both the individual and course levels. The *Advanced Microsoft® Excel® 2016* course content is also available for export into any LMS system that supports (LTI) tools.

Paradigm Education Solutions provides technical support for SNAP through 24-7 chat at ParadigmCollege.com. In addition, an online User Guide and other SNAP training tools are available.

Instructor eResources

All instructor resources are available digitally through a web-based ebook on the Paradigm Bookshelf. The instructor materials include the following items:

- Planning resources, such as lesson plans with teaching hints, sample course syllabi, and Microsoft Office Specialist and Microsoft Office Expert Excel 2016 objectives correlations

- Delivery resources, including discussion questions and presentations with lecture notes
- Assessment resources, including live model answers for chapter tasks and workbook activities, rubrics for open-ended student work, chapter-based Supplemental Assessments, and chapter-based exam banks

Acknowledgments

The authors and editors thank the following reviewers for their contributions to this program:

DeLynn Anderson, Aims Community College, Greeley, CO

Joshua Drivdahl, Finance Consultant, St. Paul, MN

Tom Lacksonen, University of Wisconsin–Stout, Menomonie, WI

Cherie Leiker, Johnson County Community College, Overland Park, KS

Theresa Lindsey, Lanier Technical College, Cumming, GA

Nasser Tadayon, Southern Utah University, Cedar City, UT

Sheri Valentin, Gateway Community College, New Haven, CT

About the Authors

Jan Davidson started her teaching career in 1997 as a corporate trainer and postsecondary instructor. Since 2001, she has been a faculty member of the School of Business, Creative Design, Liberal Studies, and English at Lambton College of Applied Arts and Technology in Sarnia, Ontario. In this role, she has developed curriculum and taught a variety of office technology, software applications, and office administration courses to domestic and international students in postsecondary Office Administration Executive, General, and Medical; Human Resources; and Fashion Business programs. Jan has written instructor resources and SNAP content for Paradigm Education Solutions since 2006. In addition, she was coauthor of the Level 2 *Access 2013* and *Excel 2013* books in the Benchmark Series as well as author of the Level 2 *Access 2016* and *Excel 2016* books in the Benchmark Series.

Jan Marrelli is an administrator with the Algoma District School Board, Sault Ste. Marie, Ontario. Along with teaching computer science and application courses, she has extensive experience working with educators on high-yield instructional strategies, assessment, and differentiated instruction. She has written curriculum and elearning courses for the Ontario Ministry of Education. She is also coauthor of Paradigm Education Solution's *Guidelines for Microsoft® Office 2016* and author of numerous Lawrenceville Press textbooks and their accompanying instructor resource materials.

Microsoft Office 365 and Microsoft Office 2016 (both of which include Excel) are available for computers running the Windows operating system, Office for Mac is available for Mac computers, and Microsoft Office mobile apps are available for mobile phones and tablets. This courseware was written using personal desktop computers and laptops with the Windows 10 operating system and Office 365. If you are using Office for Mac, you may be able to perform some of the activities in this textbook, but some steps may not work as written and your results may not match the model answers provided with the course materials. For example, PivotCharts and Power Pivot are not available in the Excel for Mac version. Office mobile apps allow you to view, edit, and create files on devices with screen sizes smaller than 10.1 inches; core features are offered free of charge and advanced features are available for purchase. Office Online is a free version of Office that you can use in your web browser but that offers limited features; for example, Excel Online does not contain a Formulas tab. If you do not have access to a personal desktop or laptop computer with Windows and Office 365, explore options such as using a computer lab at your institution.

Office 365 is a subscription-based suite that is delivered through a live Internet connection and installed on your computer. With an Office 365 subscription, you have the option of installing new features or versions as they are released. You can choose from among several Office 365 versions for home, school, business, and enterprise—each with a slightly different set of features. The number of computers and devices on which a license can be installed depends on the version purchased. Excel 2016 and the other Office 2016 applications are also available in desktop versions, which update while you are online and may be used when you are offline. A desktop version is available as a one-time purchase and may be installed on one PC.

With both the Office 365 and Office 2016 desktop applications, Microsoft is constantly updating features and functionality, and the user may choose to update as soon as the changes are made available or on a delayed schedule. Updates to the software may alter feature names and locations in the Excel interface and may also affect the steps required to apply Excel features. Further differences may be seen depending on the device you are using. For example, the Quick Access Toolbar will automatically display an added Touch/Mouse Mode button if you are working on a device with a touchscreen.

The authors and editors of this program took care to use the most current versions of the Excel application when writing the course materials. They will also monitor the software and update the ebook as new features and functionality become available.

Throughout this course, you will have frequent opportunities to apply the tools and features you are learning about in hands-on tasks and other assignments. This Getting Started section provides the information you will need to complete those activities. The following sections explain how to choose commands in Excel and other computer applications, work with multiple programs that are open at the same time, customize the settings on your computer to match the settings used in writing this course, download the data files needed for this course, use special features and add-ins, enter formulas that contain functions, and complete assignments for the course.

Choosing Commands with the Mouse and Keyboard

Within a computer application, you can use several methods to choose commands. A command is an instruction that tells the application to do something. You can choose a command using the mouse, touchscreen, touchpad, or keyboard. Some commands can be issued using a combination of these methods. Commands are available on the ribbon, on the Quick Access Toolbar, in dialog boxes, in task panes, and in other boxes and panes.

The Office suite also provides accelerator keys you can press to use a command in an application. Press the Alt key on the keyboard to display KeyTips that identify the accelerator key you can press to execute a command. For example, if you press the Alt key in an Excel workbook with the Home tab active, KeyTips display as shown in Figure G.1. Continue pressing accelerator keys until you execute the desired command. For example, to begin checking the spelling in a workbook, press the Alt key, press the R key on the keyboard to display the Review tab, and then press the S key on the keyboard.

Figure G.1 Home Tab KeyTips

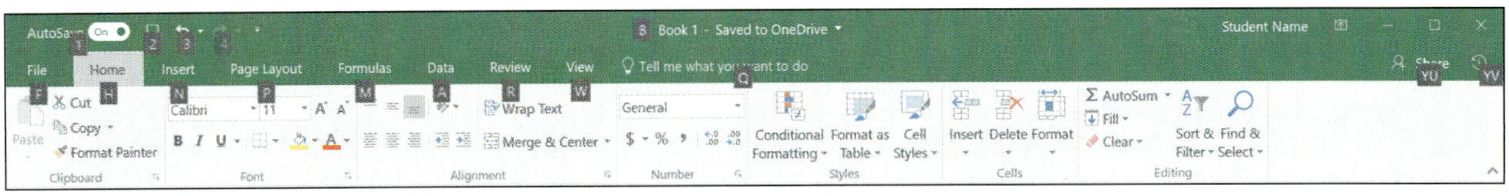

Buttons and Options on the Ribbon and on the Quick Access Toolbar

When an application such as Excel is open, the ribbon contains buttons and options for completing tasks, as well as tabs you can click to display additional buttons and options. The Quick Access Toolbar is a row of buttons on the title bar that offers quick access to frequently used commands. To choose a button or option using the mouse, point to the button or option with the mouse pointer and then click the left mouse button.

Commands at Drop-Down Lists and Palettes

A drop-down list of options displays when you click a button or arrow that offers further choices. A drop-down palette often displays for color choices. To choose an option at a drop-down list or palette with the mouse, point to the option with the mouse pointer and then click the left mouse button. To make a selection from a drop-down list with the keyboard, type the underlined letter in the option name. Some options at a drop-down list may appear grayed out (dimmed), indicating that the option is currently unavailable. If an option at a drop-down list displays preceded by a check mark, the option is currently active. If an option at a drop-down list displays followed by an ellipsis (...), clicking that option will display a dialog box.

Commands at Drop-Down Galleries (with the Live Preview Feature)

A drop-down gallery displays options with the live preview feature. To use the live preview feature, point at the option with the mouse pointer until the worksheet displays with the option applied. To choose the option, click the left mouse button.

Commands at Dialog Boxes and Task Panes

A dialog box or task pane contains options for applying formatting or otherwise modifying a file or the data within a file. The names of tabs that contain additional options display along the tops of some dialog boxes and task panes. For example, the Format Cells dialog box, shown in Figure G.2, contains six tabs: the Number tab, the Alignment tab, the Font tab, the Border tab, the Fill tab, and the Protection tab. The tab that displays in front of the others is the active tab. To make a tab active using the mouse, point to the tab name with the mouse pointer and then click the left mouse button. If you are using the keyboard, press Ctrl + Tab or press Alt + the underlined letter in the tab name.

Figure G.2 Format Cells Dialog Box

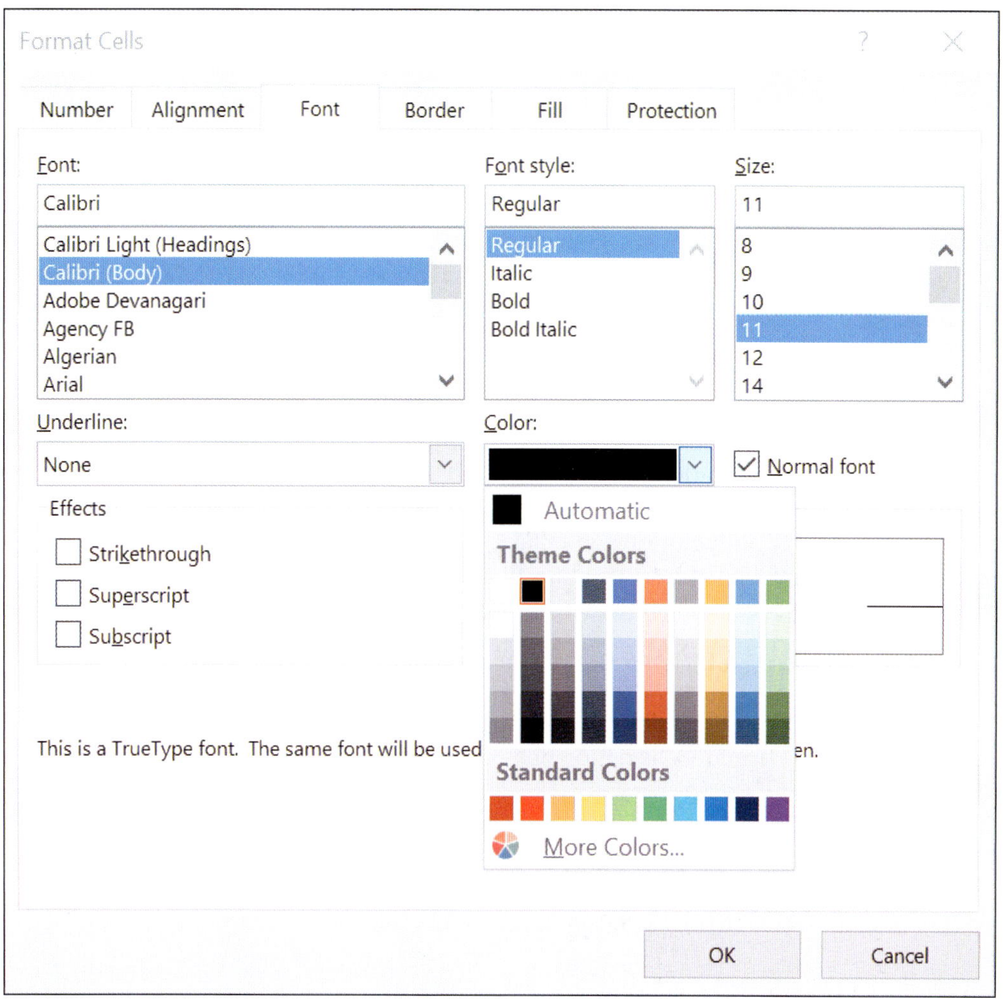

To choose an option at a dialog box or task pane with the mouse, point to the option with the mouse pointer and then click the left mouse button. If you are using the keyboard, press the Tab key to move the insertion point forward from option to option. Press Shift + Tab to move the insertion point backward from option to option. You can also press and hold down the Alt key and then press the underlined letter in the option name. When an option is selected, it displays with a blue background or surrounded by a dashed box called a *marquee*. A dialog box contains one or more of the following elements: list boxes, option boxes, check boxes, text boxes, option buttons, measurement boxes, and command buttons.

Commands in List Boxes and Option Boxes

The fonts available on the Font tab at the Format Cells dialog box, shown in Figure G.2, are contained in a list box. To make a selection from a list box with the mouse, point to the option with the mouse pointer and then click the left mouse button.

Some list boxes contain one or two scroll bars. A scroll bar displays at the right side of the list box (a vertical scroll bar) or at the bottom of the list box (a horizontal scroll bar). Use a vertical scroll bar or a horizontal scroll bar to move through the list if the list is longer (or wider) than the box. To move down a list using a vertical scroll bar, point to the down arrow with the mouse pointer, and then click and hold down the left mouse button. To scroll up through a list, point to the up arrow with the mouse pointer, and then click and hold down the left mouse button. You can also point to the area of the scroll bar above the scroll box and then click the left mouse button to scroll up the list, or point to the area of the scroll bar below the scroll box and then click the left mouse button to scroll down the list. To navigate in a list with a horizontal scroll bar, click the left arrow to scroll to the left of the list or click the right arrow to scroll to the right of the list.

To use the keyboard to make a selection from a list box, move the insertion point into the box by holding down the Alt key and then pressing the underlined letter in the desired option name. Press the Up Arrow and/or Down Arrow keys on the keyboard to move through the list, and press the Enter key when the desired option has been selected.

In some cases, options are contained in a drop-down list box and the selected option displays in an *option box*. An option box displays with a down arrow that you click to display a drop-down list, gallery, or palette of options. For example, in Figure G.2, the selected font color option (Black) displays in the option box and the option box arrow has been clicked to display a drop-down palette of color choices. If you are using the keyboard, press Alt + C.

Commands with Check Boxes

Some options are preceded by a check box, and a check mark may or may not appear in the box. The Font tab at the Format Cells dialog box, shown in Figure G.2, displays several check boxes in the *Effects* section. If a check mark appears in the box, the option is active (turned on). If the check box does not contain a check mark, the option is inactive (turned off). Any number of check boxes can be active at the same time. For example, in the *Effects* section on the Font tab at the Format Cells dialog box in Figure G.2, check marks are inserted in two of the check boxes.

To make a check box active or inactive with the mouse, point to the check box with the mouse pointer (or, in some cases, point to the option) and then click the left mouse button. If you are using the keyboard, press Alt + the underlined letter in the option name.

Commands with Text Boxes

Some options require you to enter text in a text box. For example, the boxes to the right of the *Find what* and *Replace with* options at the Find and Replace dialog box, shown in Figure G.3, are text boxes. In a text box, you type new text or edit existing text. Edit text in a text box in the same manner as you edit text in a worksheet cell. Use the Home, End, Left Arrow, and Right Arrow keys on the keyboard to move the insertion point without deleting text, and use the Delete key or Backspace key to delete text. You can also select existing text and then type to replace it with new text.

Figure G.3 Find and Replace Dialog Box

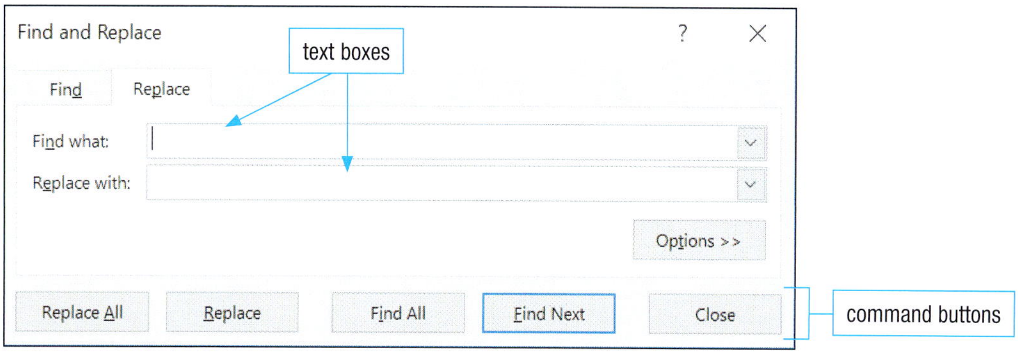

Command Buttons

The buttons at the bottom of the Find and Replace dialog box, shown in Figure G.3, are called command buttons. Use a command button to execute or cancel a command. Some command buttons display with an ellipsis (...), which indicates that another dialog box will open if you click that button. To choose a command button with the mouse, point to the button with the mouse pointer and then click the left mouse button. To choose a command button with the keyboard, press the Tab key until the command button is surrounded by a marquee and then press the Enter key. A command button may also display with a pair of greater-than symbols (>>), which indicates that the dialog box will expand if you click that button.

Radio Buttons

The Page Setup dialog box, shown in Figure G.4, contains options preceded by radio buttons. Only one radio button in a section of the dialog box can be selected at any time. When a radio button is selected, a bullet displays in the button. To select a radio button with the mouse, point to the radio button with the mouse pointer (or, in some cases, point to the option) and then click the left mouse button to insert a bullet. To make a selection with the keyboard, press and hold down the Alt key, press the underlined letter in the option name, and then release the Alt key.

Measurement Boxes

Some options allow you to increase or decrease measurements or amounts. These options are generally located in measurement boxes. For example, the Page Layout dialog box, shown in Figure G.4, contains *Adjust to* and *Fit to* measurement boxes. To increase a number in a measurement box, point to the increment (up) arrow at the right of the measurement box with the mouse pointer and then click the left mouse button. To decrease the number, point to the decrement (down) arrow with the mouse pointer and then click the left mouse button. If you are using the keyboard, press and hold down the Alt key and then press the underlined letter in the option name, press the Up Arrow key to increase the number or the Down Arrow key to decrease the number, and then release the Alt key. You can also select the value in the measurement box and then type to replace it with a new value.

Figure G.4 Page Setup Dialog Box

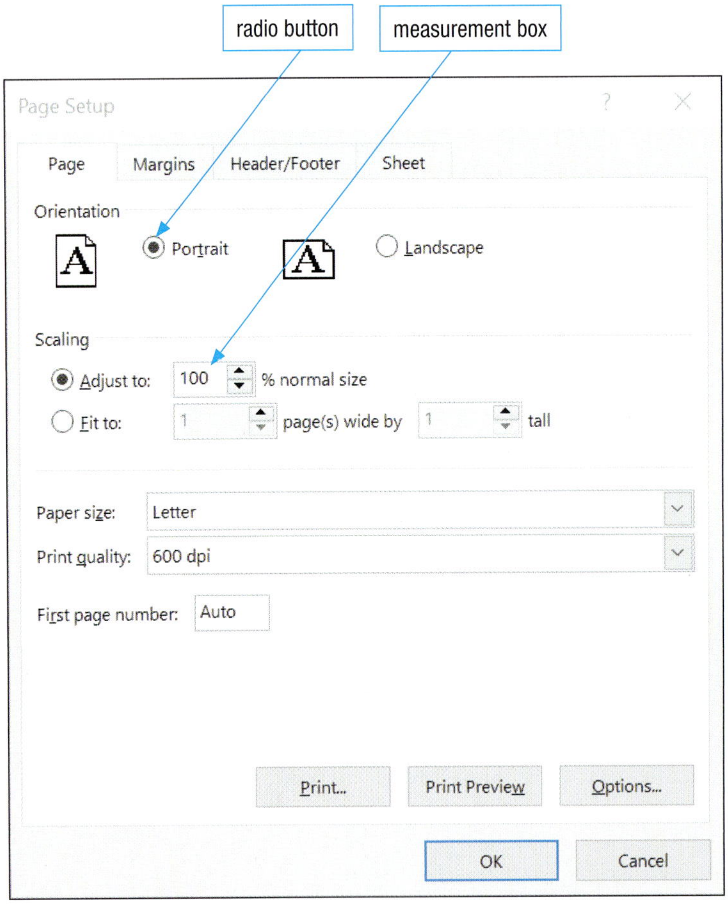

Choosing Commands with Keyboard Shortcuts

Applications in the Office suite offer a variety of keyboard shortcuts you can use to execute specific commands. A keyboard shortcut generally requires using two or more keys. For example, the keyboard shortcut to display the Open dialog box in an application is Ctrl + F12. To use this keyboard shortcut, press and hold down the Ctrl key, press the F12 function key on the keyboard, and then release the Ctrl key. For a list of keyboard shortcuts, refer to the Help files.

Choosing Commands with Pop-Up Menus

The Office applications include pop-up menus that contain commands related to different items. To display a pop-up menu, point to the item for which you want to view more options with the mouse pointer and then click the right mouse button, or press Shift + F10. The pop-up menu will appear wherever the insertion point is positioned. In some cases, the Mini toolbar will also appear with the pop-up menu. For example, if you click in any cell in an Excel worksheet, clicking the right mouse button or pressing Shift + F10 will display the pop-up menu and Mini toolbar, as shown in Figure G.5.

To select an option at a pop-up menu with the mouse, click the option. If you are using the keyboard, press the Up Arrow or Down Arrow key until the option is selected and then press the Enter key. To close a pop-up menu without choosing an option, click outside the pop-up menu or press the Esc key.

Figure G.5 Pop-Up Menu and Mini Toolbar

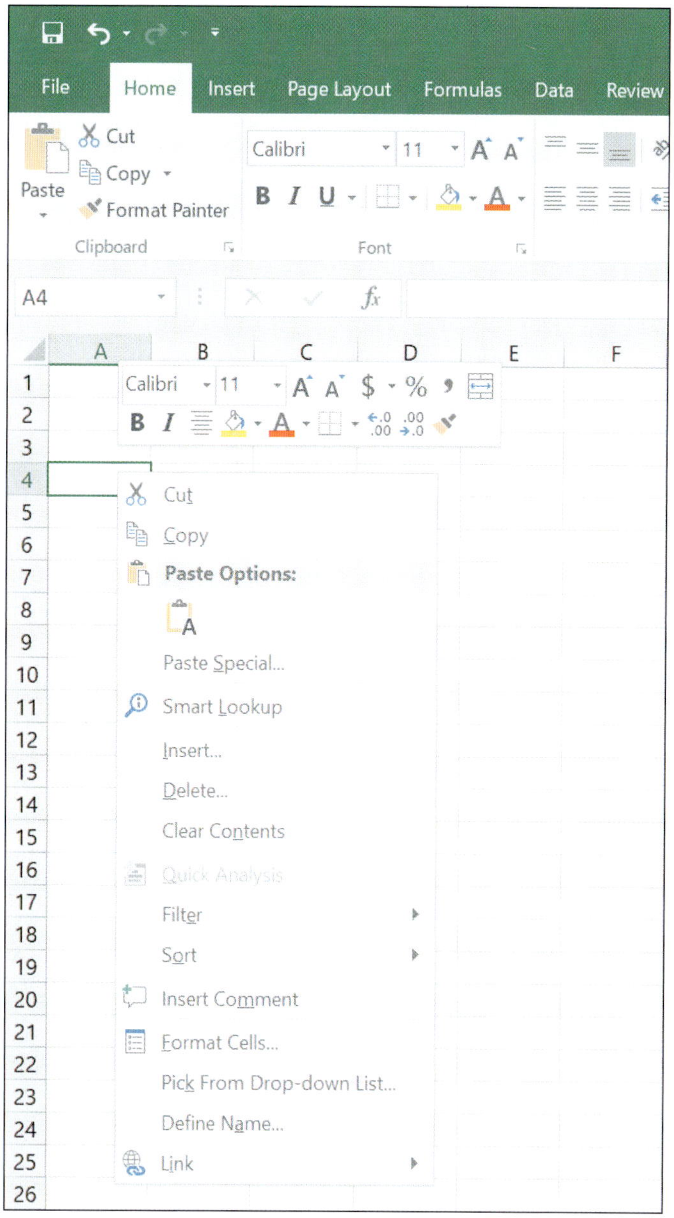

Working with Multiple Programs

In this textbook, you will work primarily with Excel, but you will also integrate content from other applications, including Word, PowerPoint, and Access. As you work with the various Office programs, you will notice many similarities among them. For example, the steps to save, close, and print are virtually the same in Word, Excel, and PowerPoint. This consistency across applications greatly enhances your ability to transfer knowledge learned in one application to another within the Office suite. Another benefit to using Microsoft Office is the ability to have more than one application open at the same time.

When you open an application, a button containing an icon representing the application displays on the Windows taskbar. If you open another application, a button containing an icon representing that application displays to the right of the first application button on the taskbar. Figure G.6 shows the Windows taskbar with Word, Excel, Access, and PowerPoint open. To move from one program to another, click the taskbar button representing the desired application.

Figure G.6 Windows Taskbar with Word, Excel, Access, and PowerPoint Open

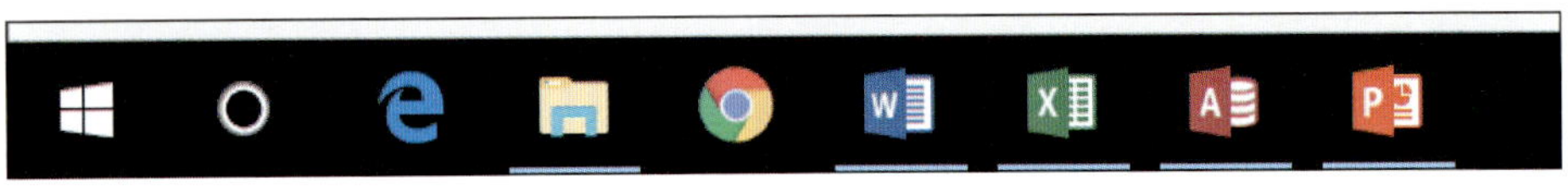

Customizing Settings

Before beginning the tasks and activities in this textbook and its accompanying workbook, you may want to customize your monitor settings, the DPI display setting, the display of file extensions, and the Windows format and location settings. The tasks and activities in the textbook and workbook assume that the monitor display is set at 1600 × 900 pixels, the DPI is set at 125%, the display of file extensions is turned off, the format is set at English (United States), and the location is set to United States.

If you are unable to change the monitor's resolution or the DPI settings, you can still complete the tasks and activities successfully. However, some references in the text might not perfectly match what you see on your screen. For example, if your monitor is set to a lower resolution, you may not see all the buttons in the Illustrations group on the Insert tab. Instead, you will see an Illustrations button with an arrow, and you will need to click the arrow to display the buttons in a drop-down list. If you do not have the monitor display settings used for this course and you have trouble locating a group on the group, look for a button with the same name.

The instructions, images, and model answers for this course have been created using the English (United States) format and United States location. The SNAP scoring feature also uses the same settings. These settings affect dates, the Accounting format, and measurements. If your computer uses a different format and/or location setting, your answers may be different from the ones your instructor and SNAP use for scoring your work. To ensure that your work is not scored incorrectly because of differences in these settings, you need to change the settings on your computer to the English (United States) format and the United States location.

Before you begin your first assignment in the Excel application, check the display settings on the computer you are using. Your monitor's display settings are important because the ribbon in the Microsoft Office suite adjusts to the screen resolution setting of your computer monitor. A computer monitor set at a high resolution will be able to show more buttons on the ribbon than a monitor set to a low resolution. The illustrations in this textbook were created with a screen resolution setting of 1600 × 900 pixels. In Figure G.7, the Excel ribbon on that monitor is shown three ways: at a lower screen resolution (1366 × 768 pixels), at the screen resolution featured throughout this textbook, and at a higher screen resolution (1920 × 1080 pixels). Note the variances in the ribbon across the three examples. If possible, set your display to 1600 × 900 pixels to match the illustrations you will see in this textbook.

Figure G.7 Excel Ribbon Displayed on a Monitor Set at Three Different Screen Resolutions

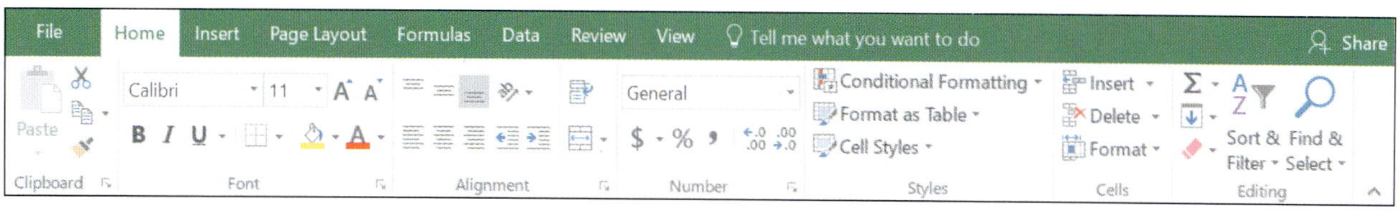

1366 x 768 Screen Resolution

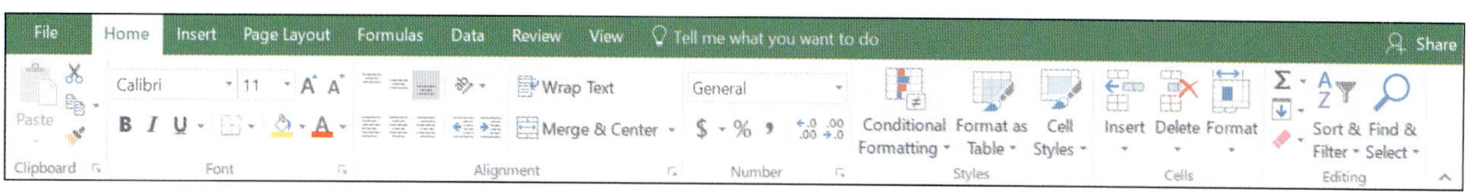

1600 x 900 Screen Resolution

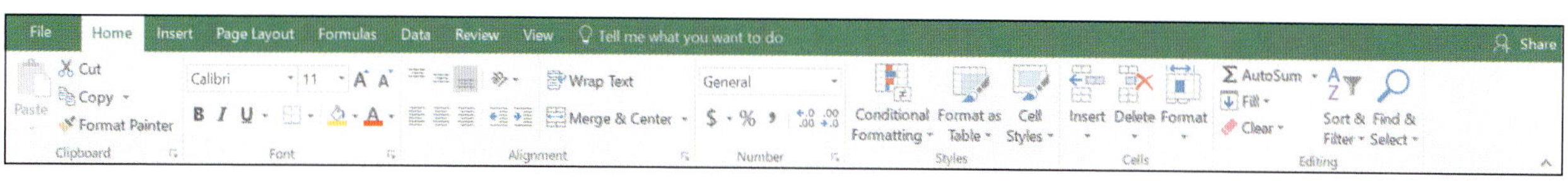

1920 x 1080 Screen Resolution

Note: Microsoft is constantly updating Windows 10. Depending on your version of Windows 10, your monitor, and other variables, the steps to accomplish Tasks G.1–G.4 may vary slightly from the ones given here.

Task G.1 Setting the Monitor Display to 1600 × 900

Note: The resolution settings may be locked on lab computers. Also, some laptop screens and small monitors may not be able to display in a 1600 × 900 resolution.

1. At the Windows 10 desktop, right-click in a blank area of the screen.
2. At the pop-up menu, click the *Display settings* option (see Figure G.8).

Figure G.8 Display settings Option

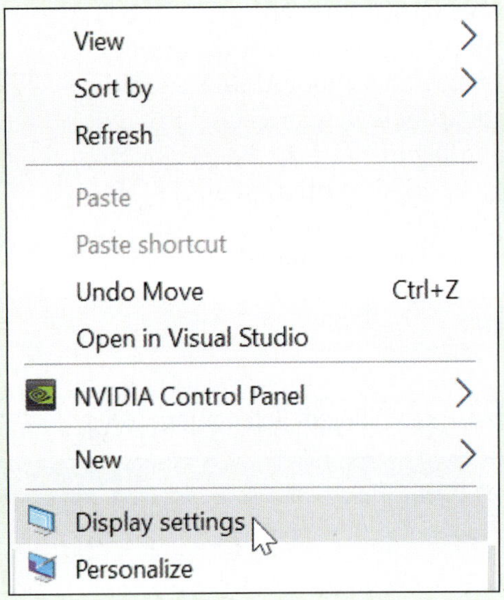

3. At the Settings window with *Display* selected in the left panel, scroll down the right panel until the *Resolution* option box is visible, and take note of the current resolution setting. If the current resolution is already set to 1600 × 900, skip ahead to Step 8.
4. Click in the *Resolution* option box and then click the 1600 × 900 option at the drop-down list (see Figure G.9). ***Note:*** *If 1600 + 900 is not listed, check with your instructor about which setting to use.*

Figure G.9 Resolution Drop-Down List

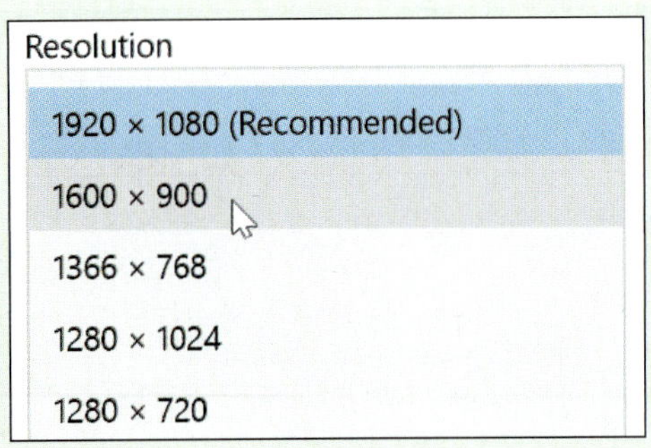

5. Click the Apply button, if necessary.
6. Click the Keep changes button.
7. Click the Close button.

Task G.2 Changing the DPI Setting

Note: *The DPI settings may be locked on lab computers. Also, some laptop screens and small monitors may not allow the DPI settings to be changed.*

1. At the Windows 10 desktop, right-click in a blank area of the screen.
2. At the pop-up menu, click the *Display settings* option.
3. At the Settings window, take note of the current DPI percentage that appears in the *Change the size of text, apps, and other items* option box. If the percentage is already set to 125%, skip to Step 5.
4. Click the *Change the size of text, apps, and other items* option box arrow and then click the *125%* option at the drop-down list (see Figure G.10).
5. Close the Settings window.

Figure G.10 *Change the size of text, apps, and other items* Option Box Drop-Down List

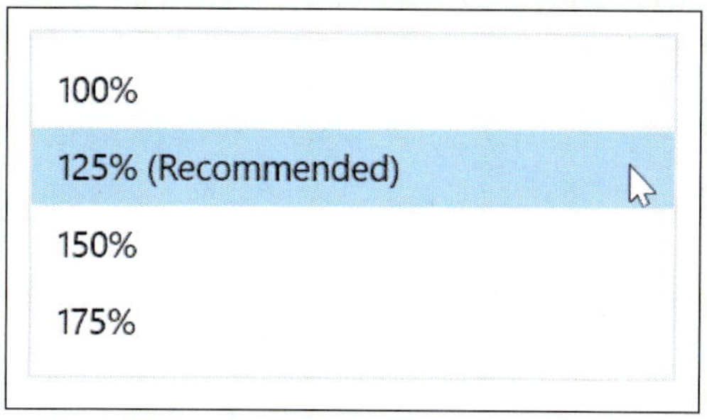

Task G.3 Hiding File Extensions

1. At the Windows 10 desktop, click the File Explorer button on the Windows taskbar (see Figure G.11).

Figure G.11 File Explorer Button on the Windows Taskbar

2. At the File Explorer window, click the View tab.
3. Click the *File name extensions* check box in the Show/hide group to remove the check mark.
4. Close the File Explorer window.

Task G.4 Changing the Country or Region

1. At the Windows desktop, click the Start button, type Control Panel, and then press the Enter key.
2. Click the *Change date, time, or number formats* option in the *Clock, Language, and Region* section at the Control Panel.
3. Click the *Format* option box arrow on the Formats tab at the Region dialog box; scroll up or down the drop-down list, if necessary; and then click the *English (United States)* option (see Figure G.12).

Figure G.12 Region Dialog Box

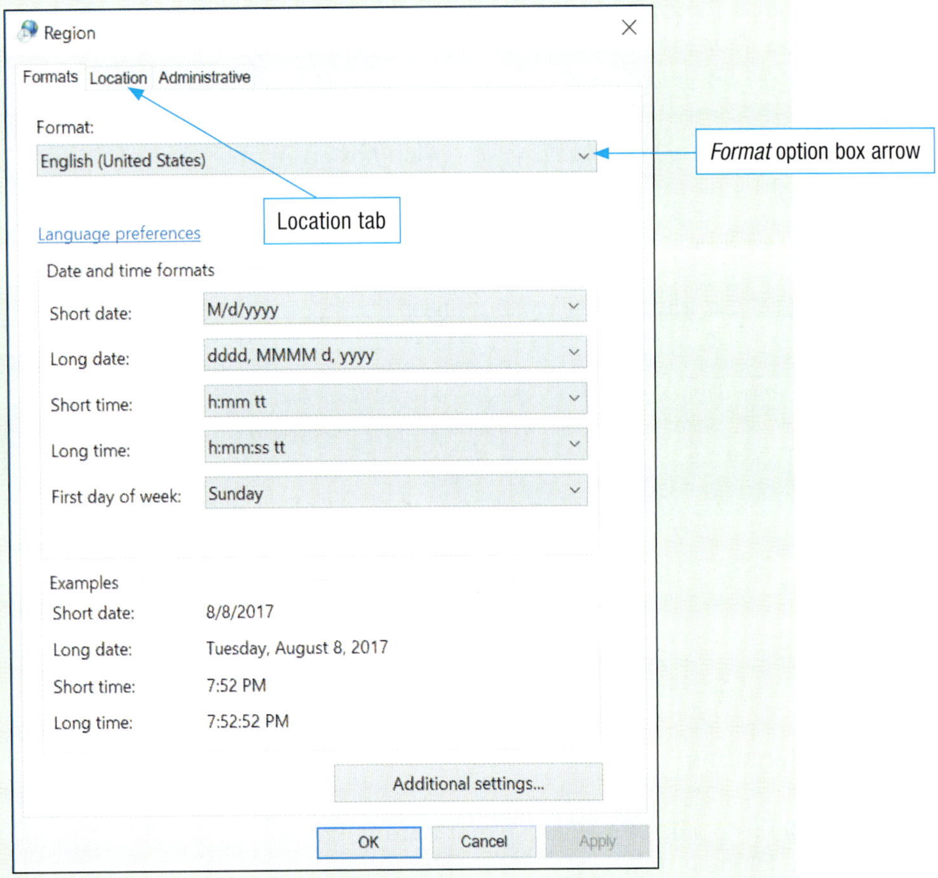

4. Click the Location tab.
5. Click the *Home location* option box arrow; scroll up or down the drop-down list, if necessary; and then click the *United States* option.
6. Click the OK button.
7. Click the Control Panel Close button.

Downloading the Data Files Needed for Tasks and Activities

Most of the tasks and activities in this textbook and workbook require that you open existing files called *data files*. You can download the data files from Paradigm's OneDrive account through links in the ebook that accompanies this textbook. You must download the files and save them to your own OneDrive account or other storage location before you can work in them. The tasks and activities are based on the assumption that you have saved the files to your OneDrive account. Complete Task G.5 to download the data files to your OneDrive account.

Task G.5 provides instructions for copying the complete folder of data files for this book. Alternatively, you may download individual folders that contain the files for a particular chapter. Links to chapter folders are available from the chapter opener pages in your ebook. Follow steps similar to the ones in Task G.5 to download the chapter folders.

In the workbook, individual data files may be downloaded from the activity pages in the ebook. Each file will open directly from the link in the ebook. You will need to save an individual file to a storage location before working in it. These individual files are also provided in the chapter folders. You may either download the individual files from the workbook pages or use the individual files from your working chapter folder, whichever is most convenient for you.

Task G.5 Downloading the Student Data Files and Copying Them to Your OneDrive Account

Data Files

Note: *Both OneDrive and the Paradigm ebook platform are updated periodically, so the steps needed to download files may vary from the ones given below. The steps in this task are based on the assumption that you are using the Microsoft Edge browser or the Chrome browser; if you are using a different browser, the steps needed to accomplish the task may vary. The steps in this task are also based on the assumption that you are copying the files to your OneDrive account. If you wish to save the files to another storage location, navigate to that location in Step 10. To save the files to a USB flash drive, start by inserting the flash drive into an available USB port on your computer.*

1. Sign in to your Microsoft Office account. ***Note:*** *See your instructor if you need help setting up a Microsoft Office account or signing in to your account.*
2. Launch your browser, navigate to the ebook for this textbook, and then open the ebook.
3. Navigate to the ebook page that corresponds to this textbook page.
4. Click the Data Files link or icon in the ebook page.
5. Click the Download button in the top left corner of the OneDrive window (see Figure G.13).

Figure G.13 Download Button

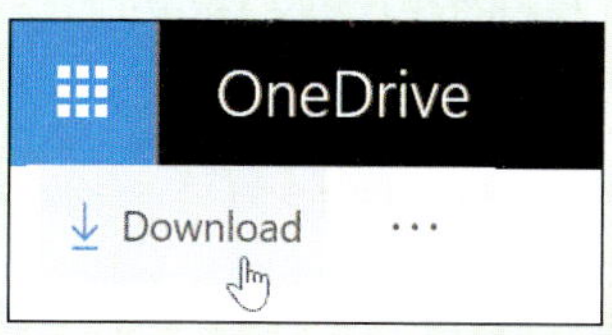

6. Click the ADE-StudentDataFiles.zip button arrow in the Download bar at the bottom of the OneDrive window when the file finishes downloading (see Figure G.14).

Figure G.14 ADE-StudentDataFiles.zip Button Arrow

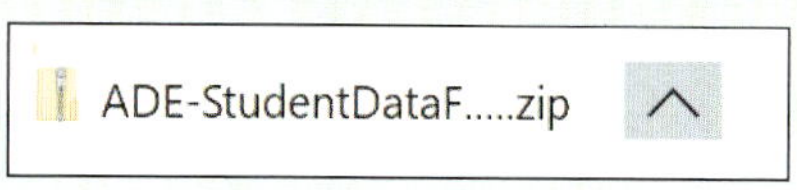

7. Click the *Open* option at the pop-up menu.
8. Select all the folders in the file list pane at the File Explorer window.

Note: *To select multiple folders: click the first folder; press and hold down the Shift key; scroll down, if necessary, and click the last folder; and then release the Shift key.*

9. Click the Home tab and then click the Copy to button in the Organize group (see Figure G.15).

Figure G.15 Copy to Button

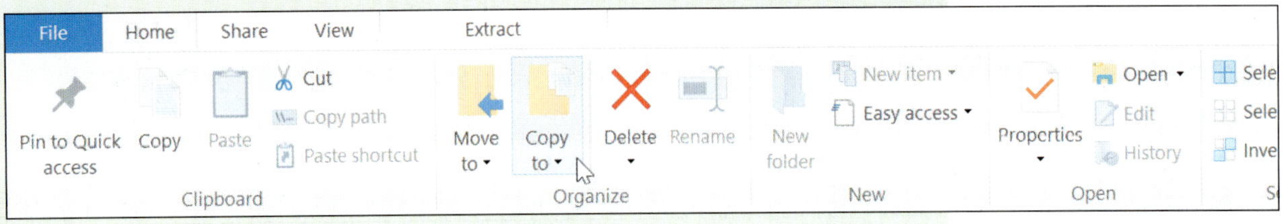

10. Click the *OneDrive* option at the drop-down list. If you do not see *OneDrive* in the list, click the *Choose location* option at the bottom of the list, navigate to your OneDrive folder in the file list box at the Copy Items dialog box, click the *OneDrive* options, and then click the Copy button. ***Note:*** *If you do not find your OneDrive account in the file list box, you may not be signed in to your Microsoft Office account. See your instructor if you need help.*
11. Click the Close button to close the File Explorer window.

Working with AutoSave

When you open a file from OneDrive, the AutoSave feature is automatically turned on. This feature saves your changes as you are working in the file. This is a nice feature to use if you have a strong and stable Internet connection. However, if your Internet connection is slow or unstable, the AutoSave operation may not function smoothly. If you have trouble with this feature, you can turn it off by clicking the AutoSave On button on the Quick Access Toolbar (see Figure G.16).

Figure G.16 AutoSave On Button on the Quick Access Toolbar

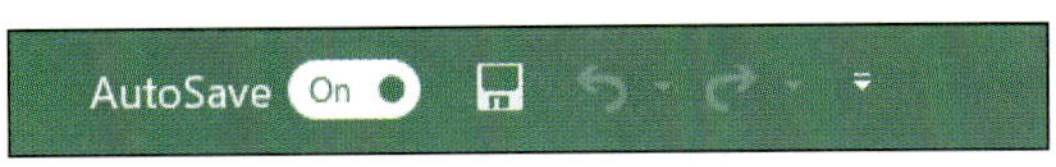

Using Special Features and Add-Ins

Some features are not available in all versions of Excel. For example, the Excel application in Office 365 ProPlus does not have the Maps feature discussed in Section 10.17 of this textbook. It does, however, come with the 3D Maps feature discussed in Sections 10.18 and 10.19. Check with your instructor if your version of Excel does not have a feature covered in a task you have been assigned.

An *add-in* is a file that can be downloaded to add functionality to an Office application. For example, Power Pivot is an add-in that can be downloaded and installed free of charge. Throughout this book, any task that requires the use of an add-in includes instructions for downloading and installing the add-in.

Entering Formulas That Contain Functions

In this book, instructions for entering a formula that contains functions do not include a space after a comma that follows an argument. The Excel interface sometimes shows such a comma and other times does not. For example, you may be instructed to type the formula *=COUNT(A1,A3,A5)*, and the Excel ScreenTip that appears while you enter the formula will show the syntax as *=COUNT(value1, [value2], ...)*.

Excel ignores spaces if you add them. However, the data files and model answer files for this course were built without spaces. In SNAP and in the Excel Compare feature (which your instructor may use to assess your work), if you include spaces, your work will not match the model answer file and could be scored as being incorrect for that reason.

Saving, Printing, and Submitting Your Completed Work

When working in a single chapter, you will generally leave a data file open at the end of one task and continue to work in it at the beginning of the next task. You will be prompted to save your work at the end of each task, and sometimes more often, to ensure that your work is not lost. You will also be instructed to save your work at the end of the final task in which you make changes to the file.

To save paper, you are encouraged to print your work only if your instructor requires it. Generally, you are prompted to print your work only at the end of the last task in which you make changes to a file. If the work you do in a later task will override the work done in the current task, you may be prompted to print the current result as well.

Check with your instructor to find out how to submit your work. Your instructor may ask you to submit hard copies or PDFs, and may ask you to insert your name, class code, and date in the footer of each worksheet, for example.

Preparing an Excel Workbook

Chapter 1

Chapter Goal

To prepare a workbook by entering data, applying formatting, checking spelling, and setting basic print options

Learning Objectives

1.1 Open, save, and close a workbook
1.2 Navigate a workbook
1.3 Change workbook views and use Zoom
1.4 Design and create a new workbook
1.5 Save and name a workbook
1.6 Add and rename worksheets and make a worksheet active
1.7 Enter, edit, copy, move, and delete data
1.8 Use AutoComplete and AutoCorrect
1.9 Wrap text in a cell
1.10 Enter numbers and dates
1.11 Use Auto Fill to copy data and fill data series
1.12 Enter a formula in a cell using the keyboard
1.13 Enter cell references in formulas by pointing
1.14 Use the AutoSum button to sum and average numbers
1.15 Use the fill handle to copy a formula
1.16 Format a worksheet
1.17 Merge and center cells
1.18 Format numbers
1.19 Adjust column width and row height
1.20 Insert and delete a cell, range, row, or column
1.21 Check spelling
1.22 Use Help and the Tell Me feature
1.23 Set basic print options and print a worksheet or workbook

Precheck

Check your understanding of the concepts, features, and skills covered in this chapter by taking the Precheck quiz.

Data Files

Before beginning the chapter work, download the AE1 folder from this page in your ebook to your storage medium and then make AE1 the active folder.

Ebook Links

Access digital resources for this course from your ebook.

SNAP

If you are a SNAP user, go to your SNAP assignments page to complete the Precheck, Tutorials, and Recheck in this chapter.

Preview

On the Job

Scenario WareBot

Jeremy Ronlin is the director of marketing and sales at WareBot, a robotics manufacturer located in Portland, Oregon. Recently, the engineers at WareBot designed a state-of-the-art robot that automates the process of moving and racking pallets in a warehouse. To increase the potential for income from this new product, WareBot has hired additional salespeople and increased the sales department budget. Jeremy has found that he is going to need better tools for monitoring the sales department's budget, payroll (including commissions), and training. He would like you to help him create an Excel workbook that can be used to gather and track budget, payroll, and training data for the department.

Visual Reference: Excel Worksheet Elements

Figure 1.1 Elements of an Excel Worksheet

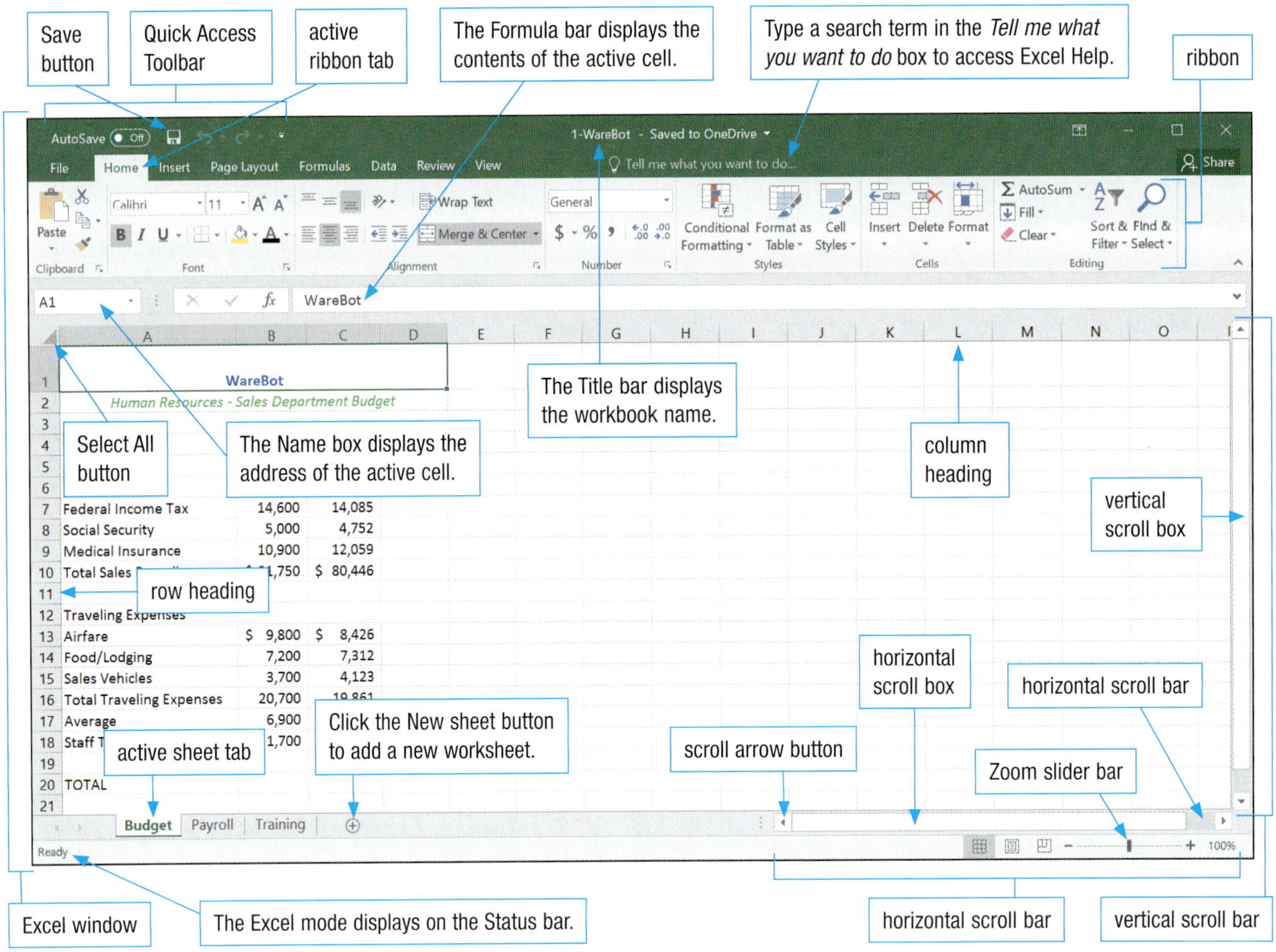

Visual Reference

Tutorial

Opening and Closing a Workbook

1.1 Opening, Saving, and Closing a Workbook

Excel is a spreadsheet application used to organize and analyze numeric and financial data. Many companies use Excel to create financial statements, prepare budgets, track inventory, and analyze data. Excel is often used to answer what-if questions. A **what-if question** asks how a value or set of values impacts results. For example, a company could use the data in an Excel spreadsheet to quickly analyze how increasing employee salaries by 1% versus 3% would impact the company's year-end profit.

Each Excel file is called a **workbook**. An Excel file is opened from the **Excel Start screen**, which displays when Excel is started, or from the Open backstage area. The **backstage area** contains file management options, including Open, Save, Print, and Close. The **Open command** transfers a copy of the workbook to the computer's **RAM (random access memory)**, where data can be read and written, and displays the active worksheet in an **Excel window**, which displays the worksheet on the computer screen. When you are finished working in an Excel file, you should save and then close the workbook. The **Save command** overwrites the original workbook file on the current storage medium, replacing it with the modified workbook file. The **Close command** closes the application window and removes the workbook from the computer's RAM.

▶ Know This about opening a saved workbook

— To open a saved workbook, type *Excel* in the Windows search box, click the *Excel 2016 Desktop app* option at the search results list, click the *Open Other Workbooks* option in the left panel at the Excel Start screen, click the storage location or Browse button in the middle panel at the Open backstage area, navigate to the file, click the file name, and then click the Open button, if necessary. ***Note:*** *Depending on your operating system and storage location, these steps may vary.*

— Saved Excel files are opened from a storage medium, such as a OneDrive account, a USB flash drive, or a hard drive.

▶ Know This about saving a modified workbook

— To save a workbook, click the File tab and then click the *Save* option.

▶ Know This about closing a workbook

— To close a workbook, click the File tab and then click the *Close* option.

— A warning box will display if the workbook has been modified since it was last saved. Click the Save button to save and then close the workbook.

On the Job

Task 1.1 Opening and Closing a Workbook

Jeremy asks you to become familiar with WareBot's sales data by opening and closing his old workbook. This is the workbook that needs to be replaced and redesigned because of the company's growth.

1. Type Excel in the Windows search box and then click the *Excel 2016 Desktop app* option.

   The Excel Start screen displays.

2. Click the *Open Other Workbooks* option.

   The Open backstage area displays (see Figure 1.2).

Figure 1.2 Excel Open Backstage Area

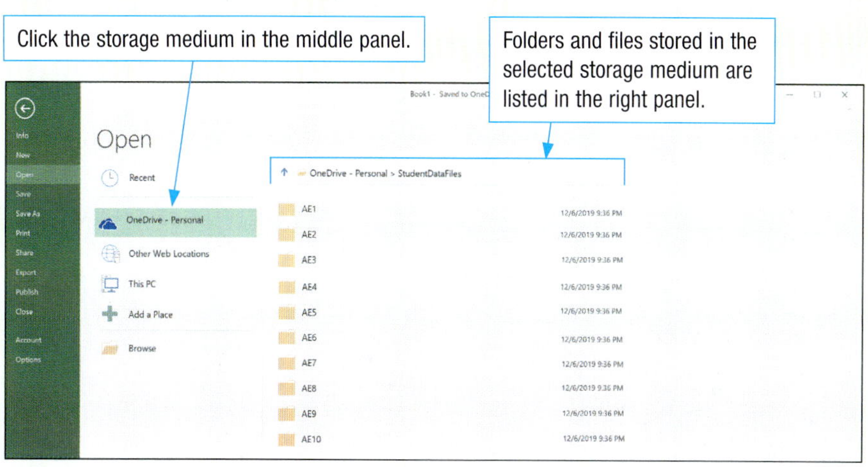

▶ Know More methods for opening a saved workbook

- If you recently opened the same workbook, click its file name in the *Recent* list at the Excel Start screen, or click the *Recent* option in the middle panel at the Open backstage area and then click the file name in the right panel.
- Press Ctrl + O to display the Open dialog box, and then navigate to the file, click the file name, and click the Open button.
- Open File Explorer, navigate to the file, and then double-click the file name.

▶ Know More methods for displaying the Open backstage area

- If Excel is already open, click the File tab and then click the *Open* option in the left panel.
- Use the Open button on the Quick Access Toolbar. If you do not see the Open button on the toolbar, add it by clicking the Customize Quick Access Toolbar button and then clicking the *Open* option.

▶ Know More methods for saving a modified workbook

- Click the Save button on the Quick Access Toolbar.
- Press Ctrl + S.

▶ Know More methods for closing a workbook

- Press Ctrl + W.
- Click the Excel window Close button.

3. Click the storage medium for your data files.

   For example, if you have stored your data files in your OneDrive account, click *OneDrive*.

4. Navigate to the data file **1-WareBot-Old**.

   The data file 1-WareBot-Old is located in the AE1 folder.

5. Click **1-WareBot-Old**.

   The workbook opens and the Sales worksheet appears in the window.

6. Click the File tab.
7. Click the *Close* option.

   The 1-WareBot-Old workbook closes. The Excel application remains open.

1.2 Navigating a Workbook

MOS 1.2.2

Tutorial

Navigating a Workbook

Each workbook contains at least one **worksheet** (also called a *sheet*), which is like a sheet of paper in a notebook. The **worksheet area** is organized into a grid of columns and rows. A **column** is a vertical set of cells, and a **row** is a horizontal set of cells. Each column is identified by a unique **column heading**, which is a letter that appears above the top of the column. Columns are lettered *A* to *Z*, *AA* to *ZZ*, and so on. Each row is identified by a unique **row heading**, which is a number that appears to the left of the row. Rows are numbered *1*, *2*, *3*, and so on.

Data is entered in a **cell**, which is the intersection of a column and a row. The **cell address**, or *cell reference*, is the combination of the column heading letter and the row heading number; for example, *B2* is the cell address for the intersection of column B, row 2. When a cell is the **active cell**, its cell address displays in the **Name box** at the top of the worksheet, the cell is highlighted with a green border, and data can be entered in the cell. You can make a cell active by clicking in it or navigating to it. You can also select a range of cells. A **range** is two or more adjacent cells, and a **range reference** consists of the address of the first cell, a colon, and the address of the last cell. For example, the range A1:A4 includes cells A1, A2, A3, and A4.

A worksheet contains a fixed number of columns and rows. The number of usable cells depends on the amount of RAM available to your computer. Not all worksheet data may be visible in the Excel window. You can **scroll**, or move, the worksheet horizontally or vertically within the window to change what cells are visible on your screen.

▸ **Know This** about navigating to a specific cell

— The active cell is highlighted with a green border.

— The active cell address displays in the Name box (see Figure 1.3 on page 6).

— To navigate to a cell using the Name box, type the cell address in the Name box and then press the Enter key.

— To navigate to a cell using the Go To dialog box, click the Find & Select button in the Editing group on the Home tab, click the *Go To* option at the drop-down list, type the cell address in the *Reference* text box at the Go To dialog box, and then click the OK button (see Figure 1.3).

▸ **Know More** ways to display the Go To dialog box

– Press the F5 function key or press Ctrl + G.

▸ **Know This** about using keyboard shortcuts to navigate to specific cells

— A **keyboard shortcut** is a key or combination of keys that you press to perform an action, issue a command, or access a feature.

— Press Ctrl + Home to navigate to cell A1.

— See Table 1.1 for other keyboard shortcuts you can use to navigate to specific cells in a worksheet.

Table 1.1 Keyboard Shortcuts for Navigating to Specific Cells

Keyboard Shortcut	Destination Cell
Enter	cell in the next row
Ctrl + Enter	active cell
Shift + Enter	cell in the previous row
Ctrl + End	last cell containing data and/or formatting in the worksheet
Home	cell at the beginning of the row
Page Down	first cell in the next page
Page Up	last cell in the preceding page
Tab	one cell to the right
Shift + Tab	one cell to the left
Up Arrow	one cell up
Down Arrow	one cell down
Left Arrow	one cell to the left
Right Arrow	one cell to the right

▸ **Know This** about scrolling a worksheet

— Scrolling does not change which cell is active.

— To shift the display left or right, drag the scroll box in the horizontal scroll bar.

— To shift the display up or down, drag the scroll box in the vertical scroll bar.

— To shift the display one column or one row, click a scroll bar arrow button or press the Right, Left, Up, or Down Arrow key.

— To scroll quickly to the last row, press the End key and then the Down Arrow key.

— To scroll quickly to the last column, press the End key and then the Right Arrow key.

▸ **Know More** ways to scroll in a worksheet

– To scroll up or down, use the **scroll wheel** (located between the left and right mouse buttons).

▸ **Know This** about the Scroll Lock feature

— The **Scroll Lock** feature toggles (switches) the keyboard Arrow keys between scrolling and nonscrolling modes.

— When the Scroll Lock feature is turned on, the Arrow keys scroll the screen without moving the active cell.

— When the Scroll Lock feature is turned off, the Arrow keys move the active cell.

— The Scroll Lock key is used to turn the Scroll Lock feature on and off.

— If your keyboard does not have a Scroll Lock key, click the Windows Start button, click the Settings button, click *Ease of Access*, click *Keyboard* in the left pane, and then click *On-Screen Keyboard* to toggle it on and display a virtual keyboard.

On the Job

Task 1.2 Navigating a Workbook

Jeremy would like you to become familiar with how he tracked warehouse sales data before you design and create a new workbook. Reopen his old WareBot sales data workbook and then use the Name box, Go To dialog box, and scrolling to explore the workbook.

1. Open the data file **1-WareBot-Old**, which you saved and closed at the end of Task 1.1.

   The workbook opens and the Sales worksheet appears in the window.

2. Click in the Name box, type B14, and then press the Enter key (see Figure 1.3).

   Cell B14 is active.

Figure 1.3 Name Box

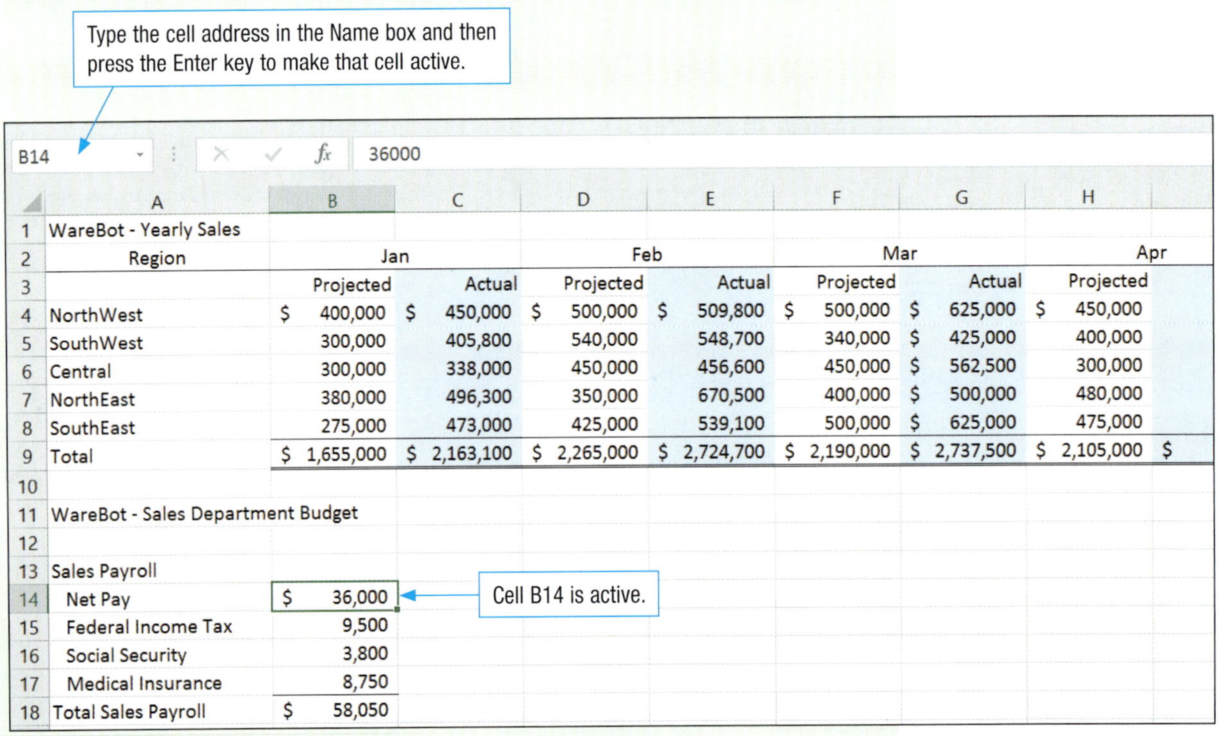

	A	B	C	D	E	F	G	H	
1	WareBot - Yearly Sales								
2	Region	Jan		Feb		Mar		Apr	
3		Projected	Actual	Projected	Actual	Projected	Actual	Projected	
4	NorthWest	$ 400,000	$ 450,000	$ 500,000	$ 509,800	$ 500,000	$ 625,000	$ 450,000	
5	SouthWest	300,000	405,800	540,000	548,700	340,000	$ 425,000	400,000	
6	Central	300,000	338,000	450,000	456,600	450,000	$ 562,500	300,000	
7	NorthEast	380,000	496,300	350,000	670,500	400,000	$ 500,000	480,000	
8	SouthEast	275,000	473,000	425,000	539,100	500,000	$ 625,000	475,000	
9	Total	$ 1,655,000	$ 2,163,100	$ 2,265,000	$ 2,724,700	$ 2,190,000	$ 2,737,500	$ 2,105,000	$
10									
11	WareBot - Sales Department Budget								
12									
13	Sales Payroll								
14	Net Pay	$ 36,000							
15	Federal Income Tax	9,500							
16	Social Security	3,800							
17	Medical Insurance	8,750							
18	Total Sales Payroll	$ 58,050							

3. Click the Find & Select button in the Editing group on the Home tab.

   A drop-down list displays.

4. Click the *Go To* option.

   The Go To dialog box displays.

5. Type A31.

   The text *A31* replaces the highlighted text in the *Reference* text box (see Figure 1.4).

6. Click the OK button.

   The Go To dialog box is removed and cell A31 is active.

7. Press Ctrl + Home.

   Cell A1 is active.

Figure 1.4 Go To Dialog Box

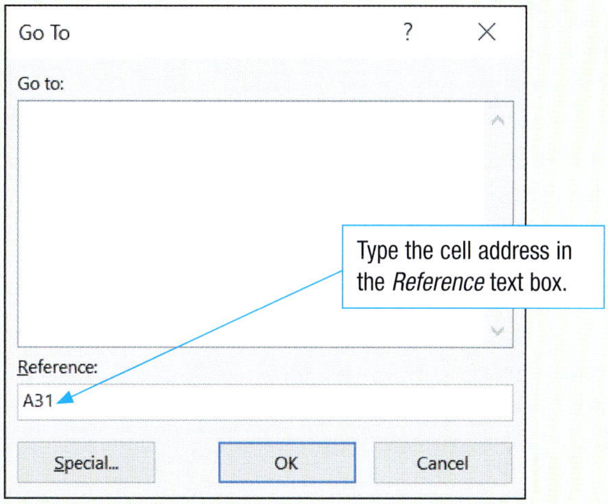

8. Press the Down Arrow key five times.

   The active cell moves down five rows and then cell A6 is active.

9. Press the Right Arrow key five times.

   The active cell moves to the right five columns and then cell F6 is active.

10. Click the down arrow button in the vertical scroll bar (see Figure 1.5).

    The display shifts down one row. Cell F6 is still active.

11. Drag the horizontal scroll box to the right until column Y is visible (see Figure 1.5).

Reminder
Scrolling does not change the active cell.

Figure 1.5 Down Arrow Button in the Vertical Scroll Bar, and the Horizontal Scroll Box

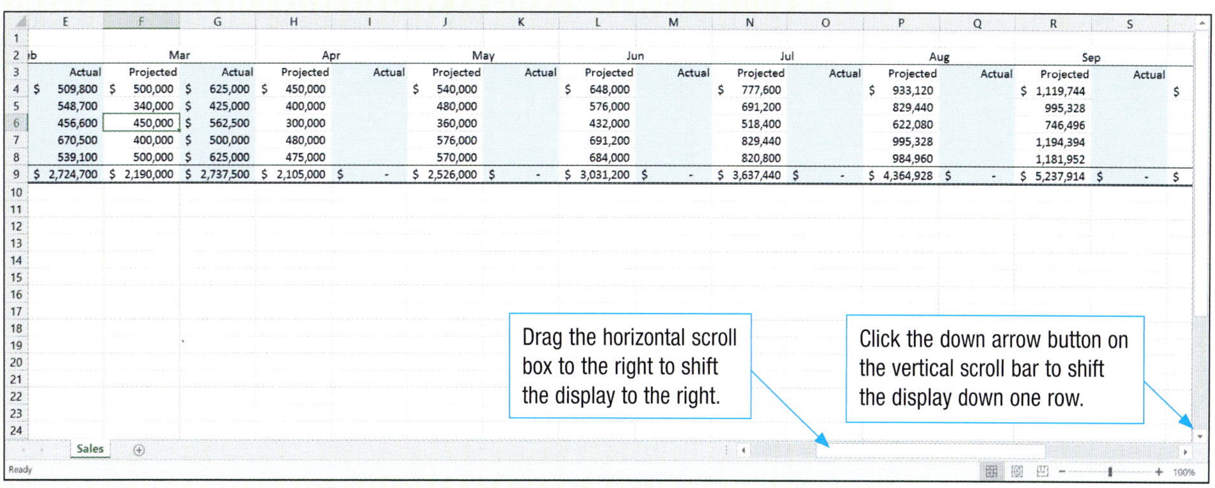

12. Click the up arrow button in the vertical scroll bar.

    The display shifts up one row.

13. Press the Home key.

    Cell A6 is active.

14. Click the Save button on the Quick Access Toolbar.

    The workbook is saved.

15. Leave the workbook open for the next task.

1.3 Changing Workbook Views and Using Zoom

MOS 1.4.4
MOS 1.4.7

Tutorial

Changing Workbook Views and Using Zoom

The **ribbon** is located at the top of the Excel application window and is organized into tabs to help you quickly find the commands you need to complete a task (see Figure 1.1 on page 2). Each **tab** contains buttons and commands that are grouped by type and activity. The View tab contains features that can be used to change how a workbook is viewed on the screen. By default, an Excel workbook is viewed in **Normal view**, which shows the main worksheet area with column and row headings near the columns and rows. Switch to **Page Break Preview** to see where pages will break when the document is printed, or switch to **Page Layout view** to see where pages begin and end and to add headers and footers. Use commands in the Zoom group to **zoom in** to get a close-up view of data at a higher magnification, or to **zoom out** to see more of the worksheet at a lower magnification. View buttons and zoom controls are also available on the **Status bar** at the bottom of the Excel window (see Figures 1.6 and 1.7).

Figure 1.6 View Buttons on the Status Bar

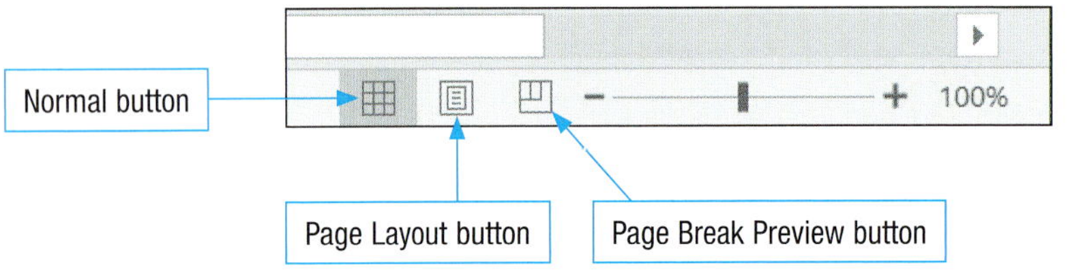

Figure 1.7 Zoom Controls on the Status Bar

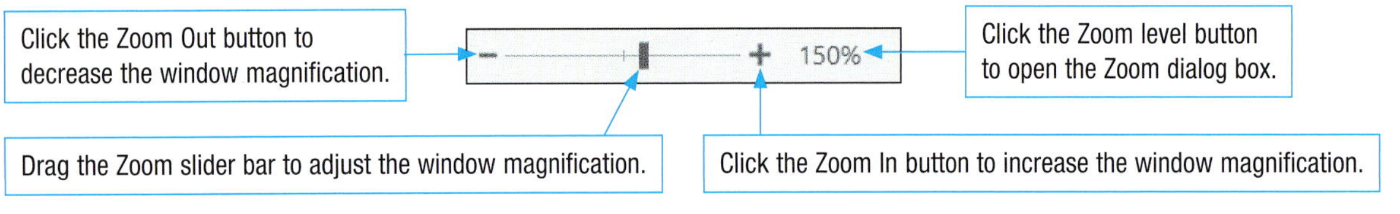

▶ Know This about changing views

— To change the view, click the Normal, Page Break Preview, or Page Layout button in the Workbook Views group on the View tab.

▶ Know This about zoom controls on the View tab

— To change the zoom level, click the Zoom button in the Zoom group on the View tab, click or enter a setting in the *Magnification* section of the Zoom dialog box, and then click the OK button.
— To quickly change the zoom setting to 100%, click the 100% button in the Zoom group on the View tab.
— To zoom in on a selected cell or range, click the Zoom to Selection button.

▶ Know This about zoom controls on the Status bar

— To adjust magnification, drag the Zoom slider bar.
— To decrease magnification, click the Zoom Out button.
— To increase magnification, click the Zoom In button.
— To display the Zoom dialog box, click the Zoom level button.

▶ Know More methods for changing views

– Click the Normal, Page Layout, or Page Break Preview button on the Status bar (see Figure 1.6).

▶ Know More about changing the zoom level

– Changing the zoom level does not affect printing. A worksheet will always print at 100% unless you change the print scaling setting. ***Note:*** *Printing is discussed later in this chapter (in Section 1.23) and in Chapter 4.*

On the Job

Task 1.3 Changing Workbook Views and Using Zoom

With WareBot's business expanding, the sales data is also going to expand. In preparation, Jeremy would like you to experiment with Excel features that make a large workbook easy to navigate. When you are done, close the file.

1. With the 1-WareBot-Old workbook open, click in cell B3.
2. Click the View tab and then click the Page Break Preview button in the Workbook Views group on the View tab.
   The worksheet displays in Page Break Preview view.
3. Click the Page Layout button on the Status bar (see Figure 1.6 on page 8).
   The worksheet displays in Page Layout view.
4. Click the Normal button in the Workbook Views group.
   The worksheet displays in Normal view. ***Note:*** *Dotted lines appear in the worksheet to indicate where the page breaks will appear when the worksheet is printed.*
5. Drag the Zoom slider bar to *150%* (see Figure 1.7 on page 8).
   The window zooms in and displays at 150% magnification.
6. Click the 100% button in the Zoom group (see Figure 1.8).
   The window zooms out and displays at 100% magnification.
7. Click the Zoom to Selection button in the Zoom group (see Figure 1.8).
   The window zooms in on the active cell.
8. Click the Zoom button in the Zoom group (see Figure 1.8).

Figure 1.8 Zoom Group on the View Tab

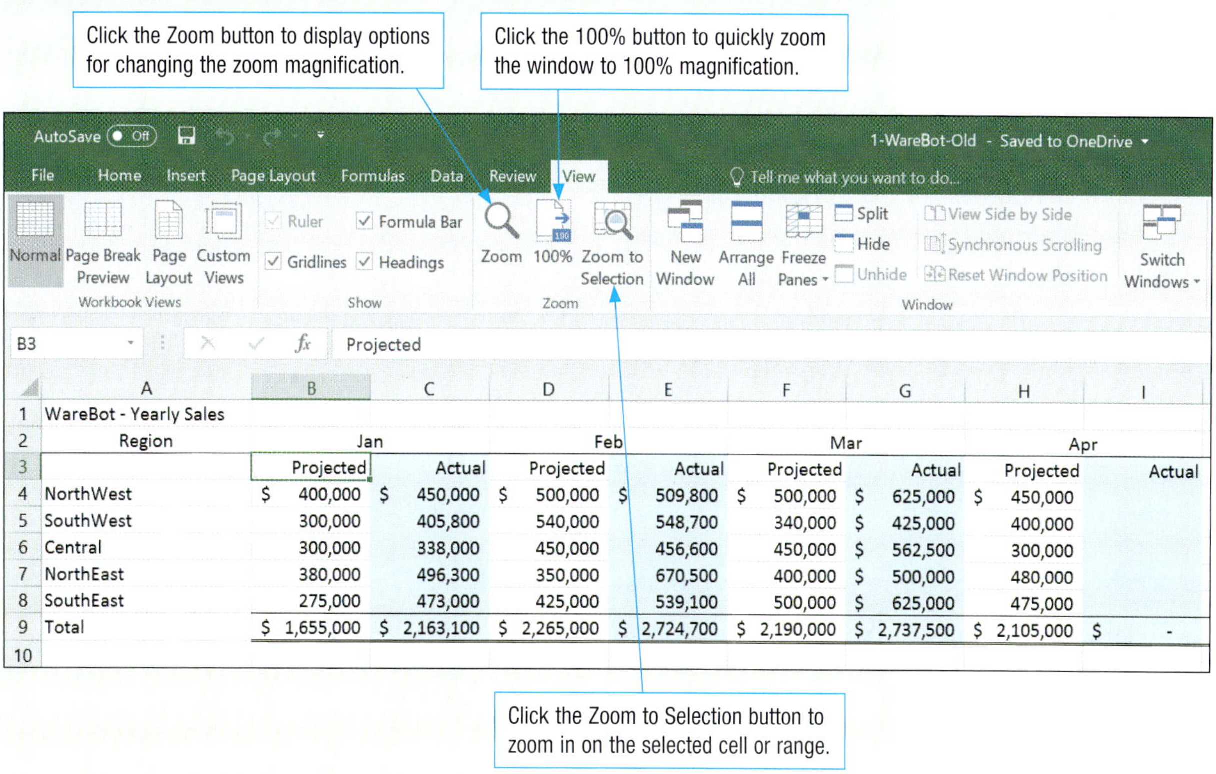

9. Click the *100%* option in the *Magnification* section of the Zoom dialog box and then click the OK button (see Figure 1.9).

   The worksheet magnification is 100%.

Figure 1.9 Zoom Dialog Box

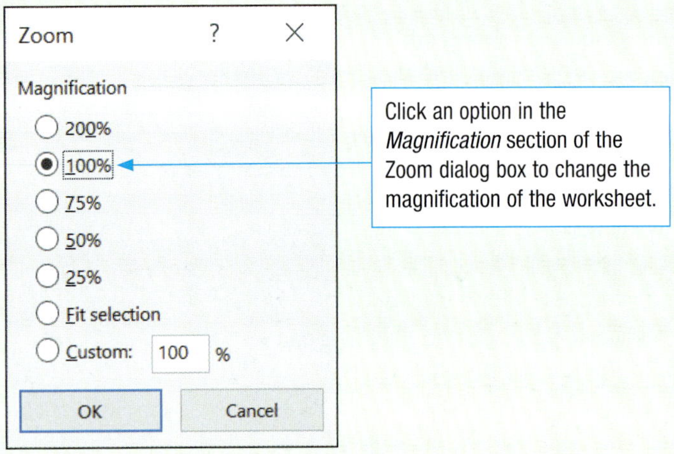

10. Click the Save button on the Quick Access Toolbar.
11. Click the Close button.

    The workbook closes.

1.4 Designing and Creating a New Workbook

MOS 1.1.1

Tutorial

Creating a New, Blank Workbook

A new workbook can be created from a blank workbook or a preformatted template. The **Blank workbook template** displays a workbook with one blank worksheet named *Sheet1*. A **preformatted template** may contain multiple worksheets, including data tables, charts and graphs, and samples.

When designing a workbook from a blank template, consider questions like these:

— What is the purpose of the workbook?

— What data should the workbook produce?

— What is the best way to organize the data in columns and rows? Designing a worksheet so that all the rows have the same types of data (e.g., January sales figures) in the same columns will make it easy to manage and analyze data.

— Should the data be organized on a single worksheet, or would it be better organized on multiple worksheets within a workbook? For example, placing sales figures for different regions in the same relative positions on different worksheets will make it easy to compare data across the worksheets.

▶ Know This about creating a new, blank workbook

— To open a new, blank workbook, type *Excel* in the Windows search box, click the *Excel 2016 Desktop app* option at the search results list, and then click the *Blank workbook* template in the right panel at the Excel Start screen. **Note:** *Depending on your operating system, these steps may vary.*

▶ Know More about creating a new, blank workbook

- If the Excel Start screen does not open when you click the *Blank workbook* template, the feature has been turned off in your version of Excel. To display the Start screen when Excel starts, open an Excel workbook, click the File tab, click the *Options* option, and then click to insert a check mark in the *Show the Start screen when this application starts* check box.
- If you are already working in an Excel file, click the File tab, click the *New* option, and then click the *Blank workbook* template.

On the Job
Task 1.4 Creating a New, Blank Workbook

Jeremy would like you to help create a new, blank Excel workbook. The purpose of the workbook will be to track budget, payroll, and training data for the sales department.

1. Type Excel in the Windows search box and then click the *Excel 2016 Desktop app* option.

    The Excel Start screen displays.

2. Click the *Blank workbook* template (see Figure 1.10).

    A new, blank workbook with one worksheet displays in the Excel window.

3. Leave the workbook open for the next task.

Figure 1.10 Excel Start screen

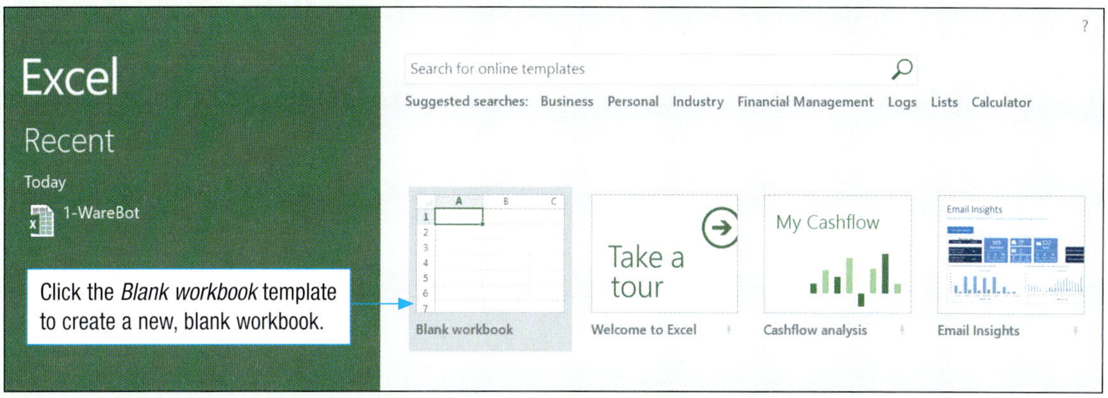

1.5 Saving and Naming a Workbook

Tutorial
Saving a Workbook with a New Name

You can save, or write, a workbook to a folder on an available storage medium, such as your OneDrive account, a USB flash drive, or the computer's hard drive. The middle panel at the Save As backstage area displays the storage locations available for the Microsoft account you are signed in to.

The **Title bar** in a workbook displays the **workbook name**, or *file name*. By default, the name of a new, blank workbook is *Book1* (or *Book2* if you open a second blank workbook, *Book3* for a third blank workbook, etc.). When saving a workbook, replace this default file name with a unique file name that describes the workbook contents.

A workbook file name and **file path** (route for reaching it, including the drive letter and any folder names) can contain up to 255 characters including spaces. Some symbols cannot be used in a file name, including the forward slash (/), back slash (\), greater-than symbol (>), less-than symbol (<), question mark (?), quotation mark ("), colon (:), asterisk (*), and pipe symbol (|). The file name is followed by the **extension** *.xlsx*, which is a set of characters that indicates the file is an Excel workbook.

The first time you save a new workbook, you will need to choose a storage location and name for the file. After you have saved a file the first time, you may open it, edit it, and then save it in the same location with the same name. Each time you do this, the modified file overwrites, or replaces, the original file.

▶ Know This about saving and naming a workbook

— To save an open file to a different location and give the file a new name: click the File tab; click the *Save As* option; click the storage location in the middle panel at the Save As backstage area; navigate to the storage folder in the right panel, if necessary, click in the file name text box at the top of the panel; type the new name; and then click the Save button (see Figure 1.11).

— If the desired storage location is not listed in the middle panel at the File backstage area, click the *Add a Place* option to add other available locations, or click the *Browse* option to display the Save As dialog box.

— To save a modified file at the same location without changing the file name, click the Save button on the Quick Access Toolbar. The modified file will overwrite the original file.

▶ Know More about saving and naming a workbook

– Depending on your version of Excel, the Save As dialog box may open when you navigate to the storage folder at the Save As backstage area.

Figure 1.11 Save As Backstage Area

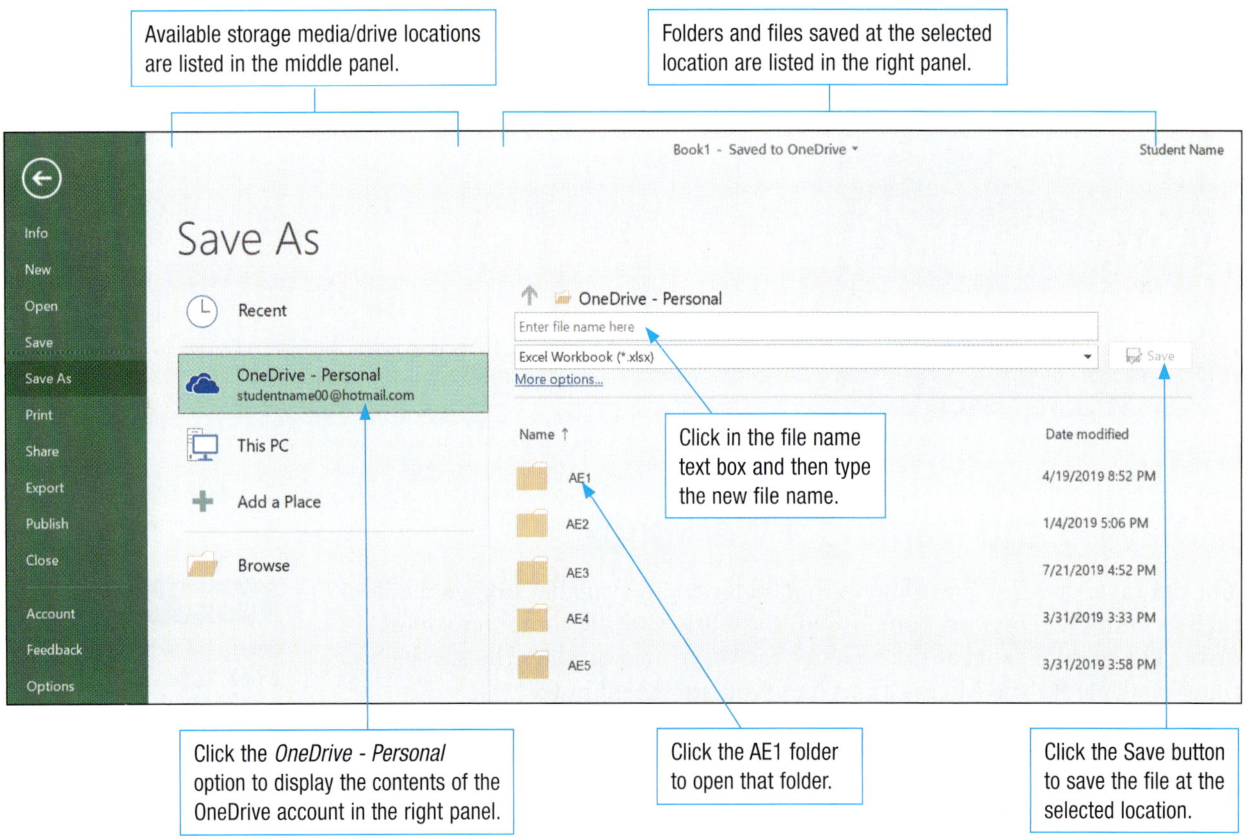

On the Job

Task 1.5 Saving a Workbook with a New Name

Jeremy explains that WareBot requires its Excel workbooks to be saved in a specific drive location and given descriptive names. This makes it easy for the IT department to back up files and for employees to quickly find the data they need. For now, however, he would like you to save the file you are preparing in your own storage location. He will copy it to the WareBot storage location and give it the appropriate file name when it is completed.

Save the workbook you created in Task 1.4 in the AE1 folder on your storage medium, and give it the descriptive name *1-WareBot-Draft*.

1. With the blank workbook you created in Task 1.4 open, click the File tab.

   The File backstage area displays.
2. Click the *Save As* option.

   The Save As backstage area displays.
3. Click the name of your storage medium.

   For example, if you have stored the data files in your OneDrive account, click *OneDrive - Personal*.
4. Click the folder name *AE1*.

   The contents of the AE1 folder display in the right panel.
5. Click in the file name text box and then type 1-WareBot-Draft.
6. Click the Save button.

   The file you created in Task 1.4 is saved in the AE1 folder on your storage medium, with the name 1-WareBot-Draft. The file remains open.

Model Answer

1.6 Adding and Renaming Worksheets and Making a Worksheet Active

MOS 1.1.3
MOS 1.3.2

Tutorial

Adding and Renaming Worksheets

Given the potential size of a worksheet (1,048,576 rows by 16,384 columns), it is possible to arrange a wide variety of data sets in ranges spread throughout a single worksheet. However, you would spend a lot of time scrolling and navigating the worksheet to find the data you want to use. Dividing data among multiple worksheets is often a more efficient way to organize the information. By default, Excel opens a new, blank workbook with just one worksheet, but you can add more as needed.

Excel assigns each new worksheet a name with a number—*Sheet1*, *Sheet2*, and so on. This name displays on the **sheet tab** at the bottom of the worksheet. When a workbook contains multiple worksheets, clicking a sheet tab makes the worksheet active. The **active worksheet** is the worksheet that will be affected by current commands and data entry. Renaming each worksheet with a unique name that identifies its contents will help users determine which sheet tab to click to find the data they need. Figure 1.12 provides examples of sheet tabs with unique names.

Figure 1.12 Sheet Tabs

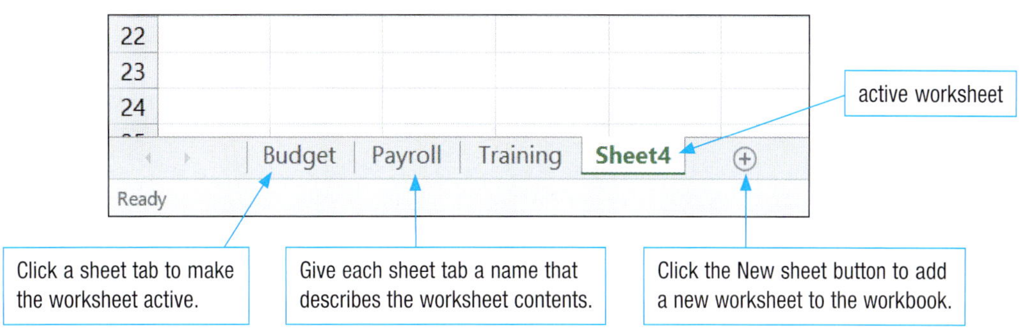

▶ Know This about adding worksheets

— To make a worksheet active, click its sheet tab.

— To add a worksheet to the right of the active worksheet, click the New sheet button on the Status bar.

— To add a worksheet to the left of the active worksheet, click the Insert button arrow in the Cells group on the Home tab and then click the *Insert Sheet* option, or press Shift + F11.

— When you add a new worksheet, Excel gives it a name with a number, such as *Sheet1*.

— Excel does not reuse worksheet numbers in an open workbook. If you create Sheet2 and then delete it before you close the workbook, the next new worksheet will be named *Sheet3*. If you close the workbook after deleting Sheet2, reopen the workbook, and then create a new worksheet, the new worksheet will be named *Sheet2*.

▶ Know More about adding worksheets

– To add multiple worksheets to a workbook that already contains several, press the Shift key, click sheet tabs until you have selected the same number of tabs as the number of worksheets you want to add, click the Insert button arrow, and then click the *Insert Sheet* option. ***Note:*** *A green line displays below each selected tab.*

▶ Know This about renaming worksheets

— To rename a worksheet, right-click the sheet tab, click the *Rename* option at the pop-up menu, type the new name, and then press the Enter key.

▶ Know More methods for renaming a worksheet

– Double-click the sheet tab to select the text on the tab, type the new name to replace the selected text, and then press the Enter key.

– To rename a worksheet, click the Format button in the Cells group on the Home tab, click the *Rename Sheet* option at the drop-down menu, type the new name, and then press the Enter key.

On the Job

Task 1.6 Adding and Renaming Worksheets

The workbook you are creating for Jeremy will track budget, payroll, and training data. To organize the data efficiently, you need three worksheets—one for each area of focus. Add two worksheets to the workbook and then name the worksheets *Budget*, *Payroll*, and *Training* so users can quickly find the data they are looking for.

1. With the 1-WareBot-Draft workbook open and the Sheet1 worksheet active, right-click the Sheet1 sheet tab.

   A pop-up menu displays.

2. Click the *Rename* option (see Figure 1.13).

   The *Sheet1* text on the sheet tab is selected.

Figure 1.13 Sheet Tab Pop-Up Menu

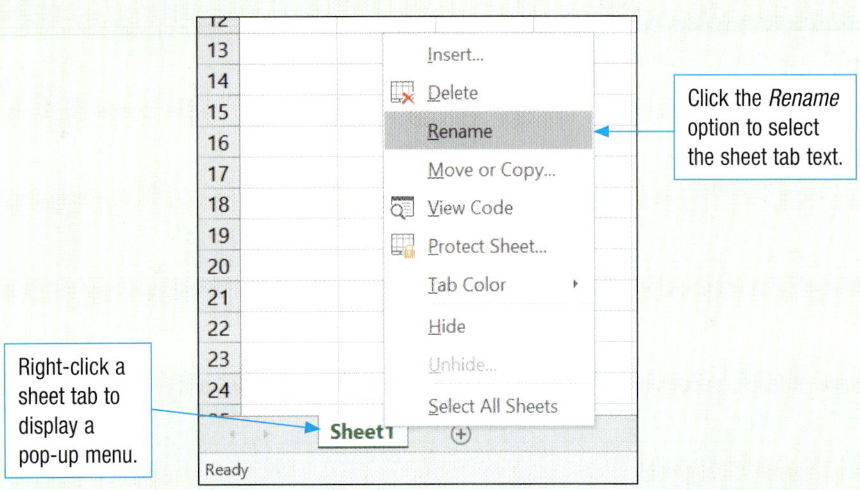

3. Type Budget and then press the Enter key.

   Budget is now the name of the first worksheet. The first worksheet remains active.

4. Click the New sheet button (see Figure 1.12 on page 13).

   Sheet1 is added to the right of the Budget worksheet and is active.

5. Double-click the Sheet1 tab.

   The text *Sheet1* on the sheet tab is selected.

6. Type Training and then press the Enter key.

   Training is now the name of the second worksheet.

7. Click the Insert button arrow in the Cells group on the Home tab.

   A drop-down list displays.

8. Click the *Insert Sheet* option.

   Sheet2 is added to the left of the Training worksheet and is active.

9. Double-click the Sheet2 tab.

   The text *Sheet2* on the sheet tab is selected.

10. Type Payroll and then press the Enter key.

    Payroll is now the name of the third worksheet.

11. Click the Budget tab.

    Budget is the active worksheet and cell A1 is the active cell.

12. Click the Save button on the Quick Access Toolbar.

Model Answer

1.7 Entering, Editing, Copying, Moving, and Deleting Data

MOS 2.1.2

Tutorial

Entering, Editing, and Copying Data

Each cell in an Excel worksheet can hold a single data entry. The **data entry** can be text, a number, a value, a date or time, or a formula that calculates a result. A **text entry** contains any combination of letters, numbers, and symbols. A **numeric entry** includes numbers that can be used in a mathematical operation. A **value entry** contains whole and decimal numbers and can also include a symbol, such as the dollar symbol ($) or percent symbol (%). A **date entry** contains a value in a standard date format, such as *4/1/2019*. A **time entry** contains a value in a standard time entry, such as *1:30:55 PM*.

After entering data, you may find that you need to edit, or change, it. You can edit the contents of a cell directly in the cell or on the **Formula bar** (between the ribbon and the column headings in an Excel worksheet).

If you want to enter similar contents in a different location in the same worksheet or in another worksheet, you can save time by copying the contents. Start by selecting the cell or range containing the contents; Table 1.2 explains how to select different types of ranges. Copy the selected contents by clicking the Copy button in the Clipboard group on the Home tab. Paste the copied contents by selecting the cell or range at the new location and then clicking the Paste button.

Copied items are placed on the **Clipboard**, which is a holding area. When you click the Paste button, the last item copied to the Clipboard is pasted in the active cell or range. You can paste a previously copied item by displaying the Clipboard task pane and then clicking the item at the list in the pane.

By default, the Paste command pastes the copied cell contents and its attributes, including formatting and formulas. To change which attributes are pasted, you can use the Paste button arrow in the Clipboard group on the Home tab before you paste the result, or the Paste Options button that displays below the result after it is pasted. Chapter 5 discusses paste options in detail.

The Delete key or Delete button can be used to delete the contents of an active cell. **Deleting** removes the contents.

Table 1.2 Methods for Selecting Cells and Ranges

Type of Range and Selection Method	Action
a range of adjacent cells using the mouse	Click in the first cell in the range, and hold down the left mouse button, drag into the last cell in the range, and then release the mouse button.
a range of adjacent cells using the keyboard	Click in the first cell in the range, press and hold down the Shift key, press one or more arrow keys in succession to extend the selection through the last cell in the range, and then release both keys.
a large range of cells	Click in the first cell in the range, click in the Name box, click in the last cell in the range or type its cell reference, press and hold down the Shift key, press the Enter key, and then release both keys.
all the cells in a worksheet	Click the Select All button (see Figure 1.1 on page 2) or press Ctrl + A.
nonadjacent cells or ranges	Click in the first cell or select the first range of cells, press and hold down the Ctrl key, click in or select the other cells or ranges, and then release the Ctrl key.
an entire row or column	Click the row or column heading.

▸ Know This about entering data

- To enter data in a cell, first click in the cell to make it active and then type the data.
- When you make a cell active, you place it in **Ready mode**, which means the cell is ready for input. A green border appears around the cell, and the word *Ready* displays at the left end of the Status bar (see Figure 1.1).
- When a cell is active and you start to type, the mode changes to Enter mode. In **Enter mode**, the insertion point is placed in the cell and the word *Ready* changes to *Enter* on the status bar.
- Refer to Table 1.1 on page 5 for keyboard shortcuts for finishing an entry and making a specific cell active.
- Text entries are aligned on the left side of the cell. Value, date, and time entries are aligned on the right side of the cell.
- To enter data on a new line in a cell, insert a manual line break by pressing Alt + Enter.
- If an entry is too long to fit in the cell, the data will overlap into the next cell to the right if that cell is empty. If the cell to the right contains data, number symbols (#####) will appear in the cell. Adjustments for displaying long entries are discussed in Sections 1.9 and 1.19 of this chapter.

▸ Know More about entering data

- The cell that becomes active when you press Enter or Shift + Enter may vary depending on the pattern you are using to enter data. For example, if you enter data in cells B1, C1, and D1, and use the Tab key to move from cell to cell, pressing the Enter key after entering the data in cell D1 will result in cell B2 becoming the active cell (not cell D2), facilitating efficient data entry.
- To change the behavior of the Enter key, click the File tab, click the *Options* option, click the *Advanced* option in the right pane at the Excel Options dialog box, click *the After pressing Enter, move selection Direction* drop-down arrow, and then click a direction.

▶ Know This about editing data

- To edit the contents of a cell directly in the cell, double-click in the cell to make it active and place the insertion point in the cell, and then make the desired changes.
- To edit the contents of a cell on the Formula bar, click in the cell to make it active, click on the Formula bar to place the insertion point on the Formula bar, and then make the desired changes.
- When you place the insertion point in a cell that contains data or on the Formula bar, the Excel mode changes to the Edit mode and the word *Edit* displays on the left side of the Status bar. In **Edit mode**, many commands are unavailable and the arrow keys move the insertion point within the cell (as opposed to moving it from cell to cell).
- To insert a character in Edit mode, click where you want to insert it and then type the new character.
- To delete data one character at a time in Edit mode, use the Backspace and Delete keys.
- To replace a character in Edit mode, select it and then type the new character.
- To exit Edit mode, press the Enter key, Tab key, or F2 function key, or click in another cell.

▶ Know More methods for editing data directly in the cell

- Click in the cell to make it active, press the F2 function key to change to Edit mode and place the insertion point in the cell, and then make the desired changes.

▶ Know This about copying cell or range contents to another location

- To copy cell or range contents to another location, click in the cell or select the range, click the Copy button in the Clipboard group on the Home tab (see Figure 1.14), click in the cell or select the range at the new location, and then click the Paste button.
- When you click the Copy button, a moving dashed line border, called a **marquee**, appears around the copied cell or range (see Figure 1.14). When the marquee is active, you can continuously click the Paste button or press the Enter key to paste the copied cell contents.
- To remove the marquee, perform another action, such as pasting the contents, entering data in another cell, or pressing the Esc key.

▶ Know More methods for copying cell or range contents to another location

- Click in the cell or select the range, press Ctrl + C, click in the cell or select the range at the new location, and then press Ctrl + V.
- Click in the cell or select the range, hover the mouse pointer over the edge of the cell or range until the pointer turns into a four-headed arrow, press and hold down the Ctrl key, and then drag the cell or range to the new location.
- To copy data from one cell into the cell below, click in the cell below and then press Ctrl + D.
- To copy the data from one cell to the cell to the left, click in the cell to the left and then press Ctrl + R.

▶ Know This about moving cell or range contents to another location

- To move cell or range contents to another location, click in the cell or select the range, click the Cut button in the Clipboard group on the Home tab (see Figure 1.14 on page 19), click in the cell or select the range at the new location, and then click the Paste button.
- When you click the Cut button, a marquee appears around the cut cell or range (see Figure 1.14).
- To remove the marquee, perform another action, such as pasting the contents, entering data in another cell, or pressing the Esc key.

▶ Know More methods for moving cell or range contents to another location

- Click in the cell or select the range, press Ctrl + X, click in the cell or select the range at the new location, and then press Ctrl + V.

continues...

▶ Know This about using the Clipboard

- To paste an item previously copied to the Clipboard, click the task pane launcher in the Clipboard group on the Home tab and then click the item in the list at the Clipboard task pane (see Figure 1.15 on page 20).

— The Clipboard is cleared when you save your workbook and exit Excel.
— To close the Clipboard task pane, click the Close button (see Figure 1.15 on page 20).

▸ Know This about deleting the contents of a cell

— To delete the contents of a cell, click in the cell to make it active and then press the Delete key.
— After you delete the contents of a cell, the cell remains active.
— If you accidentally delete the contents of a cell and want to restore it, click the Undo button on the Quick Access Toolbar (see Figure 1.15) or press Ctrl + Z.

On the Job

Task 1.7 Entering, Editing, Moving, and Copying Data

Jeremy would like you to continue to create the Budget worksheet by entering, editing, copying, moving, and deleting data.

1. With the 1-WareBot-Draft workbook open, the Budget worksheet active, and cell A1 active, type WareBot and then press the Enter key.
   Cell A2 is active.
2. Type Human Resources - Sales Department Budget and then press the Enter key.
   Cell A3 is active.
3. Click in cell B4, type Actual, and then press the Tab key.
   Cell C4 is active.
4. Type Projected and then press the Tab key.
   Cell D4 is active.
5. Type Variance and then press the Tab key.
   Cell E4 is active.
6. Type Total and then press Ctrl + Enter.
   Cell E4 is active.
7. Press the Delete key.
   The contents of cell E4 are deleted.
8. Click in cell A6, type Sales, and then press Ctrl + Enter.
   Cell A6 is active.
9. Press the F2 function key, press the spacebar, type Payroll, and then press Ctrl + Enter.
   The text *Sales Payroll* displays in cell A6 and cell A6 is active.
10. Click the task pane launcher in the Clipboard group on the Home tab.
    The Clipboard task pane displays.
11. Click the Cut button.
    A marquee appears around cell A6 and the *Sales Payroll* item displays in the Clipboard.
12. Click in cell A5 and then click the Paste button (see Figure 1.14).
    The text *Sales Payroll* displays in cell A5.

▸ Know More methods for moving cell or range contents to another location *...continued*

– Click in the cell or select the range, hover the mouse pointer over the edge of the cell until the pointer turns into a four-headed arrow, and then drag the cell(s) to the new location.

▸ Know More methods for deleting the contents of a cell

– Click in the cell to make it active, click the Clear button in the Editing group on the Home tab, and then click the *Clear Contents* option.
– Click in the cell to make it active and then press the Delete button in the Cells group.
– Right-click in the cell and then click the *Clear Contents* option.

Figure 1.14 Clipboard Group on the Home Tab

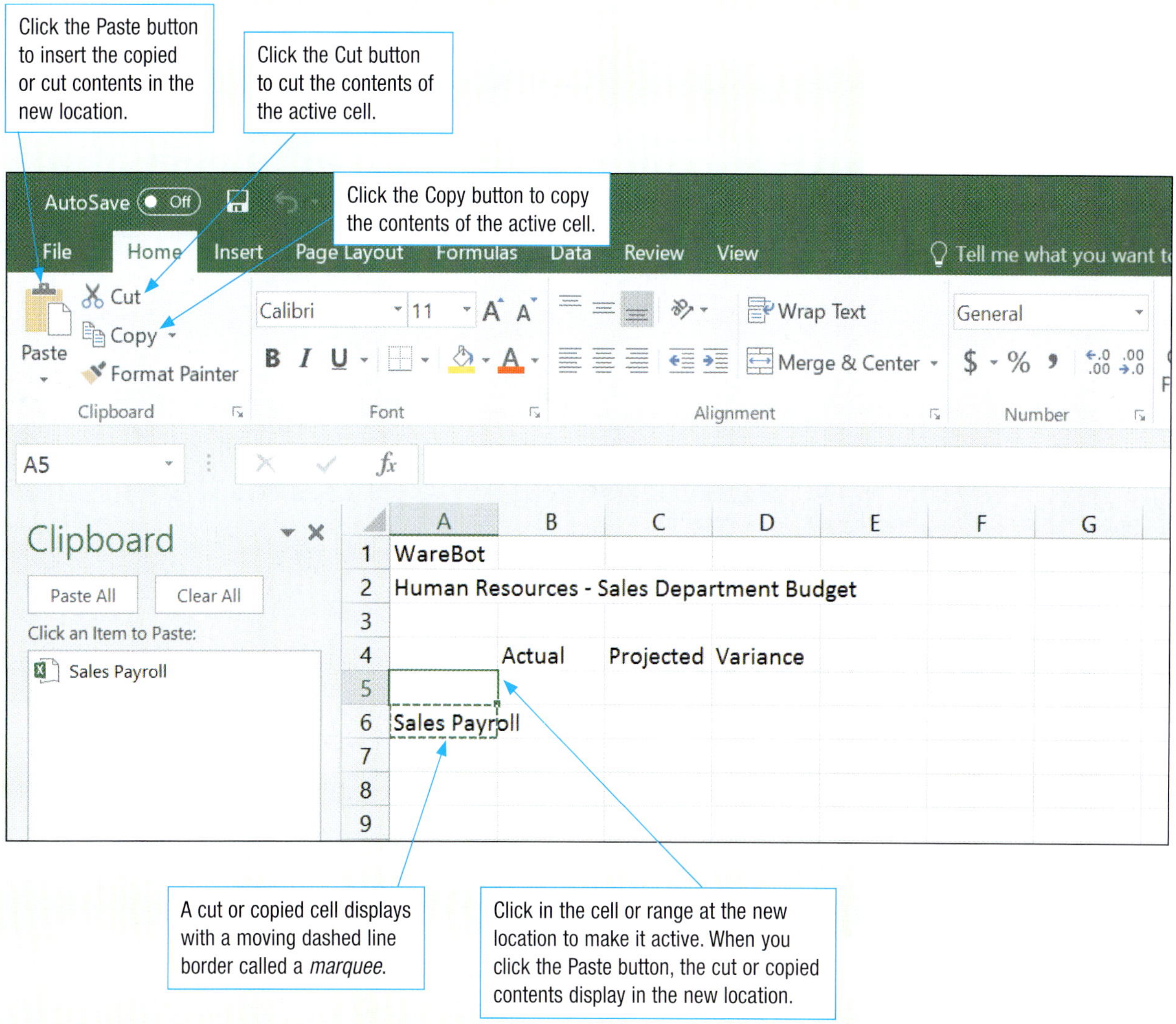

13. Select the range A1:A2.
14. Click the Copy button.

    A marquee appears around the range A1:A2 and the copied contents appear in the Clipboard task pane.

15. Click the Payroll sheet tab.

    The Payroll worksheet is active and cell A1 is active.

16. Click the Paste button.

    The text *WareBot* displays in cell A1, the text *Human Resources - Sales Department Budget* displays in cell A2, and the Paste Options button displays.

16. Click in cell A5 and then click the *Sales Payroll* item in the Clipboard task pane (see Figure 1.15).

    The text *Sales Payroll* displays in cell A5.

17. Click the Undo button on the Quick Access Toolbar (see Figure 1.15).

    The entry in cell A5 is deleted.

Figure 1.15 Clipboard Task Pane and the Undo Button on the Quick Access Toolbar

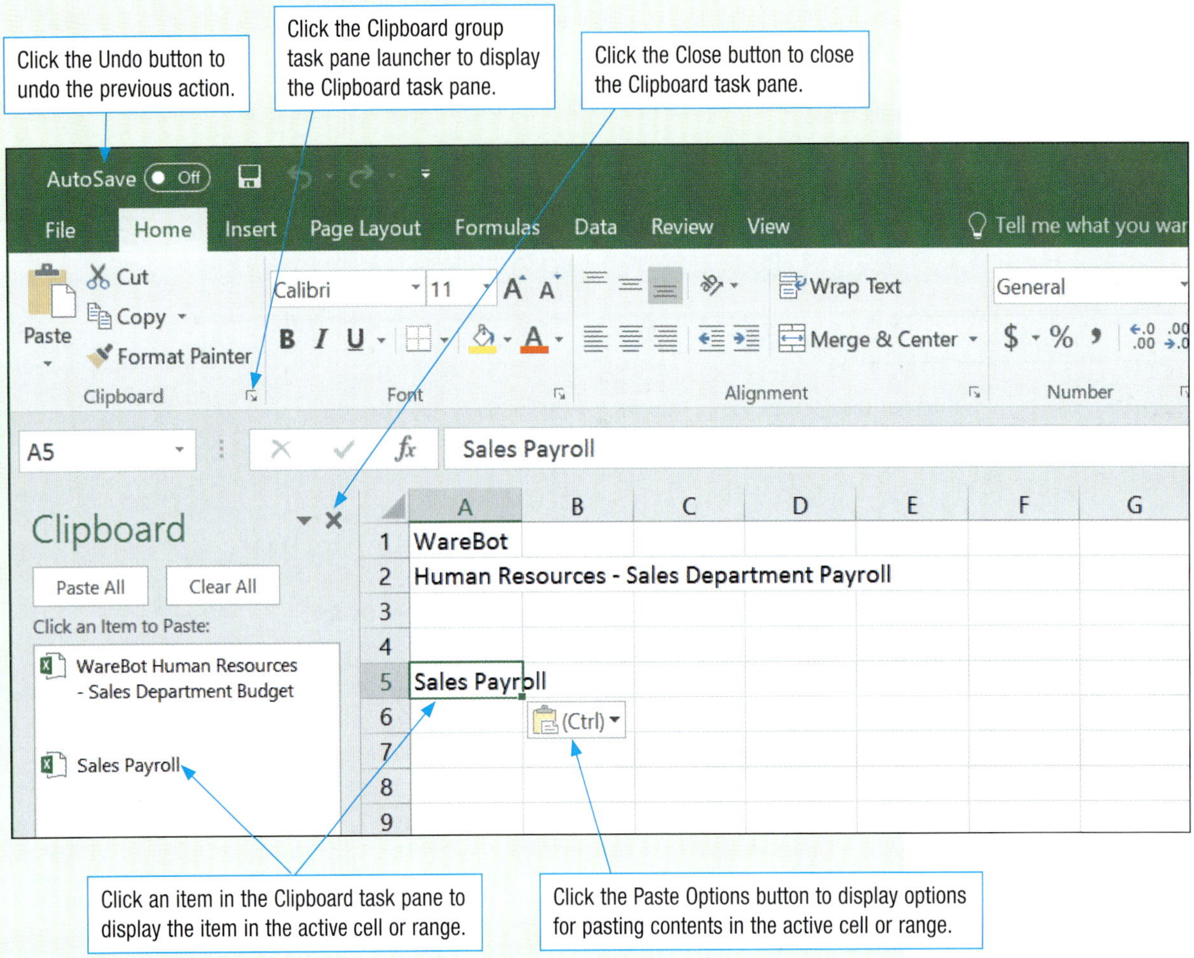

18. Click in cell A2.
19. Double-click the word *Budget* on the Formula bar, type Payroll, and then press the Enter key.
    The text *Human Resources - Sales Department Payroll* displays in cell A2.
20. Click the Budget sheet tab.
    The Budget worksheet is active.
21. Click the Close Clipboard task pane Close button (see Figure 1.15).
    The Clipboard task pane closes.
22. Click the Save button on the Quick Access Toolbar.

Model Answer

1.8 Using AutoComplete and AutoCorrect

The AutoComplete feature automatically inserts data in a cell when you start typing data that begins the same as a previous entry. This feature can save you time if a worksheet contains repetitive data entries. The AutoCorrect feature helps to ensure your text entries are spelled correctly by automatically correcting common typing errors.

Tutorial

Using AutoComplete and AutoCorrect

▶ **Know This** about using AutoComplete

- If the first few characters you type in a cell match an existing entry in that column, Excel automatically enters the remaining characters.
- To accept an AutoComplete entry, press the Enter key or the Tab key.
- To reject the AutoComplete entry and replace the data it added, keep typing.
- To reject the AutoComplete entry and delete the data if added, press the Backspace key.
- The AutoComplete feature only completes entries that contain text or a combination of text and numbers.

▶ **Know This** about using AutoCorrect

- When you make a common typing error, such as *teh* instead of *the*, the AutoCorrect feature automatically corrects the error when you enter the data.
- To see what symbols and words are included in the AutoCorrect feature, click the File tab, click the *Options* option, click *Proofing* in the left panel at the Excel Options dialog box, and then click the AutoCorrect Options button in the right panel (see Figure 1.16).

> ▶ **Know More** about using AutoCorrect
>
> – To add a word to the **exceptions list** (the set of words that AutoCorrect does not change), click the Exceptions button in the AutoCorrect dialog box.

Figure 1.16 AutoCorrect Options

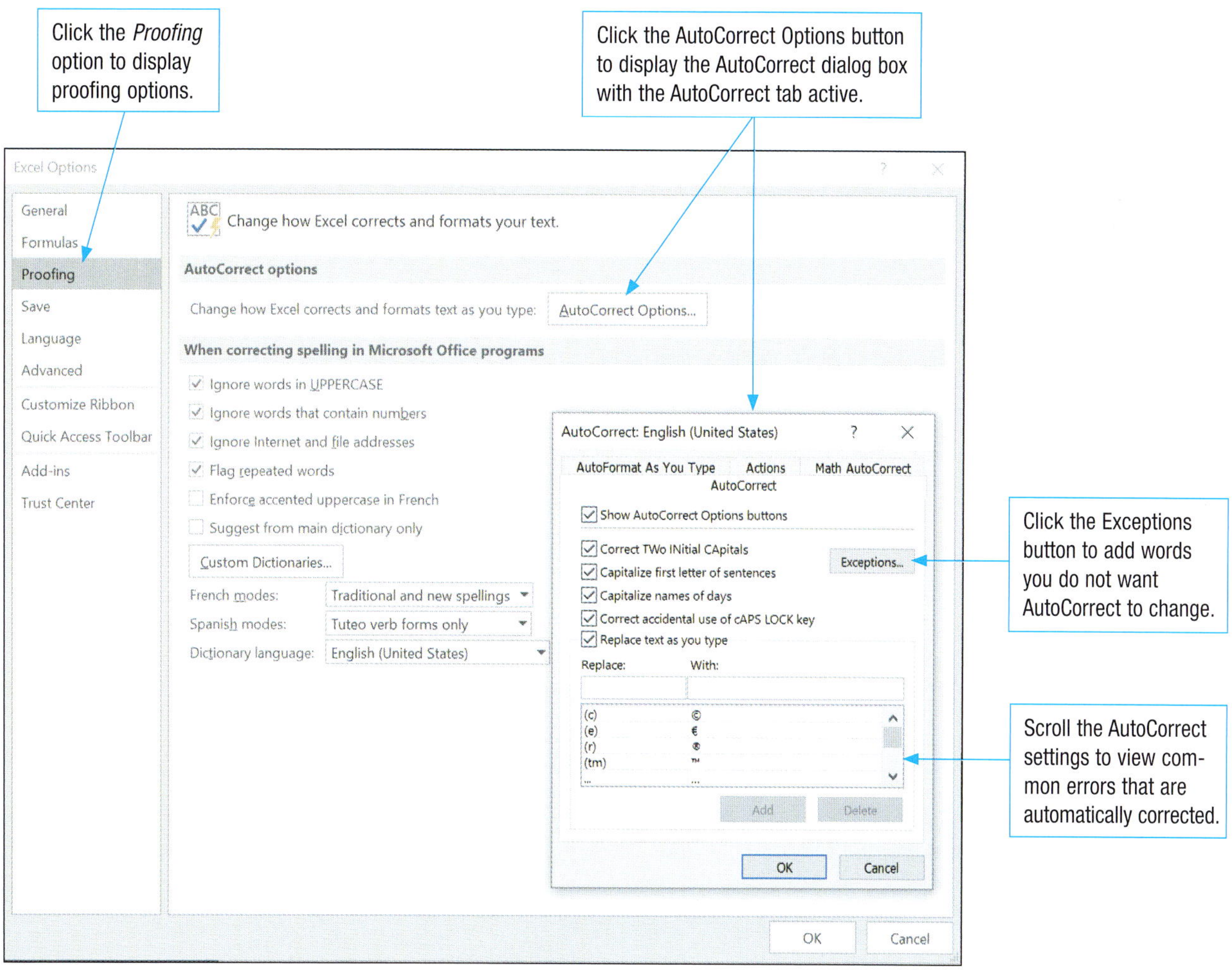

On the Job

Task 1.8 Using AutoComplete and AutoCorrect

Jeremy would like you to make a couple of changes in the Budget worksheet and then turn your draft of the workbook over to him so he can fill in the payroll and training data. Use the AutoComplete and AutoCorrect features to add and edit entries, explore AutoCorrect options, and then close the workbook so Jeremy can review your work and add data to the file.

1. With the 1-WareBot-Draft workbook open, the Budget worksheet active, and cell A1 active, click in cell A6.

   Cell A6 is active.

2. Type the entry Royalty Paymetns exactly as shown and then press the Enter key.

   The AutoCorrect feature corrects the spelling, the text *Royalty Payments* appears in cell A6, and cell A7 is active.

3. Type Overtime Pay and then press the Enter key.

   Cell A8 is active.

4. Type O (see Figure 1.17).

   The AutoComplete feature completes the entry by adding the letters *vertime Pay* and highlights them to show that they are selected.

Figure 1.17 AutoComplete Feature

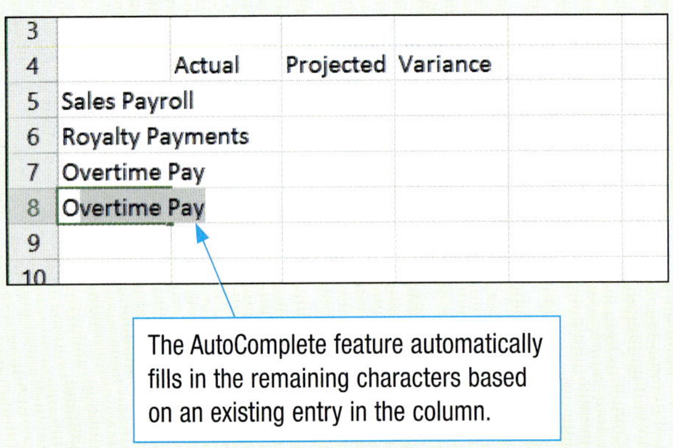

5. Press Ctrl + Enter.

   The AutoComplete entry is accepted, the text *Overtime Pay* appears in cell A8, and cell A8 is active.

6. On the Formula bar, click to the left of the letter *P*.

   The insertion point appears to the left of the letter *P*.

7. Type Premium, press the spacebar, and then press the Enter key.

   The text *Overtime Premium Pay* displays in cell A8, and cell A9 is active.

8. Click the File tab.

   The File Backstage area displays.

9. Click the *Options* option.

   The Excel Options dialog box displays.

10. Click the *Proofing* option in the left panel.
    Proofing options display in the right panel.
11. Click the AutoCorrect Options button in the right panel.
    The AutoCorrect dialog box displays (see Figure 1.16 on page 21).
12. Scroll to view the *Replace* and *With* AutoCorrect entries.
13. Click the OK button.
    The AutoCorrect dialog box disappears.
14. Click the OK button.
    The Excel Options dialog box closes.
15. Click the Save button on the Quick Access Toolbar.
16. If printed work is required by your instructor, print the workbook.
    Printing a workbook is covered in Chapter 4.
17. Click the File tab.
18. Click the *Close* option.
    The workbook closes.

Model Answer

1.9 Wrapping Text in a Cell

MOS 2.2.4

Tutorial

Wrapping Text

You can format a cell so that a text entry wraps automatically to display on multiple lines within the cell width. The **Text Wrap** feature is often applied to column headings that are longer than the longest line of data in the column. Using the Text Wrap feature is better than entering a manual line break (by pressing Alt + Enter) because if the column width changes, the text wrapping will automatically adjust to fit within the new width.

▸ **Know This** about wrapping text in a cell

— To wrap text in active or selected cells, click the Wrap Text button in the Alignment group on the Home tab.

On the Job
Task 1.9 Wrapping Text

Jeremy has edited and added data to the workbook since you completed your draft in Task 1.8. He asks you to open his new version of the file and adjust the formatting of some column headings on the Payroll tab.

1. Open the data file **1-WareBot**.
2. Click the Payroll sheet tab.
   Payroll is the active worksheet.
3. Click in cell D5.
   Cell D5 is active.
4. Click the Wrap Text button in the Alignment group on the Home tab.
   The text wraps in cell D5 (see Figure 1.18).
5. Select the range E5:F5.
   Cells E5 and F5 are selected.

Figure 1.18 Wrap Text Feature

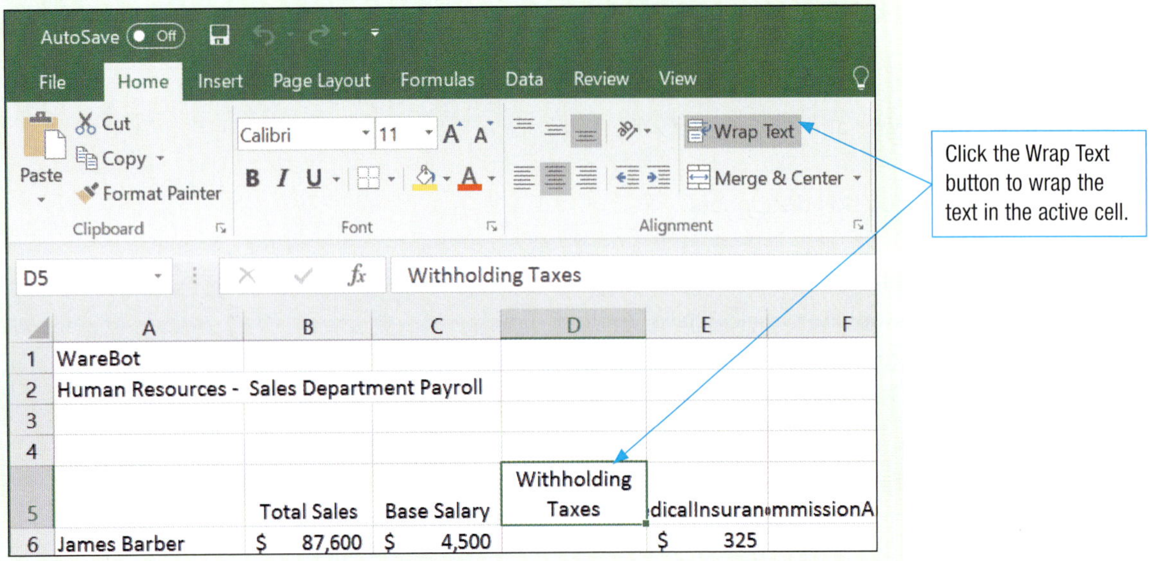

6. Click the Wrap Text button.

   The text wraps in the range E5:F5.

7. Click the Save button on the Quick Access Toolbar.

Model Answer

1.10 Entering Numbers and Dates

Tutorial
Entering Numbers and Dates

Numbers and dates are common data types in Excel workbooks. In this textbook, you will learn Excel techniques and features for entering numbers and dates quickly and accurately.

Numbers can be entered as whole numbers, decimals, or negatives. You can include a currency symbol, such as the dollar symbol ($), or you can include a percent symbol (%), but it is more efficient to apply the Currency or Percent format to the cell after the number has been entered. Excel stores currency values and percentages as decimal values—for example, it stores *$35.50* as *35.5*, and *85.05%* as *85.05*.

Dates are entered using a standard date format, such as *3-3-19* or *March 3, 2019*. Excel displays the entry using the format selected in the Date & Time section of the Windows Settings pane (e.g., *3/3/2019*) or another format (e.g., *3-Mar-2019*), but you can change the format after you finish the entry. Excel stores a date as a serial number that represents the number of days since January 1, 1900. For example, the date *March 3, 2019* converts to the serial number *43527*. This method of storing allows dates to be used in calculations.

Number and date formats are discussed in Section 1.18 in this chapter.

▸ Know This about entering numbers

— To enter a whole number, such as *1050*, type the digits and then press the Enter key.

— To enter a negative number, begin with a minus sign—for example, *-250*.

— When you enter a decimal value, Excel automatically inserts leading zeros and drops trailing zeros. For example, if you type *.55*, the entry displays a *0.55*, and if you type *100.50*, the entry displays as *100.5*.

Reminder
Number entries are aligned on the right side of the cell.

- Excel treats an entry that combines numbers with text characters (such as the phone number *206-555-0117*) as text, not a number.
- To enter a number as a text entry, type an apostrophe (') in front of the number. ***Note:*** *When you do this, an error indicator (a green triangle) displays in the upper left corner of the cell and, when the cell is active, the Error Checking button displays below the bottom right corner of the cell. Error checking is covered in Chapters 2 and 10.*
- When entering numbers, you may find it quicker to use the number pad if your keyboard has one.

▸ Know This about entering dates

- Excel recognizes common date formats, such as *March 3, 2019* and *Mar 3, 2019*.
- To enter a value that Excel will recognize as a date, type a slash (/) or a hyphen (-) after the month and the day—for example, *1-1-19* or *2/2/19*.
- If you do not include the year when entering a date (e.g., *March 3*), Excel automatically adds the current year.

On the Job

Task 1.10 Entering Numbers and Dates

Jeremy would like you to add projected budget data and a payroll date to the sales department workbook. Use whole numbers and a standard date format to enter this data.

1. With the 1-WareBot workbook open and the Payroll worksheet active, click the Budget sheet tab.

   Budget is the active worksheet.

2. Click in cell C6, type 49550, and then press the Enter key.

   Cell C7 is active and *49550* displays in cell C6.

3. Type the following entries in the range C7:C9:

   cell C7 14085
   cell C8 14752
   cell C9 112059

4. Type the following entries in the range C13:C15:

   cell C13 18426
   cell C14 17312
   cell C15 14123

5. Make cell B18 active, type 1700, and then press the Tab key.

   Cell C18 is active and *1700* displays in cell B18.

6. Type 2340 and then press the Enter key.
7. Click the Payroll sheet tab.

   The Payroll worksheet is active.

8. Click in cell H3, type March 19, 2019, and then press Ctrl + Enter.

   The date displays in the format selected in the Date & Time section of the Windows Settings pane for your computer (e.g., *3/19/2019 or 19-Mar-19*), and cell H3 remains active.

9. Click the Save button on the Quick Access Toolbar.

Model Answer

1.11 Using Auto Fill to Copy Data and Fill Data Series

MOS 2.1.4

Tutorial

Using Auto Fill to Fill a Data Series

You can use the **Auto Fill** feature to copy data to adjacent cells or to fill adjacent cells with data and formulas that follow a pattern. When a cell or range is selected, the **fill handle** displays as a small square in the lower right corner of the cell or range (see Figure 1.19). You can drag the fill handle to copy contents and formatting. For example, you can type *Jan* in a cell and then use the Auto Fill feature to enter the rest of the months (*Feb*, *Mar*, *Apr*, and so on). You can also use the **fill series** option to complete a pattern by typing data for the first few cells and then drag the fill handle to continue the pattern. Refer to Table 1.3 for fill series examples. You can even create your own fill series by entering values in two or three cells to establish a pattern.

Auto Fill can also be used to copy formulas and formatting, and to fill series using formulas. Using the fill handle to copy formulas is covered in Section 1.15 of this chapter.

Table 1.3 Examples of Data Fill Series

Data Entered*	Series Filled*
1, 2	3, 4, 5...
10, 20	30, 40, 50...
9:00 AM	10:00 AM, 11:00 AM, 12:00 PM...
Monday	Tuesday, Wednesday, Thursday...
1st Quarter	2nd Quarter, 3rd Quarter, 4th Quarter

*Commas separate data that is entered or displayed in separate cells.

▸ Know This about using Auto Fill to copy data to a range

— To copy data using Auto Fill, select the cell or range containing the data, press Ctrl + Enter, hover the mouse pointer over the fill handle until the pointer turns into a black crosshairs, click and hold down the left mouse button, drag into the last cell in the range you want to fill, and then release the mouse button.

— As you drag the fill handle, a **ScreenTip** (note) displays the entry that will appear in each cell.

— When you have completed the fill, check the result while the cells are still selected. If the fill handle filled a series instead of copying cells, click the Auto Fill Options button and then click the *Copy Cells* option (see Figure 1.19).

▸ Know More methods for using Auto Fill to copy data entered in a cell

– Select the cell or range containing the data and the other cells in the range you want to fill, click the Fill button in the Editing group on the Home tab, and then click the *Down*, *Right*, *Up*, or *Left* option at the drop-down list.

▸ Know This about using Auto Fill to fill a data series

— To fill a series using Auto Fill, enter data establishing the series pattern in the first or second cell (depending on the series), press Ctrl + Enter, hover the mouse pointer over the fill handle until the pointer turns into a black crosshairs, click and hold down the left mouse button, drag into the last cell you want to fill, and then release the mouse button.

— As you drag the fill handle, a ScreenTip displays the entry that will appear in each cell.

— When you have completed the fill, check the result while the cells are still selected. If the fill handle copied data instead of filling a series, click the Auto Fill Options button and then click the *Fill Series* option.

▸ Know More methods for using Auto Fill to fill a data series

– Select the cell or cells containing the data establishing the series pattern and the other cells in the range you want to fill, click the Fill button in the Editing group on the Home tab, and then click the *Fill Series* option at the drop-down list.

On the Job
Task 1.11 Using Auto Fill to Fill a Data Series

Jeremy would like you to enter column headings for the tests in the test groups on the Training tab. Use the Auto Fill feature to quickly enter these column headings.

1. With the 1-WareBot workbook open and the Payroll worksheet active, click the Training sheet tab.

   The Training worksheet is active.

2. Click in cell B5, type Test 1, and then press Ctrl + Enter.

   Cell B5 displays the entry *Test 1* and is active.

3. Drag the fill handle across into cell E5 (see Figure 1.19).

   The ScreenTip *Test 4* displays below cell E5 as you drag across into the cell. When you release the mouse button, the entry *Test 2* displays in cell C5, the entry *Test 3* displays in cell D5, the entry *Test 4* displays in cell E5, the range B5:E5 is selected, and the Auto Fill Options button displays.

Figure 1.19 Fill Handle and ScreenTip

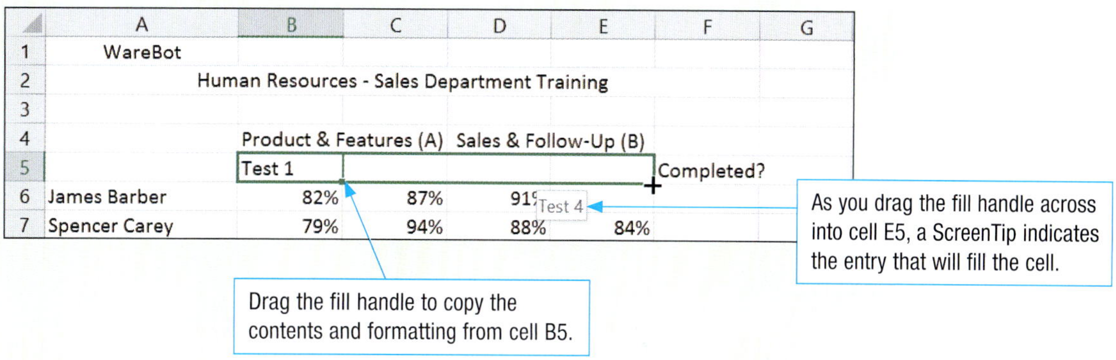

4. Click the Save button on the Quick Access Toolbar.

Model Answer

1.12 Entering a Formula in a Cell Using the Keyboard

Tutorial

Entering a Formula in a Cell Using the Keyboard

A formula is a statement entered in a cell to perform a calculation. A formula always begins with an equals sign (=) and includes arithmetic operators (symbols that specify the types of calculations to perform) and arguments (values, text, and cell references used in the calculations). For example, the formula =1+2 adds the values 1 plus 2 and returns the result 3.

In Excel, if you enter a formula in a cell, the program performs the calculation and displays the result. If a formula includes a value that may change—such as an interest rate in a formula that calculates car payments—it is a good idea to place that value in a separate cell and then use the cell reference in the formula. If the value in the referenced cell is updated, Excel automatically recalculates the value in the cell containing the formula and displays the new result.

▸ Know This about entering a formula in a cell using the keyboard

— To enter a formula in an active cell, first type an equals sign (=) and then type the rest of the formula, including numbers, cell references, and arithmetic operators.

— Column references can be entered as either lowercase or uppercase letters (e.g., *c1* or *C1*); Excel automatically converts lowercase column reference letters to uppercase.

— The result of a formula displays in the cell, and the formula displays on the Formula bar (see Figure 1.20). ***Note:*** *In Figures 1.20 to 1.37, you may see misspellings—for example,* Scial Security *in in cell A8 and and* Ttal Sales *in cell A10. These errors are included in the data file for this chapter. You will fix the spelling errors in Section 1.21.*

Figure 1.20 Display of a Formula and Its Result

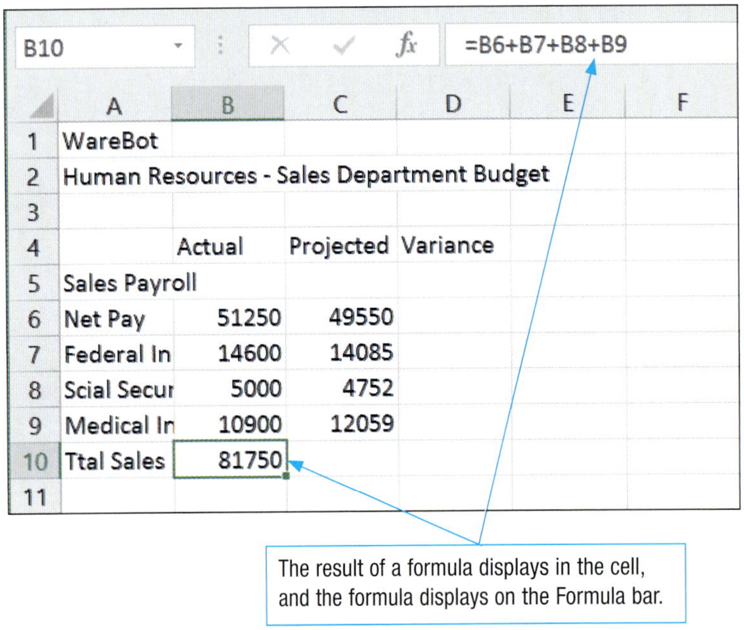

On the Job

Task 1.12 Entering a Formula using the Keyboard

Jeremy would like you to enter a formula to calculate the actual total sales payroll on the Budget worksheet. Use the keyboard and cell references to enter the formula.

1. With the 1-WareBot workbook open and the Training worksheet active, click the Budget sheet tab.

   The Budget worksheet is active.

2. Click in cell B10, type =B6+B7+B8+B9, and then press Ctrl + Enter.

   The result *81750* displays in cell B10 and cell B10 is active, and the formula displays in the Formula bar (see Figure 1.20).

3. Click the Save button on the Quick Access Toolbar.

Model Answer

1.13 Entering Cell References in Formulas by Pointing

Instead of typing a cell reference in a formula while you are typing the formula, you can click in the cell you want to reference. This method of entering cell references, called **pointing**, can be quicker than typing and can also be more accurate because it helps avoid typing errors.

Tutorial
Entering Cell References in Formulas by Pointing

▸ **Know This** about entering a formula using pointing

— To enter a formula using pointing, click in the cell that will contain the formula, type the equals sign (=), click in a cell to add its cell reference to the formula, type a mathematical operator, and then click in another cell to add its cell reference. Continue in this manner until you have entered all the necessary cell references and operators.

— As a formula is entered, each cell that is referenced displays with a different color fill and border, and its cell reference displays with the same color font in the formula (see Figure 1.21).

— The last cell that is referenced also displays with a moving dashed line border (a marquee).

— When you point to a cell to insert its reference, the mode indicator on the Status bar changes from *Enter* to *Point*.

— When you have entered the entire formula, finish the entry by pressing the Enter key to move the active cell to the next row.

Reminder
See Table 1.1 on page 5 for keyboard shortcuts that move the active cell to other locations.

Figure 1.21 Formula Entered Using Pointing

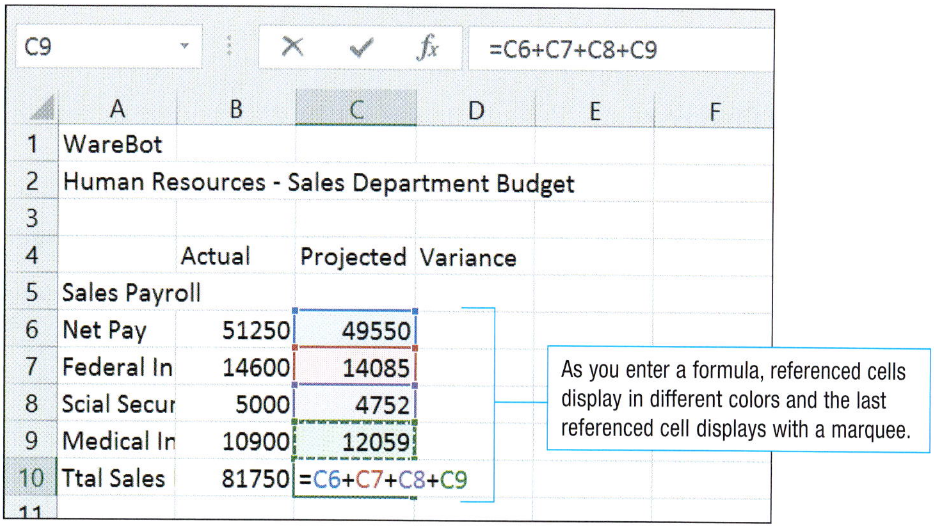

On the Job

Task 1.13 Entering Cell References in Formulas by Pointing

Jeremy would like you to enter a formula to calculate the projected total sales payroll in the Budget worksheet. Use pointing to enter cell references in the formula.

1. With the 1-WareBot workbook open and the Budget worksheet active, click in cell C10.
2. Type the equals sign (=).
3. Click in cell C6.

   The entry =*C6* displays in cell C10, the cell reference *C6* displays in a blue font color, and cell C10 is active. Cell C6 displays with a blue fill and a moving dashed line border (a marquee).
4. Type the plus sign (+).

   The entry =*C6+* displays in cell C10.
5. Click in cell C7.

   The entry =*C6+C7* displays in cell C10. The cell reference *C7* displays in a red font, and cell C7 displays with a red fill and a marquee.
6. Type + and then click in cell C8.

   The entry =*C6+C7+C8* displays in cell C10. The cell reference *C8* displays in a purple font, and cell C8 displays with a purple fill and a marquee.
7. Type + and then click in cell C9.

   The entry =*C6+C7+C8+C9* displays in cell C10. The cell reference *C9* displays in a green font, and cell C9 has a green fill and a marquee (see Figure 1.21 on page 29).
8. Press the Enter key.

   The result *80446* displays in cell C10 and cell C11 is the active cell. The referenced cells display without colors and borders.
9. Click the Save button on the Quick Access Toolbar.

Model Answer

1.14 Using the AutoSum Button to Sum and Average Numbers

Tutorial

Using the AutoSum Button to Sum and Average Numbers

The **AutoSum** feature provides a quick way to enter a function in a formula. A function simplifies the entry of a lengthy and complicated formula by performing a predefined calculation. A function consists of the function name and the arguments used in the calculation. For example, the **SUM function** SUM(A1:A3) adds the contents of cells A1 and A2 and A3, and the **AVERAGE function** AVERAGE(A1:A3) averages the contents of cells A1 and A2 and A3. You can use the AutoSum button in the Editing group on the Home tab to insert commonly used functions (see Figure 1.22).

Figure 1.22 AutoSum Button Drop-Down List

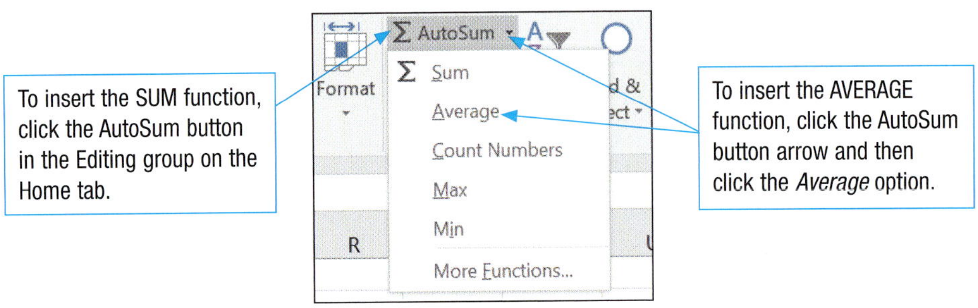

When you use the AutoSum button, Excel examines the surrounding cells and uses an appropriate range as the function's argument. For example, if you use AutoSum to insert the SUM function at the bottom of a column of data, Excel uses the range defined by the column. Always check the range suggested by Excel, and edit it, if necessary, before finishing the function.

To preview the result of an AutoSum function without entering the formula in a cell, select a range of cells and then check the Status bar (see Figure 1.23).

Figure 1.23 Status Bar AutoSum Totals

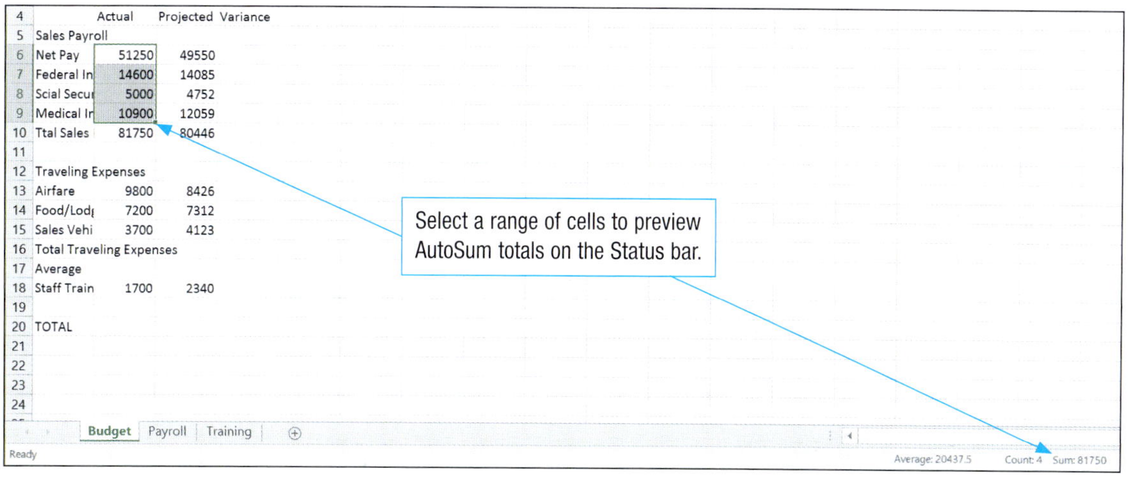

▸ **Know This** about using the AutoSum button to sum numbers

— To insert a function that sums numbers, click in a cell to make it active, click the AutoSum button in the Editing group on the Home tab, check to see whether the suggested range is correct, edit the range, if necessary, and then press the Enter key to accept the range and finish the function.

▸ **Know This** about using the AutoSum button to average numbers

— To insert a function that averages numbers, click the AutoSum button arrow in the Editing group on the Home tab, click the *Average* option at the drop-down list, check to see whether the suggested range is correct, edit the range, if necessary, and then press the Enter key to accept the range and finish the function.

— If the suggested range is not correct, you can either type the correct range or drag to select the correct range and then click the Enter key.

On the Job

Task 1.14 Using the AutoSum Button to Sum and Average Numbers

Jeremy would like you to enter a formula that calculates the actual total traveling expenses in the Budget worksheet. Use the AutoSum feature to enter this formula.

1. With the 1-WareBot workbook open and the Budget worksheet active, click in cell B16.

   Cell B16 is active.

2. Click the AutoSum button in the Editing group on the Home tab.

The formula *=SUM(B13:B15)* displays in cell B16 and the argument is selected (see Figure 1.24).

Figure 1.24 Function Inserted Using the AutoSum Feature

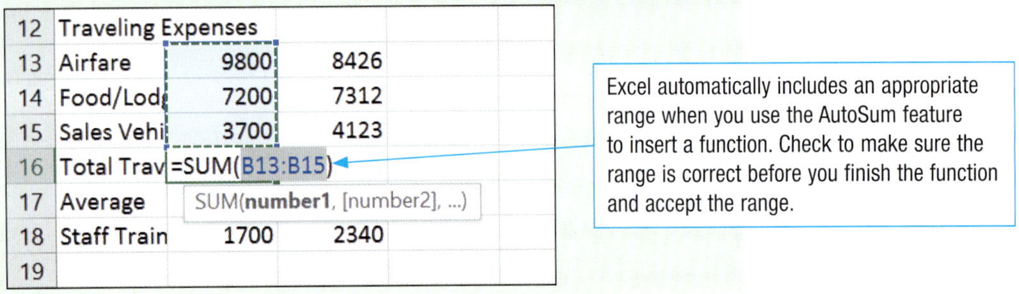

3. Press the Enter key.

The result *20700* displays in cell B16. Cell B17 is active.

4. Click the AutoSum button arrow.

A drop-down list displays.

5. Click the *Average* option.

The formula *=AVERAGE(B13:B16)* displays in cell B17 and the argument is selected. ***Note:** The range in this formula is incorrect; B16 should not be included in the range.*

6. Drag to select the correct range, B13:B15.

The formula *=AVERAGE(B13:B15)* displays in cell B17.

7. Press the Enter key.

The result *6900* displays in cell B17. Cell B18 is active.

8. Click the Save button on the Quick Access Toolbar.

Model Answer

1.15 Using the Fill Handle to Copy a Formula

Tutorial

Using the Fill Handle to Copy a Formula

The fill handle can be used to quickly copy a formula into adjacent cells. By default, cell references, such as *B13*, are relative. A relative cell reference will change if you copy a formula. For example, if you use the fill handle to copy the formula =SUM(B13:B15) to the next cell to the right, the formula will adjust to =SUM(C13:C15) in the new location (see Figure 1.25).

Figure 1.25 Copying a Formula Using the Fill Handle

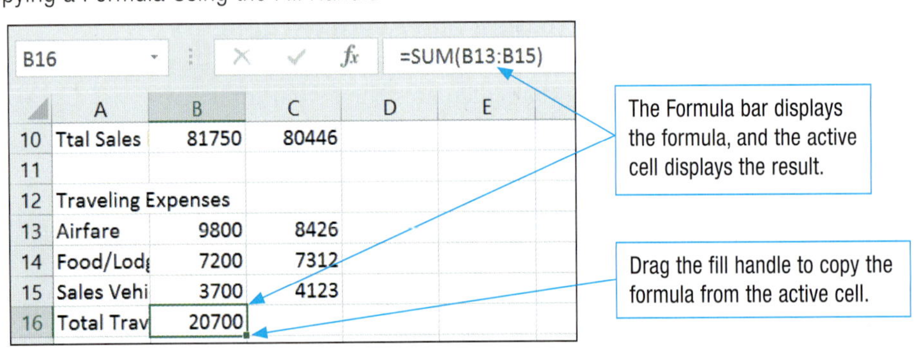

▸ Know This about using the fill handle to copy a formula

— To copy a formula using the fill handle, click in the cell containing the formula and then drag the fill handle through the adjacent cells you want to fill, ending in the last cell in the range.

— Click in any cell outside the selected range to deselect the range.

Figure 1.26 Copying a Formula by Double-Clicking the Fill Handle

5		Total Sales	Base Salary	Withholding Taxes	M In
6	James Barber	$ 87,600	$ 4,500	$ 900	$
7	Spencer Carey	94,550	4,700	$ 940	
8	Bridget Coleman	109,950	4,900	$ 980	
9	Sasha Gibson	74,200	4,650	$ 930	
10	Sam Hall	125,400	5,000	$ 1,000	
11	Adam Howard	102,010	4,750	$ 950	
12	Jarid Khalil	122,200	5,000	$ 1,000	
13	Juanita Marquez	89,700	4,600	$ 920	
14	Andrew McNiel	72,650	4,400	$ 880	
15	Natalia Pena	131,600	4,950	$ 990	
16					
17					

Double-click the fill handle to copy the formula in cell C6 down the column. The formula automatically copies to row 15—the last row containing data in the column to the left.

▸ Know More methods for using the fill handle to copy a formula

– To copy a formula down the column to the right of a column of data, click in the cell containing the formula and then double-click the fill handle. The formula will copy down to the last row containing data in the column to the left. ***Note:*** *This method works only if the column to the left of the formula contains data (see Figure 1.26).*

On the Job

Task 1.15 Using the Fill Handle to Copy a Formula

Jeremy would like you to enter a formula to calculate the projected total traveling expenses in the Budget worksheet. In Task 1.14, you used the AutoSum feature to insert a function that calculates the actual expenses in the *Actual* column. Use the fill handle to copy that function across to the *Projected* column.

1. With the 1-WareBot workbook open and the Budget worksheet active, click in cell B16.
2. Drag the fill handle across into cell C16.

   A solid green border appears around the range B16:C16.
3. Release the fill handle.

   The entry *19861* displays in cell C16 and the formula *=SUM(B13:15)* displays in the Formula bar.
4. Press the Enter key.

   Cell B16 is highlighted and the formula *=SUM(C13:C15)* displays in the Formula bar.
5. Click in cell B17.

   Cell B17 is active.
6. Drag the fill handle across into cell C17.

   A solid green border appears around the range B17:C17.
7. Release the fill handle.

   The entry *6620.333* displays in cell B17 and the formula *=AVERAGE(B13:15)* displays in the Formula bar.

8. Press the Enter key.
   Cell B17 is highlighted and the formula *=AVERAGE(C13:C15)* displays in the Formula bar.
9. Click cell B20.
   Cell B20 is active.
10. Click the Save button on the Quick Access Toolbar.

Model Answer

1.16 Formatting a Worksheet

Tutorial
Applying Text Formatting and Changing the Font Color

Formatting can be applied to cells to clarify the meaning of the data and to improve the readability of a worksheet both on the screen and on paper. For example, bold formatting can be used to differentiate the header at the top of a column from the data below the header. Commands in the Font group on the Home tab (see Figure 1.27) can be used to apply text formatting (such as bold, italic, and underlining), add borders, change the color of the background or text in a cell, and change the font and font size. These commands are also available on the **Mini toolbar**, which appears when you right-click in an active cell or range and contains buttons for common formatting options (see Figure 1.28).

Figure 1.27 Font Group on the Home Tab

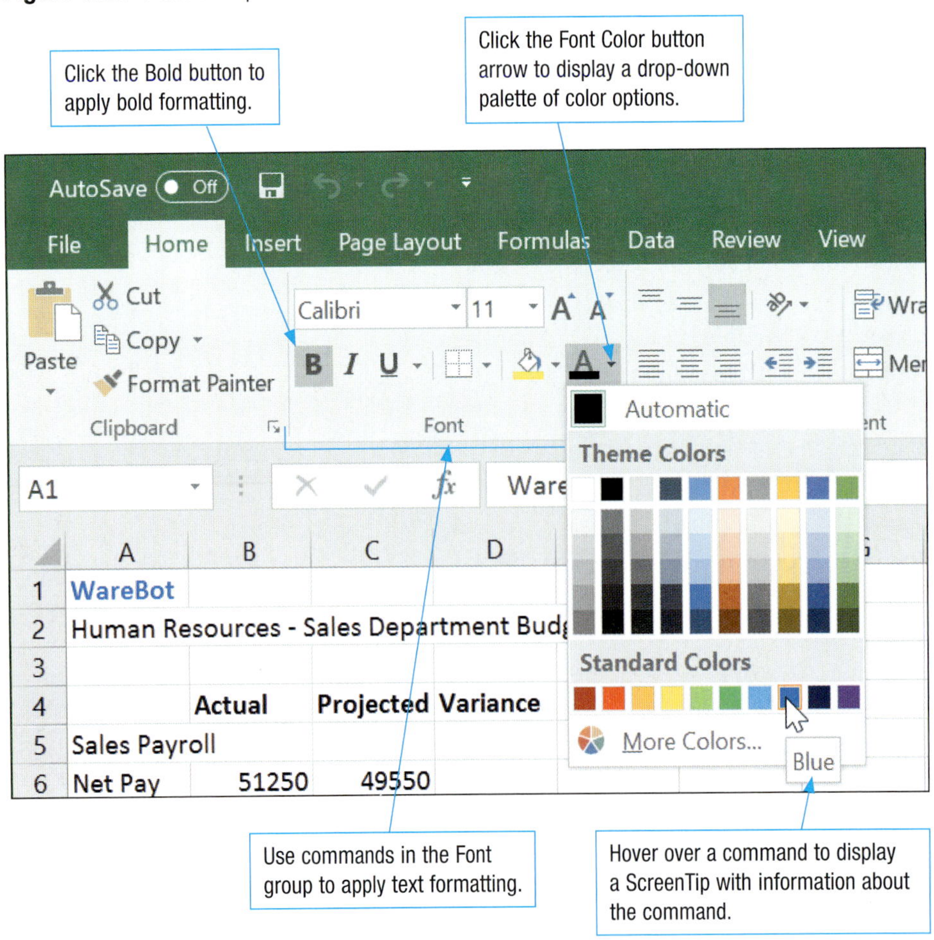

▶ Know This about applying text formatting and changing the font color

— To apply text formatting to selected cells, click the Bold, Italic, or Underline button in the Font group on the Home tab.

— To change the font color of selected cells, click the Font Color button arrow and then click a color option at the drop-down palette.

Figure 1.28 Mini Toolbar

Right-click in an active cell or range to display the Mini toolbar, which contains options for formatting the cell or range.

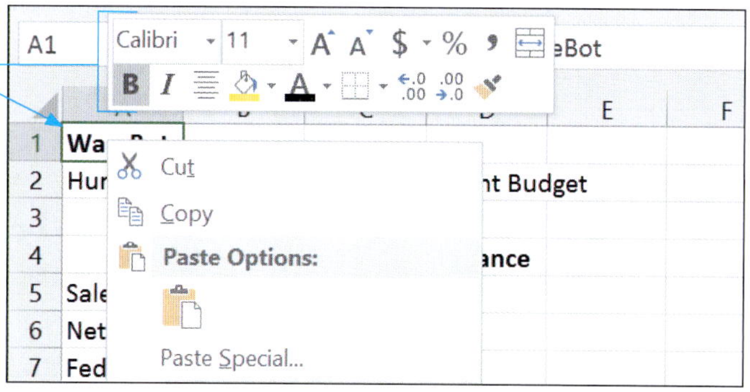

▶ **Know More** ways to apply formatting to selected cells

– Right-click in the cells and then click the command on the Mini toolbar (see Figure 1.28).

– To apply bold formatting, press Ctrl + B.

– To apply italic formatting, press Ctrl + I.

On the Job

Task 1.16 Applying Text Formatting and Changing the Font Color

Jeremy asks you to improve the readability of the Budget worksheet. Use text formatting and font colors to make the worksheet title and subtitle and the column headings stand out.

1. With the 1-WareBot workbook open and the Budget worksheet active, click in cell A1.
2. Click the Bold button in the Font group on the Home tab.

   The text in cell A1 is bold.
3. With cell A1 still active, click the Font Color button arrow.

   A drop-down palette displays.
4. Click the *Blue* option (eighth option in the *Standard Colors* section) (see Figure 1.27 on page 34).

   The text in cell A1 is blue.
5. Click in cell A2.
6. Click the Italic button.

   The text in cell A2 is italic.
7. With cell A2 still active, click the Font Color button arrow.

   A drop-down list displays.
8. Click the *Green* option (sixth option in the *Standard Colors* section).

   The text in cell A2 is green.
9. Select the range B4:D4.
10. Click the Bold button.

    The text in cells B4 through D4 is bold.
11. Click the Save button on the Quick Access Toolbar.

Model Answer

1.17 Merging and Centering Cells

MOS 2.2.1

Tutorial

Merging and Centering Cells

You can use the Merge & Center feature to **merge**, or combine, selected cells into a single cell and center text across the combined cell. This feature is often used to center a title or label across multiple columns (see Figure 1.29). Alternatively, you can use options at the Merge & Center drop-down list to merge cells without centering text, to merge selected cells, and to restore merged cells.

Figure 1.29 Results of Applying Different Merge Options

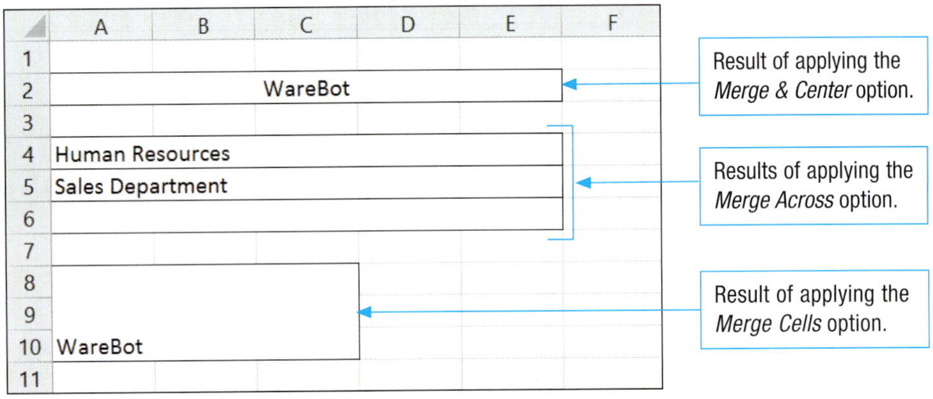

▸ Know This about merging and centering cells

— To merge and center cells, select two or more adjacent cells and then click the Merge & Center button in the Alignment group on the Home tab.

— When you merge cells, the contents of only one merged cell (the upper left cell) appear in the merged cell. The contents of the other merged cells are deleted.

— To merge cells across selected rows, select the cells, click the Merge & Center button arrow, and then click the *Merge Across* option. Note that if multiple rows are selected, the rows are not merged when this option is applied (see Figure 1.29).

— To merge multiple cells into one cell, select the cells, click the Merge & Center button arrow, and then click the *Merge Cells* option (see Figure 1.29).

— To unmerge a cell, select the cell, click the Merge & Center button arrow, and then click the *Unmerge Cells* option.

On the Job

Task 1.17 Merging and Centering Cells

Jeremy likes the changes you made in Task 1.16 to improve the readability of the Budget worksheet, but he suggests making it clearer that the title and subtitle apply to all the data in the worksheet. Use the Merge & Center feature to center the title and subtitle across all the columns containing data.

1. With the 1-WareBot workbook open and the Budget worksheet active, select the range A1:D1.

2. Click the Merge & Center button in the Alignment group on the Home tab.

   Cells A1 through D1 are combined to form a single cell, and the text from cell A1 is centered in the combined cell (see Figure 1.29 on page 36).

Figure 1.30 Merge & Center Feature

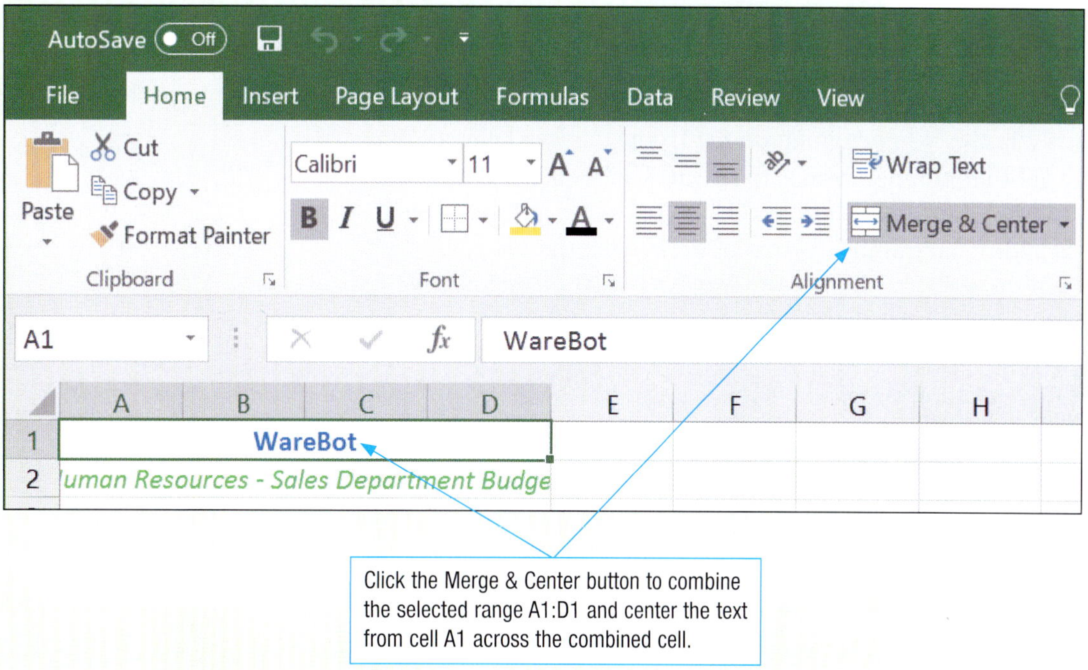

3. Select the range A2:D2.
4. Click the Merge & Center button.

   Cells A2 through D2 are combined to form a single cell, and the text from cell A2 is centered in the combined cell. ***Note:** The text in cell A2 does not fit in the cell. This will be adjusted in Task 1.19.*

5. Select the range A3:D3.
6. Click the Merge & Center button arrow.

   A drop-down list displays.

7. Click the *Merge Cells* option.

   Cells A3 through D3 are combined to form a single blank cell.

8. Select the range A5:D5.
9. Press and hold down the Ctrl key, and then select the range A12:D12.
10. Click the Merge & Center button arrow.

    A drop-down list displays.

11. Click the *Merge Across* option.

    Cells A5 through D5 are combined to form a single cell (cell A5) and cells A12 though D12 are also combined to form a single cell (cell A12).

12. Click the Save button on the Quick Access Toolbar.

Model Answer

1.18 Formatting Numbers

When you type an entry in a cell, the data is automatically assigned the General format. The **General format** usually displays numbers exactly as they are typed. You can apply different number formats to add dollar symbols, commas, and other characters to the cells. Some number formats, such as Accounting format, affect the alignment of the number in the cell. Applying a new format changes the display of an entry but not the actual number entered.

Tutorial

Formatting Numbers

▸ Know This about formatting numbers

— To apply the Accounting, Percent, or Comma format to selected cells, click the Accounting Number Format, Percent Style, or Comma Style button, respectively, in the Number group on the Home tab (see Figure 1.31).

— To apply another number format to selected cells, click the *Number Format* option box arrow and then click an option at the drop-down list.

— To access additional number format options, click the *More Number Formats* option at the bottom of the *Number Format* drop-down list to display the Format Cells dialog box.

— Refer to Table 1.4 for descriptions of available number formats.

Table 1.4 Number Formats

Number Format	Result When Format Is Applied
General	a number with no special formatting
Number	a number with two digits after the decimal point
Currency	a number with a dollar symbol and two digits after the decimal point
Accounting	a number with a currency symbol (such as a dollar symbol [$]) aligned at the left edge of the cell and two digits after the decimal point
Short Date	a date in a *3/29/2019* format
Long Date	a date in a *Friday, March 29, 2019* format
Time	a time in a *3:00:00 PM* format
Percent	a number with a percent symbol and two digits after the decimal point
Fraction	a fraction in the format *1/2*
Scientific	a very large number or very small number with a decimal point and a notation indicating the number of places that Excel has moved the decimal point—for example, *1.00E+06* for the entry *1,000,000*
Text	a number as text, exactly as typed
Comma	a number with a thousands separator and two digits after the decimal point

— Use the Increase Decimal button and the Decrease Decimal button to change the number of digits after the decimal point (see Figure 1.31).

— Date formats vary from country to country. Be sure to use a date format that will not be misinterpreted by your audience.

▸ Know More methods for formatting numbers

- Right-click in the selected cells, click the *Format Cells* option at the pop-up menu, click a format option in the *Category* section of the Format Cells dialog box, if appropriate select the number of digits after the decimal point if appropriate, and then click the OK button.
- Excel automatically applies an appropriate number format if you type a symbol with a number. For example, type *$25.50* to automatically apply the Currency format, or type *15%* to automatically apply the Percent format.

Figure 1.31 Number Group on the Home Tab

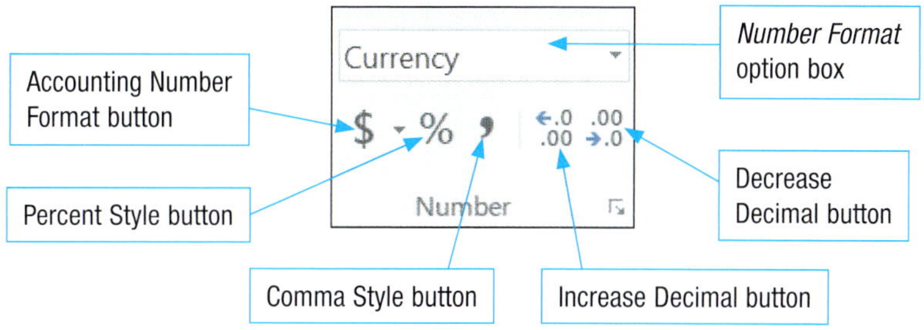

— Standard accounting practice is to apply Accounting format and display the currency symbol (e.g., $ for US dollars or £ for British pounds) at the very top and very bottom of each schedule (usually listed in a column) in a worksheet. (A schedule is a statement containing monetary information, such as a cash flow statement listing income coming in and income going out.)

On the Job

Task 1.18 Formatting Numbers

Jeremy would like you to apply formatting to clarify the meaning of the numbers in the Budget worksheet. Properly formatting a worksheet is important because it conveys professionalism and makes it easier for others to read and understand the analysis. Use options in the Number group on the Home tab to apply standard accounting formatting to the schedules in the worksheet.

1. With the 1-WareBot workbook open and the Budget worksheet active, select the range B6:C6.
2. Click the *Number Format* option box arrow in the Number group on the Home tab (see Figure 1.32).

   The *Number Format* drop-down list displays.

Figure 1.32 Accounting Option at the *Number Format* Option Box Drop-Down List

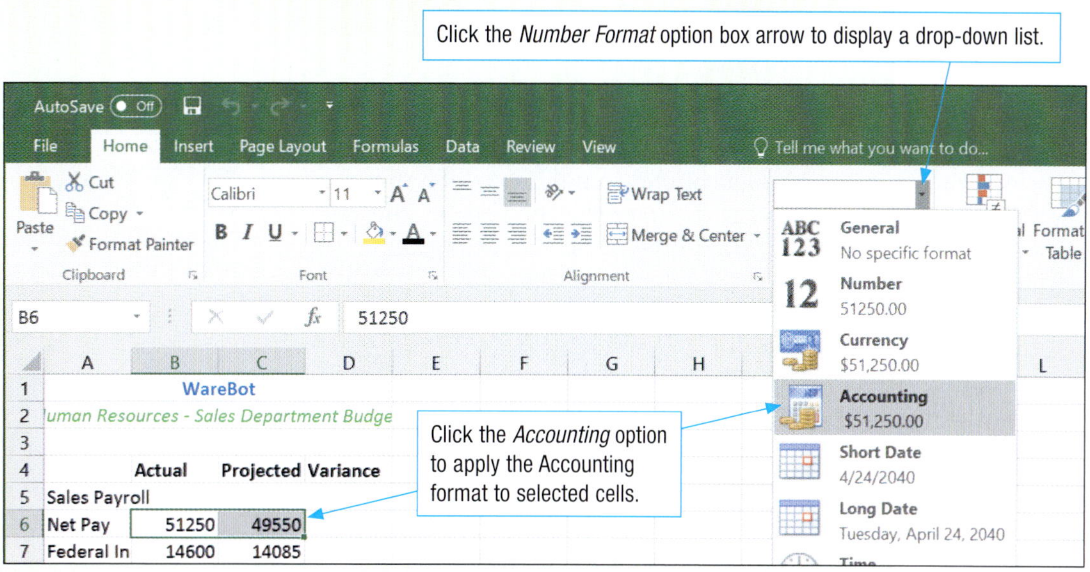

3. Click the *Accounting* option.

   The selected cells display in Accounting format with two digits after the decimal point.

4. With the range B6:C6 still selected, click the Decrease Decimal button.

   The selected cells display in Accounting format with one digit after the decimal point.

5. Click the Decrease Decimal button again.

   The selected cells display in Accounting format with no digits after the decimal point.

6. Select the range B7:C9.
7. Click the Comma Style button.

   The selected cells display in Comma format with two digits after the decimal point.

8. Click the Decrease Decimal button two times.

   The selected cells display in Comma format with no digits after the decimal point.

9. Select the range B10:C10, press and hold down the Ctrl key, and then drag to select the nonadjacent in the ranges B13:C13 and B18:C18.
10. Click the Accounting Number Format button.

    The selected cells display in Accounting format with two digits after the decimal point.

11. Click the Decrease Decimal button two times.

    The selected cells display in Accounting format with no digits after the decimal point.

12. Select the range B14:C17.
13. Click the Comma Style button.

    The selected cells display in Comma format with two digits after the decimal point.

14. Click the Decrease Decimal button two times.

    The selected cells display in Comma format with no digits after the decimal point.

15. Click the Save button on the Quick Access Toolbar.

Model Answer

1.19 Adjusting Column Width and Row Height

MOS 1.3.7

Tutorial

Adjusting Column Width and Row Height

Excel automatically adjusts the width of a column or the height of a row when you perform certain actions, such as changing the cell format. However, in some situations, entries do not fit neatly in their cells. For example, if you enter text in a cell and the cell to the right contains data, Excel displays only as much of your entry as fits in the width of the cell, hiding the rest. To display the entire entry, you can adjust the column width to fit the entry or wrap the text to multiple lines in the cell. When you wrap the text, you may also need to adjust the row height to display all the cell contents.

A string of pound symbols (#####) in a cell indicates the cell contains a number that is wider than the cell. To see the number, you need to resize the column.

You may also choose to modify column width or row height to make a worksheet more readable. For instance, you might increase the height of the row containing the worksheet title to draw attention to the title. You can adjust column width or row height to a specific number, or you can use the **AutoFit** feature to fit a column or row to its widest entry or tallest entry, respectively.

▸ **Know This** about adjusting column width

— To adjust column width, click in any cell in the column, click the Format button in the Cells group on the Home tab, click the *Column Width* option in the *Cell Size* section at the drop-down list, type to replace the selected value in the *Column width* box at the Column Width dialog box, and then click the OK button.

— Column width is measured by the number of characters that will fit the width of the column.

— Column width is also measured in pixels. The word **pixel** is short for *picture element*. A pixel is the smallest element of an image that can be displayed on a monitor.

— The default column width is 8.43 characters (64 pixels) (see Figure 1.33).

— Setting the column width for a merged cell adjusts the column width of all the merged columns. For example, if cells in the range A1:D1 are merged, clicking in cell A1 and then setting the column width to *15* will set the width of columns A, B, C, and D to 15 characters.

— You can specify a column width of 0 to 255 characters. (A column with a width of *0* will be hidden.)

▸ **Know More** methods for adjusting column width

- Right-click the column heading, click the *Column Width* option at the pop-up menu, and then change the setting at the Column Width dialog box.
- Drag the right border of the column heading. As you drag, the width displays in a ScreenTip (see Figure 1.33).
- In Page Layout view, column width can be specified in inches. To specify a column width in inches, click the File tab, click the *Options* option, click the *Advanced* option, click the Ruler Units arrow in the *Display* section, and then click the *Inches* option.
- To change the width of multiple adjacent columns at the same time, drag across the column headings to select the columns, and then set the column width. If the columns are nonadjacent, press and hold down the Ctrl key while clicking the column headings, and then set the column width.

Figure 1.33 Default Column Width

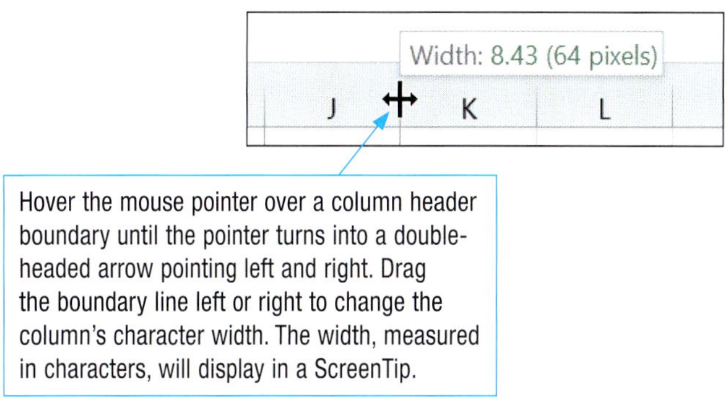

▸ **Know This** about adjusting row height

— To adjust row height, click in any cell in the row, click the Format button in the Cells group on the Home tab, click the *Row Height* option in the *Cell Size* section at the drop-down list, type to replace the selected value in the *Row height* box at the Row Height dialog box, and then click the OK button.

— Row height is measured in points. A point equals approximately 1/72 inch.

— Row height is also measured in pixels.

— The default row height is 15 points (20 pixels).

— You can specify a row height of 0 to 409 points.

▸ **Know More** methods for adjusting row height

- Right-click the row heading, click the *Row Height* option at the pop-up menu, and then change the setting at the Row Height dialog box.
- Drag the bottom border of the row heading. As you drag, the height displays in a ScreenTip.

continues...

▶ **Know This** about using the AutoFit feature

— To adjust column width or row height using the AutoFit feature, hover the mouse pointer over the gray boundary line at the right side of the column heading or below the row heading until the pointer turns into a left-and-right-pointing arrow with a vertical line in the middle and then double-click the left mouse button (see Figure 1.34).

▶ **Know More** methods for adjusting row height

...continued

– To change the height of multiple adjacent rows at the same time, drag across the row headings to select the rows and then set the row height. If the rows are not adjacent, press and hold down the Ctrl key while clicking the row headings and then set the row height.

Figure 1.34 AutoFitting the Column Width

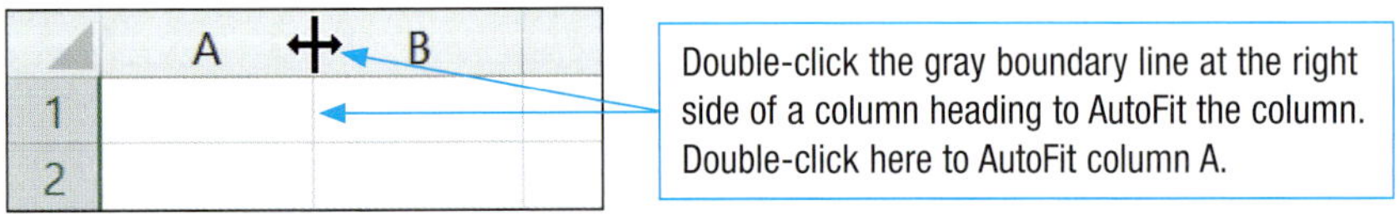

On the Job

Task 1.19 Adjusting Column Width and Row Height

Many of the entries on the Budget worksheet are cut off or overlap into the next column. Jeremy would like you to fix the cell formatting so entries are readable. He would also like you to make the worksheet title stand out at the top of the worksheet. Adjust column widths and a row height to accomplish these changes.

1. With the 1-WareBot workbook open and the Budget worksheet active, double-click the gray boundary line at the right side of the column B heading.

   The width of column B changes to fit the longest entry in the column.

2. Double-click the gray boundary line at the right side of the column C heading.

   The width of column C changes to fit the longest entry in the column.

3. Click in cell A6.
4. Click the Format button in the Cells group on the Home tab.

   A drop-down list displays.

5. Click the *Column Width* option.

   A dialog box displays.

6. Type 22 and then click the OK button.

   The width of column A changes to 22 characters.

7. Click in cell A1.
8. Click the Format button.

   A drop-down list displays.

9. Click the *Row Height* option.

   A dialog box displays.

10. Type 31 and then click the OK button.

    The height of row 1 changes to 31 points.

11. Click the Save button on the Quick Access Toolbar.

Model Answer

1.20 Inserting and Deleting a Cell, Range, Row, or Column

MOS 1.3.5
MOS 2.1.5

Tutorial

Inserting a Column, a Row, and a Cell

You can insert a blank cell or range above or to the left of the active cell or range in a worksheet. When you insert a blank cell or range, Excel shifts the other cells in the same column down or in the same row to the right to accommodate the new cell or range. Similarly, you can insert a blank row above a selected cell, range, or row, or you can insert a blank column to the left of a selected cell, range, or column. You can also delete cells, ranges, rows, and columns. When you insert or delete cells, ranges, rows, or columns, the relative references that are affected by the insertion or deletion adjust accordingly.

▸ **Know This** about inserting a cell or range

— To insert a cell or range above a selected cell or range, click the Insert button arrow in the Cells group on the Home tab, click the *Insert Cells* option at the drop-down list, click the *Shift cells down* option at the Insert dialog box (see Figure 1.35), and then click the OK button.

— To insert a cell or range to the left of a selected cell or range, click the *Shift cells right* option at the Insert dialog box.

Figure 1.35 Insert Dialog Box Options

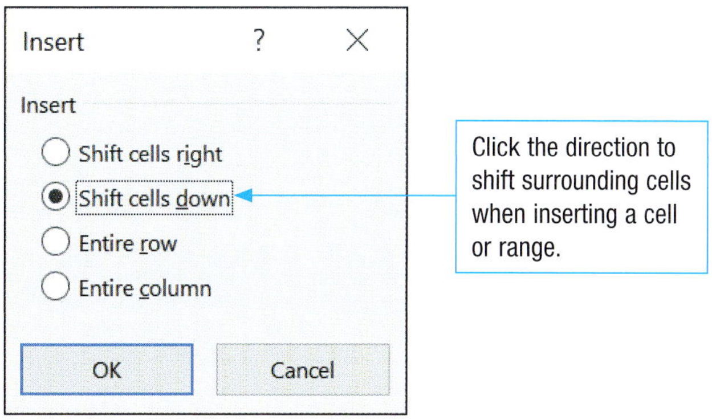

▸ **Know This** about deleting a cell or range

— To delete a cell or range, select the cell or range, click the Delete button arrow in the Cells group on the Home tab, click the *Delete Cells* option at the drop-down list, and then click the direction to shift the surrounding cells at the Delete dialog box.

▸ **Know This** about inserting a row or column

— To insert a row, click in a cell below where the new row is to appear, click the Insert button arrow in the Cells group on the Home tab, and then click the *Insert Sheet Rows* option at the drop-down list.

— To insert a column, click in a cell to the right of where the column is to appear, click the Insert button arrow, and then click the *Insert Sheet Columns* option at the drop-down list.

— Cells in the new row have the same formatting as the cells in the row above, and cells in the new column have the same formatting as the cells in the column to the left.

▸ **Know More** methods for inserting a row and column

– Right-click the row heading or column heading and then click the *Insert* option at the pop-up menu (see Figure 1.36).

▸ Know This about deleting a row or column

— To delete a row or column, select a cell in the row or column, click the Delete button arrow in the Cells group on the Home tab, and then click the *Delete Sheet Rows* or *Delete Sheet Columns* option.

— If you delete a row or column by accident, click the Undo button on the Quick Access Toolbar (or press Ctrl + Z) to restore the contents of the deleted row or column.

▸ Know More methods for deleting a row or column

– Right-click the row heading or column heading and then click the *Delete* option at the pop-up menu.

On the Job

Task 1.20 Inserting a Column and a Row

Jeremy would like to indicate whether each employee has completed all the training tests in the Training worksheet. He would also like to separate the area that displays test scores from the area that displays averages, minimums, and maximums. Insert a column and a row to make these updates.

1. With the 1-WareBot workbook open and the Budget worksheet active, click the Training sheet tab.

   The Training worksheet is active.

2. Click in cell F1.

   Cell F1 is active.

3. Click the Insert button arrow in the Cells group on the Home tab.

   A drop-down list displays.

4. Click the *Insert Sheet Columns* option.

   A new column is inserted to the left of the active cell.

5. Click in cell F5, type Exam, and then press the Enter key.

   Cell F6 is active.

6. Right-click the row 16 heading.

   Row 16 is selected and a pop-up menu displays.

7. Click the *Insert* option (see Figure 1.36).

   A new row is inserted above the selected row.

Figure 1.36 *Insert* Option at the Row Heading Pop-Up Menu

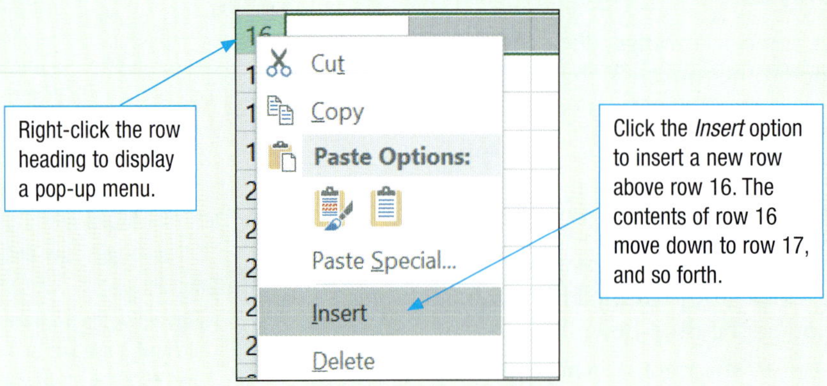

8. Click the Save button on the Quick Access Toolbar.

Model Answer

1.21 Checking Spelling

Excel provides a **spelling checker** that locates and corrects possible spelling errors. You can use this feature to check for errors in a word, a selected range, or an entire worksheet. The spelling checker compares words in the Excel worksheet with words in a dictionary file. A word that you use often but is not in the dictionary, such as a proper name, can be added to the dictionary to avoid having it flagged over and over again.

It is important for financial documents to be error free, and using the spelling checker will help achieve that. However, you still need to proofread your worksheets because the spelling checker will not catch all errors. For example, if you enter the label *Audit Tail* instead of *Audit Trail*, the spelling checker will not catch the error because both *Tail* and *Trail* are words in the dictionary.

Tutorial

Checking Spelling

▸ Know This about checking spelling

— To check the spelling in an entire worksheet, click in any cell, click the Spelling button in the Proofing group on the Review tab, review the flagged words and suggested corrections that display in the Spelling dialog box (see Figure 1.37), and then click the appropriate button (see Table 1.5).

— To check the spelling of a specific cell or range, select the cell or range before clicking the Spelling button.

— To check the spelling of a specific word, click in the cell containing the word, select the word on the Formula bar, and then click the Spelling button.

— The spelling checker starts from the active cell. When it reaches the last cell in the worksheet, it displays a message asking if you want to continue checking from the beginning of the worksheet.

— The spelling checker can check only text; it cannot check formulas and functions.

▸ Know More methods for displaying the Spelling dialog box

– Press the F7 function key.

Figure 1.37 Spelling Dialog Box

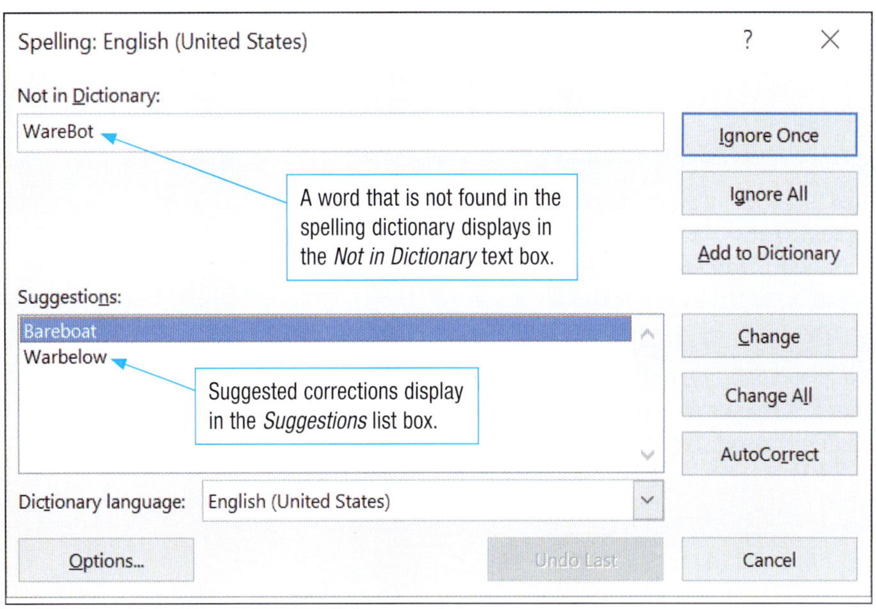

Table 1.5 Spelling Dialog Box Buttons

Click this button...	if...
Ignore Once	the flagged word is spelled correctly, such as a proper name.
Ignore All	the flagged word is spelled correctly and may appear in the worksheet multiple times.
Add to Dictionary	you want to add the flagged word to your custom dictionary so that the word will not be flagged again.
Change	the selected word in the *Suggestions* box is the correct spelling.
Change All	the selected word in the *Suggestions* box is the correct spelling and you want to change all the occurrences of the flagged word.
AutoCorrect	you want Excel to correct the flagged word with the selected word in the *Suggestions* box and also add the flagged word and suggestion to the AutoCorrect dialog box.

On the Job

Task 1.21 Checking Spelling

Jeremy regularly stresses the importance of producing professional-looking files with accurate data and text. Use the spelling checker to help ensure that the text in the Budget worksheet is error free.

1. With the 1-WareBot workbook open and the Training worksheet active, click the Budget sheet tab.

   The Budget worksheet is active.

2. Click in cell A1.

   Cell A1 is active.

3. Click the Review tab.

   The Review tab is active.

4. Click the Spelling button in the Proofing group.

   The Spelling dialog box displays. The word *WareBot* displays in the *Not in Dictionary* text box. This word is spelled correctly and may appear in the worksheet multiple times.

5. Click the Ignore All button.

   The word *Scial* displays in the *Not in Dictionary* text box and the word *Social* is selected in the *Suggestions* text box. The selected suggestion is the correct spelling.

6. Click the Change button.

   The misspelled word *Scial* is replaced with the correctly spelled word *Social* in the worksheet. The word *Ttal* displays in the *Not in Dictionary* text box and the word *Total* is selected in the *Suggestions* text box. The selected suggestion is the correct spelling.

7. Click the Change button.

   The misspelled word *Ttal* is replaced with the correctly spelled word *Total* in the worksheet. A message box says the spelling check is complete and you are good to go.

8. Click the OK button.

   The message box closes.

9. Click the Save button on the Quick Access Toolbar.

Model Answer

1.22 Using Help and the Tell Me Feature

The **Help** feature contains information about Excel commands and features. You can access Excel Help through the Microsoft Office support site or through the Help Viewer feature (see Figure 1.38). Both options allow you to enter search criteria and click links to view information on various Help topics. Use the navigation buttons provided to move between pages.

Tutorial

Using the Help Viewer Feature and the Tell Me Feature

Figure 1.38 Help Viewer Feature

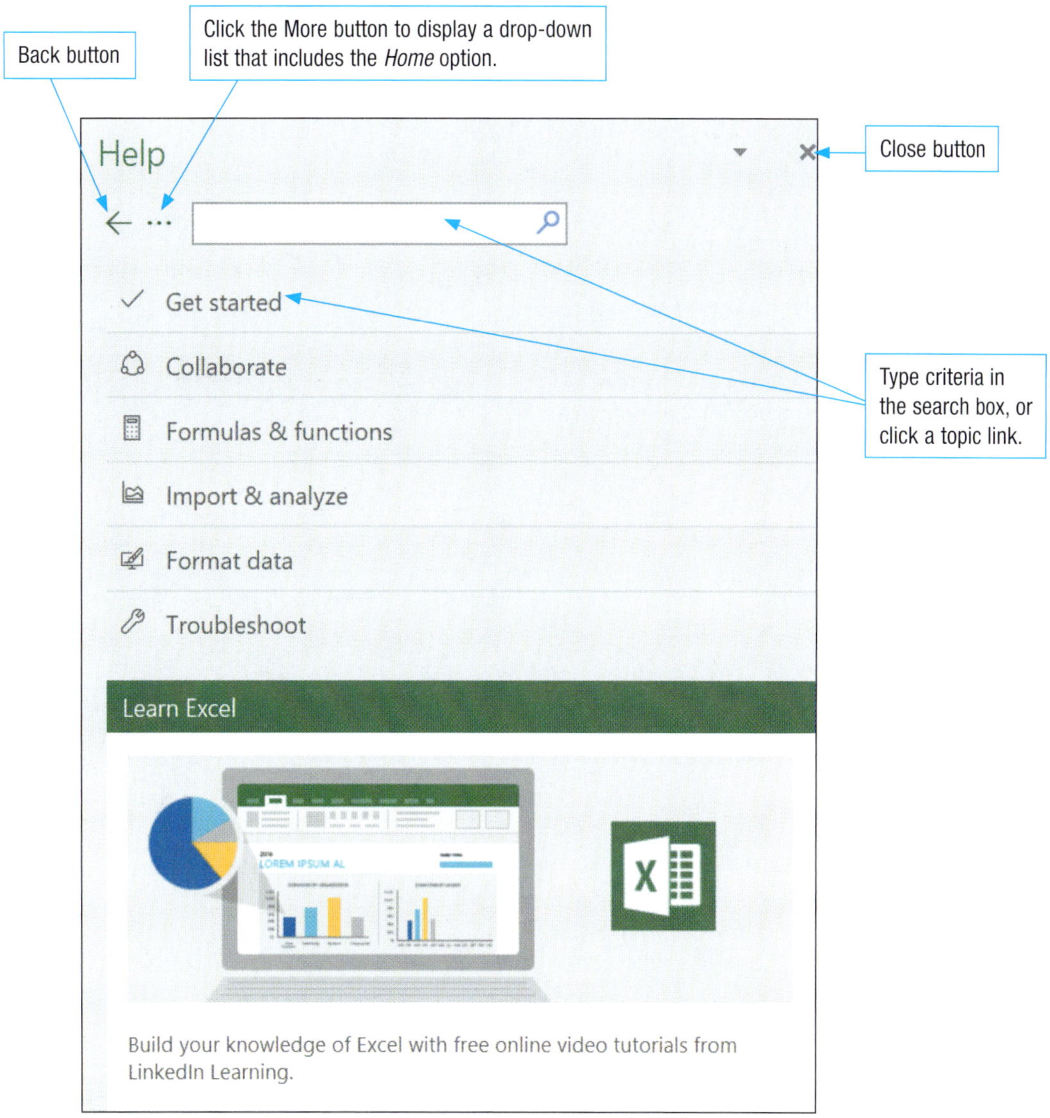

Another way to access Excel help is to use the **Tell Me** feature. If you type a word or phrase in the *Tell me what you want to do* text box on the ribbon, Excel displays a drop-down list with options for completing the action, getting help on the action, and using the **Smart Lookup** feature to find information about the action. When you click an option for completing the action, Excel activates the command sequence. For example, if you type *print* in the *Tell me* text box and then click the *Print Preview and Print* option at the drop-down list, Excel displays the Print backstage area. If you click a Help option, the Help Viewer window displays. If you click a Smart Lookup option, the Smart Lookup task pane displays with information about the action from a variety of Internet sources (see Figure 1.39). Click the Explore tab to display word usage information and entries from Wikipedia and Bing search results. Click the Define tab for definition, pronunciation, and word meaning information.

Figure 1.39 Smart Lookup Task Pane

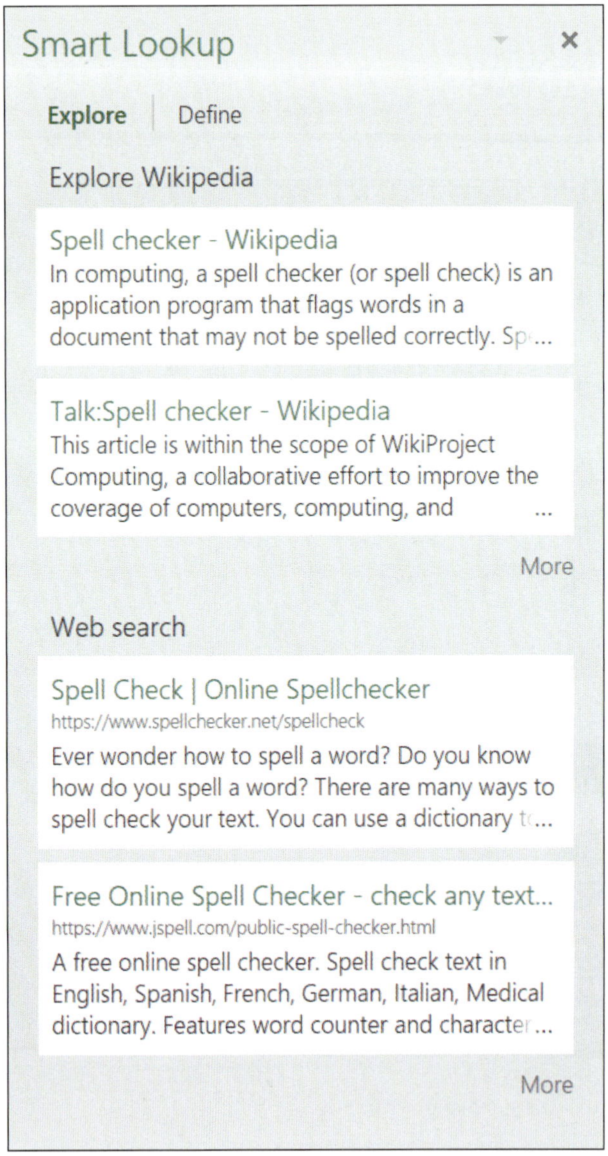

▶ **Know This** about using Help

— To access the Excel Help Viewer feature (see Figure 1.38), press the F1 function key, and then either click a topic link or else type a criterion in the search box and click a topic link.

— To access the Microsoft Office support site, click the File tab, click the Help button in the upper right corner of the File backstage area (see Figure 1.40) to display the Microsoft Office support site in a web browser, and either click a topic link or else type a criterion in the Search Office help search box and then click a topic link.

▶ **Know More** methods for displaying the Help Viewer feature

– Type *Help* in the *Tell me what you want to do* text box and then click the *Help* or *Get Help* option.

Figure 1.40 Help Button

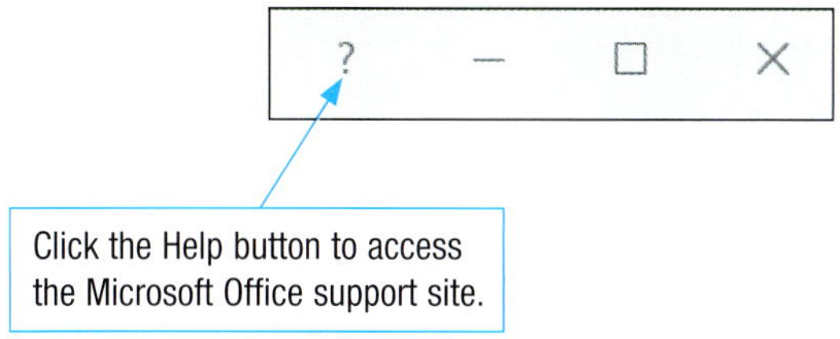

▸ **Know This** about using the Tell Me feature

— To use the Tell Me feature, click in the *Tell me what you want to do* text box on the ribbon, type a word or phrase, and then click a command, Help option, or Smart Lookup option at the drop-down list.

▸ **Know More** about using the Tell Me feature

– The Smart Lookup task pane can also be opened by clicking the Smart Lookup button in the Insights group on the Review tab.

On the Job

Task 1.22 Using the Help Viewer Feature and the Tell Me Feature

Jeremy wants you to be able to work independently—sometimes from a remote location. Therefore, you need to know how to use the Excel software and where to find help if you are unsure how to use a feature. Jeremy asks you to take some time and learn how to use the Excel Help features.

1. With the 1-WareBot workbook open and the Budget worksheet active, press the F1 function key.
   The Help Viewer feature displays (see Figure 1.38 on page 47).
2. Click in the search box, type Tell Me, and then press the Enter key.
   Links to the Tell Me information display.
3. Click the first link to read information about the Tell Me feature.
   Information about the Tell Me feature displays.
4. Click the More button and then click the Home option.
   The Help home page displays.
5. Click the first link in the topics list.
   Get started links display.
6. Click the Back button.
   The Help home page displays.
7. Click the Close button.
   The Help feature closes.
8. Click in the *Tell me what you want to do* text box and then type print. (see Figure 1.41).
   A drop-down list displays.
9. Click the *Print Preview and Print* option.
   The Print backstage area displays.
10. Click the Back button (see Figure 1.42).
    Print Preview closes.
11. Click the Save button on the Quick Access Toolbar.

Figure 1.41 Tell Me Feature

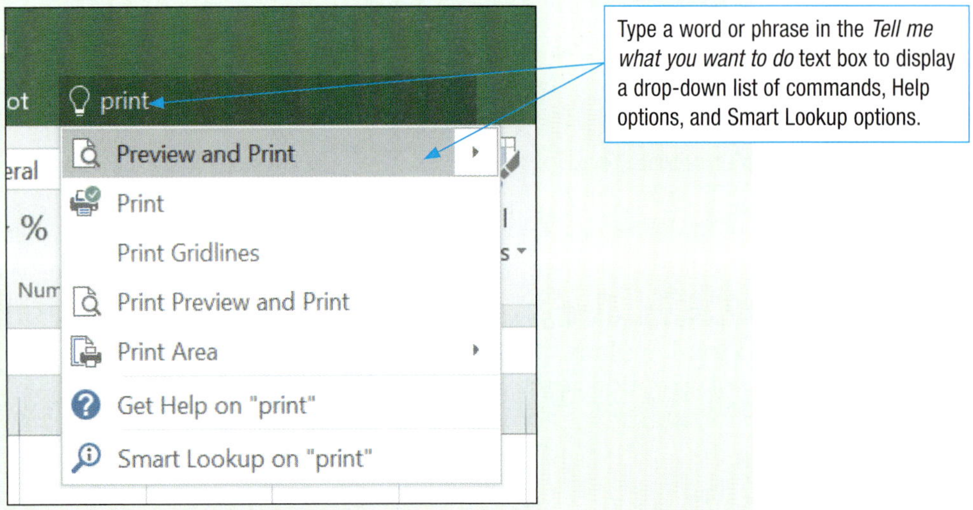

Figure 1.42 Print Backstage Area

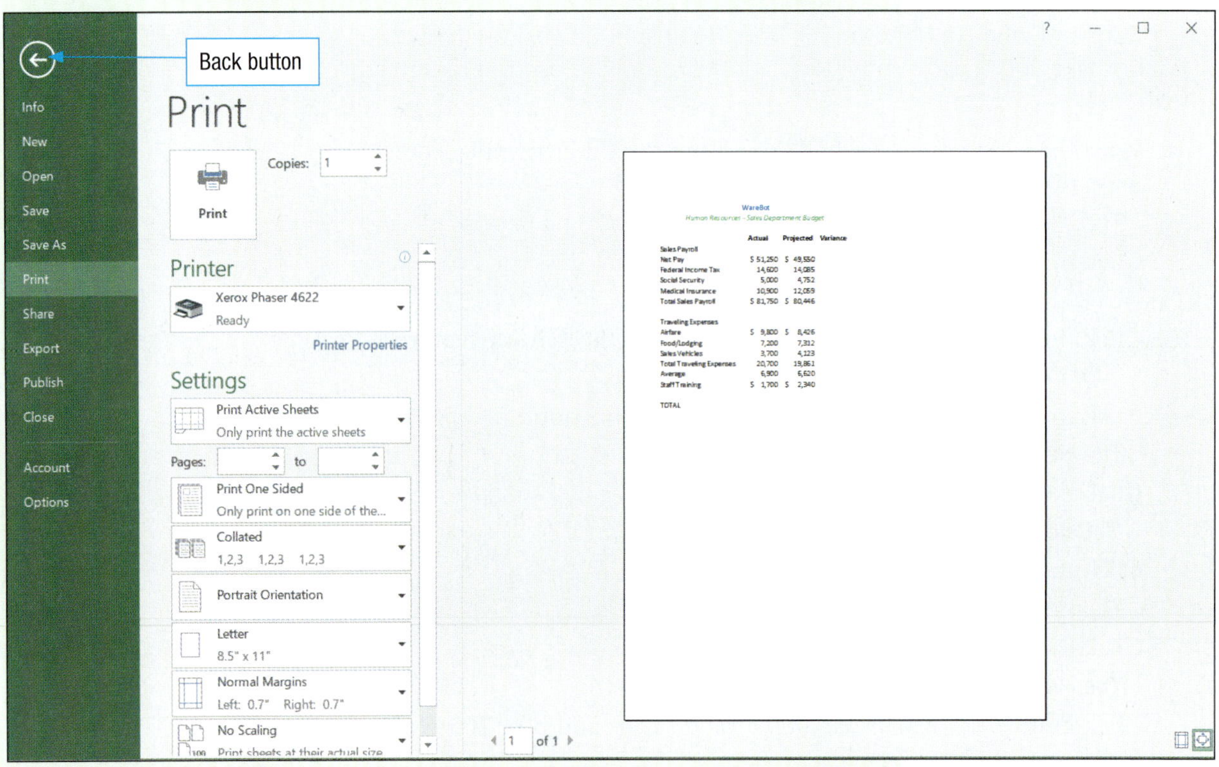

1.23 Setting Basic Print Options and Printing a Worksheet or Workbook

MOS 1.5.3

Tutorial

Printing Two Copies of a Workbook

A worksheet is printed from the Print backstage area. This area can also be used to set print options, such as what printer to use and how many copies to print. The **Print Preview** feature displays a preview of what the printed worksheet will look like in the right panel at the backstage area. By default, the active worksheet is printed. However, you can change the setting to print the entire workbook.

▸ **Know This** about printing a worksheet or workbook

— To print a worksheet, click the File tab, click the *Print* option, adjust settings in the middle panel at the Print backstage area, and then click the Print button.

— To print a workbook, click the File tab, click the *Print* option, click the *Print Active Sheets* option in the *Settings* section in the middle panel at the Print backstage area, click the *Print Entire Workbook* option, and then click the Print button.

▸ **Know More** methods for displaying the Print backstage area

– Press Ctrl + P.

▸ **Know This** about setting basic print options

— Set basic print options in the middle panel at the Print backstage area.

— Change the number of copies to print by clicking in the *Copies* box, typing to replace the selected value, and then pressing the Enter key.

— Select a printer by clicking the *Printer* option box arrow and then clicking an option at the drop-down list.

— Preview the pages that will print by clicking the Next Page arrow and the Previous Page arrow.

▸ **Know More** methods for changing the number of copies to print

– Click the *Copies* increment (up) or decrement (down) arrow.

On the Job

Task 1.23 Printing Two Copies of a Workbook

Jeremy would like you to print two copies of the 1-WareBot workbook so the two of you can review the data together and plan the remaining tasks.

1. With the 1-WareBot workbook open and the Budget worksheet active, click the File tab.
   The File backstage area displays.
2. Click the *Print* option.
   The Print backstage area displays.
3. Click in the *Copies* box and then type 2.
   The value 2 displays in the *Copies* box.
4. Click the *Print Active Sheets* option.
   A drop-down list displays.
5. Click the *Print Entire Workbook* option.
6. Click the Next Page arrow three times.
   Each page that will print displays in the Preview panel, one page at each click.
7. If printed work is required by your instructor, click the Print button.
   Two copies of the workbook print.
8. Click the Save button on the Quick Access Toolbar and then click the Close button.

Model Answer

Chapter Summary

1.1
- Excel is a spreadsheet application used to organize and analyze numeric and financial data. An Excel file is called a *workbook*.
- The open command transfers a copy of the workbook to the computer's RAM (random access memory) and displays the active worksheet in an Excel window. The Save command overwrites the original workbook file on the current storage medium. The close command closes the application window and removes the workbook from the computer's RAM.

1.2
- Each Excel workbook contains at least one worksheet, which is organized into a grid of columns and rows. A column is a vertical set of cells, and a row is a horizontal set of cells. Each column is identified by a unique column heading, which is a letter that appears above the top of the column. Each row is identified by a unique row heading, which is a number that appears to the left of the row.
- Data is entered in a cell, which is the intersection of a column and a row. The cell address, or cell reference, is the combination of the column heading letter and the row heading number. When a cell is active, its cell address displays in the Name box at the top of the worksheet, the cell is highlighted with a green border, and data can be entered in the cell.
- A range is two or more cells, and a range reference consists of the address of the first cell, a colon, and the address of the last cell.
- A worksheet contains a fixed number of columns and rows. The number of usable cells depends on the amount of RAM available to the computer. Scrolling horizontally or vertically changes what cells are visible on the screen but does not change which cell is active.

1.3
- The View tab contains features that can be used to change how a workbook is viewed on the screen. By default, an Excel workbook is viewed in Normal view. Other views include Page Break Preview, which shows where pages will break when the document is printed, and Page Layout view, which shows where pages begin and end and allows adding headers and footers.
- Commands in the Zoom group on the View tab can be used to zoom in to get a close-up view of data at a higher magnification or to zoom out to see more of the worksheet at a lower magnification.

1.4
- A new workbook can be created from a blank workbook or a preformatted template. The Blank workbook template displays a workbook with one blank worksheet named *Sheet1*. A preformatted template may contain multiple worksheets, including data tables, charts and graphs, and samples.

1.5
- A workbook can be saved, or written, to a folder on an available storage medium, such as a OneDrive account, a USB flash drive, or the computer's hard drive. The middle panel at the Save As backstage area displays the storage locations available for the Microsoft account the user is signed in to.
- The Title bar in a workbook displays the workbook name. By default, the name of a new, blank workbook is *Book1*. When a workbook is saved, the user should replace this default file name with a unique file

name that describes the workbook contents. A workbook file name and file path can contain up to 255 characters (including spaces), and the file name is followed by the extension *.xlsx*.

- The first time a new workbook is saved, the user needs to save a storage location and name for the file. Available storage locations are listed in the middle panel at the Save As backstage area. After a file has been saved the first time, it can be opened, edited, and then saved in the same location with the same name. The modified file overwrites the original file.

1.6
- Dividing data among multiple worksheets is often an efficient way to organize information. Excel assigns each new worksheet a name with a number; this name displays on the sheet tab at the bottom of the worksheet. Clicking the sheet tab makes the worksheet active. Renaming each worksheet with a unique name that identifies its contents will help users determine which sheet tab to click to find the data they need.

1.7
- Each cell in an Excel worksheet can hold a single data entry, which can be text, numeric, a value, a date or time, or a formula that calculates a result. The contents of a cell can be edited directly in the cell or on the Formula bar.
- If a user wants to enter similar contents from a cell or range in a different location in the same worksheet or in another worksheet, the user can save time by copying the contents. The selected contents can be copied by clicking the Copy button in the Clipboard group on the Home tab. The copied contents can be pasted by selecting the cell or range at the new location and then clicking the Paste button.
- Copied items are placed on the Clipboard, which is a holding area. When the user clicks the Paste button, the last item copied to the Clipboard is pasted in the active cell or range.
- By default, the Paste command pastes the copied cell contents and its attributes, including formatting and formulas. Which attributes are pasted can be changed by clicking the Paste Options button and then clicking an option at the pop-up gallery.
- The Delete key or Delete button can be used to delete the contents of an active cell. Deleting removes the contents from the cell.
- When you make a cell active, you place it in Ready mode, which means the cell is ready for input. A green border appears around the cell, and the word Ready displays at the left end of the Status bar.
- When a cell is active and you start to type, the mode changes to Enter mode. In Enter mode, the insertion point is placed in the cell and the word Ready changes to Enter on the status bar.

1.8
- The AutoComplete feature automatically inserts data in a cell when the user starts typing data that begins the same as a previous entry. The AutoCorrect feature helps to ensure that text entries are spelled correctly by automatically correcting common typing errors.

1.9
- A cell can be formatted so that a text entry wraps automatically to display on multiple lines within the cell width. The Text Wrap feature is often applied to column headings that are longer than the longest line of data in the column.

1.10 ▶ Excel provides techniques and features for entering numbers and dates quickly and accurately. Numbers can be entered as whole numbers, decimals, or negatives. Excel stores currency values and percentages as decimal values. Dates are entered using a standard date format. Excel displays the entry using the format selected in the Date & Time section of the Windows Settings pane or another format; the format can be changed after the entry has been finished.

1.11 ▶ Using the Auto Fill feature allows copying data to adjacent cells or to fill adjacent cells with data and formulas that follow a pattern. When a cell or range is selected, the fill handle displays as a small square in the lower right corner of the cell or range. The fill handle can be dragged to copy contents and formatting. Auto Fill can also be used to copy formulas and formatting and to fill series using formulas.

1.12 ▶ A formula is a statement entered in a cell to perform a calculation. Excel performs the calculation and displays the result. A formula always begins with an equals sign and includes arithmetic operators and arguments.

▶ If a formula includes a value that may change, it is a good idea to place that value in a separate cell and then use the cell reference in the formula. If the value in the referenced cell is updated, Excel automatically recalculates the value in the cell containing the formula and displays the new result.

1.13 ▶ When a formula is being typed, a cell reference can be entered by clicking in the cell to be referenced. This method of entering a cell reference, called *pointing*, can be quicker and more accurate than typing.

1.14 ▶ The AutoSum feature provides a quick way to enter a function in a formula. A function consists of the function name and the arguments used in the calculation. The AutoSum button can be used to insert commonly used functions, such as the SUM function and the AVERAGE function.

1.15 ▶ The fill handle can be used to quickly copy a formula into adjacent cells. By default, cell references are relative. A relative cell reference will change if a formula is copied.

1.16 ▶ Formatting is applied to cells to clarify the meaning of the data and to improve the readability of a worksheet both on the screen and on paper. Commands in the Font group on the Home tab can be used to apply text formatting (such as bold, italic, and underlining), add borders, change the color of the background or text in a cell, and change the font and font size. These commands are also available on the Mini toolbar.

1.17 ▶ The Merge & Center feature can be used to merge selected cells into a single cell and center the text across the combined cell. Options at the Merge & Center drop-down list can also be used to merge cells without centering text, to merge selected cells, and to restore merged cells.

1.18 ▶ When an entry is typed in a cell, the data is automatically assigned the General format, which usually displays numbers exactly as they are typed. Different number formats can be applied to add dollar symbols, commas, and other characters to the cells; some number formats affect the alignment of the number in the cell. Applying a new format changes the display of an entry but not the actual number entered.

1.19 ▶ Excel automatically adjusts the width of a column or the height of a row when certain actions are performed. However, in some situations, entries do not fit neatly in their cells. Excel displays only as much of an entry as fits in the width of the cell. To display the entire entry, the column width can be adjusted to fit the entry, or the text can be wrapped to multiple lines in the cell.

▶ Column width (measured in characters) or row height (measured in points) can also be modified to make a worksheet more readable—for instance, a user might increase the height of the row containing the worksheet title to draw attention to the title. Column width or row height can be adjusted to a specific number, or the AutoFit feature can be used to fit a column or row to its widest entry or tallest entry, respectively.

1.20 ▶ A blank cell or range can be inserted above or to the left of the active cell or range in a worksheet. Excel shifts other cells in the same column down or in the same row to the right to accommodate the new cell or range. Similarly, a blank row can be inserted above a selected cell, range, or row, or a blank column can be inserted to the left of a selected cell, range, or column. Cells, ranges, rows, and columns can also be deleted. When cells, ranges, rows, or columns are inserted or deleted, the relative references that are affected adjust accordingly.

1.21 ▶ Excel provides a spelling checker that locates and corrects possible spelling errors. The spelling checker compares words in the Excel worksheet with words in a dictionary file. A word that is used often but is not in the dictionary, such as a proper name, can be added to the dictionary to avoid having it flagged over and over again.

1.22 ▶ The Help feature contains information about Excel commands and features. It can be accessed through the Microsoft Office support site or through the Help Viewer window. Both options allow the user to enter search criteria and click links to view information on various Help topics.

▶ Another way to access Excel help is through the Tell Me feature. When a word or phrase is typed in the *Tell me what you want to do* text box on the ribbon, Excel displays a drop-down list with options for completing the action, getting help on the action, and using the Smart Lookup feature to find information about the action.

1.23 ▶ A worksheet is printed from the Print backstage area. This area can also be used to set print options, such as the printer and number of copies. The Print Preview feature displays a preview of what the printed sheet will look like in the right panel at the backstage area. By default, the active sheet is printed, but this setting can be changed to print the entire workbook.

Features Review

Feature	Ribbon Tab, Group	Button, Option	Keyboard Shortcut
access Excel Help	File	? or , *Get Help*	F1
access Smart Lookup		, *Smart Lookup*	
add a worksheet to the left	Home, Cells	Insert, *Insert Sheet*	Shift + F11
add a worksheet to the right	Status bar		
adjust column width	Home, Cells	, *Column Width*	
ro	Home, Cells	, *Row Height*	
apply Accounting format	Home, Number	$	
apply bold formatting	Home, Font	**B**	Ctrl + B
apply Comma format	Home, Number	,	
apply italic formatting	Home, Font	*I*	Ctrl + I
apply Percentage format	Home, Number	%	
apply underline formatting	Home, Font	U	
change Enter key behavior	File	Options	
change font color	Home, Font	A	
change view to Normal	View, Workbook Views		
change view to Page Layout	View, Workbook Views		
change view to Page Break Preview	View, Workbook Views		
change zoom level	View, Zoom *or* Status bar		
close workbook	File	*Close* or	Ctrl + W
copy cell contents	Home, Clipboard		Ctrl + C
create new, blank workbook	File	*New*	
cut cell contents	Home, Clipboard	,	Ctrl + X
decrease number of digits after decimal point	Home, Number	.00 →.0	

continues...

Feature	Ribbon Tab, Group	Button, Option	Keyboard Shortcut
delete cell contents	Home, Editing or Home, Cells	, *Clear Contents*	Delete
delete cells	Home, Cells	Delete, *Delete Cells*	
delete columns	Home, Cells	Delete, *Delete Sheet Columns*	
delete rows	Home, Cells	Delete, *Delete Sheet Rows*	
display Go To dialog box	Home, Editing	, *Go To*	F5 or Ctrl + G
go to cell A1			Ctrl + Home
increase number of digits after decimal point	Home, Number		
insert cells	Home, Cells	Insert, *Insert Cells*	
insert columns	Home, Cells	Insert, *Insert Sheet Columns*	
insert rows	Home, Cells	Insert, *Insert Sheet Rows*	
merge cells across rows	Home, Alignment	Merge & Center, *Merge Across*	
merge and center adjacent cells	Home, Alignment		
merge selected cells	Home, Alignment	Merge & Center, *Merge Cells*	
open a saved workbook	File	*Open*	Ctrl + O
paste cell contents	Home, Clipboard		Ctrl + V
print	File	*Print*	Ctrl + P
rename worksheet	Home, Cells	, *Rename Sheet*	
save modified workbook	File	*Save*	Ctrl + S
save open file with new name	File	*Save As*	
specify cell attributes to paste	Home, Clipboard	Paste	
spell check	Review, Proofing		
unmerge cells	Home, Alignment	Merge & Center, *Unmerge Cells*	
use Auto Fill to copy data or fill series	Home, Editing		
use AutoSum	Home, Editing		
use Tell Me			
wrap text	Home, Alignment		
zoom in	Status bar		

continues...

Feature	Ribbon Tab, Group	Button, Option	Keyboard Shortcut
zoom out	Status bar	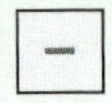	
zoom to 100%	View, Zoom		
zoom to selection	View, Zoom		

Recheck

Recheck your understanding of the concepts, features, and skills covered in this chapter by taking the Recheck quiz.

Workbook

Access the study tools, review exercises, assessments, and challenges for this chapter in the workbook available from this page in your ebook.

Entering Formulas and Inserting Functions

Chapter 2

Chapter Goal

To create useful formulas, use common functions effectively, and identify common formula/function errors.

Precheck

Check your understanding of the concepts, features, and skills covered in this chapter by taking the Precheck quiz.

Learning Objectives

2.1 Create and display Excel formulas
2.2 Type a formula in the Formula bar
2.3 Type and point to enter a formula, and use the Fill button
2.4 Determine the order of operations
2.5 Copy a formula with relative references
2.6 Use an absolute cell reference in a formula
2.7 Use a mixed cell reference in a formula
2.8 Insert functions and use the Math & Trig functions RAND, ROUND, and SUM
2.9 Use the Statistical functions AVERAGE, COUNT, COUNTA, MAX, MEDIAN, and MIN
2.10 Use Quick Analysis to enter formulas
2.11 Create and use defined names
2.12 Modify and delete defined names
2.13 Use a defined name in a formula
2.14 Use the Date functions DATE, NOW, TODAY, and WORKDAY
2.15 Use Logical functions, comparison operators, and the IF function
2.16 Use the Insert Function dialog box
2.17 Identify common formula/function errors and use the Trace Error button

Data Files

Before beginning the chapter work, download the AE2 folder from this page in your ebook to your storage medium and then make AE2 the active folder.

Ebook Links

Access digital resources for this course from your ebook.

SNAP

If you are a SNAP user, go to your SNAP assignments page to complete the Precheck, Tutorials, and Recheck in this chapter.

Preview

On the Job

Scenario WareBot

In Chapter 1, you set up the basic framework in an Excel workbook to be used to gather budget, payroll, and training data. Now Jeremy Ronlin, the director of marketing and sales at WareBot, would like you to enter the formulas and insert the functions that will provide the information he needs to track and analyze the data.

Visual Reference: Formulas and Functions

Figure 2.1 Payroll Worksheet with the Formulas Tab Active

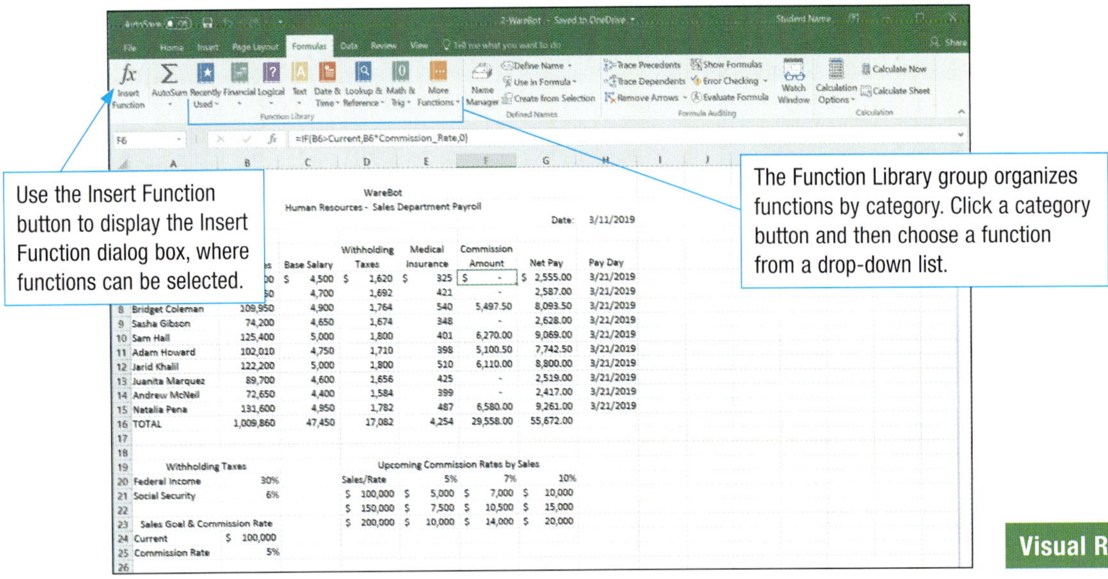

Visual Reference

Figure 2.2 Payroll Worksheet with the Show Formulas Button Active

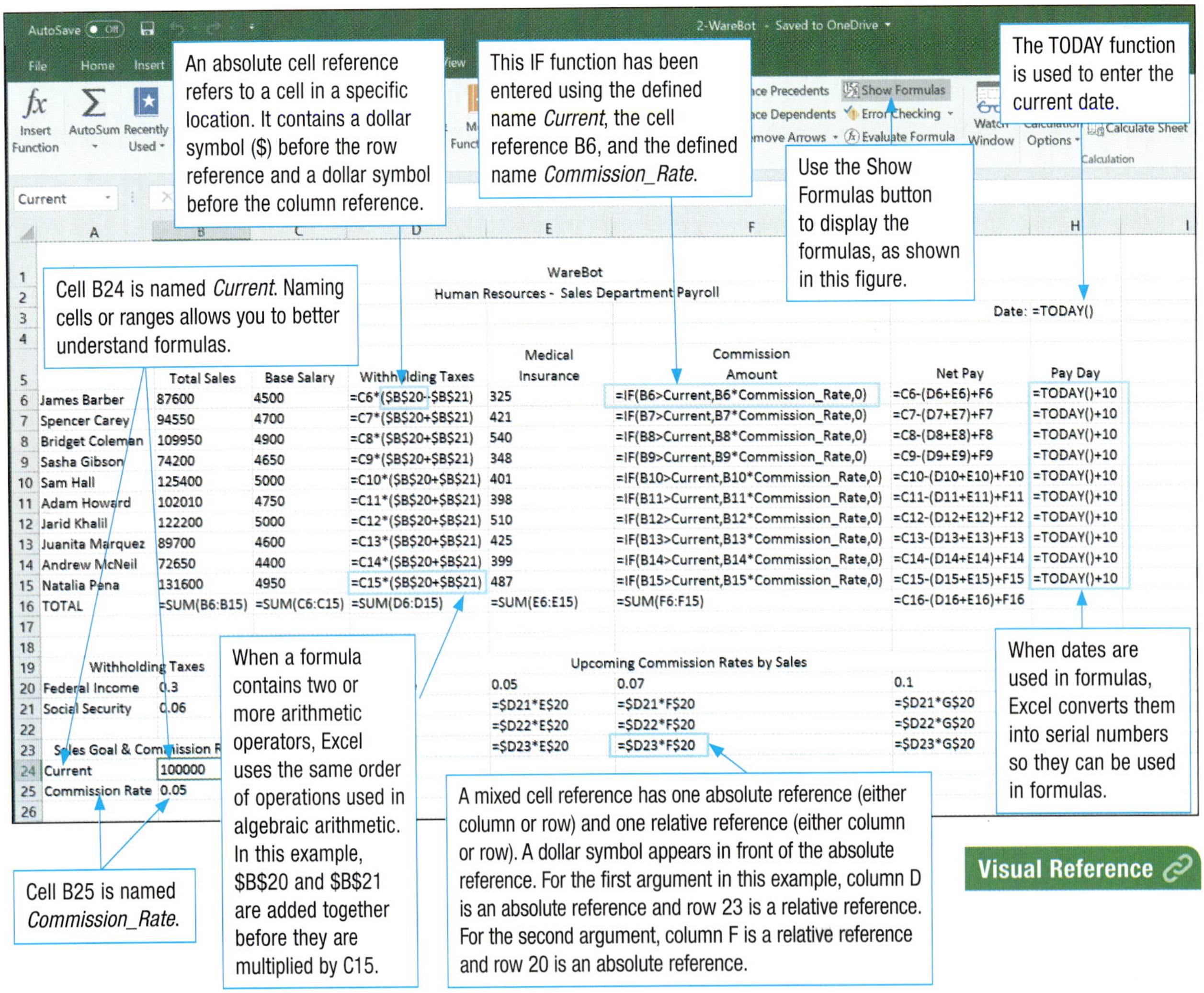

Visual Reference

2.1 Creating and Displaying Excel Formulas

Excel is often used for calculating data to assist in making business decisions and for manipulating data to create what-if situations. To calculate data, you enter formulas in a workbook. Excel is flexible, allowing you to enter formulas that calculate and summarize data in numerous ways.

A **formula** is a user-created equation that calculates data based on mathematical principles, such as the order of operations. Formulas can contain values, cell references, defined names, and operators. They can also contain functions. **Syntax** is the set of rules that outline how a formula or a function should be written. Functions are introduced in Section 2.8 of this chapter.

MOS 1.4.8

Tutorial

Creating and Displaying Excel Formulas

▶ Know This about creating formulas

- Use proper syntax to ensure that a formula calculates data correctly.
- Every formula begins with an equals sign (=).
- A formula contains values that will be calculated.
- Formulas are made up of constants and variables.
- A **constant** does not change and is usually represented as a typed-out value.
- A **variable** is generally represented as a cell or range reference, and values in the referenced cell or range can be altered.
- An example of a formula that includes both a constant and a variable is =100+C5.
- Most formulas contain cell references (variables), which allow you to easily change the values used in a formula by changing the contents of the cell being referenced rather than changing the actual formula.
- If the active cell contains a formula, the results of the formula are displayed in the cell while the actual formula is displayed in the Formula bar.
- If an equals sign is not typed at the beginning of a formula, Excel will assume that text is being entered.

▶ Know More about creating formulas

- In the formula =100+C5, the value 100 is added to the value in C5. The value 100 stays constant. The plus sign (+) is an arithmetic operator that adds the two values in the formula. The value in cell C5 may be entered by the user, or it may be the result of a formula; in either case, it can change.

▶ Know This about displaying formulas

- To display the formulas instead of the results of formulas in a worksheet, click the Show Formulas button in the Formula Auditing group on the Formulas tab.

▶ Know More ways to display formulas

- Press and hold down the Ctrl key, press the grave accent key (`), and then release the Ctrl key. (The grave accent key is generally located to the left of the 1 key.)

▶ Know This about entering formulas

- Use **arithmetic operators** (also called *mathematical symbols*) to dictate how values will be calculated in a formula. Table 2.1 identifies commonly used arithmetic operators and their purposes.
- In Excel, you can use comparison operators to compare two values. Comparison operators are explained later in the chapter, in Section 2.15.
- You can enter a formula directly in a cell or in the Formula bar. Include cell and cell range references by typing them or pointing to them.

Table 2.1 Common Arithmetic Operators

Arithmetic Operator	Purpose	Example
+ (plus sign)	Addition	=3+4
- (minus sign)	Subtraction Negation	=3-2 =-1
* (asterisk)	Multiplication	=3*4
/ (forward slash)	Division	=3/2
% (percent symbol)	Percent	=20%
^ (caret)	Exponentiation	=3^2

On the Job

Task 2.1 Typing in a Cell to Enter a Formula and Displaying Formulas

Jeremy would like to see the actual total sales department budget in cell B20 on the Budget worksheet. This total is found by adding the total values for payroll, traveling, and staff training expenses in cells B10, B16, and B18. These cells are not adjacent, so using the AutoSum button will not return the correct actual total. In this case, creating a formula using the addition operator (+) will allow you to choose the correct cells to add. To quickly verify any formulas in the worksheet, turn on the display of formulas, review the formulas, and then turn off the display of formulas.

1. Open the data file **2-WareBot**.
2. Click the Budget sheet tab, if necessary, to make the worksheet active.
3. Click in cell B20, type the formula =B10+B16+B18, and then press the Enter key.

   Cell B21 (the cell below the actual total cell) is now active. Notice that the total for the actual budget is $104,150, and it includes payroll, traveling, and staff training expenses.
4. Press and hold down the Ctrl key, press the grave accent key (`), and then release the Ctrl key.

   The formulas are displayed in cells B10, C10, B16, C16, and B20.
5. Press and hold down the Ctrl key, press the grave accent key (`), and then release the Ctrl key.

   The results are redisplayed in cells B10, C10, B16, C16, and B20.
6. Click the Save button on the Quick Access Toolbar.

Model Answer

2.2 Typing a Formula in the Formula Bar

You may type a formula directly in a cell or in the Formula bar, whichever you prefer.

Tutorial

Typing a Formula in the Formula Bar

▸ **Know This** about typing a formula in the Formula bar

— To type a formula in the Formula bar, click in the cell that will contain the formula, click in the Formula bar (see Figure 2.3), enter the formula, and then finish the formula in one of these ways:

- Click the Formula bar Enter button to keep the cell containing the formula active.
- Press the Enter key to make the next cell below the one containing the formula active.

On the Job

Task 2.2 Typing in the Formula Bar to Enter a Formula

Jeremy would also like to see the projected total sales department budget in cell C20 on the Budget worksheet. Use a formula to add the nonadjacent total values for payroll, traveling, and staff training expenses in cells C10, C16, and C18. Enter the formula by typing it in the Formula bar.

1. With the Budget worksheet active, click in cell C20 and then click in the Formula bar (see Figure 2.3).
2. Type the formula =C10+C16+C18.

   The color of each cell reference in the Formula bar matches the color of the fill and border of that cell in the worksheet.
3. Click the Formula bar Enter button (see Figure 2.3).

   The cell that contains the formula remains active. The projected total ($102,647) is slightly less than the actual total ($104,150).
4. Click the Save button on the Quick Access Toolbar.

Figure 2.3 Formula Typed in the Formula Bar

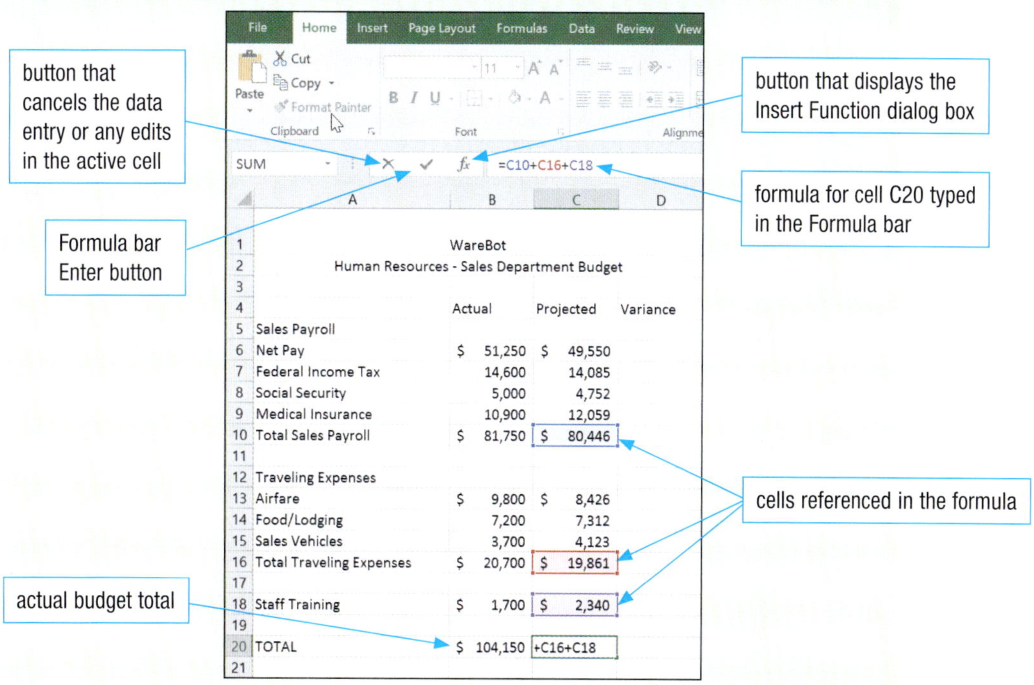

Model Answer

2.3 Typing and Pointing to Enter a Formula, and Using the Fill Button

Instead of typing a cell reference in a formula, you can enter the reference by pointing to the cell and then clicking the cell. Using this method can reduce errors due to the mistyping of cell references.

You learned in Chapter 1 that one benefit of using a formula is that it can be copied to other cells. One method of copying formulas is to use the Fill button.

MOS 4.1.1

Tutorial

Typing and Pointing to Enter a Formula, and Using the *Fill Down* Option

▸ Know This about clicking to add a cell reference to a formula

— While entering a formula, you can point to a cell and then click in the cell to add that cell's reference to the formula.

▸ Know This about using the Fill button to copy a formula

— To copy a formula using the Fill button, select the cell containing the formula, select the cells in which to copy the formula, click the Fill button in the Editing group on the Home tab, and then choose the direction in which to fill. (See Figure 2.4 for all the Fill button options.)

— The cells in which to copy the formula do not have to be adjacent to the cell containing the formula.

▸ Know More ways to copy a formula

– To copy a formula down into adjacent cells in a column, select the cell containing the formula and the cells in which to copy the formula and then press Ctrl + D.

– To copy a formula to the right into adjacent cells in a row, select the cell containing the formula and the cells in which to copy the formula and then press Ctrl + R.

On the Job

Task 2.3 Typing and Pointing to Enter a Formula, and Using the *Fill Down* Option

Jeremy is interested in determining if the formula used to calculate the projected budget gives an adequate result, or if an adjustment needs to be made in next month's budget. He would like you to find the variance in the actual and projected totals for the current month, and display them in column D on the Budget worksheet. The result in cell D20 will show the overall variance between the projected and actual totals, making it easier for him to determine how to move forward. Start by entering the correct formula in cell D6. Select all the other cells and ranges (D6:D10, D13:D16, D18, and D20) that will use this formula and then use the Fill button to copy the formula down through the required cells.

1. With the Budget worksheet active, click in cell D6, type an equals sign (=), and then click in cell B6.
2. Type a minus sign (–), click in cell C6, and then press the Enter key.

   The variance between the projected and actual totals for net pay displays. The variance number is positive, indicating that the category was over budget.
3. Click in cell D6, press and hold down the Shift key, click in cell D10, and then release the Shift key.

   The range D6:D10 is selected.
4. Press and hold down the Ctrl key, click in cell D13, release the Ctrl key, press and hold down the Shift key, click in cell D16, and then release the Shift key.

   The range D13:D16 is added to the selection.

Reminder

In Chapter 1, you learned to press and hold down the Shift key when selecting adjacent cells or a range of cells, and to press and hold down the Ctrl key when selecting nonadjacent cells.

5. Press and hold down the Ctrl key, click in cell D18, click in cell D20, and then release the Ctrl key.

   The cells D18 and D20 are added to the selection.

6. Click the Fill button in the Editing group on the Home tab and then click the *Down* option at the drop-down list (see Figure 2.4).

   The rest of the variance column populates, including the total variance in cell D20. Jeremy can use this number to determine the accuracy of the projected total.

7. Click in any cell to deselect the cells and ranges.
8. Click the Save button on the Quick Access Toolbar.

Figure 2.4 Selected Cells and Ranges, and the Fill Button Drop-Down List

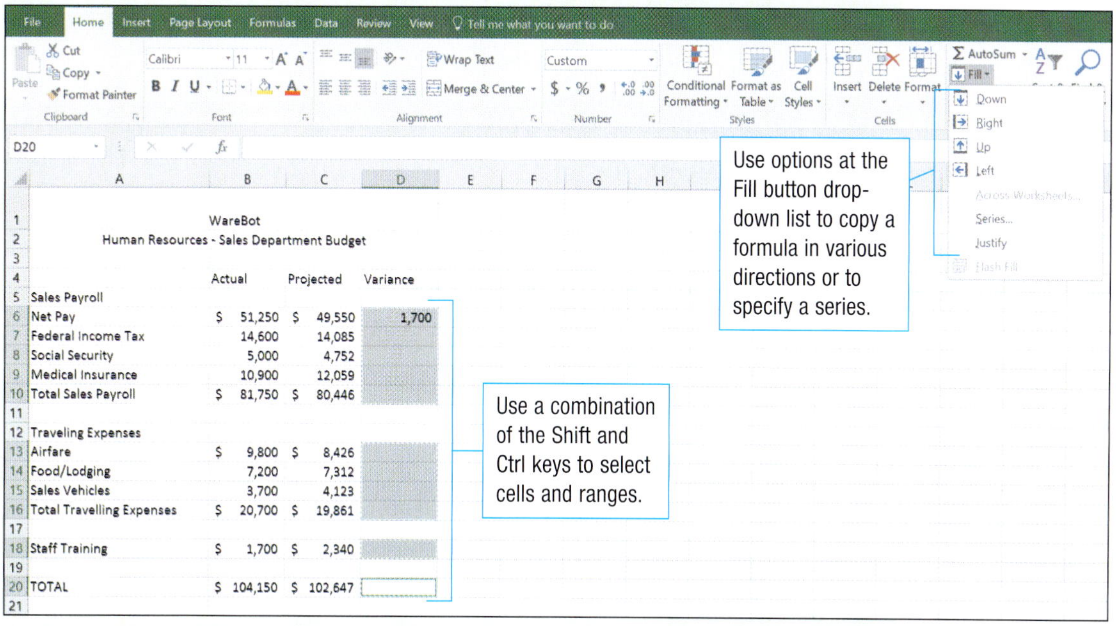

Model Answer

2.4 Determining the Order of Operations

Tutorial

Determining the Order of Operations

When you create a formula in Excel, you may need to use more than one arithmetic operator. If a formula contains two or more arithmetic operators, Excel calculates the result using the same order of operations used in algebraic arithmetic. The **order of operations** is a set of rules that defines which procedure to perform first, second, and so on, in a mathematical equation.

▸ Know This about the order of operations

— Excel reads a formula from left to right.

— By default, Excel processes a formula in the following order:

1. negations (A **negation** is a negative number—that is, a number preceded by the minus sign [–])
2. percentages (%)
3. exponentiations (^)

4. multiplications (*) or divisions (/)
5. additions (+) or subtractions (–)

— Placing parentheses around different values changes the order in which a formula is calculated, which in turn produces different results. Table 2.2 demonstrates how placing parentheses around different parts of an example formula changes the formula's result. The highlighting shows which calculation is performed first in each operation.

Table 2.2 How Parentheses Affect the Order of Operations and Result in a Formula

Formula	First Operation	Second Operation	Third Operation	Result
=4+6*3–2	=4+6*3–2	=4+18–2	=22–2	20
=(4+6)*3–2	=(4+6)*3–2	=10*3–2	=30–2	28
=4+6*(3–2)	=4+6*(3–2)	=4+6*1	=4+6	10

▸ **Know This** about nested parentheses and advanced formulas

— In an advanced formula, you can nest parentheses.
— Nested parentheses are one or more sets of parentheses placed within another set of parentheses.
— When Excel encounters nested parentheses in a formula, it calculates the values in order from the innermost set of parentheses to the outermost set.
— More advanced formulas can contain many sets of parentheses and nested parentheses.
— Here is an example of a formula that uses nested parentheses: =B5*((C9/(K6+D12))*J11).

▸ **Know More** about how Excel calculates a formula that contains nested parentheses

In the example =B5*((C9/(K6+D12))*J11), Excel calculates the result as follows:

- First, Excel adds the values in cells K6 and D12.
- Second, Excel divides the value in cell C9 by the first result.
- Third, Excel multiplies the value in cell J11 by the second result.
- Fourth, Excel completes the computation, multiplying the value in cell B5 by the third result.

On the Job

Task 2.4 Using Parentheses to Change the Order of Operations in a Formula

Jeremy likes what you have done to the Budget worksheet. Now he would like you to modify the Payroll worksheet. Start by entering a formula that determines how much of each salesperson's base salary needs to be withheld for federal income and social security taxes. Use parentheses to specify the order of operations in the formula.

1. Click the Payroll sheet tab to make the worksheet active and then click in cell D6.
2. Type the formula =C6*(B20+B21) and then press the Enter key.
   The parentheses in the formula tell Excel to add the federal income tax percentage and social security tax percentage, and then multiply the sum by the base salary. The result, $1,620, is the amount that will be withheld for federal income and social security taxes.
3. Click the Save button on the Quick Access Toolbar.

Model Answer

2.5 Copying a Formula with Relative References

MOS 4.1.1

Tutorial Copying a Formula with Relative References

In Chapter 1, you learned how to copy a formula to adjacent cells using the fill handle. You can use the fill handle to copy a formula to numerous cells without having to create a new formula for each column or row of data. When you use the fill handle to copy a formula that contains a relative reference, you can change calculations relative to their new cell locations without manually entering each formula in the adjacent cells.

▸ Know This about relative references

— A **relative reference** automatically changes in relation to the position of each cell that contains the formula.

— For example, in Figure 2.5, Excel interprets the formula in cell C1 as saying, "Multiply the value in the cell two columns to the left by the value in the cell one column to the left."

— If you use the fill handle to copy a formula containing relative references down through adjacent cells in a column, Excel automatically retains the interpretation of each reference based on each new location, as shown in Figure 2.6.

Figure 2.5 Formula with Relative References

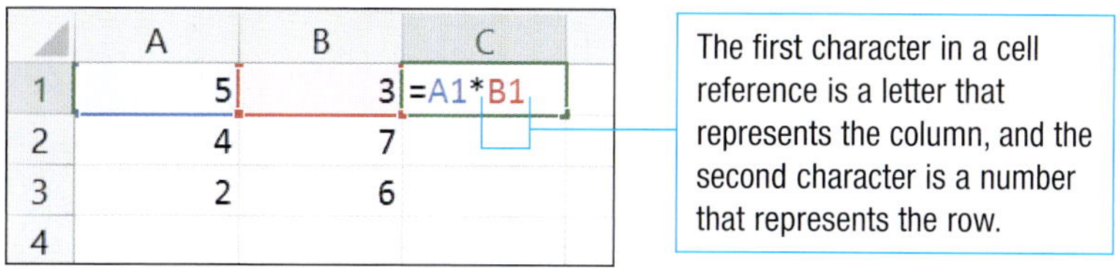

Figure 2.6 Formula with Relative References Copied Down

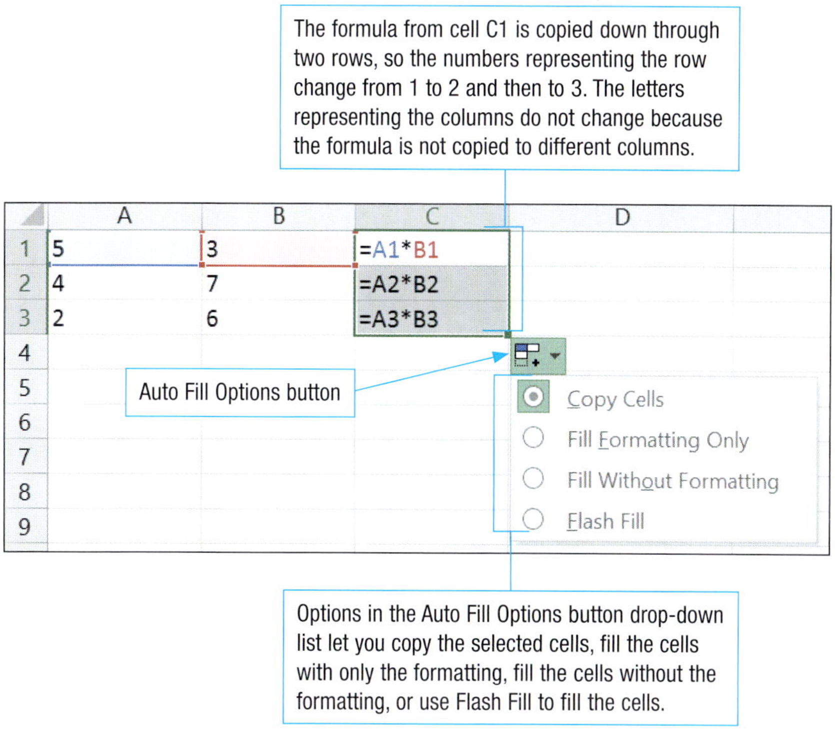

— You can also use the fill handle to copy a formula across through adjacent cells in a row, as shown in Figure 2.7. In this example, the entire argument of the SUM function (a range of cells) changes relatively.

Figure 2.7 Formula with Relative References Copied Across to the Right

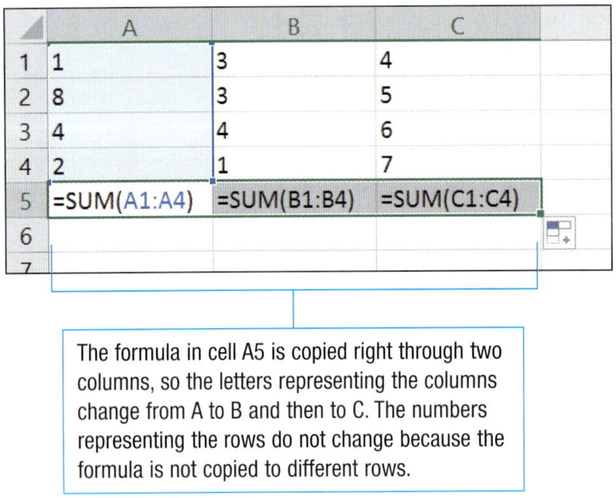

On the Job

Task 2.5 Using the Fill Handle to Copy a Formula Containing Relative References

Jeremy would like you to use the formula you created in Task 2.4 to determine how much withholding tax is owed by each salesperson. You decide to use the fill handle to copy the formula down through the *Withholding Taxes* column. Withholding taxes total 36% (federal income tax of 30% plus social security tax of 6%), so you expect the withholding taxes to be 36% of the base salary for each salesperson. After you see the results, you realize that the copied formula did not produce the correct values, and you delete the range you just filled.

1. With the Payroll worksheet active, click in cell D6.
2. Hover the mouse pointer over the fill handle at the lower right corner of cell D6 until the pointer turns into a thin black cross, click and hold down the left mouse button, drag the handle down into cell D15, and then release the mouse button.
3. Review the results in the range D7:D15 to determine whether they are what you expected.

   The results are not what you expected (see Figure 2.8). The cell references for the withholding taxes changed relative to the new cell locations, giving you incorrect results. To produce the correct results, you want the cell reference for the base salary to change but the cell references for federal income and social security taxes to remain the same.
4. Select the range D7:D15 and then press the Delete key.

   The incorrect results are removed from the worksheet.
5. Click the Save button on the Quick Access Toolbar.

Figure 2.8 Copied Formula That Produces Incorrect Results

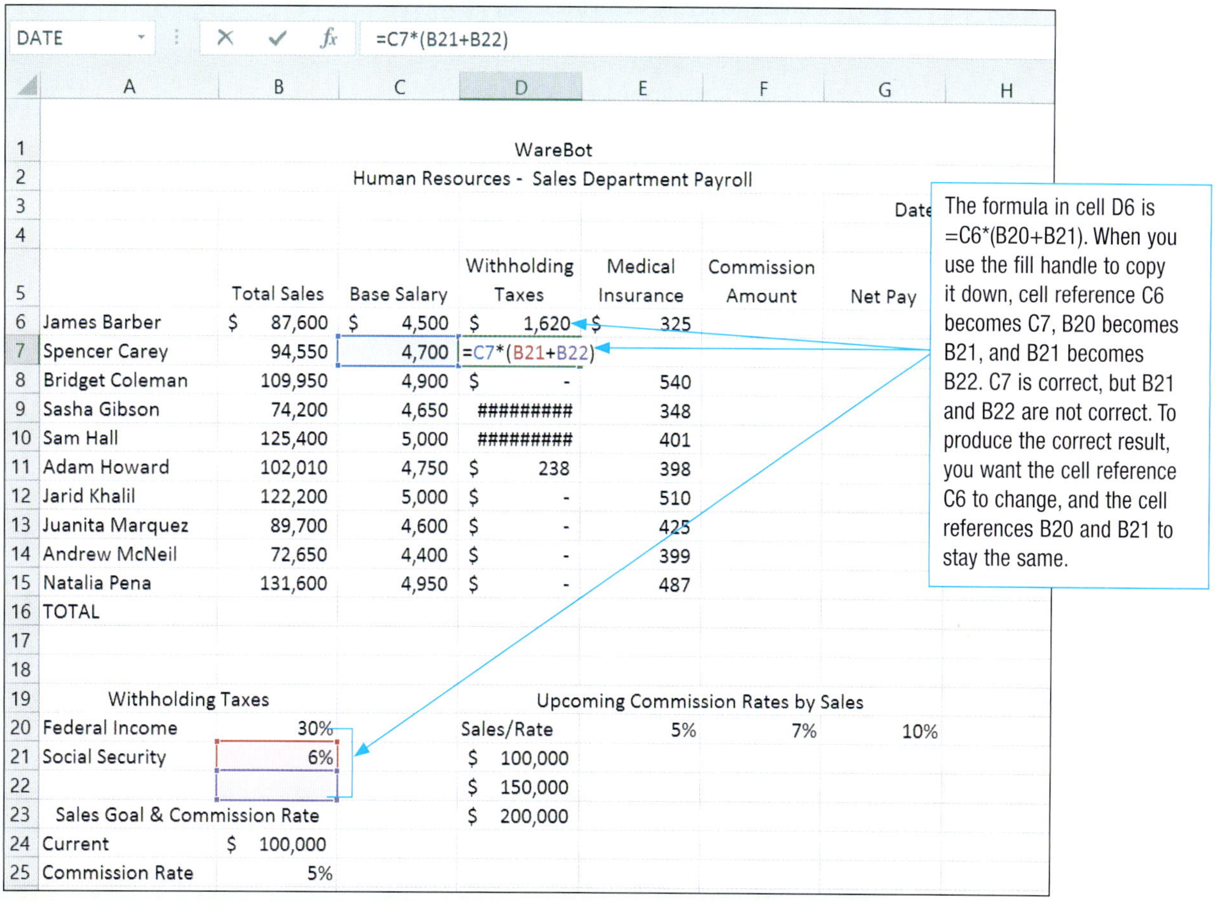

Model Answer

2.6 Using an Absolute Cell Reference in a Formula

Tutorial

Creating an Absolute Cell Reference and Copying a Formula with Absolute References

If you do not want a cell reference or range to change when you use the fill handle to copy formulas, use an absolute reference. An **absolute reference** stays the same when the formula is copied to a new cell location.

▸ Know This about absolute references

— If you include an absolute reference in a formula, the reference will not change when you copy the formula.

— To create an absolute cell reference, insert a dollar symbol in front of the column letter and a dollar symbol in front of the row number.

— For example, in the cell reference $A$5, the column (A) will stay the same and the row (5) will stay the same.

— If a formula includes a constant that may change (such as a sales commission rate), you can type the constant in its own cell and then insert an absolute reference to that cell in the formula. If you copy the formula to other cells, you can alter the constant in that one location, instead of having to edit it in each instance of the formula.

— Figure 2.9 shows an example of a formula with an absolute cell reference.

▸ Know More ways to create an absolute reference

– Type or click in a cell reference and then press the F4 function key. If you press the F4 function key multiple times, it cycles through the various types of cell referencing. For example, type *C5*, press the F4 function key, and the cell reference changes to $C$5.

continues...

Figure 2.9 Copied Formula Containing an Absolute Cell Reference

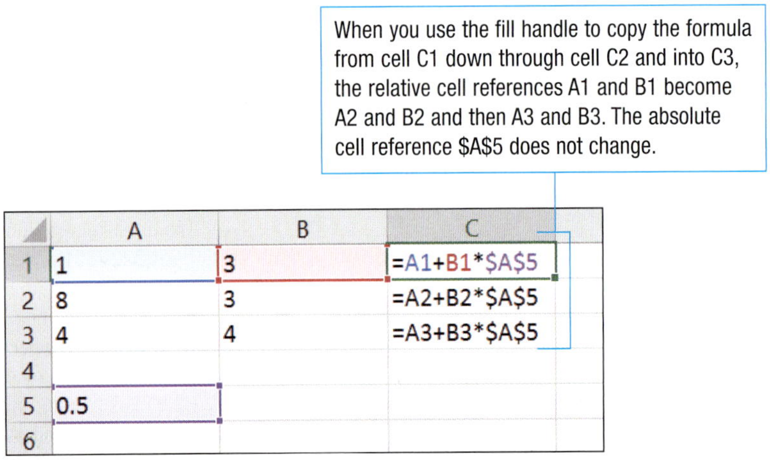

▶ **Know More** ways to create an absolute reference *...continued*

Press the F4 function key again, and the cell reference changes to C$5. Press the F4 function key again, and the cell reference changes to $C5. Press the F4 function key again, and the cell reference cycles back to C5.

On the Job

Task 2.6 Entering and Copying a Formula with an Absolute Cell Reference

You decide to try again to copy the withholding taxes formula using the fill handle. This time, you will first change the cell references for the federal income tax and social security to absolute references so that they will not change when you copy the formula. You will also apply formatting to display the results with a comma and with no digits after the decimal point.

1. With the Payroll worksheet active, click in cell D6 and then click in the Formula bar.
2. Place the insertion point immediately to the left of the cell reference B20, type a dollar symbol ($), press the right arrow key, and then type another dollar symbol ($).

   The formula appears as =C6*($B$20+B21).
3. Press the right arrow key three times and then press the F4 function key.

   The cell reference B21 changes to $B$21, and the formula now includes the two required absolute references.
4. Click the Formula bar Enter button.

   Cell D6 remains active.
5. Use the fill handle to copy the formula from cell D6 down into cell D15.
6. Review the results in the range D7:D15.

   The cells in the range D7:D15 are now populated with the correct formulas (see Figure 2.10).
7. Select the range D7:D15 and then apply comma formatting with no digits after the decimal point. Click in any cell to deselect the range.

   Comma formatting is applied to remove the unwanted dollar symbols.
8. Click the Save button on the Quick Access Toolbar.

Figure 2.10 Copied Formula Containing Absolute References

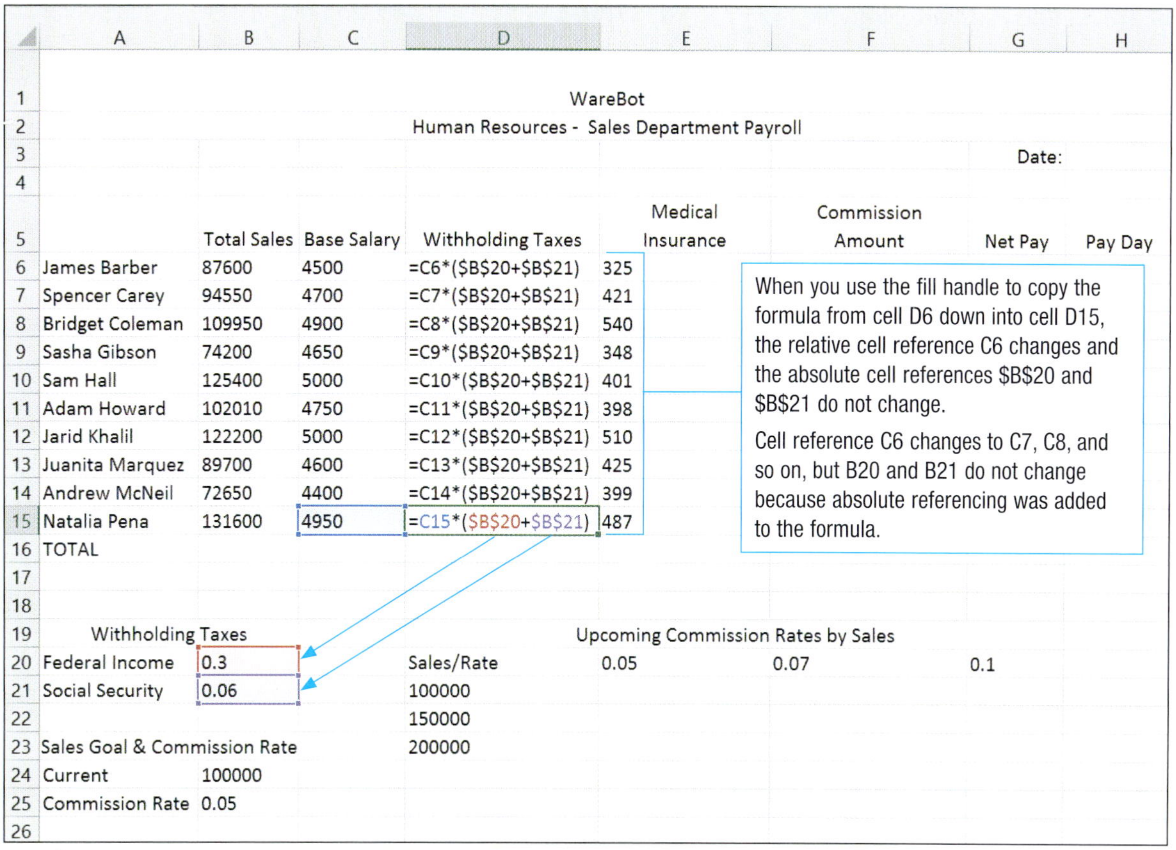

	A	B	C	D	E	F	G	H
1				WareBot				
2				Human Resources - Sales Department Payroll				
3							Date:	
4								
5		Total Sales	Base Salary	Withholding Taxes	Medical Insurance	Commission Amount	Net Pay	Pay Day
6	James Barber	87600	4500	=C6*($B$20+$B$21)	325			
7	Spencer Carey	94550	4700	=C7*($B$20+$B$21)	421			
8	Bridget Coleman	109950	4900	=C8*($B$20+$B$21)	540			
9	Sasha Gibson	74200	4650	=C9*($B$20+$B$21)	348			
10	Sam Hall	125400	5000	=C10*($B$20+$B$21)	401			
11	Adam Howard	102010	4750	=C11*($B$20+$B$21)	398			
12	Jarid Khalil	122200	5000	=C12*($B$20+$B$21)	510			
13	Juanita Marquez	89700	4600	=C13*($B$20+$B$21)	425			
14	Andrew McNeil	72650	4400	=C14*($B$20+$B$21)	399			
15	Natalia Pena	131600	4950	=C15*($B$20+$B$21)	487			
16	TOTAL							
17								
18								
19	Withholding Taxes				Upcoming Commission Rates by Sales			
20	Federal Income	0.3		Sales/Rate	0.05	0.07	0.1	
21	Social Security	0.06		100000				
22				150000				
23	Sales Goal & Commission Rate			200000				
24	Current	100000						
25	Commission Rate	0.05						
26								

Model Answer

2.7 Using a Mixed Cell Reference in a Formula

If you want only the column or row to change when you copy a formula use a mixed reference. A **mixed reference** contains both relative and absolute references. Either the column remains the same and the row changes relative to the new location, or the row remains the same and the column changes.

Tutorial

Entering and Copying a Formula with Mixed Cell References

▸ Know This about mixed cell references

— If you include a mixed reference in a formula, the relative reference will change and the absolute reference will stay the same when you copy the formula.

— You can insert a mixed cell reference that makes the column reference absolute and the row reference relative, or you can insert a mixed cell reference that makes the column reference relative and the row reference absolute.

— When entering a cell reference in a formula, press the F4 function key to change between a relative, an absolute, or a mixed cell reference.

— In the example in Figure 2.11, mixed cell references are used to create a table of commissions based on sales and on commission rates.

- The formula contains mixed cell references for both the sales and the commission rate, to ensure that the formula calculates as intended when the fill handle is used to copy it:
  - The first mixed cell reference is for the sales values in column A; the column reference will not change when the formula is copied across to the right because it is absolute.
  - The second mixed cell reference is for the commission rates in row 1; the row reference will not change when the formula is copied down because it is absolute.
- Figure 2.12 displays the worksheet with the formulas displayed. Notice that each cell contains an absolute reference to column A and row 1.
- Figure 2.13 shows the results of the calculated formulas.

Figure 2.11 Formula Containing Mixed Cell References

	A		B	C	D	E	F	G
1	Sales/Comm Rate		5%	10%	15%	20%	25%	30%
2	$	25,000	=$A2*B$1					
3	$	50,000						
4	$	75,000						
5	$	100,000						
6	$	150,000						
7	$	200,000						
8								

Column A is an absolute reference and row 2 is a relative reference. When the formula is copied down, the column reference does not change, but the row reference changes from 2 to 3 and then 4, and so on.

Column B is a relative reference, and row 1 is an absolute reference. When the formula is copied across to the right, the column reference changes from B to C and then D, and so on, but the row reference does not change.

Figure 2.12 Copied Formula Containing Mixed Cell References

	A	B	C	D	E	F	G
1	Sales/Comm Rate	0.05	0.1	0.15	0.2	0.25	0.3
2	25000	=$A2*B$1	=$A2*C$1	=$A2*D$1	=$A2*E$1	=$A2*F$1	=$A2*G$1
3	50000	=$A3*B$1	=$A3*C$1	=$A3*D$1	=$A3*E$1	=$A3*F$1	=$A3*G$1
4	75000	=$A4*B$1	=$A4*C$1	=$A4*D$1	=$A4*E$1	=$A4*F$1	=$A4*G$1
5	100000	=$A5*B$1	=$A5*C$1	=$A5*D$1	=$A5*E$1	=$A5*F$1	=$A5*G$1
6	150000	=$A6*B$1	=$A6*C$1	=$A6*D$1	=$A6*E$1	=$A6*F$1	=$A6*G$1
7	200000	=$A7*B$1	=$A7*C$1	=$A7*D$1	=$A7*E$1	=$A7*F$1	=$A7*G$1
8							

Column A is an absolute reference and the row number is a relative reference. When the formula is copied down, the column reference does not change, but the row reference changes from 2 to 3 and then 4, and so on.

The column is a relative reference, and row 1 is an absolute reference. When the formula is copied down, the column reference changes from A to B and then C, and so on, but the row reference does not change.

Figure 2.13 Results for a Copied Formula Containing Mixed Cell References

	A	B	C	D	E	F	G
1	Sales/Comm Rate	5%	10%	15%	20%	25%	30%
2	$ 25,000	$ 1,250	$ 2,500	$ 3,750	$ 5,000	$ 6,250	$ 7,500
3	$ 50,000	$ 2,500	$ 5,000	$ 7,500	$ 10,000	$ 12,500	$ 15,000
4	$ 75,000	$ 3,750	$ 7,500	$ 11,250	$ 15,000	$ 18,750	$ 22,500
5	$ 100,000	$ 5,000	$ 10,000	$ 15,000	$ 20,000	$ 25,000	$ 30,000
6	$ 150,000	$ 7,500	$ 15,000	$ 22,500	$ 30,000	$ 37,500	$ 45,000
7	$ 200,000	$ 10,000	$ 20,000	$ 30,000	$ 40,000	$ 50,000	$ 60,000
8							

On the Job

Task 2.7 Entering a Formula with Mixed Cell References

Jeremy is going to implement a new bracket system for commission rates, to encourage salespeople to not only meet their sales quota but go above and beyond them. With the new system, the more total sales a salesperson brings in, the higher his or her commission rate. Jeremy asks you to create a table of commission amounts at different levels of sales. Using this table will provide a quick way for salespeople to determine how much they can make in commissions if they increase their sales. Use a formula with mixed cell references to add this table in the range E21:G23 on the Payroll worksheet.

1. With the Payroll worksheet active, click in cell E21, type the formula =$D21*E$20, and then press the Enter key.

   Both cell references in this formula are mixed; the first reference has a fixed column, and the second reference has a fixed row.

2. Click in cell E21 and then use the fill handle to copy the formula down into cell E23.

   The second mixed cell reference in the formula provides the desired results when you copy the formula down, because the row is fixed.

3. With cells E21 through E23 still selected, use the fill handle to copy the formulas across to the right, into cell G23.

   The first cell reference in the formula has a fixed column, which makes the formula calculate the correct values when you copy the formula across to the right.

4. Click in any cell to deselect the range.
5. Click the Save button on the Quick Access Toolbar.

Model Answer

2.8 Inserting Functions and Using the Math & Trig Functions RAND, ROUND, and SUM

MOS 4.1.2

Tutorial

Using the SUM Function

A **function** is a predesigned equation that calculates data using arguments. For example, SUM is a function that you inserted in a worksheet in Chapter 1. Excel includes a number of functions, which are grouped in categories. Common categories include *Financial*, *Logical*, *Text*, *Date & Time*, *Lookup & Reference*, *Math & Trig*, and *Statistical*.

▸ Know This about functions

— The proper syntax for a function differs from the proper syntax for a formula.
— A function includes a function name (such as SUM) followed by a set of parentheses.
— The parentheses enclose arguments. An **argument** provides data needed to make a calculation.
— A **required argument** is an argument that the function needs in order to return a value.
— An **optional argument** is an additional argument that is identified by square brackets.
— An optional argument may include a default value so that Excel has a value to use if you do not specify a different value.
— Complex functions require more than one argument, with a comma between arguments.
— An example of the correct syntax for a simple SUM function is =SUM(B6:B9).

▸ Know This about inserting functions

— If you know the name and proper syntax for a function, you can type the function and arguments directly in the Formula bar.
— You must follow all the relevant syntax when creating advanced formulas and functions. If, for example, you leave out a parenthesis or forget an argument, Excel will not be able to perform the correct calculations.

The *Math & Trig* category includes functions that perform a variety of calculations, ranging from basic arithmetic to advanced trigonometry. Table 2.3 displays commonly used Math & Trig functions and their descriptions.

Table 2.3 Commonly Used Math & Trig Functions

Function	Description
RAND()	Returns a random number between 0 and 1 (changes on recalculation)
ROUND(number, num_digits)	Rounds a number to the number of digits specified by the *num_digits* argument (*num_digits* is the number of digits after the decimal point)
SUM(number1[,number2, number3, ...])	Adds the contents of the specific cells and/or ranges and any additional arguments

▸ Know This about using Math & Trig Functions

— The syntax for each Math & Trig function is slightly different.
— The **RAND function** does not require any arguments to be entered because it returns a random number from one of Excel's random number generators.
— The **ROUND function** requires that two arguments be entered: the first argument determines which number or cell to round, and the second argument determines how many digits to display after the decimal point.
— The SUM function includes optional arguments.

▸ Know More about arguments

– In the formula =SUM(B6:B9), the argument is the range of cells B6 through B9. Excel uses this argument to add all the values in the indicated cells.

▸ Know More about functions

– The SUM function in the formula =SUM(C3:C12,F3:F12,K9:L12) includes two additional ranges, which are added as optional arguments. This function adds the numbers from the three ranges referenced in the arguments.
– A function can include a formula.
– The argument of a function can be entered in the form of a formula that contains arithmetic operators. For example, the ROUND function in the formula =ROUND(C5*F3,0) uses a formula as an argument. This function multiplies the values in cells C5 and F3 and then rounds the results to the nearest whole number.
– A function can also be used as part of a larger formula, as in the example =C5*D7+SUM(J10:J20).

On the Job
Task 2.8 Using the SUM Function

Jeremy wants you to include the totals for the *Total Sales* and *Base Salary* columns in the Payroll worksheet. Use the SUM function to determine the total for each of these columns.

1. With the Payroll worksheet active, click in cell B16, type the formula =SUM(B6:B15), and then press the Enter key.
   The SUM function returns the value 1,009,860.
2. Click in cell C16, type =SUM(, select the range C6:C15, type), and then press the Enter key.
   The total for base salaries is 47,450.
3. Click in cell C16. Using the fill handle, copy the formula from cell C16 across into cell E16.
4. Click the Save button on the Quick Access Toolbar.

Model Answer

2.9 Using the Statistical Functions AVERAGE, COUNT, COUNTA, MAX, MEDIAN, and MIN

MOS 4.1.3
MOS 4.1.4
MOS 4.1.5

Tutorial
Using the COUNT Function

The *Statistical* category of functions is used to summarize sets of data into useful measures, such as averages and counts. Table 2.4 lists commonly used Statistical functions.

Table 2.4 Commonly Used Statistical Functions

Function	Description
AVERAGE(number1[,number2,number3,...])	Calculates the average of the specified cells or range(s)
COUNT(number1[,number2,number3,...])	Counts the cells in a range that contain numbers
COUNTA(value1[,value2,value3,...])	Counts the number of cells in a range that are not empty (The cells can contain text.)
MAX(number1[,number2,number3,...])	Finds the maximum value in the specified range(s)
MEDIAN(number1[,number2,number3,...])	Calculates the middle value in the specified range(s)
MIN(number1[,number2,number3,...])	Finds the minimum value in the specified range(s)

▸ Know This about inserting Statistical functions

— Statistical functions are generally used on a range or multiple ranges of data because statistical data relies on a group of values to determine the desired result.

— For example, you would not find the average or median of one value.

— Most Statistical functions include optional arguments, which are used for selecting additional ranges of data.

On the Job

Task 2.9 Using the COUNT Function

Salespeople at WareBot are required to train on product and features, and on sales and follow-up. Jeremy will use tests to track the training performance of each salesperson, and then enter the test results in the Training worksheet. He asks you to help him summarize the data he collects by inserting a function that will count the number of tests each employee has taken.

1. Click the Training sheet tab to make the worksheet active.

   Each salesperson is required to complete two product features tests and two sales and follow-up tests.

2. Click in cell F6 and then type =COUNT(.

   The COUNT function will determine how many tests each salesperson has completed.

3. Select the range B6:E6 and then press the Enter key.

   Excel automatically inserts the last parenthesis in the formula if you do not include it yourself.

4. Use the fill handle to copy the formula from cell F6 down into cell F15.
5. Click in any cell to deselect the range.
6. Click the Save button on the Quick Access Toolbar.

Model Answer

2.10 Using Quick Analysis to Enter Formulas

When you select a range of cells, the **Quick Analysis button** appears at the lower right corner of the selected cells. Click the button to display the Quick Analysis gallery (see Figure 2.14).

Tutorial

Using the Quick Analysis Button to Insert a Formula

Figure 2.14 Quick Analysis Gallery

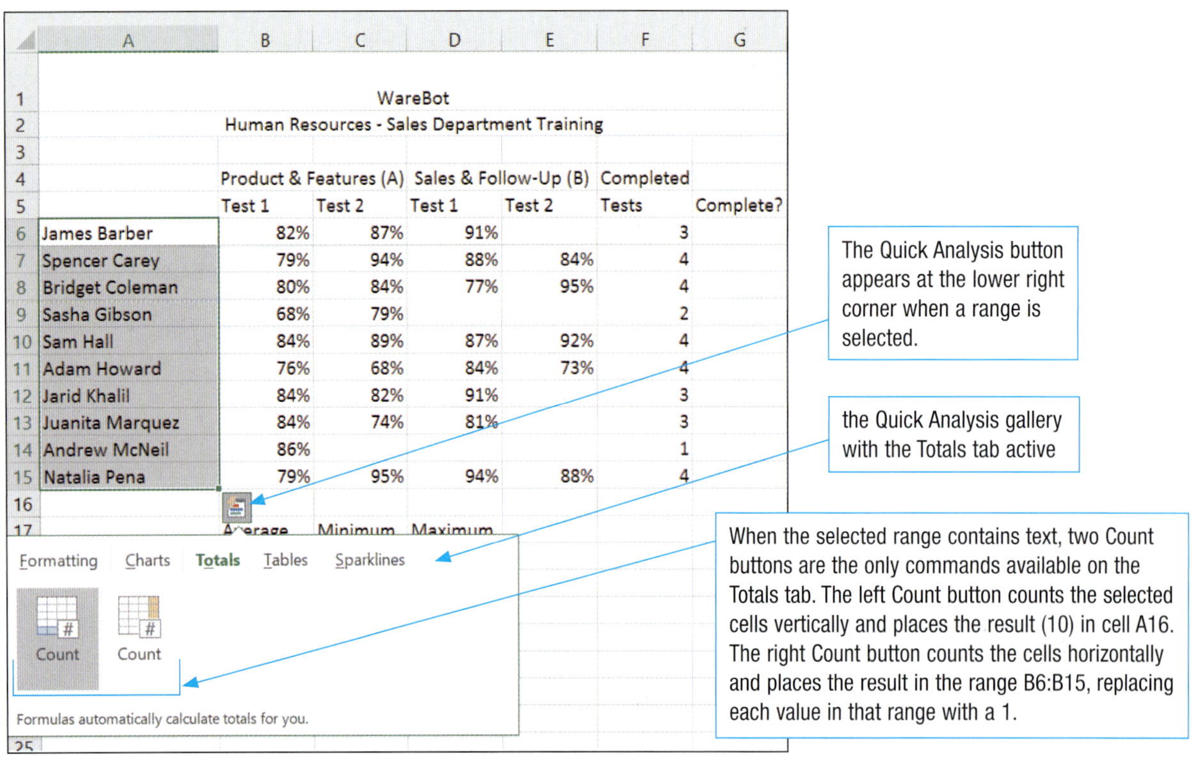

▸ **Know This** about using the Quick Analysis button

— The options under each tab of the Quick Analysis button change depending on the type of data in the selected range (e.g., numbers, text, a chart).

— To enter a formula using the Quick Analysis button, select a range, click the Quick Analysis button, click the Totals tab, and then choose an option at the Quick Analysis gallery.

▸ **Know More** ways to display the Quick Analysis gallery

– Select a range and then press Ctrl + Q.

On the Job

Task 2.10 Using the Quick Analysis Button to Enter a Formula

Jeremy asks you to add a formula that uses a function to count the number of sales department employees in cell A16. Use the Quick Analysis button to enter this formula.

1. With the Training worksheet active, select the range A6:A15.
2. Click the Quick Analysis button (see Figure 2.14).

   The Quick Analysis gallery displays.
3. Click the Totals tab.
4. Click the left Count button.

   The number 10 appears in cell A16. Bold formatting has been applied by Excel.
5. Click in any cell to deselect the range.
6. Click the Save button on the Quick Access Toolbar.

Model Answer

2.11 Creating and Using Defined Names

MOS Expert 3.6.1
MOS Expert 3.6.2

Tutorial

Creating and Using Defined Names

When you enter a formula that uses cell addresses, it may be difficult to tell what the formula is calculating. Excel includes a feature that allows you to create a **defined name** for a cell or range. Using defined names instead of cell addresses makes it easier to understand formulas, print a worksheet, and navigate in a worksheet. For example, in the Payroll worksheet, cell B20 contains the federal income tax rate and cell B21 contains the social security tax rate. If you named the cells *Federal* and *Social,* respectively, the formula to calculate the withholding taxes could be =C6*(Federal+Social) instead of =C6*($B$20+$B$21).

▸ **Know This** about defined names

— When a cell or range has been named, it will have an absolute reference in a formula or function.

— When creating a defined name, follow these rules:

- The name must begin with a letter, an underscore (_), or a backslash (\).
- The name cannot contain a space.
- The name cannot contain a symbol other than an underscore, a period, or a backslash.
- The name cannot contain a cell address (e.g., A4), the name of a function (e.g., SUM), the letter *C* alone, or the letter *R* alone.

▸ **Know More** about defined names

– A defined name is also referred to as a *named range.*

- The name will not be case sensitive (e.g., *net_sales* and *Net_Sales* reference the same cell).
- The name can be up to 255 characters long.

▶ Know This about using the Name box to name a cell or range

— To name a cell or range using the Name box, select the cell or range, click in the Name box, type the name, and then press the Enter key.

— Pressing the Enter key after typing the name is important because if you neglect to do so, the name will not be applied to the cell or range.

— You can easily navigate to a defined name by clicking the Name box arrow and then clicking the desired name at the drop-down list.

▶ Know More methods for naming a cell or range

– Use the Define Name button in the Defined Names group on the Formulas tab.

▶ Know This about creating a defined name using the Create from Selection button

— To create a defined name using the Create from Selection button, select the range and then click the Create from Selection button in the Defined Names group on the Formulas tab.

— Use the Create from Selection button to quickly define ranges if the spreadsheet is set up with the headings in the top or bottom row or in the left or right column.

On the Job

Task 2.11a Naming Ranges Using the Name Box and the Define Name Button

Jeremy would like to see the average, minimum, and maximum test scores displayed on the Training worksheet. To make it easier to enter the appropriate Statistical functions, name the range for the product features tests and the range for the sales and follow-up tests.

1. With the Training worksheet active, select the range B6:C15 and then click in the Name box.
2. Type the name TestsA (see Figure 2.15) and then press the Enter key.

   The name *TestsA* can be used as an argument standing for the range B6:C15 in a formula.
3. Select the range D6:D15 and then click in the Name box.
4. Type the name TestsB and then press the Enter key.

   This defined name includes only the scores for Test 1. In Task 2.12, you will modify the defined name to include the Test 2 scores.
5. Select the range A6:A15 and then click the Define Name button in the Defined Names group on the Formulas tab.

   The New Name dialog box displays.
6. With the text selected in the *Name* text box, type SalesEmp and then click the OK button.
7. Click in any cell to deselect the range.

   There is no visible change to the workbook.
8. Click the Save button on the Quick Access Toolbar.

Figure 2.15 Entering a Defined Name Using the Name Box

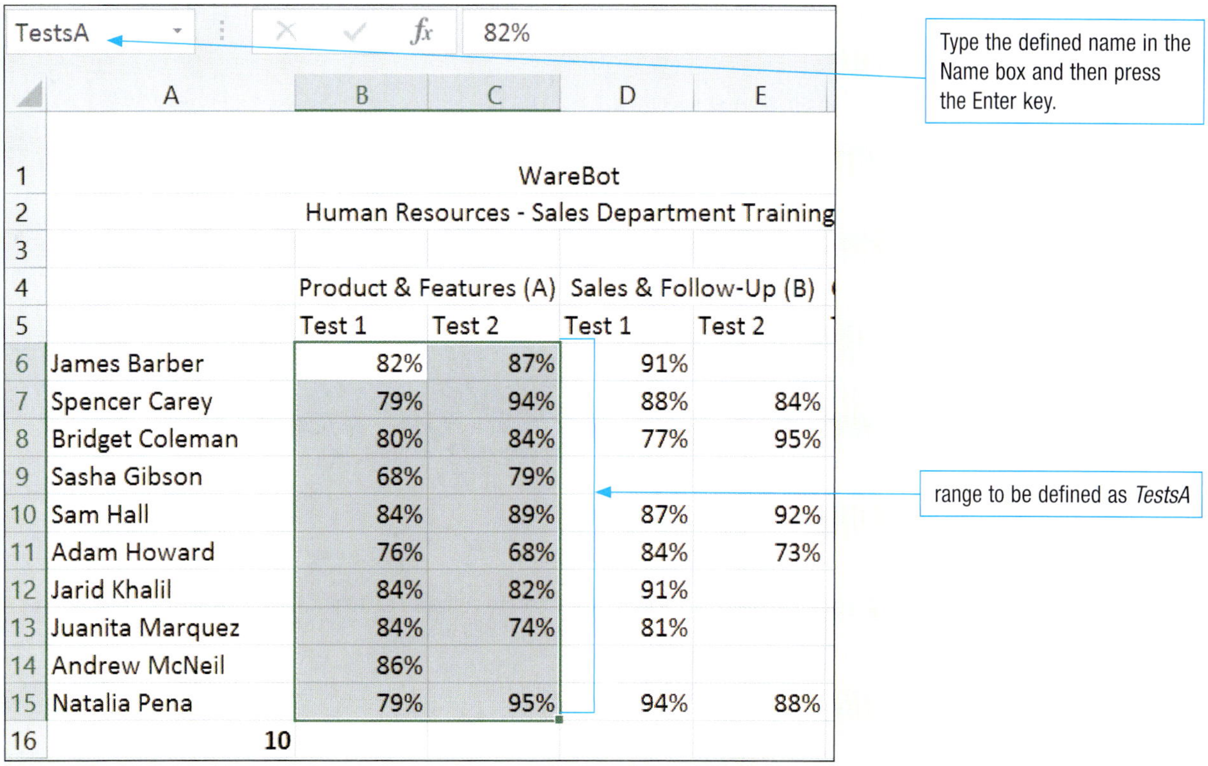

Model Answer

On the Job

Task 2.11b Naming a Range Using the Create from Selection Button

Jeremy would like you to create defined names for the *Total Sales*, *Base Salary*, *Withholding Taxes*, and *Medical Insurance* columns on the Payroll worksheet. He cautions you to include only the data in rows 5 through 15, not the totals in row 16.

1. Click the Payroll sheet tab to make the worksheet active.
2. Select the range B5:E15.
3. Click the Create from Selection button in the Defined Names group on the Formulas tab.
4. With a check mark inserted in the *Top row* check box, click the OK button.
5. Click the Name box arrow.

   The defined names *Base_Salary*, *Medical_Insurance*, *Total_Sales*, *and Withholding_Taxes*, have been added to the drop-down list in alphabetic order.

6. Click the *Total_Sales* option.

   The range B6:B15 is selected.

7. Click in any cell to deselect the range.

   There is no visible change to the workbook.

8. Click the Save button on the Quick Access Toolbar.

2.12 Modifying and Deleting Defined Names

MOS Expert 3.6.4

Tutorial

Modifying and Deleting Defined Names

A defined name can be modified by changing the name itself or the cell address associated with it. A defined name can also be deleted.

▸ Know This about modifying and deleting defined names

— The Name Manager dialog box contains options for creating, editing, and deleting cell or range names (see Figure 2.16).

— You can delete a defined name, but use extra caution when doing so.

— A cell containing a formula that uses a deleted cell or range name displays the error text *#NAME?*

Figure 2.16 Name Manager Dialog Box

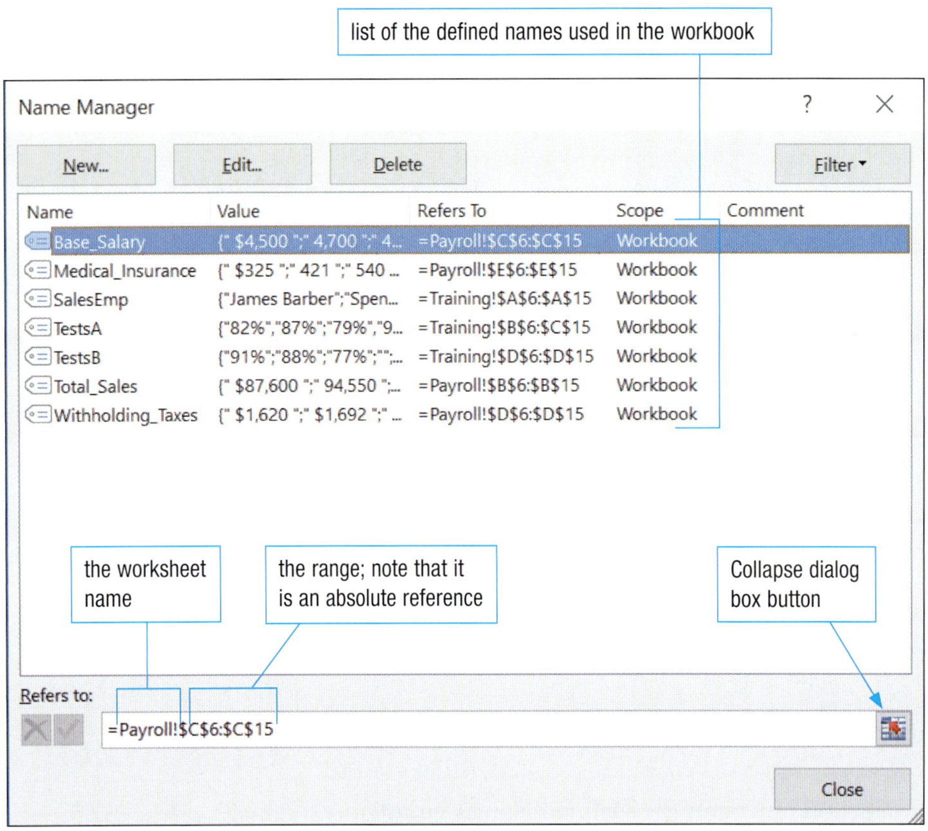

On the Job

Task 2.12 Modifying and Deleting a Defined Name

Jeremy would like you to determine whether the *TestsA* and *TestsB* defined names are correct, make any necessary changes, and then delete the *SalesEmp* defined name.

1. Click the Training sheet tab to make the worksheet active.
2. Click the Name box arrow and then click the *TestsA* option.

   The range B6:C15 is selected. The defined name *TestsA* is correct, as it selects the results for all the Product & Features (A) tests.

3. Click the Name box arrow and then click the *TestsB* option.

   The range D6:D15 is selected. The defined name *TestsB* is incorrect, as it selects the results for only one of the two Sales & Follow-Up (B) tests.

4. Click the Name Manager button in the Defined Names group on the Formulas tab.

   The Name Manager dialog box displays (see Figure 2.16, on page 80).

5. Click the *TestsB* option in the Name Manager list box.

   The formula *=Training!$D$6:$D$15* appears in the *Refers to* text box at the bottom of the Name Manager dialog box.

6. Click the Edit button.

   The Edit Name dialog box displays.

7. Click the Collapse dialog box button.

   The dialog box collapses.

8. Select the range D6:E15 in the worksheet.

   The formula *=Training!$D$6:$E$15* appears in the *Refers to* text box in the Edit Name dialog box.

9. Click the Expand dialog box button and then click the OK button.
10. Click the *SalesEmp* option in the Name Manager list box and then click the Delete button.

    A dialog box displays, asking if you are sure you want to the delete the defined name.

11. Click the OK button.
12. Click the Close button.

    The Name Manager dialog box closes. There is no visible change to the workbook.

13. Click the Save button on the Quick Access Toolbar.

2.13 Using a Defined Name in a Formula

MOS 4.1.3
MOS 4.1.5

Tutorial

Using a Defined Name in a Formula

If you use cell addresses to write a formula that multiplies the net sales in cell H21 by the tax rate in cell K2, the formula will appear as =H21*K2. To a user who is not familiar with the worksheet and how it was created, this formula may be confusing and uninformative. If you name cell H21 *NetSales* and cell K2 *TaxRate*, and write the formula using these names, the formula will appear as =NetSales*TaxRate. For users of the worksheet, this formula will be more descriptive and easier to understand.

▸ **Know This** about using a defined name in a formula

— Once you have named a cell or range in a worksheet, you can use the defined name when creating formulas.

— If you edit a defined name, the formula will amend to use the new defined name.

On the Job
Task 2.13 Using Defined Names in Formulas

Jeremy would like you to add to the Training worksheet the average, minimum, and maximum scores for the Product & Features (A) tests and for the Sales & Follow-Up (B) tests. Insert functions to calculate those statistics, using the defined name for each set of tests so that users can easily see what each formula means.

1. With the Training worksheet active, click in cell B18, type =AVERAGE(TestsA), and then press the Enter key.

   The result 0.8178947 displays as the average score for all Product & Features (A) tests. (The number of decimal places in your worksheet may differ.) The AVERAGE function does not include empty cells in its calculations. This means that the empty cell for Test 2 for Andrew McNeil (cell C14), is not included in the average score. If you want to include an empty cell in the calculation for an average, you must type a 0 in the empty cell.
2. Click in cell C18, type =MIN(TestsA), and then press the Enter key.

   The minimum test score for the Product & Features (A) tests is 0.68.
3. Click in cell D18, type =MAX(TestsA), and then press the Enter key.

   The maximum test score for the Product & Features (A) tests is 0.95.
4. Insert the same functions for the Sales & Follow-Up (B) tests in row 19, but use the name *TestsB* for the function arguments.

   The results should be as follows: Average = 0.8653846, Minimum = 0.73, and Maximum = 0.95. (The number of decimal places in your worksheet may differ.)
5. Select the range B18:D19, click the Home tab, and then click the Percent Style button in the Number group.

   The result 0.8178947 changes to 82%, 0.68 changes to 68%, 0.95 changes to 95%, and so on. (The number of decimal places in your worksheet may differ.)
6. Click in any cell to deselect the range.
7. Click the Save button on the Quick Access Toolbar.

Model Answer

Reminder
See Table 2.4 on page 75 for information about the AVERAGE, MIN, and MAX functions.

2.14 Using the Date Functions DATE, NOW, TODAY, and WORKDAY

MOS Expert 3.3.1
MOS Expert 3.3.2

Tutorial
Using the TODAY Function

Excel includes a number of functions that are used to insert or modify dates and times. **Date functions** are often used by businesses in workbooks created for scheduling and as calendars. Table 2.5 contains commonly used Date functions.

Table 2.5 Commonly Used Date Functions

Function	Description
DATE(year,month,day)	Returns a serial number for the date entered as arguments
NOW()	Returns the current date and time and updates when the workbook is recalculated

continues...

Table 2.5 Commonly Used Date Functions *...continued*

Function	Description
TODAY()	Returns the current date and updates when the workbook is recalculated
WORKDAY (start,days[,holiday])	Returns the serial number of a date before or after a determined amount of workdays

▶ Know This about the DATE, NOW, TODAY, and WORKDAY functions

— The DATE, NOW, and TODAY functions are used to insert either a predetermined date or the current date (and time).

— Although the NOW and TODAY functions do not use arguments, you must include a set of parentheses after the function name when you enter the function.

— The WORKDAY function is used to determine what the date will be when you add or subtract workdays (Mondays through Fridays). This function is useful for operations that occur only during the workweek—such as determining when shipments will arrive (because most shipping companies do not operate on weekends or holidays).

▶ Know This about using Date functions

— Excel interprets dates by converting them into serial numbers that can then be used in formulas. A **serial number** is a number that Excel assigns to each date in a sequential order. For example, January 1, 1900, has the serial number 1.

— If you type a date using the format mm/dd/yyyy, Excel automatically converts the date to a serial number.

— Using the DATE function to insert a date will also return a serial number.

— When you enter a date in a worksheet, the cell number format automatically changes to Date, so the date appears in the format mm/dd/yyyy rather than as a serial number.

▶ Know More about using Date functions

– To enter the current date without using a function, press and hold down the Ctrl key, press the semicolon key (;), and then release the Ctrl key.

– To enter the current time without using a function, press Ctrl + Shift + :.

On the Job

Task 2.14a Using the TODAY Function

The Payroll worksheet is created after employees are paid, but Jeremy wants it to show when the payroll is calculated and when salespeople are paid. Use the TODAY function to insert the current date in the worksheet.

1. Click the Payroll sheet tab to make the worksheet active and then click in cell H3.
2. Type =TODAY() and then press the Enter key.

   The current date appears in the format mm/dd/yyyy. If you wanted to include the current time as well, you would insert the NOW function instead of the TODAY function.
3. Click the Save button on the Quick Access Toolbar.

Model Answer

▸ Know This about using dates and times in formulas

— Because dates in Excel are converted into serial numbers, you can create a formula to calculate the current date plus 15 days.

— Being able to use a date in a formula makes it easier to create schedules that change constantly.

— For example, the formula =TODAY()+15 uses a Date function to calculate the current date plus 15 days.

▸ **Know More** about using dates and times in formulas

- In the formula =TODAY()+15, the Date function TODAY is used to return the current day, which is then modified by adding 15 days.
- When you use Date functions in formulas, you will generally use only the addition and subtraction operators. (It would not make sense to multiply or divide the serial number assigned to a date.)

On the Job

Task 2.14b Using the TODAY Function in a Formula

WareBot deposits paychecks for salespeople 10 days after the payroll is calculated. Jeremy wants the Payroll worksheet to show the date that each paycheck is deposited in the *Pay Day* column. Use a formula containing a Date function that adds 10 days to the current date.

1. With the Payroll worksheet still active, click in cell H6, type the formula =TODAY()+10, and then press the Enter key.

   The result of adding 10 days to the current date displays. Alternatively, you could enter the formula as *=$H$3+10*, which uses an absolute cell reference for cell H3 (current date).

2. Use the fill handle to copy the formula from cell H6 down into cell H15.
3. Click in any cell to deselect the range.
4. Click the Save button on the Quick Access Toolbar.

Model Answer

2.15 Using Logical Functions, Comparison Operators, and the IF Function

MOS 4.2.1
MOS Expert 3.6.1

Tutorial
Using the IF Function

Using **conditional logic** in a formula requires Excel to perform a calculation based on the outcome of a logical or conditional test. One calculation is performed if the test proves true, and another calculation is performed if the test proves false. For example, the IF function in the formula =IF(Sales>Projected,Bonus,0) uses defined names to calculate a salesperson's bonus if his or her sales exceed a projected amount. Excel first tests the value in the cell named *Sales* to see if it is greater than the value in the cell named *Projected*. If the condition or test proves true, Excel returns the value of the cell named *Bonus*. If the sales value is not greater than the projected value, the condition proves false, and Excel places a *0* in the cell containing the formula.

▸ Know This about logical functions

— A Logical function performs a logical test and then returns a different value based on whether the logical test resulted in a true condition or a false condition.

— For example, a Logical function can be used to determine whether to close down a manufacturing plant based on output demand.

— Most Logical functions include a comparison between two items, such as numbers or text.

▸ **Know More** about logical functions

- Logical functions are primarily used to compare two numerical values, but they can also be used to compare text (e.g., *B* is greater than *A* and *C* is less than *D*).

— To make a comparison between two items, use a comparison operator. A **comparison operator** is a sign or symbol used to describe the relationship between two values.
— Table 2.6 lists the comparison operators available in Excel.

Table 2.6 Comparison Operators

Operator	Meaning	Example	Description
= (equals sign)	Equal to	A1=C2	Tests whether the values in cells A1 and C2 are equal
> (greater than sign)	Greater than	A1>C2	Tests whether the value in cell A1 is greater than the value in cell C2
< (less than sign)	Less than	A1<C2	Tests whether the value in cell A1 is less than the value in cell C2
>= (greater than sign followed by equals sign)	Greater than or equal to	A1>=C2	Tests whether the value in cell A1 is greater than or equal to the value in cell C2
<= (less than sign followed by equals sign)	Less than or equal to	A1<=C2	Tests whether the value in cell A1 is less than or equal to the value in cell C2
<> (less than sign followed by greater than sign)	Not equal to	A1<>C2	Tests whether the values in cells A1 and C2 are not equal

▸ Know This about IF functions

— The **IF function** is the most commonly used Logical function in Excel.
— The syntax for the IF function is =*IF(logical_test,value_if_true,value_if_false)*.
- The first argument *(logical_test)* is the logical test that compares the desired values or text.
- The second argument *(value_if_true)* is the value the function will return if the test evaluates to TRUE.
- The third argument *(value_if_false)* is the value the function will return if the test evaluates to FALSE.

— When inserting an IF function, it may help to first write out the function in sentence format using the words *if* and *then*. For example:
- *If* the demand for concrete is greater than XX loads per day, *then* start up the second concrete manufacturing plant.
- *If* the demand for concrete is not greater than XX loads per day, *then* shut down the second concrete manufacturing plant.

— Once you have written the IF statement using the words *if* and *then*, you may find it easy to understand what to use as arguments in the formula.
— For example, the formula =IF(D7=E7,10,2) compares the values in cells D7 and E7. Excel first executes the logical test to determine if the values in cells D7 and E7 are equal. If the contents of cells D7 and E7 are equal, the formula returns the value 10. If the values in D7 and E7 are not equal, the formula returns the value 2.

▸ Know This about the power of IF functions

— The second and third arguments of an IF function are not limited to just values. They can return cell references, formulas, text, and even other functions.

— To return text properly in an IF function, you must put quotation marks around the text.
— An IF function can also be used to modify one of the values being compared in the first argument.
— For example, in the formula =IF(D7>=E7,D7*A1,E7*A1), the second and third arguments contain both cell references and formulas. Excel determines if the contents of cell D7 are greater than or equal to the contents of cell E7. If the logical test returns a true condition, Excel multiplies the contents of cell D7 by the contents of cell A1. If the test returns a false condition, Excel multiplies the contents of cell E7 by the contents of cell A1. As you can see, the values compared in the first argument are modified in the second and third arguments.

▶ Know More about returning text in an IF function

- In some situations, text can provide more information than can values.
- For example, an IF function can be used to determine if a person passed or failed a test, and then return the text *PASS* or *FAIL* instead of the score.
- For example, the formula =IF(D12>=65%, "PASS","FAIL") determines if a student's test score (contained in cell D12) is greater than or equal to 65%, and then returns the text *PASS* if the condition is true or *FAIL* if it is false.

▶ **Know This** about inserting functions

— To insert a function, you can use a category button in the Function Library group on the Formulas tab (see Figure 2.1 on page 60), or you can use the Insert Function dialog box.
— To open the Insert Function dialog box, click the Insert Function button in the Function Library on the Formulas tab (see Figure 2.1) or the Insert Function button on the Formula bar (see Figure 2.3 on page 63).

On the Job

Task 2.15 Inserting an IF Function

WareBot offers each salesperson a commission on total sales when he or she reaches the goal of $100,000 in total sales. Jeremy would like you to modify the Payroll worksheet so that it calculates the commission, adds it to the base salary, subtracts withholding taxes and medical insurance fees, and displays the net pay for each salesperson. Start by creating two defined names for the *Current* and *Commission Rate* cells, and then insert an IF function using the defined names based on the following if statements:

- If the total sales for a salesperson is greater than $100,000 (*Current*), then multiply the total sales by the 5% (*Commission_Rate*) commission rate.
- If the total sales for a salesperson is not greater than $100,000, then return the value 0.

Next, use the SUM function to calculate the net pay. Finally, apply formatting to the cells containing the new data.

1. With the Payroll worksheet active, select the range A24:B25.
2. Click the Formulas tab and then click the Create from Selection button in the Defined Names group.
3. With a check mark inserted in the *Left column* check box, click the OK button.

   Two defined names, *Current* and *Commission_Rate*, have been created.
4. Click in cell F6, type =IF(B6>Current,B6*Commission_Rate,0), and then press the Enter key.

   The formula returns a zero amount for James Barber because he did not meet the sales goal.

5. Make cell F6 active and then copy the formula down into cell F15.

   Each salesperson who met the sales goal earns a commission of $5,000 or more.
6. Make cell F16 active, type =SUM(F6:F15), and then press the Enter key.
7. Make cell G6 active, type the formula =C6-(D6+E6)+F6, and then press the Enter key.

   This formula returns the net pay for James Barber, which is the base salary minus withholding taxes and medical insurance fees plus commission.
8. Make cell G6 active and then use the fill handle to copy the formula down into cell G16.
9. Select the range F7:G16 and then click the Comma Style button.

   The Payroll worksheet is now complete.
10. Click in any cell to deselect the range.
11. Click the Save button on the Quick Access Toolbar.

Model Answer

2.16 Using the Insert Function Dialog Box

So far in this chapter, you have been inserting functions by manually typing them into the cell or Formula bar. Excel includes another, more informative, way to insert functions: using the Insert Function dialog box.

Tutorial

Using the Insert Function Dialog Box

▸ **Know This** about the benefits of using the Insert Function dialog box

— At the Insert Function dialog box (see Figure 2.17), you can search for a desired function by typing in a search phrase or by browsing the different function categories.

▸ **Know More** ways to display the Insert Function dialog box

– Press Shift + F3.

Figure 2.17 Insert Function Dialog Box

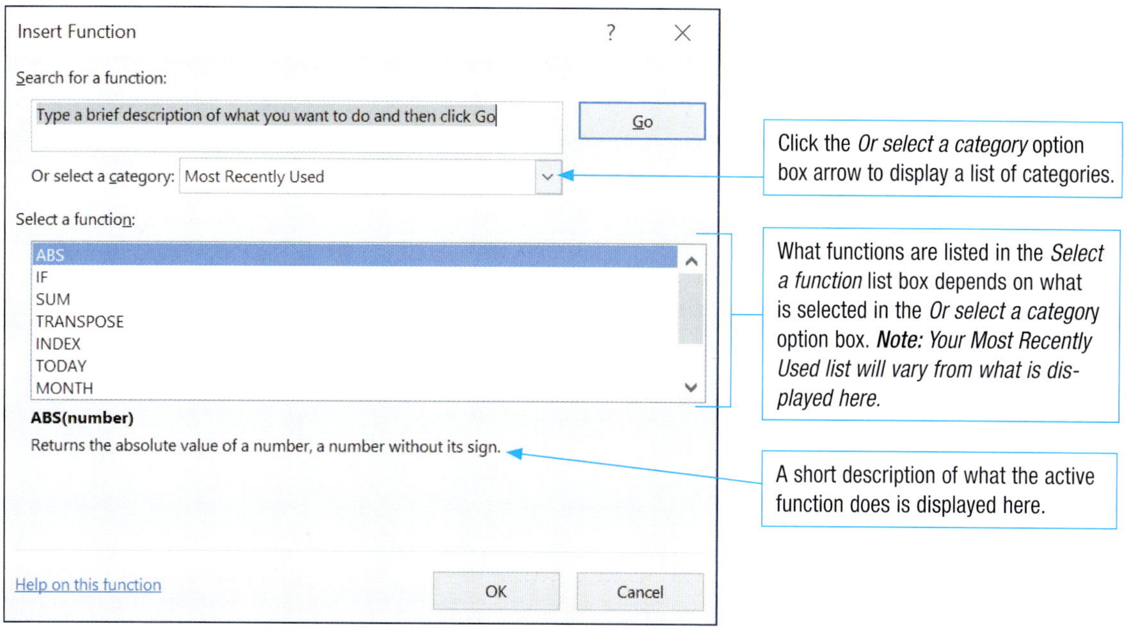

— Once you find the desired function and click the OK button, the Function Arguments dialog box displays (e.g., see the Function Arguments dialog box for the IF function in Figure 2.18 on page 89).
— To display the Insert Function dialog box, click the Insert Function button in the Function Library group on the Insert tab.
— Each argument is contained in its own text box. This structure makes it easier to enter arguments because they are separated by more than just commas.
— A short description for each argument is included; the description is particularly useful when you are inserting an unfamiliar function or a function that you have not used in a while.
— The returned value is displayed, so you can determine if you entered the arguments correctly before completely inserting the function.

On the Job

Task 2.16 Entering an IF Function Using the Insert Function Dialog Box

Jeremy now wants you to make one more change to the Training worksheet. He would like you to indicate whether each salesperson has completed all four tests in the training series. In the *Completed?* column, insert an IF function that determines if a salesperson has completed all four tests, and then returns the result *Yes* if the condition is true and *No* if it is false.

1. Click the Training sheet tab to make the worksheet active and then click in cell G6.
2. Click the Formulas tab and then click the Insert Function button in the Function Library group.

   The Insert Function dialog box displays. You can use this dialog box to search the various functions available in Excel.
3. At the Insert Function dialog box, type the search phrase if to replace the highlighted text in the *Search for a function* text box, and then click the Go button.
4. With the IF function selected in the *Select a function* list box, click the OK button.

   The Function Arguments dialog box for the IF function displays (see Figure 2.18).
5. In the *Logical_test* text box, type the logical test F6=4 and then press the Tab key.

   The logical test determines if the value in the *Completed?* column equals 4.
6. With the insertion point in the *Value_if_true* text box, type "Yes" and then press the Tab key.

   If the logical test returns a true condition, then the function will return the text *Yes*.
7. With the insertion point in the *Value_if_false* text box, type "No" and then observe the result in the section below the argument text boxes.

   If the value in the *Completed?* column does not equal 4, then the function will return the text *No* (see Figure 2.18).
8. Click the OK button.

Figure 2.18 IF Function Arguments Dialog Box

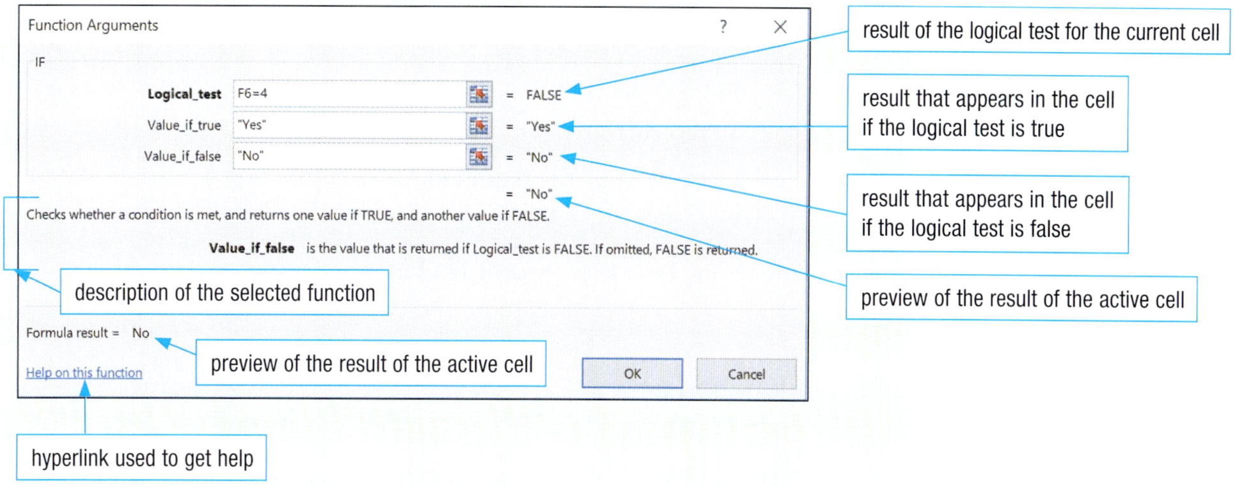

9. Click in cell G6 and then use the fill handle to copy the IF function down into cell G15.
10. Click in any cell to deselect the range.

    All three worksheets are now complete and the workbook is ready to be returned to Jeremy.

11. Click the Save button on the Quick Access Toolbar.

Model Answer

2.17 Identifying Common Formula/Function Errors and Using the Trace Error Button

MOS Expert 3.5.3

Tutorial

Using the Trace Error Button

Generally, an Excel workbook contains valuable information that is used in making business decisions, so ensuring that the data, formulas, and functions in the workbook are free of errors is very important. If a workbook is riddled with errors or data that was not entered correctly, important decisions could be based on incorrect or inaccurate information. Although the user is responsible for entering data correctly, Excel attempts to help identify errors using error codes and the Trace Error feature.

The Trace Error button appears beside an active cell that Excel has flagged as possibly containing an error. A button that pops up near an active cell is called a **smart tag**. The display of a smart tag button varies depending on the action performed.

▸ Know This about common formula/function errors

— If Excel determines that a cell may contain an error, it places an **error indicator** (a small green triangle) in the upper left corner of the cell.

— When you do not follow protocols that dictate how data or formulas and functions must be entered, Excel displays one of several error codes.

— Error codes make it easier to track down issues so you can fix them.

— Table 2.7 lists common error codes.

Table 2.7 Common Error Codes

Error Code	Meaning
#DIV/0	A formula is attempting to divide a number by 0.
#N/A	An argument parameter has been left out of a function.
#NAME?	A function name is not entered correctly.
#NUM!	An argument parameter does not meet the requirements of a function.
#REF!	A referenced cell no longer exists in the workbook.
#VALUE	The data entered is the wrong type (e.g., text instead of numbers).

▸ Know This about common function errors

— Most errors in Excel result from a user incorrectly inputting data, such as entering the wrong data or referencing incorrect cells.

— More complex errors include creating or entering an incorrect formula or function, creating a circular reference, and not using the correct order of operations in a formula.

— A **circular reference** occurs when a formula in a cell uses the results of that formula in the same cell.

— Excel displays an error message when data is being computed, not when you enter the wrong value in a cell.

— If you enter data incorrectly, you may not realize it right away. Be sure you double-check all the data you enter.

▸ Know This about using the Trace Error button

— If a small green triangle displays in the upper left corner of an active cell, the Trace Error button displays next to the cell.

— Click the Trace Error button to display a drop-down list of options for updating the formula to include specific cells, getting help with the error, ignoring the error, editing the error, and completing an error check.

— In most cases, the Trace Error button displays when a formula or function is copied to a cell near data that is structured differently or if the formulas are entered before the data. In some cases, this is not an error, and you can click the *Ignore Error* option to clear the green triangle and Trace Error button.

On the Job

Task 2.17 Investigating an Error in a Worksheet

Jeremy likes the way you have modified the Payroll worksheet, but he doesn't think you really need the defined name *Current*. He has asked you to investigate what happens if you delete this defined name and then to restore the name if you determine it is needed.

1. Click the Payroll sheet tab to make the worksheet active.
2. Click the Formulas tab, click the Name Manager button in the Defined Names group to display the Name Manager dialog box, click

the *Current* option in the Name Manager list box, click the Delete button, click the OK button, and then click the Close button.

The defined name range *Current* is deleted, *#NAME?* appears in each cell in the range F6:G16, and a green triangle appears in the upper left corner of each cell in that range.

3. Click in cell F6 and then click the Trace Error button that displays (see Figure 2.19).

   Clicking the Trace Error button displays a drop-down list of options. The highlighted text that displays at the top of the drop-down list is the error that Excel has found. Excel has highlighted the *Invalid Name Error* option because you deleted the defined name *Current*, the formula in this cell contains that defined name, and the formula does not know where to look for the value to use in the formula.

4. Click the *Ignore Error* option at the drop-down list.

   The green triangle and Trace Error button no longer display.

5. Click in cell B24, click the Define Name button in the Defined Names group on the Formulas tab, type Current in the *Name* text box, and then click the OK button.

   The correct results redisplay in the *Commission Amount* and *Net Pay* columns, and the error codes and green triangles all disappear.

6. If printed work is required by your instructor, print the workbook.
7. Click the Save button on the Quick Access Toolbar and then close the workbook.

Figure 2.19 Error Indicators and the Trace Error Button

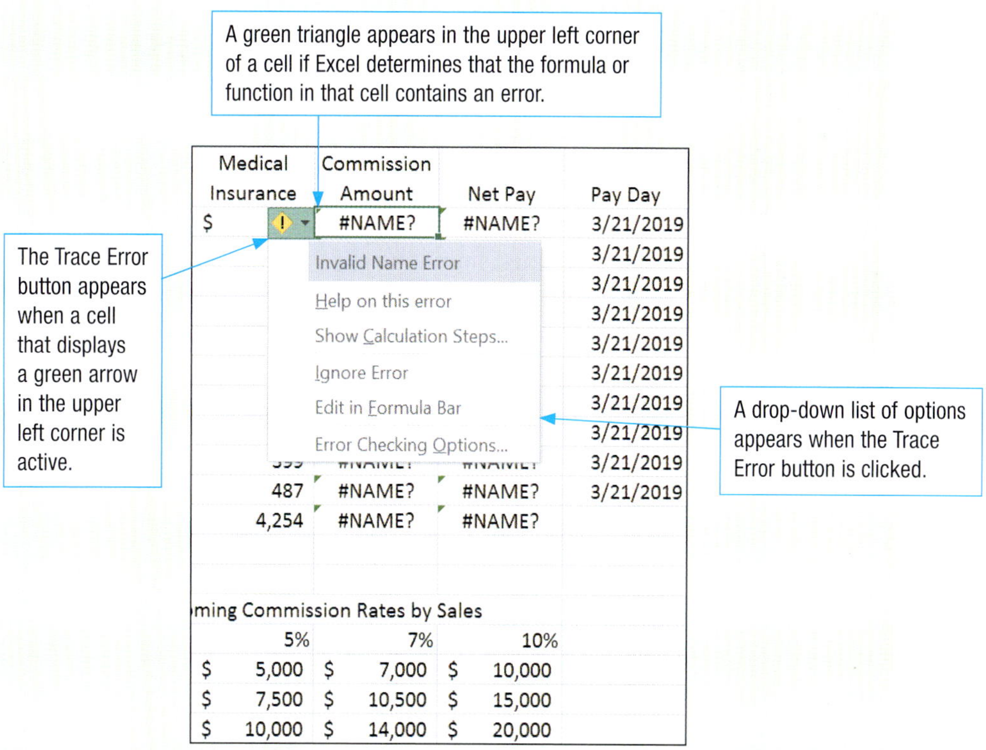

Model Answer

Chapter Summary

2.1 ▶ In Excel, a formula is a user-created equation that calculates data based on mathematical principles, such as the order of operations. A formula can contain values, cell references, defined names, and operators. A formula can also contain a function, which is a predesigned equation that calculates data using arguments.

2.2 ▶ A formula can be typed directly in an active cell or in the Formula bar.

2.3 ▶ A cell reference can be typed in a formula or entered by pointing to the cell and then clicking the cell. Using this method can reduce errors due to the mistyping of cell references.

2.4 ▶ If a formula contains two or more arithmetic operators, Excel calculates the result using the same order of operations used in algebraic arithmetic.

2.5 ▶ Use the fill handle to copy a formula into numerous cells without having to create a new formula for each column or row of data. When the copied formula contains a relative reference, calculations automatically change relative to their new cell locations without your having to manually enter each formula in the cells.

2.6 ▶ To avoid having a cell reference or range change when using the fill handle to copy formulas, use an absolute reference. It stays the same when the formula is copied to a new cell location.

2.7 ▶ To allow only the column or row to change when you copy a formula, use a mixed reference; it contains both relative and absolute references. Either the column remains the same and the row changes relative to the new location, or the row remains the same and the column changes.

2.8 ▶ Excel includes a number of functions, which are grouped in categories. Some of the common categories are *Financial*, *Logical*, *Text*, *Date & Time*, *Lookup & Reference*, *Math & Trig*, and *Statistical*.

2.9 ▶ The *Statistical* category of functions is used to summarize sets of data into useful measures, such as averages and counts.

2.10 ▶ When a range of cells is selected, the Quick Analysis button appears at the lower right corner of the selected range. Click the button to display the Quick Analysis gallery.

2.11 ▶ Excel includes a feature that allows creating a defined name for a cell or range. Using defined names instead of cell addresses makes it easier to understand formulas and functions, print a worksheet, and navigate in a worksheet.

2.12 ▶ A defined name can be modified by changing the name or the cell address associated with it. A defined name can also be deleted.

2.13 ▶ Using defined names makes formulas more descriptive and easier to understand, particularly for users who are not familiar with a worksheet.

2.14 ▶ Excel includes a number of functions that are used to insert or modify dates and times. Date functions are often used by businesses in workbooks created for scheduling and as calendars.

2.15 ▶ Using conditional logic in a formula requires Excel to perform a calculation based on the outcome of a logical or conditional test. One calculation is performed if the test proves true, and another calculation is performed if the test proves false.

2.16 ▶ Functions can be inserted by manually typing them in the cell or Formula bar, or by using the Insert Function dialog box.

2.17 ▶ Excel attempts to help identify errors using error codes and the Trace Error feature. The Trace Error button appears beside an active cell that Excel has flagged as possibly containing an error. A button that pops up near an active cell is called a *smart tag*.

Features Review

Feature	Ribbon Tab, Group	Button	Keyboard Shortcut
copy a formula	Home, Editing		Ctrl + D
create a defined name	Formulas, Defined Names		
create a defined name from a selection	Formulas, Defined Names		
delete or modify a defined name	Formulas, Defined Names		
display formulas	Formulas, Formula Auditing	15/fx	Ctrl + `
display Comma format	Home, Number	,	
display Percentage format	Home, Number	%	
display Quick Analysis gallery			Ctrl + Q
finish a formula without moving the active cell	Formula bar		
insert the current date			Ctrl + ;
insert the current time			Ctrl + Shift + :
insert or search for a function	Formulas, Function Library	*fx*	Shift + F3

Recheck

Recheck your understanding of the concepts, features, and skills covered in this chapter by taking the Recheck quiz.

Workbook

Access the study tools, review exercises, assessments, and challenges for this chapter in the workbook available from this page in your ebook.

Applying Formatting to Data

Chapter 3

Chapter Goal

To enhance the readability of a workbook by applying formatting to text and data.

Learning Objectives

3.1 Change and format fonts
3.2 Apply a workbook theme
3.3 Modify cell alignment and indentation, and rotate text
3.4 Add a fill color
3.5 Add cell borders
3.6 Format numbers using the Format Cells dialog box
3.7 Apply cell styles
3.8 Use the Format Painter and the Repeat command
3.9 Hide and unhide columns and rows
3.10 Use advanced fill series options
3.11 Use the Quick Analysis button to apply conditional formatting
3.12 Use highlight cells rules
3.13 Use top/bottom rules
3.14 Use data bars, color scales, and icon sets
3.15 Edit and delete conditional formatting rules
3.16 Use conditional formatting or cell attributes to sort and filter
3.17 Create custom number formats
3.18 Create custom date and time formats
3.19 Find and replace data and formatting

Precheck

Check your understanding of the concepts, features, and skills covered in this chapter by taking the Precheck quiz.

Data Files

Before beginning the chapter work, download the AE3 folder from this page in your ebook to your storage medium and then make AE3 the active folder.

Ebook Links

Access digital resources for this course from your ebook.

SNAP

If you are a SNAP user, go to your SNAP assignments page to complete the Precheck, Tutorials, and Recheck in this chapter.

Preview

On the Job

Scenario WareBot

In Chapter 2, you inserted formulas and functions in an Excel workbook to provide the information Jeremy Ronlin needs to analyze budget, payroll, and training data for WareBot's marketing and sales department. Now Jeremy needs to review the workbook with the vice president of marketing and sales. He would like you to add formatting that will make the text and data easy to read and interpret.

Visual Reference: Formatted Data

Figure 3.1 Excel Worksheet with Formatting Applied

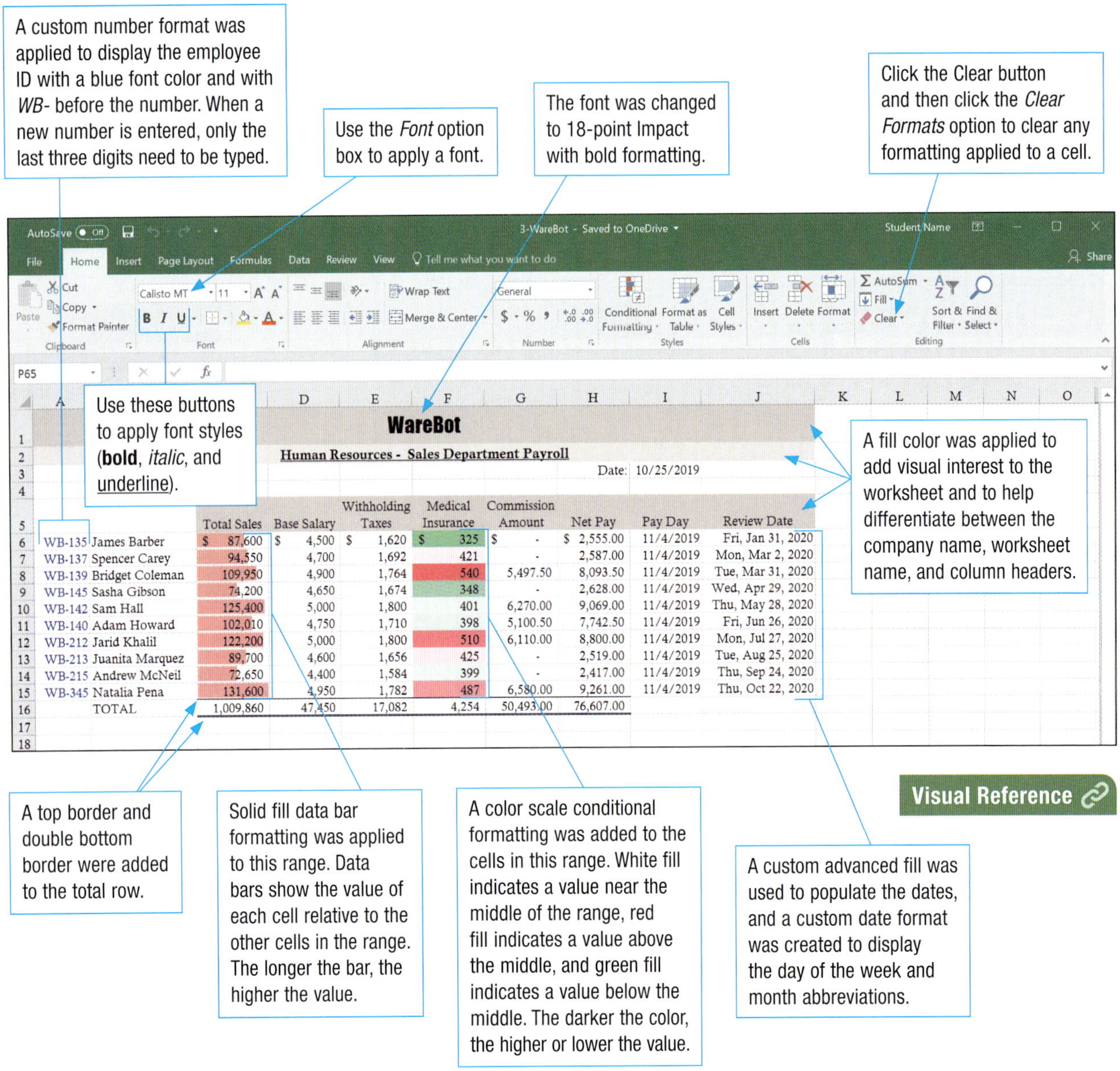

Visual Reference

3.1 Changing and Formatting Fonts

MOS 2.2.6

Tutorial

Changing and Formatting Fonts

The **formatting**, or appearance, of a worksheet can help a reader better understand its content. Using **contrast** is an effective way to draw the reader's eye to a particular point. If you apply too many contrasts, though, the reader will not know where to look first. One way to achieve contrast is through changes in font formatting, including font size, font style, and font color.

A **font** is a combination of a typeface (such as Calibri) and other attributes (such as size and style) that defines the appearance of text. The **font size** is the vertical measurement of the characters and is usually expressed in **points**. A **font style** is an attribute such as bold, italic, or underline.

▶ Know This about changing and formatting fonts

— To change the font or font formatting, use buttons and options in the Font group on the Home tab (see Figure 3.2).

— To change the font formatting of all the data in a cell, make the cell active.

— To change the font formatting of individual words or values in a cell, make the cell active, select the individual words or values, and then apply the change.

— To clear any formatting applied to a cell, click the Clear button in the Editing group on the Home tab and then click the *Clear Formats* option at the drop-down list.

Figure 3.2 Font Group on the Home Tab

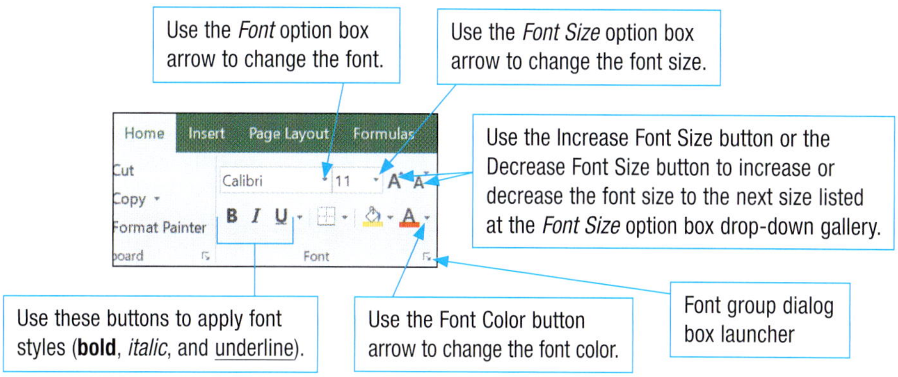

Figure 3.3 Font Tab in the Format Cells Dialog Box

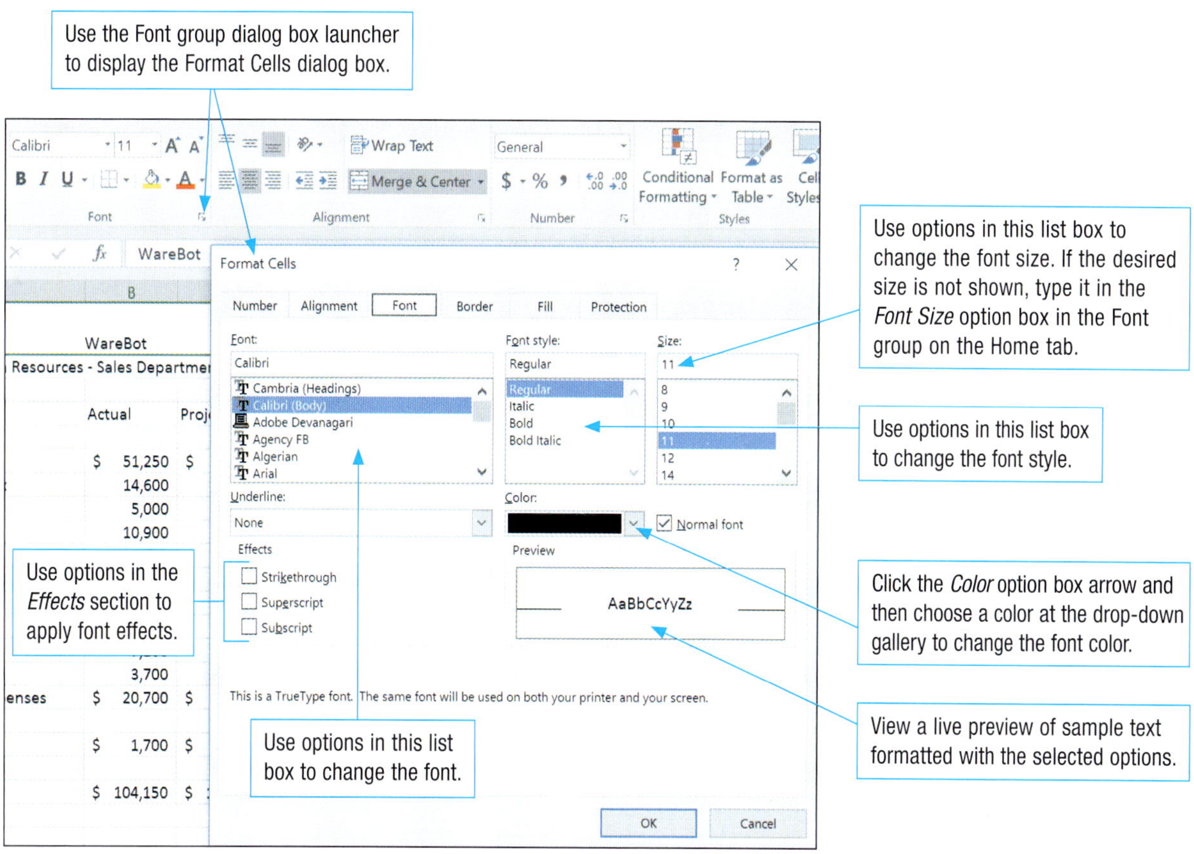

▶ Know More about changing and formatting fonts

– Another way to change the font formatting is to click the Font group dialog box launcher on the Home tab and then use buttons and options at the Format Cells dialog box (see Figure 3.3).

– The font styles listed as options in the dialog box depend on the font chosen.

– The font style options may include Regular, *Italic*, **Bold**, and ***Bold Italic***.

Reminder

In Chapter 1, you learned that you can apply formatting using the Mini toolbar, which displays when you select the contents of a cell or right-click in a cell.

▸ **Know This** about changing the font

— To change the font, click the *Font* option box arrow and then either scroll to the font name at the drop-down gallery and click it, or start typing the font name and stop when the full name replaces the highlighted text in the *Font* option box.

— A **gallery** is a drop-down or pop-up list that shows a live preview of how each option will affect the worksheet.

— The default font in Excel is Calibri.

— The fonts are listed alphabetically in the gallery.

— Each font displays as a visual representation of itself in the gallery.

— If the active cell contains data, a **live preview** will show you how an option will affect the data when you point to the option at the gallery.

▸ **Know This** about changing the font size

— To change the font size, click the *Font Size* option box arrow and then either scroll to the font size at the drop-down list and click it, or type the desired size to replace the highlighted value in the *Font Size* option box.

— If the active cell contains data, a live preview will display when you point to an option at the drop-down list.

— The default font size in Excel is 11 points.

▸ **Know More** ways to change the font size

- To increase the font size to the next larger size listed in the *Font Size* option box drop-down gallery, click the Increase Font Size button in the Font group on the Home tab.
- To decrease the font size to the next smaller size listed in the *Font Size* option box drop-down gallery, click the Decrease Font Size button.

▸ **Know This** about changing the font style or color

— To change the font style, click the Bold, Italic, or Underline button.

— To change the font color, click the Font Color button arrow to display a drop-down gallery and then click the desired color.

— When you apply the underline style, only the text or value is underlined; the underline does not extend the full width of the cell.

— When you apply the underline style, choose either a single or double underline from the drop-down list.

— The Font Color button updates to display and apply the last color added during the current session of Excel. The next time you start Excel, the font color will change back to Red.

— Use the keyboard shortcuts listed in Table 3.1 to turn font styles on and off. Similar shortcuts can be used across all the Microsoft applications (Excel, Word, PowerPoint, Access, and Outlook, for example).

Table 3.1 Font Style Keyboard Shortcuts

Style	Shortcut
Bold	Ctrl + B
Italic	Ctrl + I
Underline	Ctrl + U

On the Job

Task 3.1 Changing Font and Formatting Fonts

Jeremy would like you to format the company name, subtitle, and main row and column headers on the Budget worksheet so that they stand out and appear in a logical hierarchy. Change the font for the name of the company to 18-point Impact, and apply bold formatting to the subtitle in row 2 and to the main headers in row 4 and column A.

1. Open the data file **3-WareBot**.
2. Click the Budget sheet tab if necessary to make the worksheet active.
3. Click in cell A1 if it is not already active.
4. Click the *Font* option box arrow in the Font group on the Home tab.

   A gallery of font options displays.
5. Type I.

   The gallery scrolls down to display Impact, which is the first font that starts with the letter I, and Impact appears in the *Font* option box and is highlighted. ***Note:*** *Your font gallery may vary.*
6. Press the Enter key.
7. Click the *Font Size* option box arrow.
8. Click the *18* option.
9. Click in cell A2, click the Bold button, and then click the Underline button.

   The subtitle is boldfaced and underlined. Notice that the underline appears only under the letters and does not extend the full width of the cell.
10. Select the range B4:D4 and then click the Bold button.
11. Click in cell A5; press and hold down the Ctrl key; click in cells A10, A12, A16, A18, and A20; and then release the Ctrl key.
12. Press and hold down the Ctrl key, press the B key, and then release both keys.

    The keyboard shortcut Ctrl + B applies bold formatting.
13. Click in any cell to deselect the cells.
14. Click the Save button on the Quick Access Toolbar.

Model Answer

3.2 Applying a Workbook Theme

MOS 1.3.6

Tutorial

Applying a Workbook Theme

Excel comes with many different predefined formatting options called *themes*. Applying a **theme** can change the appearance of a workbook quickly by modifying the fonts, colors, and effects all at the same time.

Use a theme to apply a consistent look to all the worksheets in a workbook or to multiple workbooks. You can even use a theme to unify related files in different Office applications; for example, you might use the same theme for an Excel workbook containing real estate sales data, a Word document summarizing the data, and a PowerPoint file presenting the data. If a theme doesn't suit your needs 100 percent, you can customize it; creating and modifying custom themes will be examined in Chapter 11.

▸ Know This when applying a workbook theme

— To apply a theme, click the Themes button in the Themes group on the Page Layout tab and then click an option at the drop-down gallery (see Figure 3.4).

— When you point to a theme at the drop-down gallery, a live preview of the worksheet displays behind the gallery.

— When a theme is applied, it will not override prior changes made to fonts in a worksheet. For example, the font in cell A1 was changed to Impact in Task 3.1 and will remain Impact after the theme is applied in Task 3.2.

— Excel applies the Office theme as the default when you create a workbook.

— Microsoft updates its themes regularly, so sometimes a particular theme may not be available.

Figure 3.4 Themes Button Drop-Down Gallery

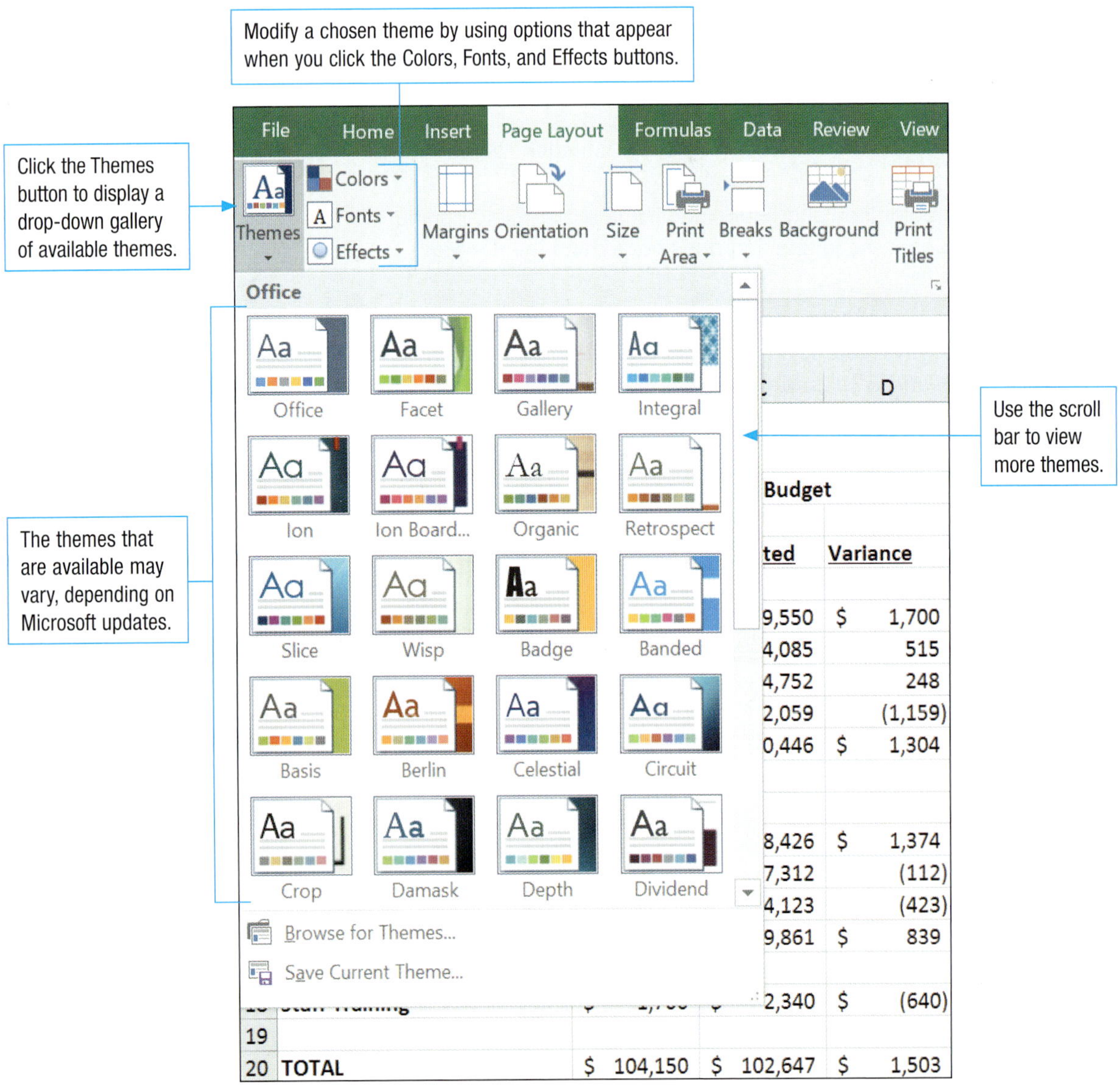

On the Job
Task 3.2 Applying a Workbook Theme

Jeremy would like to be sure all elements of the workbook are consistent and appealing. Use an option in the Themes group on the Page Layout tab to apply the Slate theme to the workbook.

1. With any worksheet active, click the Page Layout sheet tab.
2. Click the Themes button in the Themes group.
   The Themes gallery displays.
3. Scroll down and then click the *Slate* option.
   The Slate theme is applied to the entire workbook. Notice that the data in cell A1 on the Budget worksheet still displays in the Impact font, while the data in all other cells in the workbook displays in the Slate theme font Calisto MT.
4. Click the Save button on the Quick Access Toolbar.

Model Answer

3.3 Modifying Cell Alignment and Indentation, and Rotating Text

MOS 2.2.2

Tutorial

Modifying Cell Alignment and Indentation, and Rotating Text

By default, data entered as text is left aligned in a cell and data entered as a type of number (such as a general number, currency, or date) is right aligned in a cell. You can modify the **alignment** to display any type of data at the left, center, or right of a cell. Data can also be aligned vertically in a cell, at the top, middle, or bottom.

Using the **indent** feature in Excel is similar to using the Tab key or using the Increase and Decrease Indent buttons in Word. In Excel, the Increase Indent button moves the data farther away from the left cell border and the Decrease Indent button moves the data closer to the left cell border.

Changing the **rotation**, or angle, of the text in a column header allows the width of a column to be decreased. This can be beneficial if, for example, a small amount of space is needed to print the worksheet on one page. The Orientation button rotates selected text diagonally or vertically.

▸ Know This about modifying cell alignment and indentation, and rotating text

— To modify cell alignment or indentation or to rotate text, select the cell or range and then click a button in the Alignment group on the Home tab (see Figure 3.5).

— To open a drop-down list of rotation options, click the Orientation button (see Figure 3.6).

— To open the Format Cells dialog box, where you will find additional options for aligning, indenting, and rotating text, click the Orientation button and then click the *Format Cell Alignment* option.

— If the data in a cell is left aligned and you click the Increase Indent button, the data will move farther away from the left edge of the cell.

— If the data in a cell is right aligned and you click the Increase Indent button, the data will left align and then move farther away from the left edge of the cell. If you click the Decrease Indent button, the contents of the cell will left align.

▸ Know More about modifying cell alignment and rotating text

– Access additional cell alignment and rotation options by clicking the Alignment group dialog box launcher (see Figure 3.5) to display the Format Cells dialog box (see Figure 3.6).

– Use options on the Format Cells dialog box Alignment tab to apply more than one alignment option at a time or to enter a specific orientation angle.

continues...

Figure 3.5 Alignment Group on the Home Tab

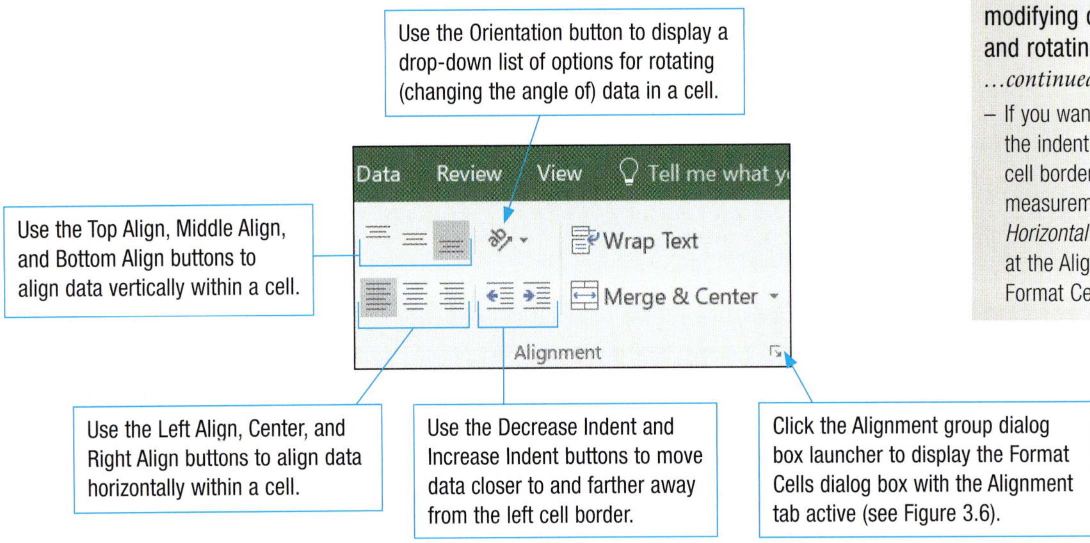

▶ **Know More** about modifying cell alignment and rotating text

...continued

– If you want to increase the indent from the right cell border, use the *Indent* measurement box and the *Horizontal* text box options at the Alignment tab at the Format Cells dialog box.

Figure 3.6 Alignment Tab in the Format Cells Dialog Box

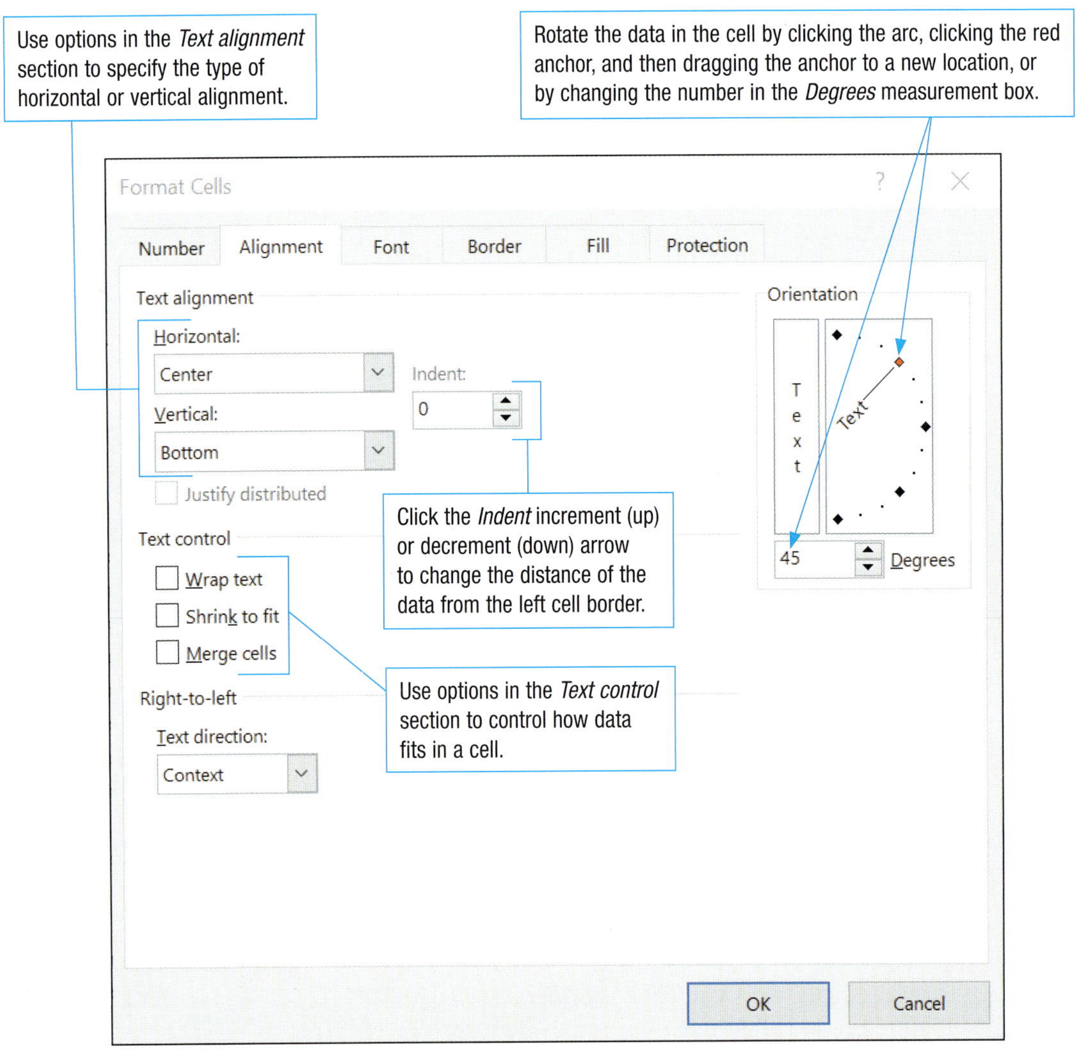

On the Job

Task 3.3 Modifying Cell Alignment and Indentation, and Rotating Text

Jeremy has asked you to change the alignment and indentation and to rotate the data in specified cells and ranges. He has also noticed that when the theme was changed in Task 3.2, some of the data in the Training worksheet was cut off. He would like you to adjust the column widths in that worksheet to fit the data in the columns.

1. With the Budget worksheet active, select the range A6:A9.
2. Click the Home tab and then click the Increase Indent button in the Alignment group.
   The text shifts slightly to the right.
3. Select the range A13:A15 and then click the Increase Indent button.
   The text shifts slightly to the right.
4. Click in cell A1 and then click the Middle Align button.
   The text aligns vertically.
5. Click the Training sheet tab.
6. Select the range B5:G5.
7. Click the Orientation button.
   The Orientation button drop-down list displays (see Figure 3.7).
8. Click the *Angle Counterclockwise* option.
   The text orients at a 45-degree angle.
9. Click the Center button.
   The text centers horizontally.
10. Select the range G6:G15 and then click the Center button.
    The text centers horizontally.
11. Right-click column heading A, click the *Column Width* option, type 19, and then press the Enter key.
12. Select column headings B through F, right-click one of the selected column headings, click the *Column Width* option, type 10, and then press the Enter key.
13. Click in any cell to deselect the range.
14. Click the Save button on the Quick Access Toolbar.

Figure 3.7 Orientation Button Drop-Down List

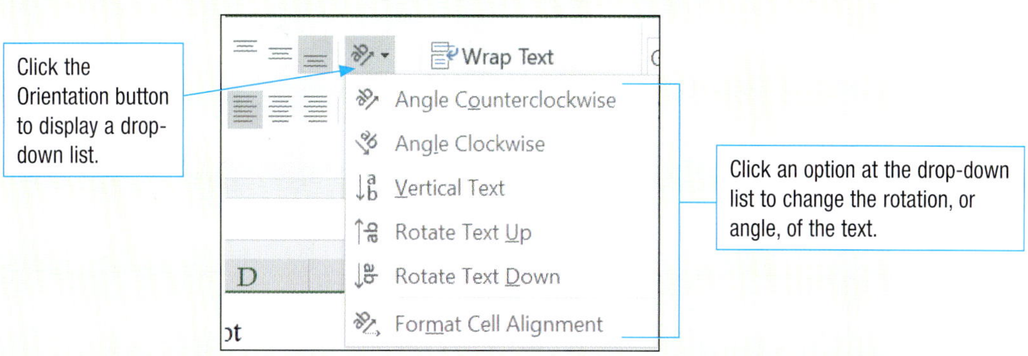

Model Answer

3.4 Adding a Fill Color

You can add a color to the background of a cell to enhance the appearance of the worksheet. The background color is also known as the **fill color**.

▸ Know This about adding fill color

- To add a fill color to a selected cell or cells, click the Fill Color button in the Font group on the Home tab.
- By default, the fill color is Yellow and the Fill Color button displays that color.
- To change the fill color, click the Fill Color button arrow and then click an option at the drop-down gallery (see Figure 3.8).
- The Fill Color button updates to display and apply the last color added during the current session of Excel. The next time you start Excel, it will change back to Yellow.
- Ensure there is enough contrast between the font color and the fill color. If you apply a dark fill, you may want to use white or a light font color.
- To avoid overpowering your workbook with too many different colors, use colors in the same column in a color gallery.
- Consider whether the workbook is being printed on a black-and-white or color printer, being viewed on a computer, or being projected onto a screen. It may be difficult to distinguish between some colors in a black-and-white print or on a computer monitor that is not calibrated the same as yours.

Tutorial

Adding a Fill Color

▸ Know More about adding fill color

- Fill color can also be added by clicking the Font group dialog box launcher to display the Format Cells dialog box, clicking the Fill tab, and then clicking an option at the gallery in the *Background Color* section (see Figure 3.9).
- The colors displayed in the *Background Color* section on the Fill tab at the Format Cells dialog box depend on the workbook's theme.

Figure 3.8 Color Button Drop-Down Gallery

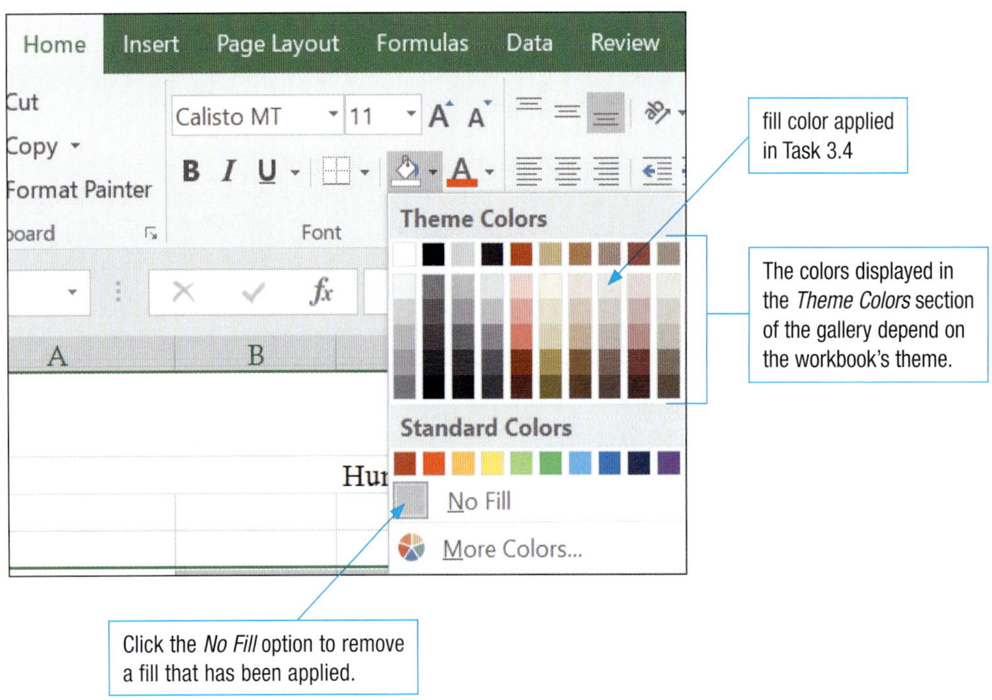

Figure 3.9 Fill Tab in the Format Cells Dialog Box

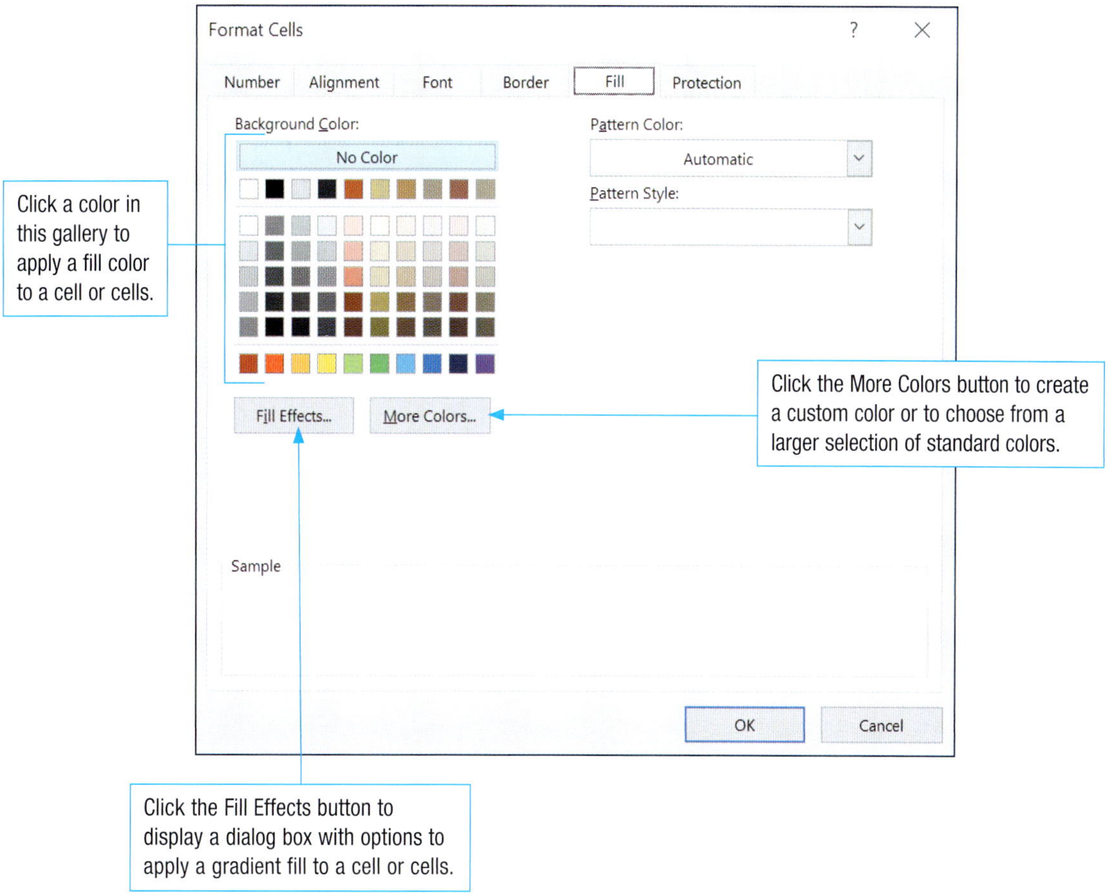

On the Job

Task 3.4 Adding a Fill Color

Jeremy would like you to emphasize the column headers in the Payroll worksheet. Use the Fill Color button to apply a fill color that is included with the Slate theme.

1. Click the Payroll sheet tab.
2. Select the range B5:H5.
3. Click the Fill Color button arrow in the Font group on the Home tab.

   A drop-down gallery displays.
4. Click the *Brown, Accent 4, Lighter 60%* option (eighth column, third row in the *Theme Colors* section).

   A light brown background is applied to the selected range.
5. Click in cell A19, press and hold down the Ctrl key, click in cells D19 and A23, and then release the Ctrl key.

   The specified cells are selected.
6. Click the Fill Color button.

   A light brown fill color is applied to the selected cells.
7. Click in any cell to deselect the cells.
8. Click the Save button on the Quick Access Toolbar.

Model Answer

3.5 Adding Cell Borders

When a worksheet is printed, the **gridlines** (intersecting vertical and horizontal lines that indicate the borders of cells) do not print by default. You can set the gridlines to print by clicking to insert a check mark in the *Print* check box in the *Gridlines* section of the Sheet Options group on the Page Layout tab.

A **border** is an outline applied to the edge of a cell or cell range. Borders print automatically when a worksheet is printed. You can add a variety of borders (including top, bottom, double bottom, and outline) to visually identify and group data.

Tutorial

Adding Cell Borders

▶ Know This about adding cell borders

— To add a border to an active cell or range, click the Borders button in the Font group on the Home tab.

— By default, the bottom border displays on the Borders button and is applied when the button is clicked.

— To change the border style, click the Borders button arrow and then click an option at the drop-down list (see Figure 3.10).

— After you choose another border at the drop-down list, that style displays on the Borders button. Just click the Borders button to apply the same border style, or click the Borders button arrow to choose and apply a different border style.

▶ Know More about adding cell borders

– To access more border style options, click the Borders button arrow and then click the *More Borders* option (see Figure 3.10) to display the Format Cells dialog box (see Figure 3.11).

– The Format Cells dialog box allows you to select more than one border style at a time or to customize borders by changing the line style or color.

Figure 3.10 Borders Button Drop-Down List

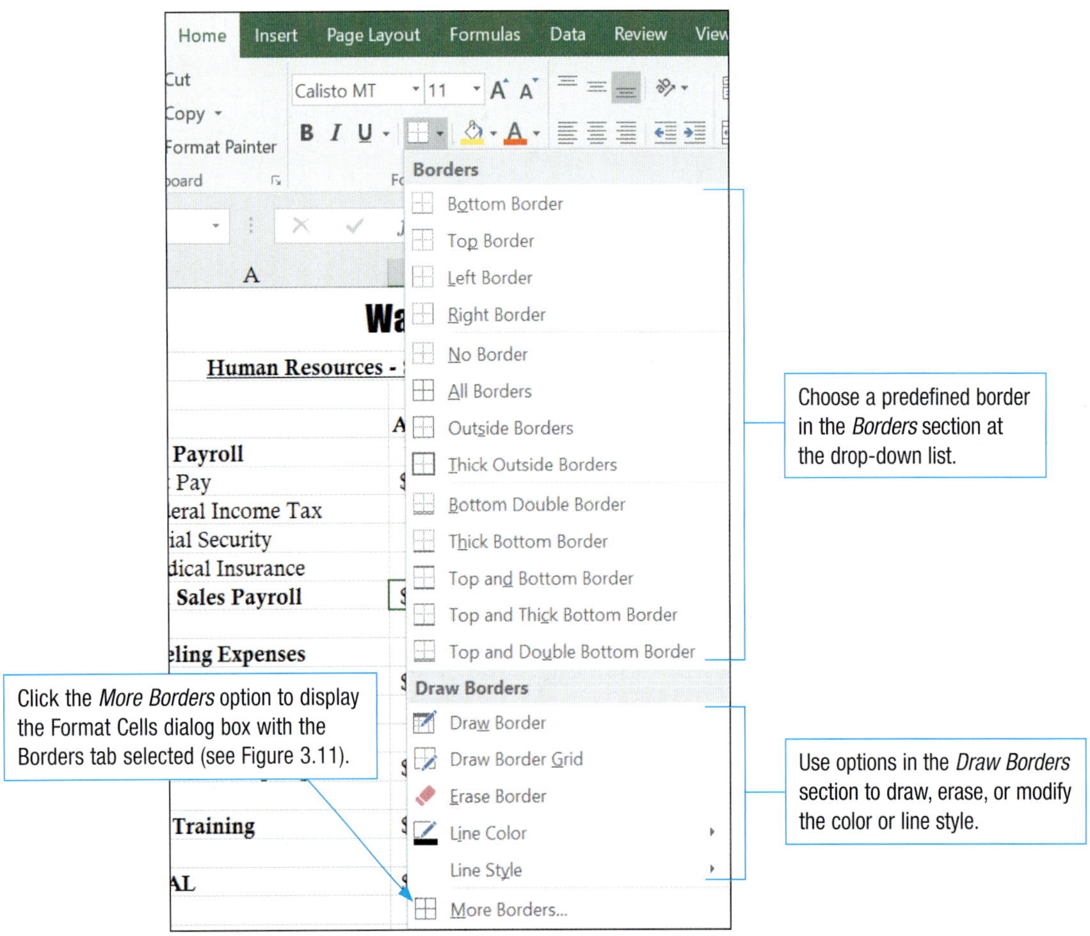

▸ **Know This** about cell borders and common accounting practices

— Use a single border above a subtotal.
— Use a double border below a total.

Figure 3.11 Border Tab in the Format Cells Dialog Box

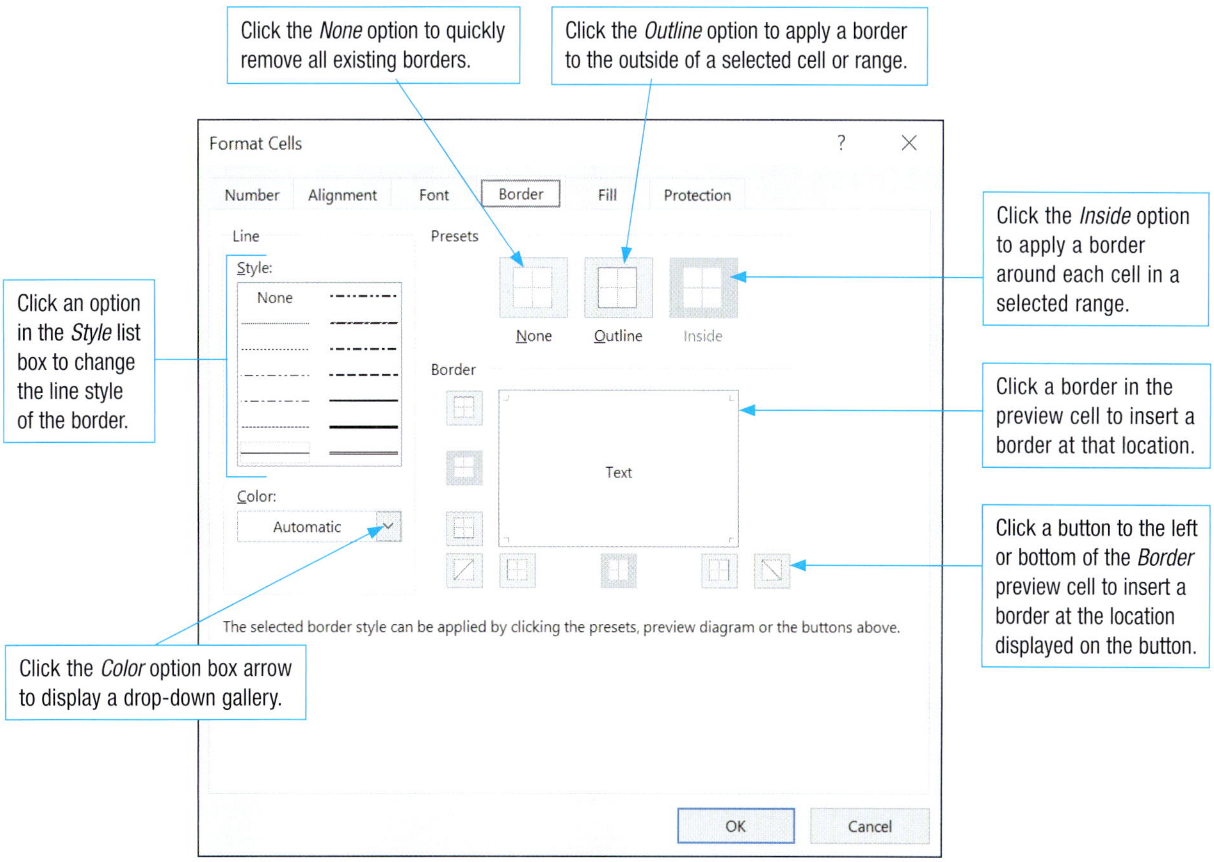

On the Job

Task 3.5 Adding Cell Borders

Jeremy wants to use common accounting practices to apply border formatting in the Budget worksheet. He has also decided it would be easier to read the employee names and test scores if borders were added around each cell containing that data. He has asked you to complete both tasks. Use options at the Borders button drop-down list and the Format Cells dialog box to add the requested borders.

1. Click the Budget sheet tab.
2. Select the range B10:D10 and then click the Borders button arrow in the Font group on the Home tab.

   A drop-down list of border options displays.
3. Click the *Top Border* option.

   A border displays at the top of each cell in the selected range.
4. Select the range B16:D16 and then click the Borders button.

   A border displays at the top of each cell in the selected range.

5. Select the range B20:D20, click the Borders button arrow, and then click the *Top and Double Bottom Border* option.

   A single top border and a double bottom border display in each cell in the selected range.
6. Click in any cell to deselect the range.
7. Click the Payroll sheet tab, select the range B16:G16, and then click the Borders button.

   A single top border and a double bottom border display in each cell in the selected range.
8. Click in any cell to deselect the range.
9. Click the Training sheet tab, select the range A5:G15, click the Borders button arrow, and then click the *All Borders* option.

   A border displays at the top, right, bottom, and left of each cell in the selected range.
10. Click in any cell to deselect the range.
11. Click the Save button on the Quick Access Toolbar.

Model Answer

3.6 Formatting Numbers Using the Format Cells Dialog Box

MOS 2.2.5

Tutorial

Formatting Numbers Using the Format Cells Dialog Box

The Format Cells dialog box offers more options for formatting numbers than you will find in the Number group and at the *Number Format* drop-down list (which were discussed in Chapter 1). Twelve categories for formatting numbers are provided on the Number tab at the dialog box. The options available for each category are explained in Table 3.2.

▶ **Know This** about formatting numbers using the Format Cells dialog box

— To format a number in an active cell, click the Number group dialog box launcher on the Home tab and then select options on the Number tab at the Format Cells dialog box (see Figure 3.12).

▶ **Know More** ways to display the Format Cells Dialog box

– Press Ctrl + 1 to display the Format Cells dialog box.

Figure 3.12 Number Tab at the Format Cells Dialog Box

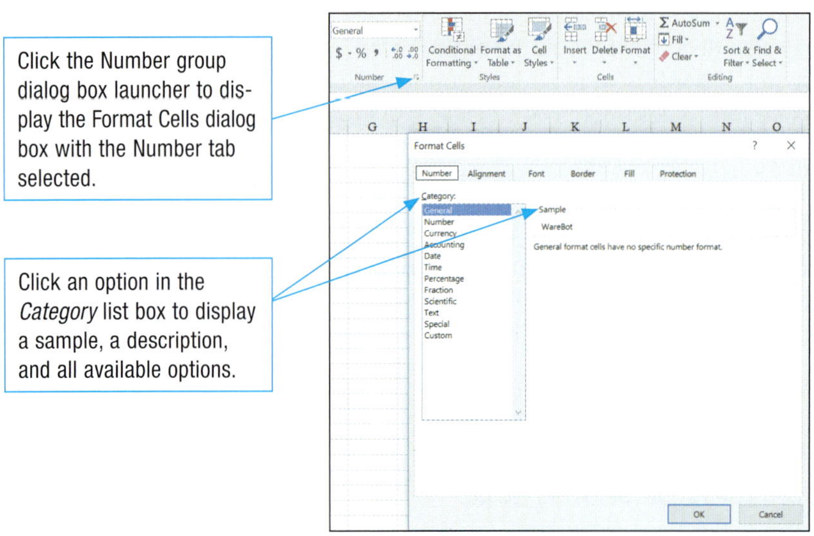

Table 3.2 Number Tab at the Format Cells Dialog Box

Category	Formatting Options
General	The *General* category has no specific number format. Numbers are right aligned and text is left aligned.
Number	You can specify the number of digits after the decimal point, whether to use the thousands separator (,), and whether to use the minus sign (–), parentheses, or the font color Red for negative numbers. Cell values display as numbers and are right aligned.
Currency	You can specify the number of digits after the decimal point, a currency symbol (such as $), and whether to use the minus sign (–), parentheses, and/or the font color Red for negative numbers. Cell values display as numbers and are right aligned.
Accounting	You can specify the number of digits after the decimal point and a currency symbol (such as $). Cell values display as numbers and are right aligned, currency symbols are left aligned, and decimal points align vertically.
Date	You can specify the type (such as *3/14/2019*) and the locale (such as *English [United States]*). Cell values display as dates and are right aligned.
Time	You can specify the type (such as *1:30:55 PM*) and the locale (such as *English [United States]*). Cell values display as times and are right aligned.
Percentage	Cell values are multiplied by 100, and the results display with the percent symbol (%) and are right aligned. You can specify the number of digits after the decimal point.
Fraction	Cell values display as fractions and are right aligned. You can specify the type.
Scientific	Cell values display using exponential notation (also called *scientific notation*), in which part of each number is replaced by *E+n*, where *E* means *exponent* and *n* represents the power (for example, *1.0E+3* stands for the exponential notation 10^3, or *1,000*). Cell values are right aligned. You can specify the number of digits after the decimal point.
Text	Both numbers and text are treated as text and are left aligned. Numbers display exactly as typed.
Special	You can specify the locale. With the locale set at *English (United States)*, you can also specify a type (including *Zip Code, Zip Code + 4, Phone Number,* and *Social Security Number*). Cell values display with the appropriate spaces and hyphens (depending on the type selected) and are right aligned.
Custom	You can specify a type from a list provided, or create your own using one of the listed codes as a starting point.

On the Job

Task 3.6 Formatting Numbers Using the Format Cells Dialog Box

Jeremy notices that in the *Variance* column in the Budget worksheet, certain cells do not have accounting formatting with zero digits after the decimal point applied. He asks you to apply consistent number formatting to this worksheet.

1. Click the Budget sheet tab.
2. Click in cell D6; press and hold down the Ctrl key; click in cells D10, D13, D16, D18, and D20; and then release the Ctrl key.
3. Click the Number group dialog box launcher on the Home tab (see Figure 3.12 on page 106).

   The Format Cells dialog box displays with the Number tab active and the *Custom* option selected in the *Category* list box.
4. Click the *Accounting* option in the *Category* list box.

   The number of decimal places is set to *0* and the *Symbol* option is set to *None* at the dialog box.
5. Click the *Symbol* option box arrow.

   A list of languages and their currency symbols displays.
6. Click the *$* option.

   The dollar symbol ($) displays in the *Symbol* option box.
7. Click the OK button.

   The contents in each selected cell display with the dollar symbol left justified, the number right justified, and no digits after the decimal point.
8. Click in any cell to deselect the cells.
9. Click the Save button on the Quick Access Toolbar.

Model Answer

3.7 Applying Cell Styles

MOS 2.2.7

Tutorial Applying Cell Styles

Formatting can be applied quickly using a predefined **cell style**, using options from the Cell Styles button drop-down gallery as shown in Figure 3.13.

Figure 3.13 Cell Styles Button Drop-Down Gallery

Click an option at the Cell Styles button drop-down gallery to apply a fill color to a cell or cells.

The colors displayed in the *Titles and Headings* and *Themed Cell Styles* sections of the gallery depend on the workbook's theme. The colors shown here reflect the options for the Slate theme.

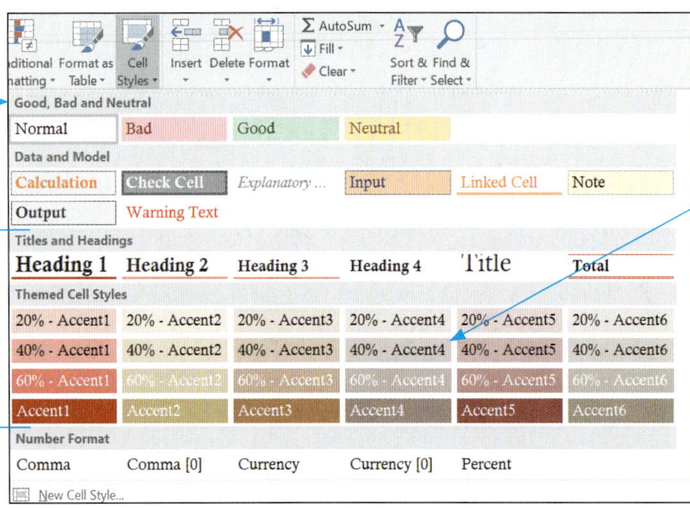

The 40% - Accent4 cell style is applied in Task 3.7.

▸ **Know This** about applying cell styles

— To apply a cell style to a selected cell or range, click the Cell Styles button in the Styles group on the Home tab and then click a style at the drop-down gallery.

— Using a predefined cell style provides consistency in the formatting of cells that contain similar information. For example, the titles on all the pages should have the same style applied. This consistency helps increase the overall understanding of a workbook.

— The colors displayed in the *Titles and Headings* and *Themed Cell Styles* sections of the Cell Styles gallery depend on the workbook's theme.

— A cell style will override some formatting previously applied to a cell. For example, a cell style will override a font choice, but it will not override a cell alignment choice.

— You can create new font styles from scratch or by editing existing styles. Creating and modifying cell styles is discussed in Chapter 11.

On the Job

Task 3.7 Applying Cell Styles

Jeremy would like you to apply a fill color to the column heads on the Training worksheet. Use a cell style to be sure the color is consistent with the theme in your workbook.

1. Click the Training sheet tab.
2. Select the range A5:G5.
3. Click the Cell Styles button in the Styles group on the Home tab.

   Depending on your monitor and window size, you may see a gallery with a More button instead of a Cell Styles button. When either button is clicked, the Cell Styles gallery displays.
4. Click the *40% - Accent4* option (fourth column, second row in the *Themed Cell Styles* section).

   A light brown fill color is added to the cells in the selected range.
5. Select the range B17:D17.
6. Click the Cell Styles button.
7. Click the *40% - Accent4* option.
8. Click in any cell to deselect the range.
9. Click the Save button on the Quick Access Toolbar.

Model Answer

3.8 Using the Format Painter and the Repeat Command

MOS 2.2.3

Tutorial

Using the Format Painter and the Repeat Command

Another method that can be used to help maintain the consistency of the formatting of a spreadsheet is the Format Painter. The **Format Painter** provides a quick and easy way to copy formatting from one cell to another without copying any data. The **Repeat command** also allows repeating the last command without copying data.

▸ **Know This** about using the Format Painter

— To copy formatting from a selected cell, click the Format Painter button in the Clipboard group on the Home tab, and then click in the target cell or select the target range.

— When you click the Format Painter button, the mouse pointer displays with a paintbrush attached.

— To apply formatting to more than one cell or range, double-click the Format Painter button and then click in the target cells and select the target ranges.

— To turn off the feature, click the Format Painter button or press the Esc key.

▸ **Know This** about using the Repeat command

— To repeat the last action performed in a selected cell, press the F4 function key or press Ctrl + Y.

On the Job

Task 3.8 Using the Format Painter and the Repeat Command

Jeremy would like you to add the same fill color to the title and subtitle rows on all three worksheets in the workbook. He also wants you to apply the same alignment formatting in the cells, but he does not want you to change any of the font formatting that has already been applied in those rows. In this case, you do not want to apply a cell style, as that would override the existing font formatting. Instead, use the Fill button to apply the fill color in the Budget worksheet, and then use the Format Painter and the Repeat command to copy the color and alignment formatting to the Payroll and Training worksheets.

1. Click the Budget sheet tab.
2. Click in cell A1.
3. Click the Fill Color button in the Font group on the Home tab.

   The Brown, Accent 4, Lighter 60% fill color should display in cell A1. If it does not, click the Fill Color button arrow and then click the *Brown, Accent 4, Lighter 60%* option (eighth column, third row in the *Theme Colors* section).
4. Click in cell A2.
5. Click the Fill Color button arrow and then click the *Brown, Accent 4, Lighter 80%* option (eighth column, second row in the *Theme Colors* section).
6. Click in cell A1.
7. Double-click the Format Painter button in the Clipboard group.
8. Click the Payroll sheet tab.
9. Click in cell A1.

   The fill color and font formatting from the Budget worksheet are both applied correctly, but the merge-and-center formatting is not. You will adjust this in a later step. If you correct it now, the Format Painter feature will stop, and you want to keep using it in Step 10.
10. Click the Training sheet tab.

11. Click in cell A1 and then press the Esc key.
    The paintbrush is no longer attached to the mouse pointer, indicating that the Format Painter is no longer active.
12. Click the Budget sheet tab and then click in cell A2.
13. Double-click the Format Painter button.
14. Click the Payroll sheet tab and then click in cell A2.
15. Click the Training sheet tab, click in cell A2, and then press the Esc key.
16. Select the range A1:G1 and then click the Merge & Center button in the Alignment group two times.
    The merge-and-center formatting in the selected range is corrected.
17. Select the range A2:G2 and then press the F4 function key.
    The last action performed is repeated, and the merge-and-center formatting in the selected range is corrected.
18. Click the Payroll sheet tab.
19. Select the range A1:H1 and then press the F4 function key.
20. Select the range A2:H2 and then press the F4 function key.
21. If printed work is required by your instructor, print the workbook.
22. Click the Save button on the Quick Access Toolbar.

Model Answer

3.9 Hiding and Unhiding Columns and Rows

MOS 1.4.2

Tutorial

Hiding and Unhiding Rows

A worksheet may contain more information than a particular reader needs at a particular time. For example, when considering staffing changes, a project manager may want to focus on internal human resource costs within the larger project budget that includes external vendor, supply, travel, and capital costs. Rows and columns can be hidden to help readers avoid scrolling and scanning through irrelevant data. **Hiding** makes rows and columns temporarily invisible, and **unhiding** makes them visible again.

▸ Know This about hiding columns and rows

— To hide selected columns or rows, click the Format button in the Cells group on the Home tab, point to the *Hide & Unhide* option, and then click the *Hide Columns* or *Hide Rows* option.

— When a row or column is hidden, its height or width is changed to 0 and a double boundary line displays between its heading and the heading for the next unhidden column or row.

▸ Know This about unhiding columns and rows

— To unhide a column, select the columns to its left and right, click the Format button in the Cells group, point to the *Hide & Unhide* option, and then click the *Unhide Columns* option.

— To unhide a row, select the rows above and below it, click the Format button in the Cells group, point to the *Hide & Unhide* option, and then click the *Unhide Rows* option.

▸ Know More ways to hide columns and rows

- Change the column width or row height to 0.
- Select the column or row heading, right-click, and then click the *Hide* option at the pop-up menu.

▸ Know More ways to unhide columns and rows

- Select the columns to the left and right of the column you want to unhide, right-click, and then click the *Unhide* option at the drop-down list.

continues...

On the Job

Task 3.9 Hiding Rows

Jeremy wants to simplify the Payroll worksheet so the vice president of marketing can focus on the payroll details for each staff member and not be distracted by the tax and commission rate information at the bottom of the worksheet. Hide the rows containing that information.

1. With the Payroll worksheet active, click in row heading 19, click and hold down the left mouse button, drag down into row heading 25, and then release the mouse button.

   Rows 19 through 25 are selected.

2. Click the Format button in the Cells group on the Home tab.
3. Point to the *Hide & Unhide* option and then click the *Hide Rows* option.

   The selected rows are hidden (see Figure 3.14).

4. Click the Save button on the Quick Access Toolbar.

Figure 3.14 Hidden Rows

	A	B	C	D	E	F	G	H
1	**WareBot**							
2	Human Resources - Sales Department Payroll							
3							Date:	10/25/2019
4								
5		Total Sales	Base Salary	Withholding Taxes	Medical Insurance	Commission Amount	Net Pay	Pay Day
6	James Barber	$ 87,600	$ 4,500	$ 1,620	$ 325	$ -	$ 2,555.00	11/4/2019
7	Spencer Carey	94,550	4,700	1,692	421	-	2,587.00	11/4/2019
8	Bridget Coleman	109,950	4,900	1,764	540	5,497.50	8,093.50	11/4/2019
9	Sasha Gibson	74,200	4,650	1,674	348	-	2,628.00	11/4/2019
10	Sam Hall	125,400	5,000	1,800	401	6,270.00	9,069.00	11/4/2019
11	Adam Howard	102,010	4,750	1,710	398	5,100.50	7,742.50	11/4/2019
12	Jarid Khalil	122,200	5,000	1,800	510	6,110.00	8,800.00	11/4/2019
13	Juanita Marquez	89,700	4,600	1,656	425	-	2,519.00	11/4/2019
14	Andrew McNeil	72,650	4,400	1,584	399	-	2,417.00	11/4/2019
15	Natalia Pena	131,600	4,950	1,782	487	6,580.00	9,261.00	11/4/2019
16	TOTAL	1,009,860	47,450	17,082	4,254	50,493.00	76,607.00	
17								
18								
26								

Rows 19 through 25 are hidden. A double boundary line displays between row heading 18 and row heading 26. The row numbering skips from 18 to 26.

Model Answer

▶ **Know More** ways to unhide columns and rows

...continued

- Select the rows above and below the row you want to unhide, right-click, and then click the *Unhide* option at the pop-up menu.

3.10 Using Advanced Fill Series Options

MOS Expert 2.1.2

Tutorial

Using Advanced Fill Series Options

Recall from Chapter 1 that a fill series can be used to quickly populate a range of cells with a sequence of numbers, dates, days of the week, months, or years—for example, *Jan*, *Feb*, *Mar*, and so on. Use either the fill handle on the cell border or the Fill button in the Editing group on the Home tab to fill cells with a series. You can create an **advanced fill series** to increase a number by a specific amount, to increase a date by a specific number of days, or to increase a day, weekday, month, or year by a specific number of days, weekdays, months, or years. For example, you can use an advanced fill series to fill a range with even numbered years—*2020*, *2022*, *2024*, and so on.

▸ **Know This** about using advanced fill series options for dates

— To create an advanced fill series for dates in a range, type the first date in the first cell of the range, select the remaining cells in the range along with the first date typed, click the Fill button in the Editing group on the Home tab, click the *Series* option to display the Series dialog box (see Figure 3.15), click the *Date* option in the *Type* section, and then click an option in the *Date unit* section (see Table 3.3).

— Excel can create a fill series based on the first or last day of the month even though the months do not all have the same number of days. (For example, January has 31 days while February has 28 or 29.)

▸ **Know More** about using advanced fill series options for dates

– To create an advanced fill series based on a sample of two dates in the series, type the two dates in the first two cells in the range, select both cells, click the fill handle, and then drag the fill handle down into the last cell in the range.

Figure 3.15 Series Dialog Box

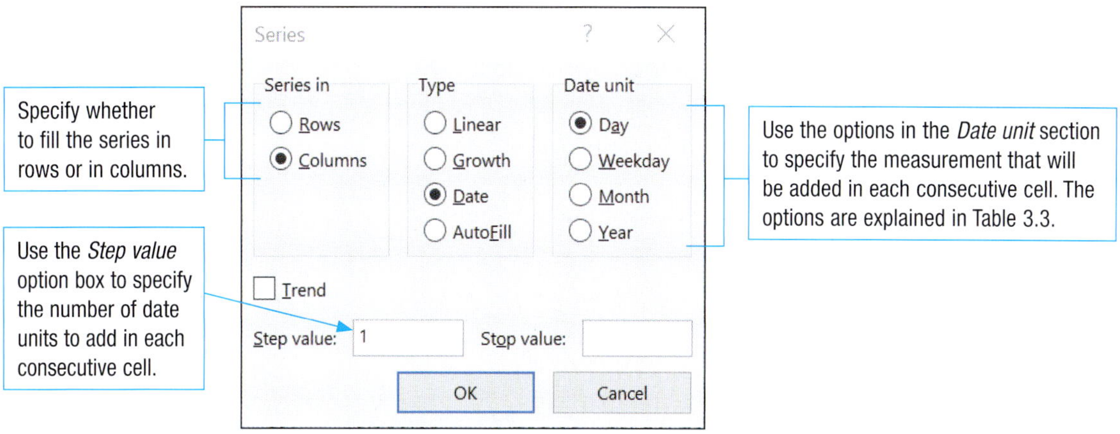

Table 3.3 *Date unit* Options at the Series Dialog Box

Option	Description
Day	Add any day during the week, including Saturday and Sunday.
Weekday	Add any day during the week, excluding Saturday and Sunday.
Month	Add one or more months, regardless of the number of days in each month.
Year	Add one or more years.

On the Job

Task 3.10 Using Advanced Fill Series Options for Dates

Jeremy needs to schedule employee performance reviews. A different employee will be reviewed every 21 weekdays (excluding Saturdays and Sundays), starting with James Barber at the end of January 2020 and progressing consecutively through the list on the Payroll worksheet. Add a *Review Date* column to the right of the *Pay Day* column in the worksheet and then use an advanced fill series to schedule the review dates for all the employees. Adjust the worksheet title and subtitle so they are merged and centered over all the columns, including the new column.

1. With the Payroll worksheet active, click in cell I5, type Review Date, and then press the Enter key.

   Excel automatically formats cell I5 with the formatting of the cell directly to the left of it.

2. Type 1/31/2020 and then press the Enter key.
3. Select the range I6:I15.
4. Click the Fill button in the Editing group on the Home tab.
5. Click the *Series* option.

   The Series dialog box displays with the *Columns* option selected in the *Series in* section and the *Date* radio button contains a bullet in the *Type* section.

6. Click the *Weekday* option in the *Date unit* section.
7. Select the number in the *Step value* text box and then type 21.

   The number *21* replaces the selected number in the text box.

8. Click the OK button.

   The reviews are scheduled so that one employee is evaluated every 21 weekdays (excluding Saturdays and Sundays).

9. Double-click the right border of the column I column heading.
10. Click in any cell to deselect the range.
11. Select the range A1:I1 and then click the Merge & Center button in the Alignment group two times.
12. Select the range A2:I2 and then press the F4 function key.
13. Click the Save button on the Quick Access Toolbar.

Model Answer

3.11 Using the Quick Analysis Button to Apply Conditional Formatting

MOS 2.3.4

Tutorial

Using the Quick Analysis Button to Apply Conditional Formatting

Conditional formatting applies formatting to cells in a selected range that meet a specified condition. Changing the appearance of a cell based on a condition can help users quickly analyze and interpret data by spotting similarities, differences, highs, lows, and trends between data entries. Consider using conditional formatting to help you answer a question such as "Which sales reps made sales above the target?" Using a different color to highlight the sales totals that exceeded the target will allow you to quickly identify the top performers. The Quick Analysis button provides access to the most common conditional formatting tools, as well as other common data analysis and formatting tools.

▸ **Know This** about using the Quick Analysis button to apply conditional formatting

— To apply common conditional formatting to a selected range, click the Quick Analysis button and then click an option on the Formatting tab at the Quick Analysis gallery (see Figure 3.16).

— When you apply conditional formatting to selected cells, the formatting of cells that do not meet the specified condition does not change.

Figure 3.16 Formatting Tab at the Quick Analysis Gallery

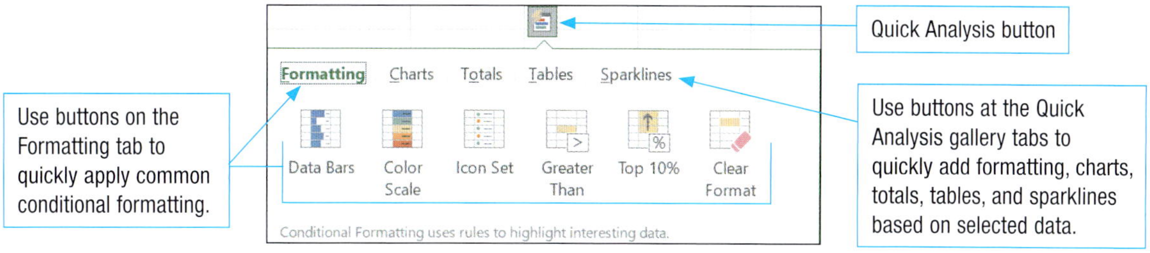

On the Job

Task 3.11 Using Quick Analysis to Apply Conditional Formatting

Jeremy would like a visual element that allows him to quickly compare the total sales data on the Payroll worksheet, showing which reps have higher and lower sales. Use the Quick Analysis gallery to add colored data bars showing the relative values in the total sales cells. (You will learn more about data bars later in this chapter.)

1. With the Payroll worksheet active, use the Name box to select the named range Total_Sales.

   The Quick Analysis button displays at the gallery right corner of the selected range.
2. Click the Quick Analysis button (see Figure 3.16).
3. Click the Data Bars button on the Formatting tab.

   Solid blue data bars are added to the selected range.
4. Click in any cell to deselect the range.
5. Click the Save button on the Quick Access Toolbar.

Model Answer

3.12 Using Highlight Cells Rules

MOS 2.3.4

Tutorial

Using the Highlight Cell Rules

If you require more conditional formatting options than the common ones available at the Quick Analysis gallery, use the Conditional Formatting button to access additional options, including a variety of rules for highlighting cells. Use **highlight cells rules** to base conditional formatting on a comparison of a cell value with a specified value. The highlight cells rules options are shown in Figure 3.17.

Figure 3.17 Highlight Cells Rules Options

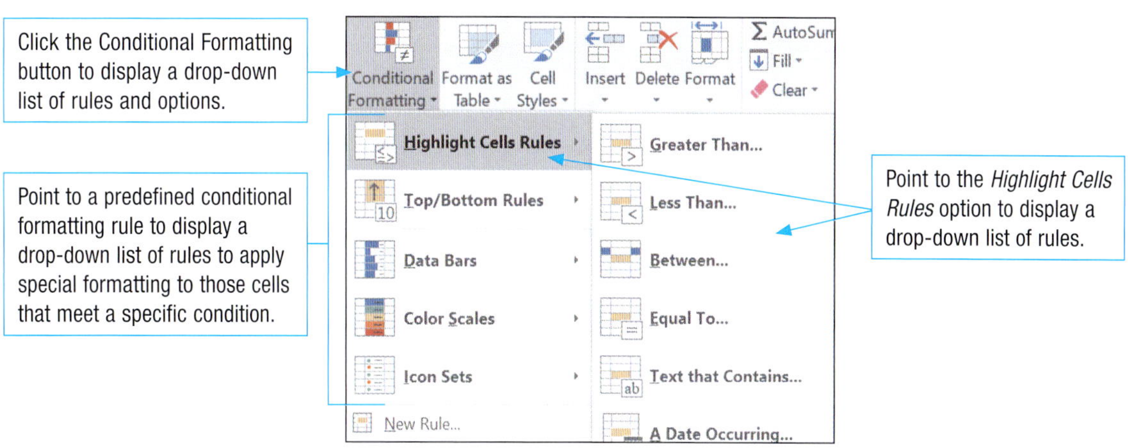

▸ Know This about using highlight cells rules

— To apply a highlight cells rule to selected cells, click the Conditional Formatting button in the Styles group on the Home tab, point to the *Highlight Cells Rules* option at the drop-down list, click a rule at the second drop-down list, enter the parameter values at the dialog box, and then click the OK button.

— The Greater Than, Less Than, Between, and Equal To rules can be used on both numbers and text. For example, *B* is greater than (>) *A*, *C* is less than (<) *D*, and *F* is between *A* and *G*.

— Add a legend to explain the conditional formatting rules applied to a worksheet.

On the Job

Task 3.12 Using Highlight Cells Rules

WareBot gives a dinner gift certificate to each employee who receives a score above 84% on a product and features test. Jeremy would like you to add a visual element that will help him identify all grades that qualify for these certificates. Use a conditional formatting rule to highlight cells that meet the 84% criterion, and add a legend to explain what the formatting means.

1. With any worksheet active, use the Name box to select the named range TestsA.

   The Training worksheet becomes active with the named range TestsA (B6:C15) selected.

Reminder
In Chapter 2, you learned that the definition for a named range includes the sheet tab. Therefore, it is not necessary to make the Training worksheet active before selecting a named range in the Name box.

2. Click the Conditional Formatting button in the Styles group on the Home tab.
3. Point to the *Highlight Cells Rules* option and then click the *Greater Than* option.

   The Greater Than dialog box displays. A live preview of the conditional formatting rule displays in the background.

4. With the value selected in the *Format cells that are GREATER THAN* text box, type 84%.

   The live preview adjusts to format cells containing values greater than 84% with a red fill and dark red text.

5. Click the *with* option box arrow and then click the *Green Fill with Dark Green Text* option (see Figure 3.18).

   The live preview adjusts to format cells containing values greater than 84% with a green fill and dark green text.

Figure 3.18 Greater Than Dialog Box

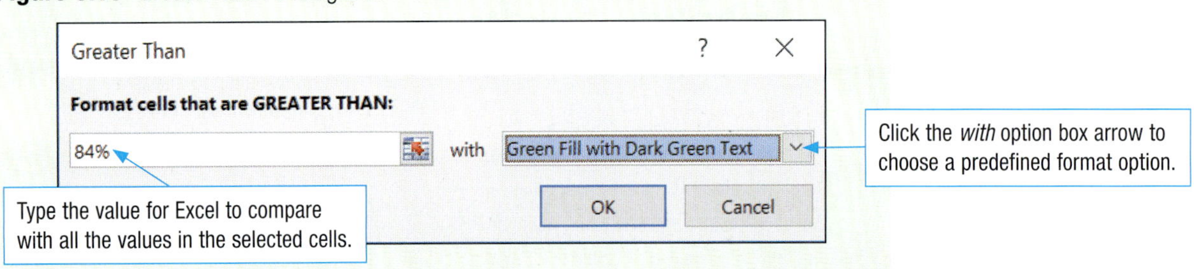

6. Click the OK button.

   Cells that meet the criterion are formatted according to the selected rule. For example, cell B14 displays the score 86% with a green fill and dark green text.

7. Click in any cell to deselect the range.
8. Click in cell A20, type Tests A >84%, and then press the Tab key.
9. Type green fill with dark green text and then press the Enter key.
10. Click in cell B20, click the Font Color button arrow in the Font group, and then click the *Green* option (sixth option in the *Standard Colors* section).
11. Click the Save button on the Quick Access Toolbar.

Model Answer

3.13 Using Top/Bottom Rules

MOS 2.3.4

Tutorial
Using Top/Bottom Rules

Excel also provides **top/bottom rules** for highlighting cells based on their values in comparison with the values of other cells. Using these comparison rules, you can highlight the cells that contain the top 10 or bottom 10 values, for example. Figure 3.19 shows the available top/bottom rules.

▸ Know This about using top/bottom rules

— To apply a top/bottom rule to selected cells, click the Conditional Formatting button, point to the *Top/Bottom Rules* option at the drop-down list, click a rule at the second drop-down list, change any parameter values at the dialog box, and then click the OK button.

— At the dialog box for the top/bottom item and top/bottom percentage rules, use the increment (up) and decrement (down) arrows to increase or decrease the number or percentage of items to highlight.

Figure 3.19 Top/Bottom Rules Options

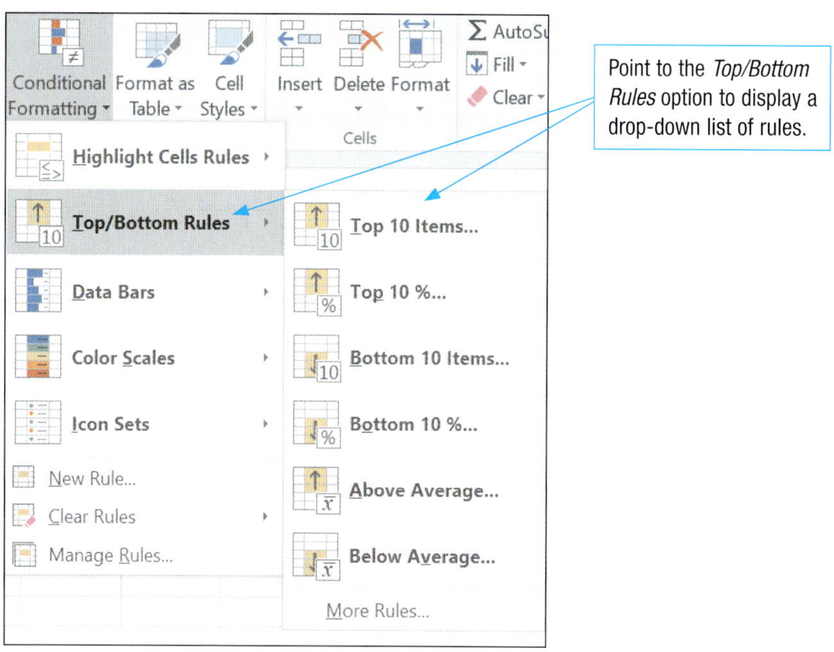

On the Job

Task 3.13 Using Top/Bottom Rules

Jeremy would also like to recognize employees who receive an above-average score on a sales and follow-up test. Use a conditional formatting rule to highlight test scores that meet this criterion, and update the legend to explain this added formatting.

1. With any worksheet active, use the Name box to select the named range TestsB.
2. Click the Conditional Formatting button in the Styles group on the Home tab.
3. Point to the *Top/Bottom Rules* option and then click the *Above Average* option.

   The Above Average dialog box displays. A live preview of the conditional formatting rule displays in the background.
4. Click the *for the selected range with* option box arrow and then click the *Yellow Fill with Dark Yellow Text* option.

   The live preview adjusts to format cells containing values that are above average with a yellow fill and dark yellow text.
5. Click the OK button.

   The cells that meet the criteria are formatted according to the selected rule. For example, cell D6 contains the score *91%* and displays with a yellow fill and dark yellow text.
6. Click in any cell to deselect the range.
7. Click in cell A21, type Tests B above average, and then press the Tab key.
8. Type yellow fill with dark yellow text and then press the Enter key.
9. Click in cell B21, click the Font Color button arrow in the Font group, and then click the *Tan, Accent 2, Darker 25%* option (sixth column, fifth row in the *Theme Colors* section).
10. Click the Save button on the Quick Access Toolbar.

Model Answer

3.14 Using Data Bars, Color Scales, and Icon Sets

MOS 2.3.4

Tutorial

Using Color Scales and Icon Sets

Excel allows you to format cells using data bars, icon sets, two-color scales, and three-color scales. These conditional formats provide visual guides for categorizing data into three to five categories, or for identifying distributions or variations within a range.

▸ Know This about using data bars, color scales, and icon sets

— To apply data bars, color scales, or icon sets, click the Conditional Formatting button in the Styles group on the Home tab; point to the *Data Bars*, *Color Scales*, or *Icon Sets* option at the drop-down list; and then click an option at the drop-down gallery.

— Be careful not to use too many data bars, color scales, and/or icon sets in a single worksheet or workbook, as readers can quickly lose focus when too many items compete for their attention.

▸ Know This about data bars

— A **data bar** is a conditional format that uses a colored bar to show the value in a cell relative to the value in other cells in a range. The longer the data bar, the higher the relative value. Figure 3.20 shows the data bars options available in Excel.

— Excel offers six colors for data bars.

— Each data bar color is available in a gradient or solid fill.

Figure 3.20 Data Bars Options

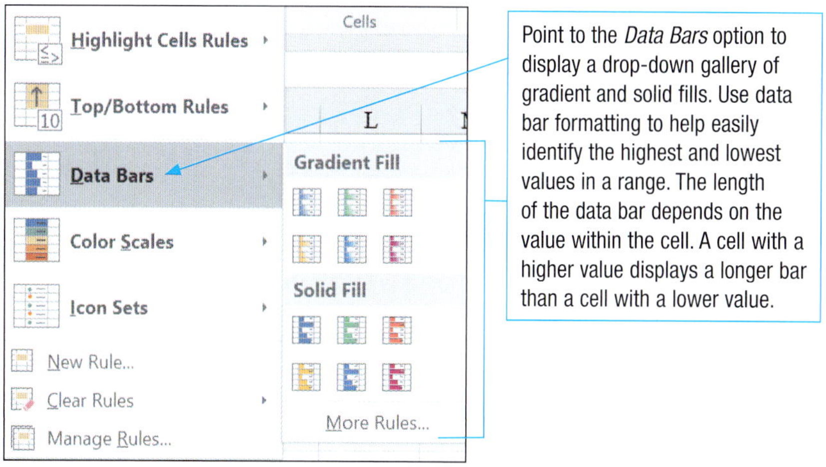

▸ Know This about color scales

— A **color scale** is a conditional format that uses a fill color to show the value in a cell relative to the values in other cells in a range. The darker the color, the higher the relative value. Figure 3.21 illustrates color scales options.

— In a two-color scale, the shade applied to a cell represents a higher or lower value in the range.

— In a three-color scale, the shade applied to a cell represents a higher, middle, or lower value in the range.

Figure 3.21 Color Scales Options

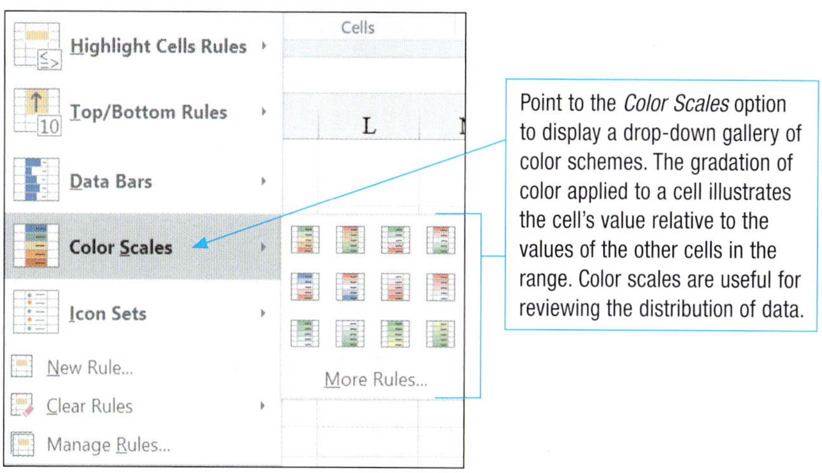

▸ Know This about icon sets

— An **icon set** is a conditional format that uses a selected icon to indicate the value in a cell relative to the values in other cells in a range. Figure 3.22 displays icon sets options.

— An icon set is used to categorize similar data so that you can easily identify high points, low points, or other trends.

— Icons are assigned to cells based on default thresholds. These thresholds can be changed.

Figure 3.22 Icon Sets Options

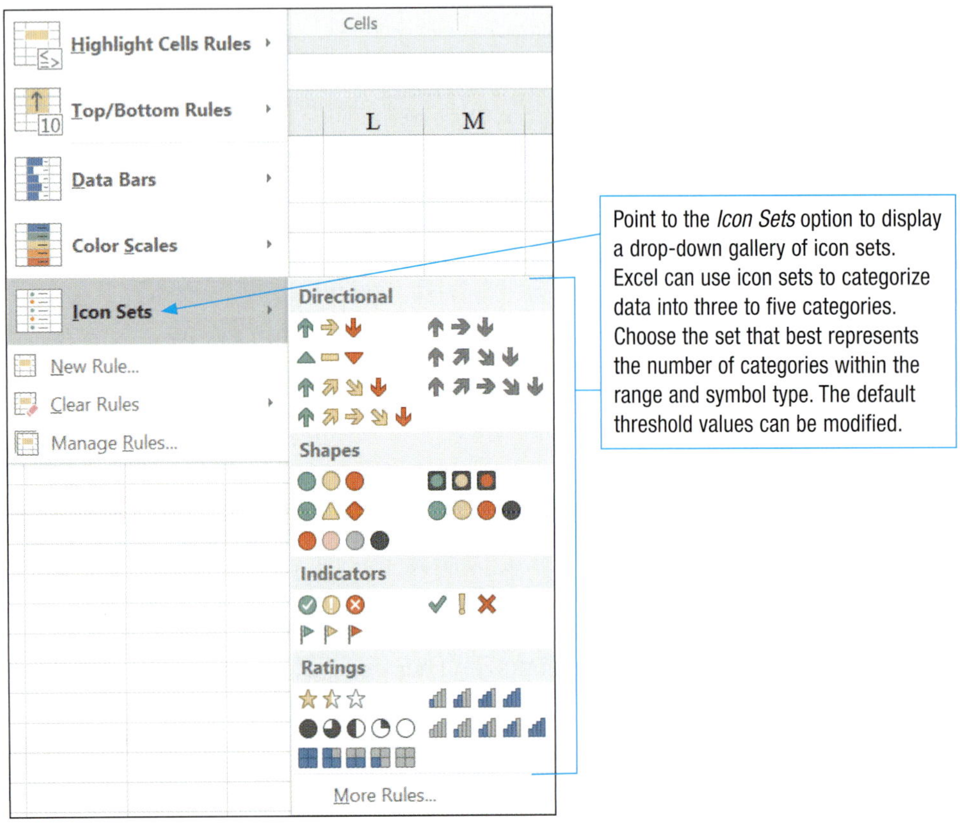

On the Job

Task 3.14 Using Color Scales and Icon Sets

Jeremy would like visual cues to help him identify how many training tests each employee has completed and to show how medical and insurance costs for employees rank, from lowest to highest. Use the icon set 4 Traffic Lights to illustrate the number of tests each employee has completed, with a green (go) light for all four tests, a yellow (caution) light for three tests, a red (stop) light for two tests, and a black light for one test. Use a color scale to compare medical and insurance costs.

1. With the Training worksheet active, select the range F6:F15.
2. Click the Conditional Formatting button in the Styles group on the Home tab.

3. Point to the *Icon Sets* option and then click the *4 Traffic Lights* option (second column, second row in the *Shapes* section).

   The selected range is formatted with icons in four colors.

4. Click in any cell to deselect the range.
5. Click the Payroll sheet tab.

   Notice the data bars in the *Total Sales* column; you added this conditional formatting in Task 3.11 using the Quick Analysis button.

6. Select the range E6:E15.
7. Click the Conditional Formatting button.
8. Point to the *Color Scales* option and then click the *Red - White - Green* option (fourth column, first row).

   Cells that meet the criteria are formatted according to the selected rule. The darker the red fill color, the higher the value, and the darker the green fill color, the lower the value. The white fill color indicates values near the middle of the range.

9. Click in any cell to deselect the range.
10. If printed work is required by your instructor, print the workbook.
11. Click the Save button on the Quick Access Toolbar.

Model Answer

3.15 Editing and Deleting Conditional Formatting Rules

MOS Expert 2.2.3

Tutorial

Editing and Deleting Conditional Formatting Rules

Once a conditional formatting rule has been applied, you can make changes to the comparison rule criteria or the formatting options. If you decide that you have applied too many conditional formatting rules and the result is visually overpowering, you can delete some rules.

▸ **Know This** about editing and deleting conditional formatting rules

— To edit a conditional formatting rule applied to selected cells, click the Conditional Formatting button in the Styles group on the Home tab, click the *Manage Rules* option, click a rule, click the Edit Rule button, make changes, and then click the OK button two times.

— When you click the *Manage Rules* option at the Conditional Formatting button drop-down list, the Conditional Formatting Rules Manager dialog box displays (see Figure 3.23).

— To delete a conditional formatting rule applied to selected cells, click the Conditional Formatting button, click the *Manage Rules* option, click a rule, click the Delete Rule button, and then click the OK button.

▸ **Know More** ways to delete conditional formatting rules from selected cells

– Click the Quick Analysis button and then click the Clear button on the Formatting tab.

– Click the Conditional Formatting button, point to the *Clear Rules* option, and then click the *Clear Rules from Selected Cells* option or the *Clear Rules from Entire Sheet* option.

Figure 3.23 Conditional Formatting Rules Manager Dialog Box

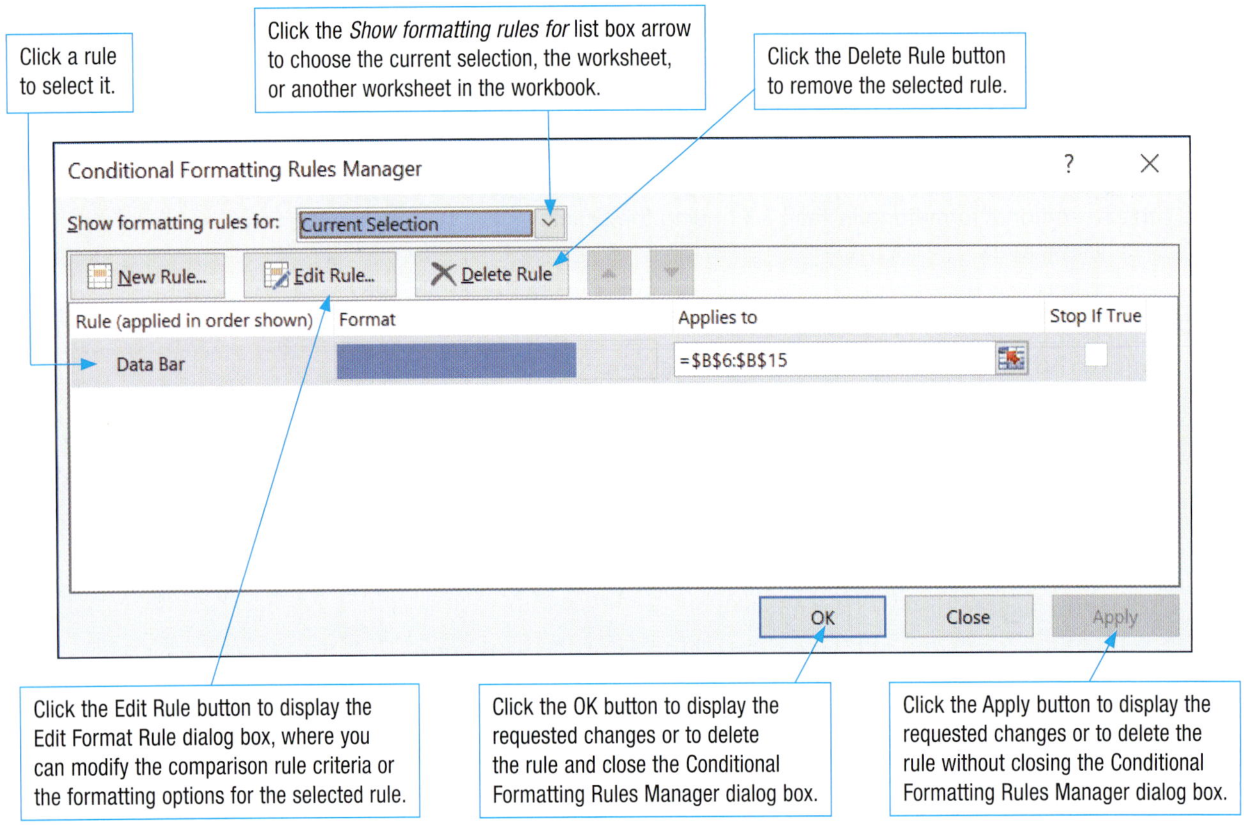

On the Job

Task 3.15 Editing and Deleting Conditional Formatting Rules

Jeremy mentions that the numbers in the *Total Sales* column are hard to read through the data bars you added in Task 3.11. He also says he has decided not to recognize employees who score above average on tests in the Tests B group. Modify the color of the data bars in the Total_Sales range, and then delete the Above Average rule and the legend describing it on the Training worksheet.

1. With any worksheet active, use the Name box to select the named range Total_Sales.

   The Payroll worksheet is active and the range B6:B15 is selected.

2. Click the Conditional Formatting button in the Styles group on the Home tab.
3. Click the *Manage Rules* option.

   The Conditional Formatting Rules Manager dialog box displays (see Figure 3.23). The *Data Bar* option appears in the list box and is selected.

4. Click the Edit Rule button.

   The Edit Formatting Rule dialog box displays.

5. Click the *Color* option box arrow in the *Bar Appearance* section and then click the *Brown, Accent 1 Lighter 60%* option (fifth column, third row).

   The color in the option box changes from blue to light brown.

6. Click the OK button.

   The Edit Formatting Rule dialog box closes.
7. Click the Apply button.

   The conditional formatting color scale changes are applied to the range B6:B15.
8. Click the *Show formatting rules for* option box arrow and then click the *Sheet: Training* option.
9. Click the *Above Average* option in the list box.
10. Click the Delete Rule button.
11. Click the Apply button.
12. Click the OK button.
13. Click the Training sheet tab.

    The top/bottom conditional formatting rule you applied in Task 3.13 is deleted.
14. Select the range A21:B21 and then press the Delete key.

    The legend for the top/bottom rule is deleted.
15. If printed work is required by your instructor, print the workbook.
16. Click the Save button on the Quick Access Toolbar.

Model Answer

3.16 Using Conditional Formatting or Cell Attributes to Sort and Filter

A **sort** temporarily displays data in a specified order, such as alphabetically by name or chronologically by date. A **filter** temporarily displays only records that match specific criteria.

If fill colors or font colors have been applied to cells either manually or using conditional formatting, the cells can be sorted and filtered by color. If cells have been formatted using an icon set, they can be sorted and filtered by icon. Cells can also be sorted and filtered by the data they contain; this type of sorting and filtering is discussed in Chapters 7 and 8.

Tutorial

Using Conditional Formatting or Cell Attributes to Filter a Range

▸ **Know This** about using conditional formatting or cell attributes to sort and filter

— To use conditional formatting or cell attributes to sort or filter a selected range, click the Sort & Filter button in the Editing group on the Home tab, click the *Filter* option, click the filter arrow at the top of the range, point to the *Sort by Color* option or *Sort by Filter* option, and then click a color or icon.

— To clear a filter, click anywhere in the filtered range, click the Sort & Filter button, and then click the *Clear* option.

— If you see an error message stating that merged cells need to be the same size when sorting, select the range and do a custom sort. Custom sorts will be examined in Chapter 7.

▸ **Know More** ways to filter formatted cells

– Right-click a cell that contains the color or icon, point to the *Filter* option, and then click the *Filter by Selected Cell's Color, Filter by Selected Cell's Font Color,* or *Filter by Selected Cell's Icon* option.

On the Job

Task 3.16 Using Conditional Formatting or Cell Attributes to Filter a Range

Jeremy would like to see the training data for only employees who have completed all four training tests and have earned a score greater than 84% on at least one of the product and features tests. Filter the data in the Tests A group by color to temporarily display these results.

1. With the Training worksheet active, select the range A5:G15.
2. Click the Sort & Filter button in the Editing group on the Home tab.
3. Click the *Filter* option.

   A filter arrow appears at the right side of each cell in the header row (see Figure 3.24).

Figure 3.24 Filter Arrows

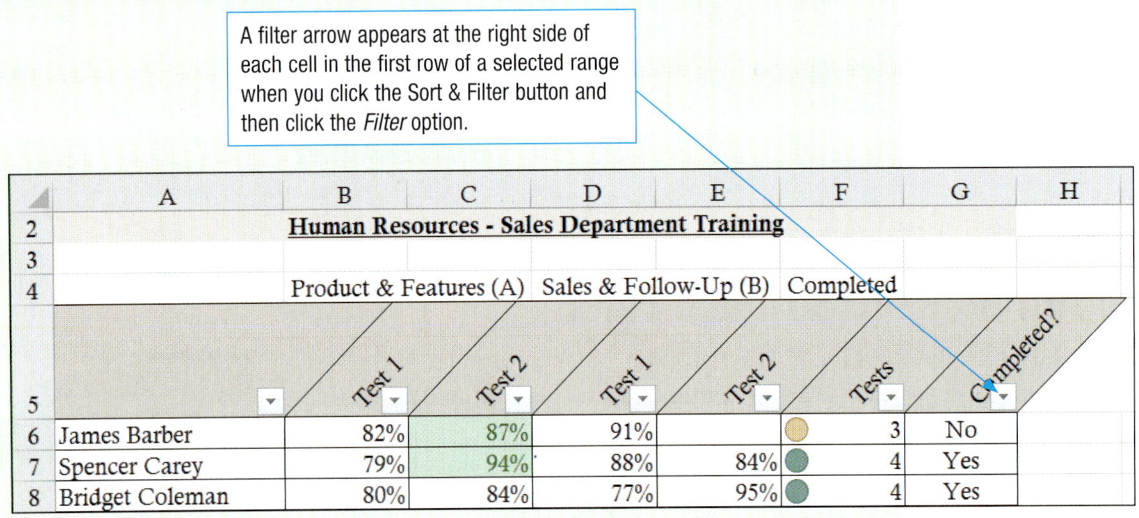

4. Click in any cell to deselect the range.
5. Click the *Tests* filter arrow.
6. Point to the *Filter by Color* option.

   A drop-down list of icons appears.
7. Click the green icon.

   The selected range is filtered to display only employees who display a green icon in the *Tests* column—that is, who have completed all four tests.
8. Right-click in cell C7, C10, or C15.
9. Point to the *Filter* option and then click the *Filter by Selected Cell's Color* option.

   The range is further filtered to display only employees who have achieved greater than 84% on any test in the Tests A group.
10. Click the Save button on the Quick Access Toolbar.

Model Answer

3.17 Creating Custom Number Formats

MOS Expert 2.1.1
MOS Expert 2.3.1

Tutorial

Creating Custom Number Formats

You can create a **custom format** for values that do not conform to predefined formats and to which you want to add consistent punctuation, text, or formatting (such as color). A custom number format uses a **format code**, or series of **placeholders**, to describe how the values should be displayed (see Table 3.4).

Table 3.4 Number Code Placeholders

Placeholder	Description	Format Code Example	Display Example
#	This placeholder represents a digit. Excel rounds numbers if necessary to fit the number of digits after the decimal point in the placeholder. If a comma placeholder is required in the format, then it is required in the code before the thousands placeholder. It is common practice to type one placeholder for each digit after the decimal point up to the hundreds placeholder.	#.## #,###.##	Typing 123.456 displays 123.46 Typing 12345678.9 displays 12,345,678.9
0	This placeholder represents a digit. Type one placeholder for each digit. Excel rounds numbers to fit the number of digits after the decimal point and also fills in leading and trailing zeros.	000.00	Typing 1.2 displays 001.20
?	This placeholder represents a digit. Type one placeholder for each digit. Excel rounds numbers to fit the number of digits after the decimal point and aligns numbers vertically on the decimal point.	???.??	Typing 123.4 .5 67.892 displays 123.40 .50 67.89
"text"	This placeholder adds the characters between the quotation marks to the cell entry.	"WB-"###	Typing 416 displays WB-416
[color]	This placeholder applies the specified font color to the cell entry.	[Blue]#.###	Typing 12.345 displays 12.345
[color];[color]	This placeholder applies the color on the left of the semicolon (;) to positive values and the color on the right to negative values.	[Blue];[Red]	Typing 12 displays 12 Typing -12 displays 12

▸ Know This about creating custom number formats

— To create a custom number format for a selected cell or cells, click the Number group dialog box launcher on the Home tab, click the *Custom* option in the *Category* list box, click a format code in the *Type* list box or select the text in the *Type* text box, edit or type the format code, and then click the OK button.

— Once a custom format has been created, it can be applied anywhere in the workbook.

— Text, numbers, and punctuation added as part of a custom number format are not saved as part of the cell value. This is important to remember when searching for or filtering data.

On the Job

Task 3.17 Creating Custom Number Formats

Jeremy would like you to add employee identification numbers in the Payroll worksheet. He gives you a list of three-digit ID numbers and asks you to add the WareBot employee code and a font color to each number. Insert a new column to the left of the employee names column in the worksheet, create a custom number format to add *WB-* at the beginning of each ID number and change the color of the number to blue, and then enter the numbers in the new column. When you are done, fix the formatting in rows 1 and 2 so that the title and subtitle are merged and centered above all the columns containing data.

1. Click the Payroll sheet tab.
2. Right-click column heading *A* and then click the *Insert* option.
3. Select the range A6:A15.
4. Click the Number group dialog box launcher on the Home tab.

   The Format Cells dialog box displays with the Number tab selected.

5. Click the *Custom* option in the *Category* list box.
6. Select the text in the *Type* text box, press the Delete key, and then type [Blue]"WB-"### (see Figure 3.25).

   The placeholder *[Blue]* tells Excel to turn the contents of the cell blue. The placeholder "*WB-*" tells Excel to add *WB-* in front of each number. The placeholder ### tells Excel to round the numbers if necessary and to not display a decimal point or any digits after a decimal point.

7. Click the OK button.
8. Click in cell A6 and then enter only the following identification numbers in cells A6 through A15. The employee names already exist in column B. Press the Enter key after you enter each number.

Employee	Identification Number
James Barber	135
Spencer Carey	137
Bridget Coleman	139
Sasha Gibson	145
Sam Hall	142
Adam Howard	140

Employee	Identification Number
Jarid Khalil	212
Juanita Marquez	213
Andrew McNeil	215
Natalia Pena	345

The numbers appear in blue and *WB-* appears in front of each number.

9. Select the range A1:J1 and then click the Merge & Center button two times.
10. Select the range A2:J2 and then click the F4 function key.
11. Click the Save button on the Quick Access Toolbar.

Figure 3.25 Format Cells Dialog Box with the Number Tab and *Custom* Category Selected

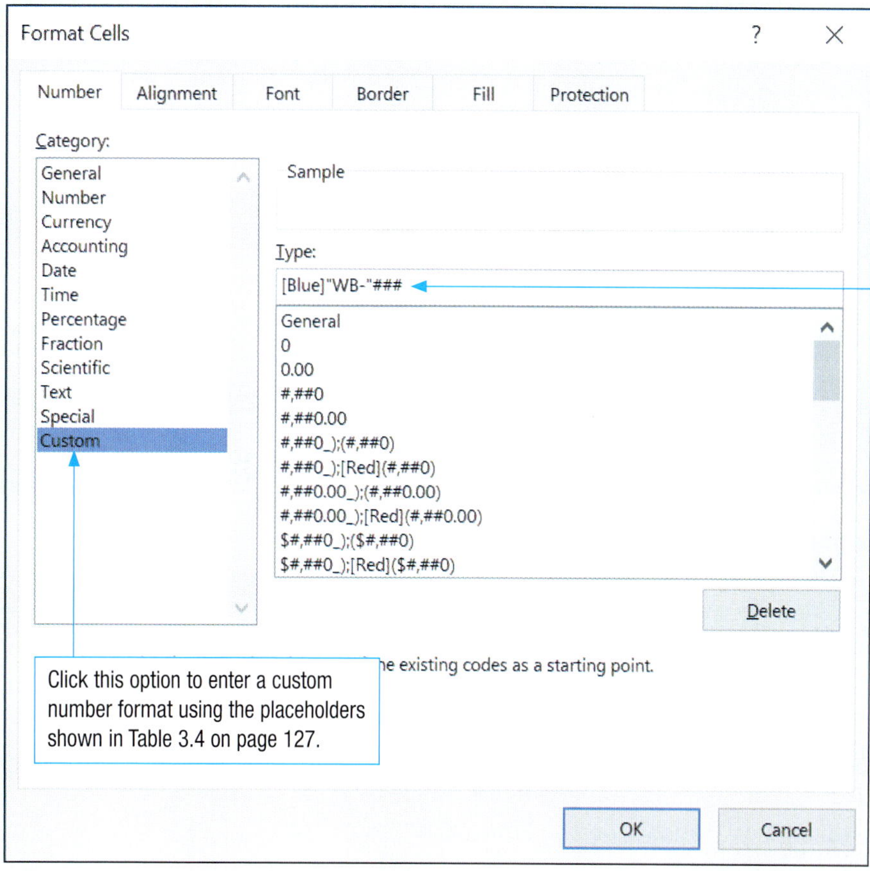

This custom number format will apply a blue font color to the text, display the text *WB-* before each number, and display each number without a decimal point.

Model Answer

3.18 Creating Custom Date and Time Formats

If none of the date and time formats provided by Excel meet your requirements, you can modify one of them or create your own. Table 3.5 lists placeholders used in custom date and time codes.

Tutorial

Creating a Custom Date Format

▸ Know This about creating custom date and time formats

— To create a custom date or time format, click the Number group dialog box launcher on the Home tab, click the *Custom* option in the *Category* list box, click a format code in the *Type* list box or select the text in the *Type* text box, edit or type the format code, and then click the OK button.

— Date formats that start with an asterisk (*) will update to any changes made to the regional date and time settings.

— To standardize the time format, select the text, press and hold down the Ctrl key, press the Shift key, and then type the at symbol (@).

Table 3.5 Date and Time Code Placeholders

Placeholder	Description
d or dd	Displays the day of the month as *1* through *31* (d) or as *01* through *31* (dd)
ddd or dddd	Displays the day of the week abbreviated (ddd) or in full (dddd)
m or mm	Displays the month as *1* through *12* (m) or as *01* through *12* (mm)
mmm or mmmm	Displays the month abbreviated (mmm) or in full (mmmm)
yy or yyyy	Displays the year as the last two digits (yy) or as all four digits (yyyy)
h	Displays the hour
mm	Displays the minutes
ss	Displays the seconds

On the Job
Task 3.18 Creating a Custom Date Format

Jeremy would like to see the day of the week that each employee review will be held. Change the format of the cells in the *Review Date* column to display the values as the day of the week abbreviated, the month abbreviated and the day of the month as *1* through *31*, and the year as all four digits—for example, *Thu, Oct 22, 2020.*

1. With the Payroll worksheet active, select the range J6:J15.
2. Click the Number group dialog box launcher on the Home tab.
3. Click the *Custom* option in the *Category* list box.
4. Select the text in the *Type* text box, press the Delete key, and then type ddd, mmm d, yyyy.
5. Click the OK button.

   The data in the selected range displays as coded—for example, cell J6 displays as *Fri, Jan 31, 2020.*
6. Click in any cell to deselect the range.
7. If printed work is required by your instructor, print the workbook.
8. Click the Save button on the Quick Access Toolbar.

Model Answer

3.19 Finding and Replacing Data and Formatting

MOS 1.2.1
MOS 2.1.1

Tutorial

Finding and Replacing Data

Use the **Find and Replace** feature to quickly locate specific data or formatting and, if required, to replace the data or formatting. Use the Find and Replace dialog box to specify the data and formatting, as shown in Figure 3.26.

▶ Know This about finding and replacing

— To find or search for data, click the Find & Select button in the Editing group on the Home tab, click the *Find* option to display the Find and Replace dialog box with the Find tab active, type the data to be found, and then click the Find All button or the Find Next button.

— To replace data, click the Find & Select button in the Editing group on the Home tab, click the *Replace* option to display the Find and Replace dialog box with the Replace tab active, type the data to be found, type the data to replace it with, and then click the Replace All button or the Replace button.

— The Find and Replace feature allows you to search for records without specifying the entire field value. You can substitute a wildcard character in each position for which the exact text is not specified. The asterisk (*) and the question mark (?) are two commonly used wildcard characters.

- Use the asterisk in a position for which one or more characters vary.
- Use the question mark in a fixed-width word for which the records with the same number of characters in the field are to be viewed.

— When using the Find and Replace feature, be careful to replace only the items you want to replace. For example, if you change the year *2019* to *2020*, be careful to change only values in cells containing dates and not values in cells containing numbers—or, for example, you might inadvertently change a salary from *201945* to *202045*.

▶ Know More about finding and replacing

– The keyboard shortcut for Find is Ctrl + F.

– The keyboard shortcut for Replace is Ctrl + H.

Figure 3.26 Find and Replace Dialog Box

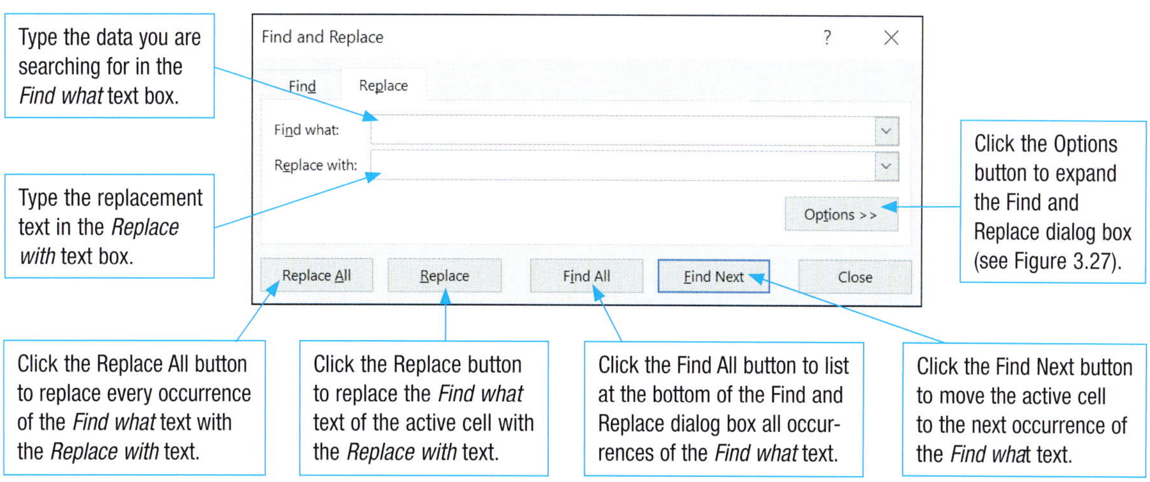

▶ Know This about replacing formatting

— Expand the Replace tab at the Find and Replace dialog box to access options for replacing formatting (see Figure 3.27).

— To expand the Replace tab, click the Options button (see Figure 3.27).

- Click the *Find what* Format button to specify formatting in the search text, click the *Replace with* Format button to specify formatting in the replacement text, and then click the Replace All button.
- Make sure the *Find what* and *Replace with* text boxes are empty when you replace formatting.
- To specify formatting already applied to a cell in either the *Find* or *Replace* row, click the *Format* option box arrow, click the *Choose Format From Cell* option, and then click in the cell with the specific format.
- If the replacement is to be made throughout the entire workbook, change the *Within* option from *Sheet* to *Workbook*.

Figure 3.27 Expanded Find and Replace Dialog Box

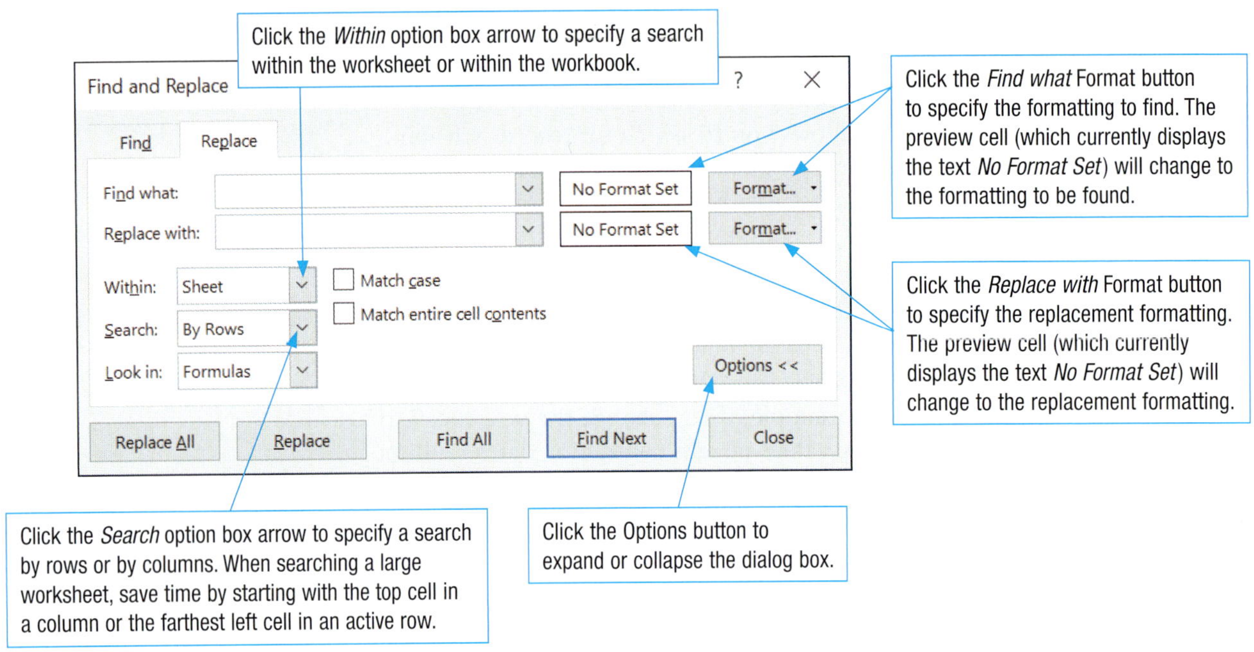

On the Job

Task 3.19a Finding and Replacing Data

Jeremy has planned a sales meeting for Wednesday, September 23, 2020, and he wants to ensure that he does not have an employee review scheduled that day. Search the review dates and change any reviews that have been scheduled for the day of the sales meeting to occur on the following day.

1. With the Payroll worksheet active, click in cell J5.
2. Click the Find & Select button in the Editing group on the Home tab.
3. Click the *Replace* option.

   The Find and Replace dialog box displays.
4. With the insertion point in the *Find what* text box, type 9/23/2020 and then press the Tab key.
5. With the insertion point in the *Replace with* text box, type 9/24/2020 and then click the Find Next button.

   The active cell moves to cell J14.

6. Click the Replace button.

   The data displayed in the active cell changes from *Wed, Sep 23, 2020* to *Thu, Sep 24, 2020*. Remember that a custom format was created for this column.
7. Click the Close button.
8. Click the Save button on the Quick Access Toolbar.

Model Answer

On the Job

Task 3.19b Finding and Replacing Formatting

The subtitles in the worksheets and the main headers in row 4 and column A in the Budget worksheet all use the same font formatting: bold 11-point Calisto MT. Jeremy would like the subtitles and headers to be slightly larger. Search for all cells that use this font formatting, and then replace the formatting in those locations with the same font and font style but a font size of 12 points.

1. With the Payroll worksheet active, click the Find & Select button in the Editing group on the Home tab.
2. Click the *Replace* option.

   The Find and Replace dialog box displays with the Replace tab active.
3. Click the Options button.

   The Find and Replace dialog expands.
4. Select the text in the *Find what* text box and then delete it.
5. Select the text in the *Replace with* text box and then delete it.
6. Click the *Find what* Format button.

   The Find Format dialog box displays.
7. Click the Font tab.
8. Scroll down the list and then click the *Calisto MT* option in the *Font* list box.
9. Click the *Bold* option in the *Font style* list box.
10. Click the *11* option in the *Size* list box.
11. Click the OK button.
12. Click the *Replace with* Format button.
13. Scroll down the list and then click the *Calisto MT* option in the *Font* list box.
14. Click the *Bold* option in the *Font style* list box.
15. Click the *12* option in the *Size* list box.
16. Click the OK button.

    The Replace Format dialog box closes.
17. Click the *Within* option box arrow and then click the *Workbook* option.
18. Click the Replace All button.

    A message box displays stating that 13 replacements were made.
19. Click the OK button.
20. Click the Close button.
21. If printed work is required by your instructor, print the workbook.
22. Click the Save button on the Quick Access Toolbar and then close the workbook.

Model Answer

Chapter Summary

3.1 ▶ A font is a combination of a typeface (such as Calibri) and other attributes (such as size and style) that defines the appearance of text. The font size is the vertical measurement of the characters and is usually expressed in points. A font style is an attribute such as bold, italic, or underline.

3.2 ▶ Excel comes with many different themes, or predefined formatting options. Applying a theme can change the appearance of a workbook quickly by modifying the fonts, colors, and effects all at the same time.

3.3 ▶ Any type of data can be displayed at the left, center, or right of a cell by changing the alignment; data can also be aligned vertically in a cell, at the top, middle, or bottom. Data can be indented to move it closer to or farther away from the left cell border, and the text in a column header can be rotated to fit the available space.

3.4 ▶ Adding a background color, or fill color, to a selected cell or cells can enhance the appearance of a worksheet.

3.5 ▶ A border is an outline applied to the edge of a cell or cell range. A variety of borders (including top, bottom, double bottom, and outline) can be added to visually identify and group data.

3.6 ▶ The Format Cells dialog box offers options for formatting numbers. Twelve categories for formatting numbers are provided on the Number tab.

3.7 ▶ Formatting can be applied quickly using a predefined cell style. A variety of cell styles for titles and headers, number formats, and more are available at the Cell Styles button drop-down gallery.

3.8 ▶ The Format Painter provides a quick and easy way to copy formats from one cell to another without copying any data. The Repeat command allows repeating the last command without copying data.

3.9 ▶ Rows and columns can be hidden to help the reader avoid scrolling and scanning through irrelevant data. Hiding makes rows and columns temporarily invisible; unhiding makes them visible again.

3.10 ▶ An advanced fill series can be created to quickly populate a range of cells by increasing a number by a specific amount, by increasing a date by a specific number of days, or by increasing a day, weekday, month, or year by a specific number of days, weekdays, months, or years.

3.11 ▶ Conditional formatting applies special formatting to cells in a selected range that meet a specified condition. Changing the appearance of a cell based on a condition can help users quickly analyze and interpret data by spotting similarities, differences, highs, lows, and trends between data entries.

3.12 ▶ Highlight cells rules (such as Greater Than and Less Than) base conditional formatting on a comparison of a cell value with a specified value.

3.13 ▶ Top/bottom rules are used to highlight cells based on their values in comparison with the values of other cells—for example, cells that contain the top 10 or bottom 10 values.

3.14 ▸ Cells can be formatted using data bars, icon sets, two-color scales, and three-color scales. These conditional formats provide visual guides for grouping data into three to five categories or for identifying distributions or variations within a range.

3.15 ▸ Once a conditional formatting rule has been applied, changes can be made to the comparison rule criteria or the formatting options. If too many conditional formatting rules have been applied and the result is visually overpowering, it may be helpful to delete some rules.

3.16 ▸ If fill colors or font colors have been applied to cells either manually or using conditional formatting, the cells can be sorted and filtered by color. If cells have been formatted using an icon set, they can be sorted and filtered by their icon.

3.17 ▸ A custom format can be created for values that do not conform to predefined formats and to which consistent punctuation, text, or formatting (such as color) is to be added. A custom number format uses a format code, or series of placeholders, to describe how the values should be displayed.

3.18 ▸ Custom formats can be created by modifying the date and time formats provided by Excel and adding new formats.

3.19 ▸ The Find and Replace feature can be used to quickly locate specific data or formatting features and, if required, to replace the data or formatting.

Features Review

Feature	Ribbon Tab, Group	Button, Option	Keyboard Shortcut
advanced fill series	Home, Editing	Fill, *Series*	
bold	Home, Font	B	Ctrl + B or Ctrl + 2
borders	Home, Font		
bottom-align	Home, Alignment		
cell styles	Home, Styles		
center-align	Home, Alignment		
color scales	Home, Styles	, *Colors Scales*	
data bars	Home, Styles	, *Data Bars*	
decrease indent	Home, Alignment		
edit or delete a conditional formatting rule	Home, Styles	, *Manage Rules*	
fill colors	Home, Font		
filter data	Home, Editing	, *Filter*	
find data	Home, Editing	, *Find*	Ctrl + F

continues...

Feature	Ribbon Tab, Group	Button, Option	Keyboard Shortcut
font colors	Home, Font	A	
fonts	Home, Font	Calisto MT	
font sizes	Home, Font	11	
Format Painter	Home, Clipboard		
gridlines	Page Layout, Sheet Options	*Gridlines*, *View* and *Print* checkboxes	
hide columns or rows	Home, Cells	, *Hide & Unhide*, *Hide Columns* or *Hide Rows*	Ctrl + 9 (rows) Ctrl + 0 (columns)
highlight cells rules	Home, Styles	, *Highlight Cells Rules*	
icon sets	Home, Styles	, *Icon Sets*	
increase indent	Home, Alignment		
italic	Home, Font	*I*	Ctrl + I or Ctrl + 3
left-align	Home, Alignment		
middle-align	Home, Alignment		
repeat last action			F4 or Ctrl + Y
replace data	Home, Editing	, *Replace*	Ctrl + H
right-align	Home, Alignment		
rotate data in a cell	Home, Alignment		
sort data	Home, Editing	, *Filter*	
themes	Page Layout, Themes		
top-align	Home, Alignment		
top/bottom rules	Home, Styles	, *Top/Bottom Rules*	
underline	Home, Font	**U**	Ctrl + U or Ctrl + 4
unhide columns or rows	Home, Cells	, *Hide & Unhide*, *Unhide Columns* or *Unhide Rows*	

Recheck

Recheck your understanding of the concepts, features, and skills covered in this chapter by taking the Recheck quiz.

Workbook

Access the study tools, review exercises, assessments, and challenges for this chapter in the workbook available from this page in your ebook.

Inserting Visual Elements and Modifying Page Setup

Chapter 4

Chapter Goal

To enhance the appearance of worksheets and communicate additional information by adding visual elements and modifying page setup.

Learning Objectives

4.1 Insert and size images, and add alternative text
4.2 Add picture styles and borders to images
4.3 Modify image properties
4.4 Insert and modify shapes
4.5 Apply shape styles
4.6 Insert SmartArt graphics
4.7 Modify the design and formatting of SmartArt graphics
4.8 Insert text boxes and icons
4.9 Insert and modify WordArt
4.10 Arrange objects
4.11 Add headers and footers
4.12 Add watermarks
4.13 Modify page setup
4.14 Insert and remove page breaks
4.15 Print row and column headers on multiple pages
4.16 Set print scaling
4.17 Insert background images
4.18 Print gridlines and row and column headings
4.19 Set print areas

Precheck

Check your understanding of the concepts, features, and skills covered in this chapter by taking the Precheck quiz.

Data Files

Before beginning the chapter work, download the AE4 folder from this page in your ebook to your storage medium and then make AE47 the active folder.

Ebook Links

Access digital resources for this course from your ebook.

SNAP

If you are a SNAP user, go to your SNAP assignments page to complete the Precheck, Tutorials, and Recheck in this chapter.

Preview

On the Job

Scenario WareBot

In Chapter 3, you increased the readability of an Excel workbook by applying formatting to text and data that the director of marketing and sales at WareBot (a robotics manufacturing company) needs to analyze budget, payroll, and training data. Now the director, Jeremy Ronlin, has created a new Excel workbook that includes sales figures for the first quarter and projections for the entire year. Jeremy plans to present this workbook to regional managers at next month's meeting. He has set up the basic framework, and he would like you to add visual elements and modify the page setup to help the managers understand and interpret the data.

Visual Reference: Visual Elements and Page Setup

Figure 4.1 Excel Worksheet with Visual Elements Added and Page Setup Modified

Use options in the Shape Styles group to apply a predefined style to a shape.

The Drawing Tools Format tab is a contextual tab that displays when an object is selected.

The company name in this worksheet was inserted using WordArt and formatted using options in the WordArt Styles group on the Drawing Tools Format tab.

The company name WordArt and the arrow shape were aligned using an Align button option in the Arrange group on the Drawing Tools Format tab.

To display the Format Shape task pane, right-click any shape in the worksheet and then click the *Format Shape* option.

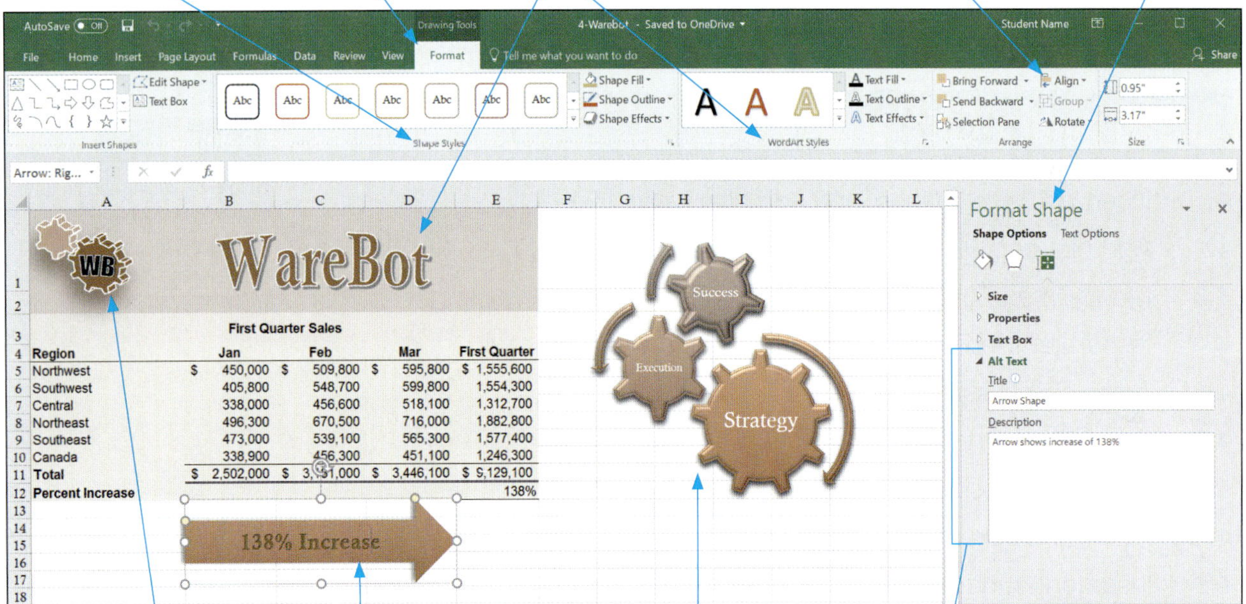

The company logo in this worksheet was formatted using options at the Format Picture task pane, where a specific color was chosen for the shadow.

This arrow shape was inserted and formatted using options on the Drawing Tools Format tab.

The Gear SmartArt graphic was inserted using the SmartArt button in the Illustrations group on the Insert tab. It was then formatted using options in the SmartArt Styles group on the SmartArt Tools Design tab and the Shape Effects button on the SmartArt Tools Format tab.

Visual Reference

Add alternative text to an object to help people using an assistive technology understand what the object depicts.

4.1 Inserting and Sizing Images and Adding Alternative Text

MOS 5.3.2
MOS 5.3.4

Tutorials

Inserting and Resizing an Image from OneDrive

Adding Alternative Text to an Image or Other Object

Pictures can make worksheets more attractive and reinforce the message conveyed by the data. You may insert images from your OneDrive account, from the results of an online search, or from a local folder on your computer or a storage medium connected to your computer.

An **object** is a table, image, shape, SmartArt graphic, WordArt, or other graphic element that appears on a worksheet page. When an object is inserted in a workbook, it is not inserted in a cell or range. Instead, it is placed on top of the worksheet and can be selected, sized, and moved without restrictions. When an object is selected, one or more contextual tabs display. A **contextual tab** provides access to tools for manipulating the object. For example, the contextual Table Tools Design tab includes commands for modifying the design of a selected table.

Some Excel users take advantage of an assistive technology that provides an audio description of an Excel spreadsheet. This program reads the text and values in a spreadsheet, along with additional information that is not readily visible to users. For example, adding a title and a description to an object, such as an image, can help users know what the image is portraying when the added information is read aloud. If this **alternative text** is missing when you run the Excel Accessibility Checker, you will get an error message. Accessibility errors should be corrected before a workbook is distributed. Running the Accessibility Checker is discussed in Chapter 14.

▸ **Know This** about inserting images using the Online Pictures button

— To insert a picture from your OneDrive account, make sure you are signed in to your Microsoft account, click the Online Pictures button in the Illustrations group on the Insert tab, click the location option box arrow (see Figure 4.2), click the *OneDrive* option, locate and select the image, and then click the Insert button.

— To insert an image from an online search, click the Online Pictures button, click in the *Bing Image Search* text box, type the topic, click the search button, locate and select the image, and then click the Insert button.

— To insert an image from a Bing category: click the Online Pictures button; click the category thumbnail at the gallery; choose the *Size*, *Type*, *Color*, *Layout*, and *License* options, if necessary; click the image; and then click the Insert button.

▸ **Know This** about copyrights and permissions

— Images from online and other sources may be copyrighted. You are responsible for respecting all forms of copyright, including restrictions on distributing or changing an image, and requirements for obtaining permission or crediting the work.

▸ **Know More** about copyrights and permissions

– By default, only images with Creative Commons licenses display when you perform an online image search. A **Creative Commons license** defines the permission granted by the creator of a work. The creator may stipulate certain conditions, such as allowing the work to be used only as it is, with no changes, and with credit to the creator.

– To see images that do not have Creative Commons licenses, click the Show all results button at the search results dialog box. Be aware that images without Creative Commons licenses may have other forms of copyright protection.

Figure 4.2 Insert Pictures Dialog Box

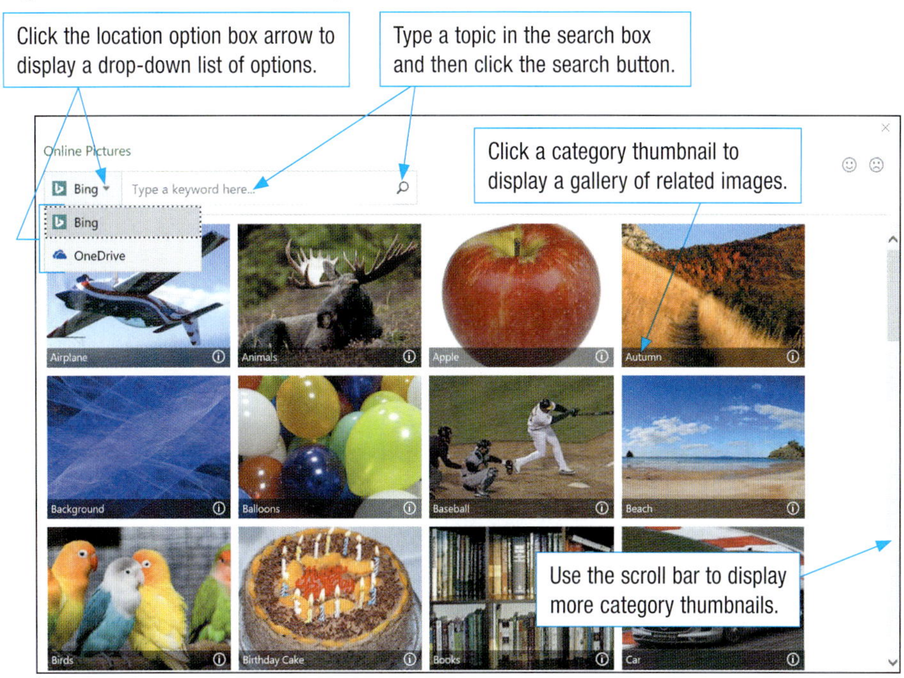

▶ Know This about inserting images using the Pictures button

— To insert an image from your local computer or a removable drive connected to the computer, click the Pictures button in the Illustrations group on the Insert tab (see Figure 4.3), locate and select the image, and then click the Insert button.

▶ Know This about adding alternative text

— To add alternative text to an image, right-click the image, click the *Format Image* option at the pop-up menu, click the Size & Properties icon at the Format Picture task pane, click the *Alt Text* section name, and then type a meaningful title and description in the *Title* and *Description* text boxes.

— An image inserted from the Internet may already have a title and/or description attached to it. If this title or description is not relevant for your use, you can modify or replace it. Be careful not to remove text that is required for copyright purposes.

▶ Know This about sizing and cropping an image

— To size an image, select the image and then use the *Height* and *Width* measurement boxes in the Size group on the Picture Tools Format tab.

— By default, the **Lock Aspect Ratio** feature is turned on, so that when the height is adjusted the width changes proportionally and when the width is adjusted the height changes proportionally.

— To turn off the Lock Aspect Ratio feature for an image, select the image, right-click, click the *Format Image* option at the pop-up menu, click the Size & Properties icon at the Format Picture task pane, click the *Size* section name, and then click the *Lock aspect ratio* check box to insert a check mark.

— To remove part of a picture, select the picture and then use options at the Crop button drop-down list in the Size group.

On the Job

Task 4.1a Inserting an Image from OneDrive or a Local Storage Medium, Sizing an Image Proportionally, and Adding Alternative Text to an Image

Jeremy would like you to add the WareBot company logo to the Sales worksheet. Insert the logo from the folder containing your student data files for Chapter 4. After inserting the logo, adjust the size and then add alternative text, including both a title and a description.

1. Open the data file **4-WareBot**.
2. With cell A1 in the Sales worksheet active, click the Insert tab.
3. If your data files are stored in your OneDrive account, click the Online Pictures button in the Illustrations group. If your data files are stored locally (on your computer or on a USB flash drive or other removable storage medium connected to your computer), click the Pictures button. See Figure 4.3.

   If you clicked the Online Pictures button, the Insert Pictures dialog box displays as shown in Figure 4.2 on page 139. If you clicked the Pictures button, the Insert dialog box displays with your folders and drives.

▶ Know More about inserting images

- You can also insert images from OneDrive using the Pictures button. At the Insert Pictures dialog box, navigate to your OneDrive account, select the image, and then click the Insert button.
- To replace an image that has already been inserted, right-click the image, click the *Change Picture* option, and then locate and insert the replacement image.

▶ Know More ways to size an image

- A **sizing handle** is a circle or square that displays on the edge or corner of a selected object and can be used to change the size of the object. (see Figure 4.4)
- To change size using a sizing handle, hover the mouse pointer over the top middle sizing handle until the pointer turns into a two-headed arrow, click and hold down the left mouse button, drag the handle until the desired size is achieved, and then release the mouse button.
- To change height or width using a pop-up menu, right-click the image, click the *Size and Properties* option at the pop-up menu, click the *Height* or Width measurement box arrow in the *Size* section until the new measurement displays, and then click the Close button.
- To change height or width using the Format Picture task pane, click the image, click the Picture Tools Format tab, click the Format Picture task pane launcher in the Size group, select the value in the *Height* or *Width* measurement box in the *Size* section, type the new measurement, press the Enter key, and then click the Close button.

Figure 4.3 Illustrations Group on the Insert Tab

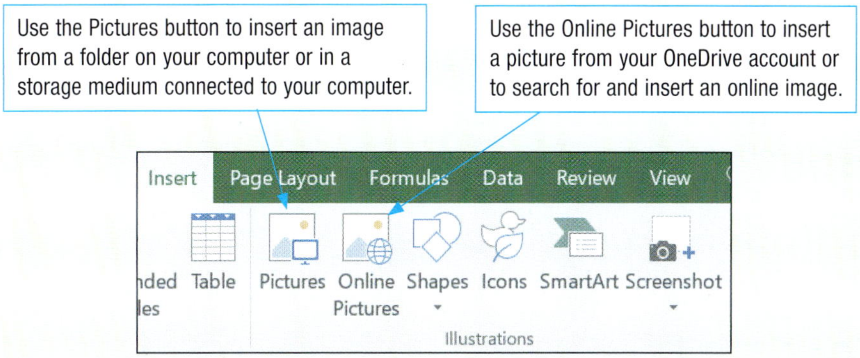

4. If you clicked the Online Pictures button, click the location option box arrow, click the *OneDrive* option, navigate to your AE4 folder, click the data file WBLogo.png, and then click the Insert button. If you clicked the Pictures button, navigate to your AE4 folder, click the data file WBLogo.png, and then click the Insert button.

   The image is inserted. The sizing handles around the image indicate that it is selected (see Figure 4.4).

Figure 4.4 Selected Image Resized with the Sizing Handles Displayed

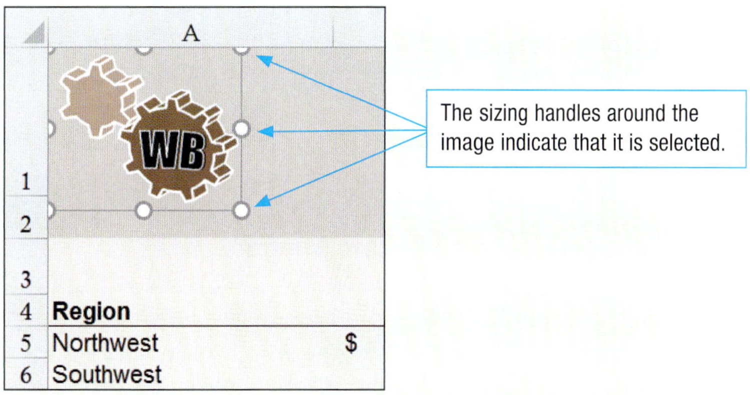

5. Click in the *Height* measurement box in the Size group on the Picture Tools Format tab, type 1, and then press the Enter key.

   The picture is resized to be 1 inch tall by 1.22 inches wide.

6. Right-click the logo and then click the *Format Picture* option.

   The Format Picture task pane displays.

7. Click the Size & Properties icon and then click the *Alt Text* section name.

   A list of *Alt Text* options displays (see Figure 4.5).

8. Click in the *Title* text box and then type Company Logo.
9. Click in the *Description* text box and then type Image of WareBot's company logo.

   Leave the Format Picture task pane displayed.

10. Click the Save button on the Quick Access Toolbar.

Figure 4.5 Format Picture Task Pane with the Size & Properties Icon Selected

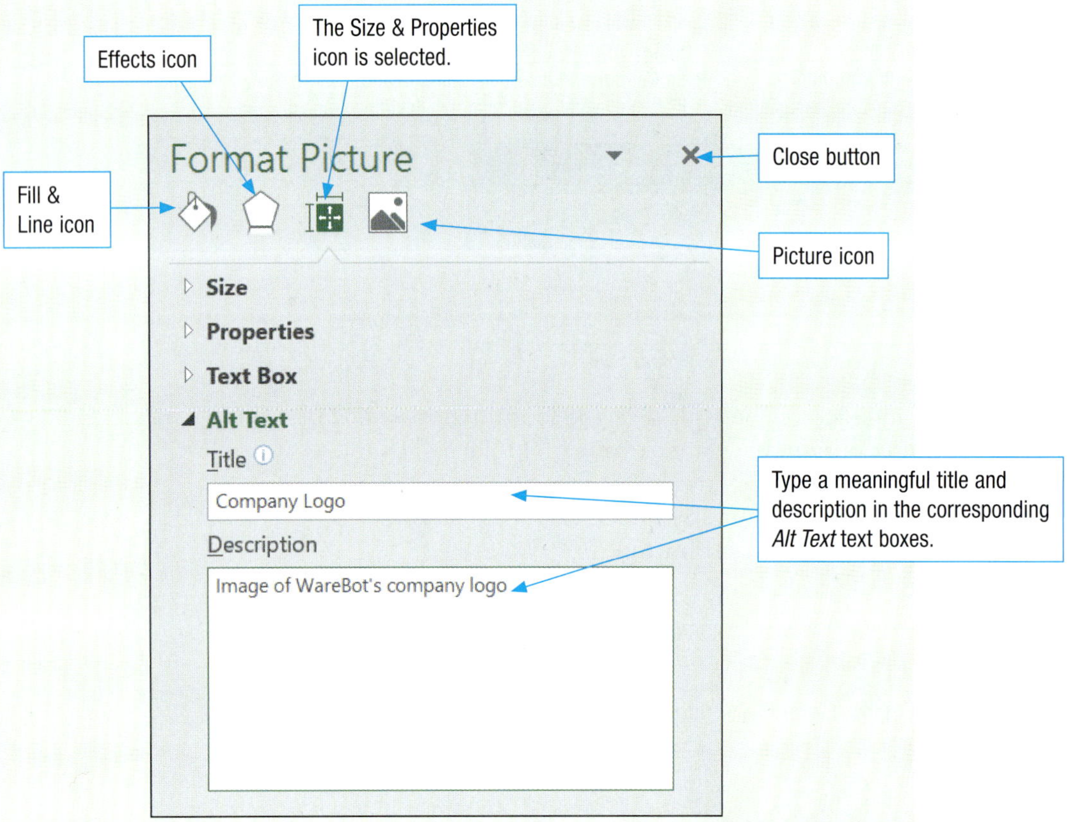

Model Answer

On the Job

Task 4.1b Searching for and Inserting an Online Image

In the Sales worksheet, Jeremy would like you to add an image showing that sales are increasing from month to month. Use the search term *sales* to find an image online, insert the image, and then use the alternative text feature to add a title and change the description.

1. With the Sales worksheet active, click in cell F1 and then click the Online Pictures button in the Illustrations group on the Insert tab.

   The Insert Pictures dialog box displays (see Figure 4.2 on page 139). If you inserted the image in Task 4.1a using the Online Pictures button, you will have to click the location option box arrow to display the *Bing* options.

2. With the insertion point in the *Bing Image Search* text box, type sales and then click the Search button.

   The Bing search results box displays (see Figure 4.6).

3. Click the sales image shown in Figure 4.6 and then click the Insert button.

   The Bing search results box closes and the sales image is inserted and selected. ***Note:*** *If the image shown in Figure 4.6 is not available online, click the Pictures button on the Insert tab,* navigate to your AE4 folder, and then double-click the data file *Sales.png*.

4. Click in the *Title* text box in the *Alt Text* section of the Format Picture task pane and then type Sales.
5. Select the text in the *Description* text box and then type Image of sales text.
6. Click the task pane Close button (see Figure 4.5 on page 142).

   The Format Picture task pane closes.
7. Click the Save button on the Quick Access Toolbar.

Figure 4.6 Sales Image

Model Answer

4.2 Adding Picture Styles and Borders to Images

When an image is selected, the contextual Picture Tools Format tab displays (see Figure 4.7). Use buttons and options on this tab to add a picture style or a border to the image.

Tutorial

Adding Picture Styles to Images

Figure 4.7 Picture Tools Format Tab

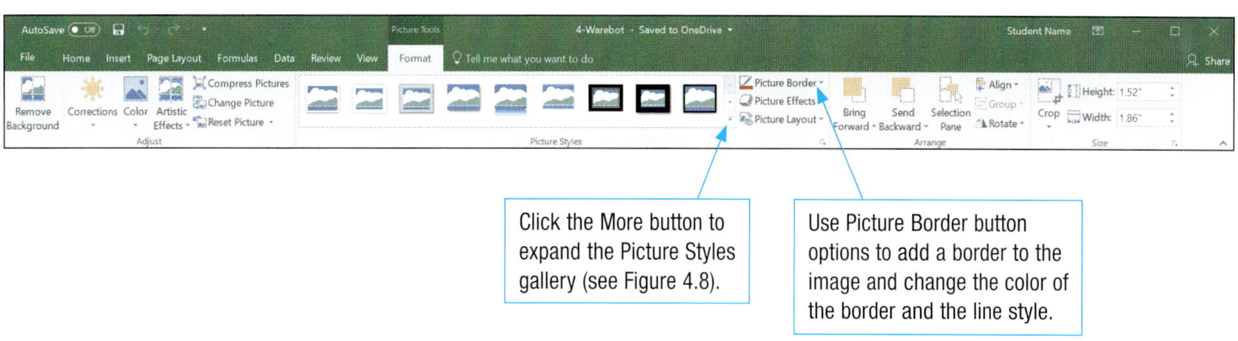

▸ **Know This** about adding or changing a style or border on an image

— To add or change a style or border on an image, crop the image within a frame, or change the perspective of the image, select the image and then use buttons and options in the Picture Styles group on the Picture Tools Format tab (see Figure 4.7 on page 143).

— To expand the Picture Styles gallery, click the More button.

— To display a drop-down list where you can choose the color as well as a line style and weight, click the Picture Border button.

On the Job

Task 4.2 Applying Pictures Styles to Images

Jeremy would like you to modify the images you inserted in the Sales worksheet in Tasks 4.1a and 4.1b. Use options and buttons on the Picture Tools Format tab to add a shadow to the company logo and a picture style to the sales text image.

1. With the Sales worksheet active, click the WareBot logo.
2. Click the Picture Tools Format tab if necessary to make it active.
3. Click the *Drop Shadow Rectangle* option (fourth column, first row) at the Picture Styles gallery (see Figure 4.8).

   A drop shadow appears behind the WareBot logo.
4. Click the sales image.
5. Click the More button in the Picture Styles group (see Figure 4.7).

   The Picture Styles gallery expands.
6. Click the *Bevel Perspective Left, White* option(fourth column, third row).

   The image displays with the Bevel Perspective Left, White style applied.
7. Click the Save button on the Quick Access Toolbar.

Figure 4.8 Expanded Picture Styles Gallery

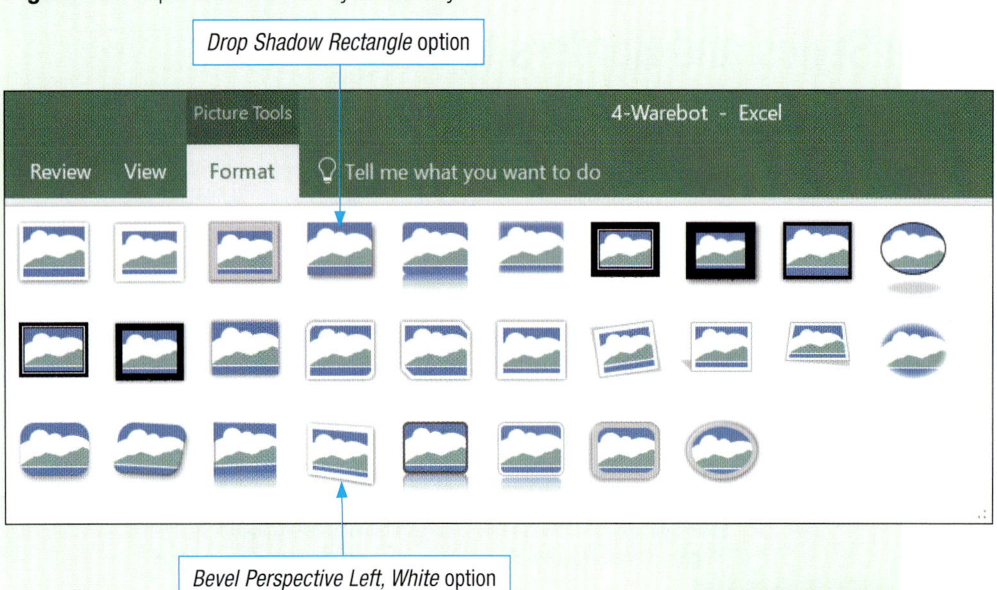

Model Answer

MOS 5.3.3

Tutorial

Modifying Image Properties

4.3 Modifying Image Properties

Image properties can be modified using options on the Picture Tools Format tab or at the Format Picture task pane. For instance, you can remove unwanted parts of an image or correct the brightness, contrast, and tint of an image.

▸ Know This about formatting image properties

— To modify an image using the Picture Tools Format tab, select the image, click the tab if necessary to make it active, and then use buttons and options in the Adjust group.

— To change the sharpness, brightness, and contrast of an image, use Corrections button options.

— To adjust the color, use Color button options.

— To apply an artistic effect such as Watercolor Sponge or Glass, use Artistic Effects button options.

— To restore the image back to its original properties, click the Reset Picture button.

▸ Know More ways to format image properties

– To modify an image using the Format Picture task pane, right-click the image, click the *Format Picture* option (see Figure 4.9), to display the task pane, click an icon to display a list of section names, and then click a section name to display a list of options (see Figure 4.10).

– Options at the Format Picture task pane not only allow you to choose the same formatting presets found on the Picture Tools Format tab, but also allow you to choose more specific properties such as the color of a shadow.

Figure 4.9 Image Pop-Up Menu

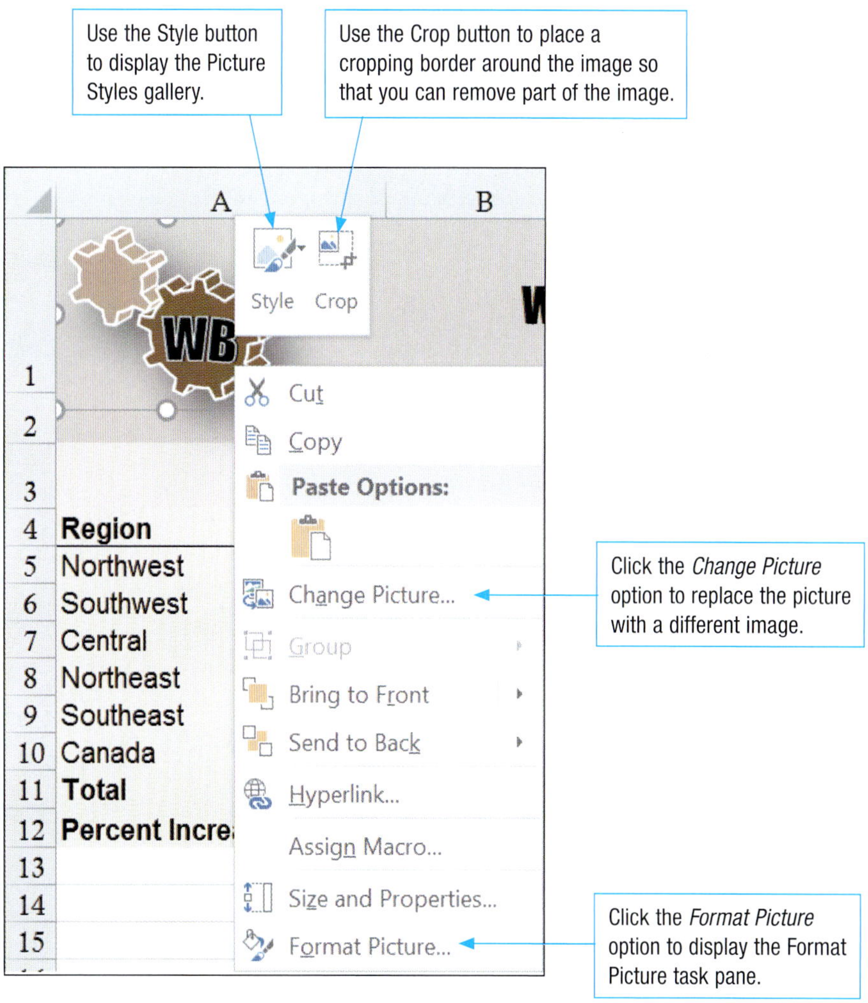

Figure 4.10 Shadow Options in the *Effects* Area of the Format Picture Task Pane

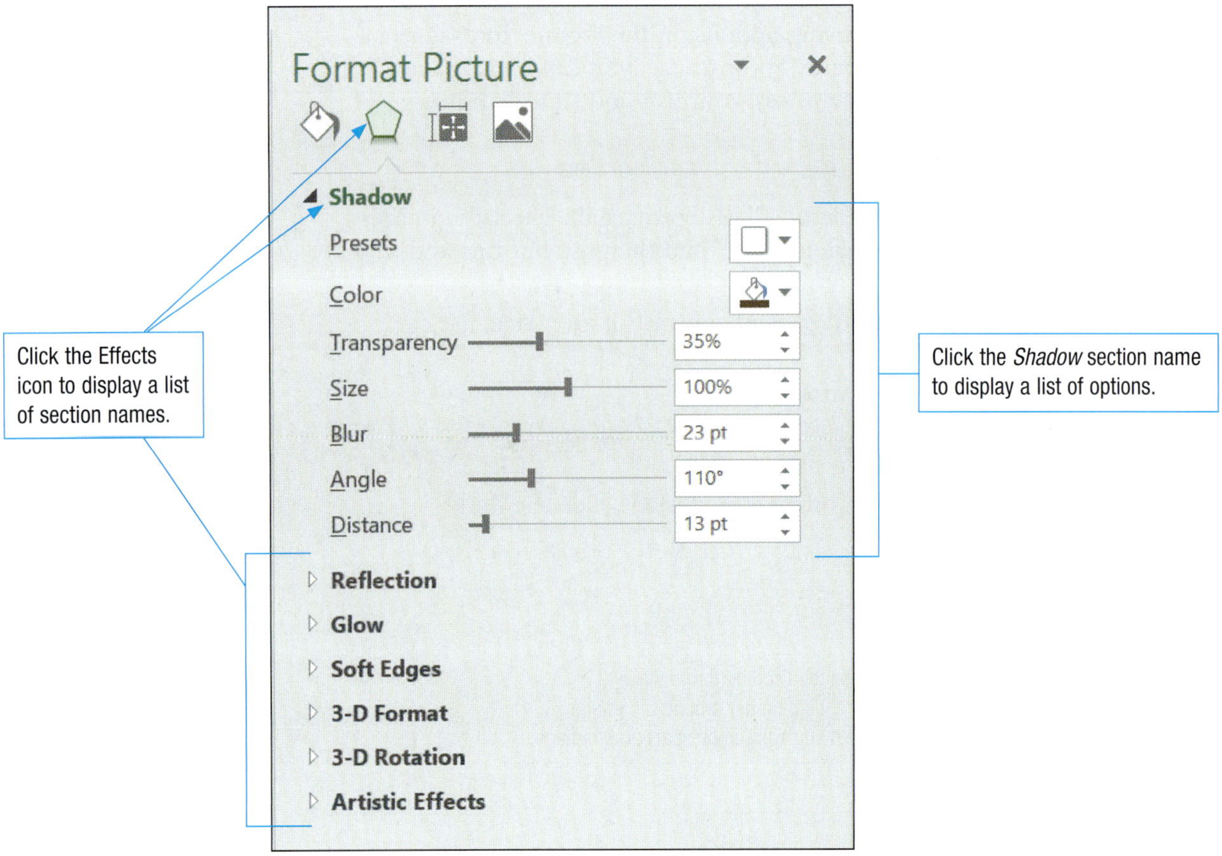

On the Job
Task 4.3 Modifying Image Properties

Jeremy would like the properties of the images in the Sales worksheet to coordinate with the workbook theme. Use the Picture Tools Format tab to recolor and adjust the contrast of the sales image and the Format Picture task pane to change the color of the shadow in the WareBot logo.

1. With the Sales worksheet active and the sales image selected, click the Color button in the Adjust group on the Picture Tools Format tab.
   The Color drop-down gallery displays.
2. Click the *Tan, Accent color 3 Light* option (fourth column, third row in the *Recolor* section).
   The letters change to tan.
3. Click the Corrections button.
   A drop-down gallery displays.
4. Click the *Brightness: 0% (Normal) Contrast: -40%* option (third column, first row in the *Brightness/Contrast* section).
5. Right-click the WareBot logo.
   A pop-up menu displays (see Figure 4.9 on page 145).
6. Click the *Format Picture* option.
   The Format Picture task pane displays (see Figure 4.10).

7. With the Effects icon selected, click the *Shadow* section name.
   The list of *Shadow* options expands.
8. Click the *Color* option box arrow and then click the *Tan, Accent 3, Darker 50%* option (seventh column, sixth row in the *Theme Colors* section).
   The shadow changes to dark tan.
9. Select the number in the *Angle* measurement box and then type 110.
   The shadow moves to the bottom left of the image.
10. Select the number in the *Distance* measurement box and then type 13.
    The shadow moves slightly away from the image.
11. Click the task pane Close button.
    The Format Picture task pane closes.
12. Click the Save button on the Quick Access Toolbar.

Model Answer

4.4 Inserting and Modifying Shapes

MOS 5.3.1
MOS 5.3.4

Tutorial

Inserting and Modifying Shapes

A **shape** can add visual interest to a worksheet. For example, shapes can illustrate overall trends, such as sales increases or decreases. You can choose from a variety of shape options, add text to the shape, and format the shape and text to match the theme of the workbook. When a shape is selected, the contextual Drawing Tools Format tab is active.

▸ **Know This** about inserting shapes

— To insert a shape, click the Shapes button in the Illustrations group on the Insert tab, click an option at the drop-down list (see Figure 4.11), and then click the worksheet.

— When you click an option at the Shapes drop-down list, the mouse pointer displays as crosshairs. Use the crosshairs to help position the shape in the worksheet.

— To add the same shape multiple times, right-click the option and then click the *Lock Drawing Mode* option at the pop-up menu (see Figure 4.12).

▸ **Know This** about sizing shapes

— To adjust the size of a shape, select the shape and then use the *Height* and *Width* measurement boxes in the Size group on the Drawing Tools Format tab.

▸ **Know This** about inserting and sizing shapes at the same time

— To insert and size a shape at the same time, click the option at the Shapes button drop-down list, hover the mouse pointer over the worksheet where the shape is to begin, click and hold down the left mouse button, drag to create and size the shape, and then release the mouse button.

— To keep a line on the same path or maintain the proportions of the shape, press and hold down the Shift key while dragging the mouse.

▸ **Know More** about sizing shapes

- To change size using one of the sizing handles that display around a selected shape, hover the mouse pointer over the sizing handle until the pointer turns into a two-headed arrow, click and hold down the left mouse button, drag the handle to achieve the desired size, and then release the mouse button.

Figure 4.11 Insert Shapes Options

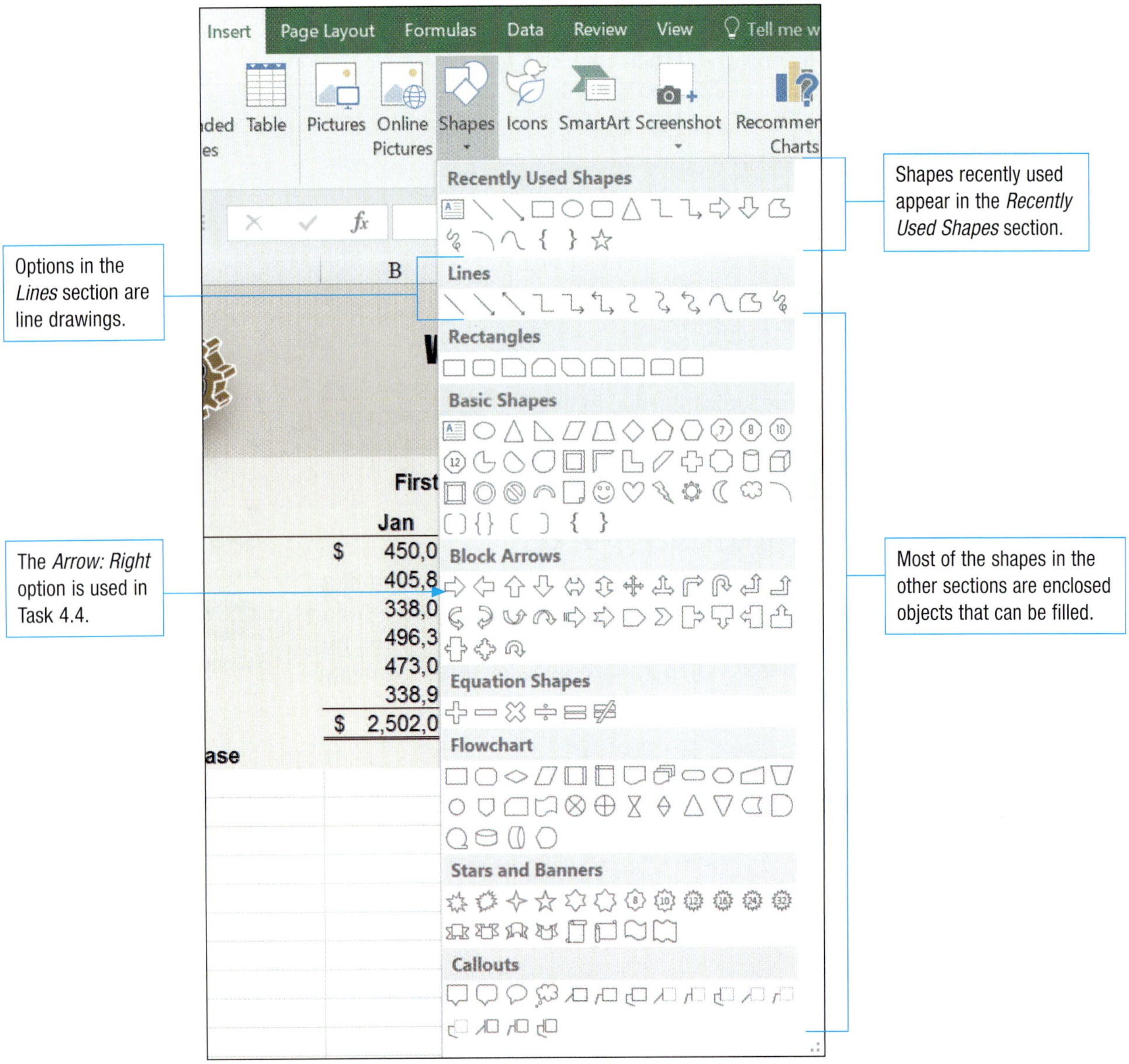

Figure 4.12 Shapes Button Pop-Up Menu

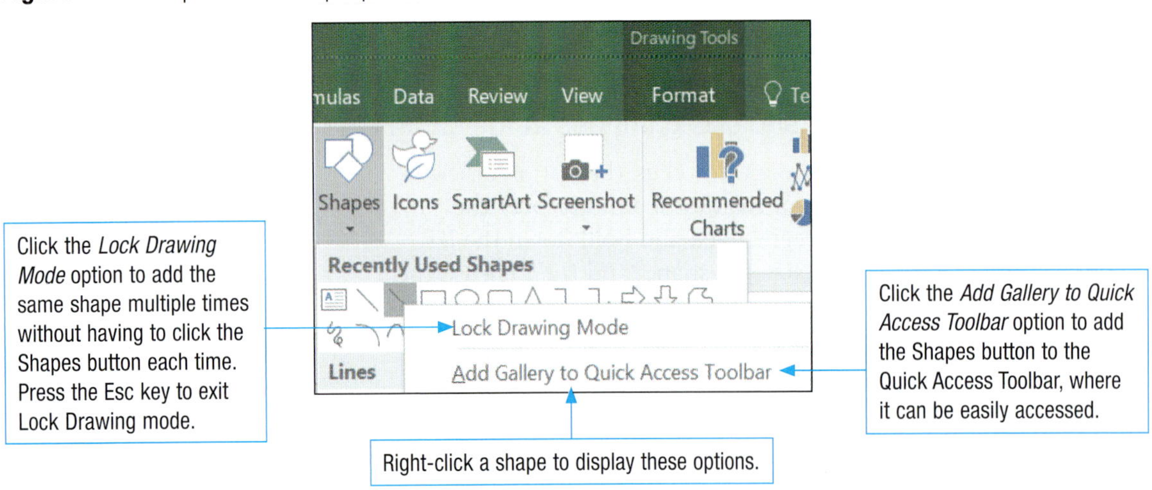

▶ Know This about modifying a shape and adding text inside a shape

— To modify a shape using the Picture Tools Format tab, select the shape, click the tab if necessary to make it active, and then use buttons and options in the Shape Styles group.
— To add text inside a shape, select the shape and then type the text.
— To modify text inside a shape, use options in the Font and the Alignment groups on the Home tab or in the WordArt Styles group on the Drawing Tools Format tab.

▶ Know More ways to add text inside a shape

- Right-click the shape, click the *Edit Text* option at the pop-up menu, and then type the text.

▶ Know This about copying a shape

— To copy a shape to another part of the workbook using keyboard shortcuts, select the shape, press Ctrl + C, click in the cell where the shape is to be copied, and then press Ctrl + V.

▶ Know More about copying a shape

- You can also copy a shape to another part of the workbook by pressing and holding down the Ctrl key while dragging the shape to the new location.
- Other ways to copy a shape to a new location are to use the Copy and the Paste buttons in the Clipboard group on the Home tab, or use the *Copy* and the *Paste* options at the pop-up menu that displays when you right-click a shape.

On the Job

Task 4.4 Inserting and Modifying Shapes

Jeremy would like you to emphasize the 138% sales figure in a visual element. Replace the sales image with an arrow shape that contains the text *138% Increase*, position the shape below the *First Quarter Sales* columns and size it to stretch from the beginning to the end of the first quarter, and then format the text to fit in the resized image. Finish by adding alternative text, including a title and a description.

1. With the Sales worksheet active, click the sales image and then press the Delete key.

   The sales image is deleted.

2. Click the Shapes button in the Illustrations group on the Insert tab.
3. Click the *Arrow: Right* option (first column, first row in the *Block Arrows* section; see Figure 4.11 on page 148).

   The mouse pointer displays as crosshairs.

4. Hover the mouse pointer over the upper left corner of cell B13 and then click.

   A right-pointing arrow is inserted.

5. Type 138% Increase.

   The text appears within the arrow. The word *Increase* is on the second line and cannot be seen.

6. Hover the mouse pointer over the right middle sizing handle until the pointer turns into a two-headed arrow, click and hold down the left mouse button, drag the shape until it meets the right border of column D, and then release the mouse button.
7. Position the mouse over the bottom middle sizing handle until the pointer turns into a two-headed arrow and then drag the shape until the widest part of the arrow touches the bottom border of row 17.
8. Select the text inside the arrow, click the Home tab, change the font size to 18 points, center the text horizontally, and then middle-align the text.

Reminder
To add alternative text to a shape, click the *Format Shape* option at the pop-up menu to display the Format Shape task pane and then follow steps similar to those described in Section 4.1.

Reminder
Triple-click to select a line or paragraph of text.

9. Right-click the arrow shape and then click the *Format Shape* option.
   The Format Shape task pane displays.
10. Click the Size & Properties icon.
11. Click the *Alt Text* section name if the *Alt Text* section is not already expanded.
   A list of *Alt Text* options display.
12. Click in the *Title* text box and then type Arrow Shape.
13. Click in the *Description* text box and then type Arrow shows increase of 138%.
14. Click the task pane Close button.
   The Format Picture task pane closes.
15. Click the Save button on the Quick Access Toolbar.

Model Answer

4.5 Applying Shape Styles

MOS 5.3.3

Tutorial

Applying and Modifying Shape Styles

You can add further interest to a shape by applying and then modifying a style using buttons and options in the Shape Styles group on the Drawing Tools Format tab (see Figure 4.13).

Figure 4.13 Shape Styles Group on the Drawing Tools Format Tab

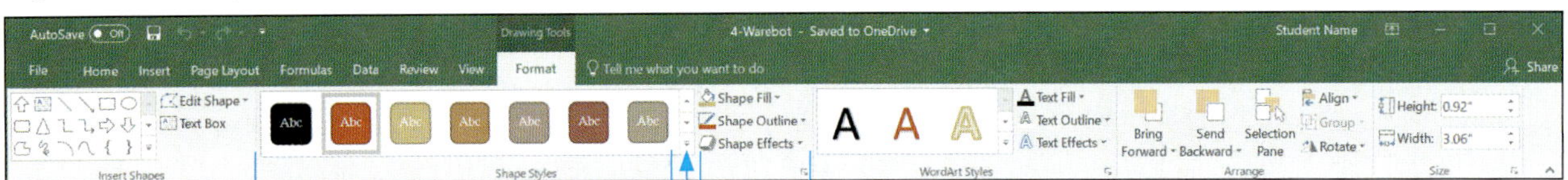

▸ **Know This** about applying shape styles

— To apply a preset style to a selected shape, click an option at the gallery in the Shape Styles group on the Drawing Tools Format tab.

— To expand the Shape Styles gallery, click the More button.

— To apply a fill such as a color, gradient, or picture, click the Shape Fill button in the Shape Styles group and then select an option.

— To apply an outline, click the Shape Outline button and then select options to set the color, weight, and other attributes.

— To apply a shape effect such as a shadow, reflection, glow, soft edges, bevel, or 3-D rotation, click the Shape Effects button and then select an option at the drop-down list (see Figure 4.14).

▸ **Know This** about formatting text in a shape

— To apply a style, fill, outline, or effect to text that has been inserted in a shape, use buttons in the WordArt Styles group.

▸ **Know More** about formatting shapes

- To modify a shape using the Format Shape task pane, right-click the shape, click the *Format Shape* option to display the task pane, click an icon to display a list of section names, and then click a section name to display a list of options.
- Options at the Format Shape task pane not only allow you to choose the same formatting presets found on the Drawing Tools Format tab, but also allow you to choose more specific properties such as the colors of a gradient fill.

Figure 4.14 Shape Effects Drop-Down List with the Shadow Gallery Displayed

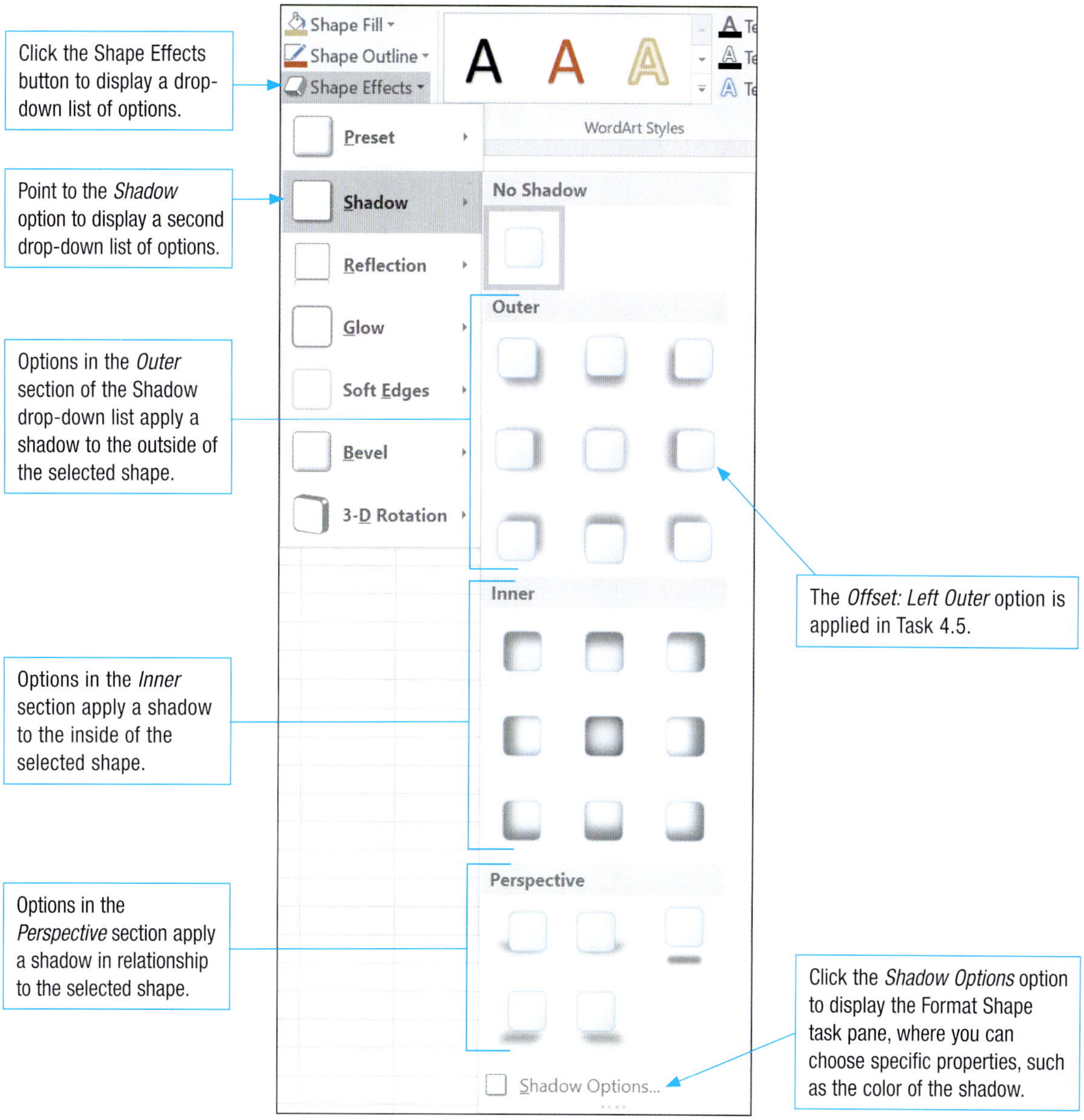

On the Job

Task 4.5 Applying and Modifying Shape Styles

Jeremy would like you to add more visual interest to the arrow. Use options and buttons on the Drawing Tools Format tab to apply a shape style that coordinates with the theme of the workbook and to add a shadow to the shape.

1. With the Sales worksheet active, click the arrow shape to select it.
2. Click the Drawing Tools Format tab if necessary to make it active and then click the More button in the Shape Styles group.

   The Shape Styles gallery expands.

3. Click the *Intense Effect - Tan, Accent 3* option (fourth column, sixth row in the *Theme Styles* section).

   The arrow shape changes to a tan color with a double border and a drop shadow.

4. Click the Shape Effects button in the Shape Styles group.

   The Shape Effects drop-down list displays (see Figure 4.14 on page 151).

5. Point to the *Shadow* option and then click the *Offset: Left* option (third column, second row in the *Outer* section).

   The drop shadow moves to the outer left side of the arrow.

6. Click in any cell to deselect the shape.
7. Click the Save button on the Quick Access Toolbar.

Model Answer

4.6 Inserting SmartArt Graphics

MOS 5.3.4

Tutorial

Inserting a SmartArt Graphic

A **SmartArt graphic** is a predesigned visual element that allows you to easily create a professional-looking illustration such as a flowchart, organizational chart, or cycle chart (see Figure 4.15).

Figure 4.15 Choose a SmartArt Graphic Dialog Box

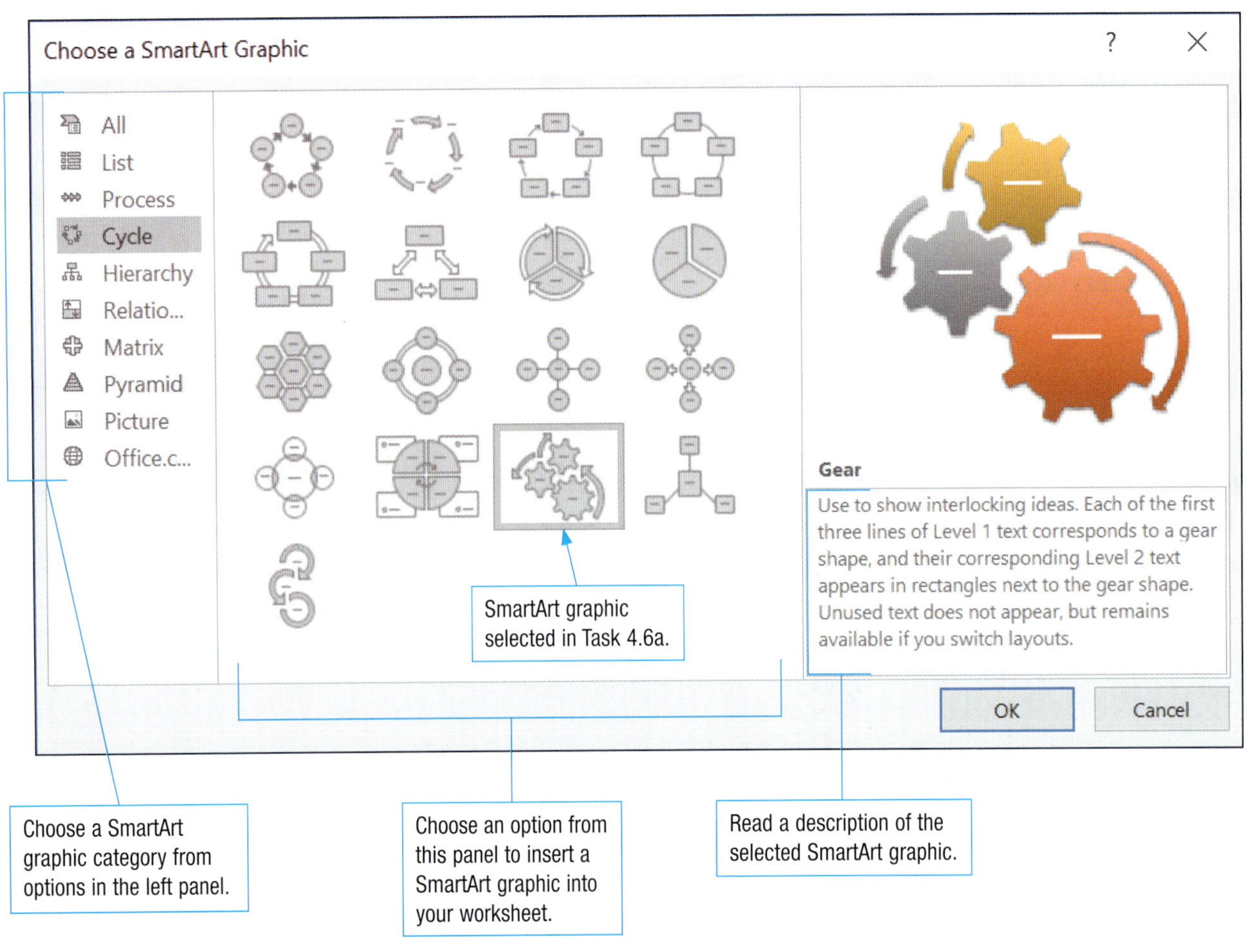

▸ Know This about inserting a SmartArt graphic

— To insert a SmartArt graphic, click the SmartArt button in the Illustrations group on the Insert tab, click a category in the left panel, click an option in the middle panel, and then click the OK button.
— If the SmartArt graphic has more shapes than you need, delete each unused shape by clicking it and then pressing the Delete key.

▸ Know This about entering and editing text in a SmartArt graphic

— To enter text in a SmartArt graphic, select a shape in the graphic or display the Text pane, and then type the text.
— To display the Text pane, click the Text Pane button in the Create Graphic group on the SmartArt Tools Design tab.
— To close the Text pane, click the Text Pane button in the Create Graphic group or click the Close button in the upper right corner of the pane.
— You can edit the text either in the shape or at the Text pane.
— As you type or edit the text in a selected shape, the font size will increase or decrease so that the text fits within the shape.
— The font size will also adjust when the SmartArt graphic is resized.
— To modify the font, use options on the Mini toolbar that appears when text is selected or use options in the Font group on the Home tab.
— Table 4.1 describes how to use different keys when entering text at the Text pane.

▸ Know More ways to display the Text pane

– To expand or collapse the Text pane, click the Expand or Collapse button on the left edge of the selected SmartArt graphic (see Figure 4.16).
– To display the Text pane, right-click the SmartArt graphic and then click the *Show Task Pane* option.

Reminder

To add alternative text to a SmartArt graphic, click the *Format Object* option at the pop-up menu to display the Format Shape task pane and then follow steps similar to those in Section 4.1.

Table 4.1 Keys to Use When Entering Text at the Text Pane

Key(s)	Description of Use
Enter	Add a new shape to the SmartArt graphic.
Tab	Demote the shape down to the next level.
Backspace	Promote the shape up to the next level.
Shift + Enter	Insert a new row in the selected shape.
Up Arrow, Down Arrow	Move between shapes without adding any new shapes.

▸ Know This about resetting, deleting, moving, and sizing a SmartArt graphic

— To restore a SmartArt graphic to its default layout, click the Reset Graphic button in the Reset group on the SmartArt Tools Design tab.
— To delete a SmartArt graphic, select the graphic and then press the Delete key.
— To move a SmartArt graphic, select the graphic, hover the mouse pointer over the graphic border until the pointer turns into a four-headed arrow, click and hold down the left mouse button, drag the graphic to the correct position, and then release the mouse button.
— To size a SmartArt graphic, use the *Height* and *Width* measurement boxes in the Size group on the SmartArt Tools Format tab.

▸ Know More about sizing a SmartArt graphic

– To change size using one of the sizing handles that display around a selected SmartArt graphic, hover the mouse pointer over the sizing handle until the pointer turns into a two-headed arrow, click and hold down the left mouse button, drag the handle to achieve the desired size, and then release the mouse button.

On the Job

Task 4.6a Inserting a SmartArt Graphic

Jeremy is planning to show the Sales worksheet to regional managers at an upcoming meeting. He would like you to add to the worksheet a graphic illustrating the inspirational message "Strategy plus Execution leads to Success." Insert a SmartArt graphic that is similar to the company logo, and label the shapes in the SmartArt graphic using key words from the inspirational message.

1. With the Sales worksheet active, click the Insert tab.
2. Click the SmartArt button in the Illustrations group.
   The Choose a SmartArt Graphic dialog box displays.
3. Click the *Cycle* category in the left panel.
   The options in the middle panel change to display the SmartArt graphics available in the *Cycle* category.
4. Click the *Gear* option (third column, fourth row) in the middle panel.
   A preview and description of the gear graphic display in the right panel.
5. Click the OK button.
   The gear graphic is inserted in the worksheet and the Text pane displays. **Note:** *If the Text pane does not display, click the Text Pane button in the Create Graphic group on the SmartArt Tools Design tab.*
6. With the insertion point in the first bullet item at the Text pane, type Strategy (see Figure 4.16).
   The text *Strategy* appears in the largest shape in the gear graphic.
7. Press the Down Arrow key.
   The insertion point moves to the second bullet item at the Text pane.
8. Type Execution and then press the Down Arrow key.
   The text *Execution* appears in the second shape in the gear graphic, and the insertion point moves to the last bullet item at the Text pane.
9. Type Success.
   The text *Success* appears in the third shape in the gear graphic.
10. Click the Text pane Close button.
    The Text pane closes.
11. Click the Save button on the Quick Access Toolbar.

Figure 4.16 SmartArt Gear Graphic with the Text Pane Displayed and Shapes Labeled

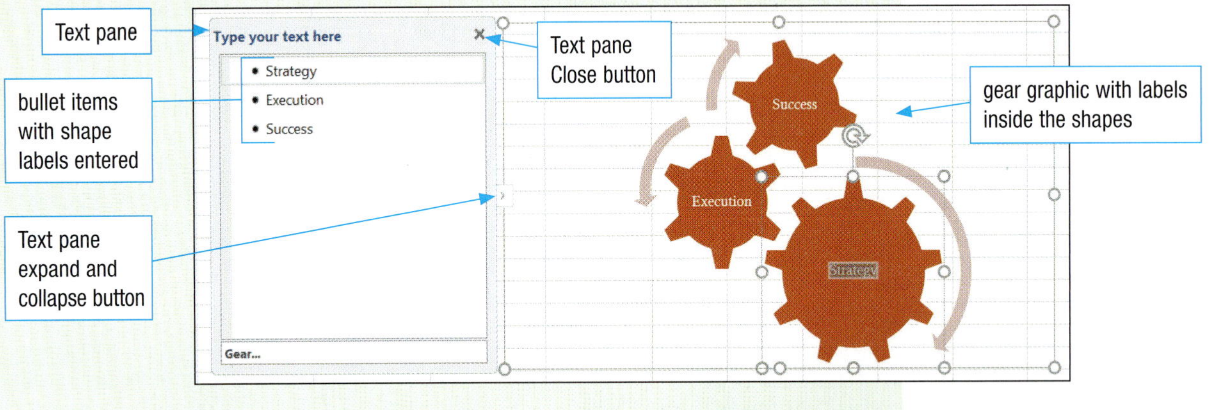

Model Answer

On the Job

Task 4.6b Moving, Editing, and Adding Alternative Text to a SmartArt Graphic

Now that you have inserted the SmartArt graphic, Jeremy would like you to make some adjustments to enhance its effectiveness. Position the graphic at the right of the First Quarter Sales chart, change the font sizes of the labels, and then add alternative text, including a title and a description.

1. With the Sales worksheet active, hover over the border of the gear graphic until a four-headed arrow appears, click and hold down the left mouse button, drag the graphic until it is positioned as shown in Figure 4.17, and then release the mouse button.

   After releasing the mouse button, check the position of your graphic against the example in Figure 4.17, and adjust the position of your graphic if necessary.

Figure 4.17 SmartArt Gear Graphic Position

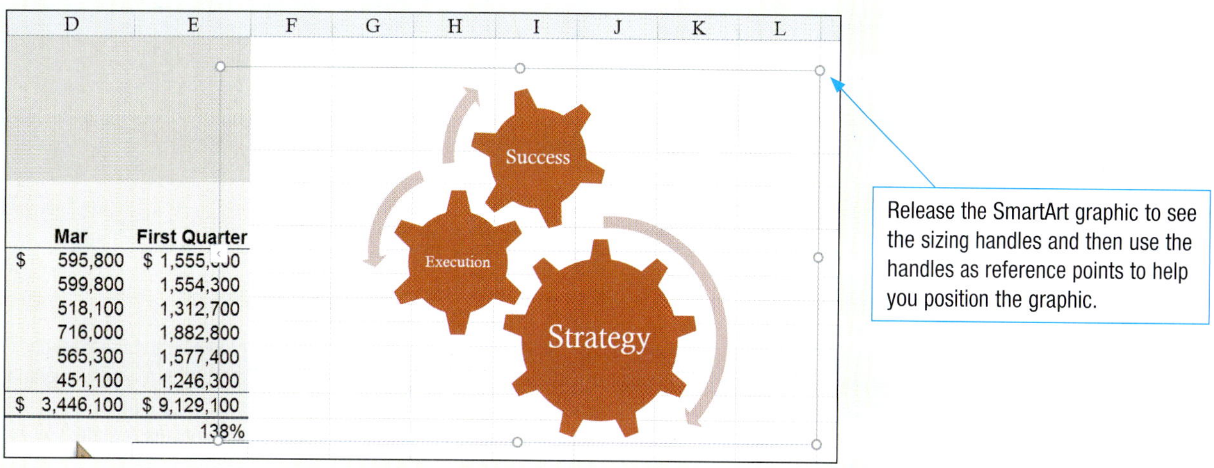

2. Click the SmartArt Tools Format tab, select the text in the *Width* measurement box in the Size group, then type 4.5 and then press the Enter key.

   The SmartArt graphic resizes.

3. Double-click the text *Strategy* in the gear graphic.

   The text is selected and the Mini toolbar displays.

4. Use the Mini toolbar to change the font size to 18 points.
5. Double-click the text *Success* and then use the Mini toolbar to change the font size to 12 points.
6. Right-click the Gear SmartArt graphic and then click the *Format Object* option.

   The Format Shape task pane displays.

7. Click the Size & Properties icon.
8. Click the *Alt Text* section name if necessary to expand the section.

   The *Alt Text* section expands.

9. Click in the *Title* text box and then type Inspirational Message.
10. Click in the *Description* text box and then type Image depicting the message "Strategy plus Execution leads to Success".
11. Click the task pane Close button.
12. Click the Save button on the Quick Access Toolbar.

Model Answer

4.7 Modifying the Design and Formatting of SmartArt Graphics

Tutorial

Changing the Style, Colors, and Effects in a SmartArt Graphic

The design and formatting of a SmartArt graphic can be modified to coordinate with the overall appearance of a workbook. Use features on the SmartArt Tools Design tab (see Figure 4.18) to add and move shapes as well as change the layout and apply a style. Use features on the SmartArt Tools Format tab to modify shapes and WordArt styles within a SmartArt graphic.

Figure 4.18 SmartArt Tools Design Tab

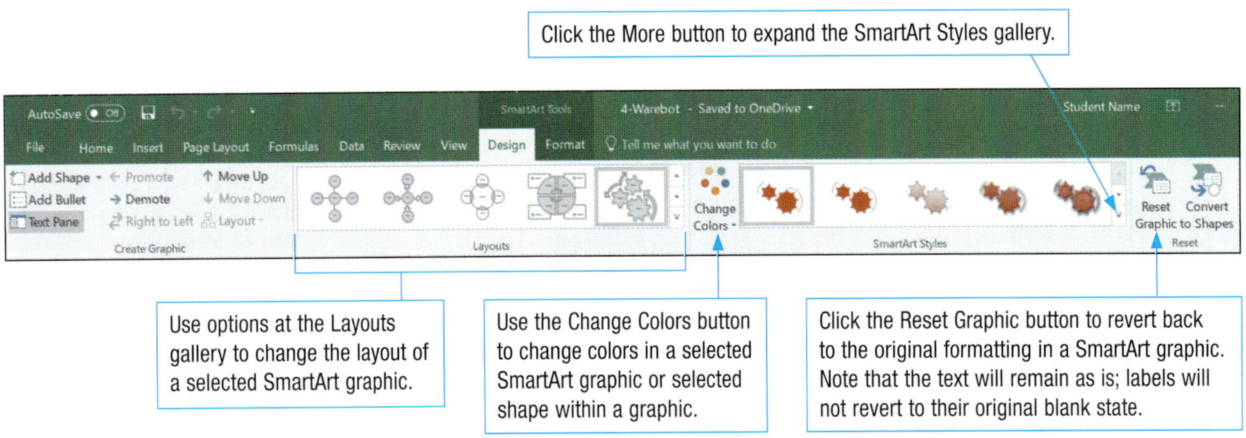

▸ Know This about modifying the design of a SmartArt graphic

— To modify the design of a SmartArt graphic, use features on the SmartArt Tools Design tab.

— To apply a style to a selected graphic, click an option at the SmartArt Styles gallery. To expand the SmartArt Styles gallery and see more options, click the More button.

— To change the colors in a selected graphic, click the Change Colors button in the SmartArt Styles group and then click an option at the drop-down gallery. It is a good idea to choose a color option that coordinates with the theme of your workbook.

— To change the layout of a selected graphic, click an option at the Layouts gallery. To expand the Layouts gallery and see more options, click the More button.

— To make other changes—such as adding, promoting, demoting, and moving shapes within a selected graphic—use options in the Create Graphic group.

▶ Know This about formatting a SmartArt graphic

— To format a SmartArt graphic, use features on the SmartArt Tools Format tab. This contextual tab offers the same formatting features as the contextual Drawing Tools Format tab that displays when you select a shape (see Sections 4.4 and 4.5).

▶ **Know More** about formatting a SmartArt graphic

- To format a SmartArt graphic using the Format Shape task pane, right-click the graphic, click the *Format Shape* option to display the task pane, click an icon to display a list of section names, and then click a section name to display a list of options.
- Options at the Format Shape task pane not only allow you to choose the same formatting presets found on the SmartArt Tools Format tab, but also allow you to choose more specific properties such as setting a specific 3-D rotation on individual shapes within the graphic.

On the Job

Task 4.7 Changing the Style, Colors, and Effects in a SmartArt Graphic

Jeremy would like to modify the gear graphic you added in Task 4.6 so that its design and format tie in with the theme of the workbook. Use features on the SmartArt Tools Design tab and SmartArt Tools Format tab to apply a SmartArt style, change the colors in the graphic, and apply a bevel effect.

1. With the Sales worksheet active and the gear graphic selected, click the SmartArt Tools Design tab and then click the More button in the SmartArt Styles group.

   The SmartArt Styles gallery expands.

2. Click the *Intense Effect* option (fifth column, first row in the *Best Match for Document* section).

   The style is applied to the graphic.

3. Click the Change Colors button.

   A drop-down gallery displays.

4. Click the *Colorful Range - Accent Colors 3 to 4* option (third column, first row in the *Colorful* section).

   The colors change to better match the colors in the workbook theme.

5. Click the SmartArt Tools Format tab.
6. Click the Shape Effects button in the Shape Styles group.

   A drop-down list displays.

7. Point to the *Bevel* option and then click the *Round Convex* option (fourth column, third row in the *Bevel* section of the *Bevel* gallery).

   A convex rounded bevel effect is applied to the shapes in the graphic.

8. Click the Save button on the Quick Access Toolbar.

Model Answer

4.8 Inserting Text Boxes and Icons

MOS 5.3.1
MOS 5.3.4

Tutorial

Inserting and Sizing a Text Box

Cells can be resized and merged to fit varying amounts of text in a worksheet. However, Excel limits the amount of text that can be entered in a given cell. When you need to include a large block of text or to put text in a specific location, consider using a text box. A **text box** is an object, which means it is placed on top of the cells, where it can be selected and manipulated. A text box allows you to add any amount of text and can be sized and positioned to fit your specific needs.

Icons is a new feature available to Office 365 users. An **icon** is provided as a Scalable Vector Graphic (SVG) file, which means that it maintains its appearance when printed or viewed on different screens with different resolutions. Excel provides 26 categories of icons, including *People*, *Analytics*, and *Signs and symbols*.

▸ Know This about inserting text boxes

— To insert a text box, click the Text Box button in the Text group on the Insert tab (see Figure 4.19), click or drag in the worksheet to create the text box, and then type the required text.

— When you click the Text Box button, the mouse pointer displays as an upside-down cross. Use the cross to position the upper left corner of the text box in the worksheet.

— When you click in the worksheet, the upside-down cross changes to crosshairs. If you release the mouse button, Excel places a small text box at this location. If you drag and then release the mouse button, you can draw a box of the desired size.

Figure 4.19 Text Group on the Insert Tab

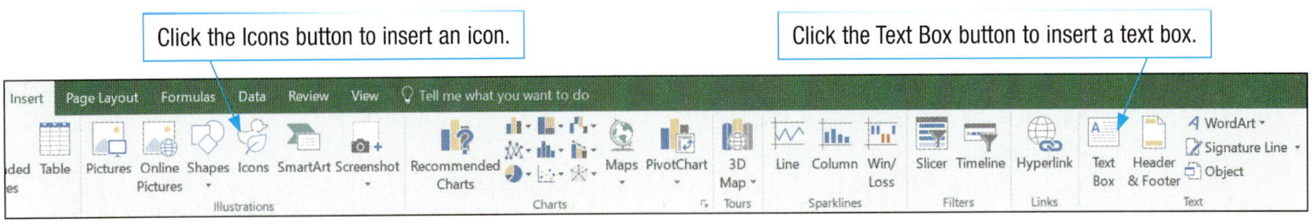

▸ Know This about sizing text boxes

— To change size using one of the sizing handles that display around a selected text box, hover the mouse pointer over the sizing handle until the pointer turns into a two-headed arrow, click and hold down the left mouse button, drag the handle to achieve the desired size, and then release the mouse button.

— Using sizing handles allows you to easily see when you have adjusted the size of a text box to fit all the text.

▸ Know More ways to size text boxes

– To size a selected text box, use the *Height* and *Width* measurement boxes in the Size group on the Drawing Tools Format tab.

▸ Know This about formatting text boxes

— To modify a text box, select the box and then use features on the Drawing Tools Format tab.

— The features available and the steps for applying them are similar to those for other objects, such as shapes.

— For example, you can apply a shape fill and shape effect to a text box, and a WordArt style and text effect to the data within the text box.

▸ Know More about formatting text boxes

– To modify a text box using the Format Picture task pane, right-click the text box, click the Format Shape option to display the task pane, click an icon to display a list of section names, and then click a section name to display a list of options.

– Options at the Format Shape task pane not only allow you to choose the same formatting presets found on the Drawing Tools Format tab, but also allow you to choose more specific properties such as the text direction and the distance of the text from the edge of the box.

▸ Know This about inserting and formatting icons

— To insert an icon, click the Icons button in the Illustrations group on the Insert tab (see Figure 4.19), click a category in the left panel at the Insert Icon dialog box, click an icon in the right panel to display a check box containing a check mark, and then click the Insert button.

— To insert more than one icon at the same time, click more than one icon before clicking the Insert button.

— To format an icon after inserting it, select the icon and then use features in the Graphics Styles group on the Graphics Tools Format tab.

— To align and rotate icons, move icons up one or more layers, or send icons back one or more layers, use features in the Arrange group.

— To resize or crop an icon, use features in the Size group.

▸ Know More ways to resize an icon

– Use the icon's sizing handles.

On the Job

Task 4.8 Inserting and Sizing a Text Box and an Icon

Jeremy would like you to insert a note in the Training worksheet, indicating that the training is almost complete for the employees and that it will be completed by the end of the second quarter. Jeremy would also like you to insert an icon to the left of the title that depicts teamwork. Use a text box so that you can size and position this note easily. After the text box is created, insert an icon that represents teamwork in cell A1. You will also need to add appropriate alternative text to the icon.

1. Click the Training sheet tab to make the worksheet active.
2. Click the Insert tab if necessary and then click the Text Box button in the Text group.

   The mouse pointer changes to display as an upside-down cross.
3. Click in the upper left corner of cell I7 and then drag to create a box two columns wide by three rows high, as shown in Figure 4.20.

   A text box appears, with the insertion point in the box.

Figure 4.20 Text Box Position

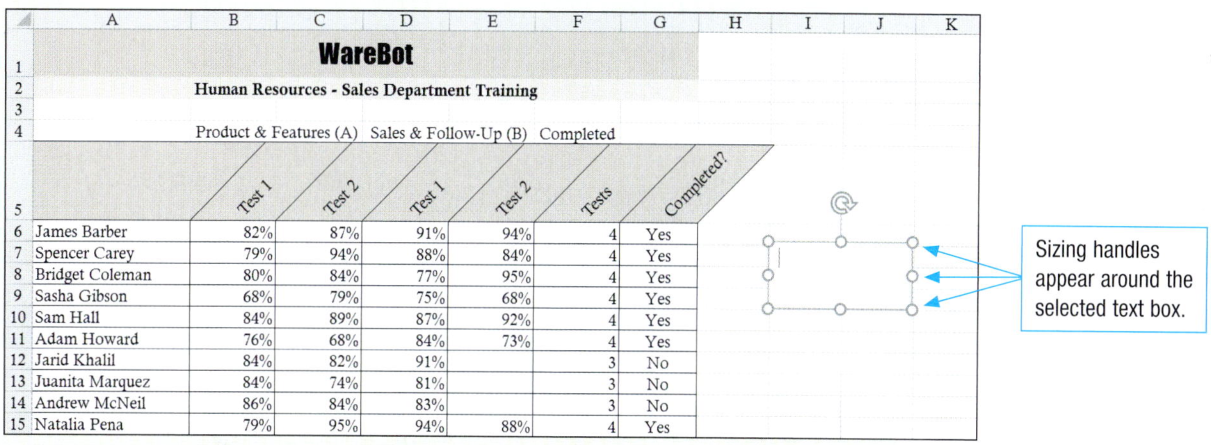

	A	B	C	D	E	F	G	H	I	J	K
1	WareBot										
2	Human Resources - Sales Department Training										
3											
4		Product & Features (A)		Sales & Follow-Up (B)		Completed					
5		Test 1	Test 2	Test 1	Test 2	Tests	Completed?				
6	James Barber	82%	87%	91%	94%	4	Yes				
7	Spencer Carey	79%	94%	88%	84%	4	Yes				
8	Bridget Coleman	80%	84%	77%	95%	4	Yes				
9	Sasha Gibson	68%	79%	75%	68%	4	Yes				
10	Sam Hall	84%	89%	87%	92%	4	Yes				
11	Adam Howard	76%	68%	84%	73%	4	Yes				
12	Jarid Khalil	84%	82%	91%		3	No				
13	Juanita Marquez	84%	74%	81%		3	No				
14	Andrew McNeil	86%	84%	83%		3	No				
15	Natalia Pena	79%	95%	94%	88%	4	Yes				

4. Type Training is almost complete for all employees. The remaining tests are expected to be completed by the end of the second quarter.

   The text is too large to fit within the text box, but it still displays.
5. Click outside the text box.

   Most of the text is hidden.
6. Click the text box to select it, hover the mouse pointer over the bottom middle sizing handle until the pointer turns into a two-headed arrow, click and hold down the left mouse button, drag the handle down until all the text can be seen, and then release the mouse button.

   The text box is about two columns wide by eight rows tall, and all the text displays within it. If some of the text remains hidden, click the text box again and drag the bottom middle sizing handle down a bit more.
7. Click in cell A1 and then click the Icons button in the Illustrations group.

   The Insert Icon dialog box displays.

8. Click the fourth icon in the *People* category (see Figure 4.21).

   A check box containing a check mark appears on the icon.

Figure 4.21 Insert Icon Dialog Box

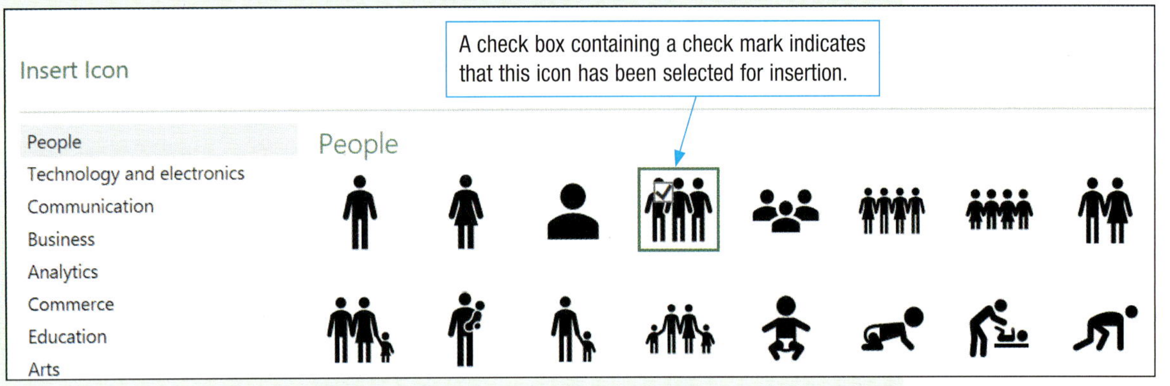

9. Click the Insert button.

   The icon is inserted in cell A1 and the Graphics Tools Format tab is active.

10. Click in the *Height measurement* box in the Size group and then type 0.7.

    The lock aspect ratio is turned on, so the width automatically changes to 0.7 inches.

11. Right-click the icon and then click the *Format Graphic* option.

    The Format Graphic task pane displays.

12. Click the Size & Properties icon and then click the *Alt Text* section name.

    A list of *Alt Text* options displays. *Team* is already entered into the *Description* text box.

13. Click in the *Title* text box, type Icon, and then press the Tab key.

    The text in the *Description* text box is selected.

14. Type Image of three team members.
15. Click the Format Graphic task pane Close button.
16. Click the Save button on the Quick Access Toolbar.

Model Answer

4.9 Inserting and Modifying WordArt

Tutorial

Inserting, Modifying, and Moving WordArt

The **WordArt** feature alters the shape, alignment, and style of text. It can be used to create company logos and to draw attention to headers.

▸ Know This about using WordArt

— To insert WordArt, click in a cell at the desired location, click the WordArt button in the Text group on the Insert tab, click an option at the drop-down gallery, and then start typing text. The text will appear in a WordArt placeholder in the worksheet.

— To size WordArt, use the white sizing handles that appear when the WordArt is selected.

— To move a WordArt object, hover the mouse pointer over the border of the WordArt object until the pointer turns into a four-headed arrow, click and hold down the left mouse button, drag the text box to the desired location, and then release the mouse button.
— To modify WordArt, use options in the WordArt styles group on the Drawing Tools Format tab. For example, you can change the fill and outline, or apply a text effect such as a shadow, reflection, glow, bevel, 3-D rotation, or transformation.
— Use WordArt with a transformation effect to insert text around a circle.
— To modify a transformation that has been applied to WordArt text, use the yellow circle that appears on the border of the WordArt object (see Figure 4.22, for example). The exact location of the yellow circle depends on the transformation chosen.

Figure 4.22 WordArt

▸ Know This about removing WordArt

— To remove a WordArt style but keep the typed text, select the WordArt object, click the More button in the WordArt Styles group on the Drawing Tools Format tab, and then click the *Clear WordArt* option.

On the Job

Task 4.9 Inserting, Modifying, and Moving WordArt

Jeremy would like you to modify the name of the company in the Sales worksheet to reflect the design of the other visual elements you have added to the worksheet. Replace the existing company name with a WordArt object and then modify the WordArt style to align with the workbook theme. Also use WordArt styling to modify the text in the arrow shape below the First Quarter Sales chart.

1. Click the Sales sheet tab to make the worksheet active, click to the right of the company logo in cell A1, and then press the Delete key.
   The company logo is an object that sits in the worksheet. Be sure you click to the right of the image to select the cell behind it.
2. Click the Insert tab and then click the WordArt button in the Text group.
   A drop-down gallery displays.
3. Click the *Fill: Black, Text color 1; Outline: White, Background color 1; Hard Shadow: White, Background color 1* option (first column, third row).
   A WordArt placeholder displays in the worksheet.
4. Type WareBot.

5. Select the WordArt text, click the Text Fill button in the WordArt Styles group, and then click the *Tan, Accent 3, Darker 25%* option (seventh column, fifth row in the *Theme Colors* section).
6. Click the Text Effects button, point to the *Transform* option, and then click the *Inflate: Top* option (first column, seventh row in the *Warp* section).
7. Hover the mouse pointer over the yellow circle on the left border of the WordArt object (see Figure 4.22 on page 161), click and hold down the left mouse button, drag the yellow circle up until it is centered between the left middle and top left sizing handles, and then release the mouse button.

   When you hover the mouse pointer over the yellow circle, the pointer turns into a white arrow. When you drag the yellow circle, the top warp of the WordArt text changes.
8. Click the Drawing Tools Format tab if necessary, select the value in the *Height* measurement box in the Size group, type 0.7, and then press the Enter key.

   The WordArt height adjusts.
9. Select the value in the *Width* measurement box in the Size group, type 2.5, and then press the Enter key.

   The WordArt width adjusts.
10. Drag the WordArt object so the bottom of the text aligns with the bottom border of row 1 and the left edge of the text aligns with the left edge of the column B heading (see Figure 4.23).

Figure 4.23 Positioning of WordArt

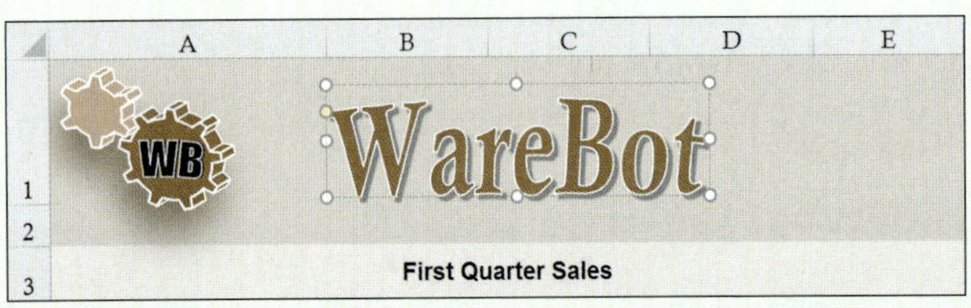

11. Select the text inside the arrow shape below the First Quarter Sales chart, click the Drawing Tools Format tab, and then click the More button in the WordArt Styles group.

    A drop-down gallery displays.
12. Click the *Fill: Light Gray, Background color 2; Inner Shadow* option (fifth column, third row).

    The selected WordArt style is applied to the text.
13. Click the Text Fill button in the WordArt Styles group and then click the *Tan, Accent 2, Darker 50%* option (sixth column, sixth row in the *Theme Colors* section).

    The text changes to the selected color.
14. Click in the worksheet to deselect the text in the arrow.
15. Click the Save button on the Quick Access Toolbar.

Model Answer

4.10 Arranging Objects

Objects such as images, shapes, SmartArt, text boxes, and WordArt are placed in different layers in a worksheet. If more than one object is placed in the same location, the last object inserted is placed on the top layer. Arrangement tools allow you to select, align, group, and rotate objects, as well as bring objects up one or more layers, or send them back one or more layers.

Tutorial

Aligning Objects

▸ **Know This** about arranging objects

— To arrange objects, select the objects and then use tools in the Arrange group on the Picture Tools Format tab, Drawing Tools Format tab, or SmartArt Tools Format tab, depending on the type of objects selected.

— To select multiple objects, click the first object, press and hold down the Shift key, click the additional objects, and then release the Shift key.

— To align two or more objects, select the objects, click the Align button, and then click an option at the drop-down list. Figure 4.24 shows the alignment options, and Table 4.2 describes them.

— If three or more objects are selected, you can arrange them equal distances from each other by clicking the Align button and then clicking the *Distribute Horizontally* option or *Distribute Vertically* option at the drop-down list.

— To move an object up one layer, click the Bring Forward button; to move an object back one layer, click the Send Backward button.

— When you align objects, Excel may slightly adjust the size of an object.

▸ **Know More** ways to select objects

– Click the Selection Pane button and then click the name of an object at the Selection pane (see Figure 4.25).

– To select multiple objects at the Selection pane, press and hold down the Ctrl key, click the names of the objects, and then release the Ctrl key.

Figure 4.24 Align Button Drop-Down List

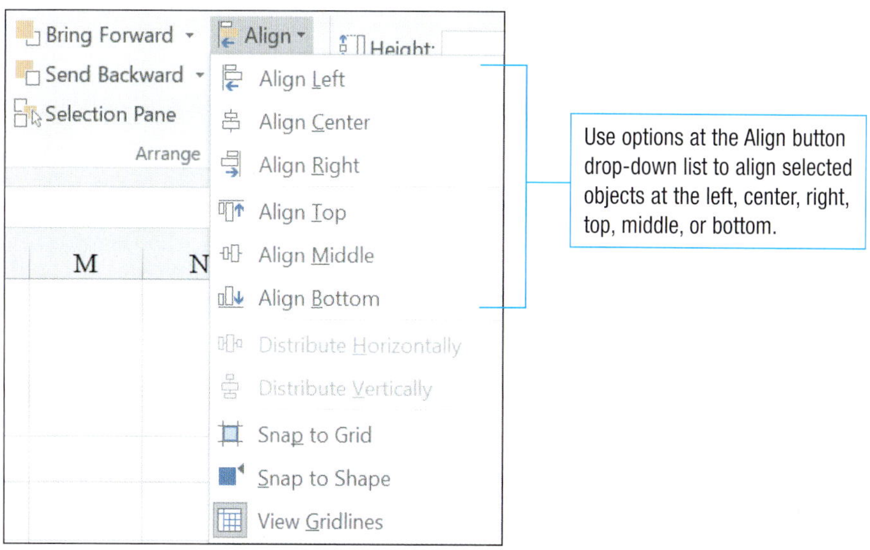

Table 4.2 Alignment Options

Option	Description
Align Left	Aligns the edges of the selected objects at the left using the edge of the leftmost object as a guide
Align Center	Aligns the selected objects horizontally using the average of their original positions

continues...

Table 7.3 Alignment Options *...continued*

Option	Description
Align Right	Aligns the edges of the selected objects at the right using the edge of the rightmost object as a guide
Align Top	Aligns the top edges of the selected objects
Align Middle	Aligns the selected objects vertically using the average of their original positions
Align Bottom	Aligns the bottom edges of the selected objects

Figure 4.25 Selection Pane

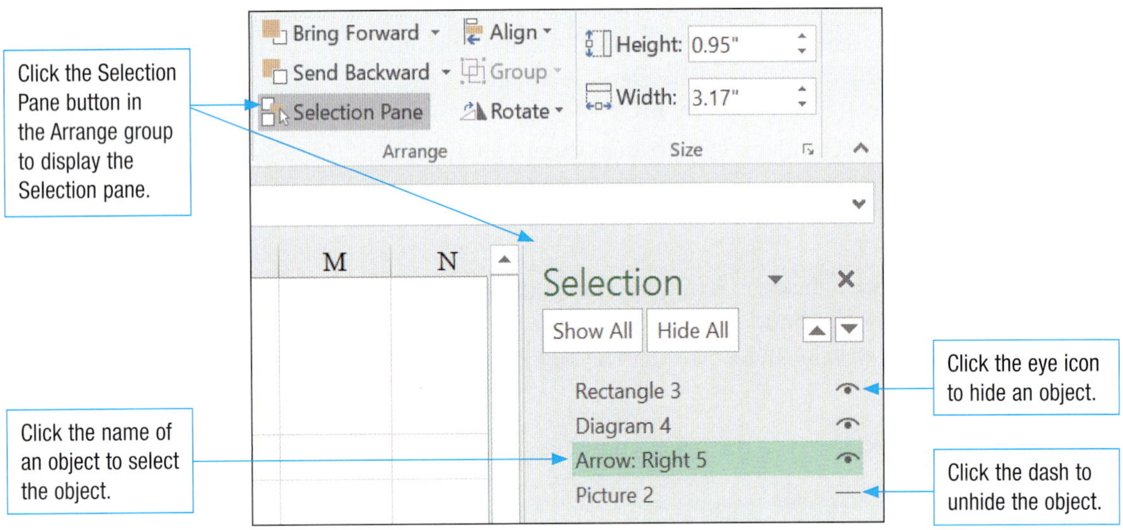

On the Job

Task 4.10 Aligning Objects

Jeremy likes the way you have styled the company name in the Sales worksheet. He would like to emphasize the connection between the company name and the sales increase figure. Use a tool in the Arrange group to align these objects so there is a visual connection between them.

1. With the Sales worksheet active, click the arrow shape, press and hold down the Shift key, click the company name, and then release the Shift key.
2. Click the Drawing Tools Format tab if necessary to make it active.
3. Click the Align button in the Arrange group.

   The alignment options display (see Figure 4.24 on page 163).
4. Click the *Align Center* option.

   The horizontal center of each object is in the same horizontal position in the worksheet.
5. Click in any cell to deselect the objects.
6. Click the Save button on the Quick Access Toolbar.

Model Answer

4.11 Adding Headers and Footers

MOS 1.3.8

Tutorial

Adding a Footer

The **header** is the area at the top of a worksheet where you can insert text and/or elements. The **footer** is the area at the bottom of a worksheet where you can insert text and/or elements. Headers and footers can appear on every page of a worksheet. Worksheets can have different first-page headers and footers or different odd and even headers and footers.

To preview the header and footer, click the File tab and then click the *Print* option to display the Print backstage area. When you enter or edit a header or footer in Page Layout view, you must click back in the worksheet area before you can change the view to either Normal or Page Break Preview.

▸ **Know This** about adding headers and footers using the Header & Footer Tools Design tab

— To display the Header & Footer Tools Design tab, click the Header & Footer button in the Text group on the Insert tab.

— The worksheet displays in Page Layout view with three sections (left, center, and right) in the header and in the footer and with the insertion point in the center section of the header. Click in a different section to position the insertion point at that location.

— At the insertion point, enter text by typing, and/or enter elements using features on the Header & Footer Tools Design tab (see Figure 4.26).

— Use buttons in the Header & Footer group to insert predesigned headers and footers.

— Use buttons in the Header & Footer Elements group to insert built-in elements such as page numbers, the current date and time, and the file path and name.

— Use check boxes in the Options group to designate a different header and/or footer for the first page as well as different headers and/or footers for odd and even pages.

— Use the Go to Header button and Go to Footer button to navigate between the header and footer.

Figure 4.26 Header & Footer Tools Design Tab

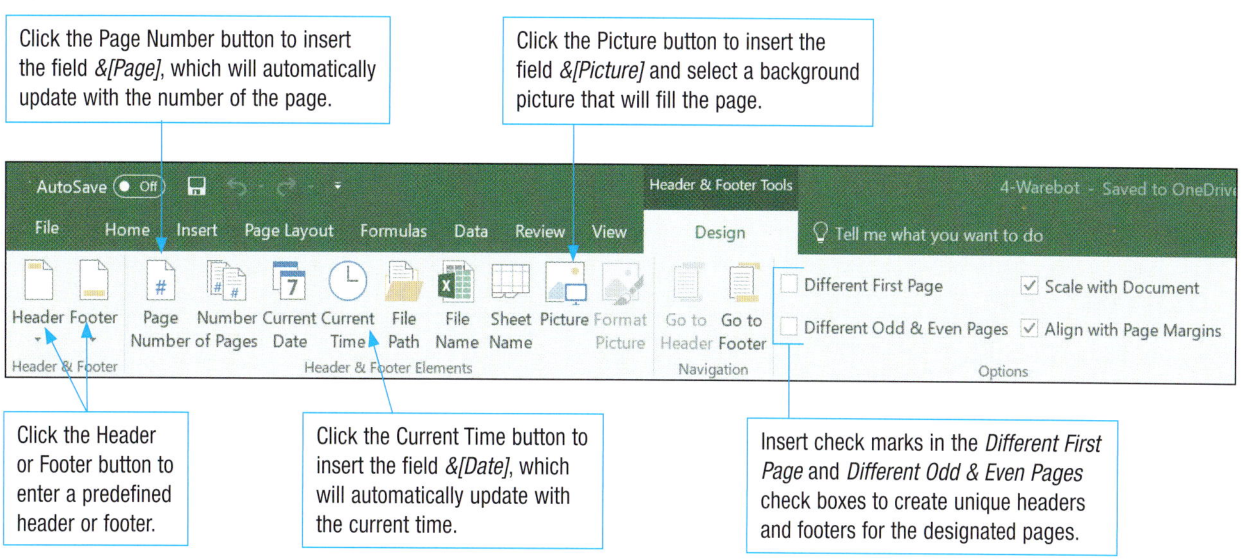

▸ **Know This** about inserting headers and footers using the Page Setup dialog box

— To display the Page Setup dialog box, click the Page Setup group dialog box launcher on the Page Layout tab or the Page Setup hyperlink at the Print backstage area.

— To insert a predefined header or footer, click the Header/Footer tab at the Page Setup dialog box, click the *Header* or *Footer* option box arrow, and then click an option at the drop-down list.

— To insert a custom header or footer, click the Header/Footer tab at the Page Setup dialog box and then click the Custom Header or Custom Footer button (see Figure 4.27).

— Use check boxes to designate a different header or footer for the first page as well as a different header or footer for odd and even pages.

— If a worksheet contains headers and/or footers, they will display at the Page Setup dialog box.

▸ **Know This** about inserting headers and footers using the Page Layout view

— To display Page Layout view, click the Page Layout button in the Workbook Views group on the View tab.

— To add text in a center section, click the *Add header* or *Add footer* placeholder and then type.

— To add text in a left or right section, click in the section and then type.

Figure 4.27 Page Setup Dialog Box

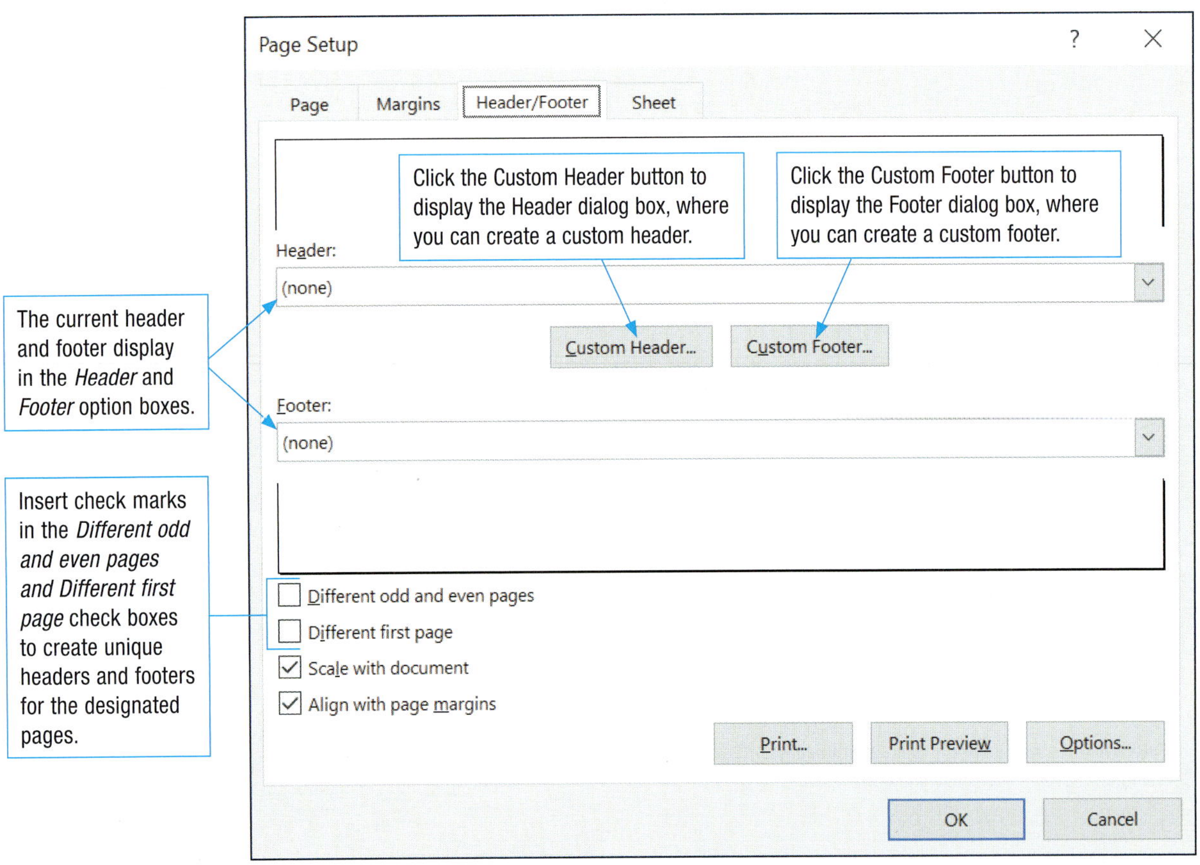

On the Job

Task 4.11 Adding a Footer

Jeremy would like to see the current date, company name, file name, and sheet name on every page in the Sales worksheet. Insert a custom footer that shows the current date at the left margin, the name of the company in the center, and the file name and sheet name at the right margin.

1. With the Sales worksheet active, click the Insert tab.
2. Click the Header & Footer button in the Text group.

   The worksheet changes to Page Layout view, the Header & Footer Tools Design tab displays and is active, and the insertion point is in the center section of the header.
3. Click the Go to Footer button in the Navigation group on the Header & Footer Tools Design tab.

   The footer displays, with the insertion point in the center section.
4. Type WareBot.

   The text *WareBot* is centered in the center section.
5. Click in the right section, click the File Name button in the Header & Footer Elements group, type a slash (/), and then click the Sheet Name button.
6. Click in the left section and then click the Current Date button in the Header & Footer Elements group.

   The footer displays as shown in Figure 4.28.
7. Click in any cell in the worksheet.

Figure 4.28 Completed Footer

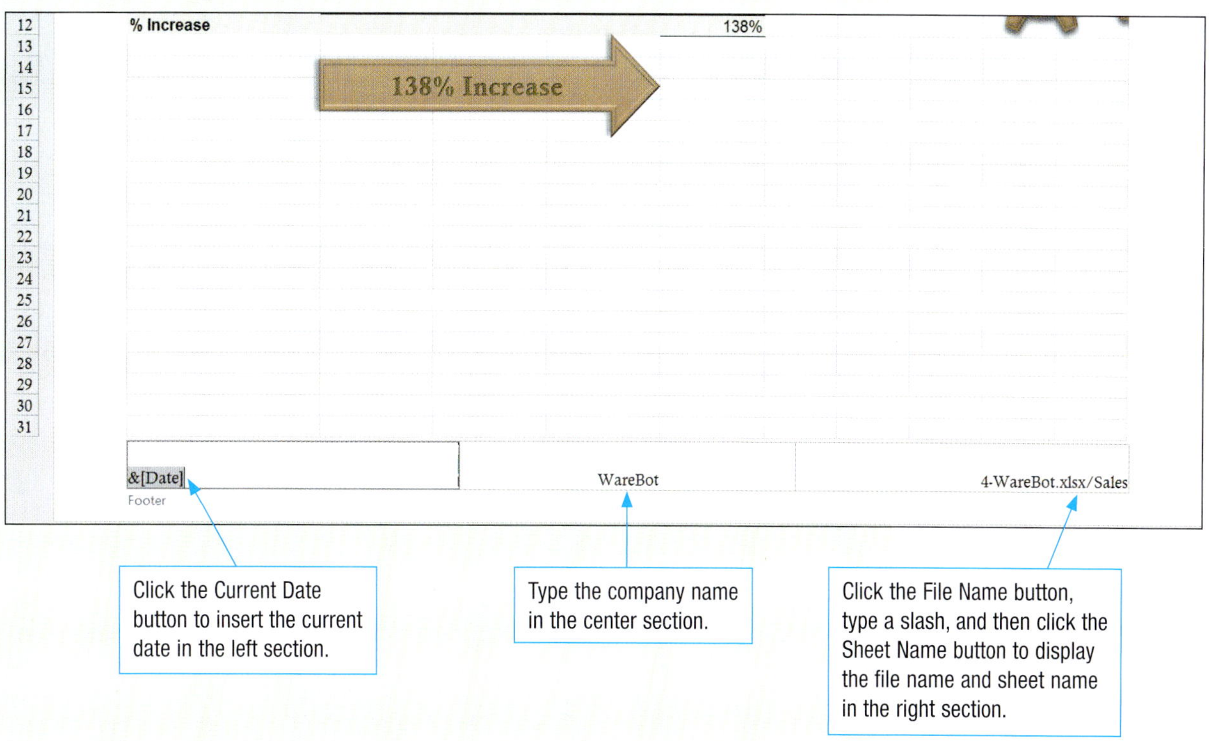

8. Click the Normal button in the View area on the Status bar (see Figure 4.29).

   The view changes from Page Layout view to Normal view.

9. Click the Save button on the Quick Access Toolbar.

Figure 4.29 Buttons in the View Area on the Status Bar

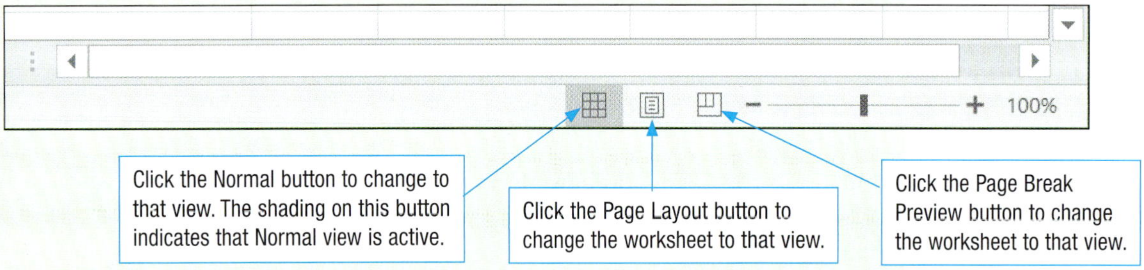

Model Answer

4.12 Adding Watermarks

A **watermark** is a faint picture that appears behind the data in a worksheet. Unlike Word, Excel does not offer tools for creating text as a watermark; it only allows an image file to be inserted. If you require a watermark that contains text, use a program such as Microsoft Paint to create a custom graphic and then save it in a standard picture format, such as PNG or JPG.

A watermark is inserted in the header or footer section. It displays in Page Layout view, but not in Normal view or Page Break Preview. It appears on screen and in print.

Tutorial

Adding a Watermark from OneDrive

▸ Know This about inserting a watermark

— To insert a watermark, click the Header & Footer button in the Text group on the Insert tab, click the Picture button in the Header & Footer Elements group on the Header & Footer Tools Design tab, navigate to the folder that contains the picture, and then double-click the picture.

— To change the size of the picture, crop the picture, or add alternative text, click the Format Picture button in the Header & Footer Elements group and then use options at the Format Picture dialog box.

— If the watermark overpowers the data in your worksheet, display the Format Picture dialog box, click the Picture tab, and then change the *Color* option to *Washout* or adjust the brightness and contrast levels.

— To keep the watermark's optimal balance, make sure the brightness and *contrast* levels add up to 100%; for example, if you set the Brightness measurement box to *75%*, set the *Contrast* measurement box to *25%*.

On the Job
Task 4.12 Adding a Watermark

Jeremy wants people who view the Budget worksheet to be aware that the information it contains is confidential. Insert an image that displays the text *Confidential* as a watermark in the worksheet.

1. Click the Budget sheet tab to make the worksheet active.
2. Click the Insert tab and then click the Header & Footer button in the Text group.

   The worksheet switches to Page Layout view. The insertion point is in the center section of the header.
3. Click the Picture button in the Header & Footer Elements group (see Figure 4.26 on page 165).

   The Insert Pictures dialog box displays.
4. Click the *From a file* Browse button, navigate to your AE4 folder, click the **Confidential.png** file, and then click the Insert button.
5. Click in any cell in the worksheet.

   The text *Confidential* appears diagonally across the page as a watermark.
6. Click the Save button on the Quick Access Toolbar.

Model Answer

4.13 Modifying Page Setup

MOS 1.3.4

Tutorial

Modifying Page Setup

When you create a new workbook, it comes with predefined settings, including default settings for margins, page orientation, and page size. A **margin** is an area of white space at the top, bottom, left, or right of a document. **Orientation** refers to the way a worksheet is laid out on the page. In **portrait orientation**, the page is taller than it is wide; in **landscape orientation**, the page is wider than it is tall.

Predefined settings for margins, orientation, and size are as follows. These page settings can be changed using options on the Page Layout tab or options at the Page Setup dialog box.

— By default, the left and right margins are each set at 0.7 inch, and the top and bottom margins are each set at 0.75 inch.

— By default, each page is laid out in portrait orientation, with the text or data beginning in the upper left corner of the page.

— The default page size is 8.5 inches by 11 inches.

▸ Know This about modifying page setup using the Page Layout tab

— To change any of the margins, click the Margins button in the Page Setup group on the Page Layout tab (see Figure 4.30) and then click an option at the drop-down list of predefined settings or click the *Custom Margins* option to display the Page Setup dialog box, where you can set a custom margin (see Figure 4.31).

— To change the page orientation, click the Orientation button and then click the *Landscape* or *Portrait* option.

— To change the page size, click the Size button and then click an option such as *Legal* or *A4* at the drop-down list.

▸ **Know This** about modifying page setup using the Page Setup dialog box

— To display the Page Setup dialog box, click the Page Setup group dialog box launcher on the Page Layout tab.

— Use the Margins tab to modify margin settings (see Figure 4.31).

- To change margin sizes, use the measurement boxes.
- To center a page in the worksheet automatically between the left and right margins, click to insert a check mark in the *Horizontally* check box in the *Center on page* section.
- To center a page in the worksheet automatically between the top and bottom margins, click to insert a check mark in the *Vertically* check box in the *Center on page* section.
- Any changes made to the margin settings are reflected in the sample worksheet, displayed in the center of the Page Setup dialog box.

— Use the Page tab to modify page settings.

- To change the page orientation, click the *Portrait* or *Horizontal* radio button.
- To change the page size, click the *Paper size* option box arrow and then select an option at the drop-down list.

Figure 4.30 Page Setup Group on the Page Layout Tab

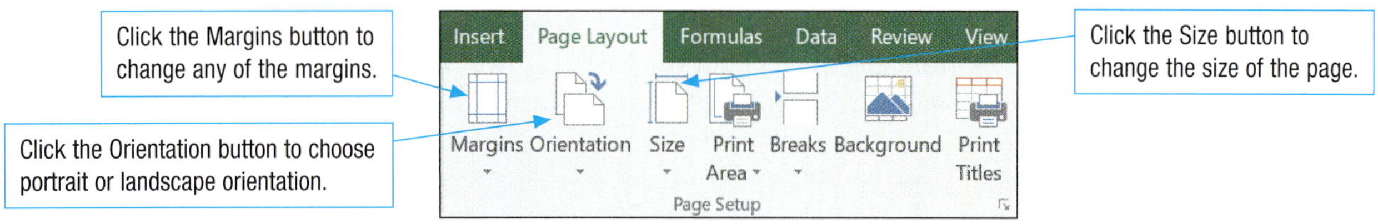

Figure 4.31 Margins Tab at the Page Setup Dialog Box

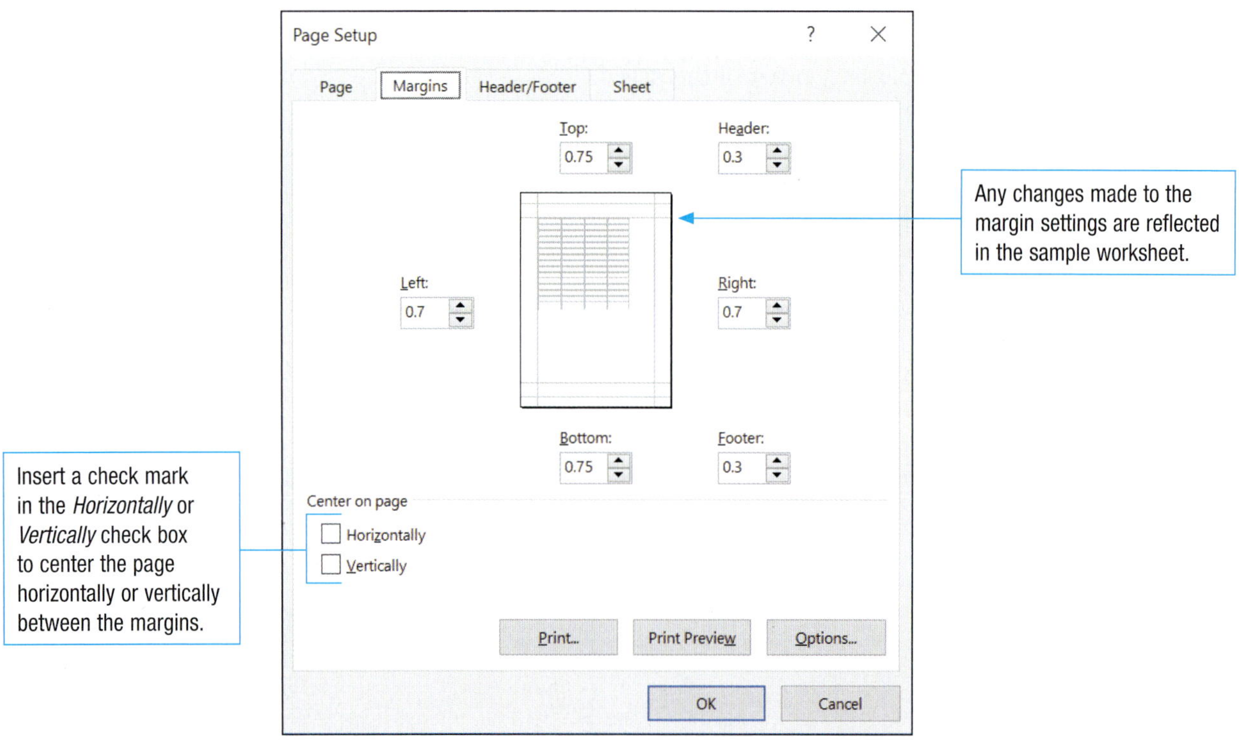

On the Job

Task 4.13 Modifying Page Setup

Jeremy would like you to ensure that the Training worksheet will print on one page when all the changes to the workbook have been completed. Adjust the page setup as necessary so that the Training worksheet will print in landscape orientation on one page.

1. Click the Training sheet tab to make the worksheet active.
2. Click the File tab and then click the *Print* option.

   Notice in Figure 4.32 that the worksheet will print on two pages.

Figure 4.32 Print Backstage Area

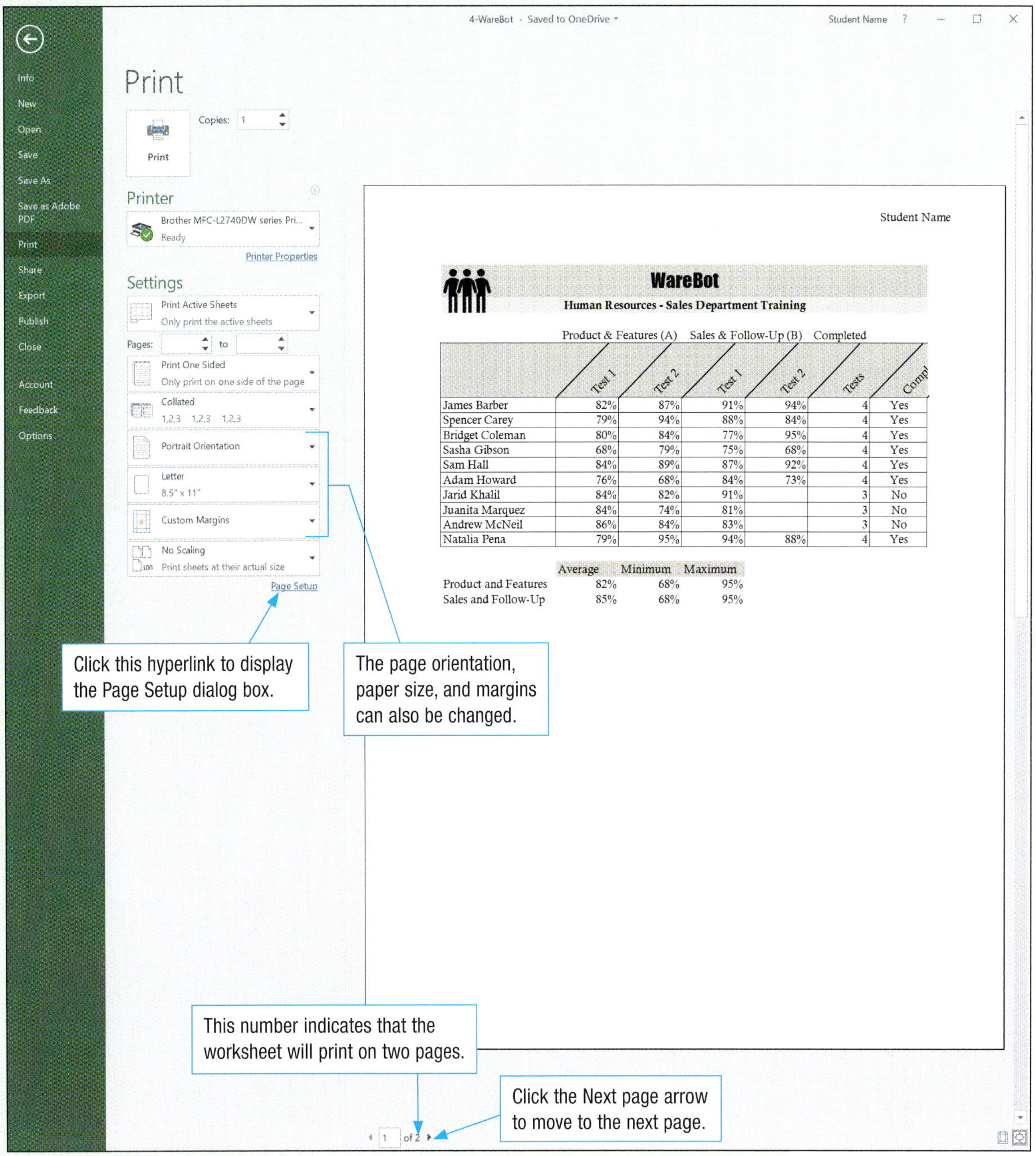

3. Click the Page Setup hyperlink in the middle panel (see Figure 4.32 on page 171).

   The Page Setup dialog box displays with the Page tab active.
4. Click the *Landscape* radio button.
5. Click the Margins tab.

   The Margins tab is active and the preview displays in landscape orientation.
6. Click the *Top* measurement box increment (up) arrow.

   The measurement in the box changes from *0.75* to *1*.
7. Click the *Horizontally* check box in the *Center on page* section to insert a check mark.
8. Click the Header/Footer tab.
9. Click the Custom Header button.
10. Click in the right section, type your name, and then click the OK button.
11. Click the OK button.

    The Page Setup dialog box closes and your name appears as a header in the upper right corner of the worksheet. Notice that the worksheet will now print on one page; the changes that you made to the margins and orientation will allow you to save a page each time you print the worksheet.
12. Click the Back button.

    The worksheet redisplays in Normal view.
13. Click the Save button on the Quick Access Toolbar.

Model Answer

4.14 Inserting and Removing Page Breaks

Excel inserts an **automatic page break** in a worksheet when the data will not fit on one page. If an inserted page break does not suit your needs, you can insert a **manual page break** where a break is better suited.

Tutorial
Moving a Page Break

▸ Know This about inserting and removing page breaks

— To insert a page break, select the column to the right of or the row below the desired location, click the Breaks button in the Page Setup group on the Page Layout tab, and then click the *Insert Page Break* option.

— A page break is inserted to the left of a selected column or above a selected row, and displays as a dashed line on the cell borders (see Figure 4.33).

— To insert a horizontal page break and a vertical page break simultaneously, click in a cell instead of selecting a column or row.

— If you click in the first cell in a column and insert a page break, Excel will insert a break to the left of the entire column. If you click in the first cell in a row, Excel will insert a break above the whole row.

— By default, page breaks inserted automatically by Excel are not visible. To display page breaks inserted by Excel, display the worksheet at the Print backstage area and then return to the worksheet.

Figure 4.33 Horizontal and Vertical Page Breaks in Normal View

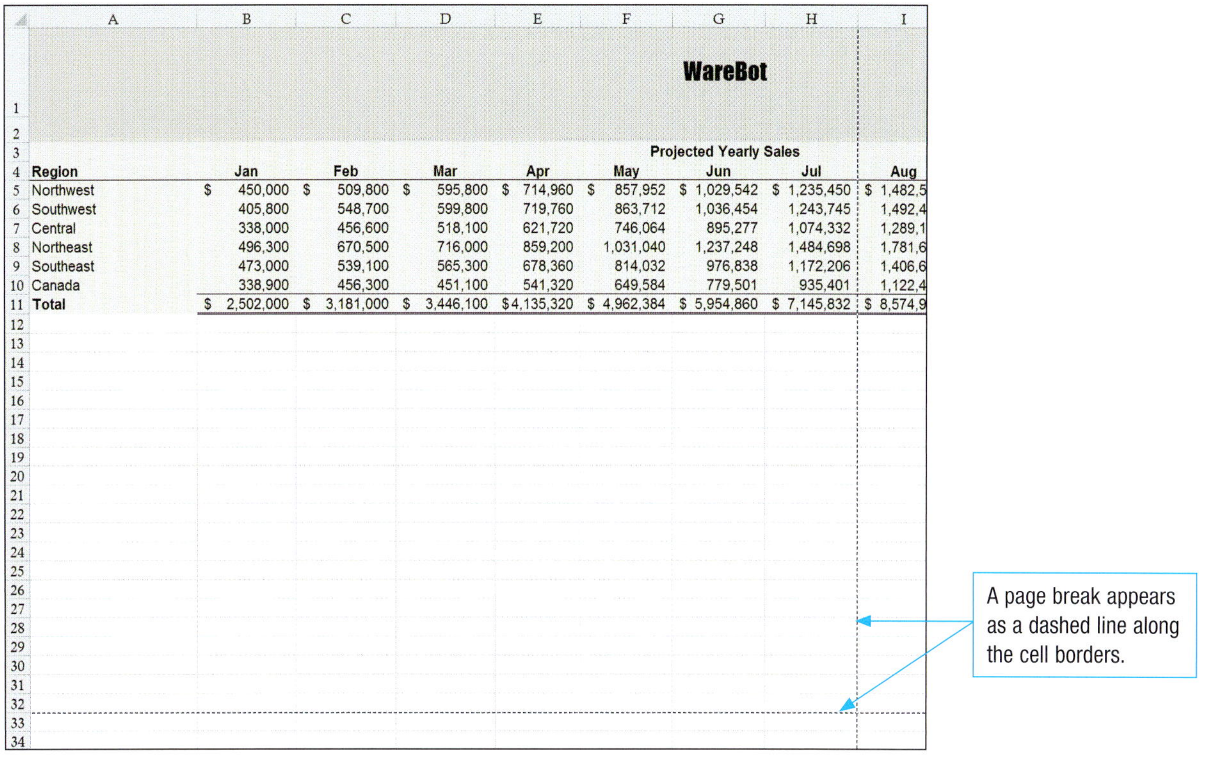

	A	B	C	D	E	F	G	H	I
1							WareBot		
2									
3							Projected Yearly Sales		
4	**Region**	**Jan**	**Feb**	**Mar**	**Apr**	**May**	**Jun**	**Jul**	**Aug**
5	Northwest	$ 450,000	$ 509,800	$ 595,800	$ 714,960	$ 857,952	$ 1,029,542	$ 1,235,450	$ 1,482,5
6	Southwest	405,800	548,700	599,800	719,760	863,712	1,036,454	1,243,745	1,492,4
7	Central	338,000	456,600	518,100	621,720	746,064	895,277	1,074,332	1,289,1
8	Northeast	496,300	670,500	716,000	859,200	1,031,040	1,237,248	1,484,698	1,781,6
9	Southeast	473,000	539,100	565,300	678,360	814,032	976,838	1,172,206	1,406,6
10	Canada	338,900	456,300	451,100	541,320	649,584	779,501	935,401	1,122,4
11	**Total**	$ 2,502,000	$ 3,181,000	$ 3,446,100	$4,135,320	$ 4,962,384	$ 5,954,860	$ 7,145,832	$ 8,574,9

— To remove a page break, select the column to the right of or the row below the break, or make the cell to right of or below the break active; click the Breaks button; and then click the *Remove Page Break* option at the drop-down list.

▸ **Know This** about page sizes

— An 8.5-inch-wide page with the default left and right margin settings of 0.7 inch will have approximately 7.1 inches of available horizontal printing space.

— An 11-inch-tall page with the default top and bottom margins settings of 0.75 inch will have approximately 9.5 inches of vertical printing space.

▸ **Know This** about Page Break Preview view

— To display a worksheet in Page Break Preview view, click the Page Break Preview button in the View area on the Status bar (see Figure 4.29 on page 168).

— Page Break Preview view displays page breaks and worksheet pages, with the word *Page* and the page number in a gray font behind the contents of each worksheet (see Figure 4.34).

— A dashed blue line denotes a page break inserted automatically by Excel, and a solid blue line denotes a page break inserted manually by a user.

— To move a page break, click the blue line and hold down the left mouse button, drag to the required location, and then release the mouse button.

— You can edit a worksheet in Page Break Preview view.

— To return to Normal view, click the Normal button in the View area on the Status bar.

▸ **Know More** ways to display a worksheet in Page Break Preview view and return to Normal view

– To display a worksheet in Page Break Preview view, click the Page Break Preview button in the Workbook View group on the View tab.

– To return to Normal view, click the Normal button.

Figure 4.34 Page Break Preview View

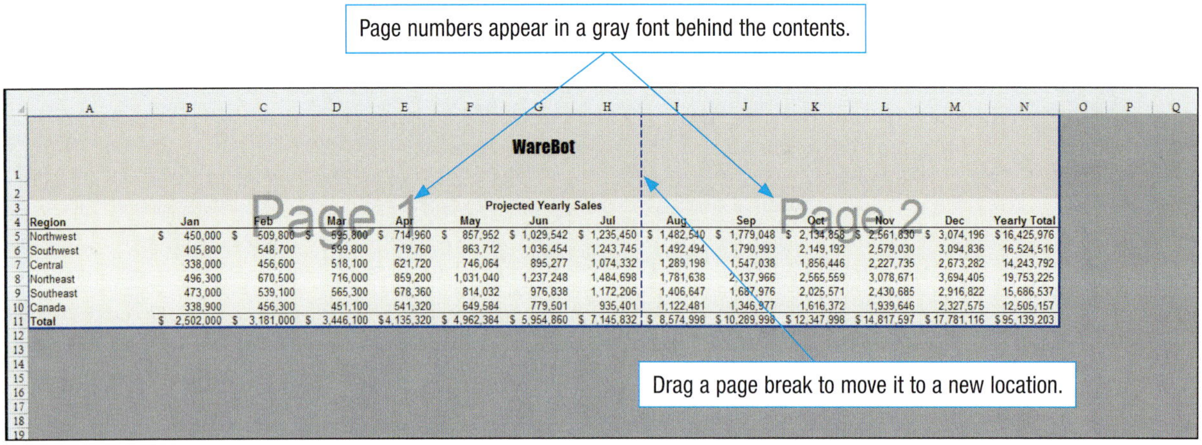

On the Job

Task 4.14 Moving a Page Break

Jeremy wants to print the Yearly Projection worksheet so he can analyze the numbers in the taxi on the way to his meeting. Adjust the page breaks so that when the worksheet is printed, he can view projected sales for the first half of the year on one page, and for the second half of the year on a second page. ***Note:*** *In Task 4.15, you will apply additional modifications to make the printed worksheet easy to read.*

1. Click the Yearly Projection sheet tab to make the worksheet active.
2. Click the Page Break Preview button in the View area on the Status bar.

   The view changes to Page Break Preview (see Figure 4.34).
3. Click the blue page break line and drag it one column to the left so that it is between the June and July columns.

   The page break line changes from a dashed blue line to a solid blue line.
4. Click the Save button on the Quick Access Toolbar.

Model Answer

4.15 Printing Row and Column Headers on Multiple Pages

MOS 1.5.5

Tutorial

Printing Column Headers on Multiple Pages

When a worksheet prints on more than one page, row and column headers print on only the first page by default. You can set these titles to print on all the pages to help readers understand the data as they view each page.

▸ Know This about printing row and column headers on multiple pages

— To print row and column headers on multiple pages, click the Print Titles button in the Page Setup group on the Page Layout tab, enter the reference for the row(s) and column(s) in the *Rows to repeat at top* and *Columns to repeat at left* text boxes on the Sheet tab at the Page Setup dialog box, and then click the OK button (see Figure 4.35).

▸ Know More about printing row and column headers on multiple pages

– The Print Titles button is unavailable (grayed out) if a worksheet cell is active, a chart is selected, or no printer is installed.

continues...

— All references in the *Rows to repeat at top* and *Columns to repeat at left* text boxes must be entered as ranges. For example, to repeat row 5, enter *5:5* in the *Rows to repeat at top* text box.
— You can enter references in the text boxes by typing or pointing.
— To enter a reference by pointing, click the Collapse Dialog button to collapse the Page Setup dialog box, select the row(s) or column(s) in the worksheet, and then click the OK button.

▶ **Know More** about printing row and column headers on multiple pages *...continued*

– The *Rows to repeat at top* and *Columns to repeat at left* features are unavailable if more than one worksheet is selected.

Figure 4.35 Sheet Tab at the Page Setup Dialog Box

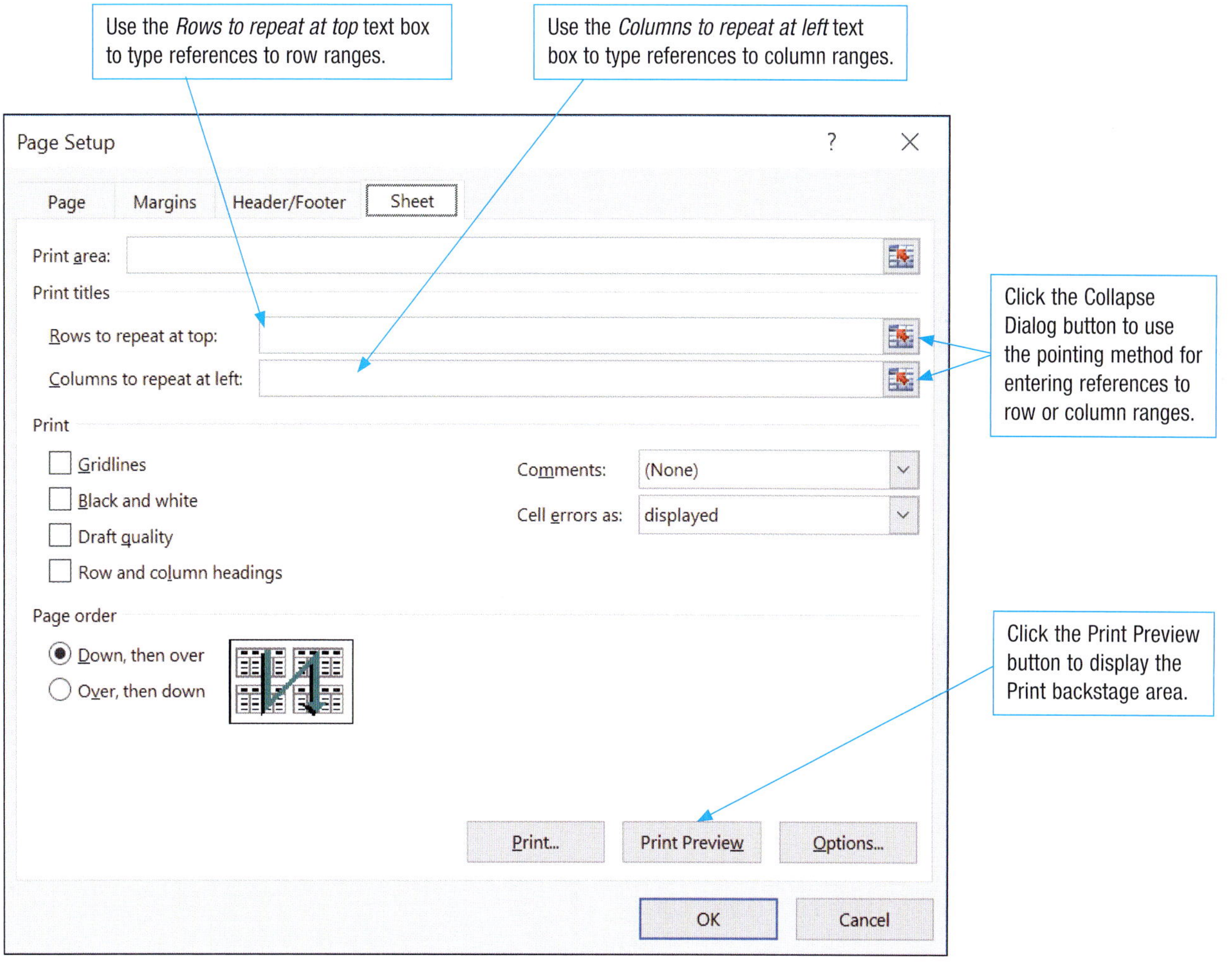

On the Job

Task 4.15 Printing Column Headers on Multiple Pages

In Task 4.14, you started formatting the Yearly Projection worksheet so that Jeremy could easily review a printed copy. Notice that because of the way the page break is set, it would be helpful to repeat column A on the second page of the printed worksheet. Set the worksheet to print with the repeated column and then preview the printout to verify your change.

1. With the Yearly Projection worksheet active, click the Page Layout tab.
2. Click the Print Titles button in the Page Setup group.
   The Page Setup dialog box displays with the Sheet tab active (see Figure 4.35 on page 175).
3. Click in the *Columns to repeat at left* text box.
4. Type A:A.
5. Click the Print Preview button.
   The view changes to the Print backstage area.
6. Click the Next Page arrow at the bottom of the right panel.
   Page 2 displays with the headers in column A repeated.
7. Click the Back button.
8. Click the Save button on the Quick Access Toolbar.

Model Answer

4.16 Setting Print Scaling

MOS 1.5.4

Tutorial
Changing Print Scaling

Changing the **scaling** of an active worksheet quickly adjusts the size of the worksheet on the printed page. You can use scaling to quickly set a worksheet to print on one page, for example. Scaling affects only the appearance of the worksheet on the printed page; it does not affect how the worksheet displays on your monitor.

▸ Know This about setting print scaling

— To adjust print scaling, use options in the Scale to Fit group on the Page Layout tab (see Figure 4.36).
— To define how many pages wide a worksheet will print, click the *Width* option box arrow and then click an option at the drop-down list.
— To define how many pages tall a worksheet will print, click the *Height* option box arrow and then click an option at the drop-down list.
— To manually increase or decrease the scale of a worksheet, click the *Scale* increment (up) or decrement (down) arrow, or type a percentage in the *Scale* measurement box and then press the Enter key.

▸ Know More ways to set print scaling

– Click the Page Setup group dialog box launcher on the Page Layout tab or the Page Setup hyperlink at the Print backstage area, and then use options in the *Scaling* section.

Figure 4.36 Scale to Fit Group on the Page Layout Tab

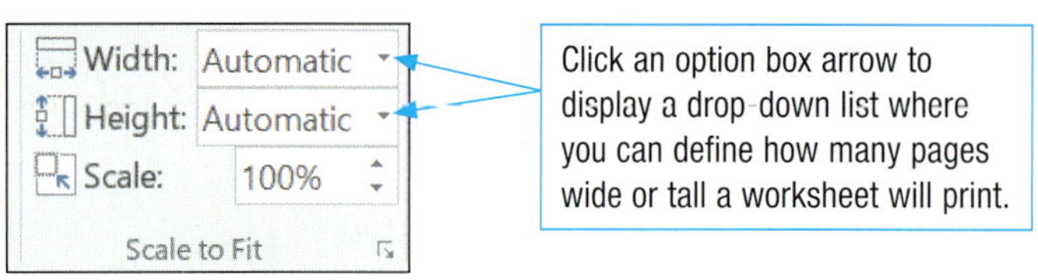

On the Job
Task 4.16 Changing Print Scaling

Jeremy wants to print the Training worksheet as a one-page handout with space for notes at the bottom of the page. Adjust the page orientation and scaling to create the best layout for this handout and then preview the printout to verify your changes.

1. Click the Training sheet tab to make the worksheet active.
2. Click the Page Layout tab if necessary to make it active.
3. Click the Orientation button in the Page Setup group and then click the *Portrait* option at the drop-down menu.
4. Click the *Width* option box arrow in the Scale to Fit group.
   A drop-down list of options displays.
5. Click the *1 page* option.
6. Click the File tab and then click the *Print* option.
   The worksheet displays on one page with plenty of room for notes on the bottom.
7. Click the Back button.
8. Click the Save button on the Quick Access Toolbar.

Model Answer

4.17 Inserting Background Images

A **background image** provides texture or other visual interest to the appearance of a worksheet. Like a watermark, a background image displays behind the data in a worksheet. Unlike a watermark, it is visible only on the screen and does not print.

Tutorial

Inserting a Background Image from OneDrive

▸ Know This about inserting a background image

— To insert a background image, click the Background button in the Page Setup group on the Page Layout tab and then add an image from a file on your computer, from the results of an online search, or from an external storage medium such as your OneDrive account.

— A background image is **tiled**, or repeated, through the entire worksheet.

— A background image is placed behind the contents of a cell, so fill colors and data appear on top of the image.

— A background image can easily overpower a worksheet; be sure all the data in the worksheet is clearly visible over the image.

— A background image displays only in Normal view and Page Layout view. It does not display in Print Preview and it does not print.

— Once a background image has been inserted, the Background button changes to a Delete Background button. Click the Delete Background button to remove the image.

▸ Know More about using background images

– If you want an image to print in the background, insert it as a watermark.

On the Job

Task 4.17 Inserting a Background Image

Jeremy is going to display the Sales worksheet on a screen during his meeting. He asks you to add visual interest to the worksheet by adding a background image. He is also going to distribute the worksheet as a printed handout without the background image. Add a background image that is visible only on the screen, and adjust the layout so the data will print across the width of one page.

1. Click the Sales sheet tab to make the worksheet active.
2. Click the Page Layout tab if necessary to make it active.
3. Click the Background button in the Page Setup group.
4. Click the Browse button, navigate to your AE4 folder, click the **Bark25.jpg** file, and then click the Insert button.

   The bark image appears in the background of the worksheet on your computer screen. It will not display in Print Preview and it will not print.
5. Click the *Width* option box arrow in the Scale to Fit group and then click the *1 page* option.

   The data fits across the width of one page.
6. Click the Save button on the Quick Access Toolbar.

Model Answer

4.18 Printing Gridlines and Row and Column Headings

By default, gridlines, column headings (letters), and row headings (numbers) display on the screen but do not print. You can set these elements to print if a worksheet is difficult to read without them.

Tutorial

Printing Gridlines and Row and Column Headings

▸ Know This about printing gridlines and row and column headings

— To print gridlines and row and column headings using options on the Page Layout tab, click the tab to make it active and then click to insert check marks in the *Print* check boxes in the *Gridlines* and *Headings* sections of the Sheet options group on the Page Layout tab.

— To print gridlines and row and column headings using options at the Page Setup dialog box, click the Page Setup group dialog box launcher on the Page Layout tab or the Page Setup hyperlink at the Print backstage area, click the Sheet tab, and then click the *Gridlines* and *Row and column headings* check boxes to insert checkmarks in the *Print* section.

▸ Know More about printing gridlines

– Instead of printing gridlines, you can apply borders to all the edges of all the cells in a worksheet.

Reminder

Borders print automatically when a worksheet is printed.

On the Job

Task 4.18 Printing Gridlines and Row and Column Headings

Jeremy would like to print the Budget worksheet with the formulas displayed so that he can review the data and the formulas behind the results. Display the workbook in Normal view, display the formulas, and then set the worksheet to print with gridlines and row and column headings displayed so that Jeremy can easily review the data and formulas. Use Print Preview to confirm your changes.

1. Click the Budget sheet tab to make the worksheet active.
2. Click the Normal view button in the View area on the Status bar.
3. Press Ctrl + `.

   Data and formulas, instead of results, display in the cells. Page break lines indicate that the worksheet is too wide to print on one sheet of paper. It would be easier for Jeremy to compare and analyze the information if the worksheet were printed on one sheet.

Reminder

The grave accent key (`) is generally located to the left of the 1 key.

4. Click the Orientation button in the Page Setup group on the Page Layout tab and then click the *Landscape* option.

   The page orientation is landscape, and a page break line indicates that the worksheet will print on one sheet of paper.

5. Click the *Print* check boxes in the *Gridlines* and *Headings* sections of the Sheet Options group.

   A check mark appears in each check box.

6. Click the File tab and then click the *Print* option.

   The worksheet displays on one page in Print Preview, with data, formulas, gridlines, and row and column headings visible.

7. If printed work is required by your instructor, print the workbook.
8. Click the Save button on the Quick Access Toolbar.

Model Answer

4.19 Setting Print Areas

MOS 1.5.1

If a worksheet contains more information than you need to include in a printout, you can set a **print area** to print only a specific area of the worksheet.

Tutorial

Setting a Print Area

▸ Know This about setting a print area

— To specify a print area, select the cells to print, click the Print Area button in the Page Setup group on the Page Layout tab, and then click the *Set Print Area* option at the drop-down list.

— Excel places a border around adjacent cells in the specified print area.

— To add more specific areas to print, select the cells and then click the *Add to Print Area* option at the Print Area button drop-down list.

— To print the specified areas, click the File tab, click the *Print* option, and then click the Print button.

— Nonadjacent cells in defined print areas will print on separate pages.

— To clear all the specified print areas on a worksheet, click the Print Area button and then click the *Clear Print Area* option. Individual print areas cannot be cleared.

— To print a print area, click the File tab, click the *Print* option, and then click the Print button.

▸ Know More about setting a print area

- When you set a print area in a worksheet, Excel adds the *Add to Print Area* option to the Print Area button drop-down list.
- When you set a print area, Excel creates the defined name *Print_Area* for that area. The defined name is saved with the workbook and can be accessed at a later time.

On the Job

Task 4.19 Setting a Print Area

Jeremy would like to print the Sales worksheet without any of the graphic elements. Set a print area that includes the range A3:E12.

1. Click the Sales sheet tab to make the worksheet active.
2. Select the range A3:E12.
3. Click the Page Layout tab if necessary to make it active and then click the Print Area button in the Page Setup group.

   A drop-down menu displays.

4. Click the *Set Print Area* option.

5. Click the File tab and then click the *Print* option.

   The range A3:E12 and the footer display.

6. If printed work is required by your instructor, print the range A3:E12.
7. Click the Save button on the Quick Access Toolbar and then close the workbook.

Model Answer

Chapter Summary

4.1
- An object is a table, image, shape, SmartArt graphic, WordArt, or other graphic element that appears on a worksheet page. When an object is inserted in a workbook, it is not inserted in a cell or range. Instead, it is placed on top of the worksheet and can be selected, sized, and moved without restrictions.
- When an object is selected, one or more contextual tabs display. A contextual tab provides access to tools for manipulating the object.
- Some Excel users take advantage of an assistive technology that provides an audio description of an Excel spreadsheet. This program reads the text and values in a spreadsheet, along with additional information that is not readily visible to users, such as alternative text. If this alternative text is missing when the Excel Accessibility Checker is run, an error message is issued.
- Images can be inserted from several sources, including a OneDrive account, an online search, the local computer, or a removable drive connected to the local computer. Images can be inserted using buttons and options in the Illustrations group on the Insert tab.
- Images from online and other sources may be copyrighted. The user is responsible for respecting all forms of copyright, including restrictions on distributing or changing an image and requirements for obtaining permission or crediting the creator of the work.
- An image can be sized and cropped using options in the Size group on the Picture Tools Format tab. An image can also be sized using the sizing handles that display on the edges of the image when it is selected.

4.2
- When an image is selected, the Picture Tools Format contextual tab displays. Buttons and options on this tab can be used to add a picture style or a border to the image.

4.3
- Image properties can be modified using options on the Pictures Tools Format tab or at the Format Picture task pane. For instance, unwanted parts of an image can be removed, or the brightness, contrast, and tint of an image can be corrected.

4.4
- A variety of shapes can be inserted to add visual interest to a worksheet. A shape can be inserted using options in the Illustrations group on the Insert tab.
- The size of a shape can be changed using options in the Size group on the Drawing Tools Format tab or using the sizing handles that display around a selected shape. A shape can also be modified using options in the Shape Styles group on the Picture Tools Format tab.

- Text can be added to a shape by selecting the shape and then typing the text. The text inside a shape can be modified using features in the Font and the Alignment groups on the Home tab or in the WordArt Styles group on the Drawing Tools Format tab.

4.5 ▶ A shape can be further modified by applying and then modifying styles using buttons and options in the Shape Styles group on the Drawing Tools Format tab or using features at the Format Shape task pane. Styles include colors, gradients, pictures, outlines, and effects (such as shadow and reflection).

- The text inserted in a shape can be formatted by applying a style, fill, outline, or effect using buttons in the WordArt Styles group.

4.6 ▶ A SmartArt graphic is a predesigned visual element that allows easily creating a professional-looking illustration, such as a flowchart, organizational chart, or cycle chart. A SmartArt graphic can be restored, deleted, moved, and sized using buttons and options on the SmartArt Tools Design tab and the SmartArt Tools Format tab. A SmartArt graphic can also be resized using the sizing handles that display around the graphic when it is selected.

- Text can be entered and edited in a SmartArt Graphic either in the selected shape or at the Text pane. As text is typed or edited inside the shape, the font size will increase or decrease so that the text fits. The font size will also adjust when the SmartArt graphic is resized.

4.7 ▶ The design and formatting of a SmartArt graphic can be modified to coordinate with the overall appearance of a workbook. Features on the SmartArt Tools Design tab can be used to add and move shapes and to change the layout and apply a style. Features on the SmartArt Tools Format tab can be used to modify shapes and WordArt styles within a SmartArt graphic. A SmartArt graphic can also be formatted using the Format Shape task pane.

4.8 ▶ A text box can be used to include a large block of text in a worksheet or to put text in a specific location in the worksheet. A text box can be inserted using buttons and options in the Text group on the Insert tab. A text box is an object, which means it is placed on top of the worksheet, where it can be selected and manipulated.

- A text box can be sized and formatted using options on the Drawing Tools Format tab or using the Format Picture task pane. It can also be sized using the sizing handles that display around the box when it is selected.
- The WordArt feature alters the shape, alignment, and style of text. It can be used to create company logos and to draw attention to headings. WordArt can be inserted using the WordArt button in the Text group on the Insert tab.

4.9 ▶ WordArt can be modified and removed using options in the WordArt Styles group on the Drawing Tools Format tab. It can also be sized using the sizing handles that display around it when it is selected.

4.10 ▶ Objects such as pictures, shapes, SmartArt, text boxes, and WordArt are placed in different layers on a worksheet. If more than one object is placed in the same location, the last object inserted is placed on the top layer. Arrangement tools allow selecting, aligning, grouping, and rotating objects and bringing objects up or sending them back one or more layers. These tools are available on the Picture Tools Format tab, Drawing Tools Format tab, or SmartArt Tools Format tab, depending on the type of objects selected. Objects can also be selected at the Selection pane.

4.11 ▶ The header is the area at the top of a worksheet where text and/or elements are inserted. The footer is the area at the bottom of a worksheet where text and/or elements are inserted. Headers and footers can appear on every page of a worksheet. Worksheets can have different first-page headers and footers or different odd and even headers and footers. Headers and footers can be inserted using buttons and options on the Header & Footer Tools Design tab or using the Page Setup dialog box.

4.12 ▶ A watermark is a faint picture that appears behind the data in a worksheet. Only an image file can be inserted as a watermark in Excel; if a watermark must contain text, a custom graphic should be created and then saved in a standard picture format. A watermark is inserted in the header or footer section.

4.13 ▶ When a new workbook is created, it comes with predefined settings, including default settings for margins, page orientation, and page size. These page settings can be changed using features on the Page Layout tab or options at the Page Setup dialog box.

4.14 ▶ Excel inserts an automatic page break in a worksheet when the data will not fit on one page. If an inserted page break is not in the proper place, a manual page break can be inserted where a break is better suited. Both horizontal and vertical page breaks can be inserted. Page breaks can be inserted and removed using buttons and options in the Page Setup group on the Page Layout tab.

▶ The page breaks in a worksheet can be displayed in Page Break Preview view by clicking the Page Break Preview button in the View area on the Status bar or in the Workbook View group on the View tab. A worksheet can also be edited in Page Break Preview view.

4.15 ▶ When a worksheet prints on more than one page, the row and/or column headers print on only the first page by default. These headers can be set to print on all the pages by clicking the Print Titles button in the Page Setup group on the Page Layout tab.

4.16 ▶ Changing the scaling of an active worksheet quickly adjusts the size of the worksheet on the printed page. Scaling affects only the appearance of the worksheet on the printed page; it does not affect how the worksheet displays on the monitor. Scaling can be adjusted using features in the Scale to Fit group on the Page Layout tab or using options in the *Scaling* section of the Page Setup dialog box.

4.17 ▶ A background image provides texture or other visual interest to the appearance of a worksheet. An image can be inserted from a file on the computer, the results of an online search, or an external storage medium using the Background button in the Page Setup group on the Page Layout tab. The image is tiled, or repeated, through the entire worksheet. Like a watermark, a background image displays behind the data in a worksheet. Unlike a watermark, a background image appears on all the pages in a worksheet and is visible only on the screen; it does not print.

4.18 ▶ By default, gridlines, column headings (letters), and row headings (numbers) display on the screen but do not print. They can be set to print using options on the Page Layout tab or at the Page Setup dialog box.

4.19 ▶ If a worksheet contains more information than needs to be included in a printout, a print area can be set that includes only a specific part. A print area is specified by selecting the cells to print, clicking the Print Area button in the Page Setup group on the Page Layout tab, and then clicking the *Set Print Area* option at the drop-down list.

Features Review

Feature	Ribbon Tab, Group	Button, Option	Keyboard Shortcut
add border to image	Picture Tools Format, Picture Styles		
adjust color of image	Picture Tools Format, Adjust		
adjust sharpness, brightness, or contrast of image	Picture Tools Format, Adjust		
apply fill to shape	Drawing Tools Format, Shape Styles		
apply fill to WordArt text	Drawing Tools Format, WordArt Styles		
apply artistic effect to image	Picture Tools Format, Adjust		
apply effect to shape	Drawing Tools Format, Shape Styles		
apply effect to SmartArt graphic	SmartArt Tools Format, Shape Styles		
apply effect to WordArt text	Drawing Tools Format, WordArt Styles		
apply outline to shape	Drawing Tools Format, Shape Styles		
align images	Picture Tools Format, Arrange		
align shapes	Drawing Tools Format, Arrange		
align SmartArt graphics	SmartArt Tools Format, Arrange		
change colors in SmartArt graphic	SmartArt Tools Design, SmartArt Styles		
change margins	Page Layout, Page Setup		
change page orientation	Page Layout, Page Setup		
change page size	Page Layout, Page Setup		
copy shape	Clipboard, Home		Ctrl + C
crop image	Picture Tools Format, Size		
display or close Text pane	SmartArt Tools Design, Create Graphic		

continues...

Feature	Ribbon Tab, Group	Button, Option	Keyboard Shortcut
display worksheet in Normal view	View, Workbook View		
display worksheet in Page Break Preview view	View, Workbook View		
format watermark	Header & Footer Tools Design, Header & Footer Elements		
insert current date in header or footer	Header & Footer Tools Design, Header & Footer Elements		
insert image from OneDrive account, social media account, or online search results	Insert, Illustrations		
insert image from local computer or storage medium connected to local computer	Insert, Illustrations		
insert page break	Page Layout, Page Setup	, *Insert Page Break*	
insert page number in header or footer	Header & Footer Tools Design, Header & Footer Elements		
insert predefined footer	Header & Footer Tools Design, Header & Footer		
insert predefined header	Header & Footer Tools Design, Header & Footer		
insert shape	Insert, Illustrations		
insert SmartArt graphic	Insert, Illustrations		
insert text box	Insert, Text		
insert WordArt	Insert, Text		
insert current time in header or footer	Header & Footer Tools Design, Header & Footer Elements		
insert file name in header or footer	Header & Footer Tools Design, Header & Footer Elements		
insert or delete background image	Page Layout, Page Setup		
insert sheet name in header or footer	Header & Footer Tools Design, Header & Footer Elements		
insert watermark	Header & Footer Tools Design, Header & Footer Elements		
move image down one layer	Picture Tools Format, Arrange		
move image up one layer	Picture Tools Format, Arrange		
move shape down one layer	Drawing Tools Format, Arrange		
move shape up one layer	Drawing Tools Format, Arrange		
move SmartArt graphic down one layer	SmartArt Tools Format, Arrange		
move SmartArt graphic up one layer	SmartArt Tools Format, Arrange		
navigate to header	Header & Footer Tools Design, Navigation		

continues...

Feature	Ribbon Tab, Group	Button, Option	Keyboard Shortcut
navigate to footer	Header & Footer Tools Design, Navigation		
paste shape	Clipboard, Home		Ctrl + V
print gridlines	Page Layout, Sheet Options	*Gridlines, Print*	
print row and column headers on multiple pages	Page Layout, Page Setup		
print row and column headings	Page Layout, Sheet Options	*Headings, Print*	
reset image	Picture Tools Format, Adjust		
reset SmartArt graphic	SmartArt Tools Design, Reset		
remove a page break	Page Layout, Page Setup	, *Remove Page Break*	
set print area	Page Layout, Page Setup	, *Set Print Area*	

Recheck

Recheck your understanding of the concepts, features, and skills covered in this chapter by taking the Recheck quiz.

Workbook

Access the study tools, review exercises, assessments, and challenges for this chapter in the workbook available from this page in your ebook.

Managing Workbooks

Chapter 5

Chapter Goal

To manage a workbook with multiple worksheets, consolidate data, and work with templates.

Learning Objectives

- **5.1** Manage a workbook with multiple worksheets
- **5.2** Move worksheets within a workbook
- **5.3** Change sheet tab color
- **5.4** Hide and unhide a worksheet
- **5.5** Group and ungroup worksheets
- **5.6** Copy worksheets within a workbook
- **5.7** Copy and move worksheets to another workbook
- **5.8** Format multiple worksheets
- **5.9** Create formulas that link to cells in other worksheets or workbooks
- **5.10** Use the Consolidate feature to summarize data
- **5.11** Use paste options
- **5.12** Split windows and manage split windows
- **5.13** Freeze and unfreeze panes
- **5.14** Manage versions of a workbook
- **5.15** Save a workbook as a custom template and create a new workbook based on a template
- **5.16** Modify existing templates
- **5.17** Use a preformatted template

Precheck

Check your understanding of the concepts, features, and skills covered in this chapter by taking the Precheck quiz.

Data Files

Before beginning the chapter work, download the AE5 folder from this page in your ebook to your storage medium and then make AE5 the active folder.

Ebook Links

Access digital resources for this course from your ebook.

SNAP

If you are a SNAP user, go to your SNAP assignments page to complete the Precheck, Tutorials, and Recheck in this chapter.

Preview

On the Job

Scenario WareBot

In Chapter 4, you added visual elements and modified the page setup in an Excel workbook that Jeremy Ronlin, director of marketing and sales at WareBot, will present to regional managers next month. The workbook contains first-quarter sales figures, annual projections, budget data, and training information. Jeremy would like you to do additional data analysis and put some finishing touches on the workbook to make it ready for the presentation. He would also like you to copy and consolidate some of the sales data in a separate workbook to be shared with other departments and for additional analysis and reports. Finally, Jeremy would like you to create a workbook that contains a travel expense template for managers who will be traveling to attend the presentation and to download a preformatted template to help with future project management.

Visual Reference: Managing Multiple Workbooks

Figure 5.1 One Excel Workbook Open in Two Windows Side by Side

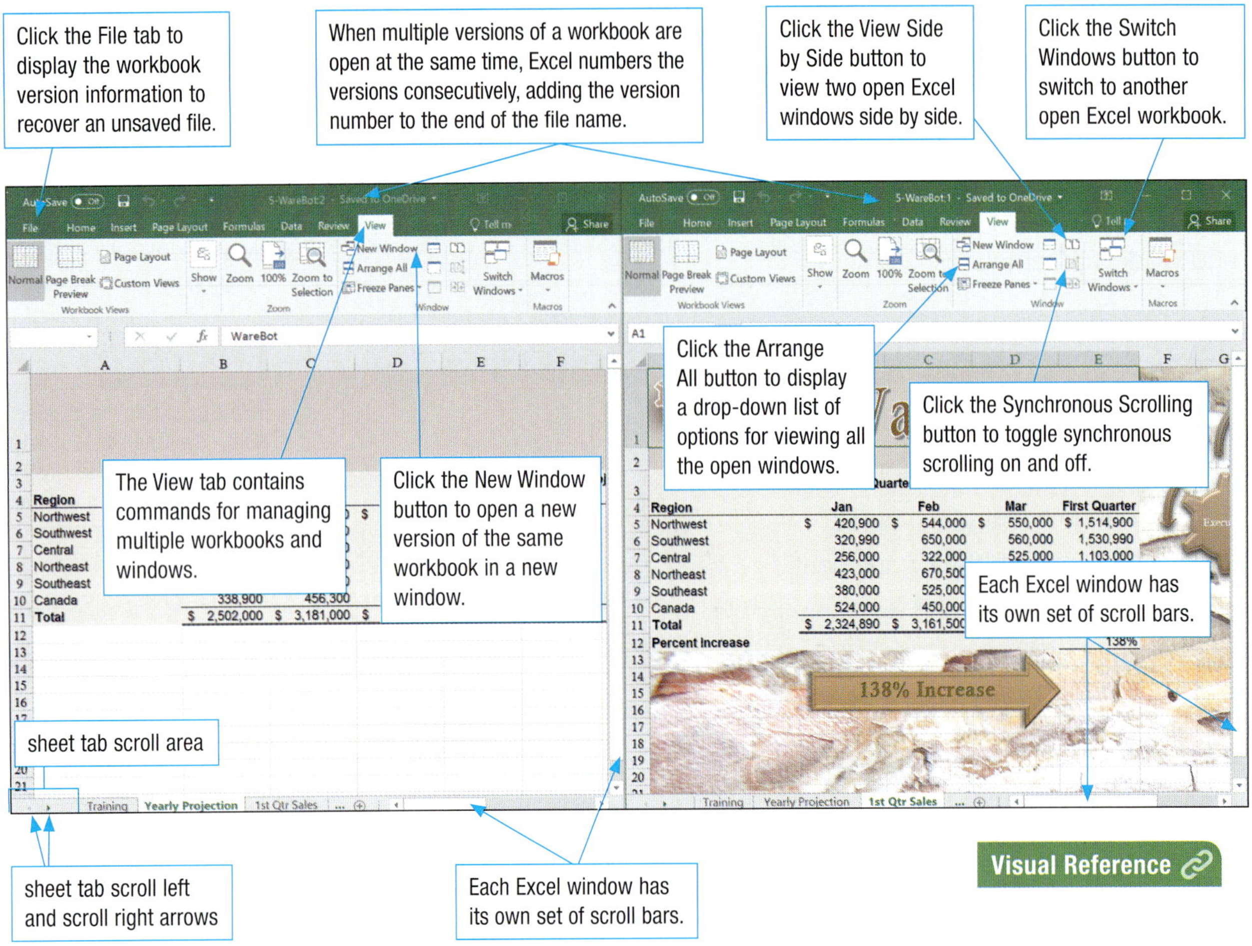

Visual Reference

5.1 Managing a Workbook with Multiple Worksheets

Tutorial

Managing a Workbook with Multiple Worksheets

A workbook can store a vast amount of data in a large number of worksheets. As a workbook grows, you will need certain tools to manage the workbook, navigate among worksheets, and view multiple worksheets.

By default, all the worksheets in a workbook appear in the same Excel window. The active worksheet is displayed in the window, while the rest of the worksheets appear as sheet tabs.

You can view more than one worksheet at a time by opening multiple versions of the workbook in separate windows, arranging all the windows so they are visible, resizing the windows for optimal viewing, and then switching between the open windows. You can set two open windows to be viewed side by side; this feature makes it easy to compare data in two worksheets.

▸ **Know This** about navigating to a worksheet

— To display a different worksheet in the Excel window, click its sheet tab.

— As worksheets are added to a workbook, some sheet tabs may not be visible in the Excel window.

— To view all the sheet tabs in a workbook, click the sheet tab scroll left and scroll right arrows (see Figure 5.1 on page 188).
— To quickly navigate to a specific worksheet, right-click the sheet tab scroll left or scroll right arrow, click the worksheet name in the *Activate* list box at the Activate dialog box, and then click the OK button (see Figure 5.2).

Figure 5.2 Activate Dialog Box

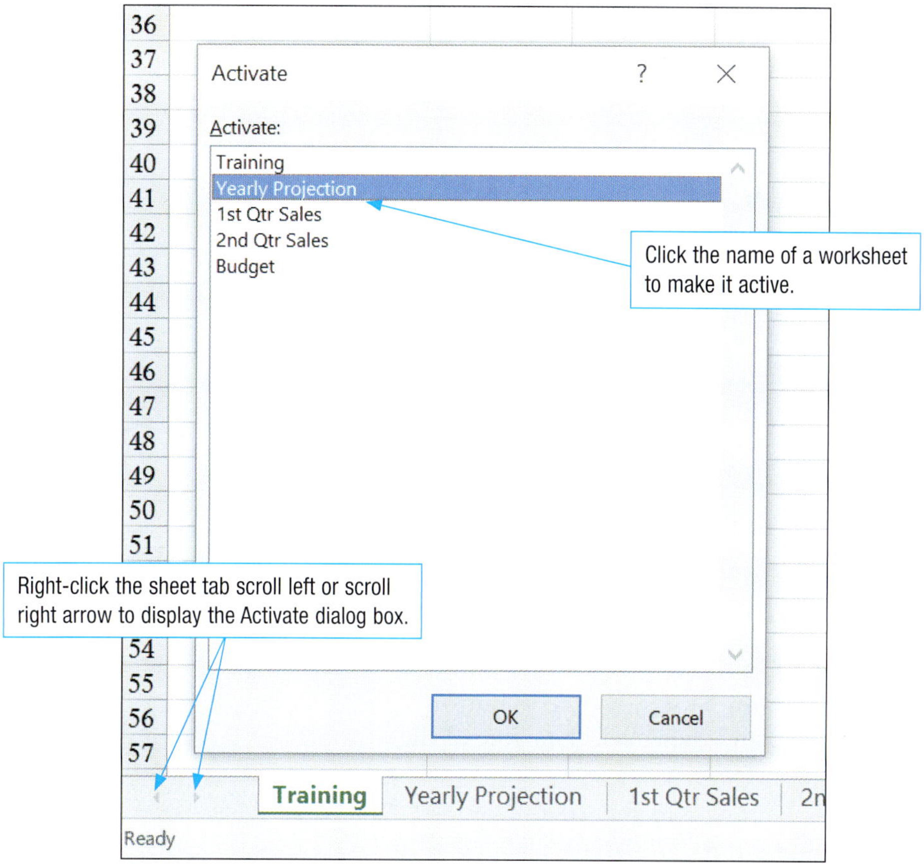

▸ Know This about opening multiple versions of a workbook

— To open a new version of a workbook in a new Excel window, click the New Window button in the Window group on the View tab.
— When more than one version of a workbook is open, Excel adds the version number to the workbook file name in the Title bar of the window (see Figure 5.1).
— Multiple windows are numbered consecutively according to the order in which they were opened. For example, if you open three versions of workbook 5-WareBot, Excel will give the first version you opened the name 5-WareBot - 1, the second version the name 5-WareBot - 2, and the third version the name 5-WareBot - 3.
— When versions of a workbook are closed, Excel automatically adjusts the version numbers in the file names. For example, if you have three versions of the workbook 5-WareBot open and you close the first version, Excel will rename the second version 5-WareBot - 1 and the third version 5-WareBot - 2.

▸ Know This about arranging open windows

— To view all open Excel windows at the same time, click the Arrange All button in the Window group on the View tab (see Figure 5.1 on page 188), select an option in the *Arrange* section at the Arrange Windows dialog box, and then click the OK button (see Figure 5.3).

Figure 5.3 Arrange Windows Dialog Box

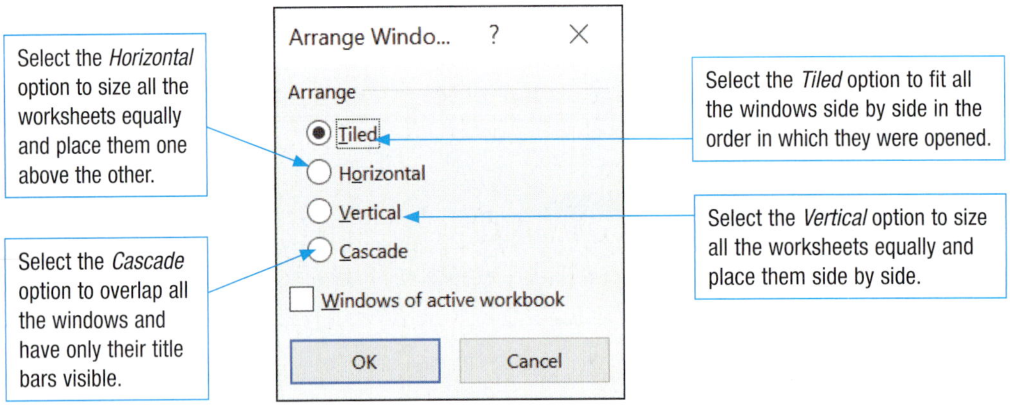

▸ Know This about resizing windows

— To resize a window for optimal viewing, drag a window border or corner.

— To restore a workbook window to full size, click the Maximize button (see Figure 5.4).

▸ Know This about switching windows

— To view a different open window, click the Switch Windows button in the Window group on the View tab and then click the name of the workbook at the drop-down menu.

▸ Know This about comparing two worksheets side by side

— To compare two worksheets in the same workbook side by side, open a second version of the workbook in a new window, click the View Side by Side button in the Window group on the View tab, click the sheet tab for one worksheet in the first window, and then click the sheet tab for the second worksheet in the second window.

— Excel automatically sizes and positions the windows so you can view both worksheets on the screen at the same time.

— By default, the Synchronous Scrolling feature is turned on when the View Side by Side feature is active. This allows you to scroll both worksheets at the same time. To turn off the Synchronous Scrolling feature, click the Synchronous Scrolling button.

— The View Side by Side feature is available only for two worksheets in the same workbook. To compare two worksheets in different workbooks, you can open the worksheets in separate windows and then manually size and position the windows so they fit side by side on the screen.

— If you resize a window when the View Side by Side feature is active, click the Reset Window Position button in the Window group on the View tab to size the workbook windows so that they share the window equally.

On the Job

Task 5.1 Managing a Workbook with Multiple Worksheets

To help him prepare for next month's presentation to the regional managers, Jeremy asks you to analyze the January sales by comparing the actual sales with the projected sales. He would also like you to identify any possible discrepancies in the January sales data.

1. Open the data file **5-WareBot**.
2. Right-click the sheet tab scroll left or scroll right arrow (see Figure 5.2 on page 189).

   The Activate dialog box displays.
3. Click the *Yearly Projection* option and then click the OK button.

   The Yearly Projection worksheet is active.
4. Click the View tab and then click the New Window button in the Window group (see Figure 5.4).

   Another version of the workbook opens in a new window in front of the first version, and the new window is active. The file name in the Title bar of the active window displays as *5-WareBot - 2*. The Home tab is active.
5. Click the View tab and then click the Arrange All button in the Window group (see Figure 5.4).

   The Arrange Windows dialog box displays (see Figure 5.3 on page 190).
6. Click the *Vertical* radio button and then click the OK button.

   The 5-WareBot - 2 and 5-WareBot - 1 windows display side by side.

Figure 5.4 Two Excel Windows Displayed Side by Side

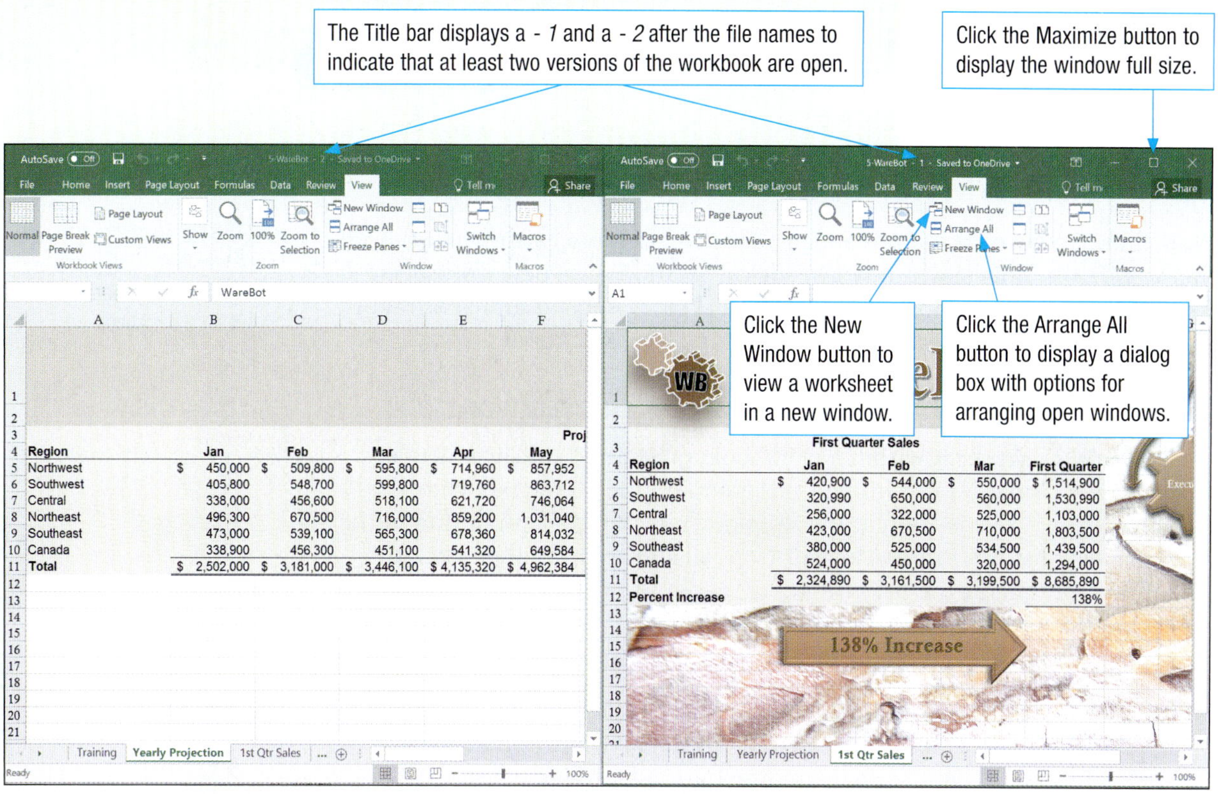

7. In the 5-WareBot - 1 window, click the 1st Qtr Sales sheet tab.
   Note: *You may need to use the sheet tab scroll arrows to display the 1st Qtr Sales sheet tab.*

   The 1st Qtr Sales worksheet is active in the 5-WareBot - 1 window (see Figure 5.4 on page 191).
8. Compare the actual January sales with the regional projections.

   Notice the underperforming results in all regions except Canada.
9. Scan the data for discrepancies.

   Notice that the January sales entry for the Southeast region is considerably lower than the sales projection. Also notice that the percent increase value in cell E12 does not match the percent increase in the arrow image. You check with Jeremy and find out that the entry in cell B9 is incorrect. Jeremy gives you the correct data for the cell and asks you to update the worksheet.
10. In the 5-WareBot - 1 window, click in cell B9, type 380000, and then press the Enter key.

    The percent increase value in cell E12 now matches the percent increase in the arrow image.
11. In the 5-WareBot - 2 window, click the Close button.

    The 5-WareBot - 2 window closes. The 5-WareBot - 1 window remains open and is renamed *5-WareBot*.
12. In the 5-WareBot window, click the Maximize button (see Figure 5.4).

    The 5-WareBot window fills the screen.
13. Click the Save button on the Quick Access Toolbar.
14. If printed work is required by your instructor, print the workbook.
15. Leave the 5-WareBot workbook open and the 1st Qtr Sales worksheet active for the next task.

Model Answer

5.2 Moving Worksheets within a Workbook

MOS 1.3.3

Tutorial

Moving Worksheets within a Workbook

By default, a new worksheet is added to the right of any existing worksheets in a workbook. This may not be the logical location for a new worksheet. Rearranging the sheet tabs to follow a logical order, such as alphabetical or sequential, can make it easier to find data in a large workbook.

▸ Know This about moving worksheets within a workbook

— To move a worksheet within a workbook, make the worksheet active, click the Format button in the Cells group on the Home tab, click the *Move or Copy Sheet* option at the drop-down menu, click an option in the *Before sheet* list box at the Move or Copy dialog box, and then click the OK button (see Figure 5.5).

▸ Know This about ways to move worksheets within a workbook

— To move a worksheet within a workbook, click the sheet tab, click and hold down the left mouse button, drag to the new location in the row of sheet tabs, and then release the mouse button (see Figure 5.6).

— Right-click the sheet tab, click the *Move or Copy* option at the pop-up menu, click an option in the *Before sheet* list box at the Move or Copy dialog box, and then click the OK button (see Figure 5.5).

Figure 5.5 Move or Copy Dialog Box with Settings for Moving a Worksheet

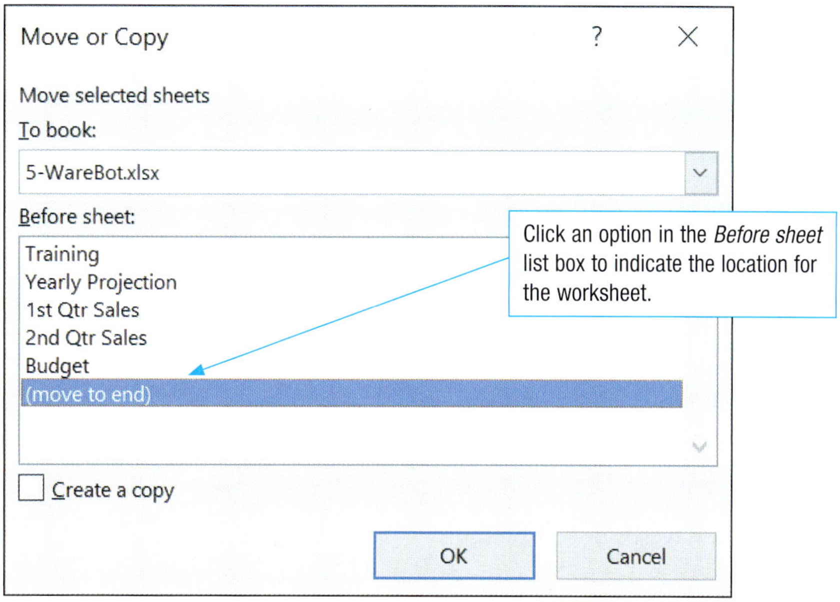

Figure 5.6 Sheet Tab Being Dragged to a New Location

On the Job

Task 5.2 Moving Worksheets within a Workbook

In next month's presentation to the regional managers, Jeremy is going to cover first-quarter sales, second-quarter sales, projected annual sales, budget figures, and training expenses, in that order. He would like you to change the order of the worksheets in the 5-WareBot workbook to match the order of topics in his presentation.

1. With the 5-WareBot workbook open and the 1st Qtr Sales worksheet active, click the Yearly Projection sheet tab.
2. Drag the Yearly Projection sheet tab to the right of the 2nd Qtr Sales sheet tab (see Figure 5.6).

   The Yearly Projection sheet tab appears to the right of the 2nd Qtr Sales sheet tab.

3. Right-click the Training sheet tab.
   A pop-up menu displays.
4. Click the *Move or Copy* option.
   The Move or Copy dialog box displays.
5. Click the *(move to end)* option and then click the OK button (see Figure 5.5 on page 193).
   The Training sheet tab appears to the right of all the other sheet tabs, and the Training worksheet is active.
6. Click the Save button on the Quick Access Toolbar.

Model Answer

5.3 Changing Sheet Tab Color

MOS 1.3.1

Tutorial
Changing Sheet Tab Color

Applying colors to sheet tabs allows you to visually differentiate between worksheets and groups of worksheets, making it easier to find data in a workbook. For example, if a workbook tracks demographic data for major cities and has multiple worksheets for each city, you might use a different sheet tab color for each city. Color can also be used to provide quick visual clues as to the statuses of projects, such as green for the sheet tabs of projects that are in progress and gray for the sheet tabs of projects that have been completed.

▸ Know This about changing sheet tab color

— To change the color of a sheet tab, right-click the sheet tab, point to the *Tab Color* option at the pop-up menu, and then click a color option at the pop-up palette (see Figure 5.7).

— Point to a color option at the *Tab Color* option pop-up palette to view a live preview of the color and to display a ScreenTip with the color name.

— Click the *No Color* option at the *Tab Color* option pop-up palette to remove the tab color.

— Click the *More Colors* option at the *Tab Color* option pop-up palette to display a dialog box with additional options for standard and custom colors.

Figure 5.7 *Tab Color* Option Pop-Up Palette

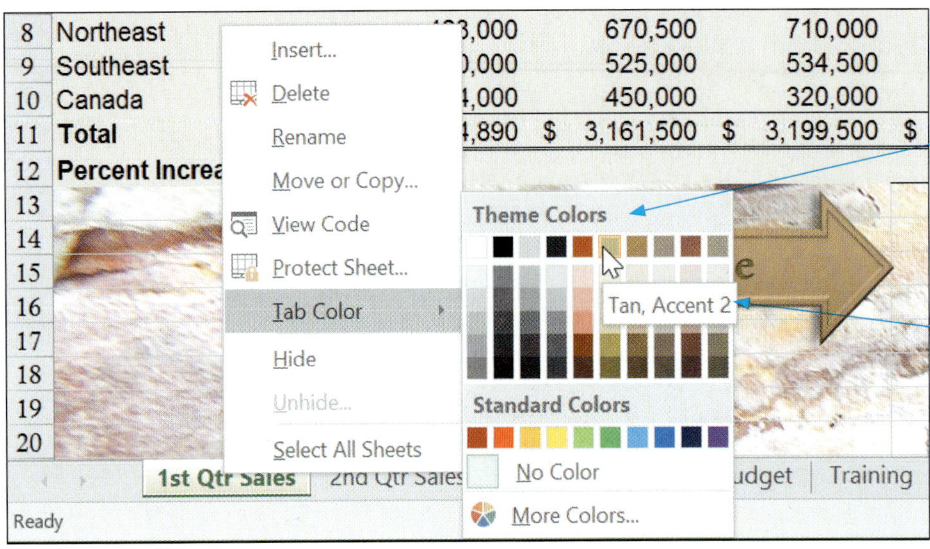

▸ **Know This** about methods for changing sheet tab color

— Click the sheet tab, click the Format button in the Cells group on the Home tab, point to the *Tab Color* option at the drop-down list, and then click a color option at the drop-down palette.

On the Job

Task 5.3 Changing Sheet Tab Color

Jeremy would like you to color code the sheet tabs to enhance the data analysis. Use theme colors to visually connect the sheet tabs of worksheets that contain similar and related sales data, and use a standard color to differentiate worksheets that do not contain financial data.

1. With the 5-WareBot workbook open and the Training worksheet active, right-click the 1st Qtr Sales sheet tab.

   A pop-up menu displays.
2. Point to the *Tab Color* option.

   A pop-up palette displays.
3. Click the *Tan, Accent 2* option (sixth column, first row in the *Theme Colors* section) (see Figure 5.7 on page 194).

   The Tan, Accent 2 color is applied to the 1st Qtr Sales sheet tab.
4. Right-click the 2nd Qtr Sales sheet tab.

   A pop-up menu displays.
5. Point to the *Tab Color* option.

   A pop-up palette displays.
6. Click the *Tan, Accent 2* option.

   The Tan, Accent 2 color is applied to the 2nd Qtr Sales sheet tab.
7. Right-click the Yearly Projection sheet tab.
8. Point to the *Tab Color* option.
9. Click the *Tan, Accent 3* option (seventh column, first row in the *Theme Colors* section).

   The Tan, Accent 3 color is applied to the Yearly Projection sheet tab.
10. Click the Budget sheet tab.
11. Click the Home tab, if necessary, and then click the Format button in the Cells group.

    A drop-down list displays.
12. Point to the *Tab Color* option.

    A drop-down palette displays.
13. Click the *Brown, Accent 4* option (eighth column, first row in the *Theme Colors* section).

    The Brown, Accent 4 color is applied to the Budget sheet tab.
14. Right-click the Training sheet tab.

    A pop-up menu displays.
15. Point to the *Tab Color* option.

    A pop-up palette displays.
16. Click the *Green* option (sixth column in the *Standard Colors* section).

    The Green color is applied to the Training sheet tab.
17. Click the Save button on the Quick Access Toolbar.

Model Answer

5.4 Hiding and Unhiding a Worksheet

MOS 1.4.1

You may want to temporarily hide a worksheet in a workbook if you are sharing the data in a presentation or meeting. For example, you may want to hide a worksheet that contains employee bonuses when sharing budget figures in the same workbook at a department meeting.

Tutorial

Hiding and Unhiding a Worksheet

▸ Know This about hiding a worksheet

- To hide a worksheet, click the sheet tab, click the Format button in the Cells group on the Home tab, point to the *Hide & Unhide* option in the *Visibility* section at the drop-down list, and then click the *Hide Sheet* option at the second drop-down list.
- When a worksheet is hidden, the data it contains is hidden from view but not deleted.
- Data on a hidden worksheet can still be referenced on another worksheet.

▸ Know More methods for hiding a worksheet

- Right-click the sheet tab and then click the *Hide* option at the pop-up menu.

▸ Know This about unhiding a worksheet

- To unhide a worksheet, click the Format button in the Cells group on the Home tab, point to the *Hide & Unhide* option in the *Visibility* section at the drop-down list, click the *Unhide Sheet* option at the second drop-down list, click the name of the worksheet in the *Unhide sheet* list box at the Unhide dialog box, and then click the OK button.

▸ Know More methods for unhiding a worksheet

- Right-click any visible sheet tab, click the *Unhide* option at the pop-up menu, click the name of the worksheet in the *Unhide Sheet* list box, and then click the OK button.

On the Job

Task 5.4a Hiding a Worksheet

The sales manager has asked to meet with Jeremy this afternoon to discuss the status of employee training. Jeremy would like you to hide the 1st Qtr Sales and 2nd Qtr Sales worksheets for this meeting because the sales data has not yet been approved for release to managers.

1. With the 5-WareBot workbook open and the Training worksheet active, click the 1st Qtr Sales sheet tab.
2. Click the Format button in the Cells group on the Home tab.

   A drop-down list displays.
3. Point to the *Hide & Unhide* option in the *Visibility* section.

   A second drop-down list displays.
4. Click the *Hide Sheet* option.

   The 1st Qtr Sales sheet tab is hidden.
5. Right-click the 2nd Qtr Sales sheet tab.

   A pop-up menu displays.
6. Click the *Hide* option.

   The 2nd Qtr Sales sheet tab is hidden.
7. Click the Save button on the Quick Access Toolbar.
8. If printed work is required by your instructor, print the workbook.

Model Answer

On the Job

Task 5.4b Unhiding a Worksheet

Jeremy's meeting about employee training has ended, and he asks you to unhide the 1st Qtr Sales and 2nd Qtr Sales worksheets.

1. With the 5-WareBot workbook open, right-click the Yearly Projection sheet tab.

   A pop-up menu displays.

2. Click the *Unhide* option.

   A dialog box displays with *1st Qtr Sales* selected in the *Unhide sheet* list box.

3. Click the OK button.

   The 1st Qtr Sales sheet tab is visible.

4. Click the Format button in the Cells group on the Home tab.

   A drop-down list displays.

5. Point to the *Hide & Unhide* option in the *Visibility* section.

   A second drop-down list displays.

6. Click the *Unhide Sheet* option.

   A dialog box displays with *2nd Qtr Sales* selected in the *Unhide sheet* list box.

7. Click the OK button.

   The 2nd Qtr Sales sheet tab is visible.

8. Click the Save button on the Quick Access Toolbar.

Model Answer

5.5 Grouping and Ungrouping Worksheets

Tutorial

Grouping and Ungrouping Worksheets

Workbooks are often organized into multiple worksheets that use a similar layout and contain similar data. For example, a company's expense workbook may contain monthly worksheets that track expenses for each month in the fiscal year. When worksheets have a similar data structure, you can perform tasks on multiple worksheets at the same time by first grouping the worksheets. A **worksheet group** is a set of multiple worksheets that are all selected together. Any changes you make in one worksheet in the group are also made in all the other worksheets in the group.

▸ Know This about grouping and ungrouping worksheets

— To group and ungroup worksheets, perform the actions described in Table 5.1.

— When multiple worksheets are grouped, the text *[Group]* appears after the workbook file name in the Title bar of the Excel window, and a solid line appears under the sheet tabs of the grouped worksheets (see Figure 5.8).

— Grouping worksheets is an efficient method of ensuring consistency between worksheets.

Table 5.1 Grouping and Ungrouping Worksheets

To group...	...take this action:
two or more adjacent worksheets	click the first sheet tab, press and hold down the Shift key, click the last sheet tab, and then release the Shift key.
two or more nonadjacent worksheets	click one of the sheet tabs, press and hold down the Ctrl key, click the other sheet tabs, and then release the Ctrl key.
all the worksheets in a workbook	right-click a sheet tab and then click the *Select All Sheets* option at the pop-up menu.
To ungroup...	**...take this action:**
grouped worksheets	click any sheet tab outside the group or right-click any sheet tab in the group and then click the *Ungroup Sheets* option at the pop-up menu.

Figure 5.8 Grouped Worksheets

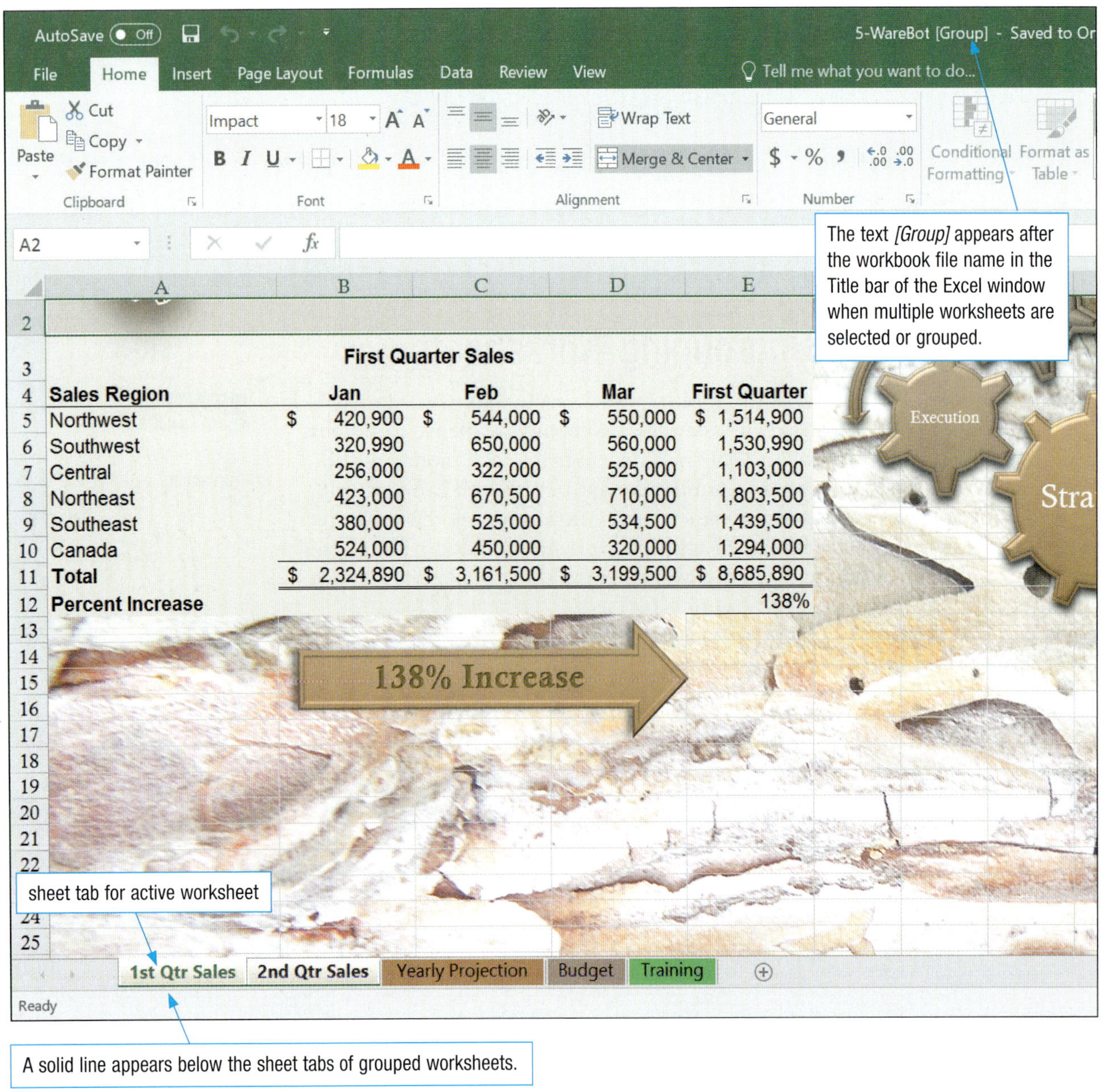

▸ **Know This** about entering and deleting data in grouped worksheets

— If multiple worksheets are grouped, entering data in a cell in one worksheet automatically enters the data in the same cell in the other selected worksheets.

— Similarly, if multiple worksheets are grouped, deleting the contents of a cell in one worksheet automatically deletes the contents of the same cell in the other selected worksheets.

▸ **Know This** about changing the worksheet structure or view in grouped worksheets

— If multiple worksheets are grouped, any change to the worksheet structure—such as inserting a row or column or changing the margins—will affect all the worksheets in the group.

— Similarly, if multiple worksheets are grouped, changing the view in one worksheet will affect all the worksheets in the group.

▸ **Know This** about printing grouped worksheets

— All grouped worksheets can be printed at the same time using the same print settings.

On the Job

Task 5.5 Using Grouped Worksheets

Jeremy would like you to make the same edit in the 1st Qtr Sales and 2nd Qtr Sales worksheets. Group the worksheets to complete this task efficiently and then double-check that the edit was made in both worksheets.

1. With the 5-WareBot workbook open, click the 1st Qtr Sales sheet tab, press and hold down the Shift key, click the 2nd Qtr Sales sheet tab, and then release the Shift key.

   The text *[Group]* appears after the file name in the Title bar of the Excel window, and a solid line appears under the 1st Qtr Sales and 2nd Qtr Sales sheet tabs.
2. Click in cell A4, type Sales Region, and then press Ctrl + Enter.

   The text *Sales Region* displays in cell A4.
3. Click the View tab and then click the Zoom button in the Zoom group.

   The Zoom dialog box displays.
4. Click the *75%* option in the *Magnification* section of the Zoom dialog box and then click the OK button.

   The window zooms out and displays at 75% magnification.
5. Click the 2nd Qtr Sales sheet tab.

   The text *Sales Region* displays in cell A4, and the window displays at 75% magnification.
6. Click the 1st Qtr Sales sheet tab.
7. Click the 100% button in the Zoom group.

   The window zooms in and displays at 100% magnification.
8. Click the Save button on the Quick Access Toolbar.

Model Answer

5.6 Copying Worksheets within a Workbook

MOS 1.1.4

Tutorial

Copying a Worksheet within a Workbook

Copying a worksheet can save time if you want to create multiple worksheets with similar data, such as sales figures for consecutive quarters. A copied worksheet displays all the same data as the original worksheet, and you can simply edit the data as necessary and then easily compare the data in the related worksheets. A worksheet that is copied or moved within a workbook keeps the same formatting at its new location.

▶ **Know This** about copying worksheets within a workbook

- To copy a worksheet within a workbook, click the sheet tab or group the worksheets, click the Format button in the Cells group on the Home tab, click the *Move or Copy Sheet* option in the *Organize Sheets* section at the drop-down list, click an option in the *Before sheet* list box at the Move or Copy dialog box, click the *Create a copy* check box to insert a check mark, and then click the OK button (see Figure 5.9).
- When you copy a worksheet within a workbook, Excel adds a copy number to the end of the new sheet tab name—for example, *Sales (2)*.
- When you copy a worksheet within a workbook, the new sheet tab displays with the same formatting as the original tab. The matching formatting is a visual cue that the data in the new worksheet is similar to the data in the original worksheet.

▶ **Know More** methods for copying worksheets within a workbook

- Right-click the sheet tab or grouped sheet tabs, click the *Move or Copy* option at the pop-up menu, click an option in the *Before sheet* list box at the Move or Copy dialog box, click the *Create a copy* check box to insert a check mark, and then click the OK button.
- Press and hold down the Ctrl key, click the sheet tab or grouped sheet tabs, click and hold down the left mouse button, drag the tab or group to the new location, and then release the Ctrl key and the mouse button.

On the Job

Task 5.6 Copying Worksheets within a Workbook

The workbook currently contains first-quarter and second-quarter sales data. Jeremy would like you to create two new worksheets to display third- and fourth-quarter sales data. Use the Copy feature in Excel to create two new worksheets with the same layout and headers as in the 1st Qtr Sales and 2nd Qtr Sales worksheets. Jeremy would also like you to use the Copy feature to create a new worksheet with the same layout and headers as in the Training worksheet to track level-2 company training.

1. With the 5-WareBot workbook open, the 1st Qtr Sales and 2nd Qtr Sales worksheets grouped, and the 1st Qtr Sales worksheet active, click the Home tab and then click the Format button in the Cells group.

   A drop-down list displays.
2. Click the *Move or Copy Sheet* option.

   A dialog box displays.
3. Click the *Yearly Projection* option in the *Before sheet* list box.
4. Click the *Create a copy* check box (see Figure 5.9).

   A check mark appears in the check box.
5. Click the OK button.

   The 1st Qtr Sales (2) and 2nd Qtr Sales (2) sheet tabs display before the Yearly Projection sheet tab. The 1st Qtr Sales, 2nd Qtr Sales, 1st Qtr Sales (2), and 2nd Qtr Sales (2) sheet tabs are the same color.
6. Double-click the 1st Qtr Sales (2) sheet tab, type 3rd Qtr Sales, and then press the Enter key.

Figure 5.9 Move or Copy Dialog Box with Settings for Copying a Worksheet within a Workbook

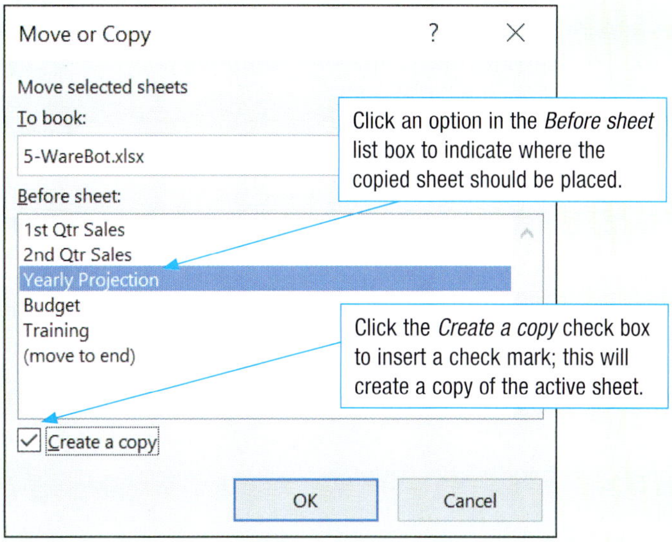

7. Double-click the 2nd Qtr Sales (2) sheet tab, type 4th Qtr Sales, and then press the Enter key.
8. Right-click the Training sheet tab.

   A pop-up menu displays.
9. Click the *Move or Copy* option.

   A dialog box displays.
10. Click the *(move to end)* option in the *Before sheet* list box.
11. Click the *Create a copy* check box to insert a check mark.
12. Click the OK button.

    The Training (2) sheet tab displays at the end of the sheet tabs.
13. Double-click the Training (2) sheet tab, type Level 2 Training, and then press the Enter key.
14. Click the Save button on the Quick Access Toolbar.
15. If printed work is required by your instructor, print the workbook.

Model Answer

5.7 Copying and Moving Worksheets to Another Workbook

MOS 1.1.4

Tutorial

Copying a Worksheet to Another Workbook

Worksheets can also be copied from one workbook to another. Doing this can save time if you need to enter similar data in a new workbook. The data copies exactly from the source workbook to the destination workbook, and you can then edit it as necessary. You can also move worksheets to another workbook. You can copy or move more than one worksheet at a time by first selecting, or grouping, the worksheets (see Table 5.1 on page 198). A worksheet that is copied or moved to another workbook uses the theme formatting that is applied to the destination workbook.

▶ Know This about copying worksheets to another workbook

- Worksheets can be copied to another open workbook or to a new workbook.
- To copy one or more worksheets to another workbook, click the sheet tab or grouped sheet tabs, click the Format button in the Cells group on the Home tab, click the *Move or Copy Sheet* option in the *Organize Sheets* section at the drop-down list, click the *To book* option box arrow at the Move or Copy dialog box, click the name of the workbook at the drop-down list, click an option in the *Before sheet* list box, click the *Create a copy* check box to insert a check mark, and then click the OK button (see Figure 5.10).
- If the name of the destination workbook does not appear in the *To book* option drop-down list at the Move or Copy dialog box, click the Cancel button, open the destination workbook, make the source worksheet or worksheets active, and then repeat the steps to copy the worksheet or worksheets.
- To copy a worksheet to a new, blank workbook, click the *(new book)* option at the *To book* option drop-down list.

▶ Know This about moving worksheets to another workbook

- To move one or more worksheets to another workbook, click the sheet tab or grouped sheet tabs, click the Format button in the Cells group on the Home tab, click the *Move or Copy Sheet* option at the drop-down list, click the *To book* option box arrow at the Move or Copy dialog box, click the name of the workbook at the drop-down list, click an option in the *Before sheet* list box, and then click the OK button.

On the Job
Task 5.7 Copying a Worksheet to Another Workbook

The Budget worksheet for the sales department contains data that is similar to the budget data required for the marketing department. Jeremy would like you to copy the Budget worksheet to the Excel workbook used by the marketing department. Notice that the marketing department workbook uses different formatting than the sales department workbook.

1. With the 5-WareBot workbook open, also open the data file **5-WareBot-Marketing**.

   The 5-WareBot-Marketing workbook opens in front of the 5-WareBot workbook and is active.

2. Click the View tab and then click the Switch Windows button in the Window group.

   A drop-down list displays.

3. Click the *5-WareBot* option at the drop-down list.

   The 5-WareBot window is active.

4. Click the Budget sheet tab.

   The Budget worksheet is active.

5. Click the Format button in the Cells group on the Home tab.

   A drop-down list displays.

▶ Know More methods for copying worksheets to another workbook

- Right-click the sheet tab or grouped sheet tabs, click the *Move or Copy* option at the pop-up menu, click the *To book* option box arrow at the Move or Copy dialog box, click the name of the workbook at the drop-down list, click an option in the *Before sheet* list box, click the *Create a copy* check box to insert a check mark, and then click the OK button.
- Open both workbooks, click the Arrange All button in the Window group on the View tab, click the Vertical radio button at the Arrange Windows dialog box, click the OK button, click the sheet tab or grouped sheet tabs, press and hold the Ctrl key, and drag to the new location in the row of sheet tabs in the other workbook, and then release the Ctrl key.

▶ Know More methods for moving worksheets to another workbook

- Right-click the sheet tab or grouped sheet tabs, click the *Move or Copy* command at the pop-up menu, click the *To book* option box arrow at the Move or Copy dialog box, click the name of the workbook at the *To book* drop-down list, click an option in the *Before sheet* list box, and then click the OK button.
- Open both workbooks, click the Arrange All button in the Window group on the View tab, click the *Vertical* radio button at the Arrange Windows dialog box, click the OK button, click the sheet tab or grouped sheet tabs, and then drag to the new location in the row of sheet tabs in the other workbook.

6. Click the *Move or Copy Sheet* option.

   A dialog box displays.

7. Click the *To book* option box arrow and then click the *5-WareBot-Marketing* option (see Figure 5.10).
8. Click the *Campaigns* option, if necessary, in the *Before sheet* list box.
9. Click the *Create a copy* check box and then click the OK button.

   A copy of the Budget worksheet appears before the Campaigns worksheet in the 5-WareBot-Marketing workbook and is active. The copied worksheet displays the theme formatting applied to the 5-WareBot-Marketing workbook.

10. Click the Save button on the Quick Access Toolbar.
11. If printed work is required by your instructor, print the 5-WareBot-Marketing workbook.
12. Click the Close button.

    The 5-WareBot-Marketing workbook closes. The 5-WareBot workbook remains open and is active.

13. Close the workbook.

Figure 5.10 Move or Copy Dialog Box with Settings for Copying a Worksheet to Another Workbook

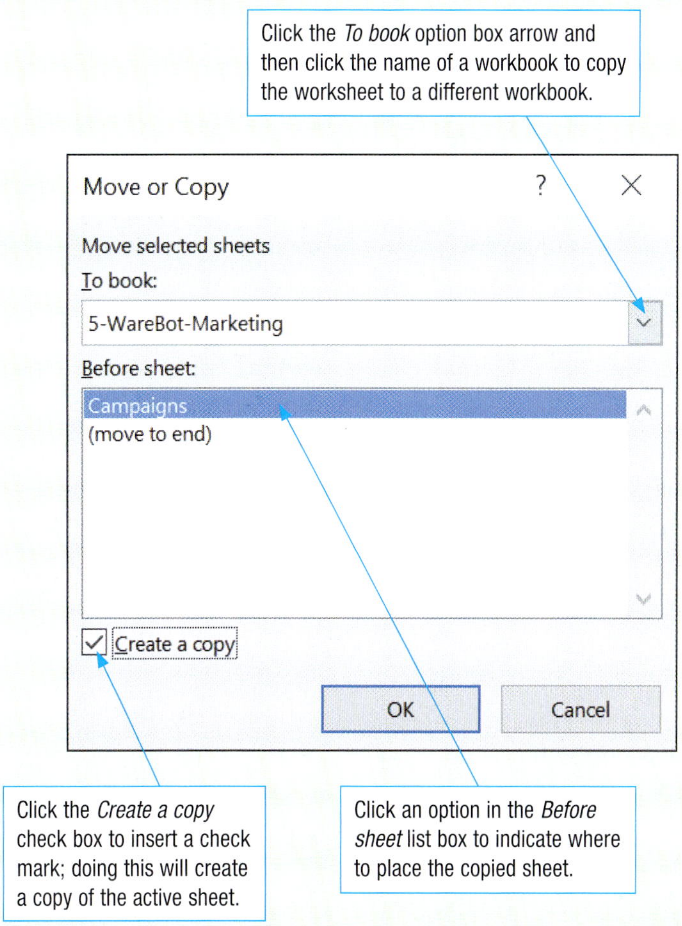

Model Answer

5.8 Formatting Multiple Worksheets

Formatting can be applied simultaneously to multiple worksheets in a workbook by first grouping the worksheets (see Table 5.1 on page 198) and then applying the formatting to cells in one of the grouped worksheets. For example, if you group Sheet1 and Sheet2 and then apply bold formatting to cell A1 in Sheet1, the same formatting is automatically applied to cell A1 in Sheet2. This feature saves development time and helps ensure that formatting is consistent throughout a workbook.

Tutorial

Formatting Multiple Worksheets Simultaneously

▸ **Know This** about formatting multiple worksheets

— To format multiple worksheets simultaneously, group the worksheets to format (see Table 5.1) and then apply the formatting to the active worksheet.

On the Job

Task 5.8 Formatting Multiple Worksheets Simultaneously

Jeremy has created a new workbook, named *5-WareBot-Sales*, that contains updated sales data for all four sales quarters. He would like you to apply consistent formatting to the worksheets that contain quarterly sales data.

1. Open the data file **5-WareBot-Sales**.
2. Group the 1st Qtr Sales, 2nd Qtr Sales, 3rd Qtr Sales, 4th Qtr Sales, and Total Sales sheet tabs.

   The text *[Group]* displays after the file name in the Title bar of the Excel window, and a solid line appears under the grouped sheet tabs.
3. With the 1st Qtr Sales worksheet active, click in cell A3.

   Cell A3 is active.
4. Click the More button in the Styles group on the Home tab.

   The Styles gallery displays.
5. Click the *Heading 2* style.

   The Heading 2 style is applied to cell A3.
6. Select the range A4:E4.
7. Click the More button in the Styles group.

   The Styles gallery displays.
8. Click the *Heading 3* style.

   The Heading 3 style is applied to the range A4:E4.
9. Select the range A3:E11.
10. Click the *Font* option box arrow in the Font group on the Home tab.

    A drop-down list displays.
11. Scroll the list and then click the *Calibri* option.

    The Calibri font is applied to the range A3:E11.
12. Click in cell A12.

    The range is deselected.
13. Right-click the Total Sales sheet tab.

    A pop-up menu displays.

14. Click the *Ungroup Sheets* option.

    The worksheets are ungrouped.

15. Click the sheet tabs for the five grouped worksheets one at a time and view the formatting.

    Each worksheet displays the same formatting applied in the 1st Qtr Sales worksheet.

16. Click the Save button on the Quick Access Toolbar.

Model Answer

5.9 Creating Formulas That Link to Cells in Other Worksheets or Workbooks

When entering formulas in Excel, you may need to include references to cells or ranges in another worksheet or workbook. You can do that by creating an **external reference**, which is also called a *link*. The worksheet that contains the original data is called the **source worksheet**, and the worksheet that relies on the source worksheet for the linked data is called the **dependent worksheet**. Using an external reference eliminates the need to enter or copy existing data and to update multiple worksheets. If the value in the referenced cell or range changes, the value returned by the external reference automatically updates.

External references can be used to merge data from several workbooks to create a summary workbook. For example, sales data from several employees or products can be linked to create a sales summary workbook. (You will learn more about summarizing data in Section 5.10 of this chapter.) External references can also be used to create a report that pulls specific data from several workbooks, simplifying and streamlining the presentation of data.

▸ Know This about inserting external references

- An external reference can be entered by typing or pointing. Pointing is recommended because it helps avoid typing errors and inaccurate cell references.
- An external reference can use a cell or range address, or a defined name.
- It is good practice to use a defined name in an external reference. An external reference that uses a defined name does not change when you move or copy it, because the defined name refers to a specific cell or range. Using a defined name also eliminates the need to include the worksheet name in an external reference, because defined names are unique within a workbook.

▸ Know This about inserting an external reference to a worksheet in the same workbook

- To insert an external reference to a worksheet in the same workbook, type the worksheet name followed by an exclamation point (!) and the cell or range address or defined name. (If the external reference is to a defined name, the worksheet name is not required.)
- An example using cell addresses is =Budget!D7+Budget!E7.
- An example using a range address is =SUM(Budget!A10:A15).
- An example using a defined range name is =SUM(Expenses).

MOS Expert 1.1.3

Tutorials

Creating a Formula That Links to Cells in Other Worksheets

Creating a Formula That Links to a Defined Name in Another Workbook

▸ Know More about using a defined name in an external reference

- To enter a defined name in an external reference, you can type the defined name, click the Name box arrow in the source workbook and then click the defined name option at the drop-down list, or select the cell or cells that contain the original data in the source worksheet.

▸ Know More about inserting external references to a worksheet in the same workbook

- The formula =SUM(Budget!A1+A3) adds the values in cells A1 and A3 in the Budget worksheet in the same workbook.
- The formula =SUM(Budget!A10:A15) adds the values in the range A10:A15 in the Budget worksheet in the same workbook.
- The formula =SUM(Expenses) adds the values in the defined range name *Expenses* in the Budget worksheet in the same workbook.

▸ Know This about inserting an external reference to another workbook that is open

— To insert an external reference to a cell or range in another workbook that is open, enter an opening square bracket ([), the workbook name, a closing square bracket (]), the worksheet name, an exclamation point (!), and then the cell or range address.

— An example using a range is =SUM([WareBot.xlsx]Budget!A10:A15).

— To insert an external reference to a defined name in another workbook that is open, enter an opening square bracket ([), an exclamation point (!), and then the defined name.

— An example using a defined range name is =SUM([WareBot.xlsx]!Expenses).

▸ Know This about inserting an external reference to another workbook that is closed

— To insert an external reference to a cell or range in another workbook that is closed, enter an opening single quotation mark ('), the entire path to the closed workbook, an opening square bracket ([), the workbook name, a closing square bracket (]), the worksheet name, a closing single quotation mark ('), an exclamation point (!), and then the cell or range address or the defined name.

— When you enter the formula containing the external reference, the Update Values dialog box displays. At the dialog box, click the workbook containing the external reference and then click the OK button.

— An example using a range is =SUM('C:\Finance\[WareBot.xlsx]Budget'!A10:A15).

▸ Know More about inserting an external reference to another workbook that is open

– The formula =SUM([WareBot.xlsx]Budget!A10:A15) adds the values in the range A10:A15 from the Budget worksheet in the open workbook WareBot.xlsx.

– To insert an external reference to a defined range name in another workbook that is open, click the Switch Windows button in the Window group on the View tab, click the source workbook, click the worksheet that contains the cells you want to link to, press the F3 function key, click the defined range name, and then click the OK button.

▸ Know More about inserting an external reference to a workbook that is closed

– The formula =SUM('C:\Finance\[WareBot.xlsx]Budget'!A10:A15) adds the values in the range A10:A15 from the Budget worksheet in the closed workbook WareBot.xlsx, which is saved in the Finance folder on the C: drive.

▸ Know More about inserting external references to another worksheet or workbook

– If the name of the other worksheet or workbook contains spaces, symbols, or numbers, you must enclose the name in single quotation marks.

– If the path to the other workbook contains symbols or numbers, you must enclose the path in single quotation marks.

On the Job

Task 5.9a Creating a Formula That Links to Cells in Other Worksheets within the Same Workbook

Jeremy would like to have a summary of the quarterly sales data in a separate worksheet within the 5-WareBot-Sales workbook. Use the Total Sales worksheet for this summary, inserting formulas with external links to the quarterly sales worksheets in the same workbook.

1. With the 5-WareBot-Sales workbook open, click the Total Sales sheet tab, if necessary, to make the worksheet active.
   The Total Sales worksheet is active.
2. Click in cell B5.
   Cell B5 is active.
3. Type an equals sign (=) and then click the 1st Qtr Sales sheet tab.
   The 1st Qtr Sales worksheet is active and the formula *='1st Qtr Sales'!* displays in the Formula bar.
4. Click in cell E5.
   The formula *='1st Qtr Sales'!E5* displays in the Formula bar and a marquee appears around cell E5.
5. Type a plus sign (+) and then click the 2nd Qtr Sales sheet tab.
   The 2nd Qtr Sales worksheet is active and the formula *='1st Qtr Sales'!E5+'2nd Qtr Sales'!* displays in the Formula bar.

6. Click in cell E5.

   The formula *='1st Qtr Sales'!E5+'2nd Qtr Sales'!E5* displays in the Formula bar and a marquee appears around cell E5.

7. Type + and then click the 3rd Qtr Sales sheet tab.

   The 3rd Qtr Sales worksheet is active and the formula *='1st Qtr Sales'!E5+'2nd Qtr Sales'!E5+'3rd Qtr Sales'!* displays in the Formula bar.

8. Click in cell E5.

   The formula *='1st Qtr Sales'!E5+'2nd Qtr Sales'!E5+'3rd Qtr Sales'!E5* displays in the Formula bar and a marquee appears around cell E5.

9. Type + and then click the 4th Qtr Sales sheet tab.

   The 4th Qtr Sales worksheet is active and the formula *='1st Qtr Sales'!E5+'2nd Qtr Sales'!E5+'3rd Qtr Sales'!E5+'4th Qtr Sales'!* displays in the Formula bar.

10. Click in cell E5.

    The formula *='1st Qtr Sales'!E5+'2nd Qtr Sales'!E5+'3rd Qtr Sales'!E5+'4th Qtr Sales'!E5* displays in the Formula bar and a marquee appears around cell E5.

11. Press Ctrl + Enter.

    The Total Sales worksheet is active, cell B5 is active, and the value *4,797,400* displays in cell B5.

12. Use the fill handle to copy the formula from cell B5 down into cell B10.

    The cells in the range B6:B10 contain the formula from cell B5.

13. Click the 4th Qtr Sales sheet tab.
14. Click in cell D5, type 295000, and then press the Enter key.

    The value in cell D5 increases by 100000 (from 195000 to 295000).

15. Click the Total Sales sheet tab.

    The value in cell B5 increases by 100000 (from 4,797,400 to 4,897,400).

16. Click the Save button on the Quick Access Toolbar.

Model Answer

On the Job

Task 5.9b Creating a Formula That Links to a Defined Name in Another Workbook

Jeremy would like you to edit the Budget worksheet that was copied from the 5-Warebot workbook to the 5-WareBot-Marketing workbook by adding the annual sales total to the worksheet. Use an external reference from the 5-WareBot-Sales workbook to enter the annual sales total.

1. With the 5-WareBot-Sales workbook open and the Total Sales worksheet active, click in cell B11.
2. Click in the Name box, type SalesTotal, and then press the Enter key.

   The text *SalesTotal* appears in the Name box.

3. Open the data file **5-WareBot-Marketing**, which you closed at the end of Task 5.7.

   The workbook 5-WareBot-Marketing is open and active.

4. Click the Budget sheet tab, if necessary, to make the worksheet active, click in cell A3, type Annual Sales, and then press the Tab key.

   The text *Annual Sales* appears in cell A3 and cell B3 is active.

5. Type =, use the taskbar to switch to the workbook 5-WareBot-Sales, click in cell B11, and then press Ctrl + Enter.

   The value *27348800* displays in cell B3 and the formula *='5-WareBot-Sales.xlsx'!SalesTotal* displays in the Formula bar.

6. Click the Accounting Number Format button in the Number group on the Home tab.

   A series of number symbols (#####) displays in cell B3.

7. Click the Decrease Decimal button two times.
8. Use the AutoFit feature to adjust the width of column B.

   The value *$27,348,800* displays in cell B3.

9. Click the Save button on the Quick Access Toolbar.
10. If printed work is required by your instructor, print the workbook.
11. Click the Close button.

    The 5-WareBot-Marketing workbook closes. The 5-WareBot-Sales workbook remains open and active.

Model Answer

5.10 Using the Consolidate Feature to Summarize Data

MOS Expert 3.4.2

Tutorial

Using the Consolidate Feature to Summarize Data

The **Consolidate** feature is used to summarize **source data** from other worksheets in a **master worksheet**. The source data can be located in the same workbook as the master worksheet or in a separate workbook. Data can be consolidated by position or by category. Consolidate data by **position** when the data in the source worksheets is arranged in the same order and uses the same labels. Consolidate data by **category** when the data in the source worksheets is not arranged in the same order but uses the same labels. For example, consolidate data by category if you have several inventory worksheets that use the same layout, but each worksheet contains a different number of entries.

Before consolidating source data, be sure it meets the following criteria:

— Each range must be in a list format with a label in the first row or left column.
— Each range must contain similar data.
— Each range must include no blank rows or columns.
— Each range must be in a separate worksheet.
— All the ranges must use the same layout.

▸ **Know This** about using the Consolidate feature to summarize data

— To consolidate data, follow these steps:

1. Click the master worksheet sheet tab.
2. Click the upper left cell of the range where you want the consolidated data to appear. Make sure enough empty cells are available to the right of

and below the active cell, because Excel populates the rows and columns based on the size of the source data.

3. Click the Consolidate button (see Figure 5.11) in the Data Tools group on the Data tab to display the Consolidate dialog box.
4. By default, the *Sum* option displays in the *Function* option box. To change the function, click the *Function* option box arrow and then click an option at the drop-down list (see Figure 5.12).
5. Type the range reference for the first unit of source data in the *Reference* text box, or click the Collapse Dialog button, navigate to the range, and then select the range. If the range is located in another workbook, use the Browse button to navigate to the workbook.
6. Click the Add button at the Consolidate dialog box and then repeat Step 5 for each unit of data to be summarized.
7. Click the *Top row* or *Left column* check box in the *Use labels in* section to insert a check mark if you want to use labels from the source ranges in the master worksheet.
8. Click in the *Create links to source data* check box to insert a check mark if you want Excel to update the data in the master worksheet automatically when the source data changes.
9. Click the OK button.

— When data is consolidated, the formatting from the source worksheet does not transfer and the data on the master worksheet will display as unformatted.

▶ **Know More** methods for using the Consolidate feature to summarize data

- Open the master worksheet, click in the upper left cell of the range where you want the consolidated data to appear, and then type a formula that uses external references.
- For example, to consolidate data from the range B6:B7 in the Budget worksheet, the range F6:F7 in the Training worksheet, and the range B9:B10 in the Sales worksheet, type *=SUM(Budget!B6:B7, Training!F6:F7,Sales! B9:B10)*.

Figure 5.11 Consolidate Button

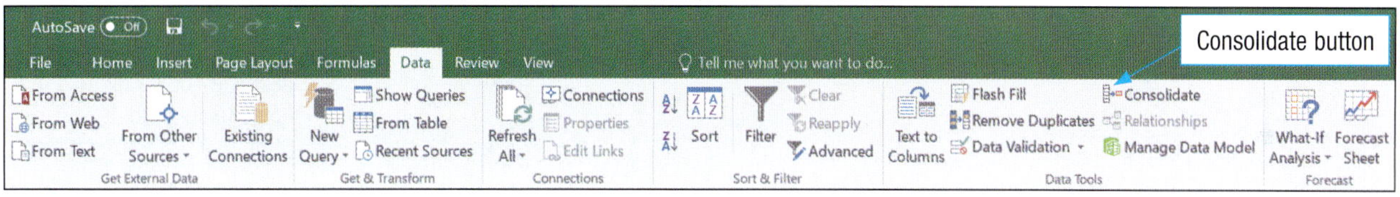

On the Job

Task 5.10 Using the Consolidate Feature to Summarize Data

Jeremy asks you to summarize the quarterly sales data in a single worksheet so he can easily compare quarterly sales. Use the Consolidate feature to summarize the data in a new worksheet positioned after the 4th Qtr Sales worksheet in the 5-WareBot-Sales workbook. You can consolidate the data by position because it is in the same range in each quarterly sales worksheet.

1. With the 5-WareBot-Sales workbook open, click the 4th Qtr Sales sheet tab.

   The 4th Qtr Sales worksheet is active.

2. Click the New sheet button.

   Sheet1 appears to the right of the 4th Qtr Sales worksheet and is active. Cell A1 is active.

3. Double-click the Sheet1 sheet tab, type Summary, and then press the Enter key.

   The sheet tab is renamed *Summary*.

4. Click the Data tab and then click the Consolidate button in the Data Tools group.

   A dialog box displays.

5. Click the Collapse Dialog button (see Figure 5.12).

   The dialog box collapses so that only the *Reference* text box displays.

6. Click the 1st Qtr Sales sheet tab.

   The 1st Qtr Sales worksheet is active, and the reference *'1st Qtr Sales'!* displays in the *Reference* text box.

7. Select the range E4:E11.

   The reference *'1st Qtr Sales'!$E$4:$E$11* displays in the *Reference* text box (see Figure 5.13).

Reminder
You can drag the dialog box Title bar, if necessary, to make worksheet data visible.

Figure 5.12 Consolidate Dialog Box

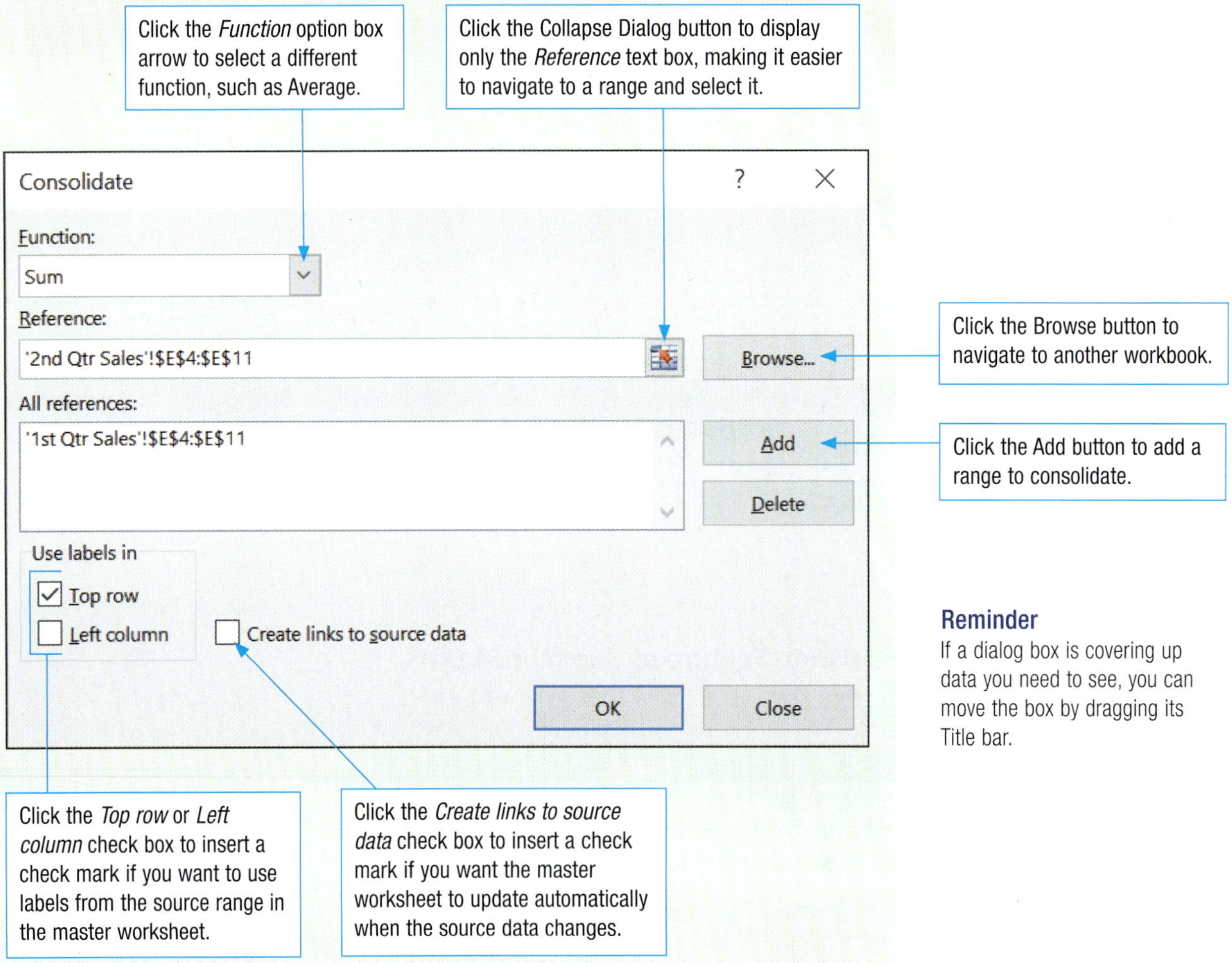

Reminder
If a dialog box is covering up data you need to see, you can move the box by dragging its Title bar.

Figure 5.13 Collapsed Consolidate Dialog Box

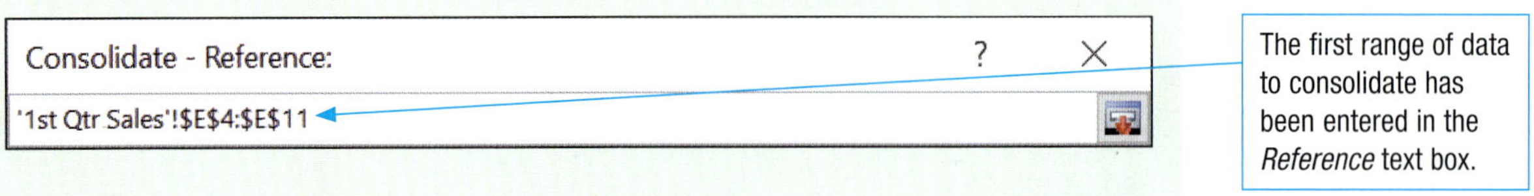

8. Press the Enter key.

   The dialog box expands.

9. Click the Add button.

   The reference *'1st Qtr Sales'!$E$4:$E$11* appears in both the *Reference* and *All references* text boxes.

10. Click the 2nd Qtr Sales sheet tab.

    The 2nd Qtr Sales worksheet is active and a marquee automatically appears around the range E4:E11—the same range you selected in the 1st Qtr Sales worksheet. The reference *'2nd Qtr Sales'!$E$4:$E$11* appears in the *Reference* text box.

11. Click the Add button.

    The reference *'2nd Qtr Sales'!$E$4:$E$11* appears in both the *Reference* and *All references* text boxes.

12. Click the 3rd Qtr Sales sheet tab.

    The 3rd Qtr Sales worksheet is active and a marquee automatically appears around the range E4:E11. The reference *'3rd Qtr Sales'!$E$4:$E$11* appears in the *Reference* text box.

13. Click the Add button.

    The reference *'3rd Qtr Sales'!$E$4:$E$11* appears in both the *Reference* and *All references* text boxes.

14. Click the 4th Qtr Sales sheet tab.

    The 4th Qtr Sales worksheet is active and a marquee automatically appears around the range E4:E11. The reference *'4th Qtr Sales'!$E$4:$E$11* appears in the *Reference* text box.

15. Click the Add button.

    The reference *'4th Qtr Sales'!$E$4:$E$11* appears in both the *Reference* and *All references* text boxes.

16. Click the *Top row* check box in the *Use labels in* section, if necessary, to insert a check mark.
17. Click the OK button.

    The consolidated data displays in the Summary worksheet with the labels from the source data in the top row.

18. AutoFit columns A through D.
19. Click the Save button on the Quick Access Toolbar.
20. If printed work is required by your instructor, print the workbook.

Model Answer

5.11 Using Paste Options

MOS 2.1.3

Tutorial

Using Paste Options

In Chapter 1, you learned that if similar cell or range contents need to be entered in a different location, you can save time by copying and pasting the contents. By default, the Paste command pastes the copied cell contents and its attributes, including formatting and formulas. You can use Paste options to change the attributes in the pasted results. Access those options at the Paste button drop-down gallery, the Paste Options button pop-up gallery, or the Paste Special dialog box.

▸ Know This about using the Paste button

— To change the attributes before a result is pasted, click the Paste button arrow in the Clipboard group on the Home tab and then click an option at the drop-down gallery (see Figure 5.14).

▸ Know This about using the Paste Options button

— To change the attributes after a result is pasted, click the Paste Options button and then click an option at the pop-up gallery (see Figure 5.15).

— The Paste Options button displays below the lower right corner of the cell at the new location after you click the Paste button and the contents are pasted.

▸ Know This about the Paste options

— Table 5.2 lists the options that appear in the Paste button drop-down gallery and the Paste Option pop-up gallery, and describes the pasted result for each option. Note that the options are similar in both galleries.

— The label for each option in the galleries displays in a ScreenTip.

— The galleries include a live preview of how the contents will display for each option.

Figure 5.14 Paste Button Drop-Down Gallery

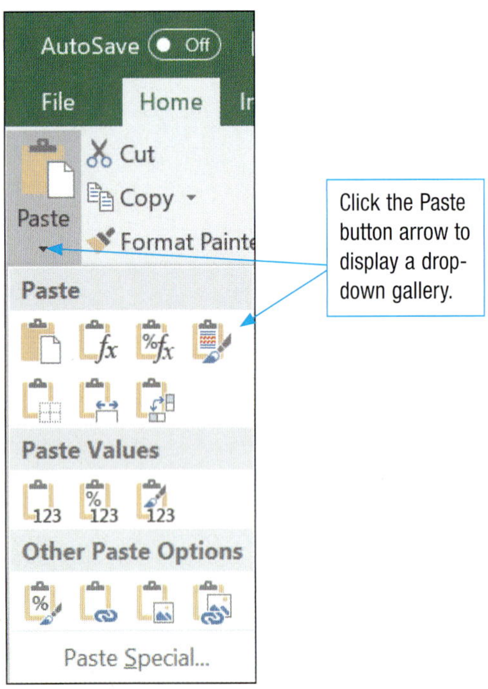

Figure 5.15 Paste Options Button Pop-Up Gallery

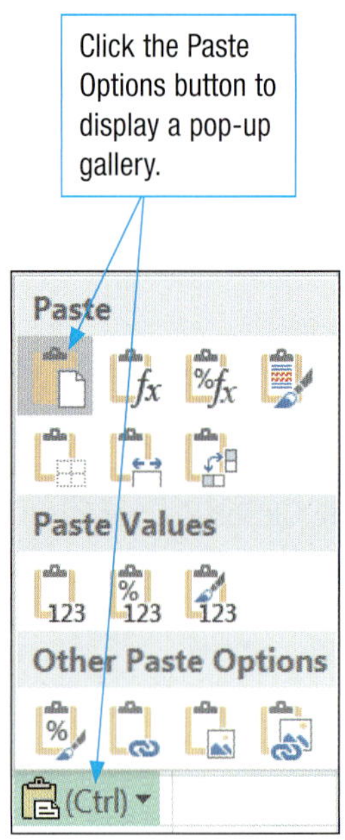

Table 5.2 Paste Options

Image	ScreenTip Label	Pasted Result
Paste **Section**		
	Paste	All cell contents and formatting, including linked data
	Formulas	Only formulas
	Formulas & Number Formatting	Only formulas and number formatting
	Keep Source Formatting	All cell contents and formatting
	No Borders	All cell contents and formatting except cell borders
	Keep Source Column Widths	Only column widths
	Transpose	Data from rows pasted in columns, and data from columns pasted in rows
Paste Values **Section**		
	Values	Only the values displayed in the cells
	Values & Number Formatting	Only the values and the number formatting
	Values & Source Formatting	Only the values and the number color and font size formatting
Other Paste Options **Section**		
	Formatting	All cell formatting, including number and source formatting
	Paste Link	A link from the pasted data to the original data
	Picture	A copy of the image
	Linked Picture	A copy of the image with a link to the original cell

▶ **Know This** about using the Paste Special dialog box

— The Paste button drop-down gallery includes the *Paste Special* option (see Figure 5.14 on page 212), which displays the Paste Special dialog box (see Figure 5.16).

— Use options at the Paste Special dialog box to paste specific attributes of the source data, perform a mathematical operation in the destination range based on values in the source range, and carry out a more complex paste sequence.

▶ **Know More** methods for opening the Paste Special dialog box

– Press Ctrl + Alt + V.

Figure 5.16 Paste Special Dialog Box

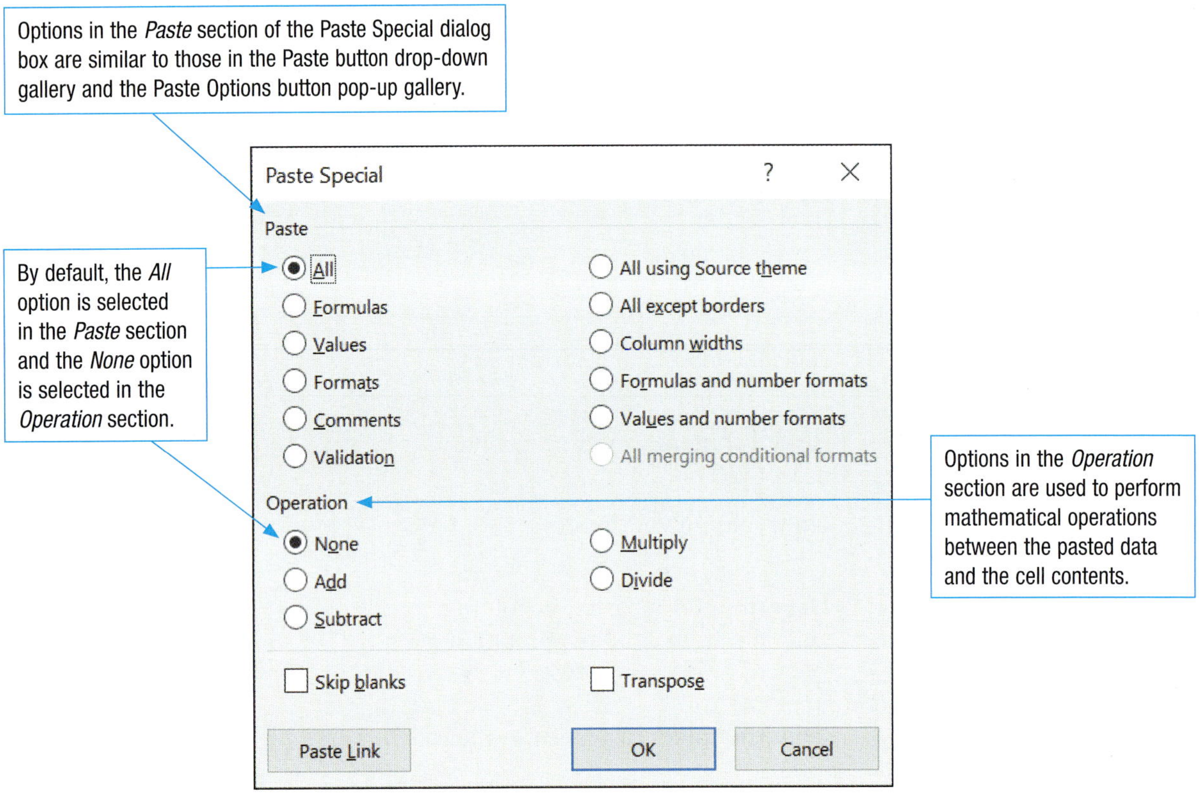

On the Job

Task 5.11 Using Paste Options

Jeremy would like you to add the row labels from the quarterly sales worksheets to the Summary worksheet so he can analyze the consolidated data by region. In addition, he has realized that all the December sales figures in the 4th Qtr Sales worksheet are short by $10,000. Copy the row labels from the 4th Qtr Sales sheet tab and then use the Paste Options button to adjust the column width in the pasted result to match the column width in the source. Use options at the Paste Special dialog box to quickly add $10,000 to each sales figure for December in the 4th Qtr Sales worksheet.

1. With the 5-WareBot-Sales workbook open and the Summary worksheet active, right-click the column A column heading and then click the *Insert* option.
   A column is inserted to the left of column A.
2. Click the 4th Qtr Sales sheet tab.
3. Select the range A4:A11.
4. Click the Copy button in the Clipboard group on the Home tab.
5. Click the Summary sheet tab.
6. Click in cell A1 and then click the Paste button.
   The copied data is pasted in cells A1:A8 and the Paste Options button displays.
7. Click the Paste Options button.
   The Paste Options button pop-up gallery displays.

8. Click the *Keep Source Column Widths* option (second column, second row in the *Paste* section).

   The column width adjusts to the source column width.

9. Click the 4th Qtr Sales sheet tab.
10. Click in cell F5, type 10000, and then press Ctrl + Enter.

    The value *$10,000* displays in cell F5.

11. Click the Copy button.

    A marquee appears around cell F5.

12. Select the range D5:D10.
13. Click the Paste button arrow.

    A drop-down list displays.

14. Click the *Paste Special* option.

    A dialog box displays.

15. Click the *Add* option in the *Operation* section and then click the OK button.

    The copied value, $10,000, is added to each value in the selected range.

16. Click in cell F5.
17. Click the Clear button in the Editing group.

    A drop-down list displays.

18. Click the *Clear All* option.

    The value and formatting in cell F5 are deleted.

19. Click the Save button on the Quick Access Toolbar.
20. If printed work is required by your instructor, print the workbook.
21. Click the File tab.
22. Click the *Close* option.

    The workbook closes in the Excel window.

Model Answer

5.12 Splitting Windows and Managing Split Windows

MOS 1.4.5

Tutorial

Splitting Windows and Managing Split Windows

Comparing data in a large worksheet may be difficult because not all the cells display at one time in the worksheet area. You can compare data at different locations in the worksheet by using a **split window**. Start by splitting the Excel window into two or four resizable sections, each called a **pane**. You can then scroll the worksheet in each pane to display the parts you want to compare. The panes in a split window are separated by movable gray lines, each called a **split line**. You can resize a pane by moving one or more of its split lines.

▸ Know This about splitting a window

— To split a worksheet window into four panes, click in the cell below and to the right of where you want the panes to intersect and then click the Split button in the Window group on the View tab (see Figure 5.17 on page 217).

— To split the window into two vertical panes, click in row 1 to the right of where you want to place the split line and then click the Split button.

- To split the window into two horizontal panes, click in column A below the row where you want to place the split line and then click the Split button.
- To deactivate a split, click the Split button.

▸ **Know This** about scrolling in a split window

- Each pane in a split window has its own set of vertical and horizontal scroll bars (see Figure 5.17).
- Use the scroll bars to shift different parts of the worksheet into the pane, where you can view them.

▸ **Know This** about displaying the active cell

- When you first split a window, the active cell displays in only one pane.
- As you scroll, the active cell may become visible in additional panes (see Figure 5.17).
- To avoid displaying the active cell in a pane, you can freeze the pane (refer to Section 5.13).

▸ **Know This** about using split lines to resize panes

- To move a split line, hover the mouse pointer over the line until the pointer turns into a left-and-right-pointing arrow with a double line in the middle, click and hold down the left mouse button, drag the split line to the new location, and then release the mouse button.
- To move the horizontal and vertical split lines at the same time, hover the mouse pointer over the intersection of the split lines until the pointer turns into a four-headed arrow, click and hold down the left mouse button, drag the split lines to the new location, and then release the mouse button.

On the Job

Task 5.12 Splitting Windows and Managing Split Windows

In next month's presentation, Jeremy will highlight projected sales and growth in the Northeast and Northwest regions. Use the Split Panes feature to review the January and December sales projections for these regions, and note any similarities and differences to help Jeremy prepare for his presentation.

1. Open the data file **5-WareBot**, which you saved and closed at the end of Task 5.7.
2. Click the Yearly Projection sheet tab.

   The Yearly Projection worksheet is active.
3. Click in cell D6.

   Cell D6 is active.
4. Click the View tab and then click the Split button in the Window group (see Figure 5.17).

   The window splits into four panes.

Figure 5.17 Window Split into Four Panes

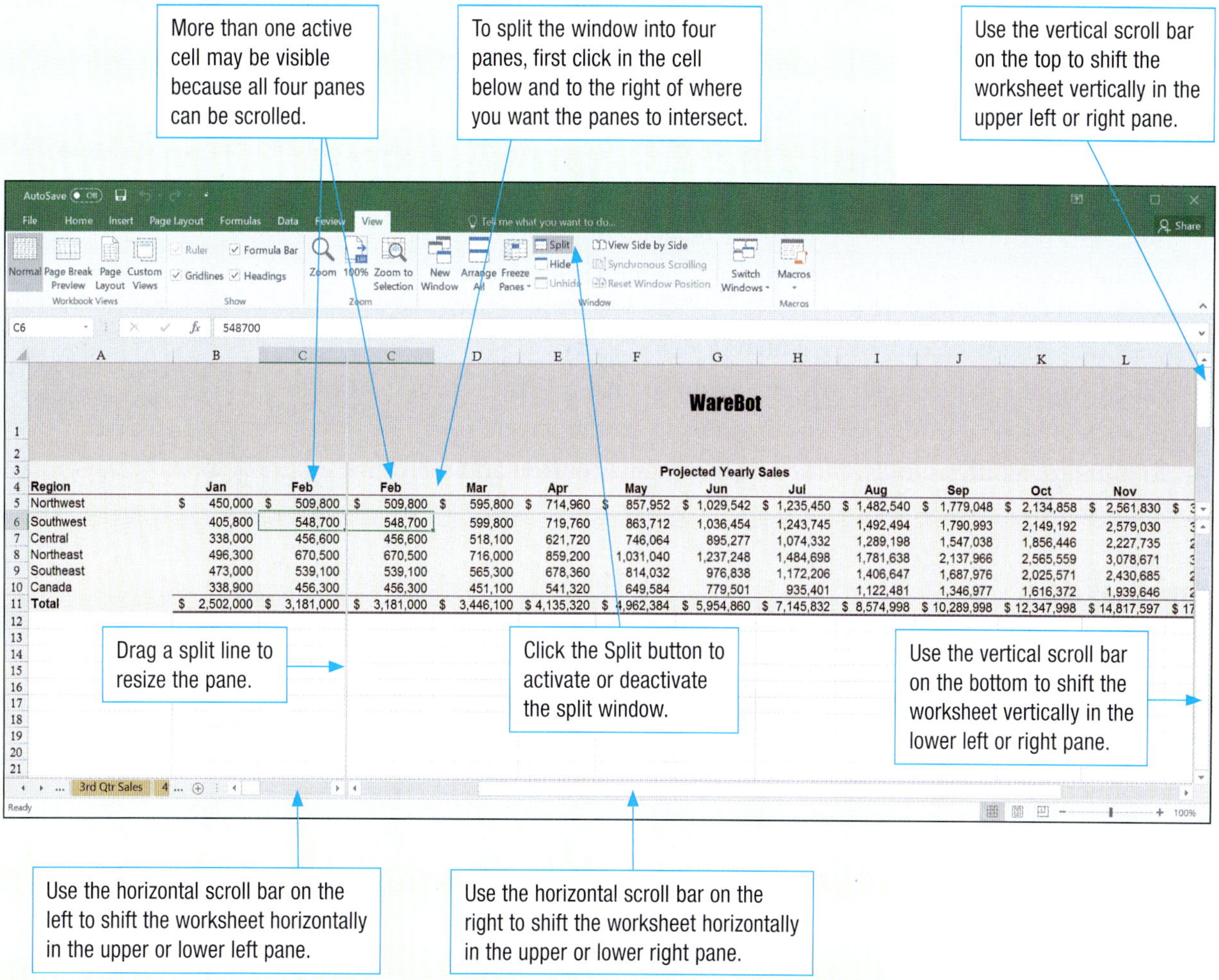

5. Scroll the worksheet in the lower right pane horizontally until column M is directly to the right of column C.
6. Drag the vertical split line one column to the left so it is positioned to the right of column B.
7. Scroll the worksheet in the lower right pane vertically until row 8 is directly below row 5.
8. Click the Split button in the Window group.

   The split window is deactivated.

9. Click the Save button on the Quick Access Toolbar.

5.13 Freezing and Unfreezing Panes

When you scroll a large worksheet, row and column labels or titles may not be visible in the current window, making it difficult to analyze the data. The **Freeze Panes** feature keeps designated rows or columns visible while you move around in the worksheet. In comparison, the Split Windows feature, discussed in Section 5.12, allows you to scroll freely through the worksheet in

Tutorial

Freezing and Unfreezing Panes

each separate pane. The Freeze Panes feature is useful when you need to keep column or row headings visible to help interpret data and guide data entry in a large worksheet. The Split Windows feature is useful when comparing various areas of a large worksheet.

▸ **Know This** about freezing and unfreezing panes

— To freeze every row above the active cell and every column to the left of the active cell, click the Freeze Panes button in the Window group on the View tab and then click the *Freeze Panes* option.

— A solid line above a row or to the left of a column indicates which cells are frozen (see Figure 5.18).

— Cells that are frozen cannot be edited or made active.

— When scrolling horizontally, frozen columns remain on the screen.

— When scrolling vertically, frozen rows remain on the screen.

— To unfreeze all frozen cells, click the Freeze Panes button and then click the *Unfreeze Panes* option.

▸ Know More options for freezing panes

- To freeze just the top row, click the Freeze Panes button in the Windows group on the View tab and then click the *Freeze Top Row* option.
- To freeze just the first column, click the *Freeze First Column* option.

On the Job

Task 5.13 Freezing and Unfreezing Panes

In next month's presentation, Jeremy will also highlight the yearly totals for each sales region. Use the Freeze Panes feature to review the yearly totals for all regions, noting which regions were the highest and lowest performers.

1. With the 5-WareBot workbook open and the Yearly Projection worksheet active, click in cell B5.
2. Click the Freeze Panes button in the Window group on the View tab.
3. Click the *Freeze Panes* option.

   A solid line appears above row 5 and another solid line appears to the left of column B. These lines indicate that the cells above row 5 and to the left of column B will always remain visible on the screen (see Figure 5.18).
4. Click the right scroll arrow on the horizontal scroll bar.

   The display shifts to show column C to the right of the solid line. Column A remains visible to the left of the solid line. Column B is not visible.
5. Continue to scroll to the right until column N is directly to the right of column A.
6. Click the Freeze Panes button.
7. Click the *UnFreeze Panes* option.

   The solid lines disappear, indicating that the panes are no longer frozen.
8. Click the Save button on the Quick Access Toolbar.

Figure 5.18 Freeze Panes

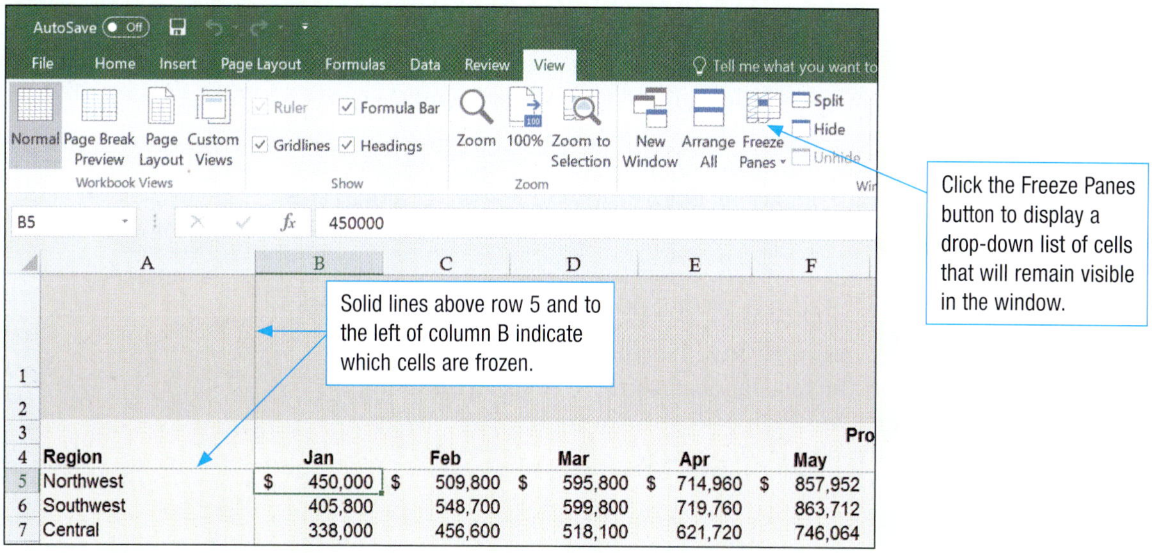

5.14 Managing Versions of a Workbook

MOS Expert 1.2.5

Tutorial

Using the AutoRecover Feature

The AutoRecover feature in Excel saves versions of your work at a specified time interval. This feature allows you to recover an earlier version of a workbook if Excel closes unexpectedly (such as during a power outage) or you accidentally close the workbook without saving changes. AutoRecover will also save your workspace (if possible), opening your worksheet in the same view with the same active cell. By default, the AutoRecover feature is turned on and will automatically save AutoRecover information every 10 minutes. Also by default, the option *Keep the last autosaved version if I close without saving* is turned on.

▸ Know This about recovering an AutoSaved workbook

— If Excel unexpectedly closes and you have not saved your most recent changes, the AutoSave feature opens the Document Recovery task pane if Excel automatically restarts (see Figure 5.19).

— If Excel does not automatically restart, a message will display the next time you start Excel (see Figure 5.20). Click the *Show Recovered Files* option to open the Document Recovery task pane.

Figure 5.19 Document Recovery Task Pane

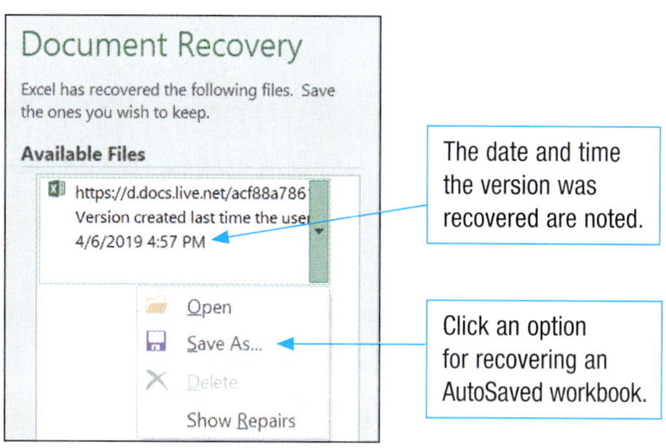

▸ Know This about recovering an unsaved workbook

— To recover an unsaved workbook, open Excel, click the File tab, click the *Open* option in the left panel if necessary, click the *Recent* option in the middle panel if necessary, click the Recover Unsaved Workbooks button in the right panel (scroll down as needed to find this button), and then click the workbook name at the Open dialog box (see Figure 5.21).

— By default, unsaved files are saved at the file location C:/Users/*sname*/AppData/Local/Microsoft/Office/UnsavedFiles (where *sname* is the name of your user folder).

Reminder

Do not rely on the AutoRecover feature to save your work. Saving regularly to minimize data loss and protect against unforeseen events is the best practice.

▸ Know This about accessing a workbook that was never saved

— To access a workbook that was never saved, open Excel, click the File tab, click the *Info* option in the left panel, click the Manage Workbook button in the middle panel, and then click the *Recover Unsaved Workbooks* option at the drop-down list (see Figure 5.22).

Figure 5.20 Show Recovered Files

Figure 5.21 Recover Unsaved Workbooks

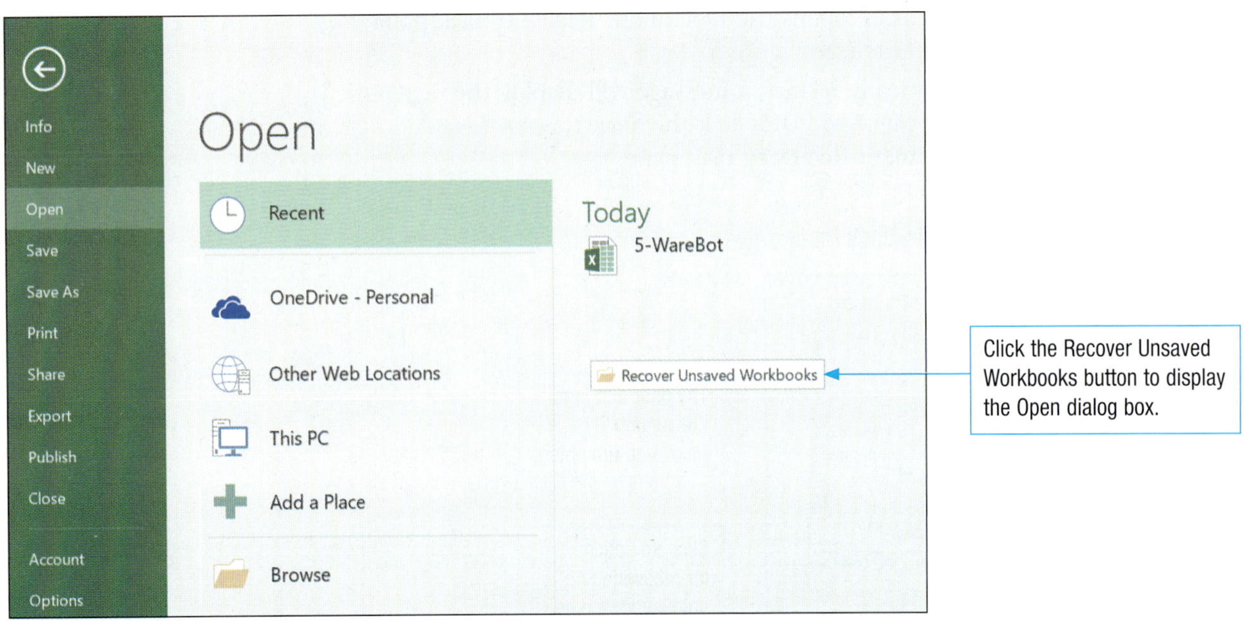

▶ Know This about accessing an earlier version of a workbook

— To open an earlier version of a workbook, open Excel, click the File tab, click the *Info* option in the left panel, and then click the version in the middle panel. If the version is not listed, click the Manage Workbook button and then click the *Recover Unsaved Workbooks* option (see Figure 5.22).

— When you open an earlier version of a workbook, click the Restore button to overwrite any previously saved versions.

▶ Know This about customizing the AutoRecover feature

— To change the AutoRecover time interval, open Excel, click the File tab, click the *Options* option in the left panel, click the *Save* option at the Excel Options dialog box, and then enter a value in the *Save AutoRecover information every...minutes* measurement box (see Figure 5.23).

— To change the AutoRecover file location, open Excel, click the File tab, click the *Options* option in the left panel, click the *Save* option at the Excel Options dialog box, and then type the new path in the *AutoRecover file location* text box.

▶ Know More about accessing an earlier version of a workbook

– To open an earlier version of a workbook saved in OneDrive or SharePoint, open the current version of the workbook from you OneDrive or SharePoint account, click the Activity button (looks like a clock) at the far right on the ribbon, and then click the earlier version in the list at the Activity task pane. ***Note:*** *The Activity button displays on the ribbon only when the workbook is saved in OneDrive or SharePoint.*

Figure 5.22 Manage Workbook Button

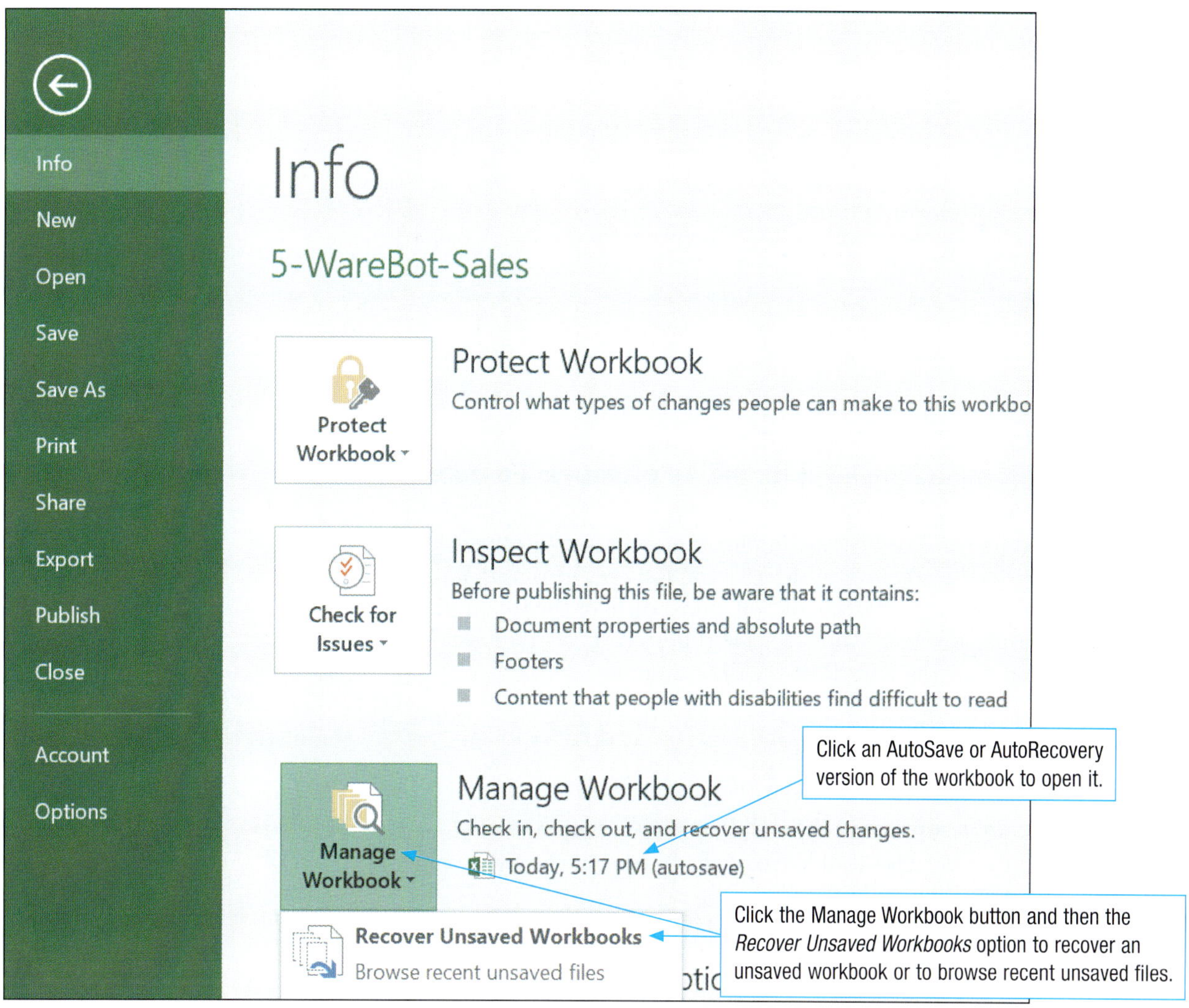

Figure 5.23 Excel Options Dialog Box

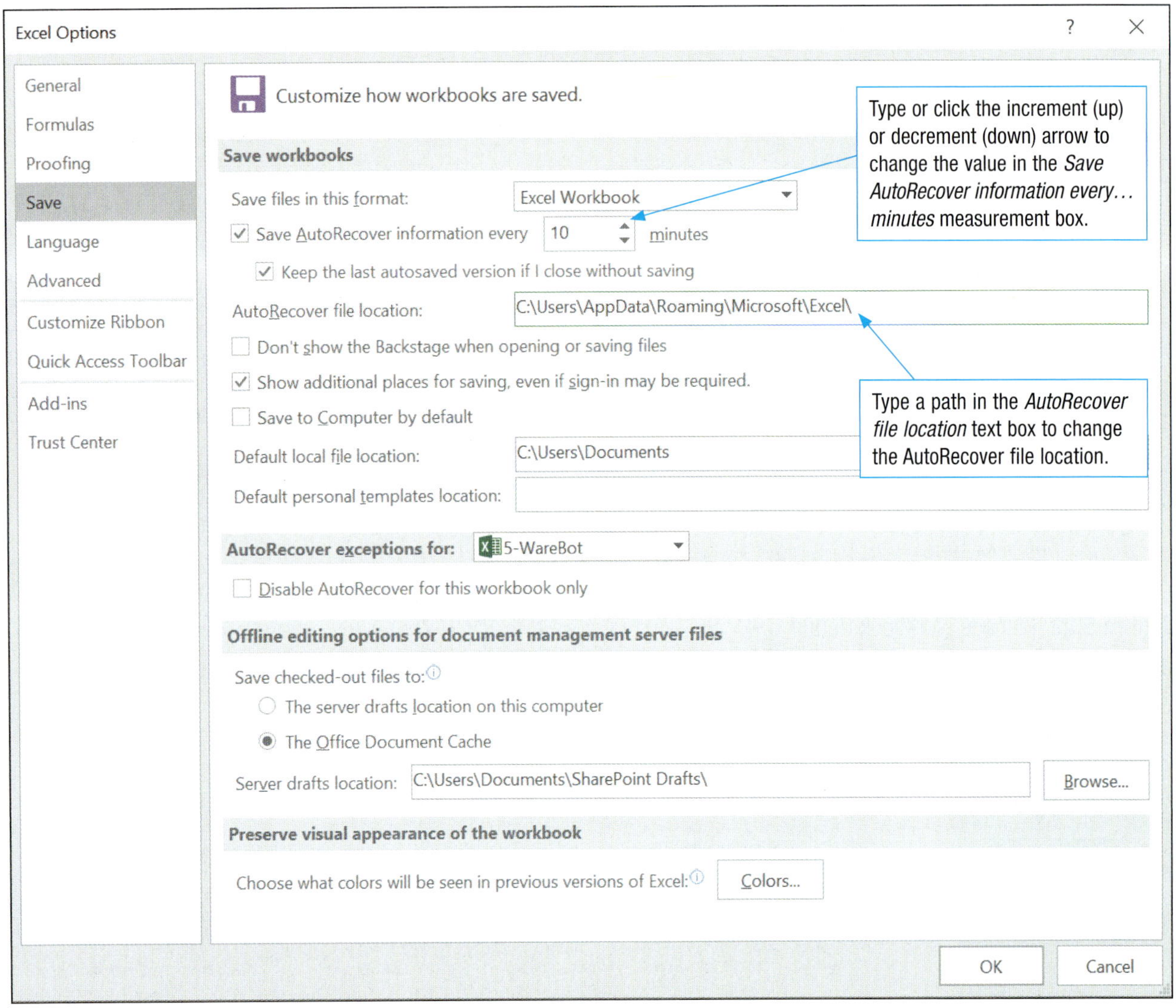

On the Job

Task 5.14 Becoming Familiar with the AutoRecover Feature

Jeremy would like you to become familiar with the AutoRecover feature in case you ever need to recover a file. Use the Recover Unsaved Workbooks button and the Manage Workbook button to display the Open dialog box and view any unsaved workbooks and then display the Excel Options dialog box and view the AutoRecover time interval.

1. With the 5-WareBot workbook open and the Yearly Projection worksheet active, click the File tab.
2. Click the *Open* option in the left panel, if necessary.
3. Click the *Recent* option in the middle panel, if necessary.
4. Click the Recover Unsaved Workbooks button in the right panel.

   The Open dialog box displays.

5. View any unsaved workbooks and then click the Cancel button.
   Note: *You may not have any unsaved files.*

   The Open dialog box disappears.
6. Click the File tab.
7. Click the *Info* option in the left panel, if necessary.
8. Click the Manage Workbook button in the middle panel.

   A drop-down list displays.
9. Click the *Recover Unsaved Workbooks* option.

   The Open dialog box displays.
10. View any unsaved workbooks and then click the Cancel button.

    The Open dialog box disappears.
11. Click the File tab.
12. Click the *Options* option in the left panel.

    The Excel Options dialog box displays.
13. Click the *Save* option in the left panel.
14. View the value in the *Save AutoRecover information every…minutes* measurement box (see Figure 5.23 on page 222).
15. Click the Cancel button.

    The Excel Options dialog box disappears.
16. Click the Save button on the Quick Access Toolbar.
17. Click the File tab.
18. Click the *Close* option.

5.15 Saving a Workbook as a Custom Template and Creating a New Workbook Based on a Template

MOS Expert 1.1.1

Tutorial

Saving a Workbook as a Template

In Excel, a **template** is a predesigned workbook that can be used over and over again. A **custom template** is a workbook template that you create by entering the data, formulas, and formatting that stay the same each time you use it. For example, all a company's invoices usually contain the same data (invoice number, quantity, service, unit price, total). Instead of adding labels, formulas, and formatting for every new invoice, a more efficient approach is to create a custom template that contains the unchanging data and formatting, and then use the template to create a new invoice each time one is needed.

▸ **Know This** about creating a workbook that will be used as a template

— To create a workbook that will be used as a template, enter the data, formulas, and formatting that will not change.

— Leave cells that will contain variable information empty, but apply any formatting that will not vary.

▸ **Know This** about saving a workbook as a custom template

— To save a workbook as a template, click the File tab, click the *Save As* option in the left panel, click the storage drive or *Browse* option in the middle panel, navigate to the folder location in the right panel or the

Save As dialog box, type the file name in the *File name* text box, click the *Save as type* option box arrow, click the *Excel Template (*.xltx)* option at the drop-down list, and then click the Save button.

— By default, custom templates are saved in the Custom Office Templates folder, which is located in your Documents folder (C:\Users\[User-Name]\Documents\Custom Office Templates).

— To change the default location for custom templates, click the File tab, click the *Options* option, click the *Save* option, and then type a location in the *Default personal templates location* box.

▸ **Know This** about creating a new workbook based on a custom template

— To open a custom template you have saved, open Excel, click the File tab, click the *New* option in the left panel, click the PERSONAL link, and then click the name of the template.

— A new workbook based on a custom template opens with the name of the template followed by a number indicating the version—for example, *Invoice1*. Save the workbook with a new descriptive name—such as *Invoice-2019-1479*.

On the Job

Task 5.15a Saving a Workbook as a Custom Template

Jeremy has created a workbook that can be used by all WareBot employees to submit their travel expenses. He would like you to save the workbook as a custom template in the default storage location.

1. Open the data file **5-WareBot-Travel**.
2. Click the File tab.
3. Click the *Save As* option.

   The Save As backstage area displays.
4. Click the *Browse* option.

   The Save As dialog box displays and the text *5-WareBot-Travel* appears in the *File name* box.
5. Click the *Save as type* option box arrow.
6. Click the *Excel Template (*.xltx)* option.
7. Click the Save button.
8. Click the File tab.
9. Click the *Close* option.

Model Answer

On the Job

Task 5.15b Creating a New Workbook Based on a Saved Template

Jeremy asks you to create a sample expense statement for employees to use as a model. Create a new workbook based on the custom template you saved in Task 5.15a and then fill in sample data.

1. Open Excel and then click the File tab.
2. Click the *New* option in the left panel.

   The New backstage area displays.

3. Click the PERSONAL link.
   Saved templates display.
4. Click the template *5-WareBot-Travel*.
   A workbook named *5-WareBot-Travel1* opens.
5. Click in cell B4, type Yasmin Mathis, and then press the Enter key.
6. Type 3405 and then press the Enter key.
7. Type March 12, 2019 and then press the Enter key.
8. Type Dallas and then press the Enter key.
9. Type Mar 8-10, 2019 and then press the Enter key.
10. Type 389 and then press the Enter key.
11. Type 350 and then press the Enter key.
12. Click the Save button on the Quick Access Toolbar.
    The Save As backstage area displays.
13. Click the storage medium for your data files.
    For example, if you have stored your data files in your OneDrive account, click *OneDrive—Personal*.
14. Navigate to your AE5 folder.
    The Save As dialog box displays. *5-WareBot-Travel1* appears in the file name box and is highlighted.
15. Type 5-WareBot-Travel-Sample and then click the Save button.
    The workbook name *5-WareBot-Travel-Sample* displays in the Title bar.
16. If printed work is required by your instructor, print the workbook.
17. Click the File tab.
18. Click the *Close* option.

Model Answer

5.16 Modifying Existing Custom Templates

An existing custom template can be updated by opening the template, making changes, and then saving the template.

Tutorial

Modifying an Existing Template

▸ **Know This** about modifying an existing custom template

— To modify an existing custom template, open Excel, click the File tab, click the *Open* option, click the *This PC* option, click the Browse button, navigate to the Custom Office Templates folder at the Open dialog box, click the name of the template, click the Open button, make the changes, click the Save button on the Quick Access Toolbar, and then close the template.

On the Job

Task 5.16 Modifying an Existing Custom Template

Jeremy would like you to modify the custom travel expenses template to include a row for entering taxi and Uber expenses.

1. With Excel open but no workbooks open, click the File tab.
2. Click the *Open* option in the left panel, if necessary.
   The Open backstage area displays.
3. Double-click the *This PC* option in the middle panel.
   The Open dialog box displays.
4. Navigate to the Custom Office Templates folder and then open the folder.
5. Click the template *5-WareBot-Travel*.
6. Click the Open button.
   The 5-WareBot-Travel template opens.
7. Right-click row heading 14.
8. Click the *Insert* option.
9. Click in cell A14, type Taxi/Uber, and then press the Tab key.
10. Click in cell B13 and then drag the fill handle from cell B13 down into cell B14.
11. Click the Save button on the Quick Access Toolbar.
12. If printed work is required by your instructor, print the template.
13. Click the File tab.
14. Click the *Close* option.

Model Answer

Reminder
The Custom Office Templates folder is located in your Documents folder (C:\Users\[UserName]\Documents\Custom Office Templates).

5.17 Using Preformatted Templates

Excel has many preformatted templates (see Figure 5.24). It may be quicker to download a preformatted template and modify it as necessary than to create your own custom template.

Tutorial
Using a Preformatted Template

Figure 5.24 Preformatted Templates

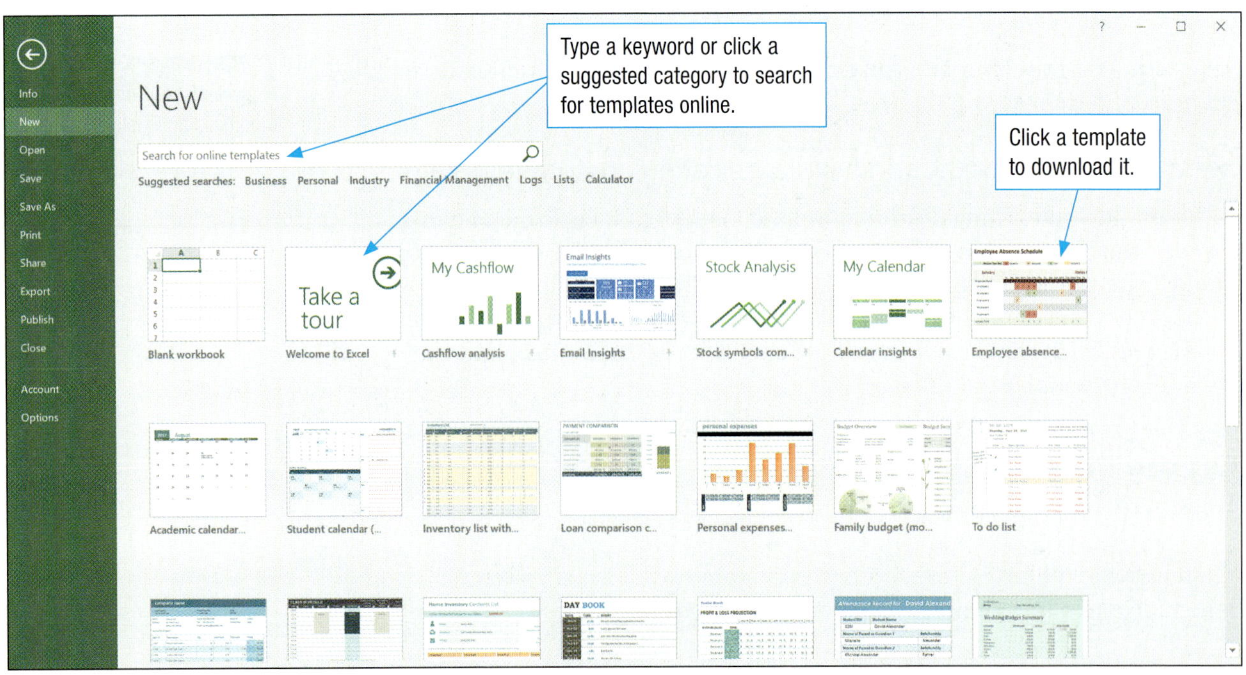

▶ **Know This** about creating a workbook based on a preformatted template

— To create a new workbook based on a preformatted template, click the File tab, click the *New* option, click a preformatted template, and then click the Create button, if necessary.

— Search for additional templates online by typing a keyword in the *Search for online templates* box or by clicking a template category, such as *Business* or *Industry*.

On the Job

Task 5.17 Using a Preformatted Template

Jeremy asks you to create a workbook that will help track the progress of the WareBot projects he is managing. Find a preformatted template, create a workbook based on the template, and add sample data before you show him the workbook.

1. Click the File tab.
2. Click the *New* option in the left panel.

   The New backstage area displays (see Figure 5.24 on page 226).
3. Scroll the list of FEATURED templates and then click the template *Project tracker*.

   A dialog box displays.
4. Click the Create button.

   A workbook named *Project tracker1* opens.
5. Click the Setup sheet tab.
6. Click in cell B5, type Marketing, and then press the Tab key.
7. Type Jeremy Ronlin and then press Ctrl + Enter.
8. Click the Project Tracker sheet tab.
9. Click in cell B5, type Ad Campaign, and then press the Tab key.
10. In cell C5, click the arrow and then click the *Marketing* option.
11. Click in cell D5, click the arrow, and then click the *Jeremy Ronlin* option.
12. Click the Save button on the Quick Access Toolbar.

    The Save As backstage area displays.
13. Click the storage medium for your data files.

    For example, if you have stored your data files in your OneDrive account, click *OneDrive—Personal*.
14. Navigate to your AE5 folder.

    The Save As dialog box displays. *Project tracker1* appears in the *File name* box and is highlighted.
15. Type 5-WareBot-ProjectTracker and then click the Save button.

    The workbook name *5-WareBot-ProjectTracker* displays in the Title bar.
16. If printed work is required by your instructor, print the template.
17. Click the File tab.
18. Click the *Close* option.

Model Answer

Chapter Summary

5.1 ▶ By default, all the worksheets in a workbook appear in the same Excel window. The active worksheet is displayed in the window, while the rest of the worksheets appear as sheet tabs.

▶ More than one worksheet can be viewed at a time by opening multiple versions of the workbook in separate windows, arranging all the windows so they are visible, resizing the windows for optimal viewing, and then switching between the open windows. Two open windows can be viewed side by side, making it easy to compare data in two worksheets.

5.2 ▶ By default, a new worksheet is added to the right of any existing worksheets in a workbook, but this may not be the logical location for a new worksheet. Rearranging the sheet tabs to follow a logical order, such as alphabetical or sequential, can make it easier to find data in a large workbook.

5.3 ▶ Applying colors to sheet tabs allows visually differentiating between worksheets and groups of worksheets. Color can also be used to provide quick visual clues as to the statuses of projects.

5.4 ▶ Temporarily hiding a worksheet in a workbook might be advised if not all the data should be shared—say, during a meeting or presentation. When a worksheet is hidden, the data it contains is hidden from view but not deleted.

5.5 ▶ When multiple worksheets have a similar data structure, tasks can be performed on them at the same time by first grouping them. A worksheet group is a set of multiple worksheets that are all selected together. Any changes made in one worksheet in the group are also made in all the other worksheets in the group.

5.6 ▶ Copying a worksheet can save time if you need to create multiple worksheets with similar data. A copied worksheet displays all the same data as the original worksheet; the data can be edited as necessary and then easily compared with the data in the related worksheets. A worksheet that is copied or moved within a workbook keeps the same formatting at its new location.

5.7 ▶ Worksheets can also be copied from one workbook to another. The data copies exactly from the source workbook to the destination workbook, and it can be edited as necessary. In addition, worksheets can be moved to another workbook. More than one worksheet can be copied or moved at a time by first grouping the worksheets. A worksheet that is copied or moved to another workbook uses the theme formatting that is applied to the destination workbook.

5.8 ▶ Formatting can be applied simultaneously to multiple worksheets in a workbook by first grouping the worksheets and then applying the formatting to cells in one of the grouped worksheets. This feature saves time and helps ensure that formatting is consistent throughout a workbook.

5.9 ▶ When entering formulas, it may be necessary to include references to cells or ranges in another worksheet or workbook. This can be done by creating an external reference, which is also called a *link*. Using an external reference eliminates the need to enter or copy existing data and to update multiple worksheets. If the value in the referenced cell or range changes, the value returned by the external reference automatically updates.

5.10 ▶ The Consolidate feature is used to summarize source data from other worksheets in a master worksheet. The source data can be located in the same workbook as the master worksheet or in a separate workbook. Data can be consolidated by position or by category.

5.11 ▶ By default, the Paste command pastes the copied cell contents and its attributes, including formatting and formulas. A variety of Paste options can be used to change the attributes in the pasted results.

5.12 ▶ The Split Windows feature allows comparing data at different locations in a large worksheet by splitting the window into two or four resizable sections. Each section is called a *pane*, and scrolling in each pane allows displaying the parts to be compared. The panes in a split window are separated by movable gray lines called *split lines*. A pane can be resized by moving one or more of its split lines.

5.13 ▶ The Freeze Panes feature keeps designated rows or columns visible while the user moves around in the worksheet. The Freeze Panes feature is useful when you need to keep column or row headings visible to help interpret data and guide data entry in a large worksheet.

5.14 ▶ The AutoRecover feature saves versions of a workbook at a specified time interval; the default is every 10 minutes. Using this feature allows recovering an earlier version of a workbook if Excel closes unexpectedly or the workbook is mistakenly closed without saving changes.

5.15 ▶ In Excel, a template is a predesigned workbook that can be used repeatedly. A custom template is a workbook template that is created by entering the data, formulas, and formatting that remain the same each time the workbook is used—for example, you might create a custom template for invoices.

5.16 ▶ An existing template can be updated by opening the template from the Custom Office Templates folder, making changes, and then saving the template.

5.17 ▶ Excel offers many preformatted templates. It may be quicker to download a preformatted template and modify it as necessary than to create a custom template.

Features Review

Feature	Ribbon Tab, Group	Button, Option	Keyboard Shortcut
access workbook that was never saved or earlier version of workbook	File, *Info*		
change cell attributes before pasting a result	Home, Clipboard		
change sheet tab color	Home, Cells	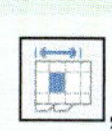, *Tab Color*	
compare two worksheets in same workbook side by side	View, Window	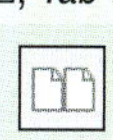	

continues...

Feature	Ribbon Tab, Group	Button, Option	Keyboard Shortcut
consolidate data from range	Data, Data Tools		
copy or move worksheet within workbook	Home, Cells	, *Move or Copy Sheet*	
copy worksheets to other workbook	Home, Cells	, *Move or Copy Sheet*	
customize AutoRecover feature	File, *Options*		
display the Paste Special dialog box	Home, Clipboard	Paste, *Paste Special*	Ctrl + Alt + V
freeze rows above and columns to left of active cell	View, Window	, *Freeze Panes*	
freeze first column	View, Window	, *Freeze First Column*	
freeze top row	View, Window	, *Freeze Top Row*	
hide or unhide worksheet	Home, Cells	, *Hide & Unhide*	
modify existing template	File, *Open*	*This PC*, Browse	
move worksheets to other workbook	Home, Cells or View, Window	, *Move or Copy Sheet* or , *Vertical*	
open new workbook based on template	File, *New*		
open new version of workbook in new window	View, Window		
open saved template	File, *New*	PERSONAL	
place workbooks side by side to share screen equally	View, Window		
recover unsaved workbook	File, *Open*	*Recent*, Recover Unsaved Workbooks	
restore window to full size			
scroll two worksheets simultaneously when viewing side by side	View, Window		
split window into panes or deactivate split	View, Window		
unfreeze frozen cells	View, Window	, *Unfreeze Panes*	
view different open window	View, Window		
view all open windows at same time	View, Window		

Recheck

Recheck your understanding of the concepts, features, and skills covered in this chapter by taking the Recheck quiz.

Workbook

Access the study tools, review exercises, assessments, and challenges for this chapter in the workbook available from this page in your ebook.

Working with Charts and Hyperlinks

Chapter 6

Chapter Goal

To create charts that best represent different types of data visually and to add hyperlinks that open other items, such as web pages.

Learning Objectives

6.1 Create charts

6.2 Choose and change a chart type and subtype

6.3 Resize and move charts

6.4 Add, modify, and remove chart elements and apply chart layouts

6.5 Apply chart styles and modify chart colors and formatting

6.6 Use Quick Analysis to create a chart

6.7 Add, modify, and filter chart data

6.8 Switch between rows and columns in source data, and change an axis scale

6.9 Use recommended charts

6.10 Use trendlines

6.11 Use a combination chart

6.12 Work with Chart Templates

6.13 Insert, modify, use, and remove hyperlinks

6.14 Print a chart

Precheck

Check your understanding of the concepts, features, and skills covered in this chapter by taking the Precheck quiz.

Data Files

Before beginning the chapter work, download the AE6 folder from this page in your ebook to your storage medium and then make AE6 the active folder.

Ebook Links

Access digital resources for this course from your ebook.

SNAP

If you are a SNAP user, go to your SNAP assignments page to complete the Precheck, Tutorials, and Recheck in this chapter.

Preview

On the Job

Scenario ProDiagnostics Medical Laboratories

Kaelan Rogers is the director of ProDiagnostics Medical Laboratories (PDML). PDML is a diagnostic laboratory with numerous testing centers located in southwestern Ontario, Canada. Doctors send their patients to a PDML center for blood work and other diagnostic testing. Kaelan is preparing a summary of the previous year's revenue at the five collection centers in the city of London. He will present the summary at a business development meeting next week, and he feels that providing a visual representation of the data will help the managers attending the meeting understand the trends and analyze the data. He asks you to create charts and then modify them.

Visual Reference: Formatted Charts and Hyperlinks

Figure 6.1 An Excel Worksheet with a Column Chart, a Pie Chart, and a Hyperlink

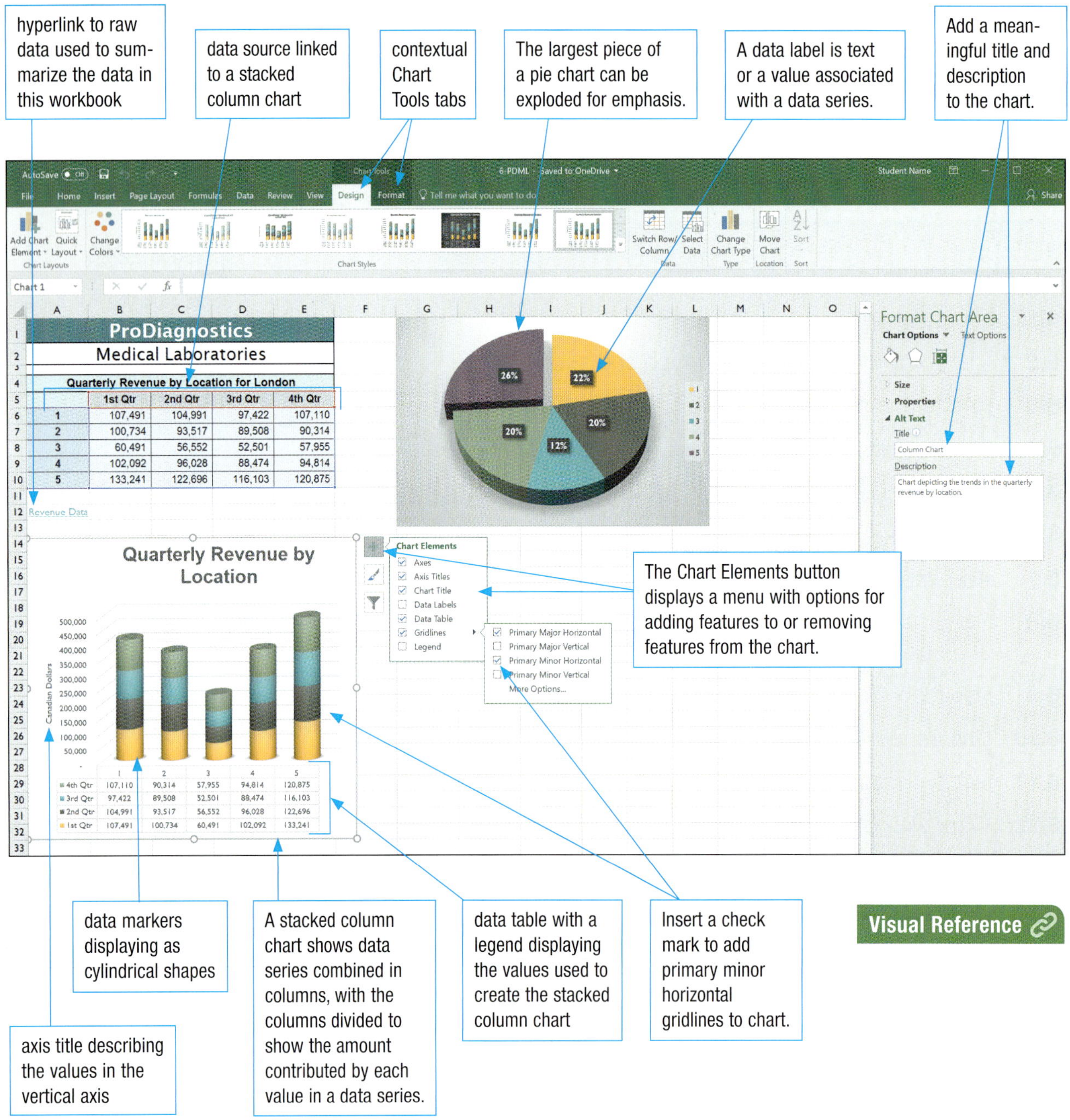

Visual Reference

Figure 6.2 An Excel Worksheet with a Combination Chart and a Treemap Chart

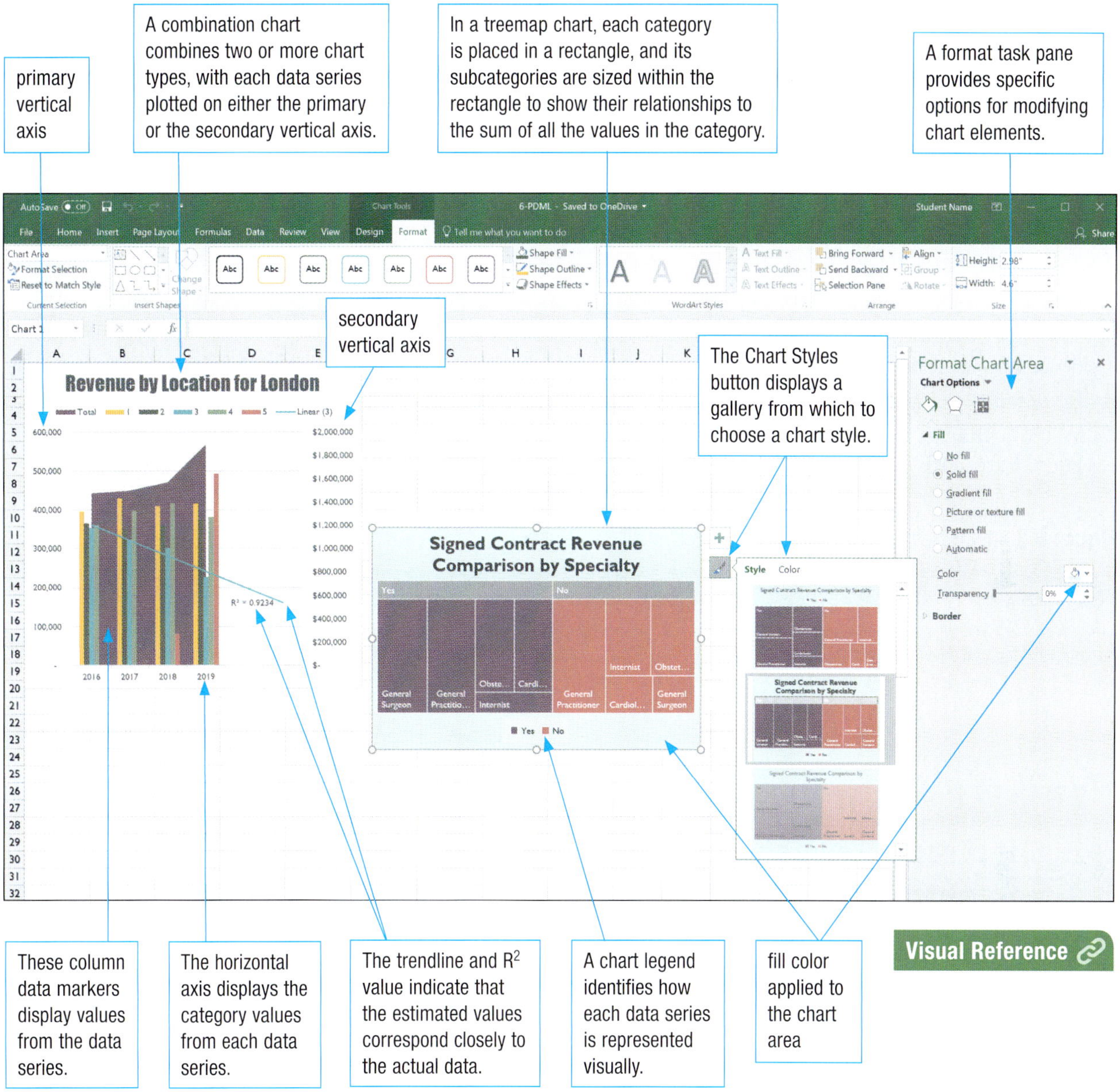

Visual Reference

6.1 Creating Charts

MOS 5.1.1
MOS 5.3.4

To easily analyze data in a worksheet, consider using a chart. A **chart** (also called a *graph*) presents data in a visual format. A chart can depict relationships and trends that may be difficult to see by just looking at the numbers.

Tutorial

Creating a Chart

▸ Know This about creating charts

— To create a chart, select the range containing the chart data, click the Insert tab, click a chart button in the Charts group, and then click a chart subtype at the drop-down gallery (see Figure 6.3).

— Excel organizes the different charts by **chart type**.

— A **chart subtype** offers a variation within a chart type.

— The range used to create the chart is called the **source data** or *data source.*
— The source data is linked to the chart. Any changes in the source data are immediately reflected in the chart.
— The source data contains values and categories. A **value** is a numerical quantity or measurement. The **data series** is the range that contains the values. A category is the group that series values belong to.
— Each value from the source data is plotted on the **value axis**, and the categories that appear in the row or column headers are used as labels on the **category axis**.
— Each value from a data series displays a **data marker**.
— The area of the chart that contains the data markers is the **plot area**.
— The row or column headers and the values that are plotted on the chart do not have to be adjacent.
— By default, a chart is inserted in the same worksheet as the selected range.
— When a chart is created or selected, the contextual Chart Tools Design and Chart Tools Format tabs become available.

▶ **Know More** ways to create charts

– Select the range containing the data, click the Insert tab, click the Charts group dialog box launcher, click the All Charts tab at the dialog box, click a chart type, and then click a chart subtype.
– To automatically insert a clustered column chart in the same worksheet as the data source, select the range and then press Alt + F1.

Figure 6.3 Insert Column or Bar Chart Button Drop-Down Gallery

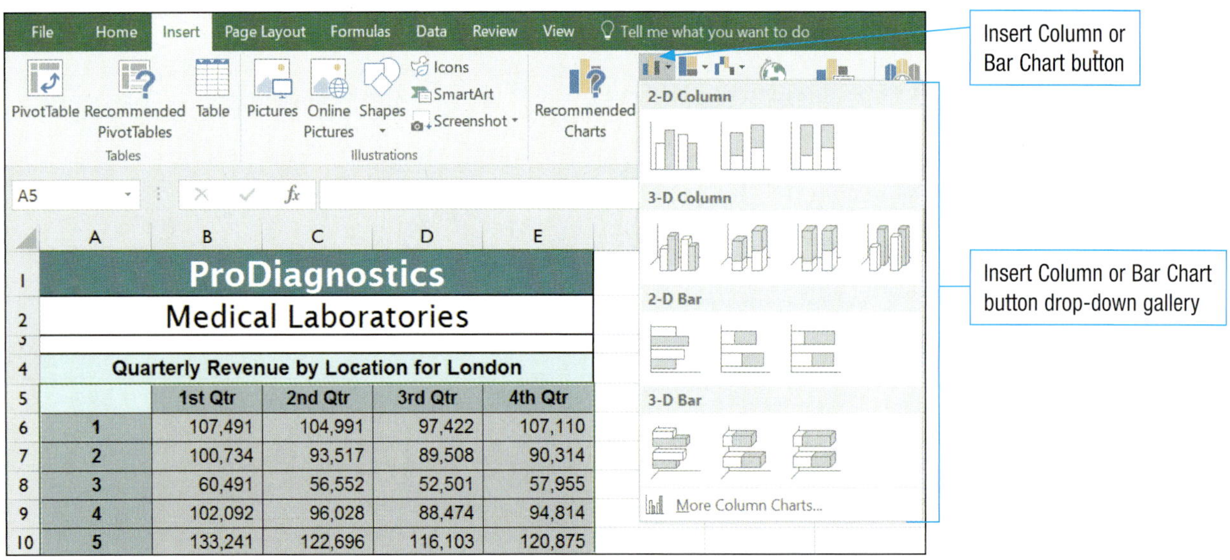

▶ **Know This** about verifying chart content

— Table 6.1 lists common chart errors and how to verify that your chart is correct.

Table 6.1 Common Chart Errors

What to Verify	How to Verify It
The correct data series are being used.	Look at the category axis and the value axis.
The chart is sized properly to show all the data series.	Compare the category axis against the source data.
The entries are typed correctly.	Look for any data markers that are not consistent with the rest of the chart.

▸ Know This about adding alternative text to a chart

— To add alternative text to a chart, point to an empty area of the chart until the ScreenTip *Chart Area* displays, right-click, click the *Format Chart Area* option at the pop-up menu, click the Size & Properties icon at the Format Chart Area task pane, click the *Alt Text* section name, and then type a meaningful title and description in the *Title* and the *Description* text boxes.

▸ Know This about deleting charts

— To delete a chart on the same worksheet as other objects or data, click the chart to select it and then press the Delete key.

— To delete a chart on its own worksheet, right-click the sheet tab, click the *Delete* option at the pop-up menu, and then click the Delete button.

▸ Know This about column and bar charts

— A **column chart** displays the data series along the **horizontal axis** and the values along the **vertical axis** (see Figure 6.4).

— A **bar chart** switches the data series and the values, displaying the data series along the vertical axis and the values along the horizontal axis.

— The height of the column or the width of the bar is dependent on the value.

— A **clustered column chart** groups the data along the horizontal axis by the data series, with each value in the data series represented by a column data marker.

— Choose a column or bar chart when there are many data series or when there is a small variance in the data values.

Figure 6.4 Column Chart versus Bar Chart

On the Job

Task 6.1 Creating a 2-D Clustered Column Chart

Kaelan wants you to create a chart to organize the data in the Quarterly Revenue worksheet. Create a 2-D column chart using the range A5:E10. Once the chart is inserted, add alternative text, including both a title and a description.

1. Open the data file **6-PDML**.
2. With the Quarterly Revenue worksheet active, select the range A5:E10.
3. Click the Insert tab and then click the Insert Column or Bar Chart button in the Charts Group.

   The Insert Column or Bar Chart button drop-down gallery displays.
4. Click the *Clustered Column* option (first column, first row in the *2-D Column* section).

   A 2-D clustered column chart is inserted in the Quarterly Revenue worksheet.
5. Right-click an empty area of the chart and then click the *Format Chart Area* option.

   The Format Chart Area task pane displays (see Figure 6.5).

Figure 6.5 Format Chart Area Task Pane

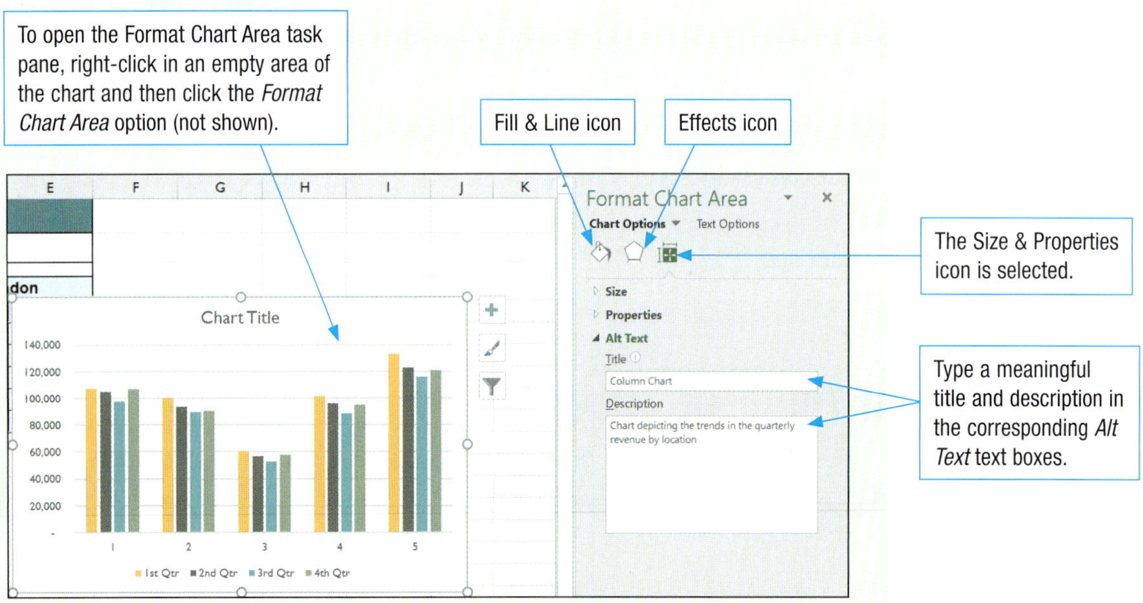

6. Click the Size & Properties icon and then click the *Alt Text* section name.

   A list of *Alt Text* options displays.
7. Click in the *Title* text box and then type Column Chart.
8. Click in the *Description* text box and then type Chart depicting the trends in the quarterly revenue by location.
9. Click the task pane Close button.
10. Click the Save button on the Quick Access Toolbar.

Model Answer

6.2 Choosing and Changing a Chart Type and Subtype

You can create different types of charts using the same data. For example, Figure 6.6 displays the same data using line, stacked column, clustered bar, and 3-D clustered column charts. Preview how a selected chart will look with a different type and subtype at the Change Chart Type dialog box.

Choose the chart type and subtype that best represent how you want the data displayed and analyzed. Do you want to show a comparison, a distribution, a relationship to the whole, a trend over time, a deviation, or a relationship? See Table 6.2 for descriptions that can help you select the best chart for interpreting your data.

After creating a chart, review it to ensure that the correct data has been used for the category axis.

Tutorial

Changing the Subtype of a Chart

Figure 6.6 Quarterly Revenue by Location Data Displayed in Four Different Charts

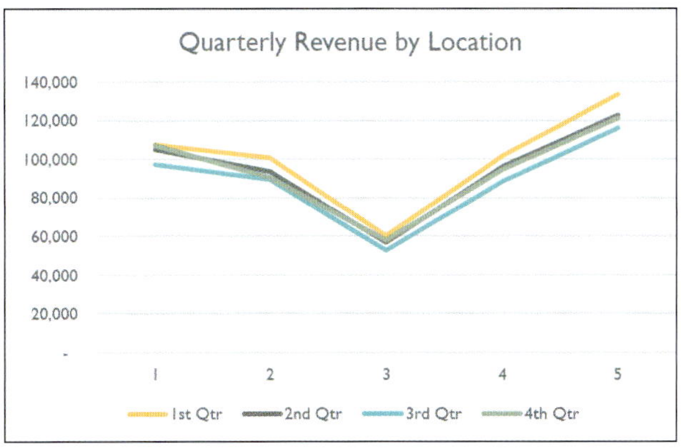

Line Chart

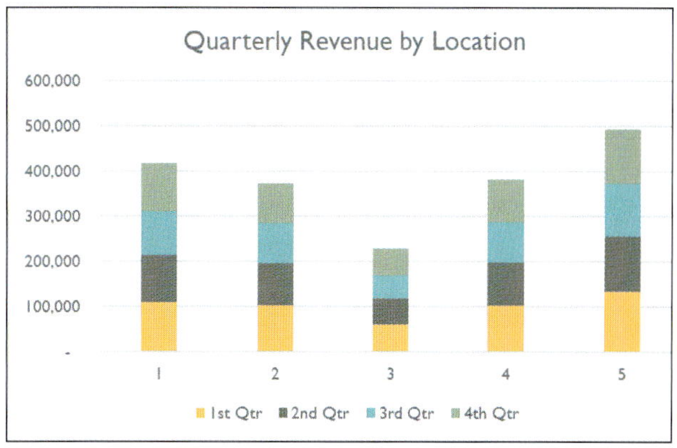

Stacked Column Chart

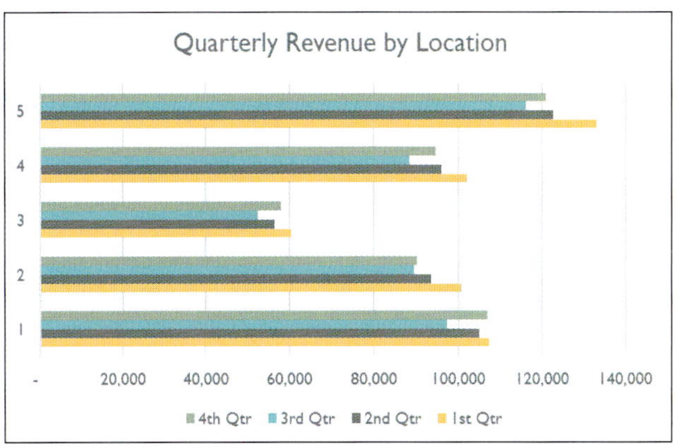

Clustered Bar Chart

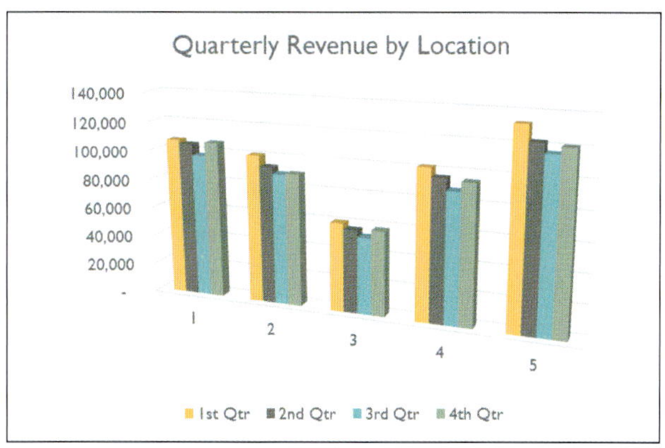

3-D Clustered Column Chart

▸ Know This about changing the chart type and subtype

— To change the chart type and subtype, select the chart in the worksheet, click the Change Chart Type button in the Type group on the Chart Tools Design tab, click the chart type in the left panel at the Change Chart Type dialog box, click the chart subtype option at the top of the right panel, and then click the chart thumbnail in the preview area of the right panel.

▸ Know More ways to display the Change Chart Type dialog box

– Right-click the chart and then click the *Change Chart Type* option at the pop-up menu.

▸ **Know This** about chart types and subtypes

— Excel offers over 60 subtypes of charts organized in 11 types (see Table 6.2). Excel continues to add more types and subtypes.

— Choose the chart subtype that best represents the data visually.

Table 6.2 Chart Types and Common Subtypes

Type	Type Description	Source Data Arrangement	Subtypes
Column or Bar	Displays data series along the horizontal axis (in columns) or vertical axis (in bars). Variations in values are indicated by the heights of the columns or the widths of the bars.	In columns or rows	2-D Column 3-D Column 2-D Bar 3-D Bar
Line or Area	Shows a trend over evenly distributed time intervals. The category is evenly distributed along the horizontal axis, and the values are evenly distributed along the vertical axis. In an area chart, the sum of the plotted values displays as the area below the line with a fill color.	In columns or rows	2-D Line 3-D Line 2-D Area 3-D Area
Pie or Doughnut	Shows individual values as they relate to the sum of all the values.	In one column or row	2-D Pie 3-D Pie Doughnut
Hierarchy	Illustrates a hierarchy. Each category and its subcategories are sized to show their relationship to the sum of all the values in the categories.	In columns or rows	Treemap Sunburst
Statistic	Groups data into intervals called *bins*. The height of each bin represents the number of values in the bin.	In columns or rows	Histogram Box & Whisker
Scatter (X, Y) or Bubble	Shows relationships between two or more sets of data. The data represents separate measurements and is plotted on both the horizontal and vertical axes. Used for analyzing scientific, statistical, and engineering data.	In columns or rows	Scatter Bubble
Waterfall or Stock	Shows fluctuations in data like daily precipitation amounts or stock prices.	In columns or rows with column headers such as *High*, *Low*, and *Average* for daily precipitation or *Open*, *High*, *Low*, and *Close* for stock prices	Waterfall Funnel Stock

continues...

Table 6.2 Chart Types and Common Subtypes *...continued*

Type	Type Description	Source Data Arrangement	Subtypes
Combo 	Combines two or more chart types and displays with a dual axis.	In columns or rows	Clustered Column - Line Clustered Column - Line on Secondary Axis Stacked Area - Clustered Column
Surface or Radar 	Shows trends in values across a 3-D surface. Similar to a topographic map. Used to compare the total values of numerous data series. Each category shows changes in values relative to a common center point.	In columns or rows	Surface Radar
Maps 	Shows values across geographical regions. A geographical region (made up of states or postal codes, for example) must be included in the data source. Variations are displayed with different colors.	In columns or rows	Filled Map
Pivot 	Visually summarizes data from a PivotTable.	In columns or rows	None

▶ Know This about stacked column and 100% stacked column charts

— A **stacked column chart** stacks the data markers in a data series on top of one another to create a column that illustrates the total for the data series.

— In a **100% stacked column chart**, each data marker in a data series is sized as a percentage of the total for the data series.

— Use a stacked column chart to visualize both the total of a data series and the value of each data marker used to create the total.

— Use a 100% stacked column chart to represent each data marker as a percentage of the total of a data series.

▶ Know This about pie charts

— A **pie chart** is a circle divided into pieces (also called *slices*). Each piece represents a percentage of the whole.

— One column or row of a spreadsheet data plus the column or row header is used as the source data.

— The headers and data do not have to be adjacent in the source data.

— Choose a pie chart when you want to represent the individual data points of one data series as percentages of the whole.

— None of the values in the source data should be zero or negative.

— Use no more than seven categories so that each piece can be easily represented as a part of the whole.

Reminder
Use the Ctrl key to select nonadjacent cells.

On the Job

Task 6.2a Changing the Subtype of a Column Chart

After reviewing the chart, Kaelan decides he would like to view the yearly revenue for each of the five locations while still viewing how much revenue each location earned each quarter. A stacked column chart is best suited to illustrate both the total year's revenue and the quarter's revenue received from each location. With this type of chart, the revenue for each of the four quarters will be stacked, one on top the other, to display the revenue for the total year. Improve the chart's presentation of the data by changing the subtype of the column chart to 3-D stacked column.

1. With the Quarterly Revenue worksheet active and the column chart selected, click the Change Chart Type button in the Type group on the Chart Tools Design tab.

   The Change Chart Type dialog box displays with the *Column* option selected in the left panel (see Figure 6.7).
2. Click the *3-D Stacked Column* option (fifth option).

   Chart previews for the 3-D Stacked Column Chart subtype display below the subtype options, and the first preview is selected.

Figure 6.7 Change Chart Type Dialog Box

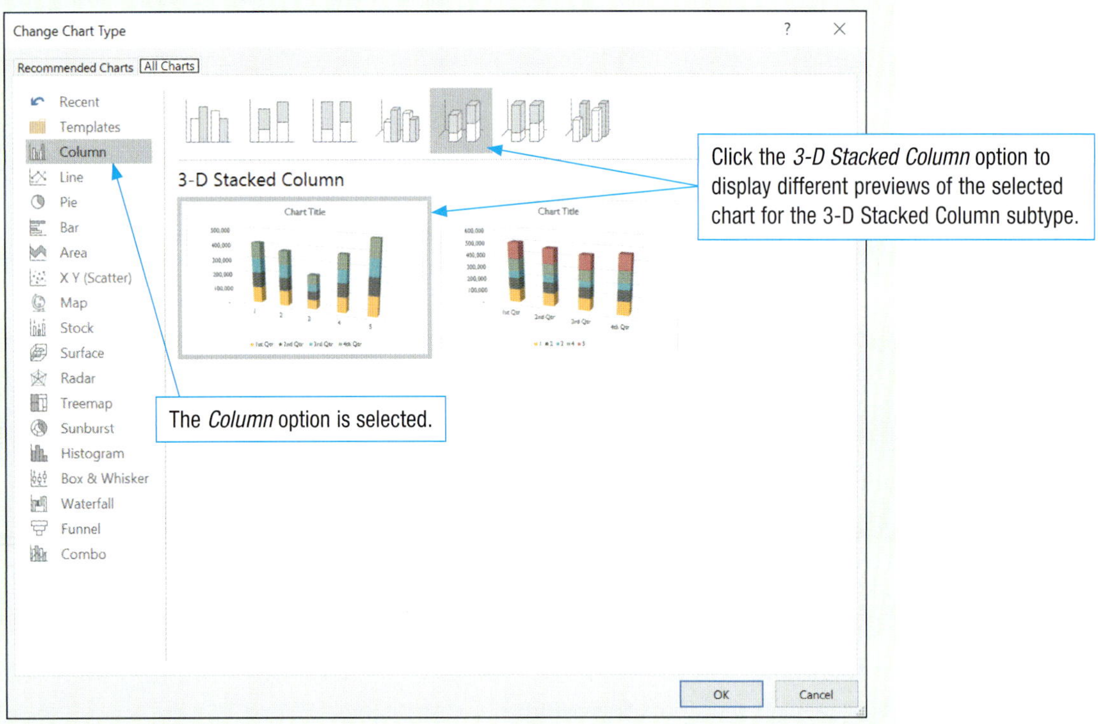

3. Click the OK button.

   The chart changes to a 3-D stacked column chart.
4. Click the Save button on the Quick Access Toolbar.

Model Answer

On the Job

Task 6.2b Creating a Chart, Changing the Chart Subtype, and Adding Alternative Text

Kaelan asks you to create a chart on the Location Total worksheet to compare the revenue from each of the five locations to the total revenue. Create a pie chart to show this comparison. After reviewing the chart, you notice that it doesn't represent the data in each cell in the range N5:N9 as a percentage of the total found in cell N10. Change the chart layout to properly represent each revenue location total as a percentage of the total revenue and then add the appropriate alternative text, including a title and a description.

1. Click the Location Total sheet tab.
2. Select the range A5:A9, press and hold down the Ctrl key, select the range N5:N9, and then release the Ctrl key.
3. Click the Insert tab.
4. Click the Insert Pie or Doughnut Chart button in the Charts group and then click the *3-D Pie* option (see Figure 6.8).

   A 3-D pie chart is inserted in the Location Total worksheet, and the Chart Tools Design tab is active.

Figure 6.8 Insert Pie or Doughnut Chart Button Drop-Down Gallery

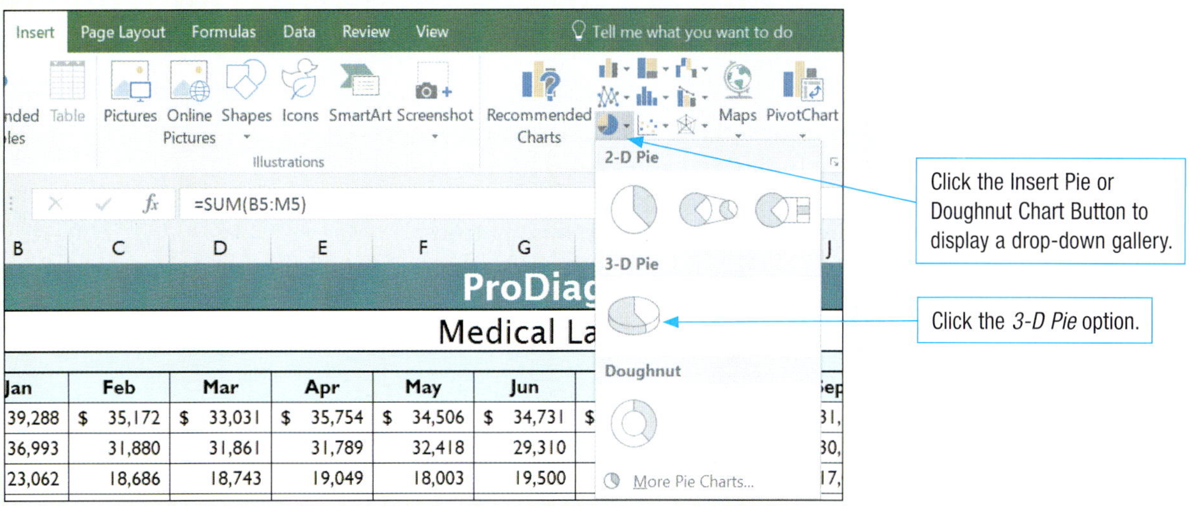

5. Review the chart to determine whether it represents the data properly.

   Notice that the area represented by the yellow data marker—the value found in cell N5 (417,014)—is approximately 22% of the total revenue found in cell N10 (1,892,909). The yellow data marker in the current chart looks like approximately 7% of the total, not approximately 22% of the total. You need to change the chart layout to represent the data properly.
6. Click the Change Chart Type button in the Type group on the Chart Tools Design tab, click the second layout option in the *3-D Pie* section, and then click the OK button.

   The chart displays with the second layout option.

7. Right-click an empty part of the chart and then click the *Format Chart Area* option.

   The Format Chart Area task pane displays.

8. Click the Size & Properties icon; click the *Alt Text* section name, if necessary; click in the *Title* text box; and then type Pie Chart.
9. Click in the *Description* text box and then type Chart depicting the revenue as a percentage of the total revenue for each location.
10. Click the task pane Close button.
11. Click the Save button on the Quick Access Toolbar.

Model Answer

6.3 Resizing and Moving Charts

MOS 5.2.1
MOS 5.2.4

Tutorial

Resizing, Positioning, and Moving Charts

By default, when a chart is inserted, it is embedded in the same worksheet as the source data. Like other objects, an **embedded chart** is placed on top of the cells in the worksheet, where it can be selected and manipulated. You may want to resize a chart or move it to a new position in the worksheet or to a different worksheet. For example, you might move a chart so you can view it along with the source data in the Excel window, or you might make a chart smaller to print it with the source data on one page.

When a chart is selected, a selection box appears around it, and sizing handles appear along the edges of the selection box. A **selection box** is used to move the chart, and a sizing handle is used to resize the chart.

Reminder

Objects are covered in detail in Chapter 4.

▸ Know This about resizing a chart

— To change the size of a chart using a sizing handle, hover the mouse pointer over the sizing handle until the pointer turns into a two-headed arrow, click and hold down the left mouse button, drag the handle until the correct size is achieved, and then release the mouse button.

— Use the corner sizing handles to simultaneously decrease or increase the width and height.

— To maintain the proportions of a chart, press and hold down the Shift key while dragging a corner sizing handle.

— By default, the Lock Aspect ratio feature is turned off, so when the height is adjusted, the width does not change.

— To turn on the Lock Aspect ratio, right-click an empty part of the chart, click the *Format Chart Area* option at the pop-up menu, click the Size & Properties icon at the Format Picture task pane, click the *Size* section name, and then click the *Lock aspect ratio* check box to insert a check mark.

▸ Know More about resizing a chart

– To resize a selected chart, use the *Height* and *Width* measurement boxes in the Size group on the Chart Tools Format tab.

▸ Know This about moving a chart in the same worksheet

— To move a chart to a new location in the same worksheet, hover the mouse pointer over the selection box or an empty part of the chart until the pointer turns into a four-headed arrow, click and hold down the left mouse button, drag the chart to the new position, and then release the mouse button.

— Be careful to move the entire chart, not a single chart element.

▶ Know This about moving a chart to a new worksheet

— To move a chart to a new worksheet, select the chart, click the Move Chart button in the Location group on the Chart Tools Design tab, click the *New sheet* radio button to insert a bullet, and then click the OK button.

— The default name for the new worksheet is *Chart1* (see Figure 6.9). If you move a chart to second new worksheet, the worksheet will be named *Chart2*.

— A worksheet containing only a chart, not its data series, is called a **chart worksheet**.

▶ Know This about moving a chart to another existing worksheet

— To move a chart to another existing worksheet, click the *Object in* radio button at the Move Chart dialog box, if necessary, to insert a bullet; click the *Object in* option box arrow; and then click the name of the worksheet at the drop-down list (see Figure 6.9).

▶ Know More ways to move a chart to a new worksheet

– Right-click an empty part of the chart and then click the *Move Chart* option at the pop-up menu.

Figure 6.9 Move Chart Dialog Box

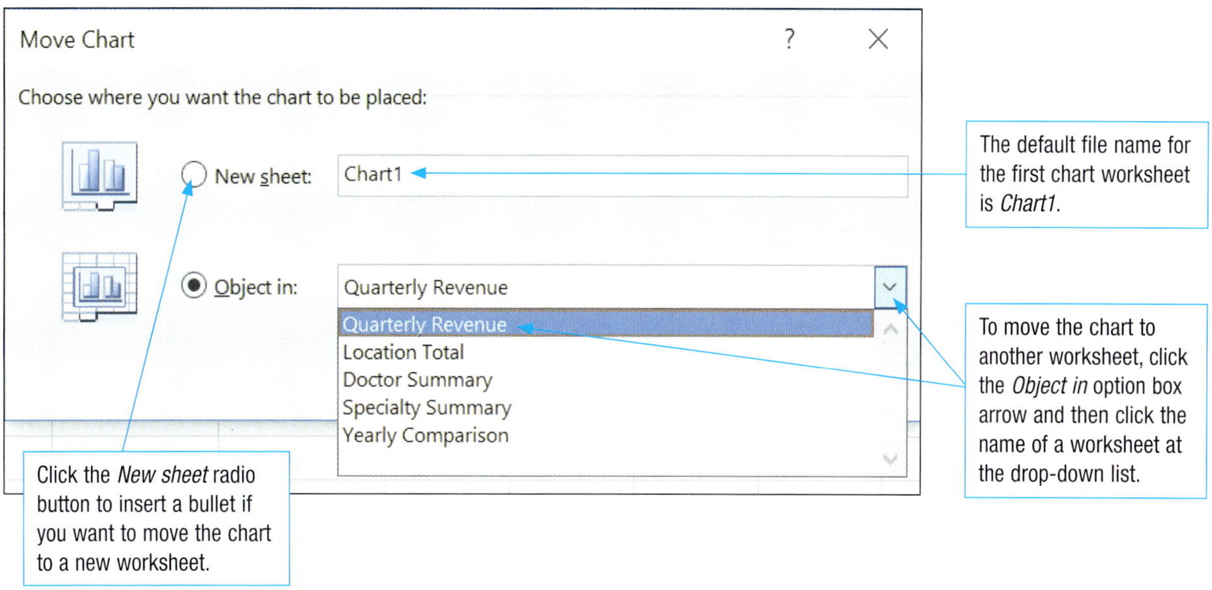

On the Job

Task 6.3 Resizing, Positioning, and Moving Charts

Kaelan wants the pie chart and source data for location revenue totals to display together in the same worksheet, with the chart sized to be read easily. In addition, he wants to show the managers at the business development meeting the column chart containing quarterly revenue data for each of the four locations in its own worksheet. Move the pie chart below the source data in the Location Total worksheet, use the sizing handles to enlarge the pie chart, and then move the column chart from the Quarterly Revenue worksheet to a new worksheet.

1. With the Location Total worksheet active and the pie chart selected, hover the mouse pointer over the chart's selection box until the pointer turns into a four-headed arrow, click and hold down the left mouse button, drag the chart until the top left corner of the chart is in the top left corner of cell D13, and then release the mouse button.

   The chart is positioned as shown in Figure 6.10.

Figure 6.10 Location Worksheet with Pie Chart Correctly Positioned

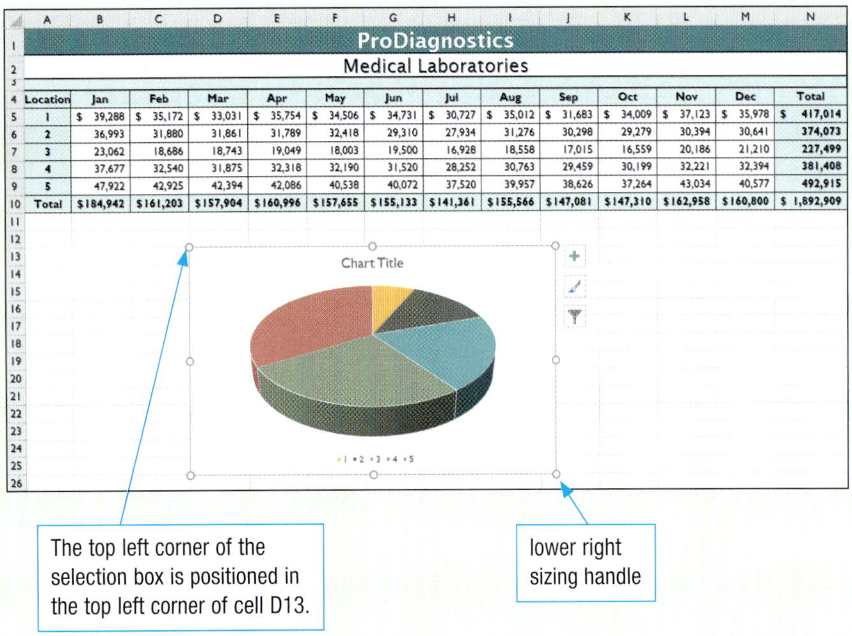

ProDiagnostics
Medical Laboratories

Location	Jan	Feb	Mar	Apr	May	Jun	Jul	Aug	Sep	Oct	Nov	Dec	Total
1	$ 39,288	$ 35,172	$ 33,031	$ 35,754	$ 34,506	$ 34,731	$ 30,727	$ 35,012	$ 31,683	$ 34,009	$ 37,123	$ 35,978	$ 417,014
2	36,993	31,880	31,861	31,789	32,418	29,310	27,934	31,276	30,298	29,279	30,394	30,641	374,073
3	23,062	18,686	18,743	19,049	18,003	19,500	16,928	18,558	17,015	16,559	20,186	21,210	227,499
4	37,677	32,540	31,875	32,318	32,190	31,520	28,252	30,763	29,459	30,199	32,221	32,394	381,408
5	47,922	42,925	42,394	42,086	40,538	40,072	37,520	39,957	38,626	37,264	43,034	40,577	492,915
Total	$184,942	$161,203	$157,904	$160,996	$157,655	$155,133	$141,361	$155,566	$147,081	$147,310	$162,958	$160,800	$ 1,892,909

2. Press and hold down the Shift key, hover the mouse pointer over the lower right sizing handle until the pointer turns into a two-headed arrow pointing diagonally, click and hold down the left mouse button, drag the sizing handle down and to the right until the bottom border of the chart is at the top of row 30, and then release the Shift key and the mouse button.

   Pressing and holding down the Shift key maintains the chart's proportions.

3. Click the Quarterly Revenue sheet tab and then click the column chart in the worksheet, if necessary.
4. Click the Chart Tools Design tab.
5. Click the Move Chart button in the Location group.

   The Move Chart dialog box displays.

6. Click the *New sheet* radio button to insert a bullet and then click the OK button.

   The chart is moved to a new worksheet named *Chart1*, the new worksheet appears to the left of the Quarterly Revenue worksheet, and the new worksheet is active.

7. Click the Save button on the Quick Access Toolbar.

Model Answer

6.4 Adding, Modifying, and Removing Chart Elements and Applying Chart Layouts

MOS 5.2.2
MOS 5.2.3

Tutorial

Removing, Modifying, and Adding Chart Elements

The **chart area** consists of a chart plus various chart elements. A **chart element** is an individual part related to the chart. The chart elements vary depending on the type of chart. For example, the elements associated with a pie chart are a **chart title** (a name describing the chart contents), **data labels** (text or values associated with the data series), and a **chart legend** (a key describing how each data series is represented visually in the chart). The elements for a column chart are the chart title, axes, **axis titles** (names describing the values in the axes), data labels, a **data table** (rows and columns listing the values used to create the chart), **tick marks** (lines that divide the axes at regular intervals), **gridlines** (major and minor vertical and horizontal extensions of the tick marks), lines, and a legend (see Figure 6.11). The **chart layout** refers to where the elements are placed in the chart area.

Figure 6.11 Chart Elements

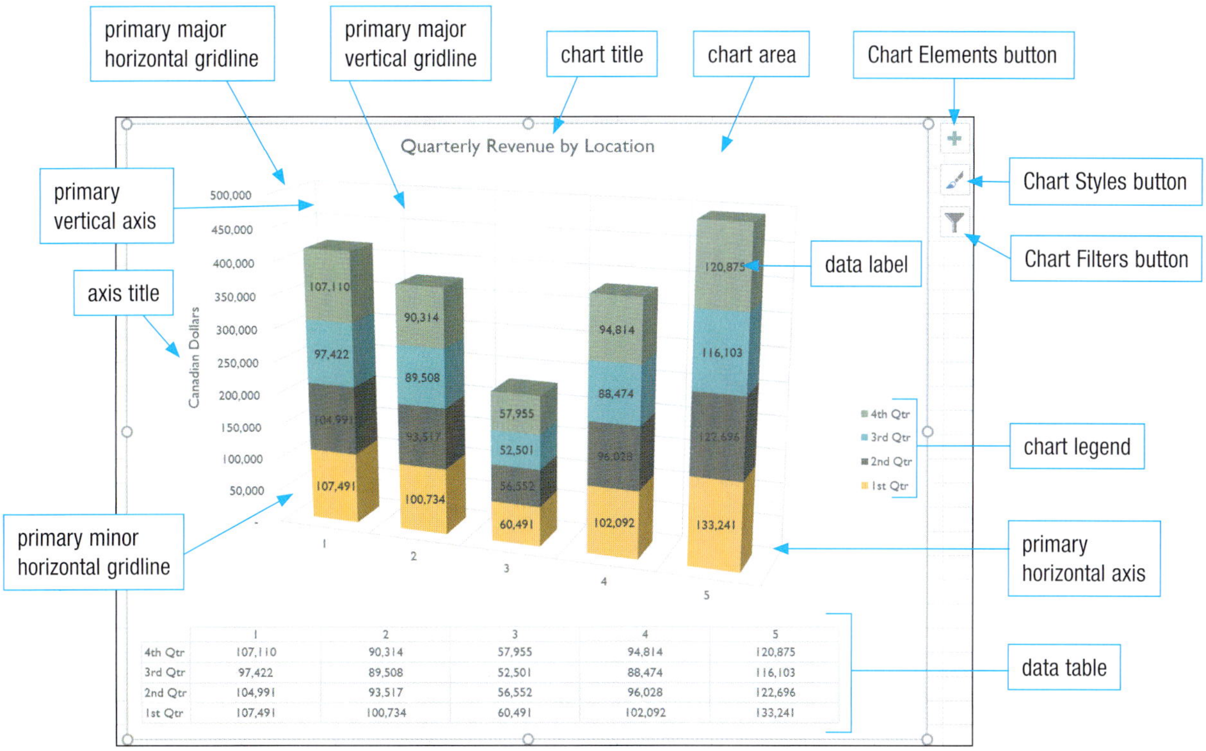

▸ Know This about chart buttons

— When a chart is selected, three buttons (Chart Elements, Chart Styles, and Chart Filters) appear at the upper right side of the chart border (see Figure 6.11). These are called *chart buttons*.

— The Chart Elements button is used to add chart elements.

— The Chart Styles button is used to modify the chart style.

— The Chart Filters button is used to filter the chart.

▶ **Know This** about using the Chart Elements button to add, modify, and delete chart elements

— To add a chart element, click the Chart Elements button, click an empty check box at the side menu to insert a check mark, and then click an option to specify attributes of the element at the second side menu (see Figure 6.12).

— To modify a chart element, click the option arrow at the side menu and then click an option at the second side menu.

— To delete a chart element, click its check box at the side menu to remove the check mark.

— To close the Chart Elements side menus, click the Chart Elements button or click in any cell in the worksheet.

Figure 6.12 Chart Elements Button Side Menus

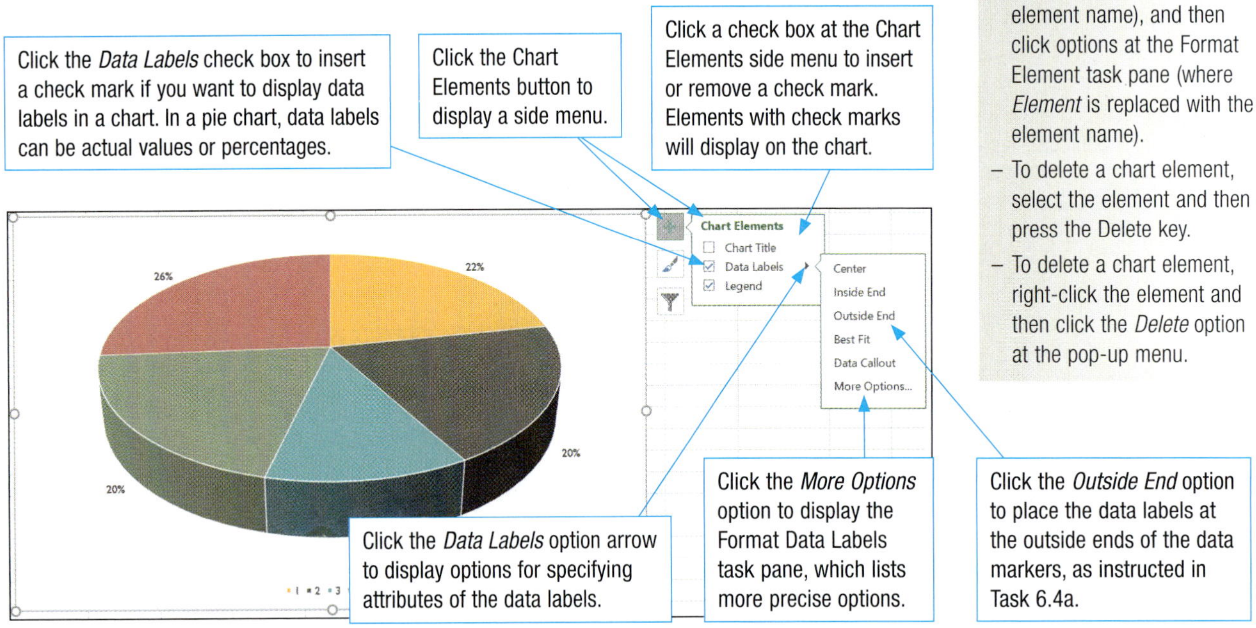

Figure 6.13 Add Chart Element Button Drop-Down List

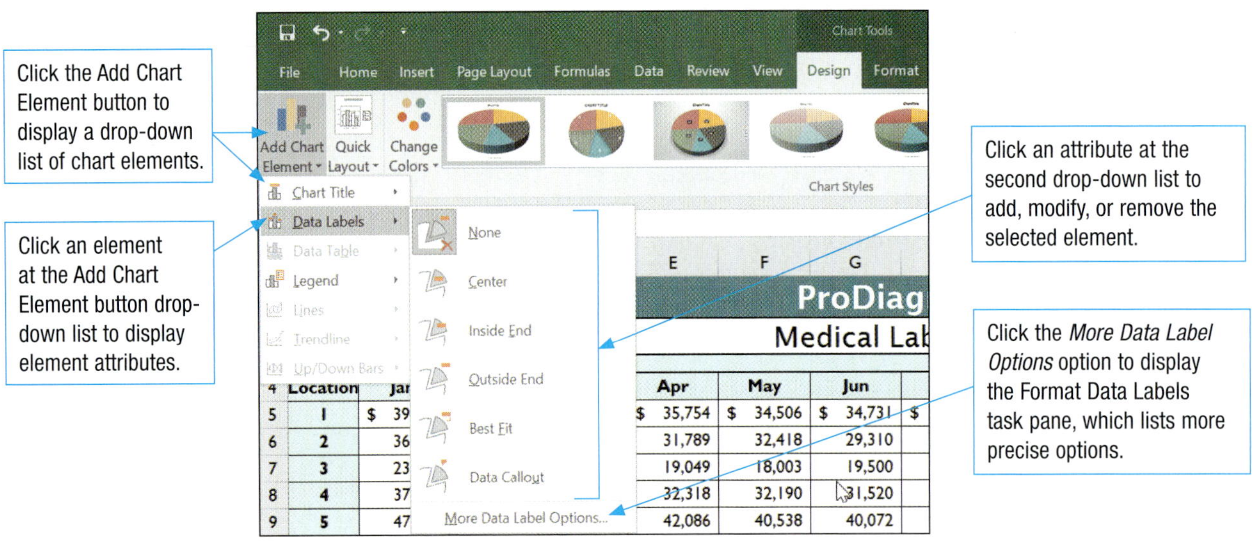

▶ **Know More** ways to add, modify, and delete chart elements

- To add a chart element, click the Add Chart Element button in the Chart Layouts group on the Chart Tools Design tab, click an option at the drop-down list, and then click options at the second drop-down list (see Figure 6.13).
- To modify a chart element, right-click the element, click the *Format Element* option (where *Element* is replaced with the actual element name), and then click options at the Format Element task pane (where *Element* is replaced with the element name).
- To delete a chart element, select the element and then press the Delete key.
- To delete a chart element, right-click the element and then click the *Delete* option at the pop-up menu.

▸ Know This about repositioning chart elements

— To reposition a chart element, select the element, hover the mouse pointer over the border of the element until the pointer turns into a four-headed arrow, click and hold down the left mouse button, drag the element to the new position, and then release the mouse button.

▸ Know This about resizing chart elements

— To resize a chart element using a sizing handle, hover the mouse pointer over the sizing handle until the pointer turns into a two-headed arrow, click and hold down the left mouse button, drag the handle until the new size is achieved, and then release the mouse button.

▸ Know This about entering text in a chart element

— Some chart elements, including the chart title and axis title, allow you to enter text.

— To enter text in an element, click to select the element, type the text, and then press the Enter key.

— When text is being typed in a chart element, it displays only in the Formula bar until the Enter key is pressed.

— The chart element will resize to fit the text.

▸ Know This about quickly modifying chart layouts

— To quickly add, delete, or move chart elements, click the Quick Layout button in the Chart Layouts group on the Chart Tools Design tab and then click a layout option at the drop-down list.

— To reposition a chart element, select the element, hover the mouse pointer over the border of the element until the pointer turns into a four-headed arrow, click and hold down the left mouse button, drag the element to the new position, and then release the mouse button.

On the Job

Task 6.4a Removing and Adding Chart Elements Using the Chart Elements Button and the Format Data Labels Task Pane

Kaelan wants you to remove the title from the pie chart in the Location Total worksheet and then add data labels showing the percentage that each location contributes to the total revenue. Use the Chart Elements button and the Format Data Labels task pane to complete these tasks.

1. Click the Location Total sheet tab and then select the pie chart, if necessary.
2. Click the Chart Elements button.

   The Chart Elements button side menu displays.
3. Click the *Chart Title* check box.

   The check mark is removed from the *Chart Title* check box, the text box containing the chart title is removed from the chart, and the chart elements resize to fit the modified chart area.

4. Click the *Data Labels* option arrow and then click the *Outside End* option (see Figure 6.12 on page 246).

   A check mark appears in the *Data Labels* check box and the total revenue for each location displays as a value outside each data marker.

5. Click the *More Options* option.

   The Format Data Labels task pane displays with the Label Options area active.

6. Click the *Percentage* check box in the *Label Contains* section.

   A check mark appears in the *Percentage* check box and the data labels in the chart display with both percentages and values.

7. Click the *Value* check box.

   The check mark is removed from the *Value* check box and values no longer display in the data labels on the chart.

8. Click the task pane Close button.

   The Format Data Labels task pane closes.

9. Click the Save button on the Quick Access Toolbar.

Model Answer

On the Job

Task 6.4b Adding Chart Elements Using Buttons in the Chart Layouts Group

Kaelan wants to show managers the quarterly revenue column chart you placed in its own worksheet in Task 6.3 and to include all the information they need to interpret the data without referring to the data table in the Quarterly Revenue worksheet. Use the Quick Layout button to add a chart title and an axis title and to replace the simple chart legend with a data table and legend combined. Also use the Add Chart Elements button to add more horizontal gridlines.

1. Click the Chart1 sheet tab and then select the chart, if necessary.
2. Click the Chart Tools Design tab if necessary; click the Quick Layout button in the Chart Layouts group; and then click the *Layout 5* option (second column, second row) (see Figure 6.14).

   The chart layout is modified to include a combined data table and legend at the bottom of the chart and a vertical axis title.

3. Click the Add Chart Element button in the Chart Layouts group, point to the *Gridlines* option, and then click the *Primary Minor Horizontal* option.

   Gridlines appear between the primary major horizontal gridlines.

4. Click the chart title element, type Quarterly Revenue by Location, and then press the Enter key.

   While you are typing, the text appears in the Formula bar. When you press the Enter key, the title *Quarterly Revenue by Location* appears in the chart title element and the element resizes to fit the text.

Figure 6.14 Quick Layout Button Drop-Down Gallery

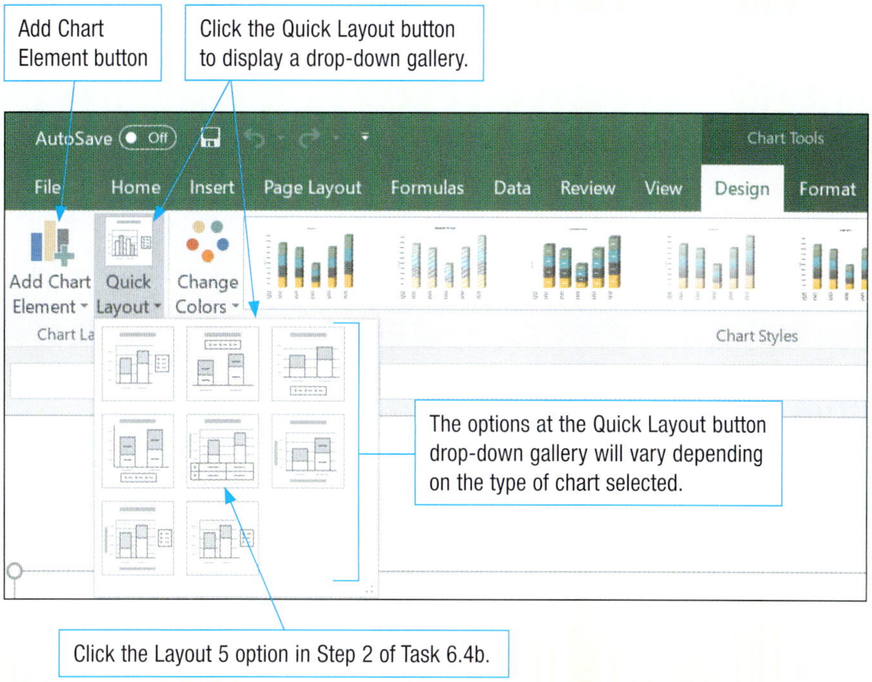

5. Click the axis title element, type Canadian Dollars, and then press the Enter key.

   When you press the Enter key, the axis title *Canadian Dollars* appears to the left of the dollar amounts in the chart area and the chart element resizes to fit the text.

6. Click the Save button on the Quick Access Toolbar.

Model Answer

6.5 Applying Chart Styles and Modifying Chart Colors and Formatting

MOS 5.2.3

Tutorial

Applying a Chart Style, Exploding a Pie Chart, and Modifying Chart Colors

Excel provides a selection of predefined format settings. Each selection, called a **chart style**, defines the overall appearance of a chart. The styles and color selections available depend on the type of chart selected. All the parts of a chart—including the chart elements, individual data markers, and chart area—can be modified by changing the style or color.

▸ Know This about applying chart styles and modifying chart colors

— To apply a chart style, select the chart, click the Chart Styles button (at the upper right side of the chart), scroll to view the available options at the pop-up gallery with the Style tab selected, and then click a chart style option (see Figure 6.15).

— To change the color of the data series for a chart, select the chart, click the Chart Styles button, click the Color tab at the pop-up gallery, and then click a color option.

▸ Know More about applying chart styles

– To display a ScreenTip showing the name of a chart style and a live preview of the style applied to the selected chart, point to the style option at the Chart Styles button pop-up gallery.

— If the chart will be viewed or printed in black and white or shades of gray, ensure there is enough contrast between the colors in the chart so all the chart elements and data markers are easy to distinguish.

Figure 6.15 Chart Styles Button Pop-Up Gallery

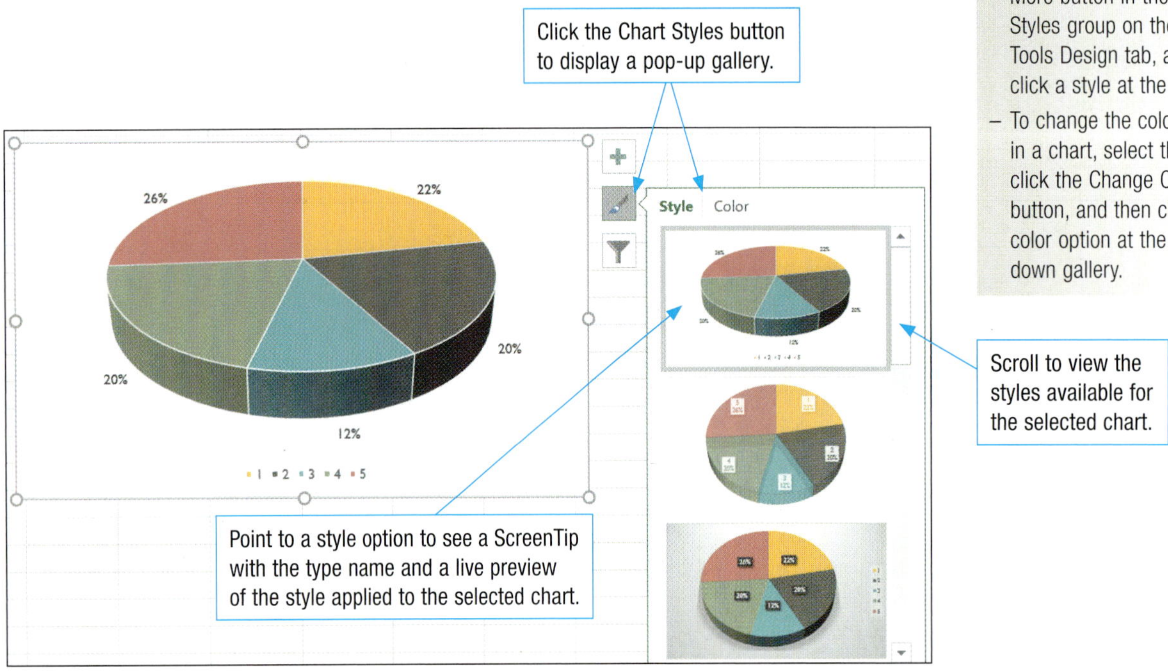

▶ Know More ways to apply chart styles and modify chart colors

– To apply a chart style, select the chart, click the More button in the Chart Styles group on the Chart Tools Design tab, and then click a style at the gallery.

– To change the colors used in a chart, select the chart, click the Change Colors button, and then click a color option at the drop-down gallery.

▶ Know This about formatting a chart

— To modify the formatting of a chart element, select the element and then use buttons and options on the Home tab and on the Chart Tools Format tab.

— Buttons and options on the Chart Tools Format tab are similar to those on the Picture Tools, Drawing Tools, and SmartArt Tools Format tabs discussed in Chapter 4.

— When a specific element of a chart is selected, selection points (see Figure 6.16 on page 252) or sizing handles display, depending on the element selected.

— To format any element of the chart using a task pane, either double-click or right-click the element and then click the specific format option at the pop-up menu. For example, double-click the chart title to display the Format Chart Title task pane.

▶ Know This about formatting data markers and data series

— To select an individual data marker, or slice, in a pie chart, click the data marker and then click it again.

— To select all the data markers in a data series in a bar or column chart, click any data marker in the series.

— To select only one data marker in a bar or column chart, click the data marker and then click it again. Be sure to click the marker two times; do not double-click it.

- To change the formatting of an individual data marker, select the data marker, click the Chart Tools Format tab, and then choose options in the Shape Styles group.
- To format a data series, select the data series and then use options in the Shape Styles group, or right-click the data series, click the *Format Data Series* option, and then use options in the Format Data Series task pane.

▸ Know This about exploding a pie chart

- To emphasize specific categories of data in a pie chart, you can explode the chart.
- An **exploded pie chart** displays one or more data markers, or slices, moved away from the center of the pie.
- To explode one slice of a pie chart, click the slice, click and hold down the left mouse button, drag the slice away from the center of the chart, and then release the mouse button.
- To explode multiple slices of a pie chart, click and drag each slice in turn.
- To explode all the slices of a pie chart, right-click any slice in the chart, click the *Format Data Point* option, and then drag the *Pie Explosion* slider in the Series Options area at the Format Data Point task pane.

▸ Know This about formatting a data series

- To change the shape of a data marker along with the width of the data marker and the space between data markers, use options at the Format Data Series task pane.

On the Job

Task 6.5 Applying Chart Styles, Exploding a Pie Chart, and Modifying Chart Colors

Kaelan wants to provide managers at the development meeting with charts that are visually compelling. He asks you to change the overall appearance of the pie chart showing total revenue by location and to emphasize the slice showing data for the location that has the highest revenue. He also asks you to update the overall appearance of the column chart showing quarterly revenue and to emphasize the title of that chart. Apply a new style to the pie chart on the Location Total worksheet and then explode the largest slice and change its fill color. After you have completed changes to the pie chart, change the style of the column chart in the Chart1 worksheet, change the data markers to be cylindrical, and modify the formatting of the chart title.

1. Click the Location Total sheet tab and then select the pie chart, if necessary.
2. Click the Chart Styles button at the upper right side of the chart.

   A pop-up gallery displays with the Style tab selected.
3. Click the *Style 3* option.

   Style 3 is applied to the chart.

4. Click the Location 5 slice two times, click and hold down the left mouse button, drag the slice away from the center of the chart, and then release the mouse button (see Figure 6.16).

   Be sure to click and drag the slice. If you double-click it instead, the Format Data Point task pane will display.

Figure 6.16 Pie Chart with the Location 5 Slice Exploded and Selected

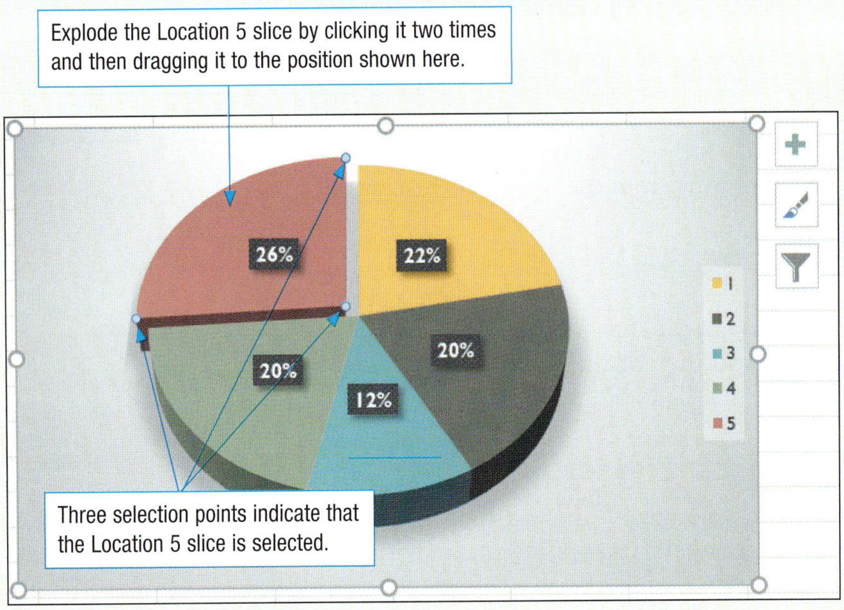

5. With the Location 5 slice still selected, click the Chart Tools Format tab, click the Shape Fill button in the Shape Styles group, and then click the *Dark Red* option (first option in the *Standard Colors* section).
6. Click the Chart1 sheet tab and then click the chart, if necessary, to select it.
7. Click the Chart Tools Design tab, click the More button in the Chart Styles group, and then click the *Style 8* option at the gallery (see Figure 6.17).

   Style 8 is applied to the chart. Applying the style removes the primary minor horizontal gridlines that you applied in Task 6.4b and changes the rotation of the horizontal axis.

Figure 6.17 Chart Styles Group

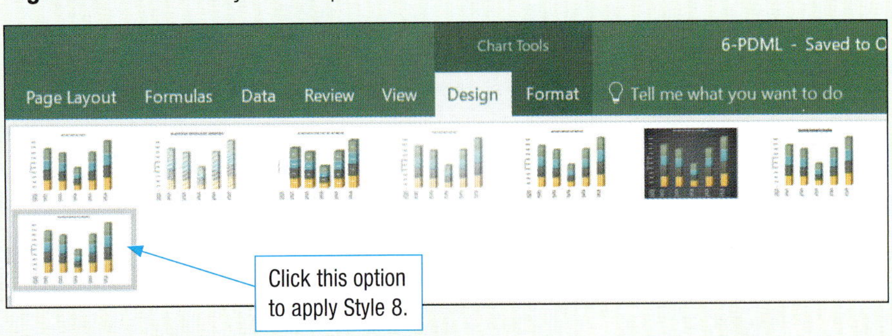

8. Click the Add Chart Element button in the Chart Layouts group, point to the *Gridlines* option, and then click the *Primary Minor Horizontal* option.

   The minor horizontal gridlines reappear between the primary major horizontal gridlines.

9. Click the chart title element, click the Home tab, change the font to Arial, and then change the font size to 20 points.
10. Double-click the center of any data marker.

    The Format Data Series task pane displays. If the Format Data Point task pane displays, leave the task pane open and click the center of another data marker.

11. Click the Series Options icon, if necessary, and then click the *Cylinder* radio button in the *Column shape* section (see Figure 6.18).

    A bullet appears in the *Cylinder* radio button and the data markers change to a cylindrical shape.

Figure 6.18 Format Data Series Task Pane

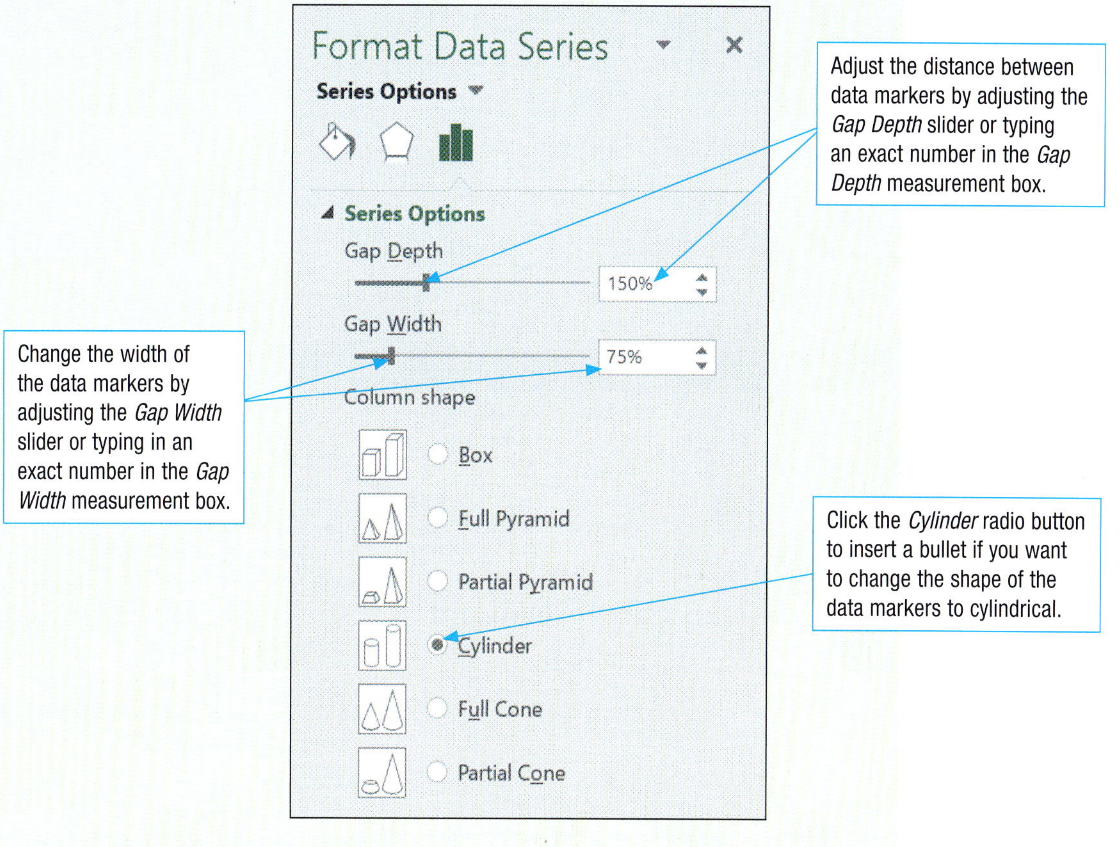

12. Select the number in the *Gap Width* measurement box, type 75, and then press the Enter key.

    A bullet appears in the *Cylinder* radio button and the data markers widen.

13. Click the task pane Close button and then click the Save button on the Quick Access Toolbar.

Model Answer

6.6 Using Quick Analysis to Create a Chart

MOS 5.1.4

Tutorial

Using Quick Analysis to Create a Chart

When a range is selected in a data source, Excel analyzes the selection and suggests various options for how best to present the data. The options can be found under the Quick Analysis button (see Figure 6.19).

Reminder

The Quick Analysis tool is also used to enter formulas and functions (see Chapter 2) and to apply conditional formatting (see Chapter 3).

▸ Know This about using Quick Analysis to create a chart

- To create a chart using Quick Analysis, select the range containing the chart data, click the Quick Analysis button, click the Charts tab at the Quick Analysis gallery, and then click an option (see Figure 6.19).
- To view a live preview of an option at the Quick Analysis gallery, point to the option.

Figure 6.19 Selected Data Source Range and Quick Analysis Button

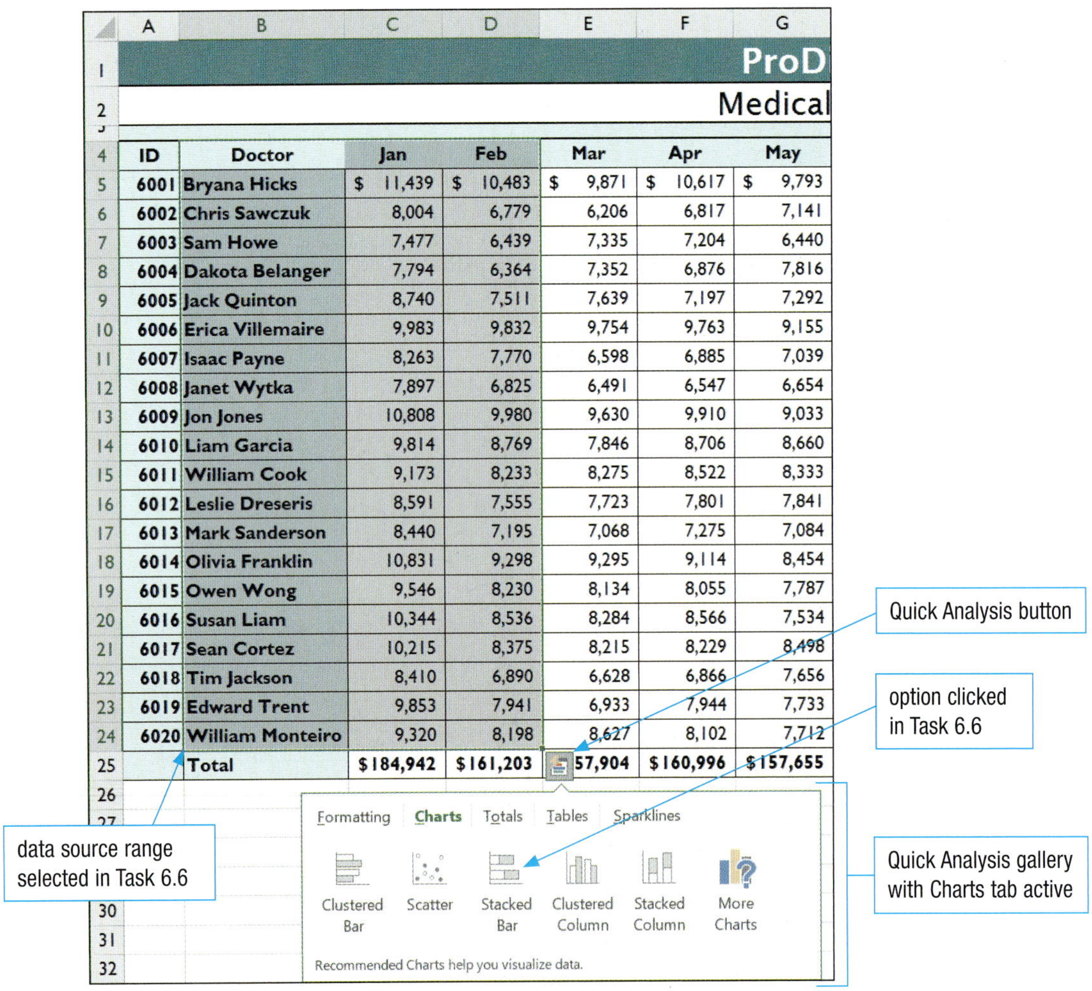

ID	Doctor	Jan	Feb	Mar	Apr	May
6001	Bryana Hicks	$ 11,439	$ 10,483	$ 9,871	$ 10,617	$ 9,793
6002	Chris Sawczuk	8,004	6,779	6,206	6,817	7,141
6003	Sam Howe	7,477	6,439	7,335	7,204	6,440
6004	Dakota Belanger	7,794	6,364	7,352	6,876	7,816
6005	Jack Quinton	8,740	7,511	7,639	7,197	7,292
6006	Erica Villemaire	9,983	9,832	9,754	9,763	9,155
6007	Isaac Payne	8,263	7,770	6,598	6,885	7,039
6008	Janet Wytka	7,897	6,825	6,491	6,547	6,654
6009	Jon Jones	10,808	9,980	9,630	9,910	9,033
6010	Liam Garcia	9,814	8,769	7,846	8,706	8,660
6011	William Cook	9,173	8,233	8,275	8,522	8,333
6012	Leslie Dreseris	8,591	7,555	7,723	7,801	7,841
6013	Mark Sanderson	8,440	7,195	7,068	7,275	7,084
6014	Olivia Franklin	10,831	9,298	9,295	9,114	8,454
6015	Owen Wong	9,546	8,230	8,134	8,055	7,787
6016	Susan Liam	10,344	8,536	8,284	8,566	7,534
6017	Sean Cortez	10,215	8,375	8,215	8,229	8,498
6018	Tim Jackson	8,410	6,890	6,628	6,866	7,656
6019	Edward Trent	9,853	7,941	6,933	7,944	7,733
6020	William Monteiro	9,320	8,198	8,627	8,102	7,712
	Total	$184,942	$161,203	57,904	$160,996	$157,655

On the Job

Task 6.6 Using Quick Analysis to Create a Chart

Kaelan asks you to create a chart showing the January and February data in the Doctor Summary worksheet. He wants to see the monthly revenue along with the total revenue. Use the Quick Analysis button to create the chart Kaelan is requesting. After reviewing the charts suggested by Excel at the Quick Analysis gallery, you decide that a stacked bar chart that illustrates the revenue for each month and the total for each doctor for the two-month period best suits Kaelan's needs. Once the chart is inserted, give the chart a useful chart title and add alternative text, including a title and a description.

1. Click the Doctor Summary sheet tab.
2. Select the range B4:D24 and then click the Quick Analysis button (see Figure 6.19 on page 254).

   The Quick Analysis gallery displays with the Formatting tab active.
3. Click the Charts tab and then click the *Stacked Bar* option.

   The chart is inserted in the same worksheet as the source data. Note that some of the doctors' names are missing in the chart. You need to enlarge the chart to display all the data. Also note that the order of the names is the reverse of how they are displayed in the chart. This option, if required, can be changed at the Format Axis task pane by clicking the *Categories in reverse order* check box.
4. With the chart selected, click the Chart Tools Format tab and then change the value in the *Height* measurement box in the Size group, typing 4.5 as the new value. Press the Enter key.

   The chart is now 4.5 inches high, and all the doctors' names can be seen.
5. Move the chart so the top left corner is in the top left corner of cell D27.
6. Click the chart title element to select it, type Monthly Revenue by Doctor, and then press the Enter key.
7. Right-click an empty area of the chart and then click the *Format Chart Area* option.

   The Format Chart Area task pane displays.
8. Click the Size & Properties icon and then click the *Alt Text* section name, if necessary.

   A list of *Alt Text* options displays.
9. Click in the *Title* text box and then type Stacked Bar Chart.
10. Click in the *Description* text box and then type Chart depicting the monthly revenue by doctor.
11. Click the task pane Close button.
12. Click the Save button on the Quick Access Toolbar.

Model Answer

6.7 Adding, Modifying, and Filtering Chart Data

MOS 5.1.2

Tutorial

Adding and Modifying Source Data

Remember that a chart is linked to the cells used to create it. You can add data to a chart by adding it to the data source or by modifying the category axis labels. You can also modify chart data by editing the corresponding data in the source. **Chart filtering** allows you to view selected data without removing any data from the chart or data source.

▸ **Know This** about adding chart data

— When a chart is selected, the source data displays with a blue fill and border and with a sizing handle in the lower right corner (see Figure 6.20).

— To add data from adjacent cells in the source data, hover the mouse pointer over the sizing handle until the pointer turns into a two-headed diagonal arrow, click and hold down the left mouse button, drag the sizing handle to include the additional data, and then release the mouse button.

▸ Know This about modifying a series name

— To modify a series name in the chart legend, click the Chart Filters button at the upper right side of the chart to display a side menu with the Values tab active, point to the name of the series to be changed in the *Series* section (see Figure 6.21), click the Edit Series button that appears at the right of the series name to display the Edit Series dialog box, type the new name in the *Series name* text box, and then click the OK button.

— For example, in the pie chart created in Task 6.2b, the series names in the legend could be changed to read *Location 1*, *Location 2*, and so on.

▸ Know This about modifying the category axis labels

— To change the category axis labels used in a chart, click the Select Data button in the Data group on the Chart Tools Design tab, click the Edit button in the *Category Axis Labels* section (see example in Figure 6.22 on page 258), and then select the range to be used as the new labels.

— For example, if a bar chart was created using the doctor's name and revenue from the Specialty Summary worksheet, you could modify the category axis labels to display the specialty instead of the doctor's name.

▸ Know This about modifying chart data

— Any changes you make to the source data are automatically shown in the chart.

Figure 6.20 Selected Data Source Range and Sizing Handle

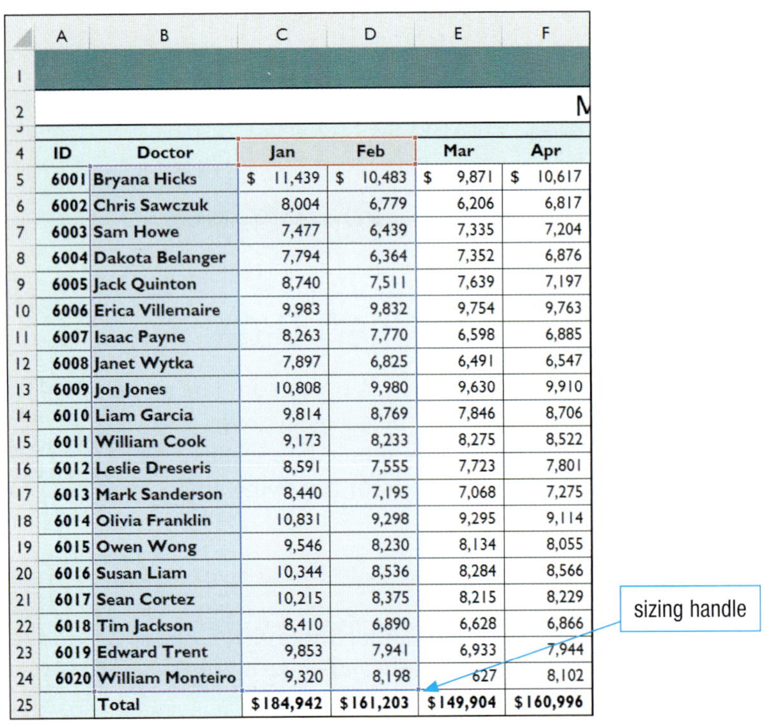

	A	B	C	D	E	F
1						
2						M
3						
4	ID	Doctor	Jan	Feb	Mar	Apr
5	6001	Bryana Hicks	$ 11,439	$ 10,483	$ 9,871	$ 10,617
6	6002	Chris Sawczuk	8,004	6,779	6,206	6,817
7	6003	Sam Howe	7,477	6,439	7,335	7,204
8	6004	Dakota Belanger	7,794	6,364	7,352	6,876
9	6005	Jack Quinton	8,740	7,511	7,639	7,197
10	6006	Erica Villemaire	9,983	9,832	9,754	9,763
11	6007	Isaac Payne	8,263	7,770	6,598	6,885
12	6008	Janet Wytka	7,897	6,825	6,491	6,547
13	6009	Jon Jones	10,808	9,980	9,630	9,910
14	6010	Liam Garcia	9,814	8,769	7,846	8,706
15	6011	William Cook	9,173	8,233	8,275	8,522
16	6012	Leslie Dreseris	8,591	7,555	7,723	7,801
17	6013	Mark Sanderson	8,440	7,195	7,068	7,275
18	6014	Olivia Franklin	10,831	9,298	9,295	9,114
19	6015	Owen Wong	9,546	8,230	8,134	8,055
20	6016	Susan Liam	10,344	8,536	8,284	8,566
21	6017	Sean Cortez	10,215	8,375	8,215	8,229
22	6018	Tim Jackson	8,410	6,890	6,628	6,866
23	6019	Edward Trent	9,853	7,941	6,933	7,944
24	6020	William Monteiro	9,320	8,198	627	8,102
25		Total	$184,942	$161,203	$149,904	$160,996

▸ Know This about filtering chart data

— To filter chart data, select the chart, click the Chart Filters button at the upper right side of the chart, remove the check marks from the check boxes for series or categories that should not be included in the chart, and then click the Apply button (see Figure 6.21).

Figure 6.21 Chart Filters Side Menu

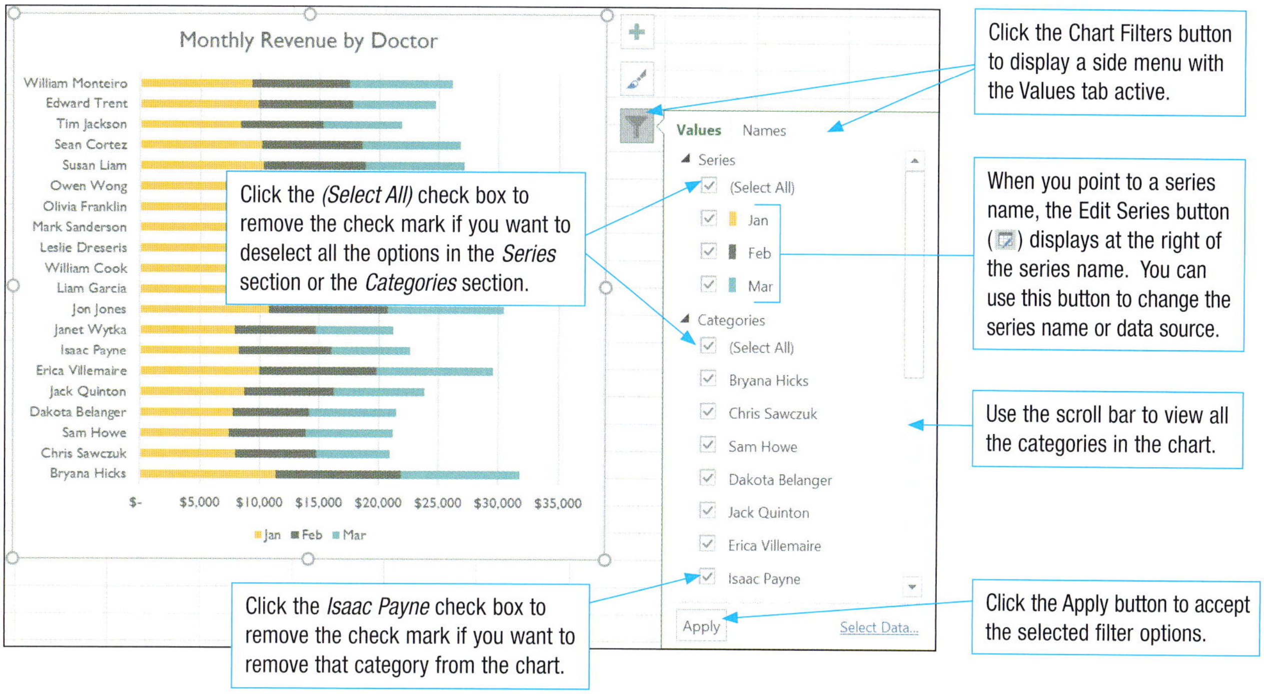

On the Job

Task 6.7a Adding and Modifying Source Data

Kaelan wants you to include the data for the entire first quarter in the Monthly Revenue by Doctor chart. Modify the source data to include the March data. After you modify the data source, you scan the data and notice that the March revenue for Dr. Monteiro is quite a bit lower than the other amounts in the selected range. You check with Kaelan, and he asks you to change the value in cell E24 to $8,627.

1. With the Doctor Summary worksheet active and the stacked bar chart selected, hover the mouse pointer over the bottom right sizing handle for the data source (see Figure 6.20 on page 256).
2. When the mouse pointer turns into a two-headed diagonal arrow, click and hold down the left mouse button, drag the sizing handle one column to the right, and then release the mouse button.

   The range now includes cells E4 through E24. The chart updates to include this additional data.
3. Change the data in cell E24, typing 8627 as the new entry, and then press the Enter key.
4. Click the Save button on the Quick Access Toolbar.

Model Answer

On the Job

Task 6.7b Filtering Source Data and Modifying Category Axis Labels

Doctors William Cook, Sean Cortez, and Tim Jackson are meeting with Kaelan next week, and Kaelan wants to show them a monthly revenue chart with only their data. Kaelan will also show this data to another group of doctors and wants to protect the anonymity of Cook, Cortez, and Jackson. Create the view Kaelan needs by filtering the Monthly Revenue by Doctor chart and then modify the category axis labels to display each doctor's ID instead of the doctor's name.

1. With the Doctor Summary worksheet active, click the stacked bar chart to select it and then click the Chart Filters button (see Figure 6.21 on page 257).

   A side menu displays.

2. Click the *(Select All)* check box in the *Categories* section.

   The check marks are removed from all the check boxes in the *Categories* section.

3. Scroll down the list of names in the *Categories* section; click the *William Cook*, *Sean Cortez*, and *Tim Jackson* check boxes to insert check marks; and then click the Apply button.

   The chart displays data only for doctors William Cook, Sean Cortez, and Tim Jackson.

4. Click the Chart Tools Design tab and then click the Select Data button in the Data group.

   The Select Data Source dialog box displays (see Figure 6.22).

Figure 6.22 Select Data Source Dialog Box

Click the Edit button to collapse the Select Data Source dialog box and then select the new range that contains the new category labels.

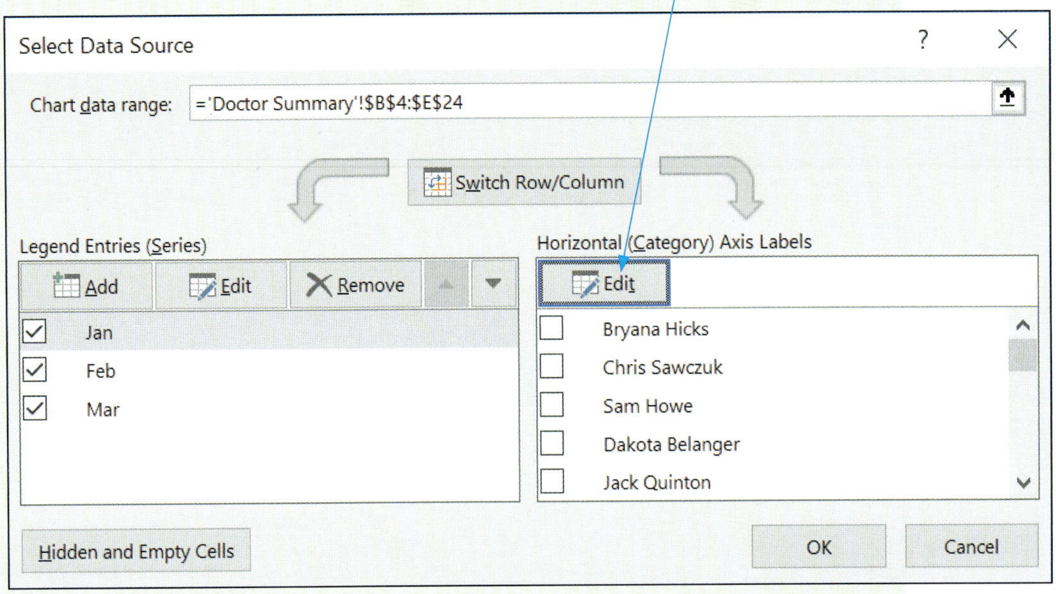

5. Click the Edit button in the *Horizontal (Category) Axis Labels* section.
   The Select Data Source dialog box collapses to display the Axis Labels dialog box.
6. Select the range A5:A24 in the worksheet and then click the OK button.
   The doctors' IDs (instead of their names) appear in the *Horizontal (Category) Axis Labels* list box and in the chart.
7. Click the OK button.
   The Select Data Source dialog box closes.
8. Click the Save button on the Quick Access Toolbar.

Model Answer

6.8 Switching between Rows and Columns in Source Data, and Changing an Axis Scale

MOS 5.1.3

Tutorial

Switching between Rows and Columns in Chart Data and Modifying the Scale or Interval on the Value Axis

By default, when a chart is created, the row headers are used to group data along the horizontal axis of the chart and the column headers are displayed in the legend. You can change the display so that the column headers are used to group data along the horizontal axis of the chart and the row headers are displayed in the legend. You can also change the **scale** (range of values) of the value axis and adjust the interval between the values.

▸ Know This about switching between rows and columns in source data

— To switch between rows and columns in the source data, select the chart, click the Chart Tools Design tab, and then click the Switch Row/Column button in the Data group.

▸ Know This about modifying the scale of the value axis

— When a chart is created, Excel automatically determines the scale and intervals of the value axis based on the data source values.

— If the data source does not contain negative values, the scale ranges from zero to the maximum value.

— To change the scale, double-click the value axis and then make the required changes in the *Axis Options* section of the Format Axis task pane (see Figure 6.23).

— The minimum and maximum values and the increment can be changed using options at the Format Axis task pane.

— Increase the maximum value to allow more blank space above the data, where you can insert any additional information required.

— Although the minimum value of the value axis can be changed, a column chart should never start above zero, because the visual representation of the data may be skewed (see Figure 6.24).

— Tick marks divide the scale at regular intervals and are classified as either major or minor depending on the interval they are identifying.

— To add major and minor tick marks, use options in the *Tick Marks* section at the Format Axis task pane.

Figure 6.23 Format Axis Task Pane with the *Axis Options* and *Tick Marks* Sections Displayed

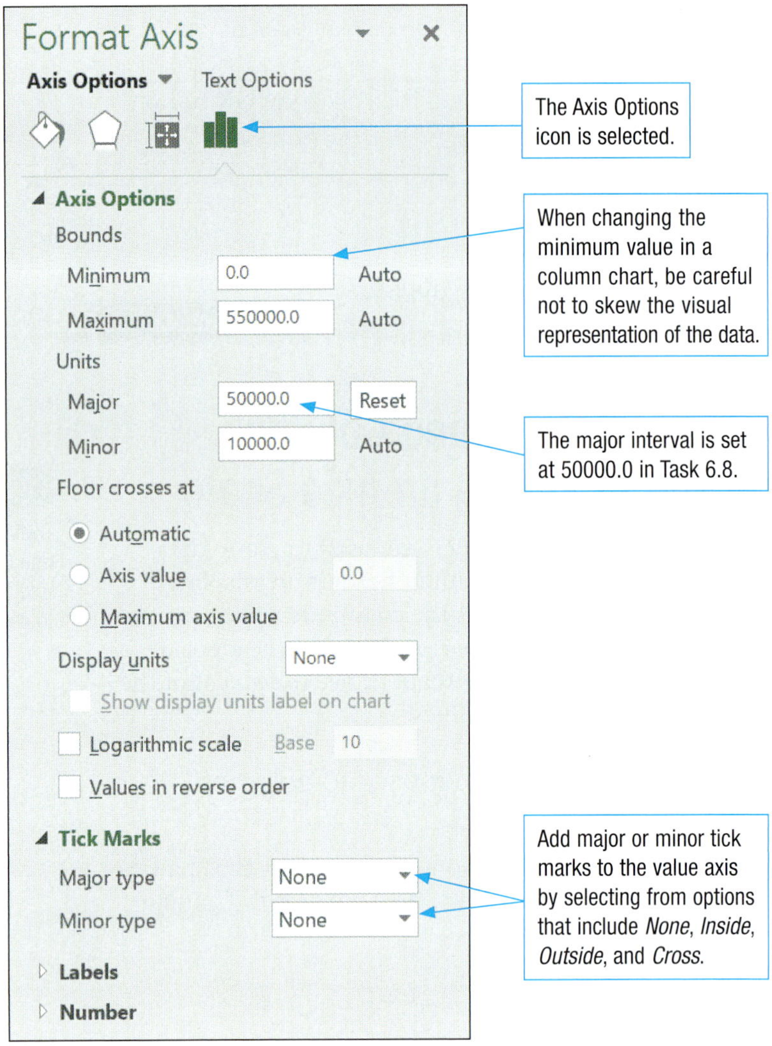

Figure 6.24 Skewing Caused by Changing the Minimum Value of the Value Axis

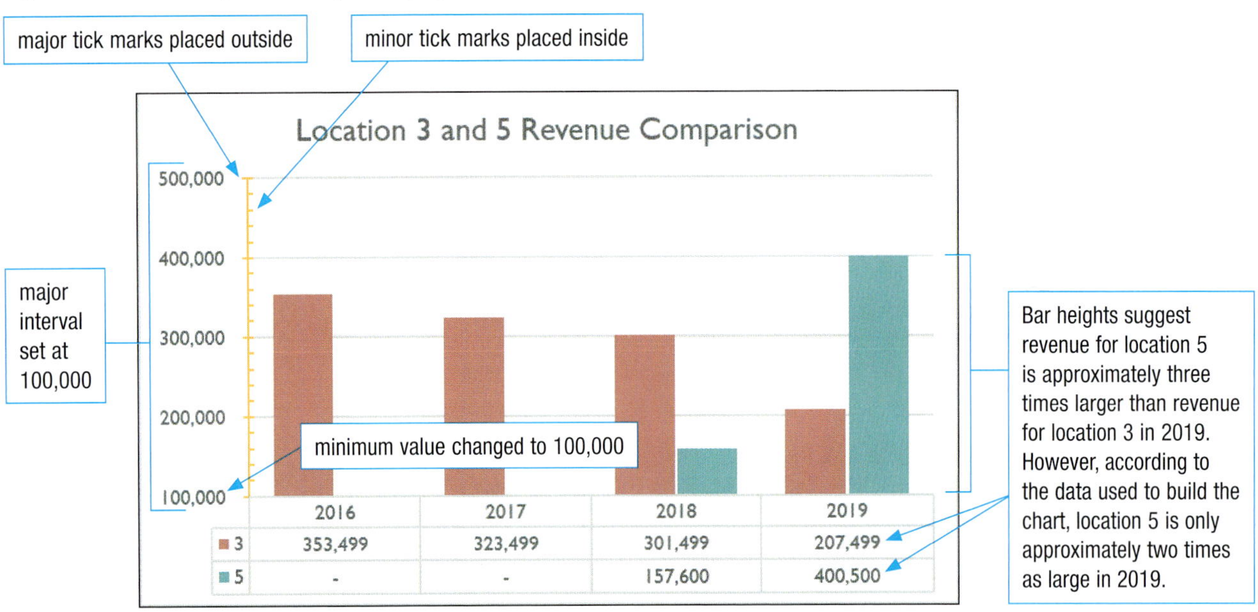

On the Job
Task 6.8 Switching between Rows and Columns in Source Data and Modifying an Axis Interval

In preparation for creating next year's budget, Kaelan wants to see a new chart with the data in the Quarterly Revenue by Location chart organized by quarters instead of by location. He plans to compare the original chart with the new chart and wants both charts to use the same major interval of $50,000 in the value axis. Start by making a copy of the chart worksheet. In the copy, switch between the rows and columns in the source data and then change the major interval of the vertical axis.

1. Click the Chart1 sheet tab.
2. Make a copy of the Chart1 worksheet and move it before the Chart1 worksheet.

   The Chart1 (2) sheet tab appears to the left of the Chart1 sheet tab.
3. Rename the copy of the Chart1 worksheet, typing Chart2 as the new sheet tab name.

   The Chart2 worksheet is active.
4. Select the column chart in the Chart2 worksheet and then click the Chart Tools Design tab.
5. Click the Switch Row/Column button in the Data group.

   The chart switches to show the four quarters as the series across the horizontal axis.
6. Change the chart title, typing Quarterly Revenue as the new title.
7. Double-click one of the values along the vertical axis.

   The Format Axis task pane displays with the *Axis Options* section expanded (see Figure 6.23 on page 260).
8. Select the value in the *Major* text box in the *Units* section, type 50000.0, and then press the Enter key.

   The scale changes to display the major horizontal gridlines at every 50,000.
9. Click the task pane Close button.
10. Click the Save button on the Quick Access Toolbar.

Model Answer

6.9 Using Recommended Charts

If you are not sure which type of chart best suits your data, Excel will provide a recommendation. A hierarchical chart is often recommended for data with several categories.

Tutorial

Using Recommended Charts

▸ Know This about using recommended charts

— To insert a recommended chart in the same worksheet as the data source, select the data, click the Recommended Charts button in the Charts group on the Insert tab, click an option in the left panel on the Recommended Charts tab at the Insert Chart dialog box, and then click the OK button.

— To automatically insert a recommended chart in a new worksheet, select the range and then press the F11 function key. Excel will insert the type of chart that it determines is best suited to the data you selected.

— Once a recommended chart is inserted, modify the chart to suit your needs using the features taught in this chapter.
— To preview any type of chart with its various category axis options, click the Recommended Charts button and then click the All Charts tab.

▸ Know This about hierarchical charts

— A **hierarchical chart** is similar to a pie chart in that it shows data values as percentages of the whole.
— There are two types of hierarchical charts: treemap charts and sunburst charts.
— In a **treemap chart**, each category is placed in a rectangle, and subcategories are placed within the category in rectangles sized to show their relationships to the sum of the values in the category (see Figure 6.25).
— In a **sunburst chart**, each level of a category is placed within a concentric ring, with the highest level at the innermost ring (see Figure 6.26).
— A treemap chart is useful for revealing patterns, such as how doctors' specialties align with revenues. The size and placement of each rectangle in the chart shows its relationship to the total.
— A sunburst chart is useful for displaying the types of patterns shown in a treemap chart at different hierarchical levels.

Figure 6.25 Treemap Hierarchical Chart

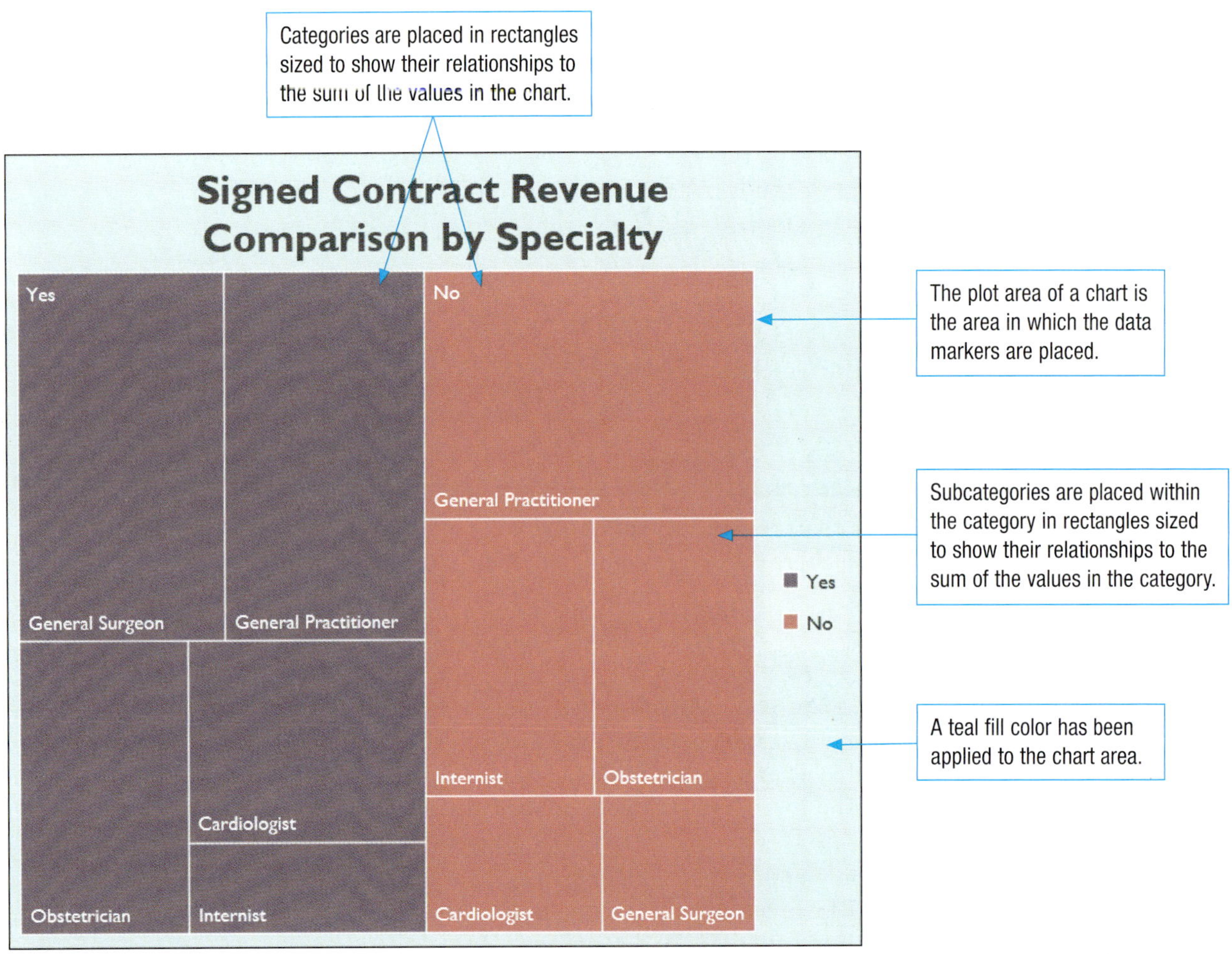

Figure 6.26 Sunburst Hierarchical Chart

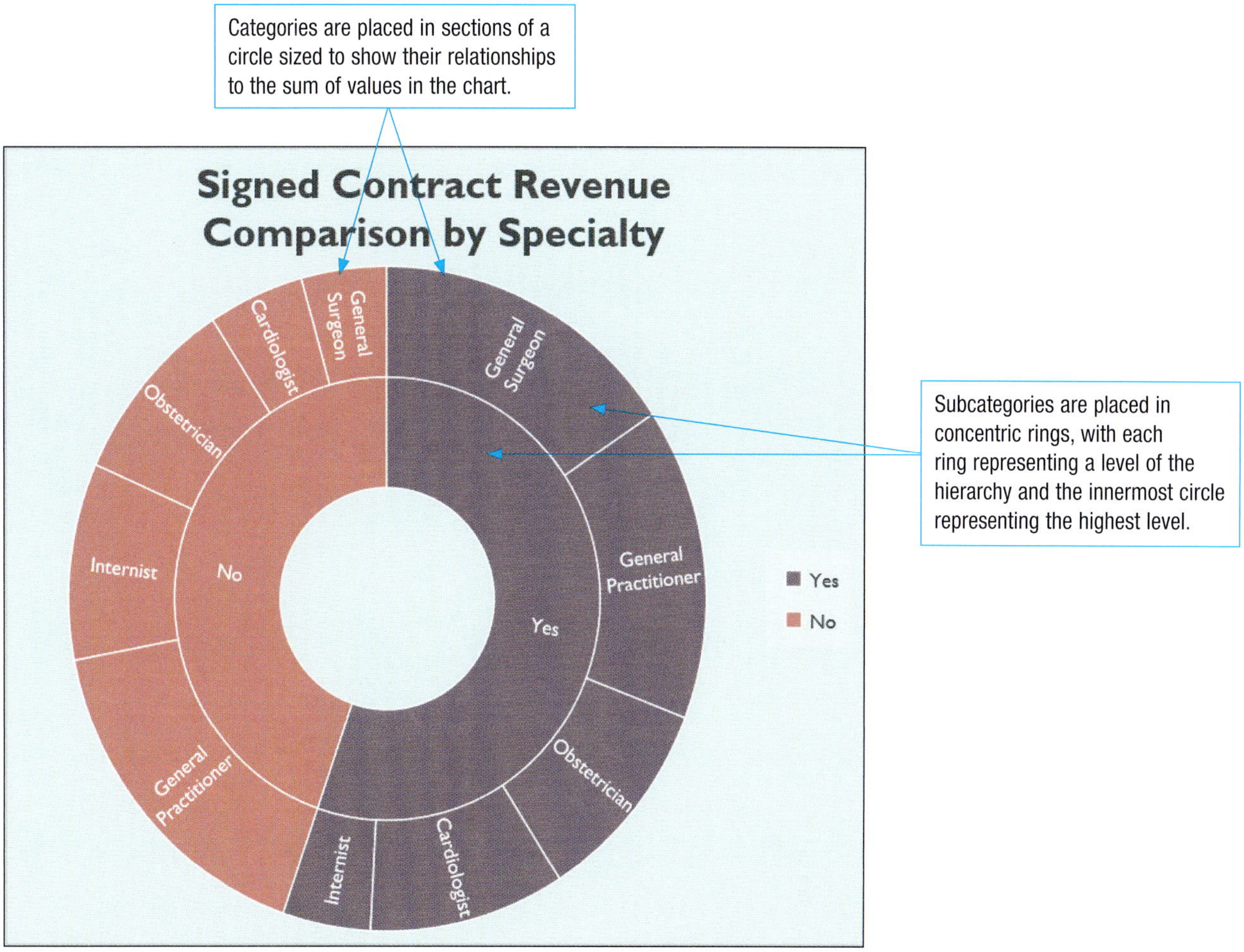

On the Job

Task 6.9 Using Recommended Charts

Kaelan asks you to create a visual representation of the Summary of Revenue data series in the Specialty Summary worksheet. He wants the visual to show two categories of doctors: those who have signed a contract and those who have not. Within each category, he wants to see how much revenue each specialty contributes to the whole. Insert an appropriate chart using a recommended chart type. After the chart is inserted, add a title, apply a style, format the chart area, and then add alternative text, including both a title and a description.

1. Click the Specialty Summary sheet tab.
2. Select the range G5:I15.
3. Click the Insert tab and then click the Recommended Charts button in the Charts group.

   The Insert Chart dialog box displays with the Recommended Charts tab active.

4. Click the *Treemap* option (fourth option in the left panel).

   A preview of the selected range formatted as a treemap chart displays in the right panel.

5. Click the OK button.

   A treemap chart with a summary of revenue data is inserted in the same worksheet as the selected data.

6. Change the chart title, typing Signed Contract Revenue Comparison by Specialty as the new title.
7. Click in an empty part of the chart area.

   The chart is selected, and the Chart Elements and Chart Styles buttons appear at the upper right side of the chart.

8. Click the Chart Styles button and then click the second style option (gray background) on the Style tab.

   The selected style is applied to the chart, and the Chart Styles button side menu continues to display.

9. Click the Color tab, click the *Colorful Palette 4* option (fourth option in the *Colorful* section), and then click the Chart Styles button.

   The selected color is applied to the chart, and the side menu closes.

10. Right-click an empty part of the chart and then click the *Format Chart Area* option.

    The Format Chart Area task pane displays with the Fill & Line area active.

11. Click the *Fill* section name.

    A list of fill options displays (see Figure 6.27).

Figure 6.27 Format Chart Area Task Pane

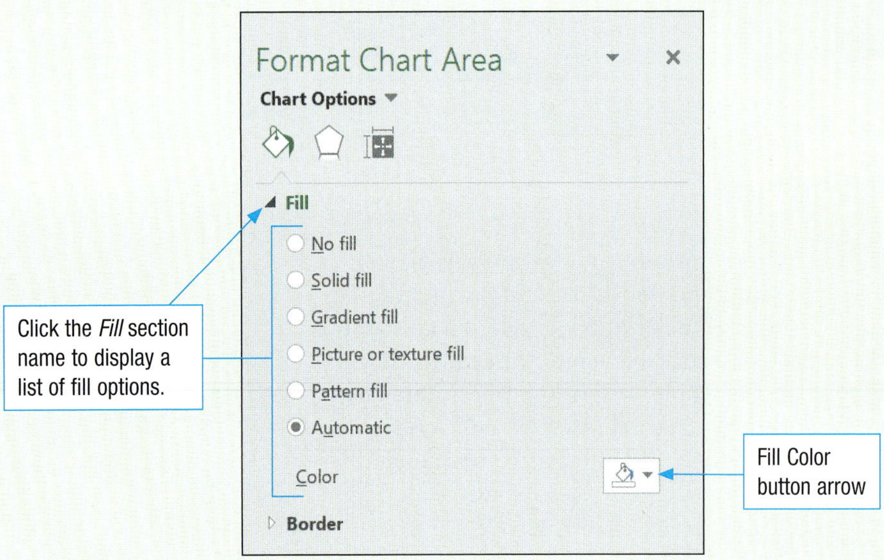

12. Click the Fill Color button arrow.

    A drop-down palette displays.

13. Click the *Teal, Accent 3, Lighter 80%* option (seventh column, second row in the *Theme Colors* section).

    The chart background changes to light teal.

14. Click the Size & Properties icon and then click the *Alt Text* section name, if necessary.

   A list of *Alt Text* options display.

15. Click in the *Title* text box and then type Treemap Chart.
16. Click in the *Description* text box and then type Revenue comparison of doctors by specialty who have signed a contract with those who have not.
17. With the task pane still displayed, double-click the plot area of the treemap chart (see Figure 6.25 on page 262).

   The Format Data Series task pane displays.

18. Click the Series Options icon, if necessary (see Figure 6.28).

   A list of series options displays.

19. Click the *Banner* radio button to insert a bullet.

Figure 6.28 Format Data Series Task Pane with Series Options Area Active

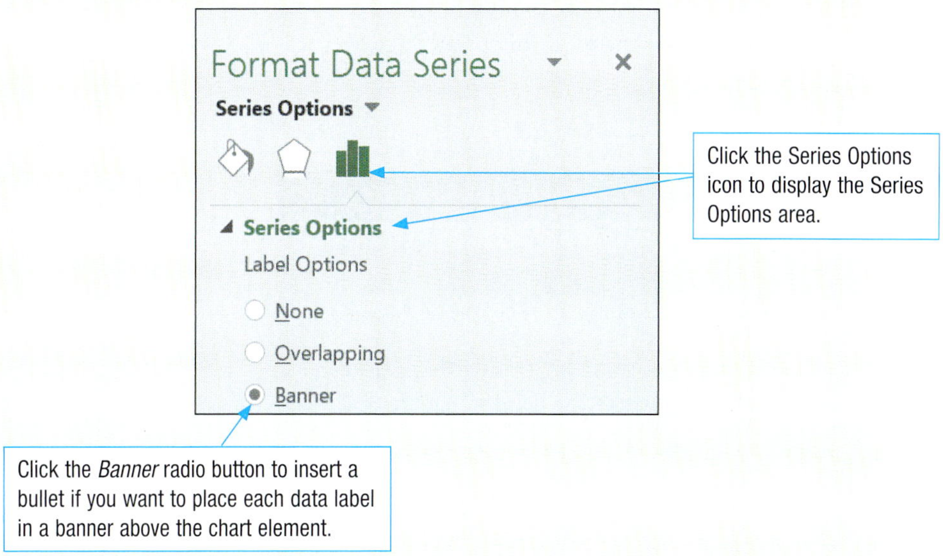

20. Click the task pane Close button.
21. Move the chart so that its upper left corner is in the upper left corner of cell G17.
22. Change the size of the chart to be approximately 3.5 inches tall by 6.5 inches wide.

   The entire label within each rectangle is now visible.

23. Click the Save button on the Quick Access Toolbar.

Model Answer

6.10 Using Trendlines

MOS Expert 4.1.1

Tutorial Adding a Trendline to a Chart

A **trendline** is used to show a data trend or a moving average in a chart, and it can be extended past the data to help predict future outcomes. A trendline is added to a specific series in a chart. After adding a trendline, you can change its type and format it.

▸ Know This about using trendlines

— To add a trendline to a data series in a chart, select the chart, click the Chart Elements button, click the *Trendlines* check box at the side menu, click the series at the Add Trendline dialog box, and then click the OK button.

— A trendline is added to a specific series and appears as a dotted line in the same color as the series it represents.

— You can add trendlines to 2-D area, bar, column, line, stock, scatter, and bubble charts.

— You cannot add trendlines to stacked, 3-D, radar, pie, surface, and doughnut charts.

▸ **Know More** ways to add trendlines to charts

– Right-click a data series, click the *Add Trendline* option at the pop-up menu, and then click options at the Format Trendline task pane.

▸ Know This about changing the type of a trendline

— After adding a trendline, you can change its type. Types of trendlines are described in Table 6.3.

— To change the type of a trendline, double-click the trendline, click the Trendline Options icon at the Format Trendline task pane, and then click the radio button for a trendline type to insert a bullet (see Figure 6.29).

Table 6.3 Types of Trendlines

Type of Trendline	Description
Exponential	Displays as a curved line; used for data sets that show large increases and decreases and that do not contain zeros or negative values
Linear	Displays as a straight line; used for trends that show constant increases or decreases
Logarithmic	Displays as a curved line; used for trends that show a quick increase or decrease and then level out
Polynomial	Displays as a curved line; used for large data sets that fluctuate
Power	Displays as a curved line; used for data sets that increase at a specific rate
Moving Average	Displays as a curved line; used to average the data points; requires entering how many points to average to create each value

▸ Know This about trendline options

— Use options in the Trendline Options area at the Format Trendline task pane to assign various attributes to a trendline (see Figure 6.29).

— To extend a trendline beyond the existing data, enter values in the *Forward* and *Backward* measurement boxes in the *Forecast* section.

— To show how closely the estimated values for the trendline correspond to the data, click the *Display R-squared value on chart* check box to insert a check mark. The value will be a number between 0 and 1, and the ideal number is close to 1.

Figure 6.29 Format Trendline Task Pane with Trendline Options Area Active

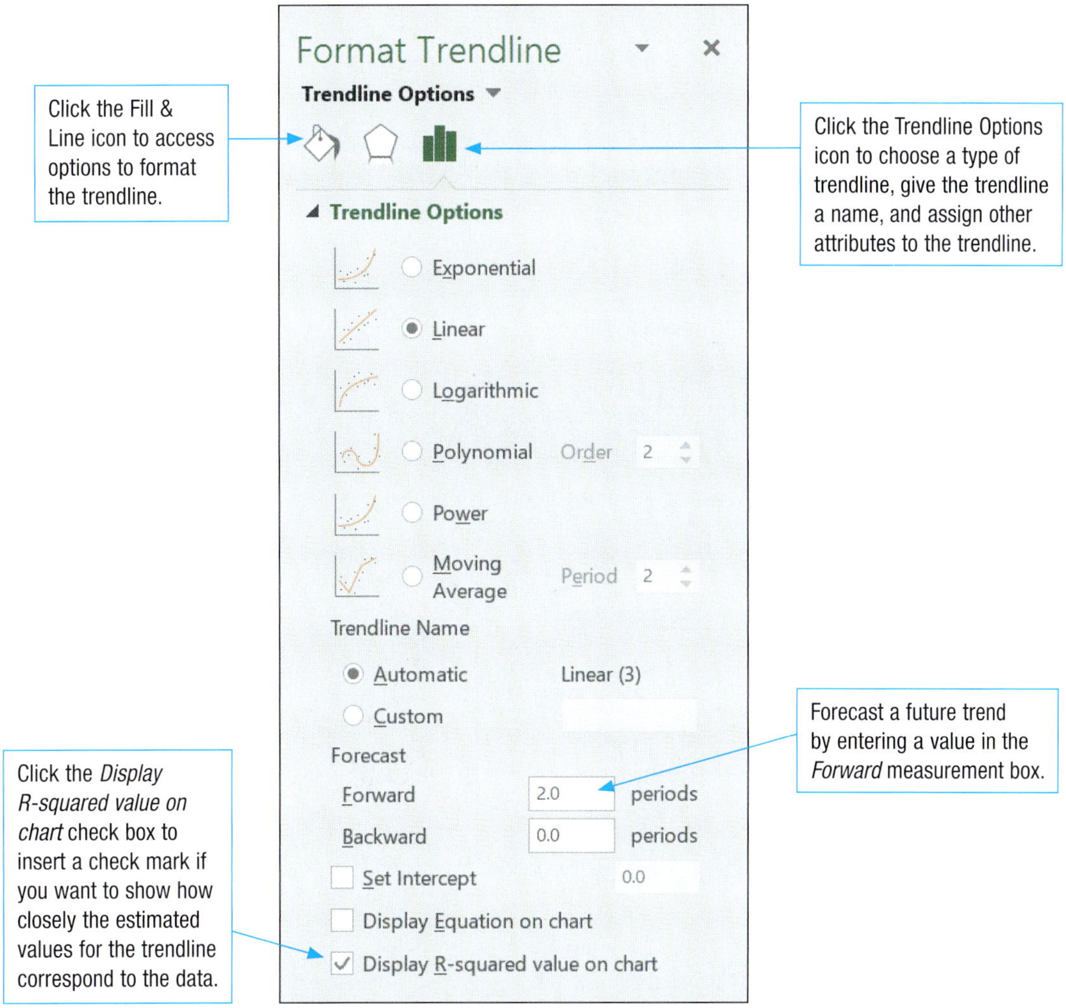

On the Job

Task 6.10 Adding a Trendline to a Chart

Kaelan wants to see how the opening of location 5 in October 2018 affected the revenue of location 3, because location 5 may be drawing some of the revenue that would have previously gone to location 3. Use the established trend to predict the effect over the next two years. Kaelan also wants to see how closely the estimated values for the trend correspond to the data. Create a clustered column chart to show how revenues from the five locations compared in 2016, 2017, 2018, and 2019 and then add a trendline to Series 3 (the revenue data for location 3). Ensure that the years are used as the data for the category axis. After the chart and trendline are inserted, extend the trendline for two years, display the R-squared value for the trendline, and then add alternative text, including a title and a description.

1. Click the Yearly Comparison sheet tab.
2. Select the range A5:E10, click the Insert tab, click the Recommended Charts button, click the All Charts tab, click the second layout option in the *Clustered Column* section in the right panel, and then click the OK button.

A clustered column chart with the years used as the category axis is inserted and selected.

3. Click the Chart Elements button and then click the *Trendline* check box (see Figure 6.30).

   The Add Trendline dialog box displays.

4. Click the *3* option and then click the OK button.

   A trendline is added to the Series 3 (Location 3) data markers in the chart and displays as a teal dotted line.

Figure 6.30 Chart Elements Side Menu and Add Trendline Dialog Box

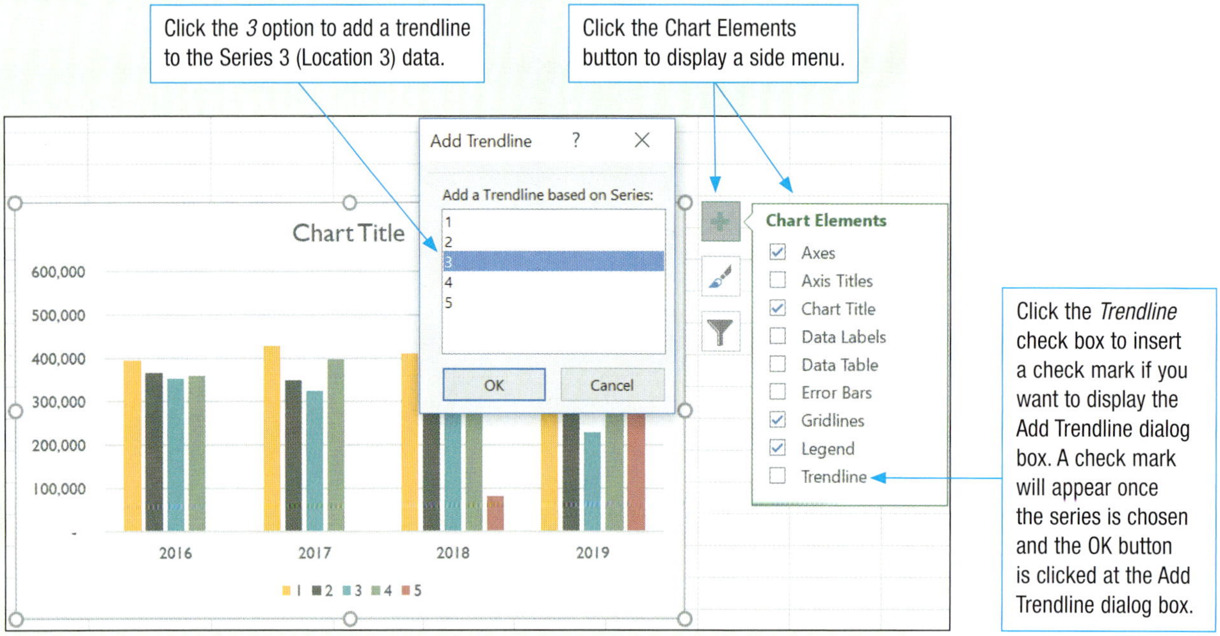

5. Double-click the trendline.

   The Format Trendline task pane displays with the Trendline Options area active. ***Note:*** *Be sure to double-click the trendline. If you click another chart element, a different task pane will display. If that happens, click another spot along the trendline.*

6. Select the value in the *Forward* measurement box in the *Forecast* section, type 2, and then press the Enter key.

   The chart adjusts and the trendline extends two years beyond the current data.

7. Click the *Display R-squared value on chart* check box.

   A check mark appears in the check box and *R^2 = 0.9234* displays below the trendline on the chart. This number is close to 1, indicating that the estimated values for the trendline correspond closely to the actual data.

8. Click in an empty part of the chart.

   The Format Trendline task pane changes to display the Format Chart Area task pane.

9. Click the Size & Properties icon, if necessary, and then click the *Alt Text* section name, if necessary.

10. Click in the *Title* text box and then type Column Chart.
11. Click in the *Description* text box and then type Chart depicting the past four years of revenue for each location.
12. Click the task pane Close button.
13. Move the chart so that its upper left corner is in the upper left corner of cell G5.
14. Click the Save button on the Quick Access Toolbar.

Model Answer

6.11 Using a Combination Chart

MOS Expert 4.1.2

Tutorial

Changing an Existing Chart to a Combination Chart

When you want to compare data series that vary greatly, consider creating a **combination chart** (also called a *dual-axis chart*). A combination chart uses two vertical axes. One data series is plotted against the **primary axis**, which usually appears along the left side of the chart. One or more additional data series are plotted against the **secondary axis**, which usually appears along the right side of the chart. A combination chart allows you to compare two sets of data that vary greatly by using the best type of chart for each data series.

▶ Know This about combination charts

— A combination chart displays data as two different chart types—for example, a column chart and a line chart—combined in one graphic.

— Each data series in a combination chart is associated with either the primary axis or the secondary axis.

— It is sometimes easier to create a chart with the data plotted on the primary axis, modify the chart to include the data for the secondary axis, and then change the chart type to a combination chart.

▶ Know This about creating a combination chart

— To create a combination chart, follow these steps:

1. Select the data.
2. Click the Insert tab and then click the Recommended Charts button in the Charts group.
3. Click the All Charts tab.
4. Click the *Combo* option.
5. Click a chart type option.
6. In the *Choose the chart type and axis for your data series* section, click the *secondary axis* check box for each data series to be plotted on the secondary axis and then click the OK button.
7. Click the Switch Row/Column button, if necessary; click the Change Chart Type button; click the *secondary axis* check box to insert a check mark for each data series to be plotted on the secondary axis; and then click the OK button.

▶ Know This about area charts

— The sum of the plotted values displays as the area below the plotted line with a fill color.

— Each series is represented by a different-colored segment.

— Area charts are useful for displaying changes over time.

— Stack one series over another to create a stacked area chart (which is similar to a stacked column chart) to create a chart that shows the individual parts used to create the total.
— Review the final chart to ensure that all the data is displayed and that no data is hidden behind another data series.
— If data is hidden, consider using a line chart.

On the Job

Task 6.11 Changing an Existing Chart to a Combination Chart

Kaelan wants to show the managers a chart that contains all the source data from the Yearly Comparison worksheet. He asks you to create a single chart that is complete, accurate, and attractive. Modify the data source in the worksheet to include the annual revenue totals and then change the chart type to a combination chart. Scan the chart and fix any errors, add a chart title, change the chart style, and then move the chart to a new worksheet.

1. With the Yearly Comparison worksheet active and the clustered column chart selected, modify the data source to include the range A11:E11.

   See Task 6.7a for instructions on how to do this.

2. Click the Chart Tools Design tab and then click the Change Chart Type button in the Type group.

   The Change Chart Type dialog box displays with the All Charts tab active.

3. Click the *Combo* option in the left panel (see Figure 6.31).

   The *Clustered Column - Line* option is selected in the right panel, and a preview of the chart with this type applied displays below the selected option.

4. Scroll down, if necessary, to display the *Total* option in the *Series Name* section of the *Choose the chart type and axis for your data series* list box.
5. Click the *Secondary Axis* check box for the Total data series.

   The preview adjusts to show the Total data series plotted against the secondary axis (on the right side of the chart).

6. Click the *Chart Type* option box for the Total data series and then click the *Area* option (first option in the *Area* section).

   The Total data series changes to an area chart.

7. Scan the chart in the preview area and note any possible errors.

   Excel shows data series 4 and 5 as lines. These series contain the same type of data as series 1, 2, and 3. You want them to display as columns in the clustered column chart.

8. Click the *Chart Type* option box for data series 4 and then click the *Clustered Column* option (first option in the *Column* section).
9. Click the *Chart Type* option box for data series 5, click the *Clustered Column* option (first option in the *Column* section), and then click the OK button.
10. Change the chart title, typing Revenue by Location for London as the new title.

Figure 6.31 Change Chart Type Dialog Box with the *Combo Clustered Column - Line* Option Selected

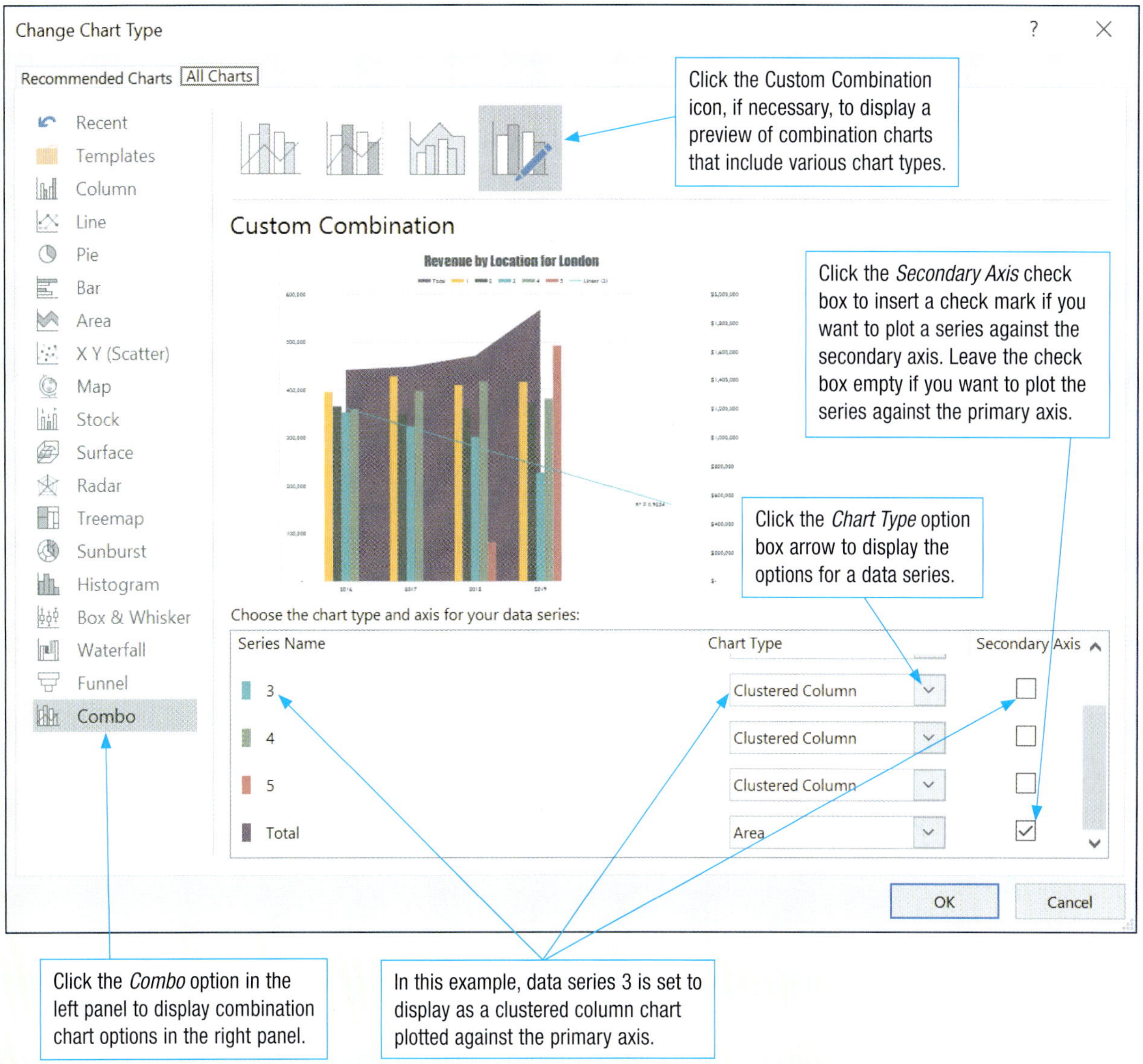

11. Change the style to Style 7.
12. Move the chart to a new worksheet named *Chart3*.

    The new worksheet appears before the Yearly Comparison worksheet by default. Leave the worksheet in this location.
13. Click the Save button on the Quick Access Toolbar.

Model Answer

6.12 Working with Chart Templates

MOS Expert 4.1.3

Tutorial

Saving and Using a Chart Template

If you find yourself creating similar charts, consider saving one of them as a template. You can then use the template to create new charts and save the time of applying all the settings to each new chart.

▸ Know This about saving a chart as a template

- To create a template from an existing chart, right-click an empty part of the chart, click the *Save as Template* option at the pop-up menu, type an appropriate name to replace the selected text in the *File name* text box at the Save Chart Template dialog box, and then click the Save button.
- The file name for the template will display the extension *.crtx*.
- The saved template will be available for all of your Excel workbooks.

▸ Know This about using a chart template

- To use a chart template, select a data range, click the Charts group dialog box launcher, click the All Charts tab at the Insert Chart dialog box, click the *Templates* option in the left panel, and then click the template in the right panel.
- When you apply a chart template to selected data, the data is formatted and styled to match the template.
- If you use a chart template in a new workbook, the theme (including colors and fonts) is retained from the original workbook.
- To apply the theme for the new workbook, right-click the chart and then click *Reset to Match Style* at the pop-up menu.

▸ Know More ways to use a chart template

- Select a data range, click the Recommended Charts button in the Charts group on the Insert tab, click the *Templates* option in the left panel at the Insert Chart dialog box, and click the template in the right panel.

▸ Know This about deleting a chart template

- To delete a template, click the Manage Templates button at the bottom of the Insert Chart dialog box, click the chart in the list, and then press the Delete key.

▸ Know This about setting a chart type as the default

- To set a chart type or template as the default for any new charts, click the Charts group dialog box launcher, locate the chart type or template at the Change Chart Type dialog box, right-click the chart, and then click the *Set as Default Chart* option at the pop-up menu.

On the Job

Task 6.12 Saving and Using a Chart Template

At the development meeting next week, Kaelan plans to share additional data with managers, including operating costs and number of patients served each quarter by location. The additional data is located in different workbooks. Kaelan asks you to help him apply the formatting from the Quarterly Revenue by Location chart to the new data. Save the chart as a template so you can use it in any workbook. Verify that the chart template works by creating a chart using the template and the range A6:E10 found in the Yearly Comparison worksheet.

1. Click the Chart1 sheet tab.
2. Right-click an empty part of the stacked column chart and then click the *Save as Template* option.

   The Save Chart Template dialog box displays with the text highlighted in the *File name* text box and the *Chart Template Files(*.crtx)* option appearing in the *Save as type* option box.
3. Click the Save button.

4. Click the Yearly Comparison sheet tab and then select the range A5:E10.
5. Click the Insert tab and then click the Recommended Charts button.

   The Insert Chart dialog box displays.
6. Click the All Charts tab and then click the *Templates* option in the left panel (see Figure 6.32).

   The available template displays.

Figure 6.32 Available Templates

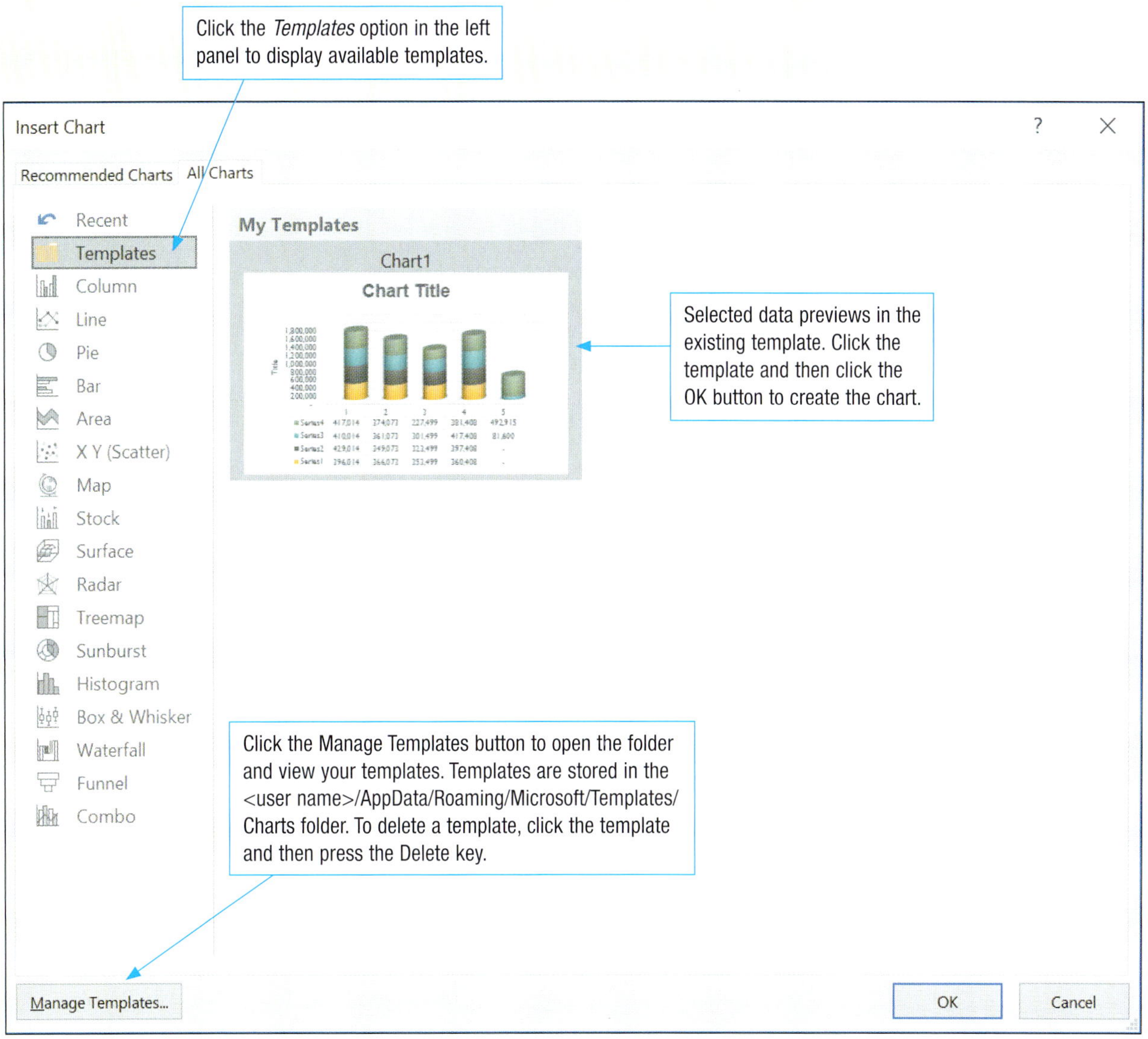

7. Click the template and then click the OK button.

   A chart is inserted in the worksheet using the data from the Yearly Comparison worksheet and the formatting of the chart in the Chart1 worksheet.
8. Move the chart so its upper left corner is in the upper left corner of cell A16.
9. Click the Save button on the Quick Access Toolbar.

Model Answer

MOS 1.2.3

Tutorial

Inserting a Text Hyperlink within an Object to a Place in the Same Document

6.13 Inserting, Modifying, Using, and Removing Hyperlinks

A **hyperlink** is a graphic or text that allows you to move to another location in the same workbook or in a new workbook, to a file (such as a PDF or a PowerPoint presentation), or to a web page. A hyperlink can also be used to open a new email message, and it can be added to text or to an object such as a chart. To create a hyperlink to a web page, you need to know the **uniform resource locator (URL)**, or address, for the web page.

▸ Know This about inserting a hyperlink

— To insert a hyperlink, click in a cell or select an object, click the Link button in the Links group on the Insert tab, make the required changes at the Insert Hyperlink dialog box, and then click the OK button (see Figure 6.33).

— By default, when a text hyperlink is created in a cell, the text is underlined and the font color is blue. After the hyperlink has been opened, it displays as purple.

— When a text hyperlink is created in an object, it appears with whatever font formatting has been applied to the shape.

— You cannot hyperlink to a chart worksheet or add a hyperlink in a chart worksheet.

▸ Know More ways to insert a text hyperlink to a web page

– Click in a cell, type the URL for the web page, and then press any key. By default, Excel displays the address as a hyperlink.

▸ Know More ways to display the Insert Hyperlink dialog box

– Click the Link button arrow and then click the *Insert Link* option at the drop-down gallery.

Reminder

A chart worksheet contains only a chart, not its data series (see Section 6.3 in this chapter).

Figure 6.33 Insert Hyperlink Dialog Box

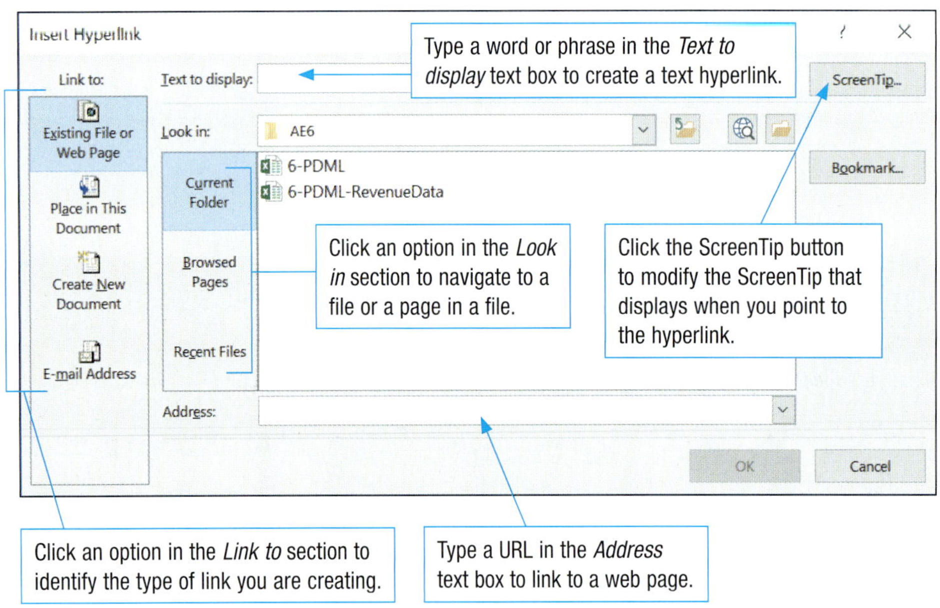

▸ Know This about email address hyperlinks

— To add an email address hyperlink, follow these steps:

1. Click in a cell.
2. Click the Link button in the Links group on the Insert tab.
3. Click the *E-mail Address* option in the *Link to* section at the Insert Hyperlink dialog box.

▸ Know More ways to insert email address hyperlinks

– Click in a cell, type the email address, and then press any key. By default, Excel displays the address as an email address hyperlink.

4. Type the email address in the *E-mail address* text box.
5. Type a subject in the *Subject* text box.
6. Select the text in the *Text to display* text box and then type the hyperlink text to display in the cell.
7. Click the OK button.

— To open a new email message with the recipient address and subject line already populated, click the email hyperlink.

— By default, Excel opens the new email message in Outlook.

— If you have more than one email account, you will be asked to choose which account to send the email from.

▸ Know This about modifying a hyperlink

— To modify a hyperlink, right-click the hyperlink text, click the *Edit Hyperlink* option at the pop-up menu, make changes at the Edit Hyperlink dialog box, and then click the OK button. *Edit Link* will display if the hyperlink is placed within an object.

▸ Know This about opening a hyperlink

— To open a hyperlink, hover the mouse pointer over the hyperlink until the pointer turns into a hand and then click the left mouse button.

▸ Know More ways to open a hyperlink

– Right-click the hyperlink and then click the *Open Hyperlink* option at the pop-up menu.

▸ Know This about selecting a hyperlink without opening the link

— To select a hyperlink without opening the link, hover the mouse pointer over the cell containing the hyperlink until the pointer turns into a hand, click and hold down the left mouse button until the pointer turns into a white cross, and then release the mouse button.

▸ Know More ways to select a hyperlink without opening the link

– Use the Up, Down, Left, and Right Arrow keys to make the cell that contains the hyperlink active.

– Press and hold down the Ctrl key, click the hyperlink, and then release the Ctrl key.

▸ Know This about removing hyperlinks

— To remove a hyperlink and the hyperlink text or object, select the hyperlink without opening the link and then press the Delete key.

— To remove a hyperlink without removing the hyperlink text, right-click the hyperlink and then click the *Remove Hyperlink* option at the pop-up menu. *Remove Link* will display if the hyperlink is placed within an object.

— To remove all the hyperlinks in a worksheet, press Ctrl + A, right-click anywhere in the worksheet, and then click the *Remove Hyperlinks* option at the pop-up menu.

▸ Know This about hyperlink ScreenTips

— To view a ScreenTip that displays the address of the hyperlinked location, point to the hyperlink.

— To modify the ScreenTip, right-click the hyperlink, click the *Edit Hyperlink* option at the pop-up menu, click the ScreenTip button, edit the text in the *ScreenTip text* text box, and then click the OK button.

▸ Know This about linking to recently used files

— The Link to Recent Items feature is available only with Office 365.

— To insert a link to a recently used file, click in a cell, click the Link button drop-down arrow in the Link group on the Insert tab, and then click the file name at the drop-down gallery.
— If you do not see the file you want to hyperlink at the drop-down list, click the *Insert Link* option and then navigate to the file at the Insert Hyperlink dialog box.
— Only files stored in the Cloud will display in the Link button drop-down gallery.

On the Job

Task 6.13a Inserting an Object Hyperlink to a Place in the Document and Modifying the Hyperlink ScreenTip

In Kaelan's presentation to the managers, he wants to move quickly from the Location Total worksheet to the Yearly Comparison worksheet. Add an object hyperlink to make this possible and then modify the hyperlink ScreenTip.

1. Click the Location Total sheet tab.
2. Insert a Rectangle: Rounded Corners shape (second option in the *Rectangles* section at the Shapes button drop-down list) that is 2.6 inches wide by 0.3 inches tall.
3. Move the shape so its lower left corner aligns with the lower left corner of cell A12.
4. Add text to the shape, typing Go to Yearly Comparison worksheet.
5. Apply the Subtle Effect - Teal, Accent 3 shape style (fourth column, fourth row in the *Theme Styles* section).
6. With the shape still selected, click the Insert tab and then click the Link button in the Links group.

   The Insert Hyperlink dialog box displays.
7. Click the *Place in This Document* option in the *Link to* section (see Figure 6.34).

Figure 6.34 Insert Hyperlink Dialog Box with the *Place in This Document* Option Selected

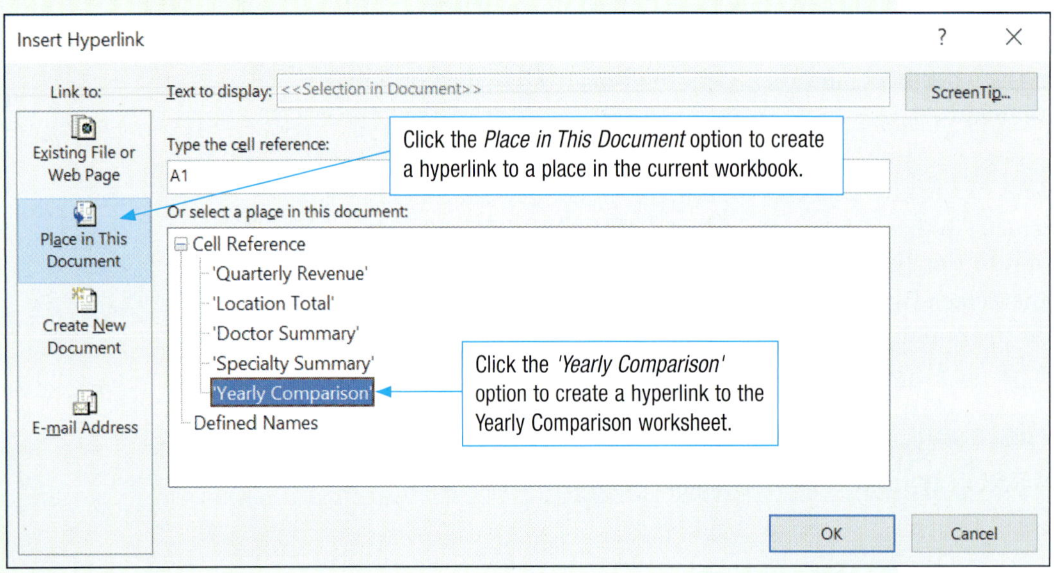

8. Click the *'Yearly Comparison'* option in the *Or select a place in this document* list box and then click the OK button.

   The Insert Hyperlink dialog box closes.

9. Right-click the shape and then click the *Edit Link* option.

   The Edit Hyperlink dialog box displays.

10. Click the ScreenTip button and then type Yearly Comparison worksheet in the *ScreenTip text* text box.

    The Set Hyperlink ScreenTip dialog box displays and the new ScreenTip text appears in the text box.

11. Click the OK button.

    The Set Hyperlink ScreenTip dialog box closes.

12. Click the OK button.

    The Edit Hyperlink dialog box closes.

13. Click in any cell in the worksheet.

    The shape is no longer selected.

14. Hover the mouse pointer over the shape until the pointer turns into a hand and then click the left mouse button.

    The ScreenTip *Yearly Comparison worksheet* displays when you point to the shape. The Yearly Comparison worksheet becomes active when you click the left mouse button.

15. Click the Save button on the Quick Access Toolbar.

Model Answer

On the Job

Task 6.13b Inserting a Text Hyperlink to a Web Page and Modifying the Hyperlink ScreenTip

After Kaelan presents the data on the Yearly Comparison worksheet, he plans to go to the company website and show information about the organization. Add a text hyperlink that opens the PDML home page and then modify the hyperlink ScreenTip.

1. With the Yearly Comparison worksheet active, click in cell A14.
2. Click the Insert tab, if necessary, and then click the Link button in the Links group.

   The Insert Hyperlink dialog box displays.

3. Click the *Existing File or Web Page* option in the *Link to* section.
4. Click in the *Text to display* text box and then type Company Information.
5. Click in the *Address* text box, type http://ADE.ParadigmEducation.com/PDML, and then click the OK button.

   The dialog box closes and the text *Company Information* appears in cell A14 as a hyperlink in blue underlined text.

6. Hover the mouse pointer over the hyperlink until the pointer turns into a hand and then click the left mouse button.

   The web page opens in your web browser.

7. Close the web browser.
8. Right-click the Company Information hyperlink and then click the *Edit Hyperlink* option.

9. Click the ScreenTip button, type View the company website in the *ScreenTip text* text box, and then click the OK button.

   The Set Hyperlink ScreenTip dialog box closes.

10. Click the OK button.

   The Edit Hyperlink dialog box closes.

11. Click the Save button on the Quick Access Toolbar.

Model Answer

On the Job

Task 6.13c Inserting a Text Hyperlink to Another Existing File

Kaelan anticipates that the managers will have questions about the quarterly revenue data. He wants to quickly access the workbook containing the data used to create the Quarterly Revenue worksheet. Add a text hyperlink that opens the other workbook.

1. Click the Quarterly Revenue sheet tab and then click in cell A12.
2. Type Revenue Data and then press Ctrl + Enter.

   The text *Revenue Data* appears in cell A12 and cell A12 is active.

3. Click the Link button in the Links group on the Insert tab.
4. Click the *Existing File or Web Page* option in the *Link to* section, if necessary.
5. Click the *Look in* option box arrow (see Figure 6.35) and then navigate to the AE6 folder in your storage medium.

Figure 6.35 Insert Hyperlink Dialog Box with the *Existing File or Web Page* Option Selected

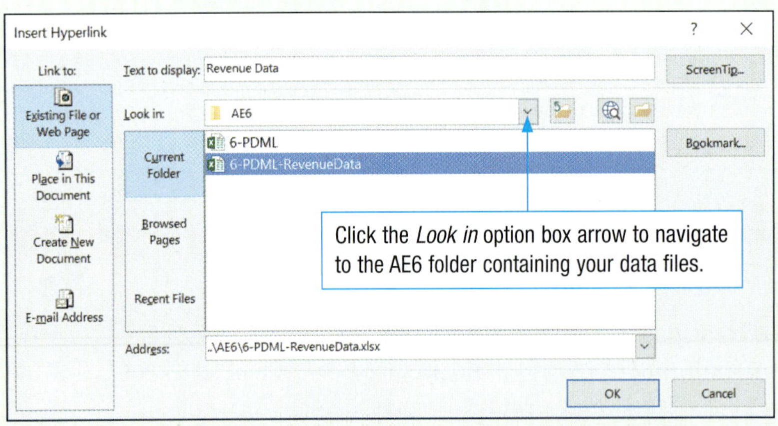

6. Double-click the data file **6-PDML-RevenueData**.

   The Insert Hyperlink dialog box closes, and the Revenue Data hyperlink displays in cell A12 with a blue font and underline formatting.

7. Hover the mouse pointer over the Revenue Data hyperlink until the pointer turns into a hand and then click the left mouse button.

   The 6-PDML-RevenueData workbook opens with the Revenue Data worksheet active.

8. Close the 6-PDML-RevenueData workbook.
9. Click the Save button on the Quick Access Toolbar.

Model Answer

6.14 Printing a Chart

Tutorial

Printing a Chart

You can print the entire worksheet containing a chart or just the embedded chart. Charts printed in color are often most effective, but if a chart has enough contrast between different data series, it may be just as effective printed in black and white or in gray tones.

▸ Know This about printing a chart

- To print only the chart from a worksheet that also contains data, select the chart, click the File tab, click the *Print* option in the left panel, verify that the option *Print Selected Chart* displays in the first option box in the *Settings* section in the middle panel, and then click the Print button in the middle panel (see Figure 6.36).
- When you select a chart that is embedded in a worksheet containing data, the option *Print Selected Chart* automatically displays in the first option box in the *Settings* section of the Print backstage area.
- A preview of the selected chart appears in the right panel of the Print backstage area.

Figure 6.36 Print Backstage Area

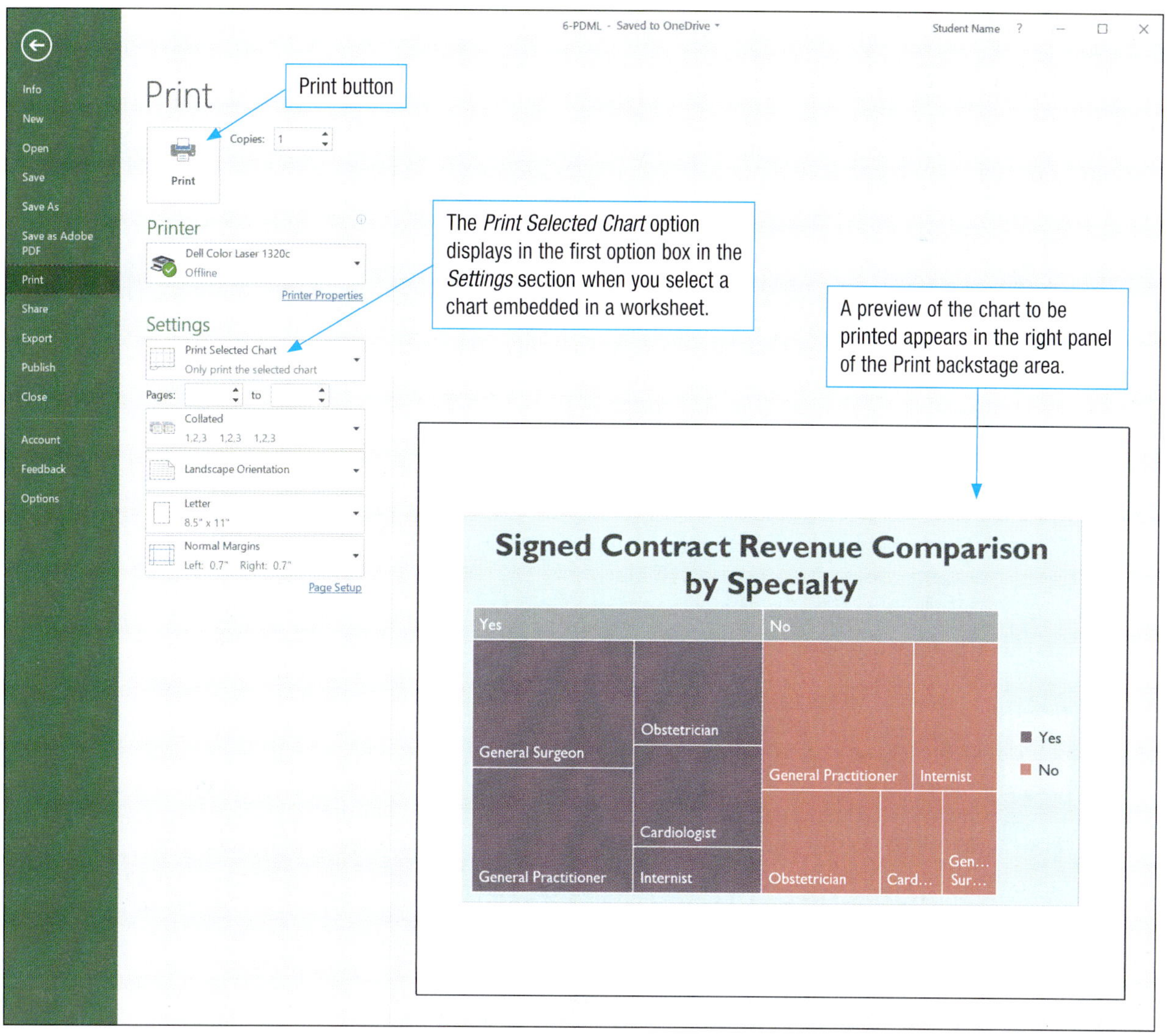

On the Job

Task 6.14 Printing a Chart

Kaelan wants to have a hard copy of the Signed Contract Revenue Comparison by Specialty chart to reference during his meeting with managers. Print only the chart, not the data that appears on the same worksheet.

1. Click the Specialty Summary sheet tab and then select the treemap chart.

   Make sure you select the entire chart, not just an element of the chart.

2. Click the File tab and then click the *Print* option.

   The Print backstage area displays (see Figure 6.36 on page 279).

3. Confirm that the *Print Selected Chart* option displays in the first option box in the *Settings* section.
4. If printed work is required by your instructor, click the Print button to print the chart.
5. If printed work is required by your instructor, also print the workbook.
6. Save and then close the workbook.

Model Answer

Chapter Summary

6.1
- A chart (or graph) presents data in a visual format. Using a chart allows for easily analyzing data in a worksheet. A chart can depict relationships and trends that may be difficult to see by just looking at the numbers.
- Different charts are organized by chart type, and a chart subtype offers variations within a chart type. The source data is the range used to create a chart, and the data series is the range that contains the values (numerical quantities or measurements). Alternative text, including a title and description, should be added to a chart.

6.2
- Different types of charts can be created using the same data—for example, column or bar, line or area, pie or doughnut, and hierarchy, to name a few. How a selected chart will look with a different type and subtype can be previewed. The chart type and subtype should be chosen that best represent the data visually.

6.3
- By default, when a chart is inserted, it is embedded in the same worksheet as the source data. A chart can be moved to a new location in the same worksheet, to a new worksheet, or to another existing worksheet.
- Like other objects, an embedded chart is placed on top of the cells in the worksheet, where it can be selected and manipulated. When a chart is selected, a selection box appears around it, and sizing handles appear along the edges of the selection box. The selection box is used to move the chart, and the sizing handles are used to resize the chart.

6.4
- The chart area consists of a chart plus various chart elements, or individual parts related to the chart. The chart layout is where the chart elements are placed in the chart area.

- ▶ The chart elements vary according to the type of chart. For example, the elements associated with a pie chart are a chart title (a name describing the chart contents), data labels (text or values associated with the data series), and a chart legend (a key describing how each data series is represented visually in the chart). Chart elements can be added, modified, and deleted.

6.5 ▶ A chart can be formatted using a selection of predefined settings. Each selection, or chart style, defines the overall appearance of a chart. The styles and color selections available depend on the type of chart selected. Any chart element can be modified by changing the color or style.

6.6 ▶ When a range is selected in a data source, the Quick Analysis feature analyzes the selection and suggests various options for how best to present the data.

6.7 ▶ A chart is linked to the cells used to create it. Data can be added to a chart by adding it to the data source or by modifying the category axis labels. Data can also be modified by editing the corresponding data in the source. Chart filtering allows viewing selected data without permanently removing any data from the chart or data source.

6.8 ▶ By default, when a chart is created, the row headers are used to group data along the horizontal axis of the chart and the column headers are displayed in the legend. This default can be changed so the column headers are used to group data along the horizontal axis of the chart and the row headers are displayed in the legend. You can also change the scale of the axes and adjust the interval between the values.

6.9 ▶ A hierarchical chart is often the best type for data with several categories. It is similar to a pie chart in that it shows data values as percentages of the whole. There are two types of hierarchical charts: treemap charts and sunburst charts.

6.10 ▶ A trendline is used to show a data trend or a moving average in a chart, and it can be extended past the data to help predict future outcomes. A trendline is added to a specific series in a chart. After a trendline has been added, its type and formatting can be changed.

6.11 ▶ A combination chart displays data as two different chart types and is useful for showing data series that vary greatly. A combination chart uses two vertical axes: one data series is plotted against the primary axis (usually along the left side of the chart), and one or more additional data series are plotted against the secondary axis (usually along the right side of the chart).

6.12 ▶ Creating similar charts can be streamlined by saving one of the charts as a template. Using the template to create new charts will save the time of applying all the settings to each new chart.

6.13 ▶ A hyperlink, whether a graphic or text, can be used to move to another location in the same workbook or in a new workbook, to a file (such as a PDF or a PowerPoint presentation), or to a web page. A hyperlink can also be used to open a new email message, and it can be added to text or to an object such as a chart.

6.14 ▶ The entire worksheet containing a chart can be printed or only the embedded chart. Charts printed in color are often most effective, but if a chart has enough contrast between different data series, it may be just as effective printed in black and white or in gray tones.

Features Review

Feature	Ribbon Tab, Group	Button, Option	Keyboard Shortcut
add chart element	Chart Tools Design, Chart Layouts		
apply chart style	Chart Tools Design, Chart Styles		
change category axis labels in chart	Chart Tools Design, Data		
change chart colors	Chart Tools Design, Chart Styles		
change chart type and subtype	Chart Tools Design, Type		
create chart	Insert, Charts		
create clustered column chart in same worksheet as data source	Insert, Charts		Alt + F1
create chart using Quick Analysis button		, Charts tab	
create combination chart	Insert, Charts	, All Charts tab, *Combo* option	
insert email address hyperlink	Insert, Links	, *E-mail Address*	
insert recommended chart in same worksheet	Insert, Charts		
insert text hyperlink	Insert, Links		
move chart to new worksheet	Chart Tools Design, Location	, *New sheet* radio button	
quickly modify chart element	Chart Tools Design, Chart Layouts		
switch between rows and columns in source data	Chart Tools Design, Data		

Recheck

Recheck your understanding of the concepts, features, and skills covered in this chapter by taking the Recheck quiz.

Workbook

Access the study tools, review exercises, assessments, and challenges for this chapter in the workbook available from this page in your ebook.

Creating Tables and Using Them to Manage Data

Chapter 7

Chapter Goal

To create tables and modify them to effectively organize, manage, and display data.

Precheck

Check your understanding of the concepts, features, and skills covered in this chapter by taking the Precheck quiz.

Learning Objectives

- **7.1** Organize data by creating tables
- **7.2** Add and remove table rows and columns
- **7.3** Name and select a table
- **7.4** Add calculated columns to a table and disable formula replication
- **7.5** Add alternative text to a table
- **7.6** Apply table styles and table style options
- **7.7** Remove duplicate records
- **7.8** Separate data using the Text to Columns feature
- **7.9** Sort data
- **7.10** Sort data on multiple columns
- **7.11** Change the sort order
- **7.12** Filter records
- **7.13** Create a custom AutoFilter
- **7.14** Clear filters and turn off AutoFilter
- **7.15** Use slicers to filter a table
- **7.16** Modify and remove table styles and formatting
- **7.17** Convert a table to a range
- **7.18** Apply advanced filters

Data Files

Before beginning the chapter work, download the AE7 folder from this page in your ebook to your storage medium and then make AE7 the active folder.

Ebook Links

Access digital resources for this course from your ebook.

SNAP

If you are a SNAP user, go to your SNAP assignments page to complete the Precheck, Tutorials, and Recheck in this chapter.

Preview

On the Job

Scenario ProDiagnostics Medical Laboratories (PDML)

Kaelan Rogers, the director of ProDiagnostics Medical Laboratories (PDML), is preparing a budget summary for the board of directors, and he needs to analyze the previous year's revenue for the five collection centers in the city of Waterloo, Ontario, Canada. Kaelan has asked the company's IT department to import into an Excel workbook the previous year's revenue data from those five centers. He would like to analyze the imported data by using an Excel table. Kaelan needs you to organize the data in a table, then modify the table to help him understand and analyze the data.

Visual Reference: An Excel Table

Figure 7.1 A Data Range Formatted as a Table, with the Table Tools Design Tab Active

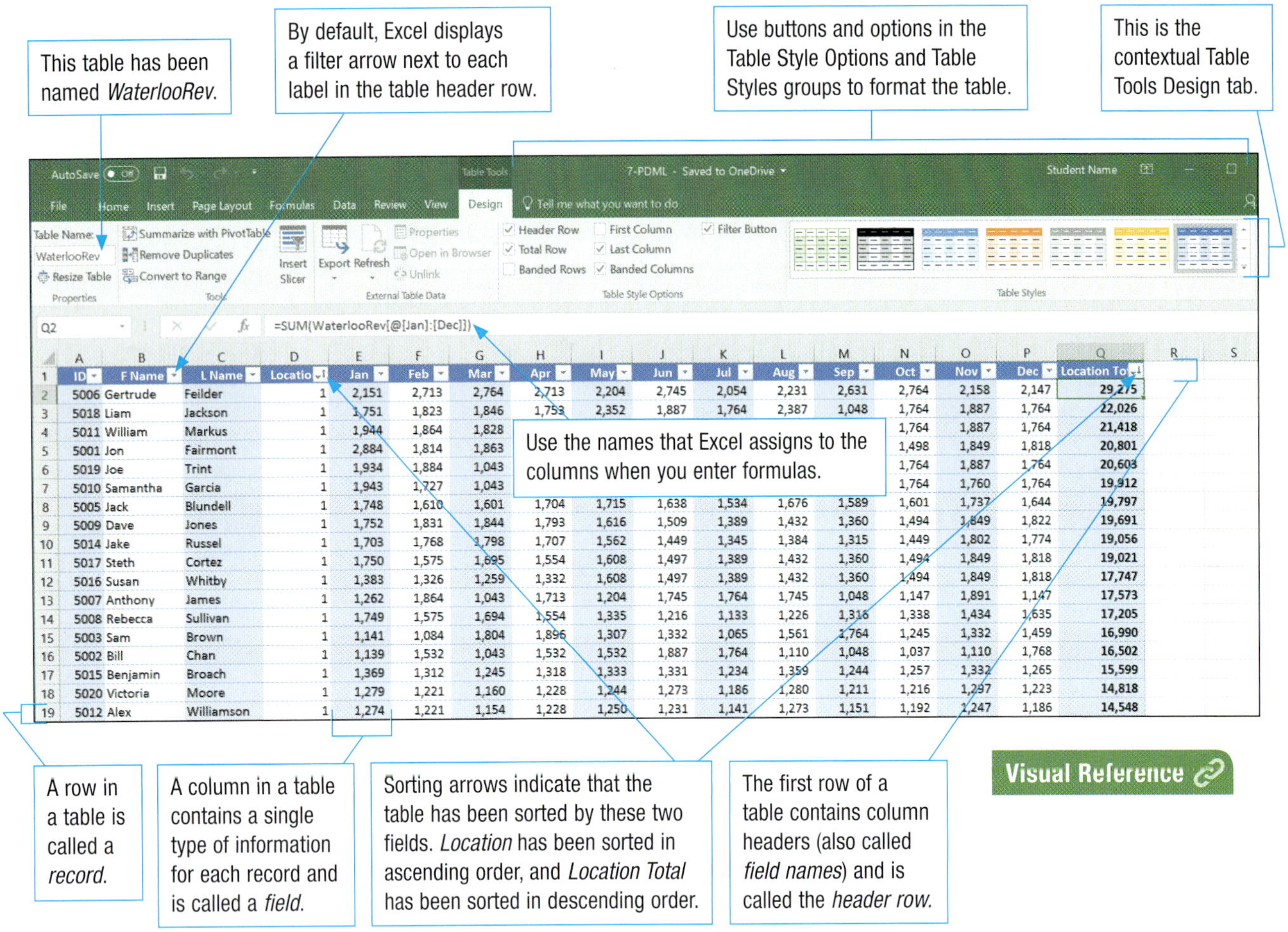

Visual Reference

7.1 Organizing Data by Creating Tables

MOS 3.1.1

Tutorial

Converting a Range to a Table

An Excel **table** is used to organize large quantities of data. A table uses the same structure as a database. Each column, commonly called a **field**, is used to store a single unit of information. Each field contains data about one aspect of the table subject, such as an employee number, first name, last name, or position. This data is found in the first row of the range. All the fields for one unit are entered in a row, which is called a **record**.

▸ Know This about planning Excel tables

- Before you create a table, consider how the data is to be used and then plan the structure of the table by creating a **data definition table** that documents the **column headers** (also called **field names**), descriptions, data types, and comments. See Table 7.1 for the data definition table for the table you will create in this chapter..
- Review the data definition table with colleagues before you create the table, to verify the information in the table is correct and complete.
- Limit your tables to one per worksheet.
- Use a unique field name/column header for each column.
- Each column or field stores a single unit of information.

Table 7.1 Data Definition Table for the PDML Table Created in Task 7.1

Field	Description	Data Type	Comments
ID	Doctor's identification number	General	Four digits
F Name	Doctor's first name	Text	Original field name is *Doctor*. Split the field into two fields called *F Name* and *L Name*. This will be completed in Task 7.8.
L Name	Doctor's last name	Text	See *F Name* comment.
City	City where testing center is located	Text	Column to be deleted as data is repeated. This will be completed in Task 7.2.
Location	Testing center location	General number	1 through 5
Jan through Dec	Monthly revenue	Number	Comma format with no decimals. This will be completed in Task 7.4
Location Total	A calculated field that sums Jan through Dec revenue	Number	Comma format with no decimals. This will be completed in Task 7.4

▸ **Know This** about creating Excel tables

— To create a table, select a range, click the Table button in the Tables group on the Insert tab, verify the range, and then click the OK button.

— Leave at least one blank row or column between a table and other data in the worksheet.

— Do not include any blank rows or columns within a table.

— When any cell or range in the table is active, the Table Tools Design tab appears. This tab is used to format and modify the table.

▸ Know More methods for creating Excel tables

- Select a range, click the Quick Analysis button in the bottom right corner of the range, click the Tables tab, and then click the Table button.
- Press Ctrl + T to display the Create Table dialog box, indicate a range and whether your table has headers, and then click the OK button.
- Select a range and then click the Format as Table button in the Styles group on the Home tab.

On the Job

Task 7.1 Converting a Range to a Table

Kaelan asks you to convert the data for last year's lab revenue into a table. Use the data found in the range A1:P101 in the Excel workbook created by the IT department.

1. Open the data file **7-PDML**.
2. Select the range A1:P101.
3. Click the Insert tab.
4. Click the Table button in the Tables group.

   The Create Table dialog box displays (see Figure 7.2). The text *=$A$1:$P$101* appears in the *Where is the data for your table?* text box, and the *My table has headers* check box contains a check mark.

Figure 7.2 Create Table Dialog Box

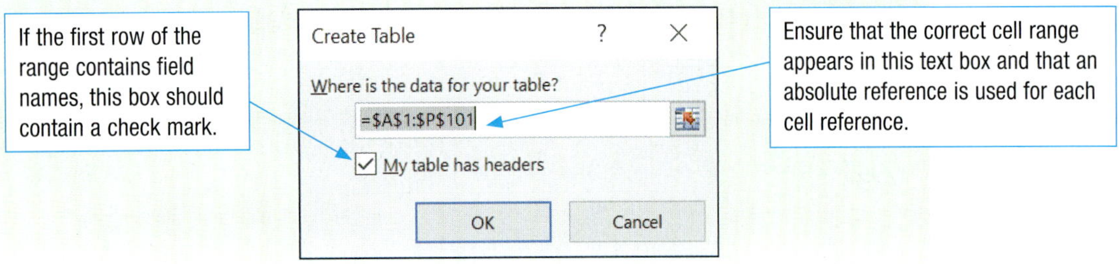

5. Click the OK button.

   The dialog box closes, the range is converted to a table with default formatting applied, and the table is selected. The contextual Table Tools Design tab appears and is active.

6. Click the Save button on the Quick Access Toolbar.

Model Answer

7.2 Adding and Removing Table Rows and Columns

MOS 3.1.3

Tutorial

Adding and Removing Rows and Columns

Once a table has been defined, typing new data immediately below or at the right of the table causes the table to automatically expand. If you enter new data that is not to be included in the table, leave a blank row or column between the table and the new data. When a row or column is removed from or added to a table, the table is resized to include this change.

▸ **Know This** about adding and removing table rows and columns

- Tables automatically expand (using the Excel **AutoExpansion** feature) when new data is entered in the row immediately below the last row of the table or in the column immediately to the right of the last column.
- To shut off AutoExpansion, click the AutoCorrect Options button and then click the *Stop Automatically Expanding Tables* option (see Figure 7.3).
- When entering a record, use the Tab key to move from cell to cell within a row. To avoid creating a blank row at the bottom of the table, press the Enter key after typing the data in the last column.
- To delete a row or column, select the row or column heading and then press Ctrl + -.
- To insert a row or column in the middle of the table, right-click a row heading or a column heading and then click the *Insert* option.

▸ **Know More** ways to add and remove table rows and columns

- To delete a row or column, right-click the row or column heading and then click the *Delete* option.
- To delete a row or column, right-click a cell, point to the *Delete* option, and then click either the *Table Columns* or the *Table Row* option.
- To insert a row or column, right-click in a cell, point to the *Insert* option, and then click either the *Table Rows Above* or the *Table Columns to the Left* option.

On the Job

Task 7.2 Deleting a Column and Adding a Row

In reviewing the table you created in Task 7.1, Kaelan notices that two changes need to be made. First, the *City* column is not necessary because all the centers are located in Waterloo, so that column can be deleted. Second, the revenue for Dr. Victoria Moore in location 5 did not transfer over when the data was imported into Excel and needs to be added manually. Kaelan would like you to make these two changes.

1. Click the column C column heading.

   Column C is selected.
2. Press Ctrl + -.

   The selected column is deleted, and the data shifts one column to the left.
3. Scroll down the document and then click in cell A102.
4. Type 5020 and then press the Tab key.

   Excel automatically expands the table to include the new row and displays the AutoCorrect Options button (see Figure 7.3).

Figure 7.3 AutoCorrect Options Button

The AutoCorrect Options button appears after the data is entered in a cell adjacent to the table.

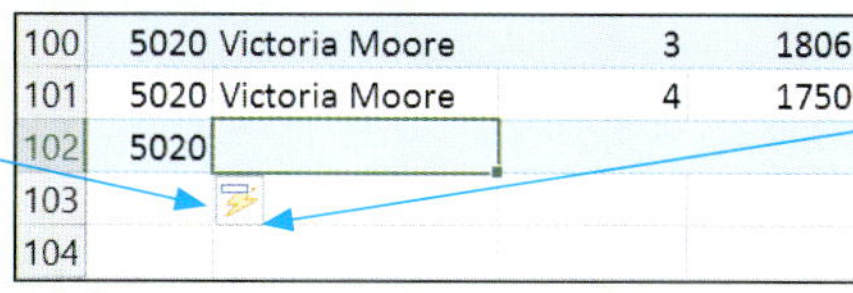

Options available at the AutoCorrect Options button include *Undo Table AutoExpansion*, *Stop Automatically Expanding Tables*, and *Control AutoCorrect Options*.

5. With cell B102 active, type the remainder of the record as follows. Press the Tab key to move from column to column in the table until you reach cell O102.

Doctor	Victoria Moore
Location	5
Jan	1234
Feb	1345
Mar	1456
Apr	1567
May	1678
Jun	1789
Jul	1987
Aug	1876
Sep	1765
Oct	1654
Nov	1543

6. With cell O102 active, type 1432 and then press the Enter key.
7. Click the Save button on the Quick Access Toolbar.

Model Answer

7.3 Naming and Selecting a Table

MOS Expert 3.6.3

Tutorial

Naming and Selecting a Table

A table name is used to reference an entire table. The table name appears in the *Table Name* text box and the Name box on the Table Tools Design tab, and at the Name Manager dialog box.

When you create a new table in a workbook, Excel uses the default name *Table1* to name the table and assigns a name to each column in the table using the row headings. If you create additional tables in the same workbook, Excel names them *Table2*, *Table3*, and so on. Giving a table a unique name that is relevant to its contents will help users easily identify it if the workbook contains more than one table.

▶ **Know This** about naming and selecting a table

- To give a table a unique name, click in any cell in the table, type the name in the *Table Name* text box in the Properties group on the Table Tools Design tab, and then press the Enter key.
- Start the name with a letter, an underscore (_), or a backslash (\).
- Don't include cell references.
- Don't use the individual letter *C* or *R* as a table name, as these letters are shortcuts for *column* or *row*, respectively.
- Don't use spaces.
- Excel doesn't differentiate between uppercase and lowercase letters in a table name, although you might want to use a combination of the two for ease of reading.
- A table can be selected using its name in the Name box.

▶ **Know More** methods for naming a table

- Click the Name Manager button in the Defined Names group on the Formulas tab, click the name of the table to be renamed, click the Edit button, edit the text in the *Name* text box, and then click the OK button.

On the Job

Task 7.3 Naming and Selecting a Table

Kaelan would like you to name the table *WaterlooRev*. After naming the table, ensure that it is named correctly by selecting it using the Name box.

1. Click in any cell in the table and then click the Table Tools Design tab.
2. Click in the *Table Name* text box in the Properties group.
3. Type WaterlooRev and then press the Enter key.
4. Click the Name box arrow and then click the *WaterlooRev* option.

   The entire table is selected (see Figure 7.4).

Figure 7.4 Table Name

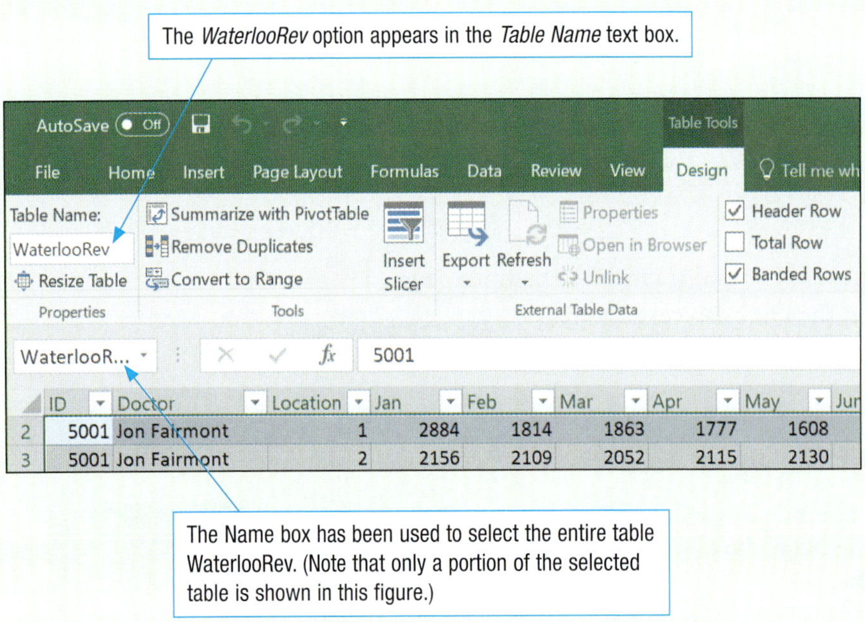

5. Click in any cell to deselect the table.

   There is no visible change to the worksheet.
6. Click the Save button on the Quick Access Toolbar.

7.4 Adding Calculated Columns and Disabling Formula Replication

MOS Expert 1.1.4

Tutorial

Adding Calculated Columns

Along with assigning a name to a table, Excel assigns a name to each column within the table. **Column names** are used in a **calculated column** much like named ranges are used in a formula. (Refer to Chapter 2 for more information on named ranges.) To add a calculated column, enter a formula by clicking in a cell or selecting a range to enter a column name or names.

▶ **Know This** about adding a calculated field or disabling formula replication

— To create a calculated column, enter the formula in the first blank column for the first record and then press the Enter key. The formula you entered in the first cell of the column is copied into the remaining cells in the column immediately after the formula is entered.

— To enter a cell or range in the formula, you must click in the cell or select the range, instead of typing it.

— When you enter a cell or range by clicking or selecting it, Excel inserts a **structured reference** (a combination of the table name and column name) instead of the cell or range reference. For example, it uses *=SUM(WaterlooRev[@[Jan]:[Dec]])* instead of *=SUM(D2:O2)*.

— To stop Excel from automatically copying a formula, click the AutoCorrect Options button and then click the *Stop Automatically Creating Calculated Columns* option. This disables **formula replication** in a table. See Figures 7.5 and 7.6 for replication options in a table.

▶ **Know More** methods for displaying the AutoCorrect dialog box and disabling formula replication

Click the File tab, click the *Options* option in the left panel at the Excel Options dialog box, click the *Proofing* option, click the AutoCorrect Options button in the right panel, click the AutoFormat As You Type tab at the AutoCorrect dialog box, click the *Fill formulas in tables to create calculated columns* check box to remove the check mark in the *Automatically as you work* section (see Figure 7.6), and then click the OK button.

Figure 7.5 AutoCorrect Options Button Expanded

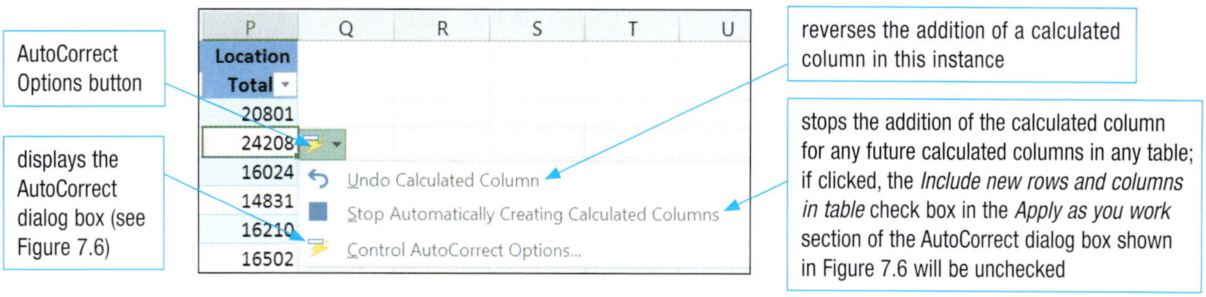

Figure 7.6 AutoCorrect Dialog Box

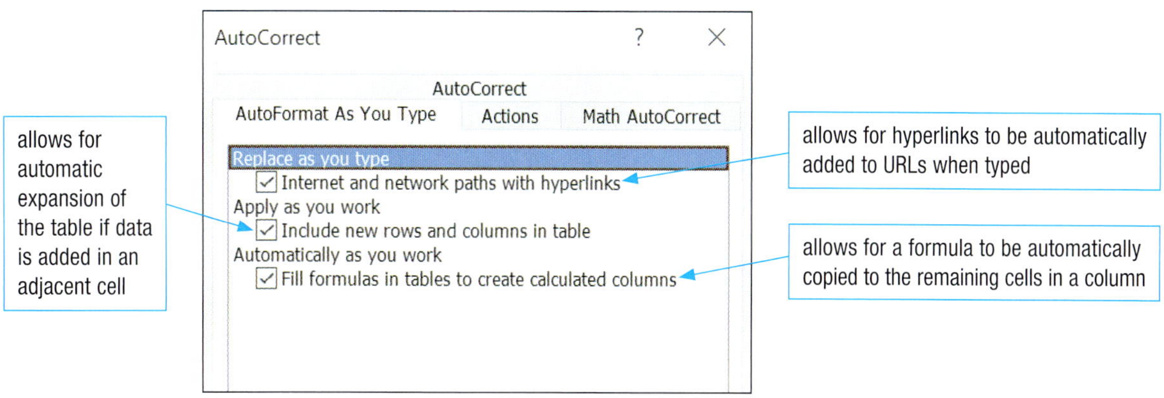

On the Job
Task 7.4 Adding a Calculated Column to a Table

Kaelan would like to see the sum of the revenue that the doctors sent to each of the five Waterloo locations the previous year. Add *Location Total* as a column header in cell P1, wrap the text in that cell, and then add a formula in cell P2 to sum Dr. Fairmont's revenue for the year for location 1. Click in the cells to enter the column names when creating the formula.

1. Click in cell P1.
2. Type Location Total and then press the Enter key.
   Excel automatically expands the table to include the new column.
3. Click in cell P1 and then click the Wrap Text button in the Alignment group on the Home tab.
   The header text appears on two lines.
4. Click in cell P2 and then type =sum(.
5. Select the range D2:O2 and then press the Enter key.
   Excel creates a calculated column and copies the formula to the rest of the rows in the table. The formula *=SUM(WaterlooRev[@[Jan]:[Dec]])* appears in each row. Note that the formula uses the structured reference, including the name of the table assigned in Task 7.3 and the names assigned to the columns when the table was created.
6. Click the Save button on the Quick Access Toolbar.

Model Answer

MOS 5.3.4

Tutorial

Adding Alternative Text

7.5 Adding Alternative Text

Recall from Chapter 4 that adding alternative text to Excel objects helps users who take advantage of an assistive technology that provides an audio description of an Excel spreadsheet. Adding alternative text to a table will help users comprehend the contents of a table when they are read out loud.

▸ Know This about adding alternative text to a table

— To display the Alternative Text dialog box, right-click in any cell in the table, hover over the *Table* option, and then click the *Alternative Text* option.

— Type a meaningful title and description to help people using assistive technology understand the contents of the table.

On the Job
Task 7.5 Adding Alternative Text to a Table

It is company policy at PDML that all Excel workbooks must comply with the requirements of the Accessibility for Ontarians with Disabilities Act (AODA). To ensure that your workbook complies, you need to make sure it passes the Excel Accessibility Check with no errors. Use the Excel Alternative Text feature to add an appropriate title and description for the WaterlooRev table.

1. Right-click in any cell in the table.
2. Hover over the *Table* option and then click the *Alternative Text* option.

   The Alternative Text dialog box displays.
3. Click in the *Title* text box, type PDML 2018 Revenue, and then press the Tab key.

   The insertion point is now in the *Description* text box.
4. Type Monthly revenue for the five centers in Waterloo by doctor. See Figure 7.7.
5. Click the OK button.

   There is no visible change to the worksheet.
6. Click the Save button on the Quick Access Toolbar.

Figure 7.7 Alternative Text Dialog Box

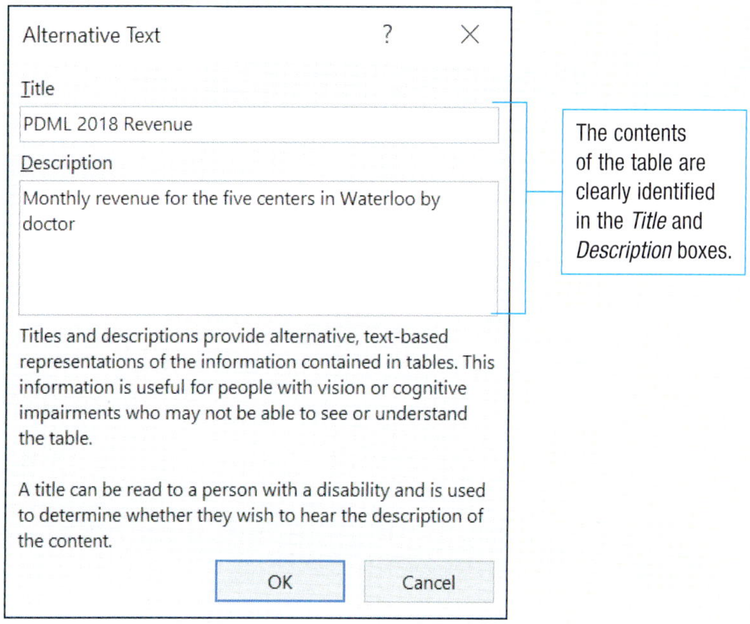

7.6 Applying Table Styles and Table Style Options

MOS 3.2.1
MOS 3.2.2
MOS 3.2.3

Tutorial

Applying Table Styles and Table Style Options

The contextual Table Tools Design tab contains options for formatting a selected table (see Figure 7.8). The Table Styles group includes a gallery that is divided into Light, Medium, and Dark color themes. By default, when a table is created, Excel applies a **table style** that **bands** the rows; this means that it formats even-numbered rows differently from odd-number rows, making the table easier to read.

You can use features in the Table Style Options group to remove banding from rows, add banding to columns, or emphasize the header row, first column, or last column (see Table 7.2). The **header row** displays as the first row in a range or table and contains field names and filter arrows. The **filter arrows** in the header row can be removed by selecting the *Filter Button* option. Adding a **total row** causes Excel to add the word *Total* in the leftmost cell of a new row at the bottom of the table and a SUM function at the end of the last numeric column in the table. Click in a cell in the total row to display an option box arrow and then click the arrow to display a list of functions from which to choose.

Figure 7.8 Table Style Options and Table Styles Groups

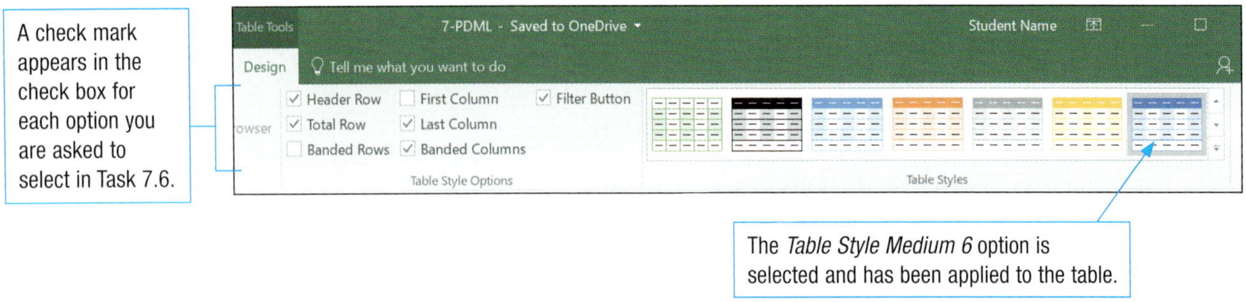

Table 7.2 Features in the Table Style Options Group

Option	Default Setting	Result When This Option Is Selected
Header Row	Checked	When this box is checked, the header row displays as the first row in the table, containing field names and filter arrows.
Total Row	Unchecked	When this box is checked, a row is added at the bottom of the table with the word *Total* in the leftmost cell and a SUM function in the last numeric column.
Banded Rows	Checked	When this box is checked, even-numbered rows are formatted differently from odd-numbered rows; the formatting depends on the table style in effect.
Banded Columns	Unchecked	When this box is checked, even-numbered columns are formatted differently from odd-numbered columns; the formatting depends on the table style in effect.
First Column	Unchecked	When this box is checked, emphasis is added to the first column; the formatting depends on the table style in effect.
Last Column	Unchecked	When this box is checked, emphasis is added to the last column; the formatting depends on the table style in effect.
Filter Button	Checked	When this box is checked, the filter arrows are displayed in the header row.

▸ **Know This** about applying table styles and table style options

- To apply table styles and table style options, start with the Table Tools Design tab active.
- To apply a different table style, click the More button in the Table Styles group and then click an option at the Table Styles gallery.
- The options that appear at the Table Styles gallery depend on the theme chosen (themes are discussed in Chapter 3).
- To add or remove emphasis from rows or columns, insert or remove check marks in the check boxes for options in the Table Style Options group.
- To add a total row to the bottom of the table, click the *Total Row* check box to insert a check mark. A SUM function is added to the last numeric column in the table. Copy the formula to other cells if required.
- Microsoft constantly updates themes and styles, so the format of a theme may change or a theme may be unavailable for a while.

On the Job

Task 7.6 Applying Table Styles and Table Style Options

Kaelan would like you to make visual changes to the WaterlooRev table by applying Table Style Medium 6, removing banding from rows, adding banding to columns, adding emphasis to the last column, and then changing the font color of the header row to White, Background 1. He would also like you to add the total revenue for each month summed at the bottom of the table, and to display all the revenue numbers with commas and no decimals. Make all the changes Kaelan has requested, in the order listed.

1. With any cell in the table active, click the Table Tools Design tab.
2. Click the More button in the Table Styles group.

   The Table Styles gallery displays.
3. Click the *Blue, Table Style Medium 6* option (sixth column, first row in the *Medium* section).
4. Click the *Banded Rows* check box in the Table Style Options group to remove the check mark (see Figure 7.8).
5. Click the *Banded Columns* check box to insert a check mark.
6. Click the *Last Column* check box to insert a check mark.
7. Click the *Total Row* check box to insert a check mark.

   The worksheet displays row 103 with *Total* in cell A103 and the sum of the location revenue in cell P103.
8. Click in cell P103.

   The column P heading displays the column name, which is *Location Total*. You see only the word *Location* because the column is not wide enough to display the entire column name.
9. Using the fill handle, copy the formula to the range D103:O103

   The column D header displays *Jan*.
10. Select the range A1:P1, click the Home tab, click the Font Color button arrow, and then click the *White, Background 1* option (first column, first row in the *Theme Colors* section at the drop-down palette).

11. Select the range D2:P103, click the Comma Style button in the Number group on the Home tab, and then click the Decrease Decimal button two times.

    The revenue numbers are now formatted with a comma and no decimals.

12. Deselect the range D2:P103.
13. Click the Save button on the Quick Access Toolbar.

Model Answer

7.7 Removing Duplicate Records

MOS 3.3.4

Tutorial

Removing Duplicate Records

Excel can compare records within a worksheet and automatically delete duplicate rows based on the selected columns that might contain duplicate values. All the columns are selected by default.

▶ Know This about removing duplicates

- To remove duplicates, click the Remove Duplicates button in the Tools group on the Table Tools Design tab to display the Remove Duplicates dialog box, select the columns to compare, and then click the OK button two times.
- At the Remove Duplicates dialog box, select the columns that might contain duplicate values. Excel compares the data and determines if duplicate records exist.
- After you click the OK button, Excel deletes any rows that contain duplicate values. A message displays indicating the number of duplicate rows that were removed and the number of remaining records.
- To undo a deletion, click the Undo button on the Quick Access Toolbar.
- In some cases, you can apply conditional formatting before using the Remove Duplicates feature to visually identify any duplicate values.
- The Duplicate Values conditional formatting feature compares the contents of a cell with the contents of all the other cells selected. The Remove Duplicates table feature is more precise and can compare the combination of two cells with all the other cells in the table. (Refer to Chapter 3 for more information on conditionally formatting duplicative values.)

▶ Know More methods for removing duplicates

- The Remove Duplicates button is also located in the Data Tools group on the Data tab.

On the Job

Task 7.7 Removing Duplicates

In Task 7.2, Kaelan noted that some data was missing from the workbook created by the IT department. He is also concerned that data might have been duplicated when it was imported into Excel. He would like you to compare the records in the *Doctor* and *Location* columns and confirm that each doctor has only one record for each location. Records are duplicates if the same values exist in the two columns that store the doctor and location information. Kaelan would like you to remove all duplicate records.

1. With any cell in the table active, click the Table Tools Design tab.

2. Click the Remove Duplicates button in the Tools group.

   The table is selected and the Remove Duplicates dialog box displays (see Figure 7.9).

Figure 7.9 Remove Duplicates Dialog Box

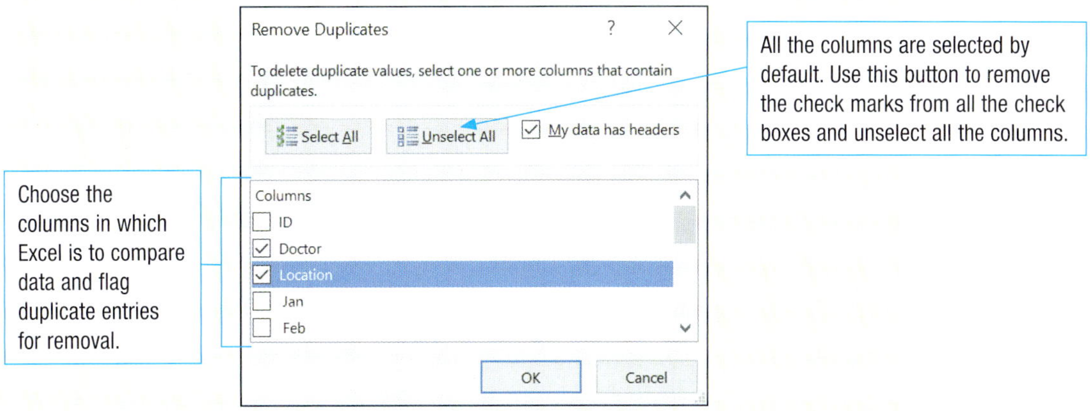

3. Click the Unselect All button to remove the check marks from all the check boxes in the *Columns* list box.
4. Click the *Doctor* check box to insert a check mark.
5. Click the *Location* check box to insert a check mark.
6. Click the OK button.

   A message box appears stating that 1 duplicate value was found and removed and 100 unique values remain.

7. Click the OK button.
8. Click the Save button on the Quick Access Toolbar.

Model Answer

7.8 Separating Data Using the Text to Columns Feature

A column that contains data for more than one field can be separated, or split, into multiple columns using the Text to Columns feature. For example, a column that has first and last names in the same cell can be split so that the first name appears in one column and the last name appears in a separate column. Separating data from one cell into multiple cells of smaller units is called **parsing**.

Tutorial

Separating Data Using the Text to Columns Feature

▸ Know This about separating data using the Text to Columns feature

— For every field you add using the Text to Columns feature, you will need one blank column immediately to the right of the column you are separating.

— To start the Convert Text to Columns Wizard, select the data to be separated and then click the Text to Columns button in the Data Tools group on the Data tab.

Reminder

To insert a column, right-click the column heading and then click the *Insert* option.

— Work through the three dialog boxes in the wizard to separate the data:
  - At the first dialog box, if the *Delimited* option is selected, the data has characters such as commas, tabs, or spaces separating items, and the fixed width is a specific width that you define.
  - At the second dialog box, select the delimiter that separates the data to display a data preview showing how the text is affected (see Figure 7.10).
  - At the third dialog box, the data format appears in a separate row at the top of each column in the *Data preview* box.
  - You can set the data format at the third dialog box of the wizard, or you can change it later.

▶ Know More methods for separating data

- Another method to insert a table column is to right-click the field name in the header row, point to the *Insert* option, and then click the *Table Columns to the Left* option.
- The Flash Fill feature can also be used to separate data. This feature will be discussed in Chapter 12.
- Some Text functions, discussed in Chapter 12 (such as LEFT, RIGHT, and MID) can also be used to separate data.

On the Job

Task 7.8 Separating Data Using the Text to Columns Feature

When the data was imported into Excel, the doctors' first and last names came over in a single field. Kaelan would like to see two separate fields: one containing the doctors' first names and one containing the doctors' last names. Using the Text to Columns feature, split the *Doctor* field into two columns. The first column header will be *F Name*, and the second column header will be *L Name*.

1. Right-click the column C column heading and then click the *Insert* option.

   A column is inserted at the right of the *Doctor* field.
2. Select the range B2:B101.
3. Click the Data tab.
4. Click the Text to Columns button in the Data Tools group.

   The Convert Text to Columns Wizard—Step 1 of 3 dialog box displays.
5. Confirm that the *Delimited* option is selected in the *Choose the file type that best describes your data* section and then click the Next button.

   The Convert Text to Columns Wizard—Step 2 of 3 dialog box displays.
6. Click the *Space* check box in the *Delimiters* section to insert a check mark.

   The *Data preview* box shows the names being split into two columns. See Figure 7.10.

Figure 7.10 Convert Text to Columns Wizard—Step 2 of 3

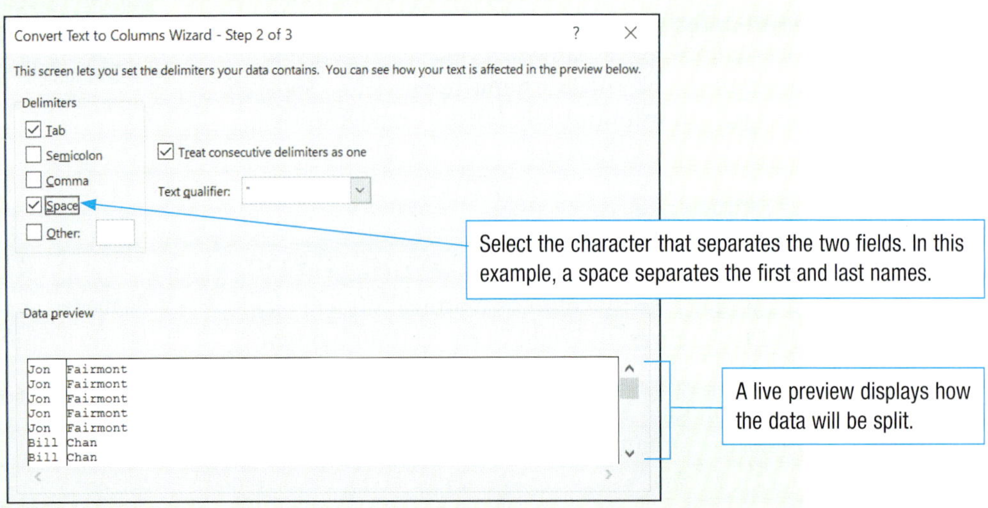

7. Click the Next button.

   The Convert Text to Columns Wizard—Step 3 of 3 dialog box displays.

8. Verify that the data format for each new column is General. Click the Finish button.
9. Click in cell B1, type F Name, and then press the Tab key.
10. Type L Name and then press the Enter key.
11. Select columns B and C. Double-click the boundary line at the right side of either column heading to AutoFit the contents of both columns.
12. Click in any cell in the table to deselect the range.
13. Click the Save button on the Quick Access Toolbar.

Model Answer

7.9 Sorting Data

Tutorial

Sorting Data in a Table

Records are organized in an Excel table in the order that they are entered. Use the sort feature to arrange the records in a particular order. For example, sort a table by last names or revenue. A sort can be done using either a button in the Sort & Filter group on the Data tab (see Figure 7.11), or the *Sort* option in the Sort & Filter button drop-down list in the Editing group on the Home tab. The options for sorting in **ascending order** or **descending order** vary depending on the type of data being sorted.

Figure 7.11 Sort & Filter Group on the Data Tab

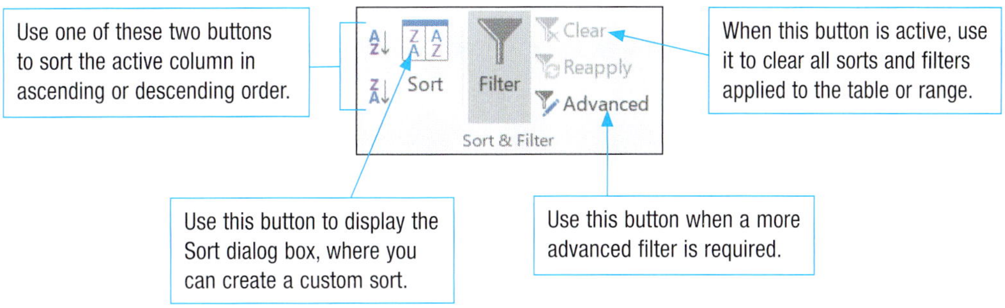

▸ Know This about sorting data in a table

— To perform a sort, click in any cell in the column to be sorted and then click a button in the Sort & Filter group on the Data tab.

— To perform a simple sort, use the ascending or descending sort button:
- If the active column contains text, the buttons will be Sort A to Z (ascending) and Sort Z to A (descending).
- If the active column contains numbers, the buttons will be Sort Smallest to Largest (ascending) and Sort Largest to Smallest (descending).
- If the active column contains dates, the buttons will be Sort Oldest to Newest (ascending) and Sort Newest to Oldest (descending).

— To sort the table on more than one field, click the Sort button to display the Sort dialog box, where you can create a custom sort (see Section 7.10, "Sorting Data on Multiple Columns").

▸ Know More methods for sorting data in a table

- Click the filter arrow in the header row for the column to be sorted and then click an option at the drop-down list.
- Right-click in any cell in the column to be sorted, hover over the *Sort* option, and then click an option in the second drop-down list.

— A directional arrow indicating the sort order will appear in the header row of a sorted column. An up-pointing arrow indicates an ascending sort; a down-pointing arrow indicates a descending sort.
— To clear all the sorts and filters in a table, click anywhere in the table and then click the Clear button in the Sort & Filter group on the Data tab.
— When you are sorting in ascending order, blank cells are placed at the bottom of the table.

▸ Know This about sorting data that is not in a table

— To sort data that is not in a table, select the range and then use the same steps as for sorting data in a table. The range will be sorted by the data in the first selected column.

On the Job

Task 7.9 Sorting Data in a Table

Kaelan would like the table sorted alphabetically by the doctors' last names. He has asked you to complete this task.

1. Click in any cell in column C.
2. Click the Data tab.
3. Click the Sort A to Z button in the Sort & Filter group.
   The table is sorted alphabetically by the doctors' last names. An up-pointing arrow appears in cell C1.
4. Click the Save button on the Quick Access Toolbar.
5. If printed work is required by your instructor, print the workbook.

Model Answer

7.10 Sorting Data on Multiple Columns

MOS 3.3.2

Tutorial
Sorting Data on Multiple Columns

To sort data in a table by more than one column, create a custom sort using options at the Sort dialog box (see Figure 7.12). When you perform a sort on multiple columns, the entire table is sorted, so it is not necessary to select the range before sorting.

Figure 7.12 Sort Dialog Box

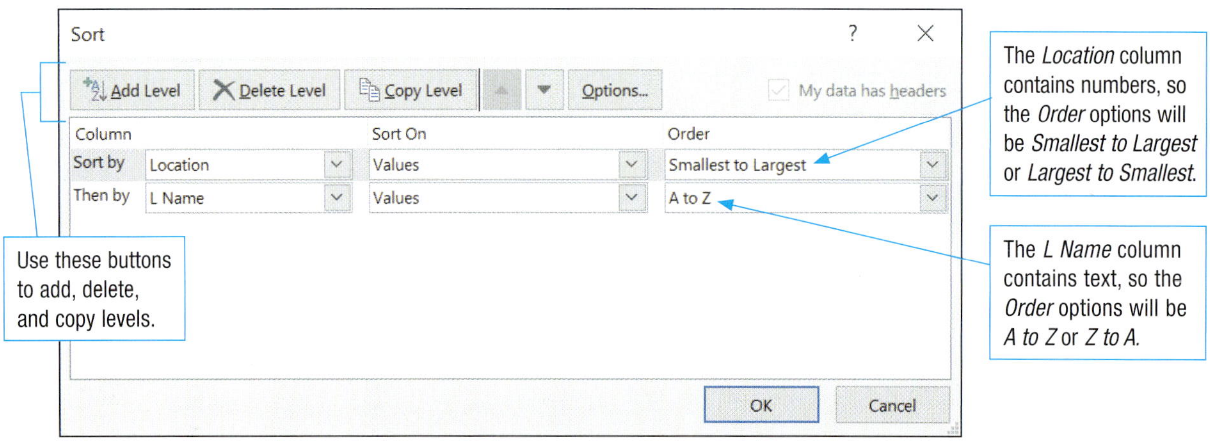

▶ Know This about sorting data on multiple columns

- To display the Sort dialog box, click the Sort button in the Sort & Filter group on the Data tab.
- Use the option box arrows at the dialog box to select the column, the sort type, and the order.
- The options at the *Order* drop-down list will vary depending on the type of data in the column.
- The first field by which the table is sorted is called the **primary sort field** and the criterion is the **primary sort criterion**. The second sort field by which the table is sorted is called the **secondary sort field** and the criterion is the **secondary sort criterion**.
- In Excel 2013 or later, up to 64 sort levels can be applied. Prior to Excel 2013, only three levels could be included in a sort.
- Use a **custom list** to sort by either a predefined list (such as days of the week or months of the year) or a custom list that you create. For example, if you had three membership categories, you could create a custom list to sort the categories in logical order (bronze, silver, and gold) instead of alphabetical order (bronze, gold, silver).
- The custom list option can be found by clicking the *Order* option box arrow, clicking the *Custom List* option, and then clicking an option at the custom list.

▶ Know More methods for sorting data in a table

- To display the Sort dialog box, click the Sort & Filter button in the Editing group on the Home tab, and then click the *Custom Sort* option.
- To clear a sort, click the Sort & Filter button on the Home tab and then click the *Clear* option at the drop-down menu.

On the Job

Task 7.10 Sorting Data on Multiple Columns

Kaelan would like to see which doctor generates the highest revenue at each of the five Waterloo locations. Clear the existing sort in the table, sort the table by location, and then sort the table by the *Location* total using the highest-to-lowest option.

1. With any cell in the table active, click the Clear button in the Sort & Filter group on the Data tab.

   The table is still sorted, but the down-pointing arrow is removed from cell C1.

2. Click the Sort button in the Sort & Filter group.

   The Sort dialog box displays.

3. Click the *Sort by* option box arrow and then click the *Location* option. Leave the default settings in the *Sort On* and *Order* option boxes.
4. Click the Add Level button.
5. Click the *Then by* option box arrow and then click the *Location Total* option.

   You may need to scroll down to see this option.

6. Click the *Order* option box arrow for the *Location Total* column (the second *Order* option box arrow) and then click the *Largest to Smallest* option.
7. Click the OK button.

   The table is sorted first by location in ascending order, and then by location total in descending order. An up-pointing arrow appears in the *Location* column header and a down-pointing arrow appears in the *Location Total* column header.

8. Click the Save button on the Quick Access Toolbar.
9. If printed work is required by your instructor, print the workbook.

Model Answer

7.11 Changing the Sort Order

MOS 3.3.3

Tutorial

Changing the Sort Order

You can modify a custom sort using options at the Sort dialog box.

▶ **Know This** about changing the sort order

— To change the sort order, display the Sort dialog box and then choose a different option in the *Order* option box.

On the Job

Task 7.11 Changing the Sort Order

Kaelan would like to see which doctor generates the least amount of revenue at each of the five Waterloo locations. Modify the sort order for the *Location Total* column to display the revenue amounts from smallest to largest.

1. With any table cell active, click the Sort button in the Sort & Filter group on the Data tab.

   The Sort dialog box displays.

2. Click the *Order* option box arrow for the *Location Total* column and then click the *Smallest to Largest* option.
3. Click the OK button.

   The table is sorted first by location in ascending order, and then by location total in ascending order.

4. Click the Save button on the Quick Access Toolbar.
5. If printed work is required by your instructor, print the workbook.

Model Answer

7.12 Filtering Records

MOS 3.3.1

Tutorial

Filtering Records

A filter temporarily displays only records that match the criteria you have chosen. By default, Excel displays a filter arrow next to each label in the table header row. If a range is not formatted as a table, the filter arrows do not display.

▶ **Know This** about displaying the filter arrows

— To display the filter arrows, click the Filter button in the Sort & Filter group on the Data tab to display.

▶ **Know More** methods for displaying the filter arrows

– Click the Sort & Filter button in the Editing group on the Home tab and then click the *Filter* option.

▶ **Know This** about filtering records by text and by numbers

— To filter a record, click the filter arrow in the column header and then click a filter option at the drop-down list.

— To remove the check marks from all the check boxes at the drop-down list, click the *(Select All)* check box. You can then click the empty check boxes to insert check marks for the items to be displayed in the filtered list.

— The filter arrow changes to a funnel icon in a column that has been filtered.

— If a total row has been added, the total is recalculated to include only the visible numbers.

— The filter arrows do not display on Print Preview or when the worksheet is printed.

▶ **Know More** methods for filtering records

– Right-click in the filtered column, hover over the *Filter* option, and then click an item at the drop-down list.

On the Job

Task 7.12 Filtering Records

Kaelan would like to see only the revenue for Dr. Fairmont. Filter the table by the last name *Fairmont*.

1. Click the filter arrow in cell C1.

   The filter drop-down list for the *L Name* column displays. See Figure 7.13. ***Note:*** *The check boxes will all contain check marks.*

2. Click the *(Select All)* check box to remove all the check marks from the check boxes in the list.
3. Click the *Fairmont* check box to insert a check mark.

Figure 7.13 Filter Drop-Down List for the *L Name* Column

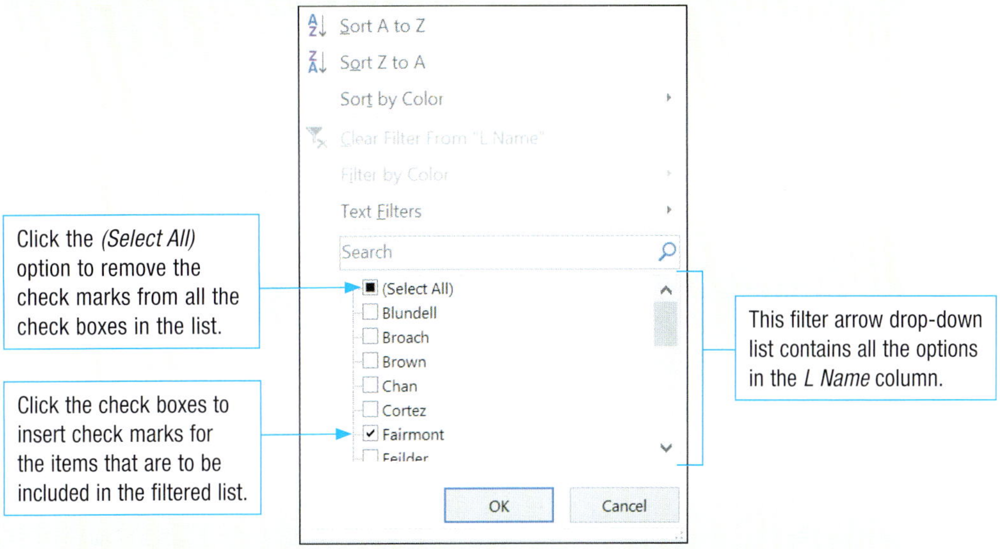

4. Click the OK button.

   The list is filtered to show only the revenue from Dr. Fairmont. The total row has been recalculated.

5. Click the Save button on the Quick Access Toolbar.
6. If printed work is required by your instructor, print the workbook.

Model Answer

7.13 Creating a Custom AutoFilter

Tutorial

Creating a Custom AutoFilter

To filter a table or range by more than one criterion using a comparison operator and/or a logical operator, use options at the Custom AutoFilter dialog box. A **logical operator** is a symbol or function that combines expressions in conditional statements. For example, the logical operator *And* requires both expressions to be true before the condition can be met.

Recall from Chapter 3 that wildcard characters can be used to find data without specifying the entire field value. The asterisk (*) is used in a position for which one or more characters vary, and the question mark (?) is used in a fixed-width word for which the records with the same number of characters in the field are to be viewed. The Custom AutoFilter dialog box also allows you to create custom criteria with the same wildcard characters. For example, you could filter the WaterlooRev table to show doctors whose last names begin with *W* by setting *W** as the criterion in the *L Name* field, or you could filter the table to show doctors with IDs that start at 5020 and end at 5029 by setting *502?* as the criterion in the *ID* field.

▸ Know This about creating a custom AutoFilter

— To create a custom AutoFilter, click the filter arrow in the header for the column to be filtered, hover over the filter option (*Text Filters, Number Filters,* or *Dates Filters*, depending on the type of data in the column), and then click an option at the second drop-down list.

— The options at the second drop-down list will vary depending on the type of data in the column, as shown in Table 7.3.

— Clicking any option at the second drop-down list displays the Custom AutoFilter dialog box.

— Select options at the dialog box to set up a custom filter and then click the OK button to apply the filter.

— After you apply a filter, Excel looks in each cell in the column to see if the data in the cell matches the filter criterion. It displays only records with cells that match the criterion.

Reminder
To display the filter arrows, click the Sort & Filter button in the Editing group on the Home tab and then click the *Filter* option.

Table 7.3 Custom AutoFilter Options

When you select the option...	the displayed data....
If the column contains text, the following options are available:	
Equals	matches the indicated text exactly
Does Not Equal	does not match the indicated text
Begins With	begins with the indicated string of text
Ends With	ends with the indicated string of text
Contains	contains the indicated string of text
Does Not Contain	does not contain the indicated string of text
Custom Filter	matches the custom criteria set at the Custom AutoFilter dialog box
If the column contains numbers, the following options are available:	
Equals	matches the indicated number exactly
Does Not Equal	does not match the indicated number
Greater Than	is greater than the indicated number
Greater Than Or Equal To	is greater than or equal to the indicated number
Less Than	is less than the indicated number
Less Than Or Equal To	is less than or equal to the indicated number
Between	is greater than or equal to and less than or equal to the indicated numbers
Top 10	is the top 10 or bottom 10 items by default; the range can be modified
Above Average or *Below Average*	is greater than or less than average
Custom Filter	matches the custom criteria set at the Custom AutoFilter dialog box

continues...

Table 7.3 Custom AutoFilter Options *...continued*

When you select the option...	the displayed data....
If the column contains dates, the following options are available:	
Equals	matches the indicated date exactly
Before	falls before the indicated date
After	falls after the indicated date
Between	is greater than or equal to and less than or equal to the indicated dates
Tomorrow	is tomorrow's date
Today	is the current date
Yesterday	is yesterday's date
Next Week, Next Month, Next Quarter, Next Year	includes any date that falls in the next week, month, quarter, or year
This Week, This Month, This Quarter, This Year	includes any date that falls in the current week, month, quarter, or year
Last Week, Last Month, Last Quarter, Last Year	includes any date that falls in the previous week, month, quarter, or year
Year to Date	includes any date since January 1 of the current year
All Dates in the Period	includes all the dates in the specified quarter or month
Custom Filter	matches the custom criteria set at the Custom AutoFilter dialog box

▸ **Know This** about *And* and *Or* logical operators

— At the Custom AutoFilter dialog box, use the operator *And* when both options need to be true—for example, if you want to show the records for which the location total is between 18,000 and 20,000.

— At the Custom AutoFilter dialog box, use the operator *Or* when only one option needs to be true—for example, if you want to show the records for either location 1 or location 4. Note that only one number exists in each location cell (1, 2, 3, 4, or 5). If you used the *And* operator (asking Excel to display the records for location 1 and location 4), no records would be displayed because location 1 and location 4 do not both appear in one cell.

On the Job

Task 7.13 Creating a Custom AutoFilter

Kaelan would like to further filter the WaterlooRev table to display only the records for locations 1 and 4 for Dr. Fairmont. Be sure to use the *Or* operator in the filter criterion to display records in both locations.

1. Click the filter arrow in the *Location* column header (cell D1).
2. Hover over the *Number Filters* option and then click the *Equals* option.
   The Custom AutoFilter dialog box displays (see Figure 7.14).

3. Click the upper right option box arrow and then click the *1* option.
4. Click the *Or* radio button.
5. Click the left option box arrow in the second *Location* row and then click the *equals* option.
6. Click the right option box arrow in the second *Location* row and then click the *4* option.

Figure 7.14 Customer AutoFilter Dialog Box

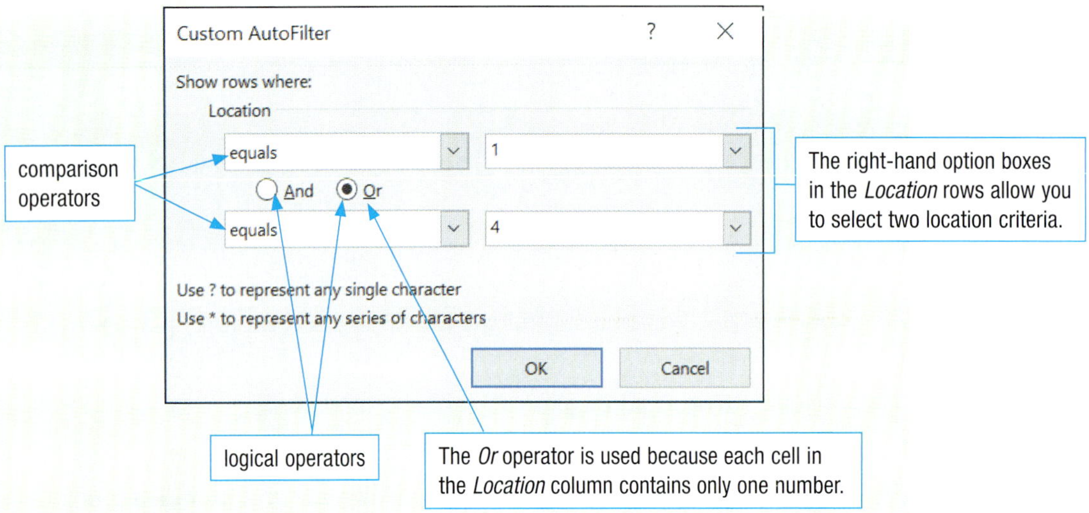

7. Click the OK button.

   The WaterlooRev table is further filtered to show only the revenue for locations 1 or 4. The total row has been recalculated.
8. Click the Save button on the Quick Access Toolbar.
9. If printed work is required by your instructor, print the workbook.

Model Answer

7.14 Clearing Filters and Turning Off AutoFilter

When a filter is applied, you see only part of the data in the table. To view all the data in a particular column, you need to clear the filters from that column. To view all the data in the table, you need to clear all the filters or turn off AutoFilter.

Tutorial

Clearing Filters and Turning Off AutoFilter

▶ **Know This** about clearing filters and turning off AutoFilter

— To clear a filter from a specific column, click the funnel icon and then click the *Clear Filter From Column Header* option (where *Column Header* is the field name).

— To clear a filter from all the columns, click the Sort & Filter button in the Editing group on the Home tab and then click the *Clear* option.

— To turn off AutoFilter, click the *Filter Button* check box to remove the check mark in the Table Style Options group on the Table Tools Design tab.

▶ **Know More** methods for clearing filters and turning off AutoFilter

– To clear a filter from a specific column, right-click anywhere in the column, hover over the *Filter* option, and then click the *Clear Filter From Column Header* option.

continues...

On the Job
Task 7.14 Clearing Filters and Turning Off AutoFilter

Kaelan would like to see all the data in the WaterlooRev table, with no filter arrows displayed. Remove all the filters to redisplay all the data and then remove the filter arrows.

1. With any cell in the table active, click the Sort & Filter button in the Editing group on the Home tab and then click the *Clear* option.

   The filters are removed from the table. The Sort arrows are removed as well, but the table remains sorted by location and then by location total.

2. Click the Table Tools Design tab and then click the *Filter Button* check box in the Table Style Options group to remove the check mark.

   The filter arrows are removed from the column headers.

3. Click the Save button on the Quick Access Toolbar.
4. If printed work is required by your instructor, print the workbook.

Model Answer

▶ **Know More** methods for clearing filters and turning off AutoFilter *...continued*

- To clear a filter from all the columns, click the Clear button in the Sort & Filter group on the Data tab.
- To turn off AutoFilter, click the Sort & Filter button in the Editing group on the Home tab and then click the *Filter* option.

7.15 Using Slicers to Filter Tables

MOS 3.3.1

Tutorial Using Slicers to Filter Tables

A table can also be filtered using the **slicer** feature. A slicer allows you to filter a table without displaying filter arrows or dialog boxes. A slicer also allows you to see what criteria are being used to filter the table.

▶ Know This about using slicers to filter a table

— To use a slicer to filter a table, start by clicking the Insert Slicer button in the Tools group on the Table Tools Design tab to display the Insert Slicers dialog box.

— At the dialog box, click the check box to insert a check mark for each field to be filtered and then click the OK button to display the Slicer pane.

— At the Slicer pane, select one option that Excel should use to filter the list. To select more options, press and hold down the Ctrl key, click each additional option, and then release the Ctrl key.

— To remove a slicer filter, click the Clear Filter button at the top right of the Slicer pane.

— To delete a Slicer pane, select the Slicer pane and then press the Delete key.

▶ **Know More** ways to select multiple slicer options

- Select one option, click the Multi-Select button at the Slicer pane or press Alt + S, and then click each additional option.

On the Job
Task 7.15 Using Slicers to Filter a Table

Kaelan would like to see the data for locations 2 and 3. Use a slicer to filter the table to display only the data for locations 2 and 3. Leave the Slicer pane displayed at the end of the task.

1. With any cell in the table active, click the Insert Slicer button in the Tools group on the Table Tools Design tab.

   The Insert Slicers dialog box displays.

2. Click the *Location* check box to insert a check mark.

3. Click the OK button.

   The Location Slicer pane displays (see Figure 7.15).

Figure 7.15 Slicer Pane

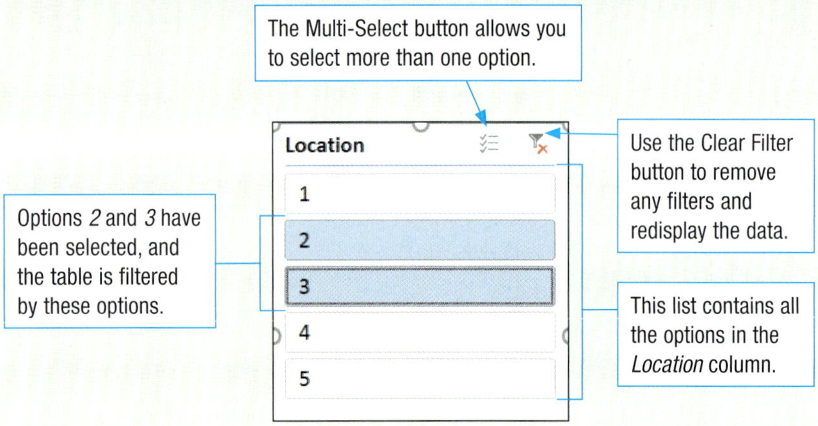

4. Click the *2* option. Excel filters the table by location 2.
5. Press and hold down the Ctrl key, click the *3* option, and then release the Ctrl key.

   Excel adds location 3 to the filter.
6. Leave the Slicer pane displayed.
7. Click the Save button on the Quick Access Toolbar.
8. If printed work is required by your instructor, print the workbook.

Model Answer

7.16 Modifying and Removing Table Styles and Formatting

After a table has been sorted and filtered, the styles and formatting that were previously applied to it may not be visually appropriate. You can modify existing styles and formatting, or remove them entirely.

Tutorial

Modifying and Removing Table Styles and Formatting

▸ Know This about removing table styles and formatting

— To remove unwanted table formatting, click check boxes in the Table Style Options group on the Table Tools Design tab to remove the check marks.

— To remove a table style, click apply the *None* option in the *Light* section of the Table Styles gallery.

▸ **Know More** ways to remove a table style

– Click the Clear button in the Editing group on the Home tab, and then click the *Clear Formats* option.

On the Job

Task 7.16 Removing a Slicer Filter, the Slicer Pane, and Table Formatting

After Kaelan sees the filtered table data for locations 2 and 3, he asks you to redisplay all the data (unfiltered) and close the Location Slicer pane. He also asks you to remove the banding from the columns and to remove the total row at the bottom of the table. Use the Location Slicer pane to remove the location filter, delete the Slicer pane, and then modify the table formatting as requested.

1. Click the Clear Filter button at the Location Slicer pane (see Figure 7.15 on page 306).

   All the data in the spreadsheet is redisplayed.
2. Click the Location Slicer pane and then press the Delete key to close the Slicer pane.
3. Click the *Banded Columns* check box in the Table Style Options group on the Table Tools Design tab to remove the check mark and remove banding from the columns.
4. Click the *Total Row* check box to remove the check mark and remove the total row.
5. Click the Save button on the Quick Access Toolbar.
6. If printed work is required by your instructor, print the workbook.

Model Answer

7.17 Converting a Table to a Range

MOS 3.1.2

Tutorial

Converting a Table to a Range and Sorting a Range

Some Excel features, such as subtotaling, cannot be accomplished using an Excel table. If a table format cannot be used or is no longer required, convert the table back to a range.

▸ Know This about converting a table to a range

— To convert a table to a range, position the insertion point anywhere within the table, and then click the Convert to Range button in the Tools group on the Table Tools Design tab.

— It is easier to modify or remove styles from a table than from a range; therefore, remove styles before converting a table to a range.

On the Job
Task 7.17 Converting a Table to a Range and Sorting a Range

In preparation for another project, Kaelan needs the data from the WaterlooRev table formatted as a range and sorted by doctor ID and then by location. Convert the table back to a range and then sort the range on the required fields.

1. With any cell in the table active, click the Table Tools Design tab.
2. Click the Convert to Range button in the Tools group.

   A message box asks if you want to convert the table to a normal range.
3. Click the Yes button.

   The table is converted to a range.
4. Click the Home tab if it is not already selected and then click the Sort & Filter button in the Editing group.
5. Click the *Custom Sort* option.
6. Click the *Sort by* option box arrow and then click the *ID* option.

7. Click the Add Level button.
8. Click the *Then by* option box arrow and then click the *Location* option.
9. Click the OK button.

   The range is sorted by ID and then by location.
10. Click the Save button on the Quick Access Toolbar.
11. If printed work is required by your instructor, print the workbook.

Model Answer

7.18 Applying an Advanced Filter

Tutorial

Applying an Advanced Filter

When a range needs to be filtered on complex criteria, apply an advanced filter. An **advanced filter** allows you to filter the data using the *And* or *Or* logical operator over more than one field. For example, in Task 7.18a, you are asked to filter the data to show the records for location 3 that have total revenue greater than 18,000 or the records for location 5 that have revenue greater than 20,000.

The criteria in an advanced filter are entered directly in the worksheet and establish the **criteria range**. After inserting five or six rows above the range, copy the row containing the field names to row 1.

▸ Know This about applying advanced filters

— To filter a range using an advanced filter, start by doing the following:
- Insert five or six rows at the top of the worksheet and then copy the column header row to the new row 1. You need enough rows at the top of the worksheet to enter all the required criteria plus at least one blank row between the criteria range and the data to be filtered.
- Enter the filter criteria under the appropriate column headers.
- Click the Data tab and then click the Advanced button in the Sort & Filter group to display the Advanced Filter dialog box (see Figure 7.16).

Figure 7.16 Advanced Filter Dialog Box

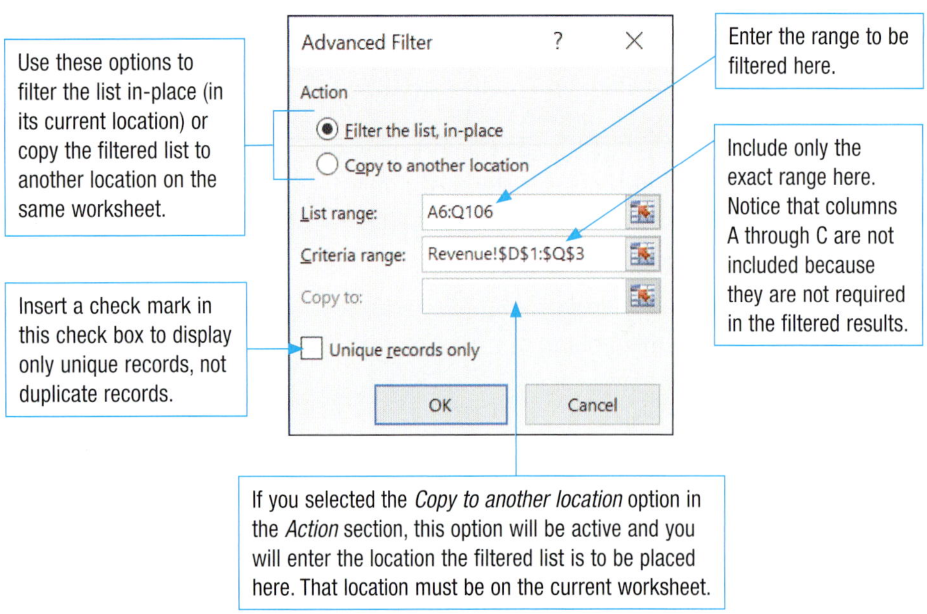

▸ Know More about applying advanced filters
- At the Advanced Filter dialog box and then the *Criteria range* text box, include only the necessary range. For example, in Task 7.18a, the range is D1:Q3. Columns A through C are not required (see Figure 7.16).
- When you insert a check mark in the *Unique records only* check box, duplicate records are listed only once (not multiple times).
- Unique records can only be copied to the active sheet.
- Enter only the top left cell in the *Copy to* location.

- Use options at the dialog box to indicate the filter criteria and then click the OK button.

— Criteria found in the same row use the *And* operator.

— Criteria found in separate rows use the *Or* operator.

▸ **Know This** about applying the between filter

— If you need to filter a range using a criterion that falls between two values in the same field, copy the field name and place it in the first empty cell in row 1. The worksheet in Figure 7.17 has been filtered to show the location totals between 23,000 and 26,000.

Figure 7.17 Between Filter Applied Using the Advanced Filter Feature

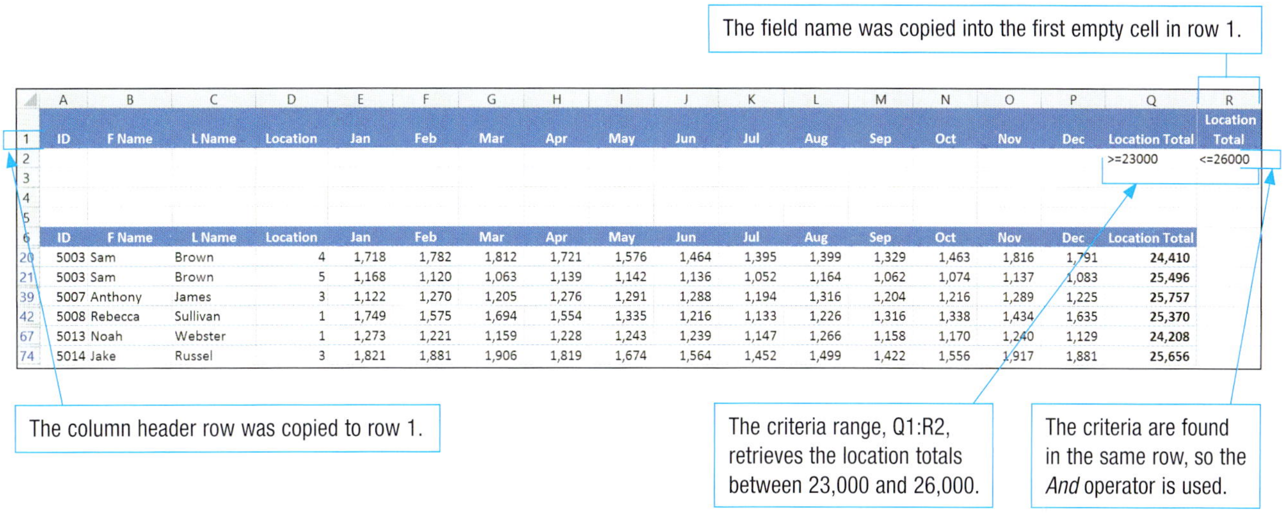

	A	B	C	D	E	F	G	H	I	J	K	L	M	N	O	P	Q	R
1	ID	F Name	L Name	Location	Jan	Feb	Mar	Apr	May	Jun	Jul	Aug	Sep	Oct	Nov	Dec	Location Total	Location Total
2																	>=23000	<=26000
3																		
4																		
5																		
6	ID	F Name	L Name	Location	Jan	Feb	Mar	Apr	May	Jun	Jul	Aug	Sep	Oct	Nov	Dec	Location Total	
20	5003	Sam	Brown	4	1,718	1,782	1,812	1,721	1,576	1,464	1,395	1,399	1,329	1,463	1,816	1,791	**24,410**	
21	5003	Sam	Brown	5	1,168	1,120	1,063	1,139	1,142	1,136	1,052	1,164	1,062	1,074	1,137	1,083	**25,496**	
39	5007	Anthony	James	3	1,122	1,270	1,205	1,276	1,291	1,288	1,194	1,316	1,204	1,216	1,289	1,225	**25,757**	
42	5008	Rebecca	Sullivan	1	1,749	1,575	1,694	1,554	1,335	1,216	1,133	1,226	1,316	1,338	1,434	1,635	**25,370**	
67	5013	Noah	Webster	1	1,273	1,221	1,159	1,228	1,243	1,239	1,147	1,266	1,158	1,170	1,240	1,129	**24,208**	
74	5014	Jake	Russel	3	1,821	1,881	1,906	1,819	1,674	1,564	1,452	1,499	1,422	1,556	1,917	1,881	**25,656**	

On the Job

Task 7.18a Apply an Advanced Filter In-Place

Kaelan would like you to filter the range in its current location to show the records for location 3 that have revenue greater than 18,000 and the records for location 5 that have revenue greater than 20,000. Apply an advanced filter with the following criteria: Location equals 3 and revenue is greater than 18000 or location equals 5 and revenue is greater than 20,000.

1. Select rows 1 through 5.
2. Right-click and then click the *Insert* option.

   Five rows are inserted at the top of the worksheet.
3. Select the range A6:Q6.
4. Press Ctrl + C.
5. Click in cell A1 and then press Ctrl + V.

   The column headers are copied and pasted into the new row 1.
6. Click in cell D2 and then type 3.
7. Click in cell D3 and then type 5.
8. Click in cell Q2 and then type >18000.
9. Click in cell Q3, type >20000, and then press the Enter key.

10. Click the Data tab and then click the Advanced button in the Sort & Filter group.

    The Advanced Filter dialog box displays.

11. Verify that the *Filter the list, in-place* radio button contains a bullet.
12. Select the text in the *List range* text box, if necessary, and then type A6:Q106.
13. Click in the *Criteria range* text box, scroll up the worksheet if necessary, to display row 1, and then select the range D1:Q3.

    The text *Revenue!$D$1:$Q$3* appears in the *Criteria range* text box.

14. Click the OK button.

    The list is filtered to display only records in which the location is 3 and the revenue is greater than 18,000, or the location is 5 and the revenue is greater than 20,000.

15. Click the Save button on the Quick Access Toolbar.
16. If printed work is required by your instructor, print the workbook.

Model Answer

On the Job

Task 7.18b Apply an Advanced Filter in Another Location

Kaelan would like you to remove the filter and criteria you added in Task 7.18a, and to add a list of only the first and last names of all the doctors in Waterloo locations. Clear the filter, delete the criteria you added to the worksheet, and then apply a new advanced filter to copy the requested unique records to another location on the same worksheet.

1. Click the Clear button in the Sort & Filter group on the Data tab.

    The filter from Task 7.18a is removed.

2. Delete the contents of cells D2, D3, Q2, and Q3.
3. Click the Advanced button.

    The Advanced Filter dialog box displays. If a Microsoft Excel message displays stating that Excel cannot determine which row in your selection contains column labels, it is because you have more than one cell selected. Click the Ok button to close the message.

4. Click the *Copy to another location* option button to insert a bullet.
5. Click in the *List range* text box and then type B6:C106.

    This range holds the doctors' first and last names.

6. Delete the text in the *Criteria range* text box.
7. Click in the *Copy to* text box and then type S6.
8. Click the *Unique records only* check box to insert a check mark.
9. Click the OK button.

    A list of doctors' first and last names appears, starting in cell S6.

10. Click the Save button on the Quick Access Toolbar.
11. If printed work is required by your instructor, print the workbook.
12. Close the workbook.

Model Answer

Chapter Summary

7.1 ▸ An Excel table is used to organize large quantities of data, and it can be managed separately from other rows and columns in a worksheet. A table uses the same structure as a database and contains columns (or fields) and rows (or records).

▸ To create a table, select a range, click the Table button in the Tables group on the Insert tab, verify the range, and then click the OK button. Leave at least one blank row or column between a table and other data in the worksheet.

7.2 ▸ Once a table has been defined, typing new data immediately below or at the right of the table causes the table to automatically expand using Excel's AutoExpansion feature. When a row or column is removed from or added to a table, the table is resized to include this change.

7.3 ▸ A table name is used to reference an entire table. It appears in the *Table Name* text box and the Name box on the Table Tools Design tab and at the Name Manager dialog box. Giving a table a unique name that is relevant to its contents will help users easily identify it if a workbook contains more than one table.

7.4 ▸ Excel assigns a name to each column within a table. Column names are used in a calculated column much like named ranges are used in a formula.

7.5 ▸ An assistive technology reads aloud the text and values in a spreadsheet, along with additional information that is not readily visible to users. If this alternative text is missing when the Excel Accessibility Checker is run, an error message will appear.

7.6 ▸ The contextual Table Tools Design tab contains options for formatting a selected table. By default, when a table is created, Excel applies a table style that bands the rows. Features in the Table Style Options group allow removing bands from rows, adding bands to columns, and emphasizing the header row, first column, or last column.

7.7 ▸ Excel can compare records within a worksheet and automatically delete duplicate rows based on the selected columns that might contain duplicate values. All the columns are selected by default.

7.8 ▸ A column that contains data for more than one field can be separated (or split) into multiple columns using the Text to Columns feature.

7.9 ▸ Use the sort feature to arrange records in a particular order; options for sorting in ascending order or descending order vary depending on the type of data being sorted. A sort can be done using one of several buttons in the Sort & Filter group on the Data tab or using the *Sort* option in the Sort & Filter button drop-down list in the Editing group on the Home tab.

7.10 ▸ To sort data in a table by more than one column, create a custom sort using options at the Sort dialog box. When a sort is performed on multiple columns, the entire table is sorted, so it is not necessary to select the range before sorting.

7.11 ▸ Modify a custom sort using options at the Sort dialog box. To change the sort order, choose a different option in the *Order* option box.

7.12 ▶ A filter temporarily displays only records that match the criteria, and by default, Excel displays a filter arrow next to each label in the table header row. Click the Filter button in the Sort & Filter group on the Data tab to display the filter arrows.

7.13 ▶ To filter a table or range by more than one criterion using a comparison operator and/or a logical operator, use options at the Custom AutoFilter dialog box. Use the operator *And* when both options need to be true, and use the operator *Or* when only one option needs to be true. Use wildcard characters to find data without specifying the entire field value.

7.14 ▶ When a filter is applied, only part of the data in the table is visible. To view all the data in a column, clear the filters from that column. To view all the data in the table, clear all the filters or turn off AutoFilter.

7.15 ▶ Use a slicer to filter a table without displaying filter arrows or dialog boxes and to see what criteria are being used to filter the table.

7.16 ▶ Modify existing table styles and formatting or remove them entirely at the Table Style Options group on the Table Tools Design tab.

7.17 ▶ If a table format cannot be used or is no longer required, convert the table back to a range. Do so by clicking the Convert to Range button in the Tools group on the Table Tools Design tab.

7.18 ▶ Apply an advanced filter when a range needs to be filtered on complex criteria. An advanced filter allows filtering the data using the *And* or *Or* logical operator over more than one field. The criteria in an advanced filter are entered directly in the worksheet and establish the criteria range.

Features Review

Feature	Ribbon Tab, Group	Button, Option	Keyboard Shortcut
apply advanced filter	Data, Sort & Filter		
clear all filters	Home, Editing	, *Clear*	
clear sorts and filters	Data, Sort & Filter		
convert table to range	Table Tools Design, Tools		
create custom sort	Data, Sort & Filter		
create table	Insert, Tables		Ctrl + T
filter records	Data, Sort & Filter		
modify table style	Table Tools Design, Table Styles AND Table Tools Design, Table Style Options		
name table	Table Tools Design, Properties	*Table Name text box*	
remove duplicates	Table Tools Design, Tools		
separate data	Data, Data Tools		
sort data in ascending order	Data, Sort & Filter		
sort data in descending order	Data, Sort & Filter		
insert slicer	Table Tools Design, Tools		

Recheck

Recheck your understanding of the concepts, features, and skills covered in this chapter by taking the Recheck quiz.

Workbook

Access the study tools, review exercises, assessments, and challenges for this chapter in the workbook available from this page in your ebook.

Using PivotTables and PivotCharts to Analyze Data

Chapter 8

Chapter Goal

To summarize and analyze data using PivotTables and PivotCharts.

Learning Objectives

- **8.1** Create and refresh a PivotTable
- **8.2** Modify a PivotTable layout
- **8.3** Format a PivotTable
- **8.4** Filter and Sort a PivotTable
- **8.5** Filter a PivotTable using slicers
- **8.6** Create and modify multilevel PivotTables
- **8.7** Filter a PivotTable using timelines
- **8.8** Use calculated fields and calculated items in PivotTables
- **8.9** Use Quick Analysis and Recommended PivotTables to create a PivotTable
- **8.10** Create a PivotChart
- **8.11** Apply PivotChart styles and modify PivotChart formatting
- **8.12** Filter a PivotChart
- **8.13** Modify a PivotChart layout
- **8.14** Group and ungroup PivotTable data
- **8.15** Reference data in a PivotTable by using the GETPIVOTDATA function
- **8.16** Use Power Pivot
- **8.17** Create and manage relationships between tables
- **8.18** Create a hierarchy
- **8.19** Drill down into PivotChart details
- **8.20** Use Power View and drill down in a data visualization
- **8.21** Use Cube functions

Precheck

Check your understanding of the concepts, features, and skills covered in this chapter by taking the Precheck quiz.

Data Files

Before beginning the chapter work, download the AE8 folder from this page in your ebook to your storage medium and then make AE8 the active folder.

Ebook Links

Access digital resources for this course from your ebook.

SNAP

If you are a SNAP user, go to your SNAP assignments page to complete the Precheck, Tutorials, and Recheck in this chapter.

Preview

On the Job

Scenario: ProDiagnostics Medical Laboratories (PDML)

In Chapter 7, you used a table to organize and analyze revenue data from the previous year for Kaelan Rogers, director of ProDiagnostics Medical Laboratories (PDML). Kaelan needs to analyze the revenue from the previous year and from January of this year in depth, because he is considering adding locations and expanding the services PDML offers. He asks you to create PivotTables and PivotCharts to summarize the data. He also asks you to create visuals that make it easy to spot patterns and trends in the summarized data. With an expansion, it will be necessary to manage a larger data set. To accommodate this need, Kaelan wants you to start building a Data Model in Power Pivot.

Visual Reference: A PivotTable and a PivotChart

Figure 8.1 PivotTable and a PivotChart with the PivotTable Fields Task Pane Displayed

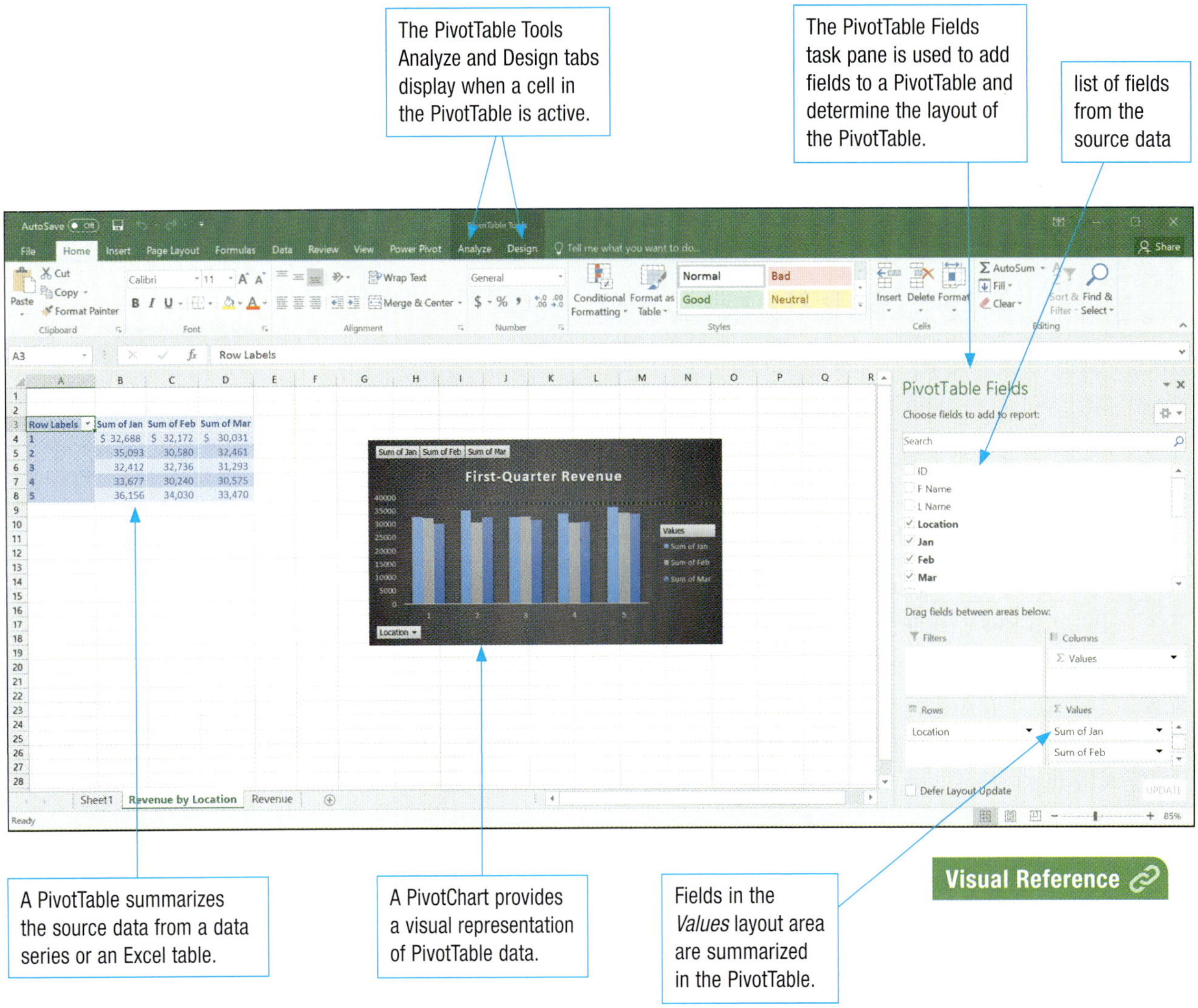

Visual Reference

8.1 Creating and Refreshing a PivotTable

MOS Expert 4.2.1

Tutorial

Creating a PivotTable

When you have a large worksheet, analyzing all the data can be challenging and time consuming. Creating a **PivotTable** can make a large worksheet more manageable by summarizing the data and allowing you to manipulate it in different ways. When you create a PivotTable, you turn, or *pivot*, the data so you can view it from a different perspective. For example, suppose a sales manager has created a worksheet that tracks monthly sales for each inventory item. To determine which items are the best sellers in a specific financial quarter, the manager can use a PivotTable to quickly reorganize the data and create a summary for each item for that quarter.

To display data in a PivotTable, you add fields from the source data to the PivotTable and indicate what layout area to place the fields in. The placement of the fields determines the layout of the PivotTable.

▸ **Know This** about creating a PivotTable

— A PivotTable can be created from a range or table in the current worksheet. It can also be created from an external source, such as an Access database.

— Creating a PivotTable does not change the range or table. Like a sort or filter, a PivotTable provides a different view of the data.

— A PivotTable can be placed in a new worksheet or in a specific location in the current worksheet.

— To create a PivotTable from a range or table in the current worksheet, follow these steps:

1. Select the range, or click in any cell in the table.
2. Click the PivotTable button in the Tables group on the Insert tab to display the Create PivotTable dialog box (see Figure 8.2).
3. Verify that the range of data you want to analyze appears in the *Table/Range* text box.
4. Specify the location for the PivotTable by clicking the *New Worksheet* radio button to insert a bullet or by clicking the *Existing Worksheet* radio button to insert a bullet and then entering the cell address for the upper left corner of the PivotTable.
5. Click the OK button to close the dialog box and display the PivotTable Fields task pane (see Figure 8.3).

▸ Know More ways to display the PivotTable Fields task pane

– Click in any cell in a PivotTable and then click the Field List button in the Show group on the PivotTable Tools Analyze tab.

Figure 8.2 Create PivotTable Dialog Box

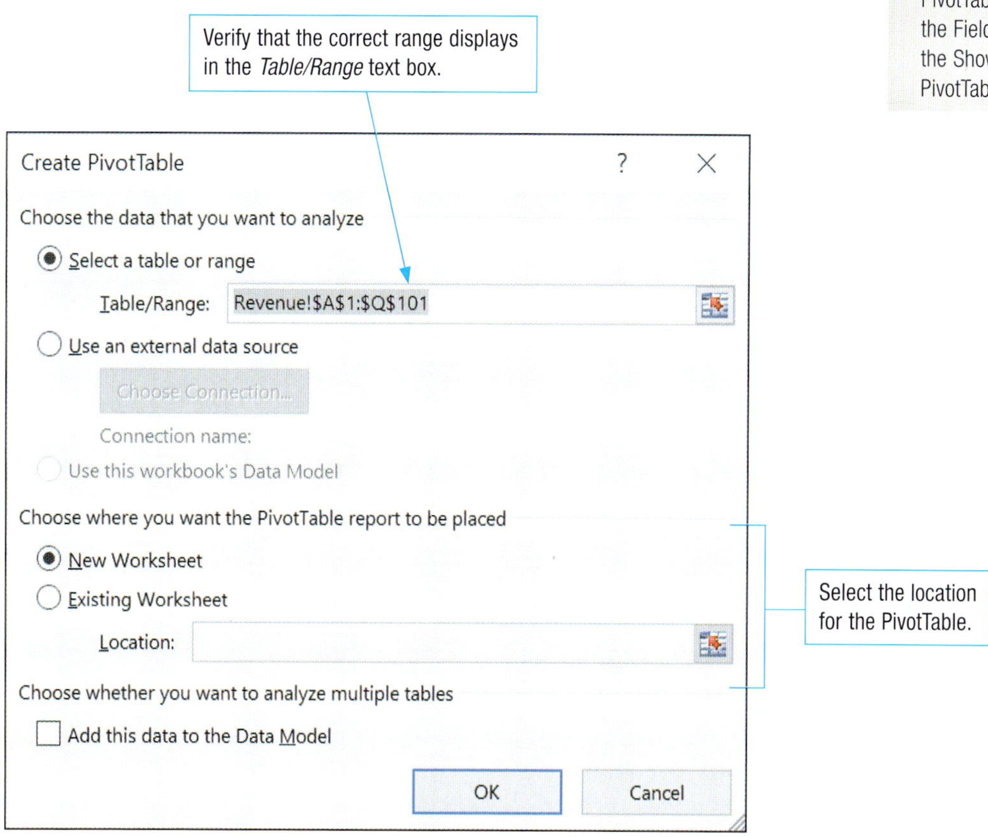

Figure 8.3 PivotTable Fields Task Pane

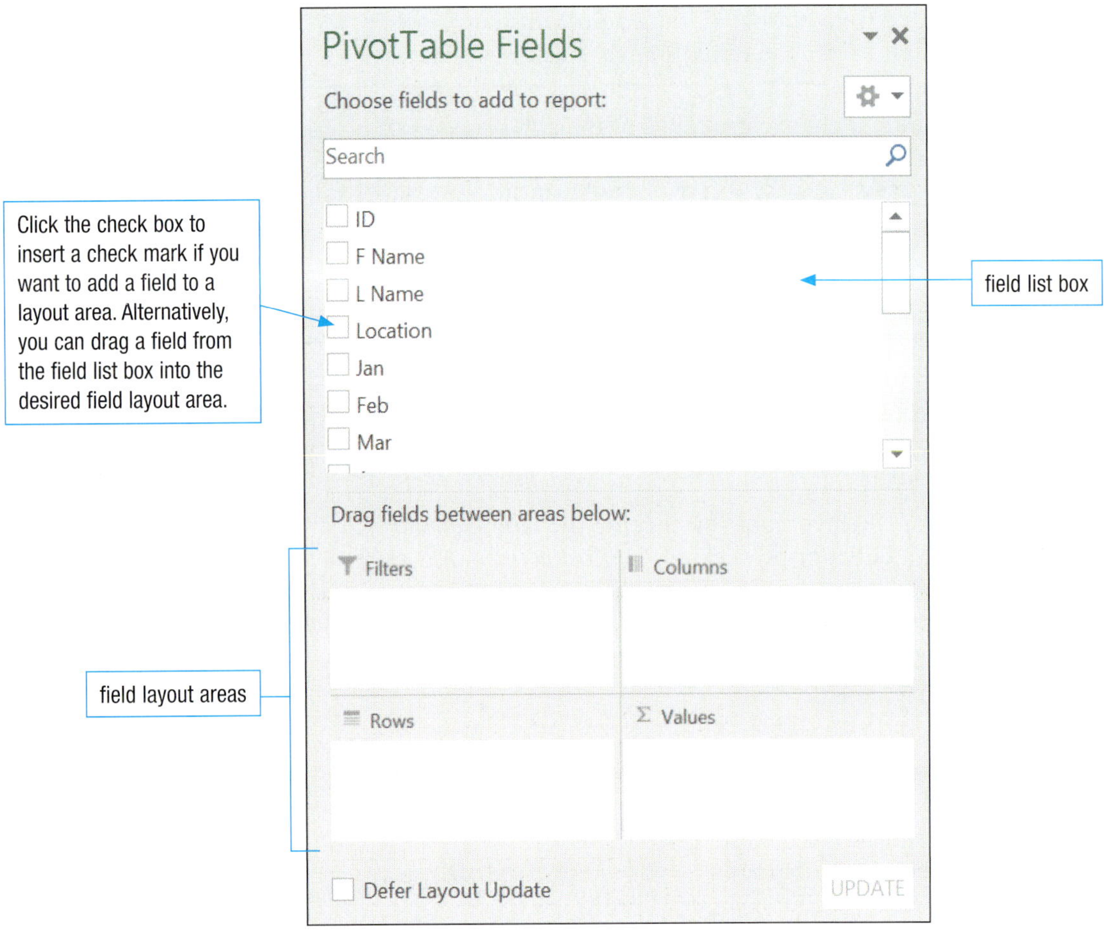

▸ **Know This** about adding fields to a PivotTable

— To add a field to a layout area and a PivotTable, click the field name check box in the field list at the PivotTable Fields task pane to insert a check mark (see Figure 8.3).

— By default, the selected field displays as a field button in the layout area that corresponds to its field type.

— The layout area determines how the data appears in the PivotTable.

— Drag a field button to move it from one layout area to another.

▸ **Know More** ways to add a field to a PivotTable

– Drag a field from the field list box to a layout area at the PivotTable Fields task pane.

▸ **Know This** about the *Columns* layout area

— Fields placed in the *Columns* layout area display as column headers in the top row of the PivotTable (see Figure 8.4).

— Each unique piece of data, or **item**, in a field displays in a separate column. For example, in Figure 8.4, the *Location* field contains five unique items: locations 1, 2, 3, 4, and 5. Each location number displays as a separate column header in the PivotTable.

— By default, date and time fields are added to the *Columns* layout area at the PivotTable Fields task pane.

▸ **Know This** about the *Filters* layout area

— Fields placed in the *Filters* layout area display as filters with arrows above the PivotTable (see Figure 8.5).

— You can use filter fields to display selected items in the PivotTable.

— Click a filter arrow and then select items at the drop-down list to display only those items in the PivotTable.

Figure 8.4 *Columns* Layout Area

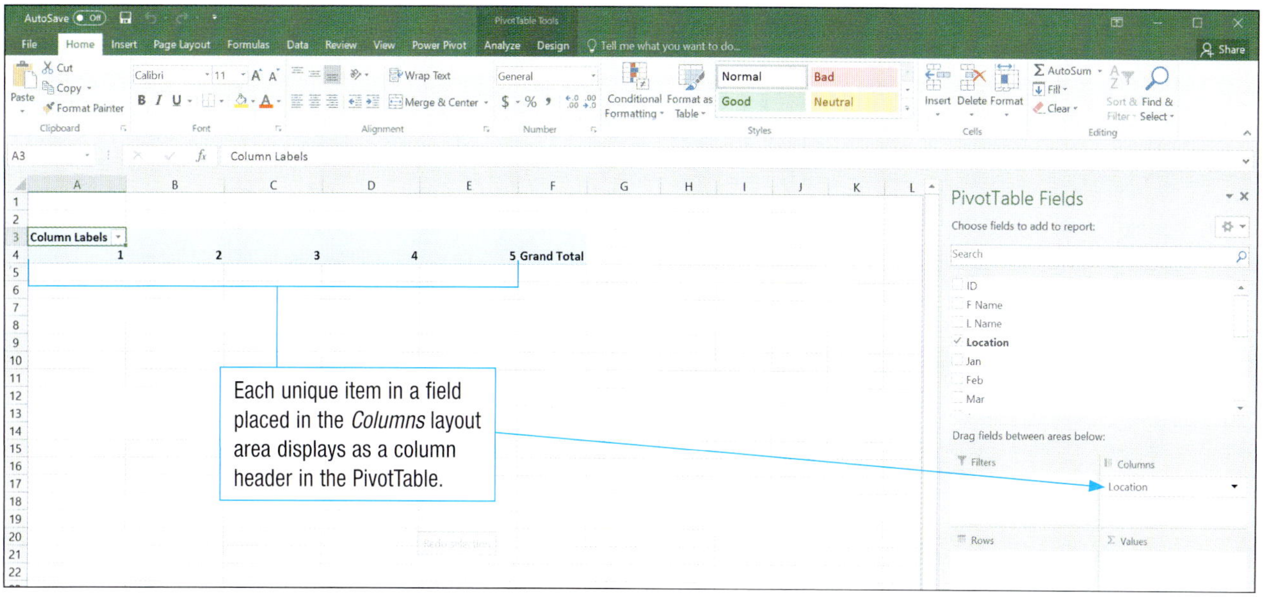

Figure 8.5 *Filters* Layout Area

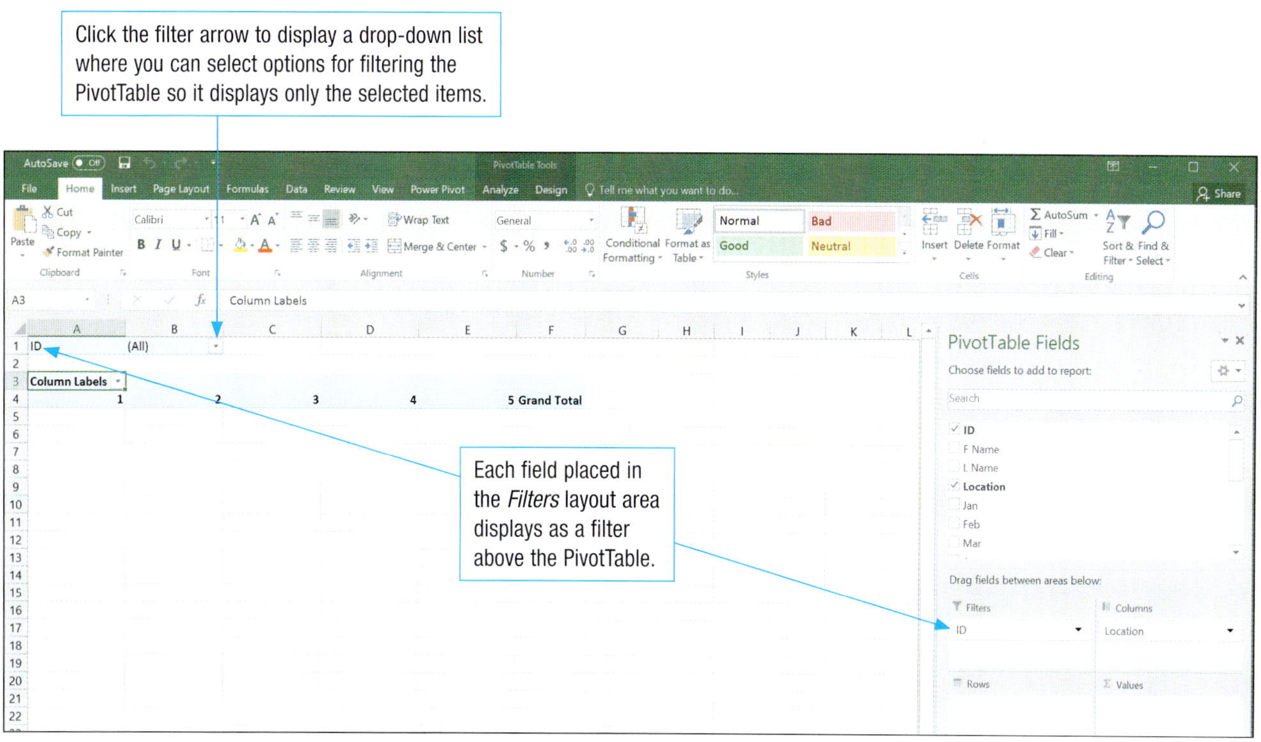

▸ Know This about the *Rows* layout area

— Fields placed in the *Rows* layout area display as row headers in the left-most column of the PivotTable (see Figure 8.6).

— Each unique item in the field displays in a separate row. For example, in Figure 8.6, the *Location* field contains five unique items: locations 1, 2, 3, 4, and 5. Each location number displays as the header of a separate row in the PivotTable.

— By default, text fields are added to the *Rows* layout area.

Figure 8.6 *Rows* Layout Area

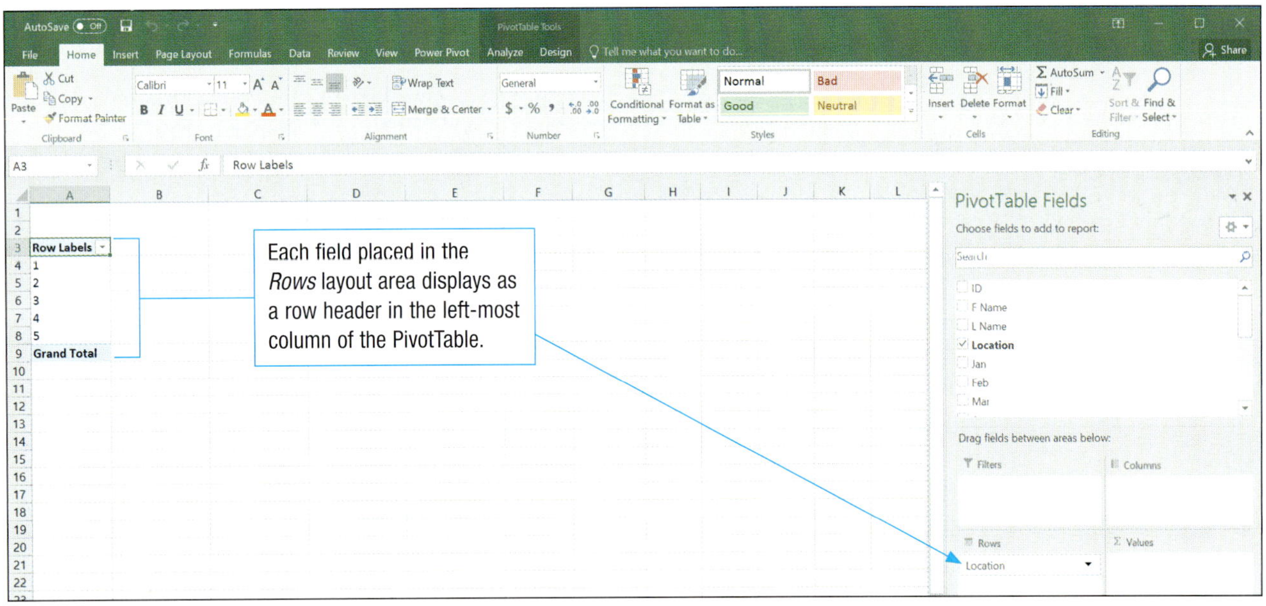

▸ Know This about the *Values* layout area

— Fields placed in the *Values* layout area are summarized in the PivotTable (see Figure 8.7).

— A field placed in the *Values* layout area is called a **value field**.

— If a field containing numeric data is placed in the *Values* layout area, it displays as a SUM value in the PivotTable.

— If a field containing text data is placed in the *Values* layout area, it displays as a COUNT value in the PivotTable.

— By default, numeric fields are added to the *Values* layout area.

▸ Know This about refreshing PivotTables

— By default, PivotTables do not update automatically when the source data is edited.

— To show changed source data in a related PivotTable, you must **refresh** (update) the PivotTable.

— To refresh all the PivotTables in a workbook manually, click the Refresh button in the Data group on the PivotTable Tools Analyze tab.

— To refresh all the PivotTables in a workbook automatically every time you open the workbook, click in any cell in the PivotTable, click the

▸ Know More methods for refreshing PivotTables manually

– Press Alt + F5.

PivotTable Tools Analyze tab, click the Options button arrow in the PivotTable group, click the *Data* tab, and then select the *Refresh data when opening the file* check box to insert a check mark.

Figure 8.7 *Values* Layout Area

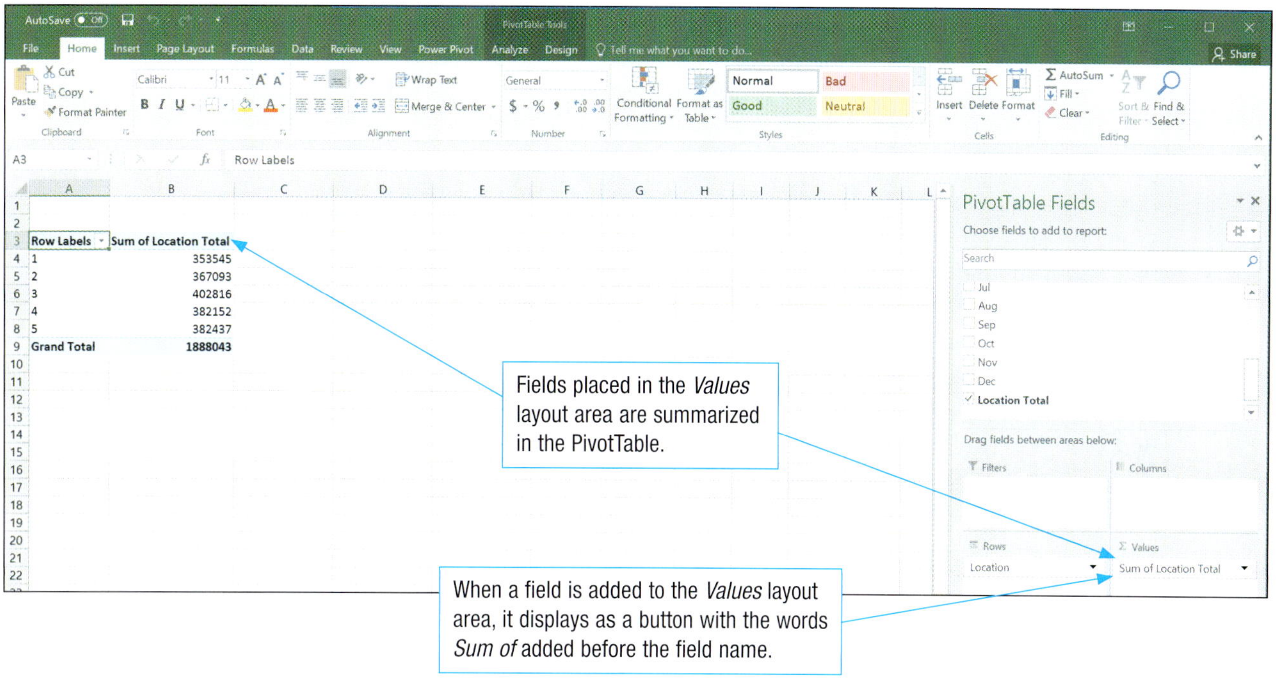

▸ **Know This** about adding alternative text to a PivotTable

— To add alternative text to a PivotTable, right-click in any cell in the PivotTable, click the *PivotTable Options* option at the pop-up menu to display the PivotTable Options dialog box, and then click the Alt Text tab.

— Type a meaningful title and description to help people using assistive technology such as screen readers understand the contents of the PivotTable.

On the Job

Task 8.1 Creating a PivotTable

Kaelan wants you to reorganize the data in the PDML workbook to summarize the annual revenue generated by each of the company's locations. To provide this summary, use a PivotTable that displays the *Location* field data in the *Rows* layout area. To ensure that your workbook passes the Excel Accessibility Check, also add alternative text to the PivotTable.

1. Open the Excel data file **8-PDML**.
2. Click in any cell in the table.
3. Click the Insert tab and then click the PivotTable button in the Tables group.

   The Create PivotTable dialog box displays (see Figure 8.2 on page 317).

4. Click the OK button.

   A blank PivotTable displays in a new worksheet named *Sheet1* and the PivotTable Fields task pane displays (see Figure 8.3 on page 318).

5. Click the *Location* check box in the field list box.

   A check mark displays in the *Location* check box, the Sum of Location button is added to the *Values* layout area, and a summary of the location data displays in cell A4 of the PivotTable.

6. Drag the Sum of Location button from the *Values* layout area into the *Rows* layout area.

   The Location button appears in the *Rows* layout area and the location data displays in range A4:A8 of the PivotTable.

7. Scroll down the field list box, if necessary, and then click the *Location Total* check box.

   A check mark displays in the *Location Total* check box, the Sum of Location Total button appears in the *Values* layout area, and a summary of the total revenue for each location displays in range B4:B8 of the PivotTable (see Figure 8.7 on page 321).

8. Right-click in any cell in the PivotTable and then click the *PivotTable Options* option at the pop-up menu.

   The PivotTable Options dialog box displays.

9. Click the Alt Text tab.
10. Click in the *Title* text box, type Annual Revenue, and then press the Tab key.
11. Type Annual revenue for each of the five company locations in the *Description* text box.
12. Click the OK button.
13. Double-click the Sheet1 tab, type Revenue by Location, and then press the Enter key.
14. Click the Save button on the Quick Access Toolbar.

Model Answer

8.2 Modifying a PivotTable Layout

MOS Expert 4.2.2

Tutorial

Modifying a PivotTable Layout

A **PivotTable report layout** is the visual display of data organized and summarized in a PivotTable. Excel offers three report layouts: Compact Form, Outline Form, and Tabular Form.

When a PivotTable is created, the default report layout, Compact Form, is applied. The Compact Form layout is designed to optimize the readability of a PivotTable. You can change the layout of a PivotTable by adding, removing, and rearranging fields at the PivotTable Fields task pane. The ability to manipulate fields makes a PivotTable a powerful tool for exploring, summarizing, and analyzing data in an interactive manner.

Other ways of modifying the layout of the PivotTable include changing the report layout, changing the way subtotals and grand totals are displayed, and inserting blank rows between items in the PivotTable to improve readability and to help group items visually.

▶ Know This about adding fields to a PivotTable

— To add a field to a PivotTable, click the field name check box in the field list box at the PivotTable Fields task pane to insert a check mark.

Reminder
To display the PivotTable Fields task pane, click in any cell in a PivotTable and then click the Field List button in the Show group on the PivotTable Tools Analyze tab.

▶ Know This about removing fields from a PivotTable

— To remove a field from a PivotTable, click the field name check box in the field list box at the PivotTable Fields task pane to remove the check mark.

▶ Know More methods for removing fields from a PivotTable

- Click the field button arrow in the layout area at the PivotTable Fields task pane and then click the *Remove Field* option at the pop-up menu (see Figure 8.8).
- Drag the field button out of the layout area at the PivotTable Fields task pane.

Figure 8.8 Field Button Arrow Drop-Down List

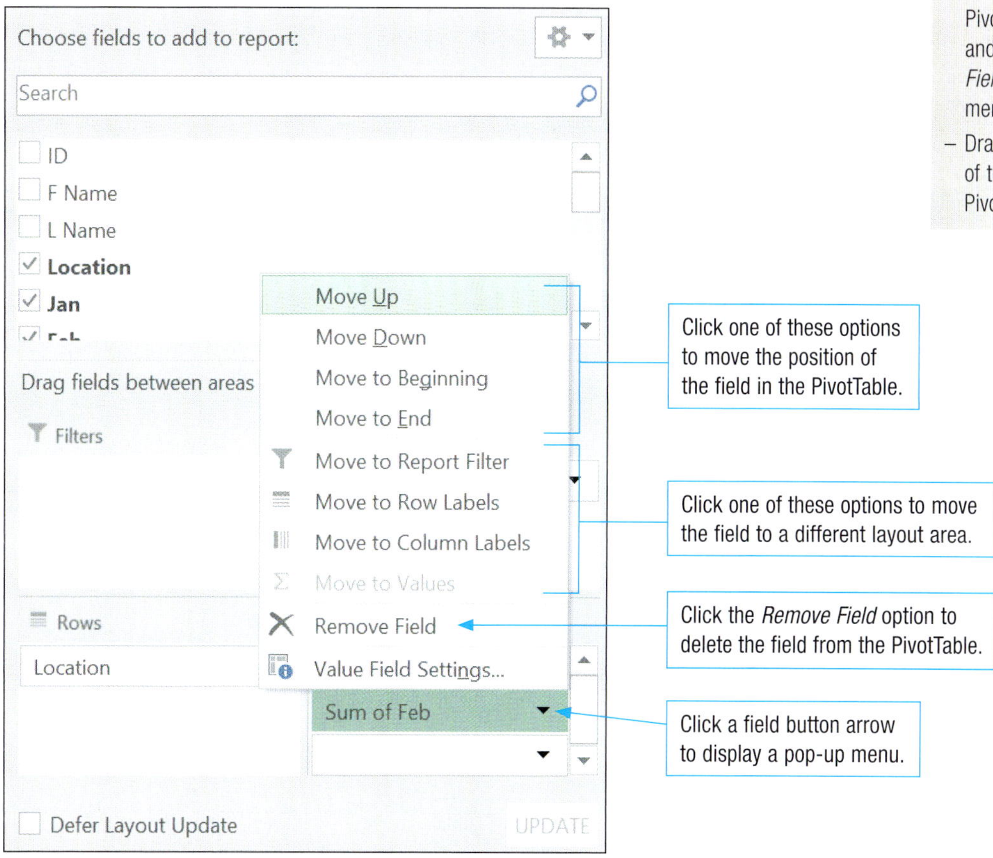

▶ Know This about rearranging fields in a PivotTable

— To change where a field is positioned in a PivotTable, click the field button arrow in the layout area at the PivotTable Fields task pane and then click the *Move Up*, *Move Down*, *Move to Beginning*, or *Move to End* option at the pop-up menu (see Figure 8.8).

— To move a field to a different layout area, click the field button arrow and then click the *Move to Report Filter*, *Move to Row Labels*, *Move to Column Labels*, or *Move to Values* option area.

Reminder
You can also move a field to a different layout area by dragging the field button to that layout area at the PivotTable Fields task pane (see Section 8.1).

▶ Know This about changing the PivotTable layout

— To show or hide subtotals, click the Subtotals button in the Layout group on the PivotTable Tools Design tab and then click an option at the drop-down list (see Figure 8.9).

— To show or hide grand totals, click the Grand Totals button and then click an option at the drop-down list.
— To change the report layout, click the Report Layout button and then click an option at the drop-down list.
— Grouping data in a PivotTable can help show a subset of data to analyze as it places fields in a hierarchy that is adjacent and subordinate to a summary row or column.
— To insert a blank line after each grouped item in a PivotTable, click the Blank Rows button and then click the *Insert Blank Line after Each Item* option at the drop-down list.

Figure 8.9 PivotTable Layout Group and Report Layout Button Drop-Down List

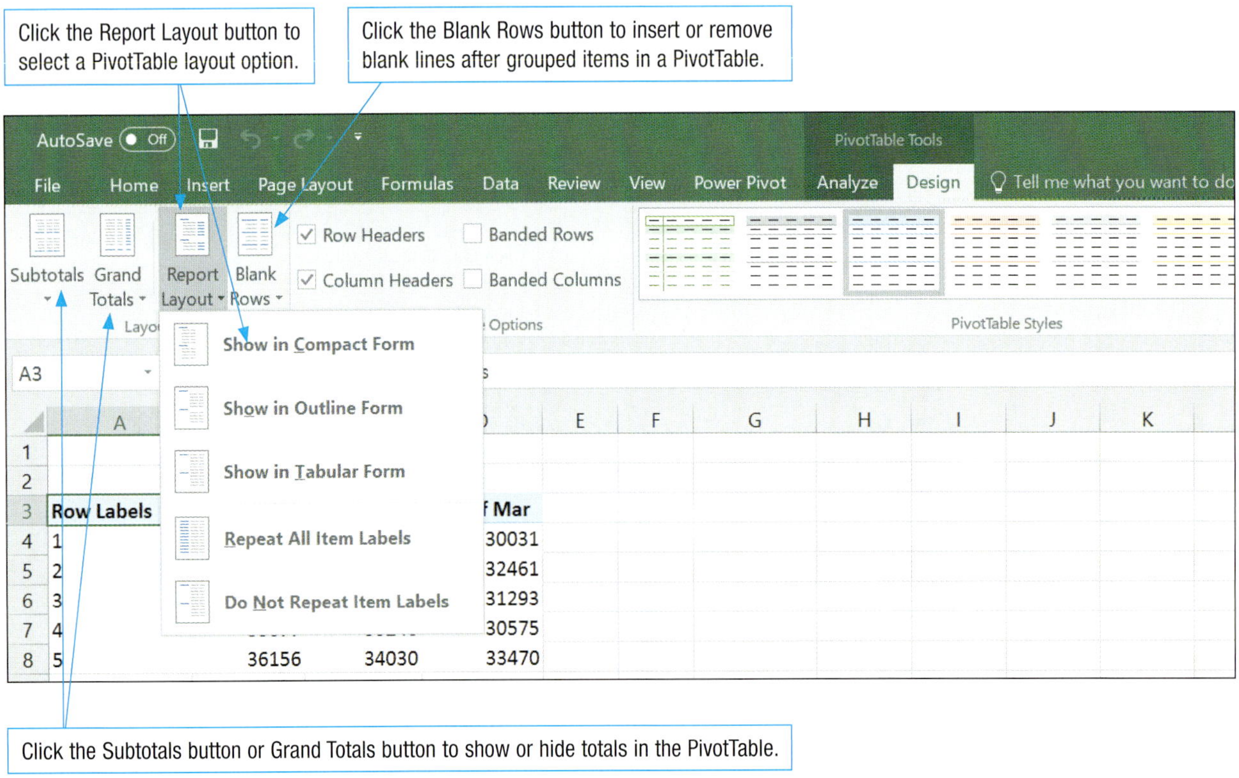

On the Job

Task 8.2a Rearranging Fields in a PivotTable Layout

After reviewing the PivotTable you created in Task 8.1, Kaelan asks you to rearrange the layout to display the *Location* field data in columns instead of rows.

1. With the 8-PDML workbook open and the Revenue by Location worksheet active, any cell in the PivotTable active, and the PivotTable Fields task pane displayed, drag the Location button from the *Rows* layout area to the *Columns* layout area at the task pane.

   The PivotTable rearranges and the location data displays in columns.

2. Click the Save button on the Quick Access Toolbar.
3. If printed work is required by your instructor, print the workbook.

Model Answer

On the Job

Task 8.2b Modifying a PivotTable Layout

After reviewing the rearranged PivotTable you created in Task 8.2a, Kaelan asks you to rearrange the layout again to display the *Location* field in rows instead of columns. Kaelan also realizes that his analysis needs to focus on first-quarter data for the previous year. He asks you to modify the PivotTable to display last year's first-quarter revenue totals for each location by month instead of the annual revenue totals.

1. With the 8-PDML workbook open and the Revenue by Location worksheet active, click the Location button arrow in the *Columns* layout area and then click the *Move to Row Labels* option.

   The PivotTable rearranges so the location data displays in rows.
2. Click the *Jan* check box in the field list box.

   The Sum of Jan button displays in the *Values* layout area and the summarized January data displays in the PivotTable.
3. Scroll down the field list box, if necessary, and then click the *Location Total* check box.

   The check mark is removed from the check box and the *Location Total* field is removed from the PivotTable.
4. Scroll up the field list box, if necessary, and then click the *Mar* check box.

   A check mark is inserted in the check box and the Sum of Mar button displays in the *Values* layout area, and the summarized March data displays in the PivotTable.
5. Click the *Feb* check box.

   A check mark is inserted in the check box, the Sum of Feb button displays in the *Values* layout area and the summarized February data displays in the PivotTable.
6. Click the Sum of Feb button arrow in the *Values* layout area.

   A pop-up menu displays.
7. Click the *Move Up* option (see Figure 8.8 on page 323).

   The Sum of Feb button moves above the Sum of Mar button in the *Values* layout area and the data in the PivotTable rearranges.
8. Click the PivotTable Tools Design tab and then click the Grand Totals button in the Layout group.

   A drop-down list displays.
9. Click the *Off for Rows and Columns* option.

   The *Grand Total* row is hidden.
10. Click the Save button on the Quick Access Toolbar.

Model Answer

8.3 Formatting a PivotTable

MOS Expert 4.2.7

Tutorial

Formatting a PivotTable

A PivotTable can be formatted quickly by applying a built-in style in the PivotTable Styles gallery. Like a table style, a PivotTable style applies a group of formatting settings together in one action. The applied style can then be modified using options in the PivotTable Style Options group on the PivotTable Tools Design tab (see Figure 8.10). Value fields can be formatted in the Value Field Settings dialog box (see Figure 8.8). A PivotTable can also be formatted using any of the formatting options that can be applied to a worksheet.

Figure 8.10 PivotTable Formatting Options

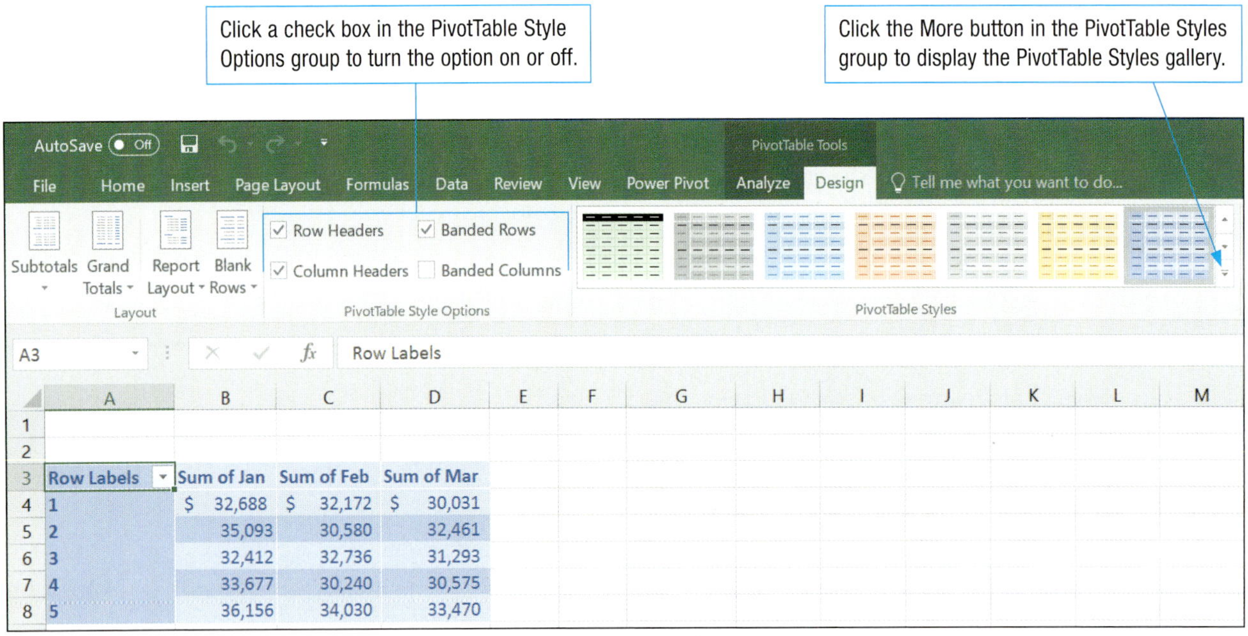

▸ **Know This** about applying a PivotTable style

— To apply a PivotTable style, click in any cell in the PivotTable, click the More button in the PivotTable Styles group on the PivotTable Tools Design tab (see Figure 8.10), and then click a style at the drop-down gallery.

— Point to a PivotTable style option to see a live preview of the style.

— Using a predefined PivotTable style provides consistency in formatting.

▸ **Know This** about applying PivotTable style options

— To turn on or off the display of row or column headers, click the *Row Headers* check box or *Column Headers* check box in the PivotTable Style Options group on the PivotTable Tools Design tab to insert or remove a check mark.

— To turn on or off the display of banded rows or columns, click the *Banded Rows* check box or *Banded Columns* check box to insert or remove a check mark.

▸ **Know This** about formatting value fields

— To change the formatting for a value field, display the PivotTable Fields task pane, click the field button arrow in the *Values* layout area, and then click the *Value Field Settings* option at the pop-up menu to display the Value Field Settings dialog box (see Figure 8.11).

— Use options at the Value Field Settings dialog to specify how the field is named and displayed, the type of calculation used to summarize the data, and the number format that will be applied to the field.

— Click the Number Format button to display options for applying a number format, such as Accounting or Percentage, to the field.

Reminder

To display the PivotTable Fields task pane, click in any cell in the PivotTable and then click the Field List button in the Show group on the PivotTable Tools Analyze tab.

Figure 8.11 Value Field Settings Dialog Box

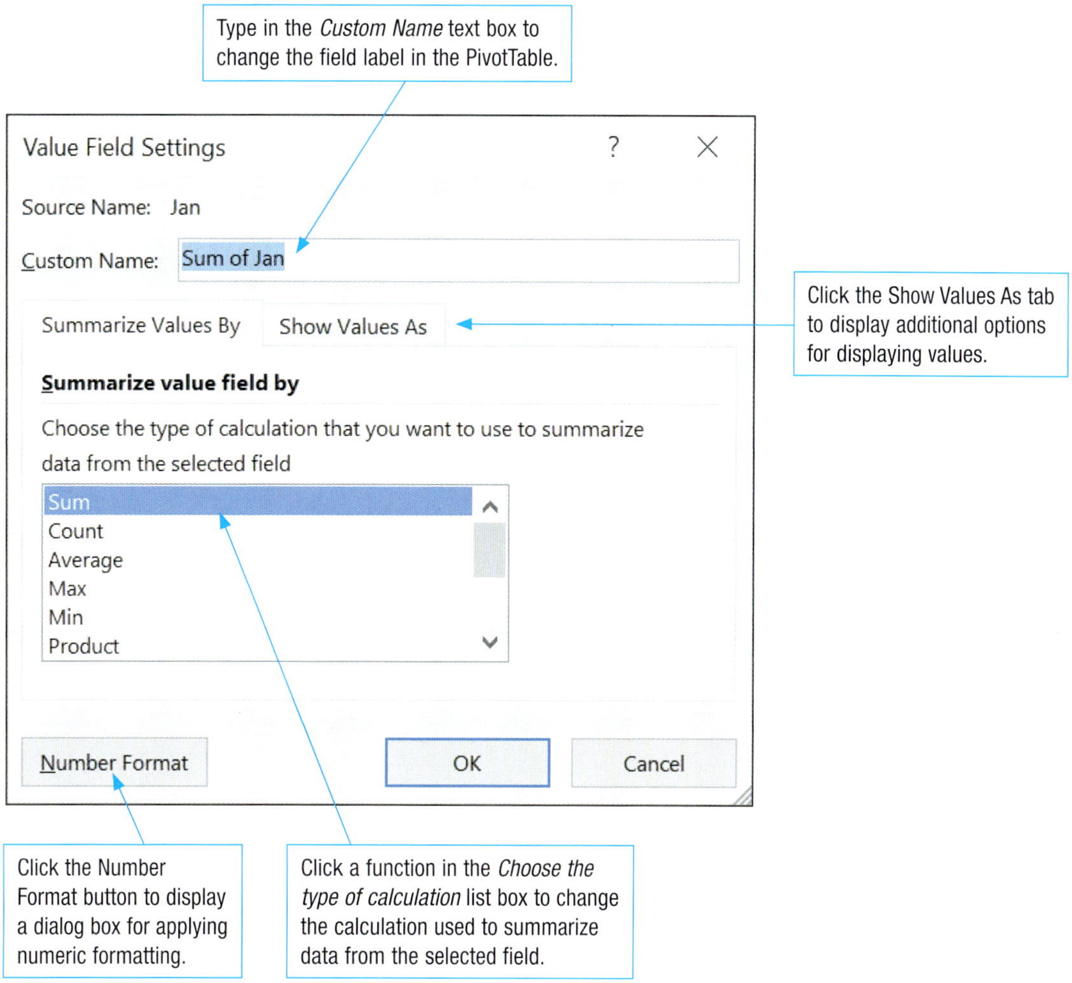

On the Job

Task 8.3 Formatting a PivotTable

Kaelan wants you to modify the PivotTable that summarizes the first-quarter revenue by location to improve its readability and to use standard accounting formatting.

1. With the 8-PDML workbook open and the Revenue by Location worksheet active, cell C6 active, and the PivotTable Fields task pane displayed, click the PivotTable Tools Design tab and then click the More button in the PivotTable Styles group.

   A drop-down gallery displays.

2. Click the *Light Blue, Pivot Style Medium 27* option (sixth column, fourth row in the *Medium* section).
3. Click the *Banded Rows* check box in the PivotTable Style Options group (see Figure 8.10 on page 326).

   A check mark displays in the *Banded Rows* check box and banded rows are applied to the PivotTable.

4. Click the Sum of Jan button arrow in the *Values* layout area at the PivotTable Fields task pane.

   A pop-up menu displays.

5. Click the *Value Field Settings* option.

   The Value Field Settings dialog box displays (see Figure 8.11 on page 327).

6. Click the Number Format button.

   The Format Cells dialog box displays.

7. Click the *Number* option in the *Category* list box, click the *Use 1000 Separator (,)* check box, and then click the *Decimal places* decrement (down) arrow two times.

   The value in the *Decimal places* measurement box displays as *0* and *32,736* displays in the *Sample* field.

8. Click the OK button.

   The Format Cells dialog box closes.

9. Click the OK button.

   The Value Field Settings dialog box closes and the formatting chosen in Step 7 is applied to the values in the *Sum of Jan* column in the PivotTable.

10. Select the range C5:D8.
11. Click the Home tab and then click the Comma Style button in the Number group.
12. Click the Decrease Decimal button two times.
13. Select the range B4:D4 and then click the Accounting Number Format button.
14. Click the Decrease Decimal button two times.
15. Click the Save button on the Quick Access Toolbar.

Model Answer

8.4 Filtering and Sorting a PivotTable

Tutorial

Filtering a PivotTable

When using a PivotTable to analyze data, you may want to drill down and focus on only a portion, or subset, of the data. An easy way to do this is to apply a filter. When a filter is applied, selected items are displayed in the PivotTable and unselected items are hidden.

Fields added to the *Filters* layout area at the PivotTable Fields task pane appear above the PivotTable in the worksheet (see Figure 8.12). You can use the filter arrow for each field to add and remove items in the filter. You can also use the *Row Labels* filter arrow or *Column Labels* filter arrow in the PivotTable to filter data by a specific item—similarly to how you would filter a table (see Figure 8.13).

Options at a field filter arrow or field button arrow drop-down list are also used to sort the data in a PivotTable. By default, the data in a PivotTable is sorted the same way as the source data.

Figure 8.12 PivotTable Filter Options

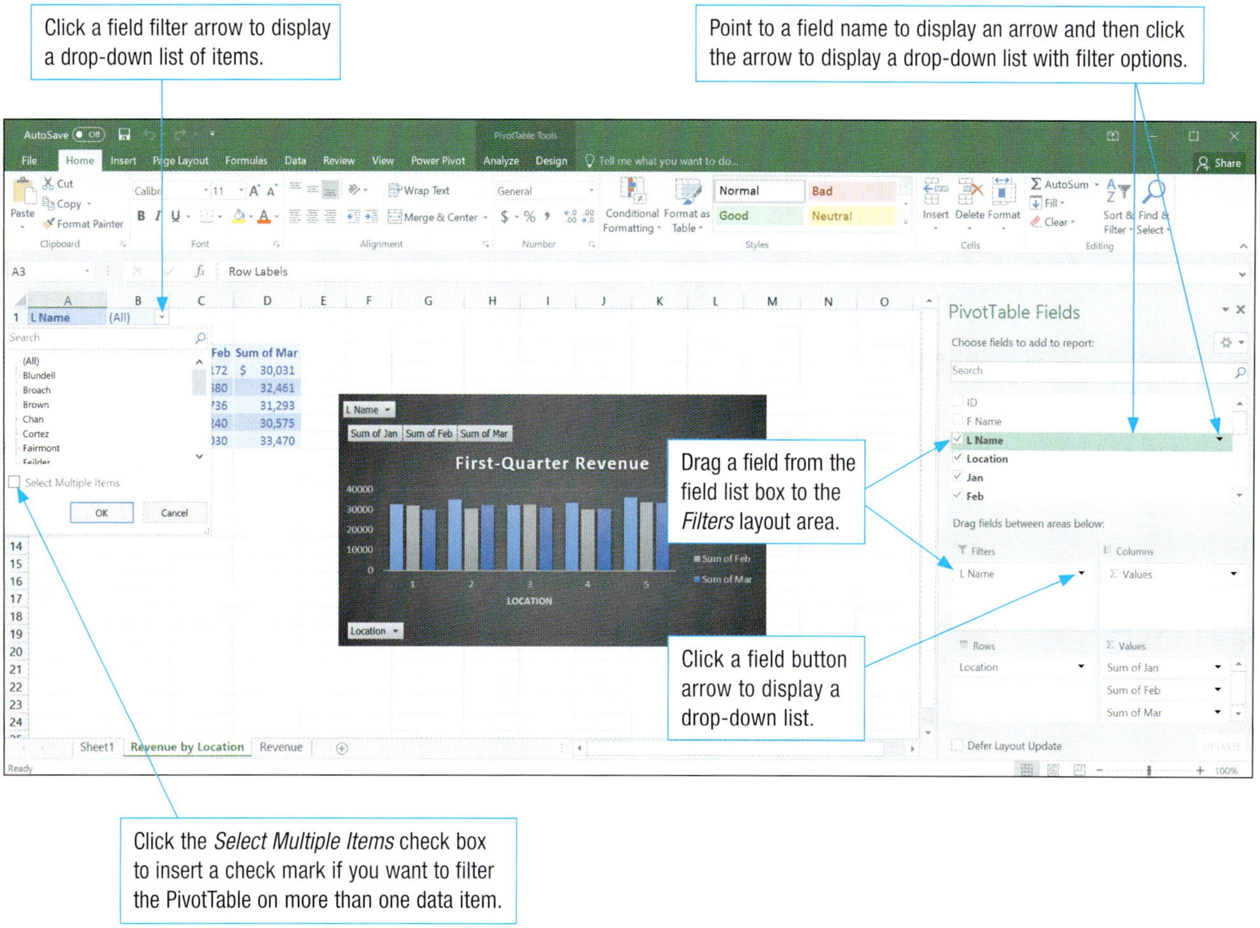

Figure 8.13 *Row Labels* Filter Arrow Drop-Down List

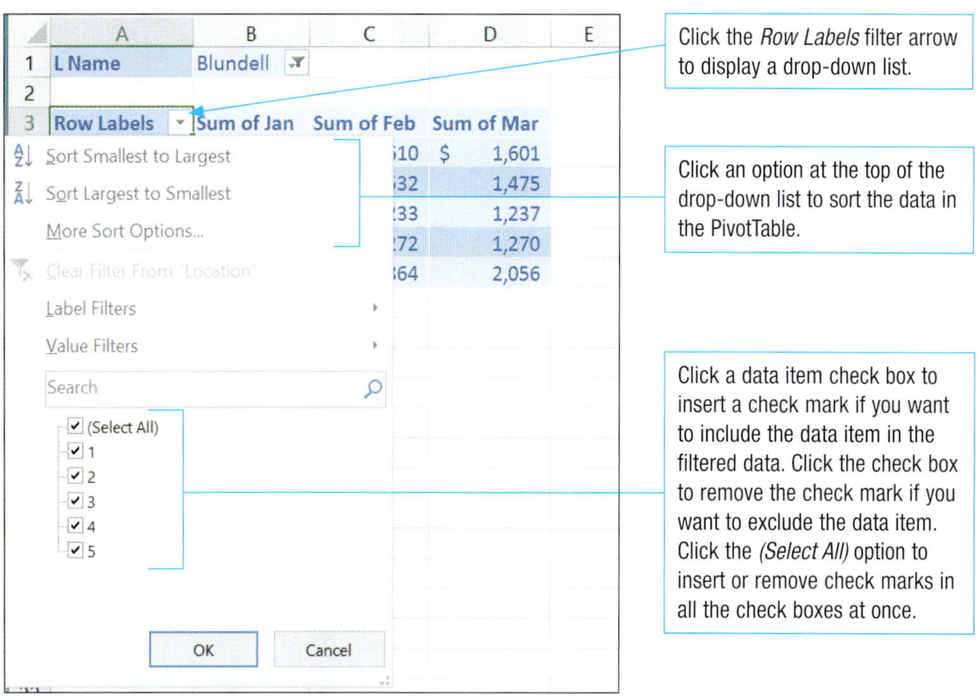

▶ Know This about adding and removing filter fields in a PivotTable

— To add a filter field to a PivotTable, drag the field from the field list box to the *Filters* layout area at the PivotTable Fields task pane (see Figure 8.12 on page 329).
— To add multiple filter fields, drag multiple fields to the *Filters* layout area.
— To remove a field from the filter, drag it out of the *Filters* layout area.

▶ Know More methods for removing a filter field in a PivotTable

– To remove a filter field from a PivotTable, click the field name arrow in the field list at the PivotTable Fields task pane and then click the *Remove Field* option or click the field button arrow in the *Filters* layout area and then click the *Remove Field* option.

▶ Know This about filtering a PivotTable

— To filter a PivotTable, click a field filter arrow in the worksheet (see Figure 8.12), select an option at the drop-down list and then click the OK button.
— To filter multiple items, click a field filter arrow in the worksheet, click the *Select Multiple Items* check box at the drop-down list to remove the check mark, click the item check boxes to insert check marks, and then click the OK button.
— To clear an applied filter, click the field filter arrow in the worksheet and then click the *(All)* option.

▶ Know This about filtering a PivotTable using a *Row Labels* filter arrow or *Column Labels* filter arrow

— To filter a PivotTable using a *Row Labels* filter arrow or a *Column Labels* filter arrow, click the filter arrow in the worksheet, click an item check box to insert a check mark, and then click the OK button (see Figure 8.13 on page 329).

▶ Know More methods for filtering a PivotTable using a *Row Labels* filter arrow or *Column Labels* filter arrow

– Point to a field name at the PivotTable Fields task pane field list to display an arrow, click the arrow (see Figure 8.12), and then click an item check box at the drop-down list.

▶ Know This about sorting a PivotTable

— To sort a PivotTable, click a field filter arrow in the worksheet (see Figure 8.12) and then click the *Sort Smallest to Largest* option or the *Sort Largest to Smallest* option at the drop-down list.
— To change the sort field location, click a field filter arrow in the worksheet, click the *More Sort Options* option at the drop-down list, select sort options at the Sort (Location) dialog box, and then click the OK button.

On the Job

Task 8.4a Using the PivotTable Fields Task Pane to Filter a PivotTable

Kaelan wants to go a little deeper with his analysis of last year's first-quarter revenue data. He wants to know how much Dr. Blundell contributed to the revenue for each location for that quarter.

1. With the 8-PDML workbook open and the Revenue by Location worksheet active, any cell in the PivotTable active, and the PivotTable Fields task pane displayed, drag the *L Name* field from the field list box to the *Filters* layout area.

   The L Name field appears in the *Filters* layout area of the task pane and in row 1, above the PivotTable, in the worksheet.

2. Click the *L Name* filter arrow in cell B1.

   A drop-down list displays (see Figure 8.12).

3. Click the *Blundell* option and then click the OK button.

   The PivotTable filters the data to display only the revenue generated by Dr. Blundell.

4. Click the Save button on the Quick Access Toolbar.
5. If printed work is required by your instructor, print the workbook.

Model Answer

On the Job

Task 8.4b Using a Filter Arrow to Filter Multiple Items a PivotTable

Kaelan wants to know how Dr. Blundell and Dr. Garcia together contributed to the revenue for each location for the first quarter.

1. With the 8-PDML workbook open and the Revenue by Location worksheet active, click the *L Name* filter arrow in cell B1 and then click the *Select Multiple Items* check box.

   A check box appears to the left of every data item in the drop-down list. The *Blundell* check box contains a check mark. The other check boxes do not contain check marks.

2. Scroll down, if necessary, click the *Garcia* check box, and then click the OK button.

   The PivotTable filters the data to display only the revenue generated by Dr. Blundell and Dr. Garcia.

3. Click the Save button on the Quick Access Toolbar.
4. If printed work is required by your instructor, print the workbook.

Model Answer

On the Job

Task 8.4c Using a Filter Arrow to Filter One Item a PivotTable

Kaelan wants to know how much location 3 contributed to the first-quarter revenue.

1. With the 8-PDML workbook open and the Revenue by Location worksheet active, click the *L Name* filter arrow in cell B1, click the *(All)* check box, and then click the OK button.

   The filter is removed and all the PivotTable data displays.

2. Click the *Row Labels* filter arrow in cell A3.

   A drop-down list displays (see Figure 8.13 on page 329).

3. Click the *(Select All)* check box.

   The check marks are removed from all the check boxes in the drop-down list.

4. Click the *3* check box and then click the OK button.

   The PivotTable is filtered to display only the data for location 3.

5. Click the Save button on the Quick Access Toolbar.
6. If printed work is required by your instructor, print the workbook.

Model Answer

On the Job
Task 8.4d Removing a Filter from a PivotTable

Kaelan has the data he needs for his analysis and wants you to remove the filter.

1. With the 8-PDML workbook open and the Revenue by Location worksheet active, click the *Row Labels* filter button in cell A3.
2. Click the *(Select All)* check box and then click the OK button.

   The filter is removed and all the PivotTable data displays.
3. With the Revenue by Location worksheet active, any cell in the PivotTable active, and the PivotTable Fields task pane displayed, click the L Name button in the *Filters* layout area and hold down the left mouse button, drag the button out of the *Filters* layout area, and then release the mouse button.

   The filter is removed from the worksheet.
4. Click the Save button on the Quick Access Toolbar.

Model Answer

8.5 Filtering a PivotTable Using Slicers

MOS Expert 4.2.3

Tutorial

Using a Slicer to Filter a PivotTable

Chapter 7 explained how to filter a table using the slicer feature. You can also use the slicer feature to filter a PivotTable without displaying filter arrows or dialog boxes.

▸ Know This about using slicers to filter a PivotTable

— To use a slicer to filter a PivotTable, start by clicking the Insert Slicer button in the Filters group on the PivotTable Tools Analyze tab to display the Insert Slicers dialog box.

— At the dialog box, click the check box to insert a check mark for each field to be filtered and then click the OK button to display the Slicer pane.

— At the Slicer pane, select one item that Excel should use to filter the list. To select more items, press and hold down the Ctrl key, click each additional item, and then release the Ctrl key.

— To remove a slicer filter, click the Clear Filter button at the top right of the Slicer pane.

— To delete a Slicer pane, select the Slicer pane and then press the Delete key.

▸ Know More ways to select multiple slicer items

– To select multiple slicer items, select one option, click the Multi-Select button at the Slicer pane or press Alt + S, and then click each additional option.

On the Job
Task 8.5a Using a Slicer to Filter a PivotTable

Dr. Russel and Dr. Sullivan will be on leave during the first quarter of this year. Kaelan wants to see how much revenue those two doctors generated for the first quarter of last year. He will use that information to help forecast revenue for the first quarter of this year and to help the board of directors decide whether to hire replacements while the doctors are on leave. Use slicers to filter the PivotTable to display the requested data.

1. With the 8-PDML workbook open and the Revenue by Location worksheet active, click the PivotTable Tools Analyze tab and then click the Insert Slicer button in the Filter group.

   The Insert Slicers dialog box displays.

2. Click the *L Name* check box to insert a check mark and then click the OK button (see Figure 8.14).

   The L Name Slicer pane displays with all the items selected.

Figure 8.14 Insert Slicers Dialog Box

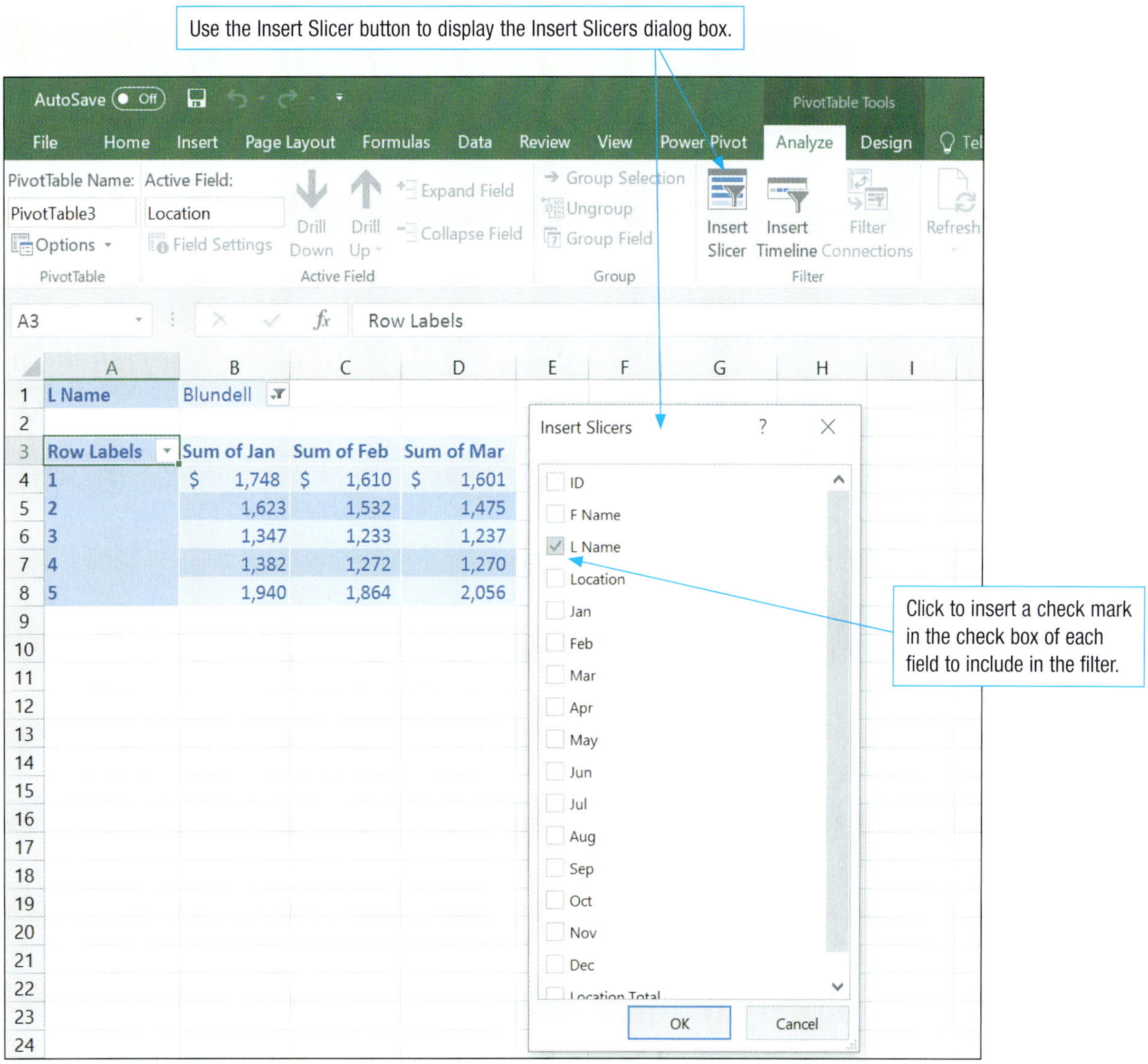

3. Scroll down, if necessary, and then click the *Russel* option.

   The data in the PivotTable filters to display only the revenue generated by Dr. Russel.

4. Press and hold down the Ctrl key, click the *Sullivan* option, and then release the Ctrl key (see Figure 8.15).

   The data in the PivotTable filters to display only the revenue generated by Dr. Russel and Dr. Sullivan.

Reminder
You can also use the Multi-Select button to add multiple items to a slicer.

Figure 8.15 L Name Slicer Pane

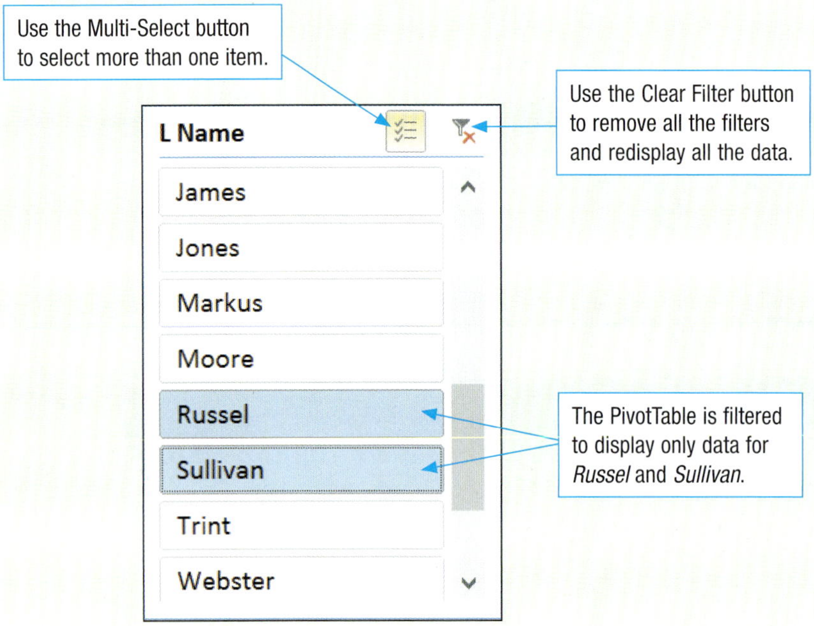

5. If printed work is required by your instructor, print the workbook.
6. Save and then close the workbook.

Model Answer

On the Job

Task 8.5b Removing a PivotTable Slicer

Kaelan has the data he needs for his analysis and wants you to remove the filter and delete the Slicer pane.

1. With the 8-PDML workbook open and the Revenue by Location worksheet active, click the Clear Filter button at the Slicer pane.
2. With the Slicer pane selected, press the Delete key.
   The Slicer pane is removed and a cell in the PivotTable is active.
3. If printed work is required by your instructor, print the workbook.
4. Save and then close the workbook.

Model Answer

8.6 Creating and Modifying Multilevel PivotTables

Tutorial

Creating and Modifying a Multilevel PivotTable

More than one field can be placed in a layout area at the PivotTable Fields task pane to create a multilevel PivotTable. By default, multiple fields added to the *Rows* layout area display as indented levels in the same column in the PivotTable. This type of layout can be used to illustrate data relationships, which may be helpful when analyzing data. Figure 8.16 shows the relationship between the date and doctor-generated revenue. The layout can be modified to show each field in a separate column (see Figure 8.17).

▸ **Know This** about using multilevel PivotTables

— By default, multiple fields added to the *Rows* layout area at the PivotTable Fields task pane display as levels in the same column in the PivotTable. The levels in the PivotTable appear in the same order as the field buttons in the *Rows* layout area, and each level is indented below the preceding level (see Figure 8.16).

— Multiple fields added to the *Columns* layout area display in separate rows in the PivotTable as a series of levels based on the order of the field buttons in the *Columns* layout area (see Figure 8.17).

— Multiple fields added to the *Values* layout area display in separate summary columns in the PivotTable (see Figure 8.12 on page 329).

Figure 8.16 Multilevel PivotTable Using Multiple Row Fields

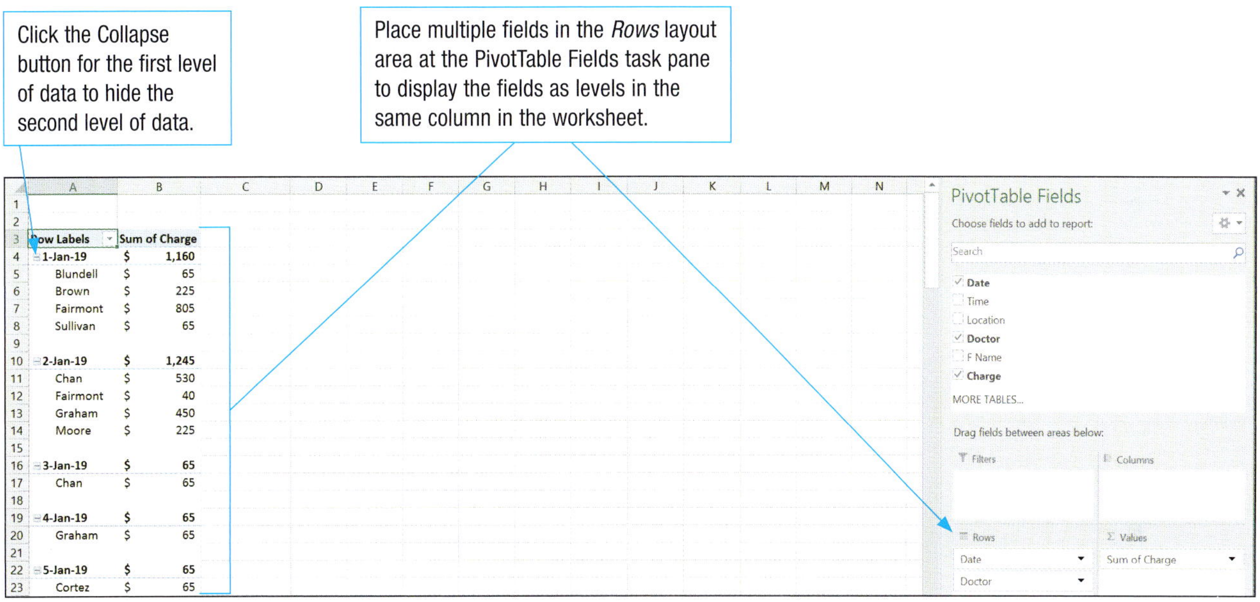

Figure 8.17 Multilevel PivotTable Using Multiple Column Fields

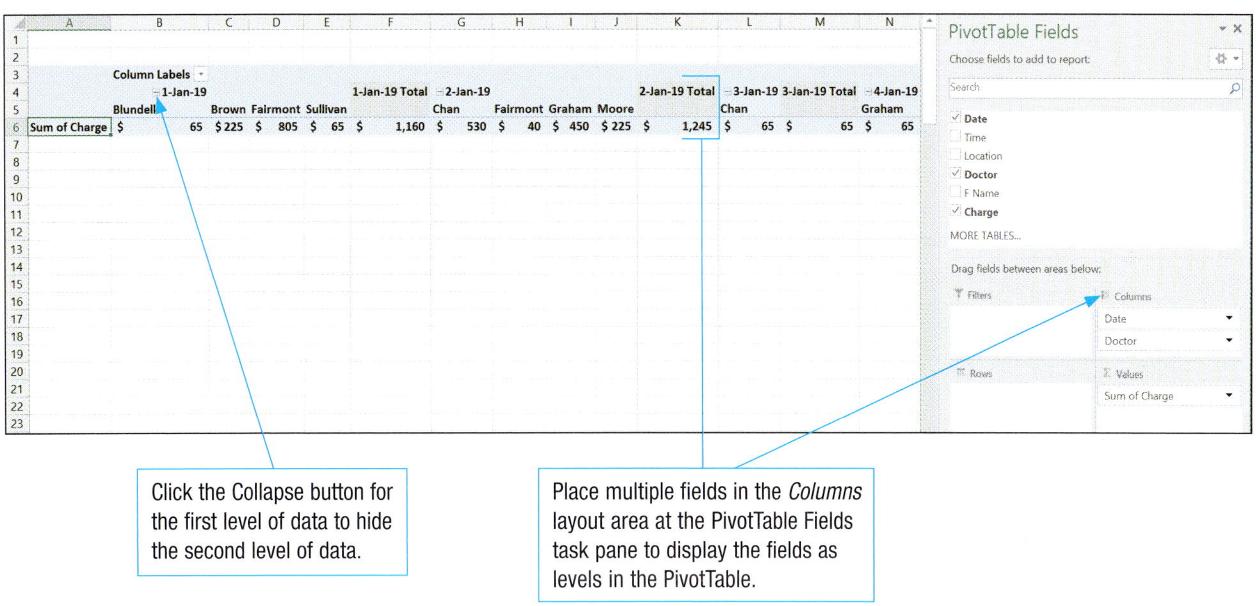

▶ **Know This** about placing multilevel fields in separate columns in a PivotTable

— To place multilevel fields in separate columns, click the top field button arrow in the *Rows* layout area, click the *Field Settings* option to display the Field Settings dialog box, click the Layout & Print tab, click the *Show items in tabular form* radio button to insert a bullet, click the *Repeat item labels* check box to insert a check mark, and then click the OK button (see Figure 8.18).

▶ **Know More** methods for placing multilevel fields in separate columns in a PivotTable

– Click the Report Layout button in the Layout group on the PivotTable Tools Design tab and then click the *Show in Tabular Form* option.

Figure 8.18 Field Settings Dialog Box with the Layout & Print Tab Active

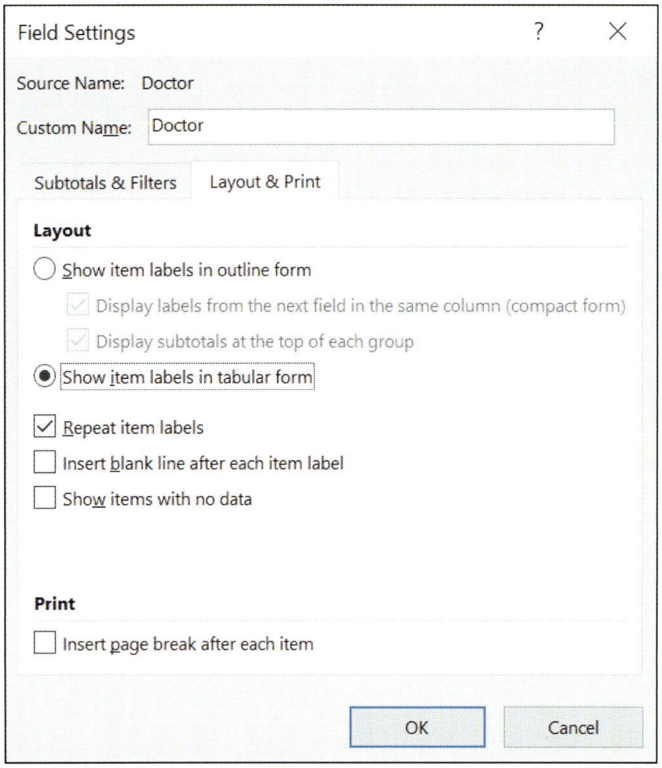

On the Job

Task 8.6 Creating and Modifying a Multilevel PivotTable

This is the first year the PDML lab has been open seven days a week. Kaelan wants to analyze which doctors booked appointments on which days in January of this year and how much revenue the appointments generated. He asks you to summarize this data in the Appointments workbook he created. Use a multilevel PivotTable to summarize the data.

1. Open the data file **8-PDML-Appointments**.
2. With the Appointments worksheet active, click in any cell in the table, click the Insert tab, and then click the PivotTable button in the Tables group.

   The Create PivotTable dialog box displays.
3. Click the OK button.

   A blank PivotTable displays on a new worksheet called *Sheet1* and the PivotTable Fields task pane displays.

4. Click the *Date* check box in the field list box.

   The Date button appears in the *Rows* layout area at the task pane and the *Row Labels* column and date items display in the PivotTable.

5. Click the *Doctor* check box.

   The Doctor button appears below the Date button in the *Rows* layout area, and doctor items display as indented items under the corresponding date items in the PivotTable.

6. Click the *Charge* check box.

   The Charge button appears in the *Values* layout area, and the charge items are summarized for individual days and for individual doctors in the PivotTable.

7. Click the Sum of Charge button arrow in the *Values* layout area and then click the *Value Field Settings* option.

   The Value Field Settings dialog box displays.

8. Click the Number Format button.

   The Format Cells dialog box displays.

9. Click the *Accounting* option in the *Category* list box, click the *Decimal places* decrement (down) arrow two times, and then click the OK button.

   The Format Cells dialog box closes.

10. Click the OK button.

    The Value Field Settings dialog box closes and the selected formatting is applied to the values in the *Sum of Charge* column in the PivotTable.

11. Click the PivotTable Tools Design tab, click the Report Layout button in the Layout group, and then click the *Show in Tabular Form* option.

    The report layout changes to display the *Date* and *Doctor* fields in separate columns.

12. Click the Blank Rows button and then click the *Insert Blank Line after Each Item* option.

    A blank row is added after each subtotal item in the PivotTable.

13. If printed work is required by your instructor, print the workbook.
14. Click the Save button on the Quick Access Toolbar.

Model Answer

Reminder

You can also drag a field name from the field list box to place it in the *Rows* layout area at the PivotTable Fields task pane.

8.7 Filtering a PivotTable Using Timelines

Another way to filter a PivotTable is to use a timeline. This feature filters by time, allowing you to analyze the data in a specific time frame. A **timeline** is similar to a slicer but filters only by date and time fields.

Tutorial

Filtering a PivotTable Using Timelines

▸ Know This about using a timeline to filter a PivotTable

— To filter a PivotTable using a timeline, start by clicking in any cell in the table, click the PivotTable Tools Analyze tab, and then click the Insert Timeline button in the Filter group to display the Insert Timelines dialog box.

— At the Insert Timelines dialog box, click the check box to insert a check mark for a date or time field to be filtered and then click the OK button to display a Date pane or Time pane.
— At the Date pane or Time pane, click the time level arrow and then click an option at the drop-down list to change the time level (see Figure 8.19).
— Also at the Date pane or Time pane, drag the timeline scroll box to view available time periods. Click a time period to add it to the filter. Drag a timespan control to add multiple adjacent time periods to the filter.
— To remove a timeline filter without closing the Date or Time pane, click the Clear Filter button at the top right of the Timeline pane.
— To remove a timeline filter and close the Date or Time pane, click an empty area of the pane, if necessary, to make it active and then press the Delete key.

Figure 8.19 Date Pane

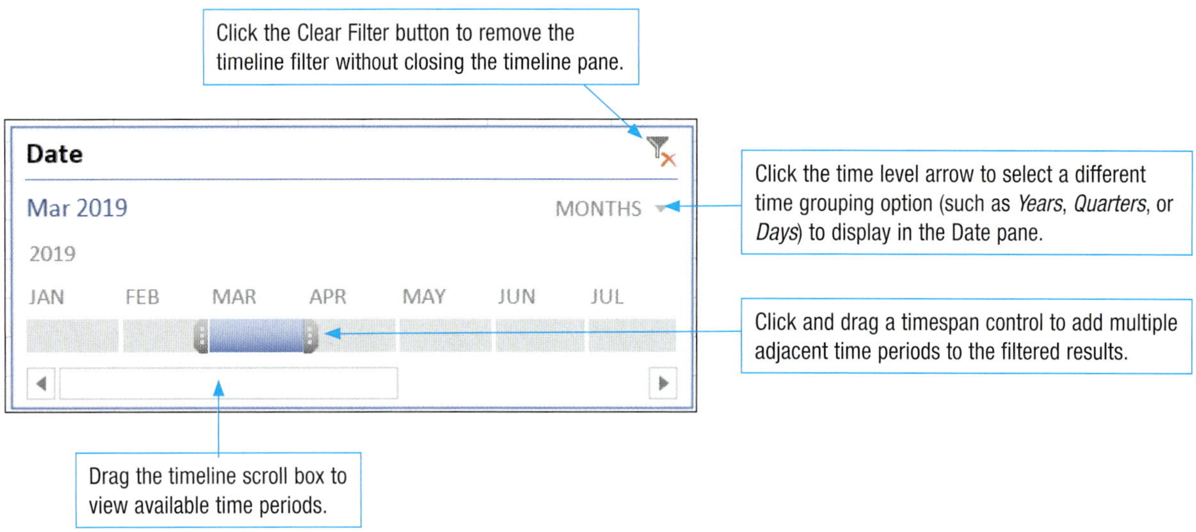

▸ Know This about using multiple timelines to filter a PivotTable

— To filter a PivotTable using multiple timelines, click multiple check boxes to insert check marks for date and time fields at the Insert Timelines dialog box. If you click both date and time fields, both the Date pane and Time pane will display. Set options for all date fields in the Date pane, and set options for all time fields in the Time pane.

On the Job

Task 8.7a Filtering a PivotTable Using Timelines

Many doctors take vacations during the first week of January. Kaelan wants to see the total revenue earned by appointment during that time period in the current year (January 1–7, 2019) to see whether it covers PDML's operating costs for the same time period, which are $2,650. If revenue does not cover operating costs, PDML may want to add staff or adjust its vacation policy to increase revenue during the same period next year. Apply timeline filters to the PivotTable you created in Task 8.6 to help Kaelan with this analysis. After applying the filter, show Kaelan the grand revenue total for this period.

1. With the 8-PDML-Appointments workbook open, the Sheet1 worksheet active, and any cell in the PivotTable active, click the PivotTable Tools Analyze tab and then click the Insert Timeline button in the Filter group.

   The Insert Timelines dialog box displays.

2. Click the *Date* check box and then click the OK button.

   The Date pane displays.

3. Click the time level arrow (see Figure 8.19 on page 338).

   A drop-down list displays.

4. Click the *DAYS* option.

   The timeline displays as a series of days.

5. Drag the timeline scroll box to the left to display the *1* box for the time period *Jan 2019*.

6. Click the *1* box on the timeline and hold down the left mouse button, drag the timespan control into the *7* box, and then release the mouse button.

   The boxes for January 1 through 7 of 2019 are selected in the Date pane and the PivotTable is filtered to display only data for the first week of January.

7. Scroll down, if necessary, and note the total revenue in cell C31.

   The grand revenue total *$2,730* displays in cell C31. Kaelan notes that the revenue is higher than operating costs for the same period, so PDML may not need to make any changes to staffing or its vacation policy.

8. If printed work is required by your instructor, print the workbook.

9. Click the Save button on the Quick Access Toolbar.

Model Answer

On the Job

Task 8.7b Clearing a Timeline Filter

Kaelan asks you to remove the filter you applied in Task 8.7a so he can see all the revenue data for 2019 the next time he looks at the worksheet.

1. With the 8-PDML-Appointments workbook open, the Sheet1 worksheet active, the Date pane open, and the PivotTable filtered to show only revenue data for January 1–7, 2019, click the Clear Filter button.

   The filter is removed and all the revenue data displays in the PivotTable.

2. Click any empty area of the Date pane.

   The Date pane is selected.

3. Press the Delete key.

   The Date pane is removed.

4. Click the Save button on the Quick Access Toolbar.

Model Answer

8.8 Using Calculated Fields and Calculated Items in PivotTables

MOS Expert 4.2.6

Tutorial

Adding a Calculated Field to a PivotTable

You can also add formulas that use calculated fields and calculated items to a PivotTable, allowing you to perform quick calculations within the PivotTable without altering the source data. A **calculated field** uses data from another field and inserts a new column in the PivotTable. A **calculated item** uses data from one or more specific items within a field and provides an alternative to adding additional row items to the source data.

Reminder
To refresh PivotTable data automatically when opening the workbook, click in any cell in the PivotTable, click the PivotTable Tools Analyze tab, click the *Options* button arrow in the PivotTable group, click the *Data* tab, and then select the *Refresh data when opening the file* check box.

▸ Know This about adding a calculated field to a PivotTable

— To add a calculated field to a PivotTable, click in any cell in the PivotTable; click the PivotTable Tools Analyze tab; click the Fields, Items, & Sets button in the Calculations group; and then click the *Calculated Field* option at the drop-down list to display the Insert Calculated Field dialog box.

— At the Insert Calculated Field dialog box, type a name for the calculated field in the *Name* text box; enter the formula in the *Formula* text box, using the *Fields* list box and Insert Field button to insert fields in the formula; click the Add button; and then click the OK button (see Figure 8.20).

— Calculated fields are automatically added to the field list box and *Values* layout area at the PivotTable Fields task pane and appear as columns of summarized data in the PivotTable.

— Calculated fields are formatted the same as fields referenced in the formula you enter.

Figure 8.20 Insert Calculated Field Dialog Box

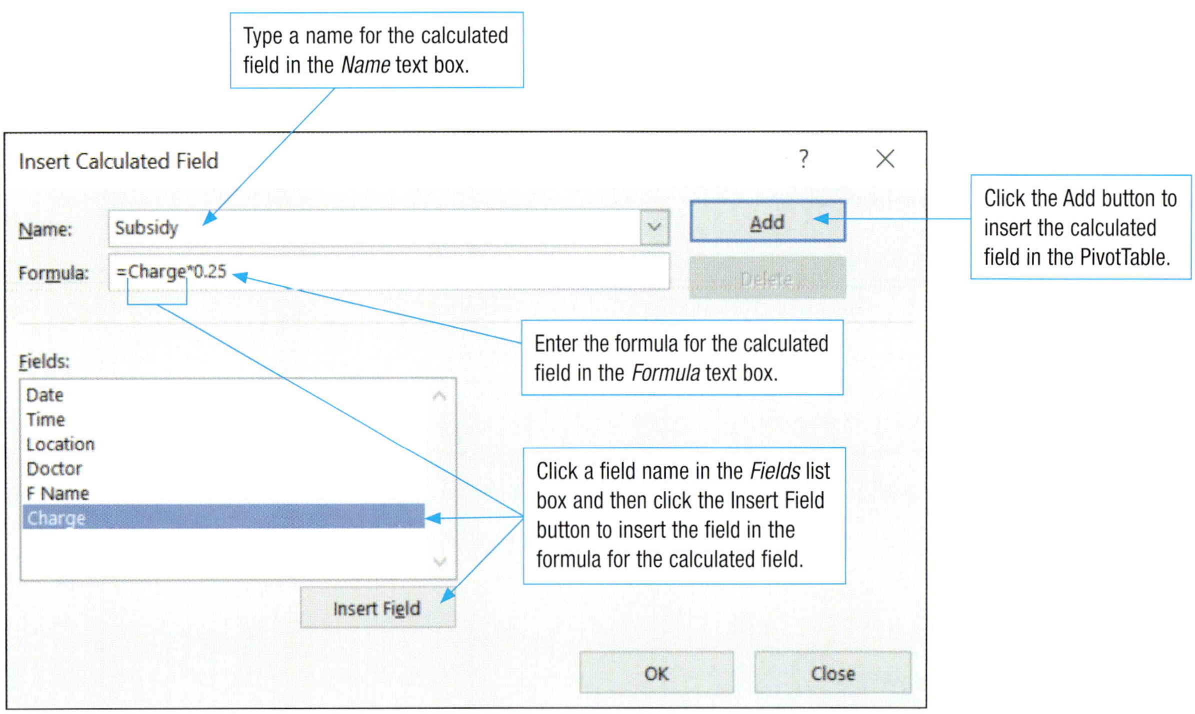

▸ Know This about adding a calculated item

— If items are grouped, click the Ungroup button in the Group group before adding a calculated item. Grouped items display with an Expand button. Grouped data is discussed in Section 8.14.

— To add a calculated item to a PivotTable, click in any cell in the PivotTable; click the PivotTable Tools Analyze tab; click the Fields, Items, & Sets button in the Calculations group; and then click the *Calculated Item* option at the drop-down list to display the Insert Calculated Item dialog box.

— At the Insert Calculated Item dialog box, type a name for the calculated item in the *Name* text box; enter the formula in the *Formula* text box, using the *Fields* list box and Insert Field button to insert fields in the formula and using the *Items* list box and Insert Item button to insert items in the formula; click the Add button; and then click the OK button (see Figure 8.21).

— Calculated items are displayed in new rows in the PivotTable.

— The calculated items can be filtered in the PivotTable to show results for different combinations of items.

— For example, if two doctors (Sullivan and Fairmont) are considering sharing a practice and you want to see what their combined revenue would be, you can add a calculated item for the shared practice to a PivotTable showing revenue data for individual doctors. The calculated item will display in a new row in the PivotTable (see Figure 8.22).

Figure 8.21 Insert Calculated Item Dialog Box

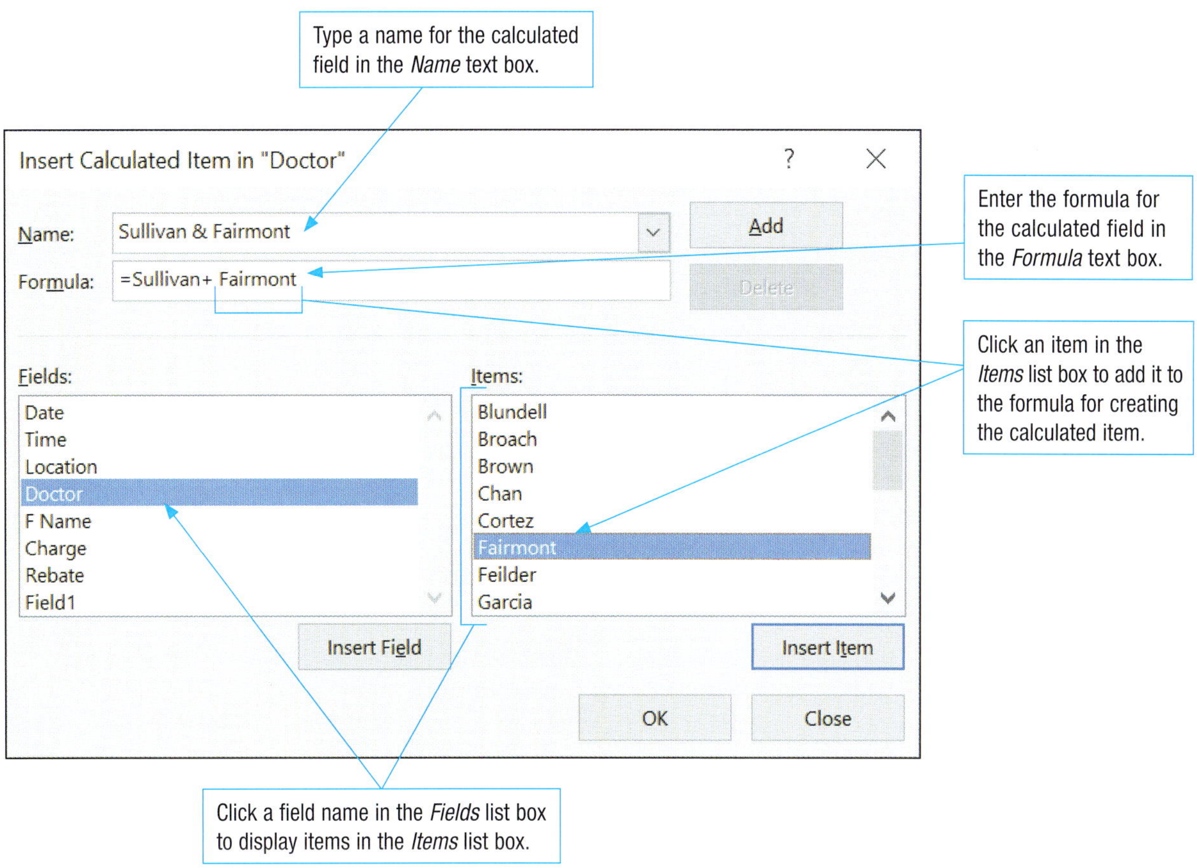

Figure 8.22 PivotTable with Calculated Item Added

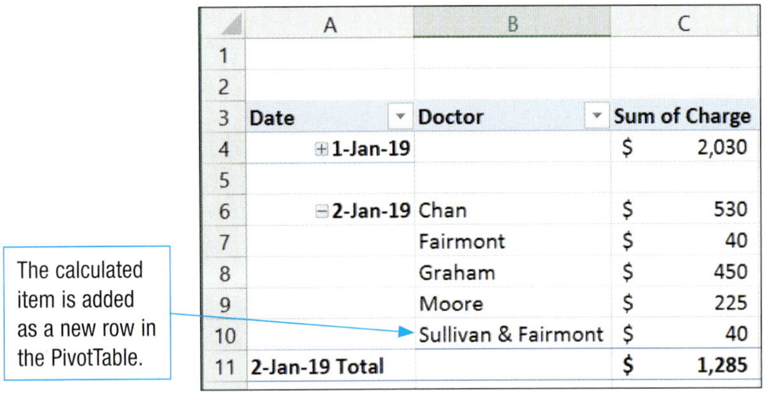

On the Job

Task 8.8 Adding a Calculated Field to a PivotTable

The federal government is considering providing a subsidy for services at medical laboratories, such as PDML. With the subsidy, PDML would reduce the amount billed to patients and insurance companies by 25% and bill the government for the difference, leaving the revenue generated by PDML unchanged. Kaelan wants you to add the subsidy to the PivotTable in the PDML-Appointments workbook. Use a calculated field to add the information.

1. With the 8-PDML-Appointments workbook open, the Sheet1 worksheet active, and any cell in the PivotTable active, click the PivotTable Tools Analyze tab and then click the Fields, Items, & Sets button in the Calculations group.

   A drop-down list displays.
2. Click the *Calculated Field* option.

   The Insert Calculated Field dialog box displays with the text *Field1* in the *Name* text box selected.
3. Type Subsidy and then press the Tab key.

   The text *Subsidy* appears in the *Name* text box and the text *= 0* is selected in the *Formula* text box.
4. Click the *Charge* field name in the *Fields* list box and then click the Insert Field button.

   The text *=Charge* displays in the *Formula* text box and the insertion point appears after the text in the text box.
5. Type *0.25.

   The text *=Charge*0.25* displays in the *Formula* text box.
6. Click the Add button.

   The field *Subsidy* displays in the *Fields* list box.
7. Click the OK button.

   The *Sum of Subsidy* calculated field is added in the field list box and *Values* layout area at the PivotTable Fields task pane and displays as the *Sum of Subsidy* column in the PivotTable.
8. Double-click the Sheet1 tab, type Revenue, and then press the Enter key.
9. If printed work is required by your instructor, print the workbook.
10. Click the Save button on the Quick Access Toolbar.

Model Answer

8.9 Using Quick Analysis and Recommended PivotTables to Create a PivotTable

Other ways to create a PivotTable include using Quick Analysis and using **Recommended PivotTables**. These features offer quick ways to create a PivotTable by suggesting PivotTable options that suit the source data. You can then choose the best option for the analysis you need to perform. Even if you want to build a custom PivotTable without using these features, suggested options provide a helpful reference by illustrating how the source data can be summarized in a PivotTable.

Tutorial

Using Quick Analysis to Create a PivotTable

▸ Know This about using Quick Analysis to create a PivotTable

— To create a PivotTable using Quick Analysis, select the range in the source data, click the Quick Analysis button that appears at the bottom right of the selected range to display the Quick Analysis gallery, click the Tables tab, and then click a PivotTable option (see Figure 8.23).

— To view a thumbnail preview of a recommended PivotTable, point to a PivotTable option at the Quick Analysis gallery.

— The number and type of options in the Quick Analysis gallery will vary depending on the data selected.

— To create a PivotTable using Quick Analysis, a range of data that includes column headers must be selected even if the source data is formatted as a table.

▸ Know This about using Recommended PivotTables to create a PivotTable

— The Recommended PivotTables feature analyzes the source data and then suggests PivotTable options from which you can choose.

— To create a PivotTable using Recommended PivotTables, click in the table or select the data range, click the Recommended PivotTable button in the Tables group on the Insert tab, click a PivotTable option at the Recommended PivotTables dialog box, and then click the OK button.

On the Job

Task 8.9 Using Quick Analysis to Create a PivotTable

Kaelan wants to see the total charges for doctors' appointments by location. Use the Quick Analysis button to quickly create a PivotTable from the table in the Appointments worksheet.

1. With the 8-PDML-Appointments workbook open and the Revenue worksheet active, click the Appointments sheet tab.
2. Select the range A1:F48.
3. Click the Quick Analysis button.

   The Quick Analysis gallery displays.

4. Click the Tables tab.
5. Point to the first *PivotTable* option (see Figure 8.23).

   The ScreenTip *Sum of Charge by Location* appears and a thumbnail preview of the PivotTable displays.

6. Click the first PivotTable option.

   The Sum of Charge by Location PivotTable opens in a new worksheet named *Sheet1*.

7. Save and then close the workbook.

Reminder

Excel does not reuse sheet numbers in an open workbook. If you left the 8-PDML-Appointments workbook open after creating Sheet1 in Task 8.5, the new worksheet you create in Task 8.9 will be named *Sheet2*.

Figure 8.23 Thumbnail Preview of a Recommended PivotTable Using the Quick Analysis Gallery Tables Tab

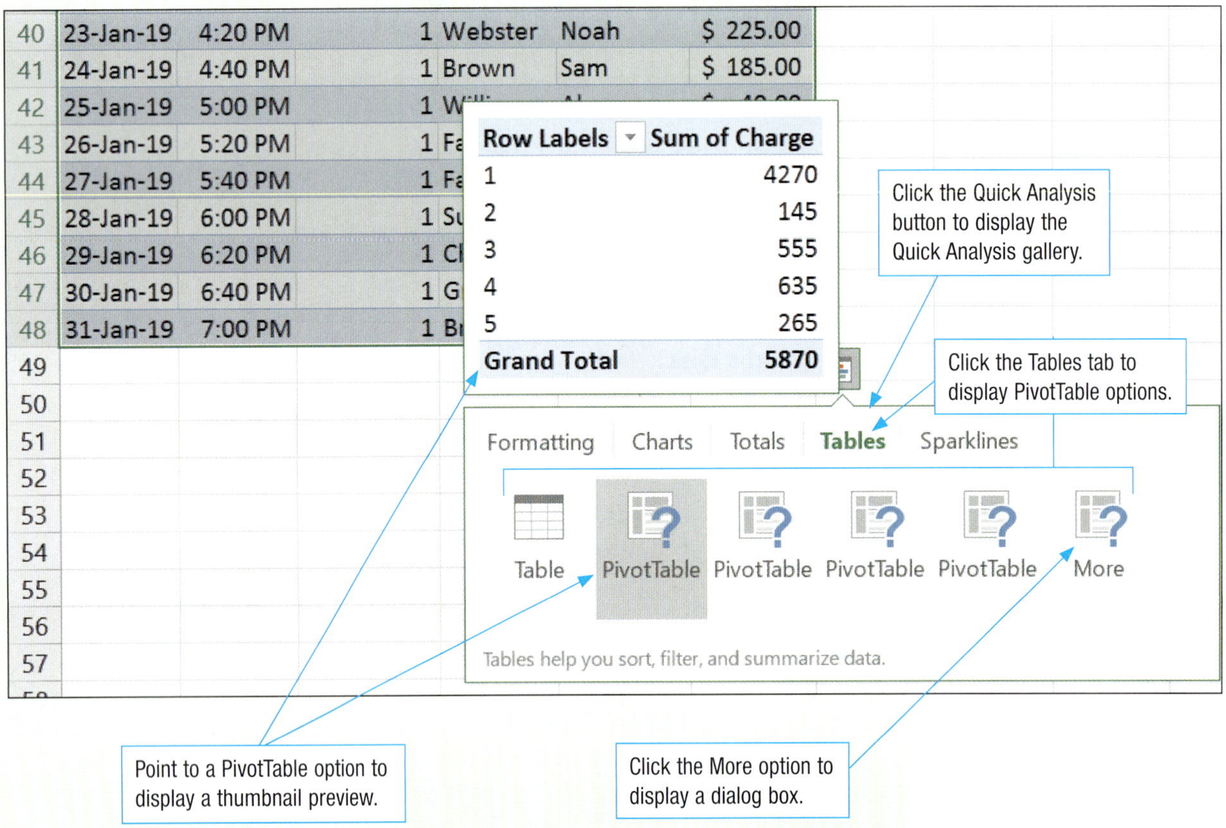

Model Answer

8.10 Creating a PivotChart

MOS Expert 4.3.1

Tutorial

Creating a PivotChart

A **PivotChart** is a visual representation of the summary data in a PivotTable. A PivotChart can enhance the readability and analysis of the data in a PivotTable by clearly illustrating patterns and trends. A PivotChart has all the features of a standard chart, such as a data series, categories, type, subtype, and axes.

A PivotChart that has both an *x*-axis and a *y*-axis—such as a column, bar, or line PivotChart—displays the values from the Rows fields from the PivotTable along the *x*-axis (horizontal axis). The values from the column fields create the data series listed in the chart legend. The values from the value fields are represented on the *y*-axis (vertical axis) (see Figure 8.24).

Figure 8.24 PivotChart

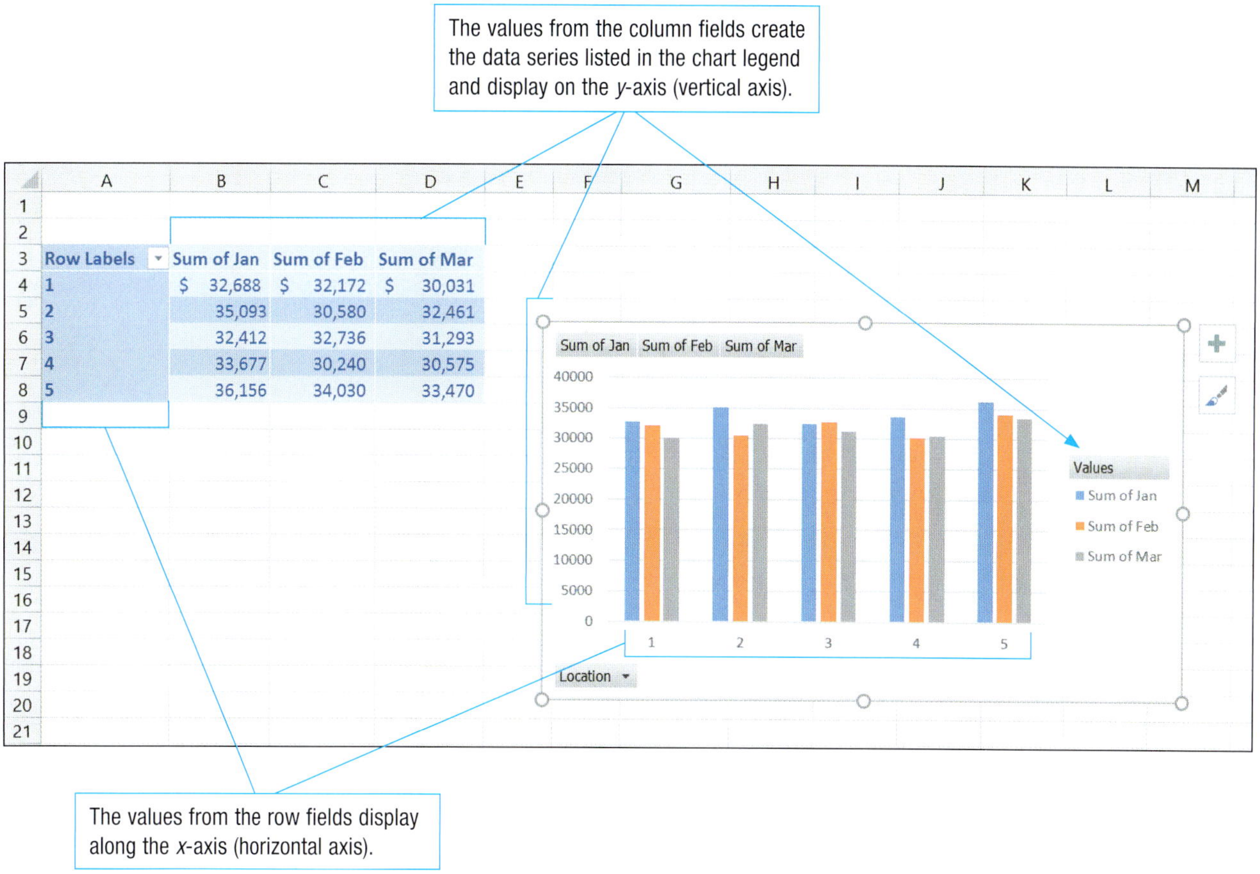

▸ **Know This** about creating a PivotChart

— A PivotChart is created from a PivotTable.

— To create a PivotChart, click in any cell in the PivotTable, click the PivotChart button in the Tools group on the PivotTable Tools Analyze tab to display the PivotChart dialog box, click a chart type in the left panel, click a chart subtype in the right panel, and then click the OK button.

— By default, the PivotChart displays in the same worksheet as the PivotTable.

— A PivotChart can display in a variety of chart types. However, some chart types—including XY (scatter), bubble, map, and stock chart types—cannot be created from the data in a PivotTable.

— When a PivotChart is selected, the layout area names change at the PivotChart Fields task pane: *Rows* becomes *Axis (Categories)* and *Columns* becomes *Legend (Series)* (see Figure 8.25).

▸ **Know More** methods for creating a PivotChart

– With any cell in the PivotTable active, click the Recommended Charts button in the Charts group on the Insert tab and then click an available chart option.

– Click the PivotChart button in the Charts group on the Insert tab, click the *PivotChart* option, click a chart type, and then click the OK button.

▸ **Know This** about adding alternative text to a PivotChart

— To add alternative text to a PivotChart, right-click a blank area of the PivotChart, click the *PivotChart Options* option at the pop-up menu to display the PivotTable Options dialog box, and then click the Alt Text tab.

— If alternative text has been added to the related PivotTable, the same alternative text will automatically apply to the PivotChart.

Figure 8.25 PivotChart Layout Areas at the PivotChart Fields Task Pane

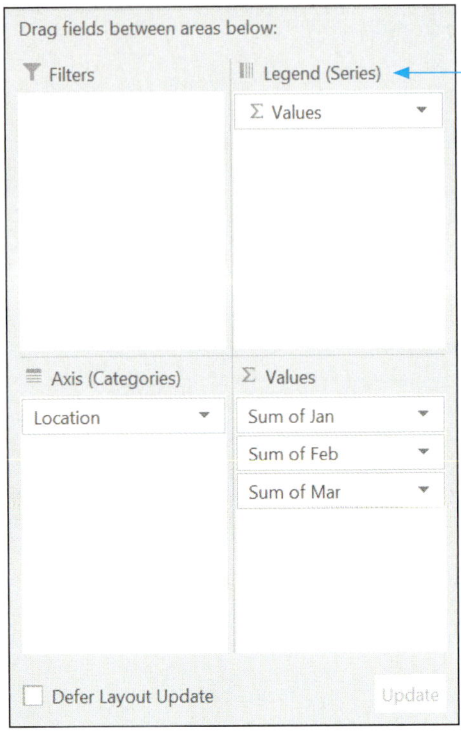

When a PivotChart is selected, the PivotChart layout areas appear at the PivotChart Fields task pane. Note that the layout area names for a PivotChart are not the same as the layout area names for a PivotTable.

On the Job

Task 8.10 Creating a PivotChart

Kaelan wants to look for trends and patterns in the revenue data by location for the first quarter of the previous year. Create a PivotChart based on the PivotTable in the Revenue by Location worksheet of the PDML workbook to provide a visual tool he can use.

1. Open the Excel data file **8-PDML**, which you saved and closed at the end of Task 8.5b.
2. Click the Revenue by Location sheet tab, if necessary.
3. With any cell in the PivotTable active, click the PivotTable Tools Analyze tab and then click the PivotChart button in the Tools group.

   The Insert Chart dialog box displays with the *Column* option selected in the left panes and the *Clustered Column* option (first option) selected in the right panes (see Figure 8.26).
4. Click the OK button at the pop-up menu.

   A clustered column PivotChart displays in the Revenue by Location worksheet.
5. Right-click a blank area of the PivotChart and then click the *PivotChart Options* option at the pop-up menu.

   The PivotTable Options dialog box displays.
6. Click the Alt Text tab.

   The alternative text that was added to the PivotTable displays in the *Title* and *Description* text boxes.
7. Click the OK button.
8. Click the Save button on the Quick Access Toolbar.

Figure 8.26 Insert Chart Dialog Box with the *Clustered Column* Option Selected

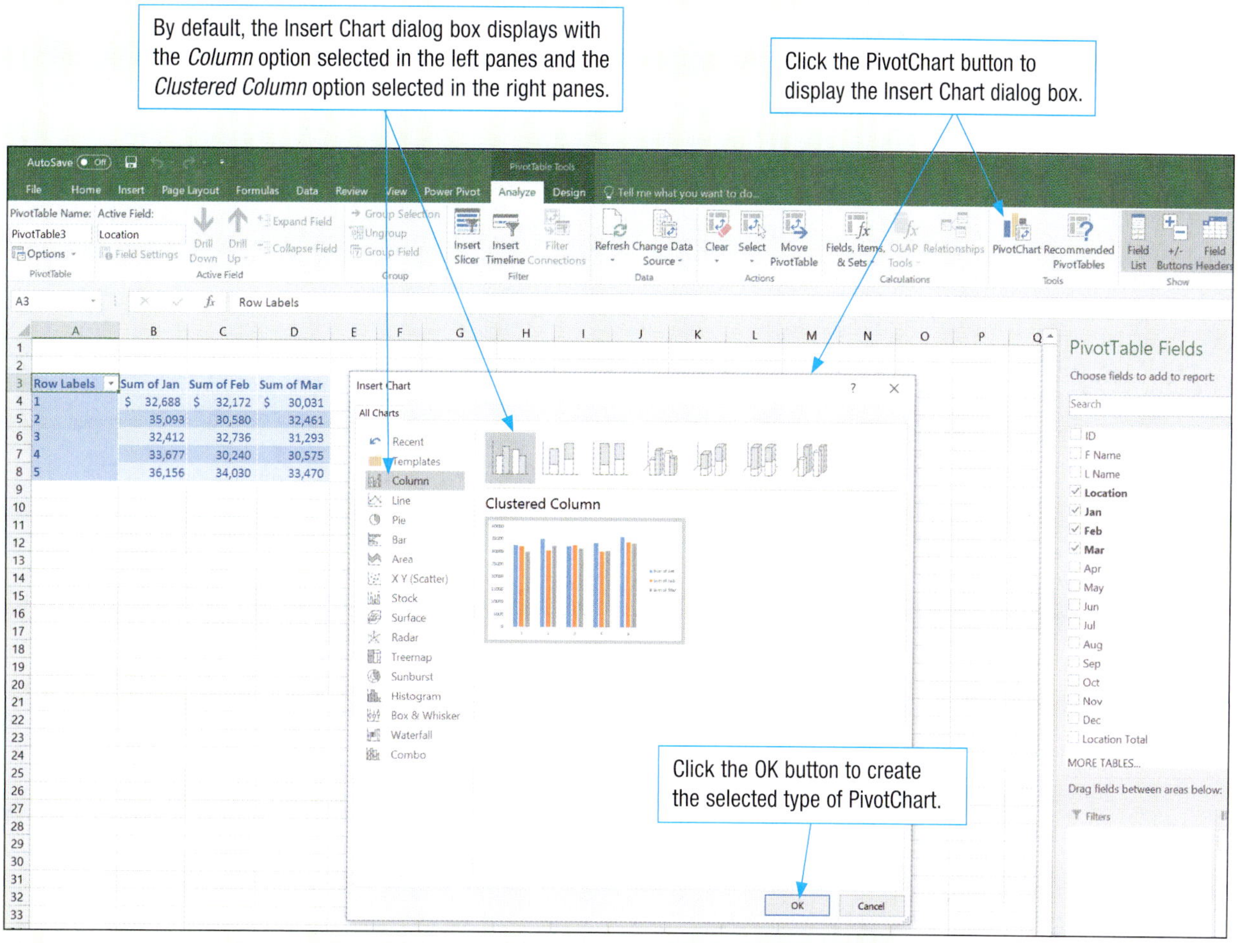

Model Answer

8.11 Applying PivotChart Styles and Modifying PivotChart Formatting

MOS Expert 4.3.3

Tutorial

Applying a PivotChart Style and Modifying PivotChart Formatting

Applying a PivotChart style is a quick way to format a PivotChart and give it a professional appearance. You can then use options on the PivotChart Tools Analyze, Design, and Format tabs to apply formatting, as you learned to do with a standard chart in Chapter 6. You can also use the same tools to size and move a PivotChart as you would a standard chart.

▸ **Know This** about applying a PivotChart style

— When a PivotChart is selected, two chart buttons appear at the upper right side of the PivotChart border: the Chart Elements button and the Chart Styles button (see Figure 8.27 on page 349).

— To modify the chart style of the PivotChart, click the PivotChart area or border, click the Chart Styles button, scroll to view the available options at the pop-up gallery with the Style tab selected, and then click a chart style option.

▸ **Know More** about applying PivotChart styles

– To apply a PivotChart style, click the PivotChart area or border, click the More button in the Chart Styles group on the PivotChart Tools Design tab, and then click a chart style at the drop-down gallery.

continues...

▸ Know This about modifying PivotChart formatting using chart buttons

— To add or modify chart elements, such as titles and data labels, click the Chart Elements button (see Figure 8.27).

— To change the color of the data series for a chart, select the PivotChart area or border, click the Chart Styles button, click the Color tab at the pop-up gallery, and then click a color option.

▸ Know This about modifying PivotChart formatting using the ribbon

— To modify the formatting of a chart element, select the element and then use buttons and options on the Home tab, PivotChart Tools Design tab, and PivotChart Tools Format tab.

— Use buttons and options on the PivotChart Tools Design tab to select a new chart style or change the chart type.

— Use buttons and options on the PivotChart Tools Format tab to add graphics to the PivotChart and change the PivotChart appearance.

— Buttons and options on the PivotChart Tools Format tab are similar to those on the Chart Tools, Picture Tools, Drawing Tools, and SmartArt Tools Format tabs discussed in Chapters 4 and 6.

▸ Know This about modifying PivotChart formatting using task panes

— To format a PivotChart element using a task pane, double-click the PivotChart element and then use options at the task pane that displays. For example, double-click the PivotChart title element to display the Format PivotChart Title task pane.

▸ Know More about applying PivotChart styles

...continued

– To display a ScreenTip showing the name of a chart style and a live preview of the style applied to the selected PivotChart, point to the style option at the Chart Styles gallery.

On the Job

Task 8.11 Applying a PivotChart Style and Modifying PivotChart Formatting

Kaelan asks you to format the PivotChart you created in Task 8.10 to make it easier for him to interpret the trends he is seeing. Change the chart style, add chart elements, and modify the chart colors to improve the appearance and readability of the PivotChart.

1. With the 8-PDML workbook open, the Revenue by Location worksheet active, and the PivotChart selected, click the Chart Styles button (see Figure 8.27).

   A pop-up gallery displays with the Styles tab selected.

2. Scroll down and then click the *Style 8* option.
3. Click the PivotChart Tools Design tab and then click the Add Chart Element button in the Chart Layouts group.

   A drop-down list displays.

4. Point to the *Chart Title* option and then click the *Above Chart* option.

   The chart title element appears near the top of the PivotChart.

5. Type First-Quarter Revenue and then press the Enter key.

   The text *First-Quarter Revenue* appears in the chart title element.

6. Click the Add Chart Element button.
7. Point to the *Axis Titles* option and then click the *Primary Horizontal* option.

   The axis title element appears near the bottom of the PivotChart.
8. Type Location and then press the Enter key.

   The text *LOCATION* appears in the axis title element.
9. Click the PivotChart area or border, if necessary; click the Chart Styles button; click the Color tab; and then click the *Colorful Palette 2* option (second option in the *Colorful* section) (see Figure 8.28).

Figure 8.27 Chart Styles Button with the Pop-Up Gallery Displayed

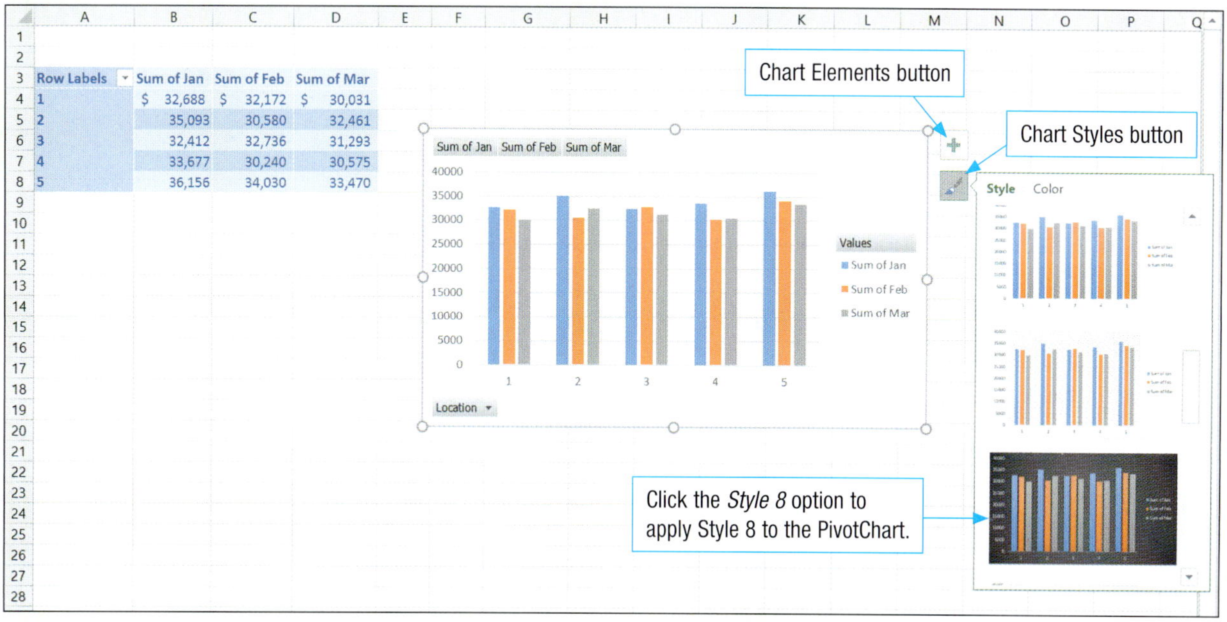

Figure 8.28 Chart Styles Button with the Color Tab Active

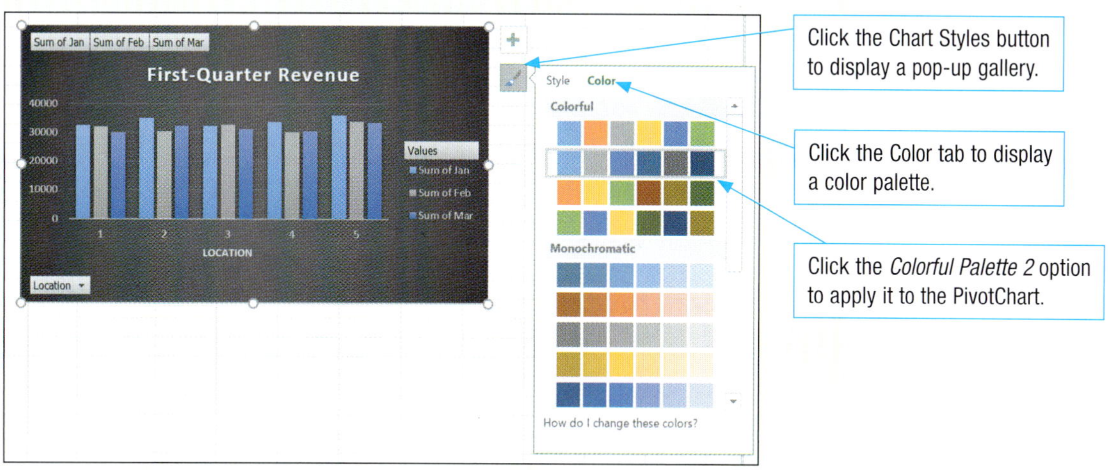

10. If printed work is required by your instructor, print the workbook.
11. Click the Save button on the Quick Access Toolbar.

Model Answer

8.12 Filtering a PivotChart

Like a PivotTable, a PivotChart can be filtered to display a specific segment of data. Filter arrows display for the filter, legend, axis, and value fields in a column, bar, or line PivotChart. The specific fields that display filter arrows vary depending on the PivotTable data and layout.

Tutorial
Filtering a PivotChart

▸ Know This about how fields are filtered in a PivotChart

- Axis fields filter the data charted along the x-axis.
- Legend fields filter the data series that display in columns, bars, and lines and are labeled in the chart legend.
- Filter fields filter the data charted along the y-axis.
- Value fields filter the values represented in the PivotChart.

▸ Know This about filtering a PivotChart

- To filter a field in a PivotChart, click the field button filter arrow in the PivotChart to display a drop-down list and then click to insert a check mark in the check box for each item you want illustrated in the PivotChart (see Figure 8.29).
- Click the *(Select All)* option to insert or remove check marks in the check boxes for all the items in the list.
- Filtering a PivotChart also filters the PivotTable.

▸ Know More about filtering a PivotChart

- To clear a filter, click the *Clear Filter From* option at the field button filter arrow drop-down list.

On the Job

Task 8.12 Filtering a Clustered Column PivotChart

Kaelan is considering an expansion project at location 1. He is concerned that the revenue from this location decreased during the first quarter of the previous year, which may result in the board of directors not approving the expansion plans. Kaelan wants to focus on this data to see if he can determine why revenue decreased at this location. Filter the PivotChart to display only the data for location 1.

1. With the 8-PDML workbook open, the Revenue by Location worksheet active, and the PivotChart selected, click the Location button filter arrow in the PivotChart.

   A drop-down list displays.
2. Click the *(Select All)* check box.

   The check marks are removed from all the check boxes in the list.
3. Click the *1* check box.

   A check mark appears in the *1* check box (see Figure 8.29).
4. Click the OK button.

   The PivotChart and PivotTable display data only for location 1.
5. If printed work is required by your instructor, print the workbook.
6. Click the Save button on the Quick Access Toolbar.

Figure 8.29 PivotChart Filter Field Button Drop-Down List

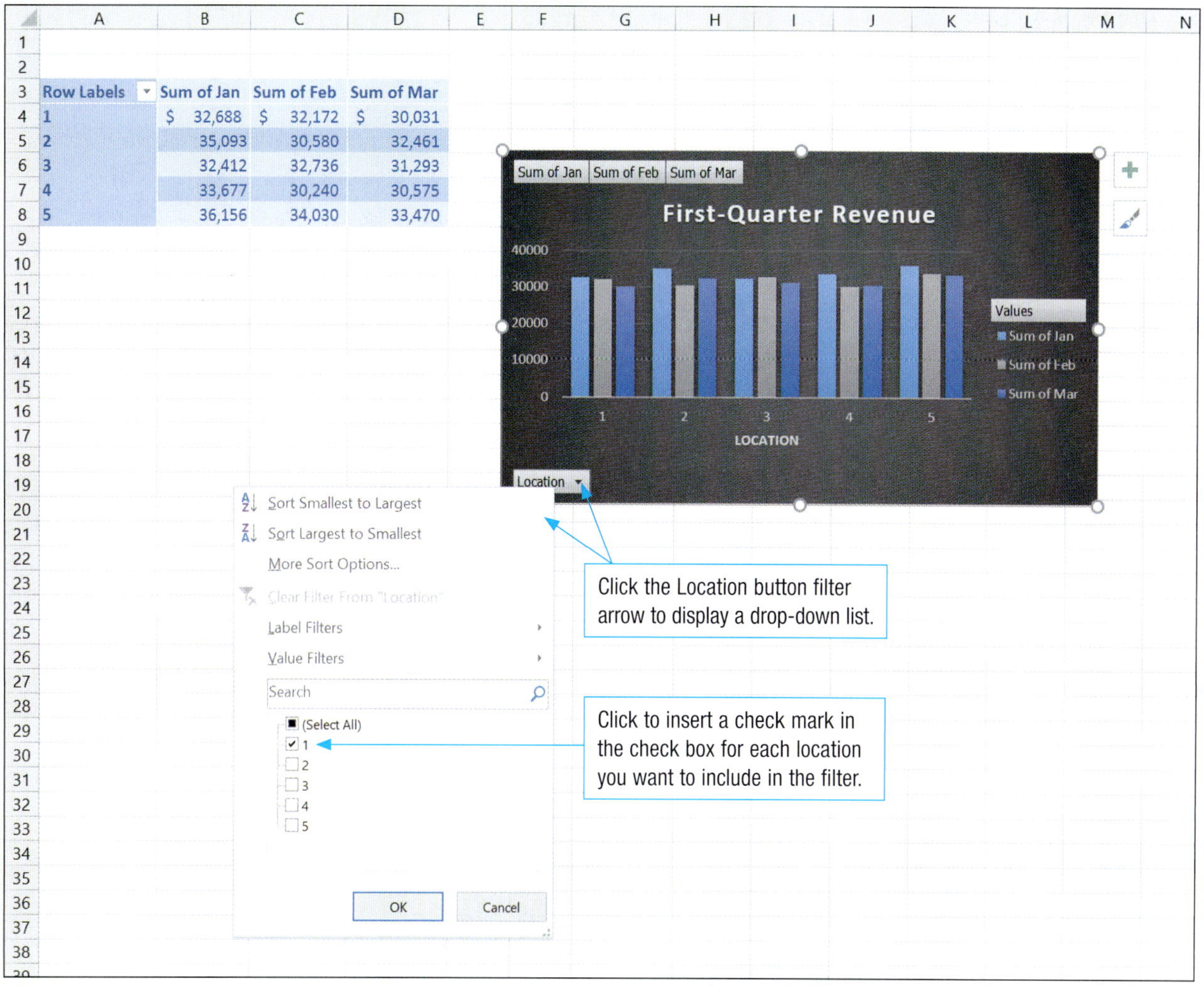

Model Answer

8.13 Modifying a PivotChart Layout

MOS Expert 4.3.2

Tutorial

Modifying a PivotChart Layout

After you create a PivotChart, you may want to modify the layout to emphasize or illustrate data patterns or trends. One way to change the layout is to **transpose**, or switch, the axis data. Other ways are to apply a **Quick Layout** and to change the chart type, subtype, and layout.

▸ **Know This** about modifying a PivotChart layout

— If you rearrange the fields in a PivotChart layout, the related PivotTable also changes. The PivotChart and related PivotTable do not function independently.

— To transpose the axis data in a PivotChart, select the PivotChart and then click the Switch Row/Column button in the Data group on the PivotChart Tools Design tab (see Figure 8.30 on page 353).

— To apply a Quick Layout, select the PivotChart, click the Quick Layout button in the Chart Layouts group, and then click a layout option at the drop-down gallery.

— To change the chart type, subtype, and layout, select the PivotChart, click the Change Chart type button in the Type group to display the Change Chart Type dialog box, click a chart type in the left panes, and then click a subtype and a layout in the right panes.

▶ Know This about adding and removing fields in a PivotChart

— To add a field to a PivotChart, click the field name check box in the field list box at the PivotChart Fields task pane to insert a check mark.

— To remove a field from a PivotChart, click the field name check box in the field list box at the PivotTable Fields task pane to remove the check mark.

▶ Know More methods for adding fields to a PivotChart

- Drag the field from the field list box into the layout area at the PivotTable Fields task pane.

▶ Know More methods for removing fields from a PivotChart

- Click the field button arrow in the layout area at the PivotChart Fields task pane and then click the Remove Field option at the pop-up menu.
- Drag the field button out of the layout area.

On the Job

Task 8.13 Modifying a PivotChart Layout

Kaelan wants to visually compare the revenue generated by all five locations in each month during the first quarter of the previous year and also to quickly see the revenue earned by location 5. Adjust the filter you applied in Task 8.12 to show all the locations and then modify the layout to provide the PivotChart Kaelan needs.

1. With the 8-PDML workbook open, the Revenue by Location worksheet active, and the PivotChart selected, click the Location button filter arrow.

   A drop-down list displays.

2. Click the *(Select All)* check box and then click the OK button.

   The location filter is removed and the first-quarter revenue for all five locations displays in the PivotChart.

3. Click the PivotChart Tools Design tab and then click the Switch Row/Column button in the Data group.

   The data transposes to display the revenue total for each location by month on the *x*-axis in the PivotChart and in the *Rows* layout area in the PivotTable.

4. Click the Quick Layout button in the Chart Layouts group.

   The Quick Layout gallery displays.

5. Point to the *Layout 10* option (first column, fourth row) (see Figure 8.30).

   A ScreenTip lists the chart elements shown in this layout. Data labels will display on the last series, which is location 5. This is the location Kaelan is focusing on in his data analysis, so this will be a good layout for him.

6. Click the *Layout 10* option.
7. If printed work is required by your instructor, print the workbook.
8. Save and close the workbook.

Figure 8.30 PivotChart Tools Design Tab with the Quick Layout Button Drop-Down Gallery Displayed

Model Answer

8.14 Grouping and Ungrouping PivotTable Data

MOS Expert 4.2.4

Tutorial

Grouping PivotTable Fields

PivotTable data can be grouped to make a subset of the data easier to analyze. Having **grouped PivotTable data** is also helpful when a lot of data needs to be illustrated in a PivotChart. You can group fields, and you can also group two or more field items, such as names in a list.

▸ Know This about grouping and ungrouping fields

— Fields in the *Rows* layout area or the *Columns* layout area of a PivotTable can be grouped if the items are values or dates.

— To group row or column fields in a PivotTable, click in any cell in the row or column, click the Group Field button in the Group group on the PivotTable Tools Analyze tab to open the Grouping dialog box, set grouping options, and then click the OK button (see Figure 8.31).

— To ungroup fields, right-click in any field in the group and then click the *Ungroup* option at the pop-up menu.

▸ Know This about grouping and ungrouping field items

— To group field items in a PivotTable, select the items and then click the Group Selection button in the Group group on the PivotTable Tools Analyze tab.

— You can group items that are adjacent or nonadjacent.
— Grouped items are automatically labeled *Group1*, *Group2*, and so on (see Figure 8.32).
— Grouping selected items creates a new field based on the field you are grouping.
— To remove all the grouped field items in a field, drag the field that was created for the grouped items out of the layout area.
— To remove a single grouping, click the *Group* header in the PivotTable and then click the Ungroup button in the Group group on the PivotTable Tools Analyze tab.

Figure 8.31 Grouping Dialog Box

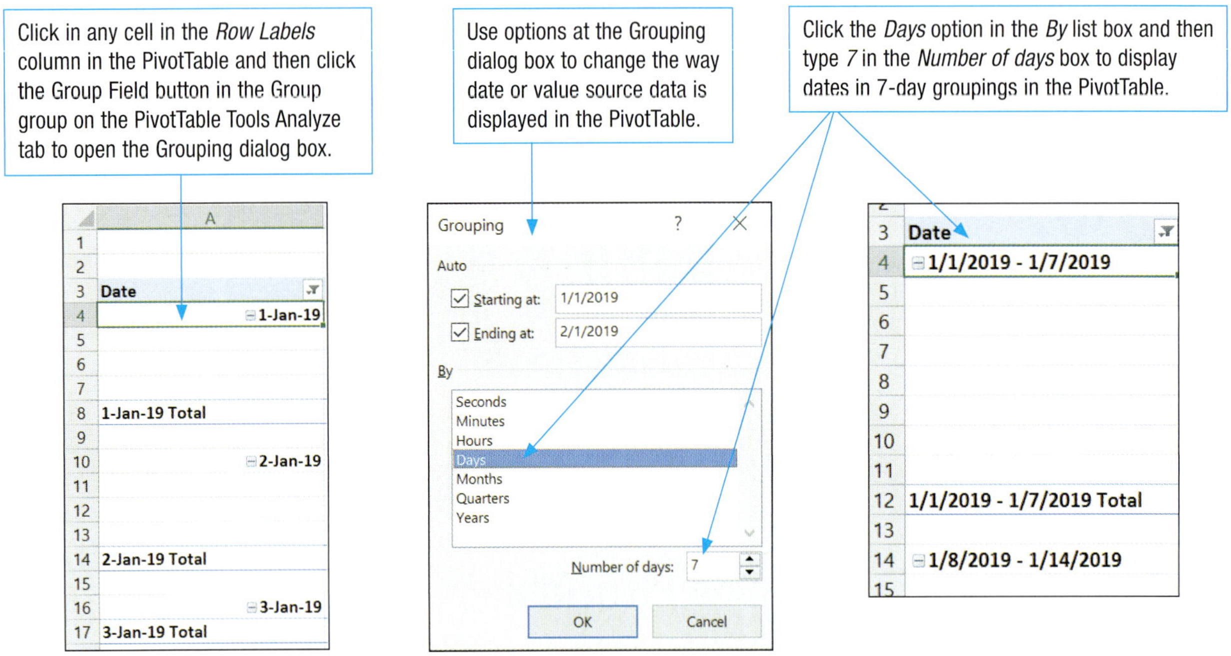

Figure 8.32 Grouped Field Items

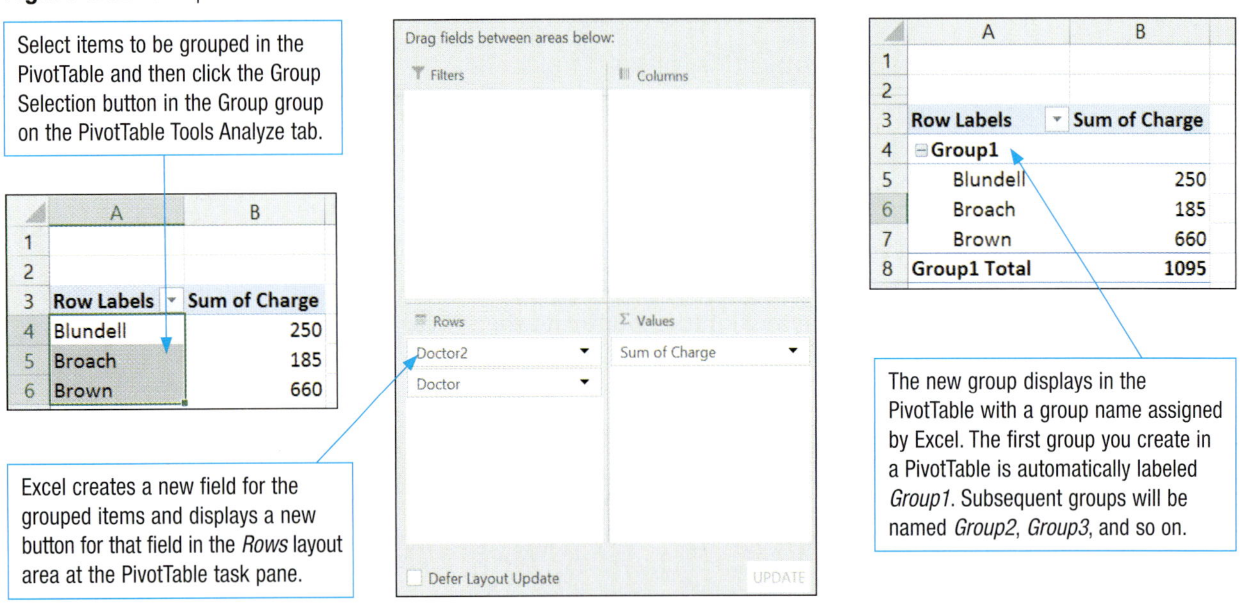

On the Job

Task 8.14 Grouping PivotTable Data

Kaelan asks you to display data in the *Date* field in the PivotTable in groups of seven days starting January 1, 2019, so he can analyze revenue on a weekly basis and analyze which doctors are generating revenue during which weeks. Making this change will also help to condense the presentation of the data and improve the readability of the PivotTable.

1. Open the Access data file **8-PDML-Appointments**, which you saved and closed at the end of Task 8.9.
2. Click the Revenue sheet tab and then click in any table cell in column A.
3. Click the PivotTable Tools Analyze tab and then click the Group Field button in the Group group.

   The Grouping dialog box displays.
4. Click the *Days* option in the *By* list box.

   The *Days* option is selected.
5. Click the *Months* option in the *By* list box.

   The *Months* option is unselected.
6. Double-click the value in the *Number of days* measurement box, type 7, and then click the OK button.

   The dates display grouped by sevens in column A (see Figure 8.31 on page 354).
7. AutoFit column A.
8. If printed work is required by your instructor, print the workbook.
9. Click the Save button on the Quick Access Toolbar.

Model Answer

8.15 Referencing Data in a PivotTable by Using the GETPIVOTDATA Function

MOS Expert 4.2.5

Tutorial

Using the GETPIVOTDATA Function

The **GETPIVOTDATA function** returns data stored in a PivotTable report. The function arguments describe the data that will be extracted. The GETPIVOTDATA function is useful for displaying summary data and other types of data that you want to highlight or focus on.

▸ **Know This** about the GETPIVOTDATA function

— To use the GETPIVOTDATA function in a worksheet, click in any blank cell and then type a formula containing the function, using the syntax *GETPIVOTDATA(data_field,pivot_table,[field1,item1],[field2,item2],...).*

— The argument *data_field* (required) is the name of the value field to query.

— The argument *pivot_table* (required) is a reference to any cell, range of cells, or named range of cells in the PivotTable report.

— The arguments *[field1,item1]*, *[field2,item2]*, and so on (optional) are pairs of field names and item names that describe the data you want to retrieve. The pairs act like filters to limit the data retrieved. The number of *[field1,item1]*, *[field2,item2]*,... arguments is limited to 126.

— In the example =GETPIVOTDATA("Sum of Charge",$A$5), the formula returns the total *Sum of Charge* value.
— In the example =GETPIVOTDATA("Sum of Charge",$A$5,"Doctor",A5), the formula returns only the total *Sum of Charge* value for the doctor in cell A5.

▸ **Know This** about using the GETPIVOTDATA function

— The GETPIVOTDATA function can be used to retrieve summary data from a PivotTable report as long as the summary data is visible in the report.
— Calculated fields are included in GETPIVOTDATA calculations.
— If the *pivot_table* argument in a GETPIVOTDATA function is not a range in which a PivotTable report is found, the function returns the *#REF!* error value.
— If the arguments in a GETPIVOTDATA function do not describe a visible field or if they include a report filter in which the filtered data is not displayed, the function returns the *#REF!* error value.

On the Job

Task 8.15 Using the GETPIVOTDATA Function

Kaelan wants to see the total charges and subsidy values at one glance while he is reviewing the PivotTable in the Revenue worksheet of the Appointments workbook. In addition, he is analyzing the charges during the first seven days in January compared with the overall charges for the month, and he wants to see these values at a glance. Use the GETPIVOTDATA function to display this data near the PivotTable at the top of the worksheet.

1. With the 8-PDML-Appointments workbook open and the Revenue worksheet active, click in cell F3, type Charge, and then press the Tab key.
2. Type =GETPIVOTDATA("Sum of Charge",$A$4) and then press Ctrl + Enter.

   The value *5870* displays in cell G3 and *=GETPIVOTDATA("Sum of Charge",$A$4)* displays in the Formula bar.
3. Click in cell F4, type Subsidy, and then press the Tab key.
4. Type =GETPIVOTDATA("Sum of Subsidy",$A$4) and then press Ctrl + Enter.

   The value *1467.5* displays in cell G4 and *=GETPIVOTDATA("Sum of Subsidy",$A$4)* displays in the Formula bar.
5. Click in cell F6, type 1/15/2019 - 1/21/2019 and then press the Tab key.
6. Type =GETPIVOTDATA("Sum of Charge",$A$4,"Date",A23) and then press Ctrl + Enter.

   The value *710* displays in cell G6 and *=GETPIVOTDATA("Sum of Charge",$A$4,"Date",A23)* displays in the Formula bar.
7. AutoFit column F.
8. If printed work is required by your instructor, print the workbook.
9. Save and close the workbook.

Model Answer

8.16 Using Power Pivot

The **Data Model** is a database attached to an Excel workbook that allows you to use database tools within Excel. A **database** is an organized collection of related data. A **database application**, such as Microsoft **Access**, uses table objects to enter and organize data. Data stored in the Data Model can be accessed and formatted using Excel tools, including PivotTables and PivotCharts. The Data Model stores data in a compressed format, resulting in a smaller file size than if the data was stored in an Excel table. When you are working with a large data set, having this smaller file size allows PivotTables to load faster and queries to run faster. The contents of the Data Model are visible in Excel only if you use the Excel add-in Power Pivot.

Power Pivot is a **business intelligence (BI) tool** used to perform powerful data analysis within Excel. Power Pivot allows you to access and combine data from multiple sources—including SQL Server, Oracle, XML, Excel, and Access—within a single data structure. You are then able to build a Data Model, integrating data from multiple tables and building a relational data source inside an Excel workbook. Because Power Pivot is an add-in, you must enable it before you can use it.

Tutorial

Importing External Data into a Data Model

▸ Know This about Excel add-ins

— An **Excel add-in** is a file that can be loaded to add functionality to the Excel application.

— To manage view a list of active and inactive add-ins and manage add-ins, open Excel, click the File tab, click the Options option, and then click the Add-ins option in the left panel at the Excel Options dialog box.

▸ Know This about enabling Power Pivot

— To install the Power Pivot add-in and enable Power Pivot, click the Manage Data Model button in the Data Tools group on the Data tab and then if prompted click the Enable button. The Power Pivot tab appears on the ribbon, and the Power Pivot window opens.

— Not all versions of Excel 2016 include the Power Pivot add-in. Check the Microsoft Office website for information on which versions include this add-in.

▸ Know More methods for enabling Power Pivot

– To enable Power Pivot if the add-in is installed, click the File tab, click the *Options* option, click the *Add-ins* option, click the *Manage* option box arrow, click the *COM Add-ins* option, click the Go button, click the *Microsoft Power Pivot for Excel* check box to insert a check mark, click the OK button, and then confirm that the Power Pivot tab appears on the Excel ribbon.

▸ Know This about opening the Power Pivot window

— To open the Power Pivot window, click the Manage button in the Data Model group on the Power Pivot tab.

▸ Know This about importing external data from a database

— To import external data from a database, click the From Database button in the Get External Data group on the Home tab of the Power Pivot window, click the *From Access* option at the drop-down list (see Figure 8.33), and then select options at the Table Import Wizard dialog box.

— If the Power Pivot window opens in Restored Down mode, the Get External Data group displays as a button. Click the Get External Data button to display the group.

▸ Know This about viewing imported data in the Power Pivot window

— Imported tables are added to the Data Model in the Power Pivot window and display in **Data view** (see Figure 8.34 on page 359).

— The contents of each table open in a separate worksheet in the Power Pivot window.

— The PowerPoint window contains the **Data Area**, which displays the contents of each table, and the **Calculation Area**, which is used to create customized functions and formulas.

Figure 8.33 From Database Button Drop-Down List

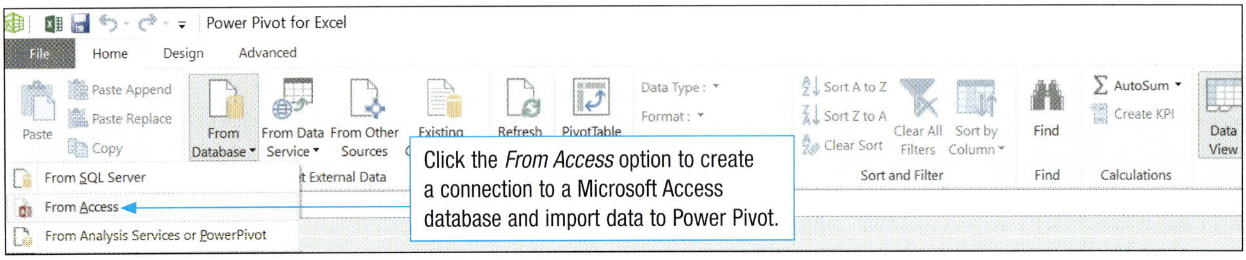

▸ Know This about opening a workbook linked to external data

— To allow a workbook to link to external data, click the Enable Content button in the yellow warning bar below the Excel ribbon, if it displays, and then click the Yes button at the security warning dialog box asking if you want to make this file a trusted document, if it displays.

On the Job

Task 8.16 Enabling Power Pivot and Importing External Data into a Data Model

A few PDML employees work at more than one PDML location in specialized departments. Data about those employees has been entered in two tables in an Access database. Kaelan asks you to import this data into the Data Model so he can determine how many employees work at multiple locations and then develop a plan to expand this work model.

Note: *Check with your instructor if you have trouble opening the Power Pivot window in Step 2.*

1. Open the data file **8-PDML-Employees**.
2. Open the Power Pivot window:
   a. If you *do not* see the Power Pivot tab on the Excel ribbon, click the Data tab, click the Manage Data Model button in the Data Tools group, and then, if prompted, click the Enable button.

      The Power Pivot tab appears on the ribbon and the Power Pivot window opens.

   b. If you *do* see the Power Pivot tab on the Excel ribbon, click the Power Pivot tab and then click the Manage button in the Data Model group.

      The Power Pivot window opens.
3. Click the From Database button in the Get External Data group.

   A drop-down list displays.
4. Click the *From Access* option.

   The Table Import Wizard dialog box displays.

Reminder

Not all versions of Excel include the Power Pivot add-in. Check the Microsoft Office website if you get an error message when you try to enable Power Pivot.

5. Click the *Database name* Browse button, navigate to the Access data file **PDML**, click the data file to select it, and then click the Open button.

   The path to the data file displays in the *Database name* text box.

6. Click the Next button.

   The Choose How to Import the Data screen displays in the dialog box.

7. With the *Select from a list of tables and views to choose the data to import* radio button selected, click the Next button.

   The Select Tables and Views screen displays in the dialog box.

8. Click the *Departments* check box.

   A check mark appears in the check box.

9. Click the *Employees* check box.

   A check mark appears in the check box.

10. Click the Finish button.

    The Importing screen displays in the dialog box. When you see the message *Success* at the top of the screen, proceed to Step 11.

11. Click the Close button.

    The imported Departments and Employees tables open in separate worksheets in the Data Model in the Power Pivot window. The Departments worksheet is active (see Figure 8.34).

Figure 8.34 Power Pivot Window in Data View

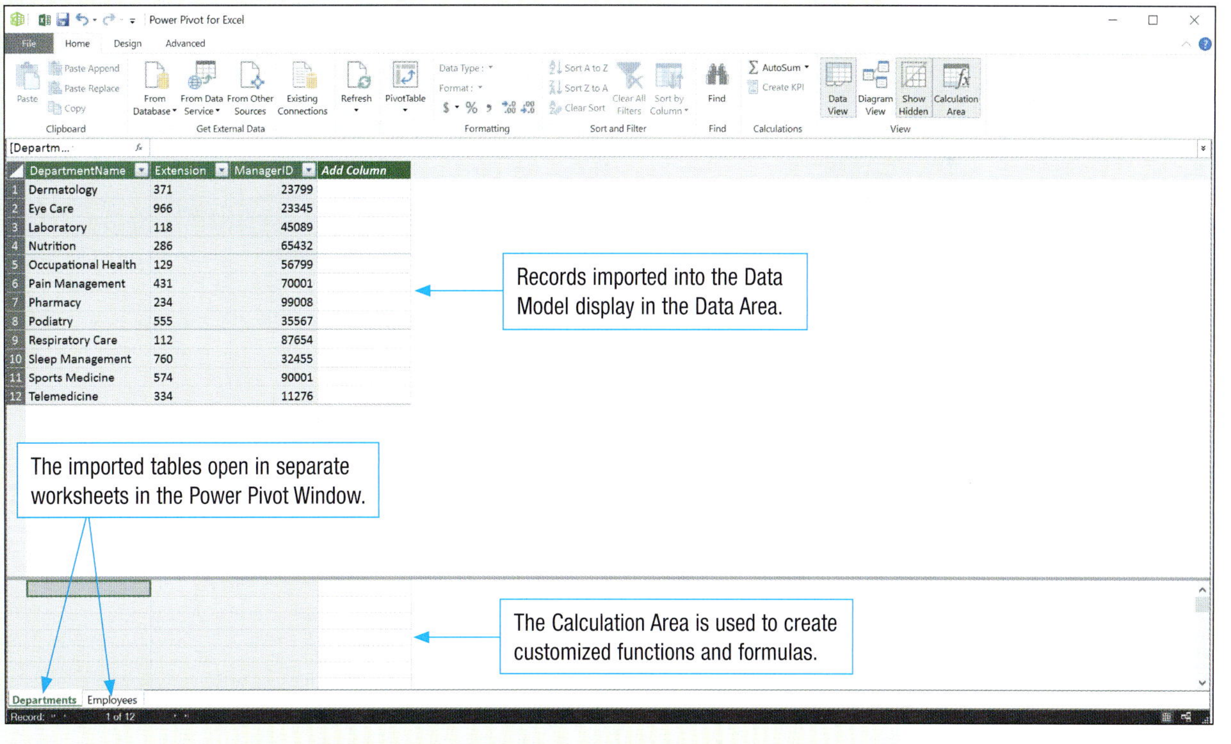

12. Click the Employees sheet tab.

    The Employees worksheet is active and the contents of the Employees table display in the Data Area.

13. Leave the Power Pivot window open for the next task. *Do not* save your work.

    If you accidentally click the Save button on the Quick Access Toolbar of the Power Pivot window, the window will collapse. If this happens, click the collapsed window and it will reopen.

Model Answer

8.17 Creating and Managing Relationships between Tables

Tutorial

Creating and Managing Relationships between Tables

In Section 8.16, you viewed the Data Model in Data view. You can view the Data Model in **Diagram view** to see the structure of each table and its table fields (see Figure 8.35). Using Diagram view also allows you to define the relationships that connect the tables.

Figure 8.35 Power Pivot Window in Diagram View

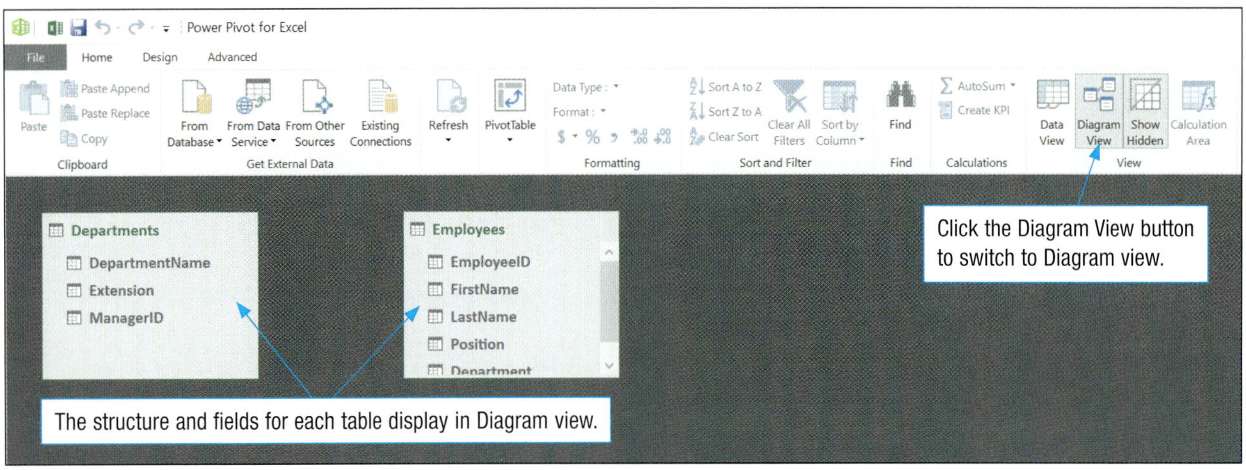

In a **relational database**, a relationship is created between tables when a field in one table corresponds to a field in another table. Every table in a relational database is related to at least one other table in the database. This allows the data in the related tables to be combined into a single data structure while avoiding **data redundancy**, or duplication of data between tables.

Every table in a relational database assigns a primary key field. The **primary key field** requires a unique entry in each row to ensure that each record in the table is unique. For example, in the Departments table shown in Figure 8.35, *DepartmentName* is the primary key field and contains a unique entry for each record.

A **foreign key field** is the primary key field in another table. The values in a foreign key field match values in the primary key field, creating a relationship between the fields. The values in a foreign key field do not have to be unique. For example, in the Employees table shown in Figure 8.35, *Department* is a foreign key field because its values match the *DepartmentName* values from the Departments table. The values in the *Department* field are not unique because each department can contain multiple employees.

To be related, fields have to be the same data type but do not have to have the same field name. Once a relationship is defined between the tables in the Data Model, a PivotTable can be created from the Data Model.

▸ **Know This** about switching to Diagram view

— To switch to Diagram view, click the Diagram View button in the View group on the Home tab of the Power Pivot window.

▸ **Know This** about creating a relationship between two tables

— To create a relationship between two tables, drag a common field from one table to the other.

— A **one-to-one relationship** exists between to tables when a single record in one table exactly matches a single record in the other table.

— To create a **one-to-many relationship** between two tables, drag the primary key field from one table to the foreign key field in the other (see Figure 8.36).

— A relationship is illustrated by a line connecting the two tables and symbols indicating the type of relationship.

— If relationships were predefined in the database, relationship lines appear when the tables are imported.

On the Job

Task 8.17 Creating and Managing Relationships between Tables

For Kaelan to analyze the imported department and employee data in Excel, he needs to see how the data in the two tables is related. Use the primary key field in the Departments table and the foreign key field in the Employees table to create a one-to-many relationship between the two tables. Also create a PivotTable from the Data Model that shows how many employees work at multiple locations by department.

1. With the 8-PDML-Employees workbook open, the Power Pivot window open, the Employees worksheet in the Power Pivot window active, and the Home tab active, click the Diagram View button in the View group.

   The Data Model displays in Diagram view.

2. Drag the *DepartmentName* field name in the Departments table field list box to the *Department* field name in the Employees table field list box.

   A one-to-many relationship displays between the tables (see Figure 8.36). The *DepartmentName* field in the Departments table is the primary key field and the *Department* field in the Employees table is the foreign key field.

3. Click the Close button in the Power Pivot window.

   The Power Pivot window closes. The Employees workbook remains open with the Employees worksheet active. If you see a security warning at the top of the window, click the Enable Content button to enable editing in the file.

4. Click in cell A4, click the Insert tab, and then click the PivotTable button in the Tables group.

Figure 8.36 One-to-Many Relationship between Fields in the Departments and Employees Tables

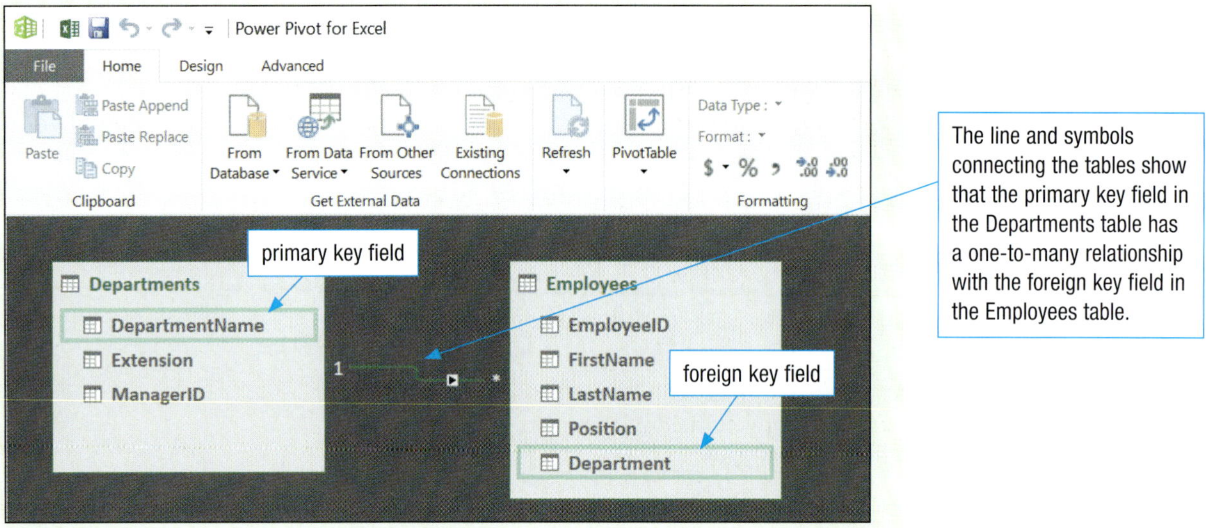

Figure 8.37 Create PivotTable Dialog Box

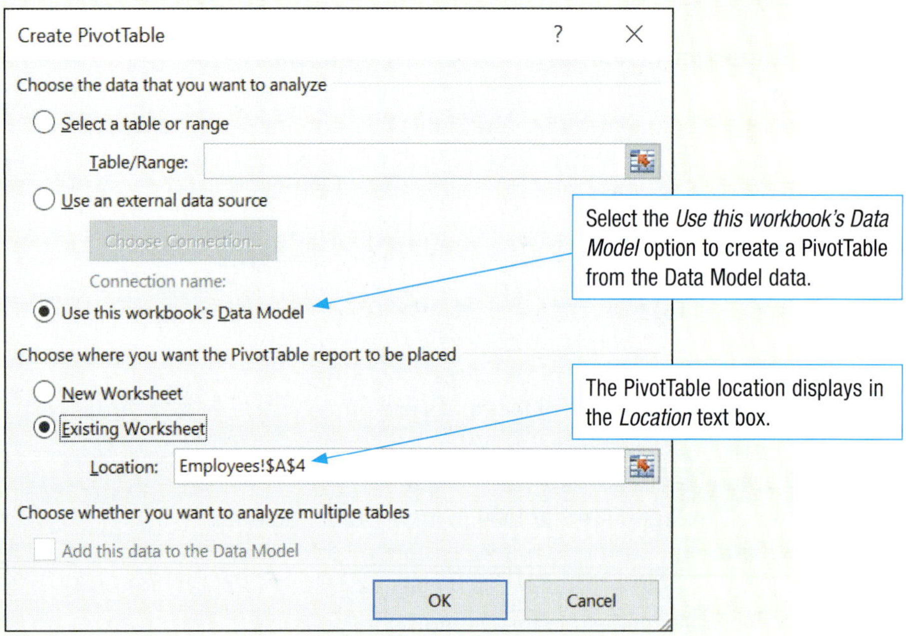

5. Verify that the *Use this workbook's Data Model* radio button is selected, the *Existing Worksheet* radio button is selected, and *Employees!$A$4* displays in the *Location* text box (see Figure 8.37).
6. Click the OK button.

   The dialog box closes and the PivotTable Fields task pane displays.
7. Click *Departments* in the field list box.

   The Departments table field check box list displays.
8. Click the *DepartmentName* field check box.

   A check mark appears in the check box. At the same time, the DepartmentName button appears in the *Rows* layout area at the task pane, and the *Row Labels* column with department name items displays in the PivotTable in the worksheet.

9. Scroll down, if necessary, and then click *Employees* in the field list box.

   The Employees table field check box list displays.

10. Click the *EmployeeID* field check box.

    A check mark appears in the check box. At the same time, the Sum of EmployeeID button is added to the *Values* layout area at the task pane and the field and corresponding data display in column B in the PivotTable.

11. Click the Sum of EmployeeID button arrow in the Values area at the PivotTable Fields task pane.

    A pop-up menu displays.

12. Click the *Value Field Settings* option.

    The Value Field Settings dialog box displays.

13. Click the *Count* option in the *Summarize value field by* list box and then click the OK button.

14. Click the *Position* field check box in the field list box.

    A check mark appears in the check box. The Position button appears in the *Rows* layout area at the task pane, and the *Row Labels* column with date items displays in the PivotTable (see Figure 8.38).

15. If printed work is required by your instructor, print the workbook.

16. Save and then close the workbook.

Figure 8.38 PivotTable Created from the Data Model

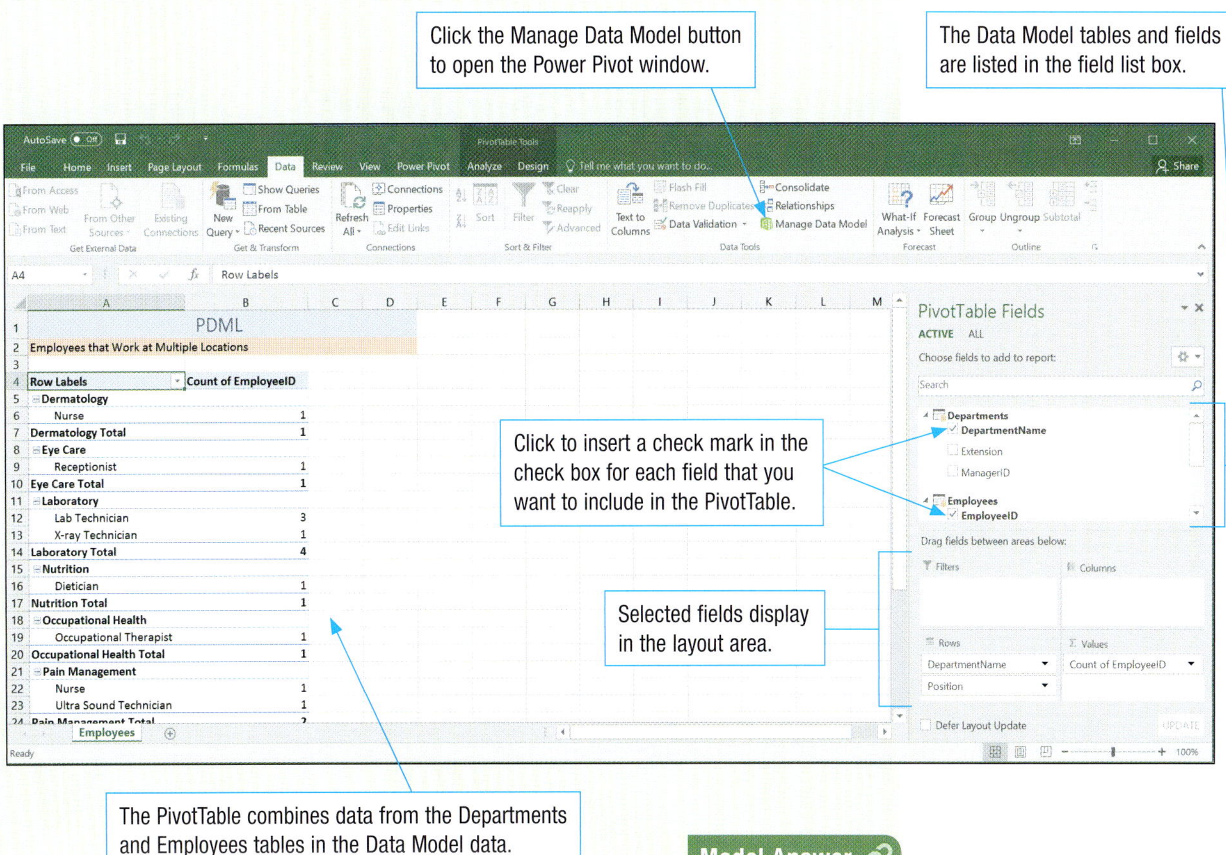

Model Answer

8.18 Creating a Hierarchy

A **hierarchy** is an organization of fields that goes from the most general to the most specific. For example, a hierarchy could consist of *Year*, *Month*, and *Day* fields. Creating a hierarchy allows you to drill down into the data to find specific information. A hierarchy can be created in Power Pivot and then added to a PivotTable.

Tutorial

Creating a Hierarchy in Power Pivot

▸ Know This about creating a hierarchy in Power Pivot

— To create a hierarchy in a table in an existing Data Model, open the Power Pivot window, click the Diagram View button in the View group on the Home tab, point to the table to display the Create Hierarchy and Maximize buttons (see Figure 8.39), click the Create Hierarchy button, type a name for the hierarchy, and then drag fields from the table into the hierarchy in order from the most general to the most specific.

▸ Know This about adding a hierarchy to a PivotTable

— To add a hierarchy to a PivotTable, click the table containing the hierarchy in the PivotTable Fields pane, and then click the hierarchy check box to insert a check mark.

— A hierarchy displays as a single object in the Field list.

— A hierarchy is considered a single item when it is added to a PivotTable.

▸ Know More ways to create a hierarchy in Power Pivot

- Right-click a field in a table, click the *Create Hierarchy* option at the pop-up menu, type a name for the hierarchy, and then drag fields from the table into the hierarchy.

▸ Know More about creating a hierarchy in Power Pivot

- To add a field to an existing hierarchy in a table, open the Power Pivot window, click the Diagram View button in the View group on the Home tab, right-click the field in the table, click the *Add to Hierarchy* option at the pop-up menu, and then click the name of the hierarchy at the pop-up list.
- To change the order of a field in a hierarchy, right-click the field and then click the *Move Up* or *Move Down* option at the shortcut menu.

On the Job

Task 8.18 Creating a Hierarchy in Power Pivot

Kaelan has learned that employees hired in 2015 are due for a special performance review. He needs to determine which departments these employees work in so he can notify their managers. He asks you to create a hierarchy in the Data Model to make it easier to navigate the data when it is added to the PivotTable.

1. Open the data file **8-PDML-DateOfHire**.

   The Date of Hire worksheet displays with a PivotTable showing the number of employees hired in 2012, 2014, 2015, 2016, and 2017.

2. Open the Power Pivot window and then click the Diagram View button in the View group on the Home tab.

   The Data Model displays in Diagram view. Existing relationships are displayed.

3. Point to the Employees table and then click the Create Hierarchy button (see Figure 8.39).

   A new hierarchy item with the default name *Hierarchy1* displays in the Employees table. The default name is highlighted.

4. Type Employee and then press the Enter key.

   The name *Employee* replaces the default name for the new hierarchy item.

5. Drag the following fields into the Employee hierarchy in the order listed: *DateOfHire (Year)*, *Department*, *Position*, *EmployeeID*, *LastName*, and *FirstName* (see Figure 8.40).
6. Close the Power Pivot window.
7. Save the workbook.

Figure 8.39 Table with the Create Hierarchy Button Displayed

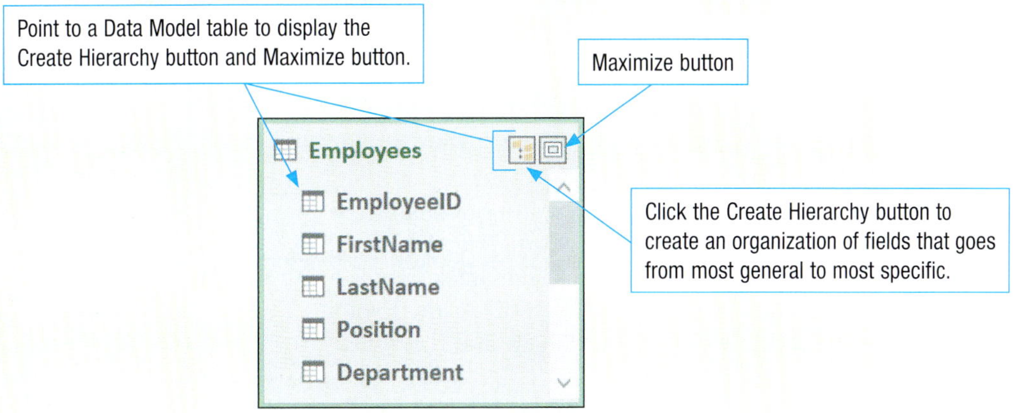

Figure 8.40 Table with a Hierarchy

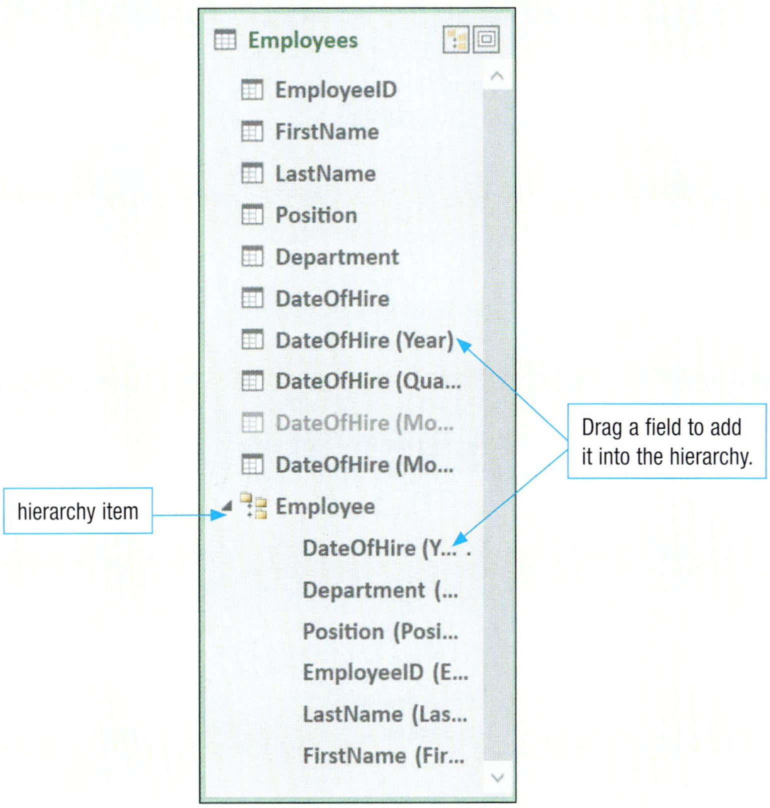

8.19 Drilling Down into PivotChart Details

MOS Expert 4.3.4

Tutorial

Drilling into PivotChart Details

When working with a Data Model, analyzing large amounts of data in a PivotTable hierarchy is a time-consuming task that involves a lot of expanding, collapsing, and filtering. You can use the **Quick Explore** feature to drill down into a PivotTable and the corresponding PivotChart hierarchy to analyze data details on different hierarchical levels.

▸ **Know This** about using the Quick Explore feature to drill down into PivotChart details

— The Quick Explore feature works with any item that contains hierarchical data.

— In a Data Model PivotTable, an item containing hierarchical data displays with an Expand button. Click the Expand button to view the next level of data in the hierarchy.

— To use the Quick Explore feature, hover the mouse pointer over an item that has an Expand button until the mouse pointer turns into a white plus sign, click the left mouse button, and then click the Quick Explore button (see Figure 8.41) to display the Explore dialog box. At the Explore dialog box, click the item you want to explore on the left and then click the drill button on the right.

— You can drill down or drill up only one item at a time.

— Continue to use the Quick Explore button and Explore dialog box until you have the data you need.

— Date fields are commonly used with the Drill Down feature because data in those fields can be viewed at smaller time intervals. For example, instead of looking at a general yearly sales summary, you can drill down to daily or hourly sales if that hierarchical data is available in the Data Model.

▸ **Know More** about drilling down into PivotChart details

- To drill down into PivotChart details, click an item that has an Expand button in the Data Model PivotTable and then click the Drill Down button in the Active Field group on the PivotTable Tools Analyze tab.
- To drill up, click the Drill Up button.

On the Job

Task 8.19 Drilling into PivotChart Details

In the previous task, you created a hierarchy to help navigate the data and locate the employees hired in 2015 that are due for a special performance review. The manager of the dermatology department has also asked Kaelan to give her the ID numbers for any employees hired in 2015. Use the Quick Explore button to display the names of all departments with employees hired in 2015. Also use the Quick Explore feature to drill down further and find the ID numbers for employees who were hired in 2015 and work in the dermatology department.

1. With the 8-PDML-DateOfHire workbook open and the PivotTable Fields task pane displayed, click the *Employee* hierarchy check box (see Figure 8.41).

   A check mark appears in the *Employee* hierarchy check box and the Employee hierarchy is added to the *Rows* layout area and to the PivotTable in the worksheet.

2. Drag the DateOfHire(Year) field button out of the *Rows* layout area.

   The DateOfHire(Year) button is removed from the *Rows* layout area and the *DateOfHire(Year)* field is removed from the PivotTable.

3. Click in cell A4.

   Cell A4 (which contains hierarchical data for employees hired in 2015) is active and the Quick Explore button displays at the lower right corner of the cell (see Figure 8.42).

4. Click the Quick Explore button.

   The Explore dialog box displays with the *Employees* option selected.

5. Click the Drill Down Department button.

   The PivotTable displays the departments that hired employees in 2015.

Figure 8.41 Hierarchy Added to PivotTable

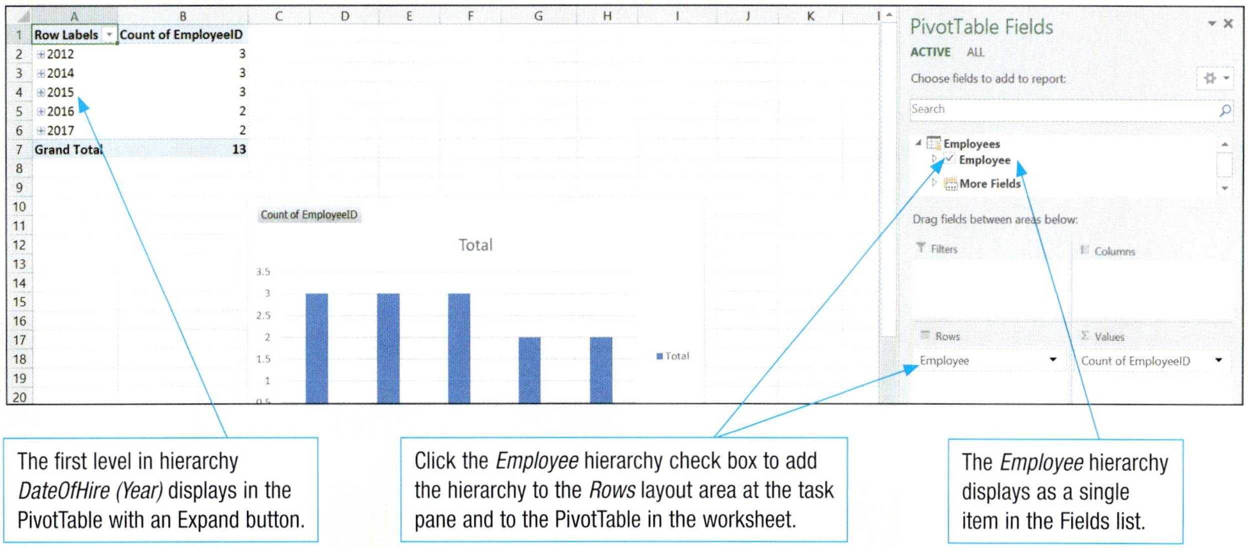

Figure 8.42 Expand Button and Quick Explore Button

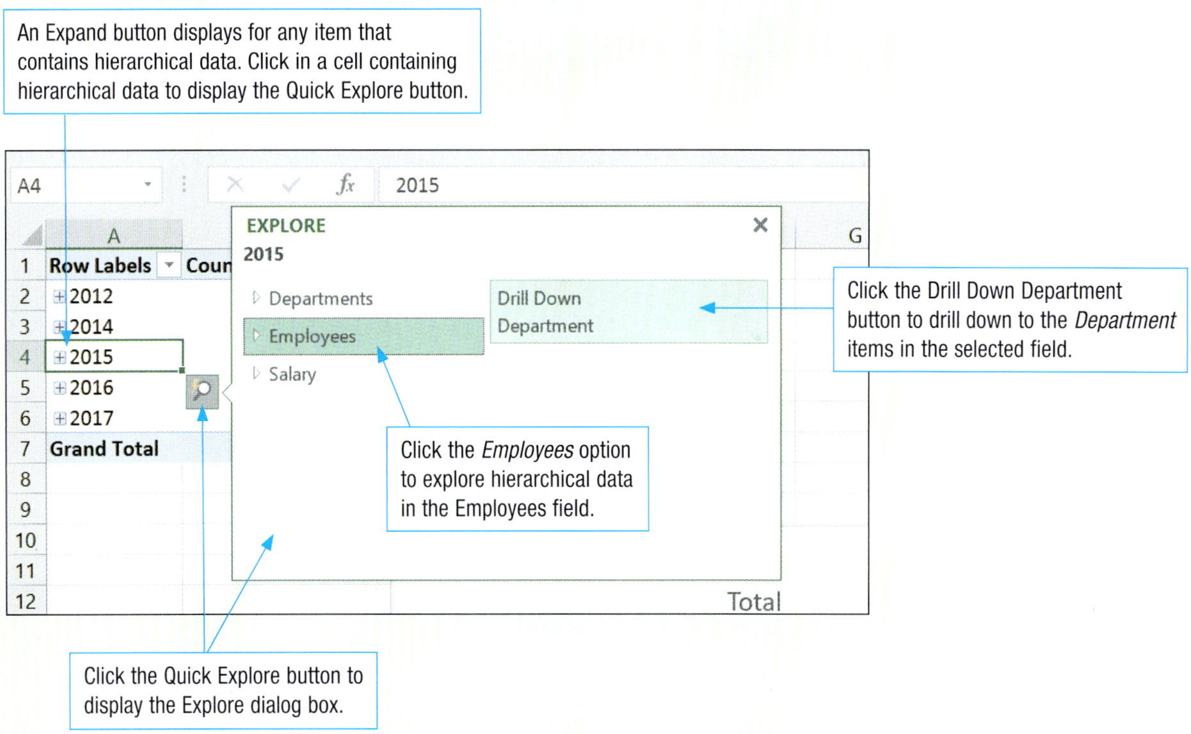

6. Click in cell A2 and then click the Quick Explore button.

   The Explore dialog box displays with the *Employees* option selected.

7. Click the Drill Down Position button.

   The PivotTable displays the position (Nurse) of the employee who was hired in the dermatology department in 2015.

8. Click the Quick Explore button.

   The Explore dialog box displays with the *Employees* option selected.

9. Click the Drill Down EmployeeID button.

   The PivotTable displays the employee ID of the nurse who was hired in the dermatology department in 2015.

10. Click the PivotTable Tools Analyze tab and then click the Drill Up button arrow in the Active Field group.

    A drop-down list displays.

11. Click the *DateOfHire (Year)* option (see Figure 8.43).

    The data with the highest level in the hierarchy displays in the PivotTable.

12. Save and then close the workbook.

Figure 8.43 Drill Up Button

Click the Drill Up button arrow and then click the *DateOfHire (Year)* option to drill up to the highest level in the hierarchy.

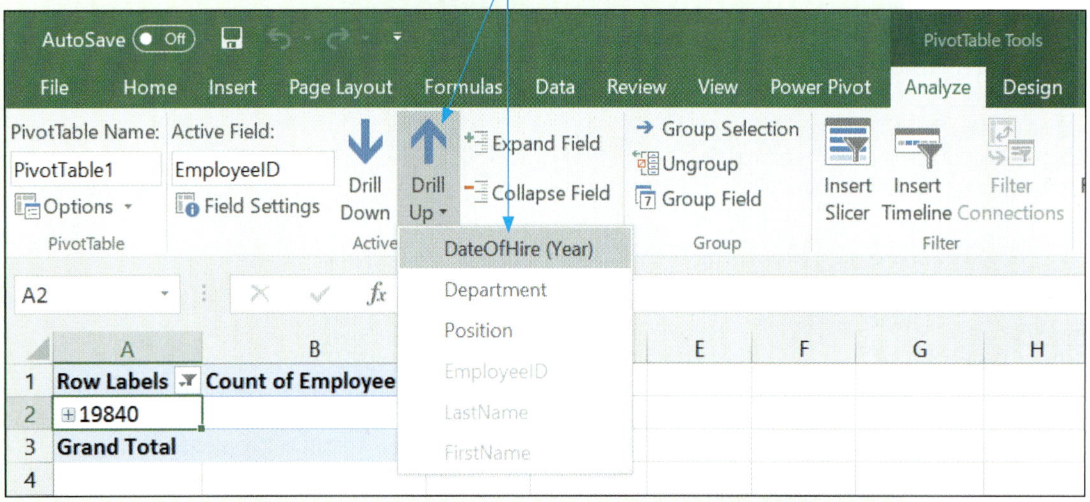

Model Answer

MOS Expert 4.3.4

Tutorial

Using Power View to Visualize Data

8.20 Using Power View and Drilling Down in a Data Visualization

Power View is a data visualization tool that is available as an Excel add-in. It is used to analyze the data from Power Pivot, and its visual interface makes it useful for finding hidden patterns and relationships in the data. A Data Model that has a hierarchy can be used to drill down into the data in Power View.

In Power View, you can create table, chart, and map visualizations. Every visualization starts with a table, and you can convert the table to the type of chart or map that best illustrates your data. A Power View visualization, or report, is designed for interactive, on-screen data analysis. You can print a Power View visualization, but it would be a static printout.

▸ **Know This** about adding Power View to the Excel ribbon

— Power View is automatically installed with Excel but it is not automatically added to the Excel ribbon.

— To add Power View to the Insert tab on the Excel ribbon, follow these steps:

1. Click the File tab.
2. Click the *Options* option.
3. Click the *Customize Ribbon* option.
4. Click the *Insert* option in the *Main Tabs* list box.
5. Click the New Group button.
6. Click the *Choose commands from* option box arrow.
7. Click the *Commands Not in the Ribbon* option.
8. Scroll down in the *Choose commands from* list box and then click the *Insert a Power View Report* option.
9. Click the Add button.
10. Click the OK button (see Figure 8.44).

Figure 8.44 Customize the Ribbon Options

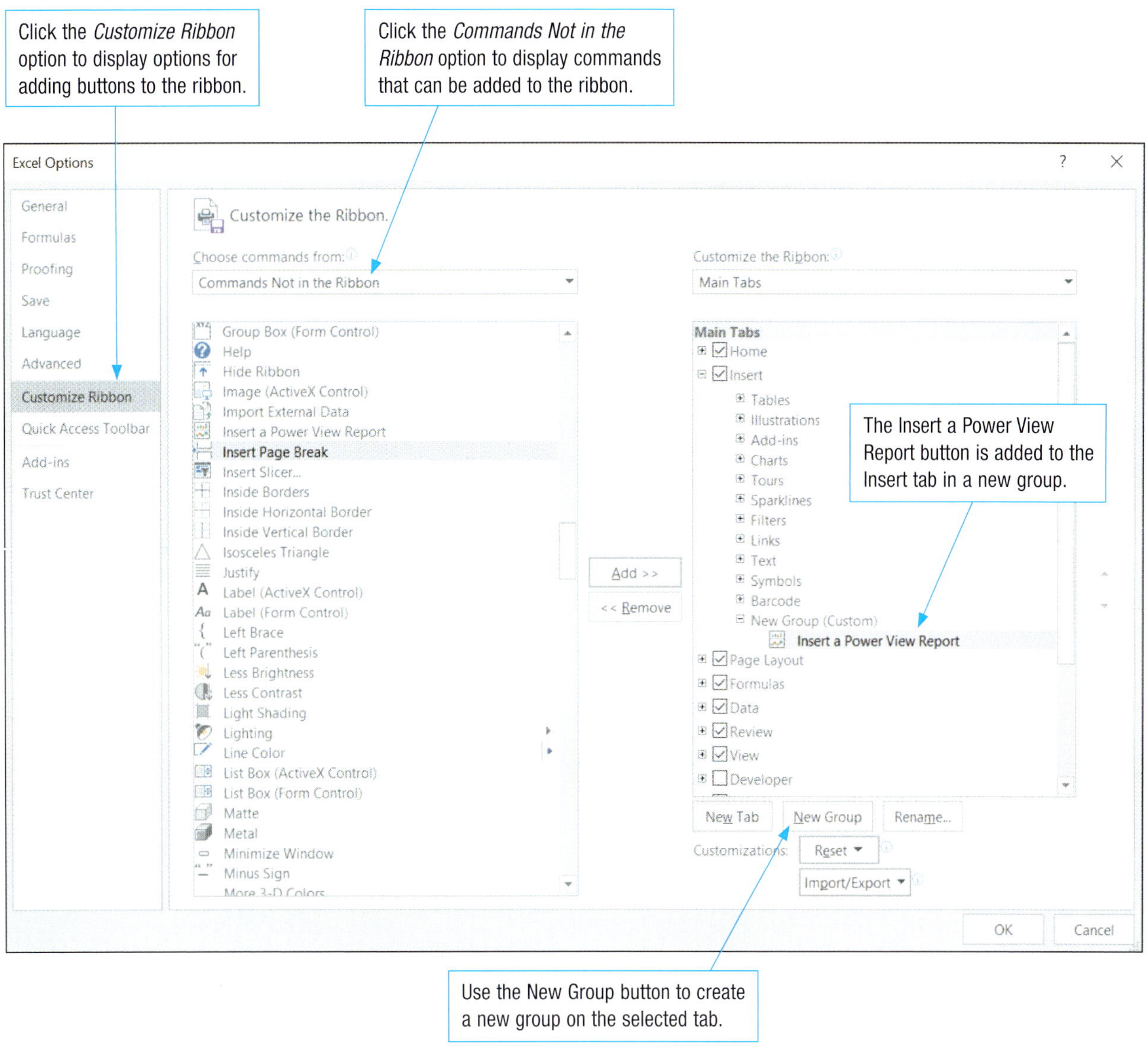

▶ Know This about creating and naming a Power View worksheet

— To add a new, blank Power View worksheet to an Excel workbook, click the Power View button in the New Group group on the Insert tab. If a message box displays, click the Enable button. You may also be prompted to install a newer version of Microsoft Silverlight before Power View opens.

— By default, the first Power View worksheet you add is named *Power View1*.

— To change the Power View worksheet name, double-click the sheet tab, type the new worksheet name, and then press the Enter key.

— To change the worksheet title, click the *Click here to add a title* placeholder and then type the new worksheet title.

▶ Know More about Silverlight

– Microsoft Silverlight is a free web browser plug-in used to create interactive experiences for media, business, and mobile applications. It is powered by the .NET framework and compatible with multiple browsers, devices, and operating systems.

▶ Know This about creating data visualizations

— To create a data visualization in a Power View worksheet, add fields to the canvas area of the worksheet by clicking the field check boxes in the field list box at the Power View Fields task pane to insert a check mark (see Figure 8.45 on page 372).

— In the field list box, fields that can be used to create a map visualization are identified with a globe icon (🌐) and fields that are numeric are identified with the sigma symbol (Σ).

— When you insert a check mark in a field check box, the field also displays in the *FIELDS* area of the Power View Fields task pane.

— By default, the fields added to the canvas are initially displayed in a table. You can modify the data visualization to display as a chart or a map.

▶ Know This about modifying data visualizations

— To modify a data visualization, use buttons and options on the contextual DESIGN tab.

— To display the contextual DESIGN tab, click in a data visualization.

— To change the data visualization from a table to a chart, click a chart button in the Switch Visualization group on the DESIGN tab and then click a chart option. Power View will only enable the buttons of charts and other visualizations that will work with the data in the table.

— To change the data visualization from a table to a map, click the Map button in the Switch Visualization group on the DESIGN tab and then click a chart option.

— By default, totals are displayed in a table visualization. To remove the display of totals, click the Totals button in the Options group on the DESIGN tab and then click the *None* option.

— To size a table or a chart, drag a sizing handle.

▸ **Know This** about chart visualizations

- To add titles and data labels to a chart visualization and to change the position of a legend in a chart visualization, use options in the Labels group on the LAYOUT tab.
- To expand the chart visualization, click the pop-out icon.

▸ **Know This** about multiple data visualizations

- Multiple data visualizations can be added to the Power View canvas. To create another visualization, drag a field to a blank area of the canvas.
- All the visualizations in a canvas are automatically linked. If you filter one chart in the canvas, the other charts are also automatically filtered on the same criteria. This is an advantage of using Power View over using a standard chart in a workbook.

▸ **Know This** about map visualizations

- Power View sends map data to Bing through a secured web connection for geocoding, so you will be prompted to enable content if you choose to create a map visualization.
- Map data can be ambiguous and it is not always correctly identified in a map visualization. For example, there are many cities named Paris in different parts of the world, and a map visualization that includes the city Paris might not identify where it is located.

▸ **Know This** about filtering a data visualization

- To filter a data visualization, click the *CHART* option at the Filters task pane, click the right-pointing arrow to the left of the filter field, and then click *filter options*.
- To change the way a filter list displays, click the List filter mode button at the Filters task pane.

▸ **Know This** about highlighting a data visualization

- Highlighting allows you to analyze a subset of the data in a visualization while still being able to see the entire visualization.
- To highlight data in a chart, click the bar, line, or slice that represents the data. The selected data is highlighted and the unselected data is dimmed.

▸ **Know This** about drilling down in a data visualization

- To drill down in a chart, add hierarchy items to the chart and then double-click a data series in the chart (a bar, line, or slice).
- Hierarchies display with an organization chart icon in the field list at the Power View Fields task pane (see Figure 8.45).
- When you drill down in a data visualization, the drill-up icon displays on the canvas and a hierarchy of fields is added to the *AXIS* area at the Power View Fields task pane.

Figure 8.45 Power View Table

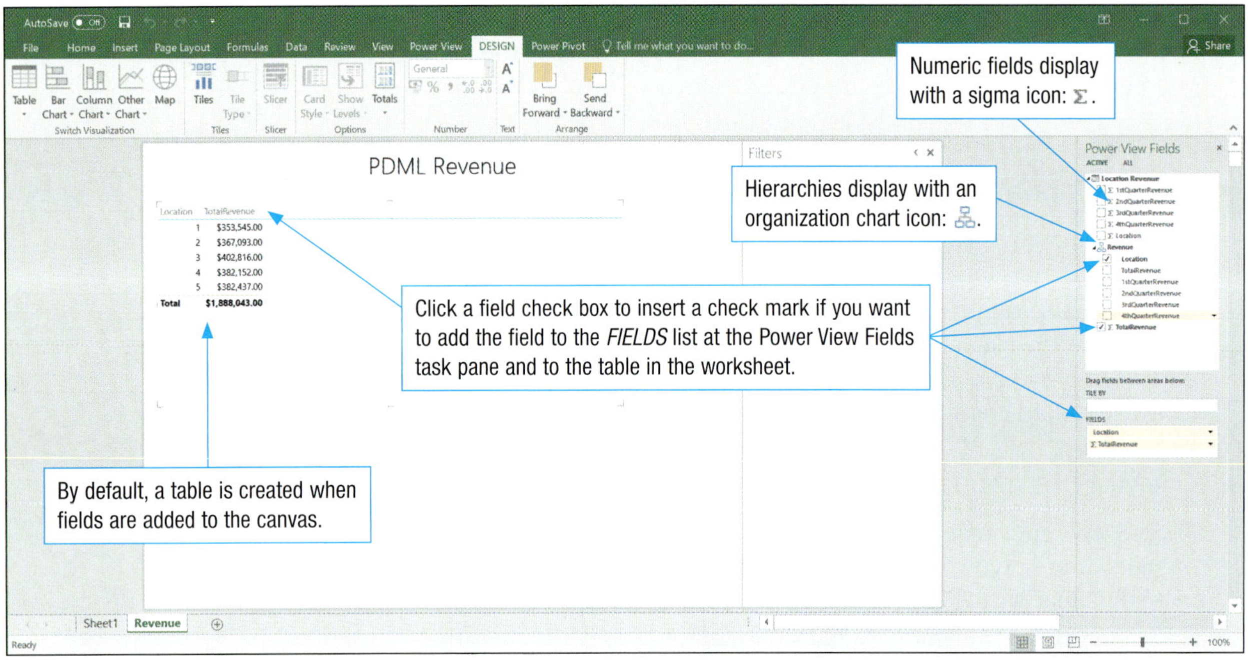

On the Job

Task 8.20 Using Power View to Visualize Data

Kaelan needs to create a staffing budget for the upcoming year. In order to do this, he needs to analyze the revenue from the previous year at all five locations. He needs to present his budget to the board of directors and feels that having visualizations of the data will help explain his budget and analysis of the data. Use Power View to create a Power View report that will allow Kaelan to illustrate and drill down in the data.

1. Open the data file **8-PDML-Revenue** and then click the Insert tab, if necessary.
2. If you see the Power View button in the new Group group, click it. If you *do not* see the Power View button, follow the steps in the Know This about adding Power View to the Excel ribbon feature (see page 369) and then click the Power View button in the New Group group on the Insert tab.

   The Power View window opens a new, blank Power View1 worksheet is added to the workbook (see Figure 8.46).
3. Double-click the Power View1 sheet tab, type Revenue, and then press the Enter key.

   The sheet tab is renamed *Revenue*.
4. Click the *Click here to add a title* placeholder and then type PDML Revenue.

   The text *PDML Revenue* displays in the title text box.
5. Click the right-pointing arrow at the left of the Location Revenue table in the field list box at the Power View Fields task pane (see Figure 8.46).

   The Location Revenue table fields display in a list. Fields that are numeric display with the sigma symbol and fields that can be mapped display with a globe icon.

Figure 8.46 Power View Window with New, Blank Power View1 Worksheet

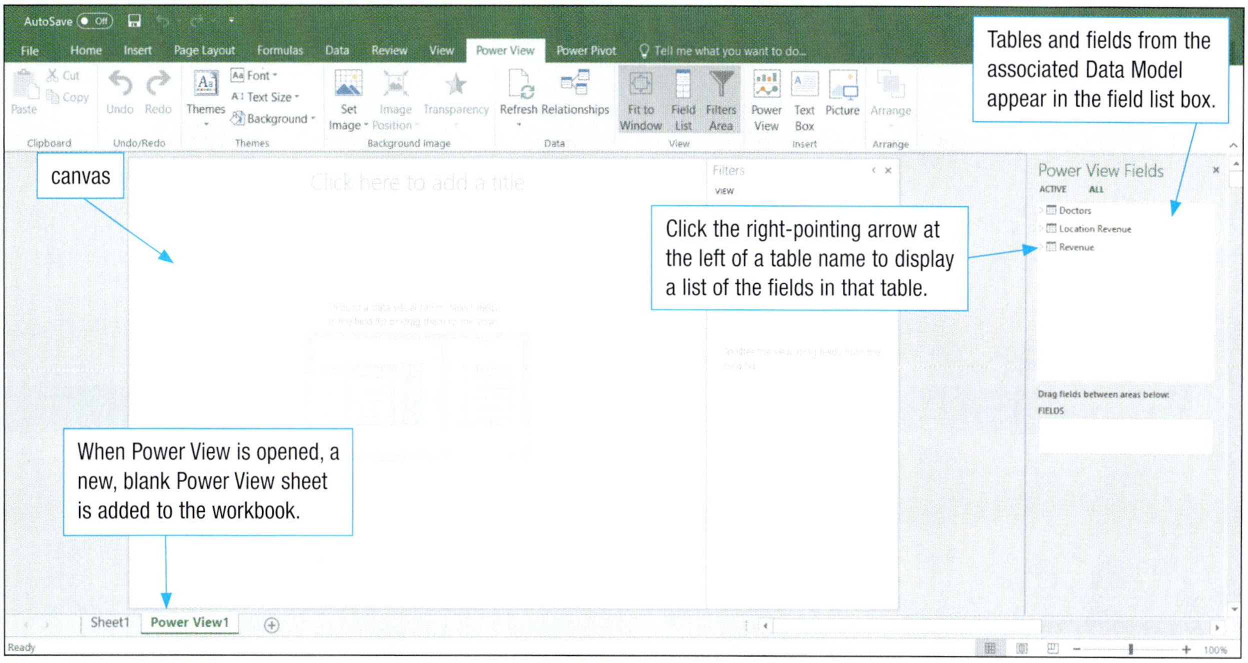

6. Click the right-pointing arrow at the left of the Revenue hierarchy item in the field list.

   The Revenue hierarchy displays with an organization chart icon. When you click the right-pointing arrow, the hierarchy fields display in a list.

7. Click the *Location* check box in the Revenue hierarchy field list.

   The check box contains a check mark. The table in the canvas area of the worksheet expands and displays the *Location* data. The *Location* field is added the *FIELDS* list at the Power View Fields task pane.

8. Click the check box for the *TotalRevenue* field that displays with the sigma symbol in the *Location Revenue* field list.

   The table in the worksheet expands and displays the total revenue data. A total of the total revenue data is automatically added to the table.

9. Click the DESIGN tab, if necessary, click the Bar Chart button in the Switch Visualization group, and then click the *Stacked Bar* option.

   The data visualization switches to a stacked bar chart.

10. Hover the mouse pointer over the lower right corner of the stacked bar chart until the pointer turns into a diagonal arrow, click and hold down the left mouse button, drag the sizing handle down and to the right until bars for all five locations are displayed and the horizontal axis displays *450K*, and then release the mouse button (see Figure 8.47).

11. Click the Other Chart button in the Switch Visualization group and then click the *Pie* option.

    The data visualization changes to a pie chart (see Figure 8.48).

12. Click the LAYOUT tab, click the Legend button in the Labels group, and then click the *Show Legend at Bottom* option.

    A legend displays below the chart, showing the color assigned to each location.

13. Click the CHART tab at the Filters task pane.

    Filter options display.

14. Click the right-pointing arrow at the left of the *Location* field at the Filters task pane and then click the *Location field's* List filter mode button.

    Filter options display in a list.

Figure 8.47 Stacked Bar Visualization

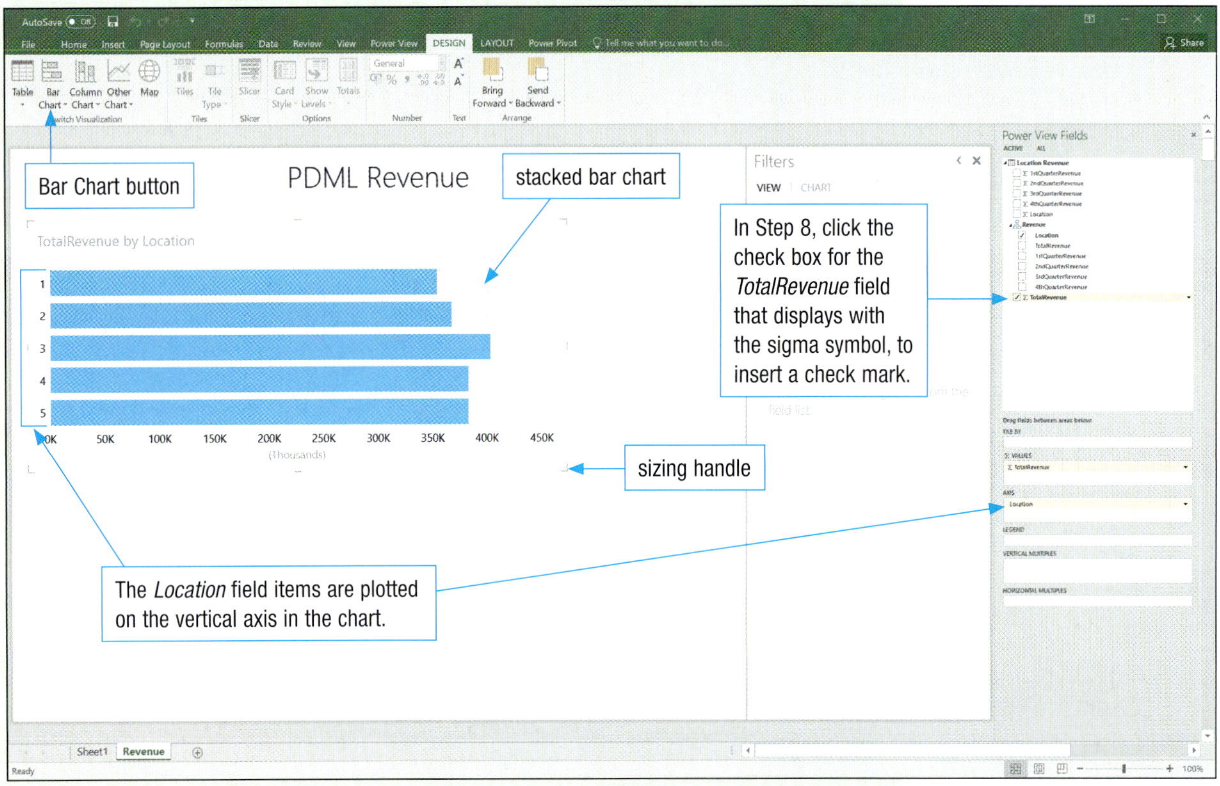

Figure 8.48 Pie Chart Visualization

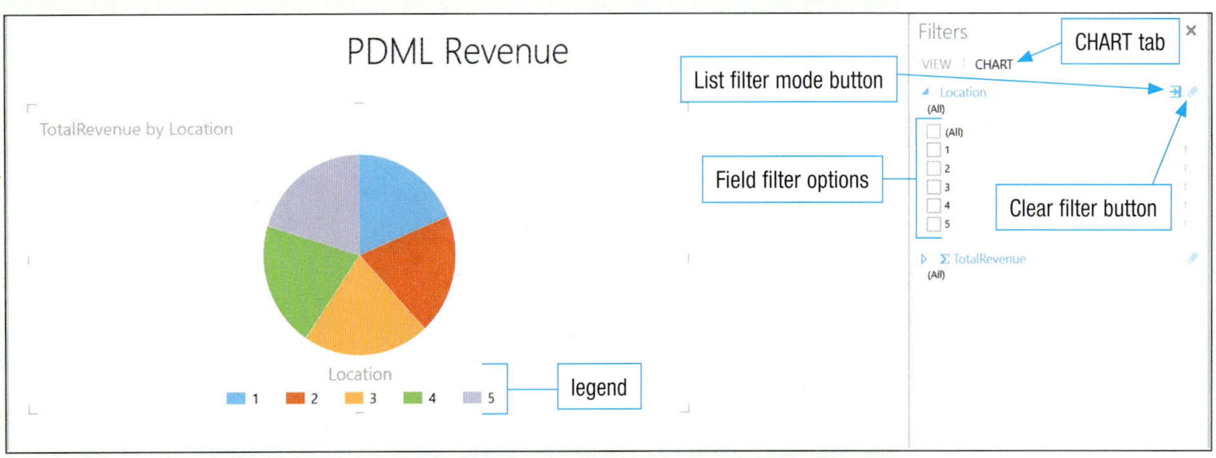

15. Click the *2*, *3*, *4*, and *5* check boxes.

    Each of the check boxes contains a check mark and the visualization shows the revenue generated at the four locations. The revenue is distributed fairly equally between the four locations.

16. Click the *Location field's* Clear filter button.
17. Click the *Location 4* pie slice (green slice).

    The *Location 4* pie slice is highlighted and the other slices are dimmed.

18. Point to the *Location 4* pie slice.

    A ScreenTip displays the data associated with the slice.

19. Click the *1stQuarterRevenue*, *2ndQuarterRevenue*, *3rdQuarterRevenue*, and *4thQuarterRevenue* check boxes in the Revenue hierarchy field list at the Power View Fields task pane.

    Each of the check boxes contains a check mark and each field is now also listed on the CHART tab at the Filters task pane.

20. Double-click the *Location 4* pie slice.

    The 1st Quarter Revenue for location 4 displays in the pie chart. This is the next level in the Revenue hierarchy.

21. Click the DESIGN tab, click the Bar Chart button, and then click the *Stacked Bar* option.

    The pie chart turns into a stacked bar chart.

22. Double-click the *Location 4 1st Quarter Revenue* bar in the chart.

    The 2nd Quarter Revenue for location 4 displays in stacked bar chart. This is the next level in the Revenue hierarchy (see Figure 8.49).

23. Click the drill-up icon.

    The 1st Quarter Revenue for location 4 displays in the stacked bar chart.

24. Save and then close the workbook.

Figure 8.49 Drill Down Visualization

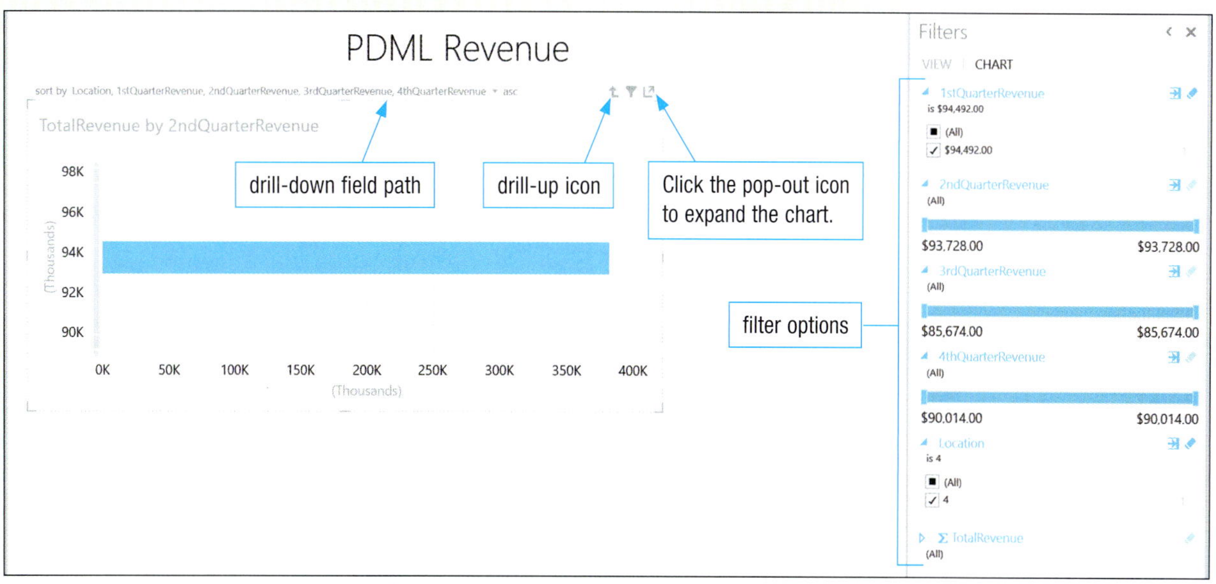

8.21 Using Cube Functions

MOS Expert 3.4.4

Tutorial

Using a Cube Function

A PivotTable is a multidimensional array of values referred to as a **Data Cube**. A Data Cube stores summary data from a combination of fields. In contrast, a database table stores summary data from records and fields.

A Data Cube is part of an **online analytic processing (OLAP) database**. OLAP is a technology used to organize large business databases and support business intelligence. OLAP databases are divided into one or more Data Cubes. In Power Pivot, you can use the Data Model as a Data Cube and extract information using Cube functions without having to build a PivotTable. A **Cube function** provides a means to summarize information from the raw data source file without having to spend a lot of time consolidating the data in Excel.

When you use the GETPIVOTDATA function, which was introduced in Section 8.15, you are treating a PivotTable as a Data Cube.

▸ Know This about Cube functions

— Cube functions are available only in a workbook that is connected to a Data Model.

— There are seven Cube functions in Excel (see Table 8.1).

Table 8.1 Cube Functions

Function Syntax	Description
CUBEKPIMEMBER (connection,kpi_name,kpi_property,caption)	Returns a **key performance indicator (KPI)** property and displays the KPI name in the cell. A KPI is a quantifiable measurement, such as monthly gross profit or quarterly employee turnover, that is used to monitor an organization's performance.
CUBEMEMBER (connection,member_expression,caption)	Returns the requested property (attribute) for a cube member.
CUBEMEMBERPROPERTY (connection,member_expression,property)	Returns the value of a member property from the Data Cube. Use to validate that a member name exists within the Data Cube and to return the specified property for this member.
CUBERANKEDMEMBER (connection,set_expression,rank,caption)	Returns the *nth*-ranked member of a set, such as the top 10 sales representatives.
CUBESET (connection,set_expression,caption,sort_order,sort_by)	Defines a set of members to create a subcube.
CUBESETCOUNT(set)	Returns the number of items in a set.
CUBEVALUE (connection,[member_expression1],[member_expression2], …)	Returns an aggregated value from the Data Cube.

▸ Know This about using a Cube function

— To use a Cube function, enter the function in a worksheet that contains a PivotTable.
— Type the Cube function in any cell outside the PivotTable.
— When you start to type the function, a ScreenTip displays the function syntax and a **connection prompt** appears below the ScreenTip asking you to confirm where the data is located (see Figure 8.50).
— Press the Tab key to accept the highlighted connection prompt.
— Use the ScreenTip to guide the rest of your entry.
— Press the Enter key or use another method to finish the entry.
— When you finish the entry, Excel creates a link between the function and the external data, and you may see a security message in a yellow warning bar below the Excel ribbon.
— To allow Excel to connect to the external data, click the Enable Content button in the yellow warning bar and then click the Yes button at the security warning dialog box, if necessary.

▸ Know This about using the CUBEVALUE function

— When the CUBEVALUE function evaluates, it temporarily displays a *"#GETTING_DATA..."* message in the cell before all the data is retrieved.

On the Job

Task 8.21 Using the CUBEVALUE Function

Kaelan has discovered that an employee who was hired in 2014 in the eye care department did not get a recent years-of-service salary increase. He asks if you can quickly find the ID number of this employee so he can work with the department manager to fix the error. Use the CUBEVALUE function to find the employee ID number.

1. Open the 8-PDML-DateOfHire workbook that you closed at the end of Task 8.19, and then click in cell A14.
2. Type =CUBEVALUE(".

   A ScreenTip displays the function syntax and a connection prompt displays below the ScreenTip (see Figure 8.50).

Figure 8.50 CUBEVALUE Function Connection Prompt

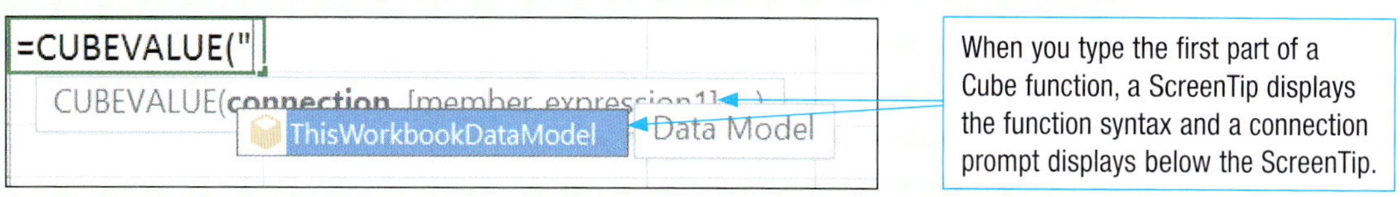

3. Press the Tab key and then type ".

   The highlighted connection is added to the function and *=CUBEVALUE("ThisWorkbookDataModel* displays in cell A14. The argument *[member_expression1]* is highlighted in the function syntax ScreenTip.

4. Type "[Sum of EmployeeID]","[DateOfHire (Year)].[2014]","[Employees].[Department].[Eye Care]") and then press the Enter key.

   The number *24789* displays in cell A14. This is the EmployeeID of the employee who was hired in 2014 in the eye care department. ***Note:*** *Type the function carefully, being sure to include the correct punctuation and spaces.*

5. Save and then close the workbook.

Model Answer

Reminder

To allow a workbook to link to external data, click the Enable Content button in the yellow warning bar below the Excel ribbon, if it displays, and then click the Yes button at the security warning dialog box asking if you want to make this file a trusted document, if it displays.

Chapter Summary

8.1 ▶ Creating a PivotTable can make a large worksheet more manageable by summarizing the data and allowing the user to manipulate it in different ways. When a PivotTable is created, the data is turned, or *pivoted*, so it can be viewed from a different perspective.

▶ Data is displayed in a PivotTable by adding fields from the source data to the PivotTable and indicating the layout area in which to place the fields. The placement of the fields determines the layout of the PivotTable. A PivotTable can be placed in a new worksheet or in a specific location in the current worksheet.

▶ A PivotTable can be created from a range or table in the current worksheet or from an external source, such as an Access database. Creating a PivotTable does not change the range or table. A PivotTable does not update automatically if the source data is edited; the PivotTable must be refreshed.

8.2 ▶ When a PivotTable is created, the default report layout Compact Form is applied. This layout is designed to optimize the readability of a PivotTable. The layout can be changed by adding, removing, and rearranging fields at the PivotTable Fields task pane. Other ways of modifying the PivotTable layout include changing the report layout, changing the way subtotals and grand totals are displayed, and inserting blank rows between items to improve readability and to help group items visually.

8.3 ▶ A PivotTable can be formatted quickly by applying a built-in style in the PivotTable Styles gallery. Like a table style, a PivotTable style applies a group of formatting settings together in one action. The applied style can then be modified using options in the PivotTable Style Options group on the PivotTable Tools Design tab. A PivotTable can also be formatted using any of the formatting options that can be applied to a worksheet.

8.4 ▶ When using a PivotTable to analyze data, the user may want to drill down and focus on only a portion, or subset, of the data. An easy way to do this is to apply a filter. When a filter is applied, selected items are displayed in the PivotTable and unselected items are hidden. The data in a PivotTable can also be sorted. By default, the data in a PivotTable is sorted the same way as the source data.

8.5 ▶ Like a regular Excel table, a PivotTable can be filtered using the slicer feature. (This feature is covered in Chapter 7.)

8.6 ▸ A multilevel PivotTable can be created by placing more than one field in a layout area at the PivotTable Fields task pane. By default, multiple fields added to the *Rows* layout area display as indented levels in the same column in the PivotTable. This type of layout can be used to illustrate data relationships.

8.7 ▸ Another way to filter a PivotTable is to use a timeline. A timeline is similar to a slicer but filters only by date and time fields; this allows analyzing data in a specific time frame.

8.8 ▸ Formulas can be added to a PivotTable that use calculated fields and calculated items, allowing the user to perform quick calculations within the PivotTable without altering the source data.

▸ A calculated field uses data from another field and inserts a new column in the PivotTable. A calculated item uses data from one or more specific items within a field and provides an alternative to adding additional row items to the source data.

8.9 ▸ Other ways to create a PivotTable include using Quick Analysis and using Recommended PivotTables. Both features provide PivotTable options that suit the source data. The user can then choose the best option for the analysis he or she needs to perform.

8.10 ▸ A PivotChart can be created from a PivotTable to provide a visual representation of the summary data. A PivotChart can enhance the readability and analysis of the data in a PivotTable by clearly illustrating patterns and trends. A PivotChart has all the features of a standard chart, such as a data series, categories, type, subtype, and axes. By default, the PivotChart displays in the same worksheet as the PivotTable.

8.11 ▸ Applying a PivotChart style is a quick way to format a PivotChart and give it a professional appearance. Options on the PivotChart Tools Analyze, Design, and Format tabs can be used to apply formatting. The same options used to size and move a standard chart can be used to size and move a PivotChart.

8.12 ▸ Like a PivotTable, a PivotChart can be filtered to display a specific segment of data. Filter arrows display for the filter, legend, axis, and value fields in a column, bar, or line PivotChart. The specific fields that display filter arrows vary depending the PivotTable data and layout.

8.13 ▸ After a PivotChart has been created, the layout can be modified to emphasize or illustrate data patterns or trends. The layout can be changed in several ways: by transposing, or switching, the axis data; by applying a Quick Layout; and by changing the chart type, subtype, and layout.

8.14 ▸ PivotTable data can be grouped to make a subset of the data easier to analyze. Having grouped data is also helpful when a lot of data needs to be illustrated in a PivotChart. Fields and field items (two or more) can be grouped.

8.15 ▸ The GETPIVOTDATA function returns data stored in a PivotTable report. The function arguments describe the data that will be extracted. The GETPIVOTDATA function is useful for displaying summary data and other types of data that the user wants to highlight or focus on.

8.16 ▶ The Data Model is a database attached to an Excel workbook that allows using database tools within Excel. Data stored in the Data Model can be accessed and formatted using Excel tools, including PivotTables and PivotCharts. The Data Model stores data in a compressed format, resulting in a smaller file size than if the data was stored in an Excel table.

▶ The contents of the Data Model are visible in Excel only if the Excel add-in Power Pivot is enabled. Power Pivot is a business intelligence (BI) tool used to perform powerful data analysis within Excel. Power Pivot allows the user to access and combine data from multiple sources within a single data structure. Building a Data Model allows integrating data from multiple tables and building a relational data source inside an Excel workbook.

8.17 ▶ A Data Model can be viewed in Data view or Diagram view. Using Diagram view allows the user to see the structure of each table and its table fields and to define the relationships that connect the tables.

▶ In a relational database, a relationship is created between tables when a field in one table corresponds to a field in another table. Every table in a relational database is related to at least one other table in the database. Once a relationship is defined between the tables in the Data Model, a PivotTable can be created from the Data Model.

▶ Every table in a relational database assigns a primary key field. The primary key field requires a unique entry in each row to ensure that each record in the table is unique. A foreign key field in one table refers to a primary key field in another table. To be related, fields have to be the same data type but do not have to have the same field name.

8.18 ▶ A hierarchy is an organization of fields that goes from the most general to the most specific. A hierarchy can be created in Power Pivot and then added to a PivotTable.

8.19 ▶ The Quick Explore feature can be used to drill down into a PivotTable and the corresponding PivotChart hierarchy to analyze data details on different hierarchical levels. This feature works with any item that contains hierarchical data. In a PivotTable, items containing hierarchical data display with an Expand button.

8.20 ▶ Power View is a data visualization tool used to find hidden patterns and relationships in the data from Power Pivot. A Data Model that has a hierarchy can be used to drill down into the data in Power View. In Power View, you can create table, chart, and map visualizations. A Power View visualization, or report, is designed for interactive, on-screen data analysis.

8.21 ▶ A PivotTable is a multidimensional array of values referred to as a *Data Cube*. A Data Cube stores summary data from a combination of fields. In contrast, a database table stores summary data from records and fields.

▶ A Data Cube is part of an online analytic processing (OLAP) database. OLAP databases are divided into one or more Data Cubes. In Power Pivot, the Data Model can be used as a Data Cube, and information can be extracted using Cube functions without having to build a PivotTable. A Cube function provides a means to summarize information from the raw data source without having to spend a lot of time consolidating the data in Excel.

Features Review

Feature	Ribbon Tab, Group	Button, Option	Keyboard Shortcut
add calculated field to PivotTable	PivotTable Tools Analyze, Calculations	, *Calculated Field*	
add calculated item to PivotTable	PivotTable Tools Analyze, Calculations	, *Calculated Item*	
apply PivotChart style	PivotChart Tools Design, Chart Styles		
apply PivotTable style	PivotTable Tools Design, PivotTable Styles		
apply PivotTable style options	PivotTable Tools Design, PivotTable Style Options	or	
add Power View button to Insert tab	File	*Options, Customize Ribbon, Insert,* New Group button, *Choose commands from* option box arrow, *Commands Not in the Ribbon, Insert a Power View Report,* Add button, OK button	
add Power View worksheet to workbook	Insert, New Group		
add or modify chart visualization titles, labels, and legends in Power View worksheet	LAYOUT, Labels		
apply Quick Layout to PivotChart	PivotChart Tools Design, Chart Layouts		
change PivotChart type, subtype, layout	PivotChart Tools Design, Type		
change report layout in PivotTable	PivotTable Tools Design, Layout		
create and manage hierarchy in Power Pivot window	Home, View		
create PivotChart		, *PivotChart*	
create PivotChart from PivotTable	PivotTable Tools Analyze, Tools	or	
create PivotTable	Insert, Tables		
create PivotTable using Recommended PivotTables	Insert, Tables		
display Get External Data group in restored down Power Pivot window	Home, Data		
display Insert Slicers dialog box	PivotTable Tools Analyze, Filters		
display PivotChart dialog box	PivotTable Tools Analyze, Tools		
display PivotTable Fields task pane	PivotTable Tools Analyze, Show	or	

continues...

Feature	Ribbon Tab, Group	Button, Option	Keyboard Shortcut
enable Power Pivot if add-in is installed	File	*Options*, *Add-ins*, *Manage* option box arrow, *COM Add-ins*, Go button, *Microsoft Power Pivot for Excel* check box, OK button	
filter PivotTable using slicer	PivotTable Tools Analyze, Filters		
filter PivotTable using timeline	PivotTable Tools Analyze, Filter		
group field items in PivotTable	PivotTable Tools Analyze, Group		
group row or column fields in PivotTable	PivotTable Tools Analyze, Group		
import external data from database in Power Pivot window	Home, Get External Data	, *From Access*	
insert blank line after grouped item in PivotTable	PivotTable Tools Design, Layout	, *Insert Blank Line after Each Item*	
install Power Pivot add-in and enable Power Pivot	Data, Data Tools		
modify data visualization in Power View window	DESIGN, Switch Visualization		
modify formatting of chart element	Home or PivotChart Tools Design or PivotChart Tools		
open Power Pivot window	Power Pivot, Data Model		
place multiple fields in separate columns in PivotTable	PivotTable Tools Design, Layout	, *Show in Tabular Form*	
refresh all PivotTables in workbook manually	PivotTable Tools Analyze, Data		Alt + F5
remove single grouping in PivotTable	PivotTable Tools Analyze, Group		
show or hide grand totals in PivotTable	PivotTable Tools Design, Layout		
show or hide subtotals in PivotTable	PivotTable Tools Design, Layout		
switch to Diagram view in Power Pivot window	Home, View		
transpose axis data in PivotChart	PivotChart Tools Design, Data		

Recheck

Recheck your understanding of the concepts, features, and skills covered in this chapter by taking the Recheck quiz.

Workbook

Access the study tools, review exercises, assessments, and challenges for this chapter in the workbook available from this page in your ebook.

Using Advanced Formulas and Functions

Chapter 9

Chapter Goal

To create formulas using advanced functions that aid in the summation and interpretation of data.

Learning Objectives

9.1 Use the COUNTIF and COUNTIFS functions

9.2 Use the AVERAGEIF and AVERAGEIFS functions

9.3 Use the SUMIF and SUMIFS functions

9.4 Use the AND, OR, and NOT functions and create nested functions with IF and IFS

9.5 Use the Evaluate Formula feature

9.6 Use the VLOOKUP function

9.7 Use the HLOOKUP function

9.8 Use the IFERROR function

9.9 Use the TRANSPOSE function

9.10 Use the MATCH function

9.11 Use the INDEX function

9.12 Configure formula calculation options

Precheck

Check your understanding of the concepts, features, and skills covered in this chapter by taking the Precheck quiz.

Data Files

Before beginning the chapter work, download the AE9 folder from this page in your ebook to your storage medium and then make AE9 the active folder.

Ebook Links

Access digital resources for this course from your ebook.

SNAP

If you are a SNAP user, go to your SNAP assignments page to complete the Precheck, Tutorials, and Recheck in this chapter.

Preview

On the Job

Scenario: ProDiagnostics Medical Laboratories (PDML)

In Chapter 8, you created PivotTables and PivotCharts to summarize data and create visuals for Kaelan Rogers, director of ProDiagnostics Medical Laboratories (PDML). Those tools made it easy for Kaelan to spot patterns and trends in revenue and appointment data. Kaelan has also put together a workbook of revenue data by location specialty, discipline, and doctor. He wants you to enter formulas using some advanced functions that will help him summarize this data and calculate bonuses for the doctors using various scenarios. You will use formulas that calculate results based on certain criteria.

Visual Reference

Figure 9.1 Worksheet Containing Advanced Formulas

The range B5:B25 has the defined name *Contract*.

The range E5:E25 has the defined name *Total_Revenue*.

Formula bar expanded to display a formula that has each argument on a separate line

Click the Evaluate Formula button to see how a formula calculates the result.

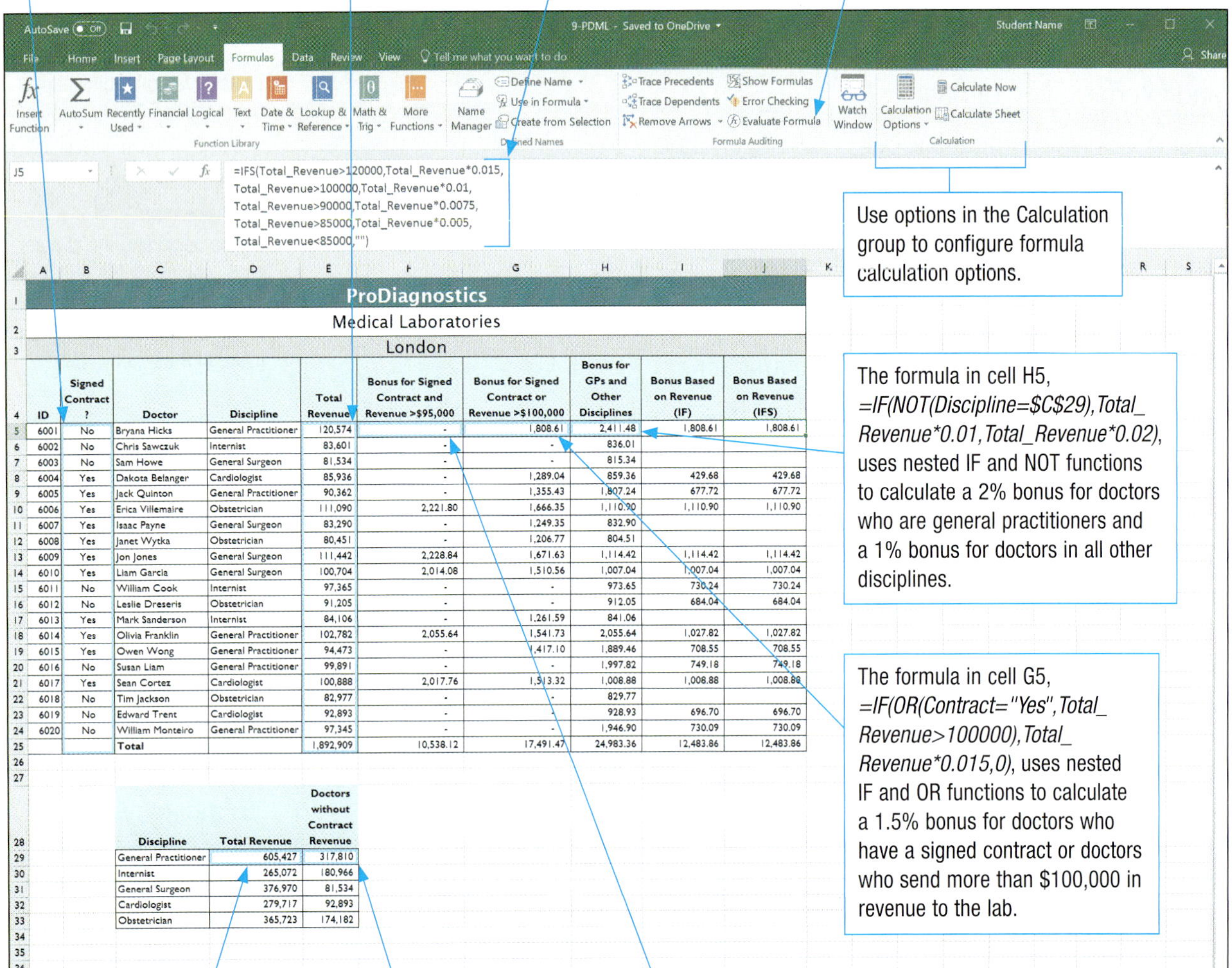

Use options in the Calculation group to configure formula calculation options.

The formula in cell H5, *=IF(NOT(Discipline=$C$29),Total_Revenue*0.01,Total_Revenue*0.02)*, uses nested IF and NOT functions to calculate a 2% bonus for doctors who are general practitioners and a 1% bonus for doctors in all other disciplines.

The formula in cell G5, *=IF(OR(Contract="Yes",Total_Revenue>100000),Total_Revenue*0.015,0)*, uses nested IF and OR functions to calculate a 1.5% bonus for doctors who have a signed contract or doctors who send more than $100,000 in revenue to the lab.

Visual Reference

The formula in cell D29, *=SUMIF(Discipline,C29,Total_Revenue)*, uses the SUMIF function to calculate the total revenue for each discipline.

The formula in cell E29, *=SUMIFS(Total_Revenue,Discipline,C29, Contract,"No")*, uses the SUMIF function to calculate the total revenue for each discipline from doctors who have not signed a contract.

The formula in cell F5, *=IF(AND(Contract="Yes",Total_Revenue>95000),Total_Revenue*0.02,0)*, uses nested IF and AND functions to calculate a 2% bonus for doctors who have signed a contract and send more than $95,000 in revenue to the lab.

9.1 Using the COUNTIF and COUNTIFS Functions

MOS 4.2.4
MOS Expert 3.1.3

Tutorial

Using the COUNTIFS Function

COUNTIF and COUNTIFS are Statistical functions. A **Statistical function** provides statistics to help facilitate analysis of the data. The **COUNTIF function** counts the number of cells in a range that meet a single criterion, or condition. The **COUNTIFS function** counts the number of cells that meet more than one condition.

The arguments of some of the functions taught in this chapter are similar to the arguments of the IF function. You may find it helpful to review Section 2.15, "Using Logical Functions, Comparison Operations, and the IF Function," in Chapter 2, before starting this chapter.

▸ Know This about the COUNTIF function

— Table 9.1 explains the syntax and arguments for the COUNTIF function.

— Each time the conditional test defined by the *criteria* argument is met, the count increases by 1.

— The syntax requires enclosing some types of criteria in quotation marks (see Table 9.2).

Table 9.1 COUNTIF Function Syntax and Arguments

Syntax
=COUNTIF(range,criteria)

Argument	Required or Optional?	Description
range	Required	The data that will be tested (where to look)
criteria	Required	The **conditional test** that must be met (what to look for)

Table 9.2 Syntax Requirements for Different Types of Criteria in a Function

Criteria Data Type	Syntax Requirement	Example
text	Enclose in quotation marks.	"Y"
cell reference, defined name	Enter a cell reference or defined name.	C5 or Revenue
number	Enter a number.	25
expression	Enclose in quotation marks.	">25"

▸ Know This about *range* arguments

— The *range* argument may be entered using cell addresses or defined names.

— For example, in the Employment Professionals worksheet shown in Figure 9.2, the formula in cell K4 is *=COUNTIF(ExcelLevel,"Advanced")*. This formula counts the number of contract employees with advanced Excel qualifications working for the Employment Professionals agency.

- *ExcelLevel* is the defined name for the range containing the criterion (range F4:F35).
- *Advanced* is the criterion.
- Each time Excel finds the data *Advanced*, the count increases by 1.

Reminder

Using defined names instead of cell addresses makes it easier for users to understand formulas and functions.

Figure 9.2 COUNTIF and COUNTIFS Formulas

	A	B	C	D	E	F	G	H	I	J	K
1					Employment Professionals						
2					Contract Employee Qualifications						
3	Employee ID	First Name	Last Name	Rate/Hr	Word Level	Excel Level	Access Level	Sage Simply Accounting (Yes/No)		Summary	
4	ZI8996	Janelle	Atkins	$23.00	Advanced	Advanced	Intermediate	Yes		Number with Advanced Excel	16
5	AE4743	Cassidy	Belanger	$16.00	Intermediate	Intermediate	Basic	No		Number with Advanced Access	3
6	AE4744	Amber	Boucher	$18.00	Advanced	Intermediate	Intermediate	Yes			
7	AF4745	Carly	Boudreault	$18.00	Intermediate	Intermediate	Basic	Yes		Number with Advanced Word	
8	PR9065	Carol-Anne	Bruno	$16.00	Basic	Advanced	Intermediate	Yes		and Advanced Excel	11
9	AE4632	Sarah	Byack	$18.00	Advanced	Intermediate	Intermediate	No			
10	PR9070	Debra	Caron	$16.00	Advanced	Intermediate	Intermediate	Yes			
11	AE4709	Heidi	Cary	$29.00	Advanced	Intermediate	Advanced	Yes			
12	PR9061	Kiera	Cook	$18.00	Advanced	Intermediate	None	Yes			
13	AE4682	Gina	Domenichino	$16.00	Intermediate	Basic	Basic	No			
14	AE4712	Bria	Galvez	$16.00	Intermediate	Basic	Basic	No			
15	AE4684	Gabriela	Gertz	$16.00	Intermediate	Intermediate	Intermediate	Yes			
16	AE4717	Celeste	Howe	$18.00	Advanced	Advanced	Intermediate	No			
17	PR9063	Violet	Kendall	$23.00	Advanced	Intermediate	None	Yes			
18	AE4688	Bella	Lajoie	$16.00	Basic	Intermediate	Intermediate	No			
19	AE4720	Brad	Lang	$18.00	Basic	Advanced	Intermediate	Yes			
20	AE4789	Sandra	Latrell	$18.00	Advanced	Advanced	Intermediate	No			
21	ZI8982	Allison	Lockwood	$29.00	Advanced	Advanced	Advanced	Yes			
22	AE4766	Taryn	Logan	$18.00	Advanced	Advanced	Intermediate	No			
23	AE4725	Braden	Michaelson	$23.00	Advanced	Advanced	Intermediate	Yes			
24	ZI8980	Abbey	Miller	$18.00	Intermediate	Advanced	Intermediate	Yes			

The formula in cell K4 is *=COUNTIF(ExcelLevel,"Advanced").*

Note: This figure shows only part of the data in the worksheet.

The range E4:E35 has the defined name *WordLevel.*

The range F4:F35 has the defined name *ExcelLevel.*

The formula in cell K8 is *=COUNTIFS(WordLevel,"Advanced",ExcelLevel,"Advanced").*

▶ Know This about inserting functions

— The method used to insert a function is based on the user's preference.

— Different methods are taught throughout this chapter.

▶ Know This about using the Insert Function button to insert the COUNTIF function

— To insert the COUNTIF function, click the Insert Function button in the Function Library group on the Formulas tab, click the *Or select a category* option box arrow at the Insert Function dialog box (see Figure 9.3), click the *Statistical* option at the drop-down list, scroll down and click the *COUNTIF* option in the *Select a function* list box, click the OK button, enter the arguments at the Function Arguments dialog box (see Figure 9.4), and then click the OK button.

— When you use the Function Arguments dialog box to insert a function, Excel automatically adds the required syntax after you finish a criterion entry. For example, it automatically puts quotation marks around text when you finish entering a text criterion.

— To finish an entry in an argument text box at the Function Arguments dialog box, press the Tab key to move to the next argument text box or click the OK button to close the dialog box.

▶ Know More ways to display the Insert Function dialog box

- Click the Insert Function button on the Formula bar.
- Click the AutoSum button arrow in the Function Library group on the Formulas tab, and then click the *More Functions* option at the drop-down list.
- Click a function category button or the More Functions button in the Function Library group, and then click the *Insert Function* option at the drop-down list.
- Click the AutoSum button arrow in the Editing group on the Home tab and then click the *More Functions* option at the drop-down list.
- Press Shift + F3.

Figure 9.3 Insert Function Dialog Box

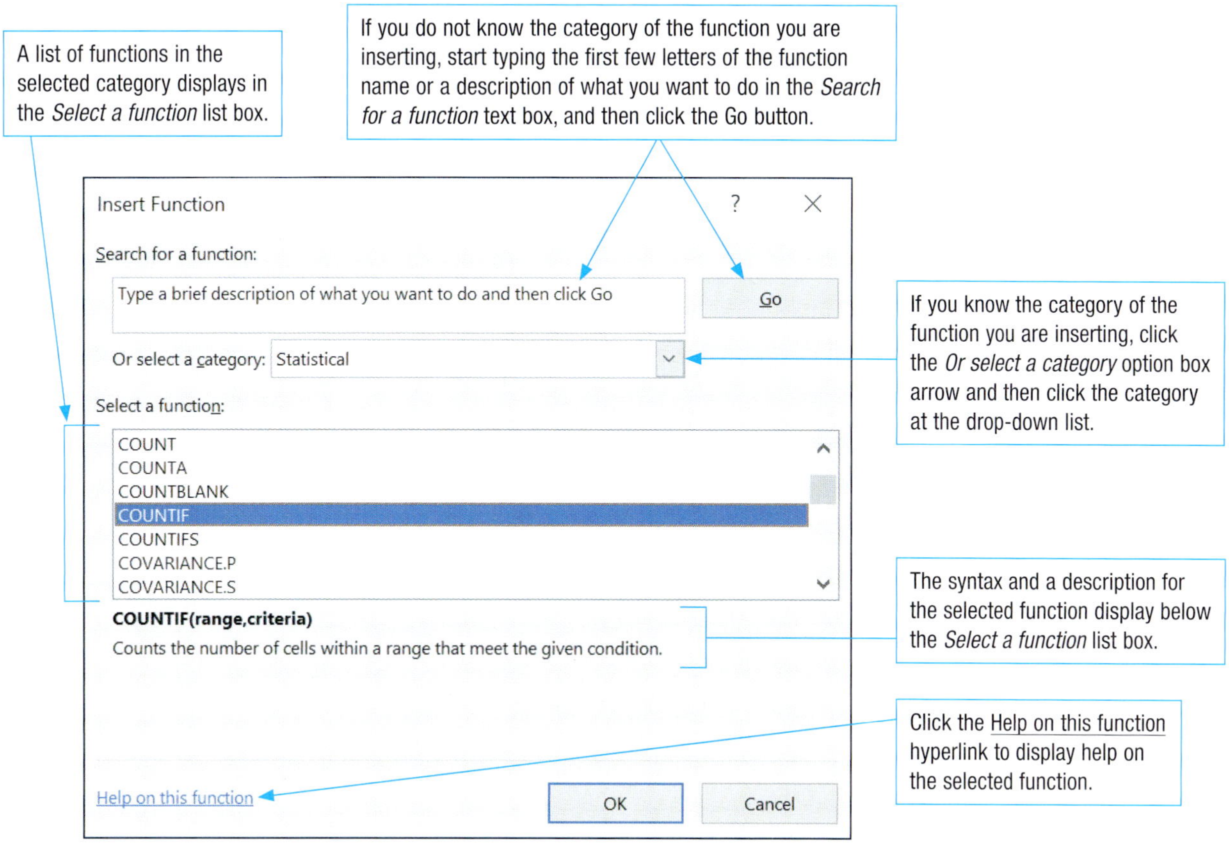

Figure 9.4 COUNTIF Function Arguments Dialog Box

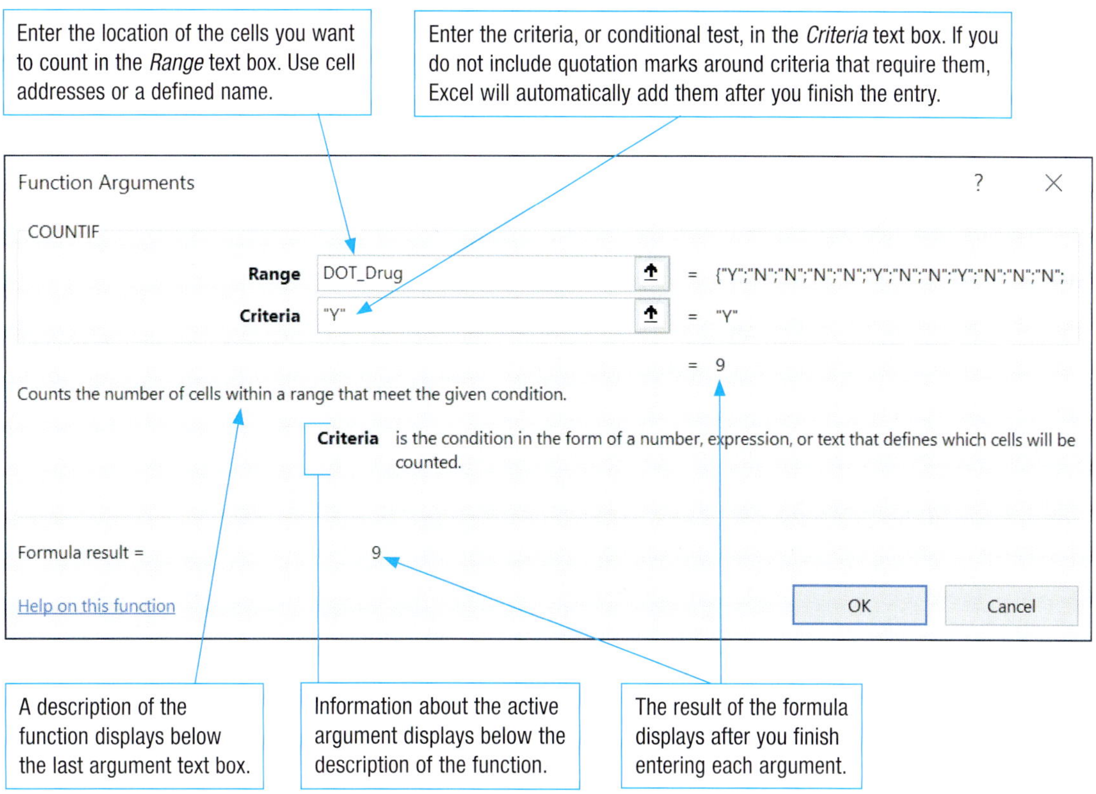

On the Job
Task 9.1a Using the COUNTIF Function

Kaelan wants to know how many PDML locations have been certified to collect samples for Department of Transportation (DOT) drug testing. In his revenue workbook, those locations are identified by the letter *Y* in the range with the defined name *DOT_Drug*. In the Location Specialty worksheet, enter a formula that uses the COUNTIF function to count the number of certified locations.

1. Open the data file **9-PDML**.
2. With the Location Specialty worksheet active, click the Formulas tab and then click in cell O5.
3. Click the Insert Function button in the Function Library group.

   The Insert Function dialog box displays (see Figure 9.3 on page 387).
4. Click the *Or select a category* option box arrow and then click the *Statistical* option, if necessary.

   The category name *Statistical* appears in the option box.
5. Scroll down in the *Select a function* list box, click the *COUNTIF* option, and then click the OK button, if necessary.

   The Function Arguments dialog box displays with the insertion point in the *Range* text box. If necessary, move the dialog box so you can see cell O5 in the worksheet.
6. Type DOT_Drug and then press the Tab key.

   The defined name *DOT_Drug* appears in the *Range* text box and the insertion point is in the *Criteria* text box.
7. Type Y.

   The text *Y* appears in the *Criteria* text box. It is not necessary to type quotation marks around the text because Excel will add them after you finish entering the argument.
8. Click the OK button.

   The dialog box closes, the result *9* displays in cell O5, and the formula *=COUNTIF(DOT_Drug,"Y")* displays in the Formula bar.
9. Click the Save button on the Quick Access Toolbar.

Model Answer

▶ Know More ways to find a function at the Insert Function dialog box

– If you do not know what category a function belongs to, type the first few letters of the function name or a brief description of the function in the *Search for a function* text box, and then click the Go button.

▶ Know More ways to display the Function Arguments dialog box

– Double-click the function name in the *Select a function* list box at the Insert Function dialog box.

Reminder

To move a dialog box, point to the title bar, click and hold down the left mouse button, drag the box to the new position, and then release the mouse button.

Reminder

To display formulas instead of results in worksheet cells, click the Show Formulas button in the Formula Auditing group on the Formulas tab, or press Ctrl + `.

▶ Know This about the COUNTIFS function

— The syntax for the COUNTIFS function is *=COUNTIFS(criteria_range1,criteria1[,criteria_range2,criteria2,...])*.
— Note that the COUNTIFS function syntax is similar to the COUNTIF function syntax but includes additional range and criteria arguments.
— For every range (where to look), there is a corresponding criterion (what to look for).
— Each range must have the same number of rows and columns.
— The ranges do not have to be adjacent to each other.
— You can have up to 127 criteria_ranges and criteria.
— Each time all the conditional tests in a COUNTIFS function are met, the count increases by 1.

— For example, in the Employment Professionals worksheet shown in Figure 9.2 (page 386), the formula in cell K7 is *=COUNTIFS(WordLevel,"Advanced",ExcelLevel,"Advanced")*. This formula counts the number of contract employees with both advanced Word and advanced Excel qualifications.

- *WordLevel* and *ExcelLevel* are the defined names of the ranges containing the criteria (ranges E4:E35 and F4:F35, respectively).
- *Advanced* is the criterion for both ranges.
- Each time Excel finds the data *Advanced* in both ranges, the count increases by 1.
- Figure 9.5 explains the formula and demonstrates how arguments are entered in the Function Arguments dialog box.

Figure 9.5 COUNTIFS Function Arguments Dialog Box

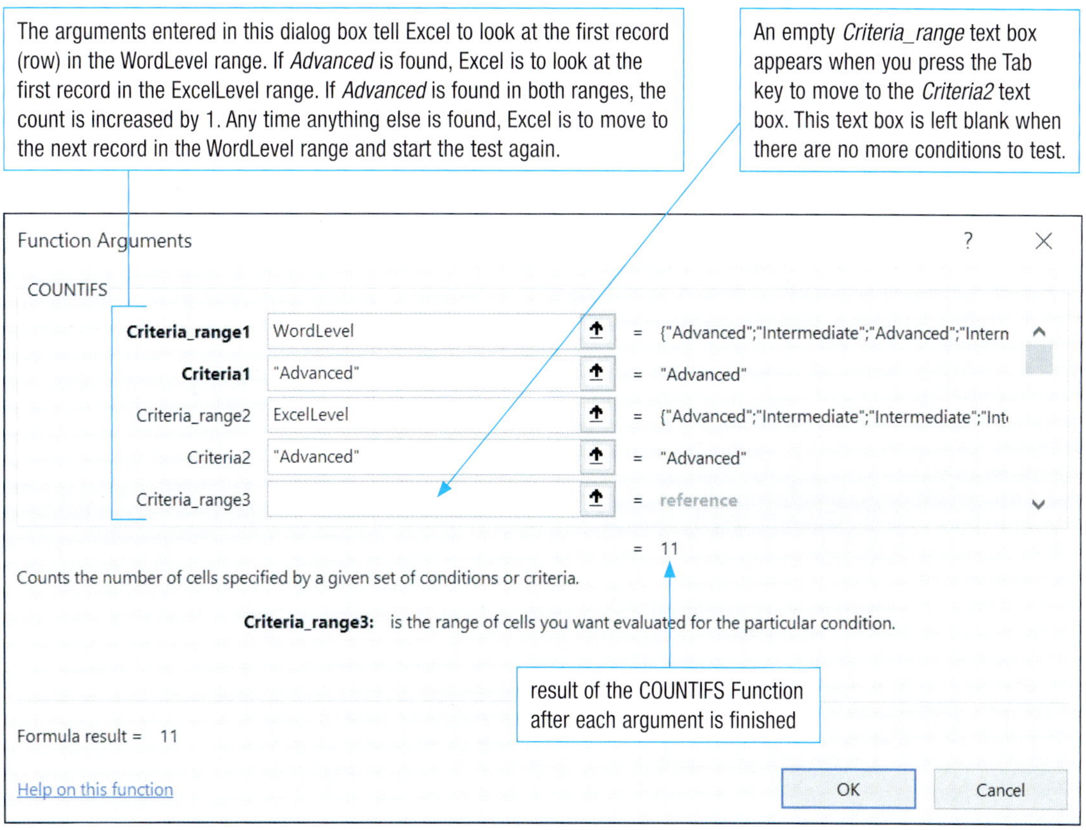

On the Job

Task 9.1b Using the COUNTIFS Function

Kaelan wants to know how many PDML locations have been certified to collect samples for DOT drug testing and can also perform alcohol breath testing. In his revenue workbook, locations certified to collect DOT drug samples are identified by the letter *Y* in the range with the defined name *DOT_Drug*, and locations able to perform alcohol breath testing are identified by the letter *Y* in the range with the defined name *Alcohol*. In the Location Specialty worksheet, enter a formula that uses the COUNTIFS function to count the number of locations that meet both criteria.

1. With the Location Specialty worksheet active and the Formulas tab active, click in cell O7.
2. Click the Insert Function button in the Function Library group.

   The Insert Function dialog box displays with the category name *Statistical* in the *Or select a category* text box.
3. Scroll down in the *Select a function* list box, click the *COUNTIFS* option, and then click the OK button.

   The Function Arguments dialog box displays with the insertion point in the *Criteria_range1* text box. See Figure 9.6 for the completed arguments entry.

Figure 9.6 COUNTIFS Function Arguments Dialog Box

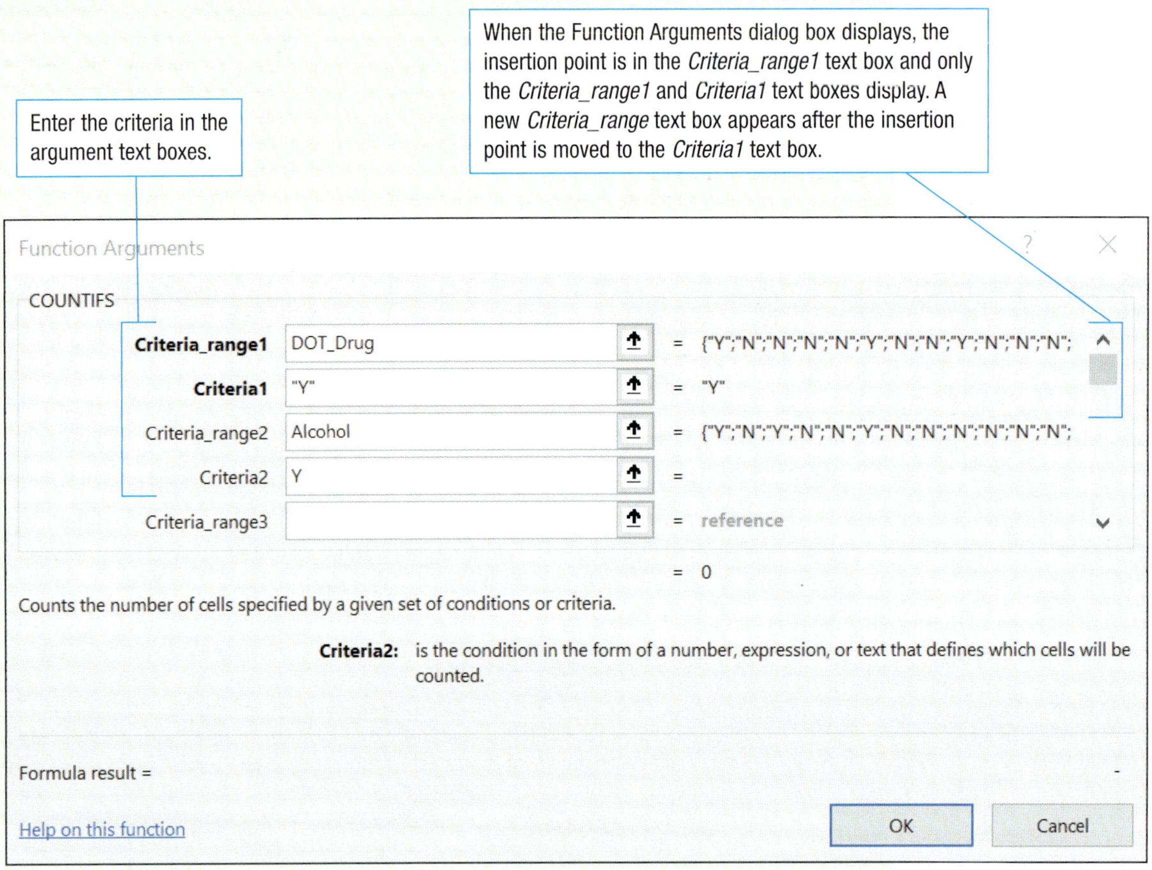

4. Type DOT_Drug and then press the Tab key.

   The defined name *DOT_Drug* appears in the *Criteria_range1* text box, the insertion point is in the *Criteria1* text box, and the *Criteria_range2* text box displays.
5. Type Y and then press the Tab key.

   The text *"Y"* appears in the *Criteria1* text box, the insertion point is in the *Criteria_range2* text box, and the *Criteria2* text box displays.

Reminder
Excel automatically adds quotation marks around text criteria when you finish entering the argument.

6. Type Alcohol and then press the Tab key.

   The defined name *Alcohol* appears in the *Criteria_range2* text box, the insertion point is in the *Criteria2* text box, and the *Criteria_range3* text box displays.

7. Type Y.

   The text *Y* appears in the *Criteria2* text box.

8. Click the OK button.

   The dialog box closes, the result *7* displays in cell O7, and the formula *=COUNTIFS(DOT_Drug,"Y",Alcohol,"Y")* displays in the Formula bar.

9. Click the Save button on the Quick Access Toolbar.

Model Answer

MOS 4.2.3
MOS Expert 3.1.3

Tutorial

Using the AVERAGEIF Function

9.2 Using the AVERAGEIF and AVERAGEIFS Functions

AVERAGEIF and AVERAGEIFS are Statistical functions. The **AVERAGEIF function** finds the arithmetic mean (average) of the data in a specified range that meet a single criterion, or condition. The **AVERAGEIFS function** calculates the average of cells that meet multiple criteria in multiple ranges.

▸ Know This about the AVERAGEIF function

— Table 9.3 explains the syntax and arguments of the AVERAGEIF function.

— For example, in the Employment Professionals worksheet shown in Figure 9.7, the formula *=AVERAGEIF(ExcelLevel,"Advanced",Rate)* calculates the average rate per hour of contract employees with advanced Excel qualifications.

- *ExcelLevel* is the defined name for the range containing the criterion (the range F4:F35).
- *Advanced* is the criterion.
- *Rate* is the defined name for the range containing the rate per hour that will be averaged (the range D4:D35).
- Each time the data *Advanced* is found in the ExcelLevel range for a record, the value in the Rate range for that record is included in the average calculation.

Table 9.3 AVERAGEIF Function Syntax and Arguments

Syntax
=AVERAGEIF(range,criteria,[average_range]).

Argument	Required or Optional?	Description
range	Required	The data that will be tested (where to look)
criteria	Required	The conditional test that must be met (what to look for)
average_range	Optional	The range containing the values that will be averaged (where to look). If this argument is left blank, the data in the *range* argument is used.

Figure 9.7 AVERAGEIF and AVERAGEIFS Formulas

	A	B	C	D	E	F	G	H	I	J	K
1	**Employment Professionals**										
2	**Contract Employee Qualifications**										
3	**Employee ID**	**First Name**	**Last Name**	**Rate/Hr**	**Word Level**	**Excel Level**	**Access Level**	**Sage Simply Accounting (Yes/No)**		**Summary**	
4	ZI8996	Janelle	Atkins	$23.00	Advanced	Advanced	Intermediate	Yes		Number with Advanced Excel	16
5	AE4743	Cassidy	Belanger	$16.00	Intermediate	Intermediate	Basic	No		Number with Advanced Access	3
6	AE4744	Amber	Boucher	$18.00	Advanced	Intermediate	Intermediate	Yes			
7	AE4745	Carly	Boudreault	$18.00	Intermediate	Intermediate	Basic	Yes		Number with Advanced Word	
8	PR9065	Carol-Anne	Bruno	$16.00	Basic	Advanced	Intermediate	Yes		and Advanced Excel	11
9	AE4632	Sarah	Byack	$18.00	Advanced	Intermediate	Intermediate	No			
10	PR9070	Debra	Caron	$16.00	Advanced	Intermediate	Intermediate	Yes		Average Rate/Hr Advanced Excel	$ 20.56
11	AE4709	Heidi	Cary	$29.00	Advanced	Intermediate	Advanced	Yes		Average Rate/Hr Advanced Word	
12	PR9061	Kiera	Cook	$18.00	Advanced	Intermediate	None	Yes		and Advanced Excel	$ 21.64
13	AE4682	Gina	Domenichino	$16.00	Intermediate	Basic	Basic	No			
14	AE4712	Bria	Galvez	$16.00	Intermediate	Basic	Basic	No			
15	AE4684	Gabriela	Gertz	$16.00	Intermediate	Intermediate	Intermediate	Yes			
16	AE4717	Celeste	Howe	$18.00	Advanced	Advanced	Intermediate	No			
17	PR9063	Violet	Kendall	$23.00	Advanced	Intermediate	None	Yes			
18	AE4688	Bella	Lajoie	$16.00	Basic	Intermediate	Intermediate	No			
19	AE4720	Brad	Lang	$18.00	Basic	Advanced	Intermediate	Yes			
20	AE4789	Sandra	Latrell	$18.00	Advanced	Advanced	Intermediate				
21	ZI8982	Allison	Lockwood	$29.00	Advanced	Advanced	Advanced				
22	AE4766	Taryn	Logan	$18.00	Advanced	Advanced	Intermediate				
23	AE4725	Braden	Michaelson	$23.00	Advanced	Advanced	Intermediate	Yes			
24	ZI8980	Abbey	Miller	$18.00	Intermediate	Advanced	Intermediate	Yes			

The formula in cell K10 is *=AVERAGEIF(Excel Level, "Advanced",Rate).*

The formula in cell K12 is *=AVERAGEIFS(Rate, WordLevel,"Advanced",ExcelLevel,"Advanced").*

The range D4:D35 has the defined name *Rate.*

The range E4:E35 has the defined name *WordLevel.*

The range F4:F35 has the defined name *ExcelLevel.*

Note: *This figure shows only part of the data in the worksheet.*

▸ **Know This** about using the More Functions button to insert the AVERAGEIF function

— To insert the AVERAGEIF function, click the More Functions button in the Function Library group on the Formulas tab (see Figure 9.8), point to the *Statistical* option at the drop-down list, click the *AVERAGEIF* option at the second drop-down list, enter the arguments at the Function Arguments dialog box, and then click the OK button.

Figure 9.8 Function Library Group

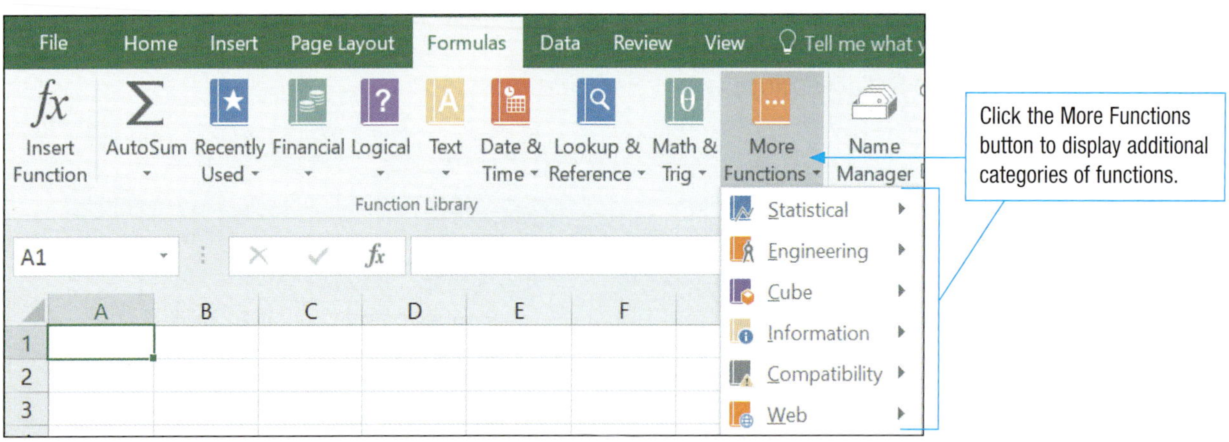

▸ **Know This** about categories of functions

— Excel organizes functions into categories (see Table 9.4).

Table 9.4 Function Categories

Category	Contains functions that...
Compatibility	are found in Excel 2010 or earlier versions of Excel and replaced with newer functions.
Cube	are used with Power Pivot to analyze data in a hierarchical manner.
Database	are used to calculate statistics when specified criteria are met.
Date & Time	store dates and times as numbers.
Engineering	perform common engineering calculations.
Financial	perform complex financial calculations.
Information	provide location and contents about cells in a spreadsheet.
Logical	test the value of a cell to be either true or false and return a different result based on the outcome of the test.
Lookup & Reference	look up the value in a row or column and return a value.
Math & Trig	perform mathematical and trigonometry calculations.
Statistical	provide statistics to help facilitate analysis of the data; includes functions such as SIN, COS, AVG, and LN.
Text	manipulate text by combining, extracting, formatting, or counting the number of characters.
Web	return results from the Internet or from XML data.

▸ **Know This** about using buttons in the Function Library group to insert functions

— Click the Insert Function button to display the Insert Function dialog box.

— Click the AutoSum button to display a drop-down list of commonly used functions.

— Click the Recently Used button to display a drop-down list of recently used functions.

— Functions in the *Financial*, *Logical*, *Text*, *Date & Time*, *Lookup & Reference*, and *Math & Trig* categories can be accessed through buttons in the Function Library group on the Formulas tab (see Figure 9.8 on page 392).

— Functions in the *Statistical*, *Engineering*, *Cube*, *Information*, *Compatibility*, and *Web* categories are accessed through the More Functions button in the Function Library group.

— Functions in the *Database* category cannot be accessed through a button in the Function Library group. To view the Database functions, click the Insert Function dialog box and switch the category to Database.

— To insert a function using a category button in the Function Library group, click the button, click the function name at the drop-down list, enter arguments at the Function Arguments dialog box, and then click the OK button.

— To insert a function using the More Functions button, click the button, point to the category name at the drop-down list, click the function name at the second drop-down list, enter the arguments at the Function Arguments dialog box, and then click the OK button.
— At the Function Arguments dialog box, arguments that are required are in bold type and arguments that are optional are not in bold type.

On the Job

Task 9.2a Using the AVERAGEIF Function

Kaelan wants to know the average revenue for the PDML locations that have been certified to collect samples for DOT drug testing. In his revenue workbook, the revenue for each location is recorded in the range with the defined name *Revenue*. In the Location Specialty worksheet, enter a formula that uses the AVERAGEIF function to calculate the average revenue for all the certified locations.

1. With the Location Specialty worksheet active and the Formulas tab active, click in cell P5.
2. Click the More Functions button in the Function Library group.
   A drop-down list displays.
3. Point to the *Statistical* option.
   A second drop-down list displays (see Figure 9.9).

Figure 9.9 More Functions Button with the *Statistical* Drop-Down List Displayed

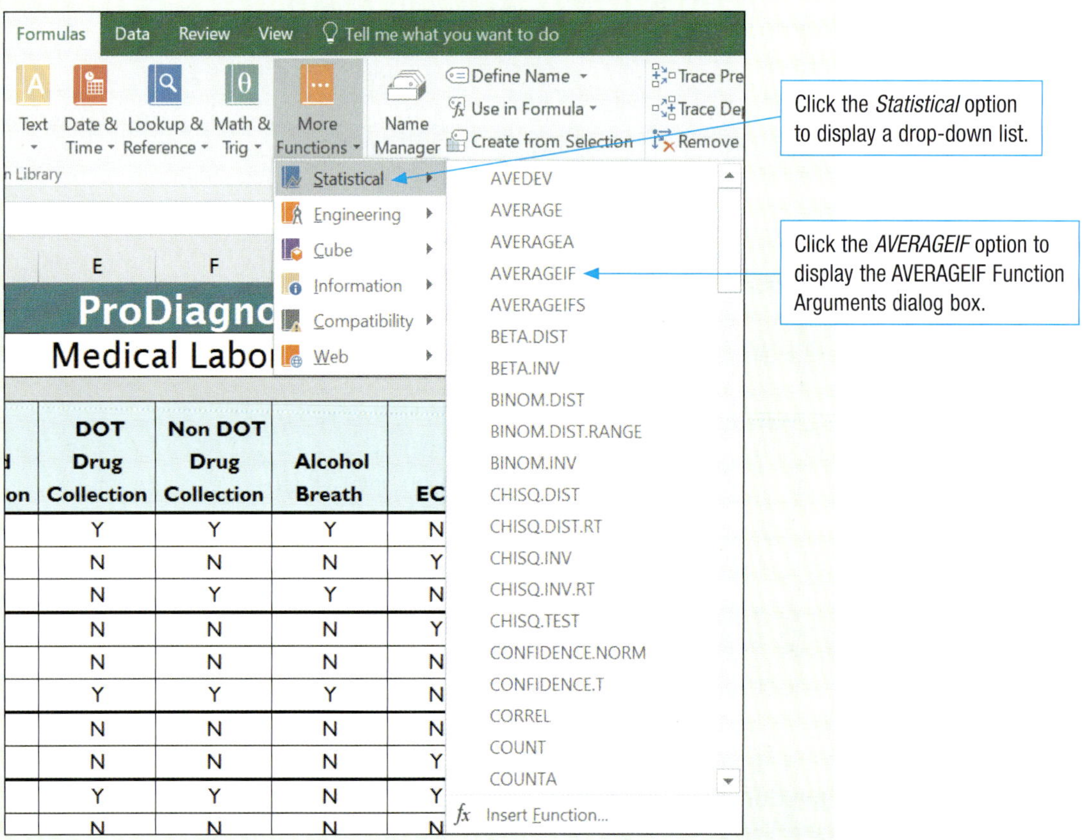

4. Click the *AVERAGEIF* option.

   The Function Arguments dialog box displays with the insertion point in the *Range* text box. *Range* is bold, which means this argument is required.

5. Type DOT_Drug and then press the Tab key.

   The defined name *DOT_Drug* appears in the *Range* text box and the insertion point is in the *Criteria* text box. *Criteria* is bold, which means this argument is required.

6. Type Y and then press the Tab key.

   The text *"Y"* appears in the *Criteria* text box and the insertion point is in the *Average_range* text box. *Average_range* is not bold, which means this argument is not always required. If it is left blank, the data in the DOT_Drug range is averaged.

7. Type Revenue and then click the OK button.

   The dialog box closes, the result *267,376* displays in cell P5, and the formula *=AVERAGEIF(DOT_Drug,"Y",Revenue)* displays in the Formula bar.

8. Click the Save button on the Quick Access Toolbar.

Model Answer

▸ **Know This** about the AVERAGEIFS functions

— The syntax for the AVERAGEIFS function is =*AVERAGEIFS(average_range,criteria_range1,criteria1[,criteria_range2,criteria2,...])*.

— The AVERAGEIFS function varies slightly from the AVERAGEIF function in that the *average_range* argument (where to look for data to average) is at the beginning of the formula instead of at the end of the formula.

— The *average_range* argument is followed by pairs of numbered *criteria_range* arguments (where to look for data to be tested) and numbered *criteria* arguments (what to look for).

— For example, in the Employment Professionals worksheet shown in Figure 9.7 on page 392, the formula =*AVERAGEIFS(Rate,WordLevel,"Advanced",ExcelLevel,"Advanced")* calculates the average rate per hour of contract employees with advanced Word and advanced Excel qualifications.

- *Rate* is the defined name of the range containing the rate per hour that will be averaged (the range D4:D35).
- *WordLevel* and *ExcelLevel* are the defined names of the ranges containing the criteria (the ranges E4:E35 and F4:F35, respectively).
- *Advanced* is the criterion for both ranges.
- Each time the data *Advanced* is found in both ranges, the value in the Rate range is included in the average calculation.
- Figure 9.10 explains the formula and demonstrates how the arguments are entered in the Function Arguments dialog box.

Figure 9.10 AVERAGEIFS Function Arguments Dialog Box

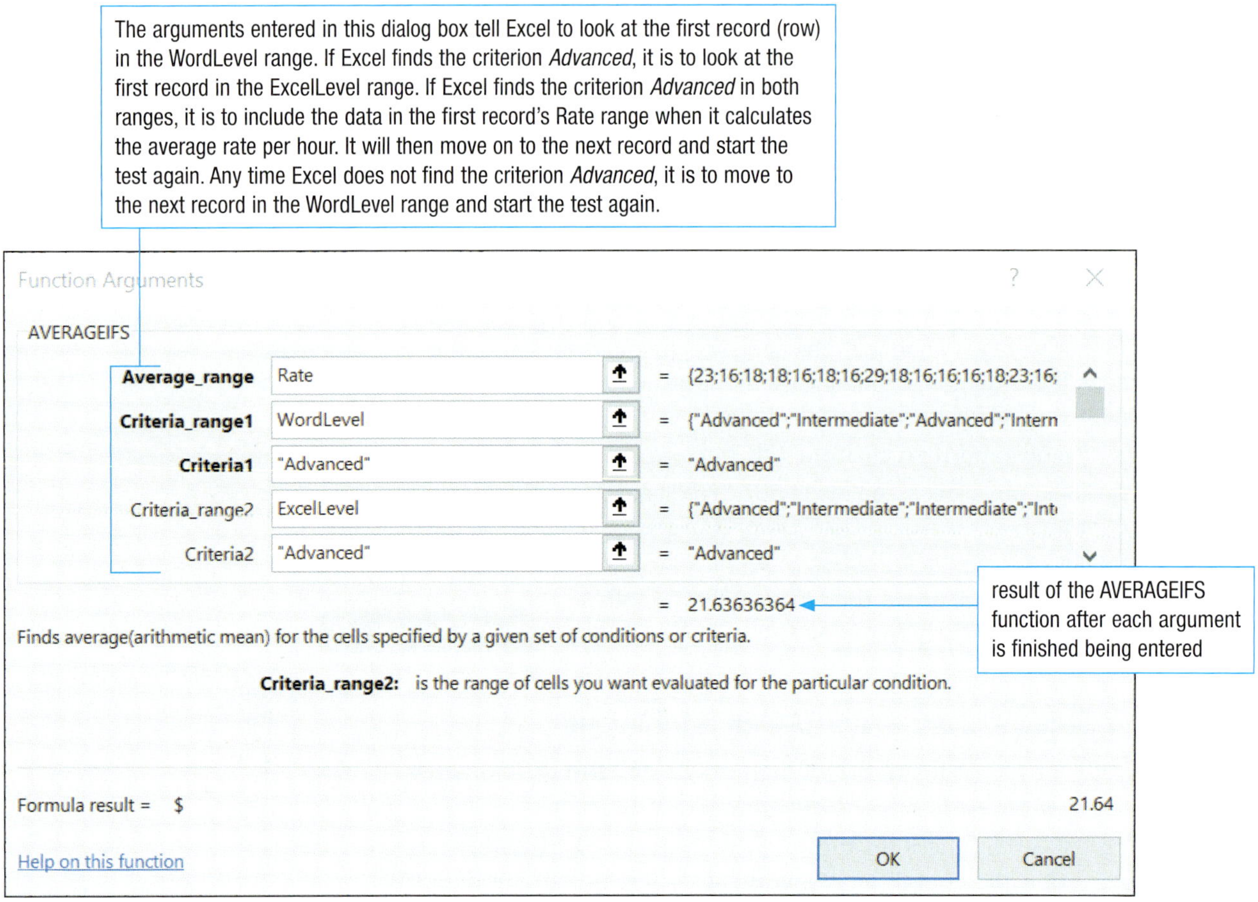

On the Job

Task 9.2b Using the AVERAGEIFS Function

Kaelan wants to know the average revenue for locations that have been certified to collect samples for DOT drug testing and can also perform alcohol breath testing. In his revenue workbook, locations certified to collect samples are identified by the letter *Y* in the range with the defined name *DOT_Drug*, and locations able to perform breath testing are identified by the letter *Y* in the range with the defined name *Alcohol*. In the Location Specialty worksheet, enter a formula that uses the AVERAGEIF function to average the revenue for the locations that meet both criteria.

1. With the Location Specialty worksheet active and the Formulas tab active, click in cell P7.
2. Click the More Functions button in the Function Library group.

   A drop-down list displays.
3. Point to the *Statistical* option.

   A second drop-down list displays.
4. Scroll down the list, if necessary, and then click the *AVERAGEIFS* option.

   The Function Arguments dialog box displays with the insertion point in the *Average_range* text box.

Reminder
In the AVERAGEIFS function, *Average_range* is the first argument. In the AVERAGEIF function, it is the last argument.

5. Type Revenue and then press the Tab key.
   The defined name *Revenue* displays in the *Average_range* text box, the insertion point is in the *Criteria_range1* text box, and the *Criteria1* text box displays.
6. Type DOT_Drug and then press the Tab key.
   The defined name *DOT_Drug* appears in the *Criteria_range1* text box, the insertion point is in the *Criteria1* text box, and the *Criteria_range2* text box displays.
7. Type Y and then press the Tab key.
   The text *"Y"* appears in the *Criteria1* text box, the insertion point is in the *Criteria_range2* text box, and the *Criteria2* text box displays.
8. Type Alcohol and then press the Tab key.
   The defined name *Alcohol* appears in the *Criteria_range2* text box and the insertion point is in the *Criteria2* text box.
9. Type Y and then click the OK button.
   The dialog box closes, the result *266,374* displays in cell P7, and the formula *=AVERAGEIFS(Revenue,DOT_Drug,"Y",Alcohol,"Y")* displays in the Formula bar.
10. Click the Save button on the Quick Access Toolbar.

Model Answer

9.3 Using the SUMIF and SUMIFS Functions

MOS 4.2.2
MOS Expert 3.1.3

Tutorial

Using the SUMIF Function

SUMIF and SUMIFS are Math & Trig functions. A **Math & Trig function** performs mathematical and trigonometry calculations. The **SUMIF function** adds the cells in a range that meet a single criterion, or condition. The **SUMIFS function** adds the data in a range that meet multiple criteria.

▸ Know This about the SUMIF function

— Table 9.5 explains the syntax and arguments for the SUMIF function.

— For example, in the Employment Professionals worksheet shown in Figure 9.11, the formula *=SUMIF(Customer,L5,Total)* calculates the sum of all the contracts for customer Z1898658.

- *Customer* is the defined name for the range containing the criterion (the range B4:B58).
- *L5* is the reference for the cell containing the criterion (Z1898658).
- *Total* is the defined name for the range containing the total that will be summed (the range J4:J58).
- Each time Excel finds the contents of cell L5 (Z1898658) in the Customer range for a record, the value in the Total range for that record is included in the sum calculation.

Table 9.5 SUMIF Function Syntax and Arguments

Syntax
=SUMIF(range,criteria,[sum_range])

Argument	Required or Optional?	Description
range	Required	The data that will be tested (where to look)

...continues

Table 9.5 SUMIF Arguments *...continued*

Argument	Required or Optional?	Description
criteria	Required	The conditional test that must be met (what to look for)
sum_range	Optional	The range containing the values that will be added (where to look). If this argument is left blank, the data in the *range* argument is used.

Figure 9.11 SUMIF and SUMIFS Functions

Employment Professionals

Contracts

	A	B	C	D	E	F	G	H	I	J	K	L	M	N
3	WR Number	Customer ID	Employee ID	Start Date	End Date	No Days	Hours/ Day	Hours/ Week	Rate	Total		Summary		
4	123476	ZI898658	AE4600	04-Mar-19	07-Mar-19	3	7.0	21	$35.00	$735.00		Customer		Total
5	123492	ZI898658	AE4607	04-Mar-19	08-Mar-19	4	6.5	26	$40.00	$1,040.00		ZI898658		$7,875.00
6	123480	PR906825	AA4575	04-Mar-19	08-Mar-19	4	5.0	20	$30.00	$600.00				
7	123472	ZI898658	AE4603	04-Mar-19	08-Mar-19	4	7.0	28	$35.00	$980.00		Customer	Employee	Total
8	123473	ZI898658	AE4611	04-Mar-19	08-Mar-19	4	7.0	28	$40.00	$1,120.00		ZI898658	AE4600	$1,855.00
9	123501	PR906825	AA4570	04-Mar-19	07-Mar-19	3	7.5	22.5	$40.00	$900.00				
10	123502	PR907564	AC4583	04-Mar-19	08-Mar-19	4	7.5	30	$35.00	$1,050.00				
11	123494	RC462556	AA4595	04-Mar-19	08-Mar-19	4	7.5	30	$25.00	$750.00				
12	123475	RC462556	AC4579	04-Mar-19	08-Mar-19	4	7.0	28	$35.00	$980.00				
13	123519	PR906825	AA4568	04-Mar-19	08-Mar-19	4	7.0	28	$30.00	$840.00				
14	123478	PR907564	AE4596	04-Mar-19	08-Mar-19	4	7.0	28	$35.00	$980.00				
15	123460	ZI898658	AE4628	04-Mar-19	08-Mar-19	4	7.5	30	$40.00	$1,200.00				
16	123459	RC461969	AA4577	04-Mar-19	08-Mar-19	4	7.5	30	$35.00	$1,050.00				
17	123479	RC462556	AA4591	04-Mar-19	06-Mar-19	2	6.5	13	$35.00	$455.00				
18	123513	ZI898658	AE4610	05-Mar-19	08-Mar-19	3	8.0	24	$35.00	$840.00				
19	123505	AE478344	AE4780	10-Mar-19	15-Mar-19	5	6.0	30	$35.00	$1,050.00				
20	123467	AE477932	AE4743	11-Mar-19	15-Mar-19	4	7.0	28	$25.00	$700.00				
21	123477	PR906779	AE4730	11-Mar-19	14-Mar-19	3	7.0	21	$25.00	$525.00				
22	123474	PR906825	PR9070	11-Mar-19	15-Mar-19	4	8.0	32	$25.00	$800.00				
23	123471	PR907564	AE4698	11-Mar-19	15-Mar-19	4	7.0	28	$40.00	$1,120.00				
24	123470	ZI898658	AE4600	11-Mar-19	15-Mar-19	4	7.0	28	$40.00	$1,120.00				

The formula in cell N5 is *=SUMIF(Customer,L5,Total).*

The formula in cell N8 is *=SUMIFS (Total,Customer,L8,Employee,M8).*

The range B4:B58 has the defined name *Customer.*

The range C4:C58 has the defined name *Employee.*

The range J4:J58 has the defined name *Total.*

***Note:** This figure shows only part of the data in the worksheet.*

▸ **Know This** about using the Math & Trig button to insert the SUMIF function

— To insert the SUMIF function, click the Math & Trig button in the Function Library group on the Formulas tab (see Figure 9.8 on page 392), click the *SUMIF* option at the drop-down list, enter the arguments at the Function Arguments dialog box, and then click the OK button.

On the Job
Task 9.3a Using the SUMIF Function

Kaelan is meeting with the marketing team tomorrow, and he will discuss the total revenue for each medical discipline at PDML. In his revenue workbook, the medical discipline for each doctor using PDML lab services appears in the range with the defined name *Discipline*. The total revenue contributed by each doctor appears in the Total_Revenue range. In the Discipline Summary worksheet, enter a formula that uses the SUMIF function to calculate the total revenue for the General Practitioner discipline, and then use the fill handle to copy the formula.

1. With the Location Specialty worksheet active, click the Discipline Summary sheet tab, click the Formulas tab, if necessary, and then click in cell D29.
2. Click the Math & Trig button in the Function Library group.

   A drop-down list displays.
3. Scroll down and then click the *SUMIF* option.

   The Function Arguments dialog box displays with the insertion point in the *Range* text box.
4. Type Discipline and then press the Tab key.

   The defined name *Discipline* appears in the *Range* text box and the insertion point is in the *Criteria* text box.
5. Type C29 and then press the Tab key.

   The cell reference *C29* appears in the *Criteria* text box and the insertion point is in the *Sum_range* text box.
6. Type Total_Revenue and then click the OK button.

   The dialog box closes, the result *605,427* displays in cell D29, and the formula *=SUMIF(Discipline,C29,Total_Revenue)* displays in the Formula bar.
7. Double-click the fill handle to copy the formula from cell D29 down into cell D33.

   The total revenue for each discipline appears in cells D29 through D33. The range D29:D33 is selected.
8. Click the Save button on the Quick Access Toolbar.

Model Answer

▸ **Know This** about the SUMIFS function

— The syntax for the SUMIFS function is *=SUMIFS(sum_range,criteria_range1,criteria1[,criteria_range2,criteria2,])*.

— The SUMIFS function is similar to the AVERAGEIFS function and varies slightly from the SUMIF function in that the *sum_range* argument (where to look for values to add) is at the beginning of the formula instead of at the end.

— The *sum_range* argument is followed by pairs of numbered *criteria_range* arguments (where to look for data to be tested) and numbered *criteria* arguments (what to look for).

— For example, in the Employment Professionals worksheet shown in Figure 9.11 on page 398, the formula *=SUMIFS(Total,Customer,L8,Employee,M8)* sums the total when employee AE4600 works for customer Z1898658.

- *Total* is the defined name of the range containing the total that will be summed (the range J4:J58).
- *Customer* and *Employee* are the defined names of the ranges containing the criteria (the ranges B4:B58 and C4:C58, respectively).
- The contents of cell L8 (Z1898658) are the criterion for the first range.

- The contents of cell M8 (AE4600) are the criterion for the second range.
- Each time the contents of cell L8 are found in the Customer range and the contents of cell M8 are found in the Employee range, the value in the Total range is included in the sum calculation.

On the Job

Task 9.3b Using the SUMIFS Function

When Kaelan meets with the marketing team, he will also discuss the total revenue for the doctors in each medical discipline who have not signed a contract. In his revenue workbook, those doctors are identified by the word *No* in the range with the defined name *Contract*. In the Discipline Summary worksheet, enter a formula that uses the SUMIFS function to calculate the total revenue for doctors without a contract.

1. With the Discipline Summary worksheet active and the Formulas tab active, click in cell E29.
2. Click the Math & Trig button in the Function Library group.

   A drop-down list displays.
3. Scroll down and then click the *SUMIFS* option.

   The Functions Arguments dialog box displays with the insertion point in the *Sum_range* text box (see Figure 9.12).

Reminder
In the SUMIFS function, *Sum_range* is the first argument. In the SUMIF function, it is the last argument.

Figure 9.12 SUMIFS Function Arguments Dialog Box

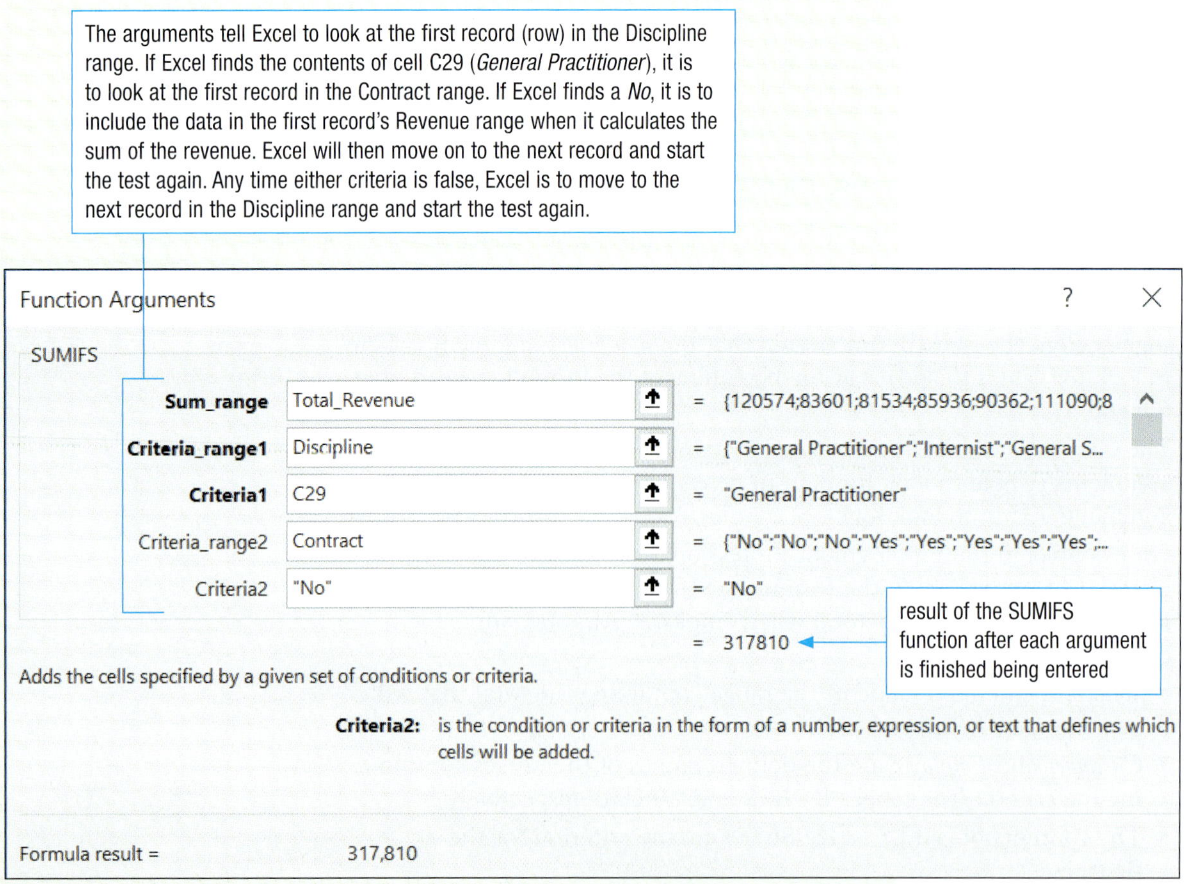

4. Type Total_Revenue and then press the Tab key.

   The range name *Total_Revenue* appears in the *Sum_range* text box, the insertion point is in the *Criteria_range1* text box, and the *Criteria1* text box displays.

5. Type Discipline and then press the Tab key.

   The range name *Discipline* appears in the *Criteria_range1* text box, the insertion point is in the *Criteria1* text box, and the *Criteria_range2* text box displays.

6. Type C29 and then press the Tab key.

   The cell reference *C29* appears in the *Criteria1* text box, the insertion point is in the *Criteria_range2* text box, and the *Criteria2* text box displays.

7. Type Contract and then press the Tab key.

   The range name *Contract* appears in the *Criteria_range2* text box and the insertion point is in the *Criteria2* text box.

8. Type No and then click the OK button.

   The dialog box closes, the result *317,810* appears in cell E29, and the formula *=SUMIFS(Total_Revenue,Discipline,C29,Contract,"No")* displays in the Formula bar.

9. Double-click the fill handle to copy the formula from cell E29 down into cell E33.

   The total revenue for doctors without a contract in each discipline appears in cells E29 through E33 and the range E29:E33 is selected.

10. Click the Save button on the Quick Access Toolbar.

Model Answer

9.4 Using the AND, OR, and NOT Functions and Creating Nested Functions with IF and IFS

MOS Expert 3.1.1
MOS Expert 3.1.2

Tutorial

Nesting the IF and AND Functions

Chapter 2 covered the IF function, which is the most commonly used Logical function in Excel. Other Logical functions offered in Excel include AND, OR, and NOT. A **Logical function** uses Boolean logic to construct a conditional test that proves either true or false. The conditional test (also called a logical test) is a **logical condition**, or expression, that returns a TRUE or FALSE result. The AND, OR, and NOT functions can be used on their own, but they are more commonly used in conjunction with other functions.

Reminder
Most Logical functions include a comparison between two items, such as numbers or text.

▸ **Know This** about the AND, OR, and NOT functions

— The syntax for the AND function is *=AND(logical1[,logical2,...])*.

— The syntax for the OR function is *=OR(logical1[,logical2,...])*.

— The syntax for the NOT function is *=NOT(logical)*.

— Table 9.6 describes how the AND, OR, and NOT functions test logical conditions and provides an example of each function.

Table 9.6 AND, OR, and NOT Logical Functions

Logical Function	Description	Example with Explanation
AND function	Returns *TRUE* if all the conditions test true Returns *FALSE* if any of the conditions test false	*=AND(Sales>Projected,NewClients>5)* Returns *TRUE* if both conditions test true Returns *FALSE* if value in Sales range is greater than value in Projected range but value in NewClients range is less than *5* Returns *FALSE* if *Sales* is less than *Projected* and *NewClients* is greater than *5*
OR function	Returns *TRUE* if any of the conditions tests true Returns *FALSE* if all the conditions test false	*=OR(Sales>Projected,NewClients>5)* Returns *TRUE* if *Sales* is greater than *Projected* or *NewClients* is greater than *5* Returns *FALSE* if *Sales* is less than *Projected* and *NewClients* is not greater than *5*
NOT function	Returns *TRUE* for *NOT(FALSE)* Returns *FALSE* for *NOT(TRUE)*	*=NOT(Sales>Projected)* Returns *TRUE* if *Sales* is less than *Projected* Returns *FALSE* if *Sales* is greater than *Projected*

▶ **Know This** about using the NOT function

— Use the NOT function to include all the options except the one you are looking for. For example, to include all the departments except administration, use the formula *=NOT(C2=Administration)*.

— A pair of less than and greater than symbols (<>) can replace the NOT function and may make a formula easier to read. For example, you can use the formula *=C2<>Administration* instead of the formula *=NOT(C2=Administration)*.

▶ **Know This** about nesting functions

— Complex conditions can be created by combining two or more functions in one formula.

— Nest an AND, OR, or NOT function with an IF function to test multiple conditions.

— Use a **nested IF function** (one IF function nested inside another IF function) to test an additional condition.

Reminder
The syntax for the IF function is *=IF(logical_test,value_if_true,value_if_false).*

▶ **Know This** about inserting nested functions

— To insert nested functions, either type the functions directly in the cell or use the Function Arguments dialog box.

— When you type a function directly in a cell, a ScreenTip displays with the syntax of the formula.

— To insert an IF function with a nested AND function, click the Logical button in the Function Library group on the Formulas tab, click the *IF* option at the drop-down list, enter the *Logical_test* argument at the Function Arguments dialog box, enter the *Value_if_true* argument, enter the *Value_if_false* argument, and then click the OK button.

On the Job

Task 9.4a Nesting the IF and AND Functions

Kaelan is working on a bonus system for the doctors who use PDML lab services. He has created four possible scenarios for the system, and he wants you to help him set up the Discipline Summary worksheet so he can compare the results of the scenarios. For the first bonus system scenario, Kaelan wants to know what PDML would pay out if it offered a 2% bonus to doctors who have a signed contract and who send more than $95,000 in revenue to PDML. Enter a formula that uses the IF and AND functions and the Contract and Total_Revenue ranges to calculate the bonus payments for individual doctors, use the fill handle to copy the formula, and then use the AutoSum button to enter a formula that calculates the total of all the individual bonus payments.

1. With the Discipline Summary worksheet active and the Formulas tab active, click in cell F5.
2. Click the Logical button in the Function Library group and then click the *IF* option.

   The Function Arguments dialog box displays with the insertion point in the *Logical_test* text box (see Figure 9.13). If necessary, move the dialog box so you can see column F.

Figure 9.13 IF Function Arguments Dialog Box for Bonus System Scenario 1

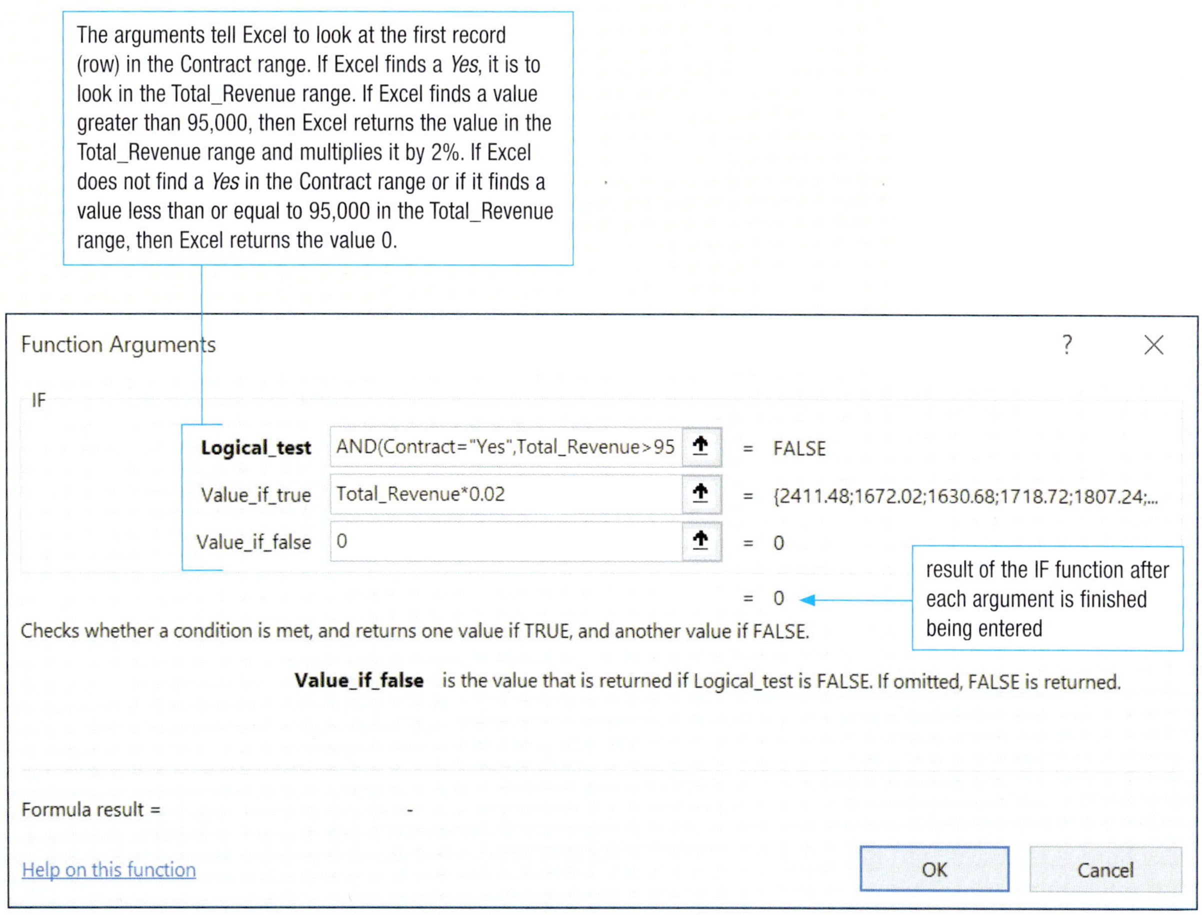

3. Type AND(Contract="Yes",Total_Revenue>95000).

   The AND function is required because both conditions must be true for PDML to pay a bonus: the doctor must have a signed contract *and* the doctor must send PDML more than $95,000 in revenue. The tests for the two conditions are separated by a comma.

4. Press the Tab key.

   The function *AND(Contract="Yes",Total_Revenue>95000)* appears in the *Logical_test* text box and the insertion point is in the *Value_if_true* text box.

5. Type Total_Revenue*0.02.

   This argument tells Excel that if the result of the logical test is true, the total revenue PDML earns from the doctor should be multiplied by 2%.

6. Press the Tab key.

   The argument *Total_Revenue*0.02* appears in the *Value_if_true* text box and the insertion point is in the *Value_if_false* text box.

7. Type 0.

   This argument tells Excel that if the result of the logical test is false, the doctor does not receive a bonus.

8. Click the OK button.

   The dialog box closes and the result - displays in cell F5. This result indicates that the doctor will not receive a bonus. ***Note:*** *The Accounting format has been applied to the cells in column F. When this formatting is applied, cells containing the value 0 display a dash (-).*

   The formula in cell F5 is *=IF(AND(Contract="Yes",Total_Revenue>95000),Total_Revenue*0.02,0)*. For the doctor Bryana Hicks, the answer to the first logical test, *Contract="Yes"*, is false. In an AND function, if the answer to any condition is false, Excel stops calculating and returns the result of the *Value_if_false* test, which in this case is 0.

9. Double-click the fill handle in cell F5.

   The formula is copied down into cell F24.

10. Click in cell F25, click the AutoSum button, and then press the Enter key.

    The result *10,538.12* displays in cell F25.

11. Click the Save button on the Quick Access Toolbar.

Model Answer

On the Job

Task 9.4b Nesting the IF and OR Functions

For the second bonus system scenario, Kaelan wants to know what PDML would pay out if it offered a 1.5% bonus for doctors who have a signed contract or doctors who send more than $100,000 in revenue to PDML. In the Discipline Summary worksheet, enter a formula that uses the IF and OR functions and the *Contract* and *Total_Revenue* defined names to calculate the bonus payments for individual doctors, use the fill handle to copy the formula, and then use copy and paste to enter a formula that calculates the total of all the individual bonus payments.

1. With the Discipline Summary worksheet active and the Formulas tab active, click in cell G5.
2. Click the Logical button in the Function Library group and then click the *IF* option.

   The Function Arguments dialog box displays with the insertion point in the *Logical_test* text box (see Figure 9.14). If necessary, move the dialog box so you can see column G.

Figure 9.14 IF Function Arguments Dialog Box for Bonus System Scenario 2

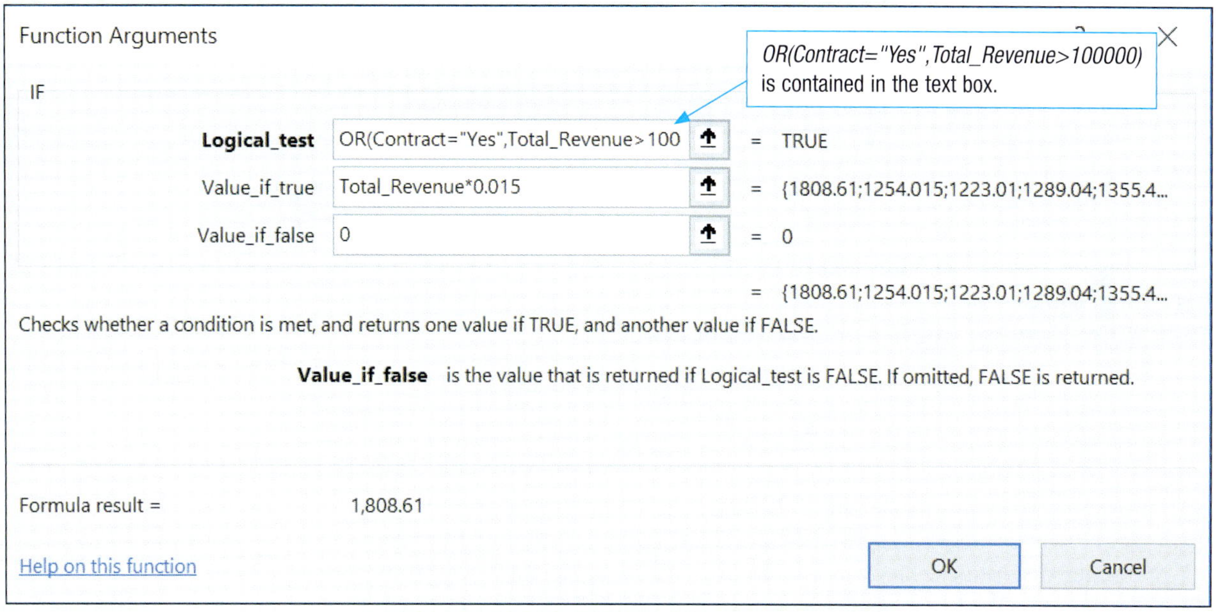

3. Type OR(Contract="Yes",Total_Revenue>100000).

   The OR function is required because only one condition must be true for PDML to pay a bonus: either the doctor must have signed a contract *or* the doctor must have sent PDML more than $100,000 in revenue. The tests for the two conditions are separated by a comma.
4. Press the Tab key.

   The function *OR(Contract="Yes",Total_Revenue>100000)* appears in the *Logical_test* text box and the insertion point is in the *Value_if_true* text box.
5. Type Total_Revenue*0.015.

   This argument tells Excel that if the result of the logical test is true, the total revenue the doctor sends to PDML is multiplied by .015 (1.5%).
6. Press the Tab key.

   The argument *Total_Revenue*0.015* appears in the *Value_if*_true text box and the insertion point is in the *Value_if_false* text box.
7. Type 0.

   This argument tells Excel that if the result of the logical test is false, the doctor does not receive a bonus.

8. Click the OK button.

   The dialog box closes and the result *1,808.61* displays in cell G5.

   The formula in cell G5 is *=IF(OR(Contract="Yes",Total_Revenue>100000),Total_Revenue*0.015,0)*. For the doctor Bryana Hicks, the answer to the first condition, *Contract="Yes"*, is false. In an OR function, only one condition needs to be true, so Excel moves on to evaluate the next condition. The answer to the next condition, *E5>95,000*, is true, so Excel returns the result of the *Value_if_true* test and multiplies the value in cell E5 by 1.5%.

9. Double-click the fill handle in cell G5.

   The formula is copied down into cell G24.

10. Copy the formula from cell F25 into cell G25.

    The result *17,491.47* (the total of the individual bonuses) displays in cell G25.

11. Click the Save button on the Quick Access Toolbar.

Model Answer

On the Job

Task 9.4c Nesting the IF and NOT Functions

For the third bonus system scenario, Kaelan wants to know what PDML would pay out if it offered a 2% bonus for doctors who are general practitioners and a 1% bonus for doctors in all other disciplines. Kaelan notes that doctors who are now using PDML services come from only five disciplines. However, PDML is growing, and in the future, doctors may come from other disciplines. He wants to be sure the third scenario will apply to all the disciplines of future customers. In the Discipline Summary worksheet, enter a formula that uses the IF and NOT functions, the *Discipline* and *Total_Revenue* defined names, and the absolute cell address $C$29 to calculate the bonus payments for individual doctors, use the fill handle to copy the formula, and then use copy and paste to enter a formula that calculates the total of all the individual bonus payments.

1. With the Discipline Summary worksheet active and the Formulas tab active, click in cell H5.
2. Click the Logical button in the Function Library group and then click the *IF* option.

   The Function Arguments dialog box displays with the insertion point in the *Logical_test* text box (see Figure 9.15). If necessary, move the dialog box so you can see column H.

3. Type NOT(Discipline=$C$29).

   The NOT function is required because Kaelan wants to be able to group doctors from all the disciplines except the General Practitioner discipline. The cell C29 reference in the function must be absolute because when the formula is copied, you want it to always reference cell C29.

4. Press the Tab key.

   The function *NOT(Discipline=$C$29)* appears in the *Logical_test* text box and the insertion point is in the *Value_if_true* text box.

Figure 9.15 IF Function Arguments Dialog Box for Bonus System Scenario 3

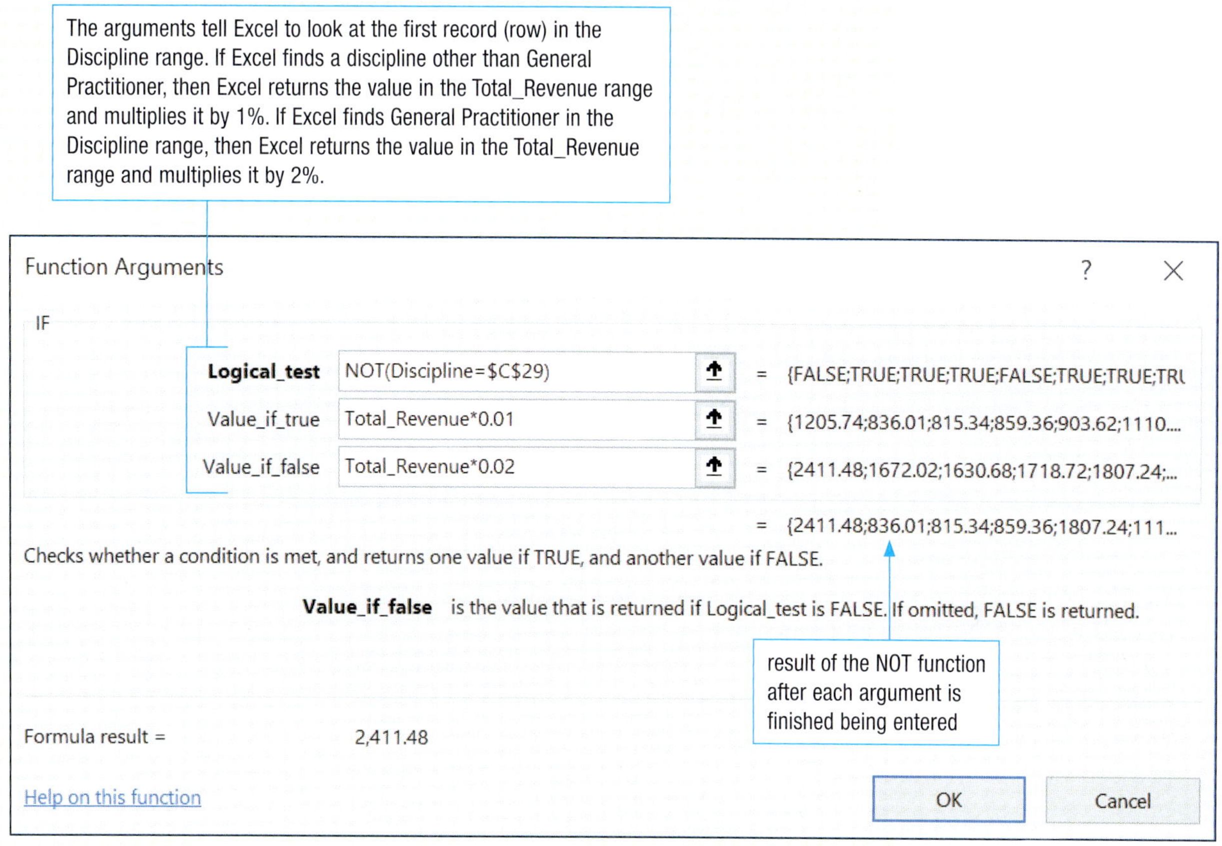

5. Type Total_Revenue*0.01.

   This argument tells Excel that if the result of the logical test is true, the total revenue the doctor sends to PDML is multiplied by 1%.

6. Press the Tab key.

   The argument *Total_Revenue*0.01* appears in the *Value_if_true* text box and the insertion point is in the *Value_if_false* text box.

7. Type Total_Revenue*0.02.

   This argument tells Excel that if the result of the logical test is false, the total revenue the doctor sends to PDML is multiplied by 2%.

8. Click the OK button.

   The dialog box closes and the result *2,411.48* appears in cell H5. The formula is *=IF(NOT(Discipline=$C$29),Total_Revenue*0.01,Total_Revenue*0.02)*. For the doctor Bryana Hicks, the answer to the first logical test, *NOT(Discipline=$C$29)*, is false, so Excel returns the result of the *Value_if_false* test and multiplies the value in cell E5 (120,574) by 2%.

9. Double-click the fill handle in cell H5.

   The formula is copied down into cell H24.

10. Copy the formula from cell G25 across into cell H25.

    The result *24,983.36* (the total of the individual bonuses) displays in cell H25.

11. Click the Save button on the Quick Access Toolbar.

Model Answer

Reminder

You can replace the NOT function in cell H5 with a pair of less than and greater than symbols (<>). The formula is then *=IF(Discipline<>$C$29,Total_Revenue*0.01,Total_Revenue*0.02)*.

▶ Know This about typing a nested IF function directly in a cell

— The number of closing parentheses needed to end a nested IF statement equals the number of times *IF* appears in the formula (see Figure 9.16).

— If you type a nested IF function directly in a cell, Excel color codes the parentheses so you can keep track of each function.

Figure 9.16 Nested IF Statement

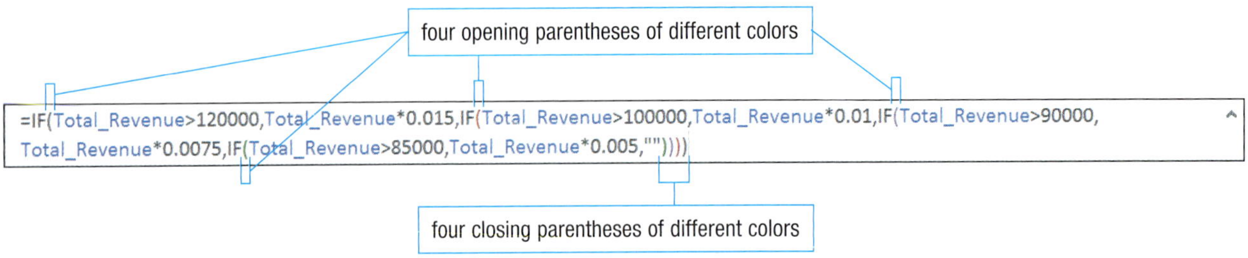

▶ Know This about viewing long formulas in the Formula bar

— Formulas containing nested functions can get quite long and be difficult to read when viewed in the Formula bar.

— To make a formula containing nested functions easier to read, place each logical test on a separate line.

— To place an argument or logical test on a new line in the Formula bar, place the insertion point immediately before the logical test and then press Ctrl + Enter.

▶ Know This about expanding and collapsing the Formula bar using the mouse

— The Formula bar can be expanded to display long formulas without scrolling.

— To expand the Formula bar using the mouse, hover the mouse pointer over the bottom of the bar until the pointer turns into a two-headed arrow, click and hold down the left mouse button, drag the border down until the new size is achieved, and then release the mouse button.

— To collapse the Formula bar using the mouse, hover the mouse pointer over the bottom of the bar until the pointer turns into a two-headed arrow, click and hold down the left mouse button, drag the bottom of the bar up until the new size is achieved, and then release the mouse button.

▶ Know More ways to expand the Formula bar

- Press Ctrl + Shift + U.
- Click the Formula Bar Expand button (down-pointing arrow) at the right of the Formula bar.

▶ Know More ways to collapse the Formula bar

- Press Ctrl + Shift + U.
- Click the Formula Bar Collapse button (up-pointing arrow) at the right of the Formula bar.

▶ Know This about leaving a cell empty

— Type a pair of double quotation marks ("") to leave a cell empty instead of entering a 0. For example, use double quotation marks as the last argument in a nested IF function when you want to leave the cell empty if none of the tests prove true.

— Use a pair of double quotation marks if you do not want to display a zero (0) or a dash (-) in a cell when the results of a test return zero.

Reminder

By default, Excel displays a dash when the results of a test return zero and the Accounting or Comma format has been applied to the cell that contains the results.

On the Job

Task 9.4d Using Nested IF Functions

For the fourth bonus system scenario, Kaelan wants to know what PDML would pay out if it offered bonuses that varied depending on the amount of revenue a doctor sends to PDML. In the Discipline Summary worksheet, enter a formula that uses nested IF functions, the revenue and bonus percentage data from Table 9.7, and the *Total_Revenue* defined name to calculate the bonus payments for individual doctors; use the fill handle to copy the formula; and then use copy and paste to enter a formula that calculates the total of all the individual bonus payments. You know it is easier to enter and verify the nested IF formula if you enter each argument on a separate line. Enter the nested IF formula in cell I5. Expand the Formula bar and review the formula. Copy the formula, and then total the bonus in cell I25.

Table 9.7 Bonus Percentages Based on Revenue Amount

Revenue	Bonus Percentage
>$120,000	1.5%
>$100,000	1%
>$90,000	0.75%
>$85,000	0.5%
<$85,000	No bonus; leave cell empty

1. With the Discipline Summary worksheet active and the Formulas tab active, click in cell I5.
2. Type =IF(Total_Revenue>120000,Total_Revenue*0.015, and then press Alt + Enter.

   When you start to type the formula, Excel displays a ScreenTip with the syntax of the function. Be sure to type the comma at the end of the logical test. When you press Alt + Enter, the insertion point moves to the start of the next line. The argument tells Excel that if the result of the logical test is true, the total revenue that the doctor sends to PDML is multiplied by 1.5%.
3. Type IF(Total_Revenue>100000,Total_Revenue*0.01, and then press Alt + Enter.

   The argument tells Excel that if the result of the logical test is true, the total revenue that the doctor sends to PDML is multiplied by 1.0%.
4. Type IF(Total_Revenue>90000,Total_Revenue*0.0075, and then press Alt + Enter.

   The argument tells Excel that if the result of the logical test is true, the total revenue that the doctor sends to PDML is multiplied by 0.75%.
5. Type IF(Total_Revenue>85000,Total_Revenue*0.005,"")))).

   The argument tells Excel that if the result of the logical test is true, the total revenue that the doctor sends to PDML is multiplied by 0.5%, and if the logical test is false, the cell is empty.

6. Press the Enter key.

   The result *1,808.61* displays in cell I5. For the doctor Bryana Hicks, the answer to the first logical test is true, so Excel returns the result of the *Value_if_true* test and multiplies the value in cell E5 (120,574) by 1.5%.

7. Click in cell I5, hover the mouse pointer over the bottom of the Formula bar until the pointer turns into a two-headed arrow, click and hold down the left mouse button, drag the bottom of the bar down until all the rows of the formula can be seen (see Figure 9.17), and then release the mouse button.

   The Formula bar expands to show the entire formula.

Reminder
Excel adds the 0 before the decimal point in the formula.

Figure 9.17 Nested IF Functions in the Expanded Formula Bar

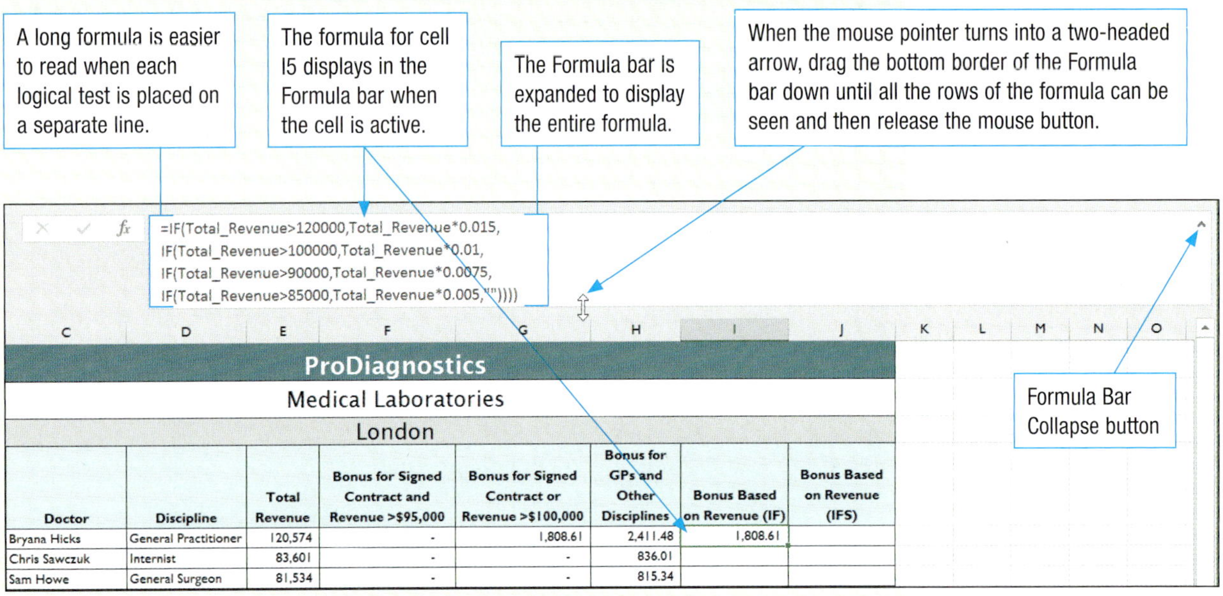

8. Double-click the fill handle in cell I5.

   The formula is copied down into cell I24.

9. Copy the formula from cell H25 across into cell I25.

   The result *12,483.86* (the total of the individual bonuses) displays in cell I25.

10. Click the Save button on the Quick Access Toolbar.

Model Answer

▸ **Know This** about the IFS function

— The result of the IFS function must test true; in contrast, the last argument of the IF function tests false.

— Table 9.8 explains the syntax and arguments for the IFS function.

— The IFS function can test up to 127 conditions.

— If you can change the last argument to test true, then the IFS function can be used instead of a nested IF function.

Table 9.8 IFS Function Syntax and Arguments

Syntax
=IFS(logical_test1,value_if_true1,logical_test2,value_if_true2,...).

Argument	Required or Optional?	Description
range	Required	The data that will be tested (where to look)
criteria	Required	The conditional test that must be met (what to look for)

— If no conditions test true, the function returns the error code #N/A.

— Unlike a nested IF function, an IFS function does not require each argument to be enclosed in parentheses. This difference makes the IFS function easier to read (see Figure 9.18).

Figure 9.18 IFS Function

```
=IFS(Total_Revenue>120000,Total_Revenue*0.0175,
Total_Revenue>100000,Total_Revenue*0.01,
Total_Revenue>90000,Total_Revenue*0.0075,
Total_Revenue>85000,Total_Revenue*0.005,
Total_Revenue<85000,"")
```

Each argument is displayed on a separate line and is separated by a comma. The IFS function does not require each argument to be enclosed in parentheses.

On the Job

Task 9.4e Using the IFS Function

In the fifth bonus system scenario, Kaelan wants to use the same bonus structure as he did in the fourth bonus system scenario but to increase the bonus percentage for doctors who send PDML revenue of more than $120,000 to 1.75%. Use the IFS function to calculate this new scenario. To save time and reduce the chance for data entry errors, copy the formula from cell I5 across into J5, modify the formula to use the IFS function, change the percentage, use the fill handle to copy the formula, and then use copy and paste to enter a formula that calculates the total of all the individual bonus payments. When you are done, collapse the Formula bar so that more of the worksheet can be seen.

1. With the Discipline Summary worksheet active and the Formulas tab active, copy the formula from cell I5 across into cell J5.
2. Click in cell J5, place the insertion point after the first *IF* in the Formula bar, and then type S.
3. Delete each instance of *IF(* in the Formula bar.

   Three instances of *IF(* are deleted.
4. Change *0.015* to *0.0175* at the end of the first line.

   The bonus percentage is increased for doctors who send more than $120,000 in revenue to PDML.
5. Place the insertion point after the comma that follows *0.005* in the last line in the Formula bar and then type Total_Revenue<85000,.

   The value_if_false has been replaced with the value if_true. Be sure to type the comma at the end of the expression. The last line in the Formula bar displays as *Total_Revenue>85000,Total_Revenue*0.005,Total_Revenue<85000,""))))*.

6. Delete three of the closing parentheses.

   The last line in the Formula bar displays as *Total_Revenue>85000,Total_Revenue*0.005,Total_Revenue<85000,"")*.

7. Place the insertion point after the comma that follows 0.005 and then press Alt + Enter.

   The last argument appears on a separate line: *Total_Revenue<85000,"")*.

8. Press the Enter key.

   The result *2,110.05* displays in cell J5 and cell J6 is active.

9. Click in cell J5 and then double-click the fill handle to copy the formula from cell J5 down into cell J24.

10. Hover the mouse pointer near the bottom of the Formula bar until the pointer turns into a two-headed arrow, click and hold down the left mouse button, drag the bottom of the bar up until only one line of the formula displays in the Formula bar, and then release the mouse button.

    More of the worksheet displays.

11. Copy the formula from cell I25 across into cell J25.

    The result *12,785.29* (the total of the individual bonuses) displays in cell J25.

12. Click the Save button on the Quick Access Toolbar.

Model Answer

9.5 Using the Evaluate Formula Feature

MOS Expert 3.5.4

Tutorial

Evaluating a Formula

Formulas containing nested functions can get quite long and complicated. If you find such a formula in a worksheet created by someone else—or even created by you at an earlier time—it may be difficult to figure out what the formula means. You can use the **Evaluate Formula** feature to discover how any formula calculates a result. This feature evaluates the parts of the formula in the order that the result is calculated.

▸ Know This about evaluating a formula

— To evaluate a formula, start by clicking in the cell containing the formula and then click the Evaluate Formula button in the Formula Auditing group on the Formulas tab (see Figure 9.19) to display the Evaluate Formula dialog box.

— The formula displays in the *Evaluation* text box and the part of the formula to be evaluated is underlined. Click the Evaluate button to look at the value of the underlined reference. Continue evaluating the formula until each part has been evaluated.

— The result of each evaluation is displayed in italics in the *Evaluation* text box.

— If a cell reference or defined name is included in the underlined part of the formula, click the Step In button to display the cell value or cell reference, respectively. Click the Step Out button to return to evaluating the formula.

— The Step In button is grayed out if the underlined part of the formula does not contain a cell reference or a defined name.
— The Step Out button becomes active when the Step In button has been clicked.
— Only one formula can be evaluated at a time.
— When the evaluation has finished, the Evaluate button turns into the Restart button. To repeat the evaluation, click the Restart button.
— Excel will stop evaluating a formula and calculate the result when a logical test returns the value True.

Figure 9.19 Formula Auditing Group

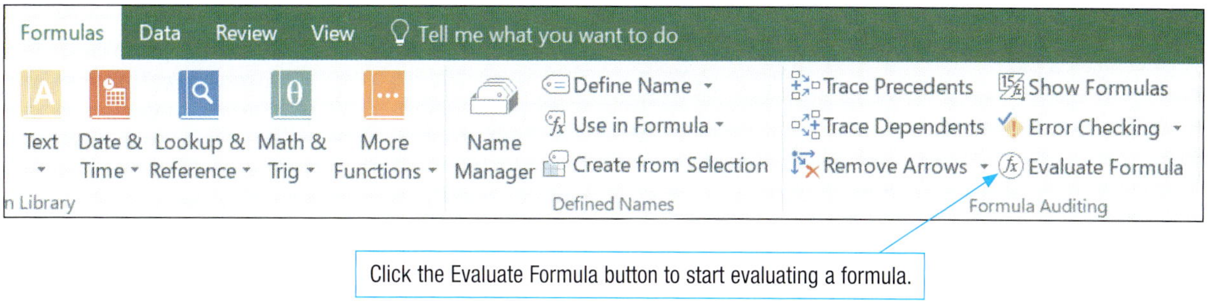

On the Job

Task 9.5 Evaluating a Formula

Kaelan wants to be sure the formula you entered in Task 9.4e calculates the correct results. He's especially concerned about the results for doctors who will not receive a bonus. Since Excel will stop evaluating this formula when a logical test returns the value True, it's beneficial to evaluate a formula where the last argument returns True. Use the Evaluate Formula feature to evaluate the formula. When you come to the first defined name *Total_Revenue*, use the Step In button to verify that the range E5:E24 is being used in the formula.

1. With the Discipline Summary worksheet active and the Formulas tab active, click in cell J6.
2. Click the Evaluate Formula button in the Formula Auditing group.

   The Evaluate Formula dialog box displays (see Figure 9.20). The formula appears in the *Evaluation* text box, the first part of the formula to be evaluated is underlined, and the Step In button is available.
3. Click the Step In button.

   The text *'Discipline Summary'!$E$5:$E$24* appears in the *Step In* text box (see Figure 9.21). This is the range referenced by the defined name *Total_Revenue*.
4. Click the Step Out button.

   The value *83601* replaces the defined name *Total_Revenue* in the formula and is italicized. This represents the value to be used from the defined range. The next part of the formula to be evaluated, the logical test *83601>120000*, is underlined. The Step In button is grayed out (not available) because the underlined part of the formula is not a cell reference or defined name.

Figure 9.20 Evaluate Formula Dialog Box with the Formula Displayed and the Step In Button Available

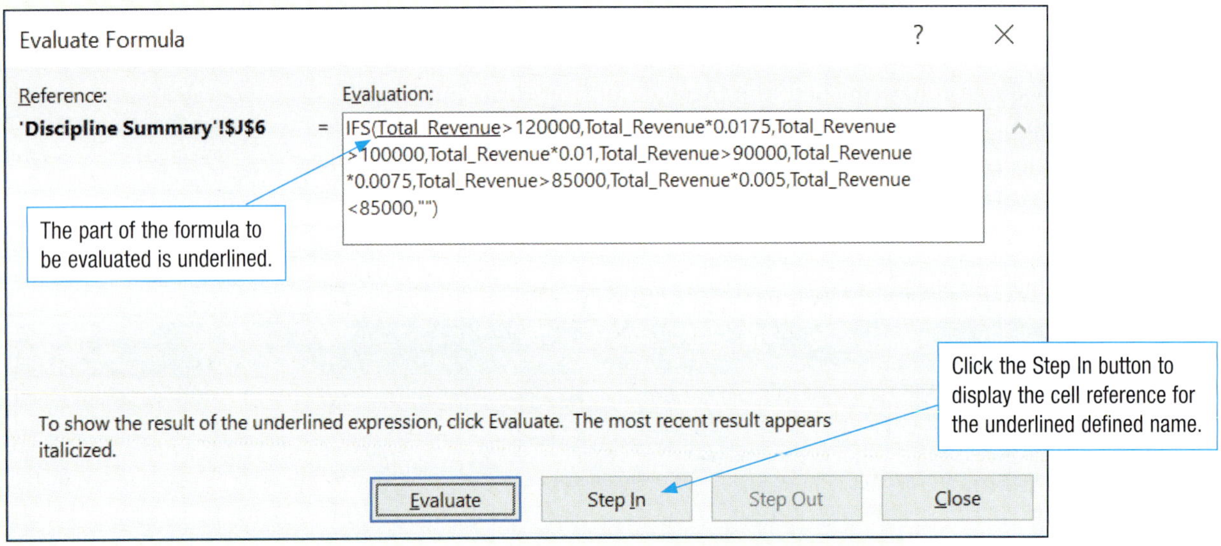

Figure 9.21 Evaluate Formula Dialog Box with the Step In Text Box Displayed and the Step Out Button Available

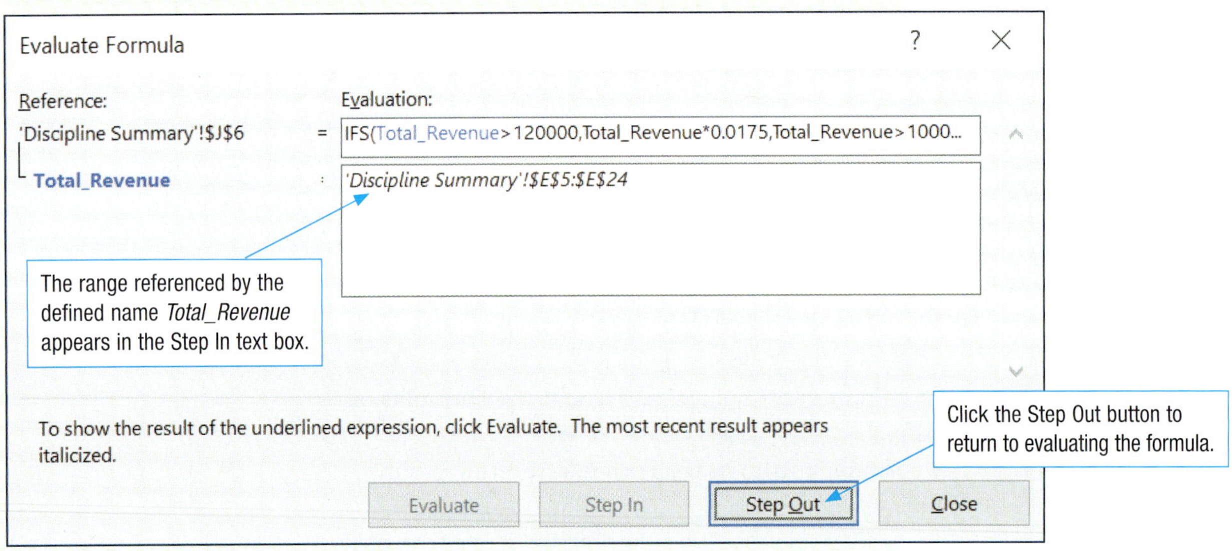

5. Click the Evaluate button.

The text *FALSE* replaces the first logical test, *83601>120000*, in the formula and is italicized. Excel has evaluated the first logical test and determined that it returns a false result. The next part of the formula to be evaluated, the defined name *Total_Revenue*, is underlined and the Step In button is available. You confirmed that the defined name was correct in Step 2. You do not need to do that again in the same formula, so you do not need to click the Step In button.

6. Click the Evaluate button.

   The value *83601* replaces the defined name *Total_Revenue* and is italicized. The operation *83,601*0.0175* is underlined.

7. Click the Evaluate button.

   The value *1463.0175* replaces the operation *83601*0.0175* and is italicized. The defined name *Total_Revenue* is underlined.

8. Click the Evaluate button.

   The value *83601* replaces the defined name *Total_Revenue* and is italicized. The logical test *83601>100000* is underlined.

9. Click the Evaluate button.

   The result *FALSE* replaces the second logical test, *83601>100000*, and is italicized. Excel has evaluated the second logical test and determined that it returns a false result. The defined name *Total_Revenue* is underlined.

10. Click the Evaluate button.

    The value *83601* replaces the defined name *Total_Revenue* and is italicized. The operation *83,601*0.01* is underlined.

11. Click the Evaluate button.

    The value *836.01* replaces the operation *83601*0.01* and is italicized. The defined name *Total_Revenue* is underlined.

12. Click the Evaluate button.

    The value *83601* replaces the defined name *Total_Revenue* and is italicized. The logical test *83601>90000* is underlined.

13. Click the Evaluate button.

    The result *FALSE* replaces the third logical test, *83601>90000*, and is italicized. Excel has evaluated the third logical test and determined that it returns a false result. The next instance of the defined name *Total_Revenue* is underlined.

14. Click the Evaluate button.

    The value *83601* replaces the defined name *Total_Revenue* and is italicized. The operation *83,601*0.0075* is now underlined.

15. Click the Evaluate button.

    The value *627.0075* replaces the operation *83601*0.0075* and is italicized. The next instance of the defined name *Total_Revenue* is underlined.

16. Click the Evaluate button.

    The value *83601* replaces the defined name *Total_Revenue* and is italicized. The logical test *83601>85000* is underlined.

17. Click the Evaluate button.

    The result *FALSE* replaces the fourth logical test, *83601>85000*, and is italicized. Excel has evaluated the fourth logical test and determined that it returns a false result. The next instance of the defined name *Total_Revenue* is underlined.

18. Click the Evaluate button.

    The value *83601* replaces the defined name *Total_Revenue* and is italicized. The operation *83601*0.005* is now underlined.

19. Click the Evaluate button.

    The value *418.005* replaces the operation *83601*0.005* and is italicized. The next instance of the defined name *Total_Revenue* is now underlined.

20. Click the Evaluate button.

    The value *83601* replaces the defined name *Total_Revenue* and is italicized. The logical test *83601<85000* is underlined.

21. Click the Evaluate button.

    The result *TRUE* replaces the last logical test, *83601<85000*, and is italicized. The entire function *IFS(FALSE,1463.0175,FALSE,836.01, FALSE,627.0075,FALSE,418.005,TRUE,"")* displays in the *Evaluation* text box and is underlined.

22. Click the Evaluate button.

    The *Evaluation* text box is empty because Excel has determined that the last logical test returns a true result, and the cell should be left empty as indicated by the pair of double quotation marks. The Restart button appears in place of the Evaluate button.

23. If you want to review Steps 3–22, click the Restart button. If not, proceed to Step 24.
24. Click the Close button.

    The Evaluate Formula dialog box closes. No changes have been made to the worksheet.

25. Leave the workbook open and the Discipline Summary worksheet active for the next task.

9.6 Using the VLOOKUP Function

MOS Expert 3.2.1

Tutorial

Using the VLOOKUP Function

A **Lookup & Reference function** is used to look up values in a range (called a **lookup range**). For example, the VLOOKUP function, which is a Lookup & Reference function, can be used in an employee worksheet, where each new hire is assigned a salary grid rating based on education and years of work experience (see Figure 9.22). The starting salary can be looked up in a range of cells that contain the salary grid rating with the corresponding salary. The salary can be returned in the formula cell by looking up the employee's salary grid rating. Being able to look up a value automates data entry in a large worksheet. When used properly, Lookup & Reference functions can prevent inaccuracies caused by data entry errors.

The **VLOOKUP function** looks up a value in the leftmost column of a table organized in a vertical order, and then returns a value that is an approximate or exact match to a corresponding value from the table. In the employee worksheet example, the **lookup table** contains the salary grid numbers with corresponding starting salaries. In the formula, range names have been included. The defined name *Rating* references the values in column E, and the defined name *SalGrid* represents the lookup table in the range H4:I7.

Figure 9.22 VLOOKUP Function in an Employee Worksheet

The error code #N/A appears in cell F6 because the VLOOKUP formula is an exact match and E is not in the lookup table.

	A	B	C	D	E	F	G	H	I
1	**Employment Professionals**								
2	**New Hires**							**Reference Table**	
3	**Employee ID**	**First Name**	**Last Name**	**Hire Date**	**Salary Grid Rating**	**Starting Salary**		**Salary Grid Rating**	**Starting Salary**
4	ZI8996	Wanda	Arthur	10/25/2018	B	$ 43,545		A	$ 49,214
5	AE4743	Tina	Babin	10/27/2018	A	49,214		B	$ 43,545
6	AE4744	Elizabeth	Bacus	10/29/2018	E	#N/A		C	$ 38,454
7	AE4745	Ally	Boucher	10/31/2018	C	38,454		D	$ 34,879
8	PR9065	Ashley	Bruno	11/2/2018	D	34,879			
9	AE4632	Jessica	Busko	11/4/2018	A	49,214			
10	PR9070	Sidney	Caron	11/6/2018	B	43,545			
11	AE4709	Erin	Cerva	11/8/2018	B	43,545			
12	PR9061	Cora	Cook	11/10/2018	C	38,454			
13	AE4682	Tracy	Davis	11/12/2018	C	38,454			
14	AE4712	Bria	Galvez	11/14/2018	B	43,5			
15	AE4684	Gabriela	Gertz	11/16/2018	A	49,2			
16	AE4717	Celeste	Howe	11/18/2018	B	43,5			
17	PR9063	Violet	Kendall	11/20/2018	B	43,545			

The range E4:E17 has the defined name *Rating*.

The lookup table has the defined name *SalGrid*.

The first column of data in the lookup table is sorted in ascending order, with A less than B, and so on.

The formula in the cells in column F is *=VLOOKUP(Rating,SalGrid,2,False)*. This formula populates the range F4:F17 by matching the salary grid rating number in column E in the lookup table named *SalGrid*. For example, the formula in cell F4 tells Excel to look up the value in cell E4 (B) in the first column of the lookup table. Excel then enters the lookup table at the top and asks, "Is A equal to B?" The answer is false, so Excel moves to the next row in the table and asks, "Is B equal to B?" The answer is true, and the third argument of the formula (2) tells Excel to take the corresponding value in the second column ($43,545) and returns it as the result.

▸ **Know This** about the VLOOKUP function

- Table 9.9 explains the syntax and arguments for the VLOOKUP function.
- A formula containing a VLOOKUP function can be set to look for an exact match or an approximate match.
- In an **exact match lookup**, Excel searches down the first column of the lookup table for a value that matches the *lookup_value* argument. When Excel finds a match, it returns the value from the same row in the column specified in the *col_index_num* argument. The employee worksheet example is an exact match because there are only four salary ratings: A, B, C, and D (see Figure 9.22). The data *E* was accidentally entered in cell E6, and the formula containing the VLOOKUP function in cell F6 returns the error code #N/A.
- In an **approximate match lookup**, Excel searches down the first column of the lookup table for the last category in which the known value fits. For example, if a lookup table (see Figure 9.23) is used to enter letter grades in a grade workbook, and Excel needs to return the letter grade for the value 68, Excel will look for the last category in

which the value existed. Excel will enter the lookup table at the first row and ask, "Is 68 greater than or equal to 0?" The answer is true, so Excel moves to the next row and asks, "Is 68 greater than or equal to 50?" The answer is true, so Excel moves to the next row and asks, "Is 68 greater than or equal to 60?" The answer is true, so Excel moves to the next row and asks, "Is 68 greater than or equal to 70?" This time the answer is false, so Excel moves back to the last category in which the answer was true (the row containing the number grade 60) and returns the letter grade result C.

Table 9.9 VLOOKUP Function Syntax and Arguments

Syntax
=*VLOOKUP(lookup_value,table_array,col_index_num,[range_lookup]).*

Argument	Required or Optional?	Description
lookup_value	Required	The value that Excel should search for in the lookup table (*table_array*) (what to look for). Enter a value, a cell or range reference, a defined name, or a structured reference.
table_array	Required	The lookup table that Excel should search (or where to look). Enter a defined name, an absolute range reference, or a table name. Do not include column headers. The table can contain text, numbers, or logical values.
col_index_num	Required	The number of the lookup table column that contains the data that will be placed in the formula cell.
range_lookup	Optional	A logical value that tells Excel whether to find approximate matches or exact matches. This argument is optional. Enter *TRUE* to instruct Excel to find approximate matches for the lookup value. Enter *FALSE* to instruct Excel to return only exact matches to the lookup value. If this argument is left out of the formula, Excel assumes the value is *TRUE*, which means that if Excel does not find an exact match, it returns the value for the last category into which the known value fits.

Figure 9.23 Lookup Table for an Approximate Match

Number Grade	Letter Grade
0	F
50	D
60	C
70	B
80	A

Data entered in the first column of the lookup table must be sorted in ascending order.

— For the VLOOKUP function to work properly, the first column of the lookup table (which contains the **lookup value**) must be sorted in ascending order.

— Do not include the lookup table headers in the *table_array* argument.
— To insert the VLOOKUP function, click the Lookup & Reference button in the Function Library group, click the *VLOOKUP* option, and then enter data in the arguments.

On the Job

Task 9.6 Using the VLOOKUP Function to Find an Approximate Match

Kaelan has designed a new system that uses the following guidelines to assign each PDML location a rating based on the amount of revenue it contributes to the company:

Revenue	Rating
up to, but not including, $100,000	D
equal to $100,000 and up to, but not including, $200,000	C
equal to $200,000 and up to, but not including, $300,000	B
equal to $300,000 and up to, but not including, $400,000	A
equal to $400,000 and above	A+

Kaelan wants you to add these ratings in the Location Specialty worksheet. In the worksheet, he has provided a vertical lookup table with the defined name *VTable* (see Figure 9.24). In cell L5, enter a formula that uses the VLOOKUP function to return the location rating, using the defined name *Revenue* as the value to look up and the defined name *VTable* as the lookup table. The data to be returned is found in the second column of the lookup table. Instruct Excel to return approximate matches. Use the fill handle to copy the formula.

Figure 9.24 Vertical Lookup Table with the Defined Name *VTable*

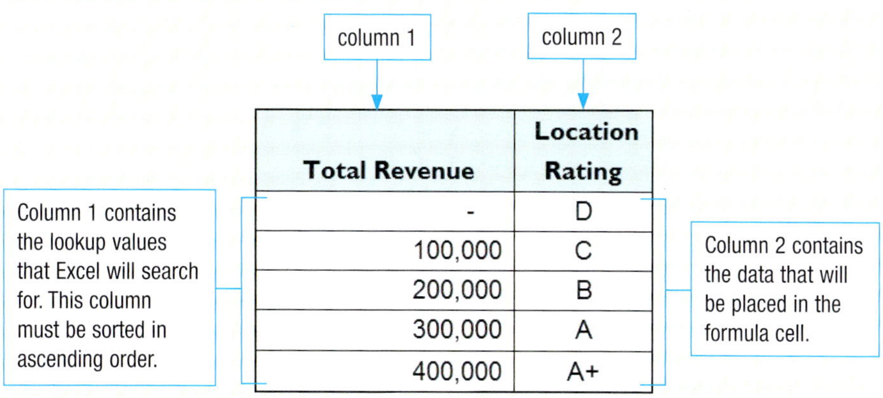

1. Click the Location Specialty sheet tab and then click in cell L5.
2. Click the Lookup & Reference button in the Function Library group on the Formulas tab and then click the *VLOOKUP* option.

   The Function Arguments dialog box displays with the insertion point in the *Lookup_value* text box (see Figure 9.25).

Figure 9.25 VLOOKUP Function Arguments Dialog Box

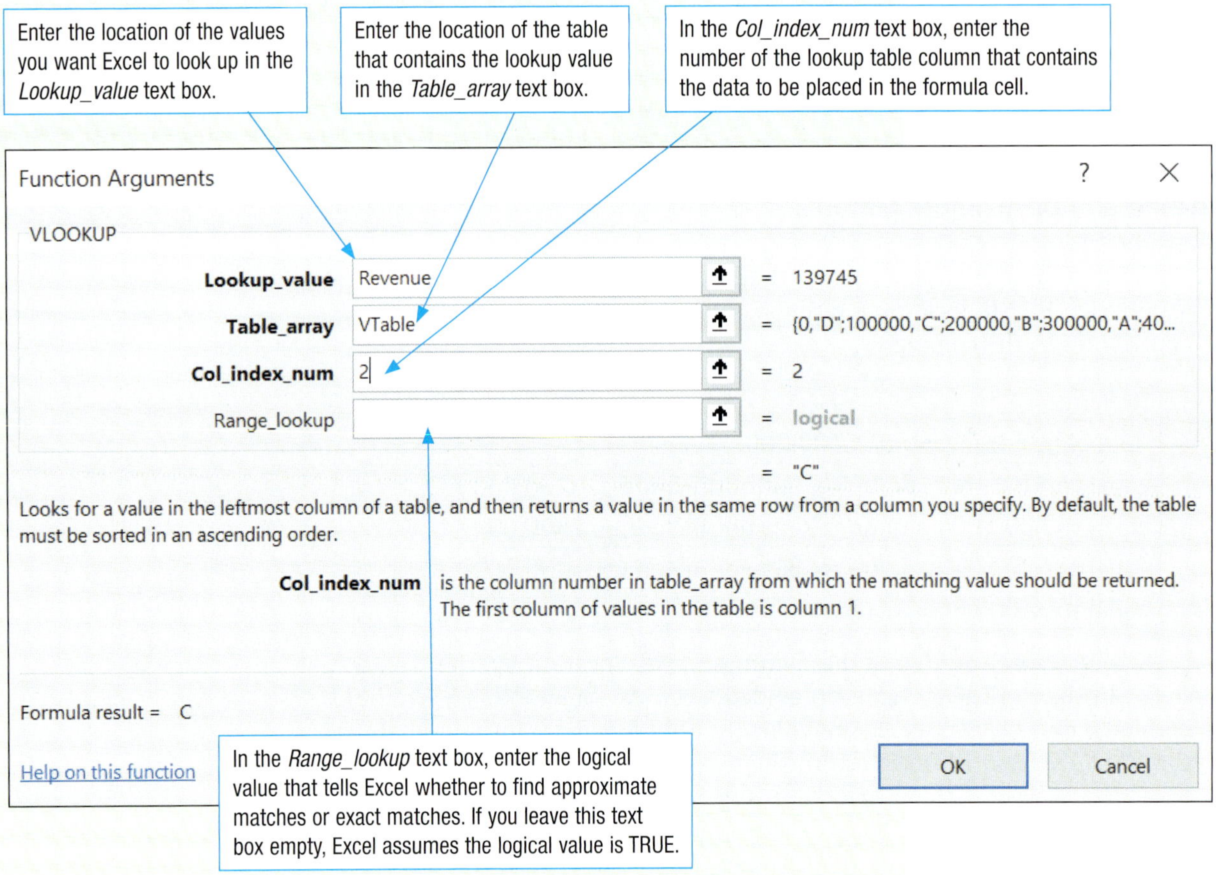

3. Type Revenue and then press the Tab key.

   The defined name *Revenue* appears in the *Lookup_value* text box. This is the reference for the range containing the values Excel will look up. The insertion point is in the *Table_array* text box.

4. Type VTable and then press the Tab key.

   The defined name *VTable* appears in the *Table_array* text box. This is the reference for the range containing the lookup table. The insertion point is in the *Col_index_num* text box.

5. Type 2.

   The value *2* appears in the *Col_index_num* text box. This is the number of the lookup table column that contains the data to be placed in the formula in cell L5. The insertion point is in the *Range_lookup* text box.

6. Leave the *Range_lookup* text box empty.

   When you leave the text box empty, Excel assumes the value is TRUE.

7. Click the OK button.

   The result *C* displays in cell L5. Excel compared the first value in the Revenue range, which is 139,745, with the first value in column 1 of the lookup table, which is 0. ***Note:*** *The Accounting format has been applied to column 1 of the lookup table, so the value* 0 *displays as a dash.*

The value 139,745 is greater than 0, so Excel went to the next value in column 1 of the lookup table, which is 100,000. The value 139,745 is greater than 100,000, so Excel went to the next value in column 1, which is 200,000. The value 139,745 is *not* greater than 200,000, so Excel went back to the previous value in column 1 (100,000) and then entered the corresponding value from column 2 (C) in cell L5. The formula is *=VLOOKUP(Revenue,VTable,2)*.

8. Double-click the fill handle in cell L5 to copy the formula from cell L5 down into cell L34.

   The range L5:L34 is filled with location ratings.

9. Click the Save button on the Quick Access Toolbar.

Model Answer

9.7 Using the HLOOKUP Function

MOS Expert 3.2.2

Tutorial

Using the HLOOKUP Function

The **HLOOKUP function** is similar to the VLOOKUP function but looks up data that is arranged horizontally rather than vertically. The contents of the worksheet in Figure 9.26 are the same as the contents of the worksheet in Figure 9.22 (on page 417) except that the lookup table is arranged horizontally rather than vertically.

Figure 9.26 HLOOKUP Function in an Employee Worksheet

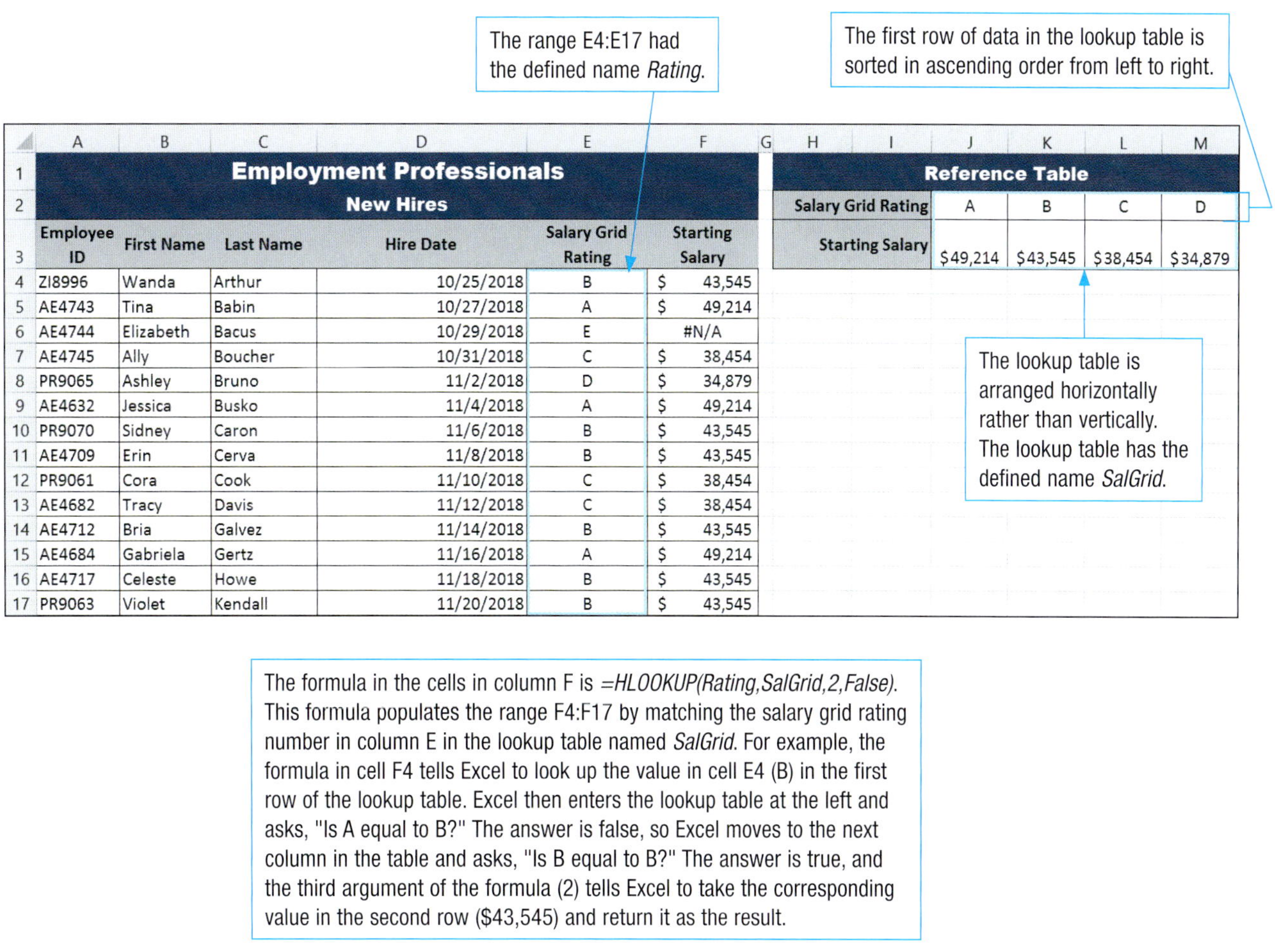

	A	B	C	D	E	F
1	Employment Professionals					
2	New Hires					
3	Employee ID	First Name	Last Name	Hire Date	Salary Grid Rating	Starting Salary
4	ZI8996	Wanda	Arthur	10/25/2018	B	$ 43,545
5	AE4743	Tina	Babin	10/27/2018	A	$ 49,214
6	AE4744	Elizabeth	Bacus	10/29/2018	E	#N/A
7	AE4745	Ally	Boucher	10/31/2018	C	$ 38,454
8	PR9065	Ashley	Bruno	11/2/2018	D	$ 34,879
9	AE4632	Jessica	Busko	11/4/2018	A	$ 49,214
10	PR9070	Sidney	Caron	11/6/2018	B	$ 43,545
11	AE4709	Erin	Cerva	11/8/2018	B	$ 43,545
12	PR9061	Cora	Cook	11/10/2018	C	$ 38,454
13	AE4682	Tracy	Davis	11/12/2018	C	$ 38,454
14	AE4712	Bria	Galvez	11/14/2018	B	$ 43,545
15	AE4684	Gabriela	Gertz	11/16/2018	A	$ 49,214
16	AE4717	Celeste	Howe	11/18/2018	B	$ 43,545
17	PR9063	Violet	Kendall	11/20/2018	B	$ 43,545

	H–I	J	K	L	M
1	Reference Table				
2	Salary Grid Rating	A	B	C	D
3	Starting Salary	$49,214	$43,545	$38,454	$34,879

▸ Know This about the HLOOKUP function

— The syntax for the HLOOKUP function is *=HLOOKUP(lookup_value,table_array,row_index_num[,range_lookup])*.

— The arguments are the same as for the VLOOKUP function except the *col_index_num* argument is replaced by the *row_index_num* argument, which is the number of the lookup table row that contains the data that will be placed in the formula cell.

— Excel searches across the first row of the table for a value that matches the *lookup_value* argument. When Excel finds a match, it returns to the formula cell the value from the same column in the row specified in the *row_index_num* argument.

— To insert the HLOOKUP function, click the Lookup & Reference button in the Function Library group, click the *HLOOKUP* option, and then enter data in the arguments.

▸ Know This about exact match lookups

— If a lookup_value does not exactly match one of the values in the first row of a horizontal lookup table or in the first column of a vertical lookup table, the error code #N/A error is returned (see Figure 9.22 on page 417).

— Enter *FALSE* as the *range_lookup* argument to instruct Excel to return only exact matches to the lookup value.

Reminder
The error code #N/A means that an argument has been left out of a function.

On the Job

Task 9.7 Using the HLOOKUP Function

The Ontario Health Insurance Plan (OHIP) uses codes to identify different medical disciplines. Kaelan wants you to add those codes in the *OHIP Code* column in the Doctor Summary worksheet. In the worksheet, he has provided a horizontal lookup table with the defined name *OHIP*. Enter a formula that uses the HLOOKUP function to compare the values in the first row of the horizontal lookup table with the values in the Discipline range in the worksheet. Instruct Excel to return only exact matches because each discipline must match a lookup value. Use the fill handle to copy the formula.

1. Click the Doctor Summary sheet tab and then click in cell D5.
2. Click the Lookup & Reference button in the Function Library group on the Formulas tab and then click the *HLOOKUP* option.

   The Function Arguments dialog box displays with the insertion point in the *Lookup_value* text box (see Figure 9.27 for the completed dialog box).
3. Type C5 and then press the Tab key.

   The cell reference *C5* appears in the *Lookup_value* text box. The insertion point is in the *Table_array* text box.
4. Type OHIP and then press the Tab key.

   The defined name *OHIP* appears in the *Table_array* text box. The insertion point is in the *Row_index_num* text box.

Figure 9.27 HLOOKUP Function Arguments Dialog Box

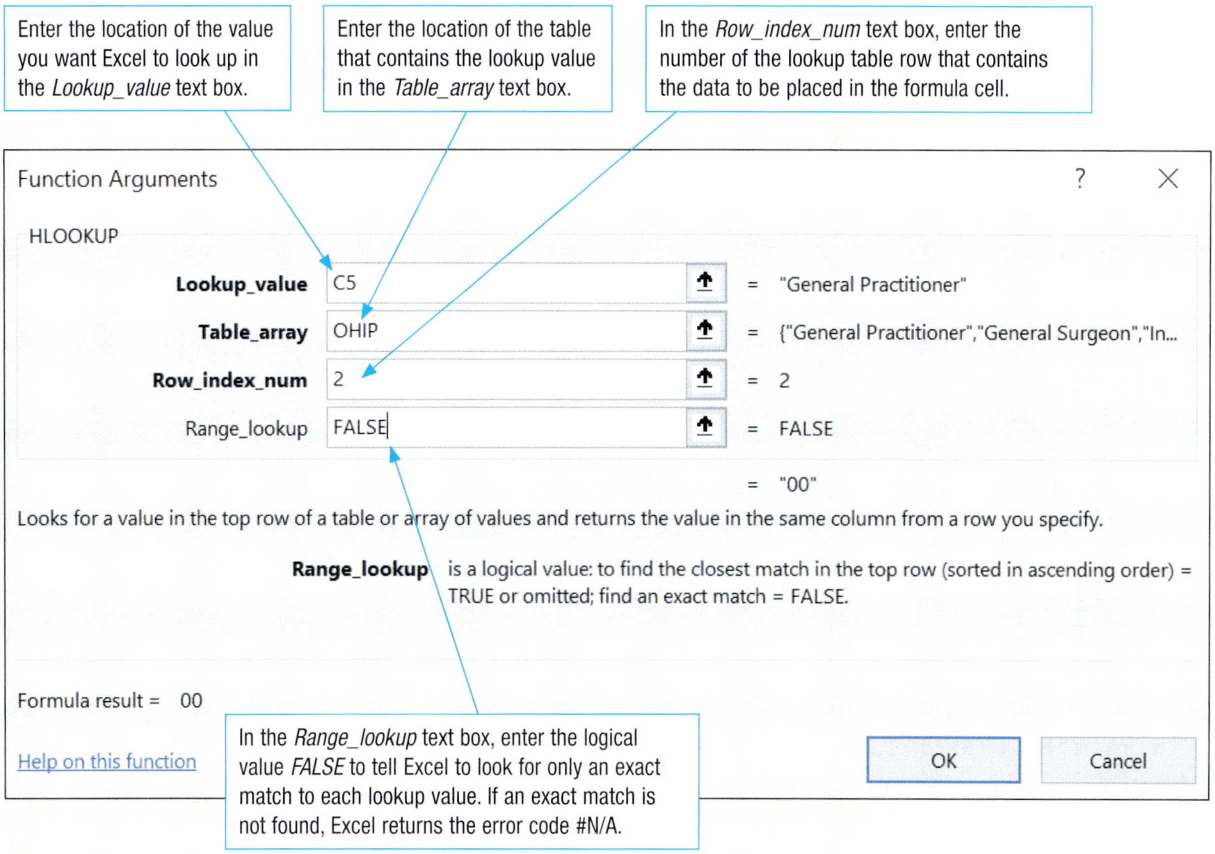

5. Type 2 and then press the Tab key.

   The value 2 appears in the *Row_index_num* text box. The insertion point is in the *Range_lookup* text box.

6. Type FALSE.

   The logical value *FALSE* appears in the *Range_lookup* text box. This value instructs Excel to look for an exact match to each lookup value.

7. Click the OK button.

   The dialog box closes and the code *00* appears in cell D5. This is the code for the General Practitioner. Excel compared the first value in the Discipline range, which is General Practitioner, with the first value in row 1 of the lookup table, which is General Practitioner. Since these values match exactly, Excel returns the value 00 in cell D5. The formula is *=HLOOKUP(C5,OHIP,2,FALSE)*.

8. Double-click the fill handle in cell D5 to copy the formula from cell D5 down into cell D24.

   The range D5:D24 is filled with location ratings. The error code *#N/A* appears in cell D8 because the value Excel found in cell C8 (Cardiac Surgeon) does not exactly match any of the lookup values in the lookup table. You will fix this error in Task 9.8.

9. Click the Save button on the Quick Access Toolbar.

Model Answer

9.8 Using the IFERROR Function

If an error occurs when Excel returns the result of a formula, Excel displays an error code in the result cell. For example, in Task 9.7, the error code *#N/A* displays in cell D8 because when Excel looked up the value in cell C8, it found Cardiac Surgeon, which does not appear in the lookup table. An Excel error code alerts you to a problem with the formula, but it may not provide useful information for fixing the error. You can use the **IFERROR function** from the *Lookup & Reference* category to display a value or text, instead of an error code, in the **result cell** (the cell containing the value returned by a formula calculation). The value or text can provide information that can be used to fix the error. For example, if you are using a VLOOKUP formula to categorize inventory and some part numbers do not fit any of the specified categories, you can enter *Miscellaneous* as the *value_if_error* argument to have Excel display the text *Miscellaneous* (instead of the error code *#N/A*) for those part numbers.

Tutorial
Nesting a Function in the IFERROR Function

Reminder
Table 2.7 on page 90 lists common error codes.

▸ Know This about the IFERROR function

— Table 9.10 explains the syntax and arguments for the IFERROR function.
— When another function is nested within the IFERROR function, the other function becomes the the *value* argument for the IFERROR funtion (see Figure 9.28).
— To insert the IFERROR function, click the Logical button in the Function Library group, click the *IFERROR* option, and then enter the data in the arguments.
— To insert the IFERROR function around an existing formula, type IFERROR(after the equals sign (=), press the End key, type a comma followed by the value to be returned if an error is found, and then type a closing parenthesis.

Table 9.10 IFERROR Function Syntax and Arguments

Syntax
=IFERROR(value,value_if_error)

Argument	Required or Optional?	Description
value	Required	The value Excel should check for errors (what to look for)
value_if_error	Required	The value that will be returned if an error is found

On the Job
Task 9.8 Nesting an HLOOKUP Function in an IFERROR Function

Kaelan notices the error code #N/A in the Doctor Summary worksheet and realizes that the discipline Cardiac Surgeon is not included in the horizontal lookup table. He asks you to edit the formula containing the HLOOKUP function so it will return the OHIP code 99 for any discipline not listed in the lookup table. Nest the HLOOKUP function in an IFERROR function to create a formula that returns the results Kaelan is looking for.

1. With the Doctor Summary worksheet active and the Formulas tab active, click in cell D5.
2. Place the insertion point after the equals sign (=) in the Formula bar, type IFERROR(, and then press the End key.
   Pressing the End key places the insertion point at the end of the formula in the Formula bar.

3. Type ,99) and then press the Enter key.
4. Click in cell D5, click at the end of the formula in the Formula bar, and then review the formula that displays in the Formula bar (see Figure 9.28).

   Clicking at the end of the formula in the Formula bar color codes the cell references and defined names in the formula and fills the corresponding cells in the worksheet with the same fill color.
5. Double-click the fill handle in cell D5 to copy the formula from cell D5 down into cell D24.

   The range D5:D24 is filled with location ratings. The error previously displayed in cell D8 is replaced with the code *99*.
6. Click the Save button on the Quick Access Toolbar.

Figure 9.28 Revised Formula with the HLOOKUP Function Nested in an IFERROR Function

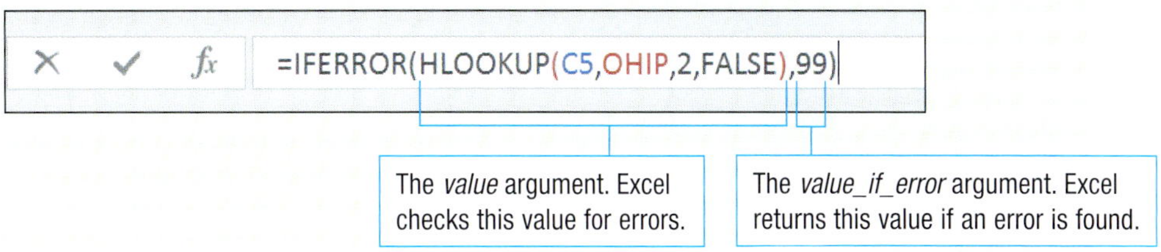

Model Answer

9.9 Using the TRANSPOSE Function

Tutorial

Using the TRANSPOSE Function

In some cases, the data in a worksheet is arranged in a way that is not suitable for performing the required analysis. For example, it may be easier to have the years or months as row headers instead of as column headers. Use the **TRANSPOSE function** from the *Lookup & Reference* category to convert columns to rows and rows to columns. A formula containing the TRANSPOSE function is an array formula.

▸ Know This about array formulas

— An **array** is a collection of data in a single row, a single column, or multiple rows and columns.
— To enter an **array formula**, such as *=TRANSPOSE(A5:E10)*, you must start by selecting the destination cells that will hold the formula results.
— To finish entering an array formula, press Ctrl + Shift + Enter.
— When you finish entering an array formula, Excel places curly brackets ({}) around the formula and enters the formula in every cell of the range into which the data is copied (see Figure 9.29).
— Curly brackets ({}) around a formula indicate that it is an array formula.
— If a cell contains an array formula, the contents of that cell cannot be changed by typing directly in the cell. If a user tries to type in the cell, a message displays, stating that you cannot change part of an array.
— An array formula can be moved or deleted as a whole, but you cannot move or delete a portion of the formula.
— Each cell in the array contains the same formula.

Figure 9.29 Worksheet Containing the TRANSPOSE Function

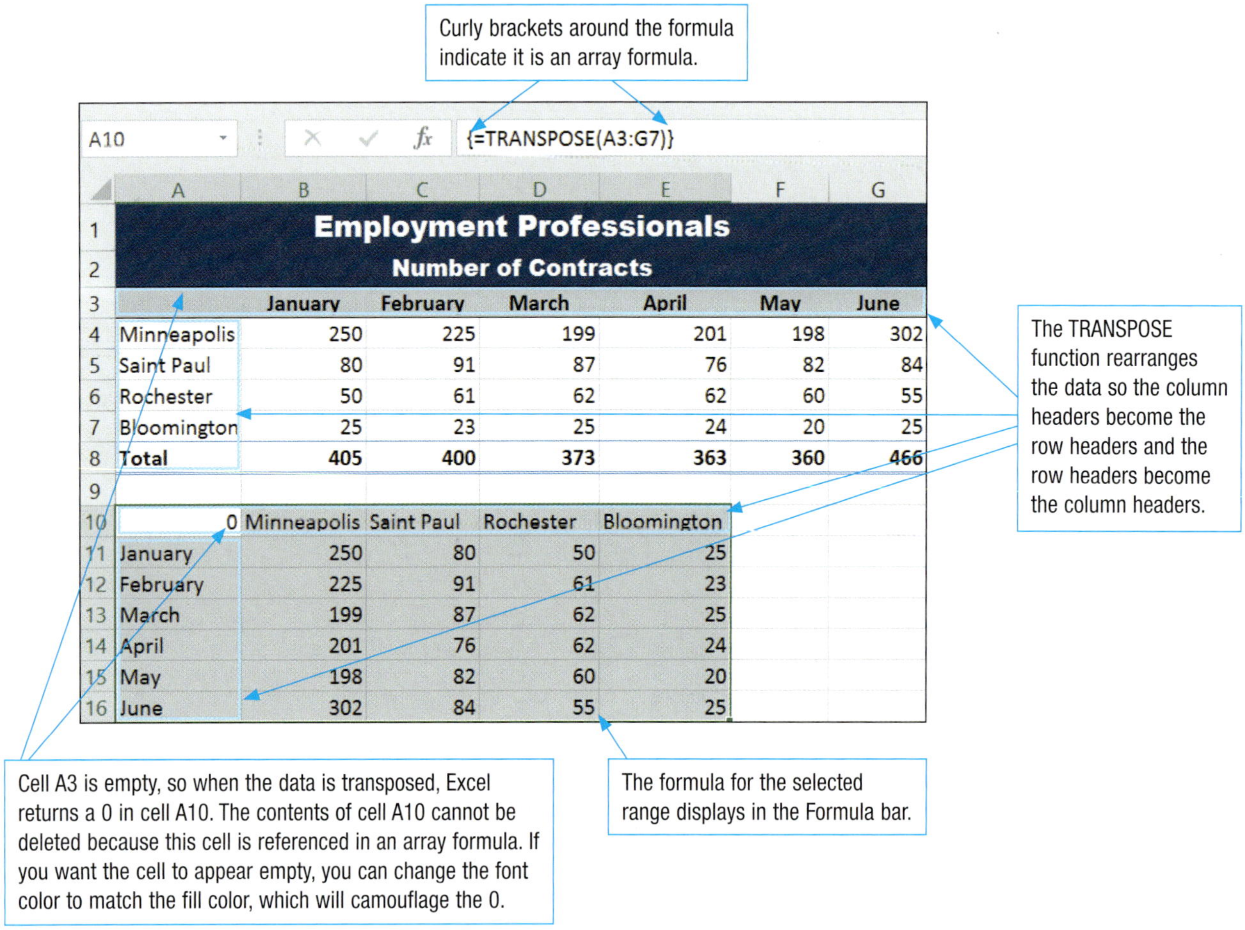

▸ **Know This** about the TRANSPOSE function

— The syntax for the TRANSPOSE function is *=TRANSPOSE(array)*.

— The TRANSPOSE function rearranges the data so the column headers become the row headers and the row headers become the column headers (see Figure 9.29).

— The *array* argument defines the range of cells that will be transposed, also called the *original range*.

— Any formatting applied to the cells in the original range is not copied to the cells in the transposed range.

— If a cell in the original range is empty, Excel returns a 0 in the corresponding cell in the transposed range.

▸ **Know This** about inserting the TRANSPOSE function

— To insert the TRANSPOSE function using the Lookup & Reference button in the Function Library group on the Formulas tab, select the cell or range where the data is to be copied, click the Lookup & Reference button, click the *TRANSPOSE* option at the drop-down list, type or type and point to enter the range that will be transposed in the *Array* text box, and then click the OK button.

— To insert the TRANSPOSE function by typing directly in a cell or the Formula bar, select the range where the data is to be copied, click in the cell

▸ **Know More** ways to transpose data

– Select the range, click the Copy button in the Clipboard group on the Home tab, click the Paste button arrow, and then click the *Transpose* option at the drop-down gallery.

continues...

or the Formula bar, type *=TRANSPOSE(*, type or type and point to enter the range that will be transposed, type *)*, and then press Ctrl + Shift + Enter.

— When you select the range where the data is to be copied, be sure to reverse the number of rows and columns. For example, if the original range has three rows and two columns, the new range needs two rows and three columns.

▶ **Know More** ways to transpose data

...continued

– Before you click the *Transpose* option, a live preview shows how the copied data will be pasted.

On the Job

Task 9.9 Using the TRANSPOSE Function

Kaelan wants the data in the Yearly Comparison worksheet to display with the location numbers across the top, location totals across the bottom, and no totals by year. He wants the new display to have the same formatting as the original display. Use the TRANSPOSE function to complete this task, typing the formula containing the function directly in the Formula bar. Place the transposed data below the current data, with the data for location 1 in column A. Add a total row and cell formatting to meet Kaelan's requirements.

1. Click the Yearly Comparison sheet tab and then select the range A14:F18.

   The original data displays in six rows and five columns. The transposed data will display in five rows and six columns.

2. Click in the Formula bar and then type =TRANSPOSE(A5:E10).

   The *array* argument A5:E10 is the reference for the original range.

3. Press Ctrl + Shift + Enter.

   The data from the original range is copied into the selected range in reverse order—with data from the rows in the original range appearing in columns in the transposed range, and vice versa. The formatting of the cells in the original range is not copied to the cells in the transposed range. The transposed range is selected.

   Cell A14 in the transposed range contains a 0 because cell A5 in the original range is empty. You would like cell A14 in the transposed range to be empty as well. You will fix this using cell formatting in Steps 9 and 10.

Reminder

Press Ctrl + Shift + Enter to finish an array formula.

4. Review the formula that displays in the Formula bar.

   The formula *{=TRANSPOSE(A5:E10)}* displays in the Formula bar when the range is selected because every cell in the range contains the same formula.

5. Click in cell A19 and then type Total.
6. Click in cell B19, insert a function that sums the revenue for location 1, and then copy the formula from cell B19 across into cell F19.
7. Add borders around all the cells in the range A14:F19.
8. Apply the Comma format with no digits after the decimal point in the range B15:F19.
9. Apply bold formatting, center alignment, and the Teal, Accent 3, Lighter 80% fill color (seventh column, second row) to the ranges A14:A19 and B14:F14.
10. Change the font color of cell A14 to Teal, Accent 3, Lighter 80% (seventh column, second row).

    Changing the font color to match the fill color masks the unwanted data that displays in cell A14.

11. Click the Save button on the Quick Access Toolbar.

Model Answer

9.10 Using the MATCH Function

MOS Expert 3.2.3

Tutorial

Using the MATCH Function

The **MATCH function** in the *Lookup & Reference* category tells where to locate a specified value in a range of data. Use the MATCH function instead of the VLOOKUP function when you want to know *where* the value is located, not *what* the value is. The MATCH function searches for a value in a range of cells and then returns the position of that value in the range. For example, if the defined name *Months* contains the values *Jan*, *Feb*, *Mar*, *Apr*, *May*, and *June*, the formula *=MATCH(Apr,Months,0)* returns the value *4* because Apr is the fourth item in the range.

▸ Know This about the MATCH function

— Table 9.11 explains the syntax and arguments for the MATCH function.

— The range of cells in the *lookup_array* argument must be a single row or column.

— If the MATCH function cannot find a match, it returns the error code #N/A.

— To insert the MATCH function, click the Lookup & Reference button in the Function Library group, click the *MATCH* option, and then enter data in the arguments.

Table 9.11 MATCH Function Syntax and Arguments

Syntax
=MATCH(lookup_value,lookup_array,[match_type])

Argument	Required or Optional?	Description
lookup_value	Required	The value that Excel should search for in the lookup range (*lookup_array*) (what to look for). Enter a value or a cell reference to a value.
lookup_array	Required	The lookup range that will be searched. Enter a range address or a defined name.
match_type	Optional	The number 1, 0, or -1, indicating how Excel should match the lookup value with values in the lookup range. Enter *1* to instruct Excel to find the largest value less than or equal to the value in the *lookup_value* argument. The lookup range must be in ascending order. Enter *0* to instruct Excel to find the first exact match. The lookup range may be in any order. Enter *-1* to instruct Excel to find the smallest value greater than or equal to the *lookup_value*. The lookup range must be in descending order or Excel will return a result of #N/A. If this argument is left out of the formula, Excel assumes the value is 1 using the same criteria as having entered 1.

On the Job

Task 9.10 Using the MATCH Function

Kaelan wants to know where the name *Sean Cortez* is located in the list of doctors in the Doctor Summary worksheet. This information will be used in Task 9.11 to quickly find the doctor's yearly revenue. Enter a formula that uses the MATCH function to locate the name and display its location.

1. Click the Doctor Summary sheet tab, click the Formulas tab, if necessary, and then click in cell B31.
2. Click the Lookup & Reference button in the Function Library group, and then click the *MATCH* option.

   The Function Arguments dialog box displays with the insertion point in the *Lookup_value* text box (see Figure 9.30).

Figure 9.30 MATCH Function Arguments Dialog Box

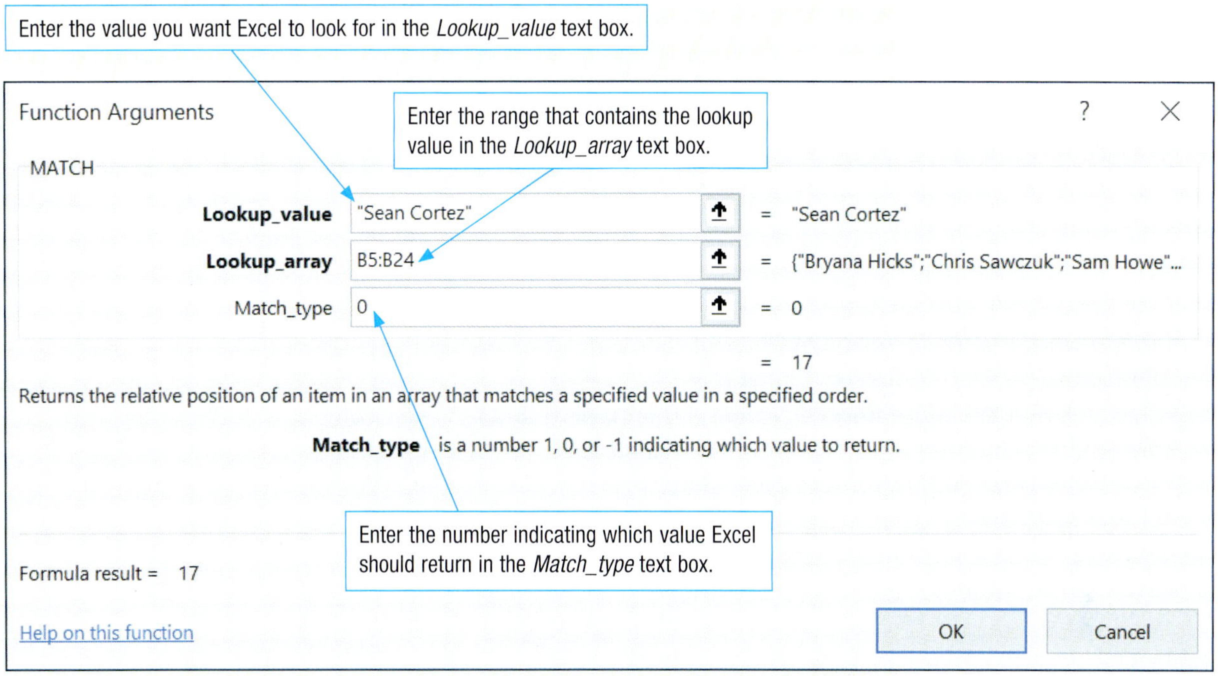

3. Type Sean Cortez and then press the Tab key.

   The text *"Sean Cortez"* appears in the *Lookup_value* text box. This is the value you want Excel to search for. The insertion point is in the *Lookup_array* text box.

4. Type B5:B24 and then press the Tab key.

   The range reference *B5:B24* appears in the *Lookup_array* text box. This is the range that contains the lookup value. The insertion point is in the *Match_type* text box.

5. Type 0.

   The value *0* displays in the *Match_type* text box. This value tells Excel to look for the first exact match.

6. Click the OK button.

   The dialog box closes, the value *17* appears in cell B31, cell B31 is active, and the formula *=MATCH("Sean Cortez",B5:B24,0)* displays in the Formula bar. Sean Cortez is the 17th person in the list. You will need to know this position for Task 9.11.

7. Click the Save button on the Quick Access Toolbar.

Model Answer

Reminder
Excel automatically places double quotation marks around the entry when you finish it because it is a text entry.

9.11 Using the INDEX Function

MOS Expert 3.2.4

Tutorial
Using the Reference INDEX Function

The **INDEX function** in the *Lookup & Reference* category returns a value or the reference to a value from a range or an array constant by telling Excel the row number to look for and the column in which to retrieve the data. There are two types of INDEX functions: array and reference. Use the INDEX function in conjunction with the MATCH function to locate a specific cell and then return its value. For example, you can use the INDEX function in conjunction with the MATCH function to find the location of a student's name and then return that student's grade.

▸ **Know This** about the array INDEX function

- The **array INDEX function** returns the value of a cell from a range or an array constant. An **array constant** is the name given to an array, like a defined name is the name given to a cell or range.
- Table 9.12 explains the syntax and arguments for the array INDEX function.
- To enter a formula containing an array INDEX function, you must start by selecting the destination cells. Select the same number of destination cells as the number of results you expect returned. For example, if you expect five values to be returned from your formula, select five cells.
- After you select the destination cells, click the Lookup & Reference button in the Function Library group on the Formulas tab, click the *INDEX* option at the drop-down list, and then enter the function arguments at the Select Arguments dialog box.
- Alternatively, click in the formula cell and then type INDEX. When you start typing the function, a ScreenTip will display, showing the syntax for the two types of INDEX functions. Refer to the syntax for the array INDEX function.
- To finish entering a formula containing an array INDEX function, press Ctrl + Shift + Enter.

Table 9.12 Array INDEX Function Syntax and Arguments

Syntax
=INDEX(array,row_num,[column_num]).

Argument	Required or Optional?	Description
array	Required	The range address or the name given to an array constant.
row_num	Required	The row number that Excel should look for. If the range address or array contains only one row, this number is optional. If the *column _num* argument is omitted the *row_num* argument is required. In the selected range, the first row is row_num1, the second row is row_num2, and so on.
column_num	Optional	The column number that Excel should look for. If the *row_num* argument is omitted, the *column_num* argument is required. In the selected range, the first column is column_num1, the second column is column_num2, and so on.

▸ **Know This** about the reference INDEX function

- The **reference INDEX function** returns the value of a cell at the intersection of a row and a column.
- If Excel is required to look in more than one range, each range will be identified with a number.
- Table 9.13 explains the syntax and arguments for the reference INDEX function.
- For example, the formula *=INDEX(B4:B35,MATCH(J4,A4:A35,0))* in the Employment Professionals worksheet shown in Figure 9.31 returns the first name of the employee in cell K4 after you enter the employee ID in cell J4. Similar formulas have been placed in the range L4:M4 to return the last name and rate per hour when the employee ID is entered.

- The range B4:B35 contains the first name of the employee where Excel will locate the data specified by the MATCH function.
- Cell J4 contains the employee ID to search for in the lookup range. It is the *lookup_value* argument of the MATCH function.
- The range A4:A35 contains the lookup range that will be searched. It is the *lookup_array* argument of the MATCH function.
- The value 0 is the *match_type* argument of the MATCH function and instructs Excel to find an exact match.
- The MATCH part of this formula finds where the information is located for the data entered in cell J4, and the INDEX part of the formula returns the value of that location in the specified range.
- To finish entering a formula containing the reference INDEX function, press the Enter key.

Table 9.13 Reference INDEX Function Syntax and Arguments

Syntax *=INDEX(reference,row_num,[column_num],[area_num])*		
Argument	**Required or Optional?**	**Description**
reference	Required	The addresses of the cells or ranges where Excel is to locate the data
row_num	Required	The row number that Excel should look for
column_num	Optional	The column number that Excel should look for. If this is omitted, the *row_num* argument is required.
area_num	Optional	If more than one cell range is defined in the *reference* argument, this number indicates which cell range to use. This number is not required if only one cell range is used. For example, if you list the range A1:B5,A7:B12 in the reference and you want Excel to look in the range A1:B5 first, enter a *1*. If you want Excel to look in the range A7:B12 first, enter a *2*.

Figure 9.31 Worksheet Containing the INDEX and MATCH Functions

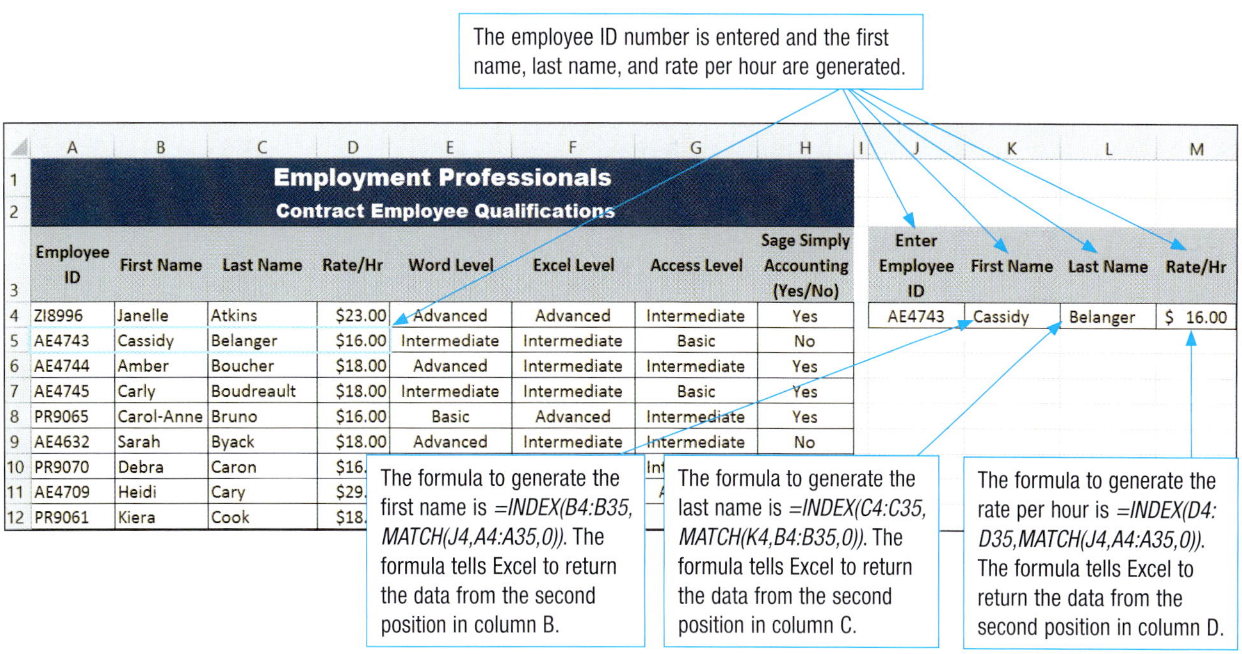

▸ Know This about the INDEX function arguments

— If both the *row_num* and the *column_num* arguments are entered in a formula, the value at their intersection will be returned.

— If *0* is entered for either the *row_num* argument or the *column_num* argument, the array of values for the entire column or row will be returned.

— If the *row_num* or the *column_num* argument points to a cell outside the array, Excel returns the error code #REF!.

Reminder
The error code #REF! indicates that a referenced cell no longer exists in the workbook.

▸ Know This about using the MATCH function with the INDEX function

— The MATCH function can be used as the *row_num* argument to indicate the row number Excel should look for.

On the Job

Task 9.11 Using the Reference INDEX Function

In meetings and while traveling, Kaelan often needs to find the yearly revenue for individual doctors on his mobile device. It's difficult to scroll through the Doctor Summary worksheet and locate that information on his device's small screen. Kaelan wants you to help him solve this problem by making it possible for him to type a doctor's name in cell B28 and see that doctor's yearly revenue in cell C28. Enter a formula that uses a MATCH function nested in a reference INDEX function to return the yearly revenue a doctor sends to the lab. The MATCH function will find the row of the doctor to look for, and the INDEX function will return the revenue.

1. With the Doctor Summary worksheet active and the Formulas tab active, click in cell B28.
2. Type Sean Cortez and then press the Tab key.

   The text *Sean Cortez* displays in cell B28 and cell C28 is active.
3. Type =INDEX(.

   A ScreenTip displays the syntax for the two types of INDEX functions (see Figure 9.32). You will be entering a reference INDEX function.
4. Type Q5:Q24,MATCH(B28,B5:B24,0)).

   The formula *=INDEX(Q5:Q24,MATCH(B28,B5:B24,0))* displays in cell C28. The range Q5:Q24 indicates where Excel will look for the data. The function MATCH(B28,B5:B24,0) replaces the *row_num* argument and tells Excel what row to search for (see Figure 9.33).
5. Press the Enter key.

   The value *$100,888* displays in cell C28. *Sean Cortez* displays in cell B21 and 108,888 is the value in cell Q21.
6. Click in cell B28, type Edward Trent, and then press the Enter key.

   The value *$92,893* displays in cell C28.
7. Click the Save button on the Quick Access Toolbar.

Model Answer

Figure 9.32 INDEX ScreenTip

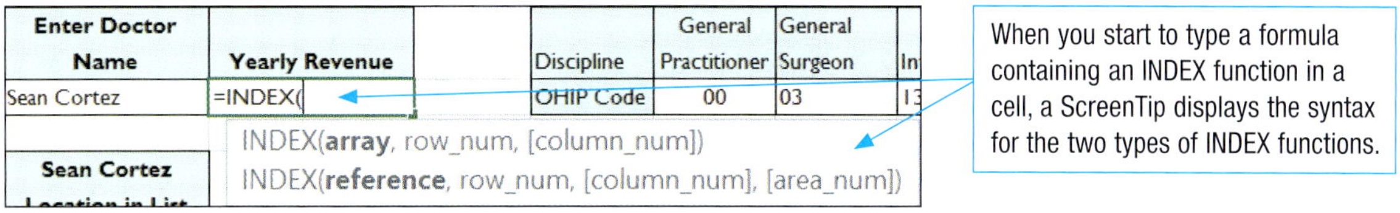

Figure 9.33 MATCH Formula Explained

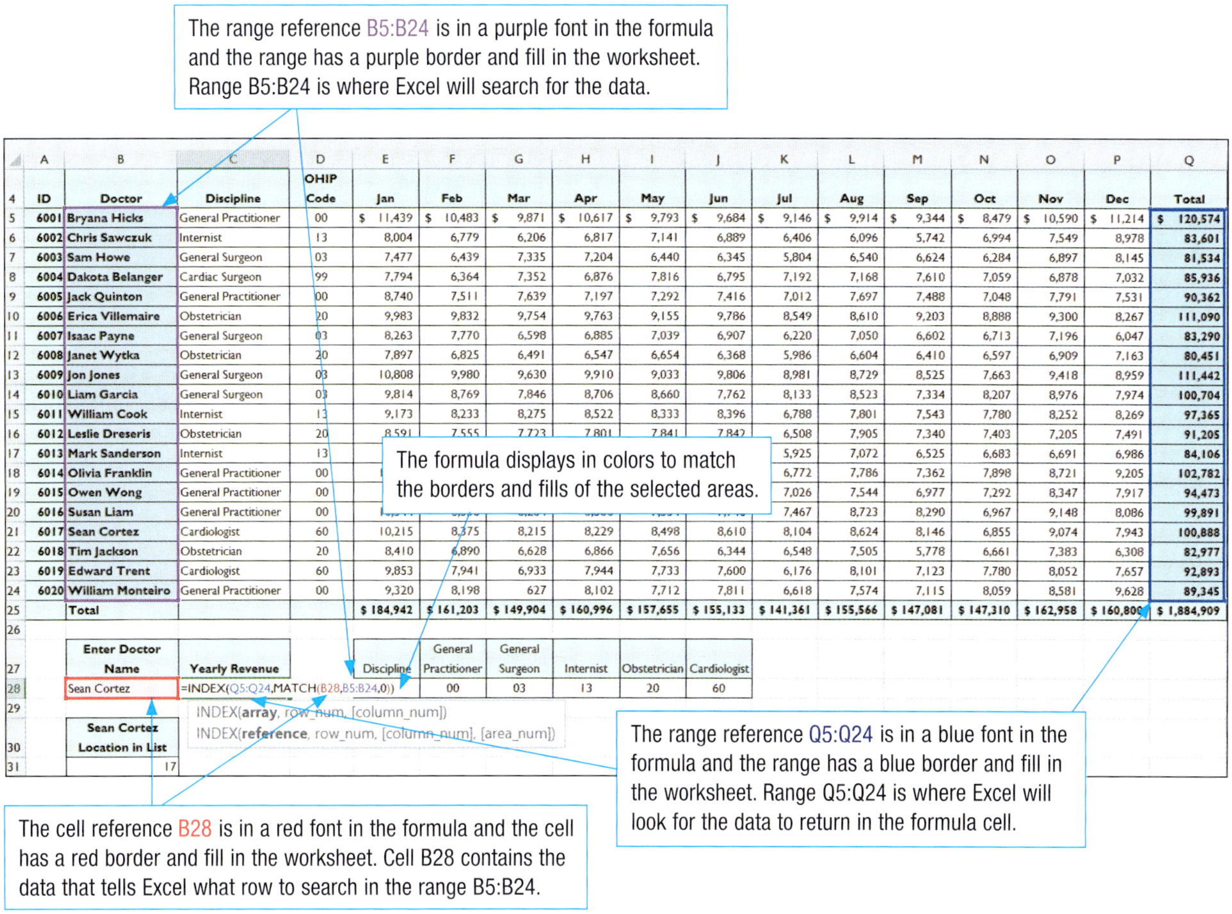

	A	B	C	D	E	F	G	H	I	J	K	L	M	N	O	P	Q
4	ID	Doctor	Discipline	OHIP Code	Jan	Feb	Mar	Apr	May	Jun	Jul	Aug	Sep	Oct	Nov	Dec	Total
5	6001	Bryana Hicks	General Practitioner	00	$ 11,439	$ 10,483	$ 9,871	$ 10,617	$ 9,793	$ 9,684	$ 9,146	$ 9,914	$ 9,344	$ 8,479	$ 10,590	$ 11,214	$ 120,574
6	6002	Chris Sawczuk	Internist	13	8,004	6,779	6,206	6,817	7,141	6,889	6,406	6,096	5,742	6,994	7,549	8,978	83,601
7	6003	Sam Howe	General Surgeon	03	7,477	6,439	7,335	7,204	6,440	6,345	5,804	6,540	6,624	6,284	6,897	8,145	81,534
8	6004	Dakota Belanger	Cardiac Surgeon	99	7,794	6,364	7,352	6,876	7,816	6,795	7,192	7,168	7,610	7,059	6,878	7,032	85,936
9	6005	Jack Quinton	General Practitioner	00	8,740	7,511	7,639	7,197	7,292	7,416	7,012	7,697	7,488	7,048	7,791	7,531	90,362
10	6006	Erica Villemaire	Obstetrician	20	9,983	9,832	9,754	9,763	9,155	9,786	8,549	8,610	9,203	8,888	9,300	8,267	111,090
11	6007	Isaac Payne	General Surgeon	03	8,263	7,770	6,598	6,885	7,039	6,907	6,220	7,050	6,602	6,713	7,196	6,047	83,290
12	6008	Janet Wytka	Obstetrician	20	7,897	6,825	6,491	6,547	6,654	6,368	5,986	6,604	6,410	6,597	6,909	7,163	80,451
13	6009	Jon Jones	General Surgeon	03	10,808	9,980	9,630	9,910	9,033	9,806	8,981	8,729	8,525	7,663	9,418	8,959	111,442
14	6010	Liam Garcia	General Surgeon	03	9,814	8,769	7,846	8,706	8,660	7,762	8,133	8,523	7,334	8,207	8,976	7,974	100,704
15	6011	William Cook	Internist	13	9,173	8,233	8,275	8,522	8,333	8,396	6,788	7,801	7,543	7,780	8,252	8,269	97,365
16	6012	Leslie Dreseris	Obstetrician	20	8,591	7,555	7,723	7,801	7,841	7,842	6,508	7,905	7,340	7,403	7,205	7,491	91,205
17	6013	Mark Sanderson	Internist	13	[illegible]	[illegible]	[illegible]	[illegible]	[illegible]	[illegible]	5,925	7,072	6,525	6,683	6,691	6,986	84,106
18	6014	Olivia Franklin	General Practitioner	00	[illegible]	[illegible]	[illegible]	[illegible]	[illegible]	[illegible]	6,772	7,786	7,362	7,898	8,721	9,205	102,782
19	6015	Owen Wong	General Practitioner	00	[illegible]	[illegible]	[illegible]	[illegible]	[illegible]	[illegible]	7,026	7,544	6,977	7,292	8,347	7,917	94,473
20	6016	Susan Liam	General Practitioner	00	[illegible]	[illegible]	[illegible]	[illegible]	[illegible]	[illegible]	7,467	8,723	8,290	6,967	9,148	8,086	99,891
21	6017	Sean Cortez	Cardiologist	60	10,215	8,375	8,215	8,229	8,498	8,610	8,104	8,624	8,146	6,855	9,074	7,943	100,888
22	6018	Tim Jackson	Obstetrician	20	8,410	6,890	6,628	6,866	7,656	6,344	6,548	7,505	5,778	6,661	7,383	6,308	82,977
23	6019	Edward Trent	Cardiologist	60	9,853	7,941	6,933	7,944	7,733	7,600	6,176	8,101	7,123	7,780	8,052	7,657	92,893
24	6020	William Monteiro	General Practitioner	00	9,320	8,198	627	8,102	7,712	7,811	6,618	7,574	7,115	8,059	8,581	9,628	89,345
25		Total			$ 184,942	$ 161,203	$ 149,904	$ 160,996	$ 157,655	$ 155,133	$ 141,361	$ 155,566	$ 147,081	$ 147,310	$ 162,958	$ 160,800	$ 1,884,909
26																	
27		Enter Doctor Name	Yearly Revenue		Discipline	General Practitioner	General Surgeon	Internist	Obstetrician	Cardiologist							
28		Sean Cortez	=INDEX(Q5:Q24,MATCH(B28,B5:B24,0))			00	03	13	20	60							
29			INDEX(array, row_num, [column_num])														
30		Sean Cortez Location in List	INDEX(reference, row_num, [column_num], [area_num])														
31		17															

9.12 Configuring Formula Calculation Options

MOS Expert 1.2.3

Tutorial

Using the *Manual* Calculation Option and Resetting the *Automatic* Calculation Option

When you are working with an Excel worksheet that contains formulas, you should consider three options:

— **Calculation** is the process Excel uses to work through a formula and return the results in the cells that contain the formula. By default, calculation occurs when a formula is entered or whenever a cell value referenced in the formula is changed.

— **Iteration** is the process Excel uses to continually work through a formula until a specific numeric condition is met. A **circular reference error** occurs when a formula refers to the cell that contains the formula. You can determine how many times the formula should recalculate. For example, you need to change the iteration if you are trying to calculate benefits when benefits are a percentage of total employee costs and total employee costs are salaries plus commissions plus benefits (see Figure 9.34).

— **Precision** measures how accurate to make the calculation. Excel stores and calculates using up to 15 digits. For example, Excel may show a result with one digit after the decimal point (10/6=1.7) or two digits ((10/6=1.67) or three digits ((10/6=1.667), and so on. The result 1.667 is more precise than the result 1.7.

Figure 9.34 Formula Containing a Circular Reference

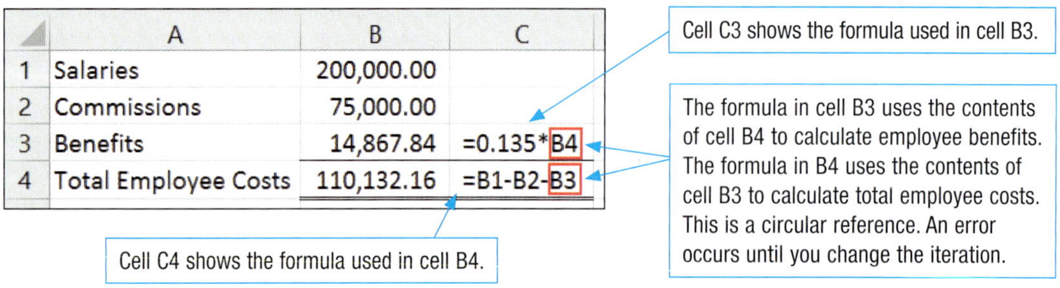

▸ Know This about configuring formula calculations

— To change how formulas recalculate, use features in the Calculation group on the Formulas tab (see Figure 9.35).

— Large array formulas may slow down calculations in a spreadsheet, so modifying the recalculation should be considered. This will allow you to make changes without Excel pausing while it recalculates.

— Split the recalculation of a complex formula over multiple processors to speed up the recalculation of the formula. The number of processors depends on your computer.

— If the *Workbook Calculation* option has been set to *Manual*, recalculate a formula that has changed since the last calculation by pressing the F9 function key.

▸ Know More ways to recalculate a formula that has changed

– If the *Workbook Calculation* option has been set to Manual, *Calculate* appears in the Status bar next to *Ready*. When you want Excel to recalculate the workbook, click the *Calculate* option on the Status bar.

▸ Know This about configuring the reiteration setting

— To modify the number of times Excel reiterates a workbook, click the File tab, click the *Options* option, click the *Formulas* category, and then modify any of the options in the *Calculation options* section (see Figure 9.36).

— The what-if analysis features addressed in Chapter 10 use iteration to obtain the required results.

— Use caution when enabling iterative calculations because this process can produce an incorrect result and slow down the calculations being performed in the workbook.

▸ Know This about configuring the precision setting

— To modify the precision of Excel, click the File tab, click the *Options* option, click the *Advanced* category, and then scroll down and modify the options in the *Formulas* or *When calculating this workbook* section (see Figure 9.37).

— By default, Excel limits the precision to 15 digits, but this number can be modified.

— By default, when completing a calculation, Excel uses the value stored in a cell, *not* the value displayed in the cell. For example, *25.005* stored in a cell formatted to show two decimal points will display as *25.01*. When the cell is used in a formula, *25.005* will be used, not *25.01*.

Figure 9.35 Calculation Group on the Formulas Tab

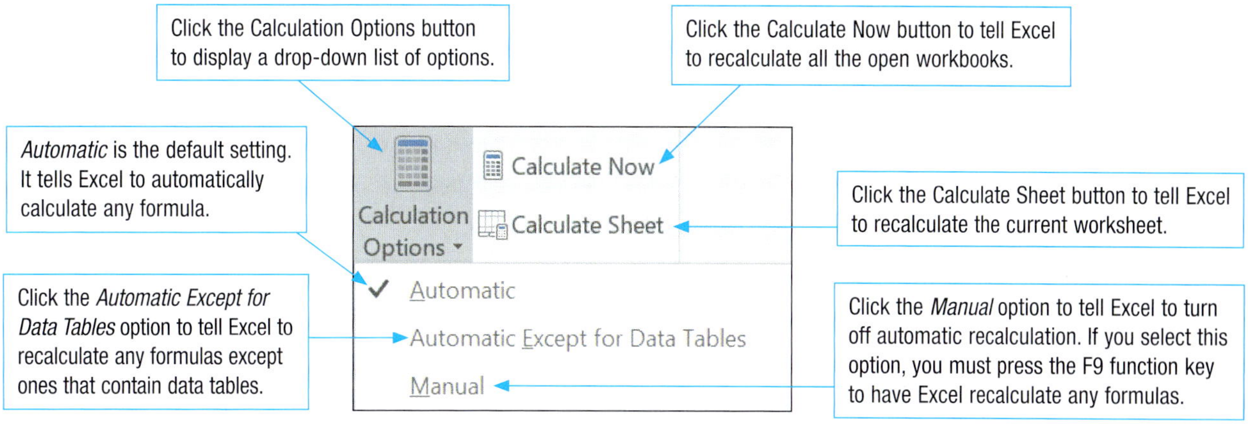

Figure 9.36 *Calculation Options* Section of the Formulas Category at the Excel Options Dialog Box

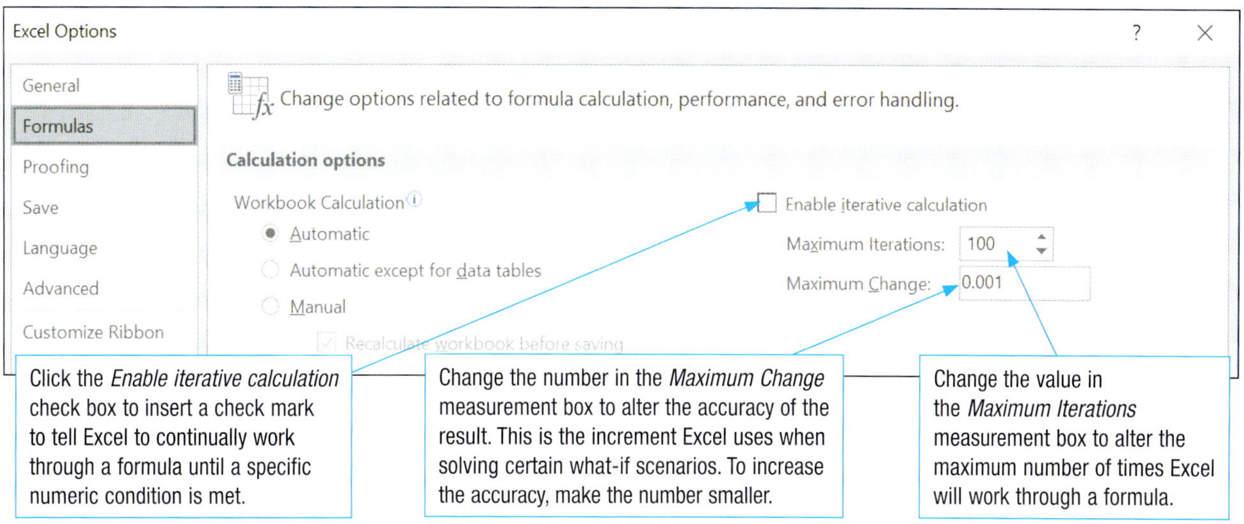

Figure 9.37 Options in the Advanced Category at the Excel Options Dialog Box

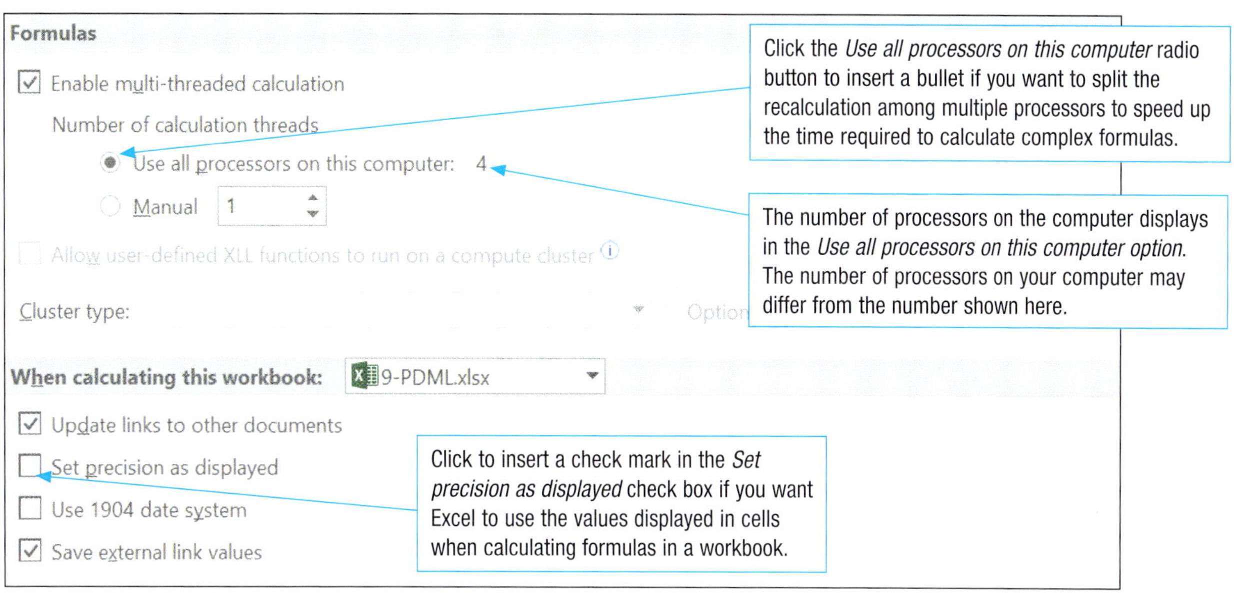

On the Job

Task 9.12a Using the *Manual* Calculation Option

Kaelan has learned that the Doctor Summary worksheet may contain an error in the total revenue listed for Edward Trent in December: the correct amount may be $10,000. Kaelan wants to see what the total revenues are for December, for Edward Trent, and for the entire year if you correct this possible error. Kaelan wants to see only the possible changes in the Doctor Summary worksheet, not in the rest of the workbook. Set the workbook to calculate manually, edit the amount of December revenue for Dr. Trent in the Doctor Summary worksheet, and then manually recalculate the worksheet so any formulas that appear on that worksheet and refer to the changed data will also update.

1. With the Doctor Summary worksheet active and the Formulas tab active, click in cell P24.
2. Click the Calculation Options button in the Calculation group and then click the *Manual* option (see Figure 9.35 on page 435).
3. Type 10000 and then press the Enter key.

   The value in cell P24 changes to 10,000 and cell P25 is active. No other values in the worksheet change because you set the workbook to calculate manually in Step 2.
4. Click the Calculate Sheet button.

   The formulas in cells Q24, Q25, and P25 recalculate and the results update to reflect the change in cell P24.
5. Click the Save button on the Quick Access Toolbar.

Model Answer

On the Job

Task 9.12b Resetting the *Automatic* Calculation Option

Kaelan has confirmed that the Doctor Summary worksheet did *not* contain an error: the total revenue for Edward Trent in December was in fact $9,628. Kaelan asks you to update the entire workbook with this information. Before you do that, reset the default calculation option so that the workbook will be recalculated automatically when you make the change. Once you have reset the default calculation, any future changes to the workbook will be recalculated automatically.

1. With the Doctor Summary worksheet active and the Formulas tab active, click the Calculation Options button and then click the *Automatic* option.

   From now on, formulas in the workbook will update automatically any time the value in a cell referenced by the formulas changes.
2. Click in cell P24, type 9628, and then press the Enter key.

   The formulas in cells Q24, Q25, and P25 recalculate and the results update to reflect the change in cell P24. Any other formulas in the workbook that reference cell P24 also update.
3. If printed work is required by your instructor, print the workbook.
4. Save and then close the workbook.

Model Answer

Chapter Summary

9.1 ▸ COUNTIF and COUNTIFS are Statistical functions. A Statistical function provides statistical analysis of data. The COUNTIF function counts the number of cells in a range that meet a single criterion, or condition. The COUNTIFS function counts the number of cells that meet more than one condition.

▸ The phrase *returning a result* is used to describe what happens when a value is calculated by a formula and is inserted in a cell. The term *returning* refers to the process of calculating the formula, and the term *result* refers to the value inserted in the cell.

▸ The *range* argument may be entered using cell addresses or defined names. Using defined names instead of cell addresses makes it easier for users to understand formulas and functions.

▸ Several methods can be used to insert functions. You can click the Insert Function button in the Function Library group, click the name of the function at the drop-down list, and then enter arguments at the Insert Function dialog box. Alternatively, you can click a button in the Function Library group, click the name of the function at the drop-down list, and then enter arguments at the Insert Function dialog box. Or you can type a formula containing the function directly in the Formula bar. You can choose a method based on personal preference.

9.2 ▸ AVERAGEIF and AVERAGEIFS are Statistical functions. The AVERAGEIF function finds the arithmetic mean (average) of the data in a specified range that meet a single criterion, or condition. The AVERAGEIFS function finds the average of cells that meet multiple criteria in multiple ranges.

9.3 ▸ SUMIF and SUMIFS are Math & Trig functions. The SUMIF function adds the cells in a range that meet a single criterion, or condition. The SUMIFS function adds the data in a range that meet multiple criteria.

9.4 ▸ A Logical function uses Boolean logic to construct a conditional test that proves either true or false. The conditional test is a logical condition, or expression, that tells Excel to return one value if the test proves true and another value if the test proves false. The IF function (covered in Chapter 2) is the most commonly used Logical function in Excel. Other Logical functions include AND, OR, and NOT. The AND, OR, and NOT functions can be used on their own, but they are more commonly used in conjunction with other functions.

▸ Complex conditions can be created by combining two or more functions in one formula. Nest an AND, OR, or NOT function with an IF function to test multiple conditions. Use a nested IF function (one IF function nested inside another IF function) to test an additional condition.

9.5 ▸ Formulas containing nested functions can get quite long and complicated. The Evaluate Formula feature can be used to discover how any formula calculates a result. This feature evaluates the parts of the formula in the order that the result is calculated.

9.6 ▸ A Lookup & Reference function is used to look up values in a range (called a *lookup range*). Being able to look up a value automates data entry in a large worksheet. When used properly, Lookup & Reference functions can prevent inaccuracies caused by data entry errors. A formula containing a LOOKUP function can be set to look for an exact match or an approximate match.

- ▶ The VLOOKUP function is a Lookup & Reference function that looks up a value in the leftmost column of a table organized in a vertical order. For this function to work properly, the first column of the lookup table (which contains the lookup value) must be sorted in ascending order.

9.7 ▶ The HLOOKUP function is a Lookup & Reference function that searches for a comparison value when the lookup table is arranged horizontally rather than vertically.

9.8 ▶ If an error occurs when Excel returns the result of a formula, Excel displays an error code in the result cell—for example, #N/A. An Excel error code alerts the user to a problem with the formula, but it may not provide useful information for fixing the error.

9.8 ▶ The IFERROR function from the *Lookup & Reference* category can be used to display a value or text, instead of an error code, in the result cell (the cell containing the value returned by a formula calculation). The value or text can provide information that can be used to fix the error.

9.9 ▶ In some cases, the data in a worksheet is arranged in a way that is not suitable for performing the required analysis. The TRANSPOSE function from the *Lookup & Reference* category can be used to convert columns to rows and rows to columns.

- ▶ A formula containing the TRANSPOSE function is an array formula. An *array* is a collection of data in a single row, a single column, or multiple rows and columns.

9.10 ▶ The MATCH function in the *Lookup & Reference* category tells where to locate a specified value in a list of data. The MATCH function can be used instead of the VLOOKUP function to determine *where* the value is located, not *what* the value is.

9.11 ▶ The INDEX function in the *Lookup & Reference* category returns the value of a cell from a table or range by telling Excel the row number to look for and the column in which to retrieve the data. There are two types of INDEX functions: array and reference. The INDEX function can be used in conjunction with the MATCH function to locate a specific cell and then return its value.

9.12 ▶ Calculation is the process Excel uses to work through a formula and return the results in the cells that contain the formula. By default, calculation occurs when a formula is entered or whenever a cell value referenced in the formula is changed.

- ▶ Iteration is the process Excel uses to continually work through a formula until a specific numeric condition is met. A circular reference error occurs when a formula refers to the cell that contains the formula. If you get this error, you can determine how many times the formula should recalculate.
- ▶ Precision measures how accurate to make the calculation.

Features Review

Feature	Ribbon Tab, Group	Button, Option	Keyboard Shortcut
display calculation options	Formulas, Calculation		
display list of commonly used functions	Formulas, Function Library	Σ	
display formulas in worksheet cells	Formulas, Formula Auditing		Ctrl + `
display list of recently used functions	Formulas, Function Library		
display Insert Function dialog box	Formulas, Function Library or Formulas, Function Library or Home, Editing	*fx* or , *Insert Function* or Σ, *More Functions*	Shift + F3
evaluate formula	Formulas, Formula Auditing		
expand or collapse Formula bar			Ctrl + Shift + U
insert AVERAGEIF function	Formulas, Function Library	, *Statistical, AVERAGEIF*	
insert Compatibility functions	Formulas, Function Library		
insert COUNTIF function	Formulas, Function Library	*fx*	
insert Cube functions	Formulas, Function Library		
insert Date & Time functions	Formulas, Function Library		
insert Engineering functions	Formulas, Function Library		
insert Financial functions	Formulas, Function Library		
insert HLOOKUP function	Formulas, Function Library	, *HLOOKUP*	
insert IF function	Formulas, Function Library	, *IF*	
insert IFERROR function	Formulas, Function Library	, *IFERROR*	
insert Information functions	Formulas, Function Library		
insert Logical functions	Formulas, Function Library		
insert Lookup & Reference functions	Formulas, Function Library		
insert MATCH function	Formulas, Function Library	, *MATCH*	
insert Math & Trig functions	Formulas, Function Library		
insert Statistical functions	Formulas, Function Library		

continues...

Feature	Ribbon Tab, Group	Button, Option	Keyboard Shortcut
insert SUMIF function	Formulas, Function Library	, *SUMIF*	
insert SUMIFS function	Formulas, Function Library	, *SUMIFS*	
insert Text functions	Formulas, Function Library		
insert TRANSPOSE function	Formulas, Function Library	, *TRANSPOSE*	
insert VLOOKUP function	Formulas, Function Library	, *VLOOKUP*	
insert Web functions	Formulas, Function Library		
modify calculation settings (e.g., precision, reiteration)	File	*Options, Formulas, Calculation options*	
recalculate all open workbooks now	Formulas, Calculation		F9
recalculate current worksheet now	Formulas, Calculation		F9
transpose data	Home, Clipboard	, *Transpose*	

Recheck

Recheck your understanding of the concepts, features, and skills covered in this chapter by taking the Recheck quiz.

Workbook

Access the study tools, review exercises, assessments, and challenges for this chapter in the workbook available from this page in your ebook.

Using Financial Functions and Analysis Features

Chapter 10

Chapter Goal

To use Financial functions to calculate and analyze data, to use data validation and formula auditing tools to identify and correct errors, to use Goal Seek and Scenario Manager for what-if analysis, and to use sparklines, map features, and infographics to represent data visually.

Learning Objectives

10.1 Understand financial functions
10.2 Find the periodic payments for a loan (PMT)
10.3 Find the future value of a series of payments (FV)
10.4 Find the present value of a series of payments (PV)
10.5 Find the interest rate of a loan (RATE)
10.6 Find the number of periods in a loan (NPER)
10.7 Insert depreciation functions (SLN, SYD, DB, and DDB)
10.8 Use the net present value (NPV)
10.9 Find the internal rate of return (IRR)
10.10 Validate and restrict data entry
10.11 Identify errors and troubleshoot formulas using formula auditing tools
10.12 Illustrate data with sparklines
10.13 Customize sparklines
10.14 Use the Goal Seek feature for what-if analysis
10.15 Use the Scenario Manager for what-if analysis
10.16 Use a Watch Window
10.17 Insert a map chart
10.18 Use the 3D Maps feature
10.19 Create an infographic using People Graph

Precheck

Check your understanding of the concepts, features, and skills covered in this chapter by taking the Precheck quiz.

Data Files

Before beginning the chapter work, download the AE10 folder from this page in your ebook to your storage medium and then make AE10 the active folder.

Ebook Links

Access digital resources for this course from your ebook.

SNAP

If you are a SNAP user, go to your SNAP assignments page to complete the Precheck, Tutorials, and Recheck in this chapter.

Preview

On the Job

Scenario: DV Auto Parts

Devon Varey is an auto mechanic with 20 years of experience who wants to open his own business, DV Auto Parts, in Miami, Florida. To get started, he needs a business plan. Devon asks you to help him compile and assess the financial and market data he needs to prepare the plan. This involves calculating loan payments, comparing investment and loan options, depreciating equipment, displaying data visually, and analyzing different financial scenarios.

Visual Reference: Financial Functions and Analysis Features

Figure 10.1 Financial Functions and Formula Auditing Tools

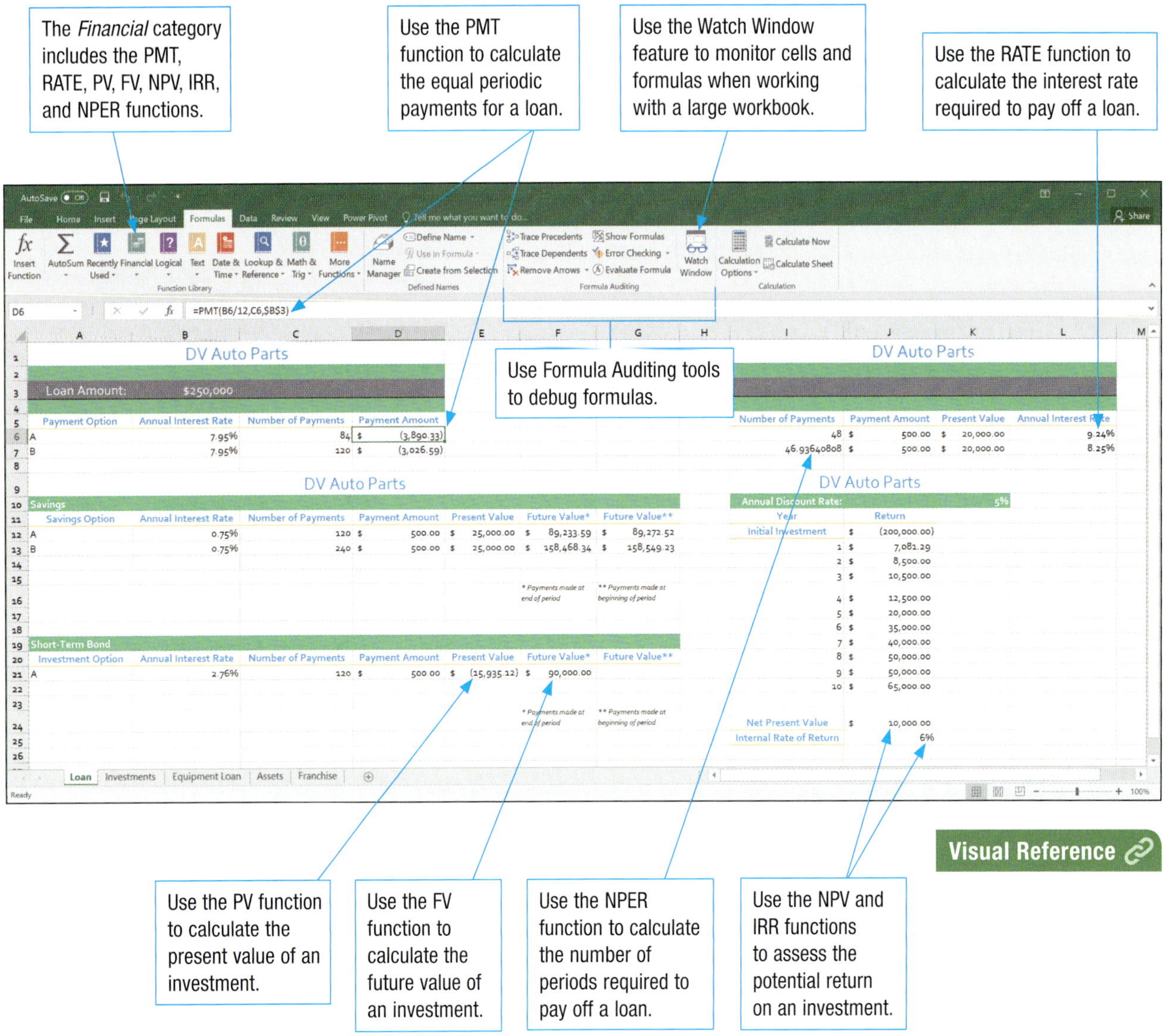

Figure 10.2 Maps and Sparklines

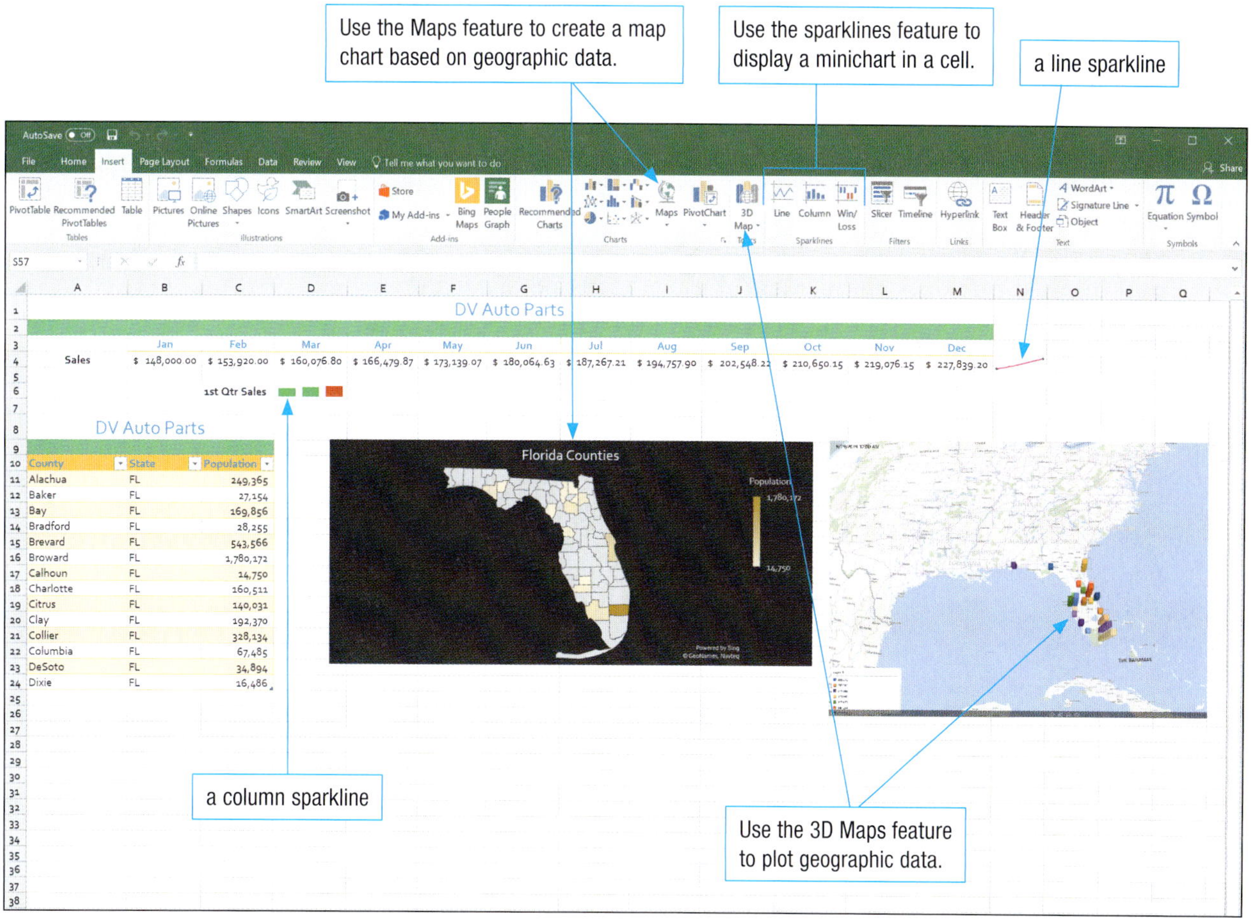

Visual Reference

10.1 Understanding Financial Functions

The Function Library group on the Formula tab offers access to Excel functions. The *Financial* category of functions in Excel includes a variety functions related to business and finance that can be used to produce financial data such as loan payments, the future value of an investment, the rate of return on an investment, or the depreciation of an asset. To understand Financial functions, it is helpful to first become familiar with some basic financial terminology and understand how to enter accurate arguments, as many Financial functions use similar arguments.

▸ Know This about financial terminology

— **Amortization** refers to the process of paying off a debt, such as a mortgage or a car loan, with a fixed repayment schedule in regular installments over a specific period of time. *Amortization* also refers to allocating the cost of an intangible asset over the useful life of the asset for accounting and tax purposes.

— An **asset** is a resource owned by an organization or individual, such as inventory or equipment. Assets are purchased to increase the value of a business or to contribute to the operation of a business, or to add to the property owned by an individual.

- **Cash flow** refers to the movement of money in and out of a business, including income and expenses. A **positive cash flow** (also called a *cash inflow*) is a positive value that represents money flowing to an organization or individual. A **negative cash flow** (also called a *cash outflow*) is a negative value that represents money leaving an organization or individual.
- An **expense** is the cost an organization or individual incurs in the course of day-to-day operation, such as rent, salary, and advertising costs. (Expenses are covered in more detail in Chapter 12.)
- A **fixed interest rate** does not fluctuate during the period of a loan, allowing the borrower to accurately calculate future payments.
- The **future value** is the value of an investment after a specified period of time, assuming a constant interest rate and consistent payments on a periodic basis.
- **Income** is money received in exchange for providing a product or service or from investments. **Net income** is the total earnings or profit calculated by subtracting costs—such as depreciation, tax, and expenses—from total revenue. **Gross income** refers to total earnings before deducting the cost of goods sold and operating expenses. (Cost of goods sold and operating expenses are discussed in Chapter 12.)
- An **intangible asset** is an asset that is not physical in nature, such as a trademark or a patent.
- **Interest** is the amount a lender charges for borrowing money.
- The **interest rate** is the amount a lender charges for borrowing money expressed as a percentage of the principal.
- The interest rate is typically listed as an annual rate, known as the **annual percentage rate (APR)**.
- An **investment** is an asset, such as a stock or bond, or an item, such as a piece of land, that is purchased with the hope that it will generate income (e.g., earn interest) or will appreciate in value over time.
- A **liability** is a debt, such as a bank loan, credit card balance owed, or payment owed to vendors and product manufacturers.
- A **liquid asset** is cash or property that can easily be converted to cash.
- The **payback period** is the length of time required to recover the principal amount of an investment. The term *payback period* also refers to the time between the first and last payment on a loan.
- The **present value** is the total amount that a series of future payments is worth today.
- The **principal** is the amount borrowed or the amount still owed on a loan, separate from the interest that is owed. *Principal* can also refer to the original amount invested.
- **Profit/loss** is a comparison used to measure how financially healthy an organization or individual is. Profit must exceed loss for the organization or individual to be financially healthy. (Profit/loss is discussed in Chapter 12.) The profit/loss ratio is sometimes called the *bottom line* because it represents the money left over after all the expenses and taxes have been deducted.

▶ Know More about interest rates

- The **nominal APR** is the annual interest rate that is typically disclosed by a lender and is the simple interest rate the borrower pays over 1 year. For example, if the borrower pays 1% interest on a loan every month, then the nominal APR is 12%.
- The **effective APR** is the annual interest rate the borrower actually pays after fees and compound interest are added. For example, if the nominal APR is 12%, fees and charges may result in an effective APR of 15.9%.
- In the United States, the federal Truth in Lending Act requires that every consumer loan agreement list the effective APR along with the nominal APR.

▶ **Know This** about Financial functions

- The RATE and IRR functions automatically apply the Percent format to the result.
- All other Financial functions automatically apply the Currency format to the result; by default, when the Currency format is applied, negative values display inside parentheses and in a red font color.
- The Accounting format is typically applied to financial spreadsheets, replacing the default Currency format. By default, when the Accounting format is applied, negative numbers display inside parentheses and in a black font color.
- Many Financial functions have matching arguments that are used in other Financial functions. For example, the *pmt* argument is used in the PMT, FV, PV, and RATE functions.

▶ **Know This** about Financial function arguments

- Some arguments can be positive or negative, depending on the direction of the cash flow. For example, if you make monthly payments on a loan, the money you pay out each month is represented by *pmt* with a negative value.
- Arguments in a Financial function must use consistent units for the function to return accurate results. For example, if you are calculating the number of monthly payments required to pay off a loan, the interest rate also needs to be expressed in months. The interest rate is typically expressed as an annual percentage rate, or APR, which needs to be divided by 12 to give the monthly interest rate.
- To facilitate what-if analysis, enter the formula containing a Financial function in its own cell and enter the data for each argument (such as the amount of a loan) in its own cell. The cell that contains the data for an argument is called the **input cell**.
- Financial functions typically have multiple arguments. If you are using cell references for arguments, you can avoid data entry errors by pointing instead of typing to enter the cell references. When using pointing, you do have to be aware of whether you are entering a positive or negative value, and this may require typing a minus sign (–) in front of the argument to indicate a negative value.

▶ **Know More** about nominal and effective interest rates

- To convert a nominal interest rate to an effective interest rate, use the EFFECT function. The syntax for this function is *=EFFECT(nominal_rate,npery)*.
- To convert an effective rate to a nominal rate, use the NOMINAL function. The syntax for this function is *=NOMINAL(effect_rate,npery)*.
- In both functions, the *npery* argument stands for the number of compounding periods per year.

10.2 Finding the Periodic Payments for a Loan (PMT)

MOS Expert 3.4.5

Tutorial

Using the PMT Function to find Equal Periodic Payments for a Loan

The **PMT function** is a Financial function used to calculate the equal periodic payments required to pay off a loan or an investment with a fixed interest rate over a specified period of time. You can use the PMT function to calculate mortgage payments and other types of loan payments that have a fixed rate of interest. Table 10.1 explains the syntax and arguments for the PMT function.

Table 10.1 PMT Function Syntax and Arguments

Syntax *=PMT(rate,nper,pv,[fv],[type])*		
Argument	**Required or Optional?**	**Description**
rate	Required	Interest rate
nper	Required	Total number of payments
pv	Required	Present value, or principal; the amount of the loan or investment
fv	Optional	Future value, or cash balance after the last payment is made. If the *fv* argument is not included, it is assumed to be 0.
type	Optional	Indication of when payments are due. A 0 indicates payments are due at the end of the period, and a 1 indicates payments are due at the beginning of the period. If the *type* argument is not included, it is assumed to be 0.

Reminder
Optional arguments display in square brackets.

For example, if you purchase a $32,000 vehicle and finance it over 5 years with an annual interest rate of 3.5%, the formula for calculating your monthly loan payments is *=PMT((3.5/12),(5*12),32000))*. The *rate* argument is divided by 12 and the *nper* argument is multiplied by 12 so that both will be expressed in the same units (months). The result is a loan payment of $633.64. In an Excel worksheet, the payment displays as a negative value—($633.64) with Currency format applied—because a payment represents an expense.

An **amortization schedule** is a table of periodic loan payments, showing the principal and interest for each loan payment until the loan is paid off at the end of its term. In an amortization schedule, the percentage of each payment that goes toward interest reduces with each payment and the percentage that goes toward the principal increases.

The **PPMT function**, which calculates the principal part of the payment, and the **IPMT function**, which calculates the interest part of the payment, are used along with the PMT function to create an amortization schedule.

The **CUMPRINC function** is used to calculate the cumulative principal paid on a loan between a start period and an end period. The **CUMIPMT function** is used to calculate the cumulative interest paid on a loan between a start period and an end period.

▸ Know This about loans

- A loan is calculated using three main variables: principal, interest, and time.
- The *principal* is the amount of the loan.
- The *interest* is the amount charged by the lender. It is often expressed as an annual percentage rate, or APR.
- The *time* allowed for repaying the loan is expressed as the number of payment periods. It is often expressed as a number of monthly payments.

▶ **Know This** about using the PMT function

— Use the same units for the *rate* and *nper* arguments. For example, to calculate the amount of each monthly payment on a 3-year loan at an annual interest rate of 10%, use 10%/12 for the *rate* argument and 3*12 for the *nper* argument. The expression 10%/12 gives the monthly interest rate, and the expression 3*12 gives the number of monthly payments in a 3-year loan.

— You can enter an interest rate as a percentage with the percent symbol (e.g., 8.25%), or you can enter it as a decimal value (e.g., 0.0825).

— The PMT function returns a negative value because loan payments are an expense to the borrower.

— The payment returned by the PMT function includes principal and interest but does not include other fees sometimes associated with loans, such as taxes or service fees.

Reminder

You can insert a function using a button in the Function Library group on the Formulas tab.

Reminder

If you know the name for a function, you can enter a formula containing the function directly in a cell. Type an equals sign (=) followed by the function name to display a ScreenTip showing the function syntax, and then enter the arguments, using the ScreenTip as a guide.

▶ **Know This** about the PPMT function

— The syntax of the PPMT function is *=PPMT(rate,per,nper,pv,[fv],[type])*.

— The arguments are the same as for the PMT function with the exception of the *per* argument, which is the period for which the payment on the principal is to be calculated and must be an integer between 1 and *nper* (number of payments).

▶ **Know This** about the IPMT function

— The syntax of the IPMT function is *=IPMT(rate,per,nper,pv,[fv],[type])*.

— Like the PPMT function, the arguments are the same as for the PMT function with the exception of the *per* argument, which is the period for which the interest payment is to be calculated and must be an integer between 1 and *nper* (number of payments).

▶ **Know This** about the CUMPRINC function

— The syntax of the CUMPRINC function is *=CUMPRINC(rate,nper,pv,start_period,end_period,type)*.

— The arguments are the same as for the PPMT function with the exception of the *start_period* and *end_period* arguments, which are the payment period number and must each be an integer between 1 and number of payments. The *nper* argument is the number of payments. The *type* argument is required in the CUMPRINC function.

▶ **Know This** about the CUMIPMT function

— The syntax of the CUMIPMT function is *=CUMIPMT(rate,nper,pv,start_period,end_period,type)*.

— The arguments are the same as for the IPMT function with the exception of the *start_period* and *end_period* arguments, which are the payment period number and must be an integer between 1 and the number of payments. The *nper* argument is the number of payments. The *type* argument is required in the CUMIPMT function.

On the Job

Task 10.2a Using the PMT Function to Find Equal Periodic Payments for a Loan

Devon has determined he will need to borrow $250,000 to fund his start-up. His bank will charge an annual interest rate of 7.95% for a 7- or 10-year loan at that amount. Devon wants to compare the monthly payments for a 7-year loan (payment option A) with the monthly payments for a 10-year loan (payment option B). Use the PMT function to calculate the monthly payments for each loan. Be sure to use the same units for the *rate* and *nper* arguments.

1. Open the data file **10-DVAutoParts**.
2. With the Loan worksheet active, click in cell B6, type 7.95%, and then press Ctrl + Enter.

   The value *7.95%* displays in cell B6. This is the interest rate charged for a 12-month period for both payment options.
3. Drag the fill handle from cell B6 down into cell B7.

   The value *7.95%* displays in cell B7.
4. Click in cell C6, type =7*12, and then press the Enter key.

   The value *84* appears in cell C6 and cell C7 is active. The formula you entered calculates the number of months in 7 years.
5. Type =10*12 and then press the Enter key.

   The value *120* appears in cell C7 and C8 is active. The formula you entered calculates the number of months in 10 years.
6. Click in cell D6 and then enter =PMT(B6/12,C6,$B$3).

   The formula *=PMT(B6/12,C6,$B$3)* displays in cell D6. This formula calculates the monthly payment for a 7-year (84-month) loan. You divide the annual interest rate in cell B6 by 12 to give a monthly interest rate, so the units for the *rate* argument will be the same as the units for the *nper* argument. You use an absolute reference for cell B3 because the loan amount is the same regardless of the number of payments, and you do not want the cell reference for this value to change when you copy the formula.
7. Press Ctrl + Enter.

   The value *($3,890.33)* displays in cell D6 and cell D6 remains active. The value is negative because the loan payment is an expense to Devon. It is automatically formatted with the Currency format and displays in a red font color.
8. With cell D6 active, apply the Accounting format.

   The negative value changes from a red font color to a black font color when you apply the Accounting format.
9. Drag the fill handle from cell D6 down into cell D7.

   The value *($3,026.59)* displays in cell D7 (see Figure 10.3). The formula in cell D7 calculates the monthly payment for a 10-year (120-month) loan.
10. Click the Save button on the Quick Access Toolbar.

Figure 10.3 Monthly Payments Calculated Using the PMT Function

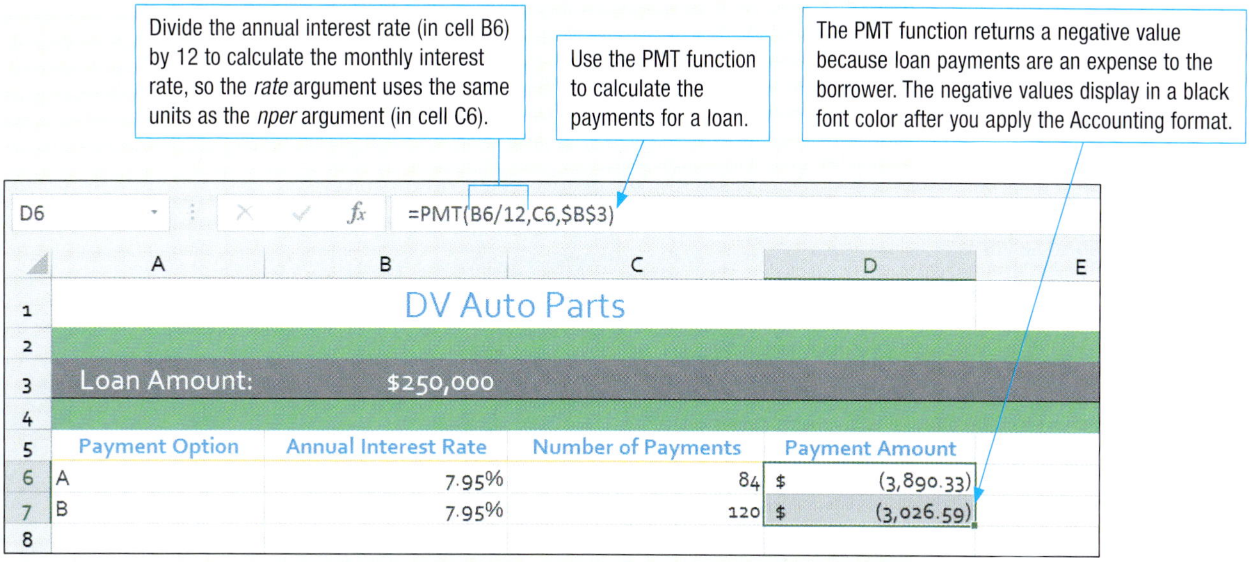

Model Answer

On the Job

Task 10.2b Creating an Amortization Schedule

In Task 10.2a, you calculated the monthly payments for a 7-year loan and a 10-year loan. Devon wants to go with the 7-year loan so that he can pay less interest in the long run, but he would like to see the payments in an amortization schedule so that he can see how much interest he is paying throughout the term of the loan. Use the PMT, PPMT, and IPMT functions to create an amortization schedule.

1. With the 10-DVAutoParts workbook open and the Loan worksheet active, click in cell A12, type 1, and then press the Tab key.
2. Type =PMT($B$6/12,$C$6,$B$3) and then press the Tab key.

   The formula to calculate the monthly payment is entered in cell B12. Absolute addresses have been used to ensure the references to the loan amounts do not change when copied.
3. Type =PPMT($B$6/12,A12,$C$6,$B$3) and then press the Tab key.

   The PPMT function calculates the principal part of the payment and is entered in cell C12. The second argument specifies the payment number.
4. Type =IPMT($B$6/12,A12,$C$6,$B$3) and then press the Tab key.

   The IPMT function calculates the interest part of the payment and is entered in cell C12. The second argument specifies the payment number.
5. Type =$B$3+C12 and then press the Enter key.

   The balance after the first payment is calculated by subtracting the amount of principal paid from the amount of the loan. Because the principal is a negative value, the formula has an addition operator in the formula. After the first payment, Devon has paid $2,234.08 of the principal of the loan.

6. Select the range A12:E12 and then use the fill handle to copy the selected range down into row 13.
7. Click in cell E13, type =E12+C13, and then press the Enter key.

   The Balance formula is updated to accurately calculate the balance after the second payment. The balance after the second payment is calculated by subtracting the principal paid in the second payment from the balance after the first payment. Again, an addition sign (+) is used in the formula because the principal is a negative value.
8. Select the range A13:E13 and then use the fill handle to copy the selected range down into row 95.

   It will take 84 payments to pay off the loan. The amortization schedule shows Devon how much interest he is paying and how the interest decreases with each payment.
9. Select the range B12:E12 and apply the Accounting format.
10. Select the range B13:E95 and apply the Comma format.
11. Click the Save button on the Quick Access Toolbar.

Model Answer

10.3 Finding the Future Value of a Series of Payments (FV)

MOS Expert 3.4.5

Tutorial

Using the FV Function to Find the Future Value of an Investment

The **time value of money** is the idea that money is worth more when it is received earlier, because of its potential to earn interest. Just how much a specific amount of money could be worth in the future can be determined in Excel using the FV function. The **FV function** is a Financial function used to calculate the future value of an investment or a loan based on a fixed interest rate. The *future value* is the amount to which the investment or loan will grow over time. You can use the FV function to calculate the future value of an investment such as an individual retirement account (IRA). Table 10.2 explains the syntax and arguments for the FV function.

Table 10.2 FV Function Syntax and Arguments

Syntax
=*FV(rate,nper,pmt,[pv],[type])*

Argument	Required or Optional?	Description
rate	Required	Interest rate
nper	Required	Total number of payment periods
pmt	Required unless the *pv* argument is included	Payment made each period
pv	Optional, but if not included, the *pmt* argument is required	Present value of the investment or loan. If the *pv* argument is not included, it is assumed to be 0.
type	Optional	Indication of when payments are due. A 0 indicates payments are due at the end of the period, and a 1 indicates payments are due at the beginning of the period. If the *type* argument is not included, it is assumed to be 0.

For example, if you invest $500 a month for 3 years in a savings account with an annual interest rate of 1.25%, the formula for calculating the future value of the investment is *=FV(1.25%/12,3*12,-500)*. The *rate* argument is divided by 12 and the *nper* argument is multiplied by 12 so that both will be expressed in the same units (months). The *pv* argument is omitted because the present value is 0. The result is a future value of $18,332.03. In an Excel worksheet, it will appear as a positive value because it represents income.

The FV function can be used to calculate the future value of a loan if the loan has not been completely paid off. For example, if you borrow $10,000 at a 7% annual interest rate and make monthly payments of $300, you could use the FV function to determine how much you will still owe on the loan after 1 year (after making 12 payments in 12 months). The formula is *=FV(7%/12,12,-300,10000)*. The *pv* argument represents the present value of the loan. The result is a future value of $7,005.13. It displays as a negative value—($7,005.13) in the Currency format—because it represents an expense (an amount that still needs to be paid).

▸ **Know This** about using the FV function

- Use the same units for the *rate* and *nper* arguments.
- Use negative values for the *pmt* argument if cash is being paid out or invested.
- Use positive values for the *pv* argument if cash is being received or borrowed.
- The calculated future value of an investment is positive because the money will be received.
- The calculated future value of a loan that is not completely paid off is negative because money still needs to be paid out.

On the Job

Task 10.3 Using the FV Function to Find the Future Value of an Investment

Devon knows the importance of having liquid assets in case equipment needs to be replaced or an emergency occurs. He plans to invest $25,000 in a savings account and add $500 a month. He will earn an annual interest rate of 0.75% on his savings. Devon wants you to help him calculate the future value of his savings account after 10 years (savings option A) and after 20 years (savings option B) at that interest rate. He also wants to see how changing the type of payment to the account will affect each option—that is, what the future value will be if he makes each payment at the start of the period versus the end of the period. Use the FV function to return the information Devon is looking for. Be sure to use the same units for the *rate* and *nper* arguments. Also be sure to use negative values for cash invested and positive values for cash received.

1. With the 10-DVAutoParts workbook open and the Loan worksheet active, click the Investments sheet tab.
2. Click in cell B4, type 0.75%, and then press Ctrl + Enter.

   The value *0.75%* displays in cell B4 and cell B4 remains active.
3. Drag the fill handle from cell B4 down into cell B5.

   The value *0.75%* displays in cell B5.

4. Click in cell C4, type =10*12, and then press the Enter key.

   The value *120* displays in cell C4 and cell C5 is active. The formula you entered in cell C4 calculates the number of months in 10 years.

5. Type =20*12 and then press the Enter key.

   The value *240* displays in cell C5 and cell C6 is active. The formula you entered in cell C5 calculates the number of months in 20 years.

6. Click in cell D4, type 500, and then press Ctrl + Enter.

   The value *$500.00* displays in cell D4 and cell D4 remains active. The formula you entered calculates the amount that Devon plans to add to his savings account each month.

7. Drag the fill handle from cell D4 down into cell D5.

   The value *$500.00* displays in cell D5.

8. Click in cell E4, type 25000, and then press Ctrl + Enter.

   The value *$25,000* displays in cell E4 and cell E4 remains active. The present value of Devon's savings account is equal to his initial payment of $25,000.

9. Drag the fill handle from cell E4 down into cell E5.

   The value *$25,000* displays in cell E5.

10. Click in cell F4 and then enter =FV(B4/12,C4,-D4,-E4).

    The formula *=FV(B4/12,C4,-D4,-E4)* displays in cell F4. This formula calculates the future value of Devon's initial payment plus his monthly payments after a period of 10 years. You divide the annual interest rate in cell B4 by 12 to give a monthly interest rate, so the units for the *rate* argument are the same as the units for the *nper* argument. Cell C4 contains the value for the *nper* argument. Cells D4 and E4 contain the values for the *pmt* and *pv* arguments, respectively. You enter these as negative arguments because they represent expenses. You omit the *type* argument to indicate that each payment will be made at the end of the period—at the end of the month.

11. Press Ctrl + Enter.

    The value *$89,233.59* displays in cell F4 and cell F4 remains active. This is the value of Devon's savings account after 10 years if payments are made at the end of the month.

12. Drag the fill handle from cell F4 down into cell F5.

    The value *$158,468.34* displays in cell F5. This is the value of Devon's savings account after 20 years if payments are made at the end of the month.

13. Click in cell G4 and then enter =FV(B4/12,C4,-D4,-E4,1).

    The formula *=FV(B4/12,C4,-D4,-E4,1)* displays in cell G4. This is the same formula you entered in cell F4 but with the *type* argument 1 added. Adding the *type* argument 1 indicates that each payment will be made at the beginning of the period—at the beginning of the month.

14. Press Ctrl + Enter.

    The value *$89,272.52* displays in cell G4 and cell G4 remains active. This is the value of Devon's savings account after 10 years if payments are made at the beginning of the month.

15. Drag the fill handle from cell G4 down into cell G5.

    The value *$158,549.23* displays in cell G5. This is the value of Devon's savings account after 20 years if payments are made at the beginning of the month. Notice that making payments to his savings account at the beginning of the period will give Devon a slightly higher future value than making payments at the end of the period.

16. Select the range F4:G5 and apply the Accounting format (see Figure 10.4).
17. Click the Save button on the Quick Access Toolbar.

Figure 10.4 Investment Returns Calculated Using the FV Function

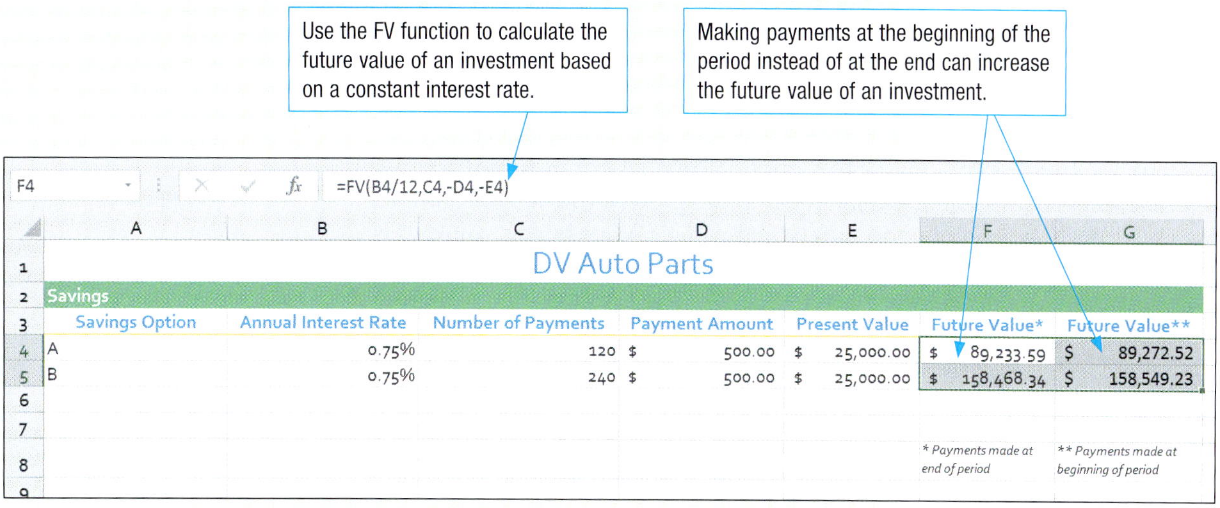

Model Answer

10.4 Finding the Present Value of a Series of Payments (PV)

MOS Expert 3.4.5

Tutorial

Using the PV Function to Find the Present Value of an Investment

The **PV function** is a Financial function used to calculate the present value of an investment or a loan. The *present value* is the amount that must be invested or borrowed now to reach a desired amount in the future. Table 10.3 explains the syntax and arguments for the PV function.

Table 10.3 PV Function Syntax and Arguments

Syntax
=PV(rate,nper,pmt,[fv],[type])

Argument	Required or Optional?	Description
rate	Required	Interest rate
nper	Required	Total number of payment periods
pmt	Required	Payment made each period

continues...

Table 10.3 PV Function Syntax and Arguments *...continued*

Syntax *=PV(rate,nper,pmt,[fv],[type])*		
Argument	**Required or Optional?**	**Description**
fv	Optional	Future value of the investment or loan, or cash balance after the last payment is made. If the *fv* argument is not included, it is assumed to be 0.
type	Optional	Indication of when payments are due. A 0 indicates payments are due at the end of the period, and a 1 indicates payments are due at the beginning of the period. If the *type* argument is not included, it is assumed to be 0.

The PV function calculates the amount you can afford to borrow given a specified number of equal payments at a fixed interest rate. For example, if you want to borrow money to purchase a vehicle, your budget allows for a maximum monthly payment of $450, and you want to pay the loan off in 4 years at an annual interest rate of 4%, then the formula for calculating the amount of loan you can afford is *=PV(4%/12,4*12,-450)*. The rate argument is divided by 12 and the nper argument is multiplied by 12 so that both will be expressed in the same units (months). The pmt argument is entered as a negative value because it is an expense. The result is a present value of $19,929.98. In an Excel worksheet, it will appear as a positive value because it represents income.

Another application of the PV function is to calculate the initial investment required to reach a savings goal. For example, if you save $200 a month for 17 years in a college savings account that earns a 3% annual interest rate, you can use the PV function to calculate the initial investment required to reach a $50,000 saving goal. The formula for calculating the initial investment is *=PV(3%/12,17*12,-200,50000)*. The result is a present value of $5,035.16. It displays as a negative value—($5,035.16) in the Currency format—because it represents the initial investment (an amount that needs to be paid).

▸ **Know This** about using the PV function

— Use the same units for the *rate* and *nper* arguments.

— Use negative values for the *pmt* and *fv* arguments if cash is being paid out or invested.

— Use positive values for the *pmt* and *fv* arguments if cash is being received or borrowed.

— The calculated present value of an investment is negative because the money will be paid out or invested.

— The calculated present value of a loan is positive because the money will be received.

On the Job

Task 10.4 Using the PV Function to Find the Present Value of an Investment

In Task 10.3, you helped Devon calculate the future value of a potential investment in a savings account. You determined that if Devon makes an initial investment of $25,000 and adds $500 at the end of each month, he will have $89,233.59 at the end of 10 years. Now Devon wants to know how much he would need to invest initially if he instead invests $500 at the end of each month for 10 years in a short-term bond fund that returns a rate of 2.76% annually. Use the PV function to calculate the present value, or initial investment, that will give him a future value of $90,000.

1. With the 10-DVAutoParts workbook open and the Investments worksheet active, click in cell B13.
2. Type 2.76% and then press the Tab key.

   The value *2.76%* displays in cell B13 and cell C13 is active.
3. Type =10*12 and then press the Tab key.

   The value *120* displays in cell C13 and cell D13 is active.
4. Type 500 and then press the Tab key two times.

   The value *$500.00* displays in cell D13 and cell F13 is active.
5. Type 90000 and then press the Enter key.
6. Click in cell E13 and then type =PV(B13/12,C13,-D13,F13).

   The formula *=PV(B13/12,C13,-D13,F13)* displays in cell E13. This formula calculates the present value of Devon's short-term bond after he makes monthly payments at the end of the month for 10 years. You divide the annual interest rate in cell B13 by 12 to give a monthly interest rate, so the units used in the *rate* argument are the same as the units used in the *nper* argument. Cell C13 contains the value for the *nper* argument. Cell D13 contains the value for the *pmt* argument; you enter this as a negative argument because it represents an expense. You omit the *type* argument to indicate that each payment will be made at the end of the payment period—at the end of the month. Cell F13 contains the value for the *fv* argument; this is the savings goal Devon wants to reach, and you enter it as a positive argument because it represents money received.
7. Press Ctrl + Enter.

   The value *($15,935.12)* displays in cell E13 and the formula *=PV(B13/12,C13,-D13,F13)* displays in the Formula bar (see Figure 10.5). The value in cell E13 is the initial amount Devon must invest to reach the future goal of $90,000 if he pays $500 a month for 10 years in a short-term bond fund that returns a rate of 2.76% annually. It is a negative amount and displays with a red font color in the default Currency format.
8. With cell E13 active, apply the Accounting format.

   The negative value displays in a black font after you appy the Accounting format.
9. Click the Save button on the Quick Access Toolbar.

Figure 10.5 Present Value of an Investment Calculated Using the PV Function

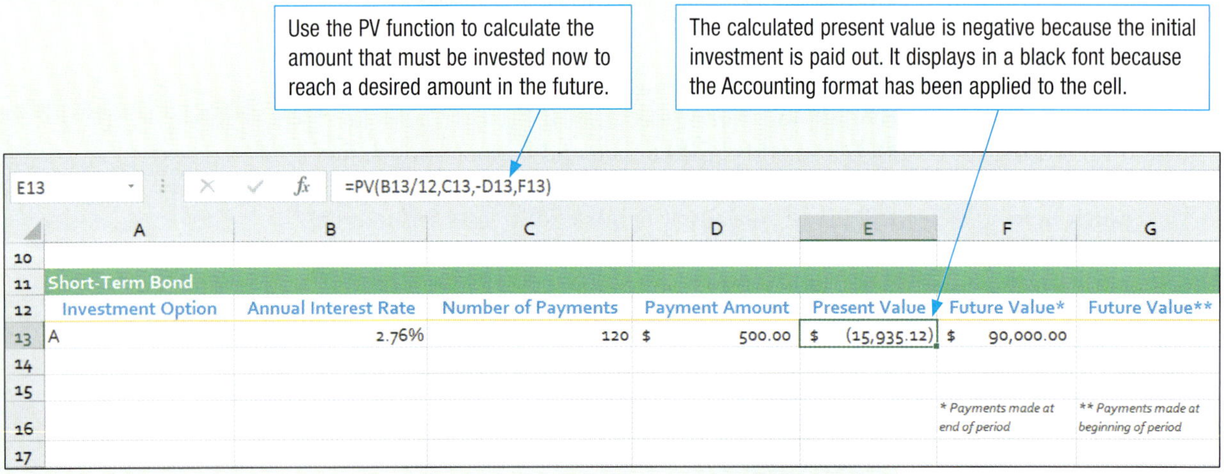

Model Answer

10.5 Finding the Interest Rate of a Loan (RATE)

MOS Expert 3.4.5

Tutorial

Using the RATE Function to Find the Interest Rate of a Loan

The **RATE function** is a Financial function used to calculate the interest rate required to pay off a loan or reach a target amount on an investment, given a fixed number of periods and a specified payment amount. It can also be used to calculate the rate of return on an investment. The **rate of return**, or *discount rate*, is the gain or loss on an investment over a specified amount of time and expressed as a percentage of the investment cost. Table 10.4 explains the syntax and arguments for the RATE function.

Table 10.4 RATE Function Syntax and Arguments

Syntax
=RATE(nper,pmt,pv,[fv],[type],[guess])

Argument	Required or Optional?	Description
nper	Required	Total number of payment periods
pmt	Required	Payment made each period
pv	Required	Present value of the investment or loan
fv	Optional	Future value of the investment or loan, or a cash balance after the last payment is made. If the *fv* argument is not included, it is assumed to be 0.
type	Optional	Indication of when payments are due. A 0 indicates payments are due at the end of the period, and a 1 indicates payments are due at the beginning of the period. If the *type* argument is not included, it is assumed to be 0.
guess	Optional	Your guess for what the rate will be. If the *guess* argument is not included, it will start with the default value of 10% and then use an iterative procedure to converge to the correct rate.

The RATE function calculates the interest rate needed for a loan when you know how much you can afford to pay monthly and want to pay the loan off in a specific amount of time. For example, if you want to borrow $10,000 and pay it off in 2 years by making monthly payments of $450, the formula for calculating the interest rate is *=RATE(2*12,-500,10000)*. The *nper* argument is multiplied by 12 so that it will be expressed in the same units as the *pmt* argument. The *pmt* argument is negative because it is money paid out. The *pv* argument is positive because it is money received. The result is 0.63%. This is a monthly rate because it uses the same units as the *nper* and *pmt* arguments. Multiply the result by 12 to find the annual interest rate: 7.5%.

You can also use the RATE function to calculate the rate of return on an investment. For example, if you invest $25,000 in a start-up company and then receive a payment of $2,500 every 6 months for 7 years, the formula for calculating the rate of return on your investment is *=RATE(2*7,2500,-25000)*. In this example, the *pv* argument is negative because the investment is an expense. The result, 4.84%, is a 6-month interest rate because it uses the same units as the *pmt* argument. Multiply the result by 2 to give the annual interest rate. The rate of return on your investment is 9.68%.

▸ **Know This** about using the RATE function

— Use the same units for the *nper* and *guess* arguments.

— Use negative values for the *pmt* argument if cash is being paid out or invested.

— Use positive values for the *pmt* argument if cash is being received or borrowed.

— The result uses the same units as the *nper* argument.

— Display the result of the RATE function with two digits after the decimal point.

— The result of the RATE function is calculated by iteration. If the function does not find a value after 20 iterations, it returns the error code #NUM!

Reminder

The RATE function automatically applies the Percent format with no digits after the decimal point to the result.

▸ **Know This** about iteration

— Iteration is the process Excel uses to continually work through a formula until a specific numeric condition is met (see Chapter 9).

— If the conditions specified in the formula are met, each successive iteration returns a result that is progressively closer to the solution. This process is called convergence.

— If the conditions specified in the formula are not met, each successive iteration produces a result that progressively moves away from the solution. This process is called divergence.

On the Job

Task 10.5 Using the RATE Function to Find the Interest Rate of a Loan

Devon wants to take out a $20,000 short-term loan to purchase equipment. He wants to make monthly payments of $500 at the end of each month for 4 years. Use the RATE function to calculate the interest rate for the loan.

1. With the 10-DVAutoParts workbook open and the Investments worksheet active, click the Equipment Loan sheet tab.
2. Click in cell A6, type =4*12, and then press the Tab key.

   The value *48* displays in cell A6 and cell B6 is active.
3. Type 500 and then press the Tab key.

   The value *$500.00* displays in cell B6 and cell C6 is active.
4. Type 20000 and then press the Tab key.

   The value *$20,000.00* displays in cell C6 and cell D6 is active.
5. Type =RATE(A6,-B6,C6) and then press Ctrl + Enter.
6. Click the Increase Decimal button in the Number group two times.

   The value *0.77%* displays in cell D6 and the formula *=RATE(A6,-B6,C6)* displays in the Formula bar. Cell A6 contains the value for the *nper* argument. Cell B6 contains the value for the *pmt* argument; you enter this as a negative argument because a loan payment is an expense to Devon. Cell C6 contains the value for the *pv* argument; it is positive because the loan is cash received by Devon. You omit the *type* argument because Devon wants to make each payment at the end of the period. The result is a monthly interest rate because the *nper* argument uses month as the unit. You need to multiply the result by 12 to get the annual interest rate.
7. Press the F2 function key, place the insertion point at the end of the formula in cell D6, type *12, and then press Ctrl + Enter.

   The formula *=RATE(A6,-B6,C6)*12* displays in the Formula bar and the value *9.24%* displays in cell D6 (see Figure 10.6). This is the annual interest rate for the loan.
8. Click the Save button on the Quick Access Toolbar.

Figure 10.6 Annual Interest Rate Calculated Using the RATE Function

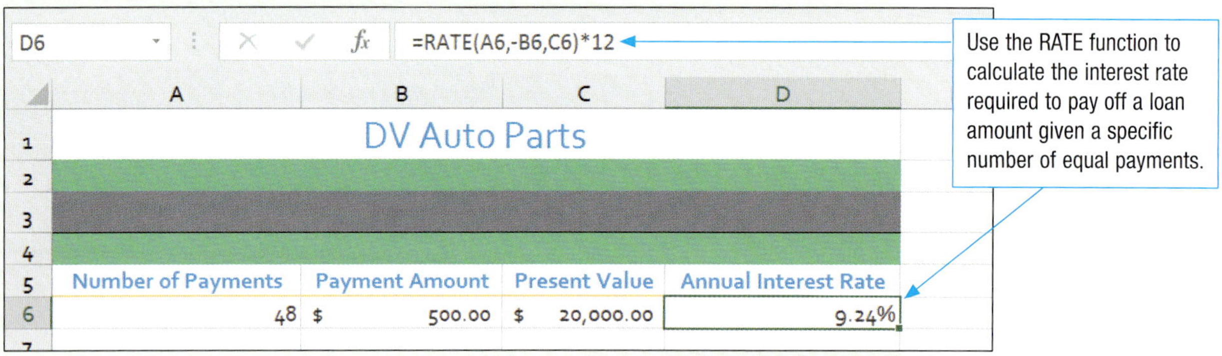

Model Answer

10.6 Finding the Number of Periods in a Loan (NPER)

MOS Expert 3.4.5

Tutorial

Using the NPER Function to Find the Number of Payments Required to Pay Off a Loan

The **NPER function** is a Financial function used to calculate the number of periods required to pay off a loan or to reach a target amount on an investment, given a fixed interest rate and a specified payment amount. Table 10.5 explains the syntax and arguments for the NPER function.

Table 10.5 NPER Function Syntax and Arguments

Syntax
=NPER(rate,pmt,pv,[fv],[type])

Argument	Required or Optional?	Description
rate	Required	Interest rate
pmt	Required	Payment made each period
pv	Required	Present value of the investment or loan
fv	Optional	Future value of the investment or loan, or a cash balance after the last payment is made. If the *fv* argument is not included, it is assumed to be 0.
type	Optional	Indication of when payments are due. A 0 indicates payments are due at the end of the period, and a 1 indicates payments are due at the beginning of the period. If the *type* argument is not included, it is assumed to be 0.

For example, if you want to purchase a vehicle for $24,000 and make payments of $200 biweekly (every 2 weeks) at an annual interest rate of 7.5%, the formula for calculating the number of payments is *=NPER(7.5%/26,200, -24000)*. You divide the annual interest rate by 26 to get the biweekly interest rate (52 weeks per year divided by 2 weeks per biweekly period equals 26 biweekly periods). The result, 68.4, is the number of biweekly periods for the loan. You can divide the result by 26 to calculate the number of years for the loan: 5.7.

When using the NPER function to calculate the number of periods required to reach a target amount on an investment, include the future value of the investment. For example, if you put $250 in an account that earns 2% interest that is compounded monthly, the formula for calculating the number of payments to reach a target goal of $4,000 is *=NPER(2%/12,-250,0,4000)*. The result, 15.84, is the number of monthly payments required to reach the investment goal. The *pv* argument is 0 because no initial investment was made prior to making the monthly deposits of $250.

▸ **Know This** about using the NPER function

- Use the same units for the *rate* and *pmt* arguments.
- Use negative values for the *pmt* argument if cash is being paid out or invested.
- Use positive values for the *pmt* argument if cash is being received or borrowed.
- The result uses the same units as the *pmt* argument. For example, if payments are made monthly, the result is the number of monthly periods.

On the Job

Task 10.6 Using the NPER Function to Find the Number of Payments Required to Pay Off a Loan

Devon's bank has offered him a $20,000 loan at an annual interest rate of 8.25% for up to 46 months. This is a better rate than you calculated for a 4-year loan in Task 10.5. Devon wants to get this rate, but he doesn't want to commit to monthly payments higher than $500 and still wants to make each payment at the end of the month. He asks you to help him determine whether he can pay off the loan in 46 months or less. Use the NPER function to calculate the number of monthly payments Devon will have to make to pay off a $20,000 loan at an 8.25% annual interest rate.

1. With the 10-DVAutoParts workbook open and the Equipment Loan worksheet active, copy the range B6:C6 and then paste it in cell B7.

   The range B6:C6 is copied into the range B7:C7.

2. Click in cell D7, type 8.25%, and then press the Enter key.

   The value *8.25%* displays in cell D7.

3. Click in cell A7, type =NPER(D7/12,-B7,C7), and then press Ctrl + Enter.

   The value *46.93640808* displays in cell A7 and the formula *=NPER(D7/12,-B7,C7)* displays in the Formula bar (see Figure 10.7). The result is the number of monthly payments because the *pmt* argument uses months as the unit. The last (47th) payment will be for $468.20, which is 93.640808% of $500. Devon will not be able to pay off the 8.25% loan in the required number of months.

4. Click the Save button on the Quick Access Toolbar.

Figure 10.7 Number of Payment Periods Calculated Using the NPER Function

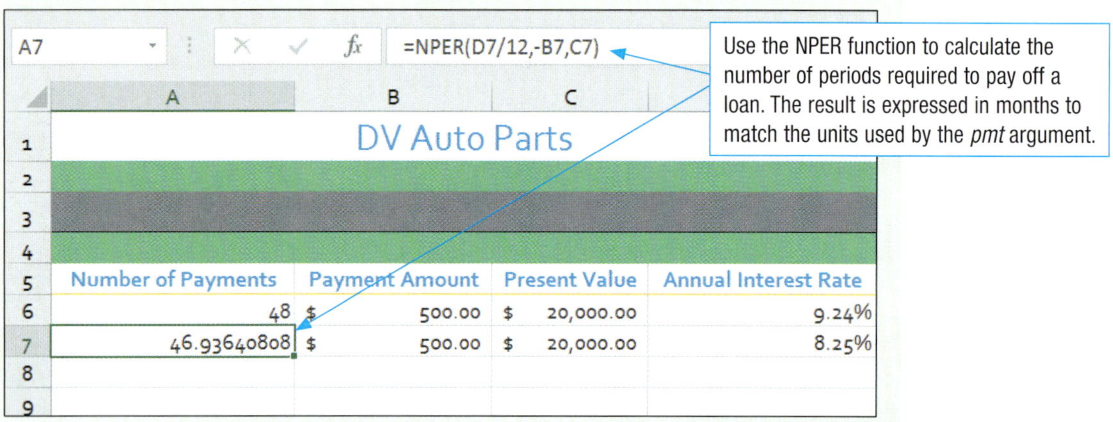

Model Answer

10.7 Inserting Depreciation Functions (SLN, SYD, DB, and DDB)

MOS Expert 3.4.5

Tutorial

Using the SLN Function to Calculate Straight-line Depreciation

Depreciation is an accounting method for allocating the cost of a tangible asset over its useful life. Organizations and individuals depreciate long-term assets for both tax and accounting purposes.

A **tangible asset** is an asset that has a physical form. Tangible assets include both fixed assets, such as buildings and machinery, and current assets, such as inventory. Depreciation only applies to fixed assets.

A **fixed asset** is a tangible piece of property that an organization or individual owns, that is used in the production of income, and that is not expected to be consumed or converted into cash within 1 year. (In comparison, a **current asset**

▶ **Know More** about depreciation

– Some assets, such as vehicles, are subject to income taxation depreciation limits.

is cash or property that can reasonably be expected to be converted to cash within 1 year. Current assets can include inventory [raw materials, work in process, and finished goods] and accounts receivable [money owed by customers].)

To calculate the depreciation of an asset, you need to know the original cost of the asset, the length of the useful life of the asset, the **salvage value** of the asset (the value at the end of the asset's useful life), and the rate at which the asset is depreciated over time.

Excel has four depreciation functions, each of which uses a slightly different method for depreciating an asset over time:

— The **SLN function** is used to calculate straight-line depreciation.

— The **SYD function** is used to calculate sum-of-the-years'-digits depreciation.

— The **DB function** is used to calculate declining balance depreciation.

— The **DDB function** is used to calculate double-declining balance depreciation.

Table 10.6 explains the syntax and arguments for the depreciation functions. It is important to note that regardless of the method used to calculate depreciation, the total depreciation over the life of an asset does not vary.

Table 10.6 Syntax and Arguments for Depreciation Functions

Syntax
= *SLN(cost,salvage,life)*
= *SYD(cost,salvage,life,per)*
= *DB(cost,salvage,life,period,[month])*
= *DDB(cost,salvage,life,period,[factor])*

Argument	Required or Optional?	Description
cost	Required	Initial cost of the asset
salvage	Required	Value of the asset after depreciation
life	Required	Number of periods over which the asset is depreciated (also referred to as the *useful life* of the asset)
per or *period*	Required	Number of the period for which you want to calculate the depreciation
month	Optional	Number of months the asset is in use in the first year. If the *month* argument is not included, it is assumed to be 12.
factor	Optional	Rate at which the value declines in the depreciation schedule. If the *factor* argument is not included, it is assumed to be 2.

Straight-line depreciation takes the estimated salvage value of an asset at the end of its life, subtracts it from the asset's original cost, and then divides the result by the estimated number of useful years of the asset. When you use straight-line depreciation, an asset depreciates by an equal amount each year until the salvage value is reached. For example, to depreciate a $15,000 die-cutting press that will have a salvage value of $3,000 after 5 years, the formula is *=SLN(15000,3000,5)*. The result, $2,400, is the amount the machine will depreciate every year for 5 years using the straight-line depreciation method (see Table 10.7).

Sum-of-the-years'-digits depreciation is an accelerated form of depreciation that results in higher depreciation in the early years of an asset's useful life and lower depreciation in later years. You include the *per* or *period* argument at the end of the SYD function to indicate which year should be used in the calculation. For example, if you depreciate the $15,000 die-cutting press using the sum-of-the-years'-digits depreciation, the formula *=SYD(15000,3000,5,1)* calculates the depreciation in the first year of the machine's useful life. The result, $4,000, is the depreciation value in year 1 using the sum-of-the-years'-digits depreciation method. The formula for the fifth year of depreciation is *=SYD(15000,3000,5,5)* and the result is $800.

With **declining balance depreciation**, an asset depreciates by a fixed percentage applied to the prior year's undepreciated value as opposed to an equal amount every year. This results in the depreciation value being higher in the early life of the asset and then decreasing with the age of the asset. The DB function includes the *per* or *period* argument, which lets you specify the period for which you want to calculate the depreciation. For example, if you depreciate the $15,000 die-cutting press using declining balance depreciation, the formula *=DB(15000,3000,5,2)* calculates the depreciation in year 2 of the machine's useful life. The result, $2,990.63, is less than the depreciation value in year 1 and higher than the value in year 3.

Double-declining balance depreciation is a commonly used accelerated form of depreciation that results in higher depreciation in the early years of an asset's useful life and lower depreciation in the later years. It is also referred to as the *200% declining balance method of depreciation* because the depreciation percentage is double what it would be under the straight-line method of depreciation. Instead of using the asset's original cost to calculate the depreciation, this method uses the asset's beginning-of-the-year book value. The *per* or *period* argument is included at the end of the DBB function to indicate which year should be used in the calculation. For example, if you depreciate the $15,000 die-cutting press using double-declining balance depreciation, the formula *=DDB(15000,3000,5,2)* calculates the depreciation in year 2 of the machine's useful life. The result, $3,600.00, is less than the depreciation value in year 1 and higher than the value in year 3.

Table 10.7 Depreciation Methods

Depreciation Method	Year 1	Year 2	Year 3	Year 4	Year 5
Straight-line depreciation	$2,400.00	$2,400.00	$2,400.00	$2,400.00	$2,400.00
Sum-of-the-years'-digits depreciation	$4,000.00	$3,200.00	$2,400.00	$1,600.00	$800.00
Declining balance depreciation	$4,125.00	$2,990.63	$2,168.20	$1,571.95	$1,139.66
Double-declining balance depreciation	$6,000.00	$3,600.00	$2,160.00	$240.00	$0.00

▸ **Know This** about using depreciation functions

— Use the same units for the *per* or *period* argument and the *life* argument.

On the Job

Task 10.7 Using the SLN Function to Calculate Straight-line Depreciation

Devon has purchased a vehicle and a computer system for his new business. He purchased the vehicle for $32,000 and its salvage value after

7 years will be $10,000. The computer system cost $15,000 and has a useful life of 2 years and a salvage value of $2,000. Devon wants you to help him calculate the depreciation value for each item using the straight-line method of depreciation. Use the SLN function to do the calculations.

1. With the 10-DVAutoParts workbook open and the Equipment Loan worksheet active, click the Assets sheet tab.
2. Click in cell B4, type 32000, and then press the Tab key.

   The value *32000* displays in cell B4 and cell C4 is active.
3. Type 10000 and then press the Tab key.

   The value *10000* displays in cell C4 and cell D4 is active.
4. Type 7 and then press the Tab key.

   The value *7* displays in cell D4 and cell E4 is active.
5. Type =SLN(B4,C4,D4) and then press Ctrl + Enter.

   The result *$3,142.86* displays in cell E4 and the formula *=SLN(B4,C4,D4)* displays in the Formula bar. The result is the amount the vehicle depreciates each year using the straight-line depreciation method.
6. Click in cell B5, type 15000, and then press the Tab key.

   The value *15000* displays in cell B5 and cell C5 is active.
7. Type 2000 and then press the Tab key.

   The value *2000* displays in cell C5 and cell D5 is active.
8. Type 5 and then press the Tab key.
9. Click in cell E4 and then use the fill handle to copy the formula from cell E4 down into cell E5.

   The result *$2,600.00* displays in cell E5 and the formula *=SLN(B4,C4,D4)* continues to display in the Formula bar (see Figure 10.8). The result is the amount the computer system depreciates each year using the straight-line depreciation method.
10. Apply the Accounting format to the range B4:C5 and the range E4:E5.
11. Click the Save button on the Quick Access Toolbar.

Figure 10.8 SLN Function

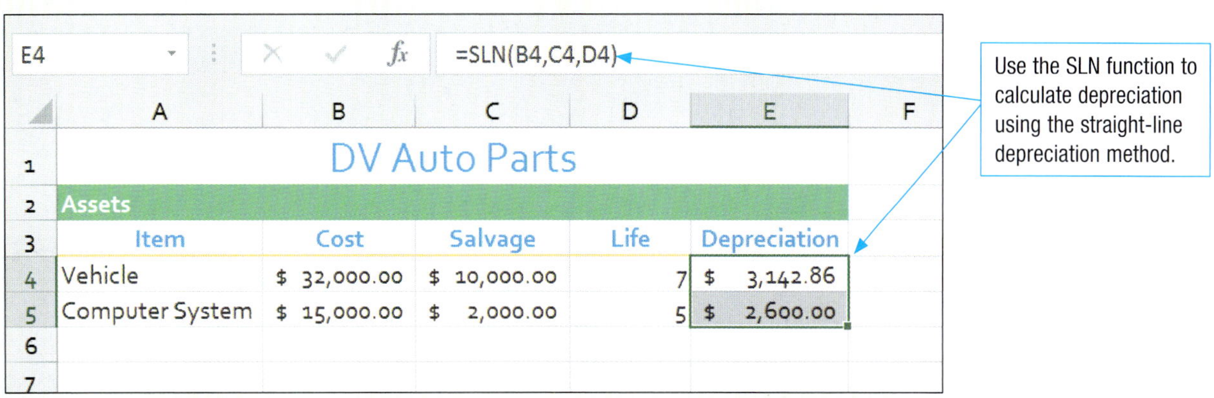

Model Answer

10.8 Using the Net Present Value (NPV)

MOS Expert 3.4.5

Tutorial

Using the NPV Function to Assess the Net Present Value of an Investment

The **net present value (NPV)** is a profitability measure used to assess the potential return on an investment by adding the present value of all future cash inflows (income) and then subtracting the present value of all future cash outflows (payments). Essentially, it compares the amount invested to the future cash inflows after they are discounted by a specified rate of return, which is the interest rate you would earn if the money were placed in an alternative investment, such as a high-yield savings or money market account. The rate of return, or discount rate, provides a method of comparing present value to future value.

The **NPV function** is similar to the PV function. One difference is that the PV function allows cash flows to be made at either the end or beginning of the period, while the NPV function assumes cash flows (income and payments) are made at the end of the period. Another difference is that with the PV function, cash flows must be constant throughout the investment, whereas the NPV function allows for unequal cash flows. Table 10.8 explains the syntax and arguments for the NPV function.

Table 10.8 NPV Function Syntax and Arguments

Syntax *=NPV(rate,value1,[value2],...)*		
Argument	**Required or Optional?**	**Description**
rate	Required	Discount rate over the length of one period
value1	Required	Cash flow from first period
value2	Optional	Cash flow from second period
...	Optional	Cash flow from subsequent periods. Up to 254 payment variables can be entered.

For example, to calculate the net present value of an investment that pays $500 every year for 3 years assuming a discount rate of 6%, use the formula *=NPV(6%,500,500,500)*. The result, $1,336.51, means that the $1,500 paid from the investment is the same as receiving $1,336.51 today.

▸ Know This about using the NPV function

- Use the same units for the *rate* and *value* arguments.
- Use negative values for the *value* arguments if cash is being paid out (payments).
- Use positive values for the *value* arguments if cash is being received (income).
- NPV uses the order of the *value* arguments to interpret the order of cash flows. Therefore, you need to enter the *value* arguments in the correct sequence, beginning with the first payment or income.
- *Value* arguments are calculated to occur at the end of the period.

— The NPV calculation is based on future cash flows. If the first cash flow (such as the initial investment) occurs at the beginning of the first period, the first value must be added to the NPV result, not included as a *value* argument.
— If the NPV function returns a positive value, the cost of the investment is less than the present value of its cash inflows.

On the Job

Task 10.8 Using the NPV Function to Assess the Net Present Value of an Investment

Devon has investigated buying an auto parts franchise. This would offer many advantages to his new business, but it would also be costly. It would require a $200,000 initial investment at the start of the first period. After discussing the investment with a franchise company and a financial analyst, Devon has estimated the return, or net cash inflow, he would receive each year for a 10-year period if he purchased the franchise. He has recorded the estimates in range B5:B14 in the Franchise worksheet of his business plan workbook. He has also estimated that he would earn a 5% rate of return if he placed the $200,000 in an alternative investment. He wants you to help him determine which investment would be most profitable. Use the NPV function to calculate the net present value of the franchise investment, including the return values Devon has provided.

1. With the 10-DVAutoParts workbook open and the Investments worksheet active, click the Franchise sheet tab.
2. Click in cell C2, type 5%, and then press the Enter key.

   The value *5%* displays in cell C2 and cell C3 is active.
3. Click in cell B4, type -200000, and then press Ctrl + Enter.
4. With cell B4 active, apply the Accounting format.

   The value *$(200,000.00)* displays in cell B4. The initial investment of $200,000 is a negative value because it is an expense, or money paid out. It is not entered as a *value* argument in the NPV function because it is paid at the beginning of the period; instead, it will be added to the result of the NPV function when you calculate the total net present value in Step 5. The negative value displays in a black font because you applied the Accounting format to the cell containing it.
5. Click in cell B16, type =NPV(C2,B5:B14)+B4, and then press Ctrl + Enter.

   The value *$8,017.82* displays in cell B16 and the formula *=NPV(C2,B5:B14)+B4* displays in the Formula bar (see Figure 10.9). The formula includes the NPV function, which calculates the result of the estimated returns assuming a return rate of 5%, plus the initial investment of $200,000. The positive value result indicates the franchise investment would give Devon a better return than the alternative investment.
6. Click the Save button on the Quick Access Toolbar.

Figure 10.9 Net Present Value of an Investment Calculated Using the NPV Function

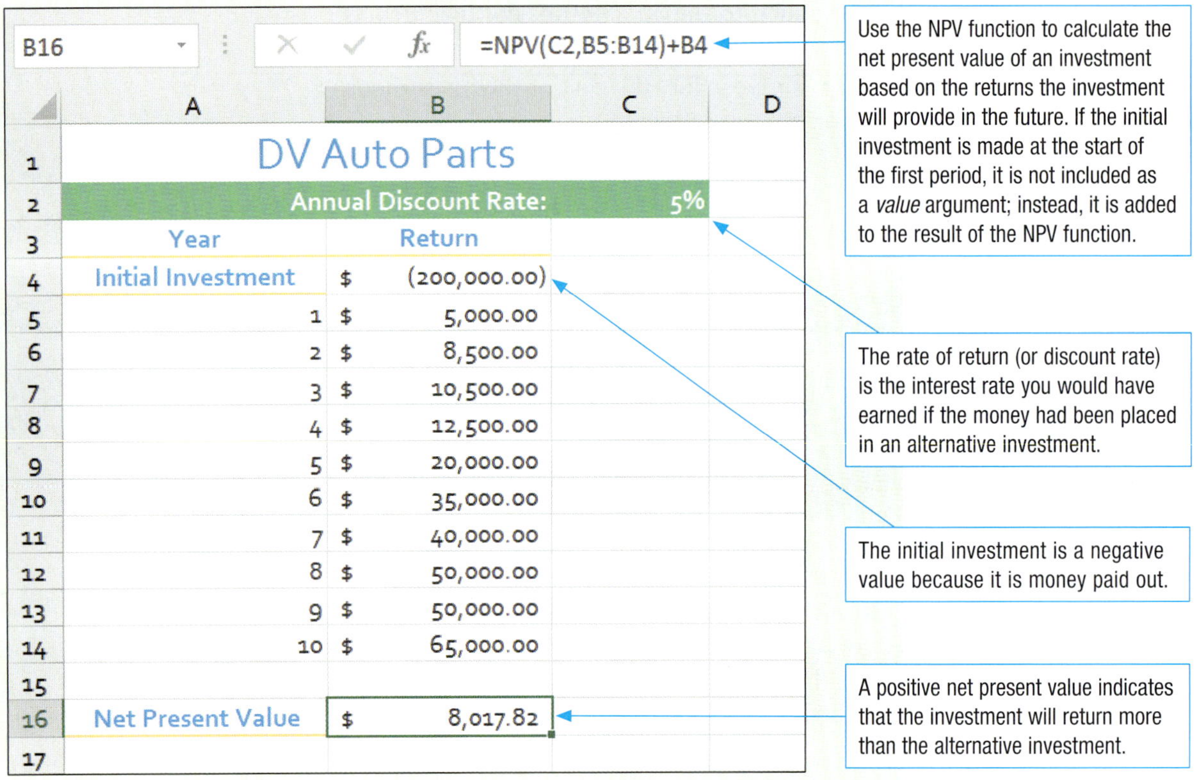

Model Answer

10.9 Finding the Internal Rate of Return (IRR)

MOS Expert 3.4.5

Tutorial

Using the IRR Function to Find the Internal Rate of Return

The **internal rate of return (IRR)** is a profitability measure used to determine which investments or projects are likely to yield the greatest return per dollar of capital investment. IRR is similar to net present value but calculates the expected gains as a percentage of the initial investment, rather than as a net dollar amount.

The **IRR function** returns the internal rate of return for a set of values, including an initial investment value and a series of net income values. Table 10.9 explains the syntax and arguments for the IRR function.

Table 10.9 IRR Function Syntax and Arguments

Syntax
=*IRR(values,[guess])*

Argument	Required or Optional?	Description
values	Required	An array or reference to the range of cells containing the series of cash flows.
guess	Optional	A number you guess that is close to the result of internal rate of return. In most cases, this argument is not needed. If the *guess* argument is not included, it is assumed to be 10%.

For example, to calculate the internal rate of return for a $1,000 investment (entered as a negative value in cell B2) that paid $200 in the first year, $250 in the second year, $350 in the third year, and $350 in the fourth year (entered as positive values in the range B3:B6), use the formula *=IRR(B2:B6)*. The result is a 5% internal rate of return. This indicates that the investment was as profitable as an alternate investment that paid 5% annual interest.

▸ **Know This** about using the IRR Function

- Use a negative value for a *values* argument if cash is being paid out or invested.
- Use a positive value for a *value* argument if cash is being received or borrowed.
- The *values* arguments must include at least one positive value and one negative value.
- The IRR function uses the order of the *values* arguments to interpret the order of cash flows. Be sure to enter the payment and income values in the correct sequence, starting with the initial expense or income.
- If a cell referenced in a *values* argument contains a logical value or text, or is empty, it is ignored.
- Excel uses an iterative technique for calculating IRR. Starting with the *guess* argument (if provided), the IRR function cycles through the calculation until the result is accurate within 0.00001%. If the IRR function cannot find a result that works after 20 tries, the error code #NUM! is returned.
- The value returned by the IRR function is a percentage.

On the Job

Task 10.9 Using the IRR Function to Find the Internal Rate of Return

In Task 10.8, you helped Devon analyze the potential profitability of a franchise investment by calculating the net present value. Devon also wants to know the expected gains after 10 years as a percentage of the initial investment. Again, he wants to know whether the franchise investment will be more profitable than the alternative investment that might earn a 5% rate of return. Use the IRR function to calculate this result.

1. With the 10-DVAutoParts workbook open and the Franchise worksheet active, click in cell A17, type Internal Rate of Return, and then press Ctrl + Enter.

   The text *Internal Rate of Return* displays in cell A17.
2. Use the Format Painter to copy the formatting from cell A16 into cell A17.

   The formatting from cell A16 is applied to cell A17.
3. AutoFit Column A.
4. Click in cell B17, type =IRR(B4:B14), and then press Ctrl + Enter.

   The value 6% displays in cell B17 and the formula *=IRR(B4:B14)* displays in the Formula bar. The formula includes the IRR function, which calculates the internal rate of return. The result indicates that the franchise investment would be more profitable than an alternate investment that pays 5% annual interest (see Figure 10.10). However, the franchise investment is a high-risk investment and involves a considerable work commitment.

5. If printed work is required by your instructor, print the workbook.
6. Save and then close the workbook.

Figure 10.10 Internal Rate of Return Calculated Using the IRR Function

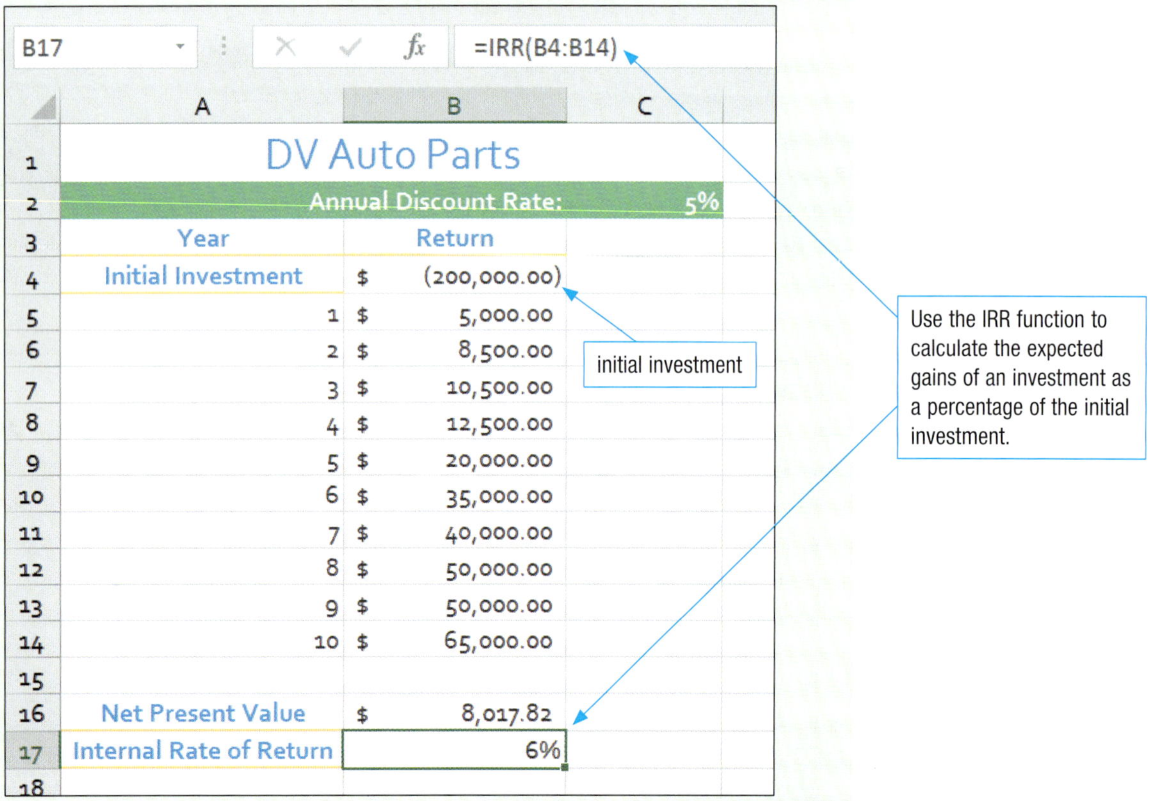

Model Answer

10.10 Validating and Restricting Data Entry

MOS Expert 2.1.

Tutorials

Creating a Validation Rule to Restrict Data Entry

Adding an Input Message and an Error Alert to a Validation Rule

You can use the **Data Validation** feature to validate and restrict the types of data or values that can be entered in a cell. An entry can be restricted to a predefined item or value, a specified range, a certain timeframe, and a maximum number of text characters. Data can also be validated based on formulas or values in other cells. The Data Validation feature prevents data entry errors and saves time with repetitive data entry.

A **validation rule** defines the criteria for the data that can be entered into a cell or range. For example, a validation rule could specify the **validation criteria** that only dates between 2019/01/01 and 2019/12/31 can be entered into the range A4:A20 (see Figure 10.11) or it can take the form of a drop-down list of allowable entries. You can also specify an **input message**, such as *yyyy/mm/dd format* (see Figure 10.12), to indicate what data is allowed in the cell and an **error alert message** to indicate that incorrect data has been entered (see Figure 10.13).

Figure 10.11 Data Validation Criteria

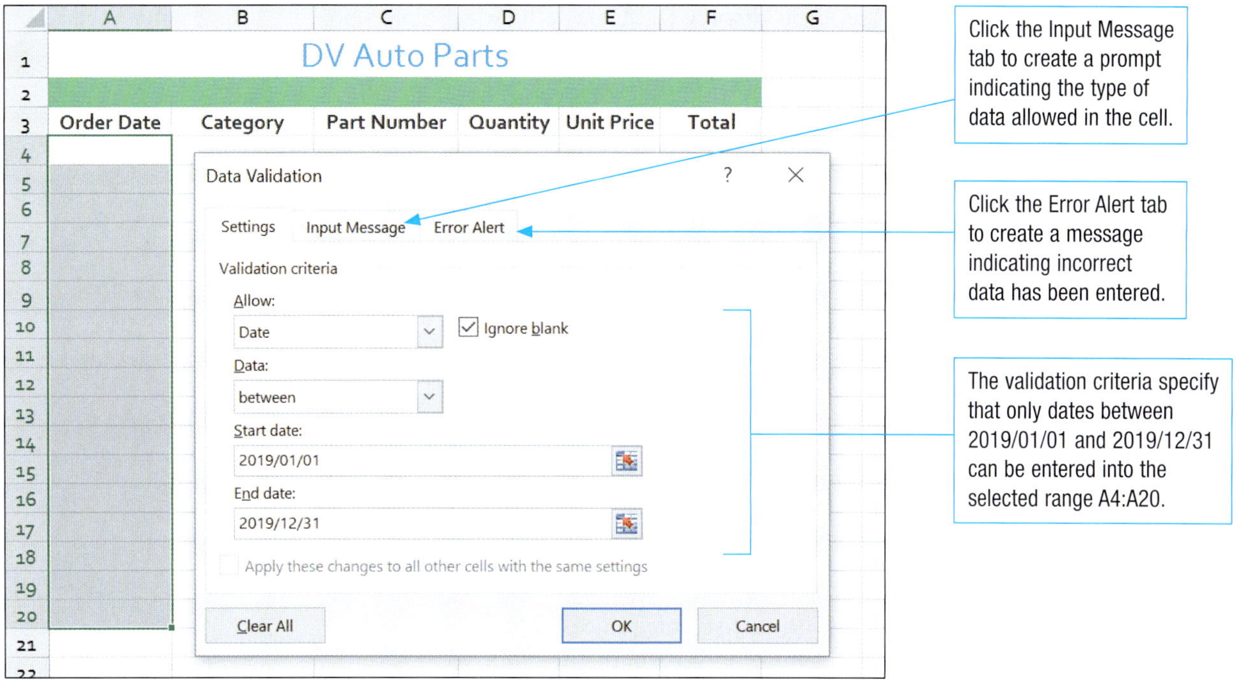

Figure 10.12 Input Message Prompt

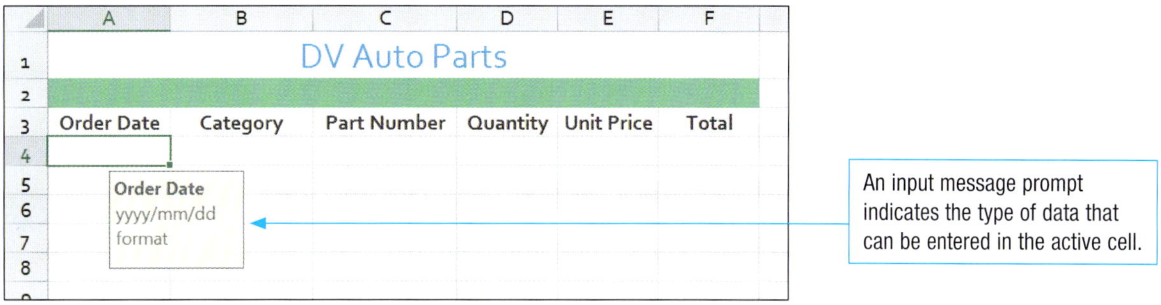

Figure 10.13 Error Alert

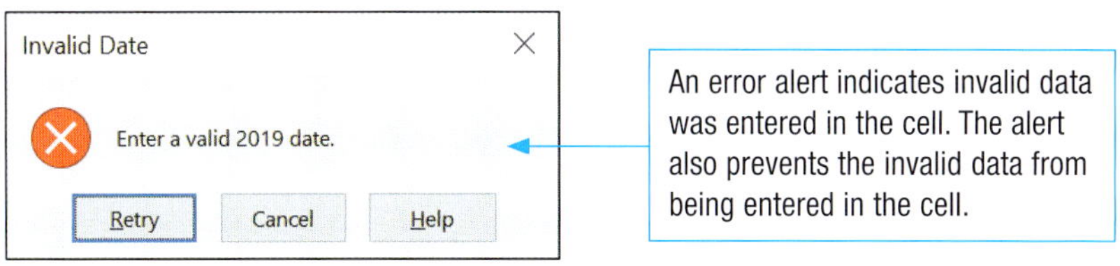

▸ **Know This** about using the Data Validation feature

— To display the Data Validation dialog box, where you can select options for setting data validation rules, click the Data Validation button in the Data Tools group on the Data tab.

— Data validation options are grouped on three tabs at the Data Validation dialog box: Settings, Input Message, and Error Alert (see Figure 10.11).

— To create a validation rule, select a cell or cells, click the Settings tab in the Data Validation dialog box, click the *Allow* option box arrow, select an option at the drop-down list, and then specify the validation criteria.

▸ **Know More** ways to display the Data Validation dialog box

– Click the Data Validation button arrow in the Data Tools group on the Data tab and then click the *Data Validation* option at the drop-down list.

▸ **Know This** about creating an input message prompt

— To create an input message prompt, display the Data Validation dialog box, click the Input Message tab, type a title in the *Title* box, type a prompt in the *Input message* box, and then click the OK button.

— The prompt displays when a cell with the validation rule is active (see Figure 10.12 on page 469).

▸ **Know This** about creating an error alert

— To create an error alert: display the Data Validation dialog box; click the Error Alert tab; click the *Style* option box arrow; click a style option at the drop-down list; type a title in the *Title* text box, (optional); type an error message in the *Error message* text box, (optional); and then click the OK button.

— If invalid data is entered in a cell with a validation rule that contains an error alert, the error alert displays in the worksheet (see Figure 10.13 on page 469) and the invalid data is cleared from the cell.

▸ **Know This** about creating a data validation drop-down list

— To create a data validation drop-down list, select a cell or cells that will display the list, click the Data Validation button in the Data Tools group on the Data tab, click the *Allow* option box arrow on the Settings tab at the Data Validation dialog box, click the *List* option at the drop-down list, type the entries that will display in the drop-down list separated by commas in the *Source* text box, and then click the OK button.

— Entries for the drop-down list can also be created by typing an equals sign (=) followed by the defined name for a cell or range in the *Source* text box, or by clicking the Collapse button to the right of the *Source* text box, and then selecting a range in the worksheet.

— Be sure the cell containing a drop-down list is wide enough to display the list entries.

— Select the *Ignore blank* check box to insert a check mark if you want the Data Validation feature to ignore blank cells.

▸ **Know This** about data validation

— If you create a validation rule and apply it to cells that already contain invalid data, Excel will not display an error message.

— To flag cells that already contain invalid data, click the Data Validation button arrow in the Data Tools group on the Data tab and then click the *Circle Invalid Data* option at the drop-down list.

— To remove circles around invalid data, click the Data Validation button arrow and then click the *Clear Validation Circles* option.

— To find worksheet cells that have data validation settings applied, click the Find & Select button in the Editing group on the Home tab and then click the *Data Validation* option.

▸ **Know This** about removing data validation from a cell or cells

— To remove data validation from a cell or cells, select the cell or cells, click the Data Validation button in the Data Tools group on the Data tab, and then click the Clear All button.

▸ **Know This** about editing data validation settings for a cell or cells

— To edit data validation settings for a cell or cells, select a cell that contains data validation, click the Data Validation button in the Data Tools group on the Data tab, edit the settings, and then click the *Apply these changes to all other cells with the same settings* check box to insert a check mark.

On the Job

Task 10.10 Validating and Restricting Data Entry

Devon has created a workbook to track orders for his new business. Several sales associates will be entering data in this workbook, and Devon wants to be sure the data entered is accurate and consistent. He wants order dates to be entered in the format *yyyy/mm/dd* and to limit entries to dates within the calendar year (2019). He also wants to use the same categories in this workbook as in his inventory workbook, so he can match orders to inventory. Use the Data Validation feature to apply settings that validate and restrict the date and category entries. Include an input message prompting users with the correct date format, an error message prompting users to enter a date for the current year, and a drop-down list for entries in the *Category* column. Test the settings to see if they behave the way Devon wants them to.

1. Open the data file **10-DVAutoParts-Orders**.
2. With the Orders worksheet active, select the range A4:A20.
3. Click the Data tab and then click the Data Validation button in the Data Tools group.

   The Data Validation dialog box displays.
4. Click the *Allow* option box arrow.

   A drop-down list displays.
5. Click the *Date* option.
6. Click in the *Start date* text box, type 2019/01/01, and then press the Tab key.

   The insertion point is in the *End date* text box.
7. Type 2019/12/31 (see Figure 10.11 on page 469).
8. Click the Input Message tab.
9. Click in the *Title* text box, type Order Date, and then press the Tab key.

   The insertion point is in the *Input message* text box.
10. Type yyyy/mm/dd format (see Figure 10.14).
11. Click the Error Alert tab.
12. Click in the *Title* text box and then type Invalid Date.
13. Click in the *Error message* text box, type Enter a valid 2019 date., and then click the OK button.

    The Data Validation dialog box closes, cell A4 is active, and the input message displays below the cell.
14. Select the range B4:B20.
15. Click the Data Validation button.
16. Click the Settings tab, click the *Allow* option box arrow, and then click the *List* option.

17. Click in the *Source* text box; type Batteries, Belts, Brakes, Exhaust, Filters, Ignition; and then click the OK button (see Figure 10.15).

Figure 10.14 Input Message

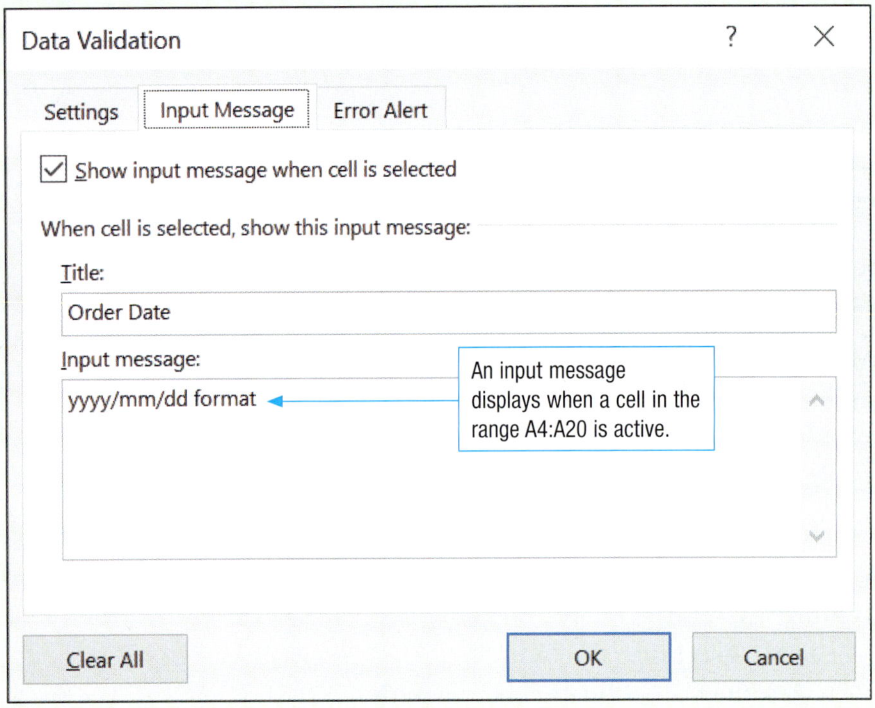

Figure 10.15 Data Validation Dialog Box with Settings for Creating a Drop-Down List of Cell Entries

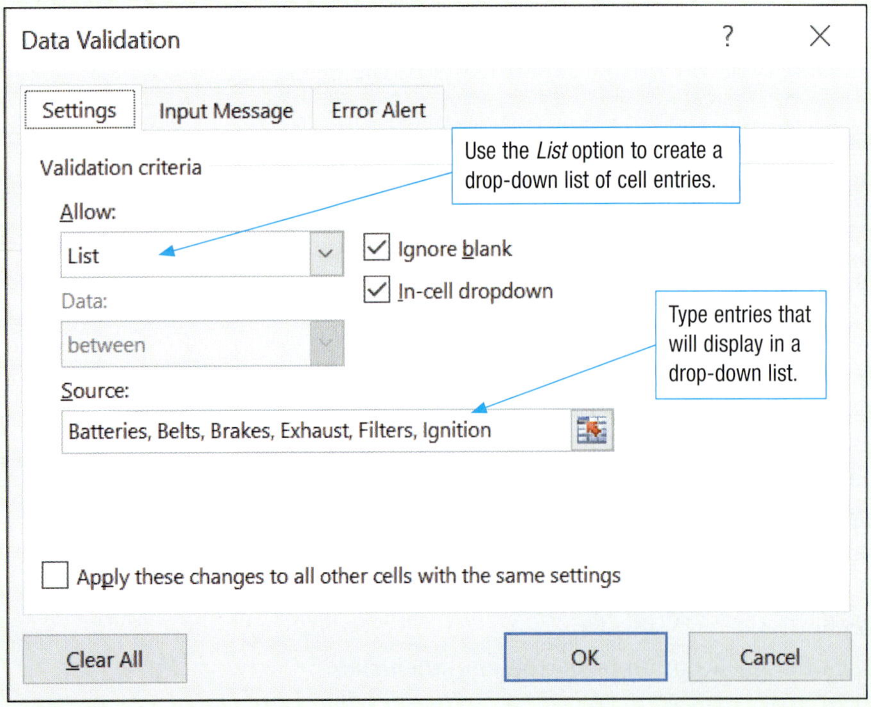

18. Click in cell A4.

    The input message displays.

19. Type 2018/01/01 and then press the Enter key.

    A dialog box displays with the error message you created in Step 13 (see Figure 10.13 on page 469).

20. Click the Cancel button.

    The dialog box is closed and the entry is cleared from the cell.

21. Click in cell B4 and then click the arrow that appears.

    A drop-down list displays with the categories you entered in Step 17 (see Figure 10.16).

Figure 10.16 Excel Worksheet with a Drop-Down List of Cell Entries

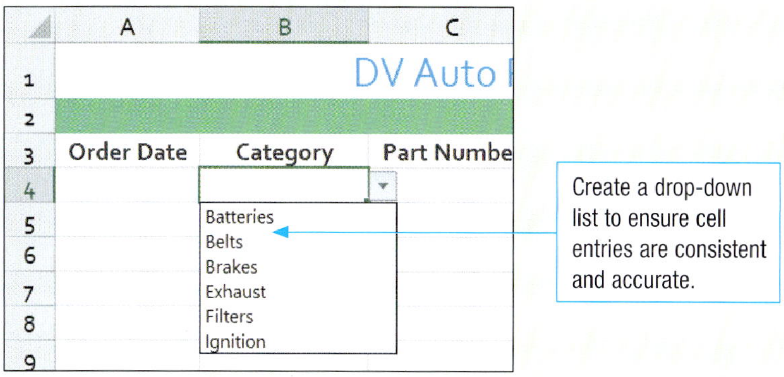

22. Click the *Brakes* option.

    The category *Brakes* appears in cell B4.

23. If printed work is required by your instructor, print the workbook.
24. Save and then close the workbook.

Model Answer

10.11 Identifying Errors and Troubleshooting Formulas Using Formula Auditing Tools

MOS Expert 3.5.1
MOS Expert 3.5.3

Tutorial

Checking for Errors and Tracing Precedents

Excel automatically displays formula and function error codes, error codes, and the Trace Error button to help you locate and debug errors in formulas and functions (see Chapter 2). Other methods for finding and fixing errors include using the Error Checking feature, tracing errors to their sources, and using the Evaluate Formula feature. It may be helpful to show formulas in the worksheet when finding and fixing formula errors.

The **Error Checking** feature displays a dialog box with buttons similar to the options at the Trace Error drop-down list. This feature checks all the formulas in the worksheet, like the spelling checker checks all the text in the worksheet.

The Trace Precedents and Trace Dependents features display the relationships between formulas and cells. A **formula auditing tool** can be used to find the source of an error by tracing precedent or dependent cells. A **precedent cell** is a cell that is referred to by a formula in another cell, and a **dependent cell** contains a formula that refers to other cells. For example, if cell G20 contains the formula =*G1*, cell G1 is a precedent to cell G20 and cell G20 is a dependent of cell G1. A cell can be both a precedent and a dependent cell.

If a complex formula contains an error, the Evaluate Formula feature can be used to evaluate each part of the formula individually (see Chapter 9). This feature can help pinpoint where the calculation error occurs.

Reminder
To show all the formulas in the worksheet, click the Show Formulas button in the Formula Auditing group on the Formulas tab or press Ctrl + `.

▸ Know This about using the Error Checking feature

— To run the error checker, click the Error Checking button in the Formula Auditing group on the Formulas tab and then click a button at the Error Checking dialog box (see Figure 10.17).

— Use the Error Checking button to access the same options as the Trace Error button and correct multiple errors without having to locate cells with the Trace Error button.

— The Error Checking feature will locate syntax errors; it will not locate logic errors. A **syntax error** is an error that violates the set of rules that describe how a formula or function should be written, such as forgetting a matching parenthesis in a function or dividing by 0. A **logic error** occurs when a formula works but produces an incorrect result, such as calculating the tax rate using a value of 6 instead of 6% (.06).

Figure 10.17 Error Checking Dialog Box

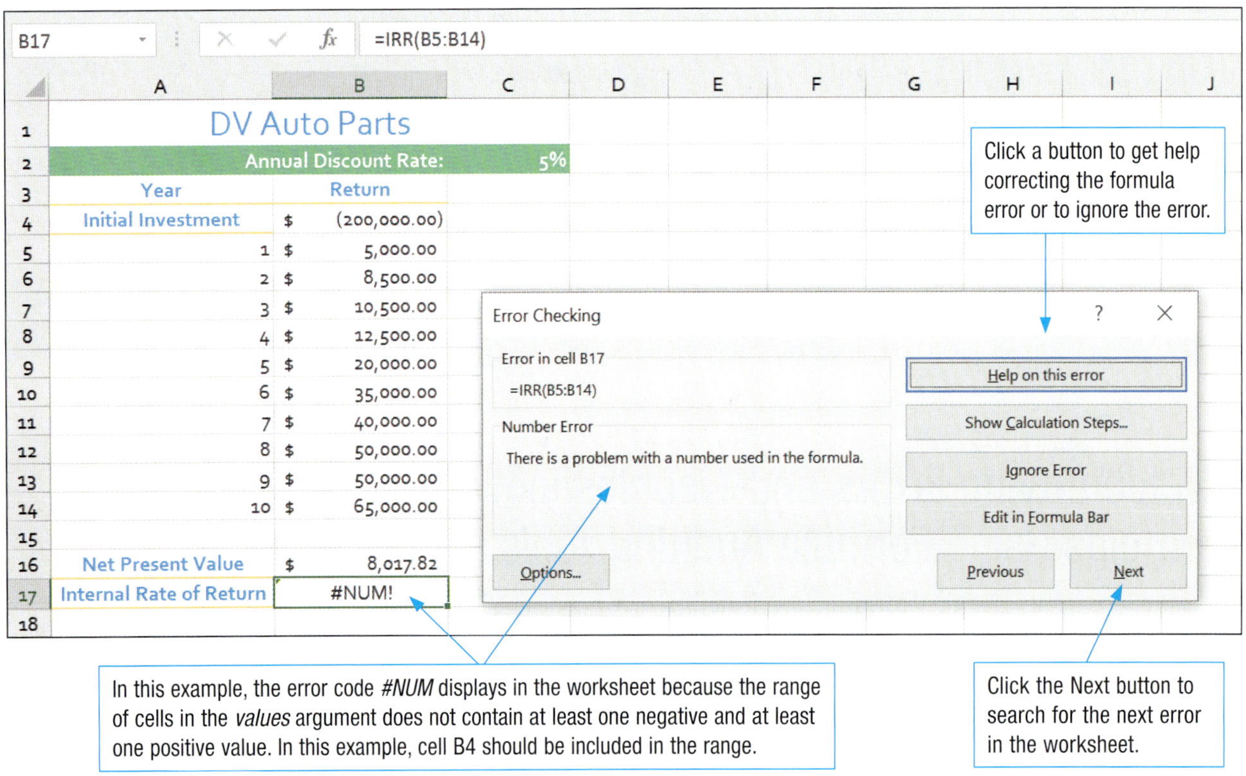

▸ Know This about tracing an error to its source

— Use **tracer arrows** to provide visual clues when locating the source of an error in a formula. Click the cell with an error value and then trace the error through the line of its precedent cells. If any of the precedent cells has an error value, trace that cell's precedent values. Repeat this process until you locate an error cell with no precedents. That cell will be the source of the error in all of its dependent cells.

— To trace precedents, click a cell containing a formula and then click the Trace Precedents button in the Formula Auditing group on the Formulas tab (see Figure 10.18).
— To trace dependents, click in a cell containing a formula and then click the Trace Dependents button.
— A blue tracer arrow points to a cell with no errors. A blue bullet in a cell with an arrow going through the cell indicates that cell is referenced in the formula.
— A red tracer arrow points to a cell that causes errors (see Figure 10.19).
— A black tracer arrow displays if the selected cell is referenced by a cell in another worksheet or another workbook that is open (see Figure 10.20). Use a tracer arrow to navigate to the sheet.
— To remove all the tracer arrows in a worksheet, click the Remove Arrows button.

Figure 10.18 Trace Precedents Button, Trace Dependents Button, and Tracer Arrows

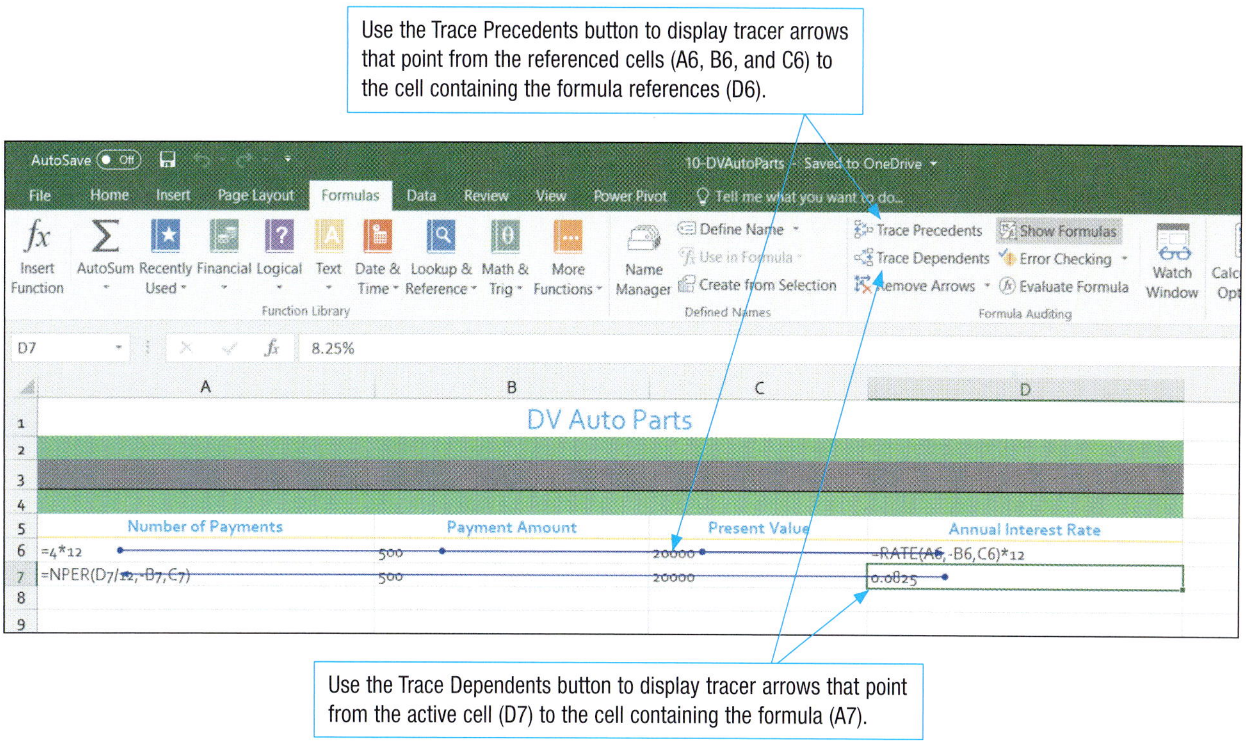

Figure 10.19 Red Tracer Arrow

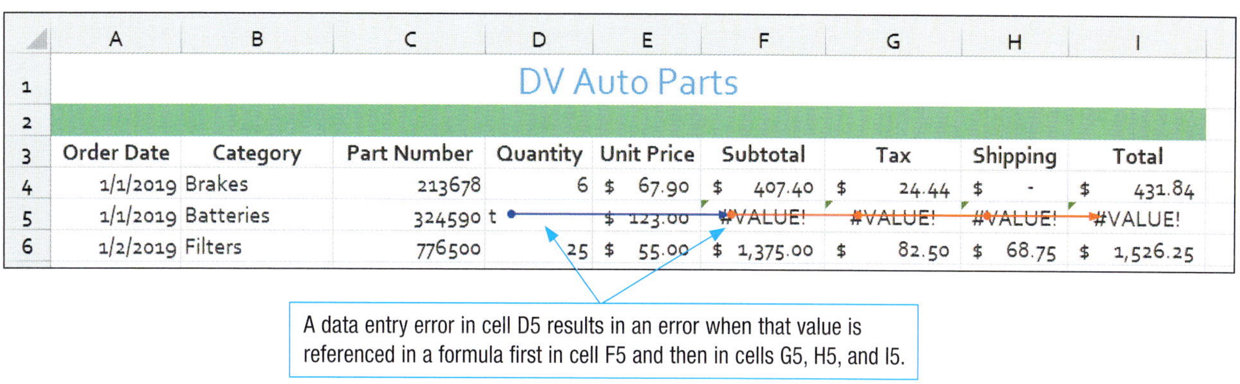

Figure 10.20 Black Tracer Arrow

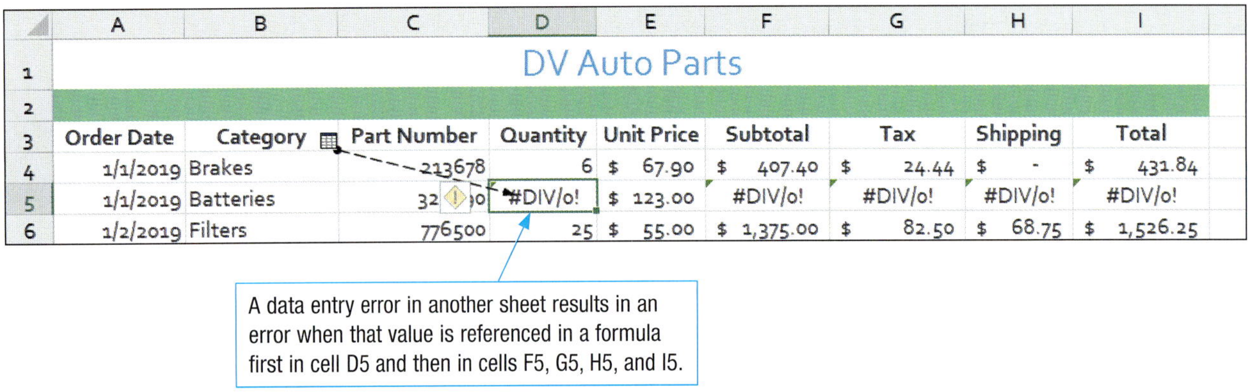

▸ Know This about using the Evaluate Formula feature

— To evaluate a formula using the Evaluate Formula feature, click the Evaluate Formula button in the Formula Auditing group on the Formulas tab and then work step by step through the formula at the Evaluate Formula dialog box.

— The Evaluate Formula feature is helpful for debugging complex formulas such as nested formulas (e.g., *=IF(AVERAGE(A2:A25)<2500,COUNT(B2:B25),0))*.

— This feature is covered in detail in Chapter 9, Section 9.5.

On the Job

Task 10.11 Checking for Errors and Tracing Precedents

Devon has created a new sales workbook including test data and formulas that calculate subtotal, tax, shipping, and total values for orders. A 6% tax is charged on all the orders. Shipping is free if the order is $500 or greater, or 5% of the subtotal if the order is less than $500. The total values in the worksheet are clearly too high, and Devon wants you to debug the formulas in the worksheet. Use the Error Checking feature to search for syntax errors in the worksheet. Use the Trace Precedents button to trace errors in the total formulas back to their source.

1. Open the data file **10-DVAutoParts-Sales**.
2. Click the Formulas tab, and then click the Error Checking button in the Formula Auditing group.

   A message box displays indicating the error check is complete for the entire sheet. This is an indication that the errors in the worksheet are logical, not syntax, errors.
3. Click the OK button.

   The dialog box closes.
4. Click in cell I4 and then click the Trace Precedents button.

   Tracer arrows display from the referenced cells (F4, G4, and H4) pointing to the active cell (I4), illustrating which cells may be causing the total formula to be inaccurate. Notice that the tax value is more than the subtotal value; it should be 6% of the subtotal.

5. Press the Left Arrow key two times.

   Cell G4 is active and the formula displays on the Formula bar. Notice the subtotal value is multiplied by 6 instead of 6%.

6. Click at the end of the formula on the Formula bar, type the percent symbol (%), and then press Ctrl + Enter.

   The value *$24.44* displays in cell G4. This is 6% of the subtotal.

7. Use the fill handle to copy the formula from cell G4 down into cell G13.

   The tax values are corrected and the tracer arrows disappear.

8. If printed work is required by your instructor, print the workbook.
9. Save and close the workbook.

Model Answer

10.12 Illustrating Data with Sparklines

MOS 2.3.1

Tutorial

Illustrating Data with Sparklines

A **sparkline** is a type of information graphic (or *infographic*) that is inserted in a cell and is used to illustrate data trends and patterns. A sparkline is small, but it efficiently creates a visual representation of the data without having to create a standard chart and add chart elements. The Quick Analysis feature can be used to quickly add sparklines to a worksheet. Sparklines can also be created using buttons in the Sparklines group on the Insert tab (see Figure 10.21). This method gives you more flexibility in placing sparklines in the worksheet.

Figure 10.21 Sparklines Group on the Insert Tab

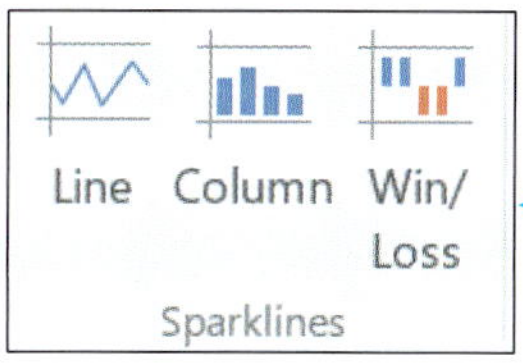

▸ Know This about sparklines

- A sparkline can take the form of a line chart, a column chart, or a win/loss chart (see Figure 10.21).
- A sparkline is not an object like an image or standard chart, which is positioned on top of the worksheet; it is a minichart inserted in the background of a cell.
- Text can be entered in the same cell as a sparkline and display in front of the sparkline.
- To copy a sparkline down a column or across a row, drag the fill handle or use the copy and paste commands to copy the sparkline into nonadjacent cells.
- Sparklines are printed with the worksheet.

▸ Know This about creating sparklines using Quick Analysis

- To insert a sparkline using Quick Analysis, select the cells that contain the data you want to chart, click the Quick Analysis button, click the Sparklines tab, and then click the type of sparkline at the Quick Analysis gallery (see Figure 10.22).

— You can point to a type of sparkline at the Quick Analysis gallery to display a live preview.
— When you use Quick Analysis to insert a sparkline, Excel automatically places the sparkline in a cell adjacent to the selected data. Be sure the adjacent cell is empty or the sparkline will be placed in the same cell as existing data.

▸ Know This about creating sparklines using buttons in the Sparklines group

— To insert a sparkline using a button in the Sparklines group, select the cells that contain the data you want to chart, click the Line, Column, or Win/Loss button in the Sparklines group on the Insert tab, type the cell address where you want the sparklines to appear (or click the Collapse button and click the location cell), and then click the OK button.
— When you use a button in the Sparklines group to insert a sparkline, you can select the location where the sparkline will appear in the worksheet.

On the Job

Task 10.12a Illustrating Data with Sparklines Using Quick Analysis

Devon has compiled the sales projection data that he needs for his business plan. He's anticipating a steady growth in sales (4% each month) as the first year progresses. He would like to illustrate the steady growth in the 2019 Sales Projections worksheet that contains the data he has compiled so that investors can quickly see the growth pattern. Use Quick Analysis to quickly insert a line sparkline in a cell adjacent to the sales growth data that illustrates this growth in the worksheet.

1. Open the data file **10-DVAutoParts-Projections**.
2. With the 2019 Sales Projections worksheet active, select the range B4:M4.
3. Click the Quick Analysis button.

   The Quick Analysis gallery displays.
4. Click the Sparklines tab (see Figure 10.22).

Figure 10.22 Quick Analysis Gallery with the Sparklines Tab Active

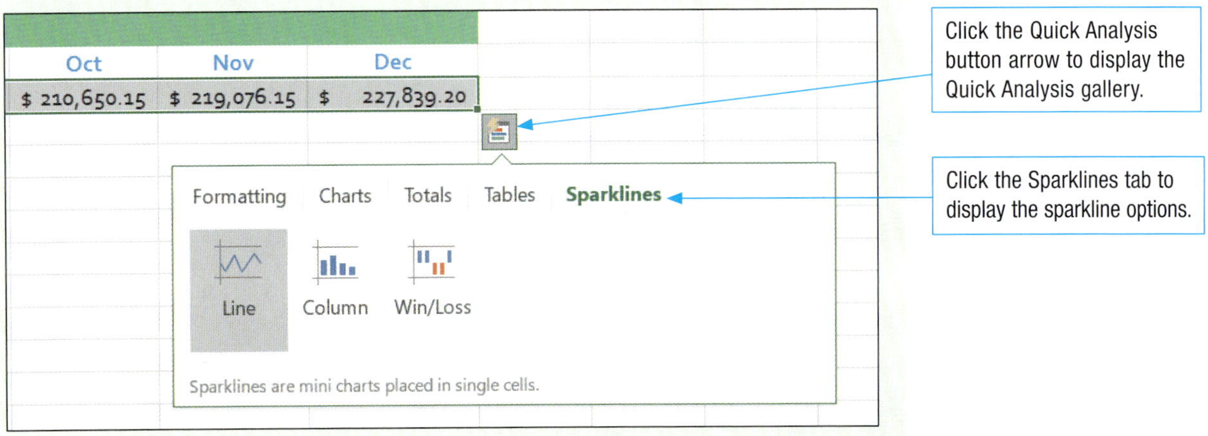

5. Click the *Line* option.

   A line sparkline displays in cell N4, the adjacent cell. The sparkline clearly illustrates the upward growth trend in the sales projections.

6. Click the Save button on the Quick Access Toolbar.

Model Answer

On the Job

Task 10.12b Creating Sparklines Using the Buttons in the Sparklines Group

Devon also wants to highlight the projected growth in the first quarter. Use a button in the Sparklines group to insert a column sparkline in a nonadjacent cell that illustrates the growth in the 2019 Sales Projections worksheet.

1. With the 10-DVAutoParts-Projections workbook open and the 2019 Sales Projections worksheet active, select the range B4:D4.
2. Click the Insert tab and then click the Column button in the Sparklines group.

   The Create Sparklines dialog box displays with the range reference *B4:D4* appearing in the *Data Range* text box and the insertion point in the *Location Range* text box.

3. Type D6.

   The cell reference *D6* appears in the *Location Range* text box.

4. Click the OK button.

   A column sparkline displays in cell D6. The sparkline shows steady growth from one month to the next in the first quarter of 2019.

5. Click in cell C6, type 1st Qtr Sales, and then press Ctrl + Enter.
6. Apply bold formatting to cell C6.
7. Click the Save button on the Quick Access Toolbar.

Model Answer

10.13 Customizing Sparklines

Tutorial

Customizing Sparklines

The amount of formatting that can be applied to a sparkline is limited, but a sparkline can be customized by changing the chart type and style and adding markers. Chart types are limited to line, column, and win/loss. When changing the chart type, keep in mind that line charts are best for illustrating trends over time, column charts are best for comparing data, and win/loss charts are best for illustrating positive and negative values. Chart styles are predefined styles that can be applied to change the appearance of a sparkline, and markers can be added to highlight specific value points.

The axis settings can also be customized. By default, a sparkline axis ranges from the minimum to the maximum value. If you have a series of sparklines down a column or across a row, the vertical axis could vary from cell to cell, resulting in the data being misinterpreted. To avoid this, you can scale the vertical axis to be the same in all the sparklines. When working with multiple sparklines, you can group them. **Grouped sparklines** are a collection of sparklines that can be formatted all together at the same time.

▶ Know This about changing the chart type, style, color, and weight of a sparkline

— To change the chart type, click in the cell containing the sparkline, click the Sparkline Tools Design tab, and then click the button for the new chart type in the Type group.

— To apply a different style, click in the cell containing the sparkline, click the Sparkline Tools Design tab, click the More button in the Style group, and then click the new style option at the drop-down gallery.

— To change the sparkline color, click in the cell containing the sparkline, click the Sparkline Tools Design tab, click the Sparkline Color button in the Style group, and then click the new color option at the drop-down palette.

— To change the sparkline weight in a line chart, click in the cell containing the sparkline, click the Sparkline Tools Design tab, click the Sparkline Color button in the Style group, click the *Weight* option at the drop-down list, and then click the new weight option at the second drop-down list.

▶ Know This about adding and customizing sparkline markers

— To add markers, click in the cell containing the sparkline, click the Sparkline Tools Design tab, and then click one or more check boxes in the Show group to insert check marks (see Figure 10.23).

— To change a marker color, click in the cell containing the sparkline, click the Sparkline Tools Design tab, click the Marker Color button in the Style group, point to the marker option at the drop-down list, and then click the new color option at the drop-down palette.

Figure 10.23 Sparkline Marker Options and the Marker Color Button

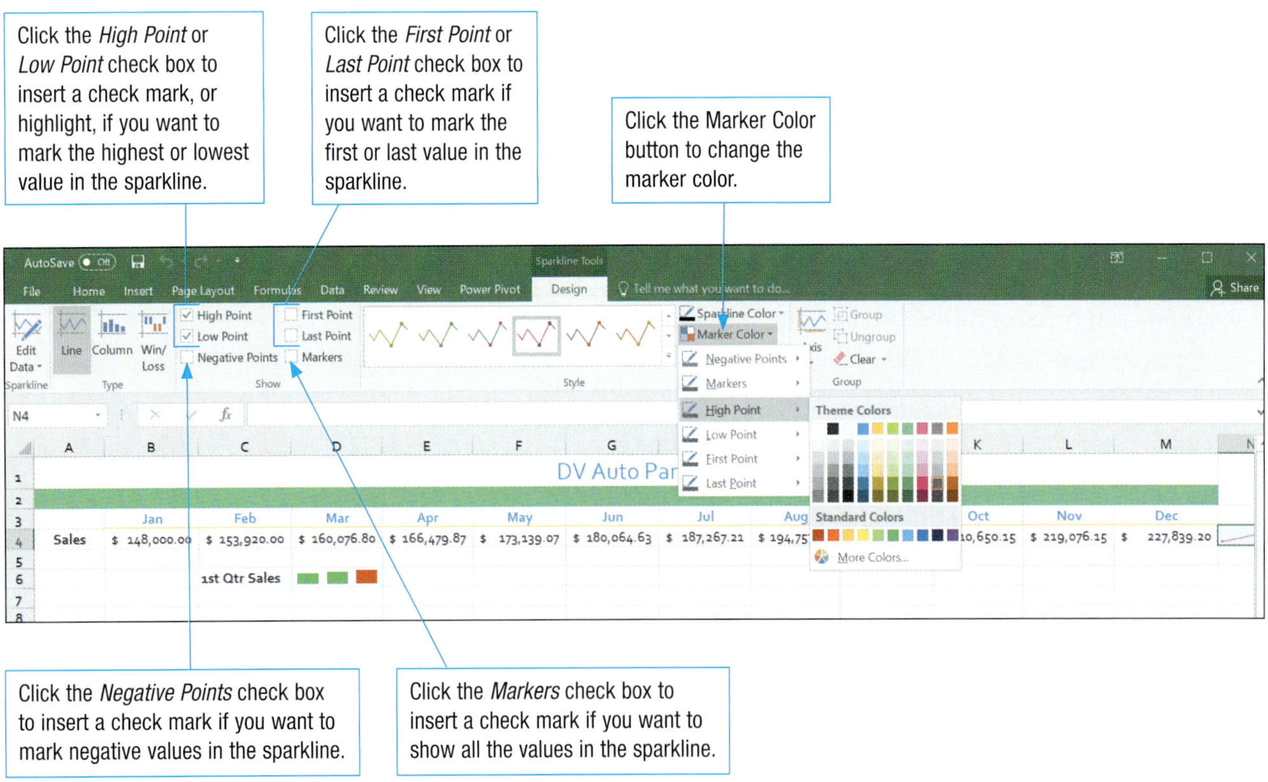

▸ **Know This** about customizing axes settings for a sparkline

— To customize the minimum value on the vertical axis, click in the cell containing the sparkline, click the Sparkline Tools Design tab, click the Axis button in the Group group, click the *Custom Value* option in the Vertical Axis Minimum Value Options section, type the minimum value, and then click the OK button.

— To customize the maximum value on the vertical axis, click in the cell containing the sparkline, click the Sparkline Tools Design tab, click the Axis button in the Group group, click the *Custom Value* option in the Vertical Axis Maximum Value Options section, type the maximum value, and then click the OK button.

— To customize axis settings for the horizontal axis, use options at the *Axis* drop-down menu (see Figure 10.24).

Figure 10.24 Horizontal and Vertical Axis Options

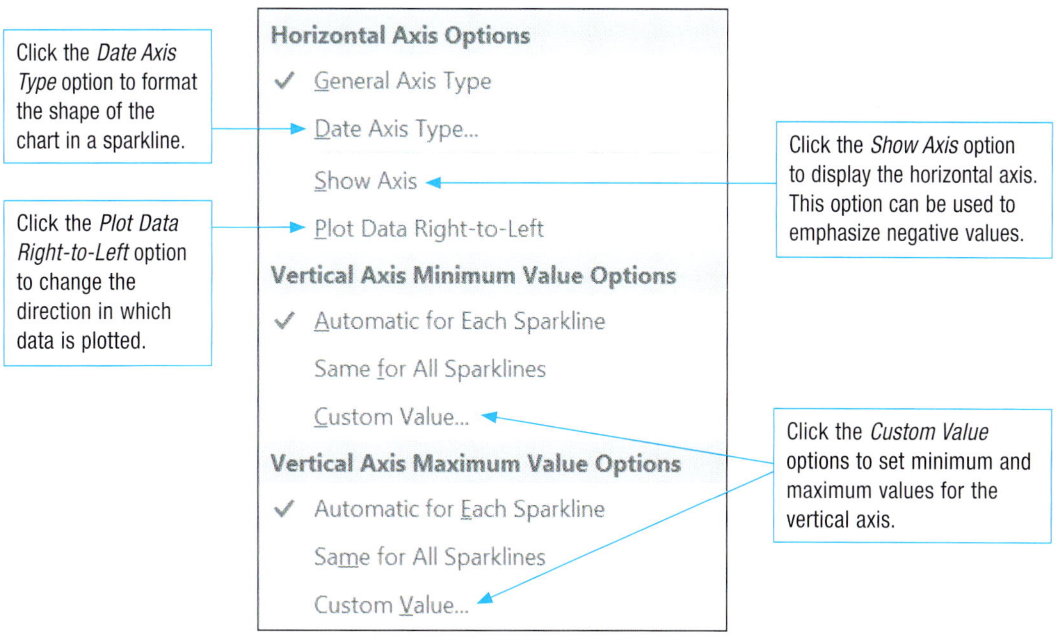

▸ **Know This** about grouping sparklines

— To group sparklines, select the sparklines' cells, click the Sparkline Tools Design tab, and then click the Group button in the Group group.

— To ungroup sparklines, select a grouped sparkline cell, click the Sparkline Tools Design tab, and then click the Ungroup button in the Group group.

On the Job

Task 10.13 Customizing Sparklines

Devon likes the addition of the sparklines to his projection worksheet, but he wants you to improve the appearance and make the charts easier to understand. Use buttons and options on the Sparkline Tools Design tab to customize the line sparkline by changing the style and adding markers, and to customize the column sparkline by changing the color and adding a marker to highlight the highest sales value. Devon also wants you to change the vertical axis in the column sparkline so that the comparison of the values is more realistic, illustrating gradual growth.

1. With the 10-DVAutoParts-Projections workbook open and the 2019 Sales Projection worksheet active, click in cell N4.
2. Click the More button in the Style group on the Sparkline Tools Design tab.

   A drop-down gallery displays.
3. Click the *Pink, Sparkline Style Accent 4, Darker 25%* (fourth column, second row) option.

   The sparkline color changes to pink.
4. Click the *High Point* check box in the Show group to insert a check mark.

   A marker displays at the highest point on the sparkline.
5. Click the *Low Point* check box.

   A marker displays at the lowest point.
6. Click in cell D6.
7. Click the Sparkline Color button arrow in the Style group.

   A drop-down palette displays.
8. Click the *Green* option (sixth option in the *Standard Colors* section).

   The sparkline color changes to green.
9. Click the *Last Point* check box in the Show group.

   The color of the last column in the sparkline changes to red.
10. Click the Axis button in the Group group.

    A drop-down list displays.
11. Click the *Custom Value* option in the *Vertical Axis Minimum Value Options* section.

    A dialog box displays.
12. Select the value in the *Enter the minimum value for the vertical axis* text box, type 100000, and then click the OK button.

    The sizes of the columns adjust to a minimum value of 100,000 on the vertical axis.
13. If printed work is required by your instructor, print the workbook.
14. Save and close the workbook.

Model Answer

10.14 Using the Goal Seek Feature for What-if Analysis

MOS Expert 3.4.3

Tutorial

Using the Goal Seek Feature for What-if Analysis

In Excel, what-if analysis tools are used to quickly change worksheet values and assess the impact of those changes in the worksheet results. The **Goal Seek** feature is a what-if analysis tool that is used when you know the result you want from a formula, but you are unsure what value the formula needs to get that result. For example, assume you sell handmade picnic tables online at $400 each and you sell 20 tables a month for a profit of $2,000 (25% of sales). You would like to increase your profit to $2,600 a month. You can use Goal Seek to determine how much you need to raise the price of a picnic table to meet your goal (see Figure 10.25).

Figure 10.25 Goal Seek Example and Solution

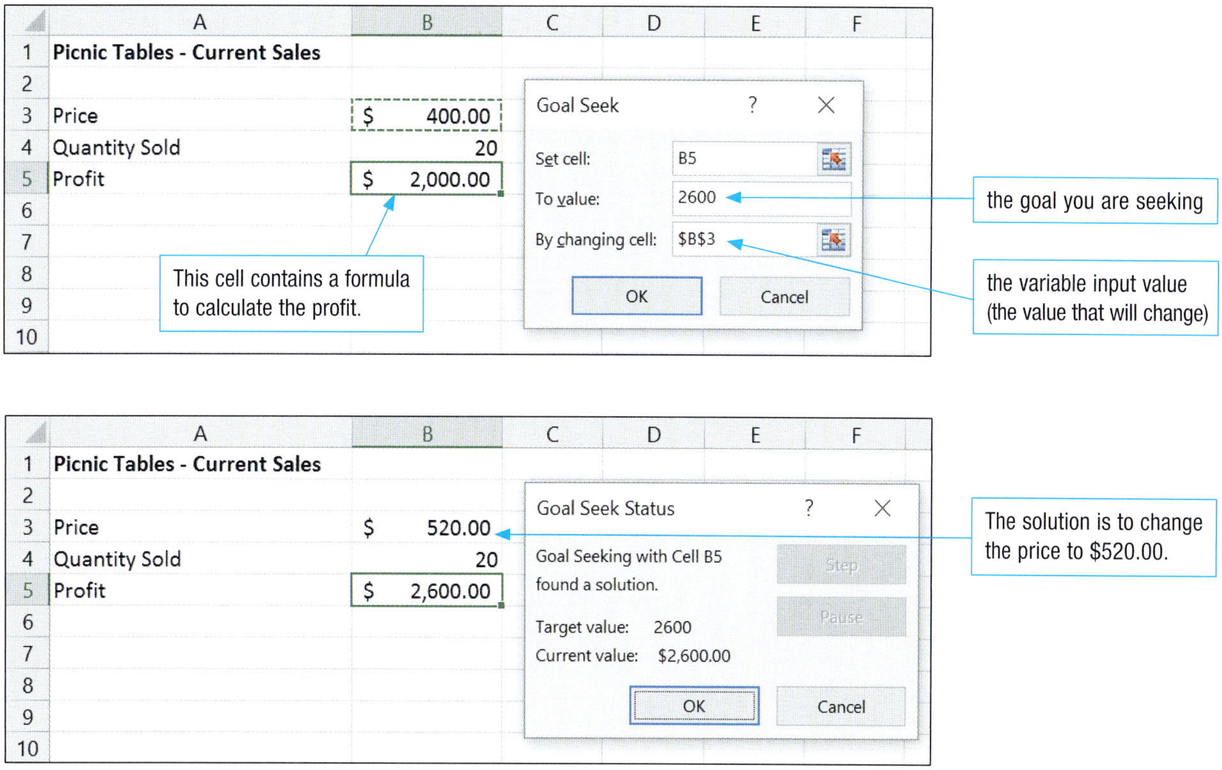

▸ Know This about the Goal Seek feature

— You can only use one variable input value with the Goal Seek feature. An **input value** is a value that is provided in a data table and used in the argument of a formula. A **variable input value** is a value that will change to give the desired result.

— The Goal Seek feature requires you to start with a formula.

▸ Know This about using the Goal Seek feature for what-if analysis

— Before using the Goal Seek feature, enter the values you know in a worksheet (see Figure 10.25).

— Also enter a formula to calculate your goal, including the variable input value. For example, to determine the profit for the picnic table scenario described in the introduction to this section, you would multiple the price (variable input value) of the picnic table times the quantity times the profit rate of 25%.

— To set Goal Seek options, click the What-If Analysis button in the Forecast group on the Data tab, click the *Goal Seek* option at the drop-down list, set options at the Goal Seek dialog box, and then click the OK button to close the Goal Seek dialog box and display the Goal Seek Status dialog box.

— To update the worksheet with the solution data, click the OK button at the Goal Seek Status dialog box; to close the dialog box without updating the worksheet, click the Cancel button.

— If you click cells to add them to the Goal Seek dialog box instead of typing them, they will be entered as absolute references.

On the Job

Task 10.14 Using the Goal Seek Feature for What-if Analysis

Devon wants to revisit the franchise data he compiled in the 10-DVAutoParts workbook. In Task 10.8, you calculated the net present value for the franchise to be $8,017.82 based on Devon's estimated annual returns over a 10-year period. Devon has asked a friend to invest in the business, and the friend has agreed to do so if Devon can increase the net present value to $10,000. Devon has also been talking with a potential customer who anticipates placing large orders in year 1 but does not have any order forecasts for years 2 through 10. Devon wants to know what the year 1 return would have to be to give a net present value of $10,000, assuming his estimates for the returns in years 2 through 10 do not change. Use Goal Seek to calculate that result for Devon.

1. Open the data file **10-DVAutoParts**, which you saved and closed in Task 10.9.
2. Click the Franchise sheet tab, if necessary, and then click in cell B16.
3. Click the Data tab, click the What-If Analysis button in the Forecast group, and then click the *Goal Seek* option.

   The Goal Seek dialog box displays with the cell reference *B16* in the *Set cell* text box (see Figure 10.26).

Figure 10.26 Goal Seek Dialog Box

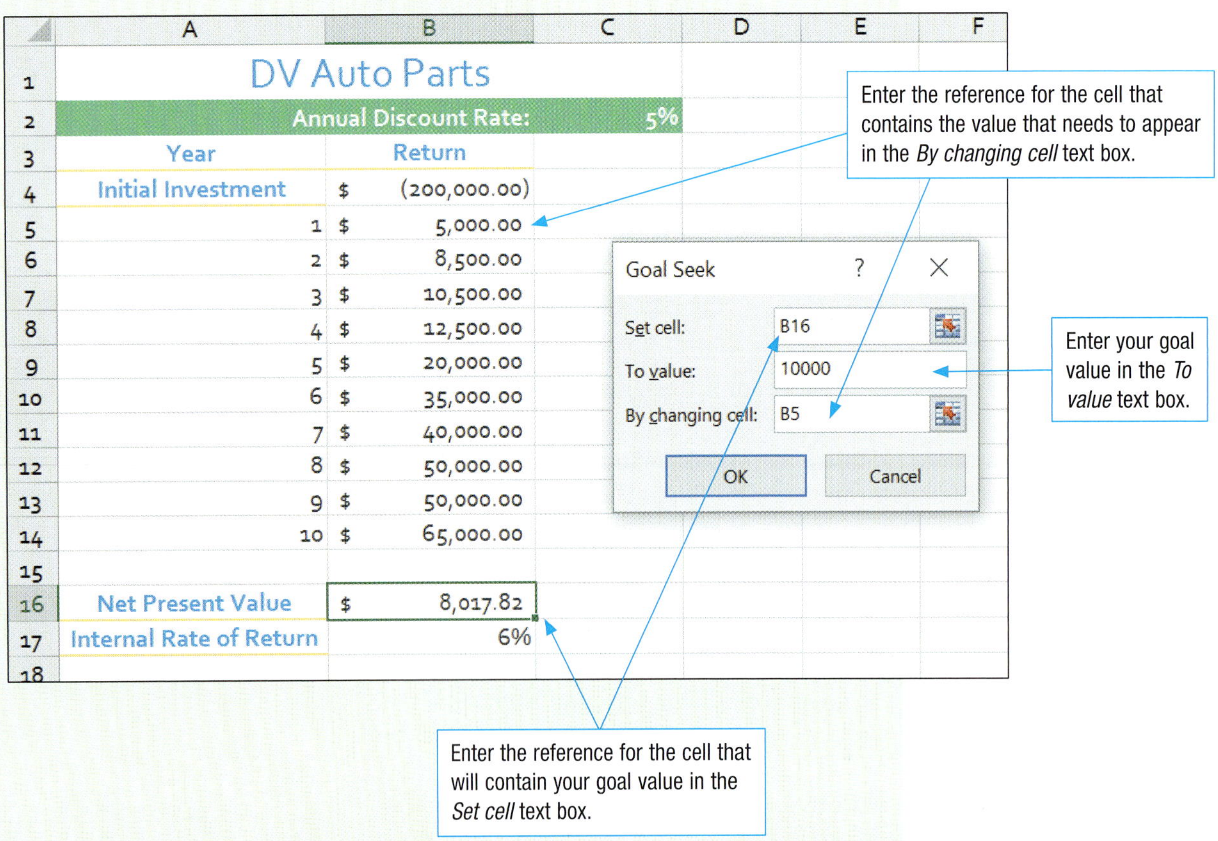

4. Click in the *To value* text box, type 10000, and then press the Tab key.

   The insertion point is in the *By changing cell* text box.

5. Type B5.
6. Click the OK button.

   The Goal Seek Status dialog box displays a solution (see Figure 10.27) and the solution appears in the worksheet: the goal year 1 return value *$7,081.29* displays in cell B5 and the goal net present value *$10,000.00* displays in cell B16. If the projected return for year 1 increases to $7,018.29, Devon's friend will invest in the business.

7. Click the OK button.

   The dialog box is closed and the solution continues to display in the worksheet.

8. If printed work is required by your instructor, print the workbook.
9. Save and close the workbook.

Figure 10.27 Goal Seek Status Dialog Box

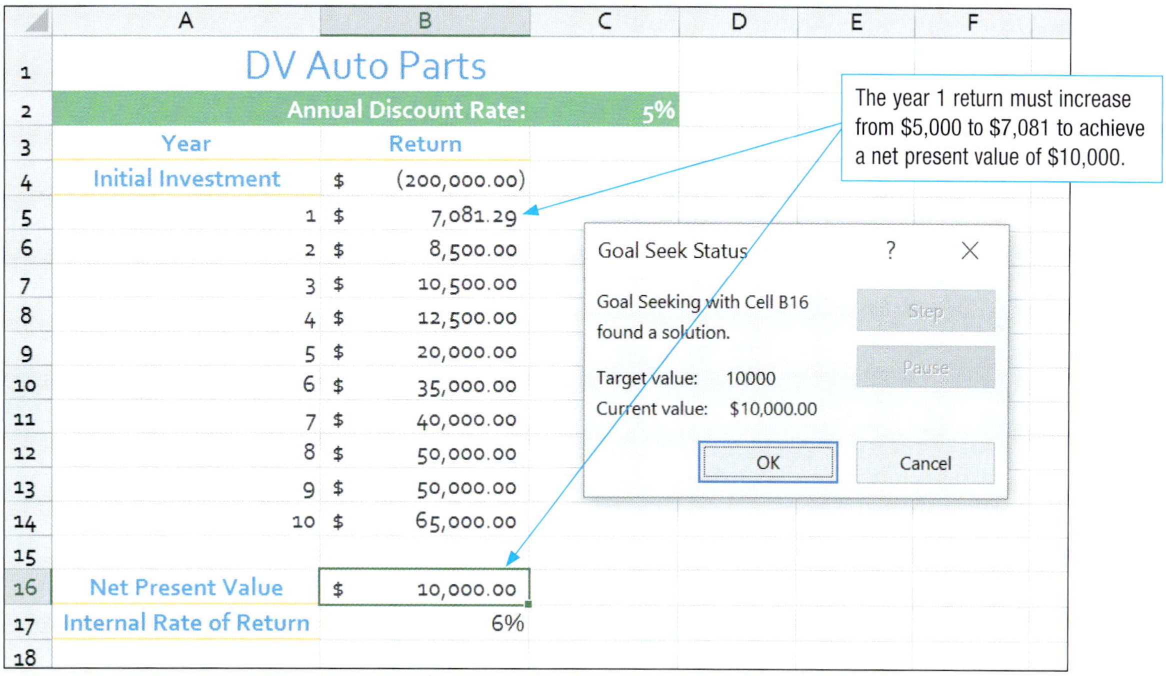

Model Answer

10.15 Using the Scenario Manager for What-if Analysis

MOS Expert 3.4.3

Tutorials

Adding a Scenario

Applying a Scenario and Compiling a Scenario Summary Report

The **Scenario Manager** is a what-if analysis tool that allows you to create different scenarios. A **scenario** is a set of values that can be substituted in cells to view different results. For example, you can create scenarios for two budget forecasts, with each scenario assuming a different amount of revenue. Once scenarios have been created, a scenario report can be generated that summarizes the data from all the scenarios.

▸ Know This about scenarios

— A scenario can contain up to 32 changing cells. A **changing cell** is a cell containing a value that will change in each scenario. In the example about budget forecast scenarios, the revenue value would be different in each scenario.

▸ Know This about creating scenarios

— Enter the worksheet data with the values for the first scenario.

— To create the first scenario, follow these steps:

1. Select the changing cell or cells.
2. Click the What-If Analysis button in the Forecast group on the Data tab.
3. Click the *Scenario Manager* option at the drop-down list.
4. Click the Add button at the Scenario Manager dialog box.
5. Type the scenario name in the *Scenario name* text box at the Add Scenario dialog box (see Figure 10.28).
6. Verify that the references for the changing cells appear in the *Changing cells* text box and then click the OK button.
7. Click the OK button at the Scenario Values dialog box (see Figure 10.29) to accept the original worksheet values and redisplay the Scenario Manager dialog box.

— To create each subsequent scenario, repeat Steps 4 and 5, type different values in the *Changing cells* text box at the Scenario Values dialog box, and then click the Add button to add another scenario or the OK button if you are done adding scenarios.

Reminder
If a dialog box covers up data you need to see, move the box by dragging its Title bar.

Figure 10.28 Add Scenario Dialog Box

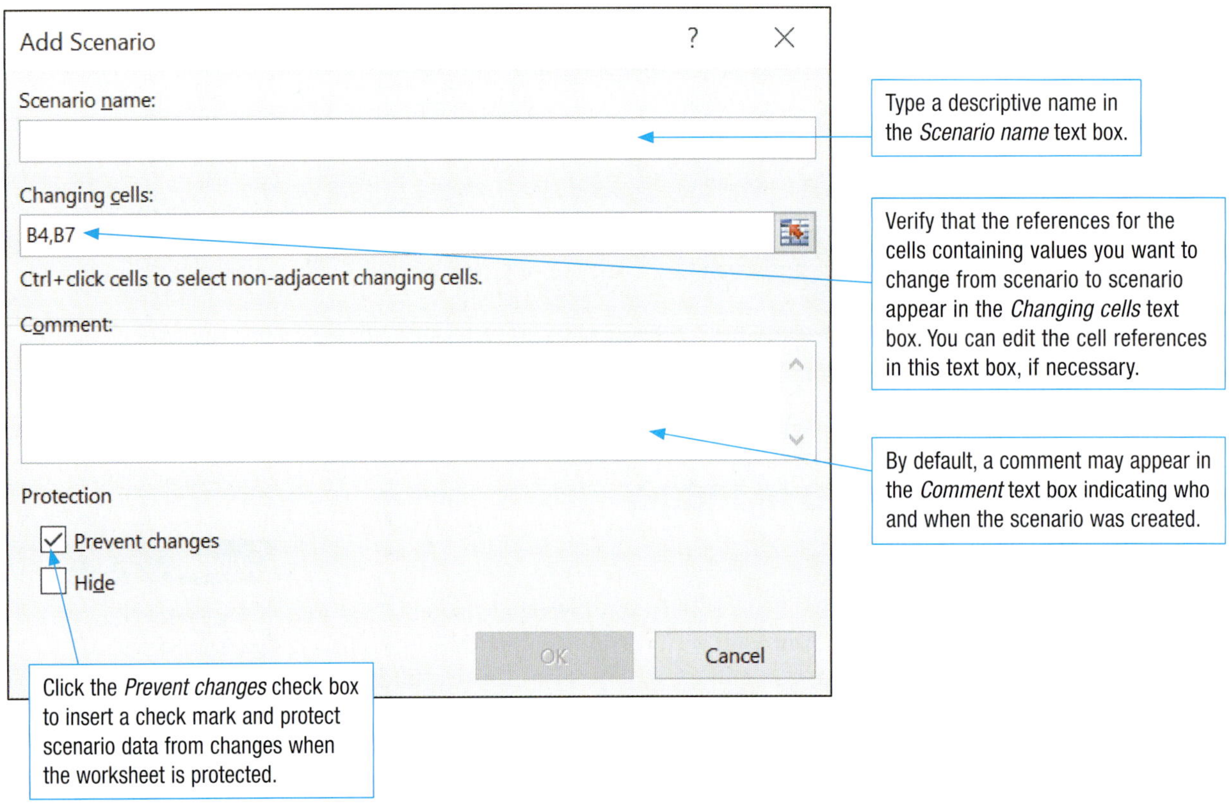

Figure 10.29 Scenario Values Dialog Box for the First Scenario

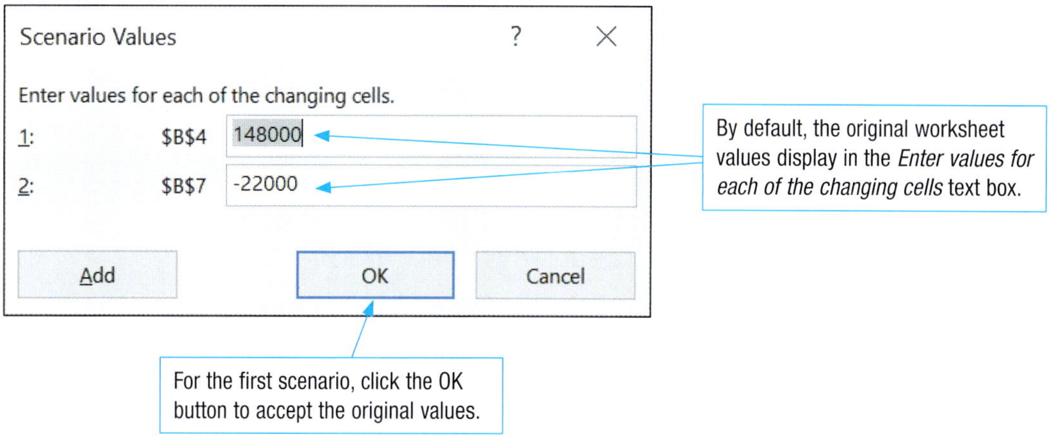

▸ Know This about creating and using scenarios

— The value entered for the changing cell in the Scenario Values dialog box can be a formula. For example, if the changing cell is 90% of the original value of 10,000, enter the formula =*10000*0.90*.

▸ Know This about viewing scenarios

— Scenarios are saved with the workbook.

— To view a saved scenario, click the What-If Analysis button and then click the *Scenario Manager* option at the drop-down list.

▸ Know This about protecting scenarios from changes

— To protect saved scenarios from changes in a protected worksheet, click the *Prevent changes* or *Hide* check box to insert a check mark in the *Protection* section of the Add Scenario dialog box (see Figure 10.28 on page 486).

▸ Know This about showing scenario values in the worksheet

— To show scenario values in the worksheet, click the What-If Analysis button in the Forecast group on the Data tab, click the *Scenario Manager* option at the drop-down list, click the scenario name in the *Scenario* list box at the Scenario Manager dialog box, and then click the Show button (see Figure 10.29).

— The changing cells in the worksheet update to reflect the values assigned to the scenario.

— Cells that contain references to the changing cells also update to reflect the scenario values.

▸ Know This about deleting scenarios

— To delete a scenario, click the What-If Analysis button in the Forecast group on the Data tab, click the *Scenario Manager* option at the drop-down list, click the scenario name in the *Scenario* list box at the Scenario Manager dialog box, and then click the Delete button.

▸ Know This about editing scenarios

— To edit a scenario, click the What-If Analysis button in the Forecast group on the Data tab, click the *Scenario Manager* option at the drop-down list, click the scenario name in the *Scenario* list box at the Scenario Manager dialog box, click the Edit button, and then click the OK button. In the Scenario Values dialog box, change references or values and then click the Show button to view the edited scenario.

▸ Know This about creating a scenario summary report

— A **scenario summary report** displays the values of all the changing cells and results for each scenario and can be used to easily compare scenarios.

— To create a scenario summary report: display the Scenario Manager dialog box; click the Summary button; click the *Scenario summary* radio button in the *Report type* section to insert a bullet, if necessary; type or click in the result cell, if necessary; and then click the OK button.

— A scenario summary report can list scenarios side by side for comparison purposes or summarize the scenarios in a PivotTable report.

— A scenario summary report automatically includes grouping levels that can be collapsed and expanded to hide and expand different parts of the scenario summary report.

— Scenario summary reports display on a separate worksheet and do not automatically recalculate. You will need to generate a new scenario summary report if you change the values of a scenario.

— A **Scenario PivotTable report** displays on a separate worksheet named *Scenario PivotTable* (see Figure 10.30). The report can be filtered and edited using PivotTable features.

Figure 10.30 Scenario PivotTable Report

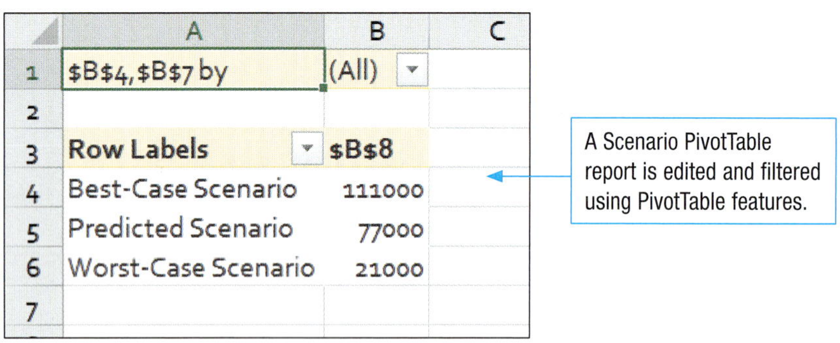

▸ Know This about merging scenarios

— Scenarios from different workbooks can be merged into the active worksheet in a workbook. You may want to do this if more than one person has been working on different scenarios with the same data.

— To merge scenarios, click the What-If Analysis button in the Forecast group on the Data tab, click the *Scenario Manager* option at the drop-down list, and then click the Merge button. In the Merge Scenarios dialog box, select the workbooks and sheets from which to merge the scenarios.

▸ **Know This** about using the Solver add-in for what-if analysis

— Another way to conduct what-if analysis in Excel is to use the Solver add-in.

— To download the Solver add-in, click the File tab, click the *Options* option, click the *Add-ins* option in the left panel at the Excel Options dialog box, click the *Manage* option box arrow in the right panel, click the *Excel Add-ins* option at the drop-down list, click the Go button, click the *Solver Add-in* check box in the *Add-ins available* list box at the Add-ins dialog box to insert a check mark, and then click the OK button.

— The Solver button is added in the Analyze group on the Data tab.

— The Solver allows you to find an optimal solution for a formula in one cell (called the *objective cell*), given variable (changing) cells and subject to constraints (limits) on the values in the variable cells and/or objective cell.

On the Job

Task 10.15 Using the Scenario Manager for What-if Analysis

Devon has created a worksheet that includes sales and expense estimates for 2019 that reflect his best guess at what will happen over the year. The worksheet also includes income estimates based on the sales and expense values. Devon knows that his estimates are subject to change depending on factors such as the economy, competition, supplier prices, bank rates, and so forth. Devon's investors have asked him to provide a report that shows two additional scenarios: a worst-case scenario and a best-case scenario. The investors want to compare sales, expense, and income values under the three scenarios. (Income is based on sales and expense values and is the bottom-line value used for comparison.) Use the Scenario Manager to set up the three scenarios and display a summary report that compares sales, expense, and income values for the three scenarios side by side on a separate worksheet.

1. Open the data file **10-DVAutoParts-Forecast**.
2. Click in cell B4, press and hold down the Ctrl key, click in cell B7, and then release the Ctrl key.

   Cells B4 and B7 are selected.
3. Click the Data tab, click the What-If Analysis button in the Forecast group, and then click the *Scenario Manager* option.

   The Scenario Manager dialog box displays.
4. Click the Add button.

   The Add Scenario dialog box displays with the insertion point in the *Scenario name* text box (see Figure 10.28 on page 486).
5. Type Predicted Scenario and then click the OK button.

   The Scenario Values dialog box displays with the values from the selected cells displaying in the *Enter values for each of the changing cells* text boxes (see Figure 10.29 on page 487).
6. Click the OK button.

   The Scenario Values dialog box closes and the Scenario Manager dialog box displays. The scenario name *Predicted Scenario* appears and is selected in the *Scenarios* list box. This is the first scenario, and it uses the original worksheet values.

7. Click the Add button.

   The Add Scenario dialog box displays with the insertion point in the *Scenario name* text box.

8. Type Best-Case Scenario and then click the OK button.

   The Scenario Values dialog box displays with the value in the *$B$4* text box selected.

9. Type 180000 and then press the Tab key.

10. Type -20000 and then click the Add button.

    The Add Scenario dialog box displays with the insertion point in the *Scenario name* text box.

11. Type Worst-Case Scenario and then click the OK button.

    The Scenario Values dialog box displays with the value in the *$B$4* text box selected.

12. Type 110000 and then press the Tab key.

13. Type -40000 and then click the OK button.

    The Scenario Manager dialog box displays.

14. Click the *Best-Case Scenario* option in the *Scenarios* list box and then click the Show button (see Figure 10.35).

    The *Best Scenario* values display in the changing cells in the worksheet. Cells containing formulas that reference the changing cells update to reflect the scenario values.

Figure 10.35 Scenario Manager Dialog Box

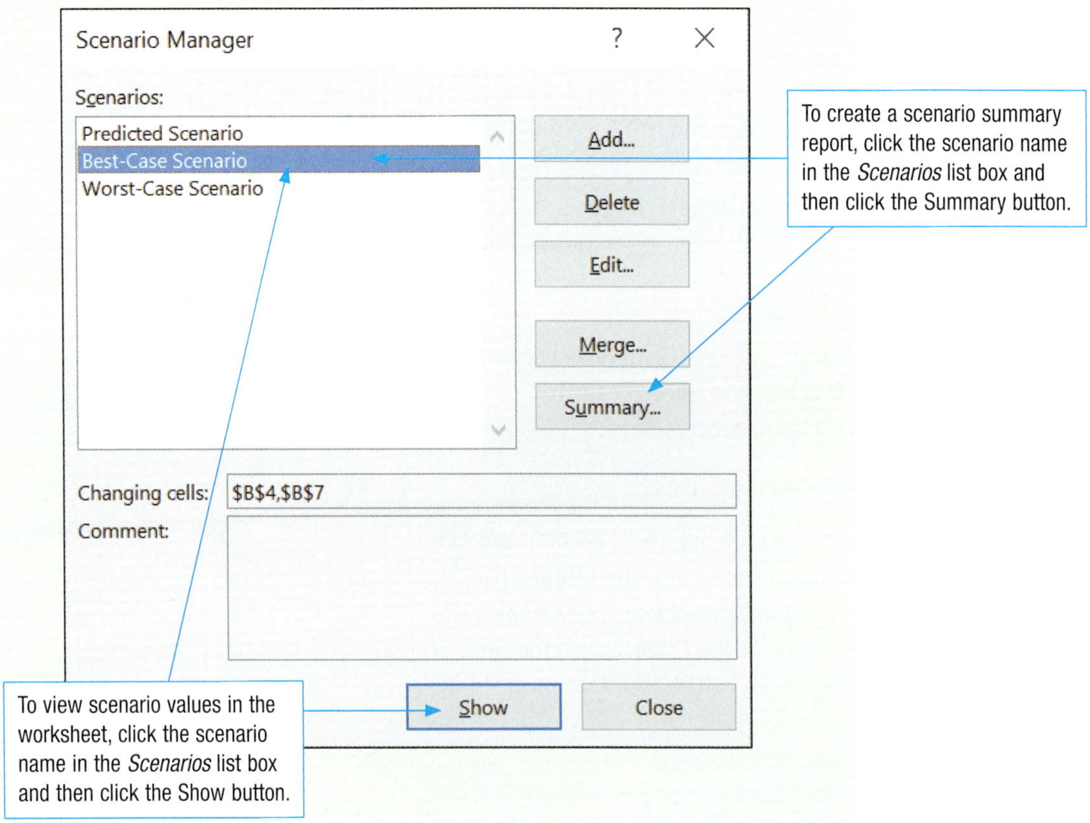

15. Click the Summary button.

    The Scenario Summary dialog box displays with the *Scenario summary* radio button selected in the *Report type* section (see Figure 10.36).

16. Click in the *Result cells* text box, if necessary, and then type B8.

    Cell B8 contains the income value, which is the bottom-line result for comparison purposes. This is the value you want to compare between scenarios.

17. Click the OK button.

    The scenario summary report displays in a new worksheet named *Scenario Summary* (see Figure 10.37).

18. Click the Save button on the Quick Access Toolbar.

Figure 10.36 Scenario Summary Dialog Box

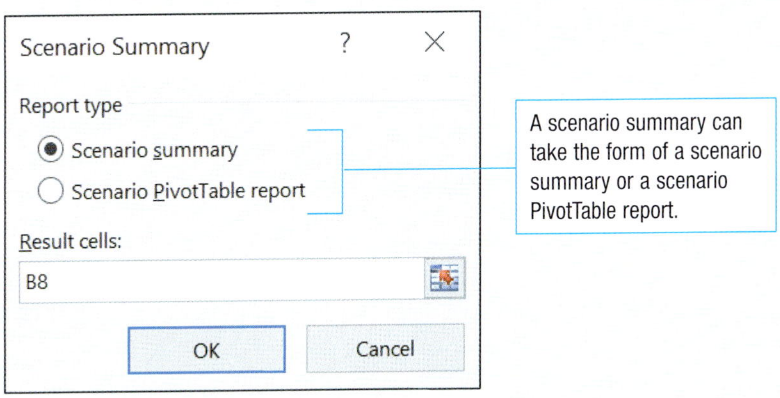

Figure 10.37 Scenario Summary Report

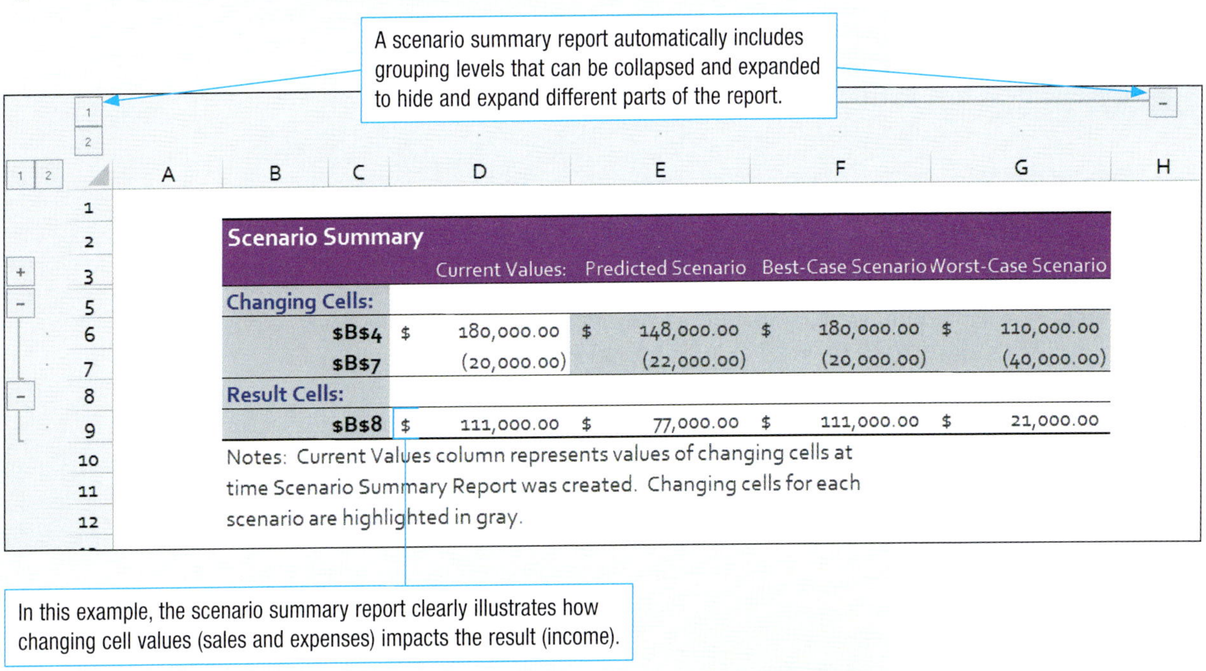

Model Answer

10.16 Using a Watch Window

MOS Expert 3.5.2

Tutorial

Using a Watch Window

A **Watch Window** can be created to display values of cells located throughout a workbook. You can create a Watch Window to monitor cells and formulas when you are going to change the values in cells that they reference. The Watch Window feature allows you to view the impact of changes without having to scroll or switch worksheets. It is useful when working with a large workbook and when a workbook contains nested formulas.

▸ Know This about a Watch Window

— A Watch Window displays information about a selected cell or cells, including the workbook name, worksheet name, cell reference, value, and formula (see Figure 10.38).

— Any changes to the value or formula in a selected cell automatically display in the Watch Window.

— A Watch Window can display information about cells from any worksheet in the workbook. It cannot display information about cells from another workbook.

▸ Know This about using a Watch Window

— To create a Watch Window, click in any cell in any worksheet, click the Watch Window button in the Formula Auditing group on the Formulas tab, click the Add Watch button at the Watch Window, type or select the cells to watch, and then click the Add button.

— The Watch Window displays in the Excel window and remains open until you close it. It remains in place when you scroll the worksheet or change worksheets.

— To remove a cell from the Watch Window, click the cell reference in the Watch Window, and then click the Delete Watch button.

— To move, size, or close a Watch Window, click the Watch Window arrow (see Figure 10.38) and then click an option at the drop-down list. A Watch Window can also be moved by dragging the title bar and closed by clicking the Close button.

On the Job

Task 10.16 Using a Watch Window

Devon is continuing to analyze his sales projections to make sure they are realistic. Recent economic trends indicate he can increase his original sales projection for January 2019 from $148,000 to $155,400. Devon wants to know how that change will affect annual sales and income totals. Create a Watch Window to monitor the annual sales and income totals so that you can easily see how they are affected when you update the sales value for the month of January.

1. With the workbook 10-DVAutoParts-Forecast open, click the Formulas tab, and then click the Watch Window button in the Formula Auditing group.

   The Watch Window displays.

2. Click the Add Watch button.

   The Add Watch dialog box displays.

3. Click in cell N4, press and hold down the Ctrl key, click in cell N8, and then release the Ctrl key.

   Cells N4 and N8 are selected (display a rolling green marquee) in the worksheet and the text *='2019 Sales Projections'!$N$4,'2019 Sales Projections'!$N$8* appears in the *Select the cells that you would like to watch the value of* text box.

4. Click the Add button.

   The information about the selected cells displays in the Watch Window list box (see Figure 10.38).

Figure 10.38 Watch Window

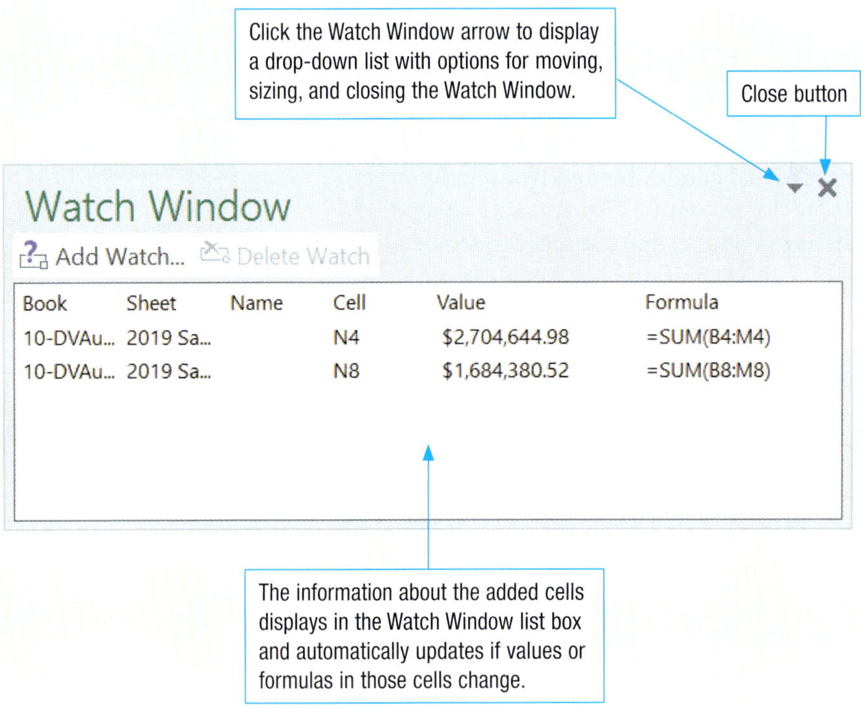

5. Scroll to the left in the worksheet, if necessary; click in cell B4; type 155400; and then press the Enter key.

   The value *$155,400* displays in cell B4 and all the cells containing formulas that reference cell B4 update—including the watched cells N4 and N8. Cells N4 and N8 may not be visible without scrolling to the right in the worksheet, but the values for these cells automatically update in the Watch Window, so you can easily see them without scrolling (see Figure 10.39).

6. Click the Watch Window Close button.

   The Watch Window closes.

7. If printed work is required by your instructor, print the workbook.
8. Save and close the workbook.

Figure 10.39 Updated Watch Window

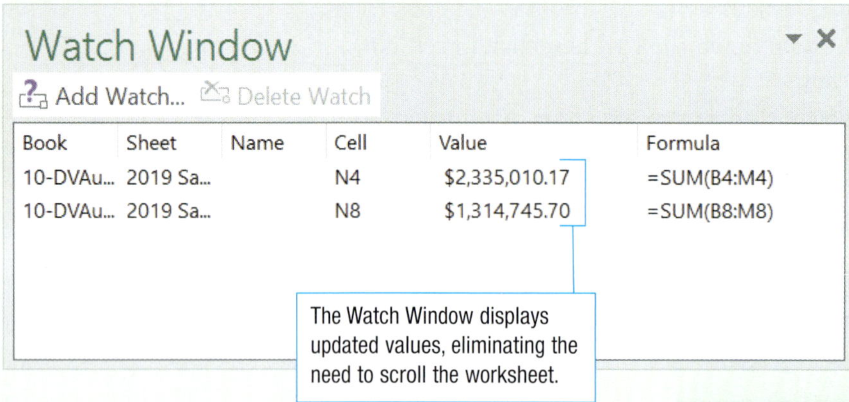

Model Answer

10.17 Inserting a Map Chart

You can compare values and illustrate categories across geographical regions by inserting a map chart. This type of visual can be created from data for geographical areas such as countries, regions, counties, states, and zip codes. A map chart puts data in a geographical context that can clearly illustrate factors such as population, markets, sales regions, and distance, making data easier to understand and analyze.

Tutorial

Inserting and Customizing a Map Chart

▸ Know This about inserting a map chart

- To insert a map chart, select the range or click in the table containing the data, click the Maps button in the Charts group on the Insert tab, and then click the *Filled Map* option at the drop-down list.
- To customize a map chart, use options and buttons on the Chart Tools Design tab and the Chart Tools Format tab, as you would with other chart types (see Chapter 6).
- An active Internet connection is necessary to use the map chart feature because the feature uses Bing to geocode the data based on its geographic properties.

On the Job

Task 10.17 Inserting a Map Chart

Devon has identified 14 counties in Florida that are currently underserved by auto parts suppliers and listed them along with population data in a new workbook. He plans to market his new business in those counties, focusing especially on the largest counties. He asks you to help him locate the underserved counties and determine in which part of Florida he should focus marketing and sales efforts. Devon will use the resulting information to help project future revenue and to set sales goals and targets. Use a map chart to create a visual Devon can use to quickly locate the area he should target.

Note: *The Map feature is only available with some Office 365 subscriptions. Check with your instructor if your version of Excel does not have this feature.*

1. Open the data file **10-DVAutoParts-Markets**.
2. With the Florida Counties sheet active, click in any cell in the table.
3. Click the Insert tab, click the Maps button in the Charts group, and then click the *Filled Map* option. If a warning dialog box displays, click the Accept button.

   A map chart displays in the worksheet and the Chart Tools Design tab is active. It appears that Devon should focus marketing and sales efforts in the southeastern part of Florida.
4. Click the chart title element and then type Florida Counties.
5. Click the fourth option in the Chart Styles gallery.
6. Drag the chart so that the top left corner is positioned in cell E2 (see Figure 10.40).
7. If printed work is required by your instructor, print the workbook.
8. Save and close the workbook.

Figure 10.40 Map Chart

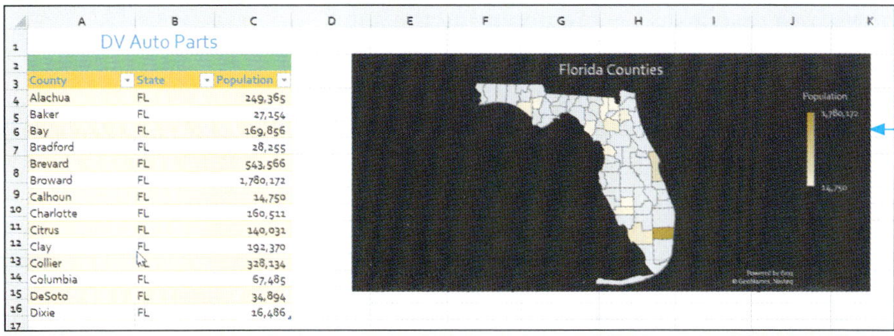

Use a map chart to compare values and illustrate categories across geographical regions.

Model Answer

10.18 Using the 3D Maps Feature

The **3D Maps** feature is a three-dimensional data visualization tool you can use to plot geographic data on a 3-D globe map or 3-D custom map. If dates or times are included in the plotted data, you can view a **3D Maps tour** that illustrates a time-based relationship between the geographic locations and their associated data, such as population numbers. For example, you could create a 3D Maps tour that shows sales growth in different geographic locations over a three-year period.

Tutorial

Creating a 3-D Map

▸ Know This about the 3D Maps feature

— An active Internet connection is necessary to use the 3D Maps feature because the feature uses Bing to geocode the data based on its geographic properties.

— The data plotted in a 3-D map must be in an Excel table or Data Model.

— Similar to a PivotTable, for a 3-D map, you determine the fields that are displayed on the map when you build it.

— Each record (row of data) must include at least one geographic field, such as *Latitude/Longitude*, *City*, *Country*, *Zip Code*, *Postal Code*, or *State*.

— If you want to view a 3D Maps tour showing the data over time, you also must include one date or time field in each record.

▸ Know This about creating a 3-D map

— To create a 3-D map, follow these steps:

1. Click in any cell in the table or Data Model containing the data you want to map.
2. Click the 3D Map button arrow in the Tours group on the Insert tab and then click the *Open 3D Maps* option at the drop-down list. ***Note:*** *The first time the 3D Maps feature is used, Excel automatically enables the feature and it takes a few seconds to display.*
3. At the Launch 3D Maps window (see Figure 10.41), drag fields from the Field List pane to areas at the Layer task pane to build the 3-D map.
   a. Fields placed in the *Location* area are plotted on the map. Location fields must contain geographic data (e.g., latitude, longitude, city, county, zip code, postal code). After a field has been dragged to the Location area, click the field arrow that appears and then click the correct geographic type at the drop-down list. For example, select the State/Province type for a field named State. ***Note:*** *You may have to add several fields to clarify the data to map. For example, when you add a city field, you may also need to add a state or province field.*
   b. Fields placed in the *Height* area display as bars representing the sum of the value.
   c. Fields placed in the *Category* area display as categories.
   d. Fields placed in the *Time* area are used to animate the 3-D map. After a field has been dragged to the Time area, click the field arrow that appears and then select the date and time fields to animate your data over time.

Figure 10.41 Launch 3D Maps Window

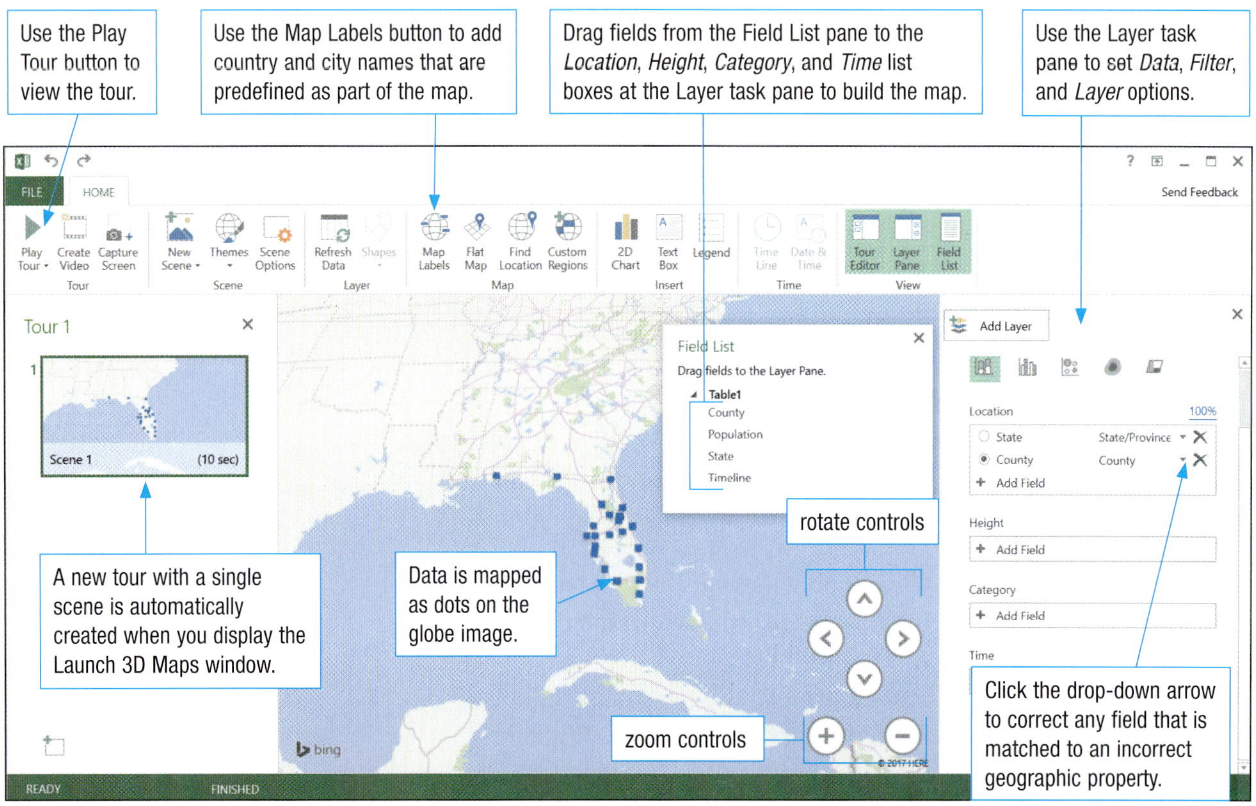

- The rotate and zoom controls enable you to rotate the globe and zoom in and zoom out as you are building the map.
- To add a filter, click the Expand arrow to the left of the *Filters* option in the Field List pane, click the *Add Filter* option, click a field, and then click the filter check boxes to filter the data displayed on the 3-D map.
- To add labels for major cities, states, and countries, click the Map Labels button in the Map group.

▸ **Know This** about modifying the Layer Options

- To change the scale of the bars on the map, click the Expand arrow to the left of the *Layer Options* option in the Field List pane and then adjust the *Height* and *Thickness* settings.
- To change the opacity of the bars on the map, click the Expand arrow to the left of the *Layer Options* option in the Field List pane and then adjust the *Opacity* setting.
- To change the color of a data series (represented by a bar on the map chart), click the Expand arrow to the left of the *Layer Options* option in the Field List pane, click the Series drop-down arrow, click a data series, click the Color drop-down arrow, and then click a color.

▸ **Know This** about viewing a 3D Maps tour

- A 3D Maps tour is automatically created when you display the Launch 3D Maps pane (see Figure 10.42).
- A tour can have a single scene, or it can have multiple scenes that play sequentially to show different views of the data.
- Tours are saved automatically.
- To play a 3D Maps tour, click the Play Tour button in the Tour group on the HOME tab in the Launch 3D Maps window.
- A 3D Maps tour plays in full-screen mode.
- To create another tour, display the Launch 3D Maps window and then click the New Tour button.
- Point to a bar on the 3-D map to display the corresponding data in a ScreenTip.

On the Job
Task 10.18 Creating a 3-D Map and Viewing a 3D Maps Tour

Devon has devised a plan to start marketing his business to the counties in Florida with the highest populations. He plans to roll out his marketing campaign in 90-day blocks. He wants you to use the 3D Maps feature to present this data visually so he can share it with sales representatives when discussing sales projections and targets.

1. Open the data file **10-DVAutoParts-Counties**.
2. Click the Insert tab, click the 3D Maps button arrow, and then click the *Open 3D Maps* option.

   The Launch 3D Maps window displays (see Figure 10.41 on page 498) with the HOME tab active.

3. Drag the *County* field from the Field List pane to the *Location* area at the Layer task pane.
4. Click the *County* field arrow in the *Location* area and then click the *County* option at the drop-down list.
5. Drag the State field from the Field List pane to the Location area at the Layer task pane.
6. Click the *State* field arrow in the *Location area* and then click the *State/Province* option at the drop-down list.
7. Drag the *Population* field from the Field List pane to the *Heigh*t area at the Layer task pane.

   Bars representing the population appear on the 3-D map.

8. Drag the *Population* field to the *Category* area.

   Population data displays in the legend.

9. Drag the *Timeline* field to the *Time* area.
10. Click the *Timeline* arrow and then click the *Day* option.

    Timeline (Day) displays in the *Time* option box, the date and time display in the upper left corner of the window, and the Timeline control displays at the bottom of the window.

11. Click the Map Labels button in the Map group.
12. Click the Play button on the Timeline control.

Figure 10.42 3D Maps Tour

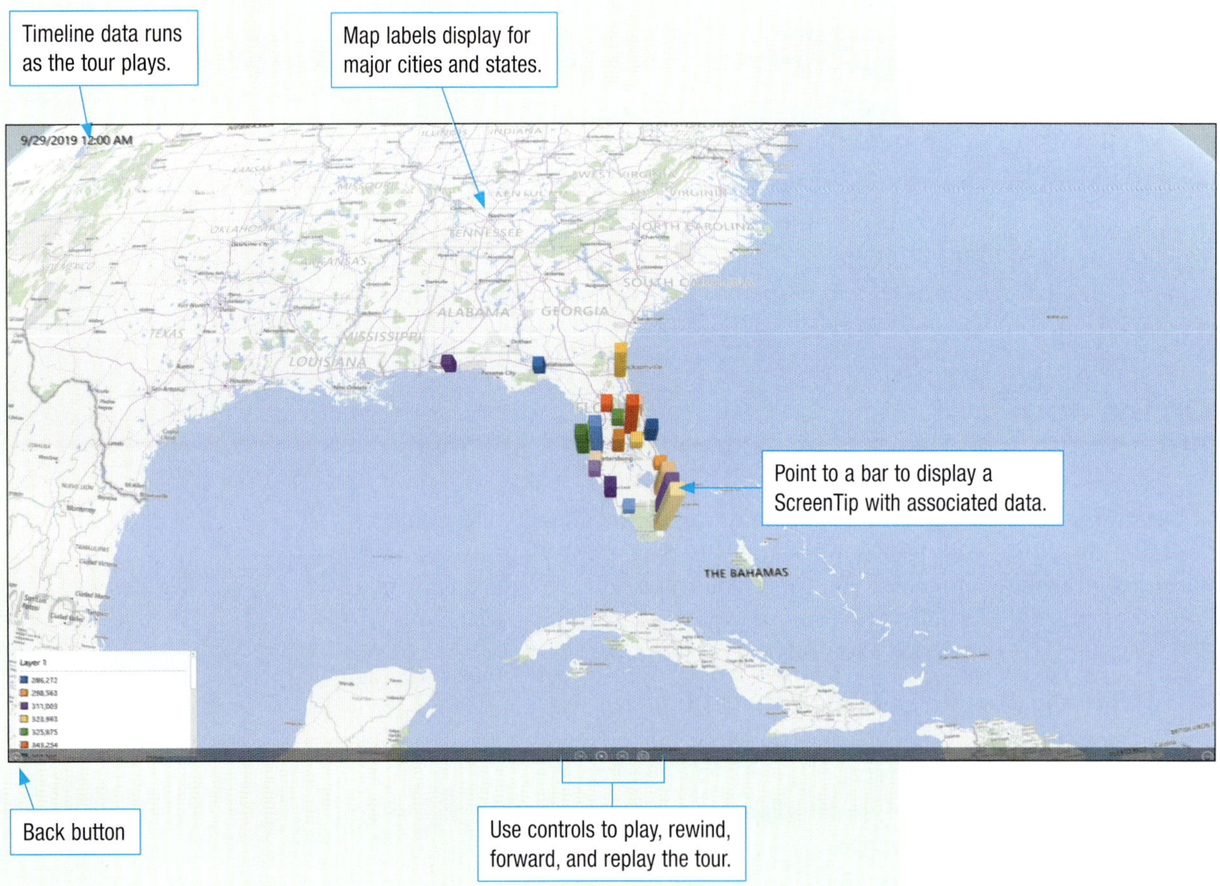

13. Click the Play Tour button in the Tour group.

    Counties display in the tour according to their timeline dates.

14. Point to a bar of data.

    A ScreenTip displays with corresponding data.

15. Click the Back button.
16. Click the File tab and then click the *Close* option.

    The worksheet displays. The *3D Maps Tours* text box displays, indicating the workbook has 3D Maps tours available.

17. If printed work is required by your instructor, print the workbook.
18. Click the Save button on the Quick Access Toolbar.

Model Answer

10.19 Creating and Formatting an Infographic Using People Graph

An **infographic** is a form of data visualization that presents data in an easy-to-understand image such as a chart or graph (see Figure 10.45). Infographics are widely used in content marketing and are an engaging way to communicate data and information. You can create and format an infographic using the Excel add-in **People Graph**.

Tutorial

Creating and Formatting an Infographic Using People Graph

▸ Know This about downloading and installing People Graph

— The People Graph feature is accessed using the People Graph button in the Add-ins group on the Insert tab.

— If you do not see the People Graph button in your version of Excel, you can download the add-in for free from the Office Store (https://store.office.com).

— The first time you use the People Graph feature, you may need to click the Trust this add-in button and sign in with your Microsoft account.

▸ Know This about creating an infographic using People Graph

— To create an infographic using People Graph, follow these steps:

1. Arrange the data that will be used in the infographic in two adjacent columns, with the first column containing labels and the second column containing values.
2. With any cell in the worksheet active, click the People Graph button in the Add-ins group on the Insert tab.
3. Click the Data button in the sample infographic.
4. Click in the *Title* text box at the Data pane, select the text in the box, and then type a title for the infographic (see Figure 10.43).
5. Select the data for the infographic in the worksheet.
6. Click the Select your data button.
7. Click the Create button.

Figure 10.43 People Graph Data Pane

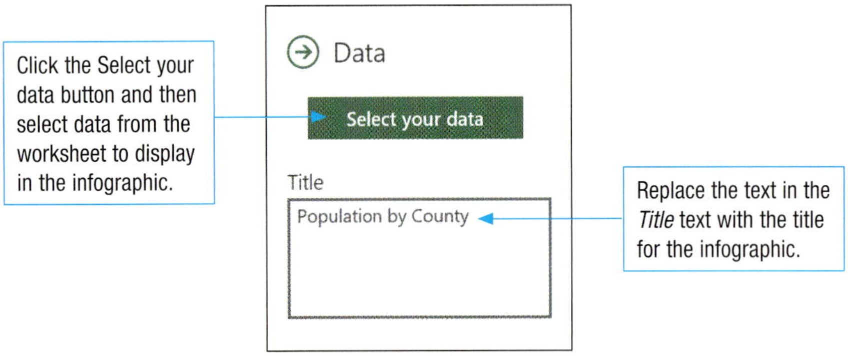

▸ Know This about formatting an infographic

— Use the Settings pane to format an infographic.
— To display the Settings pane, click the Settings button (see Figure 10.44).
— To change the appearance of an infographic, click the *type* or *theme* category and then select type or theme options (see Figure 10.45).
— To change the shape of the figure representing the data in the infographic, click the *shape* category and then select a shape option.
— To remove the Settings pane, click the Back button.

Figure 10.44 People Graph Settings Pane

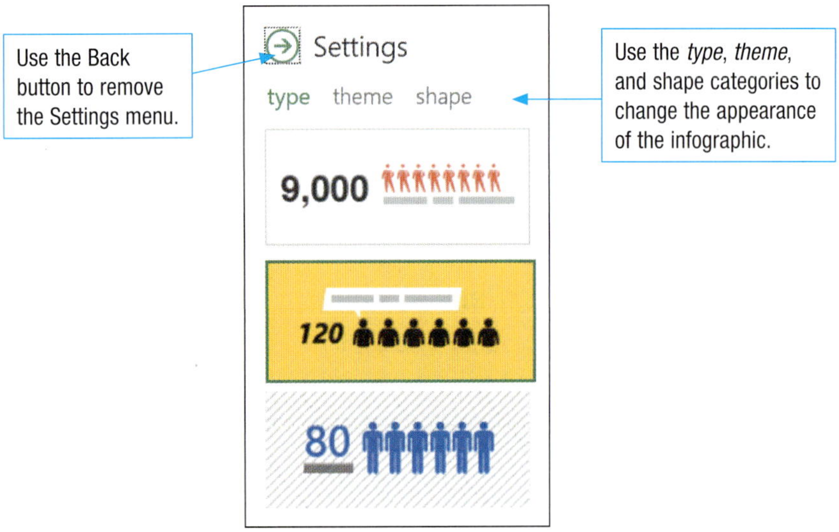

On the Job

Task 10.19 Creating an Infographic Using People Graph

Devon is preparing a presentation to introduce his new marketing campaign to his sales representatives. He would like an engaging visual to emphasize the importance of targeting the Florida counties with the highest population so the sales representatives can easily correlate the sales projections and targets to Devon's marketing campaign. Use the population data Devon provides to create an infographic for his presentation.

1. Open the data file **10-DVAutoParts-Population**.
2. With the Florida Counties worksheet active, click the Insert tab and then click the People Graph button in the Add-ins group.

   A sample infographic window displays.
3. Click the Data button (see Figure 10.43 on page 502).

   The Data pane displays.
4. Click in the *Title* text box, if necessary; select the text in the box; and then type Population by County.
5. Select the range A1:B6 in the worksheet.

   The population data is selected for the five most highly populated counties in the state of Florida.
6. Click the Select your data button.
7. Click the Create button.
8. Click the Settings button and then click the *Type 2* option.
9. Click the *theme* option and then click the *Theme 4* option.
10. Click the *shape* option and then click the *Shape 4* option.
11. Click the Back button.

    The Settings pane is removed and the data displays with the chosen settings in the infographic window.
12. If printed work is required by your instructor, print the workbook.
13. Save and then close the workbook.

Figure 10.45 People Graph Infographic Window

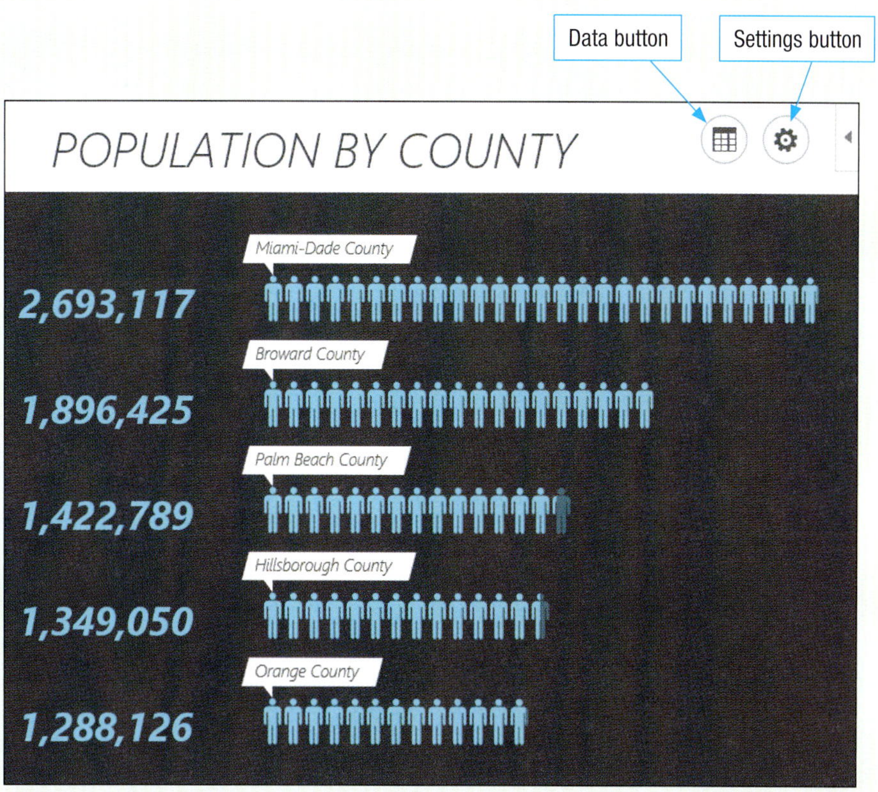

Model Answer

Chapter Summary

10.1 ▶ The *Financial* category in Excel includes a variety of functions related to business and finance that can be used to determine financial data such as loan payments, the future value of an investment, the rate of return on an investment, and the depreciation of an asset. To understand Financial functions, it is helpful to first become familiar with some basic financial terminology and understand how to enter accurate arguments, as many Financial functions use similar arguments.

10.2 ▶ The PMT function is used to calculate the equal periodic payments required to pay off a loan or an investment with a fixed interest rate over a specified period of time. The PMT function can be used to calculate mortgage payments and other types of loan payments that have a fixed rate of interest.

▶ The PPMT function, which calculates the principal part of the payment, and the IPMT function, which calculates the interest part of the payment, are used along with the PMT function to create an amortization schedule.

10.3 ▶ The FV function is used to calculate the future value of an investment or a loan based on a fixed interest rate. The *future value* is the amount to which the investment or loan will grow over time.

10.4 ▶ The PV function is used to calculate the present value of an investment or a loan. The *present value* is the amount that must be invested or borrowed now to reach a desired amount in the future. Another application of the PV function is to calculate the initial investment required to reach a savings goal.

10.5 ▶ The RATE function is used to calculate the interest rate required to pay off a loan or reach a target amount on an investment, given a fixed number of periods and a specified payment amount. It can also be used to calculate the rate of return on an investment.

10.6 ▶ The NPER function is used to calculate the number of periods required to pay off a loan or to reach a target amount on an investment, given a fixed interest rate and a specified payment amount. When using the NPER function to calculate the number of periods required to reach a target amount on an investment, the future value of the investment should be included.

10.7 ▶ Excel has four depreciation functions, each of which uses a slightly different method for depreciating an asset over time. The SLN function is used to calculate straight-line depreciation. The SYD function is used to calculate sum-of-the-years'-digits depreciation. The DB function is used to calculate declining balance depreciation. The DDB function is used to calculate double-declining balance depreciation.

10.8 ▶ Net present value (NPV) is a profitability measure used to assess the potential return on an investment. The NPV function is similar to the PV function with two exceptions: The NPV function assumes cash flows (income and payments) are made at the end of the period, and the NPV function allows for unequal cash flows.

10.9 ▶ The internal rate of return (IRR) is a profitability measure used to determine which investments or projects are likely to yield the greatest return per dollar of capital investment. IRR is similar to NPV but calculates the expected gains as a percentage of the initial investment, rather than as a net dollar amount. The IRR function returns the internal rate of return for a set of values, including an initial investment value and a series of net income values.

10.10 ▶ The Data Validation feature is used to validate and restrict the types of data or values that can be entered in a cell. An entry can be restricted to a predefined item or value, a specified range, a certain timeframe, and a maximum number of text characters. Data can also be validated based on formulas or values in other cells. A validation rule defines the criteria for the data that can be entered into a cell or range. In addition, the user can specify an input message to indicate what data is allowed in the cell and an error alert message to indicate that incorrect data has been entered.

10.11 ▶ Excel automatically displays formula and function error codes, error codes, and the Trace Error button to help the user locate and debug errors in formulas and functions. Other troubleshooting methods include finding and fixing errors using the Error Checking feature, tracing errors to their sources using the Trace Precedents and Trace Dependents features, and evaluating individual parts of a formula using the Evaluate Formula feature.

10.12 ▶ A sparkline is a type of information graphic (or *infographic*) that is inserted in a cell and is used to illustrate data trends and patterns. Although a sparkline is small, it efficiently creates a visual representation of the data without having to create a standard chart and add chart elements.

10.13 ▶ A sparkline can be customized by changing the chart type and style and adding markers. Chart types are limited to line, column, and win/loss. Chart styles are predefined styles that can be applied to change the appearance of a sparkline, and markers can be added to highlight specific value points.

10.14 ▶ What-if analysis tools are used to quickly change worksheet values and assess the impact of those changes in the worksheet results. The Goal Seek feature is used when the user knows the result that is wanted from a formula but is unsure what value the formula needs to get that result.

10.15 ▶ The Scenario Manager is a what-if analysis tool that allows the user to create different scenarios. A *scenario* is a set of values that can be substituted in cells to view different results. Once scenarios have been created, a scenario report can be generated that summarizes the data from all the scenarios.

▶ Instead of using the Scenario Manager to create scenarios, you can use a data table. A data table is a range of cells in which you can change values to view different scenarios. A one-variable data table allows you to change the value of one variable in a formula. A two-variable data table allows you to change the values of two variables in a formula.

10.16 ▸ A Watch Window can be created to display values of cells located throughout a workbook. The user can create a Watch Window to monitor cells and formulas when he or she is going to change the values in cells that they reference. The Watch Window feature allows viewing the impact of changes without having to scroll or switch worksheets.

10.17 ▸ Inserting a map chart allows comparing values and illustrating categories across geographical regions. This type of visual can be created from geographical data such as countries, regions, counties, states, and postal codes.

10.18 ▸ The 3D Maps feature is a three-dimensional data visualization tool that can be used to plot geographic data on a 3-D globe map or 3-D custom map. If dates or times are included in the plotted data, the user can view a 3D Maps tour that illustrates a time-based relationship between the geographic locations and their associated data.

10.19 ▸ An infographic is a form of data visualization that presents data in an easy-to-understand image such as a chart or graph. Infographics are widely used in content marketing and are an engaging way to communicate data and information. You can create and format an infographic using the Excel add-in People Graph.

Features Review

Feature	Ribbon Tab, Group	Button, Option	Keyboard Shortcut
add sparkline markers	Sparkline Tools Design, Show	insert check marks in check boxes	
change sparkline chart type	Sparkline Tools Design, Type		
change sparkline color	Sparkline Tools Design, Style		
change sparkline line weight	Sparkline Tools Design, Style	, *Weight*	
change sparkline marker color	Sparkline Tools Design, Style		
change sparkline style	Sparkline Tools Design, Style		
create column sparkline	Insert, Sparklines	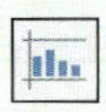	
create data validation drop-down list	Data, Data Tools		
create line sparkline	Insert, Sparklines	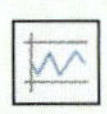	
create scenario	Data, Forecast	, *Scenario Manager*	
create 3-D map	Insert, Tours	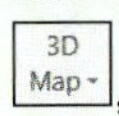, *Open 3D Maps*	
create Watch Window	Formulas, Formula Auditing		
create win/loss sparkline	Insert, Sparklines		

continues…

Feature	Ribbon Tab, Group	Button, Option	Keyboard Shortcut
customize map chart	Chart Tools Design or Chart Tools Format		
customize sparkline axes settings	Sparkline Tools Design, Group		
delete scenario	Data, Forecast	, *Scenario Manager*	
display Data Validation dialog box	Data, Data Tools		
display Launch 3D Maps window	Insert, Tours	3D Map, *Open 3D Maps*	
edit data validation settings	Data, Data Tools	, *Apply these changes to all other cells with the same settings check box*	
edit scenario	Data, Forecast	, *Scenario Manager*	
evaluate formula	Formulas, Formula Auditing		
find cells that have data validation settings applied	Home, Editing	, *Data Validation*	
flag cells containing invalid data	Data, Data Tools	Data Validation, *Circle Invalid Data*	
group sparklines	Sparkline Tools Design, Group		
insert function	Formulas, Function Library		
insert infographic	Insert, Add-ins		
insert map chart	Insert, Charts	, *Filled Map*	
insert sparkline	Insert tab, Sparklines		
merge scenarios	Data, Forecast	, *Scenario Manager*	
play 3D Maps tour	HOME, Tours (in Launch 3D Maps window)		
remove data validation from selected cells	Data, Data Tools	, *All Clear button*	
remove data validation circles from selected cells	Data, Data Tools	Data Validation, *Clear Validation Circles*	
remove tracer arrows	Formulas, Formula Auditing		
run error checker	Formulas, Formula Auditing		
set data validation rules	Data, Data Tools		
set Goal Seek options	Data, Data Tools	, *Goal Seek*	
show all formulas in worksheet	Formulas, Formula Auditing		Ctrl + `

continues...

Feature	Ribbon Tab, Group	Button, Option	Keyboard Shortcut
trace dependents	Formulas, Formula Auditing		
trace precedents	Formulas, Formula Auditing		
ungroup sparklines	Sparkline Tools Design, Group		
view scenarios	Data, Forecast	, *Scenario Manager*	
view 3D Maps tour	Home, Tours		

Recheck

Recheck your understanding of the concepts, features, and skills covered in this chapter by taking the Recheck quiz.

Workbook

Access the study tools, review exercises, assessments, and challenges for this chapter in the workbook available from this page in your ebook.

Working with Subtotals, Outlines, Groups, and Advanced Formatting

Chapter 11

Chapter Goal

To enhance the readability of a workbook by applying advanced formatting to text and data, and to analyze data using grouping, summarizing, and outlining tools.

Learning Objectives

11.1 Insert subtotals

11.2 Modify subtotals and print groups with subtotals

11.3 Work with outline levels

11.4 Group and ungroup data without adding subtotals

11.5 Create custom conditional formats

11.6 Apply conditional formatting using a formula

11.7 Modify theme colors and create a custom color

11.8 Modify theme fonts and manage options for body and heading fonts

11.9 Modify theme effects

11.10 Work with custom themes

11.11 Work with cell styles

Precheck

Check your understanding of the concepts, features, and skills covered in this chapter by taking the Precheck quiz.

Data Files

Before beginning the chapter work, download the AE11 folder from this page in your ebook to your storage medium and then make AE11 the active folder.

Ebook Links

Access digital resources for this course from your ebook.

SNAP

If you are a SNAP user, go to your SNAP assignments page to complete the Precheck, Tutorials, and Recheck in this chapter.

Preview

On the Job

Scenario: DV Auto Parts

Devon Varey is an auto mechanic who opened his own business, DV Auto Parts, in Miami, Florida, in January 2019. Devon is meeting with his investors next week to review the progress his business made during the first two weeks of October 2019. He wants to summarize the sales data for the business in one worksheet of the workbook he's using for the business, update the look of the workbook, and ensure that all the files for the business have a consistent look. Use advanced formatting grouping, summarizing, and outlining tools to help Devon achieve these goals.

Visual Reference: Subtotals and Conditional Formatting

Figure 11.1 Excel Worksheet with Subtotals

When subtotals have been inserted in a data range, Outline buttons, Show Details buttons, and Hide Details buttons display in the outline area to the left of the data range.

Use the Outline buttons to display levels of detail in the data range. In this example, the worksheet displays level 4 with two part numbers expanded.

The *Count* subtotal was added above the *Average* subtotal to count the number of orders for a particular part number.

Use the Group and Ungroup buttons to group and ungroup data by rows or columns.

Use the Subtotal button to recalculate subtotals in the worksheet after a change has been made in a group.

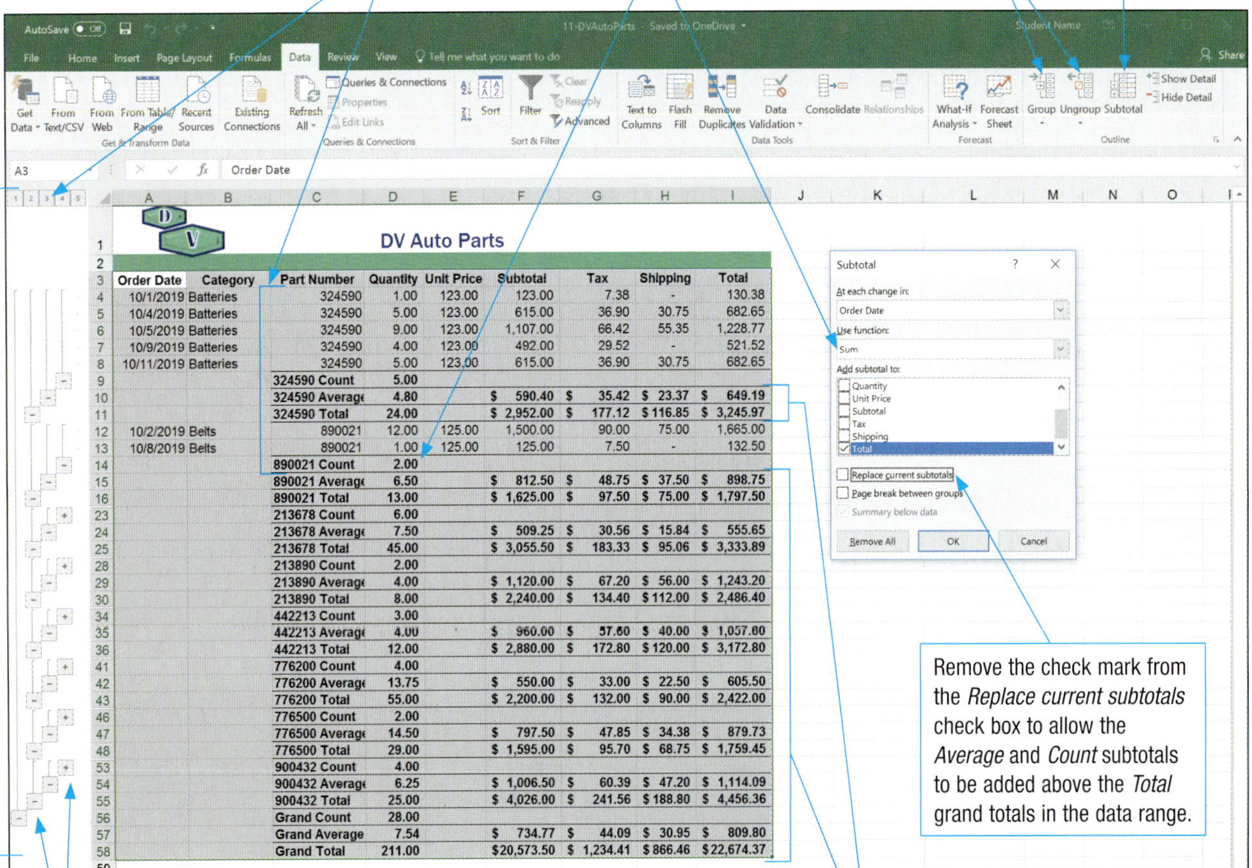

Remove the check mark from the *Replace current subtotals* check box to allow the *Average* and *Count* subtotals to be added above the *Total* grand totals in the data range.

Use the Hide Detail buttons (-) and Show Detail buttons (+) to collapse and expand the levels of detail in the worksheet.

The subtotals and grand totals were formatted with bold formatting and top, middle, and bottom borders using the *Go To Special* and *Visible cells only* options at the Find & Select drop-down menu.

Visual Reference

Figure 11.2 Excel Worksheet with Conditional Formatting and Cell Styles

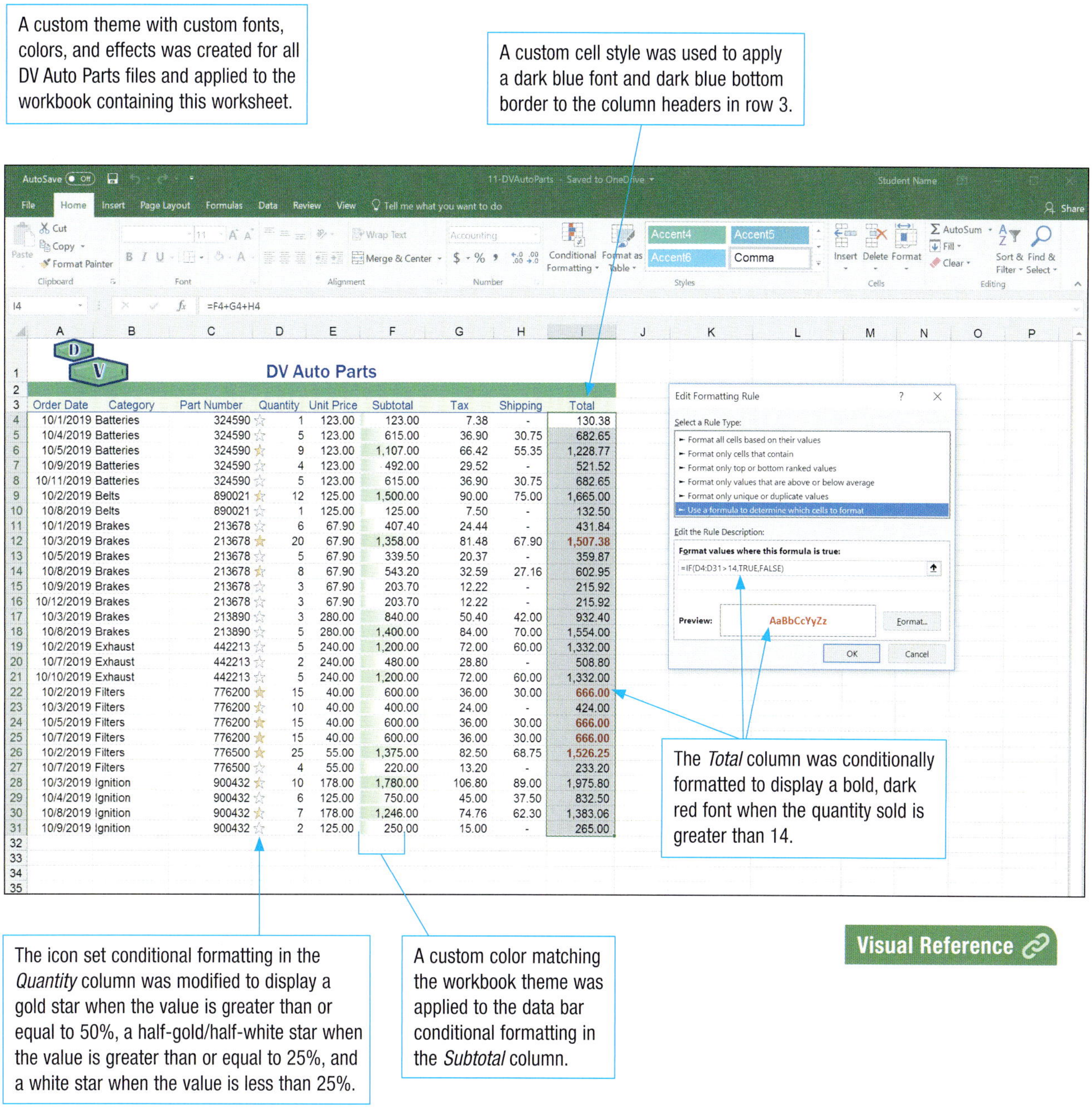

Order Date	Category	Part Number	Quantity	Unit Price	Subtotal	Tax	Shipping	Total
10/1/2019	Batteries	324590	1	123.00	123.00	7.38	-	130.38
10/4/2019	Batteries	324590	5	123.00	615.00	36.90	30.75	682.65
10/5/2019	Batteries	324590	9	123.00	1,107.00	66.42	55.35	1,228.77
10/9/2019	Batteries	324590	4	123.00	492.00	29.52	-	521.52
10/11/2019	Batteries	324590	5	123.00	615.00	36.90	30.75	682.65
10/2/2019	Belts	890021	12	125.00	1,500.00	90.00	75.00	1,665.00
10/8/2019	Belts	890021	1	125.00	125.00	7.50	-	132.50
10/1/2019	Brakes	213678	6	67.90	407.40	24.44	-	431.84
10/3/2019	Brakes	213678	20	67.90	1,358.00	81.48	67.90	**1,507.38**
10/5/2019	Brakes	213678	5	67.90	339.50	20.37	-	359.87
10/8/2019	Brakes	213678	8	67.90	543.20	32.59	27.16	602.95
10/9/2019	Brakes	213678	3	67.90	203.70	12.22	-	215.92
10/12/2019	Brakes	213678	3	67.90	203.70	12.22	-	215.92
10/3/2019	Brakes	213890	3	280.00	840.00	50.40	42.00	932.40
10/8/2019	Brakes	213890	5	280.00	1,400.00	84.00	70.00	1,554.00
10/2/2019	Exhaust	442213	5	240.00	1,200.00	72.00	60.00	1,332.00
10/7/2019	Exhaust	442213	2	240.00	480.00	28.80	-	508.80
10/10/2019	Exhaust	442213	5	240.00	1,200.00	72.00	60.00	1,332.00
10/2/2019	Filters	776200	15	40.00	600.00	36.00	30.00	**666.00**
10/3/2019	Filters	776200	10	40.00	400.00	24.00	-	424.00
10/5/2019	Filters	776200	15	40.00	600.00	36.00	30.00	**666.00**
10/7/2019	Filters	776200	15	40.00	600.00	36.00	30.00	**666.00**
10/2/2019	Filters	776500	25	55.00	1,375.00	82.50	68.75	**1,526.25**
10/7/2019	Filters	776500	4	55.00	220.00	13.20	-	233.20
10/3/2019	Ignition	900432	10	178.00	1,780.00	106.80	89.00	1,975.80
10/4/2019	Ignition	900432	6	125.00	750.00	45.00	37.50	832.50
10/8/2019	Ignition	900432	7	178.00	1,246.00	74.76	62.30	1,383.06
10/9/2019	Ignition	900432	2	125.00	250.00	15.00	-	265.00

Visual Reference

11.1 Inserting Subtotals

MOS 2.3.3

Tutorial

Inserting Subtotals

The **Subtotal** feature helps you group and summarize your data by inserting a subtotal row for a range of data, adding a grand total row below the last row of data, and displaying the worksheet in outline view. **Outline view** allows you to collapse and expand a worksheet to display various levels of detail (see Section 11.3).

▸ Know This about inserting subtotals

— A subtotal can be inserted only in a data range, not in a table. If your data resides in a table, convert the table to a data range before inserting a subtotal.

— Excel inserts a subtotal after a change in a specific field value. For this reason, you must first sort the data range by the field to which the subtotal is to be added. For example, if you want to subtotal the benefit costs for employees by department and the worksheet is arranged by hire date, you must first sort the worksheet by department.

— To insert a subtotal, complete these steps:

1. Select the range.
2. If necessary, sort the data in the range to arrange the data.
3. Click the Subtotal button in the Outline group on the Data tab to display the Subtotal dialog box (see Figure 11.3).
4. Identify the common field in which Excel will search for a change in the *At each change in* option box.
5. Select the function in the *Use function* option box.
6. Select the field or fields to subtotal in the *Add subtotal to* list box. ***Note**: By default, Excel inserts a check mark in the check box for the field farthest to the right.*
7. Click the OK button to close the Subtotal dialog box.

— When you close the Subtotal dialog box, the specified subtotals display in the worksheet.

— A grand total is automatically added at the bottom of the range.

— Functions available at the *Use functions* drop-down list include, but are not limited to, sum, average, count, minimum, and maximum.

Figure 11.3 Subtotal Dialog Box

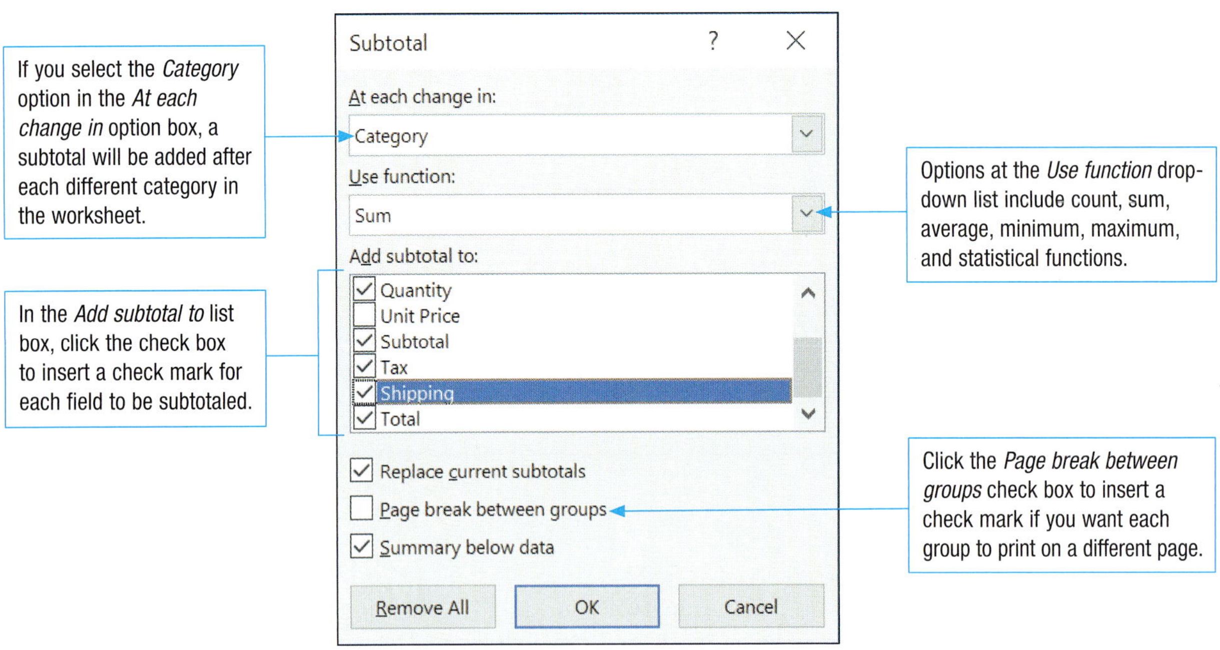

On the Job

Task 11.1 Inserting Subtotals

Devon wants to see sales details for each category of parts sold by DV Auto Parts in the first two weeks of October 2019. He wants to see sums for the number of units sold and for the subtotal, tax, shipping, and total amounts. To display the data Devon wants to see in the Orders worksheet, sort the data by category and then by part number, and then insert subtotals for the *Quantity*, *Subtotal*, *Tax*, *Shipping*, and *Total* fields.

Note: *Tasks 11.1 and 11.2 should be completed at the same time, without closing the file between tasks.*

1. Open the data file **11-DVAutoParts**.
2. With the Orders worksheet active, select the range A3:I31.
3. Sort the range by category and then by part number. ***Hint:*** *Click the Sort & Filter button in the Editing group on the Home tab, click the* Custom Sort *option, click the* Sort by *option box arrow, and then click the* Category *option. Click the Add Level button, click the* Then by *option box arrow, click the* Part Number *option, and then click the OK button.*

   The range is sorted by category and then by part number. Keep the range selected.
4. Click the Data tab and then click the Subtotal button in the Outline group.

   The Subtotal dialog box displays.
5. Click the *At each change in* option box arrow and then click the *Category* option (see Figure 11.4).

   Category appears in the option box, indicating a subtotal will be added after each group of items in the *Category* field.

Figure 11.4 Subtotal Dialog Box with *At each change in* Drop-Down List Displayed

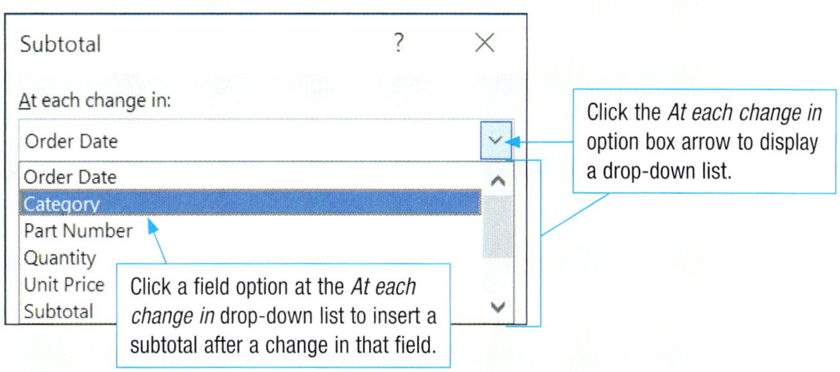

6. Click the *Quantity*, *Subtotal*, *Tax*, and *Shipping* check boxes in the *Add subtotal to* list box, scrolling down the list box as necessary.

   Check marks appear in the *Quantity*, *Subtotal*, *Tax*, and *Shipping* check boxes. There is already a check mark in the *Total* check box. Do not insert a check mark in the *Unit Price* check box. Subtotals will be added for the selected fields.
7. Click the OK button.

   The dialog box closes. A sum subtotal is inserted after each change in category in the data range (in rows 9, 12, 21, 25, 32, and 37), and a grand total is inserted at the bottom of the data range (in row 38).
8. Click the Save button on the Quick Access Toolbar. Leave the file open for the next task.

Model Answer

11.2 Modifying Subtotals and Printing Groups with Subtotals

You can modify subtotals to include more than one type of calculation. For example, if you have inserted subtotals that sum data, you can add subtotals that count and average the same data. You can also replace and delete subtotals. Suppose that after totaling the benefit costs for each department in a company, you want to find out the average benefit costs across all the departments. You can print the statistics for each department on a separate page so that you can forward the information to each department head.

Tutorial

Modifying Subtotals

▸ Know This about adding additional subtotals

— To add a subtotal to a data range that already has one or more subtotals, follow these steps:

1. Select a cell in the range that has been subtotaled.
2. Display the Subtotal dialog box.
3. Select the field to insert the new subtotal at the *At each change in* drop-down list.
4. Select a function for the new subtotal at the *Use function* drop-down list.
5. Click the check box to insert a check mark for the field to which you are adding a subtotal.
6. Click the *Replace current subtotals* check box to remove the check mark.
7. Click the OK button.

— When you add a new subtotal, it is placed above the existing subtotal or subtotals.

Reminder

To display the Subtotal dialog box, select the range and then click the Subtotal button in the Outline group on the Data tab.

▸ Know This about replacing subtotals

— To replace all the subtotals, click in a cell in the range; display the Subtotal dialog box; select the location, function, and field or fields for the replacement; verify that the *Replace current subtotals* check box contains a check mark; and then click the OK button.

— If there is more than one subtotal, each will be replaced with a new subtotal.

▸ Know This about printing ranges with subtotals

— To print each group of data on a separate page, display the Subtotal dialog box and then click the *Page break between groups* check box to insert a check mark.

On the Job

Task 11.2 Modifying Subtotals

After Devon reviews the subtotals you added to the Orders worksheet in Task 11.1, he decides he wants to see the sales details by part number instead of by category. He wants to see both sums and averages for the number of units sold and for the subtotal, tax, shipping, and total amounts. He also wants to know how many orders were placed for each part number. To provide the data Devon needs, modify the existing subtotals to sum after each change in part number. Also add subtotals that average the units sold (quantity), the subtotal, the tax, the shipping, and the total, and add subtotals that count how many orders were placed for each part number.

1. With the Orders worksheet active, click in any cell in the range A3:I38 and then click the Subtotal button in the Outline group on the Data tab.

   The Subtotal dialog box displays.

2. Click the *At each change in* option box arrow and then click the *Part Number* option (see Figure 11.5).
3. Verify that the *Replace current subtotals* check box contains a check mark.

Figure 11.5 Subtotal Dialog Box

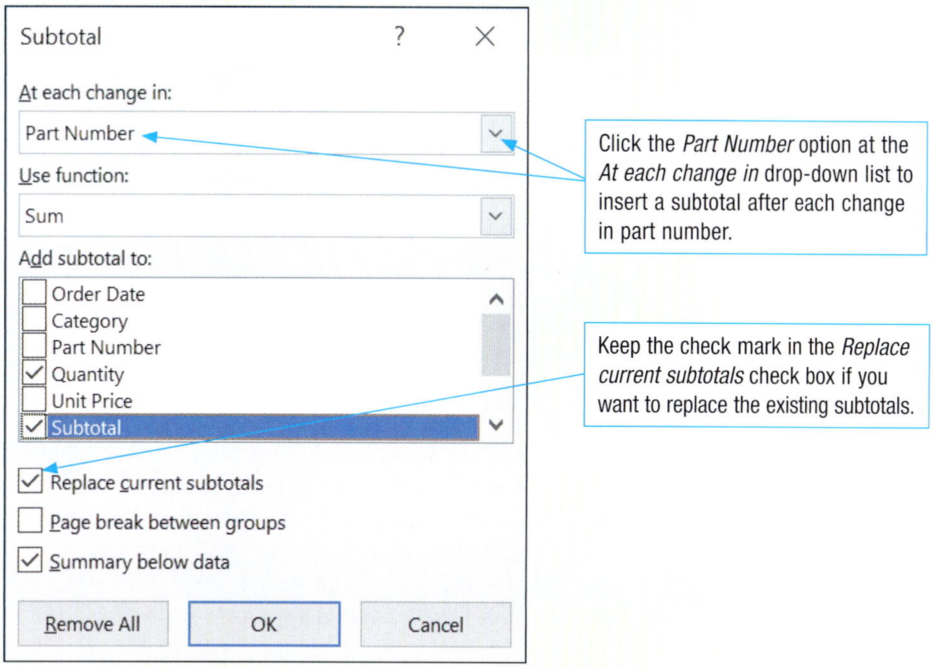

4. Click the OK button.

   The Subtotal dialog box closes and the worksheet includes a *Total* subtotal in the selected fields after each change in a part number instead of after each change in the category. The *Brakes* category has subtotals now for both part number 213678 and part number 213890.

5. Click the Subtotal button.

   The Subtotal dialog box displays.

6. Click the *Use function* option box arrow and then click the *Average* option.

   Average now appears in the *Use function* option box.

7. Click the *Replace current subtotals* check box.

   The check mark is removed from the check box.

8. Click the OK button.

   The worksheet includes an average subtotal above each sum (total) subtotal for each field selected.

9. Click the Subtotal button.

   The Subtotal dialog box displays.

10. Click the *Use function* option box arrow and then click the *Count* option.

    Count appears in the *Use function* option box.

11. Scrolling as necessary, click the *Subtotal*, *Tax*, *Shipping*, and *Total* check boxes in the *Add subtotal to* list box to remove the check marks, if necessary.

    The *Quantity* check box contains a check mark. All other check boxes in the list box are empty. ***Note:*** *If you closed the file after completing Task 11.1, the check boxes may not appear as described in this step. You may need to click the* Quantity *check box to insert a check mark, and you may or may not need to remove check marks from the other check boxes.*

12. Click the OK button.

    The number of orders appears as a count subtotal above each average subtotal in the *Quantity* field.

13. AutoFit the width of column C.

    All the data can now be seen in column C.

14. Click the Save button on the Quick Access Toolbar.

Model Answer

MOS 2.3.2

Tutorial

Working with Outlines

11.3 Working with Outline Levels

When subtotals have been added to a worksheet, the worksheet displays in outline view where the **outline area** appears along the left side of the worksheet. The outline area displays Outline buttons, Show Detail buttons, and Hide Detail buttons, which you use to control the amount of detail you see in the worksheet. Outline buttons display at the top of the outline area, and Show Detail and Hide Detail buttons appear beside data levels in the outline area.

▸ Know This about working with outlines

— A worksheet contains different levels of detail, depending on how many times a subtotal has been inserted.

— Excel can outline data with up to eight levels of detail.

— The highest level of detail shows all the data in the worksheet, all the subtotals, and all the grand totals. The lowest level of detail shows only the grand totals.

— By default, the highest level of detail is displayed in the worksheet.

— To display different levels of detail, click the Outline button for that level.

— For example, the Orders worksheet you worked with in Tasks 11.1 and 11.2 has five levels of detail:

- Level 5 is the highest level and displays all the data, all the subtotals, and all the grand totals (see Figure 11.6).
- Level 4 displays the subtotals for the sum, average, and count functions along with the grand totals for the same functions.
- Level 3 displays the subtotals for the sum and average functions along with the grand totals for the sum, average, and count functions (see Figure 11.7).

- Level 2 displays the subtotals for the sum function along with the grand totals for the sum, average, and count functions.
- Level 1 displays the grand totals for the sum, average, and count functions (see Figure 11.8 on page 518).

Figure 11.6 Orders Worksheet in Outline View with Level 5 Displayed

By default, the Level 5 Outline button is active and level 5 displays in the worksheet.

Level 5 displays all the data, subtotals, and grand totals in the worksheet. ***Note:*** *You may need to scroll to see the entire worksheet.*

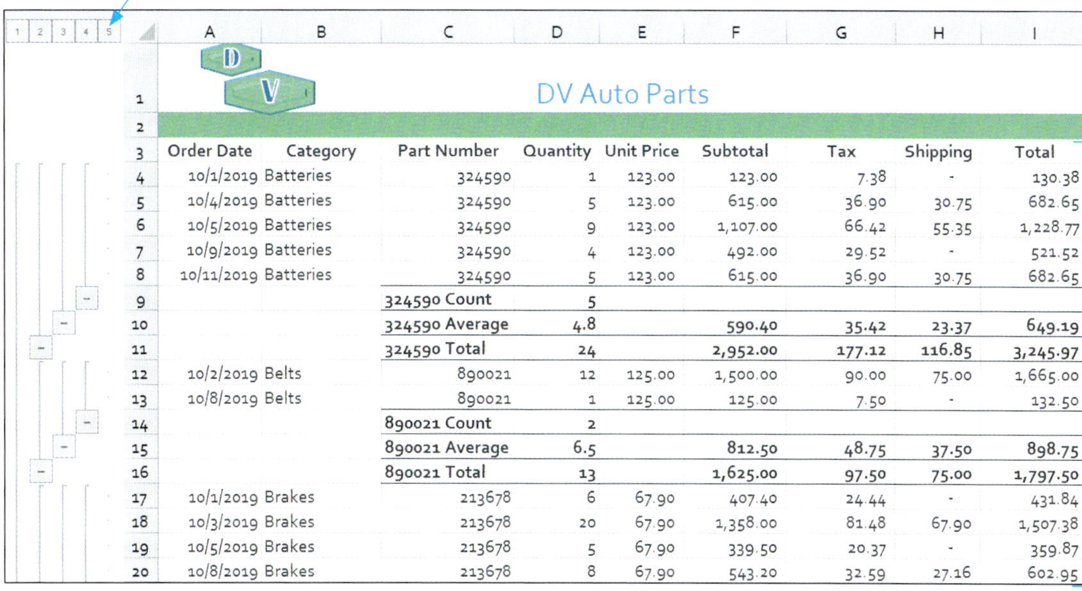

	A	B	C	D	E	F	G	H	I
1				DV Auto Parts					
2									
3	Order Date	Category	Part Number	Quantity	Unit Price	Subtotal	Tax	Shipping	Total
4	10/1/2019	Batteries	324590	1	123.00	123.00	7.38	-	130.38
5	10/4/2019	Batteries	324590	5	123.00	615.00	36.90	30.75	682.65
6	10/5/2019	Batteries	324590	9	123.00	1,107.00	66.42	55.35	1,228.77
7	10/9/2019	Batteries	324590	4	123.00	492.00	29.52	-	521.52
8	10/11/2019	Batteries	324590	5	123.00	615.00	36.90	30.75	682.65
9			324590 Count	5					
10			324590 Average	4.8		590.40	35.42	23.37	649.19
11			324590 Total	24		2,952.00	177.12	116.85	3,245.97
12	10/2/2019	Belts	890021	12	125.00	1,500.00	90.00	75.00	1,665.00
13	10/8/2019	Belts	890021	1	125.00	125.00	7.50	-	132.50
14			890021 Count	2					
15			890021 Average	6.5		812.50	48.75	37.50	898.75
16			890021 Total	13		1,625.00	97.50	75.00	1,797.50
17	10/1/2019	Brakes	213678	6	67.90	407.40	24.44	-	431.84
18	10/3/2019	Brakes	213678	20	67.90	1,358.00	81.48	67.90	1,507.38
19	10/5/2019	Brakes	213678	5	67.90	339.50	20.37	-	359.87
20	10/8/2019	Brakes	213678	8	67.90	543.20	32.59	27.16	602.95

Figure 11.7 Orders Worksheet in Outline View with Level 3 Displayed

When the Level 3 Outline button is active, level 3 displays in the worksheet. No Show Detail or Hide Detail buttons appear for levels 4 and 5.

Level 3 displays all the subtotals for the sum and average functions along with the grand totals for the sum, average, and count functions.

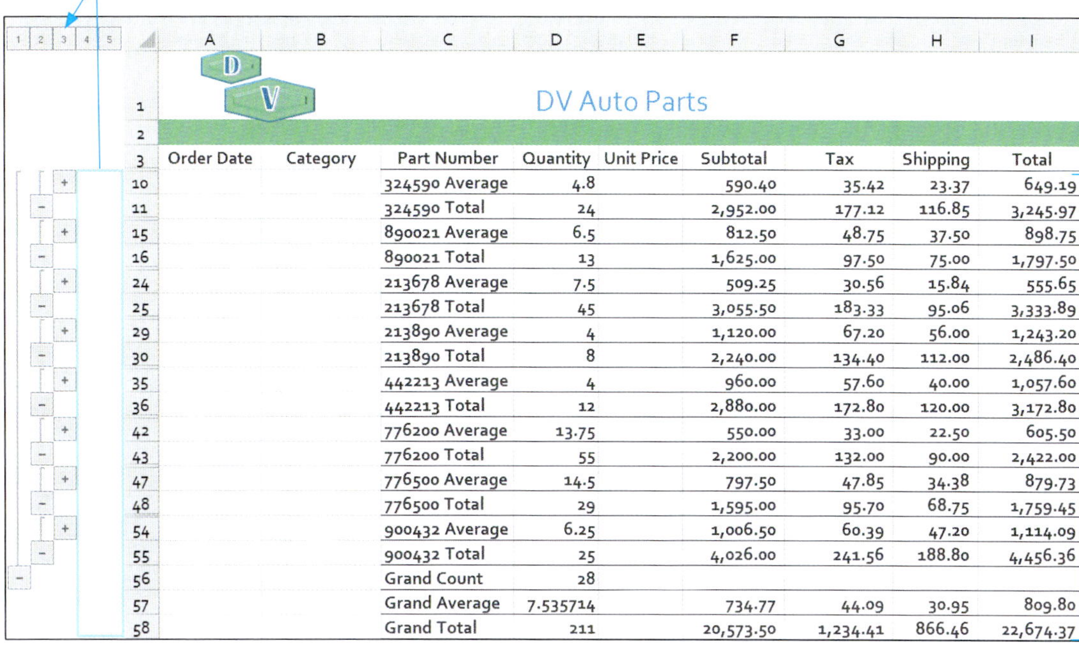

	A	B	C	D	E	F	G	H	I
1				DV Auto Parts					
2									
3	Order Date	Category	Part Number	Quantity	Unit Price	Subtotal	Tax	Shipping	Total
10			324590 Average	4.8		590.40	35.42	23.37	649.19
11			324590 Total	24		2,952.00	177.12	116.85	3,245.97
15			890021 Average	6.5		812.50	48.75	37.50	898.75
16			890021 Total	13		1,625.00	97.50	75.00	1,797.50
24			213678 Average	7.5		509.25	30.56	15.84	555.65
25			213678 Total	45		3,055.50	183.33	95.06	3,333.89
29			213890 Average	4		1,120.00	67.20	56.00	1,243.20
30			213890 Total	8		2,240.00	134.40	112.00	2,486.40
35			442213 Average	4		960.00	57.60	40.00	1,057.60
36			442213 Total	12		2,880.00	172.80	120.00	3,172.80
42			776200 Average	13.75		550.00	33.00	22.50	605.50
43			776200 Total	55		2,200.00	132.00	90.00	2,422.00
47			776500 Average	14.5		797.50	47.85	34.38	879.73
48			776500 Total	29		1,595.00	95.70	68.75	1,759.45
54			900432 Average	6.25		1,006.50	60.39	47.20	1,114.09
55			900432 Total	25		4,026.00	241.56	188.80	4,456.36
56			Grand Count	28					
57			Grand Average	7.535714		734.77	44.09	30.95	809.80
58			Grand Total	211		20,573.50	1,234.41	866.46	22,674.37

▸ **Know This** about collapsing and expanding groups of data

— The Show Detail and Hide Detail buttons allow you to control the level of detail you see for a group of data (see Figure 11.9).

— To display the data in a collapsed group, click the Show Detail button.

— To collapse the data in an expanded group, click the Hide Detail button.

— After a Show Detail button has been clicked, the group expands to show the data and the Show Detail button changes to a Hide Detail button.

Figure 11.8 Orders Worksheet in Outline View with Level 1 Displayed

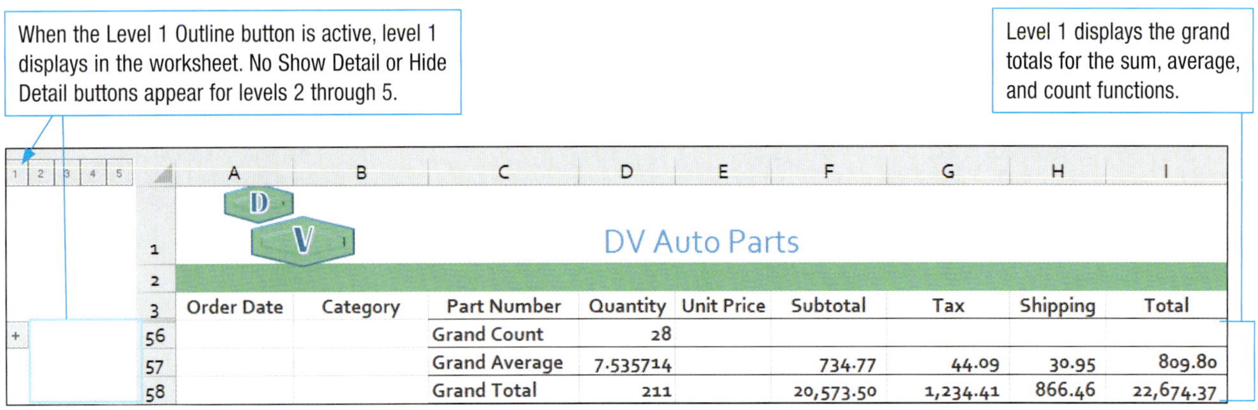

Row	Order Date	Category	Part Number	Quantity	Unit Price	Subtotal	Tax	Shipping	Total
56			Grand Count	28					
57			Grand Average	7.535714		734.77	44.09	30.95	809.80
58			Grand Total	211		20,573.50	1,234.41	866.46	22,674.37

Figure 11.9 Orders Worksheet in Outline View with Level 4 Displayed and the Part Number 324590 Group Expanded

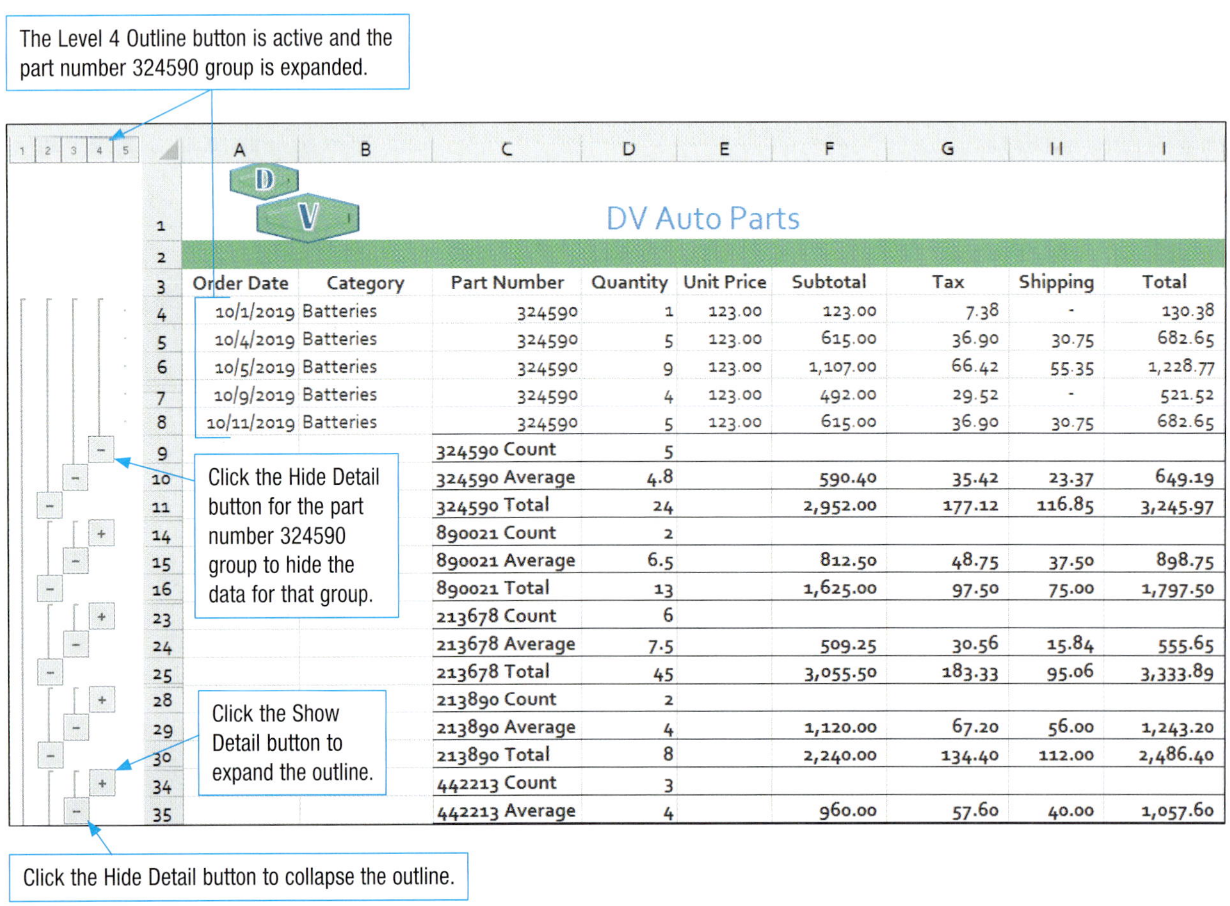

Row	Order Date	Category	Part Number	Quantity	Unit Price	Subtotal	Tax	Shipping	Total
4	10/1/2019	Batteries	324590	1	123.00	123.00	7.38	-	130.38
5	10/4/2019	Batteries	324590	5	123.00	615.00	36.90	30.75	682.65
6	10/5/2019	Batteries	324590	9	123.00	1,107.00	66.42	55.35	1,228.77
7	10/9/2019	Batteries	324590	4	123.00	492.00	29.52	-	521.52
8	10/11/2019	Batteries	324590	5	123.00	615.00	36.90	30.75	682.65
9			324590 Count	5					
10			324590 Average	4.8		590.40	35.42	23.37	649.19
11			324590 Total	24		2,952.00	177.12	116.85	3,245.97
14			890021 Count	2					
15			890021 Average	6.5		812.50	48.75	37.50	898.75
16			890021 Total	13		1,625.00	97.50	75.00	1,797.50
23			213678 Count	6					
24			213678 Average	7.5		509.25	30.56	15.84	555.65
25			213678 Total	45		3,055.50	183.33	95.06	3,333.89
28			213890 Count	2					
29			213890 Average	4		1,120.00	67.20	56.00	1,243.20
30			213890 Total	8		2,240.00	134.40	112.00	2,486.40
34			442213 Count	3					
35			442213 Average	4		960.00	57.60	40.00	1,057.60

▸ Know This about selecting data from different outline levels

— By default, when a subtotal or grand total is selected in a collapsed outline, the underlying data is also selected.

— To select only specific subtotals and/or grand totals and not the underlying data, select the subtotals and/or grand totals, click the Find & Select button in the Editing group on the Home tab, click the *Go To Special* option to display the Go To Special dialog box (see Figure 11.10), click the *Visible cells only* radio button to insert a bullet, and then click the OK button.

— After you have selected subtotals and/or grand totals, you can copy them to a new range or format the cells containing them.

▸ Know This about removing subtotals and the outline area

— To delete all the subtotals from a selected range, click the Subtotal button in the Outline group on the Data tab and then click the Remove All button.

— When the subtotals are removed, the outline area is also removed.

On the Job

Task 11.3a Working with Outlines

Devon wants the subtotals and grand totals from the Orders worksheet copied into the Total worksheet he has prepared to display summary data. He also wants the subtotals and grand totals to be formatted so they stand out from the other data in the Orders worksheet. Finally, he wants to see all the details for the part number 324590 group in the Orders worksheet. Use the Outline buttons, the Show Detail and Hide Detail buttons, and the Find & Select button to modify the workbook as Devon has requested.

1. With the Orders worksheet active, click the Level 2 Outline button (see Figure 11.7 on page 517).

   The worksheet collapses to show the subtotals for the sum function and the grand totals for the count, average, and sum functions. The other data is hidden.

2. Select the range C3:I58; click the Home tab, if necessary; and then click the Find & Select button in the Editing group.

   A drop-down menu displays.

3. Click the *Go To Special* option.

   The Go To Special dialog box displays (see Figure 11.10).

4. Click the *Visible cells only* radio button.

   The radio button contains a bullet.

5. Click the OK button.

   The dialog box closes and the range is still selected in the worksheet.

Figure 11.10 Go To Special Dialog Box

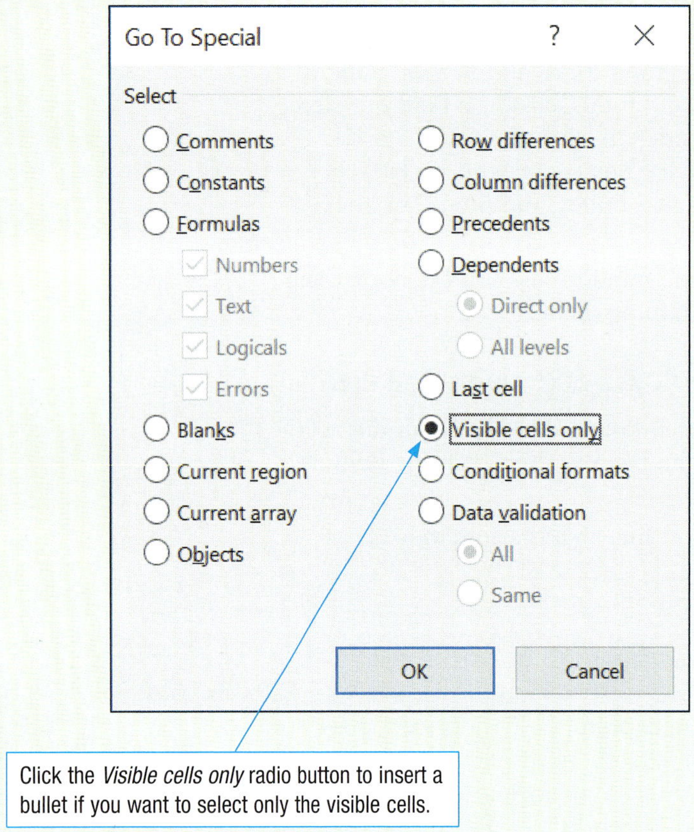

6. Press Ctrl + C, click the Total sheet tab, click in cell A3, and then press Ctrl + V.

   The subtotals for the sum function and the grand totals for the count, average, and sum function from the Orders worksheet appear in the range A3:G14 in the Total worksheet. Note that you have copied and pasted the subtotals and grand totals (not the underlying data for those totals).

7. Delete column C.

   The *Unit Price* column is removed. Devon didn't ask you to include that column in the Total worksheet.

8. Click the Orders sheet tab, click the Esc key, click in any cell in the range A3:I58, and then click the Level 4 Outline button.

   The worksheet expands to show the subtotals for the count, average, and sum functions, and the grand totals for the count, average, and sum functions. You may need to scroll to see all the subtotals and grand totals.

9. Select the range C9:I58, click the Find & Select button, click the *Go To Special* option, click the *Visible cells only* radio button, and then click the OK button.

   The contents of the visible cells have been selected in the range C9:I58.

10. Click the Bold button in the Font group.

    The bold formatting is removed from the selected cells in column C.

11. Click the Bold button.

Bold formatting is applied to all the visible cells.

12. Click the Borders button arrow and then click the *More Borders* option.

The Format Cells dialog box displays with the Border tab active.

13. Click the top, middle, and bottom borders in the *Border* preview section (see Figure 11.11).

The default line style is applied to the selected borders in the preview section.

14. Click the OK button.

The dialog box closes and the specified borders display in the selected range.

Figure 11.11 Border Tab at the Format Cells Dialog Box

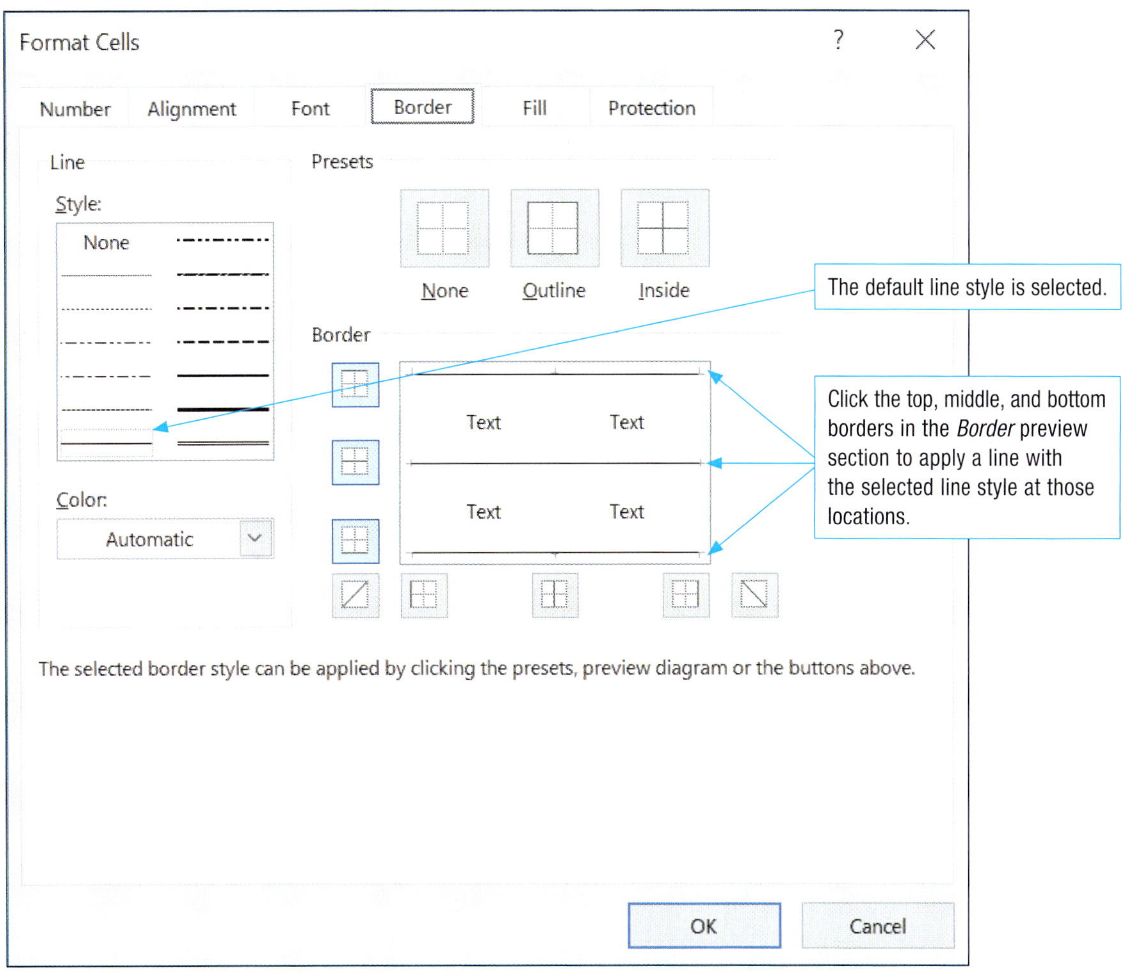

15. Select the range F10:I58. Using visible cells only, apply the Currency format to the *Average* and *Total* subtotals and grand totals.
16. AutoFit the width of column F, if necessary.
17. Click in any cell in the range A9:I58.

The range is no longer selected.

18. Click the Show Detail buttons to expand the outline for the part number 324590 group and the part number 890021 group (see Figure 11.12).

    The data displays for part numbers 324590 and 890021. The data cells have not been formatted with the bold formatting and borders that you applied to the subtotal and grand total cells.

19. Click the Save button on the Quick Access Toolbar.

Figure 11.12 Orders Worksheet in Outline View with Formatting Applied

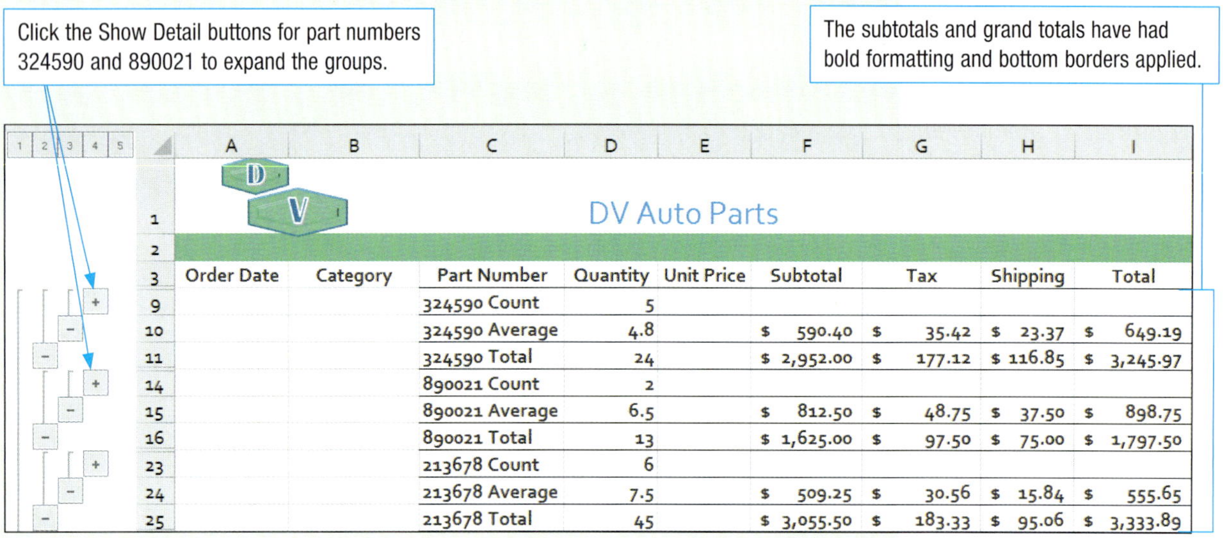

Model Answer

On the Job

Task 11.3b Removing Subtotals

Devon wants to see all the data from the Orders worksheet without any subtotals. He asks you to create a copy of the Orders worksheet, name the copy *Conditional*, and then delete the subtotals in the copy. (In later tasks, Devon will ask you to format the Conditional worksheet for an upcoming meeting with his investors.)

1. Make a copy of the Orders worksheet and place it to the right of the Total worksheet in the 11-DVAutoParts workbook.

    A copy of the Orders worksheet is placed to the right of the Total worksheet.

2. Rename the Orders (2) worksheet, typing Conditional as the new name.

    The worksheet is renamed Conditional.

3. Click the Data tab and then click the Subtotal button in the Outline group.

    The Subtotal dialog box displays (see Figure 11.13).

Reminder

To copy a worksheet within a workbook, click the sheet tab, click the Format button in the Cells group on the Home tab, click the *Move or Copy Sheet* option in the *Organize Sheets* section at the drop-down list, click an option in the *Before sheet* list box at the Move or Copy dialog box, click the *Create a copy* check box to insert a check mark, and then click the OK button.

Reminder

To rename a worksheet, right-click the sheet tab, click the *Rename* option at the pop-up menu, type the new name, and then press the Enter key.

4. Click the Remove All button.

   The dialog box closes and the subtotals and grand totals are removed from the Conditional worksheet.

5. Click the Save button on the Quick Access Toolbar.

Figure 11.13 Subtotal Dialog Box

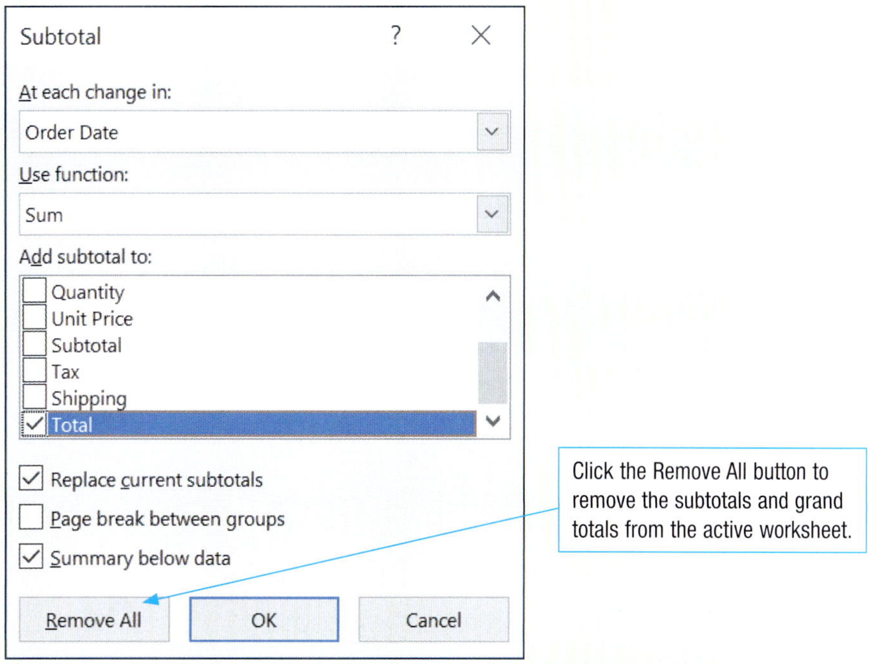

Model Answer

11.4 Grouping and Ungrouping Data without Adding Subtotals

Another way to summarize data is to use the Group feature. When data is grouped, Excel automatically creates an outline, which allows you to collapse and expand each group of data to control the level of detail you see in a worksheet. A worksheet can be grouped in rows or in columns. For example, in a worksheet in which two columns are used to arrive at a formula, the source columns can be grouped and the details hidden so that only the formula column with the calculated results is displayed. Grouping and ungrouping data is similar to hiding and unhiding rows and columns.

Tutorial

Grouping Data and Collapsing a Group of Data

Reminder

Collapsing and expanding groups is covered in Section 11.3.

▸ Know This about grouping data

— To group data by rows, select the range to be grouped, click the Group button in the Outline group on the Data tab to display the Group dialog box (see Figure 11.14), verify that the *Rows* radio button contains a bullet, and then click the OK button.

— To group data by columns, select the range to be grouped, click the Group button, click the *Columns* radio button to insert a bullet, and then click the OK button.

▸ Know This about ungrouping data

— To ungroup data that is grouped by rows, select the range that is grouped, click the Ungroup button to display the Ungroup dialog box, verify that the *Rows* radio button contains a bullet, and then click the OK button.

— To ungroup data that is grouped by columns, select the range that is grouped, click the Ungroup button to display the Ungroup dialog box, verify that the *Columns* radio button contains a bullet, and then click the OK button.

▸ Know More ways to ungroup data

– Click the Ungroup button arrow in the Outline group and then click the *Clear Outline* option.

On the Job

Task 11.4 Grouping Data and Collapsing a Group of Data

Devon wants to be able to quickly hide and unhide the *Tax*, *Shipping*, and *Total* columns in the Total worksheet. Group the data in the *Tax*, *Shipping*, and *Total* columns and then collapse the group to hide the details.

1. Click the Total sheet tab and then select the range D3:F3.
2. Click the Data tab, if necessary, and then click the Group button in the Outline group.

   The Group dialog box displays (see Figure 11.14).
3. Click the *Columns* radio button.

   The *Columns* radio button contains a bullet.

Figure 11.14 Group Dialog Box with the *Columns* Radio Button Selected

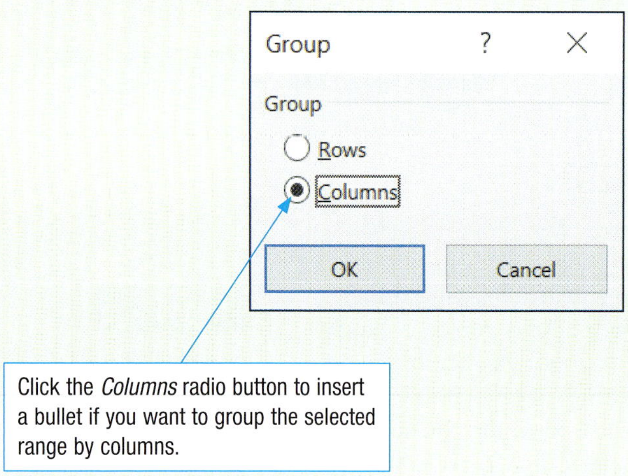

4. Click the OK button.

   The dialog box closes and an outline area containing Outline buttons and a Hide Detail button displays at the top of the worksheet (see Figure 11.15).
5. Click the Hide Detail button.

   The *Tax*, *Shipping*, and *Total* columns are hidden in the worksheet.
6. Click the Save button on the Quick Access Toolbar.

Figure 11.15 Outlined Worksheet with the Outline Area Displayed

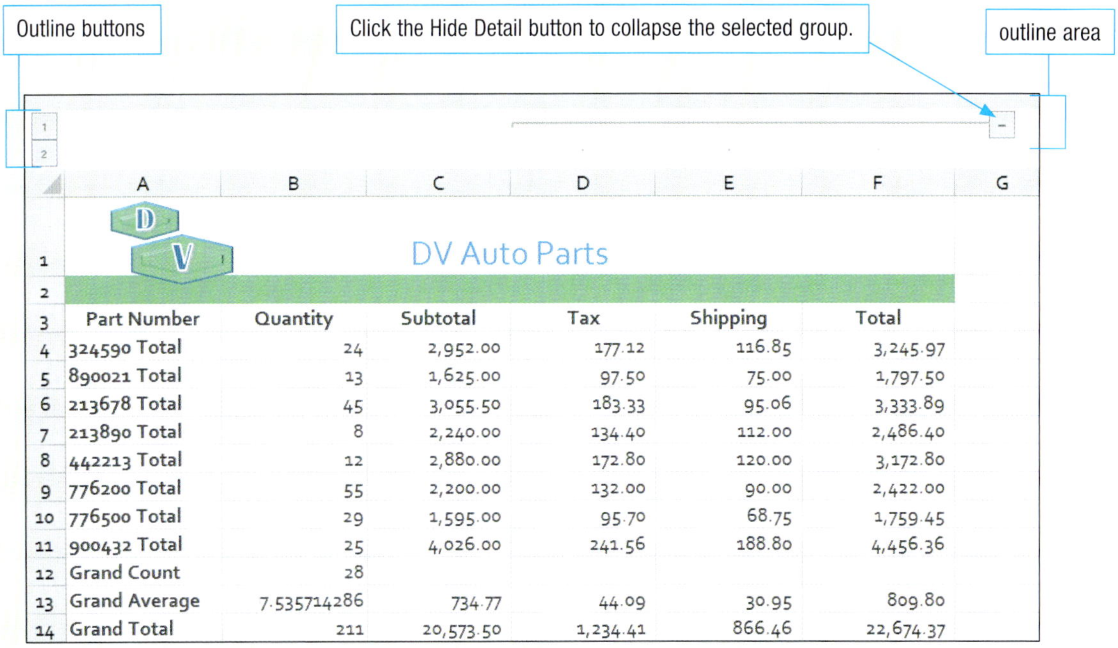

	A	B	C	D	E	F
1			DV Auto Parts			
2						
3	Part Number	Quantity	Subtotal	Tax	Shipping	Total
4	324590 Total	24	2,952.00	177.12	116.85	3,245.97
5	890021 Total	13	1,625.00	97.50	75.00	1,797.50
6	213678 Total	45	3,055.50	183.33	95.06	3,333.89
7	213890 Total	8	2,240.00	134.40	112.00	2,486.40
8	442213 Total	12	2,880.00	172.80	120.00	3,172.80
9	776200 Total	55	2,200.00	132.00	90.00	2,422.00
10	776500 Total	29	1,595.00	95.70	68.75	1,759.45
11	900432 Total	25	4,026.00	241.56	188.80	4,456.36
12	Grand Count	28				
13	Grand Average	7.535714286	734.77	44.09	30.95	809.80
14	Grand Total	211	20,573.50	1,234.41	866.46	22,674.37

Model Answer

11.5 Creating Custom Conditional Formats

MOS Expert 2.2.1

Tutorial

Creating Custom Conditional Formatting Rules

Conditional formatting applies formatting to the cells within a specified range that meet a specific condition, and leaves unchanged the formatting of cells that do not meet the condition (see Chapter 3). A conditional formatting rule can be applied to a single cell or to a range of adjacent or nonadjacent cells. Usually, it is applied to a range of cells.

Cells are conditionally formatted based on rules. A rule defines the criteria by which cells are selected for formatting and includes the formatting attributes that are applied to cells that meet the criteria. Excel provides a variety of predefined rules that specify the parameters of the criteria and formatting. It also allows users to create custom conditional formatting rules by defining all or part of the criteria and the formatting parameters. To create cohesiveness among all your business documents, a custom conditional format should apply colors similar to those already being applied.

▸ **Know This** about creating a custom conditional formatting rule

— To create a custom conditional formatting rule, complete the following steps:

1. Select the cell or range to be formatted.
2. Click the Conditional Formatting button in the Styles group on the Home tab.
3. Click the *New Rule* option (see Figure 11.16) to display the New Formatting Rule dialog box.
4. Select a rule type.
5. Edit the rule description.
6. Select formatting attributes.
7. Click the OK button.

Reminder
Be careful not to use too many conditional formats in a single worksheet. Readers can quickly lose focus when too many items compete for their attention.

— Custom conditional formatting rules allow you to apply specific formatting options not available at the Quick Access gallery or in the predefined rules at the Conditional Formatting button drop-down list. For example, you can specify the color used in a color scale or data bar, or the values used in an icon set.

Figure 11.16 Conditional Formatting Button Drop-Down List

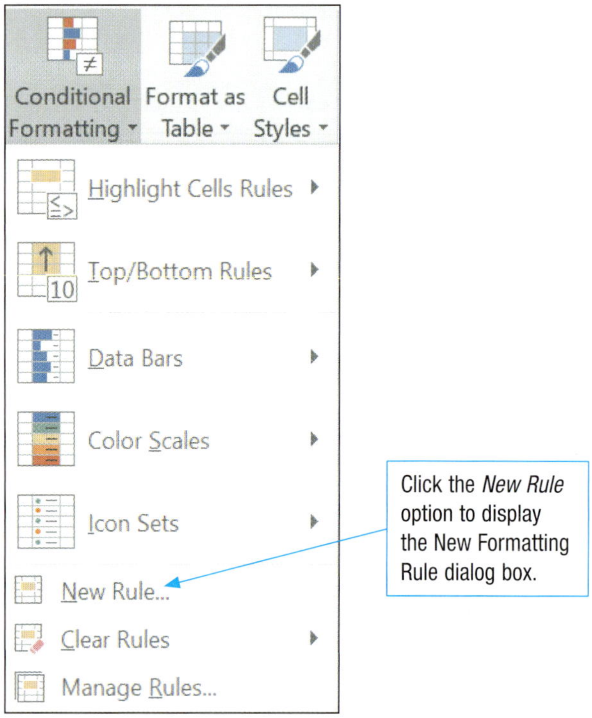

On the Job
Task 11.5a Creating and Applying a Custom Conditional Formatting Rule for Data Bars

Devon wants you to add a visual element that will allow him to compare the values in the subtotal columns in the Conditional worksheet at a glance. Create a custom conditional formatting rule that adds data bars to the *Subtotal* column in the worksheet, using a theme color for the data bars so that these visual elements are consistent with the appearance of the workbook.

1. Click the Conditional sheet tab and then select the range F4:F31.
2. Click the Home tab, click the Conditional Formatting button in the Styles group, and then click the *New Rule* option.

   The New Formatting Rule dialog box displays (see Figure 11.17).
3. Verify that the *Format all cells based on their values* option is selected in the *Select a Rule Type* list box.
4. Click the *Format Style* option box arrow and then click the *Data Bar* option.

   Data Bar appears in the *Format Style* option box, and the *Edit the Rule Description* section changes to display data bar options.

5. Click the *Fill* option box arrow and then click the *Gradient Fill* option.
6. Click the *Color* option box arrow and then click the *Lime, Accent 2, Lighter 60%* (sixth column, third row in the *Theme Colors* section) option.

   The *Preview* box shows a data bar with the specified gradient fill and theme color.
7. Click the OK button.

   The specified custom conditional formatting rule has been applied to the range F4:F31.
8. Click the Save button on the Quick Access Toolbar.

Figure 11.17 New Formatting Rule Dialog Box with the *Data Bar* Format Style Selected

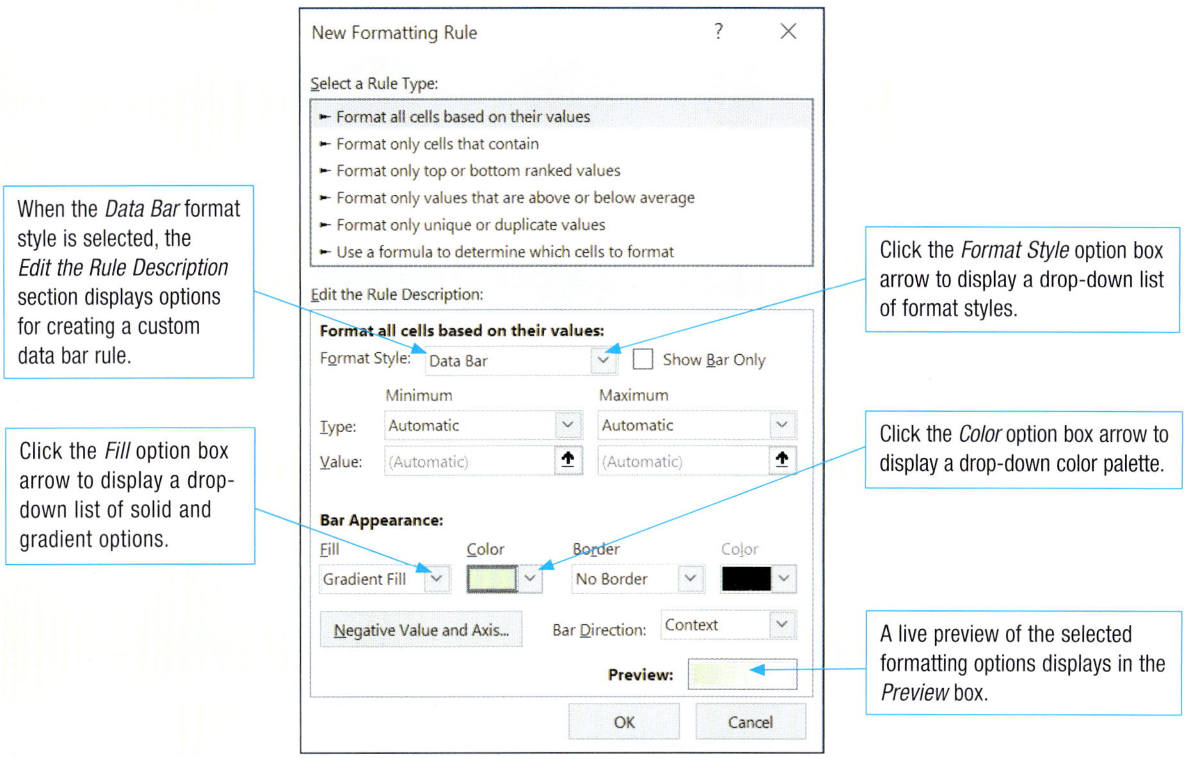

Model Answer

On the Job

Task 11.5b Creating and Applying a Custom Conditional Formatting Rule for an Icon Set

Devon wants you to add another visual element that will let him easily identify high and low points in the *Quantity* column in the Conditional worksheet. Modify the 3 Stars icon set to display a gold star when the value is greater than or equal to 50%, a half-gold/half-white star when the value is greater than or equal to 25%, and a white star when the value is less than 25%.

Reminder
An icon set is used to indicate the value in a cell relative to the values in other cells in a range.

1. With the Conditional worksheet active, select the range D4:D31.
2. Click the Home tab, click the Conditional Formatting button in the Styles group, and then click the *New Rule* option.

   The New Formatting Rule dialog box displays (see Figure 11.18).
3. Verify that the *Format all cells based on their values* option is selected in the *Select a Rule Type* list box.
4. Click the *Format Style* option box arrow and then click the *Icon Sets* option.

   Icon Sets appears in the *Format Style* option box, and the *Edit the Rule Description* section changes to display icon set options.
5. Click the *Icon Style* option box arrow and then click the *3 Stars* option (the ninth option at the drop-down list).

   The three star icons display individually in the *Icon* section, the value *67* appears in the first *Value* text box, and the value *33* appears in the second *Value* text box.
6. Select the value in the first *Value* text box and then type 50.
7. Select the value in the second *Value* text box and then type 25.
8. Click the OK button.

   The specified conditional formatting rule has been applied to the range D4:D31.
9. Click the Save button on the Quick Access Toolbar.

Figure 11.18 New Formatting Rule Dialog Box with the *Icon Sets* Format Style Selected

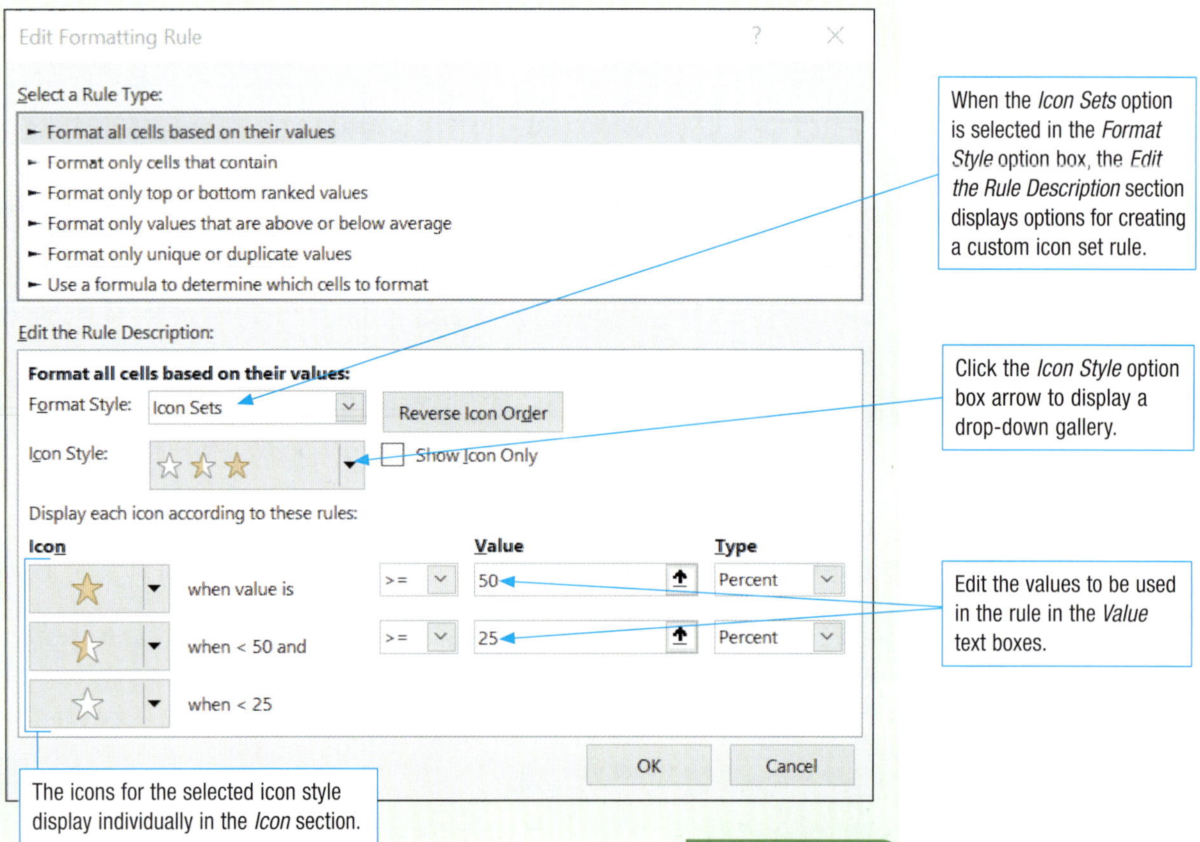

Model Answer

11.6 Applying Conditional Formatting Using a Formula

MOS Expert 2.2.2

Tutorial

Applying Conditional Formatting Using a Formula

Reminder
The logical test of an IF function returns only a true or false result.

Reminder
To edit or delete a conditional formatting rule for a selected range, click the Conditional Formatting button, click the *Manage Rules* option at the drop-down list, and then use options at the Conditional Formatting Rules Manager dialog box (see Chapter 3).

Use conditional formatting and a formula to format a cell based on the value in another cell or using a logical test. Suppose you have a worksheet that lists each employee's name in one column, the department in which each employee works in a second column, and the benefit cost for each employee in a third column. You want to format an employee's benefit cost in a bold red font if the employee works for the administration department. Enter a formula that uses an IF statement to determine whether the conditional formatting will be applied to a cell in the *Benefit Costs* column. The logical test of the IF function returns only a true or false result. Set the value in the *Department* column to either equal *Administration* (true) or not equal *Administration* (false). Excel will conditionally format only the cells in the *Benefit Costs* column for which the conditional test returns a true result. The formula is *=IF(B3:B50="Administration",TRUE,FALSE)*, where B3:B50 is the range containing each employee's department.

▸ Know This about applying conditional formatting using a formula

— To create and apply a new formatting rule using a formula, complete the following steps:
  1. Select the range to be formatted.
  2. Click the Conditional Formatting button in the Styles group on the Home tab.
  3. Click the *New Rule* option to display the New Formatting Rule dialog box.
  4. Click the *Use a formula to determine which cells to format* option.
  5. Add the formula.
  6. Click the Format button.
  7 Select the required formatting attributes.
  8. Click the OK button two times.

— If the formula returns TRUE for a cell, the conditional formatting is applied to that cell.

— If the formula returns FALSE for a cell, no formatting is applied to the cell.

— If a defined range is used in the formula, Excel treats the formula as an array formula, which means that only one rule needs to be added for the range.

— If cell or range references are used in the formula, be sure they are relative, absolute, or mixed, as needed.

On the Job

Task 11.6 Applying Conditional Formatting Using a Formula

Devon wants to quickly identify large orders so he can pay special attention to them through order fulfillment and billing. In the Conditional worksheet, use a formula to apply conditional formatting that makes the total for an order stand out if the quantity for the order is greater than 14.

1. With the Conditional worksheet active, select the range I4:I31.
2. Click the Home tab, click the Conditional Formatting button in the Styles group, and then click the *New Rule* option.

   The New Formatting Rule dialog box displays (see Figure 11.19).
3. Click the *Use a formula to determine which cells to format* option in the *Select a Rule Type* list box.

   The *Edit the Rule Description* section changes to display options for defining a conditional formatting rule that uses a formula.
4. Click in the *Format values where this formula is true* text box and then type =IF(D4:D31>14,TRUE,FALSE).

Figure 11.19 New Formatting Rule Dialog Box with the *Use a formula to determine which cells to format* Rule Type Selected

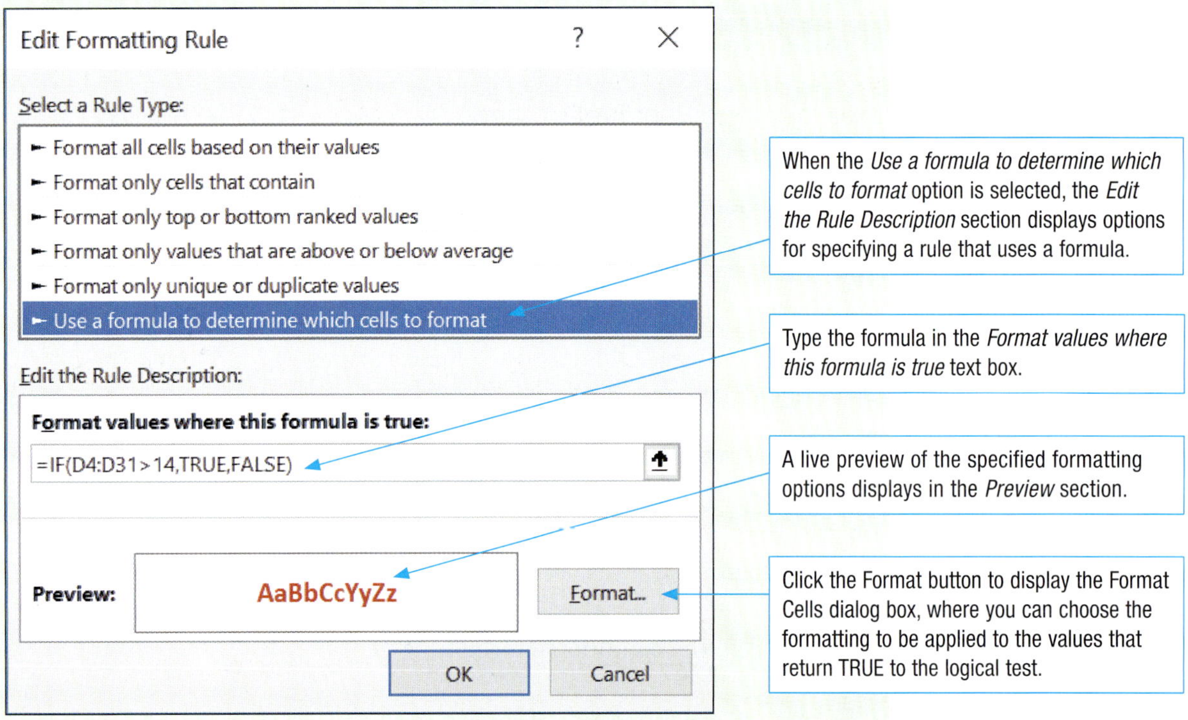

5. Click the Format button.

   The Format Cells dialog box displays with the Font tab active.
6. Click the *Bold* option in the *Font style* list box.

   The font in the *Preview* box has bold formatting applied.
7. Click the *Color* option box arrow and then click the *Dark Red* option (first option in the *Standard Colors* section).

   The font in the *Preview* box changes to Dark Red.
8. Click the OK button.

   The Format Cells dialog box closes and the *Preview* section of the Edit Formatting Rule dialog box displays a bold, dark red font.

9. Click the OK button.

   The New Formatting Rule dialog box closes and the bold Dark Red font is applied to cells in the *Total* column if the corresponding value in the *Quantity* column is greater than 14.

10. Click the Save button on the Quick Access Toolbar.

Model Answer

11.7 Modifying Theme Colors and Creating a Custom Color

MOS Expert 2.3.3

Tutorial

Changing Theme Colors and Creating a Custom Color

Microsoft offers a number of predefined themes that can be used in Excel workbooks and in other types of files (such as Word documents and PowerPoint presentations). Applying a theme can change the appearance of a workbook quickly by modifying the theme elements, including fonts, colors, and effects all at the same time (see Chapter 3). Each theme includes colors that are coordinated to provide a professional appearance and effective contrast when applied to different elements in a file. You can change the colors associated with a theme or create a custom color to suit your requirements. For example, you might want to match the colors to a company logo or modify the colors to add a unique look to a workbook.

▸ **Know This** about colors

— A **hue** is a pure color (such as red, green, or blue) with no black or white added to it.

— A **shade** is a color with black added to it.

— A **tint** is a color with white added to it.

▸ **Know This** about font colors

— Font colors can add strong visual contrast in a workbook.

— Font colors can be used to emphasize key points.

— Consistency in font colors provides cohesiveness to workbooks and other files, allowing an individual or organization to present a consistent overall image.

▸ **Know This** about theme colors

— Each theme has a set of 12 **theme colors** associated with it.

— Four theme colors are used for text and backgrounds, six theme colors are used for accents and highlights, and two theme colors are used for hyperlinks (one for links not followed and one for links followed).

— Each theme color has five variations in which tint or shading has been applied.

▸ **Know This** about standard colors

— Ten **standard colors** are also available: Dark Red, Red, Orange, Yellow, Light Green, Green, Light Blue, Blue, Dark Blue, and Purple.

— The standard colors are available with every theme.

— To display the expanded palette of 134 standard colors, click the *More Colors* option at any drop-down color palette.

▸ Know This about custom colors

- In addition to the theme colors and standard colors, custom colors can be created.
- Custom colors can be created using the **RGB Color model** in which each color is made up of different levels of red (R), green (G), and blue (B).
- An RGB color is expressed as a set of numbers that represent the intensity values of the three colors, with the lowest intensity value being 0 and the highest intensity value being 255.
- For example, the RGB color 0, 0, 255 is a high-intensity blue with no red or green in it; the RGB color 0, 100, 100 is a medium-intensity green blue with no red in it.
- All RGB colors start at black, with the values for red, green, and blue being 0.
- All RGB colors end at white, with the values for red, green, and blue being the maximum, or 255.

▸ Know This about modifying theme colors and creating custom theme colors

- To choose another set of colors to be associated with a theme, click the Colors button in the Themes group on the Page Layout tab, and then click an option at the drop-down gallery (see Figure 11.20).
- To modify a color for a theme element (text/background, accent, or hyperlink), click the Colors button, click the *Customize Colors* option at the drop-down gallery, click the color button arrow for the element at the Create New Theme Colors dialog box (see Figure 11.21), click a color option at the drop-down palette, type a name for the modified theme in the *Name* text box, and then click the Save button.
- To create a custom color for a theme element, click the Colors button, click the *Customize Colors* option at the drop-down gallery, click the color button arrow for the element at the Create New Theme Colors dialog box, click the *More Colors* option at the drop-down palette, move the color picker at the Colors dialog box, move the intensity slider to fine-tune the shade and tint, click the OK button to close the Colors dialog box, type a name for the customized theme colors in the *Name* text box, and then click the Save button.
- Custom colors display in the *Recent* section at a color palette.
- The colors at the Create New Theme Colors dialog box display as the theme colors at all the drop-down color palettes in the file (e.g., the Fill Color drop-down color palette) (see Figure 11.21).
- To change the theme colors back to the original colors, click the Reset button at the Create New Theme Colors dialog box.
- To delete custom theme colors, click the Colors button in the Themes group on the Page Layout tab, right-click the theme at the drop-down gallery, and then click the *Delete* option at the pop-up menu.

Figure 11.20 Colors Button Drop-Down Gallery

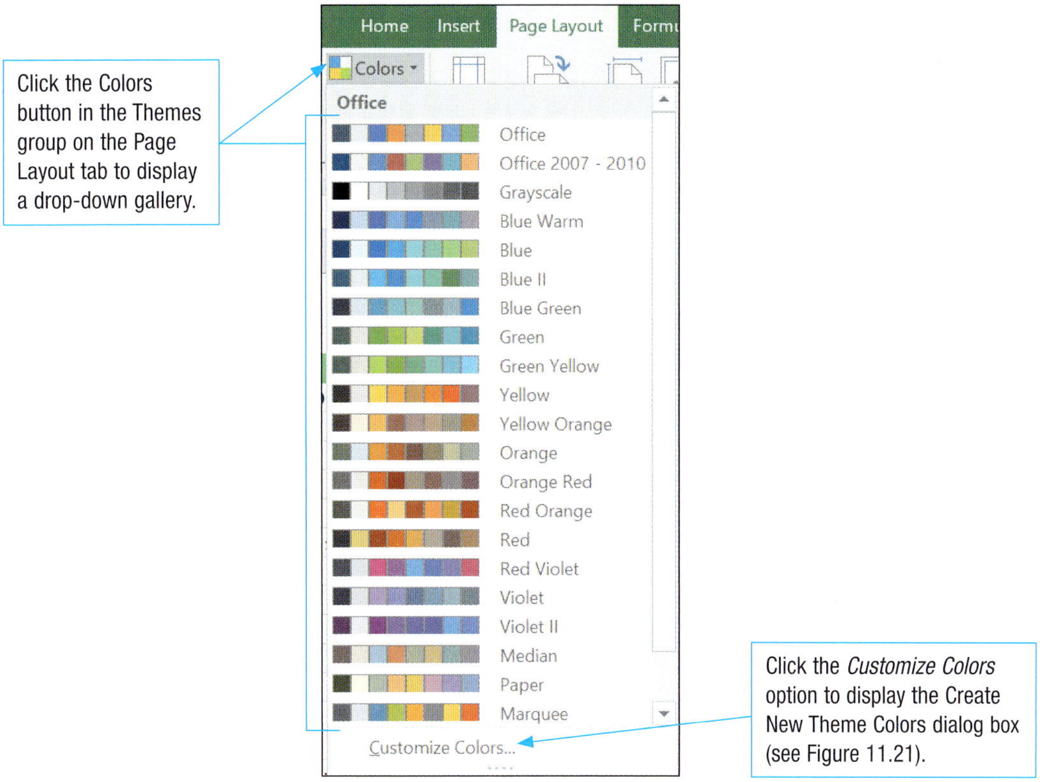

Figure 11.21 Create New Theme Colors Dialog Box Compared with the Fill Color Drop-Down Palette

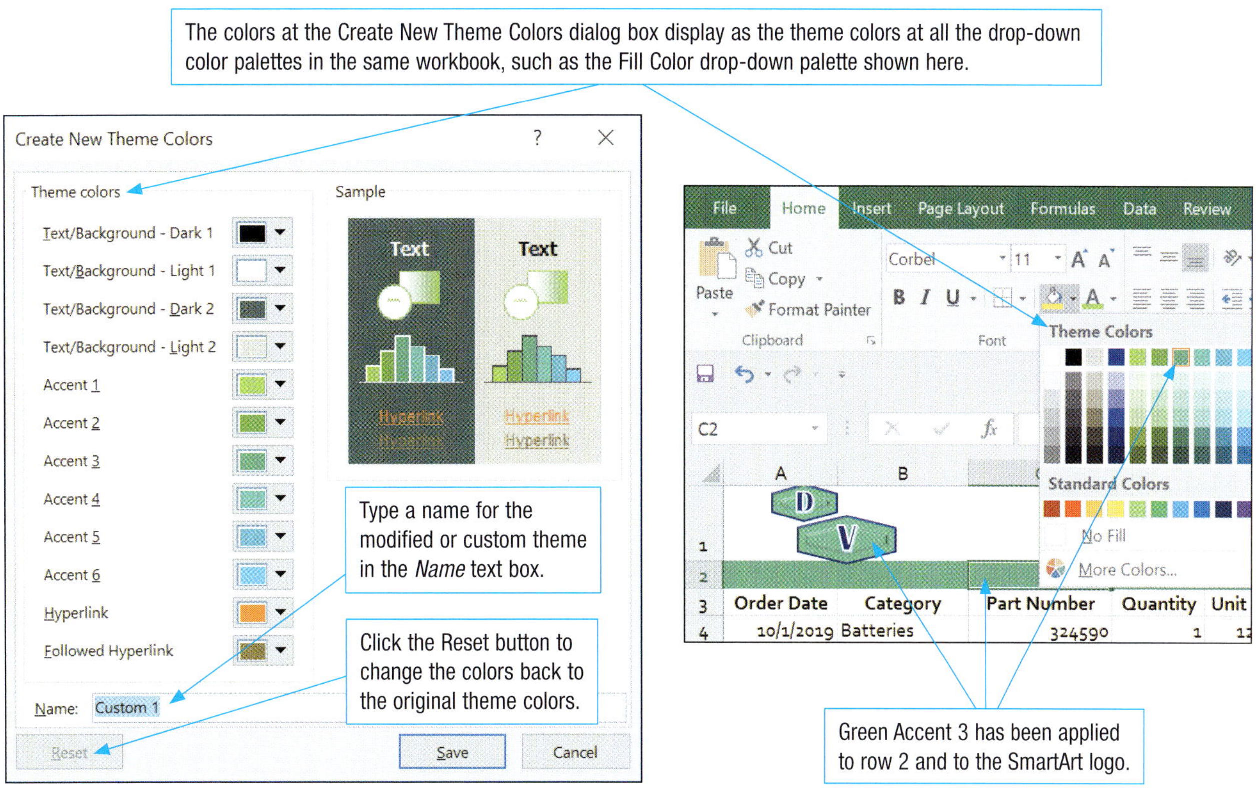

Custom New Theme Colors Dialog Box | **Fill Color Drop-Down Palette**

On the Job

Task 11.7 Creating and Modifying Theme Colors

Devon has applied the Banded theme to the 11-DVAutoParts workbook. He asks you to modify the colors in the workbook to coordinate with the colors in the DV Auto Parts logo. Change the default color of the theme to Green Yellow and then customize the theme color associated with the font so it is a dark blue, similar to the blue used for the *D* and *V* in the company logo.

1. With the Conditional worksheet active, click the Page Layout tab and then click the Colors button in the Themes group.

   A drop-down gallery displays (see Figure 11.20 on page 533).

2. Click the *Green Yellow* option.

   The SmartArt logo in cell A1, the fill color in row 2, and the data bars in the range F4:F31 change to a slightly different green.

3. Click the Colors button and then click the *Customize Colors* option.

   The Create New Theme Colors dialog box displays (see Figure 11.21 on page 533).

4. Click the *Text/Background - Dark 2* color option box arrow.

   A color palette displays.

5. Click the *More Colors* option.

   The Colors dialog box displays with the Custom tab active.

6. Position the color picker as shown in Figure 11.22, with the *Red* value set at *6*, the *Green* value set at *10*, and the *Blue* value set at *158*.

   Alternatively, you can replace the values in the *Red*, *Green*, and *Blue* measurement boxes by selecting each value and then typing the new value.

7. Click the OK button.
8. Click in the *Name* text box to select the text and then type DVAutoPartsColors.
9. Click the Save button.

   The text in row 1 and in the SmartArt logo change to the new color.

10. Click the Save button on the Quick Access Toolbar.

Figure 11.22 Colors Dialog Box with the Custom Color Tab Active

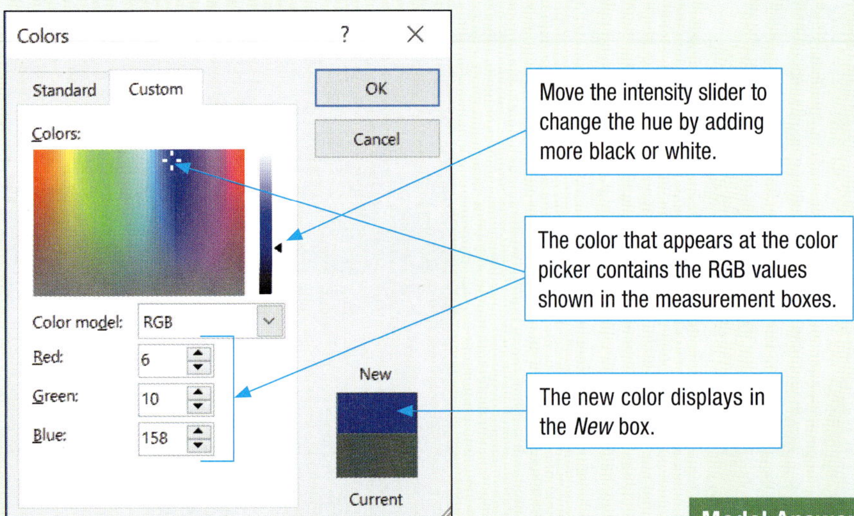

Model Answer

11.8 Modifying Theme Fonts and Managing Options for Body and Heading Fonts

MOS Expert 2.4.3

Tutorial

Modifying Theme Fonts and Managing Options for Body and Heading Fonts

A font is a combination of a typeface and other attributes (such as size and style) that defines the appearance of text, and a font style is an attribute such as bold, italic, or underline (see Chapter 3). Fonts are the basic building blocks of a workbook. When you use more than one font in a worksheet, the fonts need to be related in ways that make the worksheet appear cohesive. To quickly change the fonts in an entire workbook, change the fonts associated with the chosen theme. You can modify the fonts associated with a theme by changing the body and heading fonts.

▶ Know This about fonts

- Title and body font formatting can be applied quickly using predefined styles at the Styles gallery.
- For example, the Title style has been applied to the name of the company, DV Auto Parts, in the Conditional worksheet in the 11-DVAutoParts workbook used for the tasks in this chapter.
- The styles that appear in the Styles gallery are related to the theme of the workbook.
- Font choices can help with the readability of a workbook.
- Two main styles of font are serif and sans serif. A **serif font** has a short line attached to the end of a stroke; a **sans serif font** does not have the short line (the word *sans* means "without").
- The extra line at the end of the stroke in a serif font helps the reader's eyes move from letter to letter and from word to word.
- Times New Roman and Cambria are examples of serif fonts.
- Arial and Calibri (the default font in Microsoft Office applications) are examples of sans serif fonts.
- A sans serif font is considered a good choice for a title or heading, whereas a serif font is considered a good choice for paragraphs of body text. Using a sans serif font for titles and headings, and a serif font for body paragraphs, provides good contrast in a file.

Reminder
To display the Styles gallery, click the More button in the Styles group on the Home tab. ***Note:*** *Depending on the size of your monitor, you may need to click the Style button instead of the More button.*

▶ Know This about theme fonts

- By default, Excel applies a theme to each workbook.
- A **theme font** is a font associated with a specific theme.
- A theme contains two font settings: one for the titles and headings, and one for the body.
- The default theme in Excel is the Office theme, and the fonts associated with it are Calibri Light for the headings and Calibri for the body.
- When a theme is changed, the theme fonts automatically change.

▶ Know More about theme fonts

- To identify the theme fonts for headings and for body text in a workbook, click the Font option box arrow in the Font group on the Home tab. The default fonts display at the top of the drop-down gallery (see Figure 11.23).

▶ Know This about modifying theme fonts

- To modify the set of fonts associated with a theme, click the Fonts button arrow in the Themes group on the Page Layout tab and then click an option at the drop-down gallery (see Figure 11.24).

— If a nontheme font has been applied in a worksheet, and then the theme fonts are changed, the nontheme font does not change to either of the new fonts. For example, the nontheme font Britannic Bold has been applied to the *D* and *V* in the company logo for the 11-DVAutoParts workbook. That font will not change if the theme fonts are changed.

— Characters are different sizes in different fonts. For example, the number 1 is wider in Times New Roman than it is in Calibri. This means that if you change a font in a workbook, the data may not fit in the same column widths.

— After modifying theme fonts in a workbook, review each page in the workbook and adjust any column widths that display number symbols (#####).

Figure 11.23 Default Fonts at the *Font* Option Box Drop-Down Gallery

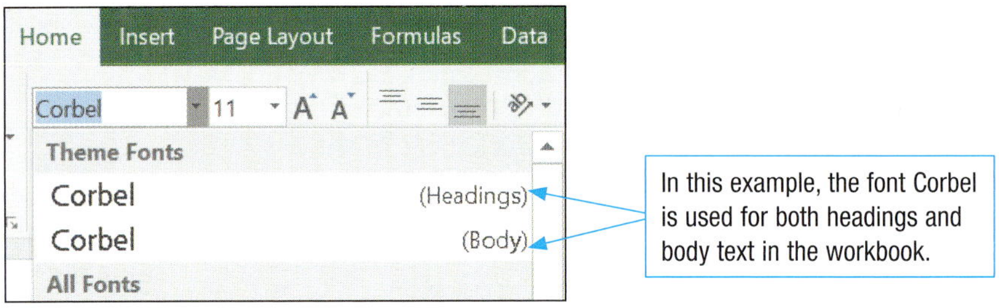

Figure 11.24 Fonts Button Drop-Down Gallery

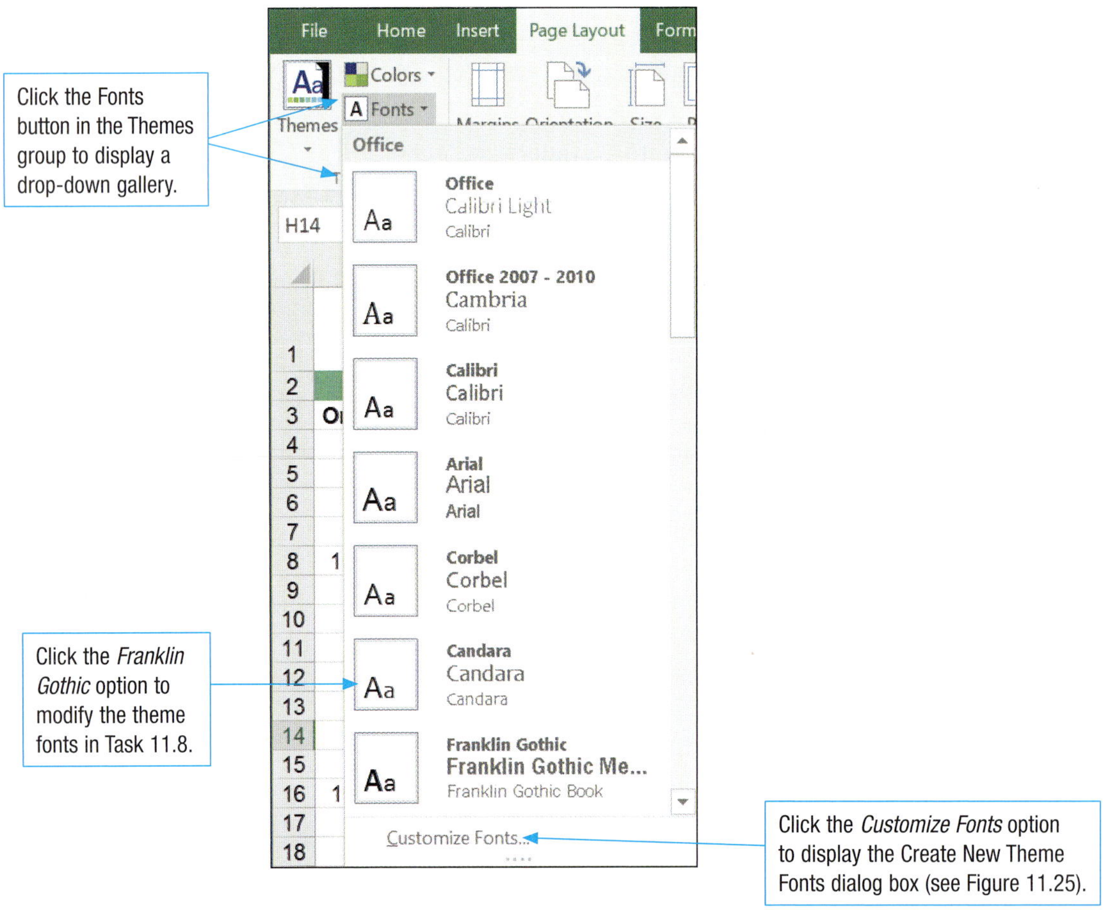

▸ **Know This** about managing the body and heading font settings for a theme

— To modify the body and heading font settings for a theme, click the Fonts button in the Themes group on the Page Layout tab, click the *Customize Fonts* option at the drop-down gallery, select the desired heading font and body font at the Create New Theme Fonts dialog box (see Figure 11.25), type a name in the *Name* box, and then click the Save button.

— To delete custom theme fonts, click the Fonts button in the Themes group on the Page Layout tab, right-click the theme at the drop-down gallery, and then click the *Delete* option at the pop-up menu.

Reminder
The Mini toolbar also contains buttons and options for applying font formatting. To display the Mini toolbar, double-click in a cell and then select the data in the cell, or right-click in a cell.

Figure 11.25 Create New Theme Fonts Dialog Box

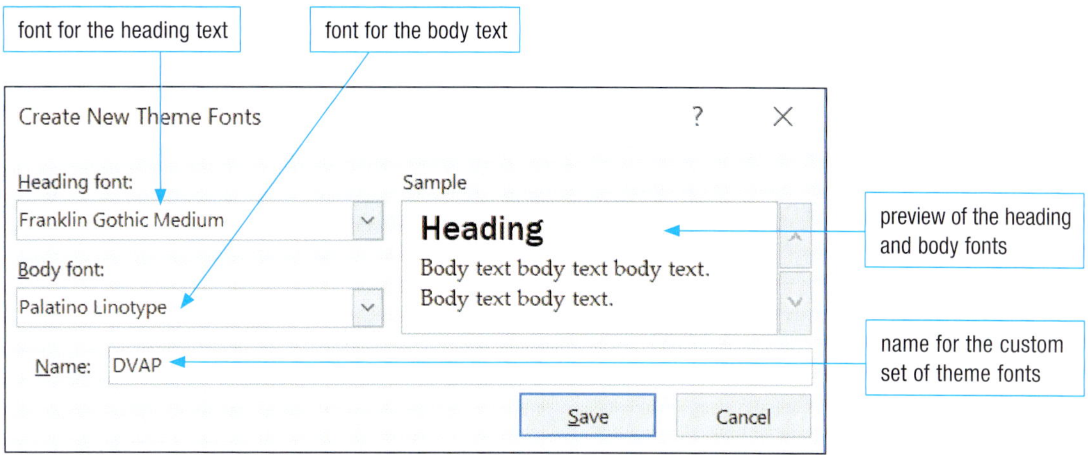

On the Job

Task 11.8 Changing Theme Fonts and Body and Heading Font Settings

Devon asks you to change the title font in the 11-DVAutoParts workbook to Franklin Gothic, to match a font used in DV Auto Parts promotional material. He also wants the rest of the data in the workbook to be in a contrasting font that is easy to read. Change the fonts associated with the workbook theme by applying the Franklin Gothic font to the headings and then changing the body font setting to create a new custom theme font for the body.

1. With the Conditional worksheet active, click the Fonts button in the Themes group on the Page Layout tab.

   A drop-down gallery displays (see Figure 11.24 on page 536).

2. Click the *Franklin Gothic* option.

   The heading and body fonts in the worksheet change to Franklin Gothic. The font in the SmartArt logo does not change because it is a nontheme font.

3. Click the Fonts button and then click the *Customize Fonts* option.

   The Create New Theme Fonts dialog box displays (see Figure 11.25).

4. Click the *Body font* option box arrow, scroll up, and then click the *Arial* option.

5. Triple-click in the *Name* text box, type DVAP, and then click the Save button.

   The font for row 1 remains Franklin Gothic because the cells in row 1 have been formatted with the Title style, which uses the theme font for headings, and you did not change the setting for the headings. The font for all the other cells in the worksheet changes to Arial because those cells have been formatted as body text and you did change the settings for the body text. The font in the SmartArt logo does not change because it is a nontheme font.

6. Click the Save button on the Quick Access Toolbar.

Model Answer

11.9 Modifying Theme Effects

Tutorial
Modifying Theme Effects

Effects add shadow, reflection, glow, soft edges, bevel, 3D rotation, and other visual features to objects such as shapes and SmartArt graphics. Excel provides 15 predefined theme effects from which to choose. Theme effects cannot be modified like theme colors and theme fonts can. Apply the same effects throughout a workbook to help promote visual consistency.

▸ Know This about modifying theme effects

— To change the theme effects, click the Effects button in the Themes group on the Page Layout tab and then click an option at the drop-down gallery (see Figure 11.26).

Figure 11.26 Effects Button Drop-Down Gallery

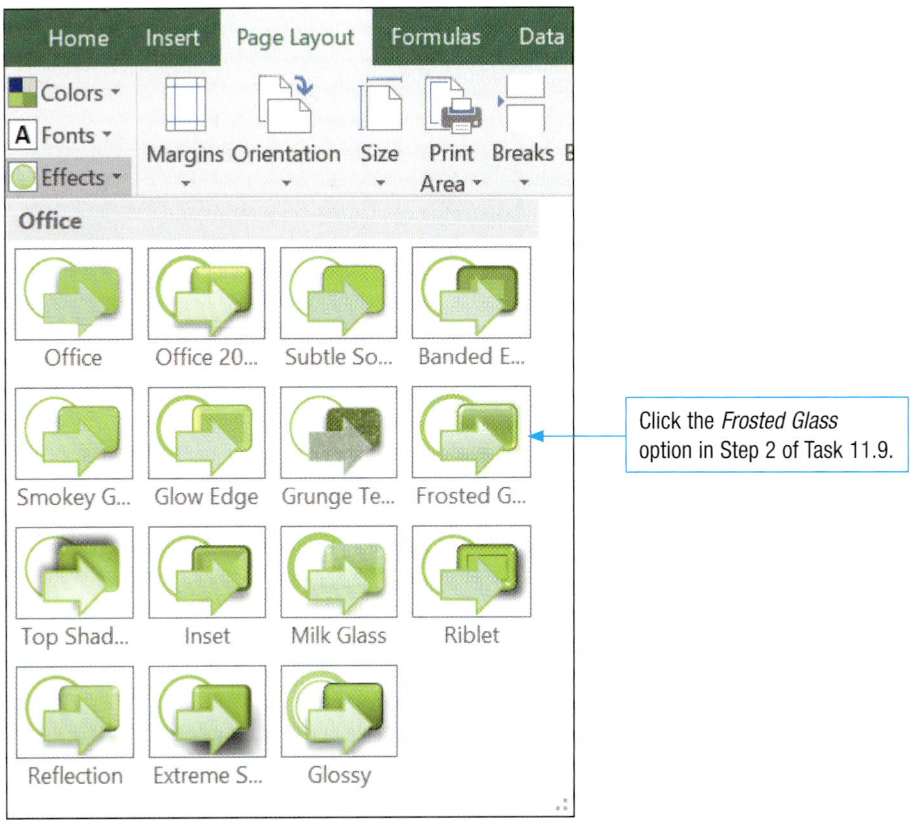

On the Job
Task 11.9 Modifying a Theme Effect

Devon wants a stronger border around the DV logo in the Conditional worksheet in the 11-DVAutoParts workbook. He explains that the logo was made from shapes and WordArt. Apply the Frosted Glass effect to strengthen the border.

1. With the Conditional worksheet active, observe the logo and then click the Effects button in the Themes group on the Page Layout tab.

   A drop-down gallery displays (see Figure 11.26 on page 538).

2. Click the *Frosted Glass* option (fourth column, second row).

   The effect applied to the SmartArt logo changes to the Frosted Glass effect.

3. Click the Save button on the Quick Access Toolbar.

Model Answer

11.10 Working with Custom Themes

Tutorial

Saving Current Formatting as a Custom Theme and Deleting a Theme

You can create a custom theme by modifying an existing theme (as described in Sections 11.7–11.10 of this chapter) and then saving the modification as a new theme. You can also create a custom theme by applying formatting to a worksheet and then saving the formatting as a new theme. Once you have saved a custom theme, you can continue to modify it until it suits your needs. When you no longer need a custom theme, you can delete it.

All themes, including the custom themes that you create, are available in all the Microsoft Office applications connected to your account. You can use a custom theme to apply visual consistency across all the types of Office files, including Word documents, PowerPoint presentations, and Access databases, as well as Excel workbooks.

▸ Know This about themes

— Every workbook has a theme applied to it.

— Office is the default theme.

— To modify theme colors, fonts, and effects, use buttons in the Themes group on the Page Layout tab.

▸ Know This about saving current formatting as a custom theme

— To save current formatting as a custom theme, click the Themes button in the Themes group on the Page Layout tab, click the *Save Current Theme* option at the drop-down gallery, type the new theme name in the *Name* text box, and then click the Save button.

▸ Know This about working with custom themes

— A custom theme is saved as a THMX file (with a *.thmx* extension) in the Document Themes folder on your local drive.

— Custom themes display at the top of the Themes button drop-down gallery.

— To apply a custom theme, click the Themes button in the Themes group on the Page Layout tab and then click the name of the theme at the drop-down gallery.

▸ Know This about deleting a custom theme

— To delete a custom theme, click the Themes button in the Themes group on the Page Layout tab, right-click the theme at the drop-down gallery, and then click the *Delete* option at the pop-up menu.

— Deleting a custom theme removes the theme name from the Themes button drop-down gallery. It does not delete or change the formatting applied to headings and body text.

On the Job

Task 11.10 Saving Current Formatting as a Custom Theme and Deleting a Theme

Devon likes the modifications you have made to the Banded theme, which was the theme originally applied to the 11-DVAutoParts workbook. He asks you to save all the modifications as a custom theme so they can be used in any Microsoft Office file connected to his account. Save the current formatting as a custom theme with the name *DVAutoParts*. Delete the theme you created for the modified fonts in Task 11.8 because the font modifications will now be saved in the DVAutoParts theme.

1. With the Conditional worksheet active, click the Themes button in the Themes group on the Page Layout tab.
2. Click the *Save Current Theme* option.

   The Save Current Theme dialog box displays with the Document Themes folder open in the file list box and the text in the *File name* text box selected.
3. Type DVAutoParts (see Figure 11.27).

   The text *DVAutoParts* replaces the selected text. Excel will automatically add the extension *.thmx* at the end of the file name.

Figure 11.27 Save Current Theme Dialog Box

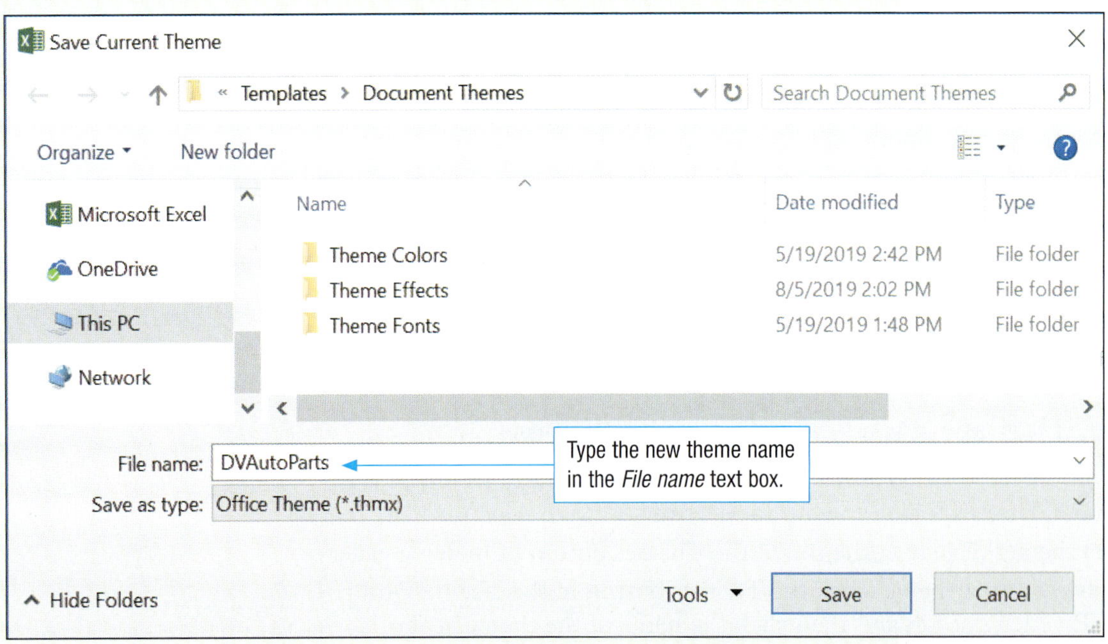

4. Click the Save button.
   The dialog box closes.
5. Click the Fonts button arrow.
   A drop-down gallery displays.
6. Right-click the *DVAP* option.
   A pop-up menu displays.
7. Click the *Delete* option.
   A message box displays (see Figure 11.28).

Figure 11.28 Microsoft Excel Delete Message

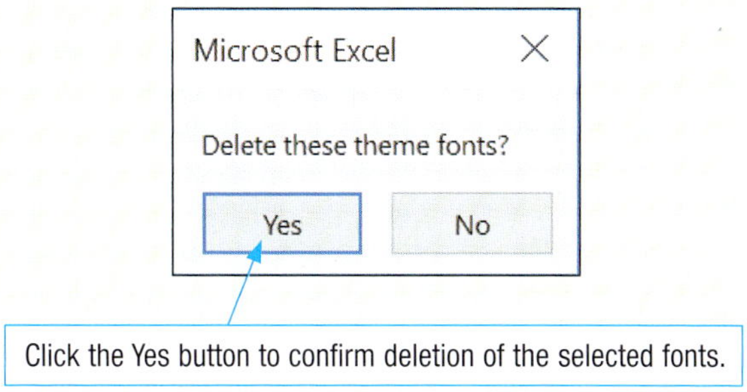

8. Click the Yes button.
   The message box closes and the *DVAP* option is deleted from the Fonts button drop-down gallery. There is no change to the appearance of the worksheet.
9. Click the Fonts button in the Themes group.
   The Fonts button drop-down gallery displays. The custom DVAP theme no longer appears in the gallery.
10. Click the Save button on the Quick Access Toolbar.

Model Answer

11.11 Working with Cell Styles

MOS Expert 2.3.2

Tutorial

Modifying a Cell Style

Reminder
Cell styles are based on the workbook theme.

Formatting can be applied quickly using a predefined cell style at the Styles drop-down gallery (see Chapter 3). If the styles at the drop-down gallery do not suit your needs, you can create a **custom cell style** by modifying a predefined cell style or creating a new style. Any cells that have been formatted with a modified style will automatically update to the new cell style.

▸ Know This about modifying cell styles

— To modify a cell style, click the More button in the Styles group on the Home tab, right-click the style at the drop-down gallery (see Figure 11.29), click the *Modify* option at the pop-up menu (see Figure 11.30 on page 544), click the Format button at the Style dialog box (see Figure 11.31 on page 544), make the formatting changes, and then click the OK button.

— The Style dialog box indicates the formatting that is included in the cell style.

Figure 11.29 Styles Drop-Down Gallery

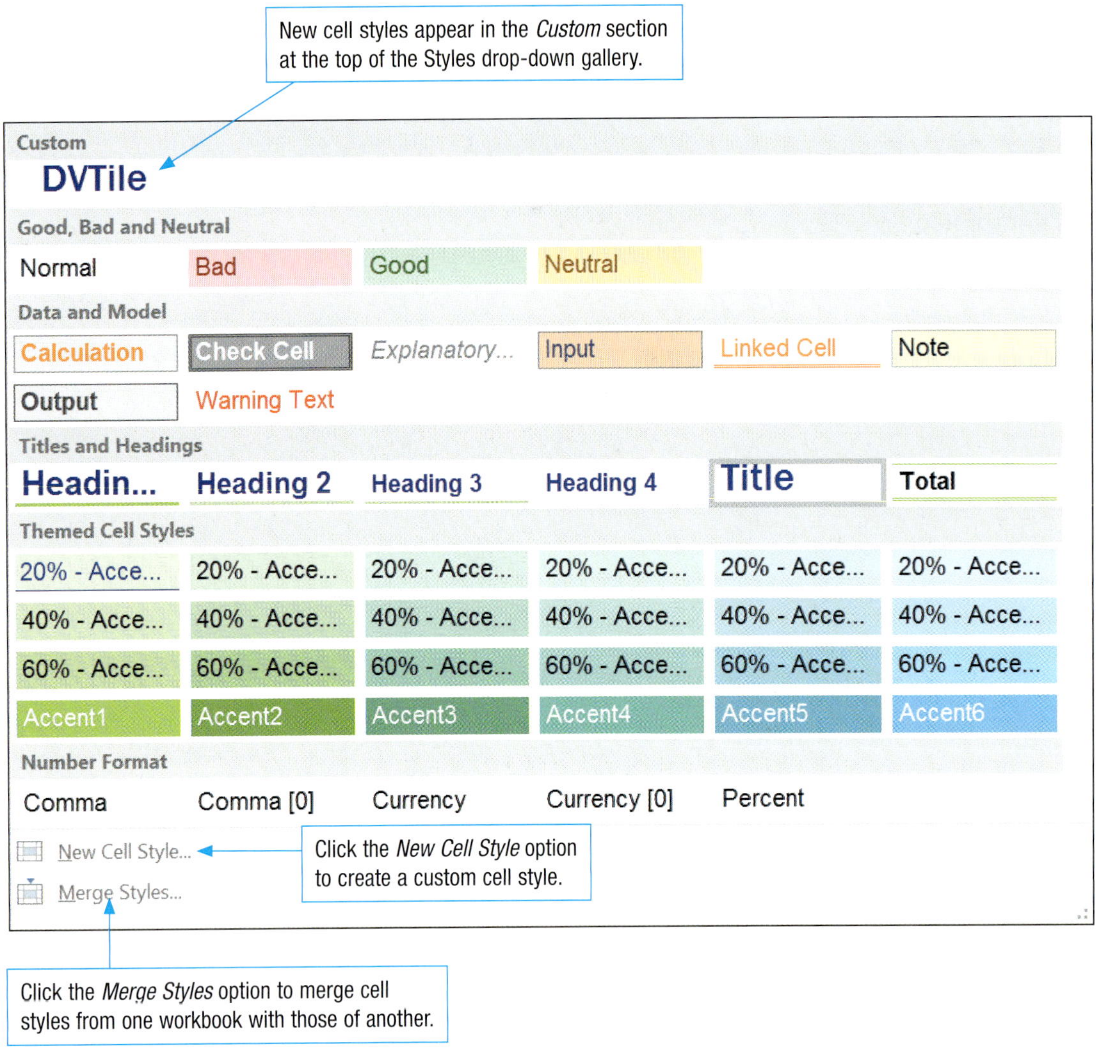

▸ Know This about creating and using custom cell styles

— To save current cell formatting as a custom style, click in the formatted cell, click the More button in the Styles group on the Home tab, click the *New Cell Style* option at the drop-down gallery (see Figure 11.29), type a name for the style in the *Style name* text box at the Style dialog box (see Figure 11.31 on page 544), and then click the OK button.

— To create a custom cell style from scratch, click the More button in the Styles group on the Home tab, click the *New Cell Style* option at the drop-down gallery, type a name for the style in the *Style name* text box at the Style dialog box, click the Format button, and then choose formatting options at the Format Cells dialog box.

— Custom styles display at the top of the Styles drop-down gallery.

— When you save current cell formatting as a custom style, the custom style is not automatically applied to the formatted cell. To apply the custom style to the formatted cell, click in the formatted cell, if necessary; click the More button in the Styles group; and then click the custom style at the drop-down gallery.

▸ **Know This** about using custom cell styles in other workbooks

— By default, custom cell styles are accessible only in the workbook in which they are created; they are not available in other workbooks.

— Custom styles can be merged from one workbook with those of another.

— To merge custom styles from one workbook with those of another, complete the following steps:

1. Open the workbook containing the custom styles and then open the other workbook.
2. Click the More button in the Styles group on the Home tab.
3. Click the *Merge Styles* option at the drop-down gallery (see Figure 11.29).
4. Double-click the name of the workbook containing the custom cell styles in the *Merge styles from* list box at the Merge Styles dialog box.

— The Undo command cannot be used to reverse the merging of styles.

— If you modify a custom cell style in one workbook, the same custom cell style in another workbook will *not* be updated.

— If you have modified an existing style or created a new style and the style name exists in the new workbook, a message box will display, asking whether you want to merge the styles that have the same names.

▸ **Know This** about removing cell style formatting from cells

— To remove cell style formatting from a cell or cells, select the cell or cells, click the More button in the Styles group on the Home tab, and then click the *Normal* option in the *Good, Bad and Neutral* section at the drop-down gallery.

▸ **Know This** about deleting a custom cell style

— To delete a cell style, click the More button in the Styles group on the Home tab, right-click the style at the drop-down gallery, and then click the *Delete* option at the pop-up menu.

— When you delete a cell style, the Normal cell style is automatically applied to any cells that were formatted with the deleted cell style.

— You cannot delete the Normal cell style.

On the Job

Task 11.11a Applying and Modifying a Cell Style

Devon wants the column headers in row 3 of the Conditional worksheet to stand out more to increase readability. To maintain consistency in the appearance of the workbook, apply an existing cell style to the column header cells and then modify the cell style by changing the font color and adding a border.

1. With the Conditional worksheet active, select the range A3:I3, click the Home tab, click the More button in the Styles group, and then click the *Lime, 20% - Accent1* option (first column, first row in the *Themed Cell Styles* section).

   The background color of the selected cells changes to a light lime green.

2. Click the More button in the Styles group and then right-click the *Lime, 20% - Accent1* option (first column, first row in the *Themed Cell Styles* section).

   A pop-up menu displays (see Figure 11.30).

3. Click the *Modify* option.

   The Style dialog box displays (see Figure 11.31).

Figure 11.30 Cell Style Option Pop-Up Menu

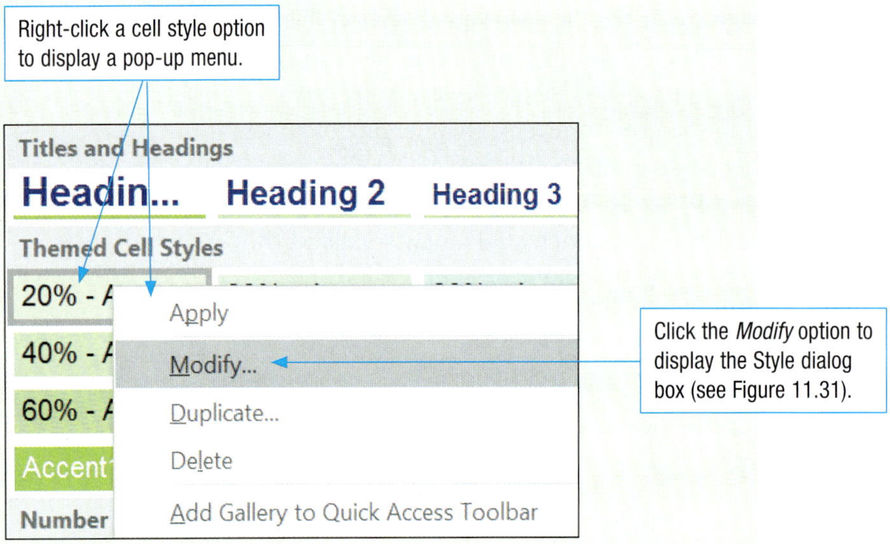

Figure 11.31 Style Dialog Box

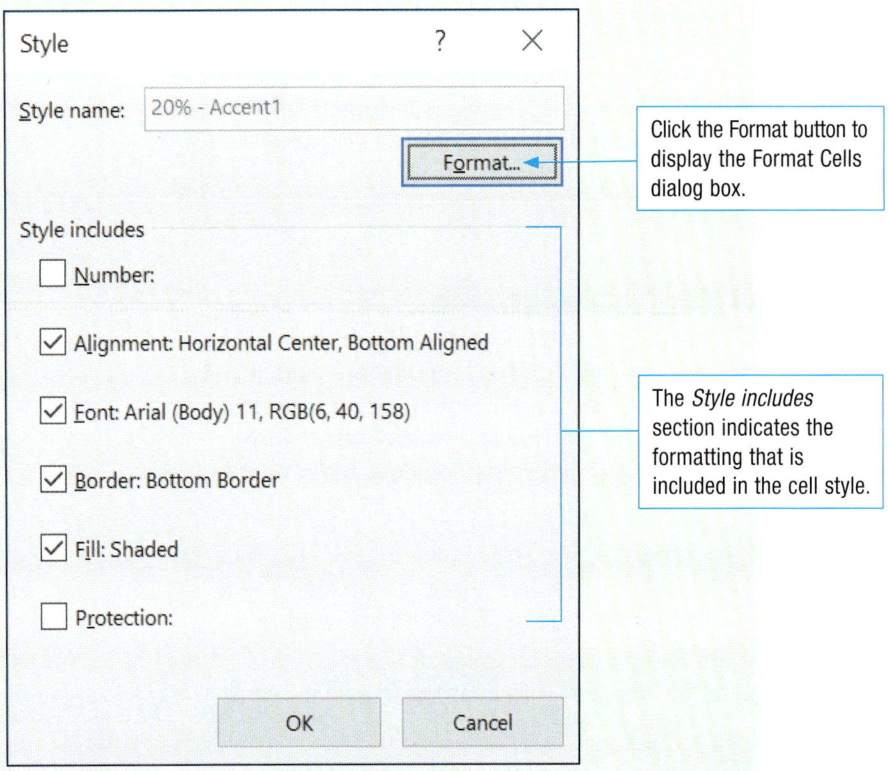

4. Click the Format button.

   The Format Cells dialog box displays.

5. Click the Font tab and then click the *Color* option box arrow.
6. Click the *More Colors* option.

   The Colors dialog box displays.

7. Click the Custom tab; type 6 in the *Red* measurement box, 10 in the *Green* measurement box, and 158 in the *Blue* measurement box; and then click the OK button.

   The Colors dialog box closes and the new font color displays in the *Color* option box at the Format Cells dialog box.

8. Click the Alignment tab, click the *Horizontal* option box arrow, and then click the *Center* option.
9. Click the Border tab and then click the *Color* option box arrow.

   A drop-down palette displays with the custom color blue added in Step 7 appearing in the *Recent Colors* section.

10. Click the custom blue color in the *Recent Colors* section.
11. Click the bottom border in the *Border* box.
12. Click the OK button.

    The Format Cells dialog box closes.

13. Click the OK button.

    The Style dialog box closes and the data in the range A3:I3 appears with the custom blue font and a custom blue bottom border.

14. Click the Save button on the Quick Access Toolbar.

Model Answer

On the Job

Task 11.11b Saving Current Cell Formatting as a Custom Cell Style

Devon wants all the workbooks for DV Auto Parts to have a consistent appearance. For this reason, he asks you to create a custom cell style based on the formatting applied to cell A1 (which contains the title *DV Auto Parts*). Create the new style and name it *DVTitle*.

1. With the Conditional worksheet active, click in cell A1 to the right of the SmartArt logo.

   Ensure that the cell, not the SmartArt logo, is selected.

2. Click the More button in the Styles group on the Home tab.

   A drop-down gallery displays.

3. Click the *New Cell Style* option.

   The Style dialog box displays with the text in the *Style name* text box selected.

4. Type DVTitle.
5. Click the OK button.

   The dialog box closes.

6. Click the More button in the Styles group and then click the *DVTitle* style in the *Custom* section.
7. Click the Save button on the Quick Access Toolbar.

On the Job

Task 11.11c Merging Cell Styles from One Workbook to Another

Devon wants to use the modified and custom cell styles you created in Tasks 11.11a and 11.11b in a new workbook. Since you created the cell styles based on theme cell styles, you will need to start by applying the DVAutoParts theme to the new workbook and then merge the modified and custom cell styles with those of the new workbook.

1. With the Conditional worksheet active, open a new workbook.
2. With the new workbook active, apply the DVAutoParts theme.
3. Click the Home tab and then click the More button in the Styles group.
4. Click the *Merge Styles* option at the drop-down gallery (see Figure 11.32).
   The Merge Styles dialog box displays (see Figure 11.33).

Figure 11.32 *Merge Styles* Option at the Styles Drop-Down Gallery

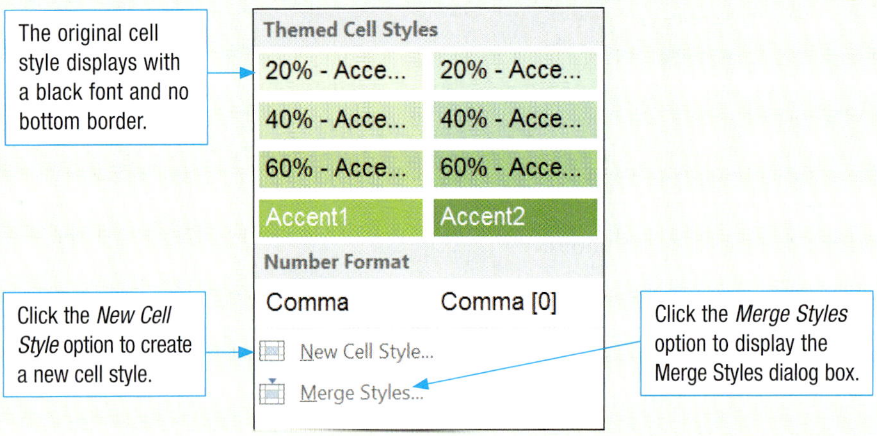

Figure 11.33 Merge Styles Dialog Box

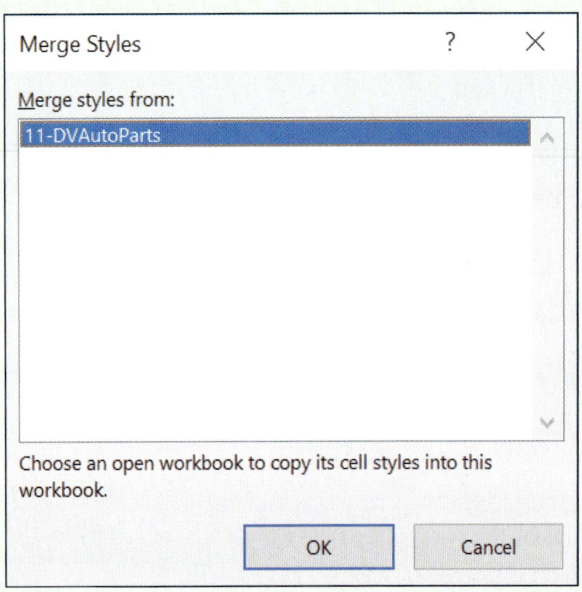

5. Click the *11-DVAutoParts* option and then click the OK button.

   A message box displays, asking whether you want to merge styles that have the same names.
6. Click the Yes button.

   The message box closes.
7. Click in cell A1, if necessary; type DV Auto Parts; and then press Ctrl + Enter.

   The text *DV Auto Parts* appears in cell A1 and cell A1 is active.
8. Click the More button in the Styles group on the Home tab.

   The cell styles created in Task 11.11a have been merged with those of the new workbook and display at the drop-down gallery.
9. Click the *Lime, 20% - Accent1* option (first column, first row in the *Themed Cell Styles* section).

   The text in cell A1 appears with the custom cell formatting you created in Task 11.11a.
10. AutoFit column A.
11. Save the new workbook in your working folder, typing 11-CellStyle as its name, and then close it.
12. If printed work is required by your instructor, print the 11-DVAutoParts workbook.
13. Save and then close the workbook.

Model Answer

Chapter Summary

11.1 ▸ The Subtotal feature helps group and summarize data by inserting a subtotal row for a range of data, adding a grand total row below the last row of data, and displaying the worksheet in outline view. Outline view allows collapsing and expanding a worksheet to display various levels of detail.

11.2 ▸ Subtotals can be modified to include more than one type of calculation. For example, if subtotals have been inserted that sum data, subtotals can be added that count and average the same data. Subtotals can also be replaced and deleted.

11.3 ▸ When subtotals have been added to a worksheet, the worksheet displays in outline view where the outline area appears along the left side of the worksheet. Outline buttons display at the top of the outline area, and Show Detail and Hide Detail buttons appear beside data levels in the outline area.

▸ A worksheet contains different levels of detail, depending on how many subtotals have been inserted. Excel can create an outline with up to eight levels of detail. The highest level of detail shows all the data in the worksheet, all the subtotals, and all the grand totals. The lowest level of detail shows only the grand totals. By default, the highest level of detail is displayed in the worksheet.

11.4 ▸ Another way to control the level of detail displayed in a worksheet is to group and ungroup data, collapse and expand data, and collapse each group of data. A worksheet can be grouped in rows or in columns. Grouping and ungrouping data is similar to hiding and unhiding rows and columns.

11.5 ▶ Conditional formatting applies special formatting to the cells within a specified range that meet a specific condition, and leaves unchanged the formatting of cells that do not meet the condition. A conditional formatting rule can be applied to a single cell or to a range of adjacent cells or to nonadjacent cells. Usually, it is applied to a range of cells.

▶ Cells are conditionally formatted based on rules. A rule defines the criteria by which cells are selected for formatting and includes the formatting attributes that are applied to cells that meet the criteria. Excel provides a variety of predefined rules that specify the parameters of the criteria and formatting. Excel also allows users to create custom conditional formatting rules by defining all or part of the criteria and the formatting parameters.

11.6 ▶ Conditional formatting and a formula are used to format a cell based on the value in another cell or using a logical test. If a defined range is used in the formula, Excel treats the formula as an array formula, which means that only one rule needs to be added for the range. If cell or range references are used in the formula, they must be relative, absolute, or mixed, as appropriate.

11.7 ▶ Microsoft offers a number of predefined themes that can be used in Excel workbooks and in other types of files (such as Word documents and PowerPoint presentations). Applying a theme can change the appearance of a workbook quickly by modifying the fonts, colors, and effects all at the same time.

▶ Each theme includes 12 theme colors that are coordinated to provide a pleasant appearance and effective contrast when applied to different elements in a file. Ten standard colors are also available with every theme. The colors associated with a theme can be changed to suit the user's requirements, and custom colors can be created using the RGB Color model.

11.8 ▶ A font is a combination of a typeface and other attributes (such as size and style) that defines the appearance of text, and a font style is an attribute such as bold, italic, or underline. A theme font is a font associated with a specific theme. Each theme contains two font settings: one for the titles and headings, and one for the body.

▶ Changing the fonts associated with the chosen theme will quickly change the fonts in an entire workbook. These options can be modified by managing the body and heading fonts. A sans serif font is considered a good choice for a title or heading, whereas a serif font is considered a good choice for paragraphs of body text.

11.9 ▶ Effects deal with shadow, reflection, glow, soft edges, bevel, and 3D rotation. They are applied to visual elements, such as shapes and SmartArt graphics. Excel provides 15 predefined sets of effects from which to choose. Applying the same effects throughout a workbook helps promote visual consistency.

11.10 ▶ A custom theme can be created by modifying an existing theme and then saving the modification as a new theme. A custom theme can also be created by applying formatting to a worksheet and then saving the formatting as a new theme. All themes, including custom themes the user creates, are available in all the Microsoft Office applications connected to the user's account.

11.11 ▸ Formatting can be applied quickly using a predefined cell style at the Styles drop-down gallery. If the styles at the drop-down gallery are not suitable, a custom cell style can be created. When a predefined cell style or a new style is modified, any cells that have been formatted with that style automatically update to the new format.

▸ By default, custom cell styles are accessible only in the workbook in which they are created; they are not available in other Office files. However, custom styles can be merged from one workbook with those of another.

Features Review

Feature	Ribbon Tab, Group	Button, Option
apply custom cell	Home, Styles	, *[custom style option]*
apply custom theme	Page Layout, Themes	, *[name of theme]*
choose new set of theme colors	Page Layout, Themes	
create custom cell style from scratch	Home, Styles	, New Cell Style
create custom color for theme element	Page Layout, Themes	, *Customize Colors*
create custom conditional formatting rule	Home, Styles	, *New Rule*
delete cell style	Home, Styles	, *Delete*
delete custom theme	Page Layout, Themes	, *Delete*
display extended palette of 134 standard colors		*More Colors* option at any drop-down color palette
display Styles gallery	Home, Styles	
group data	Data, Outline	
identify theme fonts	Home, Font	Corbel
insert, add, delete, modify, or replace subtotals	Data, Outline	
merge custom styles from one workbook with those of another	Home, Styles	, *Merge Styles*
modify cell style	Home, Styles	, *Modify*
modify theme colors	Page Layout, Themes	
modify theme effects	Page Layout, Themes	
modify theme fonts	Page Layout, Themes	A
print ranges with subtotals on separate pages	Data, Outline	, insert check mark in *Page break between groups* check box
remove cell style formatting from cell or cells	Home, Styles	, *Normal*

continues...

Feature	Ribbon Tab, Group	Button, Option
save current cell formatting as custom style	Home, Styles	, *New Cell Style*
save current formatting as custom theme	Page Layout, Themes	, *Save Current Theme*
select specific subtotals and/or grand totals	Home, Editing	, *Go To Special*
ungroup data	Data, Outline	

Recheck

Recheck your understanding of the concepts, features, and skills covered in this chapter by taking the Recheck quiz.

Workbook

Access the study tools, review exercises, assessments, and challenges for this chapter in the workbook available from this page in your ebook.

Calculating and Analyzing Business Data

Chapter 12

Chapter Goal

To create financial statements and enter, calculate, and analyze business data in financial statements.

Learning Objectives

12.1 Create income statements
12.2 Calculate the cost of goods sold and gross profit
12.3 Differentiate between fixed and variable costs
12.4 Calculate general and administrative costs, other income, and taxes
12.5 Find net profit or net loss
12.6 Identify common income statement errors
12.7 Visualize an income statement
12.8 Create balance sheets
12.9 Use the double entry accounting method in a general journal
12.10 Calculate assets
12.11 Calculate liabilities
12.12 Calculate equity
12.13 Identify common balance sheet errors
12.14 Determine the gross profit margin
12.15 Find the contribution margin ratio and the break-even point
12.16 Chart the break-even point
12.17 Use Goal Seek to determine the break-even point
12.18 Create a statement of cash flows
12.19 Project future income and expenses
12.20 Chart linear trends and growth trends
12.21 Create a Forecast Sheet

Precheck

Check your understanding of the concepts, features, and skills covered in this chapter by taking the Precheck quiz.

Data Files

Before beginning the chapter work, download the AE12 folder from this page in your ebook to your storage medium and then make AE12 the active folder.

Ebook Links

Access digital resources for this course from your ebook.

SNAP

If you are a SNAP user, go to your SNAP assignments page to complete the Precheck, Tutorials, and Recheck in this chapter.

Preview

On the Job

Scenario: DV Auto Parts

Devon Varey opened DV Auto Parts in January 2019. He needs to create financial statements—including an income statement, a balance sheet, and a statement of cash flows—and then analyze the performance of his business in its first year of operation. Devon also needs to project future sales income and chart growth trends. He asks you to help with that work.

Visual Reference: Financial Statements

Figure 12.1 Income Statement

	A	B
1		**DV Auto Parts**
2		
3		**Income Statement**
4		*for the year ended December 31, 2019*
5		
6	**Revenue**	
7	Sales	$ 1,256,296
8	Cost of Goods Sold	753,778
9	Gross Profit	502,518
10		
11	**Operating Expenses**	
12	Salaries	120,000
13	Rent	50,000
14	Utilities	10,000
15	Insurance	4,000
16	Advertising	2,500
17	Depreciation Expense	1,200
18	Total Operating Expenses	187,700
19		
20	**Other Income**	
21	Interest Revenue	5,000
22	Interest Expense	(1,400)
23	Total Other Income	3,600
24		
25	Income before Income Taxes	318,418
26	Income Tax Expense	98,000
27	**Net Income**	$ 220,418
28		

An income statement is a financial statement that reports on the performance of a company over a specific accounting period.

Net income shows the profitability of a company during a specified time interval.

Visual Reference

Figure 12.2 Waterfall Chart

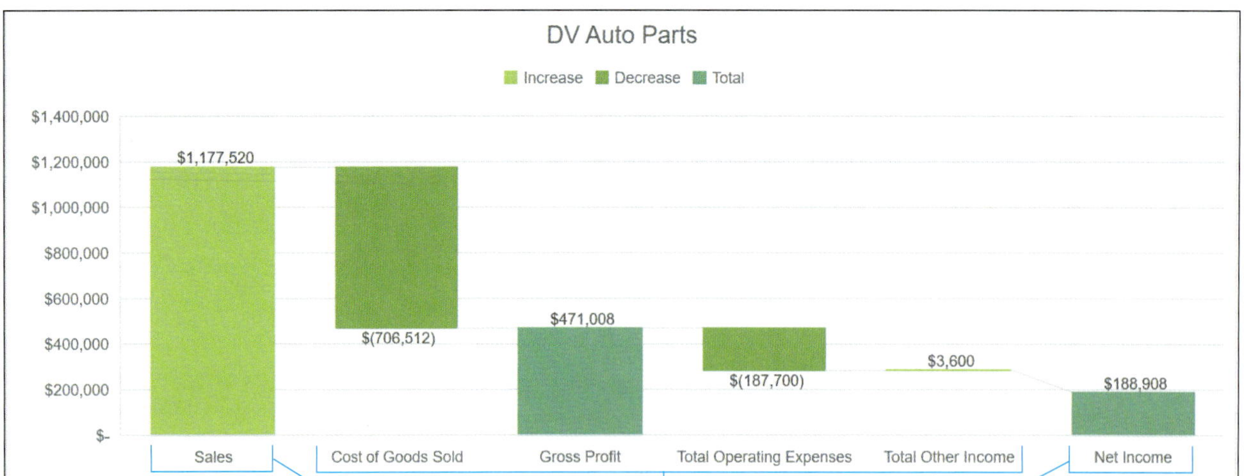

A waterfall chart shows how the starting value (sales) is affected by a series of positive and negative values (cost of goods sold, operating expenses, and total other income) to give an ending value (net income).

Visual Reference

Figure 12.3 Cost Volume Profit Chart Showing Break-Even Point

The break-even point shows how many units need to be sold before a profit can be made.

DV Auto Parts

Part #E8-978-02

Units Sold	Fixed Costs	Total Costs	Total Revenue
100	$ 1,700	$ 2,550	$ 510
200	1,700	2,950	738
300	1,700	3,200	1,088
400	1,700	3,500	1,470
500	1,700	3,750	1,988
600	1,700	4,000	2,680
700	1,700	4,250	3,783
800	1,700	4,500	4,725
900	1,700	4,750	5,344
1000	1,700	5,000	7,500

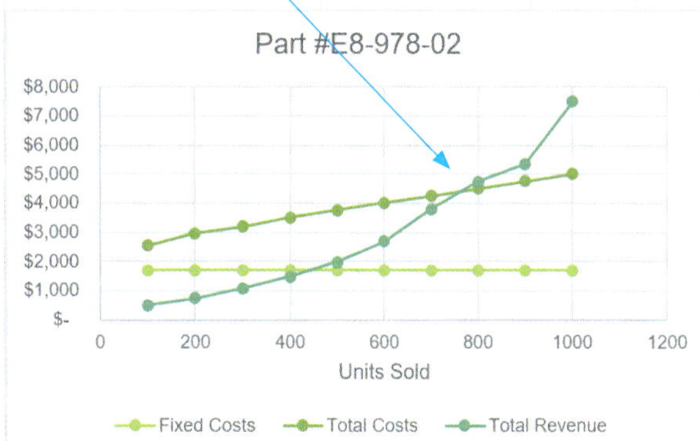

Visual Reference

Figure 12.4 Sales Projections Using a Linear Trend and a Growth Trend

DV Auto Parts

Financial Projections

Revenue	Year 1	Year 2	Year 3	Year 4	Year 5
Sales - Linear Trend	$ 1,177,520	$ 1,333,140	$ 1,488,760	$ 1,644,380	$ 1,800,000
Sales - Growth Trend	$ 1,177,520	$ 1,309,316	$ 1,455,863	$ 1,618,812	$ 1,800,000

Sales projections for years 2 through 4 are interpolated based on a starting value and ending sales goal, to show both a linear and growth trend.

A scatter chart illustrates the sales projections based on a linear and a growth trend.

Visual Reference

12.1 Creating Income Statements

MOS 4.1.1

Tutorial

Creating a Multiple-Step Income Statement and Entering Sales Revenue

An **income statement** (also referred to as a *profit and loss statement*, *profit/loss statement*, or *P&L*) is a financial statement that reports on the financial performance of a company, organization, or individual over a specific accounting period. It summarizes the revenues and expenses generated and shows the resulting net profit or loss.

The income statement is used by accountants and business owners to show the profitability of a company during a specific time interval. If a company is not profitable (shows a net loss), investors and banks will be hesitant to extend additional credit to the company.

Analysts and investors also focus on net profit because it is used to calculate earnings per share, which is a key measure of profitability for companies that issue stock. A **stock** is a share in the ownership of a company. Companies issue two main types of stocks, preferred stock and common stock, to raise capital to expand the company or fund new projects. A **common stock** pays dividends based on company profits and offers voting rights. A **preferred stock** pays a fixed dividend and offers payment priority of dividends but no voting rights. **Earnings per share** is calculated by subtracting preferred dividends from net income and then dividing by the weighted average common shares outstanding (calculation that incorporates any changes in the amount of outstanding shares over a reporting period).

Income statements can be created using a single-step format or a multiple-step format. A **single-step income statement** uses only one subtraction to arrive at net income: *Net income = (revenues & gains) – (expenses & losses)* (see Figure 12.5).

Figure 12.5 Single-Step Income Statement

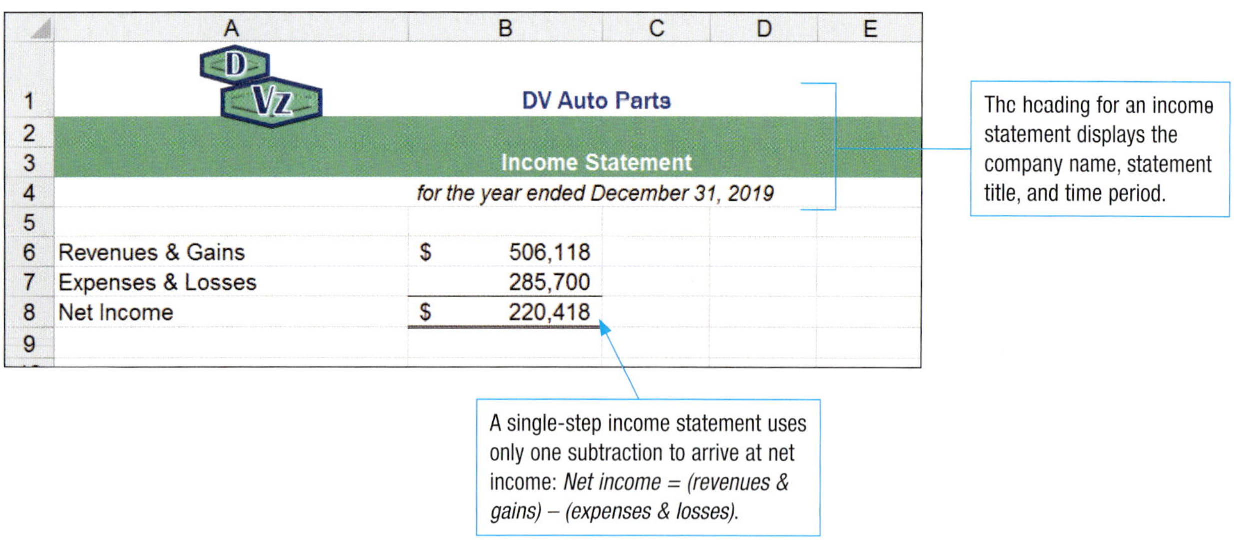

A **multiple-step income statement** calculates the gross profit, which is the amount of profit after the total cost of goods sold is subtracted from the total sales. It also separates the operating revenues and operating expenses from the nonoperating revenues and nonoperating expenses. (See Figure 12.6.) The multiple-step income statement is often preferred because of the level of detail it provides.

Figure 12.6 Multiple-Step Income Statement

	A	B	C	D	E	F
1	DV Auto Parts					
2						
3	Income Statement					
4	*for the year ended December 31, 2019*					
5						
6	**Revenue**					
7	Sales	$ 1,256,296				
8	Cost of Goods Sold	753,778				
9	Gross Profit	502,518				
10						
11	**Operating Expenses**					
12	Salaries	120,000				
13	Rent	50,000				
14	Utilities	10,000				
15	Insurance	4,000				
16	Advertising	2,500				
17	Depreciation Expense	1,200				
18	Total Operating Expenses	187,700				
19						
20	**Other Income**					
21	Interest Revenue	5,000				
22	Interest Expense	(1,400)				
23	Total Other Income	3,600				
24						
25	Income before Income Taxes	318,418				
26	Income Tax Expense	98,000				
27	**Net Income**	$ 220,418				
28						
29						

Income Statement | 2019 Sales Data

A multiple-step income statement calculates gross profit.

A multiple-step income statement also separates operating revenues and operating expenses from nonoperating revenues and nonoperating expenses.

Income statements can be generated using the cash accounting method or the accrual accounting method. **Cash accounting** calculates net income based on when the income and expenses are deposited or withdrawn from the company bank accounts. **Accrual accounting** calculates net income based on when a sale was made regardless of when payment was received.

▸ Know This about income statements

- An income statement is based on the equation *Net income = revenues – expenses*.
- Revenues are important because all companies need to generate revenue to stay in business.
- Revenues include **operating revenue**, which is revenue from primary activities such as the sale of merchandise, and **nonoperating revenue**, which is revenue from secondary activities such as interest from an investment.
- Sales (operating) revenue is reported as **net sales**, which is the amount of sales generated by a company after the deduction of returns, allowances for damaged or missing goods, and any discounts.

▸ Know More about income statements

- The income statement is one of the major financial statements that all publicly listed companies, which are regulated by the Securities and Exchange Commission, must prepare at the end of every quarter and fiscal year.

continues...

— The cost of goods sold is the accumulated total a company spends directly on producing goods and delivering services during an accounting period. It is an expense and is listed under the related sales revenue on the income statement.

— Expenses include operating expenses and nonoperating expenses. An **operating expense** is a cost directly incurred to earn operating revenue. A **nonoperating expense** is a cost incurred to earn nonoperating revenue, such as an interest expense.

— After all the costs of doing business (expenses) are paid, the difference is called the *net income* or *net loss*.

▶ Know This about creating an income statement

— The data for an income statement comes from a company's financial records. Refer to section 12.10 (page 573) for information on the basic accounting cycle.

▶ Know This about the format of an income statement

— A standard format is used for an income statement regardless of the type of business or industry (see Figure 12.1 on page 552):

- A heading displays the company name, statement title, and accounting period.
- Revenues are presented before expenses.
- Net income displays on the last line.

— Revenues and expenses can be listed alphabetically or by total dollar amount.

— Entries can also vary depending on whether the statement is a single-step or multiple-step statement and depending on the complexity of the business activities.

▶ Know More about income statements

...continued

– Creating an income statement on a regular schedule, such as quarterly or annually, helps businesses make better decisions, prepare for tax time, provide proof of profitability, and project future income and expenses.

On the Job

Task 12.1 Creating a Multiple-Step Income Statement and Entering Sales Revenue

Devon is creating an income statement to report the performance of DV Auto Parts for its first year of business, the year ending December 31, 2019. He is using a multiple-step income statement to provide detail about the current profitability of the company. Devon has started the income statement and has applied some formatting. He would like you to add a standard statement heading and insert the sales total with traditional accounting formatting. The sales total and other data that will be used for the income statement are provided in a separate worksheet in the same workbook.

1. Open the data file **12-DVAutoParts-IncomeStatement**.
2. Click the Income Statement sheet tab, if necessary, to make the worksheet active.
3. Click in cell A3, type Income Statement, and then press the Enter key.
   The text *Income Statement* displays in cell A3 and cell A4 is active.

4. Type for the year ended December 31, 2019, and then press the Enter key.

   The text *for the year ended December 31, 2019* displays in cell A4 and cell A5 is active.

5. Apply bold formatting to cells A6, A11, A20, and A27.
6. Click in cell B7, type =, and then click the 2019 Sales Data sheet tab.
7. Click in cell N4 and then press Ctrl + Enter.

   The result *$1,256,296.00* displays in cell B7 and cell B7 remains active.

8. Click the Decrease Decimal button two times.

   The result *$1,256,296* displays in cell B7 (see Figure 12.6).

9. Click the Save button on the Quick Access Toolbar.

Model Answer

12.2 Calculating the Cost of Goods Sold and Gross Profit

Tutorial

Entering the Cost of Goods Sold and Calculating the Gross Profit in a Multiple-Step Income Statement

The **cost of goods sold (COGS)** (also called the *cost of sales*) is the accumulated total that a company, organization, or individual spends directly on producing goods and delivering services during an accounting period. For example, in a business that manufactures bowling trophies, this amount will include the cost of the materials used in creating the trophies along with the labor costs associated with producing the trophies. It will not include indirect expenses such as distribution, sales, and marketing costs. In a dog-walking business, the cost of goods sold will include the labor, payroll taxes, and benefits for employees providing the service. In a grocery store, the cost of goods sold includes the food and other merchandise purchased from manufacturers and growers.

Inventory is merchandise that was purchased but has yet to be sold to customers. Inventory data is used to calculate the cost of goods sold using either the periodic or perpetual method of inventory. The **periodic method of inventory** calculates the cost of goods sold using the equation *Cost of goods sold = beginning inventory + inventory purchased – end inventory*. In the periodic inventory method, assumptions are made as to which products were sold depending on the inventory valuation method used. Under the **first-in, first-out (FIFO) method**, an assumption is made that the oldest units of inventory are always sold first. Under the **last-in, first-out (LIFO) method**, the opposite assumption is made: the newest inventory is sold before any older inventory is sold. In the **perpetual method of inventory**, inventory balances are updated with each sale of goods and each purchase of inventory rather than at the end of the accounting period. The perpetual method of inventory provides a more accurate, up-to-date balance of inventory as data is updated anytime a product is sold or received.

Gross profit is the profit a company makes after deducting the costs associated with producing and selling its products or providing its services.

▸ **Know This** about calculating the cost of goods sold and gross profit

— The cost of goods sold is considered an expense for the accounting period reported in the income statement.

— The **matching principle** requires a company to match expenses with related revenues for the same accounting period in order to report profitability for the specified time interval.
— The cost of goods sold is used to analyze how well purchasing and/or payroll costs are being controlled.
— In an income statement, the cost of goods sold is subtracted from the revenue to calculate the gross profit *(Gross profit = sales – cost of goods sold)*.
— Gross profit is used to analyze a company's efficiency at using labor and supplies.

On the Job

Task 12.2 Entering the Cost of Goods Sold and Calculating the Gross Profit in a Multiple-Step Income Statement

DV Auto Parts is a retail business. The owner, Devon Varey, uses the perpetual method of inventory. The cost of goods sold accounts for the total value of the merchandise that was purchased from manufacturers during the accounting period. Devon would like you to enter the cost of goods sold in the income statement for the year ended December 31, 2019, and then calculate the gross profit for the same year.

1. With the 12-DVAutoParts-IncomeStatement workbook open and the Income Statement worksheet active, click in cell B8, type =, click the 2019 Sales Data sheet tab, click in cell N5, and then press the Enter key.
   The result *753,778* displays in cell B8 and cell B9 is active.
2. Type =B7-B8 and then press the Enter key.
   The result *502,518* displays in cell B9. You calculated the gross profit by subtracting the cost of goods sold from sales (see Figure 12.7). The gross profit indicates how much profit DV Auto Parts has after paying direct expenses for the goods sold during the same accounting period.
3. Click the Save button on the Quick Access Toolbar.

Figure 12.7 Income Statement with Cost of Goods Sold and Gross Profit Entered

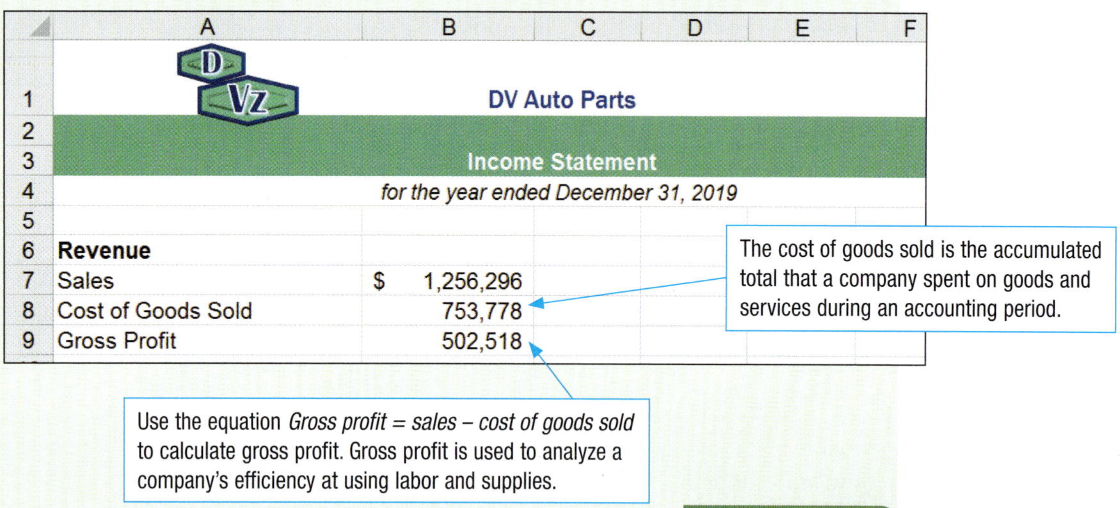

Model Answer

12.3 Differentiating between Fixed and Variable Costs

To analyze the profitability of a business or organization, you need to know which costs, or expenses, in an income statement are variable and which are fixed. A **variable cost**, or *variable expense*, varies depending on a company's production volume. Variable costs rise as production increases and fall as production decreases. A **fixed cost**, or *fixed expense*, is a cost that does not vary in the short term, regardless of changes in production or sales levels.

When a company has a large fixed-cost component, it must generate a significant amount of sales volume to pay the fixed costs. Once that sales level has been reached, this type of company generally has low variable costs, and this situation allows the company to generate large profits. For example, the oil industry is a high fixed-cost industry that generates large profits when sales are high but incurs large losses when sales decline.

In comparison, if a company has low fixed costs, it generally has high variable costs. This type of business can earn a profit at very low volume levels but does not earn large profits as sales increase. Low fixed costs and high variable costs are typical in the service industry. For example, a consulting business has low fixed costs and high variable costs because most of its costs are in the form of labor.

Tutorial

Entering Fixed Costs in a Multiple-Step Income Statement

▸ Know This about variable costs

— Variable costs fluctuate proportionally with the level of sales activity in a given period.

— Variable costs can change significantly from one period to the next.

— Common variable costs include sales commissions, transportation costs, and bank/credit card fees based on transaction usage.

— The cost of goods sold is typically the largest variable expense of a business that sells products.

▸ Know This about fixed costs

— Fixed costs do not change according to the level of sales activity in a given period.

— A fixed cost is a basic operating expense that cannot be avoided.

— A fixed cost is not directly related to sales.

— Common fixed costs include rent, salaries for employees not directly involved in production, insurance, depreciation, office supplies, and property taxes.

— Fixed costs are listed in the income statement under the heading *Expenses* or *Operating Expenses*.

— Some fixed costs, such as advertising costs and rent, are periodic fixed costs. A **periodic fixed cost** may change over time—for example, from one year to the next.

On the Job

Task 12.3 Entering Fixed Costs in a Multiple-Step Income Statement

In Task 12.2, you entered the variable expense cost of goods sold in the DV Auto Parts income statement for the year ended December 31, 2019.

Cost of goods sold is the only variable expense the company had for that accounting period. Devon is now entering the fixed costs in the income statement. He has entered row headers for each fixed cost under the heading *Operating Expenses*. He has included advertising, which is a periodic fixed cost, because he has a set annual budget for advertising. Devon would like you to enter the corresponding values for all the fixed expenses.

1. With the 12-DVAutoParts-IncomeStatement workbook open and the Income Statement worksheet active, click in cell B12, type 120000, and then press the Enter key.

   The Salaries value entered represents salaries for management employees. Cell B13 is active.
2. Type 50000 and then press the Enter key.
3. Type 10000 and then press the Enter key.
4. Type 4000 and then press the Enter key.
5. Type 2500 and then press the Enter key.
6. Type 1200 and then press the Enter key (see Figure 12.8).
7. Click the Save button on the Quick Access Toolbar.

Figure 12.8 Income Statement with Fixed Costs Entered

	A	B	C	D	E	F
1		DV Auto Parts				
2						
3		Income Statement				
4		for the year ended December 31, 2019				
5						
6	**Revenue**					
7	Sales	$ 1,256,296				
8	Cost of Goods Sold	753,778				
9	Gross Profit	502,518				
10						
11	**Operating Expenses**					
12	Salaries	120,000				
13	Rent	50,000				
14	Utilities	10,000				
15	Insurance	4,000				
16	Advertising	2,500				
17	Depreciation Expense	1,200				
18	Total Operating Expenses					

Fixed costs are often listed under the heading *Operating Expenses* in an income statement. These are costs that do not vary in the short term, regardless of changes in production or sales levels.

Model Answer

12.4 Calculating General and Administrative Costs, Other Income, and Taxes

MOS 4.1.2

Tutorial

Calculating General and Administrative Costs, Other Income, and Taxes in a Multiple-Step Income Statement

General and administrative costs are often referred to as the *overhead*, or *operating expenses*, of a company or organization. They are the operating costs or expenses a company must incur to open for business each day regardless of whether the company produces or sells anything. Examples include rent, management salaries and benefits, depreciation on office equipment, insurance, office supplies, legal fees, and utility bills.

In income statements, general and administrative costs are often grouped with selling costs in a category called **selling, general, and administrative expenses (SG&A)**. **Selling costs** include advertising and marketing costs, along with compensation paid to inside and outside salespeople.

Usually, SG&A expenses are included as operating expenses. In some cases, companies list SG&A expenses as separate line items under the heading *Operating Expenses* (see Figure 12.8 on page 560). In other cases, companies that do not want to report the details of employee salaries, pensions, insurance, marketing costs, depreciated assets, or other business expenses include SG&A expenses as a single item (see Figure 12.9) that may or may not include the heading *Operating Expenses*.

Figure 12.9 Income Statement with Selling, General, and Administrative Expenses Entered as a Single item

	A	B	C	D	E	F
1		DV Auto Parts				
2						
3		Income Statement				
4		*for the year ended December 31, 2019*				
5						
6	**Revenue**					
7	Sales	$ 1,256,296				
8	Cost of Goods Sold	753,778				
9	Gross Profit	502,518				
10						
11	Selling, General and Administrative Expenses	187,700				
12						

SG&A expenses may be entered as a single item when companies do not want to report specific detail.

Other income includes all nonoperating revenues and expenses, such as interest earned on cash or interest paid on loans.

Income taxes can include federal, state, and local government taxes on both earned income (e.g., from wages, salaries, and commissions) and unearned income (e.g., from dividends, interest, and rents). Income taxes do not include taxes that can be used as a tax deduction, such as property taxes; those are overhead costs and should be included as operating expenses.

Analysts and investors often assess the profitability of a business before subtracting the income tax expense. This is because companies use various methods to avoid or minimize taxes, and the results affect reported income but are not related to business operations. Using income before taxes are deducted provides a more accurate measure of profitability.

▸ Know This about calculating general and administrative costs

— To calculate selling, general, and administrative expenses as a single item, add all selling, general, and administrative costs together.

— General and administrative costs are fixed costs. They include expenditures related to the day-to-day operations of a business and occur independent of sales activity.

— General and administrative costs include rent/mortgage on buildings, utilities, insurance, consultant fees, depreciation on office equipment, and salaries of all nonsales personnel.

— In an income statement, general and administrative costs are deducted from the gross profit to calculate net income.

▸ **Know This** about calculating other income (nonoperating revenue and expenses)

— In an income statement, nonoperating expenses are entered as negative values.

— Nonoperating revenues are entered as positive values.

▸ **Know This** about calculating taxes

— In an income statement, a tax expense entry appears immediately before the calculation of net income.

— The income tax amount entered in an income statement is an estimate, or an account that has been created to cover what a company expects to pay.

▸ **Know This** about calculating total operating expenses

— In an income statement, the SUM function can be used to calculate the total operating expenses. All listed operating expenses are included in the argument range.

▸ **Know This** about calculating total other income

— In an income statement, the SUM function can be used to calculate the total other income. All entries for other income are included in the argument range.

▸ **Know This** about calculating income before taxes

— In an income statement, the total operating expenses are subtracted from the gross profit to calculate the income before taxes: *Income before income taxes = gross profit – total operating expenses + total other income.*

On the Job

Task 12.4 Calculating General and Administrative Costs, Other Income, and Taxes in a Multiple-Step Income Statement

In the DV Auto Parts income statement for the year ended December 31, 2019, the general and administrative costs are listed as separate line items under the *Operating Expenses* heading. Devon asks you to calculate the total operating expenses, enter and calculate the other income (nonoperating expenses and income), calculate the income before taxes, and enter the income tax expense. Use SUM functions to calculate the total operating expenses and total other income, and use a formula to calculate the income before income taxes.

1. With the DVAutoParts-IncomeStatement workbook open, the Income Statement worksheet active, and cell B18 active, type =SUM(B12:B17) and then press the Enter key.

   The result *187,700* displays in cell B18. This is the total of all operating expenses.

2. Click in cell B21, type 5000, and then press the Enter key.

   The result *5,000* displays in cell B21. This is the interest revenue (nonoperating revenue). It is a positive value because it is cash inflow.

3. Type -1400 and then press the Enter key.

   The value *(1,400)* displays in cell B22. This is the interest expense. It is a negative value because it is a cash outflow.

4. Type =SUM(B21:B22) and then press the Enter key.

   The result *3,600* displays in cell B23. This is the total other income.

5. Click in cell B25, type =B9-B18+B23 and then press the Enter key.

   The result *318,418* displays in cell B25. This is the income before income taxes *(Income before income taxes = gross profit – total operating expenses + total other income)*.

6. Type 98000 and then press the Enter key.

   The value *98,000* displays in cell B26. This is the income tax DV Auto Parts estimates it will pay for the year ended December 31, 2019 (see Figure 12.10).

7. Click the Save button on the Quick Access Toolbar.

Figure 12.10 Income Statement with Administrative Costs Calculated, Other Income Entered and Calculated, and Taxes Entered

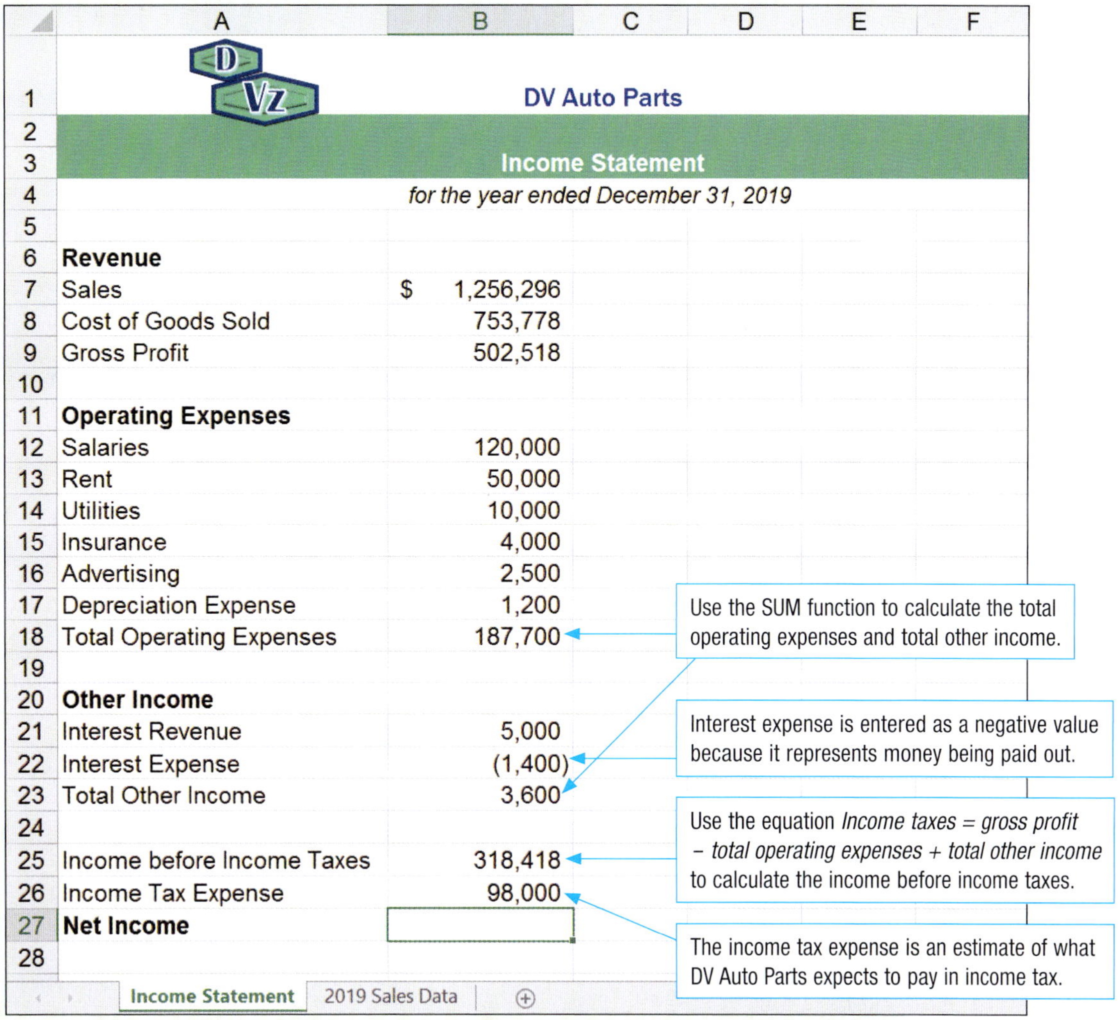

Model Answer

12.5 Finding Net Profit or Net Loss

MOS 4.1.1

A net profit or loss is often referred to as the **bottom line** because it is reported at the bottom of the income statement. **Net profit** (also called *net income* or *net earnings*) is the amount of profit remaining after total costs and expenses have been subtracted from total income and revenue. **Net loss** (also called *net operating loss*, or *NOL*) is the amount of loss remaining after total expenses are subtracted from total income and revenue. If a business earns a net profit, it is considered profitable. If a business operates at a net loss, it is considered nonprofitable.

Tutorial

Finding Net Profit in a Multiple-Step Income Statement

▶ Know More about net income

- If net income is a positive value, it may be called *net profit*.
- Conversely, if net income is a negative value, it may be called *net loss*.

▶ Know This about net profit

— Net profit is a measure of the profit remaining, not the amount of cash earned, because the values used to calculate net profit in the income statement include noncash expenses such as depreciation. To determine how much cash a company earned in a financial period, refer to the Cash Flow statement, which is introduced in Section 12.18.

— If the net profit of a corporation is healthy and growing, the value of the corporation's shares will typically increase.

▶ Know This about finding the net profit or net loss

— To calculate the net profit, subtract the income tax expense from the income before income taxes: *Net income = income before income taxes – income tax expense*.

— If income exceeds expenses, the result will be a positive value, or net profit.

— If expenses exceed income, the result will be a negative value, or net loss.

— Net profit is used to pay shareholder dividends in public or private companies that issue stocks. Any income that remains after dividends are paid becomes part of a company's equity in the form of retained earnings.

On the Job

Task 12.5 Finding Net Income in a Mutiple-Step Income Statement

Devon would like to know whether his business was profitable for the year ending December 31, 2019. He asks you to calculate the net income in the DV Auto Parts income statement for that accounting period. He would also like you to add formatting to the income statement.

1. With the 12-DVAutoParts-IncomeStatement workbook open, the Income Statement worksheet active, and cell B27 active, type =B25-B26 and then press the Enter key.

   The result *$220,418* displays in cell B27 and cell B28 is active (see Figure 12.11).

2. Select cells B8, B17, B22, and B26 and then apply a single bottom border.
3. Click in cell B27 and then apply a bottom double border.
4. Click the Save button on the Quick Access Toolbar.

Reminder

In a financial worksheet, use a single border above a subtotal and a double border below a total.

Figure 12.11 Income Statement with Net Income Calculated

	A	B	C	D	E	F
1		DV Auto Parts				
2						
3		Income Statement				
4		*for the year ended December 31, 2019*				
5						
6	**Revenue**					
7	Sales	$ 1,256,296				
8	Cost of Goods Sold	753,778				
9	Gross Profit	502,518				
10						
11	**Operating Expenses**					
12	Salaries	120,000				
13	Rent	50,000				
14	Utilities	10,000				
15	Insurance	4,000				
16	Advertising	2,500				
17	Depreciation Expense	1,200				
18	Total Operating Expenses	187,700				
19						
20	**Other Income**					
21	Interest Revenue	5,000				
22	Interest Expense	(1,400)				
23	Total Other Income	3,600				
24						
25	Income before Income Taxes	318,418				
26	Income Tax Expense	98,000				
27	**Net Income**	$ 220,418				
28						
29						

Net income is a positive value, indicating the business was profitable in its first year of operation.

Income Statement | 2019 Sales Data

Model Answer

12.6 Identifying Common Income Statement Errors

Tutorial

Identifying and Fixing Data Entry Errors in an Income Statement

The accuracy of an income statement or other financial document is extremely important because many business decisions are based on financial statement data. For example, if you fail to record a sale, the net income listed in the income statement will be low and investors may decide to stop supporting the business because it is not profitable enough.

Common errors in income statements include data entry errors and calculation errors. A **data entry error** occurs when data is entered incorrectly. A calculation error occurs when a formula is entered incorrectly.

Section 2.17, in Chapter 2, describes how to identify common formula and function errors. Section 9.5, in Chapter 9, explains how to use the Evaluate Formula feature to identify errors. Section 10.11, in Chapter 10, discusses how to identify errors and troubleshoot formulas using formula auditing tools.

▸ Know This about identifying common income statement errors

— Miscalculating sales or net income leads to an incorrect valuation for the company. **Valuation** is the process of determining the fair market value of a company or business.

— Errors in calculating operating expenses can lead a business to overspend, since these figures are used to set future budgets. It can also result in not allocating enough resources to sustain operations or not having enough inventory.

— Examples of income statement errors are forgetting to charge depreciation on a fixed asset and overstating ending inventory values when calculating the cost of goods sold.

— It is important to proofread the income statement and compare it against the source data to make sure numbers have not been transposed, decimal places are in the correct position, and all data has been entered.

▸ Know More about common income statement errors

- Generally accepted accounting principles (GAAP) are a common set of accounting principles, standards, and procedures that companies follow when creating financial statements.
- GAAP uses three classifications for accounting errors: **error of commission** (mathematical mistake), **error of omission** (transaction not recorded), and **error of principle** (mistake in applying GAAP).
- Accounting errors can also be categorized as deliberate or nondeliberate.

On the Job

Task 12.6 Identifying and Fixing Data Entry Errors in an Income Statement

Devon double-checks the sales figures in the 2019 Sales Data worksheet and realizes there are errors in the data recorded for the months of February and June. The errors are a result of product refunds due to a manufacturer recall that were not recorded. The changes to the sales data will ultimately affect the net income for DV Auto Parts because the sales data is used to calculate the cost of goods sold, those values are used to calculate the gross profit, gross profit is included in income before taxes, and income before taxes is included in net income. Devon would like you to correct the sales entry errors in the 2019 Sales Data worksheet and then report on how the changes affect the net income.

1. With the 12-DVAutoParts-IncomeStatement workbook open and the Income Statement worksheet active, note the value in cell B27.

   The value *$220,418* displays in cell B27. This is the net income for DV Auto Parts for the year ended December 31, 2019.

2. Click the 2019 Sales Data sheet tab.

   The 2019 Sales Data worksheet is active.

3. Click in cell C4, type 87500, and then press the Enter key.

   The value *$87,500.00* appears in cell C4. The values in cells C5, N4, and N5 also change because they contain formulas that refer to cell C4.

4. Click in cell G4, type 77500, and then press the Enter key.

   The value *$77,500.00* appears in cell G4. The values in cells G5, N4, and N5 also change because they contain formulas that refer to cell G4.

5. Click the Income Statement sheet tab and then note the value in cell B27.

   The value *$188,908* displays in cell B27, indicating a lower net income.

6. Click the Save button on the Quick Access Toolbar.

Model Answer

12.7 Visualizing an Income Statement

MOS 5.1.1

The data in an income statement can be illustrated in a waterfall chart to make the data easier to present and analyze. A **waterfall chart** shows a running total as values are added or subtracted. This type of chart is helpful for illustrating how a value, such as sales revenue, is affected by a series of positive and negative values, such as cost of goods sold. In a waterfall chart, data that is considered a subtotal or total can be set so that it starts on the horizontal axis instead of floating (see Figure 12.12).

Tutorials

Creating an Income Statement Summary for a Waterfall Chart

Creating a Waterfall Chart from an Income Statement Summary

Figure 12.12 Waterfall Chart Illustrating Income Statement Data

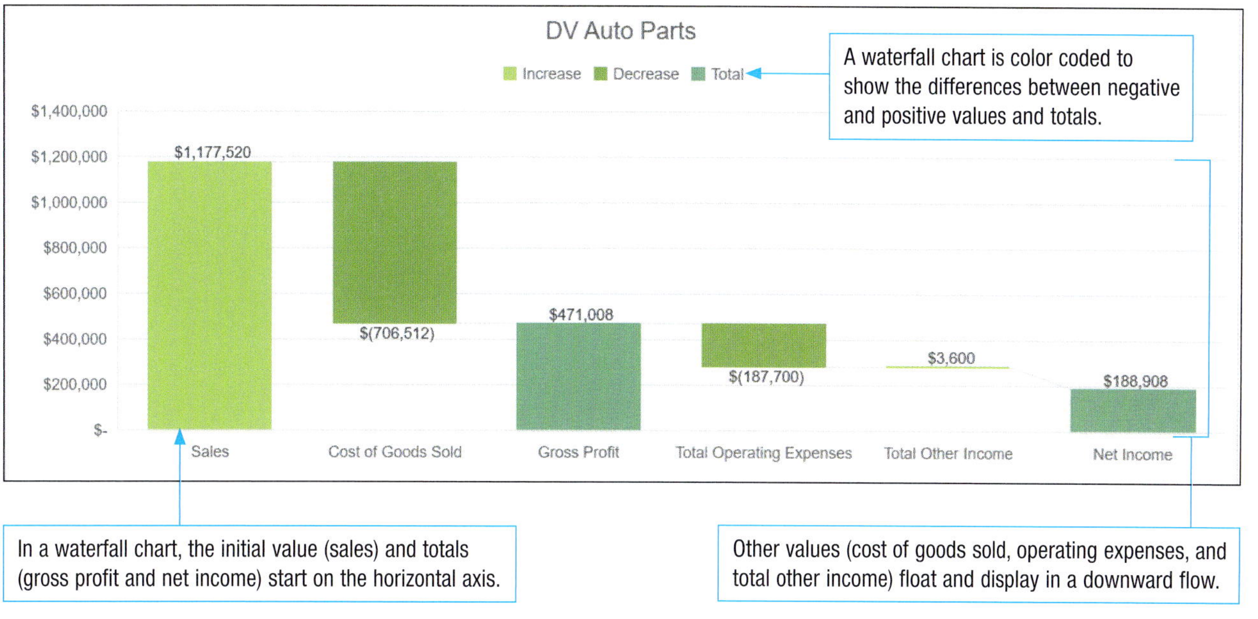

▸ Know This about creating a waterfall chart

— To create a waterfall chart from the data in an income statement, follow these steps:

1. Create a summary version of the income statement that only includes the subtotals and totals. In the summary, display values that are expenses, such as cost of goods sold, as negative values.
2. With the income statement summary created, click a cell within the summarized data, click the Insert tab, click the Insert Waterfall or Stock Chart button, and then click the *Waterfall* option.
3. To set data as a subtotal or total, click the data column on the chart two times to select it, right-click the column, and then click the *Set as Total* option at the pop-up menu.
4. Repeat Step 3 for all subtotal or total columns.

On the Job

Task 12.7 Creating a Waterfall Chart from Income Statement Data

Devon would like to present the data in the income statement in a visual format so that he can better analyze the data and share it with his investors. He asks you to summarize the data in the income statement in a separate worksheet and then create a waterfall chart.

1. With the 12-DVAutoParts-IncomeStatement workbook open and the Income Statement worksheet active, select the ranges A7:B9, A18:B18, A23:B23, and A27:B27.
2. Click the Copy button in the Clipboard group.
3. Click the New sheet button.

   A new sheet opens to the right of the Income Statement worksheet.
4. Click in cell A1, if necessary, and then click the Paste button.
5. Use the AutoFit feature to adjust the widths of columns A and B.
6. Click in cell B2, press the F2 function key, click to the left of the value in the cell, type -, and then press the Enter key.
7. Repeat Step 6 to display the value in cell B4 as a negative value.
8. With cell B5 active, click the Insert tab, click the Insert Waterfall or Stock Chart button, and then click the *Waterfall* option.

   A waterfall chart displays in the worksheet.
9. Click the gross profit column on the chart two times.

   The gross profit column is selected and the other chart columns appear faded.
10. Right-click the gross profit column and then click the *Set as Total* option at the pop-up menu.

    The gross profit starts on the horizontal axis instead of floating.
11. Repeat Steps 9 and 10 to set the net income column as a total.
12. Size the chart so that all data labels display in their entirety (see Figure 12.12 on page 567).
13. Click the chart title placeholder and type DV Auto Parts.
14. If printed work is required by your instructor, print the workbook.
15. Save and then close the workbook.

Model Answer

12.8 Creating Balance Sheets

A **balance sheet** presents the financial position of a company, organization, or individual at the end of a specified period, providing a snapshot of the company's financial position at that point in time. The most common use of the balance sheet is to determine the liquidity of a business. **Liquidity** is the ability to pay debts in a timely manner.

A balance sheet shows how the resources owned by the business (assets) are financed by debt (liabilities) or by shareholder investments (equity). Investors and creditors use a balance sheet to analyze how efficiently a company uses its resources and how effectively it finances them.

Tutorial

Creating a Balance Sheet Using the Report Format

▸ Know This about balance sheets

— A balance sheet allows investors and creditors to see what a company owns as well as what it owes as of the date indicated in the balance sheet heading.

— A balance sheet lists the ending balances in a company's asset, liability, and equity accounts as of the date stated in the balance sheet heading.

▸ Know More about balance sheets

– The balance sheet is one of the major financial statements that all publicly listed companies, which are regulated by the Securities and Exchange Commission, must prepare at the end of every quarter and fiscal year.

▶ **Know This** about balance sheet formatting

— The format of the balance sheet is not mandated by accounting standards, but businesses tend to follow one of two formats: account format or report format.
  - The **account format** uses two columns, displaying assets in the left column and liabilities and equity in the right column. The debit accounts are displayed on the left, and credit accounts are on the right (see Figure 12.13).
  - The **report format** lists all items in one column and is the traditional format used by companies (see Figure 12.14).

— The balance sheet has a heading that displays the company name, the title of the statement, and the accounting period of the report.

— Assets are always presented first, followed by liabilities and equity.

— Assets are categorized as current and long-term. A current asset is a resource that will be used in the current year, and a **long-term asset** is a resource that will last longer than one year.

— Liabilities are also categorized as current and long-term. A **current liability** is a debt or obligation that will become due in the current accounting period (often the current year), and a **long-term liability** is a debt or obligation that will become due in a future accounting period (often more than one year).

— The **equity** for a business is the amount of the funds contributed by the owners plus the retained earnings or losses. It represents the net worth of the owner or the company. Equity varies depending on the type of business. For example, corporations may list common stock, preferred stock, retained earnings, and treasury stock; partnerships may list members' capital; and sole proprietorships list the owner's capital.

Figure 12.13 Account Format

The account format displays debit accounts on the left and credit accounts on the right.

The balance sheet heading displays the company name, the title of the statement, and the reporting date.

	A	B	C	D	E	F
1	DVZ			DV Auto Parts		
2				Balance Sheet		
3				December 31, 2019		
4	**Assets**			**Liabilities**		
5	**Current Assets**			**Current Liabilities**		
6	Cash	20,000		Accounts Payable	128,000	
7	Accounts Receivable	120,000		Accrued Expenses	125,000	
8	Inventory	178,000		Total Current Liabilities	253,000	
9				Long-term Liabilities	65,000	
10	**Total Current Assets**	318,000		**Total Liabilities**	318,000	
11						
12				**Owner's Equity**		
13	**Long-term Assets**			**Owner's Equity**		
14	Equipment	140,000		Retained Earnings	84,200	
15	Accumulated Depreciation	(5,800)		Devon Varey, Capital	50,000	
16	Total Long-term Assets	134,200		Total Owner's Equity	134,200	
17	**Total Assets**	452,200		**Total Liabilities and Owner's Equity**	452,200	

Figure 12.14 Report Format

	A	B	C	D
1		DV Auto Parts		
2		Balance Sheet		
3		December 31, 2019		
4	Assets			
5	**Current Assets**			
6	Cash	20,000		
7	Accounts Receivable	120,000		
8	Inventory	178,000		
9	Total Current Assets	318,000		
10	**Long-term Assets**			
11	Equipment	140,000		
12	Accumulated Depreciation	(5,800)		
13	Total Long-term Assets	134,200		
14	**Total Assets**	452,200		
15				
16	Liabilities			
17	**Current Liabilities**			
18	Accounts Payable	128,000		
19	Accrued Expenses	125,000		
20	Total Current Liabilities	253,000		
21	**Long-term Liabilities**	65,000		
22	**Total Liabilities**	318,000		
23				
24	Owner's Equity			
25	**Owner's Equity**			
26	Retained Earnings	84,200		
27	Devon Varey, Capital	50,000		
28	Total Owner's Equity	134,200		
29	**Total Liabilities and Owner's Equity**	452,200		
30				

The report format displays all items in one column and is the traditional format used by companies.

On the Job

Task 12.8 Creating a Balance Sheet Using the Report Format

Devon has set up a balance sheet to reflect the point in time when all the transactions for DV Auto Parts through December 31, 2019, have been recorded. He has used the report format and applied formatting to make this financial document consistent with other DV Auto Parts financial documents. Devon has started the balance sheet and has applied some formatting. He would like you to add the heading.

1. Open the data file **12-DVAutoParts-BalanceSheet**.
2. With the Balance Sheet worksheet active, click in cell A2, type Balance Sheet, and then press the Enter key.

   The text *Balance Sheet* displays in cell A2 and cell A3 is active.
3. Type December 31, 2019, and then press the Enter key.

   The text *December 31, 2019* displays in cell A3 and cell A4 is active (see Figure 12.14).
4. Save and close the workbook.

Model Answer

12.9 Using the Double Entry Accounting Method in a General Journal

A **general journal** is the initial financial document in which business transactions are entered in an accounting system. It is a chronological record of all the transactions for a business, including an explanation of each transaction, identification of the accounts affected by a transaction, and the amount by which each account is increased or decreased. Data from the general journal is used to compile financial statements.

Tutorial
Using the Double Entry Accounting Method in a General Journal

An **account** is a separate, detailed record associated with a specific asset, liability, equity, revenue, expense, gain, or loss. Examples of accounts are cash, accounts receivable, inventory, and accounts payable (see Table 12.1).

Table 12.1 Common Types of Accounts

Asset Accounts	Liability Accounts	Equity Accounts
Cash	Notes Payable	Common Stock
Accounts Receivable	Accounts Payable	Preferred Stock
Inventory	Wages Payable	Retained Earnings
Supplies	Income Tax Payable	Treasury Stock

The **double entry accounting method** is commonly used for entering transactions in the general journal to help ensure that financial statements are accurate and to help identify errors. Double entry accounting is used to satisfy the equation *Assets = liabilities + equity*. This accounting method is based on the fact that every financial transaction has equal and opposite effects in at least two accounts.

▸ Know This about the double entry accounting method

- With the double entry accounting method, each transaction is recorded in the general journal first as a debit and then as a credit (see Figure 12.15).
- A **chart of accounts** is a numbered list of the accounts in a company's general ledger. It is organized according to a numerical system. For example, all assets may start with the number 1 and cash accounts may be labeled 101, accounts receivable 102, and so forth.
- A **debit** is the part of an accounting entry that either increases an asset or expense account, or decreases a liability or equity account. It is positioned to the left in an accounting entry.
- A **credit** is the part of an accounting entry that either increases a liability or equity account, or decreases an asset or expense account. It is positioned to the right in an accounting entry.
- In a transaction, the sum of all debits must be exactly equal to the sum of all credits. For example, if goods are purchased for $1,000 with the intention of reselling them, the entry is a debit to the inventory (asset) account and a credit to the accounts payable (liability) account.
- Alternatively, if goods are sold for $1,000 in cash, the entry is a debit to the cash (asset) account and a credit to the inventory (asset) account.

▸ **Know This** about entering transactions in the general journal

- Use the standard mm/dd/yyyy format for entering dates.
- Format monetary values with the standard two digits after the decimal point.
- Use the Increase Indent button to indent credit account entries in the *Account Title* column.

On the Job

Task 12.9 Using the Double Entry Accounting Method in a General Journal

Devon has set up a general journal for DV Auto Parts. He is planning to use the double entry accounting method in the journal. Devon asks you to record two transactions in the journal.

1. Open the data file **12-DVAutoParts-GeneralJournal**.
2. On January 8, 2020, DV Auto Parts purchases $250 in office supplies. Devon would like you to record a debit to the office supplies account and a credit to the cash account (see Figure 12.15).
   a. Click in cell A6, type 01/08/2020, and then press the Tab key.
   b. Type Office Supplies and then press the Tab key.
      The first account for this transaction is the office supplies account.
   c. Type 107 and then press the Tab key.
      The office supplies account number is 107.
   d. Type 250 and then press Ctrl + Enter.
      The office supplies account is debited $250.
   e. Click in cell B7, click the Increase Indent button in the Alignment group on the Home tab, type Cash, and then press the Tab key.
      The second account for this transaction is the cash account.
   f. Type 101 and then press the Tab key three times.
      The account number for the cash account is 101.
   g. Type 250 and then press the Enter key.
      The cash account is credited $250.
3. Also on January 8, 2020, DV Auto Parts purchases a $500 piece of machinery on credit. Devon would like you to record a debit to the equipment account and a credit to the accounts payable account.
   a. Click in cell A8, type 01/08/2020, and then press the Tab key.
   b. Type Equipment and then press the Tab key.
      The first account for this transaction is the equipment account.
   c. Type 109 and then press the Tab key.
      The equipment account number is 109.
   d. Type 500 and then press the Enter key.
      The equipment account is debited $500.
   e. Click in cell B9, press the Increase Indent button in the Alignment group, type Accounts Payable, and then press the Tab key.
      The second account for this transaction is the accounts payable account.

f. Type 103 and then press the Tab key three times.

The accounts payable account number is 103.

g. Type 500 and then press the Enter key.

The accounts payable account is credited $500.

4. Save and close the workbook.

Figure 12.15 General Journal with Double Entries Recorded

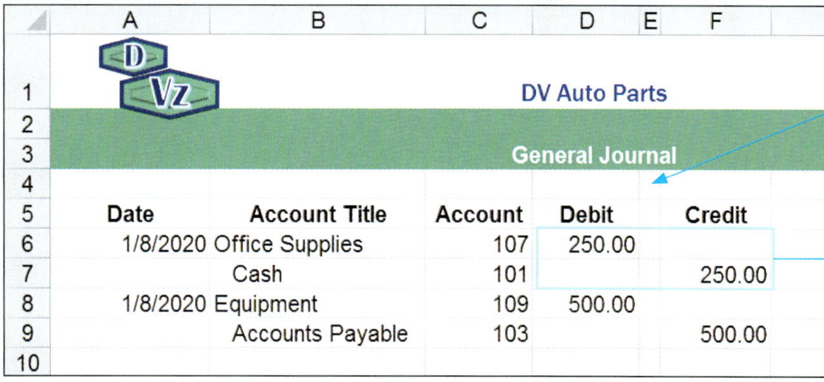

	A	B	C	D	E	F
1			DV Auto Parts			
2						
3			General Journal			
4						
5	Date	Account Title	Account	Debit		Credit
6	1/8/2020	Office Supplies	107	250.00		
7		Cash	101			250.00
8	1/8/2020	Equipment	109	500.00		
9		Accounts Payable	103			500.00
10						

Including a narrow blank column between the *Debit* and *Credit* columns makes the data easier to read.

In the double entry accounting method, each transaction is recorded in the general journal as both a debit and a credit.

Model Answer

12.10 Calculating Assets

MOS 4.1.1
MOS 4.1.2

Creating a balance sheet involves calculating the value of an organization's assets. To calculate the value of assets, it is important to understand the **basic accounting cycle** for an accounting period (see Figure 12.16).

Tutorial

Calculating Assets in a Balance Sheet

Figure 12.16 Basic Accounting Cycle for an Accounting Period

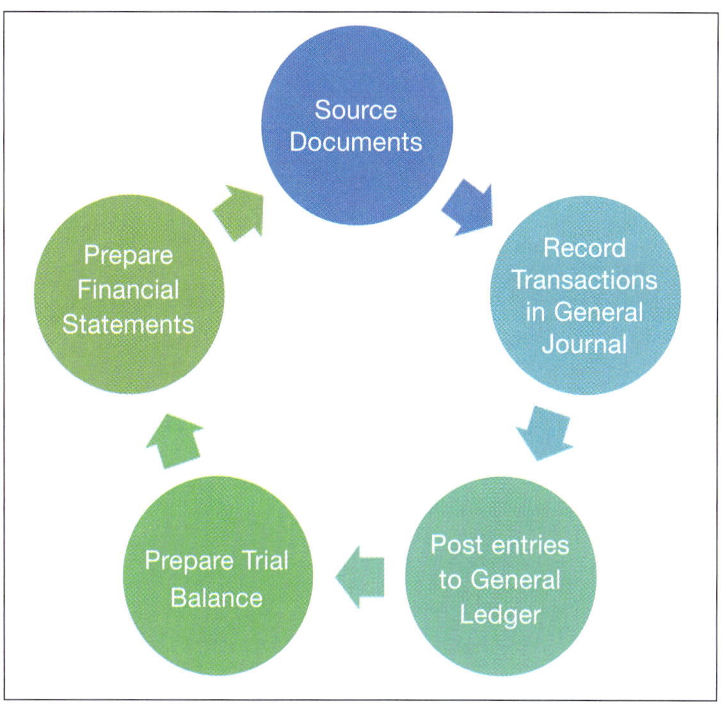

In Section 12.9, you recorded transactions in the general journal. The next step is to post the transaction data to the appropriate account in the general ledger. The **general ledger** contains all the balance sheet accounts, including cash, accounts receivable, equipment, accumulated depreciation, and accounts payable. **Posting** transfers the debit or credit balance of a transaction to the appropriate account (see Figure 12.17).

Figure 12.17 Accounts in a General Ledger

	A	B	C	D	E
1			DV Auto Parts		
2					
3			General Ledger		
4	**Account 101**		**Cash**	**Balance**	
5					
6		**Debit**	**Credit**	**(DR Bal)**	
7	1/15/2019			$ 10,000.00	
8	1/16/2019	400.00	250.00	$ 10,150.00	
9	1/17/2019	500.00		$ 10,650.00	
10	1/18/2019		500.00	$ 10,150.00	
11					
12					
13	**Account 201**	**Accounts Payable**		**Balance**	
14					
15		**Debit**	**Credit**	**(CR Bal)**	
16	1/15/2019			$ 2,500.00	
17	1/16/2019	58.00	1190.00	$ 3,632.00	
18	1/17/2019	300.00		$ 3,332.00	
19	1/18/2019		670.00	$ 4,002.00	
20					

The debit or credit balance of a transaction is transferred from the general journal to the appropriate general ledger account.

The next step is to prepare a trial balance. A **trial balance** lists all the accounts in the general ledger at the end of the accounting period with their ending credit or debit balance. A trial balance is prepared to ensure the debits equal the credits (see Figure 12.18).

Figure 12.18 Trial Balance

	A	B	C	D
1		DV Auto Parts		
2		Trial Balance		
3		December 31, 2019		
4	**Account**	**Debit**	**Credit**	
5	Cash	$ 20,000		
6	Accounts Receivable	120,000		
7	Inventory	178,000		
8	Equipment	140,000		
9	Accumulated Depreciation	(5,800)		
10	Accounts Payable		$ 128,000	
11	Accrued Expenses		125,000	
12	Long-term Liabilities		65,000	
13	Retained Earnings		84,200	
14	Devon Varey, Capital		50,000	
15	**Totals**	**$ 452,200**	**$ 452,200**	
16				

The debit and credit balances must be equal in a trial balance.

▸ Know This about assets

— Assets are purchased to increase the value of a company, generate future revenue, or maintain company operations.

▸ Know This about calculating assets

— When a balance sheet is created, the accounting cycle is followed, with asset data typically transferred from the trial balance.

— Assets should appear in the balance sheet in the order that they will be converted to cash. For example, in Figure 12.19, cash is listed first because it is most liquid, accounts receivable are listed second because they are expected to be collected in 30 to 60 days, inventory is listed third because it is expected to be sold within the year, and so forth.

— Asset accounts usually have debit balances.

— Use the SUM function to calculate the total current assets and total long-term assets.

— To calculate total assets, use the equation *Total assets = total current assets + total long-term assets*.

▸ Know More about calculating assets

– Most companies and businesses use accounting software to manage their daily transactions, general ledger, accounts receivable, accounts payable, and other financial functions. The data generated from the accounting software is used to create the financial reports. Many of these accounting software applications interface with Excel to perform data analysis activities.

On the Job

Task 12.10 Calculating Assets in a Balance Sheet

Devon would like you to continue compiling the DV Auto Parts Balance Sheet by entering data from the trial balance and then calculating the total assets.

1. Open the 12-DVAutoParts-BalanceSheet workbook, which you saved and closed in Task 12.8.
2. With the Balance Sheet worksheet active, click the Balance Sheet sheet tab, click in cell B6, type 20000, and then press the Enter key.
3. Type 120000 and then press the Enter key.
4. Type 190000 and then press the Enter key.
5. Type =SUM(B6:B8) and then press the Enter key.

   The total current assets are calculated and the result, *330,000*, displays in cell B9 (see Figure 12.19).
6. Click in cell B11, type 140000, and then press the Enter key.
7. Type -5800 and then press the Enter key.

   Accumulated depreciation is entered as a negative value because it represents a decline in the value of an asset.
8. Type =SUM(B11:B12) and then press the Enter key.

   The total long-term assets are calculated and the result, *134,200*, displays in cell B13.
9. Type =B9+B13 and then press the Enter key.

   The total assets are calculated and the result, *464,200*, displays in cell B14.
10. Select cells B8, B12, and B13 and then apply a single bottom border.
11. Click the Save button on the Quick Access Toolbar.

Figure 12.19 Balance Sheet with Assets Calculated

	A	B	C	D
1		DV Auto Parts		
2		Balance Sheet		
3		December 31, 2019		
4	**Assets**			
5	**Current Assets**			
6	Cash	20,000		
7	Accounts Receivable	120,000		
8	Inventory	190,000		
9	Total Current Assets	330,000		
10	**Long-term Assets**			
11	Equipment	140,000		
12	Accumulated Depreciation	(5,800)		
13	Total Long-term Assets	134,200		
14	**Total Assets**	464,200		
15				

Current assets are assets that a company can or will sell within one year.

Long-term assets are assets a company cannot or does not plan to sell within a year.

Total assets are the sum of all current and long-term assets owned by a company at a particular point in time.

Model Answer

12.11 Calculating Liabilities

MOS 4.1.1
MOS 4.1.2

Tutorial

Calculating Liabilities in a Balance Sheet

Creating a balance sheet also involves calculating the value of an organization's liabilities. Like assets, liabilities are transferred from the trial balance as part of the accounting cycle.

▸ Know This about calculating liabilities

- When a balance sheet is created, the accounting cycle is followed, with liability data transferred from the trial balance.
- Liabilities should appear in the balance sheet in the order that they will be paid. For example, in Figure 12.20, accounts payable is listed first as they are expected to be paid in 30 to 60 days.
- Liability accounts usually have credit balances.
- Use the SUM function to calculate the total current liabilities and total long-term liabilities.
- To calculate total liabilities, use the equation *Total liabilities = total current liabilities + total long-term liabilities*.

On the Job

Task 12.11 Calculating Liabilities in a Balance Sheet

Devon would like you to continue to create the DV Auto Parts balance sheet by entering liability data from the trial balance and then calculating the total liabilities.

1. With the 12-DVAutoParts-BalanceSheet workbook open and the Balance Sheet worksheet active, click in cell B18, type 140000, and then press the Enter key.
2. Type 125000 and then press the Enter key.

3. Type =SUM(B18:B19) and then press the Enter key.
   The total current liabilities are calculated and the result, *265,000*, displays in cell B20 (see Figure 12.20).
4. Type 65000 and then press the Enter key.
   The long-term liabilities are entered and the result, *65,000*, displays in cell B21.
5. Enter =B20+B21 and then press the Enter key.
   The total liabilities are calculated and the result, *330,000*, displays in cell B22.
6. Select cells B19 and B21 and apply a single bottom border.
7. Click the Save button on the Quick Access Toolbar.

Figure 12.20 Balance Sheet with Liabilities Calculated

	A	B	C
13	Total Long-term Assets	134,200	
14	**Total Assets**	464,200	
15			
16	**Liabilities**		
17	**Current Liabilities**		
18	Accounts Payable	140,000	
19	Accrued Expenses	125,000	
20	Total Current Liabilities	265,000	
21	**Long-term Liabilities**	65,000	
22	**Total Liabilities**	330,000	
23			

Current liabilities are liabilities a company will pay within a year.

Long-term liabilities are liabilities a company will pay more than a year in the future.

Total liabilities are the sum of all current and long-term liabilities owed to a company at a particular point in time.

Model Answer

12.12 Calculating Equity

MOS 4.1.1
MOS 4.1.2

Tutorial

Calculating Equity in a Balance Sheet

The final data that needs to be entered on the balance sheet is equity. Like assets and liabilities, equity data is transferred from the trial balance as part of the accounting cycle.

▸ **Know This** about calculating equity

— To calculate equity, subtract the total liabilities from the total assets.

— In the balance sheet, equity may be categorized as owner's equity or stockholders' equity.

- **Owner's equity** is the category used when the business is a sole proprietorship (has a single owner) or a partnership.
- **Stockholders' equity** is the category used for corporations. In the balance sheet, it may be listed as common stock or preferred stock.

— Equity is used to analyze financial risk. In general, if a company's total liabilities are a high amount when compared with their total equity, the greater the risk of being unable to repay debts.

On the Job

Task 12.12 Calculating Equity in a Balance Sheet

Devon would like you to continue compiling the DV Auto Parts balance sheet by entering data from the trial balance and then calculating the total owner's equity and the combined total liabilities and owner's equity.

1. With the 12-DVAutoParts-BalanceSheet workbook open and the Balance Sheet worksheet active, click in cell B26, type 84200, and then press the Enter key.
2. Type 50000 and then press the Enter key.
3. Type =SUM(B26:B27) and then press the Enter key.

   The total owner's equity is calculated and the result, *134,200*, displays in cell B28 (see Figure 12.21).
4. Type =B22+B28 and then press the Enter key.

   The total liabilities and owner's equity is calculated and the result, *464,200*, displays in cell B29. Total liabilities and owner's equity is the same as total assets (in cell B14).
5. Select cells B27 and B28 and then apply a single bottom border.
6. Click the Save button on the Quick Access Toolbar.

Figure 12.21 Balance Sheet with Total Owner's Equity and Total Liabilities and Owner's Equity Calculated

	A	B	C
10	**Long-term Assets**		
11	Equipment	140,000	
12	Accumulated Depreciation	(5,800)	
13	Total Long-term Assets	134,200	
14	**Total Assets**	464,200	
15			
16	**Liabilities**		
17	**Current Liabilities**		
18	Accounts Payable	140,000	
19	Accrued Expenses	125,000	
20	Total Current Liabilities	265,000	
21	**Long-term Liabilities**	65,000	
22	**Total Liabilities**	330,000	
23			
24	**Owner's Equity**		
25	**Owner's Equity**		
26	Retained Earnings	84,200	
27	Devon Varey, Capital	50,000	
28	Total Owner's Equity	134,200	
29	**Total Liabilities and Owner's Equity**	464,200	
30			

The balance sheet equation *Assets = liabilities + equity* is illustrated in the DV Auto Parts balance sheet.

Model Answer

12.13 Identifying Common Balance Sheet Errors

A balance sheet organizes a company, organization, or individual's financial data in a standardized format that can be easily understood. When a balance sheet is created, accounting errors can occur because of the large amount of data that is transferred to the balance sheet from other sources.

Tutorial

Identifying and Fixing an Error of Omission in a Balance Sheet

Errors in a balance sheet can lead to problems such as presenting a better financial picture than actually exists. While it is difficult to prevent errors, you can take precautions to catch them before they create problems. Digital copies of all financial documents should be available for quick review if a problem arises, and manual reconciliation of the financial information can help ensure the balance sheet data is accurate.

▸ **Know This** about identifying common balance sheet errors

- One common balance sheet error is the incorrect classification of assets and liabilities.
- A **transposition error** occurs when numbers are reversed, such as when 43 is entered as 34.
- A data entry error occurs when data is entered incorrectly, such as when a 5 is entered as a 4.
- An error of omission occurs when data is not entered, such as when expenses are not being reported or inventory quantities are not updated.
- An error in the balance sheet may be attributed to an earlier point in the accounting cycle, resulting in updates required to other records in the general journal, general ledger, and trial balance.

On the Job

Task 12.13 Identifying and Fixing an Error of Omission in a Balance Sheet

After a careful review of the data in the balance sheet against the source data, Devon realizes that $12,000 that was entered in the balance sheet as inventory was never actually ordered or received. This error of omission means the general journal, general ledger, and trial balance need to be updated along with the balance sheet. The inventory account needs to be credited $12,000, and the accounts payable account needs to be debited the same amount. Devon asks you to update the balance sheet.

1. With the 12-DVAutoParts-BalanceSheet workbook open and the Balance Sheet worksheet active, click in cell B8, type 178000, and then press the Enter key.

   The value in cell B8 decreases by 12,000, from 190,000 to 178,000. A decrease to the inventory asset account is a credit.

2. Click in cell B18, type 128000, and then press the Enter key.

   The value in cell B18 decreases by 12,000, changing from 140,000 to 128,000. An increase to the accounts payable account is a debit.

3. Compare the total asset result in cell B14 with the total liabilities and owner's equity result in cell B29.

   The result is the same in both cells (*452,200*). The balance sheet equation *Assets = liabilities + equity* is correct, indicating that the balance sheet was updated correctly: a debit in one account was offset by a credit in another account.

4. Click the Save button on the Quick Access Toolbar.
5. If printed work is required by your instructor, print the workbook.
6. Save and close the workbook.

Model Answer

12.14 Determining the Gross Profit Margin

The **gross profit margin** expresses the profits of a business as a percentage of the total sales revenues generated. Using a percentage, rather than a value, for this measurement allows the profits of businesses of varying sizes to be compared. Gross profit margin is used to analyze how efficiently a company utilizes labor and supplies. It is also used to analyze what percentage of revenues is available to cover operating expenses. Gross profit margin can also be used to determine the financial success of a particular product.

Tutorial

Calculating the Gross Profit Margin

▸ Know This about the gross profit margin

— A company must have a sufficient gross profit margin to pay for its operating expenses.

— Gross profit margin is used to compare a company with its competitors. If a competitor has a higher gross profit margin, it is operating more efficiently.

— To calculate the gross profit margin, use the equation *Gross profit margin = (sales – cost of goods sold) / sales*.

— The gross profit margin can be used to create budgets and forecast future activities, as it shows how profitable a product or business is.

— In general, a gross profit margin of 25% or higher is considered good by most market analysts. However, profit margins vary considerably between industries.

On the Job

Task 12.14 Calculating the Gross Profit Margin

During the first year of operation, Devon put in many hours at DV Auto Parts to avoid the high labor costs of hiring others. He was also able to take advantage of discounts from suppliers for signing on as a new customer. Going into the second year of business, he knows he needs to cut back on his hours and he also knows those discounts will no longer be available. He wonders whether his business is healthy enough to absorb those changes. Devon asks you to calculate the gross profit margin for the year ending December 31, 2019, to analyze how efficiently his company used labor and supplies in its first year of operations.

1. Open the data file **12-DVAutoParts-Analysis**.
2. With the Analysis worksheet active, click in cell D7, type Gross Profit Margin, and then press the Enter key.
3. Click in cell E7, type =(B5-B6)/B5, and then press Ctrl + Enter.

   The formula entered in cell E7 expresses the equation *Gross profit margin = (sales – cost of goods sold) / sales*.
4. Apply the Percentage format to cell E7.

   The result *40%* displays in cell E7 (see Figure 12.22). The gross profit margin for DV Auto Parts is 40%, which is very good. With this gross profit margin, Devon makes projections for the future that suggest he can consider cutting back his hours in his second year of operation and should be able to operate without all the first-year discounts.
5. Click the Save button on the Quick Access Toolbar.

Figure 12.22 Income Statement with Gross Profit Margin Calculated

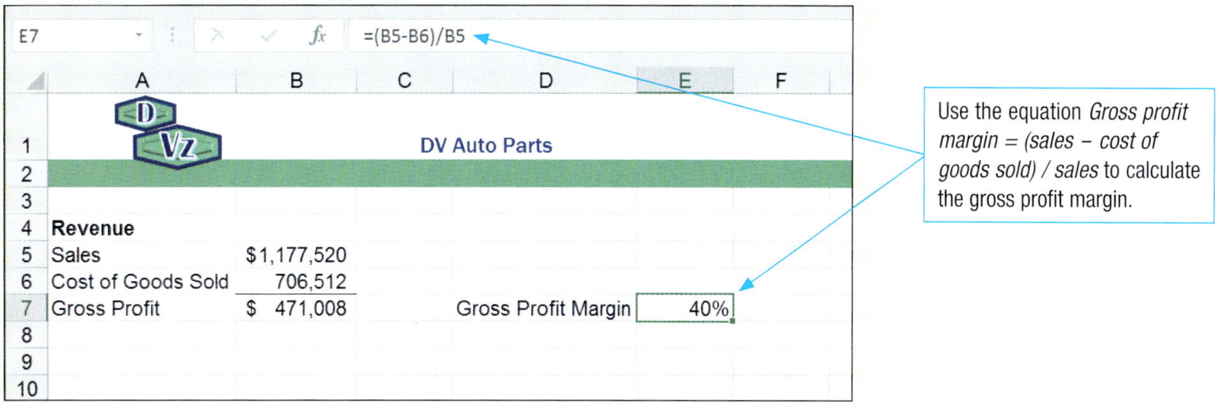

Model Answer

12.15 Finding the Contribution Margin Ratio and the Break-Even Point

Tutorial
Finding the Contribution Margin Ratio and the Break-Even Point

Break-even analysis is used to determine the amount of revenue a company must earn to cover the costs of doing business and start to make a profit. The **break-even point** of a product, service, or business is the point at which its sales exactly cover its expenses. The break-even point is used to calculate when a product, service, or business will be profitable. There are a variety of applications for the break-even point. For example, how many units of one product need to be sold for the product to be profitable or how many service calls need to be completed before a business starts to make a profit.

To calculate the break-even point, you first have to calculate the contribution margin. The contribution margin is the amount of money a company has to pay its fixed costs after it pays all of its variable costs. The contribution margin can also be used to calculate the profit contribution of a specific product. When the contribution margin is expressed as a percentage, it is referred to as the **contribution margin ratio**.

Calculating the break-even point allows companies or businesses to calculate the margin of safety. The **margin of safety** indicates the amount by which the sales of a company could decrease before the company became unprofitable.

▸ Know This about finding the break-even point and contribution margin ratio

— To calculate the break-even point in sales dollars for multiple products or services or for a business, use the equation *Break-even point = fixed costs / contribution margin*.

— To calculate the contribution margin ratio, use the equation *Contribution margin ratio = (sales – variable costs) / sales*, and then format the result as a percentage.

— To calculate the contribution margin ratio for a specific product, use the equation *Contribution margin ratio = (sales from a specific product – variable costs for the specific product) / sales from the specific product*, and then format the result as a percentage.

▸ Know This about mixed costs

— The cost of goods sold is typically the largest variable cost of a business that sells products (see Section 12.3 in this chapter). However, the cost of goods sold could include fixed costs as well as variable costs. For example, in a production business, direct labor is included in cost of goods sold, although at least part of direct labor can be considered a fixed cost because some production staff are required regardless of production volume. This is sometimes referred to as a **mixed cost** or *mixed expense*.

▸ Know This about calculating the margin of safety

— To calculate the margin of safety in sales dollars, use the equation *Margin of safety = current sales level – break-even point*.

— To express the margin of safety ratio as a percentage, use the equation *Margin of safety ratio = (current sales level – break-even point) / current sales level,* and then format the result as a percentage.

On the Job

Task 12.15 Finding the Contribution Margin Ratio and the Break-Even Point

To set projections for the coming year, Devon needs to know the point at which DV Auto Parts sales exactly covered expenses for the year ending December 31, 2019. Fixed costs are all included in the total operating expenses for the year. Use that information to calculate the variable costs (cost of goods sold), contribution margin ratio, fixed costs, and break-even point.

1. With the 12-DVAutoParts-Analysis workbook open and the Analysis worksheet active, click in cell D8, type Variable Costs, and then press the Tab key.
2. Type =B6 and then press Ctrl + Enter.

   The variable costs display in cell E8 (see Figure 12.23).
3. Click in cell D9, type Contribution Margin Ratio, and then press the Tab key.
4. Type =(B5-E8)/B5 and then press Ctrl + Enter.
5. Apply the Percentage format to cell E9.

   The contribution margin ratio is calculated as the difference between sales and variable expenses. The result, *40%*, displays in cell E9.
6. Click in cell D10, type Fixed Costs, and then press the Tab key.
7. Enter =B18 and then press the Enter key.

   The fixed costs are calculated and the result displays in cell E10.
8. With the insertion point in cell D11, type Break-Even Point, and then press the Tab key.
9. Type =E10/E9 and then press the Enter key.

   The break-even point displays in cell E11. This is the point at which DV Auto Parts sales exactly covered expenses during the year 2019 (see Figure 12.23).
10. If printed work is required by your instructor, print the workbook.
11. Save and close the workbook.

Figure 12.23 Income Statement with Variable Costs, Contribution Margin Ratio, Fixed Costs, and Break-Even Point Calculated

E11 =E10/E9

	A	B	C	D	E	F
1				DV Auto Parts		
2						
3						
4	**Revenue**					
5	Sales	$1,177,520				
6	Cost of Goods Sold	706,512				
7	Gross Profit	$ 471,008		Gross Profit Margin	40%	
8				Variable Costs	706,512	
9				Contribution Margin Ratio	40%	
10				Fixed Costs	187,700	
11	**Operating Expenses**			Break-Even Point	469,250	
12	Salaries	120,000				
13	Rent	50,000				
14	Utilities	10,000				
15	Insurance	4,000				
16	Advertising	2,500				
17	Depreciation Expense	1,200				
18	Total Operating Expenses	187,700				
19						

Use the equation *Break-even point = fixed costs / contribution margin ratio.* The break-even point indicates the point at which sales exactly cover expenses.

Model Answer

MOS 5.1.1

12.16 Charting the Break-Even Point

A **cost-volume-profit (CVP) chart** provides a visual that quickly shows the break-even point—the point at which total sales revenue equals total costs or expenses. This is the point where profit will begin to accumulate. It also illustrates the relationship between costs, sales volume, and profitability.

A CVP chart is typically used to illustrate when the total costs and total revenues intersect given different output or sales levels (see Figure 12.24). The amount of profit or loss at any sales or output level can be determined from the chart. It also shows how variable costs change with production volume but fixed costs stay the same regardless of the production volume.

Tutorial

Charting the Break-Even Point

Figure 12.24 CVP Chart Illustrating the Break-Even Point

	A	B	C	D
1		DV Auto Parts		
2				
3				Part #E8-978-02
4	Units Sold	Fixed Costs	Total Costs	Total Revenue
5	100	$ 1,700	$ 2,550	$ 510
6	200	1,700	2,950	738
7	300	1,700	3,200	1,088
8	400	1,700	3,500	1,470
9	500	1,700	3,750	1,988
10	600	1,700	4,000	2,680
11	700	1,700	4,250	3,783
12	800	1,700	4,500	4,725
13	900	1,700	4,750	5,344
14	1000	1,700	5,000	7,500
15				
16				
17				

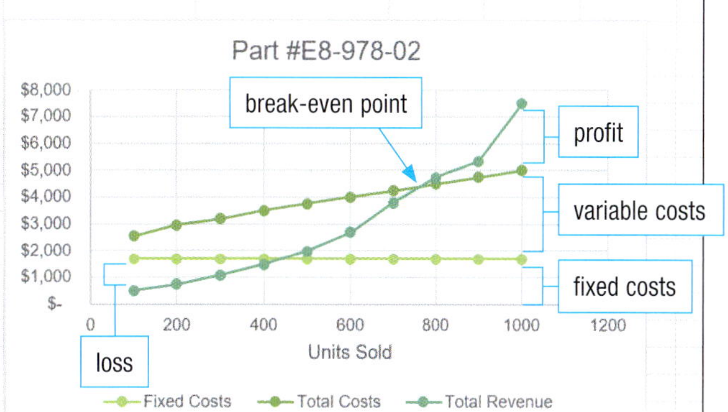

▸ Know This about charting the break-even point

— To chart the break-even point, enter product data in a worksheet. You will need to include the number of units sold or output level, fixed costs, total costs (fixed + variable costs), and revenue generated. In the example shown in Figure 12.24 on page 583, the variable costs decrease and the revenue increases with the number of units sold due to bulk pricing.

— To create a CVP chart in Excel, select the chart data in the worksheet, click the Insert Scatter (X, Y) or Bubble Chart button in the Charts group on the Insert tab, and then click a scatter chart subtype option.

— The break-even point displays as the point where the two lines or curves intersect in the chart.

▸ Know More about charting the break-even point

– An additional line illustrating the variable costs could be added to the break-even point chart by adding the data to the worksheet and then modifying the data series to include the data in the chart.

On the Job

Task 12.16 Charting the Break-Even Point

Devon is meeting with a wholesaler tomorrow to arrange a contract for purchasing inventory of part #E8-978-02 for his company's second year of operation. Before making a purchasing decision, he would like to know the quantity he needs to sell before he earns a profit on this product. He will use the result to assess whether the product will be profitable based on the previous year's sales. He has already calculated the revenue and costs associated with the product based on sales volume from the wholesaler quote and the previous year's sales, and he asks you to calculate the break-even point. Use an Excel chart to create a visual that will quickly give him that information.

1. Open the data file **12-DVAutoParts-Parts**.
2. With the Part #E8-978-02 worksheet active, select the range A4:D14 in the Part #E8-978-02 table.
3. Click the Insert tab and then click the Insert Scatter (X, Y) or Bubble Chart button in the Charts group.

   A drop-down gallery displays.
4. Click the *Scatter with Straight Lines and Markers* option (first column, second row).

   A scatter chart displays in the worksheet, illustrating where revenues and costs intersect, which is the point at which break-even occurs (see Figure 12.24 on page 583).
5. With the chart selected, click the Chart Elements button.

   A side menu displays.
6. Click the *Axis Titles* option arrow.

   A second side menu displays.
7. Click the *Primary Horizontal* check box.

   A check mark appears in the *Axis Titles* check box and in the *Primary Horizontal* check box, and the *Axis Title* text box appears below the horizontal axis in the chart.
8. Type Units Sold and then press the Enter key.

   The text *Units Sold* appears in the *Axis Title* text box.
9. Click the *Chart Title* text box, type Part #E8-978-02, and then press the Enter key.

   The text *Part #E8-978-02* appears in the *Chart Title* text box.

10. If printed work is required by your instructor, print the workbook.
11. Click the Save button on the Quick Access toolbar.

Model Answer

MOS Expert 3.4.3

Tutorial

Using the Goal Seek Feature to Determine the Break-Even Point

12.17 Using Goal Seek to Determine the Break-Even Point

In Chapter 10, Section 10.14, you learned to use the Goal Seek feature as a tool for what-if analysis. The Goal Seek feature can also be used to determine the break-even point. For example, the Goal Seek feature can be used to calculate how many units of a product need to be sold to break even.

▸ **Know This** about using the Goal Seek feature to determine the break-even point

— Enter the values in a worksheet.

— Enter a formula to calculate the net income (or net profit/loss).

— To set Goal Seek options, click in any cell in the worksheet containing the values and formula to be used, click the What-If Analysis button in the Forecast group on the Data tab, click the *Goal Seek* option at the drop-down list, set options at the Goal Seek dialog box (see Figure 12.25), and then click the OK button to close the Goal Seek dialog box and display the Goal Seek Status dialog box.

— To update the worksheet with the solution data, click the OK button at the Goal Seek Status dialog box; to close the dialog box without updating the worksheet, click the Cancel button.

On the Job

Task 12.17 Using the Goal Seek Feature to Determine the Break-Even Point

At the wholesaler meeting tomorrow, Devon is also planning on arranging a contract for purchasing inventory of part #E8-450-07 for his company's second year of operation. In the first year of operation, 850 units were sold, which generated a net income of $4,700. Before making a purchasing decision, he would like to know the quantity he needs to sell before he earns a profit on this product. He asks you to calculate the break-even point. Use the Goal Seek feature to calculate the break-even point.

1. With 12-DVAutoParts-Parts workbook open, click the Part #E8-450-07 sheet tab to make the worksheet active and then click in cell B10.
2. Click the Data tab, click the What-If Analysis button in the Forecast group, and then click the *Goal Seek* option.

   The Goal Seek dialog box displays with the cell reference *B10* in the *Set cell* text box (see Figure 12.25).
3. Click in the *To value* text box, type 0, and then press the Tab key.

   The insertion point is in the *By changing cell* text box.
4. Click in cell B4.

   $B$4 displays in the *By changing cell* text box.

5. Click the OK button.

   The Goal Seek Status dialog box displays a solution (see Figure 12.26) and the solution appears in the worksheet: *774* units would need to be sold for the company to break even on this product.

6. Click the OK button.

   The dialog box is closed and the solution continues to display in the worksheet.

7. If printed work is required by your instructor, print the workbook.
8. Save and close the workbook.

Figure 12.25 Setting Goal Seek Options to Calculate the Break-Even Point

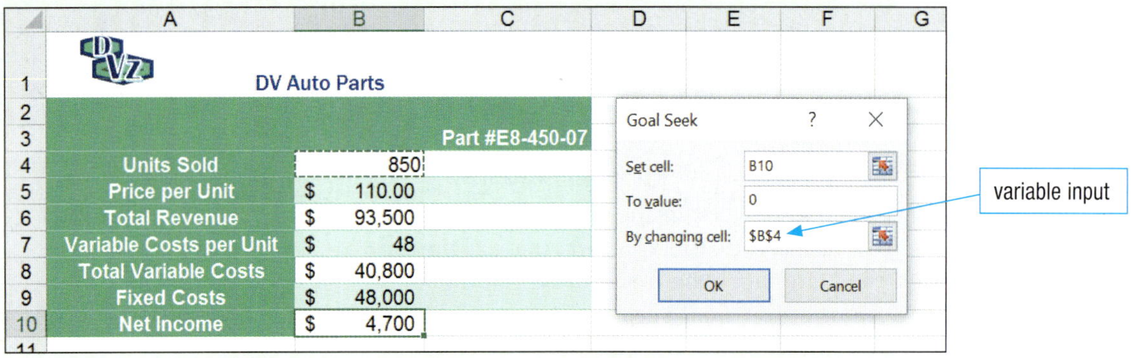

Figure 12.26 Goal Seek Feature Calculating the Break-Even Point

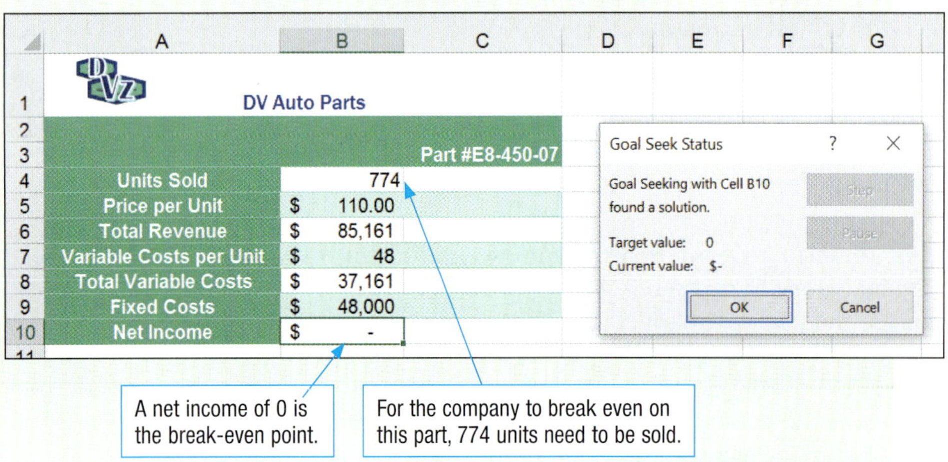

Model Answer

12.18 Creating a Statement of Cash Flows

MOS 4.1.2

Tutorial

Creating a Statement of Cash Flows Using the Indirect Method

The **statement of cash flows** is a primary financial document that records the cash flows into and out of a business or organization (see Figure 12.27). The statement of cash flows focuses on activities that generate and use cash, including the operations, investments, and financing areas of a business. Operating activities consist of cash inflows and outflows from the main business activities, such as product sales and payroll. Investing activities consist of payments for long-term assets and cash received from the sale of long-term assets. Financing activities consist of activities that will change the equity or borrowings of a business, such as the sale of company shares or dividend payments.

Figure 12.27 Statement of Cash Flows

	A	B	C
1	DV Auto Parts		
2			
3	**Statement of Cash Flows**		
4	*for the year ended December 31, 2019*		
5			
6	**Cash Flows from Operating Activities**		
7	Net income	$ 188,908	
8	Adjustments to reconcile net income to		
9	net cash provided by operating activities:		
10	Depreciation on fixed assets	5,800	
11	**(Increase) decrease in current assets:**		
12	Accounts receivable	(120,000)	
13	Inventory	(178,000)	
14	**Increase (decrease) in current liabilities:**		
15	Accounts payable	128,000	
16	Accrued expenses	125,000	
17	**Net Cash Provided by Operating Activities**	149,708	
18			
19	**Cash Flows from Investing Activities**		
20	Purchase of equipment	(140,000)	
21	**Net Cash Used in Investing Activities**	(140,000)	
22			
23	**Cash Flows from Financing Activities**		
24	Payments on line of credit	10,292	
25	**Net Cash Used in Financing Activities**	10,292	
26	**Net Increase (Decrease) in Cash**	20,000	
27			
28	Beginning Cash Balance	-	
29	**Ending Cash Balance**	$ 20,000	
30			

The statement of cash flows documents the flow of cash into and out of a business, focusing on the different activities of the business, the net increase or decrease in cash, and the resulting cash balance at the end of the period.

The statement of cash flows is used to analyze trends in business performance that are not visible in other financial statements, such as the accounts receivable turnover rate. Many investors and creditors view the statement of cash flows as the most transparent of the financial statements. It is used as an analysis tool when there is a discrepancy between the profits and the cash flow generated by a business.

▸ Know This about creating a statement of cash flows

- A statement of cash flows presents the inflows and outflows of cash in the different activities of the business, the net increase or decrease in cash, and the resulting cash balance at the end of the period.
- A statement of cash flows can be created using a direct or an indirect method. Most businesses use the indirect method.
- To create a statement of cash flows using the indirect method, begin with the net income or loss reported in the income statement and then make a series of adjustments to calculate the amount of net cash provided by operating activities.
- The direct method uses major classes of cash receipts as its starting point and is a much more complex method compared to the indirect method.

▸ Know More about creating a statement of cash flows

- The statement of cash flows is one of the major financial statements that all publicly listed companies, which are regulated by the Securities and Exchange Commission, must prepare at the end of every quarter and fiscal year.

— The cash balance at the end of the statement of cash flows is the same as the entry for the cash account in the company's balance sheet.
— Use the SUM function to calculate the subtotals of the operating activities, investing activities, and financing activities sections in the statement of cash flows.
— To calculate the net increase (decrease) in cash, add the subtotals of the operating activities, investing activities, and financing activities sections in the statement of cash flows.

On the Job

Task 12.18 Creating a Statement of Cash Flows Using the Indirect Method

Devon has started to create a statement of cash flows for the year ended December 31, 2019, so that he can analyze the cash flow into and out of the business during its first year of operations. He has entered some data and formatting. Devon would like you to add the statement heading and fill in missing data to complete the statement.

1. Open the data file **12-DVAutoParts-CashFlow**.
2. With the Statement of Cash Flows worksheet active, click in cell A3, type Statement of Cash Flows, and then press the Enter key.

   The text *Statement of Cash Flows* displays in cell A3, and cell A4 is active.
3. Type for the year ended December 31, 2019 and then press the Enter key.

   The text *for the year ended December 31, 2019* displays in cell A4, and cell A5 is active.
4. Click in cell B7, type 188908, and then press the Enter key.

   The value *$188,908* appears in cell B7. This is the net income reported in the income statement for the accounting period.
5. Click in cell B13, type -178000, and then press the Enter key.

   The value *(178,000)* displays in cell B13. This is the inventory value reported for the accounting period. It is a negative value because it represents cash outflow.
6. Click in cell B17, type =SUM(B7:B16), and then press the Enter key.

   The net cash provided by the operating expenses is calculated and the value *149,708* displays in cell B17.
7. Click in cell B20, type -140000, and then press the Enter key.

   The value *(140,000)* displays in cell B20. This is the amount of cash spent purchasing equipment for the business. It is a negative value because it represents a cash outflow.
8. Type =B20 and then press the Enter key.

   The result *(140,000)* displays in cell B21. The result equals the value in cell B20 because there is only one investing activity for this accounting period.
9. Click in cell B26, type =B17+B21+B25, and then press the Enter key.

   The net increase (decrease) in cash is calculated and the result, *20,000*, appears in cell B26. This is the sum of the net cash inflows and outflows from all the activities in the business during the accounting period.

10. Click in cell B29, type =B26+B28, and then press the Enter key.
    The ending cash balance is calculated and the result, *$20,000*, appears in cell B29. This amount matches the entry in the cash account in the balance sheet for the same accounting period.
11. If printed work is required by your instructor, print the workbook.
12. Save and close the workbook.

Model Answer

12.19 Projecting Future Income and Expenses

MOS 2.1.4

Tutorial

Using Interpolation to Project Future Income on a Linear Trend

A **financial projection** is a forecast of future income and expenses. Financial projections are used to plan and budget and measure success. Key financial documents needed when creating a projection are the balance sheet, income statement, and statement of cash flows. Economic and industry data are also required. For example, sales projections for future years will be based on the previous year(s) sales along with industry and economic data.

The Fill Series command in Excel can be used to automatically generate future values based on existing data, such as sales or expenses. It can also be used to automatically extrapolate or interpolate values based on linear trends or growth trends. An **extrapolated value** is generated from a starting value, such as the sales revenue from the previous year, and requires a **step value**, such as 15%. An **interpolated value** is generated from a starting value and a projected ending value, such as a sales goal (see Figure 12.28).

Figure 12.28 Interpolated Values

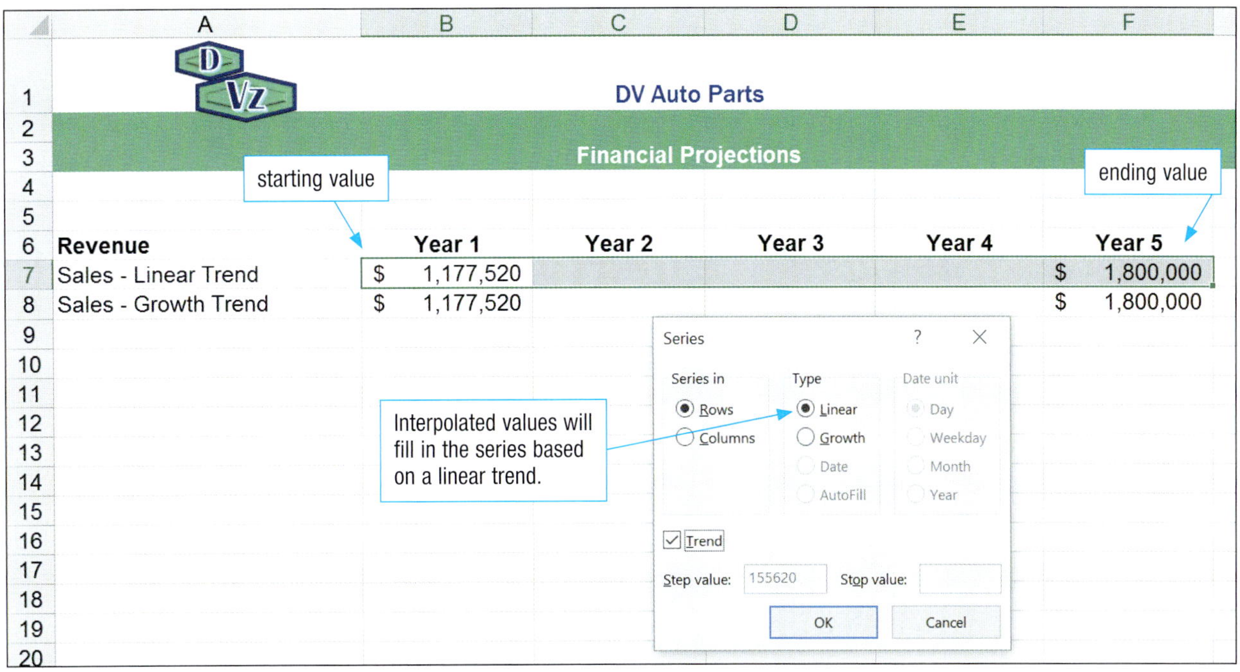

In a **linear trend**, values change by a constant amount each period. In a **growth trend**, values change by a constant percentage each period. If you use a growth trend to interpolate values, use the equation *Percentage growth = (year 2 sales – year 1 sales) / year 1 sales* to calculate the percentage growth from year to year.

▸ **Know This** about projecting future income and expenses

— To use interpolation to project future values, enter a starting value in the worksheet, enter an ending value in the worksheet, select the range including the starting and ending values, click the Fill button in the Editing group on the Home tab, click the *Series* option, select the *Rows* or *Columns* option in the *Series in* section at the Series dialog box, select the *Linear* or *Growth* option in the *Type* section, click the *Trend* check box to insert a check mark, and then click the OK button.

— To use extrapolation to project future values, enter a starting value in the worksheet, click the Fill button in the Editing group on the Home tab, click the *Series* option, select the *Rows* or *Columns* option in the *Series in* section at the Series dialog box, select the *Linear* or *Growth* option in the *Type* section, enter a step value in the *Step value* measurement box, and then click the OK button.

On the Job

Task 12.19 Using Interpolation to Project Future Income

Devon would like to project the DV Auto Parts sales for the next four years—years 2 through 5 of operation—so that he can properly staff, budget, and ensure he has enough inventory in stock. He would like to compare forecasts using a linear trend versus a growth trend. Devon has set up a sales projection worksheet with the starting and ending values. He used the sales total for year 1 (the year ended December 31, 2019) as the starting value and set an ending value sales goal of $1,800,000 for year 5. He would like you to use interpolation to calculate the projections for years 2 through 4. He would also like you to determine the percentage change from year to year for the growth trend. Use the Fill series button to interpolate linear and growth projections for Devon.

1. Open the data file **12-DVAutoParts-Projections**.
2. With the Sales Projections worksheet active, select the range B7:F7.
3. Click the Home tab, if necessary, and then click the Fill button in the Editing group.

   A drop-down list displays.
4. Click the *Series* option.

   The Series dialog box displays (see Figure 12.29).
5. Click the *Trend* check box.

   A check mark appears in the check box.
6. Verify that the *Rows* radio button in the *Series in* section contains a bullet and the *Linear* radio button in the *Type* section contains a bullet.
7. Click the OK button.

   The Series dialog box closes and future sales values appear between the starting value and the ending value in row 7. The added values are projected values for years 2, 3, and 4 based on a linear trend in sales.
8. Select the range B8:F8.
9. Click the Fill button.

Figure 12.29 Series Dialog Box

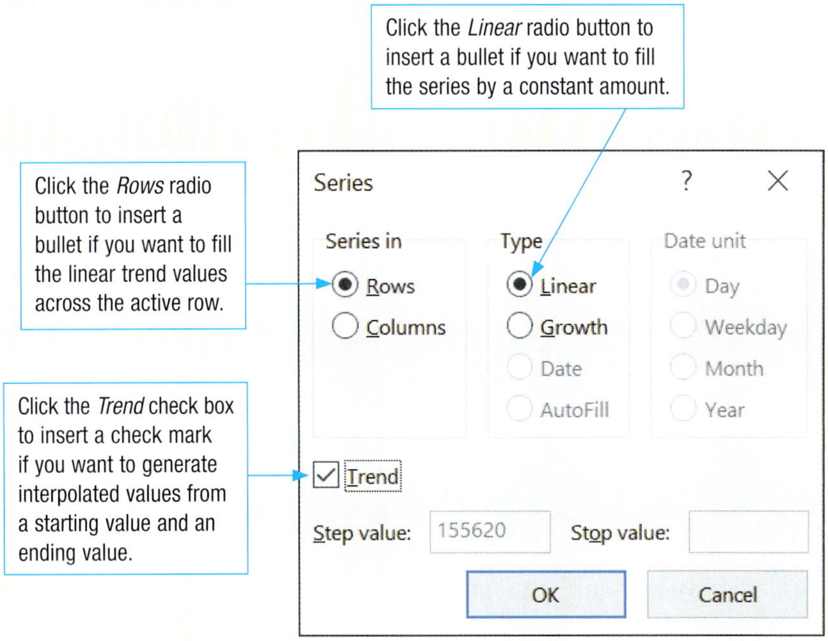

10. Click the *Series* option.

    The Series dialog box displays.

11. Verify that a bullet appears in the *Rows* radio button in the *Series in* section.
12. Click the *Growth* radio button in the *Type* section.

    A bullet appears in the radio button.

13. Click the *Trend* check box.

    A check mark appears in the check box.

14. Click the OK button.

    The Series dialog box closes and future sales values appear between the starting value and the ending value in row 8. The added values are projected values for the years 2, 3, and 4 based on a growth trend.

15. Click in cell H8, type =(C8-B8)/B8, and then press Ctrl + Enter.
16. Apply Percentage formatting to cell H8.

    The result *11%* appears in cell H8. This indicates the growth trend projections would result in an 11% growth in sales from one year to the next.

17. Click the Save button on the Quick Access Toolbar.

Model Answer

12.20 Charting Linear Trends and Growth Trends

MOS 5.1.1

Tutorial

Using a Line Chart to Compare Linear and Growth Trends

Charting linear and growth trend data can make it easier to understand the data, see patterns, and make comparisons. A linear pattern will show a steady decrease or increase in numbers over time. For example, the sale of DVDs would be charted as a straight diagonal line angled downward, illustrating that sales of DVDs are decreasing steadily over time. In comparison, a growth (also called *exponential*) pattern will show data rising (or falling) at an increasing (or decreasing) rate over time and will be charted as a curved line. For example, a growth pattern may show sales of a product were slow when it was first on the market but are expected to pick up after an advertising campaign.

▸ **Know This** about charting linear and growth trends

- To chart linear and a growth trends, select the range containing the trend data in the worksheet, click a chart button in the Charts group, and then click a chart option at the drop-down gallery.
- Select a chart type that will illustrate the trend appropriately.
- A line chart is good for showing comparisons over time.
- When you use a line chart to illustrate a linear trend, the trend appears as a straight line because the values change by a constant amount each period.
- When you use a line chart to illustrate a growth trend, the trend appears as a curve that becomes steeper each period because the values change by a constant percentage and the greatest increase occurs at the end of the series.
- If the results are difficult to compare or understand, use options at the Format Axis task pane to adjust the data points.

▸ Know More about charting linear and growth trends

- You can also use the TREND and GROWTH functions to project trends. The TREND function is used to project values that follow a linear trend, and the GROWTH function is used to project values that follow an exponential curve or growth pattern.

Reminder

To display the Format Axis task pane, double-click one of the values on the vertical axis.

On the Job

Task 12.20 Using a Line Chart to Compare Linear and Growth Trends

Devon has created two scenarios for projected sales growth. One follows a linear trend and the other is based on a growth trend. He would like you to chart the projected sales growth for the next four years based on a linear trend and a growth trend so he can compare the scenarios. Use a line chart for this comparison over time.

1. With the 12-DVAutoParts-Projections workbook open and the Sales Projections worksheet active, select the range A6:F8.
2. Click the Insert tab and then click the Insert Line or Area Chart button in the Charts group.

   A drop-down gallery displays.
3. Click the *Line* option (first option in *2-D Line* section).

   A line chart displays in the worksheet.
4. Click the *Chart Title* text box, type Sales Projections, and then press the Enter key.
5. Double-click one of the values on the vertical axis.

   The Format Axis task pane displays.
6. Triple-click in the *Minimum* text box, type 1000000, and then press the Enter key.

   The minimum value is set to 1,000,000, making it easier to compare data points and read the chart. The linear trend data is charted in a straight line and the growth trend data has a slight curve (see Figure 12.30).
7. If printed work is required by your instructor, print the workbook.
8. Save and then close the workbook.

Figure 12.30 Line Chart Showing Sales Projections for a Linear Trend and a Growth Trend

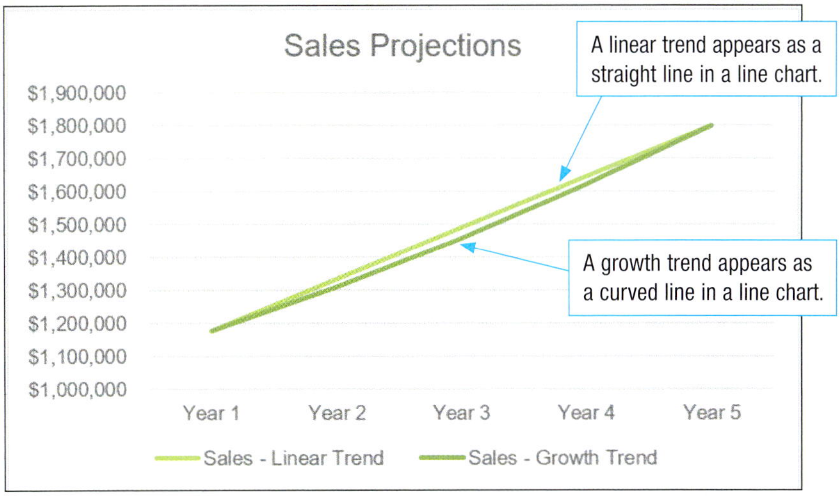

Model Answer

12.21 Creating a Forecast Sheet

Tutorial
Creating a Forecast Sheet

The **Forecast Sheet** feature creates a forecast of predicted data based on historical data. This feature provides a quick way to create a budget or sales forecast. A forecast sheet is created from two related data series, with one of the data series being consistent date or time entries (such as the last day of each month or the end of each year) and the other data series being numerical values. It is important to note that for this feature to work effectively, you should have at least two or three full seasonal cycles in the historical data.

One advantage of using the Forecast Sheet feature compared with using linear and growth projections (discussed in Section 12.19) is that the Forecast Sheet feature automatically recognizes seasonal data and accounts for that seasonality when creating a forecast. It also displays a **confidence interval**, which is the degree of confidence (accuracy) surrounding each predicted value.

▸ **Know This** about the data series for a forecast sheet

- A forecast sheet can be created from two data series that are the same size.
- One of the data series must consist of a timeline series of dates or numbers, and the other data series must be a numerical value series.
- The data series may appear as a data range in a worksheet.

▸ **Know This** about creating a forecast sheet

- To create a forecast sheet, follow these steps:
  1. Select the two related data series, or click in any cell in the data series range.
  2. Click the Forecast Sheet button in the Forecast group on the Data tab.
  3. Click the Create a column chart button at the Create Forecast Worksheet dialog box to change the chart type, or leave the Create a line chart button selected to use the default chart type.

4. Click the *Forecast End* Calendar button and then click an end date at the drop-down calendar.
5. Click the *Options* option and then select additional options at the expanded dialog box (see Figure 12.31).
6. Click the Create button.

— A new forecast sheet automatically displays in a new worksheet to the left of the active sheet.

— The forecast sheet includes the historical data, forecast values, and a line chart or column chart illustrating the trends in the historical and forecast values.

— You can filter the data in the forecast sheet using filter arrows.

— You can resize, move, and format the chart in a forecast sheet, using the same tools used to modify other charts (see Chapter 6).

Figure 12.31 Create Forecast Worksheet Dialog Box

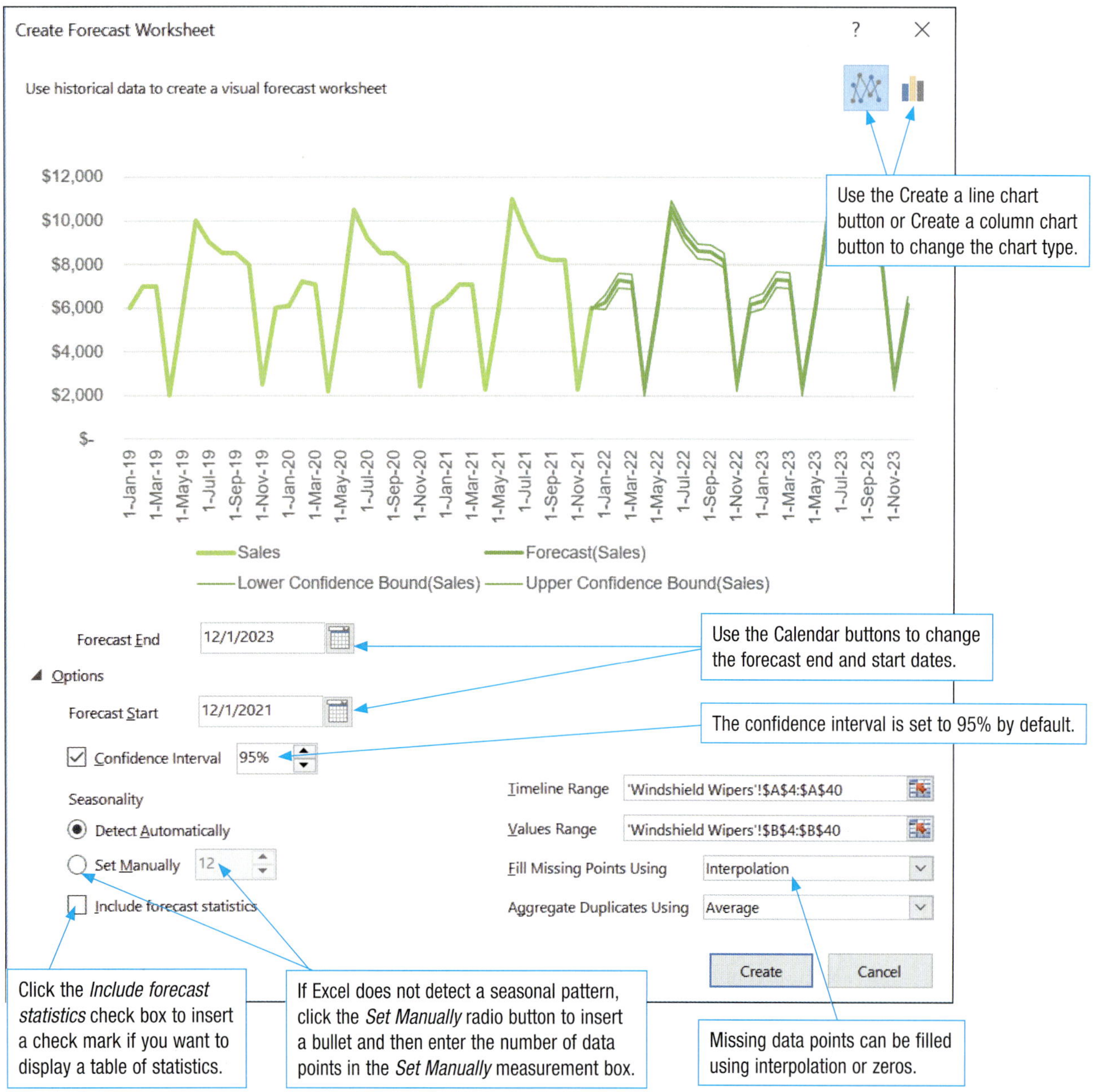

On the Job

Task 12.21 Creating a Forecast Sheet

After his first year in business, Devon is realizing the importance of forecasting sales so that he can keep sufficient product in stock without ordering too much stock. He has also noted that certain product types are subject to seasonal demand. For example, sales of windshield wipers are generally lowest in April and November, which tend to be the driest months in Miami, where Devon's business is located. In contrast, sales of windshield wipers are highest in June, which tends to be the month with the most rain. Devon asks you if there is a quick way to create a sales forecast that takes into consideration seasonal sales. You use some sample data to show Devon that once he has compiled two to three years of historical sales data, he will be able to use the Forecast Sheet feature to predict future sales.

1. Open the data file **12-DVAutoParts-ProductForecast**.

   The Windshield Wipers worksheet is active. A data series consisting of consecutive dates by month displays in the range A4:A40, and a data series consisting of the column headings and sales amounts displays in the adjacent range B4:B40.

2. Click in any cell in the range A4:B40.
3. Click the Data tab and then click the Forecast Sheet button in the Forecast group.

   The Create Forecast Worksheet dialog box displays with a preview of the forecast chart using the default line chart type.

4. Click the *Options* option.

   The dialog box expands.

5. Click the Create button.

   A data table with the historical data, forecast values, and a line chart illustrating the trends in the historical and forecast values displays in a new worksheet named *Sheet1* (see Figure 12.32). Fields in the data table can be filtered, and the forecasted values include a lower and upper confidence value. The seasonal sales pattern was automatically detected by Excel.

6. If printed work is required by your instructor, print the workbook.
7. Save and then close the workbook.

Figure 12.32 Create Forecast Worksheet Dialog Box

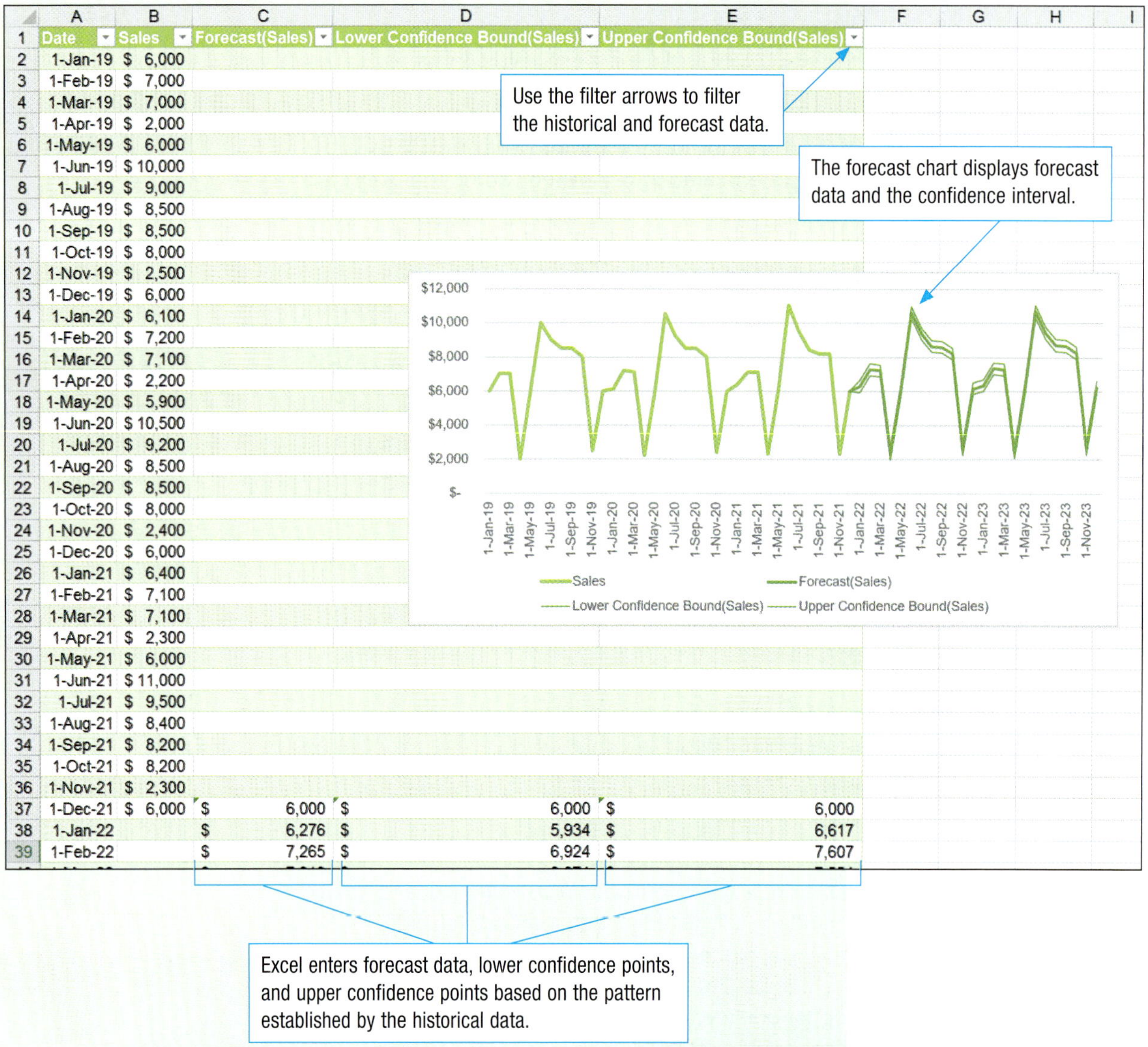

	A	B	C	D	E
1	Date	Sales	Forecast(Sales)	Lower Confidence Bound(Sales)	Upper Confidence Bound(Sales)
2	1-Jan-19	$ 6,000			
3	1-Feb-19	$ 7,000			
4	1-Mar-19	$ 7,000			
5	1-Apr-19	$ 2,000			
6	1-May-19	$ 6,000			
7	1-Jun-19	$ 10,000			
8	1-Jul-19	$ 9,000			
9	1-Aug-19	$ 8,500			
10	1-Sep-19	$ 8,500			
11	1-Oct-19	$ 8,000			
12	1-Nov-19	$ 2,500			
13	1-Dec-19	$ 6,000			
14	1-Jan-20	$ 6,100			
15	1-Feb-20	$ 7,200			
16	1-Mar-20	$ 7,100			
17	1-Apr-20	$ 2,200			
18	1-May-20	$ 5,900			
19	1-Jun-20	$ 10,500			
20	1-Jul-20	$ 9,200			
21	1-Aug-20	$ 8,500			
22	1-Sep-20	$ 8,500			
23	1-Oct-20	$ 8,000			
24	1-Nov-20	$ 2,400			
25	1-Dec-20	$ 6,000			
26	1-Jan-21	$ 6,400			
27	1-Feb-21	$ 7,100			
28	1-Mar-21	$ 7,100			
29	1-Apr-21	$ 2,300			
30	1-May-21	$ 6,000			
31	1-Jun-21	$ 11,000			
32	1-Jul-21	$ 9,500			
33	1-Aug-21	$ 8,400			
34	1-Sep-21	$ 8,200			
35	1-Oct-21	$ 8,200			
36	1-Nov-21	$ 2,300			
37	1-Dec-21	$ 6,000	$ 6,000	$ 6,000	$ 6,000
38	1-Jan-22		$ 6,276	$ 5,934	$ 6,617
39	1-Feb-22		$ 7,265	$ 6,924	$ 7,607

Model Answer

Chapter Summary

12.1

- An income statement is a financial statement that summarizes revenues and expenses generated and shows the resulting net profit or loss. The income statement is used by accountants and business owners to show the profitability of a company during a specific time interval.
- Income statements can be created using a single-step format or a multiple-step format. A single-step income statement uses only one subtraction to arrive at net income. A multiple-step income statement calculates the gross profit, which is the amount of profit after the total cost of goods sold is subtracted from the total sales. It also separates the operating revenues and operating expenses from the nonoperating revenues and nonoperating expenses.

12.2 ▶ The cost of goods sold (COGS) is the accumulated total that a company, organization, or individual spends directly on producing goods and delivering services. In an income statement, the COGS is subtracted from revenue to calculate gross profit. Gross profit is the profit a company makes after deducting the costs associated with producing and selling its products, or the costs associated with providing its services.

12.3 ▶ Variable costs, or variable expenses, and fixed costs, or fixed expenses, are used to analyze the profitability of a business or organization. Variable costs rise as production increases and fall as production decreases. Fixed costs do not vary in the short term, regardless of changes in production or sales levels.

12.4 ▶ In income statements, general and administrative costs are frequently grouped with selling costs in a category called *selling, general, and administrative expenses (SG&A)*. Sales costs include advertising and marketing costs, along with compensation paid to inside and outside salespeople. Analysts and investors often assess the profitability of a business before subtracting the income tax expense.

12.5 ▶ To determine if a business is profitable, calculate the net profit or loss (also called the *bottom line*). Net profit is the amount of profit remaining after total costs and expenses have been subtracted from total income and revenue. Net loss is the amount of loss remaining after total expenses are subtracted from total income and revenue.

12.6 ▶ Identifying common income statement errors is extremely important because many business decisions are based on financial statement data. Common errors in income statements include data entry errors and calculation errors.

12.7 ▶ The data in an income statement can be illustrated in charts to make the data easier to present and analyze. A waterfall chart shows a running total as values are added or subtracted.

12.8 ▶ A balance sheet shows how the resources owned by a business (assets) are financed by debt (liabilities) or by shareholder investments (equity). Liquidity is the ability to pay debts in a timely manner.

▶ Businesses tend to use one of two formats for balance sheets: account format or report format. The account format uses two columns, displaying assets in the left column and liabilities and equity in the right column. The report format lists all items in one column and is the traditional format used by companies.

12.9 ▶ A general journal is the initial financial document in which business transactions are entered in an accounting system. The double entry accounting method is commonly used for entering transactions in the general journal to help ensure that financial statements are accurate and to help identify errors. Double entry accounting is based on the fact that every financial transaction has equal and opposite effects in at least two accounts. It is used to satisfy the equation *Assets = liabilities + equity*.

12.10 ▶ To calculate the value of assets for the balance sheet, it is important to understand the basic accounting cycle for an accounting period, the set-up of the general ledger, and how posting transfers the debit or credit balance of a transaction to the appropriate account. The general ledger contains all the balance sheet accounts, including cash, accounts receivable, equipment, accumulated depreciation, and accounts payable.

12.11 ▶ To create a balance sheet, liabilities must also be calculated. Like assets, liabilities are transferred from the trial balance as part of the accounting cycle. Use the SUM function to calculate the total current liabilities and total long-term liabilities. To calculate the total liabilities, use the equation *Total liabilities = total current liabilities + total long-term liabilities*.

12.12 ▶ The final data that needs to be entered on the balance sheet is equity. Like assets and liabilities, equity data is transferred from the trial balance as part of the accounting cycle.

▶ In the balance sheet, equity may be categorized as owner's equity or stockholders' equity. Owner's equity is the category used when the business is a sole proprietorship (has a single owner) or a partnership. Stockholders' equity is the category used for corporations. In the balance sheet, it may be listed as common stock or preferred stock.

12.13 ▶ When a balance sheet is created, accounting errors can occur because of the large amount of data that is transferred to the balance sheet from other sources. Common balance sheet errors include incorrect classification of assets and liabilities, transposition errors (when numbers are reversed), data entry errors (when data is entered incorrectly), and errors of omission (when data is not entered).

12.14 ▶ The gross profit margin expresses the profits of a business as a percentage of the total sales revenues generated. Using a percentage, rather than a value, allows the profits of businesses of varying sizes to be compared. Gross profit margin is used to analyze how efficiently a company uses labor and supplies. To calculate the gross profit margin, use the equation *Gross profit margin = (sales – cost of goods sold) / sales*.

12.15 ▶ The break-even point of a product, service, or business is the point at which its sales exactly cover its expenses and can begin to be profitable. To calculate the break-even point, you must first calculate the contribution margin, which is the amount of money a company has to pay its fixed costs after it pays all of its variable costs.

12.16 ▶ A cost-volume-profit (CVP) chart provides a visual that quickly shows the break-even point—the point at which total sales revenue equals total costs or expenses. This is the point where profit will begin to accumulate. The CVP chart also illustrates the relationship between costs, sales volume, and profitability.

12.17 ▶ Use the Goal Seek feature to determine the break-even point. For example, the Goal Seek feature can be used to calculate how many units of a product need to be sold to break even.

12.18 ▶ The statement of cash flows is a primary financial document that records the cash flows into and out of a business or organization. The statement of cash flows focuses on activities that generate and use cash, including the operations, investments, and financing areas of a business. Operating activities consist of cash inflows and outflows from the main business activities, such as product sales and payroll.

12.19 ▶ A financial projection is a forecast of future income and expenses. Financial projections are used to plan and budget and measure success. The Fill Series command in Excel can be used to automatically generate future values based on existing data, such as sales or expenses. It can also be used to automatically extrapolate or interpolate values based on linear trends or growth trends.

12.20 ▸ A linear pattern will show a steady decrease or increase in numbers over time and will be charted as a straight line. A growth pattern will show data rising (or falling) at an increasing (or decreasing) rate over time and will be charted as a curved line.

12.21 ▸ Use the Forecast Sheet feature to create a forecast of predicted data based on historical data. This feature will recognize seasonal data and display the confidence interval.

Features Review

Feature	Ribbon Tab, Group	Button, Option
create scatter chart to illustrate cost-volume-profit (CVP) or break-even point	Insert, Charts	
create waterfall chart to illustrate income statement data	Insert, Charts	, *Waterfall*
use extrapolation to project future values	Home, Editing	, *Series*
use Goal Seek to determine break-even point	Data, Forecast	, *Goal Seek*
use interpolation to project future values	Home, Editing	, *Series*

Recheck

Recheck your understanding of the concepts, features, and skills covered in this chapter by taking the Recheck quiz.

Workbook

Access the study tools, review exercises, assessments, and challenges for this chapter in the workbook available from this page in your ebook.

Exporting, Importing, and Transforming Data

Chapter 13

Chapter Goal

To export and import data in various file types and transform imported data.

Learning Objectives

13.1 Embed and link Excel data in a Word document

13.2 Copy, embed, and link Excel data in a PowerPoint presentation

13.3 Break a link to an Excel object

13.4 Copy and append Excel data to an Access table

13.5 Export Excel data as a text file

13.6 Import data into Excel from Access

13.7 Import and append data to Excel from a delimited text file

13.8 Import data into Excel using legacy settings

13.9 Refresh, modify, and delete queries and data connections

13.10 Use the TRIM function to modify text

13.11 Use Flash Fill to transform data

13.12 Use the RIGHT, LEFT, and MID functions to extract characters

13.13 Use the CONCATENATE and CONCAT functions to join text values

13.14 Use the UPPER, LOWER, and PROPER functions to edit text

13.15 Export Excel worksheets and workbooks as PDF and XPS files

13.16 Publish an Excel worksheet as a web page

Precheck

Check your understanding of the concepts, features, and skills covered in this chapter by taking the Precheck quiz.

Data Files

Before beginning the chapter work, download the AE13 folder from this page in your ebook to your storage medium and then make AE13 the active folder. ***Note:*** *Linking between files may not work in OneDrive. You must save the AE13 folder to a computer drive, not your OneDrive account.*

Ebook Links

Access digital resources for this course from your ebook.

SNAP

If you are a SNAP user, go to your SNAP assignments page to complete the Precheck, Tutorials, and Recheck in this chapter.

Preview

On the Job

Scenario: DV Auto Parts

DV Auto Parts has been successfully selling auto parts in Florida since the company was launched in January 2019. Owner Devon Varey has put together a team of sales associates. He holds weekly meetings with the sales team to discuss the company's best-selling and worst-selling products as well as potential untapped markets. Devon asks you to help him prepare a handout and a visual presentation for the next meeting, import new data into the Excel workbook containing sales and inventory data, format the new data, and publish the workbook as a PDF file, an XPS file, and a web page.

Visual Reference: Files with Imported Data

Figure 13.1 Word Document with Data Embedded and Linked from an Excel Workbook

When data embedded from an Excel workbook is selected, the Word ribbon is temporarily replaced by the Excel ribbon.

Data embedded from an Excel workbook can be formatted using the temporary Excel ribbon.

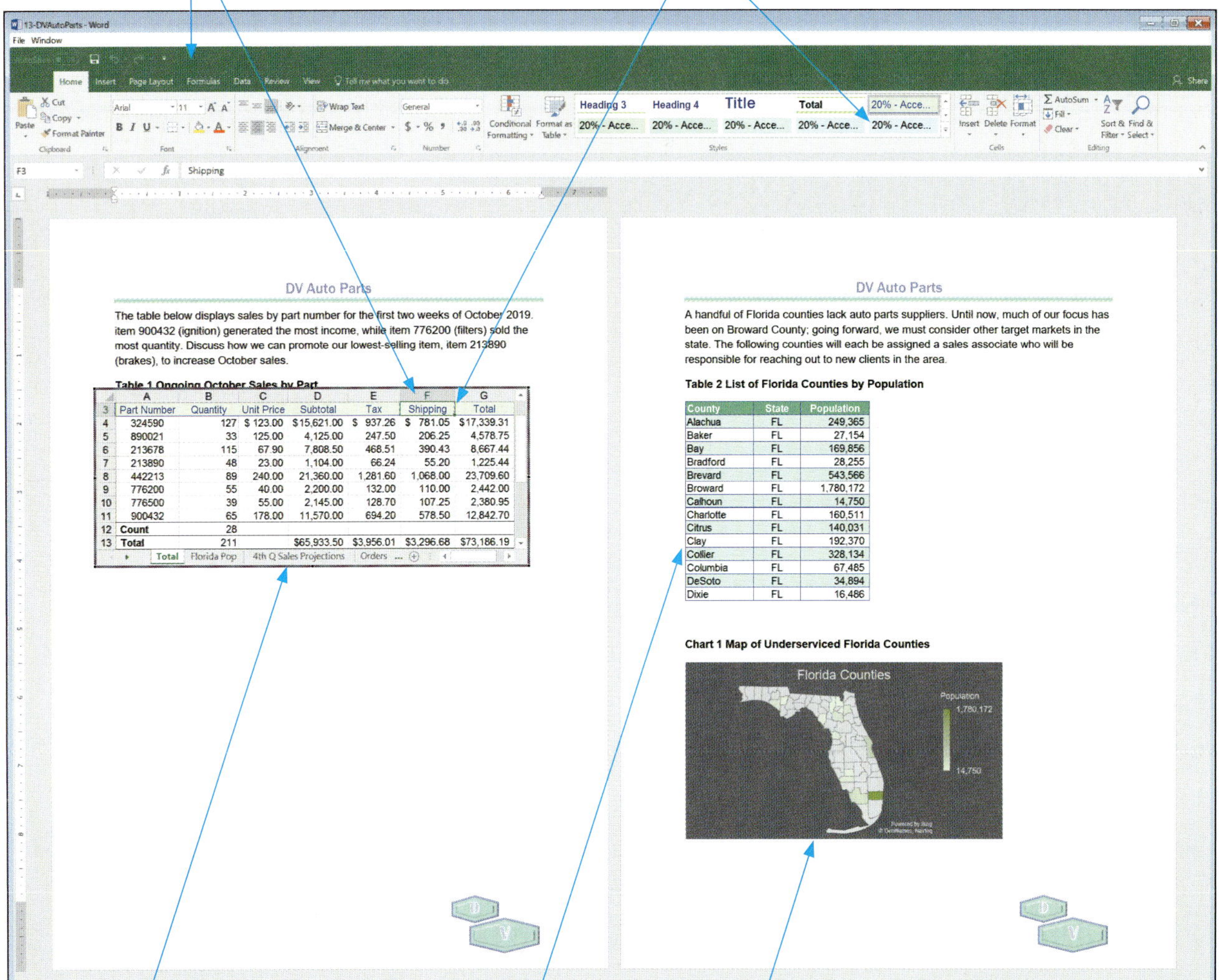

Table 1 contains data that has been embedded from an Excel workbook.

Table 2 is an object linked to data in an Excel workbook. To change the data in this linked table, you must change the data in the Excel workbook.

Chart 1 is an embedded map chart containing all the worksheets from the Excel workbook.

Visual Reference

Figure 13.2 Excel Worksheet with Data Imported from an Access Database and Transformed

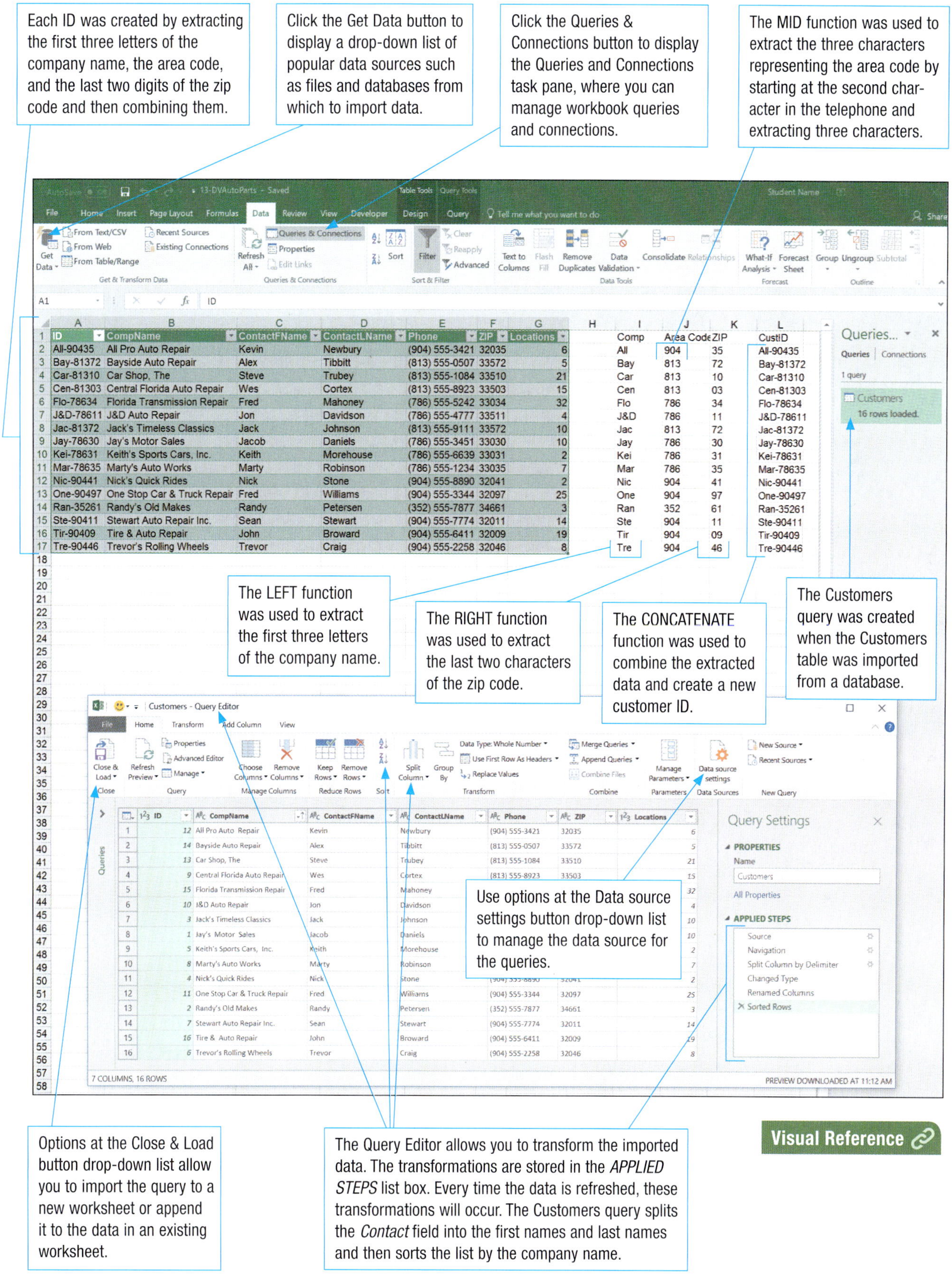

Visual Reference

13.1 Embedding and Linking Excel Data in a Word Document

Applications in Office 365 and Office 2016 by Microsoft are designed for **integration** so that you can easily create an object in one application and copy it to another application. For example, you can use Excel data in other Microsoft programs by copying cells to the Clipboard and then pasting them in the destination files. Integration is possible because the applications have a **common interface** that allows each application to understand another application's file format.

Tutorials

Copying and Pasting Excel Data in a Word Document

Copying and Embedding Excel Data in a Word Document

Copying and Linking Excel Data in a Word Document

▸ Know This about integrating data

- There are three ways to integrate data: copying and pasting, embedding, and linking.
- An **import** brings data from other applications into Excel, and an **export** copies data from Excel into another application.
- During an import or export, the file containing the original data is called the **source file**, and the file to which the original data is being copied, embedded, or linked is called the **destination file**.

▸ Know This about copying and pasting data

- When you copy data from a source file and **paste** it in a destination file as data, the destination file does not store any information about the source file.
- If you later make changes to the data in the source file, they will not be reflected in the destination file.
- To change pasted data in the destination file, you use the tools available in the destination file. For example, if you paste data from an Excel workbook in a Word document, you use Word tools to edit the pasted data.

▸ Know This about object linking and embedding (OLE)

- Linking and embedding between applications in Office 365 and Office 2016 uses a technology called **object linking and embedding (OLE)**. This technology ensures that information about the program that created the object is stored in the object when it is pasted.

▸ Know This about embedding data

- When you copy data from a source file and paste it in a destination file as an **embedded object**, the data is stored in the destination file and is not connected to the source file.
- If you later make changes to the data in the source file, they will not be reflected in the destination file.
- Embedding increases the size of the destination file because it embeds the entire source file. For example, if you select a range of data in an Excel worksheet and embed it in a Word document, you see just the selected range in the Word document. However, if you open the embedded Excel object for editing, you are able to scroll the entire Excel worksheet containing the data and click sheet tabs to move to different worksheets in the workbook.

— To change embedded data in the destination file, you use the application used to create the object. For example, if you embed data from an Excel workbook in a Word document, you double-click the embedded object to make the Excel ribbon temporarily available and then use tools on the Excel ribbon to edit the embedded data. Even though you are editing the file using the Excel ribbon, you are not changing the source file.

▸ **Know This** about linking data

— When you copy data from a source file and paste it in a destination file as a **linked object**, the data is stored in the destination file and also connected to the source file.

— If you later make changes to the data in the source file, they will be reflected in the destination file.

— To change linked data in the destination file, you either open the source file and make the changes in the source application, or double-click the object in the destination file to open the destination application and make the changes in the destination application.

▸ **Know This** about which integration method to use

— Copy and paste the data if you are not likely to update or edit it afterward.

— Embed the data if you want to be able to edit it in the application in which it was created.

— Link the data if you want it to update the data in the destination file when changes are made in the source file.

Reminder
To copy and paste, you can use commands in the Clipboard group on the Home tab or options at the pop-up menu that displays when you right-click a cell or range.

▸ **Know This** about copying and pasting Excel data in a Word document

— To copy data from an Excel workbook and paste it in a Word document, select the data in the Excel workbook, press Ctrl + C, place the insertion point in the Word document, and then press Ctrl + V.

— Data copied from Excel is pasted in Word as a Word table.

— When Excel data is copied and pasted in Word, formulas are converted to numbers.

— To edit Excel data that has been copied and pasted in Word, use the tools on the Word ribbon.

— To delete Excel data that has been pasted into a table in Word, select the table, click the Delete button in the Rows & Columns group on the Table Tools Layout tab, and then click the *Delete Table* option at the drop-down list.

Reminder
To select a table, click in the table and then click the table selector button in the upper left corner of the table.

On the Job

Task 13.1a Copying and Pasting Excel Data in a Word Document

Devon is creating a Word document that he will print as a handout for next week's sales meeting. He has written an outline of the topics he wants to cover, and he wants you to insert data from an Excel workbook in the Word document as a table to support the first topic. Copy the data from the Excel workbook and then paste it into the Word document.

Note: Be sure to open the data files for this chapter from a computer drive, not your OneDrive account.

1. Open the data file **13-DVAutoParts**.
2. Click the Total sheet tab, if necessary, to make the worksheet active.
3. Select the range A3:G13.
4. Press Ctrl + C.
5. Start Word 2016 and then open the data file **13-DVAutoPartsRpt** from the AE13 folder on your storage medium.
6. Click the Enable Editing button if a security warning displays in the message bar below the ribbon, stating that the document is in protected view.
7. Place the insertion point at the end of the heading *Table 1 Ongoing October Sales by Part* on the first page of the Word document and then press the Enter key.
   The insertion point appears at the beginning of the next line.
8. Press Ctrl + V.
   The range from Excel is pasted as a Word table below the Table 1 heading in the Word document. The insertion point is below the table.
9. Click the Save button on the Quick Access Toolbar. Leave both the Word document and the Excel workbook open for the next task.

Model Answer

▸ Know This about embedding Excel data in a Word document

— To embed data from an Excel workbook in a Word document, select the data in the Excel workbook, press Ctrl + C, place the insertion point in the Word document, click the Paste button arrow in the Clipboard group on the Home tab, click the *Paste Special* option at the drop-down gallery, click the *Microsoft Excel Worksheet Object* option in the *As* list box at the Paste Special dialog box, and then click the OK button.

— After data is copied from Excel and embedded in Word, the data in the Word document is not connected to the data in the Excel workbook, and changes made to the data in the Excel workbook are not reflected in the Word document.

— To edit Excel data that has been pasted in Word as an embedded object, open the object for editing by double-clicking it and then use tools on the Excel ribbon that is temporarily available (see Figure 13.3).

— When an embedded Excel object is selected, a border surrounds the object and the Word ribbon is temporarily replaced with the Excel ribbon. The entire workbook is available for editing.

— When you are finished editing a selected embedded Excel object, click in the document outside the object to restore the Word ribbon.

— To delete an embedded Excel object, click the object and then press the Delete key.

▸ Know More ways to display the Paste Special dialog box

- Press Alt + Ctrl + V.

▸ Know More ways to use Paste Special

- Click the Paste button arrow in the Clipboard group to open the Paste button drop-down gallery.
- See Table 13.1 for a list of options at the Paste button drop-down gallery.

Reminder

After the data is pasted, use the Paste Options button that displays below the lower right corner of the pasted cell or range to display the pop-up gallery. The gallery includes a live preview of how the contents will display. For a list of options, see Table 13.1.

Figure 13.3 Selected Excel Object Embedded in a Word Document

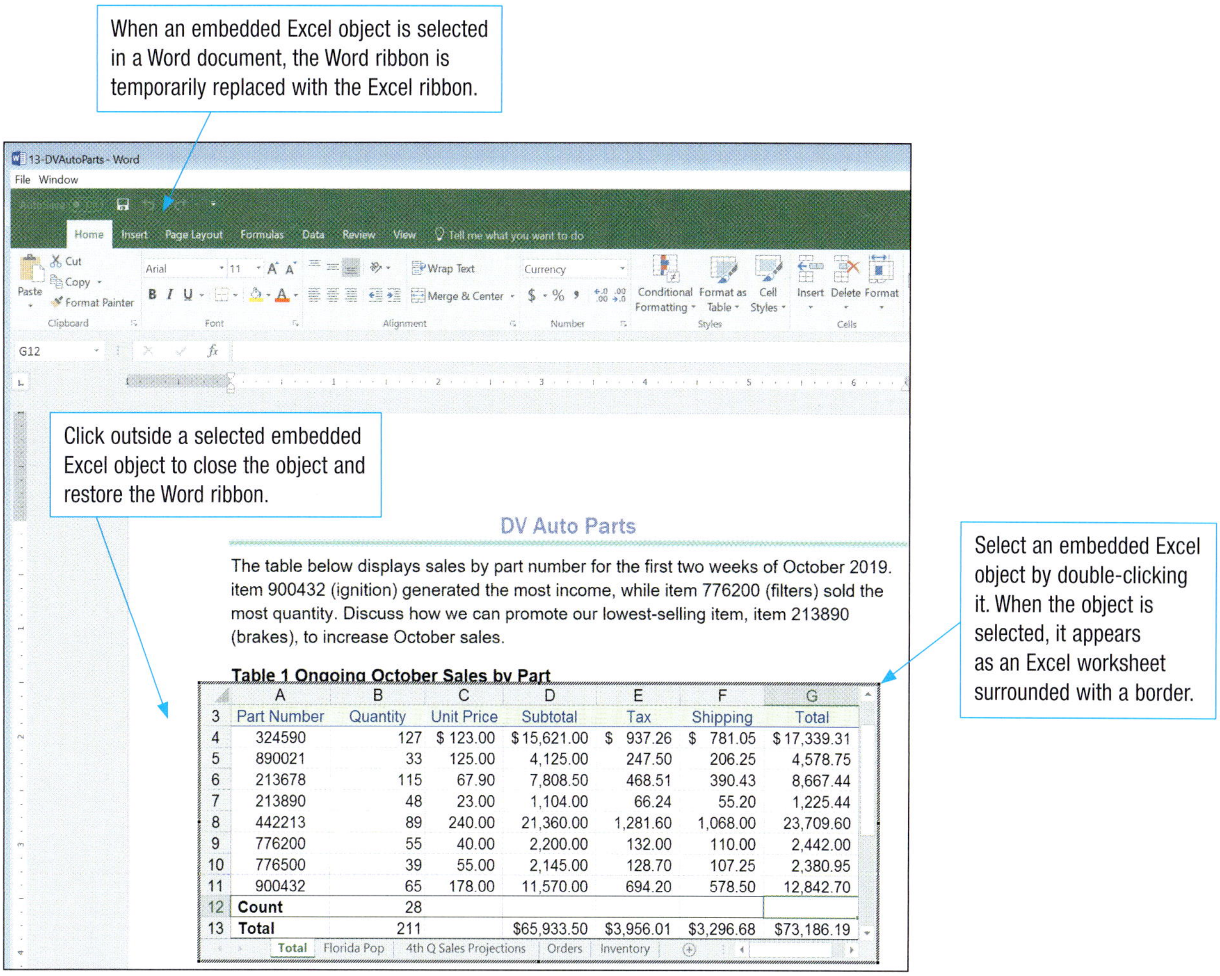

Table 13.1 Paste Options at the Paste Button Drop-Down Gallery and at the Paste Options Button Pop-Up Gallery

Image	Option	Description
	Use Destination Styles & Embed Workbook	Embeds the data and updates the data pasted in Word to match the formatting in the Word document
	Keep Source Formatting & Embed Workbook	Embeds the data in the Word document and keeps the formatting used in the Excel workbook
	Use Destination Styles & Link Data	Links the data and updates the pasted data in Word to match the formatting in the Word document
	Keep Source Formatting & Link Data	Links the data and keeps the formatting used in the Excel workbook
	Picture	Pastes the Excel data as a picture
	Keep Text Only	Pastes the data with tabs separating the columns

On the Job

Task 13.1b Copying and Embedding Excel Data in a Word Document

Devon asks you to edit the Excel data you inserted in the Word document in Task 13.1a. You want to edit it using features in Excel, but to do that, the data needs to be embedded in the Word document. Replace the copied data with embedded data and then use tools on the Excel ribbon to format the header row in the embedded data.

Note: *Be sure to open the data files for this chapter from a computer drive, not your OneDrive account.*

1. With the 13-DVAutoParts workbook open and the 13-DVAutoPartsRpt document open and active, click in the table and then click the Table Select button (see Figure 13.4).

   The table is selected.

Figure 13.4 Table Select Button

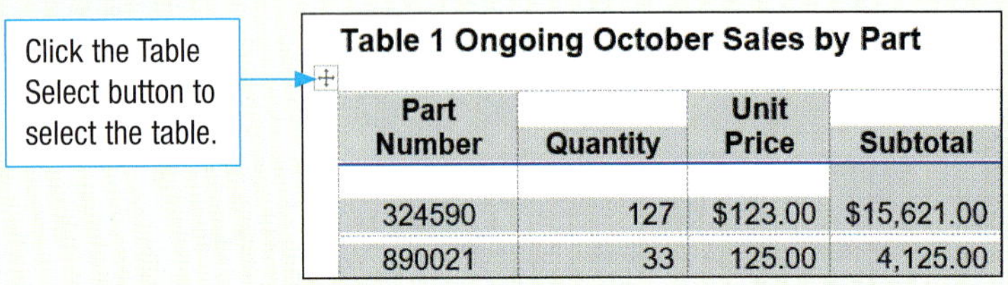

2. Click the Table Tools Layout tab, click the Delete button in the Rows & Columns group, and then click the *Delete Table* option.

   The table is removed from the Word document.

3. Click the Home tab, if necessary; click the Paste button arrow in the Clipboard group (see Figure 13.5); and then click the *Paste Special* option.

   The Paste Special dialog box displays. ***Note:*** *If the options at the Paste button arrow drop-down gallery are grayed out, point to the Excel button on the Windows taskbar and then click the* 13-DVAutoParts *thumbnail to make the workbook active; select the range A3:G13 in the Total worksheet, if necessary; press Ctrl + C; point to the Word button on the Windows taskbar and then click the* 13-DVAutoPartsRpt *thumbnail to make the Word document active; and then repeat this step.*

Figure 13.5 Paste Button Arrow Drop-Down Gallery

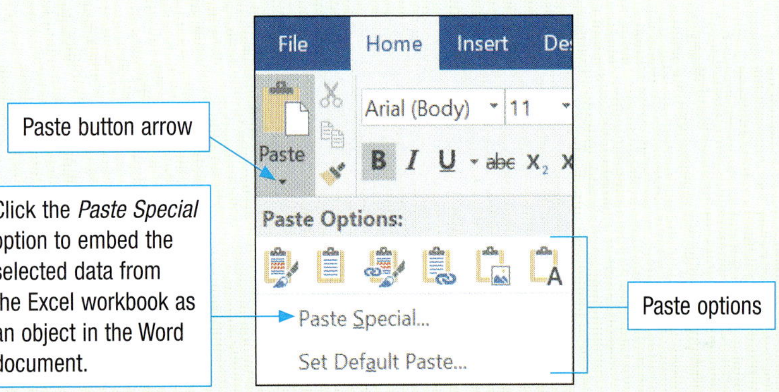

4. Click the *Microsoft Excel Worksheet Object* option in the *As* list box (see Figure 13.6).
5. Click the OK button.

   The selected data from the Excel workbook is pasted as an embedded object in the Word document and can be edited using Excel tools. Notice that the data displays with the same formatting it has in the Excel worksheet, including values aligned on decimal points.
6. Double-click in any cell in the embedded Excel object.

   The embedded object opens in an Excel window surrounded with a border and with Excel column and row headings visible. The Word ribbon is temporarily replaced with the Excel ribbon (see Figure 13.3 on page 607).
7. Select the range A3:G3 in the embedded object, click the More button in the Styles group on the Home tab of the Excel ribbon, and then click the *20% - Accent1* option (first column, first row in the *Themed Cell Styles* section).

   A dark blue font and light green fill style are applied to the selected cells.
8. Click in the document outside the embedded object.

   The Excel workbook is active. Point to the Word button on the Windows taskbar and then click the *13-DVAutoPartsRpt* thumbnail to return to the Word document.
9. Click the Save button on the Quick Access Toolbar. Leave both the Word document and the Excel workbook open for the next task.

Figure 13.6 Paste Special Dialog Box

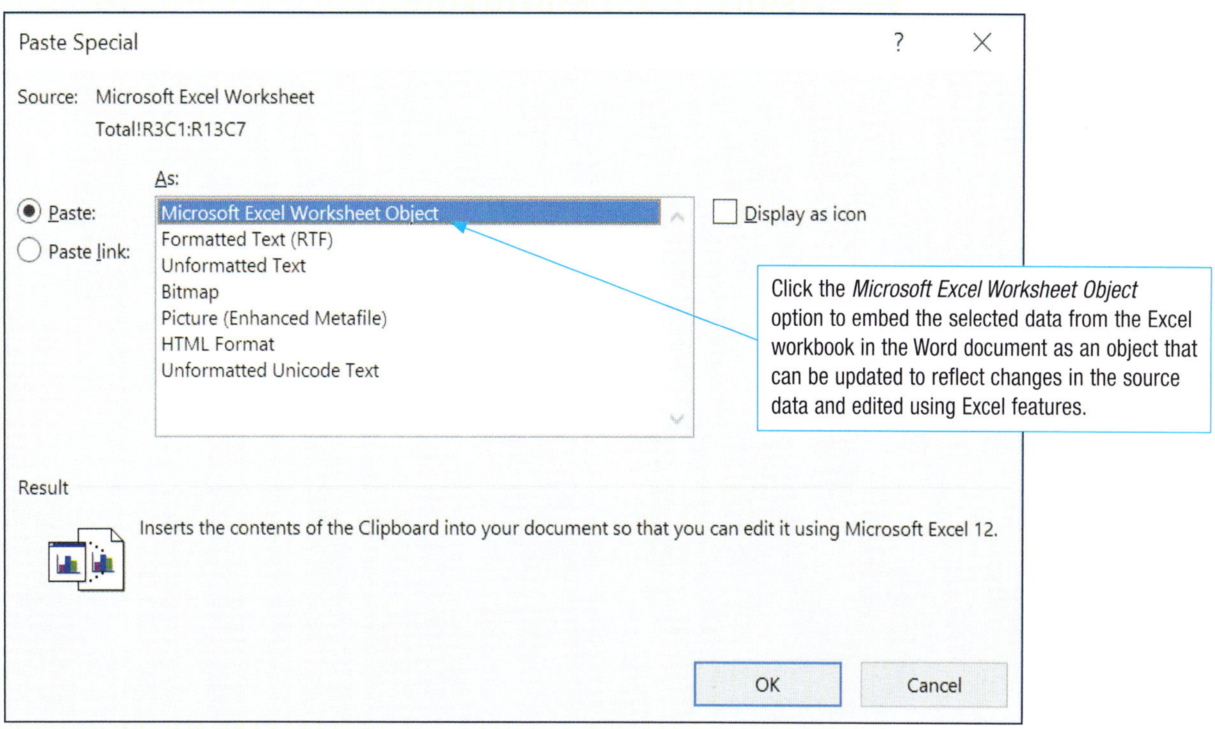

▸ **Know This** about linking Excel data in a Word document

— To link data from an Excel workbook in a Word document, select the data in the Excel workbook, press Ctrl + C, place the insertion point in the Word document, click the Paste button arrow in the Clipboard group on the Home tab, click the *Paste Special* option at the drop-down gallery, click the *Microsoft Excel Worksheet Object* option in the *As* list box at the Paste Special dialog box, click the *Paste link* radio button to insert a bullet, and then click the OK button.

— After data is copied from Excel and linked in Word, the data in the Word document is connected to the data in the Excel workbook, and changes made to the data in the Excel workbook are reflected in the Word document.

— The data exists only in the Excel workbook and cannot be edited directly in the Word document.

— Word places a shortcut to the source data file name and range in the document (see Section 13.9).

— When you open a Word document that contains one or more links, Word displays a message box asking whether you want to update the links. If you click the Yes button, any changes made directly to the Excel document will display in the Word document. If you click the No button, any changes made directly to the Excel document will not display in the Word document.

— If you want to rename or move the Excel workbook that contains the linked data, you must do so while the Word document is open. Otherwise, the link will no longer work and you will have to relink the documents (see Section 13.9).

— To edit Excel data that has been pasted in Word as a linked object, open the Excel workbook and change the source data, open the Word document, right-click the linked object in the Word document, point to the *Linked Worksheet Object* option at the pop-up menu, and then click the *Edit Link* option at the second pop-up menu to open the Excel workbook (see Figure 13.7).

— To break a link to an Excel workbook, see Section 13.3.

— To delete a linked object, select the object and then press the Delete key.

Figure 13.7 Editing Options at the Linked Object Pop-Up Menu

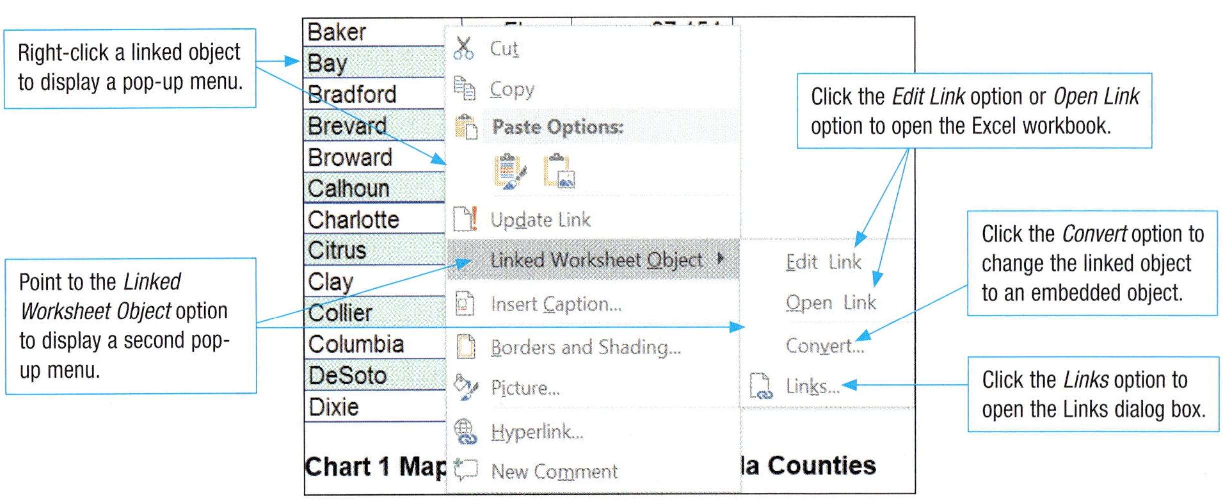

On the Job

Task 13.1c Copying and Linking Excel Data in a Word Document

Devon wants you to insert a list of Florida counties and their populations under the *Table 2* heading on the second page of the 13-DVAutoPartsRpt document. These statistics are available in the 13-DVAutoParts workbook. Devon has heard that Dixie County will issue updated population statistics at the end of the week, and he wants you to update the data in the Excel workbook after that happens. You want to be sure Devon has the most current information in his handout when he prints it next week. Copy the data from the Excel workbook and then paste it in the Word document as a linked object, so that when Devon opens the Word document to print it as a handout next week, he will be prompted to update the link.

Note: *Be sure to open the data files for this chapter from a computer drive, not your OneDrive account.*

1. With the 13-DVAutoParts workbook open and the 13-DVAutoPartsRpt document open and active, scroll to the second page of the Word document, place the insertion point at the end of the heading *Table 2 List of Florida Counties by Population*, and then press the Enter key.

   The insertion point appears at the beginning of the next line.
2. Point to the Excel button on the Windows taskbar and then click the *13-DVAutoParts* thumbnail.

   The 13-DVAutoParts workbook is active.
3. Click the Florida Pop sheet tab to make the worksheet active, select the range A2:C16, and then press Ctrl + C.
4. Point to the Word button on the Windows taskbar and then click the *13-DVAutoPartsRpt* thumbnail.

   The 13-DVAutoPartsRpt document is active.
5. Click the Home tab, if necessary; click the Paste button arrow in the Clipboard group; and then click the *Paste Special* option.

   The Paste Special dialog box displays.
6. Click the *Microsoft Excel Worksheet Object* in the *As* list box, click the *Paste link* radio button to insert a bullet, and then click the OK button.

   The selected data from the Excel workbook is pasted in the Word document as a linked object and cannot be edited in the Word document.
7. Click the Save button on the Word Quick Access Toolbar.
8. Click the File tab and then click the *Close* option.

   The 13-DVAutoPartsRpt document closes but the Word application remains open.

   At the end of the week, you check with Dixie County and get a new population statistic for the county. You are now ready to update the Excel worksheet with the new data.
9. Point to the Excel button on the Windows taskbar and then click the *13-DVAutoParts* workbook thumbnail, if necessary.

   The 13-DVAutoParts workbook is active and the Florida Pop worksheet is active.
10. Press the Esc key and then click in any cell outside the range A2:C16.

    The scrolling marquee is removed from the range A2:C16 and the range is no longer selected.

11. Click in cell C16, type 16,486, and then press the Enter key.

The value *16,486* appears in cell C16 and cell C17 is active.

12. Point to the Word button on the Windows taskbar and then open the Word document you closed in Step 8. ***Hint:*** *To open the 13-DVAutoPartsRpt document, click the File tab and then click the* 13-DVAutoPartsRpt *option in the* Recent *section at the backstage area.*

A message box displays, asking whether you want to update the document with data from the linked file (see Figure 13.8).

Figure 13.8 This document contains links... Message Box

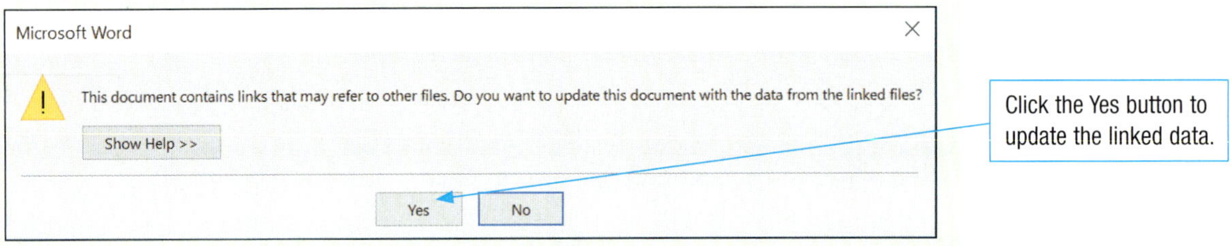

13. Click the Yes button.

The message box closes.

14. Scroll to page 2 in the Word document and verify that the population data for Dixie County has updated to match the new data in the Excel workbook.

The population data for Dixie County is 16,486, which matches the new data in the Excel workbook.

15. Click the Save button on the Quick Access Toolbar. Leave both the Word document and the Excel workbook open for the next task. ***Note:*** *If you need to close the files, be sure to save the changes to the Excel workbook before closing it.*

Model Answer

▸ **Know This** about embedding an Excel chart in a Word document or a PowerPoint presentation

— To embed a chart in a Word document, click the chart in Excel to select it, press Ctrl + C, click in the Word document where the chart is to be placed, and then either press Ctrl + V or click the Paste button in the Clipboard group and choose one of the options.

— To embed a chart in a PowerPoint presentation after you press Ctrl + C, you need to select the slide the chart is to be placed in.

— Whether you use the paste command or *Paste Special* options when you copy and paste a chart, the chart is, by default, embedded in the destination file as a **Microsoft Office Graphic Object**, which is an OLE embedded object.

— An Excel chart inserted in a Word document or PowerPoint presentation is pasted as an embedded object, and the source data used to generate the chart is stored in an Excel workbook.

— To edit the embedded chart, right-click the chart, point to the *Edit Data* option at the pop-up menu, and then click the *Edit Data* option or the *Edit Data in Excel* option at the second pop-up menu.
  - Clicking the *Edit Data* option opens the entire Excel workbook directly in the Word document (see Figure 13.9).
  - Clicking the *Edit Data in Excel* option opens Excel and then opens the workbook.

Figure 13.9 Word Document with an Embedded Excel Chart Open for Editing

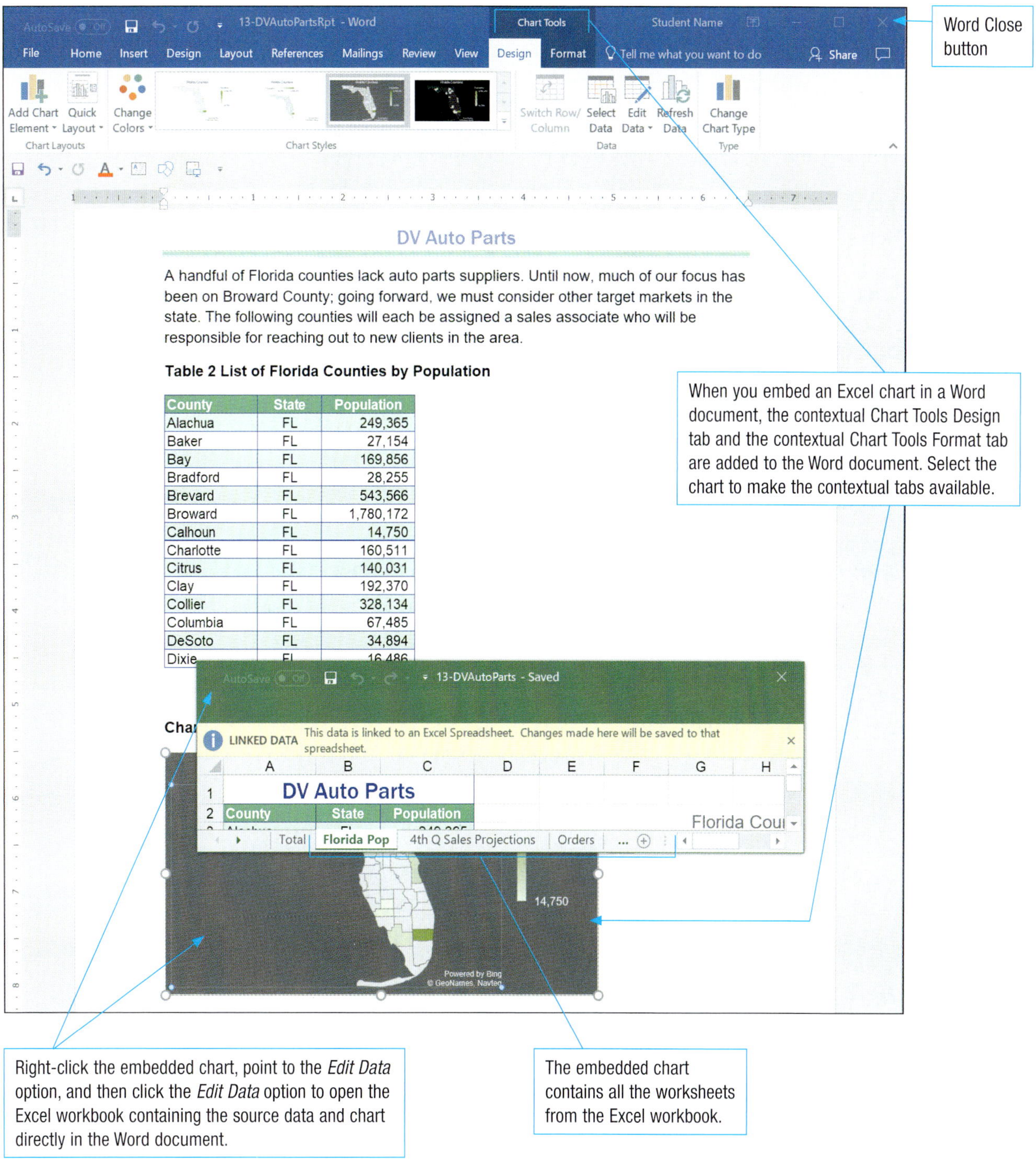

▸ **Know This** about the Office 365 and Office 2016 charting system

— In Office 365 and Office 2016, the charting system is fully integrated with Word, Excel, and PowerPoint.

— When you embed an Excel chart in a Word document or PowerPoint presentation, the Excel workbook containing the source data becomes part of the document or presentation file.

— You edit an Excel chart embedded in a Word document or PowerPoint presentation using the same techniques and tools used for editing a chart in Excel.

— Three buttons—Layout Options, Chart Elements, and Chart Styles—are available for editing.

— To edit an Excel chart embedded in a Word document or PowerPoint presentation, click the chart and then use tools on the contextual Chart Tools Design tab and contextual Chart Tools Format tab on the Word ribbon or PowerPoint ribbon. These tabs contain the same groups and buttons on the Word ribbon and PowerPoint ribbon as they do on the Excel ribbon.

On the Job

Task 13.1d Copying and Embedding an Excel Chart in a Word Document

Devon asks you to supply a visual to help the sales associates see at a glance which Florida counties have large populations and could use additional sales service in the coming months. Copy the map chart from the Florida Pop worksheet and embed it under the *Chart 1* heading on the second page of the Word document. After inserting the chart, use tools on the Word ribbon to modify the chart style.

Note: *Be sure to open the data files for this chapter from a computer drive, not your OneDrive account.*

1. With the 13-DVAutoParts workbook open and the 13-DVAutoPartsRpt document open and active, place the insertion point at the end of the heading *Chart 1 Map of Underserviced Florida Counties* on the second page and then press the Enter key.

   The insertion point appears at the beginning of the next line.

2. Point to the Excel button on the Windows taskbar and then click the *13-DVAutoParts* thumbnail.

   The 13-DVAutoParts workbook is active.

3. With the Florida Pop worksheet active, click an empty area of the Florida Counties map chart to select the chart and then press Ctrl + C.

4. Point to the Word button on the Windows taskbar and then click the *13-DVAutoPartsRpt* thumbnail.

   The 13-DVAutoPartsRpt document is active, with the insertion point in the blank line below the Chart 1 heading.

5. Click the Paste button arrow in the Clipboard group on the Home tab and then click the *Paste Special* option.

   The Paste Special dialog box displays with a bullet in the *Paste* radio button and the *Microsoft Office Graphic Object* option selected in the *As* list box (see Figure 13.10).

Figure 13.10 Paste Special Dialog Box with Options Selected for Embedding an Excel Chart

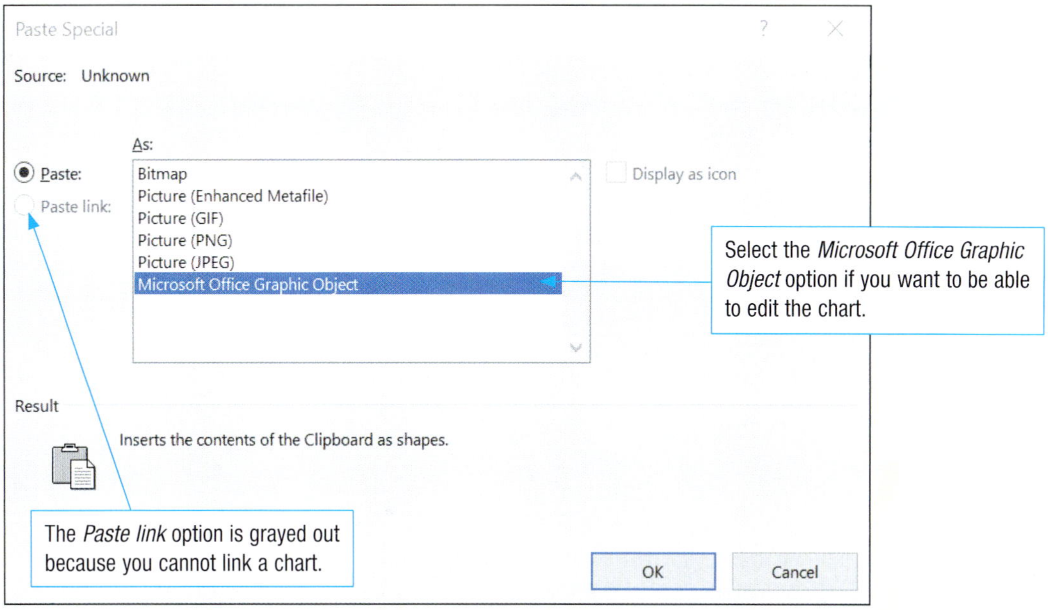

6. Click the OK button.

   The Paste Special dialog box closes and the Excel chart appears in the Word document.

7. Click an empty area of the chart.

   The chart is selected and the contextual Chart Tools Design tab and contextual Chart Tools Format tab are available on the Word ribbon.

8. Click the Chart Tools Design tab and then click the third option at the Chart Styles gallery.

   The chart area changes to a dark gray.

9. If printed work is required by your instructor, print the Word document.

10. Save and then click the Word Close button (see Figure 13.9 on page 613).

    The 13-DVAutoPartsRpt document closes and Word closes. The 13-DVAutoParts workbook remains open and is active, with the Florida Pop worksheet active.

11. Click the Save button on the Quick Access Toolbar. Leave the Excel workbook open for the next task.

Model Answer

13.2 Copying, Embedding, and Linking Excel Data in a PowerPoint Presentation

Tutorial

Copying and Embedding an Excel Chart in a PowerPoint Presentation

You can copy and paste, copy and embed, and copy and link Excel data in a PowerPoint presentation just as you can in a Word document. Charts are often incorporated in presentations to show numerical data in a graph format that is easy to understand. Charts present data in a visual format that can depict relationships and trends (see Chapter 6). Your audience may find a chart easier to understand than just data. Although numerical data and charts can be entered or created in PowerPoint slides, you may prefer to use Excel to create these items and then copy and paste, embed, or link them in PowerPoint.

▸ **Know This** about copying and pasting Excel data in a PowerPoint presentation

— To copy data from an Excel workbook and paste it in a PowerPoint presentation, select the data in the Excel workbook, press Ctrl + C, place the insertion point in the PowerPoint slide, and then press Ctrl + V.

— Excel data can be pasted in a PowerPoint presentation similar to the way it is pasted in a Word document (see Section 13.1).

▸ **Know This** about embedding Excel data in a PowerPoint presentation

— To embed data from an Excel workbook in a PowerPoint presentation, select the data in the Excel workbook, press Ctrl + C, place the insertion point in the PowerPoint slide, click the Paste button arrow in the Clipboard group on the Home tab, click the *Paste Special* option at the drop-down gallery, click the *Microsoft Excel Worksheet Object* option in the *As* list box at the Paste Special dialog box, and then click the OK button.

— Excel data can be embedded in a PowerPoint presentation similar to the way it is in a Word document (see Section 13.1).

Reminder

You can also press Alt + Ctrl + V to display the Paste Special dialog box.

▸ **Know This** about linking Excel data in a PowerPoint presentation

— To link data from an Excel workbook in a PowerPoint presentation, select the data in the Excel workbook, press Ctrl + C, place the insertion point in the PowerPoint slide, click the Paste button arrow in the Clipboard group on the Home tab, click the *Paste Special* option at the drop-down gallery, click the *Microsoft Excel Worksheet Object* option in the *As* list box at the Paste Special dialog box, click the *Paste link* radio button to insert a bullet, and then click the OK button.

— Excel data can be linked in a PowerPoint presentation similar to the way it is linked in a Word document (see Section 13.1).

▸ Know More ways to use Paste Special

- Click the Paste button arrow in the Clipboard group to open the Paste button drop-down gallery (see Figure 13.6 on page 609).
- See Table 13.1 on page 607 for a list of options at the Paste button drop-down gallery.

On the Job

Task 13.2a Copying and Embedding Excel Data in a PowerPoint Presentation

For Devon's upcoming meeting with the sales associates, he's creating a PowerPoint presentation. He has prepared the title slide and a slide outlining the meeting agenda. He has also inserted three topic slides and titled them. Devon wants you to add data from the 13-DVAutoParts workbook to the topic slides. For this task, copy the data from the Total worksheet in the Excel workbook and embed it in the third slide of the PowerPoint presentation. After you embed the object, use tools on the PowerPoint ribbon to change the size and alignment of the object and then use tools on the Excel ribbon to format the header row in the object.

Note: *Be sure to open the data files for this chapter from a computer drive, not your OneDrive account.*

1. With the 13-DVAutoParts workbook open, click the Total sheet tab and then, if necessary, select the range A3:G13.
2. Press Ctrl + C.
3. Start PowerPoint 2016 and then open the data file **13-DVAutoPartsPPT** from the AE13 folder on your storage medium.
4. Click the Enable Editing button if a security warning displays in the message bar below the ribbon, stating that the presentation is in protected view.
5. Click Slide 3 in the slide thumbnails pane of the PowerPoint presentation (see Figure 13.11).

   Slide 3 is selected in the slide thumbnails pane and displays in the slide pane.
6. Click in the Slide 3 content placeholder.

   The insertion point is at the top of the Slide 3 content placeholder.

Figure 13.11 PowerPoint Presentation with the Slide Thumbnails Pane Displayed

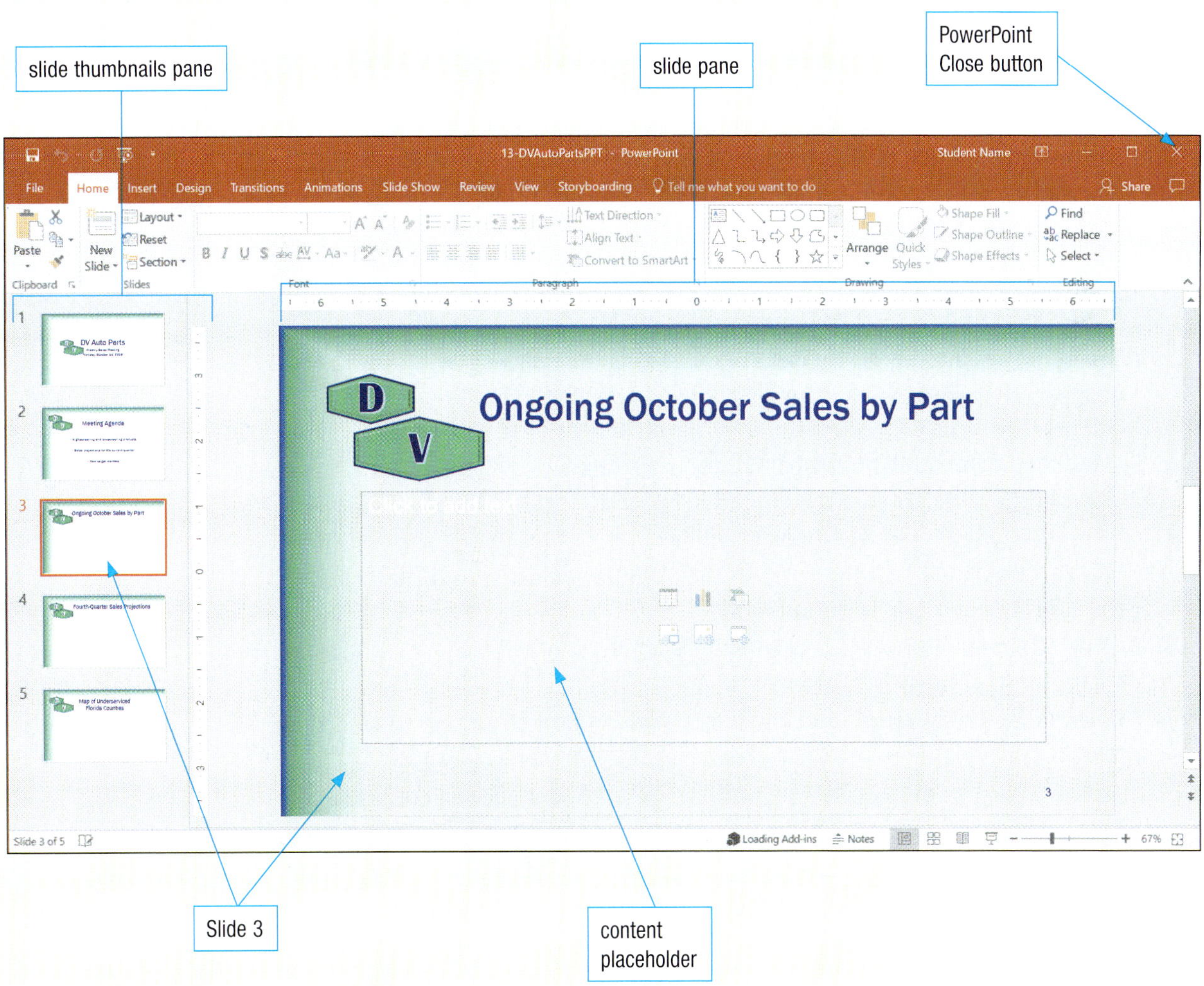

7. Click the Paste button arrow in the Clipboard group on the Home tab and then click the *Paste Special* option.

   The Paste Special dialog box displays. By default, the *Paste* radio button contains a bullet and the *Microsoft Excel Worksheet Object* option is selected in the *As* list box.

8. Click the OK button.

   The selected data from the Excel workbook is inserted as an embedded object in the PowerPoint slide. The object is selected and the contextual Drawing Tools Format tab is available on the PowerPoint ribbon.

9. Click the Drawing Tools Format tab.

10. Click in the *Height* measurement box in the Size group, type 3, and then press the Enter key.

    The embedded object changes size to be 3 inches tall by about 8.43 inches wide. ***Note:*** *Depending on your computer setup and the version of Excel you are using, your width measurement may vary.*

11. Click the Align button in the Arrange group and then click the *Align Center* option.

    The embedded object is centered horizontally in the content placeholder.

12. Double-click in any cell in the embedded object.

    The embedded object opens in an Excel window surrounded with a border and with the Excel column and row headings visible. The PowerPoint ribbon is temporarily replaced with the Excel ribbon.

13. Select the range A3:G3 in the embedded object, click the More button in the Styles group on the Home tab of the Excel ribbon, and then click the *20% - Accent1* style option (first column, first row in the *Themed Cell Styles* section).

    A dark blue font and light green fill are applied to the selected cells. Number symbols (#####) may appear in the embedded object. These indicate a column is not wide enough to fit the contents of a cell. Ignore them; they will disappear after you close and then reopen the presentation.

14. Click in the slide outside the embedded object.

    The 13-DVAutoParts workbook is active.

15. Point to the PowerPoint button on the Windows taskbar and then click the *13-DVAutoPartsPPT* thumbnail.

    The 13-DVAutoPartsPPT presentation is active.

16. Click the Save button on the Quick Access Toolbar. Leave both the PowerPoint presentation and the Excel workbook open for the next task.

Model Answer

On the Job

Task 13.2b Copying and Embedding Excel Data as a Picture in a PowerPoint Presentation

Devon asks you to continue to update his PowerPoint presentation by copying the data from the 4th Q Sales Projections worksheet in the

Excel workbook and embedding it as a picture on the fourth slide of the PowerPoint presentation. After you embed the object, use tools on the PowerPoint ribbon to change the size and alignment of the object.

Note: *Be sure to open the data files for this chapter from a computer drive, not your OneDrive account.*

1. With the 13-DVAutoParts workbook open and the 13-DVAutoPartsPPT presentation open and active, point to the Excel button on the Windows taskbar and then click the *13-DVAutoParts* thumbnail.

   The 13-DVAutoParts workbook is active.
2. Click the 4th Q Sales Projections sheet tab and then select the range A4:D5.
3. Press Ctrl + C.
4. Point to the PowerPoint button on the Windows taskbar and then click the *13-DVAutoPartsPPT* thumbnail.

   The 13-DVAutoPartsPPT presentation is active.
5. Click Slide 4 in the slide thumbnails pane of the PowerPoint presentation.

   Slide 4 is selected in the slide thumbnails pane and displays in the slide pane.
6. Click in the Slide 4 content placeholder.

   The insertion point is at the top of the Slide 4 content placeholder.
7. Click the Home tab and then click the Paste button arrow in the Clipboard group.

   A drop-down gallery displays.
8. Click the *Picture* option (fourth option; see Figure 13.12).

   The selected data from the Excel workbook is inserted as an embedded object in the PowerPoint slide. The object is selected and the contextual Picture Tools Format tab is available on the PowerPoint ribbon. If the Design Ideas task pane is open, close it.

Figure 13.12 Paste Button Arrow Drop-Down Gallery

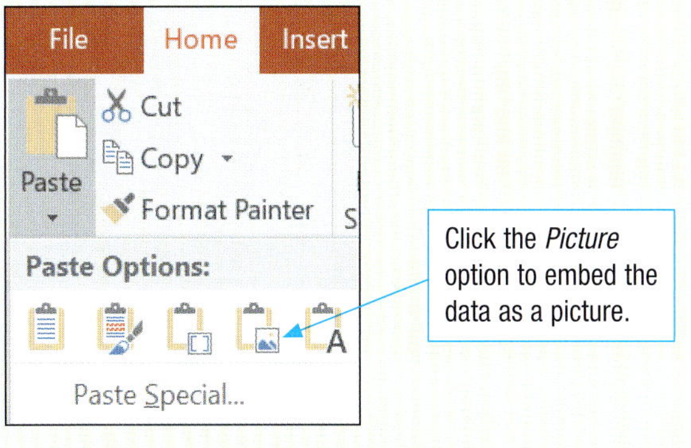

9. Click the Picture Tools Format tab.
10. Click in the *Height* measurement box in the Size group, type 0.8, and then press the Enter key.

    The embedded object changes size to be 0.8 inch tall by about 8.8 inches wide. ***Note:*** *Depending on your computer setup and the version of Excel you are using, your width measurement may vary.*

11. Click the Align button in the Arrange group and then click the *Align Center* option.

    The embedded object is centered horizontally in the content placeholder.

12. Click the Align button and then click the *Align Middle* option.

    The embedded object is centered vertically in the content placeholder.

13. Click the Save button on the Quick Access Toolbar. Leave both the PowerPoint presentation and the Excel workbook open for the next task.

Model Answer

On the Job

Task 13.2c Copying and Embedding an Excel Chart in a PowerPoint Presentation

Devon wants you to copy the map chart from the Florida Pop worksheet in the Excel workbook and embed it in Slide 5 of the PowerPoint presentation. After you embed the object, use tools on the PowerPoint ribbon to modify the chart style.

Note: *Be sure to open the data files for this chapter from a computer drive, not your OneDrive account.*

1. With the 13-DVAutoParts workbook open and the 13-DVAutoPartsPPT presentation open and active, point to the Excel button on the Windows taskbar and then click the *13-DVAutoParts* thumbnail.

    The 13-DVAutoParts workbook is active.

2. Click the Florida Pop sheet tab and then select the map chart, if necessary.
3. Press Ctrl + C.
4. Point to the PowerPoint button on the Windows taskbar and then click the *13-DVAutoPartsPPT* thumbnail.

    The 13-DVAutoPartsPPT presentation is active.

5. Click Slide 5 in the slide thumbnails pane.

    Slide 5 is selected in the slide thumbnails pane and displays in the slide pane.

6. Click in the Slide 5 content placeholder.

    The insertion point is at the top of the Slide 5 content placeholder.

7. Press Ctrl + V.

    The selected chart from the Excel workbook is pasted as an embedded object in the PowerPoint slide. The object is selected and the contextual Chart Tools Design tab and contextual Chart Tools Format tab are available on the PowerPoint ribbon.

8. Click the Chart Tools Design tab and then click the third option at the Chart Styles gallery.

    The chart area changes to a dark gray.

9. Click in the slide outside the embedded chart.

    The embedded chart is no longer selected and the contextual tabs are no longer available.

10. If printed work is required by your instructor, print the PowerPoint presentation.
11. Save and then click the PowerPoint Close button (see Figure 13.11 on page 617).
12. Close the Excel workbook.

Model Answer

13.3 Breaking a Link to an Excel Object

If the data in a linked object does not need to be updated when the data in the source file changes, you can break the link. **Breaking the link** means disconnecting the data in the destination file from the data in the source file. After you break the link between the linked object and the source file, any change made to the original data in the source file will not be reflected in the linked object. For example, you may link data from an Excel workbook to a Word document while you are preparing and revising a report that uses the Excel data. If you need to email the Word document to sales associates and do not want them to also get the Excel workbook, you will break the link before you send the document.

Tutorial

Breaking a Link to an Excel Object

Reminder

During an import or export, the file containing the original data is called the *source file* and the file to which the original data is being copied, embedded, or linked is called the *destination file.*

▸ Know This about breaking a link to an Excel object

— To break a link to an Excel object, right-click the linked object in the destination file, point to the *Linked Worksheet Object* option at the pop-up menu, click the *Links* option at the second pop-up menu, click the source object for the link to be broken in the list box at the Links dialog box, click the Break Link button, click the Yes button at the message box to confirm that the link is to be broken, and then click the OK button two times.

— When you display the Links dialog box, all the links in the workbook are listed in the dialog box.

— When a link is broken, the linked object turns into a picture object and the contextual Picture Tools Format tab is available on the ribbon when the picture object is selected.

— Once the link to an object is broken, the prompt to update the object each time the destination file is opened no longer appears.

— After a link is broken, an information message displays, stating that the linked file is not available. To reestablish the link, click the File tab, click the *Edit Links to Files* option at the Info backstage area, and then use options at the Links dialog box.

On the Job
Task 13.3 Breaking a Link to an Excel Object

Devon plans to distribute the 13-DVAutoPartsRpt document to the sales associates electronically after next week's sales meeting. He's finished updating the Excel data under the *Table 2* heading in the 13-DVAutoPartsRpt document. Delete the link between the table and the source file.

Note: *Be sure to open the data files for this chapter from a computer drive, not your OneDrive account.*

1. Start Word and then open the data file **13-DVAutoPartsRpt**, which you closed at the end of Task 13.1d.

   A message box displays, asking whether you want to update the links.

2. Click the No button.
3. Scroll down to Table 2 on page 2.
4. Right-click the linked Excel object under the Table 2 title.

   A pop-up menu displays.

5. Point to the *Linked Worksheet Object* option and then click the *Links* option.

   The Links dialog box displays (see Figure 13.13). The link to Table 2 and the link to Chart 1 appear in the *Source file* list box.

6. Click the Break Link button.

   A message box displays, asking whether you are sure you want to break the selected link (see Figure 13.14).

Figure 13.13 Links Dialog Box

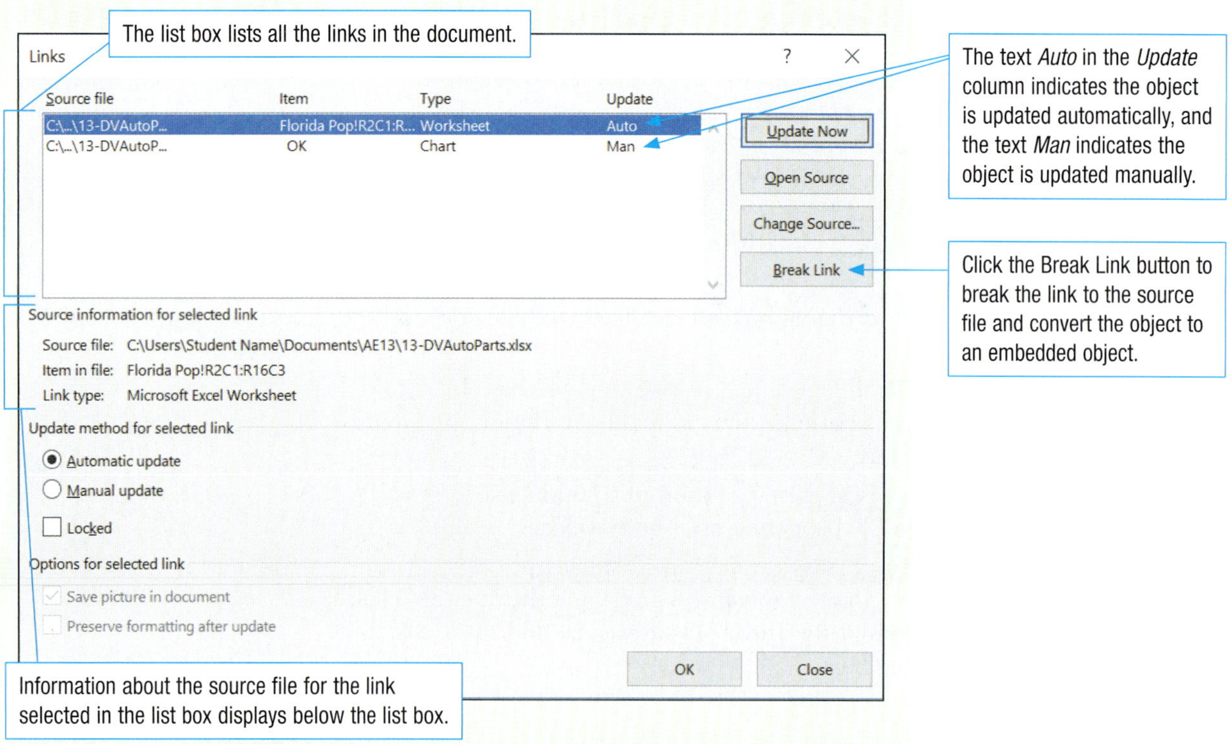

Figure 13.14 *Are you sure you want to break the selected links?* Message Box

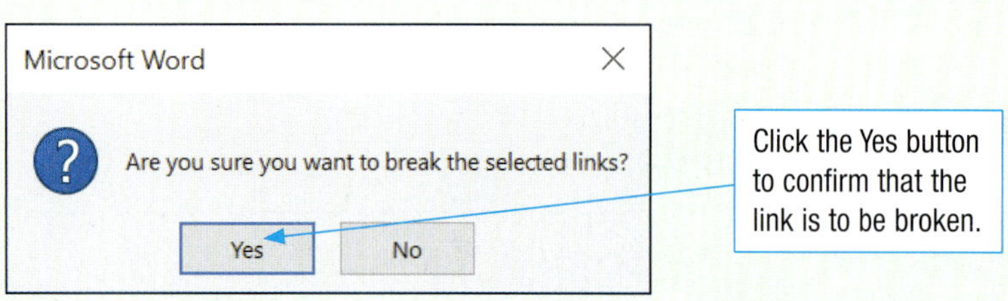

7. Click the Yes button.

   The message box closes and the Links dialog box continues to display. The link is broken and the linked object is now a picture object. The chart link is selected in the list box at the Links dialog box.

8. Click the Break Link button.

   The message box asking whether you are sure you want to break the selected link displays again.

9. Click the Yes button.

   The message box closes and the Links dialog box continues to display.

10. Click the OK button.

    An information box displays, stating the linked file is not available (see Figure 13.15).

11. Click the OK button.
12. Save and then close the Word document.

Figure 13.15 *The linked file is not available...* Information Box

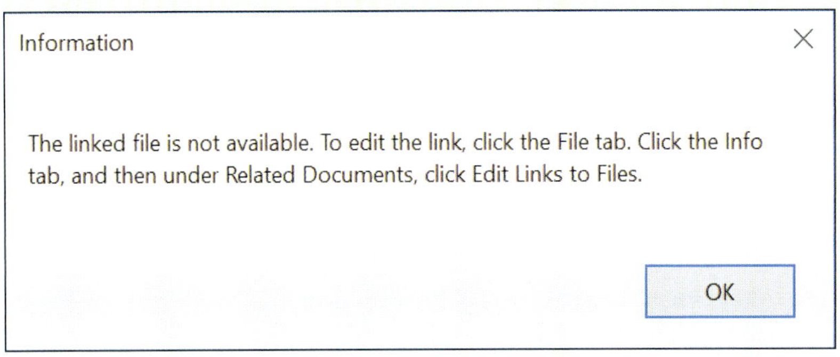

13.4 Copying and Appending Excel Data to an Access Table

Tutorial

Copying and Appending Excel Data to an Access Table

Access is a database and can be used, like Excel, to store and retrieve data. Access uses tables to store data. An Access table is similar in structure to an Excel worksheet. A field in Access, like a column in Excel, holds one piece of information about a person, an item, or an amount. A record in Access, like a row in Excel, holds the information for one item. You can extract specific information from Access through a database object called a *query* and generate a report that presents the information in a professional format that can help in decision making.

▸ **Know This** about appending Excel data to an Access table

— You can copy data from an Excel worksheet and paste it in an Access database table, query, or form.

— Before pasting Excel data in an Access table, make sure the columns in the Excel workbook match the fields in the Access table. The column headers and the field names do not have to match exactly, but the type of data in each column (for example, phone numbers) must match the type of data in the corresponding field.

▸ Know This about appending Excel data to an existing Access table

— When you copy data to an existing table, you **append** (add) the data to the table.

— To append Excel data to an Access table, select the data in the Excel workbook, press Ctrl + C, open the Access table in Datasheet view, click the Paste button arrow in the Clipboard group on the Home tab in the Access database, click the *Paste Append* option at the drop-down gallery, and then click the Yes button.

▸ Know This about copying, importing, and linking Excel data in a new Access table

— To insert data from an Excel workbook into an Access database that does not have an existing table in which to receive the data, open the Access database, click the Excel button in the Import & Link group on the External Data tab, specify the Excel workbook file name, click the *Import the source data into a new table in the current database* option, and then click the OK button.

On the Job

Task 13.4 Copying and Appending Excel Data to an Access Table

Devon has decided to start keeping track of orders in an Access database. He's set up a table in the database with the same structure as the Excel workbook and has entered the data for October 1, 2019, to October 18, 2019. He wants you to enter the data for October 19, 2019, to October 30, 2019. Copy the data from the Order worksheet in the 13-DVAutoParts workbook and append it to the OctSales table in the 13-DVAutoParts database. The *Subtotal, Tax, Shipping*, and *Total* columns don't need to be copied because they have been created as calculated fields in the database. Once the data has been copied into the table, these values will be calculated for you—just like with Excel formulas.

Note: *Be sure to open the data files for this chapter from a computer drive, not your OneDrive account.*

1. Open the data file **13-DVAutoParts**, which you closed at the end of Task 13.2c.
2. Click the Orders sheet tab and then select the range A22:F33.
3. Press Ctrl + C.
4. Start Access 2016 and then open the data file **13-DVAutoPartsDB** from the AE13 folder on your storage medium.
5. Click the Enable Content button if a security warning displays in the message bar below the ribbon, stating that some active content has been disabled.
6. Double-click the table name *OctSales* in the Tables group in the Navigation pane (see Figure 13.16).

   The OctSales table opens in Datasheet view.
7. Click the Home tab, if necessary.

8. Click the Paste button arrow in the Clipboard group and then click the *Paste Append* option.

   The data displays at the bottom of the table and a message box displays, stating that you are about to paste 12 records (see Figure 13.17).

Figure 13.16 Access Window with a Table Open in Datasheet View

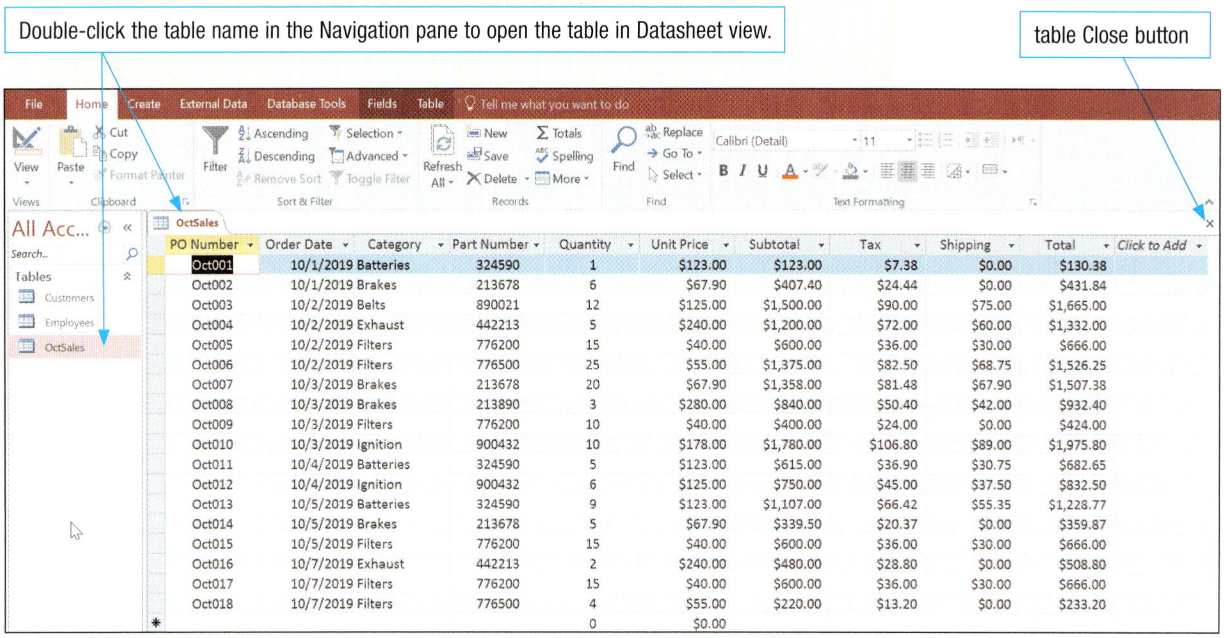

Figure 13.17 *You are about to paste 12 record(s)* Message Box

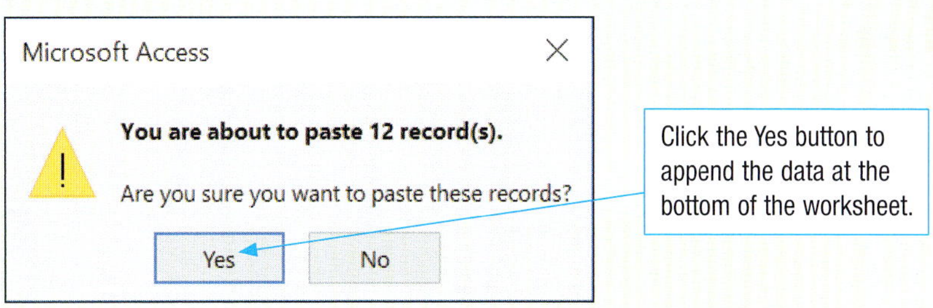

9. Click the Yes button.

   The message box closes and the data is pasted at the bottom of the table. Although you did not copy data from the *Subtotal*, *Tax*, *Shipping*, and *Total* fields in the Excel worksheet, data appears in the corresponding fields in the Access table database because they are calculated fields in the database.

10. If printed work is required by your instructor, complete the following steps to print the Access table:

    a. Click the File tab.

    b. Click the *Print* option.

    c. Click *Print Preview* option.

    The Print Preview view displays (see Figure 13.18).

d. Click the Landscape button in the Page Layout group on the Print Preview tab.
e. Click the Page Setup button.
f. Select the value in the *Left* measurement box in the *Margins (inches)* section on the Print Options tab at the Page Setup dialog box and then type 0.5.
g. Select the value in the *Right* measurement box and then type 0.5.
h. Leave the top and bottom margins set to 1 inch.
i. Click the OK button.
j. Click the Print button in the Print group.
k. Click OK at the Print dialog box.
l. Click the Close Print Preview button in the Close Preview group.

Figure 13.18 Access Print Preview Tab and Page Setup Dialog Box

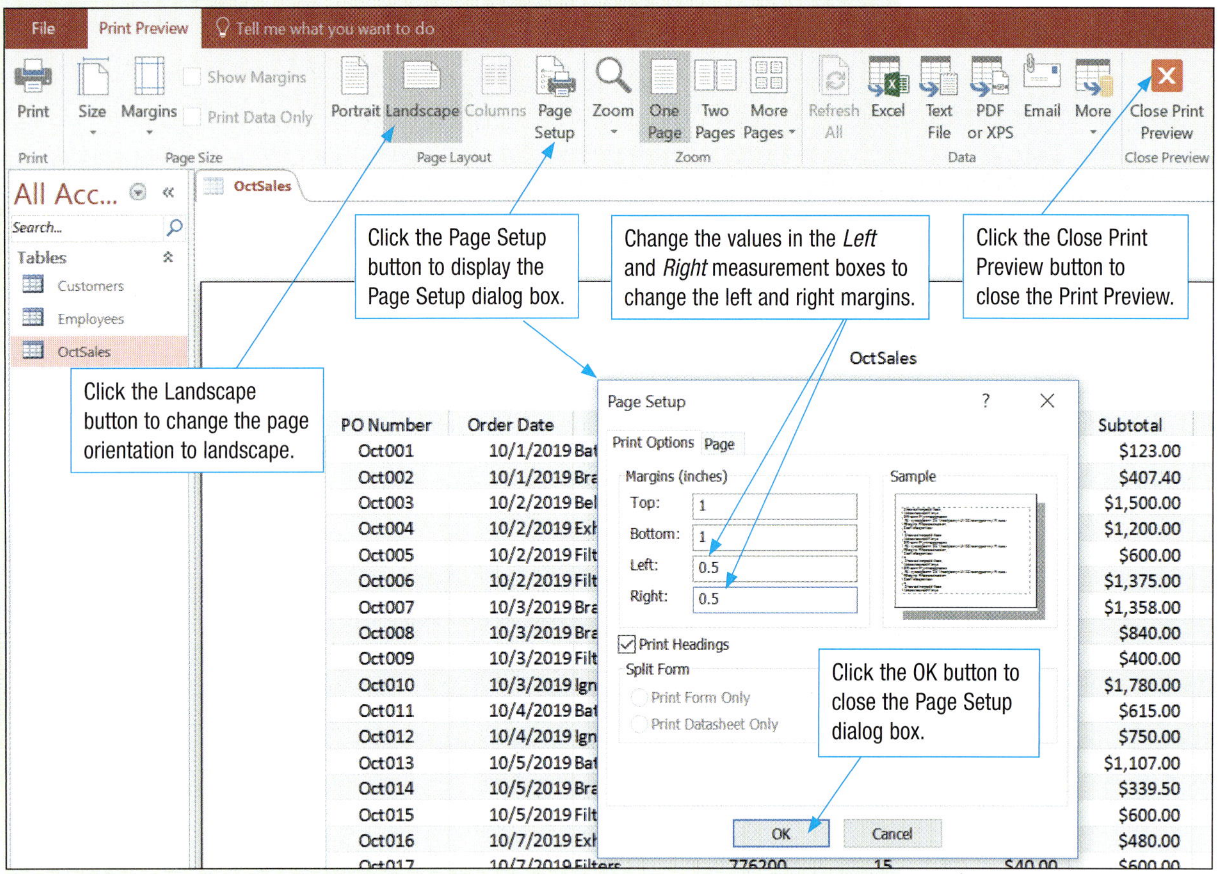

11. Click the Table Close button.

    The table is closed. ***Note:*** *Data entered in an Access table or form is saved automatically, so you do not have to save the file before closing the table or form.*

12. Click the Access Close button.

    Access closes.

13. Leave the Excel workbook open and the Orders worksheet active for the next task.

Model Answer

13.5 Exporting Excel Data as a Text File

The integration features in the Office 365 and Office 2016 make it easy to exchange Excel data with others who are using any of the programs in the suite. You may, however, run into compatibility issues with other applications when trying to copy or import Excel data. A solution is to export the Excel data as a text file that can be opened and edited by a wide variety of applications.

Tutorial

Exporting Excel Data as a Text File

▸ **Know This** about text file formats

— A **text file** is a type of file type that contains only plain text and numbers, with no special formatting or objects.

— Excel provides several text file options, including file formats suitable for computers that use the Apple's operating system (Mac OS), as shown in Table 13.2.

— There are as many text file formats as there are differences across platforms. For example, the Apple's operating system denotes the end of a line in a text file with a carriage return character, Unix uses a line-feed character, and MS-DOS inserts both a line-feed character and a carriage return character code at the end of each line.

— In a text file, a **delimiter** is a special character that separates data to be placed in separate columns. Tabs, commas, semicolons, and spaces are commonly used in text files as delimiters.

Table 13.2 Text File Formats That Excel Supports for Exporting

Text File Format	File Extension
text (tab delimited)	.txt
unicode text	.txt
CSV (comma separated values)	.csv
formatted text (space delimited)	.prn
text (Apple)	.txt
text (MS-DOS)	.txt
CSV (Apple)	.csv
CSV (MS-DOS)	.csv

▸ **Know This** about exporting Excel data as a text file

— To export data from an Excel worksheet as a text file, click the File tab; click the *Export* option; click the *Change File Type* option in the middle panel at the Export backstage area; click the *Text (Tab delimited)*, *CSV (Comma delimited)*, or *Formatted Text (Space delimited)* option in the *Other File Types* section in the right panel; click the Save As button; navigate to the storage location in the Save As dialog box; type the file name, if necessary; and then click the Save button.

— You can export up to 1,048,576 rows and 16,384 columns of data.

— When you export data from an Excel worksheet, all the data in the worksheet is exported. You cannot export selected portions of the worksheet.

▸ **Know More** ways to export Excel data as a text file

– Display the Save As dialog box; click the *Save as type* option box arrow; click the text file option at the drop-down list; navigate to the storage location; type a new file name in the *File name* text box, if necessary; click the Save button; click the OK button at the message box stating that only the active worksheet will be saved; and then click the Yes button to confirm saving the data as a text file.

- Only one worksheet can be exported as a text file at a time.
- To export an entire workbook, you must export each worksheet separately as an individual text file.
- When you export Excel data to another file format, you save a copy of the worksheet data in the other file format. You do not change the contents of the original Excel worksheet.

On the Job

Task 13.5 Exporting Excel Data as a Text File

Devon has contracted an adviser to analyze the data he's collected on orders and suggest ways the sales associates can focus their efforts to increase orders in the future. The adviser has asked Devon to supply the data in a tab delimited (.txt) file. Devon asks you to export the data from the Orders worksheet in the required format.

Note: *Be sure to open the data files for this chapter from a computer drive, not your OneDrive account.*

1. With the 13-DVAutoParts workbook open and the Orders worksheet active, click the File tab and then click the *Export* option.

   The Export backstage area displays.
2. Click the *Change File Type* option.

   The *Change File Type* section displays in the right panel.
3. Click the *Text (Tab delimited)* option in the *Change File Types* section.
4. Click the Save As button.

   The Save As dialog box displays. The text *13-DVAutoParts.txt* appears in the *File name* text box.
5. Change the file name, typing 13-DVAutoPartsText as the new name, and then click the Save button.

   A message box displays, stating that the selected file type does not support workbooks that contain multiple sheets and will save only the active sheet.
6. Click the OK button.

   The sheet tab name changes to *13-DVAutoPartsText* and the file name in the Title bar changes to *13-DVAutoPartsText.*
7. Close the Excel workbook without saving it.

   You do not need to save the workbook because you have not made any changes to it.
8. Click the Windows Start button. At the Start screen, start typing notepad. When *Notepad* appears in the *Best match* section at the search results list, press the Enter key. ***Note:*** *Depending on your operating system, these steps may vary.*

   A Notepad window opens with the title *Untitled - Notepad.*
9. Click the File command on the Notepad menu bar and then click the *Open* option.
10. Navigate to the AE13 folder on your storage medium and then double-click the data file **13-DVAutoPartsText**.

    The text file opens. Data that is arranged in columns in the Excel workbook displays as items separated by tabs in the text file.

11. If printed work is required by your instructor, click the File command on the Notepad menu bar, click the *Print* option at the drop-down list, select the printer, and then click the Print button at the Print dialog box.
12. Close the Notepad window without saving it.

    There is no need to save the text file because you did not make any changes to it.

Model Answer

13.6 Importing Data into Excel from Access

MOS Expert 3.4.1

Tutorial

Importing Data into Excel from Access

Importing data from other applications allows you to manipulate, organize, and analyze the data in a variety of ways. You can save time and money by not having to enter the information manually, and also reduce errors that may be introduced during data entry.

Since March 2017, the tools in the Get & Transform group on the Data tab have been based on Power Query technology, which provides instinctive steps for importing, combining, and refining data from a variety of sources. Previously, Excel used wizards to import data. These wizards are now called *legacy wizards*, and they are covered in Section 13.8.

Exchanging data between Access and Excel is a seamless process because the data in an Access datasheet is structured in the same row and column format as the data in an Excel worksheet.

▸ **Know This** about importing data into Excel from Access

— Data imported into Excel from Access can be appended to an existing worksheet or placed in a new worksheet.

— To import an Access table into an Excel workbook, perform the following steps:

1. With any worksheet active, click the Data tab.
2. Click the Get Data button in the Get & Transform Data group (see Figure 13.19).
3. Point to the *From Database* option at the drop-down list and then click the *From Microsoft Access Database* option at the second drop-down list.
4. Navigate to the folder containing the database at the Import Data dialog box and then double-click the database file in the file list box.
5. Click the Access table name in the left panel at the Navigator dialog box (see Figure 13.20). A preview of the data appears in the right panel.
6. Click the Load button to import the data in a new worksheet, click the Load button arrow and then click the *Load To* option at the drop-down list to import the data in a different location, or click the Edit button to edit and then import the data.

— In Step 5, to import more than one table, click the *Select multiple items* check box to insert a check mark at the Navigator dialog box and then click the check box for each table to insert a check mark. If more than one table is selected, the last table selected appears in the preview.

— In Step 6, if you click the Load button arrow and then the *Load To* option to import data in a different location, specify how you want to view the data and where you want to put the data at the Import Data dialog box and then click the OK button (see Figure 13.21 on page 631).

— In Step 6, if you click the Edit button, make the changes to the data (such as splitting the data or removing or adding rows or columns) at the Query Editor window (see Figure 13.22 on page 631) and then click the Close & Load button in the Close group on the Home tab to close the editor and load the data in a new worksheet.

Figure 13.19 Get Data Button Drop-Down List

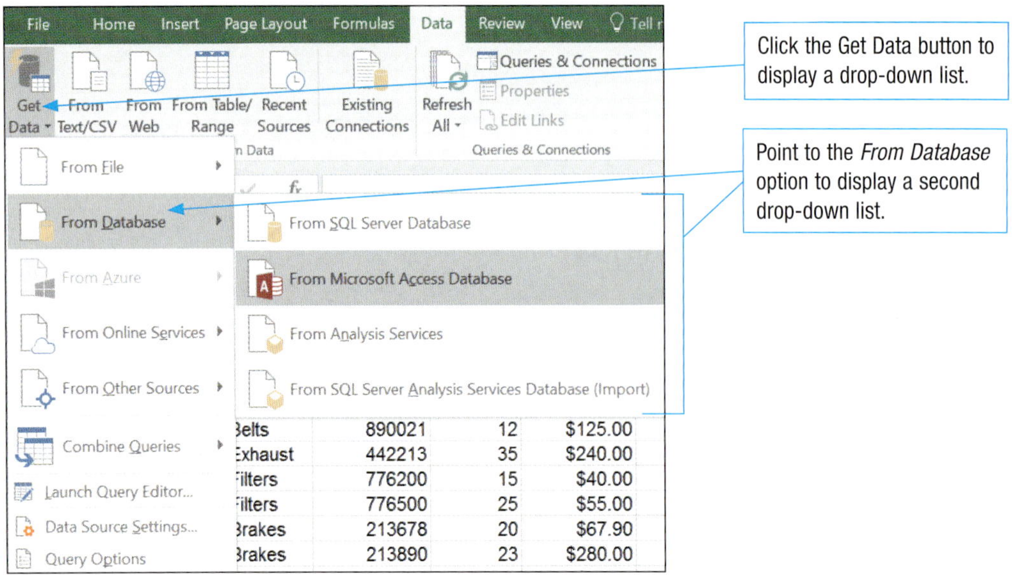

Figure 13.20 Navigator Dialog Box

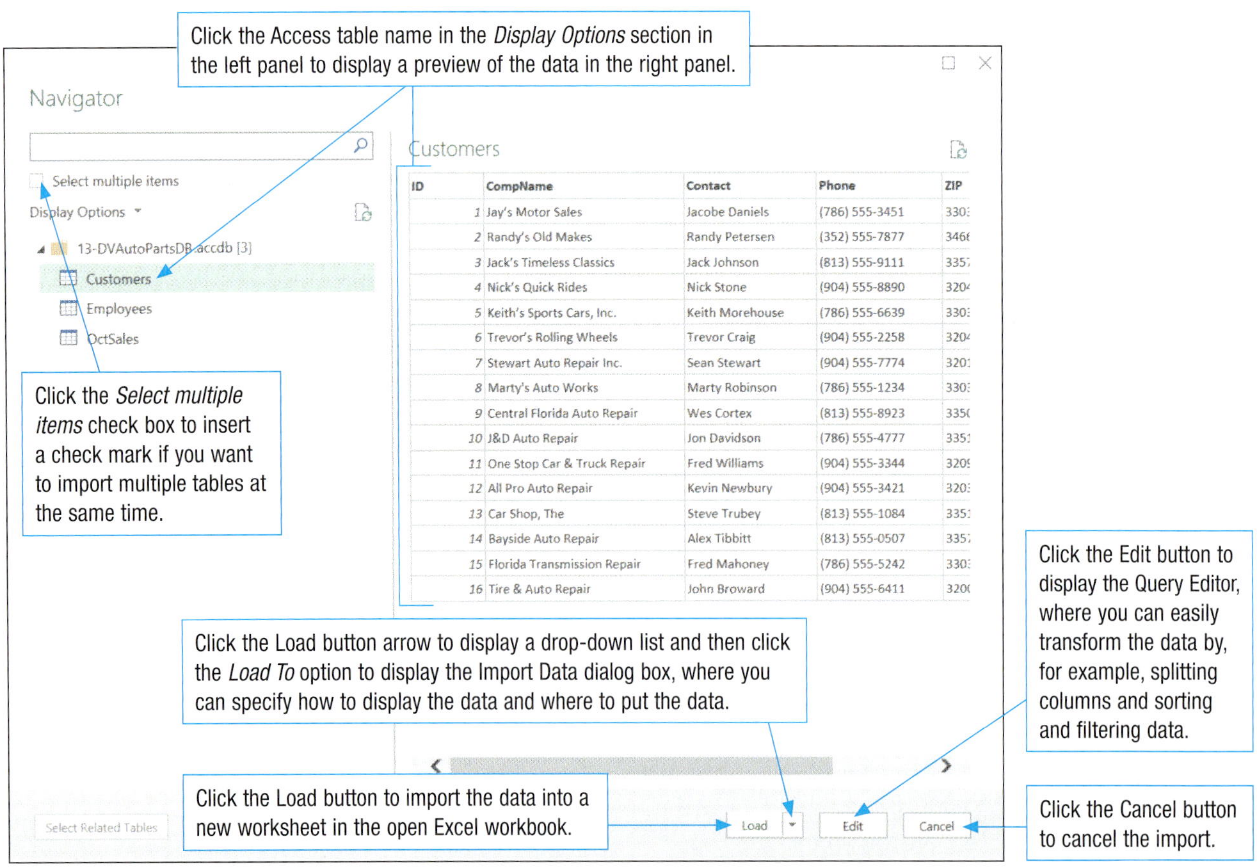

Figure 13.21 Import Data Dialog Box

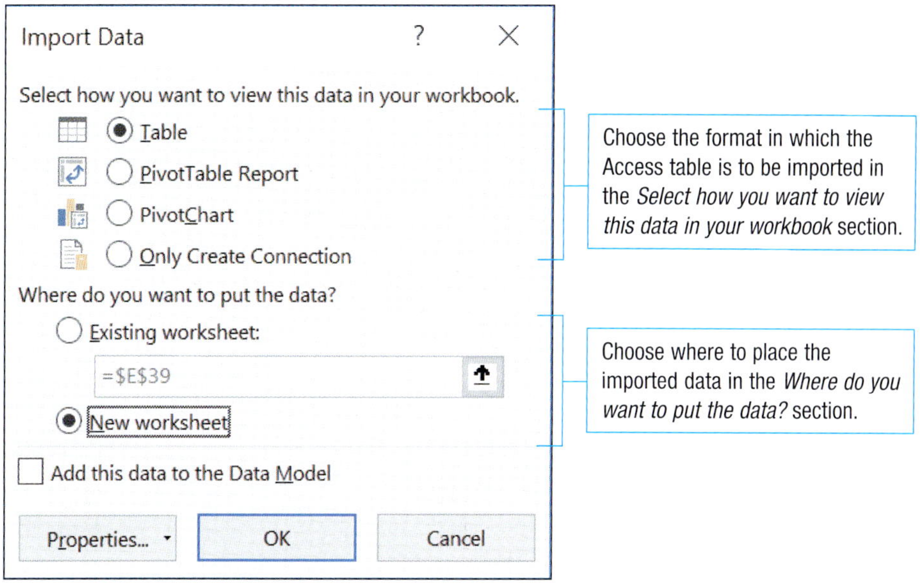

Figure 13.22 Query Editor Window

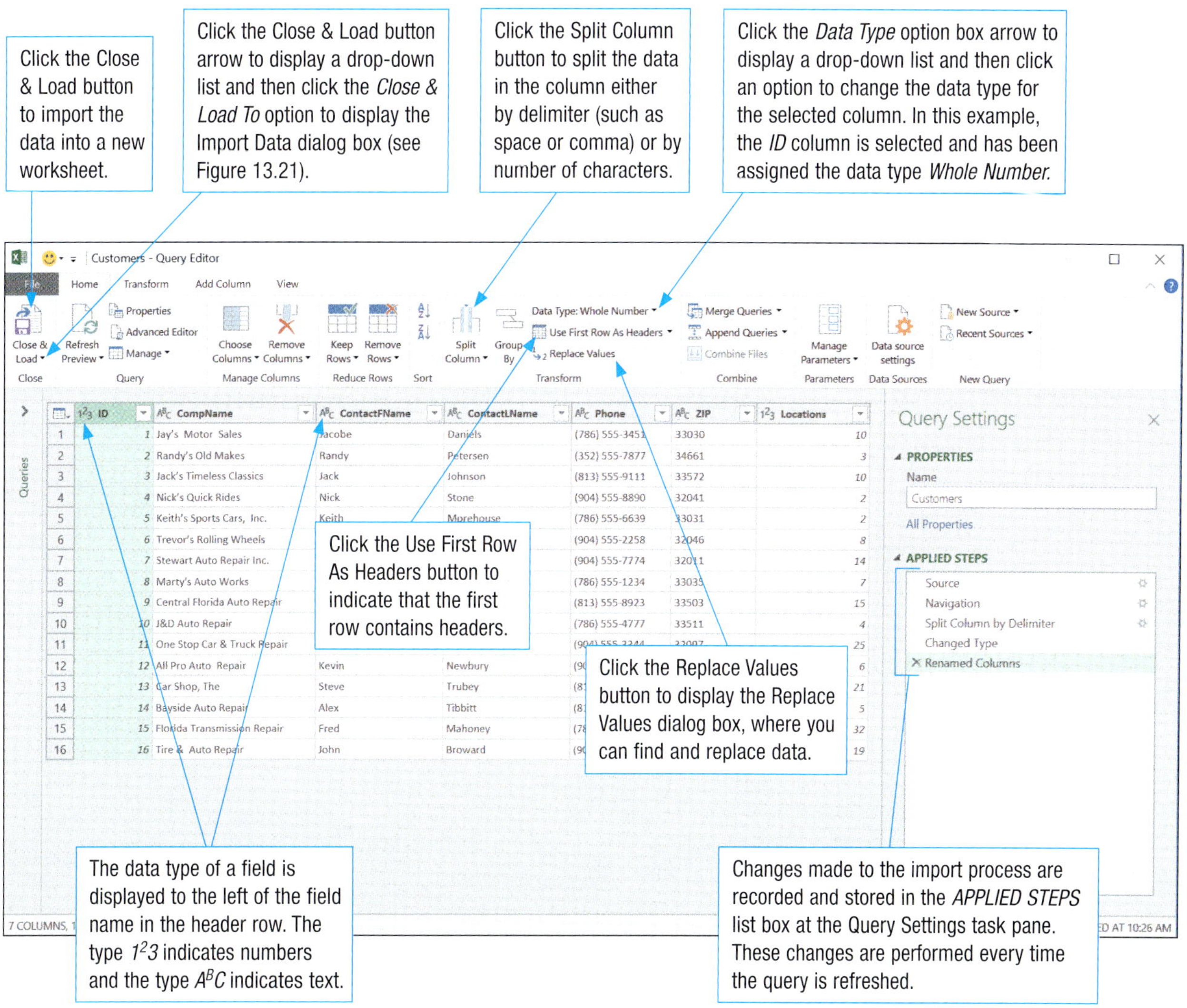

▸ **Know This** about the Query Editor

— When data is imported into Excel, a query is created. The query specifies the import steps and any modifications made to the data.

— You can use the Query Editor to transform data to display as you want it to in Excel.

— To display the Query Editor window, you can click the Edit button at the Navigator dialog box (see Figure 13.20 on page 630).

— To transform data, use tools on the Query Editor ribbon. For example, if a field contains both the first names and the last names of contacts, you can separate the field into two fields, one containing first names and the other containing last names.

— The steps you use to transform the data are saved as part of the query in the *APPLIED STEPS* section at the Query Settings task pane in the Query Editor window.

— The steps in the *APPLIED STEPS* section will be reapplied to the data every time the data is refreshed.

▸ **Know This** about transforming data using the Query Editor

— To split a database field into two fields, click in any cell in the field, click the Split Column button in the Transform group on the Home tab, click the *By Delimiter* option at the drop-down list, choose options to tell Excel how to split the field at the Split Column by Delimiter dialog box, and then click the OK button.

— To rename a field, right-click the field header, click the *Rename* option at the drop-down list, type the new name, and then press the Enter key.

▸ **Know This** about imported data

— Data is imported into Excel in a table format.

— When you click within the imported data, the contextual Table Tools Design tab and the Query Tools Query tab are available.

▸ **Know This** about the Queries & Connections task pane

— When data is imported into Excel, the Queries & Connections task pane displays with the Queries tab active and the *Customers* query item selected.

— The query item indicates the number of rows imported from the database table.

On the Job
Task 13.6 Importing Data into Excel from Access

Devon wants to add the customer identification numbers, company names, purchasing and accounting manager names, telephone numbers, zip codes, and location numbers he's been collecting in the 13-DVAutoPartsDB database to the 13-DVAutoParts workbook so he can forward the data to sales associates who aren't familiar with Access. Use the Get Data button on the Excel ribbon to import the Access data into a new worksheet in the Excel workbook, split the first and last names of the purchasing managers into two columns, and then rename the sheet tab to be *Customers*.

Note: Be sure to open the data files for this chapter from a computer drive, not your OneDrive account.

1. Open the data file **13-DVAutoParts** that you closed in Task 13.5; click the Orders sheet tab, if necessary; and then click the Data tab.
2. Click the Get Data button in the Get & Transform Data group (see Figure 13.19 on page 630).

   A drop-down list displays.
3. Point to the *From Database* option and then click the *From Microsoft Access Database* option at the second drop-down list.

   The Import Data dialog box displays.
4. Navigate to the AE13 folder on your storage medium and then double-click the data file **13-DVAutoPartsDB**.

   The Navigator dialog box displays (see Figure 13.20 on page 630).
5. Click the *Customers* table name in the left panel.

   A preview of the data appears in the right panel.
6. Click the Edit button in the right panel.

   The Query Editor window displays (see Figure 13.22 on page 631).
7. Click in any cell in the *Contact* column, click the Split Column button in the Transform group on the Home tab, and then click the *By Delimiter* option at the drop-down list.

   The Split Column by Delimiter dialog box displays (see Figure 13.23).

Figure 13.23 Split Column by Delimiter Dialog Box

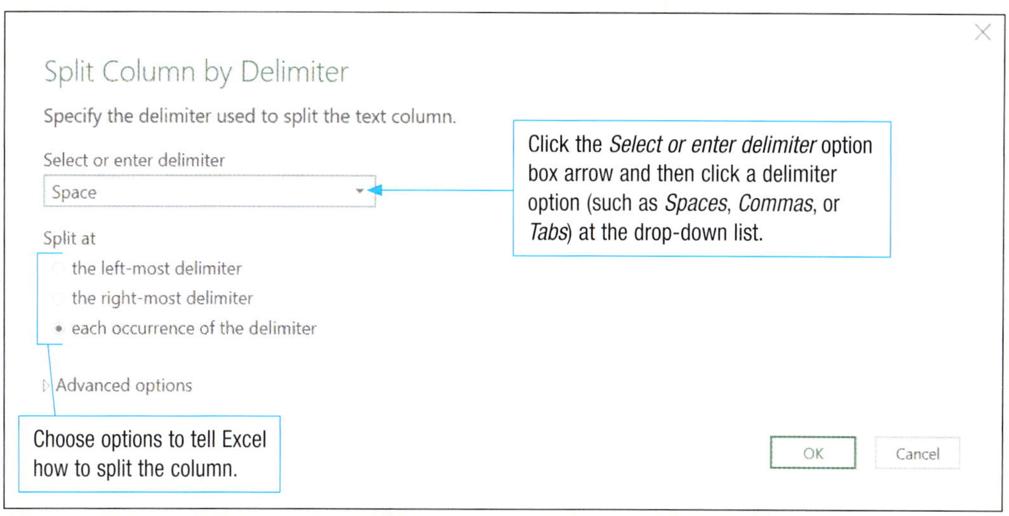

8. With the *Space* option appearing in the *Select or enter delimiter* option box and a bullet appearing in the *Each occurrence of the delimiter* radio button, click the OK button.

   The *Contact* column has been split into two columns: *Contact.1* and *Contact.2*. The *Split Column by Delimiter* and *Changed Type* steps have been added to the *APPLIED STEPS* list box at the Query Settings task pane.
9. Right-click the *Contact.1* column header, click the *Rename* option, type ContactFName, and then press the Enter key.

10. Right-click the *Contact.2* column header, click the *Rename* option, type ContactLName, and then press the Enter key.
11. Click the Close & Load button in the Close group.

    The data is inserted as a table in a new worksheet named *Sheet1*. Sheet1 is before the Orders worksheet. The Table Tools Design tab is active. The Query Tools Query tab is available. (The Query Tools Query tab is discussed in Section 13.9). The Queries & Connections task pane displays with the Queries tab active and the *Customers* query item selected (see Figure 13.24).

12. Rename the Sheet1 sheet tab, typing Customers as the new name.
13. Click the Save button on the Quick Access Toolbar.

Figure 13.24 Queries & Connections Task Pane with the Customers Query Selected

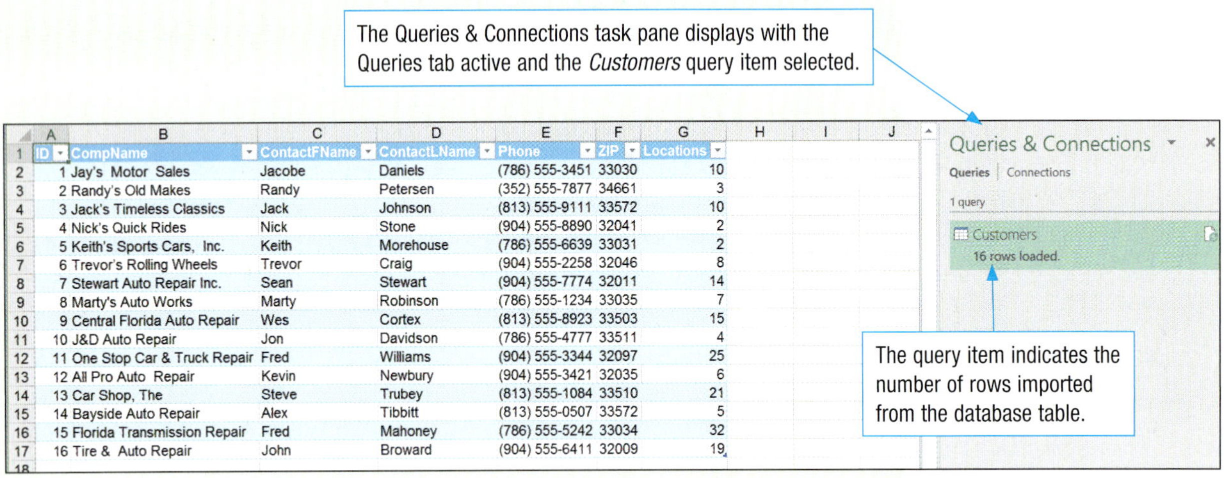

Model Answer

13.7 Importing and Appending Data to Excel from a Delimited Text File

MOS 1.1.2
MOS Expert 3.4.1

Tutorial

Importing and Appending Data to Excel from a Delimited Text File

A text file is often used to exchange data between different programs because the file format is recognized by nearly all applications. A text file contains no formatting and consists only of letters, numbers, punctuation symbols, and a few control characters. Two commonly used text file formats separate fields with tabs (**delimited file format**) and commas (**comma-separated file format**).

As with importing an Access table, when you import a text file into Excel, you can either place it in a new worksheet or append it to the end of existing data in a worksheet. When you append new data to existing data, if the formatting and organization of the appended data do not exactly match those of the existing data, leave one or more blank rows or columns between the existing data and the appended data. You can then transform and combine the appended data as required to make it fit in with the existing data (see Sections 13.11 and 13.13 later in this chapter).

▸ **Know This** about importing data into Excel from a text file

- Excel allows you to import data directly from some applications and programs.
- To use data from an application or program that cannot import directly into Excel, check the application or program's export options for a text file format.

  Most applications and programs can export data in a text file.
- Delimited files use tabs as separators, whereas fixed-width files use spaces.
- If necessary, view and edit a text file in Notepad before importing it into Excel (see Task 13.5, Steps 9–10).
- To import a text file into an existing Excel workbook, complete the following steps:
  1. With the workbook open and the worksheet active, click in the cell in which the first cell of data will be placed and then click the Data tab.
  2. Click the From Text/CSV button in the Get & Transform Data group.
  3. Navigate to the folder containing the text file at the Import Data dialog box and then double-click the text file in the file list box. ***Note:*** *By default, in the file list box, Excel displays only text files—that is, files whose names end with the extension* .prn, .txt, *or* .csv.
  4. Click the *Delimiter* option box arrow and choose a different delimiter, if necessary, at the dialog box. A preview of the data with the chosen delimiter appears in the list box.
  5. Click the Load button to import the data in a new worksheet, click the Load button arrow and then click the *Load To* option at the drop-down list to import the data in a different location, or click the Edit button to edit and then import the data.
- In Step 5, if you click the Load button arrow and then the *Load To* option to import data in a different location, specify how you want to view the data and where you want to put the data at the Import Data dialog box and then click the OK button (see Figure 13.21 on page 631).
- In Step 5, if you click the Edit button, make the changes to the data in the Query Editor window (see Figure 13.22 on page 631), click the Close & Load button arrow in the Close group on the Home tab, click the *Close & Load To* option at the drop-down list, specify how you want to view the data and where to place the data at the Import Data dialog box, and then click the OK button to import the data and close the Query Editor window.

On the Job

Task 13.7 Importing and Appending Data to Excel from a Delimited Text File

Devon has a text file containing data about new parts. He asks you to add this data to the Inventory worksheet in the 13-DVAutoParts workbook. The text file doesn't use the same formatting as the Inventory worksheet. Import the data from the text file to the bottom of the Inventory worksheet, leaving two blank lines above the new data. In Task 13.13, you will transform and combine the data to match the existing data in the worksheet.

Note: Be sure to open the data files for this chapter from a computer drive, not your OneDrive account.

1. With the 13-DVAutoParts workbook open and the Customers worksheet active, click the Inventory sheet tab and then click in cell A15.
2. Click the Data tab, if necessary, and then click the From Text/CSV button in the Get & Transform Data group.

   The Import Data dialog box displays.
3. Navigate to the AE13 folder on your storage medium and then double-click the data file **13-NewInventory** in the file list box.

   The 13-NewInventory.txt dialog box displays, with the *Tab* option in the *Delimiter* option box (see Figure 13.25).

Figure 13.25 13-NewInventory.txt Dialog Box

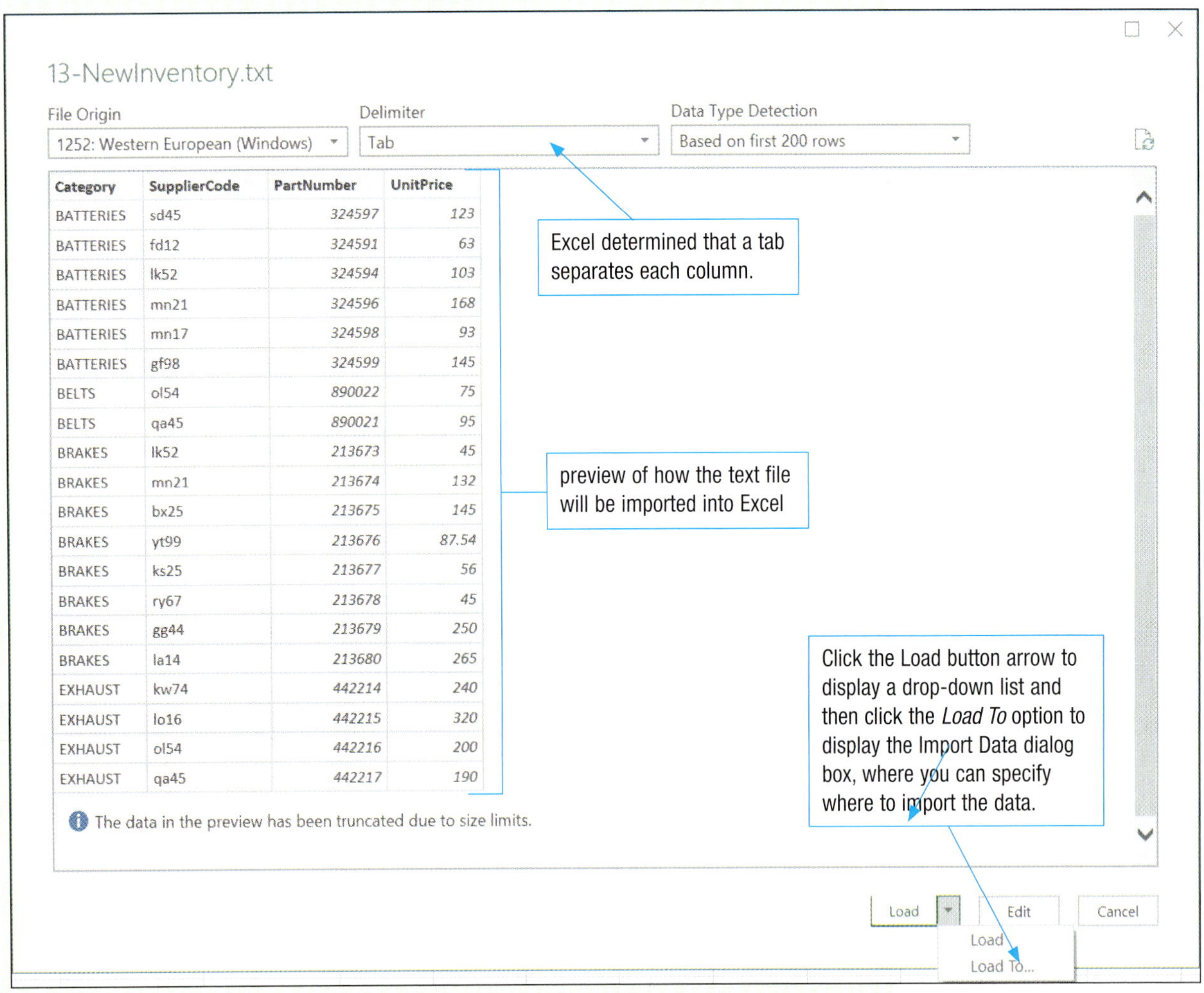

4. Click the Load button arrow and then click the *Load To* option.

   The Import Data dialog box displays.

5. Click the *Existing worksheet* radio button.

   A bullet appears in the radio button and the location *=$A$15* in the *Existing worksheet* text box appears in black font instead of being grayed out (see Figure 13.26).

Figure 13.26 Import Data Dialog Box

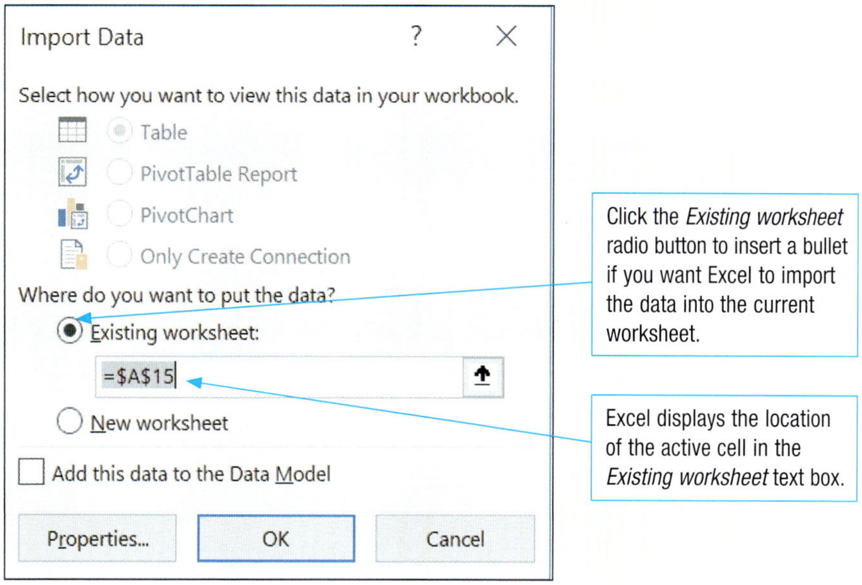

6. Click the OK button.

   The data is appended to the Inventory worksheet, starting in cell A15. The Queries & Connections task pane displays with the Queries tab active and the *13-NewInventory* query item selected. The query item indicates that 30 rows were loaded (see Figure 13.27).
7. Click the Save button on the Quick Access Toolbar. Leave the Excel workbook open for the next task.

Figure 13.27 Queries & Connections Task Pane with the *13-NewInventory* Query Item Selected

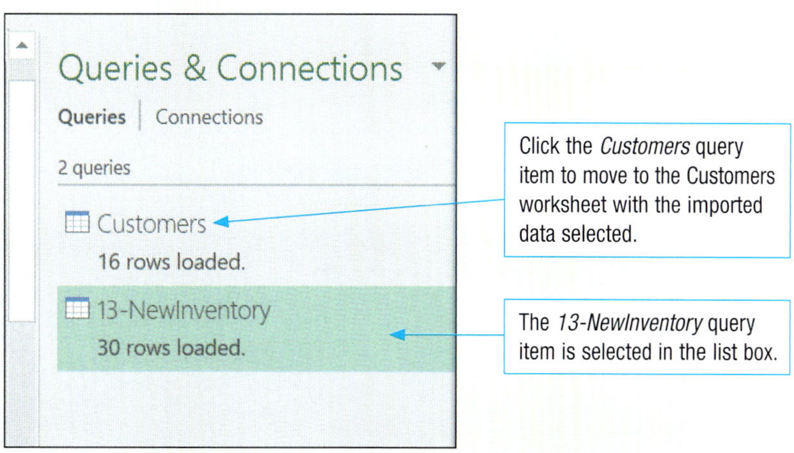

Model Answer

13.8 Importing Data into Excel Using Legacy Settings

Before March 2017, Excel used wizards instead of Power Query technology to import data. At times, you may want to use these legacy wizards instead of the Power Query features in the Get & Transform Data group. The wizards allow you to save the data source login credentials as part of the workbook. However, this method is not in line with current security standards. When you use a legacy wizard, you create a connection rather than a query. (Queries and connections are discussed in Section 13.9.) Before you can use a legacy wizard, you must add it to the Get & Transform Data group.

Tutorial

Importing Data into Excel Using the Access Legacy Wizard

▸ Know This about using a legacy wizard

— To add a legacy wizard to the Get & Transform group on the Excel ribbon, click the File tab, click the *Options* option, click the *Data* option in the left panel at the Excel Options dialog box, click the wizard check box in the *Show legacy data import wizards* section to insert a check mark (see Figure 13.28), and then click the OK button.

— To start a legacy wizard, click the Get Data button, point to the *Legacy Wizards* option at the drop-down list, and then click the *From Application (Legacy)* option at the second drop-down list (see Figure 13.29).

Figure 13.28 *Show legacy data import wizards* Section at the Excel Options Dialog Box

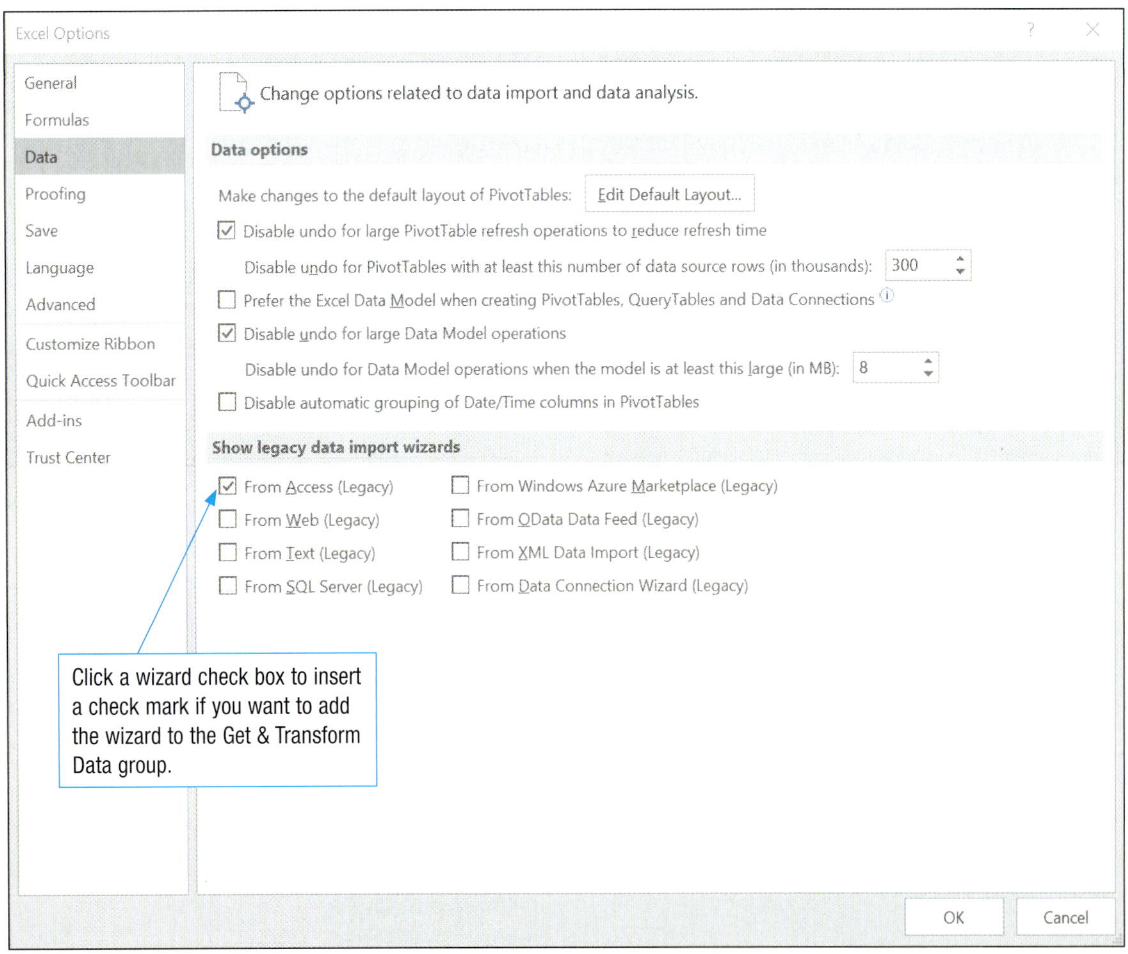

Figure 13.29 *Legacy Wizards* Option Drop-Down List

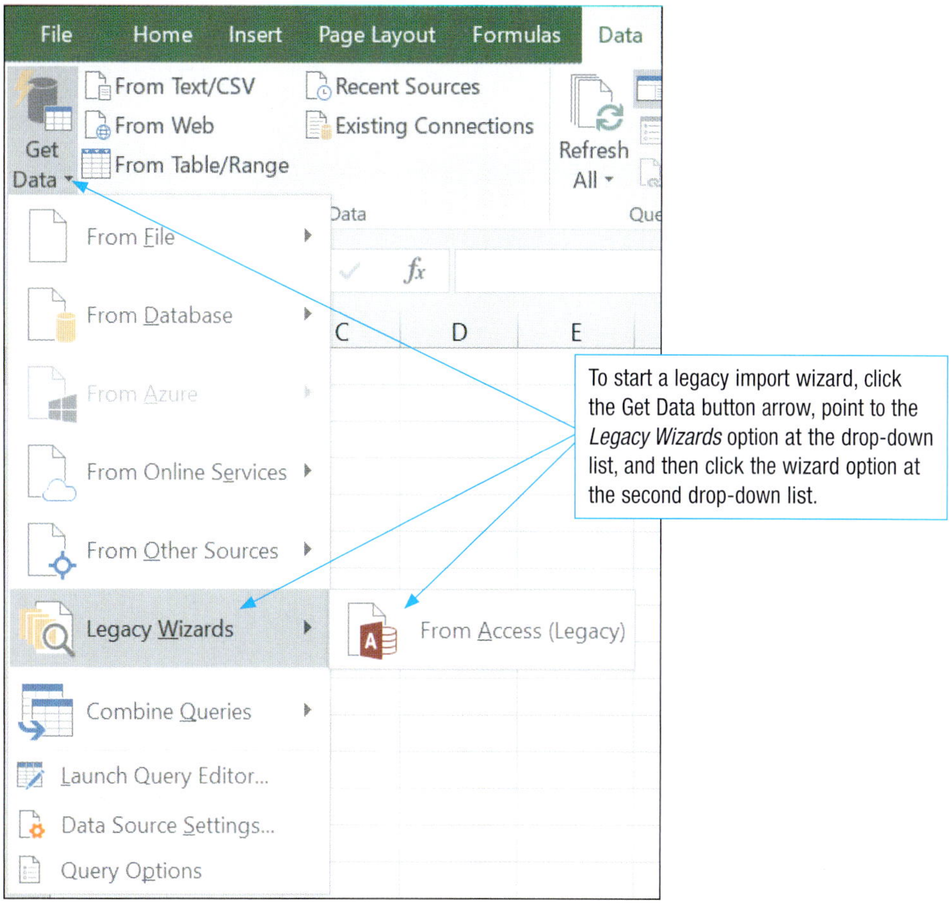

▸ **Know This** about importing data into Excel from Access using the legacy From Access wizard

— To import an Access table into an active Excel worksheet using a legacy wizard, perform the following steps:

1. Click in any cell that does not contain imported data. ***Note:*** *You cannot import new data on top of imported data.*
2. Click the Data tab.
3. Click the Get Data button in the Get & Transform Data group, point to the *Legacy Wizards* option at the drop-down list, and then click the *From Access (Legacy)* option at the second drop-down list (see Figure 13.29).
4. Navigate to the Access database at the Select Data Source dialog box and then double-click the database file in the file list box.
5. Click the Access table name in the list box at the Select Table dialog box, if it displays (see Figure 13.30). ***Note:*** *If the source database contains more than one table, the Select Table dialog box displays. If the source database contains only one table, the Select Table dialog box does not display.*
6. Choose how to view the data and where to place the data at the Import Data dialog box.
7. Click the OK button.

Figure 13.30 Select Table Dialog Box

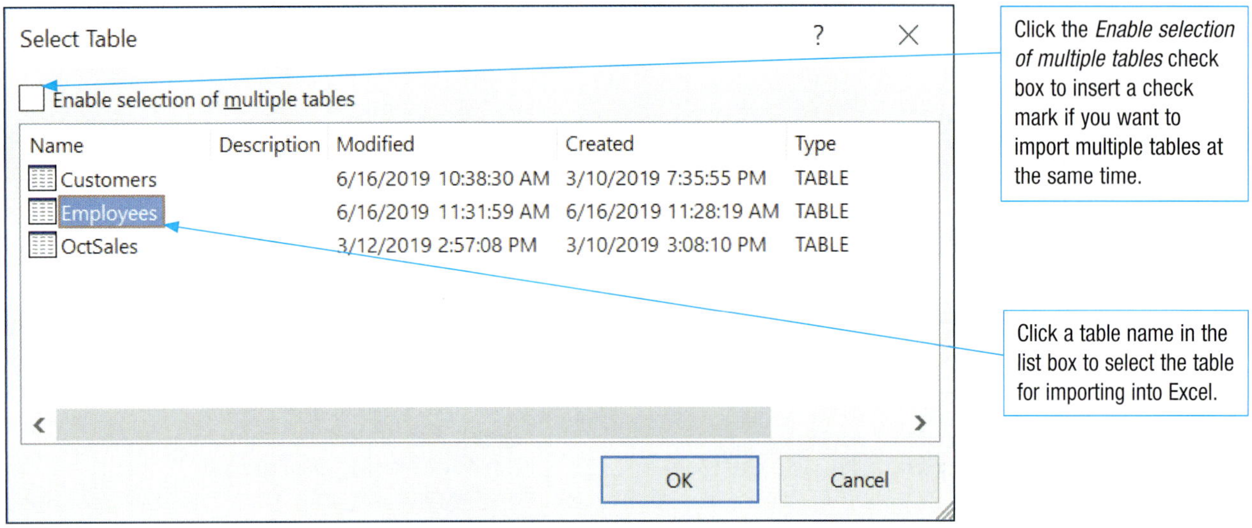

On the Job

Task 13.8 Importing Data into Excel Using the Access Legacy Wizard

Devon wants to add the employee information from the 13-DVAutoPartsDBV database in a new worksheet. You decide to use the Access legacy wizard to add them as you want to create a connection to the data instead of a query to the data. You must first add the option to use the Access legacy wizard and then import the Employees table.

Note: *Be sure to open the data files for this chapter from a computer drive, not your OneDrive account.*

1. With the 13-DVAutoParts workbook open and the Inventory worksheet active, click the File tab and then click the *Options* option.

   The Excel Options dialog box displays.

2. Click the *Data* option in the left panel.

   Data options display in the right panel (see Figure 13.28 on page 638).

3. Click the *From Access (Legacy)* check box in the *Show legacy data import wizards* section to insert a check mark, if necessary.
4. Click the OK button.

   The Excel Options dialog box closes.

5. Click in any cell that does not contain imported data.
6. Click the Data tab, if necessary; click the Get Data button; point to the *Legacy Wizards* option; and then click the *From Access (Legacy)* option (see Figure 13.29 on page 639).

   The Select Data Source dialog box displays.

7. Navigate to the AE13 folder on your storage medium and then double-click the data file **13-DVAutoPartsDB** in the file list box.

   The Select Table dialog box displays.

8. Click the *Employees* table name in the list box and then click the OK button.

   The Import Data dialog box displays.

Reminder
You cannot import new data on top of imported data.

9. Click the *New worksheet* radio button to insert a bullet and then click the OK button.

   The data is inserted as a table in a new worksheet named *Sheet2*. Sheet2 is before the Inventory worksheet. The Queries & Connections task pane displays with the Connections tab active and the 13-DVAutoPartsDB connection item selected.

10. Rename the Sheet2 sheet tab, typing Employees as the new name.
11. Click the Save button on the Quick Access Toolbar.

Model Answer

13.9 Refreshing, Modifying, and Deleting Queries and Connections

When data is imported into Excel, a connection is established between the source file and the destination file. If the file is imported using Power Query technology, the connection is created using a query. If the file is imported using a legacy wizard, the connection is called a *connection*. This connection can be refreshed, modified, or removed. Refreshing, modifying, and removing queries and connections helps you maintain the data you need to make sound business decisions. Refreshing a connection allows you to update data when you need the most current data in a destination file. Editing a query allows you to make further changes to the data. Removing a connection allows you to capture data at a specific time.

MOS Expert 3.4.1

Tutorials

Editing a Query

Refreshing Data

▸ **Know This** about the Queries & Connections task pane

— To redisplay the Query & Connections task pane, click the Queries & Connections button in the Queries & Connections group on the Data tab (see Figure 13.31).

Figure 13.31 Queries & Connections Group on the Data Tab

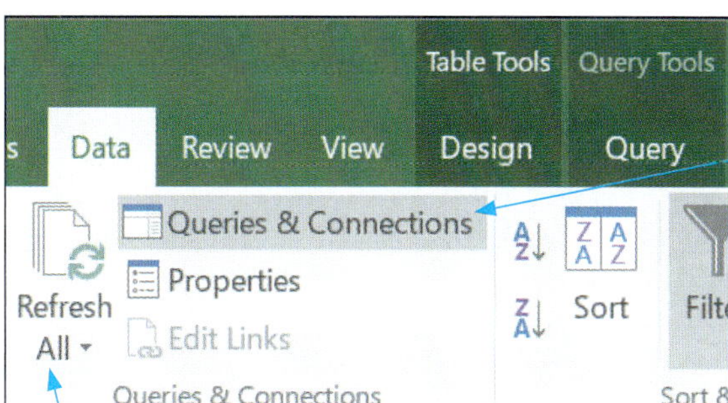

Click the Queries & Connections button to display the Queries & Connections task pane.

Click the Refresh All button to refresh all the queries and connections in the workbook.

▸ **Know This** about previewing, editing, and deleting a query

— To display a dialog box with options for previewing, editing, and deleting a query, point to the query item at the task pane (see Figure 13.32).

Figure 13.32 Query Dialog Box

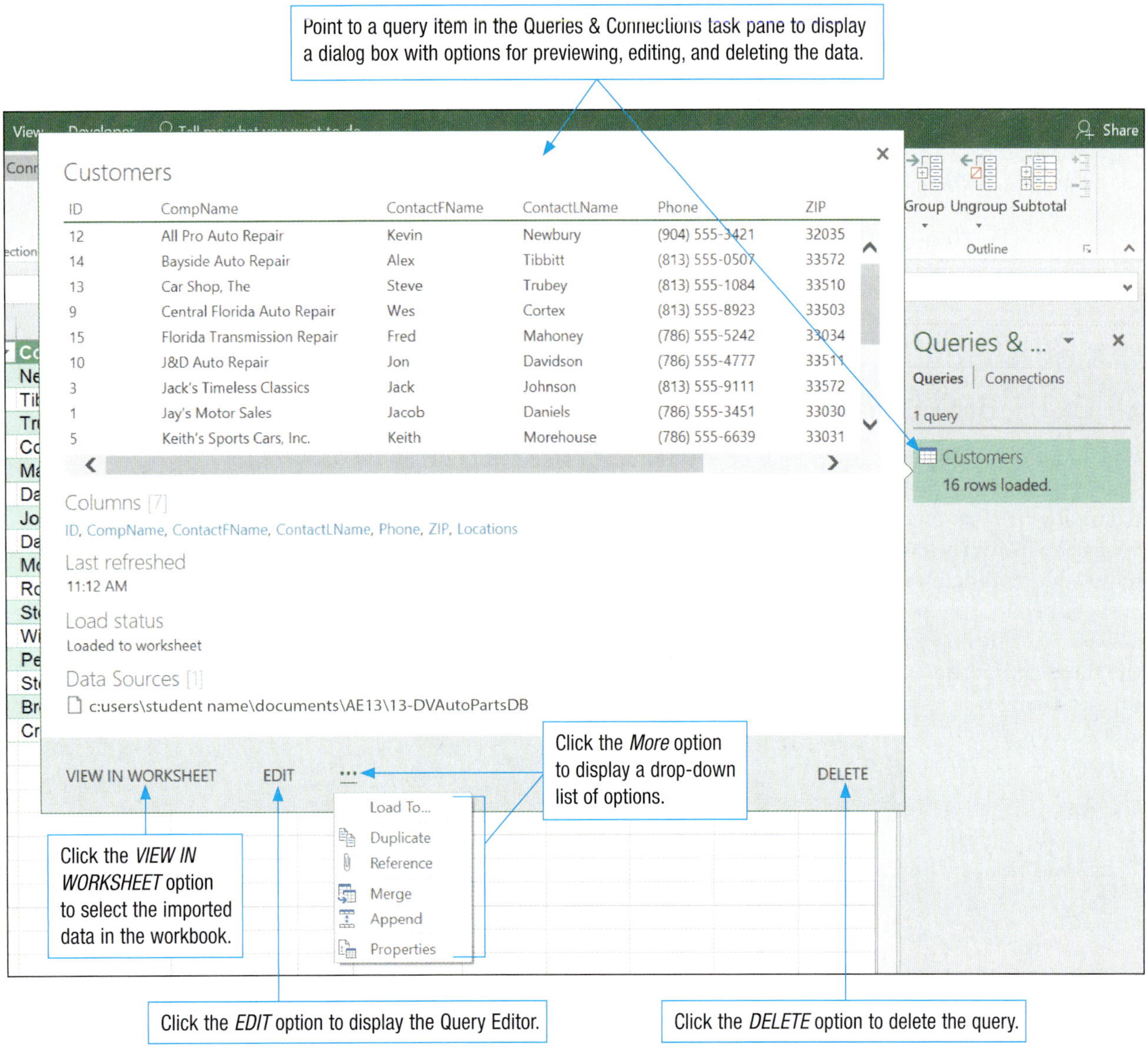

▸ Know This about refreshing data

— When you refresh data, Excel goes back to the source data to retrieve the data, applies any changes listed in the *APPLIED STEPS* list box, and then loads the data to the designated location.

▸ Know This about when to refresh or remove queries and connections

— If a query or connection is no longer being used, remove it so you do not accidentally refresh the data.

— If you make changes to data in the destination file and want to keep the changes, remove the association so you do not accidentally refresh the data and remove the changes.

— If data is frequently updated in the source file and you want to reflect those changes in the destination file, consider maintaining the query or connection and refreshing the data on a regular basis.

— You can modify the query properties to refresh the data at a specific time period (such as every 60 minutes) or when the file is opened.
— Refreshing a query may override any additional changes you have made to the imported data.

▶ **Know This** about how to refresh queries and connections

— To refresh queries and connections, click the Refresh All button in the Queries & Connections group on the Data tab.
— To refresh just the selected query or connection, click the Refresh All button arrow and then click the *Refresh* option at the drop-down list.
— To modify the data to refresh at a specific time period or when the workbook is opened, click the Refresh All button arrow, click the *Connections Properties* option at the drop-down list, and then choose options at the Query Properties dialog box (see Figure 13.33).

▶ Know More ways to refresh queries and connections

– Right-click the query or connection item at the Queries & Connections task pane and then click the *Refresh* option at the query item pop-up menu (see Figure 13.34) or connection item pop-up menu (see Figure 13.35).
– Right-click the table and then click the *Refresh* option at the pop-up menu.

Figure 13.33 Query Properties Dialog Box

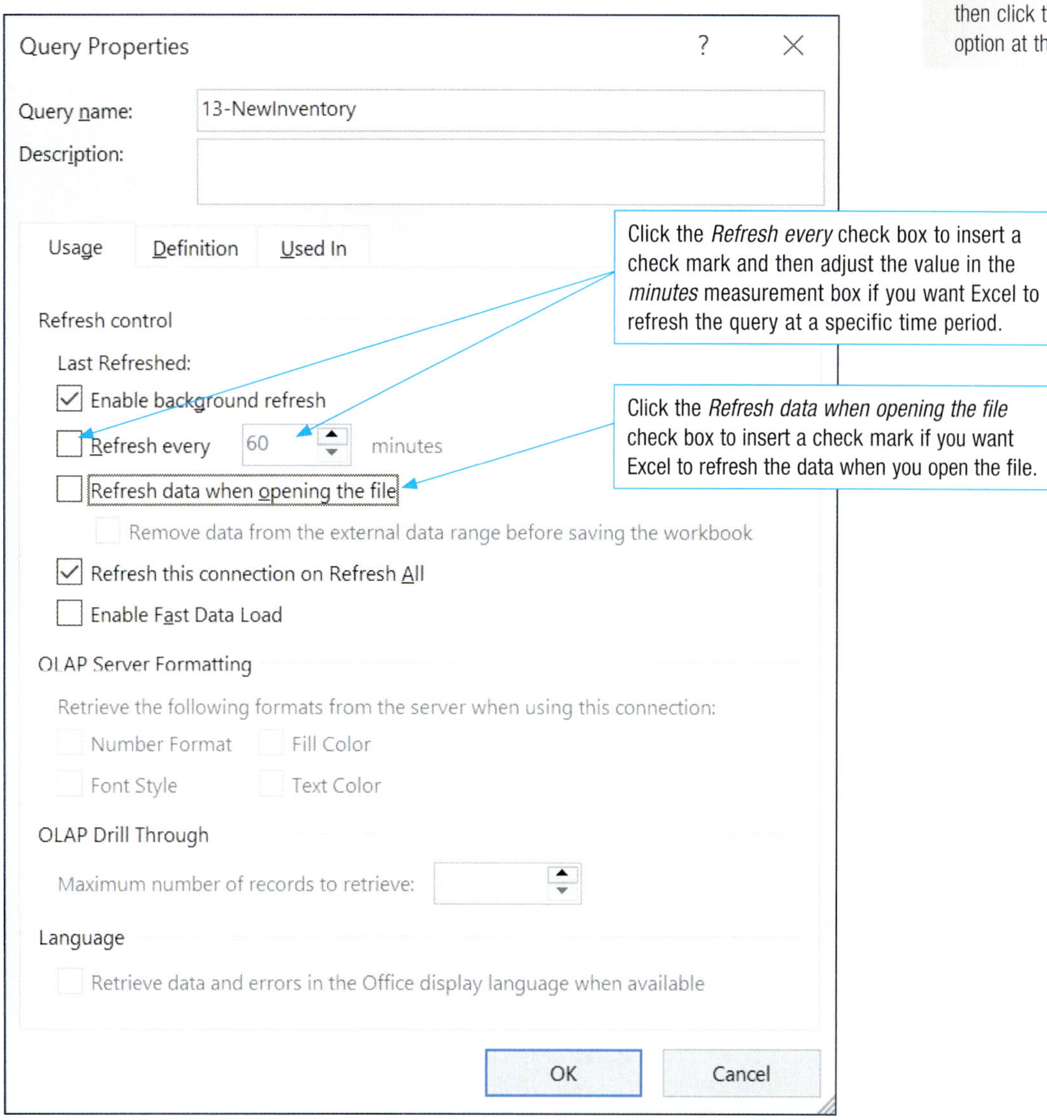

Figure 13.34 Query Item Pop-Up Menu

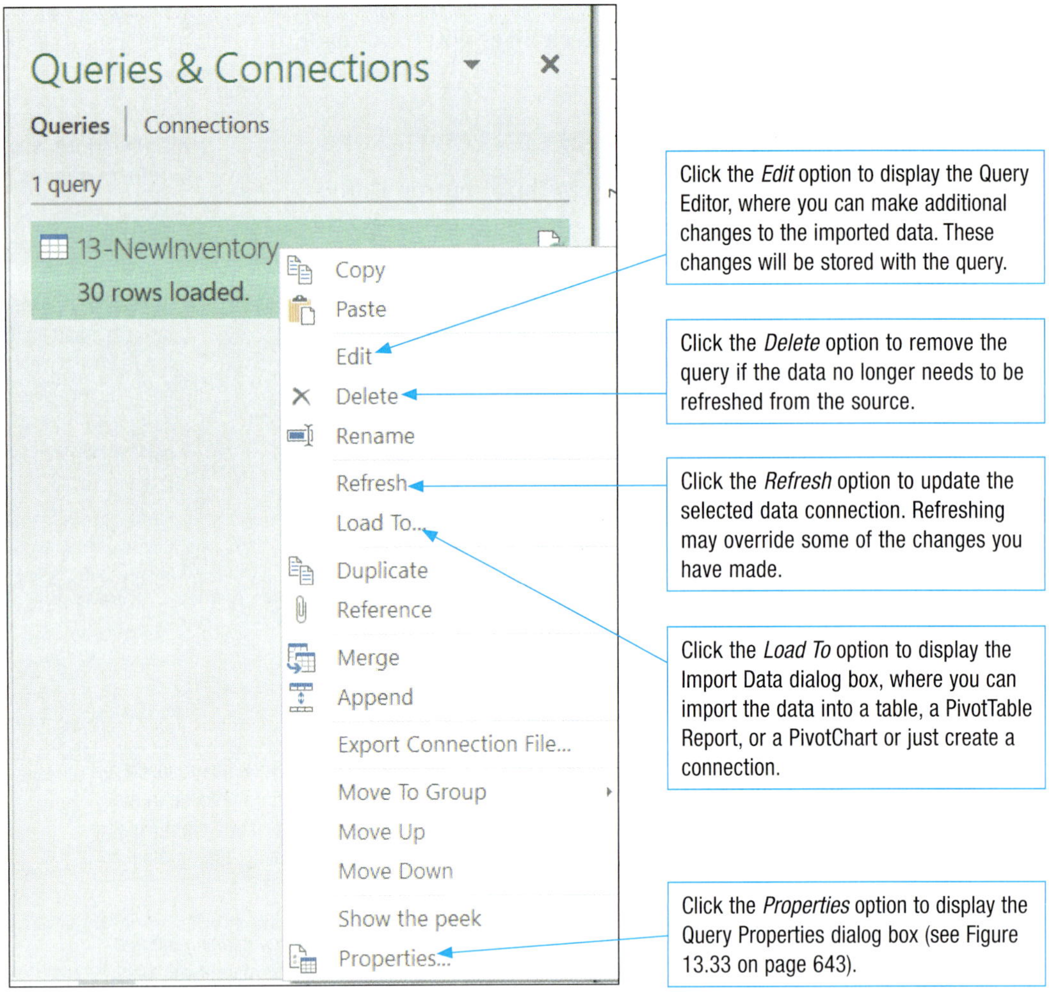

Figure 13.35 Connection Item Pop-Up Menu

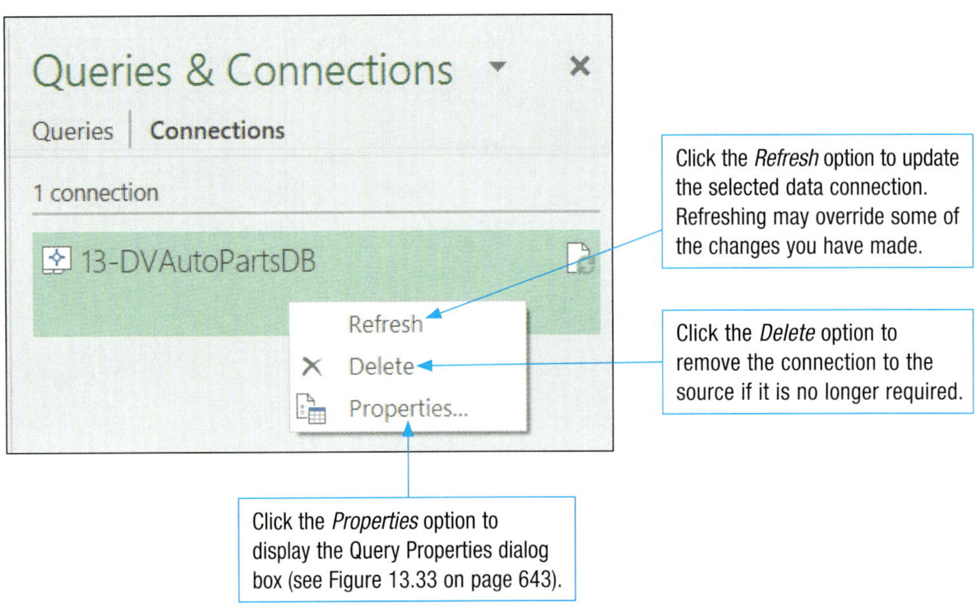

▸ Know This about managing existing workbook queries and connections

— To manage a query in an Excel workbook, open the workbook: click the Queries & Connections button in the Queries & Connections group on the Data tab; click the Queries tab at the Queries & Connections task pane, if necessary; right-click the query item in the list on the tab; and then click an option at the pop-up menu (see Figure 13.34 on page 644).

— To manage a connection in an Excel workbook: open the workbook; click the Queries & Connections button; click the Connections tab at the Queries & Connections task pane, if necessary; right-click the connection item in the list on the tab; and then click an option at the pop-up menu (see Figure 13.35 on page 644).

▸ Know This about editing a query

— Edit a query if further changes need to be made to the data.

— Changes made to a query will be incorporated when the data is refreshed.

— To edit a query, double-click the query item at the Queries & Connections task pane, make the necessary changes in the Query Editor window, and then click the Close & Load button in the Close group on the Home tab in the Query Editor window.

▸ Know More ways to edit a query

– Right-click the query item at the Queries & Connections task pane and then click the *Edit* option at the pop-up menu (see Figure 13.34).

– Click the Query Tools Query tab and then click the Edit button in the Edit group (see Figure 13.36).

▸ Know This about the Query Tools Query tab

— The features on the Query Tools Query tab are also found at the pop-up menu when you right-click a query item at the Queries & Connections task pane.

Figure 13.36 Query Tools Query Tab

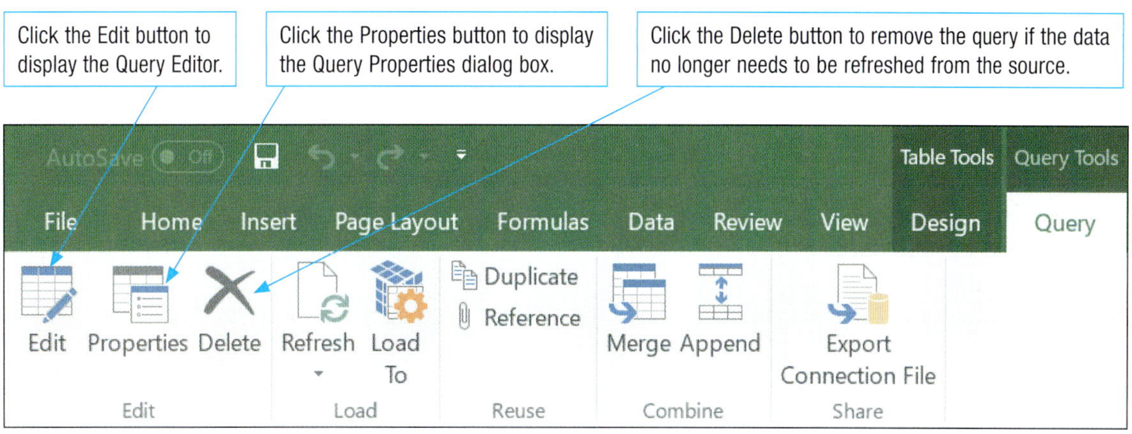

On the Job

Task 13.9a Editing a Query and Refreshing Data

Devon would like the list of customer data in the 13-DVAutoParts workbook sorted alphabetically by company name. He also mentions that customer information that he sends to the sales associates who are not familiar with Access will be imported into the workbook on a regular basis. While editing the query, you notice that Jacob's name is spelled incorrectly.

You decide to change it in the database to ensure that every time the query is refreshed, the name is spelled correctly.

Note: *Be sure to open the data files for this chapter from a computer drive, not your OneDrive account.*

1. With the 13-DVAutoParts workbook open, click the Customers sheet tab.

   The Customers worksheet is active.
2. Double-click the *Customers* query item on the Queries tab at the Queries & Connections task pane.

   The Query Editor window displays.
3. Click in any cell in the *CompName* column and then click the Sort Ascending button in the Sort group on the Home tab.

   The database data is sorted alphabetically from *A* to *Z* by company name.
4. Click the Close & Load button in the Close group.

   The worksheet data is sorted alphabetically from *A* to *Z* by company name.
5. Save and then close the workbook.
6. Start Access 2016 and then open the data file **13-DVAutoPartsDB** from the AE13 folder on your storage medium. Click the Enable Content button if a security warning displays, stating that some active content has been disabled. Click the Yes button if a message box displays, asking if you want to make this a trusted document.
7. Double-click *Customers* in the Tables group in the Navigation pane.

   The Customers table opens in Datasheet view.
8. In row 1, change the contact name *Jacobe Daniels* to *Jacob Daniels*.
9. Close the 13-DVAutoPartsDB database.

   When you close the database, the data is saved automatically.
10. Open the data file **13-DVAutoParts** and notice the name *Jacobe* in the cell C9 in the Customers worksheet.
11. Click the Data tab and then click the Refresh All button in the Queries & Connections group.

    The data refreshes and the name *Jacob* is spelled correctly in cell C9. The changes made to the query previously continue to be reflected when the data is refreshed.
12. Click the Save button on the Quick Access Toolbar.

Reminder
To redisplay the Queries & Connections task pane, click the Queries & Connections button in the Queries & Connections group on the Data tab.

▸ Know This about deleting a query or connection

— To delete a query or connection, right-click the query or connection at the Queries & Connections task pane and then click the *Delete* option at the pop-up menu.

— If you convert the table to a range, a message box displays, asking if you want to permanently remove the query definition or to break the connection. The type of message depends on whether the association with the source file is a query or a connection. Click the appropriate button to delete the query or connection.

▸ Know More ways to delete a query or connection

- Click the Delete button in the Edit group on the Query Tools Query tab.
- Point to the query or connection item at the Queries & Connections task pane and then click the *Delete* option at the drop-down list.

continues...

▸ Know This about unlinking a query

— To unlink a query, click the Unlink button in the External Table Data group on the Table Tools Design tab.

▸ Know This about editing or removing the source for a query or connection

— If you move or rename a destination workbook, Excel will not know where to locate the file and a yellow triangle with an exclamation mark will appear beside the query item at the Queries & Connections task pane (see Figure 13.37). To edit the source, you will need to remove the query or connection.

— To remove a query or connection and edit the source, perform the following steps:

1. Double-click the query or connection item at the Queries & Connections task pane.
2. Click the Data source settings button in the Data Sources group on the Home tab in the Query Editor window.
3. Click the Change Source button at the Data source settings dialog box (see Figure 13.38).
4. Click the *File path* Browse button at the source information dialog box (see Figure 13.39).
5. Navigate to the folder containing the source file, click the source file in the file list box, and then click the OK button.
6. Click the Close button at the Data source settings dialog box.
7. Click the Close & Load button in the Close group on the Home tab at the Query Editor window to import the data from the new source file.

Figure 13.37 Source File Moved or Renamed

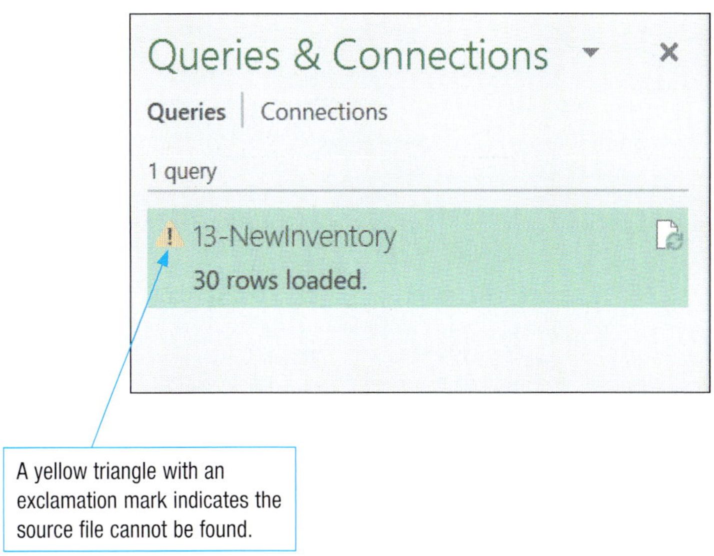

▸ Know More ways to delete a query or connection *...continued*

– If you convert the table to a range, a message box displays, asking if you want to permanently remove the query definition or to break the connection. The type of message depends on whether the association with the source file is a query or a connection. Click the appropriate button to delete the query or connection.

Figure 13.38 Data source settings Dialog Box

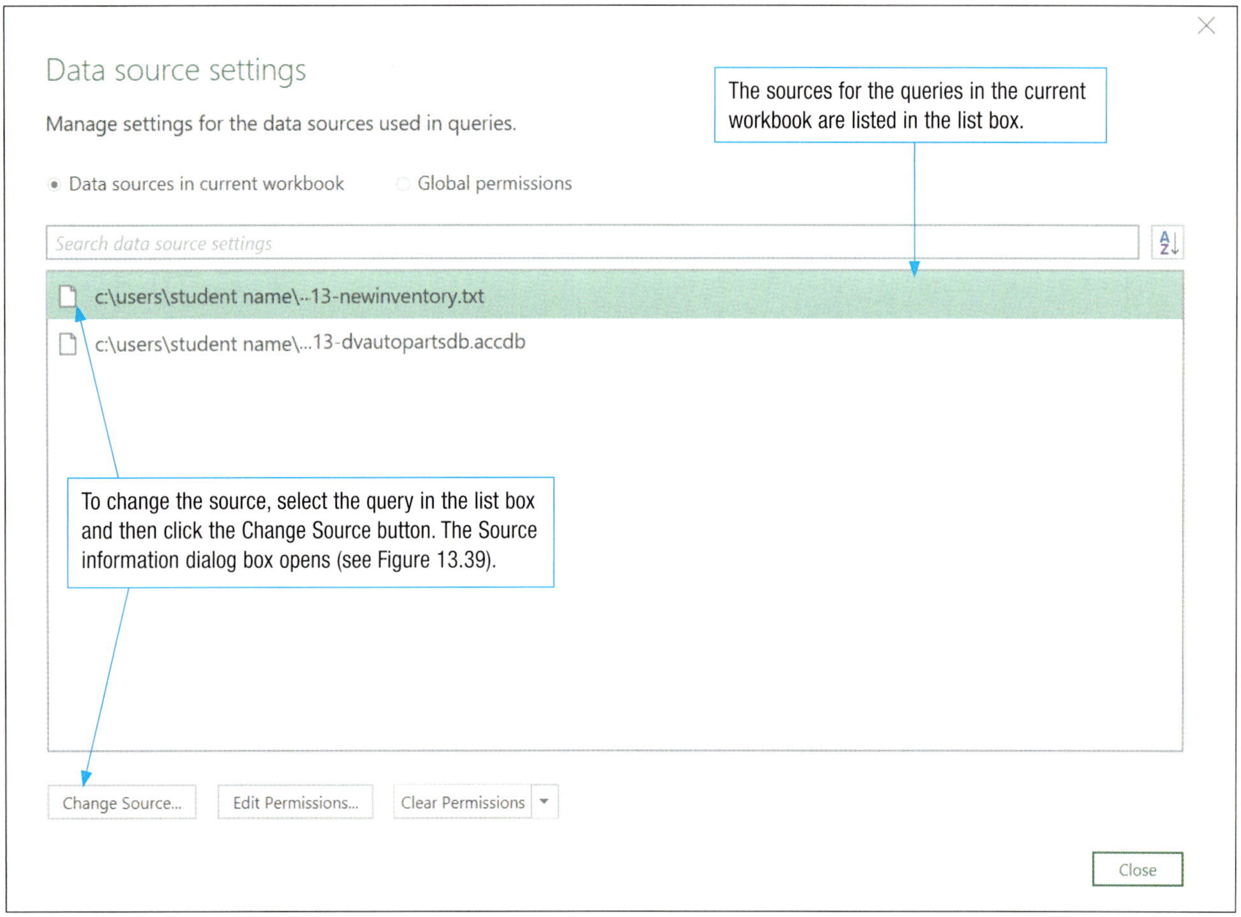

Figure 13.39 Source Information Dialog Box

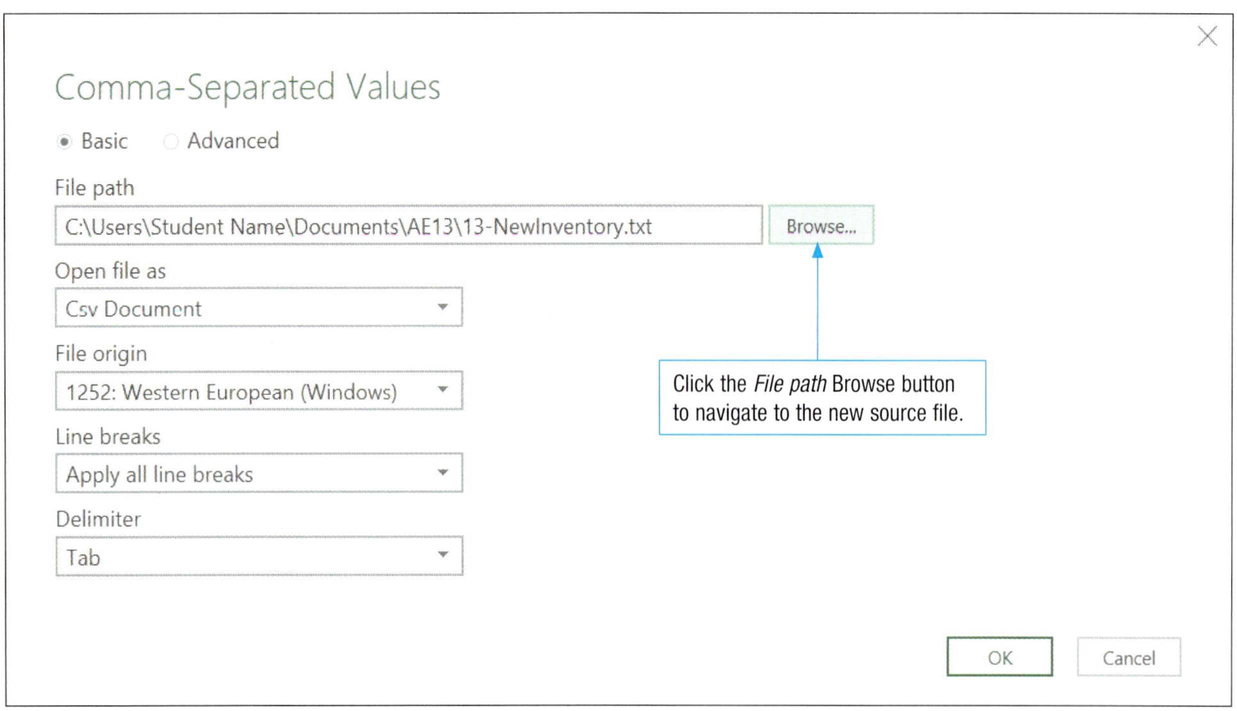

On the Job
Task 13.9b Deleting a Query

Devon is planning to make changes to the inventory data you imported into the Excel workbook from the text file. He wants to keep the changes he makes in the workbook and also keep the data in the source files unchanged. Remove the data connections to the text file.

***Note:** Be sure to open the data files for this chapter from a computer drive, not your OneDrive account.*

1. With the 13-DVAutoParts workbook open, click the Inventory sheet tab.
2. Click the Data tab, if necessary, and then click the Queries & Connections button in the Queries & Connections group.
   The Queries & Connection task pane displays with the Queries tab active.
3. Right-click the *13-NewInventory* query item at the task pane.
   A pop-up menu displays.
4. Click the *Delete* option.
   The Delete Query message box displays (see Figure 13.40).

Figure 13.40 Delete Query Message Box

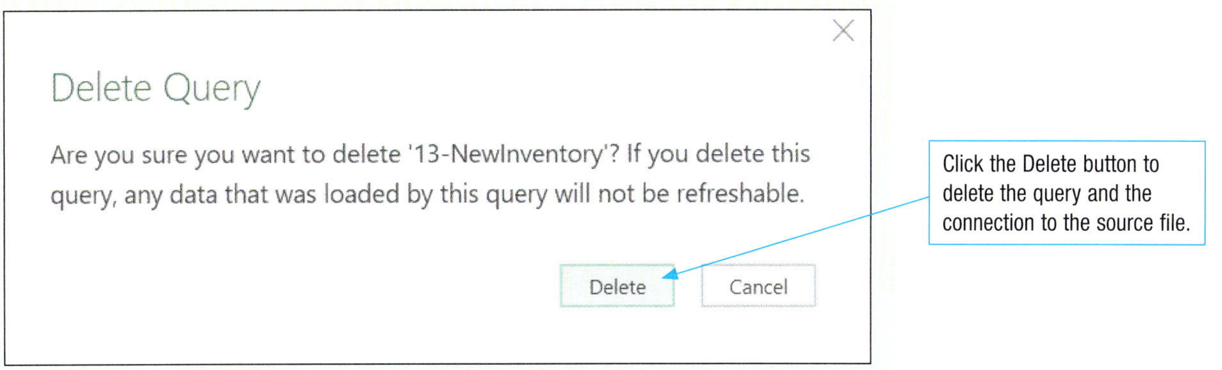

5. Click the Delete button.
   The query is removed from the Queries & Connections task pane.
6. Click the Save button on the Quick Access Toolbar. Leave the Excel workbook open for the next task.

13.10 Using the TRIM Function to Modify Text

Tutorial

Using the TRIM Function to Modify Text

After you copy and paste or import text data into Excel from another source, the data may need to be edited. Excel provides Text functions to help you manipulate, edit, and correct common text errors in any type of Excel data. For example, you can create an employee identification number by taking the first initial of an employee's first name, the first four letters of the employee's last name, and the last two digits of the employee's phone number.

The **TRIM function** is a Text function that removes extra spaces between characters. If data has been imported, extra spaces may exist in the source file. Using the TRIM function after an import removes any unwanted extra spaces.

▸ **Know This** about using the TRIM function

- The TRIM function removes extra spaces between words in text data. It does not remove a single space between words.
- The syntax for a formula using the TRIM function is *=TRIM(Text)*.
- To insert the TRIM function, click the Text button in the Function Library group on the Formulas tab, click the *TRIM* option at the drop-down list, enter the arguments at the Function Arguments dialog box, and then click the OK button.
- To apply the formula containing the TRIM function to one or more columns of data in a worksheet, leave one blank column, enter the formula in the first cell of the new column, and then use the fill handle to copy the function down into the last cell in the new column.
- To replace the original data that contains extra spaces with the formula results that do not contain extra spaces, copy the formula results and then use the *Value* option at the Paste Special gallery to paste the results (not the formula) over the original data. (You do not want to paste the formula because the formula contains references to the cells containing the extra spaces, and pasting the formula in those cells will return an Excel error code.)

On the Job

Task 13.10 Using the TRIM Function to Modify Text

Devon reviews the Excel workbook and notices extra spaces in the company names in the Customers worksheet. He asks you to remove the extra spaces. The data in the Customers worksheet was imported into the Excel workbook from an Access database. Use the TRIM function to remove the extra spaces in the Excel worksheet.

Note: *Be sure to open the data files for this chapter from a computer drive, not your OneDrive account.*

1. With the 13-DVAutoParts workbook open and the Inventory worksheet active, click the Customers sheet tab and then click in any cell in the table.

   Notice that a few company names have extra spaces (see Figure 13.41).

2. Click in cell I2, type =TRIM(B2), and then press Ctrl + Enter.

   The formula =*TRIM(B2)* displays in the Formula bar and the company name from cell B2 displays without extra spaces in cell I2.

Figure 13.41 Extra Spaces in Company Names

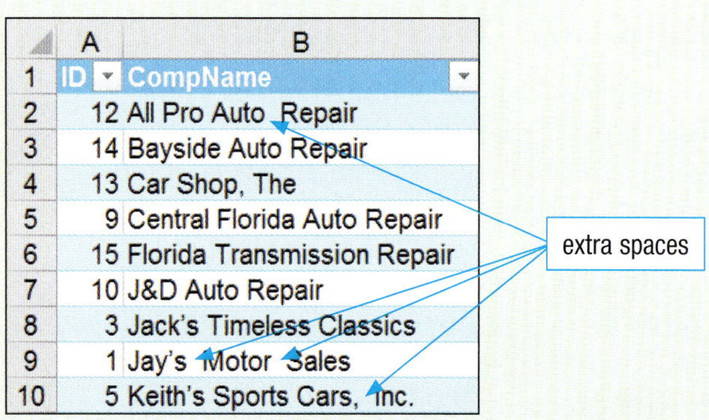

3. Use the fill handle to copy the formula from cell I2 down into cell I17.

   The company names from the range B2:B17 display without extra spaces in the range I2:I17. The range I2:I17 is selected.

4. Press Ctrl + C; click in cell B2; click the Home tab, if necessary; click the Paste button arrow in the Clipboard group; and then click the *Values* option (first option in the *Paste Values* section) (see Figure 13.42).

   The edited text values, and not the formulas, are pasted in the range B2:B17. The range B2:B17 is selected.

Figure 13.42 Paste Button Arrow Drop-Down List

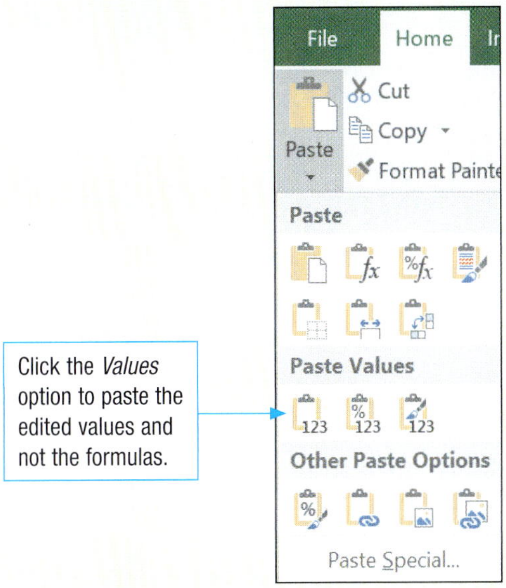

5. Click in any cell outside the range.

   The range is not selected.

6. Press the Esc key.

   The marquee is removed.

7. Delete the contents of the range I2:I17.
8. Click the Save button on the Quick Access Toolbar. Leave the Excel workbook open for the next task.

Model Answer

13.11 Using Flash Fill to Transform Data

MOS Expert 3.4.1

Tutorial

Using Flash Fill to Transform Data

The **Flash Fill** feature analyzes a column while you are entering data, detects any patterns, and suggests how the rest of the column could be completed using a detected pattern. Flash fill extracts, joins, and inserts text, numbers, dates, and times. It is useful for organizing data that has been pasted or imported into an Excel workbook from other sources. It can be used to join or extract all the contents of cells, or to join or extract parts of the contents of cells.

Flash Fill does not always recognize the pattern, but it is not the only tool for organizing data. To join the contents of two or more cells, you can use the CONCATENATE function or the CONCAT function (see Section 13.13). To separate data in a cell, you can use the Text to Columns button in the Data Tools group on the Data tab (see Chapter 7).

▶ **Know This** about using Flash Fill to transform data

— To transform data in an Excel worksheet using Flash Fill, insert one or more blank columns next to the data, if necessary; type the entry in the first row; press the Enter key; and then start typing the entry in the second row. When Flash Fill displays a sequence of suggested entries in gray text, press the Enter key to accept the suggested entries.

— You may need to enter a few rows of data before Excel recognizes the pattern.

— After you transform data, you may want to delete the original data.

▶ **Know More** ways to accept suggested entries

- Click the Fill button in the Editing group on the Home tab and then click the *Flash Fill* option at the drop-down list.
- Press Ctrl + E.

On the Job

Task 13.11 Using Flash Fill to Transform Data

Devon wants you to sort the list of employees in the Employees worksheet alphabetically from *A* to *Z* by last name so he can easily locate an employee's information. He also wants you to apply a different cell style to the table, delete column G (*StartDate*), delete column H (*Salary*), change the column E header to *Cell Phone*, adjust the widths of the columns in the table, and then convert the table to a range.

The data in the Employees worksheet was imported from an Access database, and the employee names were imported in one column with the first name followed by the last name. To sort the employees by last name, you need to reorganize the data so that first names are listed in one column and last names in another column. Use Flash Fill to separate the employee names into two columns. After you separate the names, make the other changes requested by Devon.

Note: *Be sure to open the data files for this chapter from a computer drive, not your OneDrive account.*

1. With the 13-DVAutoParts workbook open, make the Employees worksheet active and then insert two columns to the right of the *EmpName* column.
2. Click in cell C1, type First Name, press the Tab key, and then type Last Name.
3. Click in cell C2, type Devon, and then press the Enter key.
4. Type V.

   Flash Fill recognizes the pattern and suggests how to fill the rest of the column with first names (see Figure 13.43).

Figure 13.43 Sequence Suggested by Flash Fill

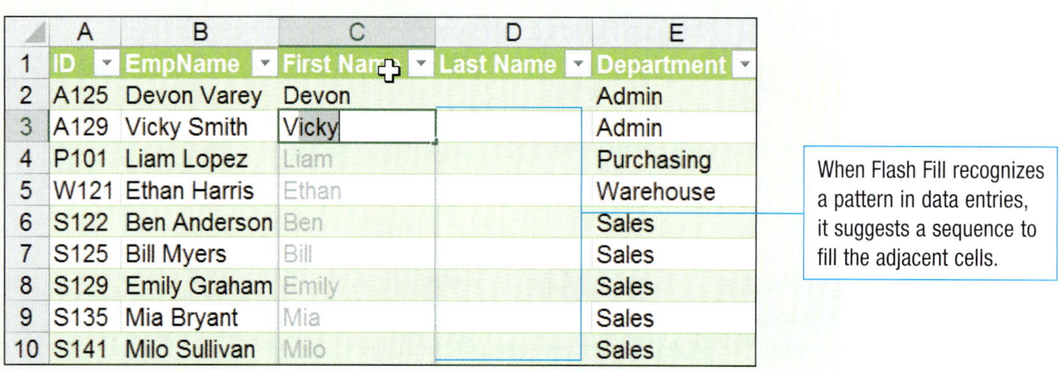

	A	B	C	D	E
1	ID	EmpName	First Name	Last Name	Department
2	A125	Devon Varey	Devon		Admin
3	A129	Vicky Smith	Vicky		Admin
4	P101	Liam Lopez	Liam		Purchasing
5	W121	Ethan Harris	Ethan		Warehouse
6	S122	Ben Anderson	Ben		Sales
7	S125	Bill Myers	Bill		Sales
8	S129	Emily Graham	Emily		Sales
9	S135	Mia Bryant	Mia		Sales
10	S141	Milo Sullivan	Milo		Sales

5. Press the Enter key.

   Column C is filled with first names.

6. Click in cell D2, type Varey, and then press the Enter key.
7. Type S.

   Flash Fill recognizes the sequence and suggests how to fill the rest of the column with last names.

8. Press the Enter key.

   Column D is filled with the last names.

9. Delete column G (*StartDate*), column H (*Salary*), and then column B (*EmpName*).
10. Sort the table alphabetically from *A* to *Z* by last name.
11. Change the table style to Green, Table Style Medium 4 (first row, fourth column in the *Medium* section at the Table Styles gallery).
12. Change cell E1 to read *Cell Phone*.
13. Adjust the column widths as you deem fit.
14. Convert the table to a range. Click the OK button to permanently remove the query definition from the sheet.
15. Click the Save button on the Quick Access Toolbar. Leave the Excel workbook open for the next task.

Model Answer

13.12 Using the RIGHT, LEFT, and MID Functions to Extract Characters

MOS 4.3.1

Tutorial

Using the LEFT Function to Extract Data

The **RIGHT function**, **LEFT function**, and **MID function** are Text functions used to extract characters from a cell when only some of the characters in a cell need to be copied. The characters can be uppercase letters, lowercase letters, numbers, symbols, or spaces. Text can be extracted from the rightmost, leftmost, and middle of a string of characters using these functions. For example, you can use these functions to extract characters from a first name, a last name, and a phone number to create a unique customer identification number.

▸ **Know This** about using the RIGHT, LEFT, and MID functions to extract data

— Use the RIGHT, LEFT, or MID function to extract a specific number of characters from the right, left, or middle, respectively, of a string of data.

— The data extracted can then be combined to create entries such as customer identification numbers and company email addresses.

— Syntax and examples for formulas using the RIGHT function, LEFT function, and MID function are found in Table 13.3.

— To insert one of these functions, click the Text button in the Function Library group on the Formulas tab, click the function option at the drop-down list, enter the arguments at the Function Arguments dialog box, and then click the OK button.

Table 13.3 Syntax and Examples for Formulas Using the RIGHT, LEFT, and MID Functions

Syntax	Description	Example
=RIGHT(text,num_chars)	Extracts the requested number of characters, starting at the rightmost character. The *text* argument can consist of text or a cell or range reference.	*=RIGHT("2019 Financial Report",16)* or *=RIGHT(A5,16)* when cell A5 contains the text *2019 Financial Report* Returns the text *Financial Report* in the formula cell
=LEFT(text,num_chars)	Extracts the requested number of characters, starting at the leftmost character. The *text* argument can consist of text or a cell or range reference.	*=LEFT("2019 Financial Report",4)* or *=LEFT(A5,4)* when cell A5 contains the text *2019 Financial Report* Returns the text *2019* in the formula cell
=MID(text,start-num,num_chars)	Extracts the requested number of characters, starting at a given position. The *text* argument can consist of text or a cell or range reference. The *start-num* argument indicates that the result should start with the first character from the left in the indicated *text* argument.	*=MID("2019 Financial Report",6,16)* or *=MID(A5,6,16)* when cell A5 contains the text *2019 Financial* Report Returns the text *Financial Report* in the formula cell

On the Job

Task 13.12 Using the RIGHT, LEFT, and MID Functions to Extract Data

When Devon started his business, he gave each new customer a simple numeric identification code (1, 2, 3, etc.). As his business grows, he realizes it would be helpful to have ID numbers that contain information he can use to quickly identify customers and group them by name or location. He asks you to create a unique ID number for each customer using the first three characters of the customer's company name, a dash (-), the area code from the customer's telephone number, and the last two characters of the customer's zip code. Create formulas that use the RIGHT, LEFT, and MID functions to extract the characters needed to create these ID numbers. In Task 13.13, you will create formulas that combine the characters to create the new customer identification numbers and you will copy the formulas to complete the table in the Customers worksheet.

Note: *Be sure to open the data files for this chapter from a computer drive, not your OneDrive account.*

1. With the 13-DVAutoParts workbook open, click the Customers sheet tab and then close the Queries & Connections task pane, if necessary.
2. Click in cell I1 and then type Comp.

   The column header *Comp* displays in cell I1. You will extract the first three characters from each company name in the *Comp* column.

3. Press the Enter key.

   Cell I2 is active. You will enter the formula for extracting the first three letters of the company name in this cell.

4. Click the Formulas tab and then click the Text button in the Function Library group.

   A drop-down list displays.

5. Click the *LEFT* option.

   The Function Arguments dialog box displays. The insertion point is in the *Text* text box.

6. Type B2 and then press the Tab key.

   The cell reference *B2* appears in the *Text* text box. This is the location of the cell containing the characters to be extracted. The insertion point is in the *Num_chars* text box.

7. Type 3.

   The number *3* appears in the *Num_chars* text box. This is the number of characters to be extracted.

8. Click the OK button.

   The dialog box closes. The result *All* appears in cell I2 and the formula *=LEFT(B2,3)* appears in the Formula bar. The formula entered in cell I2 returns the first three characters of the company name.

9. Click in cell J1, type Area Code, and then press the Enter key.
10. Click the Text button.
11. Click the *MID* option.
12. Type E2 and then press the Tab key.

    The cell reference *E2* appears in the *Text* text box. This is the location of the cell containing the characters to be extracted. The insertion point is in the *Start_num* text box.

13. Type 2 and then press the Tab key.

    The number *2* appears in the *Start_num* text box. This is the position of the first character to be extracted. The insertion point is in the *Num_chars* text box.

14. Type 3.

    The number *3* appears in the *Num_chars* text box. This is the number of characters to be extracted.

15. Click the OK button.

    The dialog box closes. The result *904* appears in cell J2 and the formula *=MID(E2,2,3)* appears in the Formula bar. The formula entered in cell J2 returns the three-character area code from the company's telephone number.

16. Click in cell K1, type ZIP, and then press the Enter key.
17. Click the Text button.
18. Click the *RIGHT* option.
19. Type F2 and then press the Tab key.

    The cell reference *F2* appears in the *Text* text box. This is the location of the cell containing the characters to be extracted. The insertion point is in the *Num_chars* text box.

20. Type 2.

    The number *2* appears in the *Num_chars* text box. This is the number of characters to be extracted.

21. Click the OK button

    The dialog box closes. The result *35* appears in cell K2 and the formula *=RIGHT(F2,2)* appears in the Formula bar. The formula entered in cell K2 returns the last two characters of the company's zip code.

22. Click the Save button on the Quick Access Toolbar. Leave the Excel workbook open for the next task.

Model Answer

13.13 Using the CONCATENATE and CONCAT Functions to Join Text Values

MOS 4.3.3

Tutorial

Using the CONCATENATE Function

The **CONCAT function** is a new function in Excel 2016 that replaces the CONCATENATE function. The **CONCATENATE function** is still available for compatibility with earlier version of Excel. These functions join the contents of two or more cells, including text, numbers, and cell references. Additional information, including spaces and characters, can also be added into the combined data. After extracting data, you can use these functions to combine the data in different ways to make unique customer numbers, employee IDs, email addresses, and other useful strings of text.

▸ Know This about using the CONCATENATE and CONCAT functions

— The syntax for the CONCATENATE function is *=CONCATENATE(Text1,Text2,Text3,...)*.

— The syntax for the CONCAT function is *=CONCAT(Text1,Text2,Text3,...)*.

— To insert the CONCATENATE function, click the Insert Function button in the Function Library group on the Formulas tab, type *CONCATENATE* in the *Search for a function* option box, click the OK button, enter the arguments at the Function Arguments dialog box, and then click the OK button.

— To insert the CONCAT function, click the Text button in the Function Library group on the Formulas tab, click the *CONCAT* option at the drop-down list, enter the arguments at the Function Arguments dialog box, and then click the OK button.

— Spaces or characters (text, numbers, or symbols) added directly to the function are enclosed in quotation marks.

- If you use the Function Arguments dialog box to enter the formula, Excel automatically adds the quotation marks when you enter spaces, text, or symbols as an argument.
- If you manually type the formula in a cell or in the Formula bar, you have to type the quotation marks.

— Numbers do not need quotation marks.

— If the error code *#NAME?* appears in a results cell, a text or symbol argument may be missing quotation marks.
— You can join up to 255 items with a total of 8,192 characters.

On the Job

Task 13.13 Using the CONCATENATE Function

Devon asks you to finish creating the customer ID numbers you started in Task 13.12. Use the CONCATENATE function to create a formula that combines the data extracted in Task 13.12. After you create the formula, copy it down column A to replace the old customer ID numbers with the new ones. Adjust the width of column A to fit the new contents.

Note: *Be sure to open the data files for this chapter from a computer drive, not your OneDrive account.*

1. With the 13-DVAutoParts workbook open and the Customers worksheet active, click in cell L1, type CustID, and then press the Enter key.
2. Click the Formulas tab, if necessary, and then click the Insert Function button in the Function Library group.

   The Insert Function dialog box displays with the text selected in the *Search for a function* option box.
3. Type CONCATENATE and then click the Go button.

   The *CONCATENATE* option is selected in the *Select a function* list box.
4. Click the OK button.

   The Function Arguments dialog box displays with the insertion point in the *Text1* text box (see Figure 13.44).

Figure 13.44 CONCATENATE Function Arguments Dialog Box

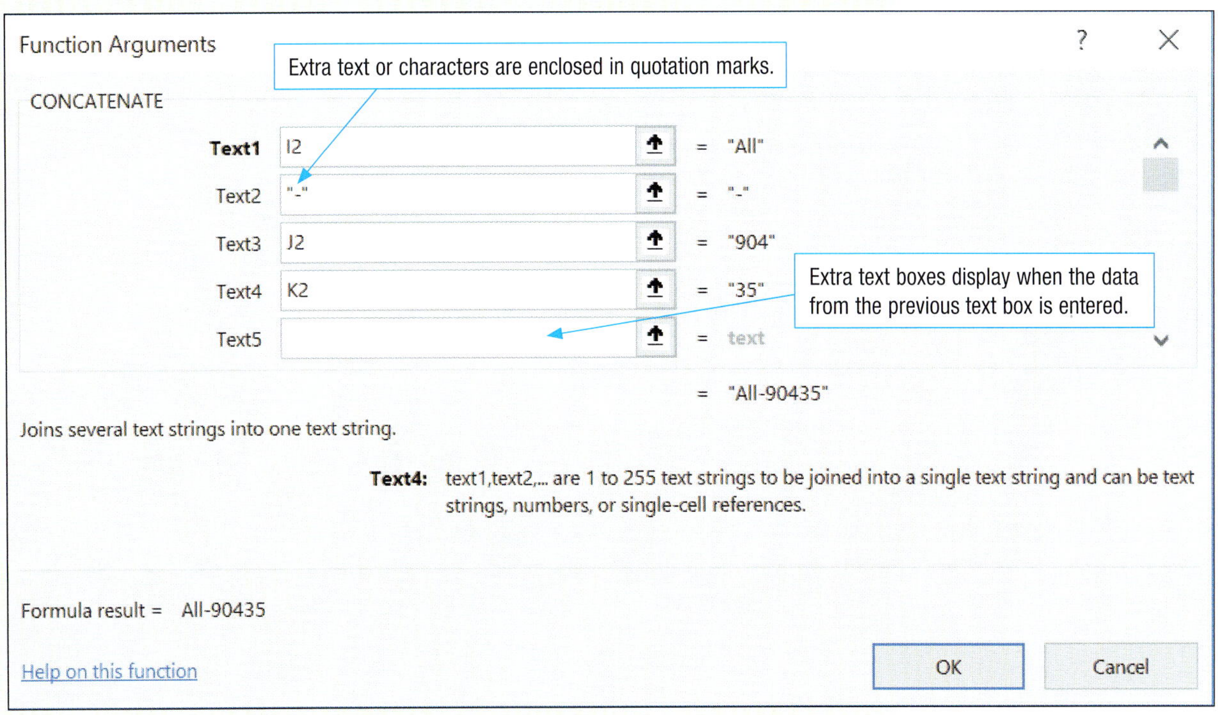

5. Type I2 and then press the Tab key.

   The cell reference *I2* appears in the *Text1* text box. This is the location of the cell containing the first value to be joined. The insertion point is in the *Text2* text box.

6. Type a dash (-) and then press the Tab key.

   The text *"-"* appears in the *Text2* text box. This is the second value to be joined. Excel automatically added the quotation marks around the dash. The insertion point is in the *Text3* text box.

7. Type J2 and then press the Tab key.

   The cell reference *J2* appears in the *Text3* text box. This is the location of the cell containing the third value to be joined. The insertion point is in the *Text4* text box.

8. Type K2.

   The cell reference *K2* appears in the *Text4* text box. This is the location of the cell containing the fourth, and last, value to be joined.

9. Click the OK button.

   The dialog box closes. The result *All-90435* appears in cell L2 and the formula *=CONCATENATE(I2,"-",J2,K2)* appears in the Formula bar. The formula entered in cell L2 returns a customer ID number consisting of the first three characters of the company name, a dash, the three-character area code from the customer's telephone number, and the last two characters of the customer's zip code. Cell L2 is active.

10. Copy the range I2:L2 in to the range I3:L17.
11. Select the range L2:L17, press Ctrl + C, click in cell A2, click the Home tab, click the Paste button arrow in the Clipboard group, and then click the *Values* option (first option in the *Paste Value* section).

    The values, and not the formulas, from the range L2:L17 are pasted in the range A2:A17.

12. AutoFit the width of column A and then change the table style to Green, Table Style Medium 4 (first row, fourth column in the *Medium* section at the Table Styles gallery).
13. Click the Save button on the Quick Access Toolbar. Leave the Excel workbook open for the next task.

Model Answer

13.14 Using the UPPER, LOWER, and PROPER Functions to Edit Text

MOS 4.3.2

Tutorial

Using the CONCAT Function with a Nested UPPER Function

The **UPPER function** and the **LOWER function** are Text functions used to convert text from uppercase to lowercase, and vice versa. The **PROPER function** is a Text function used to capitalize the first letter of each word. Being able to quickly convert text from uppercase to lowercase or title case avoids having to retype data and perhaps making errors.

▸ **Know This** about using the UPPER, LOWER, and PROPER functions to edit text

— The syntax and examples for formulas containing the UPPER function, LOWER function, and PROPER function are found in Table 13.4.

— To insert one of these functions, click the Text button in the Function Library group on the Formulas tab, click the function option at the drop-down list, enter the arguments at the Function Arguments dialog box, and then click the OK button.

— To apply the formula containing one of these functions, you may need to enter the formula in a separate column or row, leaving one or more blank columns or rows between the existing data.

▸ **Know This** about replacing original data with formula results

— To replace original data with formula results in an Excel worksheet, copy the cells containing the formula results, select the cells containing the original data, and then click the *Values* option in the *Paste Values* section at the Paste button drop-down list in the Clipboard group on the Home tab. (You do not want to paste the formula because the formula contains references to the original cells, and pasting the formula in those cells will return an Excel error code.)

▸ **Know More** ways to replace original data with formula results

- Copy the cells containing the formula results, select the cells containing the original data, click the *Paste Special* option, and then click the *Values* option in the *Paste* section at the Paste Special dialog box.
- Copy the cells containing the formula results, select the cells containing the original data, right-click one of the selected cells, and then click the *Values* option at the pop-up menu.

Table 13.4 Syntax and Examples for Formulas Using the UPPER, LOWER, and PROPER Functions

Syntax	Description	Example
=UPPER(text)	Converts text to uppercase. The *text* argument can consist of text or a cell or range reference.	*=UPPER("financial report")* or *=UPPER(A5)* when cell A5 contains the text *financial report* Returns the text *FINANCIAL REPORT* in the formula cell
=LOWER(text)	Converts text to lowercase. The *text* argument can consist of text or a cell or range reference.	*=LOWER("FINANCIAL REPORT")* or *=LOWER(A5)* when cell A5 contains the text *FINANCIAL REPORT* Returns the text *financial report* in the formula cell
=PROPER(text)	Capitalizes the first letter of each word. The *text* argument can consist of text or a cell or range reference.	*=PROPER("financial report")* or *=PROPER(A5)* when cell A5 contains the text *financial report* Returns the text *Financial Report* in the formula cell

On the Job

Task 13.14 Using the UPPER, LOWER, and PROPER Functions to Edit Text

The data you appended from a text file to the Inventory worksheet in Task 13.8 is missing the *Reorder Code* field. Devon points out that the reorder code is a combination of the supplier code, a dash (-), and the part number. He also points out that the supplier codes in the existing data use all uppercase letters, and the supplier codes in the appended data use all lowercase letters. He asks you to create reorder codes for the appended data that match the structure and formatting of the existing reorder codes. Use the CONCAT function with a nested UPPER function to create a formula that combines the text values for these codes with the correct capitalization, and then copy the formula to provide reorder codes for the appended items.

Devon also notices that the *Unit Price* column in the appended data does not line up under the *Unit Price* column in the existing data, that the full contents of each cell in column D do not display, and that the appended data uses different capitalization and formatting than the existing data. Devon wants you to fix all of these issues so all the data in the Inventory worksheet uses consistent formatting and capitalization. Use the UPPER, LOWER, and PROPER functions, along with other Excel tools, to make the requested changes.

Note: *Be sure to open the data files for this chapter from a computer drive, not your OneDrive account.*

1. With the 13-DVAutoParts workbook open and the Customers worksheet active, click the Inventory sheet tab.
2. Click in any cell in the imported table that starts in cell A15.
3. Click the Table Tools Design tab and then click the *None* option (first column, first row in the *Light* section) at the Quick Styles drop-down gallery in the Table Styles group.
4. Convert the table to a range.
5. Select the range D15:D45 and move it to the range E15:E45.
6. AutoFit the width of column D.
7. Click in cell D16, click the Formulas tab, and then click the Text button in the Function Library group.

   A drop-down list displays.
8. Click the *CONCAT* option.

   The Function Arguments dialog box displays. The insertion point is in the *Text1* text box.
9. Type UPPER(B16) and then press the Tab key.

   The argument *UPPER(B16)* appears in the *Text1* text box. The cell reference in parentheses is the location of the cell containing the first value to be joined. The nested UPPER function tells Excel to display the letters in uppercase letters. The insertion point is in the *Text2* text box.
10. Type a dash (-) and then press the Tab key.

    The text "-" appears in the *Text2* text box. This is the second value to be joined. The insertion point is in the *Text3* text box.

11. Type C16.

    The cell reference *C16* appears in the *Text3* text box. This is the location of the cell containing the third value to be joined.

12. Click the OK button.

    The dialog box closes. The result SD45-324597 appears in cell D16 and the formula *CONCAT(UPPER(B16), "- ",C16)* appears in the Formula bar. The formula entered in cell D16 returns a reorder code consisting of the supplier code using all uppercase letters, a dash, and the part number. Cell D16 is active.

13. Copy the formula in D16 down into the range D17:D45.
14. Click in cell G12, type Category, press Ctrl + Enter, and then apply the 20% - Accent1 cell style (first column, first row in the *Themed Cell Styles* section) to cell G12.

    Rows 13 to 15 will be deleted later in this task and the *Category* column header is still required, so it is being entered in row 12.

15. Click in cell G16, type =LOWER(A16), and then press Ctrl + Enter.

    The result *batteries* appears in cell G16 and the formula *=LOWER(A16)* appears in the Formula bar. The capitalization of the result does not match the capitalization of the original data in the *Category* column; the LOWER function did not give you the correct result. Cell G16 is active.

16. Type =PROPER(A16) and then press Ctrl + Enter.

    The result *Batteries* appears in cell G16 and the formula *=PROPER(A16)* appears in the Formula bar. The capitalization of the result matches the capitalization of the original data in the *Category* column; the PROPER function gave you the correct result. Cell G16 is active.

17. Click in cell H12, type Supplier Code, press Ctrl + Enter, and then apply the 20% - Accent1 cell style (first column, first row in the *Themed Cell Styles* section) to cell H12. AutoFit the width of column H.
18. Click in cell H16, type =UPPER(B16), and then press Ctrl + Enter.

    The result *SD45* appears in cell H16 and the formula *=UPPER(B16)* appears in the Formula bar. The capitalization of the result matches the capitalization of the original data in the *Supplier Code* column; the UPPER function gave you the correct result. Cell H16 is active.

19. Select the range G16:H16 and then copy it down into the range G17:H45.
20. With the range G16:H45 selected, press Ctrl + C, click in cell A16, click the Home tab, click the Paste button arrow, and then click the *Values* option (first option in the *Paste Values* section).

    The values, and not the formulas, from the range G16:H45 are pasted in the range A16:B45.

21. Delete rows 13 to 15.
22. Modify the formatting of rows 13 to 42 to match the formatting of rows 5 to 12.
23. Click the Save button on the Quick Access Toolbar. Leave the Excel workbook open for the next task.

Model Answer

MOS 1.5.2

Tutorial

Publishing a Selection from an Excel Worksheet as an XPS File

13.15 Publishing Excel Worksheets and Workbooks as PDF and XPS Files

The **PDF (portable document format) format** and **XPS (XML paper specification) format** are popular for distributing content over the Internet because they display content in a **fixed layout**—that is, in a layout that does not change depending on the settings of the viewer's computer or software. Excel offers the options of publishing a workbook as a PDF file and as an XPS file. Saving a workbook as a PDF or XPS file allows you to send the information to people who do not have Excel and cannot open and view an Excel workbook. PDFs can be easily opened on tablets and smartphones, making the data readily available.

▸ Know This about exporting Excel worksheets and workbooks as PDF and XPS files

— To export an active Excel worksheet as a PDF file or XPS file, click the File tab, click the *Export* option, click the *Create PDF/XPS Document* option in the middle panel, click the Create PDF/XPS button in the right panel, click the *Save as type* option box arrow at the Publish as PDF or XPS dialog box (see Figure 13.45), click the *PDF Document (*.pdf)* option or the *XPS Document (*.xps)* option at the drop-down list, and then click the Publish button.

— To have the PDF open automatically after it is published, click the *Open file after publishing* check box at the Publish as PDF or XPS dialog box to insert a check mark.

Figure 13.45 Publish as PDF or XPS Dialog Box

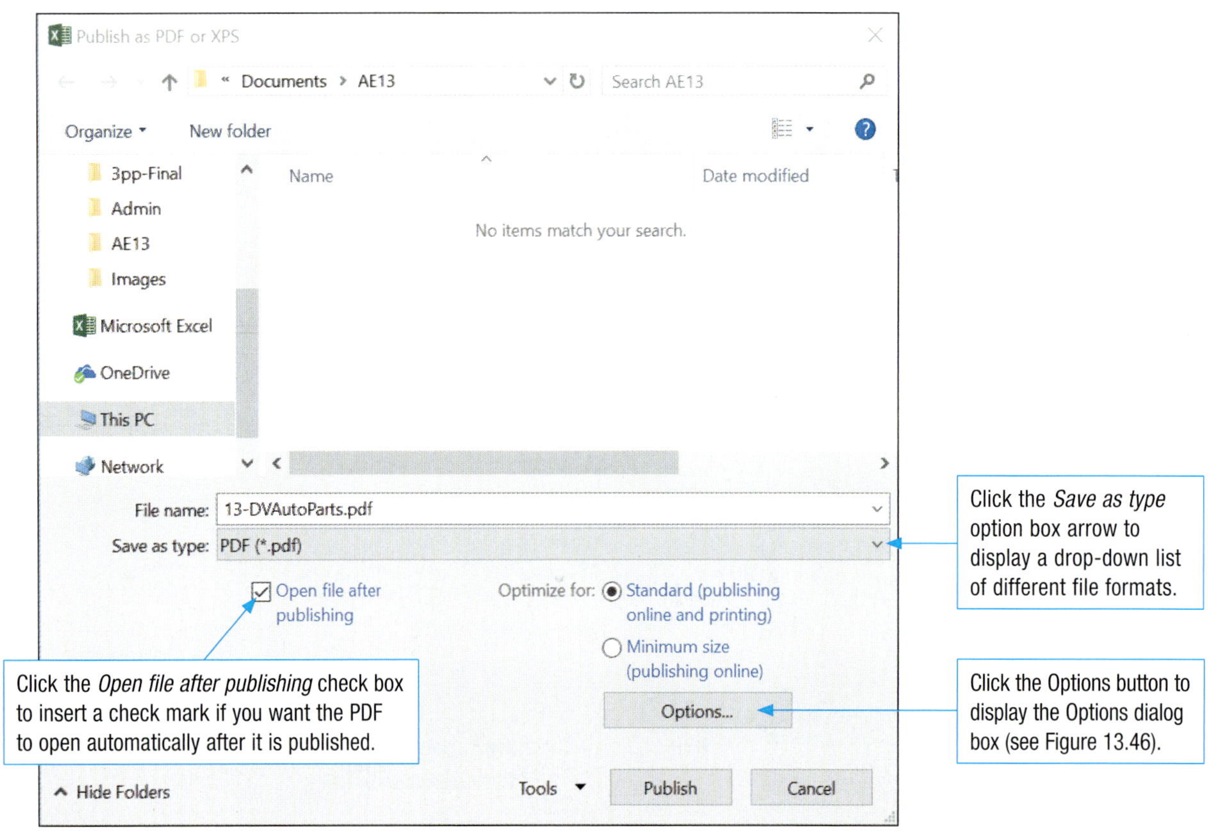

— To export a multisheet Excel workbook as a multipage PDF file, click the Options button at the Publish as PDF or XPS dialog box and then click the *Entire workbook* radio button in the *Publish what* section at the Options dialog box to insert a bullet (see Figure 13.46).

— To export selected cells in an Excel workbook, click the Options button at the Publish as PDF or XPS dialog box and then click the *Selection* radio button in the *Publish what* section of the Options dialog box to insert a bullet.

Figure 13.46 Options Dialog Box

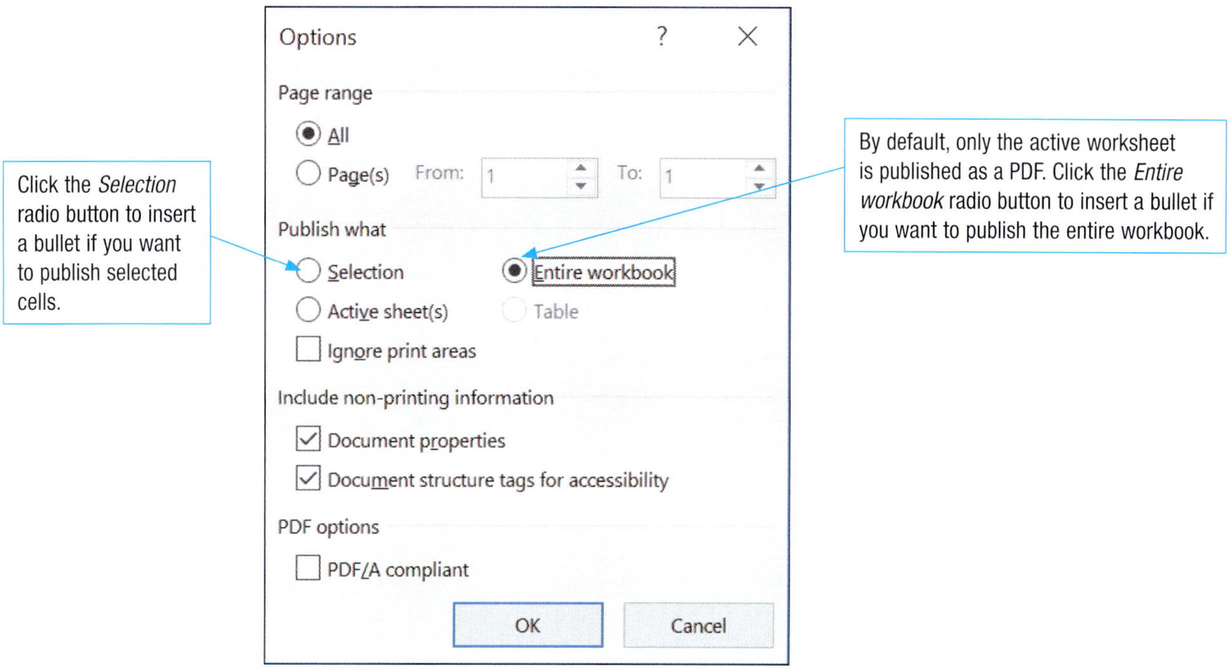

▸ **Know This** about viewing a PDF file

— A PDF file can be viewed in a web browser or using Adobe Reader or Adobe Acrobat.

— Adobe Reader is a free application that allows you to view, search, and annotate PDFs. Adobe Acrobat is a for-purchase program that allows you to edit PDFs.

— To download the latest version of the free Adobe Reader or to purchase Adobe Acrobat, go to http://adobe.com.

▸ **Know This** about viewing an XPS file

— An XPS file can be viewed in Internet Explorer or using the XPS viewer.

— The XPS viewer is provided by Microsoft and is packaged with Windows 10, Windows 8.1, Windows 7, and Windows Vista.

— To view an XPS file using Windows XP, you may need to download the viewer application.

— To download the XPS viewer, go to www.microsoft.com and use the phrase *View and Generate XPS* to search for the download page.

▸ Know This about setting the default program to open a file

— To set the default program to open a file, navigate to the file using the Windows Explorer dialog box, right-click the file name in the file list pane, click the *Choose Another App* option at the pop-up menu, select an application at the How do you want to open this file? dialog box, click the *Always use this app to open [.xxx] files* check box (where *[.xxx]* is replaced by the file extension for the active file) to insert a check mark, and then click the OK button (see Figure 13.47).

Figure 13.47 How do you want to open this file? Dialog Box

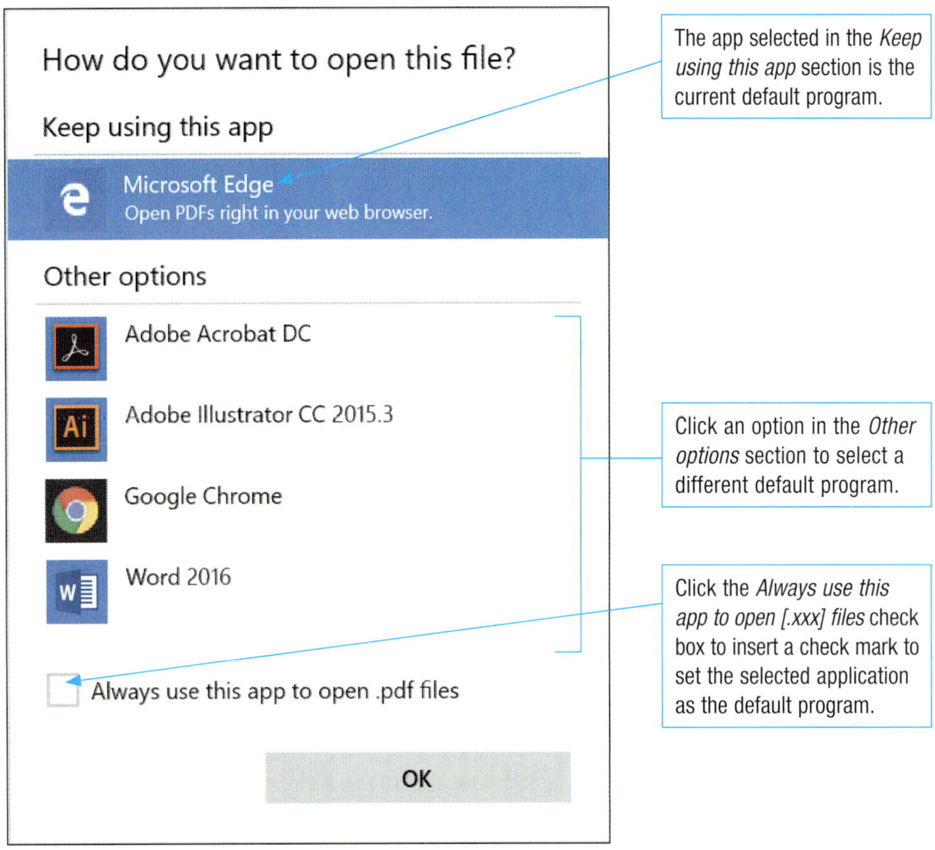

▸ Know This about opening a PDF file in Word 2016

— A PDF file can be opened with Word 2016.

— Word converts the PDF to an editable file, converting any formulas to values and any charts to objects.

— The contents of the Word file may not look exactly like the contents of the original PDF file.

— To open a PDF file in Word, open Word, click the Open Other Documents link at the bottom of the left panel, click the Browse button in the middle panel, click the file type option box arrow at the Open dialog box, click the *PDF Files (*.pdf)* option at the drop-down list, navigate to the PDF file you want to open, click the PDF file to select it, and then click the Open button. A message will appear, stating that Word will now convert your PDF to an editable Word document and that it may take a while. Click the OK button.

On the Job

Task 13.15a Publishing a Multisheet Excel Workbook as a Multipage PDF File

Devon wants to distribute the Excel workbook to the sales associates by email before next week's meeting. Adjust a few worksheets by changing the margins and orientation so that they will display as a PDF properly, and then publish the workbook as a multipage PDF.

Note: *Be sure to open the data files for this chapter from a computer drive, not your OneDrive account.*

1. With the 13-DVAutoParts workbook open and the Inventory worksheet active, click the File tab, click the *Print* option, click the *Print Active Sheets* option in the *Settings* section, and then click the *Print Entire Workbook* option.

   The workbook displays in Print Preview with nine pages.
2. Scroll through the pages to preview how the PDF will look.

   The Customers and Inventory worksheets will each print awkwardly on two pages. You can make some adjustments to improve the presentation of the data on those worksheets.
3. Click the Back button to return to the Inventory worksheet. Modify the scale so that the width will fit on one page.

   The worksheet will now print on one page.
4. Click the Customers sheet tab and then change the page orientation to landscape.
5. Click the File tab and then click the *Export* option.

   The Export backstage area displays with the *Create Adobe PDF* option selected in the middle panel. Depending on your computer's settings, you may not have a *Create Adobe PDF* option.
6. Click the *Create PDF/XPS Document* option in the middle panel, if necessary.
7. Click the Create PDF/XPS button in the right panel.

   The Publish as PDF or XPS dialog box displays (see Figure 13.45 on page 658).
8. Confirm that the *PDF (*.pdf)* option appears in the *Save as type* option box.
9. Click the *Open file after publishing* check box.

   A check mark appears in the check box.
10. Click the Options button.

    The Options dialog box displays.
11. Click the *Entire workbook* radio button in the *Publish what* section (see Figure 13.46 on page 659).

    A bullet appears in the radio button.
12. Click the OK button.

    The Options dialog box closes.
13. Click the Publish button.

    The Publish as PDF or XPS dialog box closes. The PDF file opens in your web browser, Adobe Reader, or Adobe Acrobat, depending on what you have installed on your computer and what you have set as the default viewer.

14. Scroll through the PDF and review the new page layouts.

    The Customers worksheet displays with all the customer information on page 4 and the TEXT functions on page 5. The Inventory worksheet displays on page 8. This arrangement is logical and neat.

15. Close the viewer window.
16. Click the Save button on the Quick Access Toolbar of the Excel workbook. Leave the Excel workbook open for the next task.

Model Answer

On the Job

Task 13.15b Publishing a Selection from an Excel Worksheet as an XPS File

One of Devon's sales associates has asked him to provide data from the Customers worksheet as an XPS file. Devon asks you to publish the range A1:G17 from the Customers worksheet as an XPS file.

Note: *Be sure to open the data files for this chapter from a computer drive, not your OneDrive account.*

1. With the 13-DVAutoParts workbook open and the Customers worksheet active, select the range A1:G17.
2. Click the File tab and then click the *Export* option.
3. Click the *Create PDF/XPS Document* option in the middle panel at the Export backstage area, if necessary.
4. Click the Create PDF/XPS button in the right panel.
5. Click the *Save as type* option box arrow and then click the *XPS Document (*.xps)* option.
6. Click the Options button.

    The Options dialog box displays.

7. Click the *Selection* option (see Figure 13.46 on page 663) and then click the OK button.

    The Options dialog box closes.

8. Click the Publish button.

    The Publish as PDF or XPS dialog box closes. The XPS file opens in either your web browser or the XPS viewer.

9. Close the application window.
10. Leave the Excel workbook open for the next task.

    You do not need to save the workbook because you did not make any changes to it.

Model Answer

13.16 Publishing an Excel Worksheet as a Web Page

MOS 1.5.2

Tutorial

Publishing a Worksheet as a Web Page

You can publish an Excel worksheet as a web page in the traditional **HTML (hypertext markup language) format** used for creating web pages. Using this method, you can easily publish information from an Excel workbook to the Internet without having to use more complicated software. The only difference between the HTM file format and the HTML file format is that one has a three-character extension (*.htm*) and the other has a four-character extension (*.html*). Some servers do not support the four-character extension.

▸ **Know This** about publishing a worksheet as a web page in HTM or HTML file format

— To publish an active worksheet as a web page in HTM or HTML format, complete the following steps:

1. Click the File tab.
2. Click the *Export* option.
3. Click the *Change File Type* option in the middle panel at the Export backstage area.
4. Click the *Save as Another File Type* option in the *Other Files Types* section of the right panel.
5. Click the Save As button.
6. Click the *Save as type* option box arrow at the Save As dialog box.
7. Click the *Web Page (*.htm;*.html)* option at the drop-down list (see Figure 13.48).
8. Navigate to the storage location for the new folder, if necessary.
9. Change the file name, if necessary.
10. Click the Change Title button, type a title for the web page in the *Page title* text box at the Enter Text dialog box, and then click the OK button.
11. Click the *Selection: Sheet* radio button in the *Save* section to insert a bullet.
12. Click the Publish button.
13. Choose options at the Publish as Web Page dialog box (see Figure 13.49).
14. Click the Publish button.

— When you select the *Web Page (*.htm;*.html)* option at the Save As dialog box, options for that file type appear at the bottom of the dialog box.

— After the worksheet is published as a web page, it needs to be uploaded to a web server if you would like others to be able to view the web page.

▸ **Know More** about adding a web page title

– The title you add in the *Page title* text box at the Enter Text dialog box displays in the Title bar of the browser window and as the text in a Favorites or Bookmarks list.

Figure 13.48 Bottom of the Save as Dialog Box with the *Web Page (*.htm;*.html)* File Type Selected

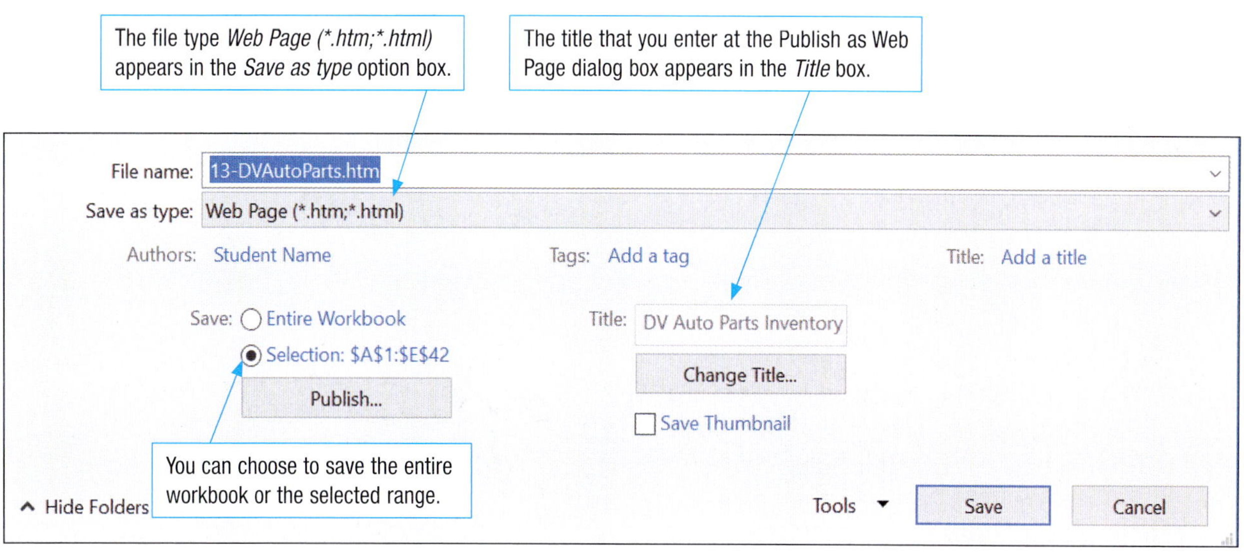

Figure 13.49 Publish as Web Page Dialog Box

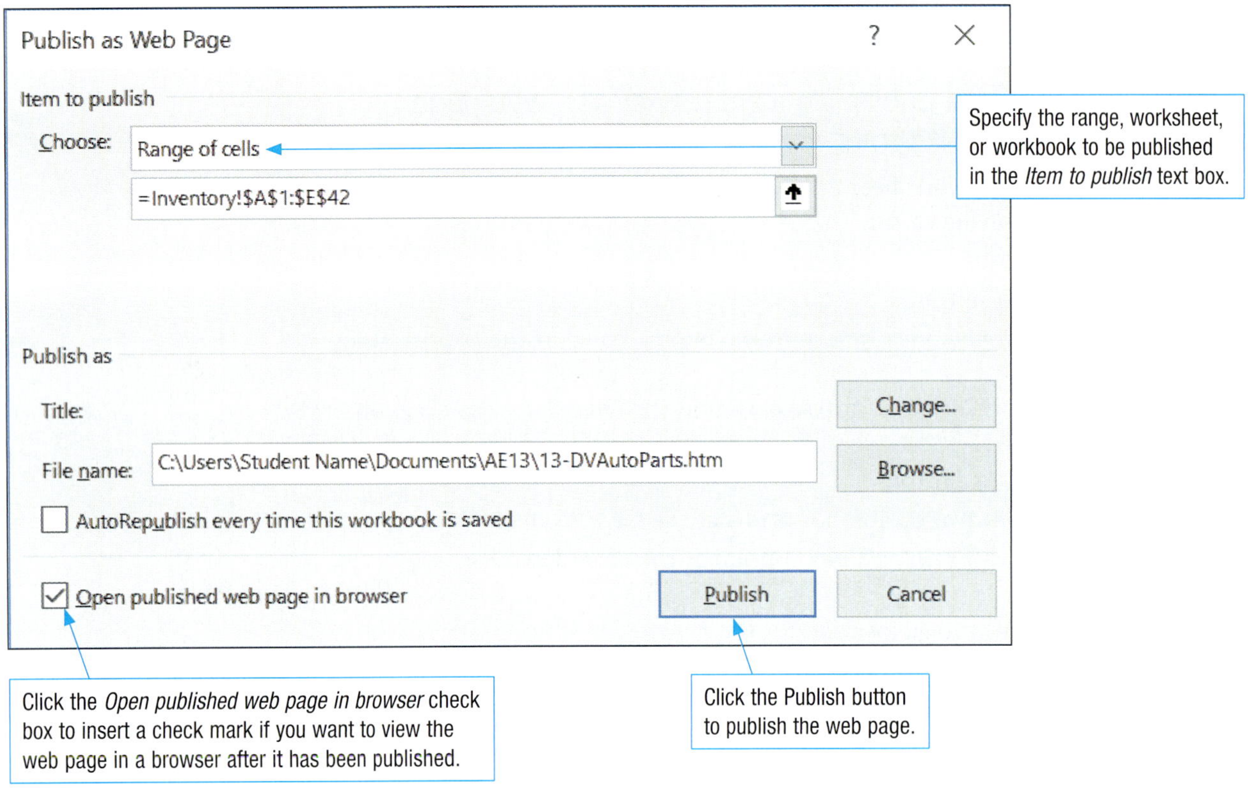

On the Job

Task 13.16 Publishing a Worksheet as a Web Page

Devon wants to publish the formatted data in the Inventory worksheet as a web page for easy use by all customers. Select the formatted data and then export it as an HTM file to post on a server.

Note: *Be sure to open the data files for this chapter from a computer drive, not your OneDrive account.*

1. With the 13-DVAutoParts workbook open and the Customers worksheet active, click the Inventory sheet tab and then select the range A1:E42.
2. Click the File tab and then click the *Export* option.
3. Click the *Change File Type* option in the middle panel.
4. Click the *Save as Another File Type* option in the right panel.
5. Click the Save As button.

   The Save As dialog box displays.
6. Click the *Save as type* option box arrow.

   A drop-down list displays.
7. Click the *Web Page (*.htm;*.html)* option.

   The options for the selected file type display at the bottom of the Save As dialog box (see Figure 13.48 on page 667).
8. Click the Change Title button.

   The Enter Text dialog box displays with the insertion point in the *Page title* text box.

9. Type DV Auto Parts Inventory and then click the OK button.

   The Enter Text dialog box closes, and the text *DV Auto Parts Inventory* appears in the *Title* box at the bottom of the Save As dialog box.

10. Click the *Selection $A$1:$E$42* radio button in the *Save* section to insert a bullet.

    Only the selected cells will be published as a web page.

11. Click the Publish button.

    The Publish as Web Page dialog box displays (see Figure 13.49 on page 668).

12. Click the *Open published web page in browser* check box, if necessary.

    A check mark appears in the check box.

13. Click the Publish button. Choose a Browser, if necessary.

    The worksheet displays in the web browser.

14. Scroll through the web page and then close the web browser window.
15. Save and then close the Excel workbook.

Model Answer

Chapter Summary

13.1

- Applications in Office 365 and Office 2016 are designed for integration so that an object created in one application can easily be copied to another application. There are three ways to integrate data: copying and pasting, embedding, and linking.
- An import routine brings data from other applications into Excel, and an export routine copies data from Excel into another application. During an import or export routine, the file containing the original data is called the *source file*, and the file to which the original data is being copied, embedded, or linked is called the *destination file*.
- When data is copied from a source file and pasted in a destination file as data, the destination file does not store any information about the source file. If changes are made later to the data in the source file, they will not be reflected in the destination file. Data pasted in the destination file can be changed using the tools available in the destination file.
- Linking and embedding between applications in Office 365 and Office 2016 uses a technology called *object linking and embedding (OLE)*. When data is copied from a source file and pasted in a destination file as an embedded object, the data is stored in the destination file and not connected to the source file. If changes are made later to the data in the source file, they will not be reflected in the destination file. Data embedded in the destination file can be changed using the application used to create the object.
- When data is copied from a source file and pasted in a destination file as a linked object, the data is stored in the destination file and also connected to the source file. If changes are made later to the data in the source file, they will be reflected in the destination file. Data in the destination file can be changed in either of two ways: by opening the source file and then making the changes in the source application,

or by double-clicking the object in the destination file to open the destination application and then making the changes in the destination application.

- ▶ Guidelines for selecting an integration method are as follows: The data should be copied and pasted if it will not likely be updated or edited later. The data should be embedded to allow editing it later in the application in which it was created. The data should be linked to allow updating it in the destination file when changes are made in the source file.
- ▶ In Office 365 and Office 2016, the charting system is fully integrated with Word, Excel, and PowerPoint. When an Excel chart is inserted in a Word document or PowerPoint presentation, the Excel workbook containing the source data becomes part of the document or presentation file. An Excel chart embedded in a Word document or PowerPoint presentation can be edited using the same techniques and tools used for editing a chart in Excel.

13.2 ▶ Excel data can be copied and pasted, copied and embedded, and copied and linked in a PowerPoint presentation, just as in a Word document. Although tables and charts can be created in PowerPoint slides, the user may prefer to use Excel to create these items and then copy and paste, embed, or link them in PowerPoint.

13.3 ▶ If the data in a linked object does not need to be updated when the data in the source file changes, the link can be broken. Breaking the link means disconnecting the data in the destination file from the data in the source file. After the link between the linked object and the source file has been broken, any change made to the original data in the source file will not be reflected in the linked object.

13.4 ▶ Access uses tables to store data. An Access table is similar in structure to an Excel worksheet. A field in Access, like a column in Excel, holds one piece of information about a person, an item, or an amount. A record in Access, like a row in Excel, holds the information for one item. Specific information can be extracted from Access through a database object called a *query*.

13.5 ▶ To exchange Excel data with someone who cannot import an Excel worksheet or cannot copy and paste using the Clipboard task pane, the data can be saved as a text file. Excel provides several text file options, including file formats suitable for computers that use the Apple operating system, among others.

13.6 ▶ Since March 2017, the tools in the Get & Transform group on the Data tab have been based on Power Query technology, which provides instinctive steps for importing, combining, and refining data from a variety of sources. The Get & Transform group on the Data tab on the Excel ribbon contains buttons for importing data into an Excel worksheet from an external source. Exchanging data between Access and Excel is a seamless process because the data in an Access datasheet is structured in the same row and column format as the data in an Excel worksheet. Data imported into Excel from Access can be appended to an existing worksheet or placed in a new worksheet.

13.7 ▶ A text file contains no formatting and consists only of letters, numbers, punctuation symbols, and a few control characters. Two commonly used text file formats separate fields with tabs (delimited file format) and commas (comma-separated file format). When a text file is imported into Excel, it can either be placed in a new worksheet or appended to the end of existing data in a worksheet.

13.8 ▶ Before March 2017, Excel used wizards instead of Power Query technology to import data. At times, you may want to use these legacy wizards instead of the Power Query features in the Get & Transform Data group. The wizards allow you to save the data source login credentials as part of the workbook. When you use a legacy wizard, you create a connection rather than a query. Before you can use a legacy wizard, you must add it to the Get & Transform Data group.

13.9 ▶ When data is imported into Excel, a query or connection is established between the source file and the destination file. This query or connection can be refreshed or removed. Refreshing a query or connection allows the user to update data when the most current data in a destination file is needed. Removing a query or connection allows the user to capture data at a specific time.

13.10 ▶ Excel provides Text functions to allow manipulating, editing, and correcting common text errors in any type of Excel data. The TRIM function can be used to remove extra spaces between characters, which sometimes occur in data that has been imported.

13.11 ▶ The Flash Fill feature is used to extract, join, and insert text, numbers, dates, and times. It is useful for organizing data that has been pasted or imported into an Excel workbook from other sources. Flash Fill analyzes a column while the user is entering data, detects any patterns, and suggests how the rest of the column could be completed using a detected pattern.

13.12 ▶ The RIGHT function, LEFT function, and MID function are Text functions used to extract characters from a cell when only some of the characters need to be copied. Text can be extracted from the rightmost, leftmost, and middle of a string of characters using these functions.

13.13 ▶ The CONCAT function is a new function in Excel 2016 that replaces the CONCATENATE function. The CONCATENATE function is still available for compatibility with earlier version of Excel. These functions join the contents of two or more cells, including text, numbers, and cell references. Additional information, including spaces and characters, can also be added into the combined data.

13.14 ▶ The UPPER function and the LOWER function are Text functions used to convert text from uppercase to lowercase, and vice versa. The PROPER function is a Text function used to capitalize the first letter of each word.

13.15 ▶ Excel offers the options of publishing a workbook as a PDF file and as an XPS file. Saving a workbook as a PDF or XPS file allows sending the information to people who do not have Excel and cannot open and view an Excel workbook. A PDF file can be viewed in a web browser or using Adobe Reader or Adobe Acrobat; it can also be opened with Word 2016. An XPS file can be viewed in Internet Explorer or using the XPS viewer.

13.16 ▶ An Excel worksheet can be published as a single web page in the traditional HTML format used for creating web pages.

Features Review

Feature	Ribbon Tab, Group	Button, Option	Keyboard Shortcut
accept entries suggested by Flash Fill	Home, Editing	, *Flash Fill*	Ctrl + E
append Excel data to Access table	Home, Clipboard	Paste, *Paste Append*	
delete Excel data pasted into table in Word	Table Tools Layout, Rows & Columns	, *Delete Table*	
display Open dialog box	File	*Open*, Browse	Ctrl + F12
display Paste Special dialog box	Home, Clipboard	Paste, *Paste Special*	Alt + Ctrl + V
edit embedded Excel chart in Word document or PowerPoint presentation	Chart Tools Design or Chart Tools Format		
embed Excel chart in PowerPoint presentation or Word document	Home, Clipboard		
embed Excel data in PowerPoint presentation or Word document	Home, Clipboard	Paste, *Paste Special*	
export Excel data as text file	File	*Export*, *Change File Type*	
import text file into Excel workbook	Data, Get & Transform Data		
import Access table into Excel worksheet	Data, Get & Transform Data		
insert Text function (CONCAT, CONCATENATE, LEFT, LOWER, MID, PROPER, RIGHT, TRIM, UPPER)	Formulas, Function Library		
link Excel data in PowerPoint presentation or Word document	Home, Clipboard	Paste, *Paste Special*	
modify data connection in Excel workbook	Query Editor Home, Data Sources		
publish Excel worksheet as single web page in HTM or HTML format	File	Export, *Change File Type*	
publish Excel worksheets and workbooks as PDF and XPS files	File	*Export*, Create PDF/XPS	
replace original data with formula results	Home, Clipboard	, *Values*	
save different type of file as Excel workbook	File	*Save As*, *Excel Workbook(*.xlsx)*	

Recheck

Recheck your understanding of the concepts, features, and skills covered in this chapter by taking the Recheck quiz.

Workbook

Access the study tools, review exercises, assessments, and challenges for this chapter in the workbook available from this page in your ebook.

Sharing a Workbook

Chapter 14

Chapter Goal

To manage collaboration in a workbook, including editing by multiple users at the same time.

Precheck

Check your understanding of the concepts, features, and skills covered in this chapter by taking the Precheck quiz.

Learning Objectives

Data Files

Before beginning the chapter work, download the AE14 folder from this page in your ebook to your storage medium and then make AE14 the active folder.

14.1 View, add, and modify workbook properties
14.2 Work with comments
14.3 Share a workbook on a network drive
14.4 Use Track Changes and open multiple instances of Excel
14.5 View changes and resolve conflicts in a shared workbook
14.6 Print a history sheet
14.7 Display, accept, and reject tracked changes
14.8 Turn off Track Changes and remove shared access
14.9 Protect a worksheet and restrict editing in a worksheet
14.10 Protect and unprotect the workbook structure
14.11 Protect a workbook with a password
14.12 Apply international number, date, and currency formats
14.13 Inspect a workbook for properties
14.14 Inspect a workbook for accessibility issues
14.15 Inspect a workbook for compatibility issues and save a workbook in the Excel 97-2003 format
14.16 Mark a workbook as final
14.17 Share a workbook in OneDrive

Ebook Links

Access digital resources for this course from your ebook.

SNAP

If you are a SNAP user, go to your SNAP assignments page to complete the Precheck, Tutorials, and Recheck in this chapter.

Preview

On the Job

Scenario: DV Auto Parts

Devon Varey, owner of DV Auto Parts, is going to discuss the Excel workbook containing October sales and inventory data with his team of sales associates at their next weekly meeting. Before the meeting, Devon wants Wes Cortez to review and edit the workbook. Devon wants you to handle the review process with Wes and then inspect the workbook and get it ready for distribution to the sales team. You will need to make sure the workbook is accessible, is compatible with older versions of Excel, and is marked as final to discourage users from editing its contents. When the file is ready, you will share it with Wes in OneDrive. Devon also wants your help preparing an invoice workbook that is protected so that only authorized users can change some of the cells in it, and formatting a sales forecast workbook to use international number and currency formatting.

Visual Reference: Shared Workbook

Figure 14.1 Excel Workbook with Accessibility and Compatibility Inspection Results

Click the New Comment button to insert a comment in the active cell.

By default, comment boxes are closed in a worksheet. Click the Show All Comments button to display all the comment boxes.

Click the Share Workbook button to allow multiple users to edit the file at the same time. Excel adds the text *[Shared]* after the file name in the Title bar of a shared workbook.

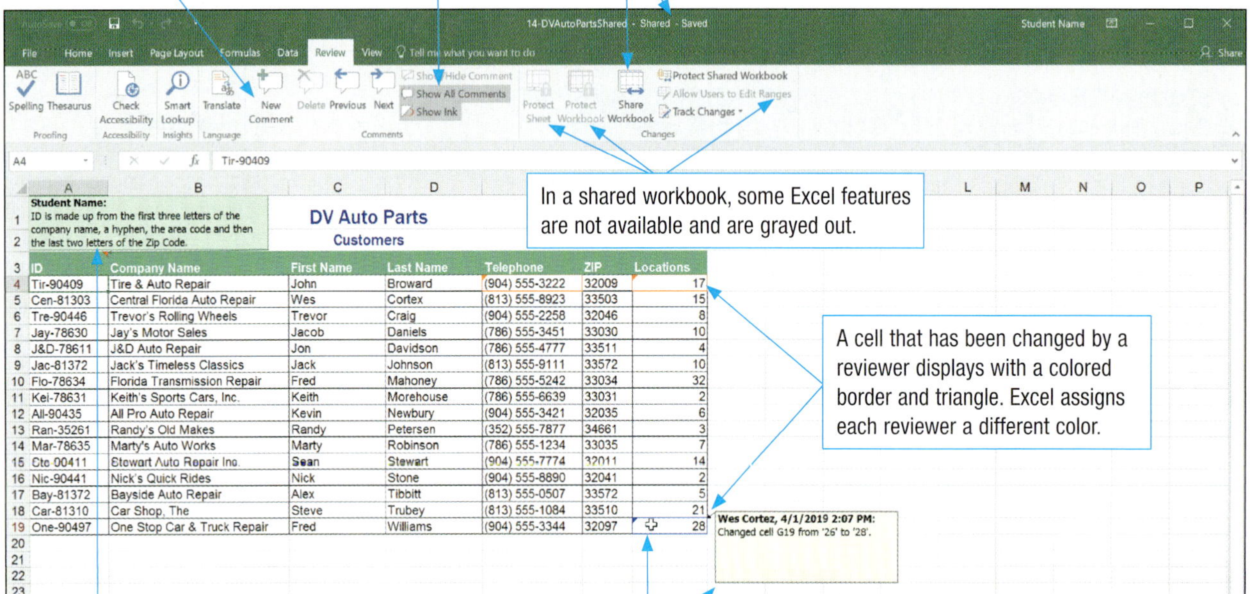

In a shared workbook, some Excel features are not available and are grayed out.

A cell that has been changed by a reviewer displays with a colored border and triangle. Excel assigns each reviewer a different color.

By default, a comment displays in a small box to the right of the cell containing it. The comment box for cell A3 has been moved and resized and its fill color has been changed.

Hover the mouse pointer over a changed cell until the pointer turns into a white cross to display a box describing the changes.

Visual Reference

Figure 14.2 Excel Workbook with Accessibility and Compatibility Inspection Results

Click an issue at the Accessibility Checker task pane to select the related item in the worksheet and to view additional information about the issue and how to fix it at the bottom of the task pane.

After the Accessibility Checker has been run, the results display at the Accessibility Checker task pane.

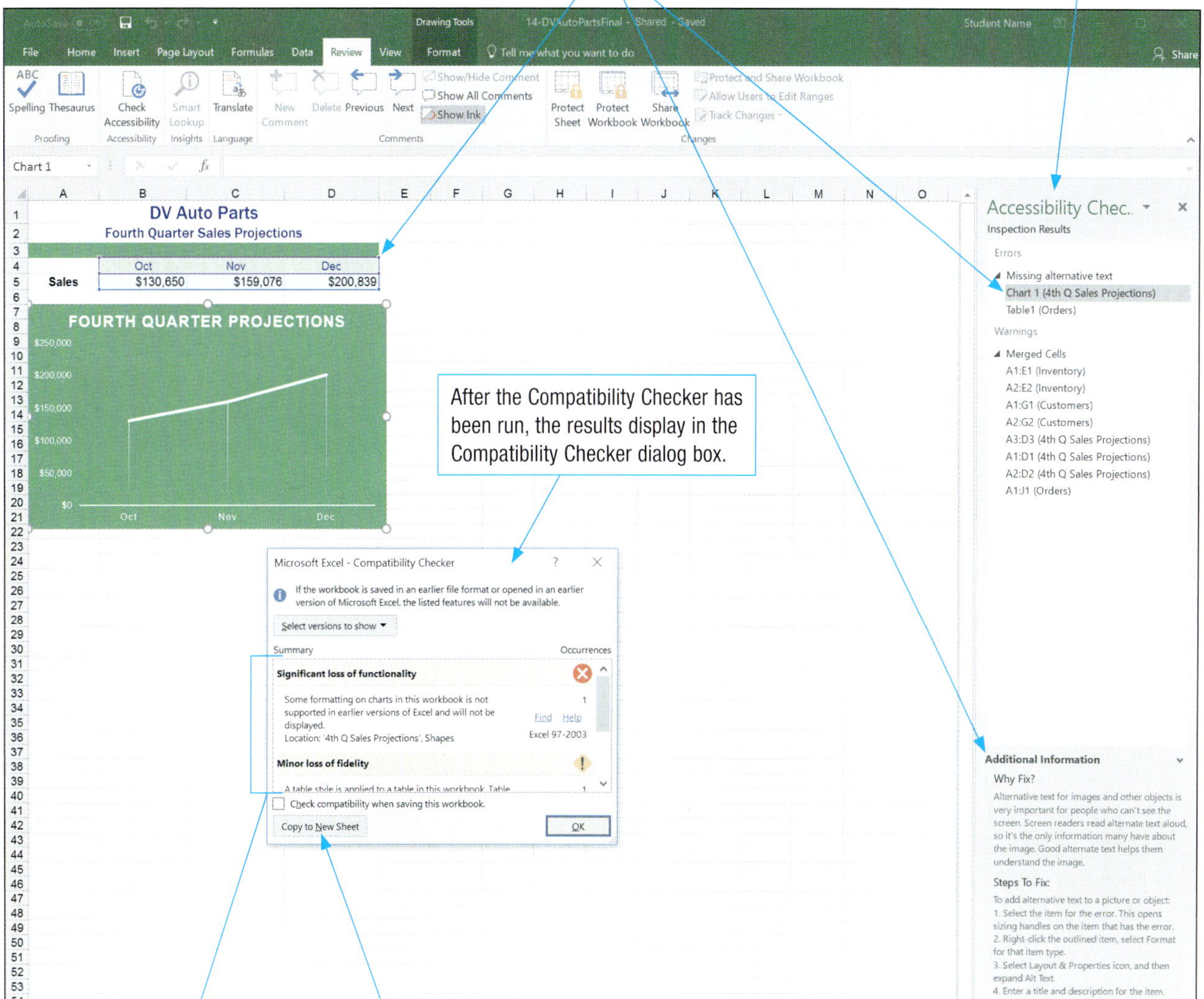

After the Compatibility Checker has been run, the results display in the Compatibility Checker dialog box.

The *Summary* list box describes features that will not be available if the workbook is saved in an earlier file format or opened in an earlier version of Excel.

Click the Copy to New Sheet button to copy the report from the *Summary* list box to a new worksheet.

Visual Reference

14.1 Viewing, Adding, and Modifying Workbook Properties

MOS 1.4.6

Tutorial

Modifying Workbook Properties

A **workbook property** provides descriptive information about the workbook data, such as the author's name, the title, the subject, the category to which the workbook is related (for example, finance), or a general comment about the workbook. Workbook properties are sometimes referred to as **metadata**. Metadata is useful if questions arise about changes made to a workbook; for instance, metadata can tell you when a workbook was last modified and who last saved it.

▸ Know This about viewing, adding, and modifying workbook properties at the Info backstage area

— To view, add, and modify information about basic workbook properties: click the File tab; click the *Info* option in the left panel, if necessary; and then see the *Properties* list in the right panel (see Figure 14.3).

— Excel automatically provides some information about workbook properties. For example, Excel supplies the size of the workbook, the date the workbook was last modified, the date the workbook was created, the date the workbook was last printed, and the name of the person who last saved the workbook.

— You can add and modify information about other workbook properties, such as the workbook title, tags, categories, and authors.

— To add information about a property, click in the placeholder text (for example, *Add a title*), type the new information in the text box that displays, and then click outside the text box.

— To modify information about a property, click in the information text, type to replace the selected text in the text box that displays, and then click outside the text box.

— To display more properties at the Info backstage area, click the Show All Properties hyperlink. After this hyperlink has been clicked, it is replaced by the Show Fewer Properties hyperlink. To display fewer properties, click the Show Fewer Properties hyperlink.

▸ Know More about workbook properties

– The document information panel found in previous versions of Excel is not available in Excel 2016.

▸ Know This about viewing, adding, and modifying workbook properties at the workbook Properties dialog box

— To view, add, and modify advanced workbook properties, click the *Properties* section head arrow at the Info backstage area, click the *Advanced Properties* option at the drop-down list, and then use options on the tabs at the workbook Properties dialog box (see Figure 14.4).

— Properties that can be edited at the workbook Properties dialog box include, but are not limited to, the date completed, the name of the editor, and the name of the person who checked the workbook.

Figure 14.3 Workbook Properties at the Info Backstage Area

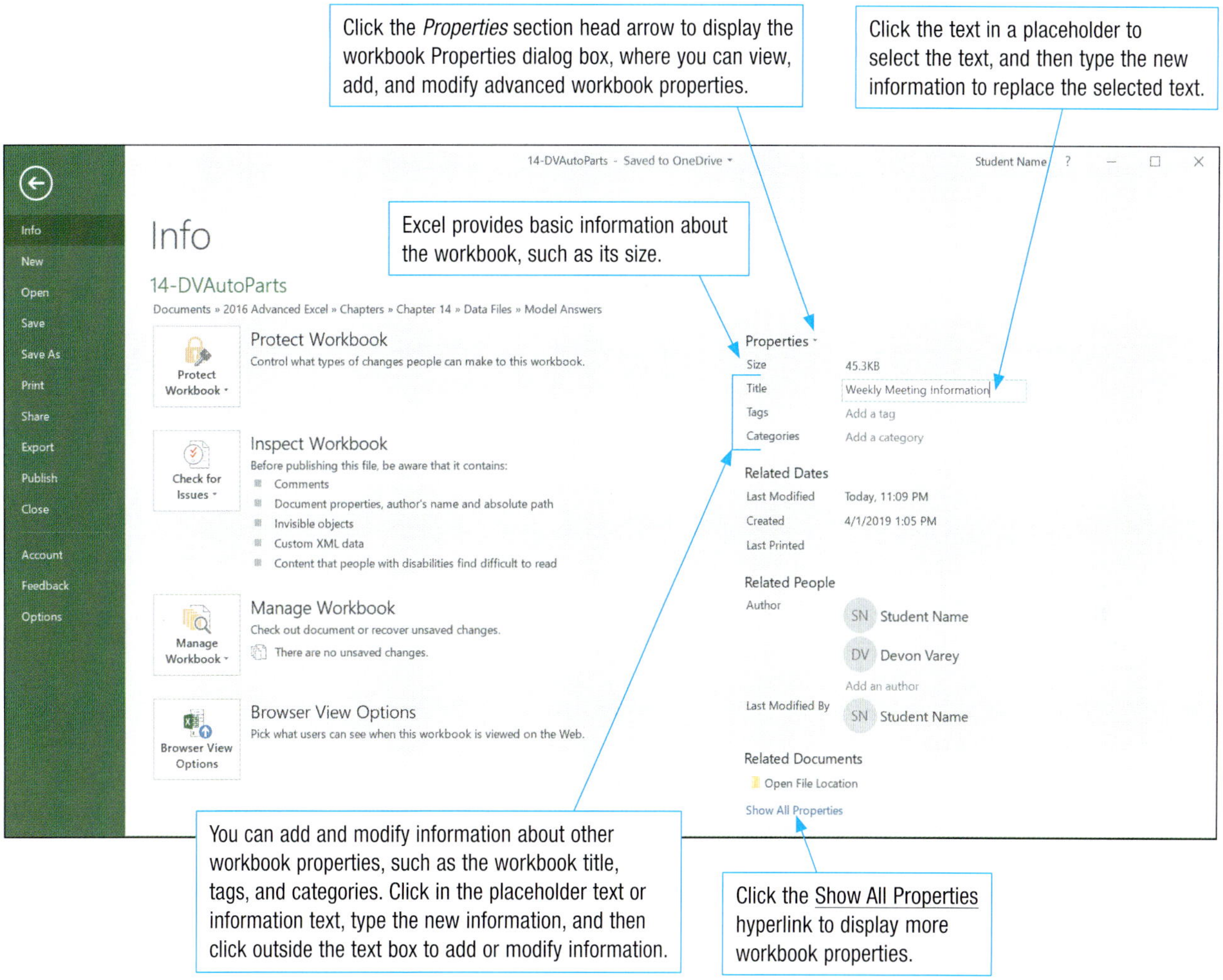

On the Job

Task 14.1 Modifying Workbook Properties

Devon asks you to add his name as author and information about other properties to the Excel workbook containing sales and inventory data. Use options at the Info backstage area and the workbook Properties dialog box to add metadata to the workbook.

1. Open the data file **14-DVAutoParts**.
2. Click the File tab.

   The Info backstage area displays.
3. Click in the placeholder text *Add an author*.

   The insertion point appears in a text box.
4. Type Devon Varey in the text box.

   If the message *We couldn't find the person you were looking for* displays, ignore it.
5. Click outside the text box.

   The text *Devon Varey* appears as information for the *Author* property (see Figure 14.3).

6. Click in the placeholder text *Add a title*, type Weekly Meeting Information in the text box, and then click outside the text box.

   The text *Weekly Meeting Information* appears as information for the *Title* property.

7. Click the Show All Properties hyperlink.

   The *Properties* section expands to display more properties for the workbook.

8. Click in the *Specify the company* placeholder text, type DV Auto Parts in the text box, and then click outside the text box.

   The text *DV Auto Parts* appears as information for the *Company* property.

9. Click the *Properties* section head arrow and then click the *Advanced Properties* option.

   The 14-DVAutoParts Properties dialog box displays with the Summary tab active.

10. Click the Custom tab.
11. Click the *Checked by* option in the *Name* list box.

    The text *Checked by* is selected in the *Name* list box and appears in the *Name* option box.

12. Click in the *Value* text box, type your name, and then click the Add button.

    The entries *Checked by*, *[your name]*, and *Text* appear in the *Name*, *Value*, and *Type* columns, respectively, in the *Properties* list box (see Figure 14.4).

Figure 14.4 Custom Tab at the 14-DVAutoParts Properties Dialog Box

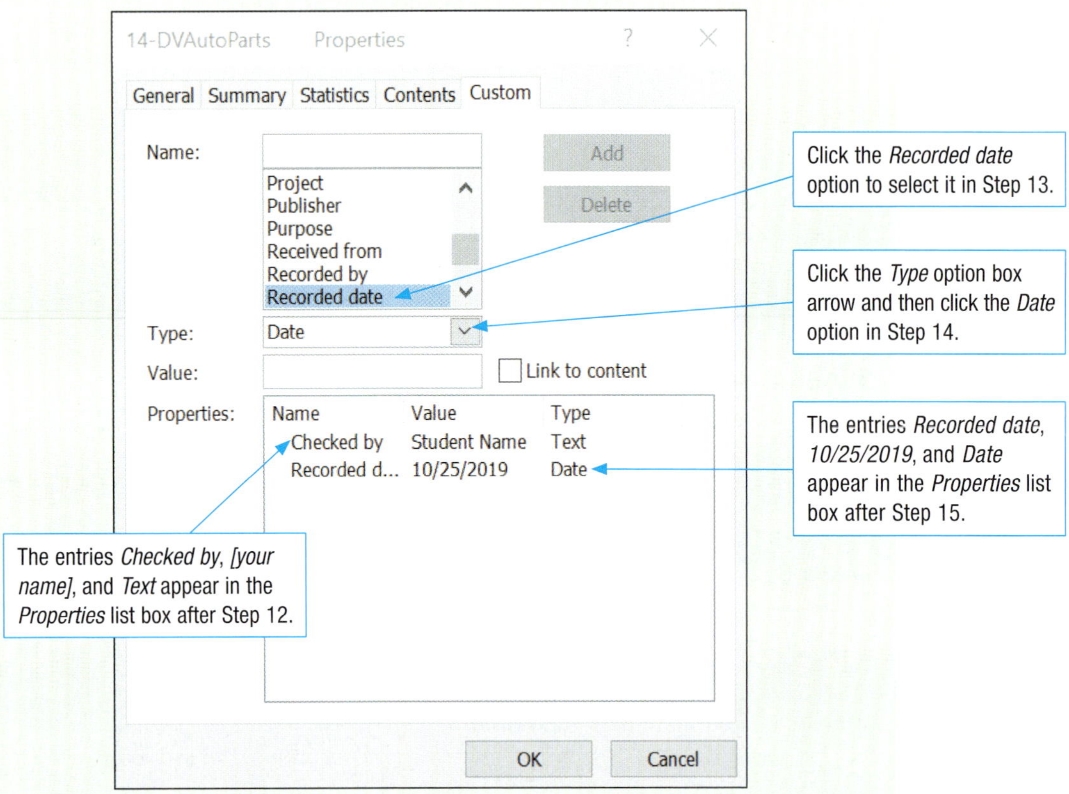

13. Scroll down in the *Name* list box and then click the *Recorded date* option.
14. Click the *Type* option box arrow and then click the *Date* option.
    The option *Date* appears in the *Type* option box.
15. Click in the *Value* text box, type 10/25/2019, and then click the Add button.
    The entries *Recorded date*, *10/25/2019*, and *Date* appear in the *Properties* list box.
16. Click the OK button.
    The 14-DVAutoParts Properties dialog box closes.
17. Click the Show Fewer Properties hyperlink.
    The *Properties* section collapses.
18. Click the Back button and then click the Save button on the Quick Access Toolbar.

14.2 Working with Comments

In Excel, a **comment** is a note that is attached to a cell and displays in a pop-up box. When a comment is attached to a cell, a colored triangle appears in the upper right corner of the cell. The comment box displays when the mouse pointer points to the cell to which the comment is attached. Comments are used to provide instructions, identify critical information, and add other explanatory information about a cell entry. They are useful when collaborating with others to create or edit a worksheet. Reviewers can use comments to add feedback and pose questions about cell entries and layout.

Tutorial

Adding, Editing, and Moving a Comment and Displaying All the Comments in a Worksheet

▸ **Know This** about inserting comments

— To insert a comment in an active cell, click the Review tab, click the New Comment button in the Comments group (see Figure 14.5), and then type the comment text.

— To start a new line in a comment box, press the Enter key.

— To close the comment box, click in the worksheet area outside the comment box.

▸ **Know More** ways to insert comments in an active cell

– Right-click and then click the *Insert Comments* option at the pop-up menu.

– Press Shift + F2.

Figure 14.5 Comments Group on the Review Tab

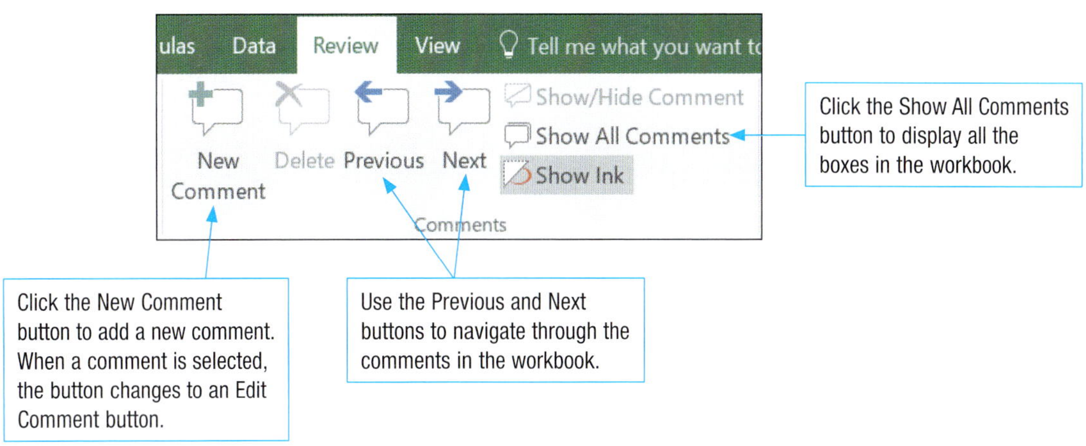

▸ Know This about viewing comments

— A small red triangle displays in the upper right corner of a cell to alert the user that a comment is attached to the cell.
— To view a comment attached to a cell, point to the cell.
— To display or hide all the comment boxes in a workbook, click the Show All Comments button in the Comments group on the Review tab. The Show All Comments button displays with a light background when it is not active and with a dark background when it is active.
— To view the next or the previous comment, click the Next button or the Previous button, respectively.

▸ Know This about resizing comment boxes

— By default, Excel opens comment boxes at a certain size. If a comment box is not large enough for you to read the entire comment, you can resize the box.
— To resize a comment box, click in the box and then drag a sizing handle.

▸ Know This about editing, formatting, and deleting comments

— When the active cell contains a comment, the Edit Comment button displays (in place of the New Comment button) in the Comments group on the Review tab.
— To edit a comment, click in the cell containing the comment, click the Edit Comment button, modify the text in the comment box, and then click in the worksheet area outside the comment box.
— The default font for comment text is Tahoma and the default font size is 9 points.
— To modify the font, font size, and other formatting for comment text, select the text and then use tools in the Font group on the Home tab. The Borders, Fill Color, and Font Color buttons in the Font group are not available for comment text and are grayed out.
— To modify the font color, fill color, and other formatting for the comment box, click the Edit Comment button, right-click the border of the comment box, click the *Format Comment* option at the pop-up menu, and then use options on the appropriate tab at the Format Comment dialog box (see Figure 14.6).
— When the Format Comment dialog box displays, if the Font tab is the only tab available, click the Cancel button and then right-click the border of the comment box again. Be careful to right-click the edge of the comment box, not inside the comment box.
— If you modify the font color and/or fill color, ensure there is enough contrast between the colors so that the comment can be easily read.
— To delete a comment, click in the cell that contains the comment and then click the Delete button in the Comments group.

▸ Know More ways to edit, format, and delete comments

- To edit a comment, right-click in the cell that contains the comment, click the *Edit Comment* option at the pop-up menu, modify the comment text, and then click in the worksheet area outside the comment box.
- To format a comment, click the Format button in the Cells group on the Home tab, click the *Format Comment* option, apply the formatting changes, and then click the OK button.
- To modify the font, font size, and other formatting for comment text, place the insertion point in the comment box, click the Format button in the Cells group on the Home tab, click the *Format Comment* option, make the formatting changes on the Font tab at the Format Comment dialog box, and then click the OK button.
- To modify the font color, fill color, and other formatting for the comment box, click the border of the comment box, click the Format button in the Cells group on the Home tab, click the *Format Comment* option, make the formatting changes on the appropriate tab at the Format Comment dialog box, and then click the OK button.
- To delete a comment, right-click in the cell that contains the comment and then click the *Delete Comment* option at the pop-up menu.

Figure 14.6 Colors and Lines Tab at the Format Comment Dialog Box

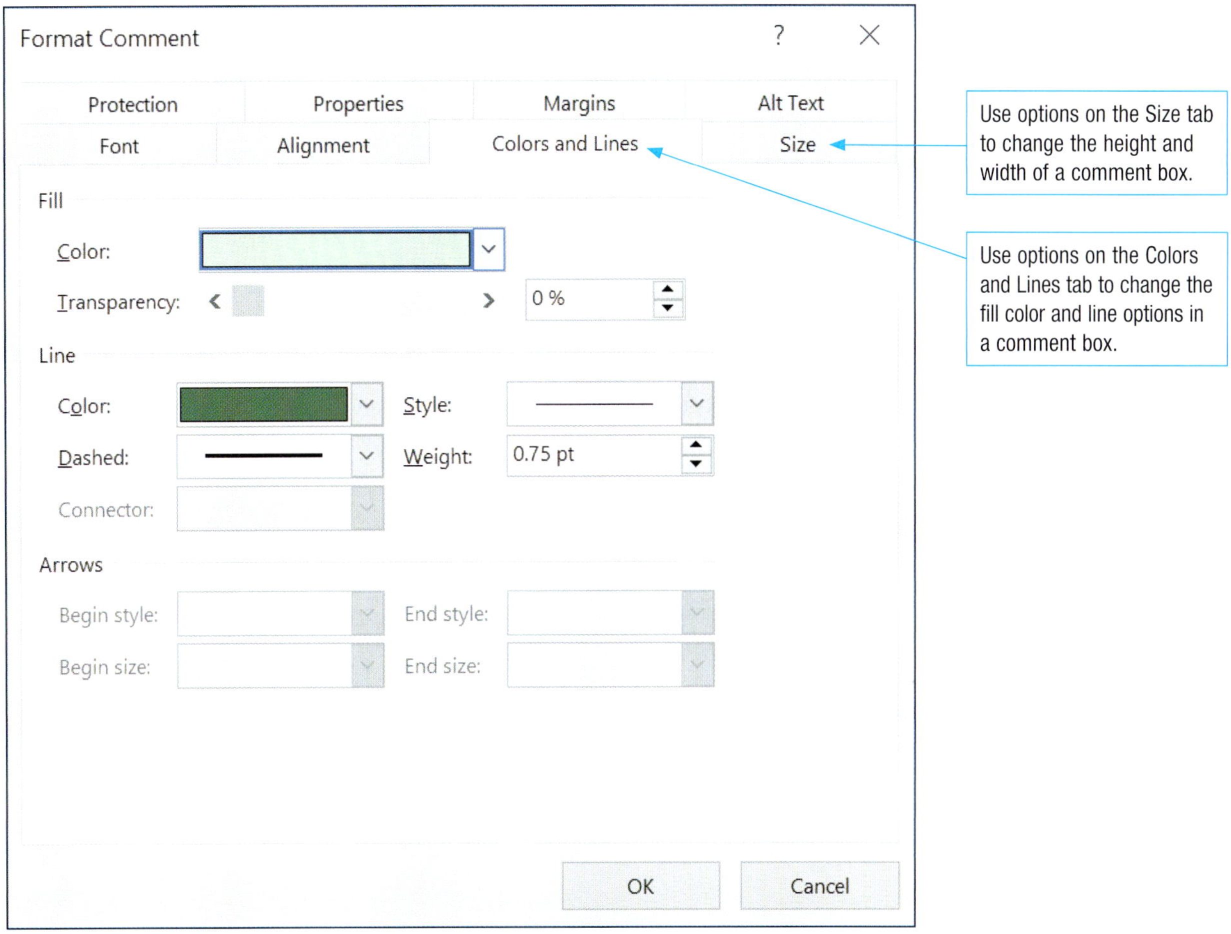

▸ **Know This** about copying and pasting comments

— A comment that has been added to a cell can be copied and pasted to one or more other cells.

— To copy and paste a comment, press Ctrl + C, click in the destination cell or select the destination cells, click the Paste button arrow in the Clipboard group on the Home tab, click the *Paste Special* option at the drop-down list, click the *Comments* radio button in the *Paste* section at the Paste Special dialog box to insert a bullet, and then click the OK button.

— If you copy a comment to a cell that already contains a comment, the original comment will be replaced.

▸ **Know This** about moving comments

— To move a comment, hover the mouse pointer over the border of the comment box until it turns into a four-headed arrow, click and hold down the left mouse button, drag the comment box to its new location, and then release the mouse button.

▸ **Know This** about printing comments

— By default, comments do not print when you print a worksheet or workbook.

— To print comments with a worksheet, click the Page Layout tab, click the Page Setup group dialog box launcher, click the Sheet tab at the Page Setup dialog box, click the *Comments* option box arrow, click the *At the end of sheet* option (to print the comments on a separate page after the cell contents) or click the *As displayed on sheet* option (to print the comments as they appear within the worksheet area), and then click the Print button.

On the Job

Task 14.2a Adding a Comment, Resizing a Comment Box, Editing a Comment, and Moving a Comment

Devon wants to provide additional information to users of the 14-DVAutoParts workbook. He asks you to add a note in the Inventory worksheet to alert users that the unit price for part number 213890 will increase to $290 in the new year. Add a comment with that information to the cell containing the 2019 price for that part.

Devon has already added a comment to cell A4 in the Customers worksheet, noting how the ID numbers were created. He realizes that he added the comment to the wrong cell (he meant to insert it in the cell containing the *ID* column header) and that he also made an error when entering the comment text. Devon asks you to fix these mistakes. When you edit the comment, start by resizing the comment box so you can read the entire comment without scrolling.

1. With the 14-DVAutoParts workbook open, click the Inventory sheet tab, if necessary, and then click in cell E8.
2. Click the Review tab, click the New Comment button in the Comments group, and then type Price increases to $290 in the new year.

   Include the period when typing the comment.
3. Click outside the comment box.

   The comment box closes and a red triangle appears in the upper right corner of cell E8.
4. Click the Customers sheet tab and then click in cell A4.
5. Click the Edit Comment button.

   The comment box displays with sizing handles.
6. Drag the bottom middle sizing handle of the comment box down until the bottom of the box touches the top of cell B10 (see Figure 14.7).

   The bottom middle sizing handle is difficult to see. To position the mouse pointer over the handle, hover the pointer over the center of the bottom border of the comment box until the pointer turns into a two-headed arrow.
7. Double-click the word *three* in the second-to-last line of the comment, type two, and then click outside the comment box.

Figure 14.7 Comment Box Selected with Sizing Handles Displayed

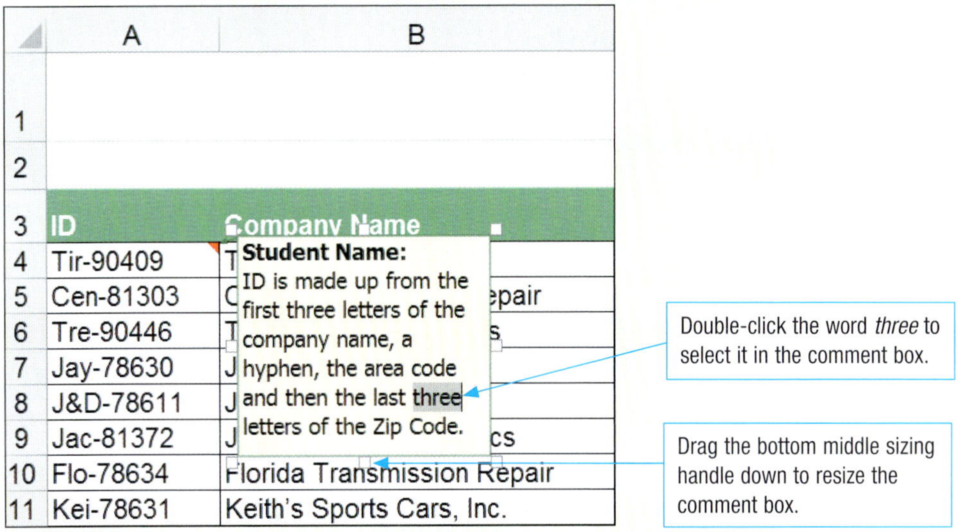

8. Click in cell A4, press Ctrl + C, click in cell A3, click the Home tab, click the Paste button arrow in the Clipboard group, and then click the *Paste Special* option.

   The Paste Special dialog box displays.

9. Click the *Comments* radio button, click the OK button, and then press the Esc key.

   A red triangle appears in the upper right corner of cell A3, indicating that the comment has been copied to that cell. You can point to cell A3 to display the comment and confirm its contents. The marquee no longer displays around cell A4.

10. Click in cell A4, click the Review tab, and then click the Delete button in the Comments group.

    The red triangle disappears from the upper right corner of cell A4, indicating the comment has been deleted.

11. Click the Save button on the Quick Access Toolbar.

Model Answer

On the Job

Task 14.2b Moving a Comment Box, Modifying the Fill Color, Resizing a Comment Box, and Displaying All the Comments in a Worksheet

Devon needs to print the Customers worksheet with all the comments displayed so he can show it to an investor. He doesn't want the comment in cell A3 to hide the contents of any cell. He also wants the fill color of the comment box to be more consistent with the colors used in the worksheet. He asks you to make changes and print the worksheet for his review. Move the comment box attached to cell A3 so it displays at the top left of the worksheet, modify the fill color of the comment box, resize the comment box, display all the comments in the worksheet, and then print the worksheet with the comments.

1. With the 14-DVAutoParts workbook open and the Customers worksheet active, click in cell A3 and then click the Edit Comment button in the Comments group on the Review tab.
2. Hover the mouse pointer over the border of the Comment box until it turns into a four-headed arrow, click and hold down the left mouse button, drag the comment box until the upper left corner of the comment box is in the upper left corner of cell A1, and then release the mouse button (see Figure 14.8).

   The comment displays in the upper left corner of cell A1.

Figure 14.8 Comment Box Positioned in Cell A1

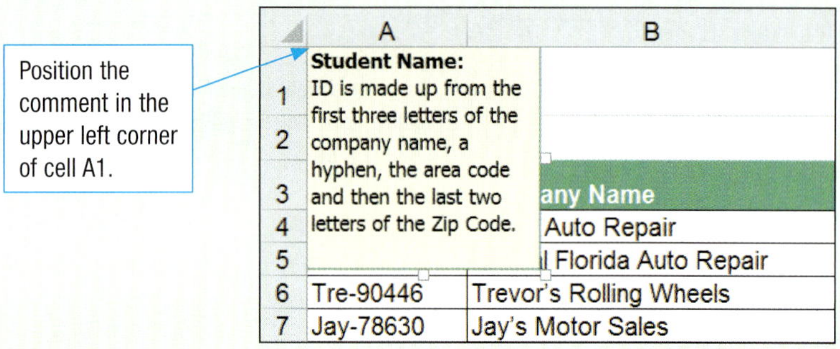

3. Right-click the edge of the comment box.

   A pop-up menu displays.
4. Click the *Format Comment* option.

   The Format Comment dialog box displays with the Font tab active. If the Font tab is the only tab at the Format Comment dialog box, click the Cancel button and then repeat Step 4. Be careful to right-click the edge of the comment box, not inside the comment box.
5. Click the Colors and Lines tab.

   The Colors and Lines tab is active (see Figure 14.6 on page 681).
6. Click the *Color* option box arrow in the *Fill* section.

   A drop-down palette displays.
7. Click the *Light Green* option (fourth column, fifth row).
8. Click the Size tab, select the value in the *Height* measurement box in the *Size and rotate* section, type 0.65, select the value in the *Width* measurement box in the *Size and rotate* section, type 3, and then click the OK button.

   The fill changes to a light green and the size adjusts to be 0.65 inches tall by 3 inches wide. The displayed comment box fits neatly above the column header row in the worksheet, without covering any cell contents, and it displays in a fill color that fits with the rest of the worksheet.
9. Click in cell A3 and then click the Show All Comments button.

   The worksheet contains only one comment: the one attached to cell A3. The comment displays.
10. Click the Page Layout tab, click the Page Setup group dialog box launcher, and then click the Sheet tab (see Figure 14.9).

    The Page Setup dialog box displays and the Sheet tab is active.

Figure 14.9 Sheet Tab at the Page Setup Dialog Box

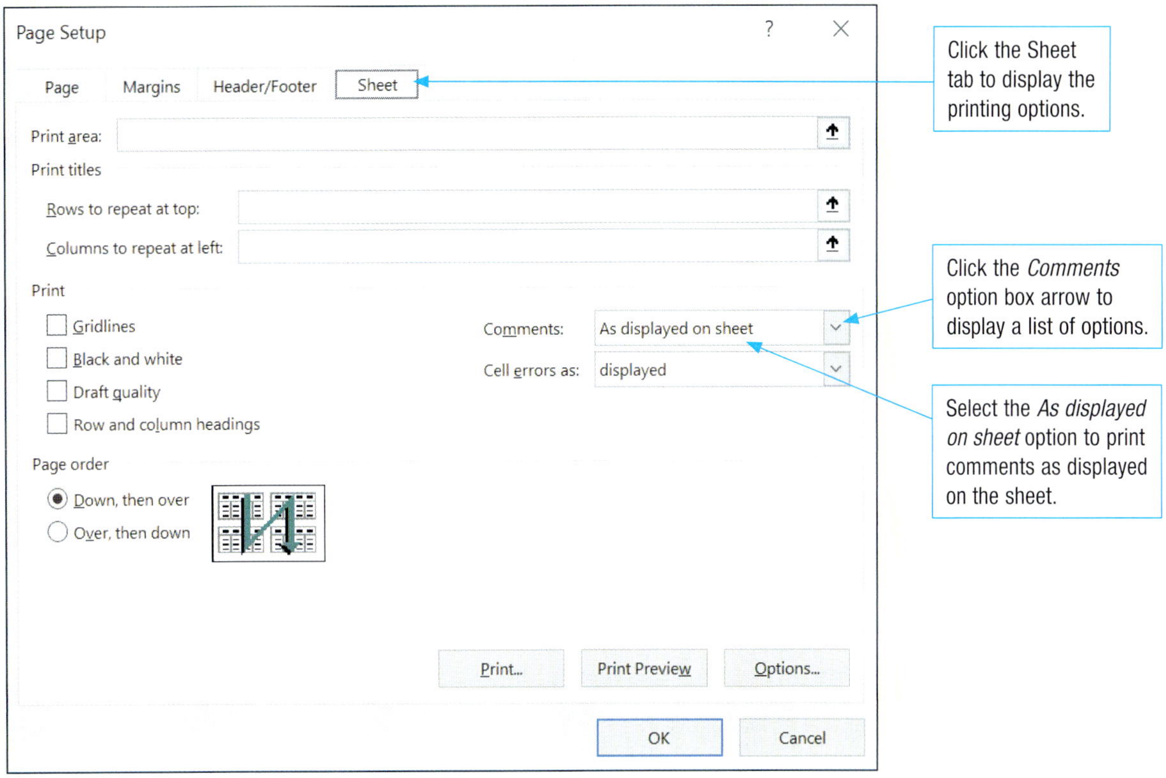

11. Click the *Comments* option box arrow.

    A drop-down list displays.

12. Click the *As displayed on sheet* option.

    The comments are set to print as displayed on the sheet.

13. Click the OK button.

    The Page Setup dialog box closes.

14. If printed work is required by your instructor, click the File tab, click the *Print* option, and then click the Print button.

    The worksheet prints with the comments displayed.

15. Click the Save button on the Quick Access Toolbar.

Model Answer

14.3 Sharing a Workbook on a Network Drive

Tutorial

Sharing a Workbook on a Network Drive

A workbook may contain data that several users need to review and modify at the same time. For example, you might create a project schedule in an Excel workbook and then ask each member of the project team to update the schedule after he or she completes an assigned task. Excel provides several options for collaborating with others. One method is to share a workbook. A **shared workbook** can be saved to a network folder that multiple users can access at the same time. Excel tracks each person's changes and displays a prompt if two or more people have the same workbook open at the same time and attempt to make changes to the same cell.

▸ Know This about sharing a workbook on a network drive

— The Share Workbook command and Track Changes command (covered in Section 14.4) are legacy tools, which means they are older tools that are no longer installed on the Excel ribbon by default but can be added by the user. In earlier versions of Excel, these tools appeared in the Changes group on the Review tab. If you do not find them in your version of Excel, see Sections 15.2 and 15.3 (on pages 744–754) for instructions on adding commands to the Review tab or the Quick Access Toolbar. Follow those instructions to add the Share Workbook (Legacy) command and the Track Changes (Legacy) command from the *All Commands* list at the Excel Options dialog box.

— To share an open workbook, click the Share Workbook button in the Changes group on the Review tab (see Figure 14.10), click the *Allow changes by more than one user at the same time* check box to insert a check mark on the Editing tab at the Share Workbook dialog box, and then click the OK button (see Figure 14.11). Click the OK button at the message box asking if you want to save the workbook and continue.

— To specify options for sharing a workbook, use the Advanced tab at the Share Workbook dialog box (see Figure 14.12).

— When a workbook is shared, Excel adds *[Shared]* in the Title bar after the workbook file name.

— Workbooks containing tables cannot be shared.

— A shared workbook cannot support all Excel features. Features that are not available are grayed out on the Excel ribbon.

— If a feature that is not available in a shared workbook is required, remove the shared access to the workbook (see Section 14.8). You can restore the shared access after using the feature. For example, to delete a worksheet from a shared file, you can remove the shared access, delete the worksheet, and then restore the shared access.

Figure 14.10 Changes Group on the Review Tab

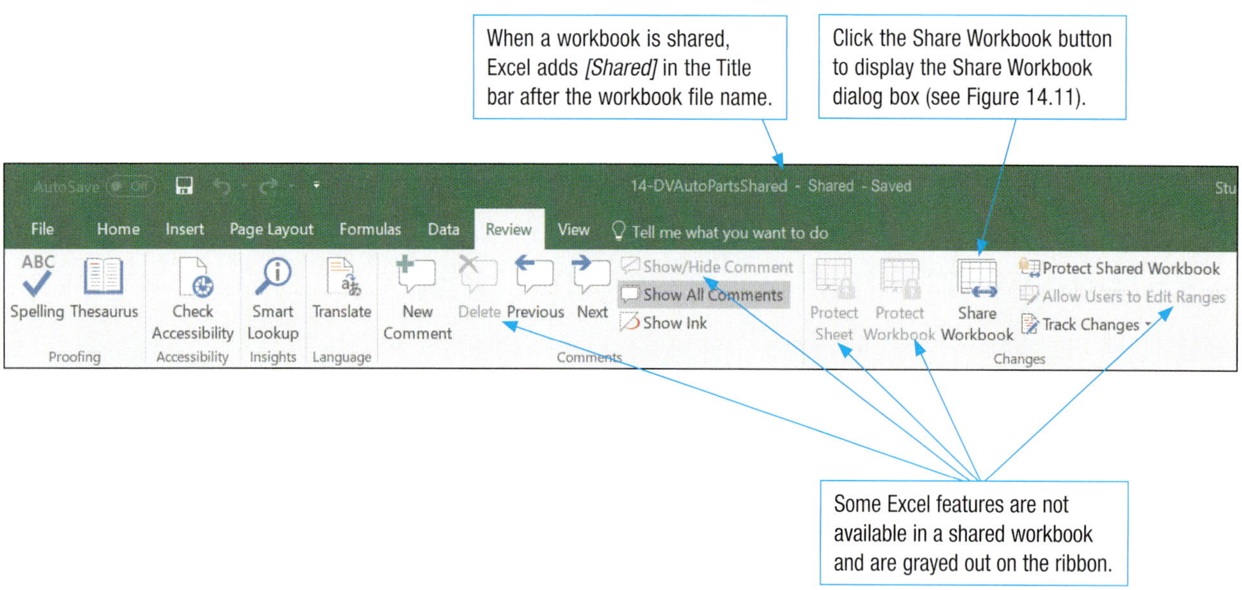

Figure 14.11 Editing Tab at the Share Workbook Dialog Box

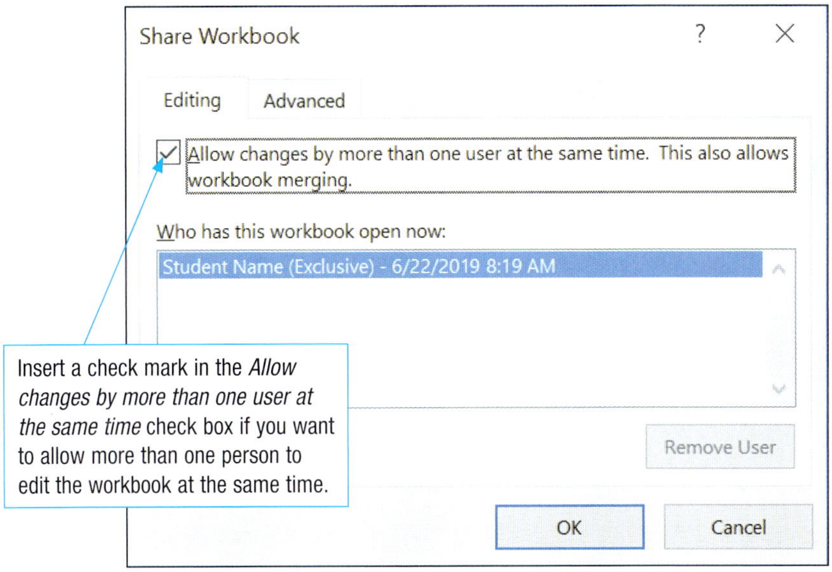

Figure 14.12 Advanced Tab at the Share Workbook Dialog Box

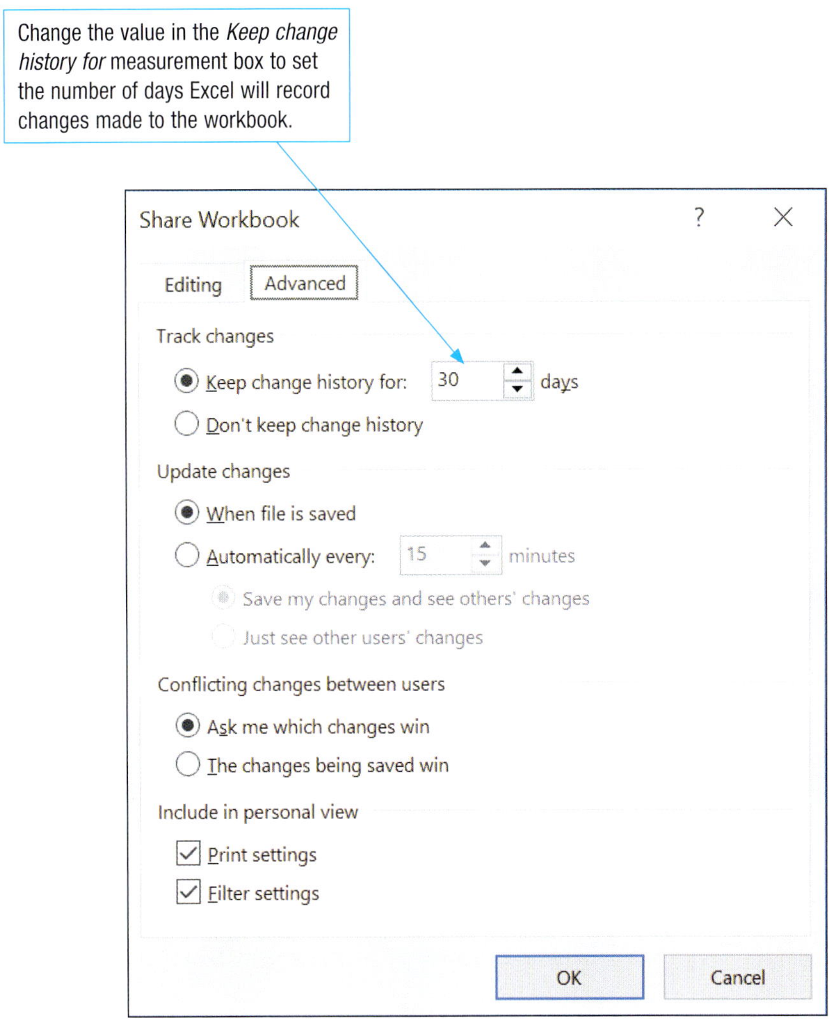

▸ **Know This** about the workbook history log

— By default, the changes made to a shared workbook are saved in a **history log** for 30 days.

— To increase or decrease the number of days changes are saved to the history log, click the Share Workbook button in the Changes group on the Review tab, click the Advanced tab at the Share Workbook dialog box, and then change the value in the *Keep change history for* measurement box in the *Track changes* section (see Figure 14.12).

— Be aware that increasing the number of days Excel saves changes to the history log increases the size of the workbook.

▸ **Know This** about sharing a workbook on a network drive

— To share a workbook on a network drive, be sure to save it to a folder that is designated as a shared folder and is accessible to the intended users.

— The network administrator is usually the person who creates a **network share**, which is a folder on a server designated with read/write access rights for multiple accounts.

— Individuals with access to the shared network folder will have full access to the shared workbook.

On the Job

Task 14.3 Sharing a Workbook on a Network Drive

Devon wants to collaborate with you so that you can both edit the workbook simultaneously. Save the workbook as a shared file with the name *14-DVAutoPartsShared* to make the workbook available for editing by multiple users at the same time.

Note: *In Tasks 14.3–14.8, you are simulating a network environment. For these tasks, you cannot save your working file to your OneDrive account. Instead, you need to save the file to a drive on your computer or to a USB flash drive. If you want to save it to the drive on a computer that is not your own, make sure you have the needed permissions to do so.*

1. With the 14-DVAutoParts workbook open and any worksheet active, click the File tab, click the *Save As* option, navigate to a drive on your computer, click the *New folder* option, type AE14, click the Open button two times, click in the *File name* text box, type 14-DVAutoPartsShared and then click the Save button.

   A copy of the workbook is saved with the new name and is open.

2. Click the Review tab and then click the Share Workbook button in the Changes group (see Figure 14.10 on page 686).

   The Share Workbook dialog box displays with the Editing tab active (see Figure 14.11 on page 686).

3. Click the *Allow changes by more than one user at the same time* check box.

   A check mark appears in the check box.

4. Click the OK button.

   A message box displays, stating that the workbook will now be saved and asking if you want to continue.

Reminder

If you added the Share Workbook (Legacy) command, you will click the Share button (instead of the Share Workbook button) to display the Share Workbook dialog box.

5. Click the OK button.

   The message box closes. Excel saves the file and adds *[Shared]* in the Title bar after the workbook file name.

6. Save and then close the workbook without closing Excel.

14.4 Using Track Changes and Opening Multiple Instances of Excel

When a workbook is shared, Excel automatically turns on Track Changes. The **Track Changes** feature records any changes made to a workbook and the names of the users who make the changes.

By default, when you open more than one workbook at the same time, all the workbooks open in the same instance of Excel. Occasionally, you may want to open each workbook in a separate instance of Excel. For example, each instance of Excel allows only one dialog box to be open at a time. If you need to compare the RGB values at the Colors dialog box for one workbook against the RGB values at the Colors dialog box for another workbook, you must open each workbook in a separate instance of Excel.

Tutorial

Changing the User Name Associated with Excel and Opening Another Instance of a Shared Workbook

▸ Know This about turning on Track Changes

— The Track Changes command and the Share command (covered in Section 14.3) are legacy tools, which means they are older tools that are no longer installed on the Excel ribbon by default but can be added by the user. In earlier versions of Excel, these tools appeared in the Changes group on the Review tab. If you do not find them in your version of Excel, see Sections 15.2 and 15.3 (on pages 744–754) for instructions on adding commands to the Review tab or the Quick Access Toolbar. Follow those instructions to add the Track Changes (Legacy) command and the Share Workbook (Legacy) command from the list All Commands list at the Excel Options dialog box.

— To turn on Track Changes in an open workbook, click the Review tab, click the Track Changes button in the Changes group, click the *Highlight Changes* option at the drop-down list, click the *Track changes while editing* check box to insert a check mark at the Highlight Changes dialog box, leave the check mark that appears by default in the *When* check box, click the OK button to close the dialog box, and then click the OK button to close the message box that displays.

— When you turn on Track Changes in a workbook that is not shared, Excel automatically saves the workbook as a shared file.

▸ Know This about using Track Changes

— To highlight changes that have not yet been reviewed in a workbook, click the Review tab, click the Track Changes button in the Changes group, click the *Highlight Changes* option at the drop-down list, click the *Track changes while editing* check box to insert a check mark at the Highlight Changes dialog box, leave the check mark that appears by default in the *When* check box, click the *When* option box arrow, click the

Not yet reviewed option at the drop-down list, click the OK button to close the dialog box, and then click the OK button to close the message box that displays.

— When changes are highlighted, a border displays around a changed cell and a black triangle appears in the upper left corner of the cell.

— To view a highlighted change in a worksheet, point to the highlighted cell to display a pop-up box containing the name of the person who changed the cell, plus the date, time, original entry, and revised entry.

— To remove highlighting from changed cells, click the *Highlight changes on screen* check box to remove the check mark.

▸ **Know This** about changing the user name and viewing the names of users

— User name information is entered when Microsoft Office is installed.

— To change the user name associated with Excel in an open workbook: click the File tab; click the *Options* option; click the *General* option in the left panel at the Excel Options dialog box, if necessary; select the text in the *User name* text box in the *Personalize your copy of Microsoft Office* section in the right panel; type the new user name; and then click the OK button.

— To view the names of users who currently have a shared workbook open, click the Review tab and then click the Share Workbook button in the Changes group. All the users who have the workbook open will be listed in the *Who has this workbook open now* list box (see Figure 14.13).

Figure 14.13 List Box with Multiple Users on the Editing Tab at the Share Workbook Dialog Box

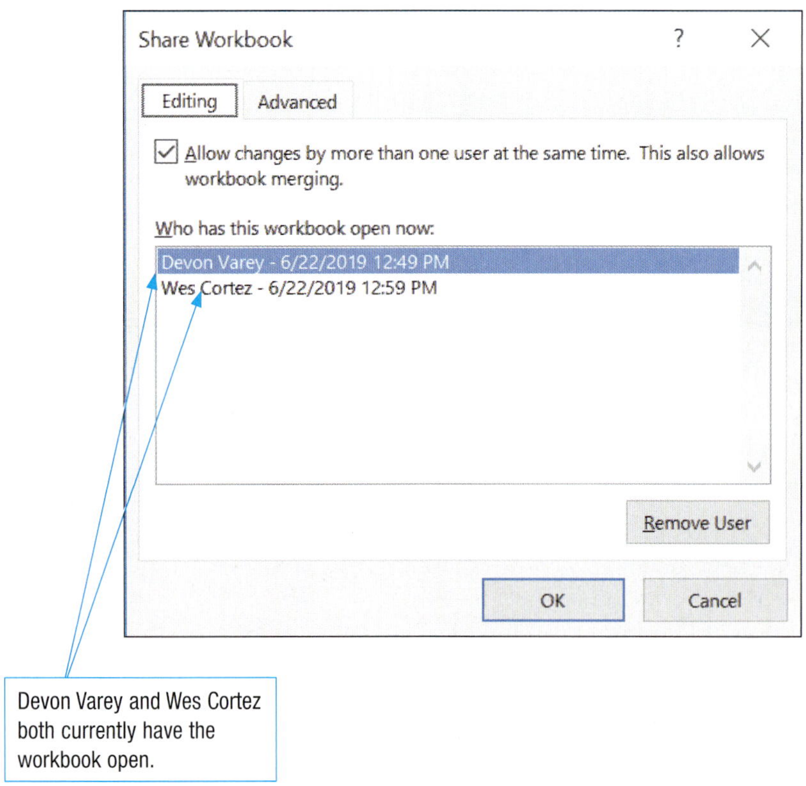

▸ **Know This** about opening multiple instances of Excel on the same computer

— By default, when multiple Excel workbooks are opened on the same computer, they are opened in the same instance of Excel. Excel does not open a new copy of the program every time a new workbook is opened.

— Opening a single instance of the program saves the computer's resources.

— At times, you may want to open multiple instances on the same computer. For example, you may want to do this so you can have more than one dialog box open at the same time.

— To open multiple instances of Excel at the same time on the same computer, open one instance of Excel, press and hold down the Alt key, right-click the Excel button on the Windows taskbar, click the *Excel 2016* option at the pop-up menu, release the Alt key when you see a message box asking if you want to start a new instance of Excel, and then click the Yes button to open the Excel Start screen.

— At the Excel Start screen, you can open an existing workbook; a new, blank workbook; or a workbook template in a new instance of Excel.

On the Job

Task 14.4a Changing the User Name Associated with Excel and Editing a Shared Workbook

Note: *To complete Tasks 14.4a through 14.6 properly, you need to keep the workbook open between tasks. Be sure to allow time for completing all four tasks without closing the workbook.*

You are traveling with Devon and Wes to a meeting. When you arrive, Devon and Wes decide they want to review the 14-DVAutoParts workbook, but they have left their computers at home. You have the workbook saved on your laptop, and you offer to help them share the file. They want to be able to track their changes separately so they can see who made what changes. Help Devon and Wes do this by opening separate instances of Excel on your computer. In the first instance of Excel, change the user name associated with Excel to *Devon Varey* and then make the changes requested by Devon.

1. With Excel open but no workbook open, click the File tab and then click the *Options* option in the left panel.

   The Excel Options dialog box displays. The *General* option is selected in the left panel.

2. Select the entry in the *User name* text box in the *Personalize your copy of Microsoft Office* section and then type Devon Varey (see Figure 14.14).
3. Click the OK button.

   The dialog box closes.

4. Open the data file **14-DVAutoPartsShared**, which you closed at the end of Task 4.3.
5. Click the Customers sheet tab, if necessary, to make the worksheet active and then make the following changes:
   a. Click in cell E4 and then change the entry from *(904) 555-6411* to *(904) 555-3222*.
   b. Click in cell G19 and then change the entry from *25* to *26*.

Figure 14.14 General Options at the Excel Options Dialog Box

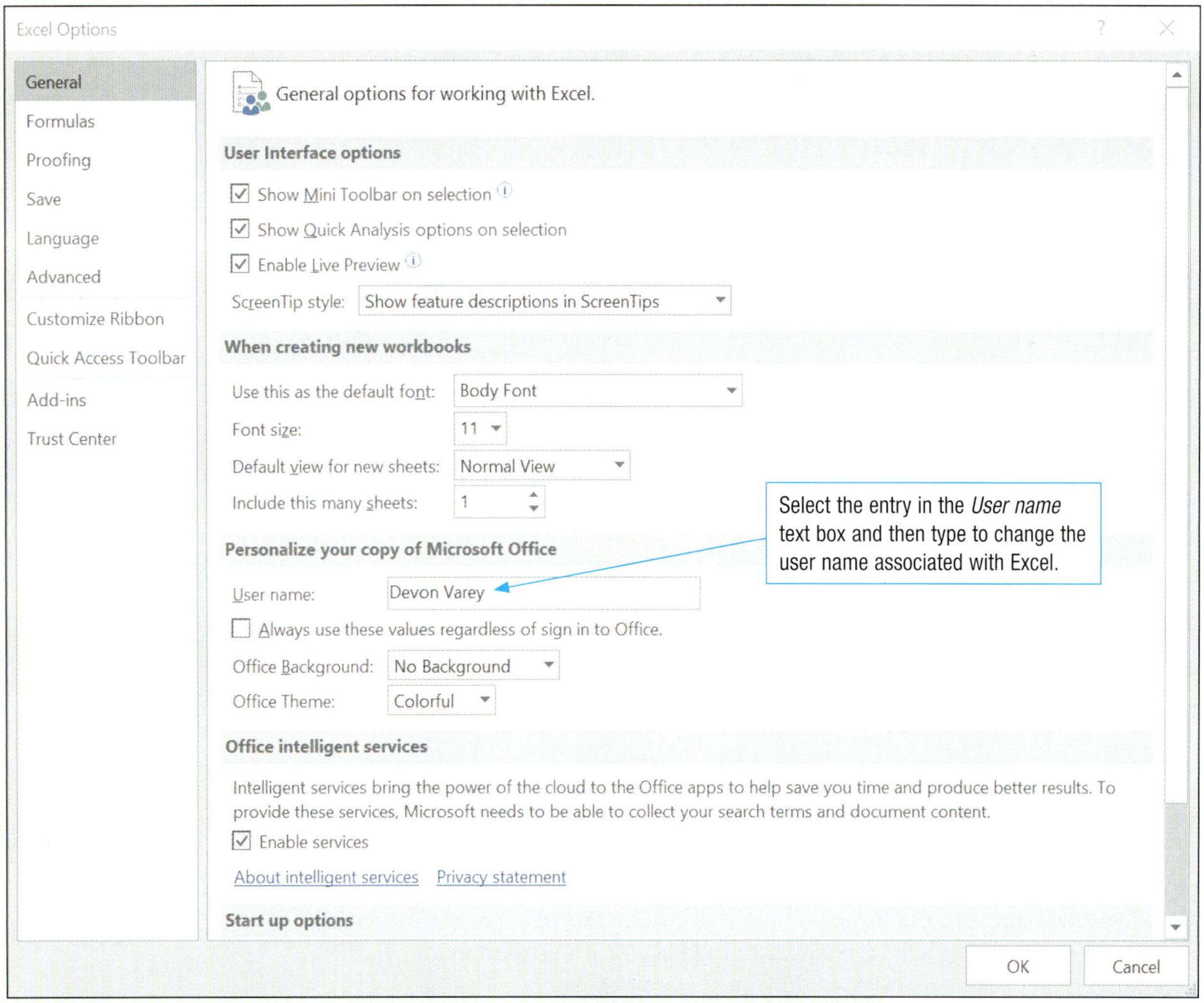

6. Click the Save button on the Quick Access Toolbar. Keep the workbook open until the end of Task 14.6 to simulate the sharing of the workbook.

On the Job

Task 14.4b Opening Another Instance of a Shared Workbook

Note: To complete Tasks 14.4a through 14.6 properly, you need to keep the workbook open between tasks. If you had to close the workbook at the end of Task 14.4a, you will need to reopen the workbook and repeat Task 14.4a before completing this task.

Devon has finished making his edits for now, and it is Wes's turn to review the workbook. Open a new instance of Excel and change the user name to *Wes Cortez*.

1. With the 14-DVAutoPartsShared workbook open and the Customers worksheet active, press and hold down the Alt key, right-click the Excel button on the Windows taskbar, click the *Excel 2016* option at the pop-up menu, release the Alt key when you see a message box

asking if you want to start a new instance of Excel, and then click the Yes button.

A second instance of Excel opens. The Excel Start backstage area displays.

2. Click the Open Other Workbooks hyperlink at the bottom of the left panel.

   The Excel Open backstage area displays.

3. Click the *Options* option in the left panel.

   The Excel Options dialog box displays with the *General* option selected in the left panel.

4. Select the entry in the *User name* text box in the *Personalize your copy of Microsoft Office* section, type Wes Cortez, and then click the OK button.

   The dialog box closes. The second instance of Excel remains open.

5. Open the data file **14-DVAutoPartsShared**.

   The data file opens in the second instance of Excel. This data file has Devon's changes incorporated because you saved the file after entering changes using the first instance of Excel (with *Devon Varey* as the user name) in Task 14.4a.

6. Click the Review tab and then click the Share Workbook button in the Changes group.

   The Share Workbook dialog box displays with the Editing tab selected. *Devon Varey* and *Wes Cortez* are listed in the *Who has this workbook open now* list box, indicating that both have the 14-DVAutoPartsShared workbook open (see Figure 14.13 on page 690).

7. Click the OK button.

   The dialog box closes.

8. Leave both instances of Excel open and the second instance (with *Wes Cortez* as the user name) active for the next task.

14.5 Viewing Changes and Resolving Conflicts in a Shared Workbook

Tutorial

Resolving Conflicts in a Shared Workbook

If two or more users have copies of a shared workbook open and each user makes a change to the same cell, a conflict will occur. The next time the workbook is saved, Excel will display a dialog box with a prompt asking the user to resolve the conflict by accepting either his or her change or the other user's change. The dialog box will show the cell address, original entry, and revised entry for each user. If multiple conflicts occur in the same workbook, the user can review each change and choose which revision to accept, or accept all of his or her changes or all the other user's changes.

▸ **Know This** about viewing changes in a shared workbook

— If you make changes in a shared workbook that is being edited by other users at the same time, you will not see their changes until you save the workbook.

— To view changes made by other users in a shared workbook, save the workbook.

- When you save a shared workbook, if a message displays, stating that your workbook has been updated with changes made by others, that means all the changes occurred in different cells and there are no conflicts in the workbook.
- Click the OK button to close the message box and view the changes in the shared workbook.
- A cell that contains changes displays with a colored border and triangle.
- Excel assigns a separate color to each user in the shared workbook.
- To view a change, point to the cell to display a pop-up box containing the name, date, and time the cell change was saved, along with the original and revised entries.

▸ **Know This** about resolving conflicts in a shared workbook

- When you save a shared workbook, if the Resolve Conflicts dialog box displays, that means one or more of the changes made in the workbook occurred in the same cell.
- To resolve a conflict in a shared workbook, review the change that displays at the Resolve Conflicts dialog box and then accept your change or accept another change.
- To resolve all conflicts at the same time, click the Accept All Mine button or the Accept All Others button.

On the Job

Task 14.5 Resolving Conflicts in a Shared Workbook

Note: *To complete Tasks 14.4a through 14.6 properly, you need to keep the workbook open between tasks. If you had to close the workbook at the end of Task 14.4b, you will need to reopen the workbook and repeat Tasks 14.4a and 14.4b before completing this task.*

Wes reviews the workbook and gives you a list of edits that are needed. Use the second instance of Excel (with *Wes Cortez* as the user name) to make the requested changes.

1. With the 14-DVAutoPartsShared workbook open and active in the second instance of Excel and the Customers worksheet active, make the following changes:
   a. Click in cell G19 and then change the entry from *26* to *28*.
   b. Click in cell G4 and then change the entry from *19* to *18*.

   The second instance of Excel has the user name *Wes Cortez*. The changes made in this instance of Excel will appear as changes made by Wes Cortez.
2. Click the Save button on the Quick Access Toolbar.
3. Click the Excel button on the Windows taskbar and then click the thumbnail on the left (see Figure 14.15).

   The 14-DVAutoPartsShared workbook in the first instance of Excel is active. The first instance of Excel has the user name *Devon Varey*.
4. Click in cell G4 and then change the entry from *19* to *17*.

   This change made in the first instance of Excel will appear as being made by Devon Varey.

Figure 14.15 Excel Button Pop-Up Menu for a Shared Workbook Open in Two Instances of Excel

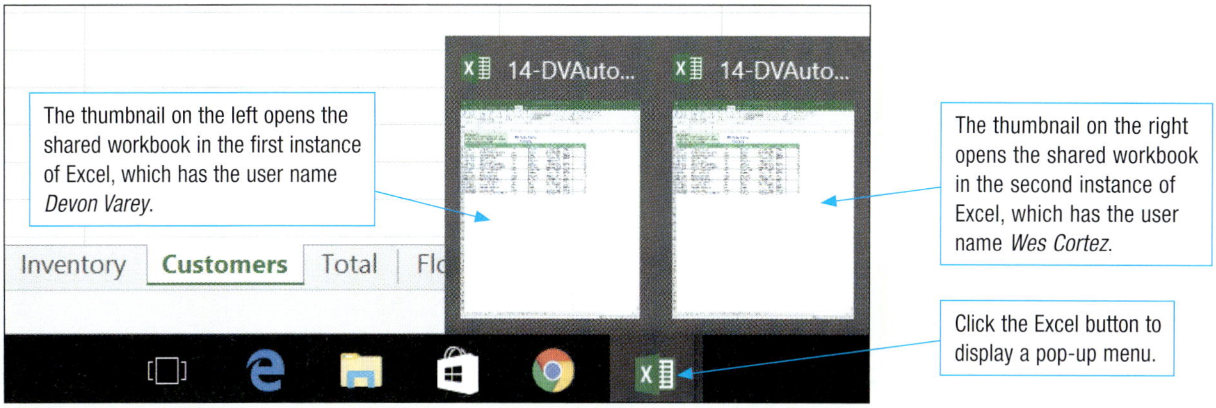

5. Click the Save button on the Quick Access Toolbar.

   The Resolve Conflicts dialog box displays (see Figure 14.16). The change made by Devon Varey in cell G4 conflicts with a change made by Wes Cortez in the same cell while both users have the workbook open.

Figure 14.16 Resolve Conflicts Dialog Box

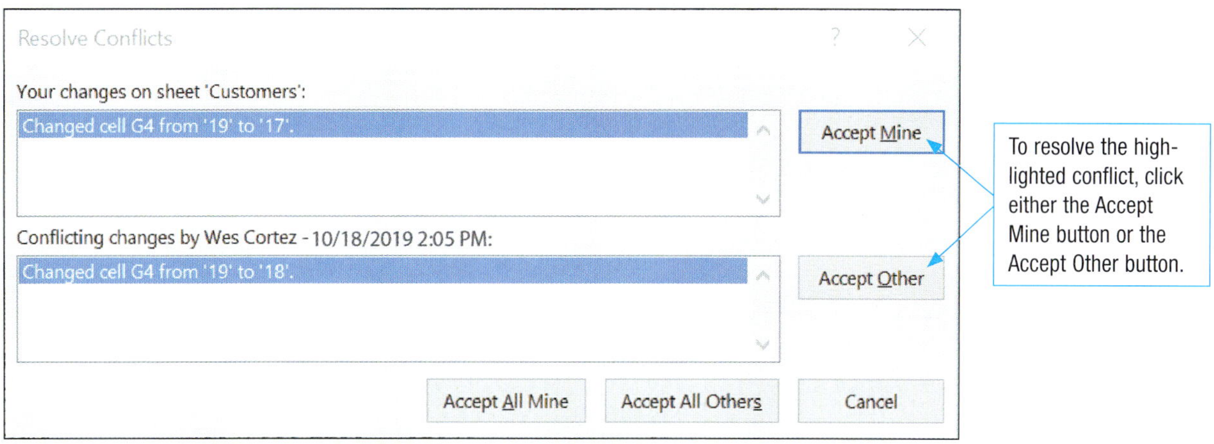

6. Click the Accept Mine button.

   A message box displays, stating the workbook has been updated with changes made by others. This message indicates that Wes Cortez (the other user who has the shared workbook open) made changes to cells that Devon Varey (the user who is saving the workbook) did not change.

7. Click the OK button.

   The dialog box closes. In the worksheet, cell G19 displays with a colored border and a triangle in the upper left corner, indicating that a change has been made.

8. Point to cell G19.

   A pop-up box displays with the name, date, and time the cell changed was saved, along with the original and revised entries (see Figure 14.17).

Figure 14.17 Change Pop-Up Box

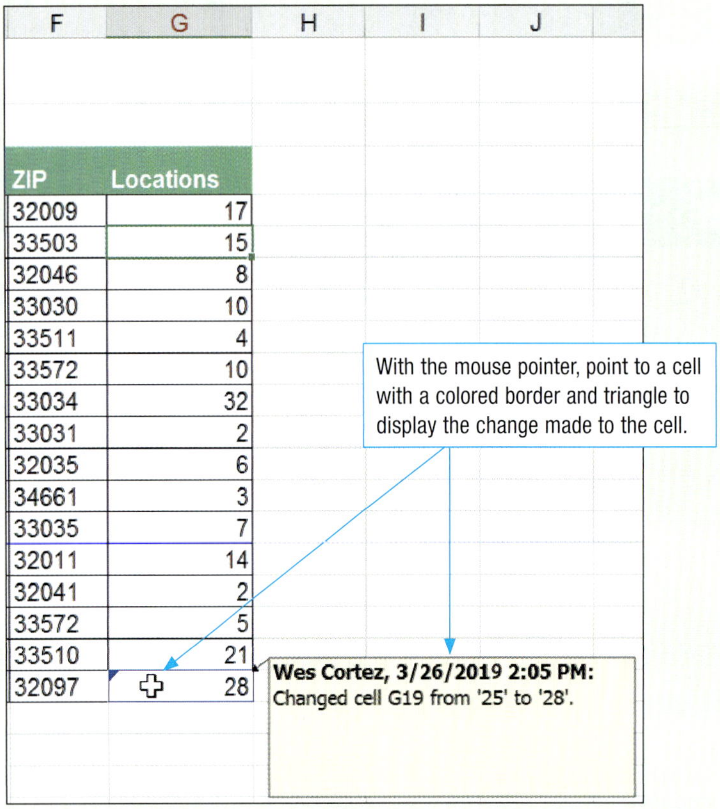

9. Click the Excel button on the Windows taskbar, click the thumbnail on the right, save the workbook, and then close the workbook and the second instance of Excel.

   The workbook that was open in the second instance of Excel (with the user name *Wes Cortez*) and the second instance of Excel are closed.

10. Leave the workbook open in the first instance of Excel (with the user name *Devon Varey*) for the next task.

14.6 Printing a History Sheet

A **history sheet** (also called a *history list*) is a new worksheet that displays all the tracked changes that have been made to a shared workbook. Create a history sheet to quickly view the changes made to a shared workbook. If you want to refer to the history sheet later, you must either print it or copy it to a new workbook, because it is automatically deleted from the original workbook when you save the workbook.

Tutorial
Creating a History Sheet

▸ **Know This** about the workbook history sheet

— A history sheet documents workbook changes as numbered actions in the order they were made. Each change is described with the date and time it was made, the name of the person who made the change, the type of change, the worksheet, the range, the new value, and the old value. If a conflict occurred in a range, the history sheet also indicates which action was accepted and which action was rejected.

— To display all workbook changes in a history sheet, click the Review tab, click the Track Changes button in the Changes group, click the *Highlight Changes* option at the drop-down list, click the *When* option box arrow at the Highlight Changes dialog box, click the *All* option at the drop-down list, click the *List Changes on a new sheet* check box to insert a check mark, and then click the OK button to close the dialog box.

▸ **Know This** about printing a history sheet

— The history sheet is not saved with the workbook.

— If you want to refer to a history sheet later, you will need to print it or copy it to a new workbook.

— To copy the history sheet to a new workbook from a shared workbook, you will need to turn off sharing because the Copy Sheet feature is not available in a shared workbook.

— A history sheet is protected and cannot be modified. Protecting a worksheet is discussed in Section 14.9.

On the Job

Task 14.6 Creating and Printing a History Sheet

Note: *To complete Tasks 14.4a through 14.6 properly, you need to keep the workbook open between tasks. If you had to close the workbook at the end of Task 14.5, you will need to reopen the workbook and repeat Tasks 14.4a, 14.4b, and 14.5 before completing this task.*

Devon wants an electronic record of the changes he and Wes made to the workbook they have been sharing. Create a history sheet and then copy it to a new workbook.

1. With the 14-DVAutoPartsShared workbook open and any worksheet active, click the Review tab, click the Track Changes button in the Changes group, and then click the *Highlight Changes* option.

   The Highlight Changes dialog box displays (see Figure 14.18).

2. Click the *When* option box arrow and then click the *All* option.

   The option *All* displays in the *When* option box.

3. Click the *List changes on a new sheet* check box.

   A check mark appears in the check box.

4. Click the OK button.

   The dialog box closes. A new worksheet called *History* is inserted at the end of the workbook and is active.

Reminder

If you added the Track Changes (Legacy) command, you will click the Track Changes button to display the drop-down list with the *Highlight Changes* and *Accept/Reject Changes* options.

Figure 14.18 Highlight Changes Dialog Box with the Settings for Printing a History Sheet

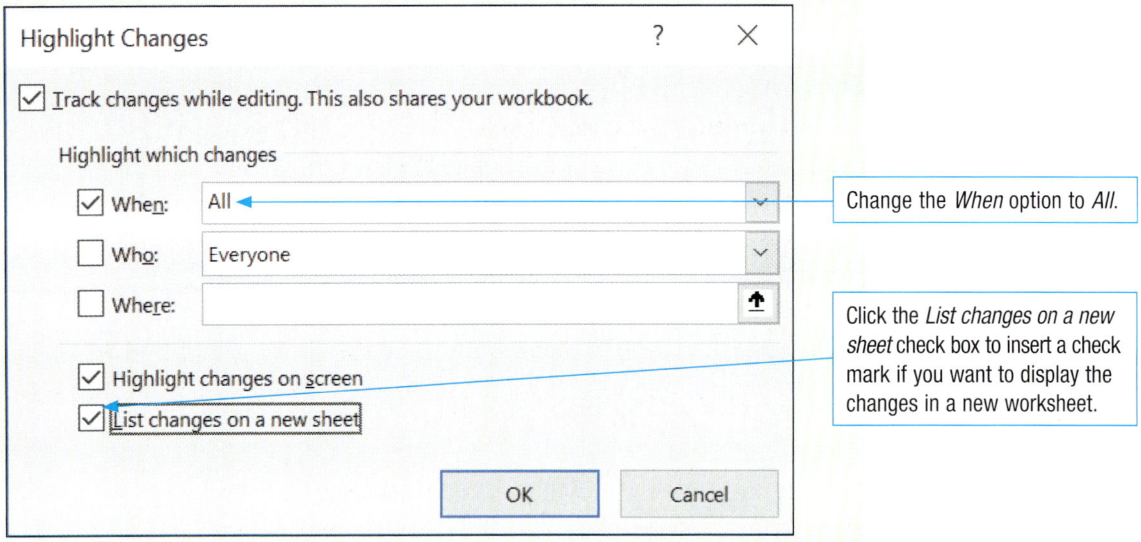

5. Review the changes in the History worksheet.

   All changes are listed as numbered actions in the order they were made. Each change is described with the date and time it was made, the name of the person who made the change, the type of change, the worksheet, the range, the new value, and the old value. If a conflict occurred in a range, the history sheet also indicates which action was accepted and which action was rejected.
6. Copy the History worksheet to a new workbook.
7. Save the new workbook, typing 14-Changes as the file name, and then close the new workbook.
8. If printed work is required by your instructor, print the History worksheet in the 14-DVAutoPartsShared workbook.
9. With the 14-DVAutoPartsShared workbook open, click the Save button on the Quick Access Toolbar.

   The History worksheet is deleted. The workbook remains open.
10. If printed work is required by your instructor, print the workbook.
11. Close the 14-DVAutoPartsShared workbook without closing Excel.
12. Change the user name associated with Excel back to your name. Leave Excel open for the next task.

Reminder
To copy a worksheet to a new workbook, right-click the sheet tab to be copied, change the *To Book* option to *(new book)*, click the *Create a copy* check box to insert a check mark, and then click the OK button.

Model Answer

14.7 Displaying, Accepting, and Rejecting Tracked Changes

It is good practice to review all tracked changes in a workbook periodically and either accept or reject each change. You can review changes by highlighting all the changed cells and then navigating to each change and either accepting or rejecting it individually. Alternatively, you can accept or reject all tracked changes at once.

Tutorial
Displaying, Accepting, and Rejecting Tracked Changes

▸ **Know This** about displaying tracked changes

— To display tracked changes, click the Track Changes button in the Changes group on the Review tab, click the *Track Changes* option at the drop-down list, click the *Highlight Changes* option at the drop-down list, click the *When* option box arrow and select an option at the drop-down list, click the *Who* option box arrow and select an option at the drop-down list (optional), and then click the OK button.

— The options at the *When* option box drop-down list are *Since I last saved*, *All*, *Not yet reviewed*, and *Since date*.

— The default option in the *Who* option box is *Everyone*. Click the *Who* option box arrow to select a specific user and limit the display to changes by that user.

— A tracked change displays in the workbook with a colored border and triangle. The color depends on the user who made the change; Excel assigns each user a different color.

▸ **Know This** about accepting and rejecting tracked changes

— To accept and reject tracked changes individually, click the Track Changes button in the Changes group on the Review tab, click the *Accept/Reject Changes* option at the drop-down list, click the *When* option box arrow, click a review option at the drop-down list, and then click the OK button to display the Accept or Reject Changes dialog box.

— The Accept or Reject Changes dialog box displays information about the first tracked change made in the workbook. Review the information and then click a button to indicate your review decision.

— Click the Accept All button or the Reject All button to make a global review decision.

— Click the Accept button or the Reject button to make a decision about the specific change displayed in the dialog box.

— If you click the Accept button or the Reject button, the dialog box displays the next tracked change that was made in the workbook.

— If you accept a change, the worksheet cell containing the change is updated to reflect the new value.

— If you reject a change, the worksheet cell is restored to its original value.

— After a change has been accepted or rejected, the colored border and triangle are removed.

— Be careful when accepting and rejecting changes because the Undo command is not available after the cells have been reviewed.

— If multiple changes were made to a cell during different sessions, the Accept or Reject Changes dialog box will display the original value and each change, along with the date and time it was made and the name of the person who made it.

— Before starting a review, press Ctrl + Home to move to cell A1. This will start the review at the top of the sheet.

On the Job

Task 14.7 Displaying, Accepting, and Rejecting Tracked Changes

Devon asks you to review and accept all the changes he and Wes made to the shared workbook. Review all the changes that have not yet been reviewed in the 14-DVAutoPartsShared workbook. (Alternatively, you could review all the changes in the workbook, since you know you have not accepted or rejected any changes to the file.)

1. Open the data file **14-DVAutoPartsShared**, which you closed at the end of Task 14.6.
2. With the Customers worksheet active, click the Track Changes button in the Changes group on the Review tab and then click the *Highlight Changes* option.

   The Highlight Changes dialog box displays with the text *Since I last saved* in the *When* option box and the text *Everyone* in the *Who* option box.
3. Click the *When* option box arrow and then click the *Not yet reviewed* option.
4. Click the OK button.
5. Point to cells E4 and G4 to verify that Devon Varey made the changes in those cells, and then point to cell G19 to verify that Wes Cortez made the change in that cell.

   Cells E4 and G4 each have a red border and triangle, indicating changes made by Devon Varey in Tasks 14.4a, 14.4b, and 14.5. Cell G19 has a blue border and triangle, indicating a change made by Wes Cortez. ***Note:*** *The colors in your workbook may differ.*
6. Press Ctrl + Home, click the Track Changes button, and then click the *Accept/Reject Changes* option.

   The Select Changes to Accept or Reject dialog box displays (see Figure 14.19). The *When*, *Who*, and *Where* options selected in the Highlight Changes dialog box are carried over to this dialog box. The *When* option should be set to *Net yet reviewed*.

Figure 14.19 Select Changes to Accept or Reject Dialog Box

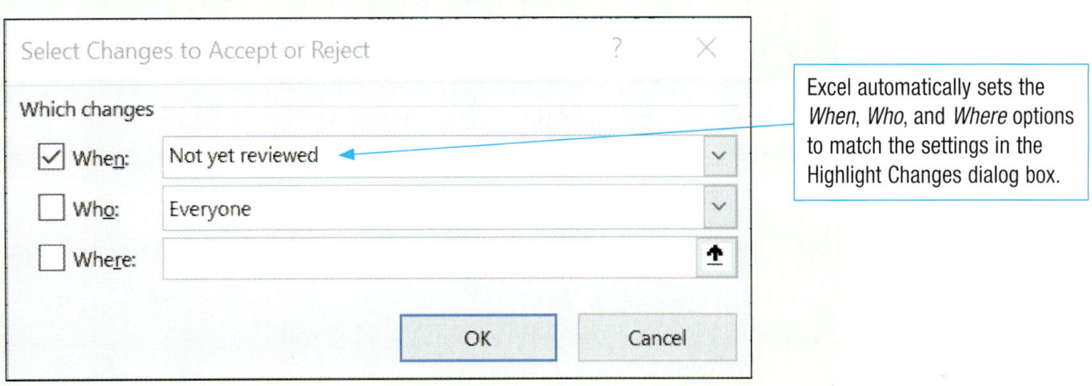

7. Click the OK button.

   The Select Changes to Accept or Reject dialog box closes. Cell G4, which contains the first change made in the workbook, is selected (displays with a green scrolling marquee) in the worksheet. The Accept or Reject Changes dialog box displays with information about the first change made in the workbook (see Figure 14.20). Only one change was made in this cell. You can either accept or reject the change.

Figure 14.20 Accept or Reject Changes Dialog Box for the First Change in the Workbook

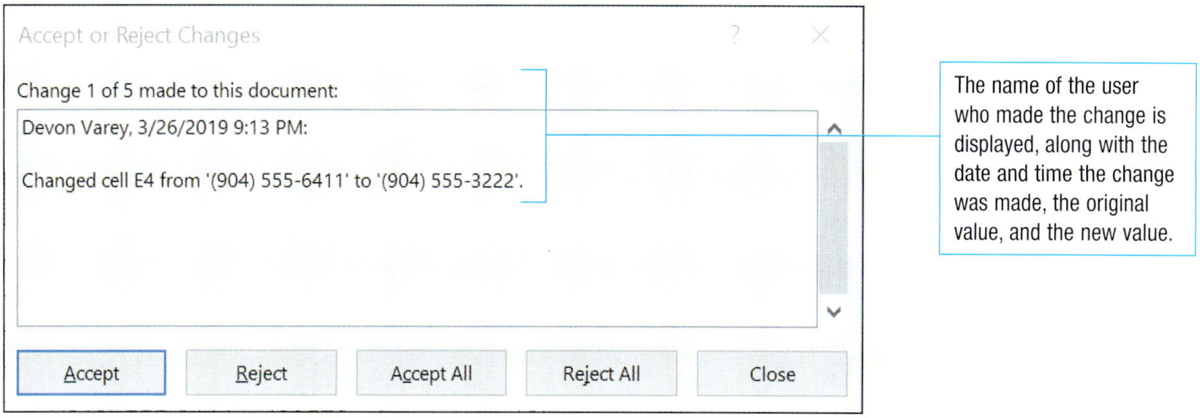

8. Click the Accept button.

   The telephone number *(904) 555-3222* remains in cell G4 in the worksheet. Cell G19, which contains the second change made in the workbook, is selected. The Accept or Reject Changes dialog box displays information about the second change (see Figure 14.21). Two changes were made in this cell. You can accept one of the changes or return the cell to its original value.

Figure 14.21 Accept or Reject Changes Dialog Box for the Second Change in the Workbook

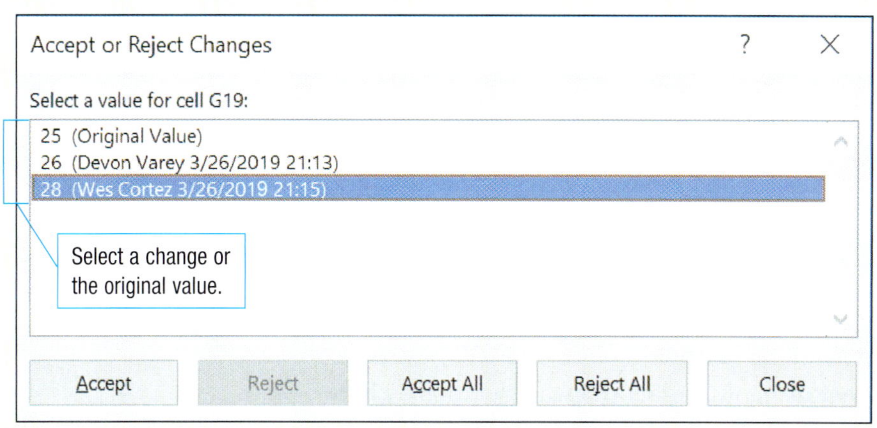

9. Click the *28* option in the *Select a value for cell G19* list box and then click the Accept button.

   The value *28* appears in cell G19 in the worksheet. Cell G4, which contains the third change made in the workbook, is selected. The

Accept or Reject Changes dialog box displays information about the third change (see Figure 14.22). Two changes were made in this cell. You can accept one of the changes or return the cell to its original value.

Figure 14.22 Accept or Reject Changes Dialog Box for the Third Change in the Workbook

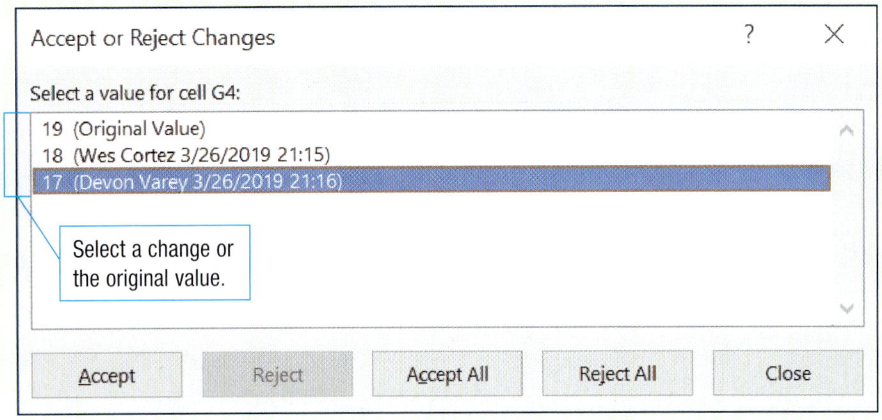

10. Click the *17* option in the *Select a value for cell G4* list box and then click the Accept button.

    The value *17* remains in cell G4 in the worksheet. No cells are selected or highlighted in the worksheet. The dialog box closes.

11. Click the Save button on the Quick Access Toolbar.

Model Answer

14.8 Turning Off Track Changes and Removing Shared Access

When you are finished collaborating in a shared workbook, you can either stop sharing the workbook or turn off the Track Changes feature. If any changes made to a workbook have not yet been reviewed, consider printing a copy of the history sheet before turning off Track Changes.

Tutorial

Turning Off Track Changes

▸ Know This about turning off Track Changes

— To turn off Track Changes in a shared workbook, click the Track Changes button in the Changes group on the Review tab, click the *Highlight Changes* option at the drop-down list, click the *Track changes while editing* check box to remove the check mark at the Highlight Changes dialog box, click the OK button to close the dialog box, and then click the Yes button at the message box that displays, stating that the workbook will no longer be shared and the change history will be erased.

▸ Know This about removing shared access

— To remove shared access to a workbook, click the Share Workbook button in the Changes group on the Review tab, click the *Allow changes by more than one user at the same time* check box to remove the check mark at the Share Workbook dialog box, click the OK button to close the dialog box, and then click the Yes button at the message box that displays, stating that changing the workbook to exclusive status will erase all the change history in the workbook and prevent users who might have the workbook open from saving their changes.

On the Job
Task 14.8 Turning Off Track Changes

Devon has finished collaborating with Wes and asks you to stop tracking changes in the 14-DVAutoPartsShared workbook. Turn off Track Changes in the workbook.

1. With the 14-DVAutoPartsShared workbook open, the Customers worksheet active, and the Review tab active, click the Track Changes button in the Changes group and then click the *Highlight Changes* option.

   The Highlight Changes dialog box displays.
2. Click the *Track changes while editing* check box.

   The check mark is removed from the check box.
3. Click the OK button.

   A message displays, stating that this action will remove the workbook from shared use and that the change history will be erased.
4. Click the Yes button.
5. Click the Save button on the Quick Access Toolbar and then close the workbook. Leave Excel open for the next task.

14.9 Protecting a Worksheet and Restricting Editing in a Worksheet

MOS Expert 1.2.1
MOS Expert 1.2.2

Tutorials

Clearing Lock Attributes and Restricting Editing

Hiding Formulas and Protecting a Worksheet

Worksheet protection prevents users from deleting or modifying cells that should not be changed in the worksheet. By default, in a protected worksheet, each cell is assigned the **lock attribute**—that is, every cell is locked. This means no one can insert, delete, or modify any of the worksheet contents. However, if some of the cells in the worksheet contain data you want other users to be able to change, you can clear the lock attribute on those cells. When a lock attribute has been cleared from a cell and you protect the worksheet, changes can be made to that cell. You can also allow specific users to edit a protected worksheet by setting a password and giving the password only to those users.

In a collaborative environment, protecting a worksheet generally involves two steps:

1. Clear the lock attribute in cells that can be edited.
2. Protect the worksheet and, if desired, set a password.

When you protect a worksheet, you can give certain users permission to edit protected cells, but you must add this permission before protecting the worksheet. For example, if you are sharing a workbook that lists part costs and sales tax rates, you might give an accountant authority to change the cells containing tax rates and then protect the worksheet so no other changes can be made in the worksheet.

If, for some reason, you do not want users to view a formula, you can hide the formula. After a worksheet has been protected, when a user clicks in a cell that contains a formula, the formula does not appear in the Formula bar.

▸ **Know This** about clearing the lock attribute in cells that can be edited

— To clear the lock attribute in cells that can be modified, select the cells, click the Home tab, click the Format button in the Cells group, and then click the highlighted *Lock Cell* option in the *Protection* section at the drop-down list.

— The highlighted icon with the *Lock Cell* option in the *Protection* section at the drop-down list indicates that the lock attribute is turned on for the selected cells

▸ **Know This** about protecting a worksheet

— To protect an active worksheet, click the Protect Sheet button in the Changes group on the Review tab, verify that the *Protect worksheet and contents of locked cells* check box contains a check mark, select options in the *Allow all users of this worksheet to* list box at the Protect Sheet dialog box, and then click the OK button (see Figure 14.23).

Figure 14.23 Protect Sheet Dialog Box

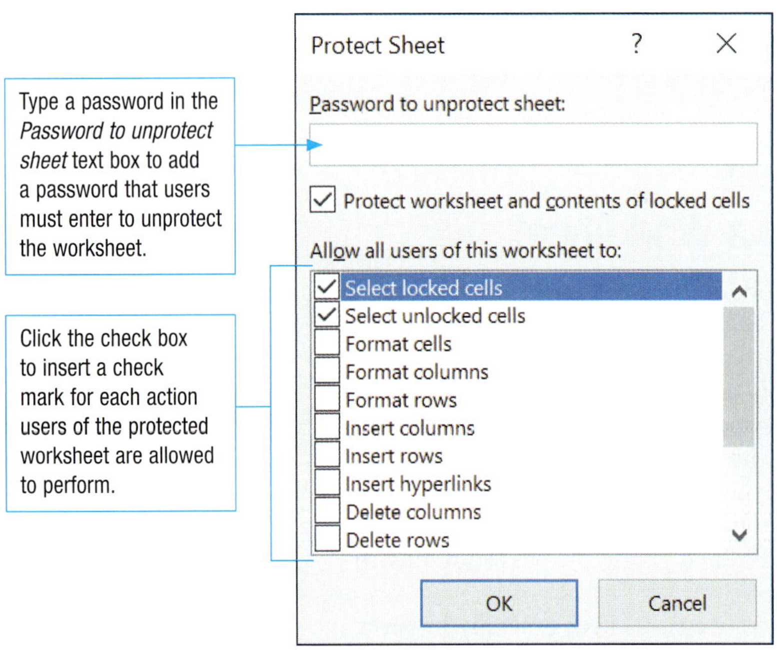

▸ **Know This** about setting a password for a worksheet

— To set a password for the worksheet, type the password in the *Password to unprotect sheet* text box at the Protect Sheet dialog box (see Figure 14.23), retype the password at the Confirm Password dialog box, and then click the OK button.

▸ **Know More** ways to clear the lock attribute in cells that can be edited

- Select the cells, click the Format button in the Cells group on the Home tab, click the *Format Cells* option, click the *Locked* check box to remove the check mark on the Protection tab at the Format Cells dialog box, and then click the OK button.

▸ **Know More** ways to protect a worksheet

- With the worksheet active, click the File tab; click the *Info* option, If necessary; click the Protect workbook button in the middle panel at the Info backstage area; and then click the *Protect Current Sheet* option at the drop-down list.
- With the worksheet active, click the Format button in the Cells group on the Home tab and then click the *Protect Sheet* option in the *Protection* section at the drop-down list.
- Right-click the sheet tab and then click the *Protect Sheet* option at the pop-up menu.

— Setting a password is optional. If you do not provide one, Excel will not require users to enter one.
— When creating a password, it is good practice to use a combination of four types of characters: uppercase letters, lowercase letters, symbols, and numbers. A password constructed using these elements is considered secure and more difficult to crack.
— A password can be up to 255 characters.
— If the password is forgotten, the worksheet cannot be unprotected. If necessary, write down the password and store it in a secure location.

▶ **Know This** about unprotecting a worksheet

— When a worksheet is protected, the Protect Sheet button in the Changes group on the Review tab changes to the Unprotect Sheet button (see Figure 14.24).
— To unprotect a worksheet, click the Unprotect Sheet button. If the Unprotect Sheet dialog box displays, enter the password and then click the OK button.
— When you need to edit a protected worksheet, unprotect the worksheet, make the edits, and then protect it again.

▶ **Know More** ways to unprotect a worksheet

– Click the File tab and then click the Unprotect hyperlink in the *Protect Workbook* section of the middle panel at the Info backstage area (see Figure 14.25). If the Unprotect Sheet dialog box displays, enter the password and then click the OK button.

Figure 14.24 Unprotect Sheet Button in the Changes Group on the Review Tab

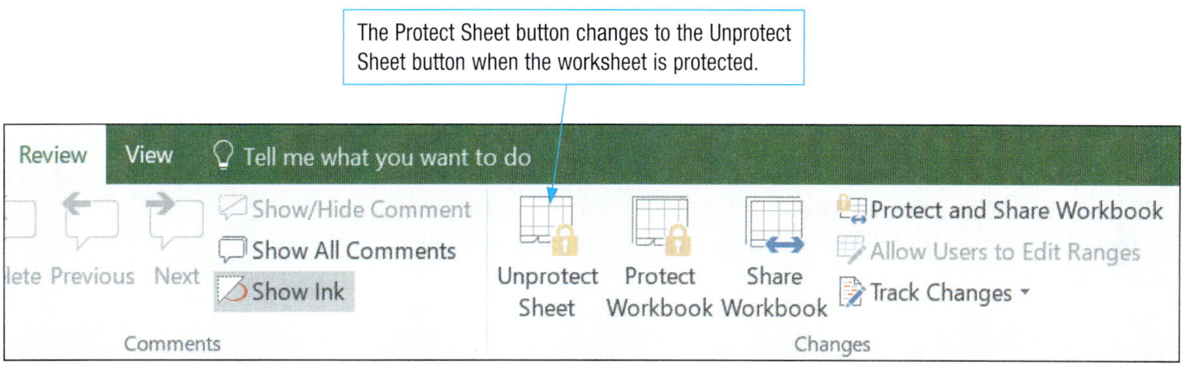

Figure 14.25 Protect Workbook Section at the Info Backstage Area

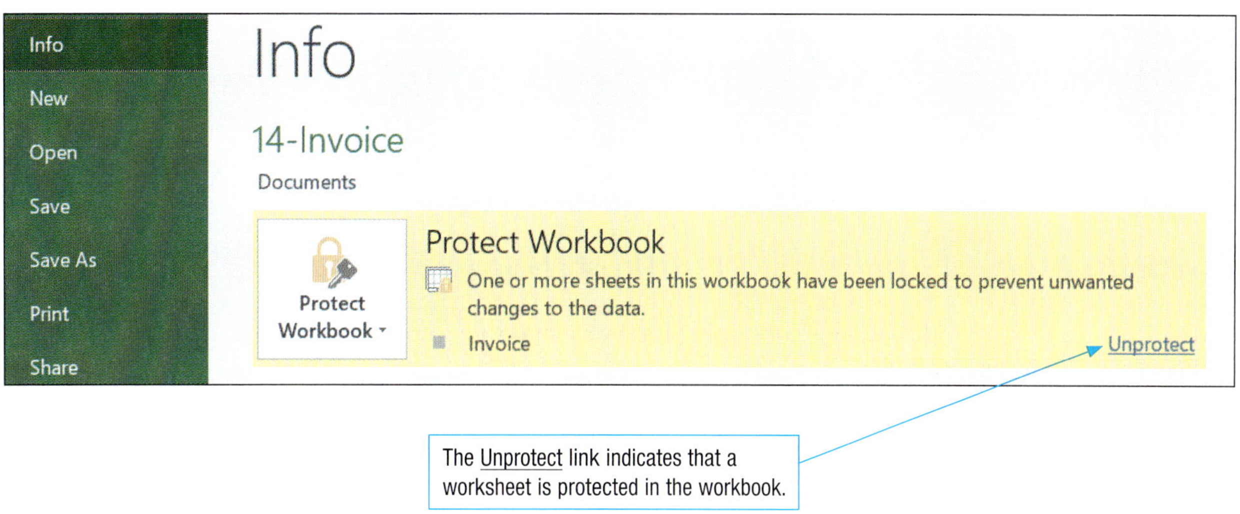

▸ Know This about giving permission to edit protected cells

- You can give users permission to edit protected cells. For example, you might give an accountant permission to change a tax rate.
- This permission must be added before the worksheet is protected.
- To give permission to edit protected cells in an active worksheet: click the Allow Users to Edit Ranges button in the Changes group on the Review tab; click the New button at the Allow Users to Edit Ranges dialog box; define the title, the range, and the range password (if required); click the OK button; reenter the password at the Confirm Password dialog box; specify who may edit the range without a password at the Allow Users to Edit Ranges dialog box; click the Protect Sheet button; and then protect the worksheet at the Protect Sheet dialog box.
- To remove permission, click the Allow Users to Edit Ranges button, select the range in the list box, click the Permissions button, select the group or user name at the Permission for Range dialog box, and then click the Remove button.

▸ Know More about giving permission to edit protected cells

- The Allow Users to Edit Ranges button changed to the Allow Edit Ranges button when the Track Changes and Share Workbook commands became legacy tools.

▸ Know This about hiding formulas in a protected worksheet

- In a protected worksheet, cells containing formulas can be hidden so that when a user clicks in a cell that contains a formula, the formula does not display in the Formula bar.
- To hide formulas, first hide the cells containing the formulas and then protect the worksheet.
- Until the worksheet is protected, the formulas remain visible in the Formula bar.
- To hide formulas in a protected worksheet, make the worksheet active, click the Format button in the Cells group on the Home tab, click the *Format Cells* option, click the Protection tab at the Format Cells dialog box, click the *Hidden* check box to insert a check mark, and then click the OK button.

On the Job

Task 14.9a Clearing Lock Attributes, Restricting Editing, Hiding Formulas, and Protecting a Worksheet

Devon has created an invoice that sales associates will fill out when they process customer orders. He wants the sales associates to be able to edit the cells containing the invoice number, bill to, attention, and phone data, as well as the number purchased, part number, category, quantity, and unit price. Devon does not want the sales associates to be able to make changes in cells that contain formulas. However, he wants you to be able to edit the cells that contain the current sales tax rate, the current shipping cost percentage, and the shipping formula. Turn off the lock attribute on the cells that can be edited by sales associates, allow editing in the three cells Devon wants you to modify, hide the cells containing formulas, and then protect the worksheet using a password.

1. Open the data file **14-Invoice**.
2. Select cells E5, E7, E8, and E10 and the range A13:E42.

   The selected cells are the cells that Devon wants the sales associates to edit.

3. Click the Format button in the Cells group on the Home tab.

A drop-down list displays. The highlighted icon with the *Lock Cell* option in the *Protection* section indicates that the lock attribute is turned on for the selected cells (see Figure 14.26). This means that if you were to protect the worksheet, you would not be able to edit the cells.

Figure 14.26 Format Button Drop-Down List

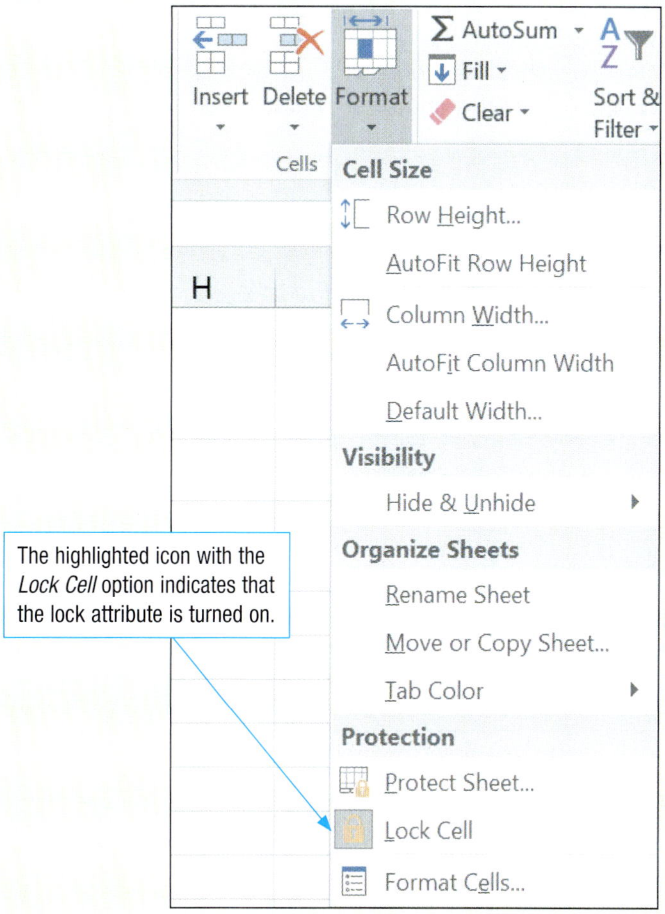

4. Click the *Lock Cell* option.

The drop-down list closes and the cells E5, E7, E8, and E10 and the range A13:E42 are selected in the worksheet. The lock attribute for the selected cells has been turned off. This means that when the worksheet is protected, users will be able to edit the selected cells.

5. Select cells C44, C45, and F45.

The selected cells contain entries that Devon wants you to be able to edit.

6. Click the Review tab and then click the Allow Users to Edit Ranges button in the Changes group.

The Allow Users to Edit Ranges dialog box displays.

7. Click the New button.

   The New Range dialog box displays with the text in the *Title* text box selected and the formula *=$C$44,$C$45,$F$45* in the *Refers to cells* text box.

8. Type Rates and Shipping Formula.
9. Click in the *Range password* text box, type AExcel14, and then click the OK button.

   The Confirm Password dialog box displays.

10. Type AExcel14 and then click the OK button.

    The Allow Users to Edit Ranges dialog box redisplays with the *Rates and Shipping Formula* range in the list box. When the worksheet is protected, users will be able to edit the cells in this range if they have the password.

11. Click the OK button.

    The dialog box closes.

12. Select cell E4 and the range F13:F46.

    The selected cells contain formulas, which Devon wants you to hide.

13. Click the Home tab, click the Format button in the Cells group, click the *Format Cells* option in the *Protection* section, and then click the Protection tab at the Format Cells dialog box.

    The Format Cells dialog box displays with the Protection tab active (see Figure 14.27).

Figure 14.27 Protection Tab at the Format Cells Dialog Box

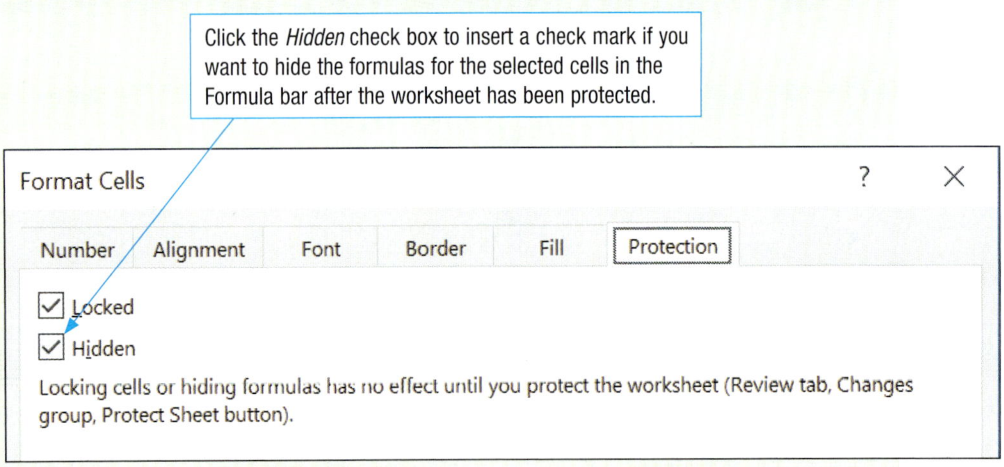

14. Click the *Hidden* check box.

    A check mark appears in the check box.

15. Click the OK button.

    The dialog box closes. After the worksheet has been protected, the formulas will not display in the Formula bar.

16. Click in any cell to deselect the range.
17. Click the Review tab and then click the Protect Sheet button in the Changes group.

    The Protect Sheet dialog box displays (see Figure 14.23 on page 704).

18. Type AExcel14 in the *Password to unprotect sheet* text box.
19. Click the OK button.

    The Confirm Password dialog box displays.
20. Type AExcel14 in the *Reenter password to proceed* text box and then click the OK button.
21. Click the Save button on the Quick Access Toolbar.

Model Answer

On the Job

Task 14.9b Editing a Protected Worksheet

Devon asks you to edit the protected worksheet by deleting the formula that displays the current date, entering an invoice number, and updating the current shipping cost percentage.

1. With the 14-Invoice workbook open and the Invoice worksheet active, click in cell E4.

   The current date displays in cell E4, but the formula for displaying this result does not display in the Formula bar (see Figure 14.28). That is because you hid the formula for this cell in Task 14.9a. The sales associates will not be able to edit this cell.

Figure 14.28 Cell E4 with the Formula Hidden

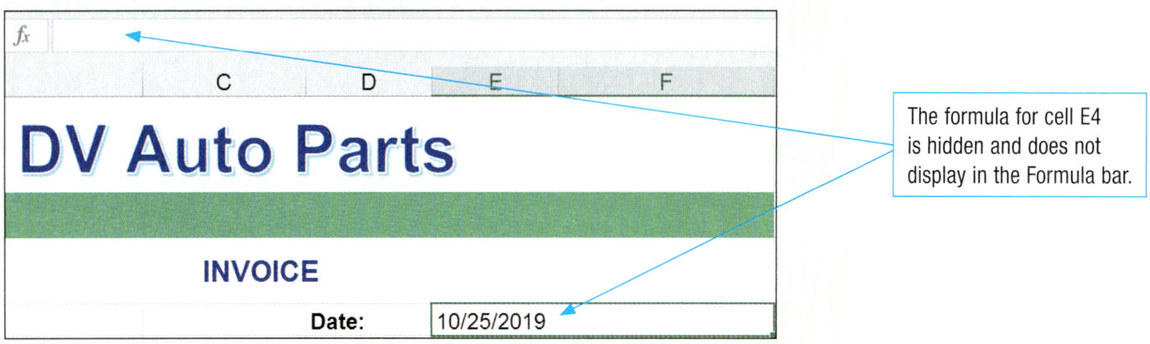

2. Press the Delete key.

   A message box displays, stating that the cell is in a protected worksheet and can be changed only if you unprotect the worksheet.
3. Click the OK button. You will keep the formula as entered.

   The message box closes.
4. Click in cell E5, type OCT033, and then press the Enter key.

   The value *OCT033* appears in the cell because you unlocked the cell in Task 14.9a. The sales associates will be able to edit this cell.
5. Double-click in cell C45.

   The Unlock Range dialog box displays (see Figure 14.29).
6. Type AExcel14 in the *Enter the password to change this cell* text box and then click the OK button.

   The dialog box closes and the insertion point is in cell C45.

Figure 14.29 Unlock Range Dialog Box

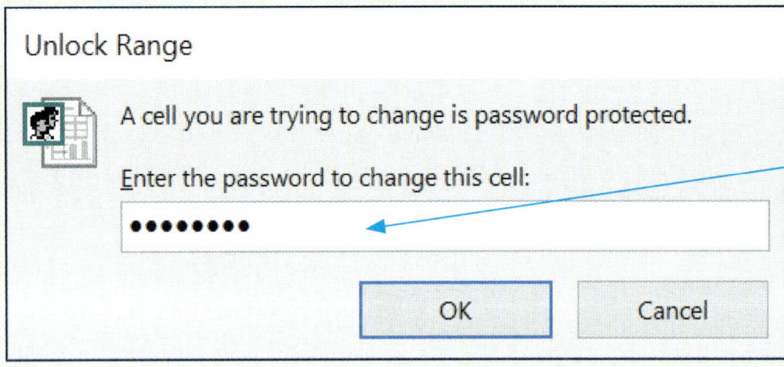

Type the password in the *Enter the password to change this cell* text box if you want to be able to change the cell.

7. Select the text in cell C45, type 5%, and then press the Enter key.

   Cell C46 is active and the value 5% appears in cell C45. You were able to edit the cell because you had the correct password. The sales associates will not be able to edit this cell unless they are given the password.

8. Click the Save button on the Quick Access Toolbar.

Model Answer

14.10 Protecting and Unprotecting the Workbook Structure

MOS Expert 1.2.4

Tutorial

Protecting the Workbook Structure

To prevent changes to the structure of a workbook—such as inserting a new sheet, deleting a sheet, and unhiding a hidden worksheet—protect the structure of the workbook.

▸ Know This about protecting and unprotecting the workbook structure

— To protect the structure of an open workbook, click the Protect Workbook button in the Changes group on the Review tab, verify that the *Structure* check box contains a check mark in the *Protect workbook for* section at the Protect Structure and Windows dialog box (see Figure 14.30), and then click the OK button.

▸ Know More ways to protect the structure of a workbook

– Click the File tab, click the Protect Workbook button in the middle panel at the Info backstage area, and then click the *Protect Workbook Structure* option at the drop-down list.

Figure 14.30 Protect Structure and Windows Dialog Box

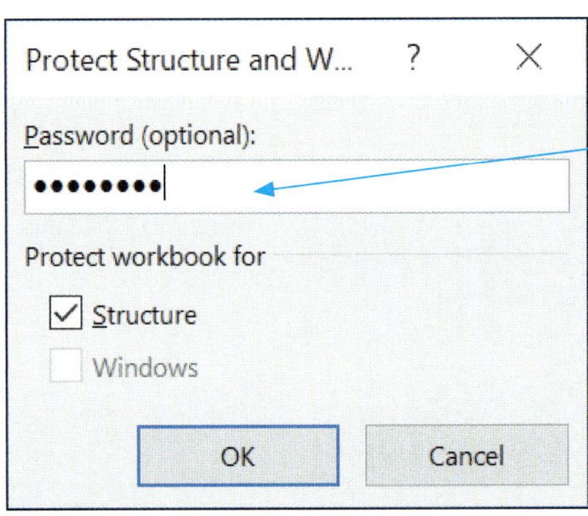

Type a password in the *Password (optional)* text box to set a password that users must enter to unprotect the structure of the workbook.

— To prevent a user from resizing or changing the positions of the windows in the workbook, click the *Windows* check box to insert a check mark in the *Protect workbook for* section at the Protect Structure and Windows dialog box.

— To set a password for the workbook structure, type the password in the *Password (optional)* text box at the Protect Structure and Windows dialog box, retype the password at the Confirm Password dialog box, and then click the OK button.

— Setting a password is optional. If you do not provide one, Excel will not require users to enter one.

— The Protect Workbook button is a toggle button. When a workbook is protected, the Protect Workbook button is active and displays with a gray background (see Figure 14.31). When a workbook is unprotected, the Protect Workbook button is inactive and displays without a gray background.

— To unprotect an open workbook, click the gray Protect Workbook button and then type the password at the Unprotect Workbook dialog box, if it displays.

Figure 14.31 Gray Protect Workbook Button in the Changes Group on the Review Tab

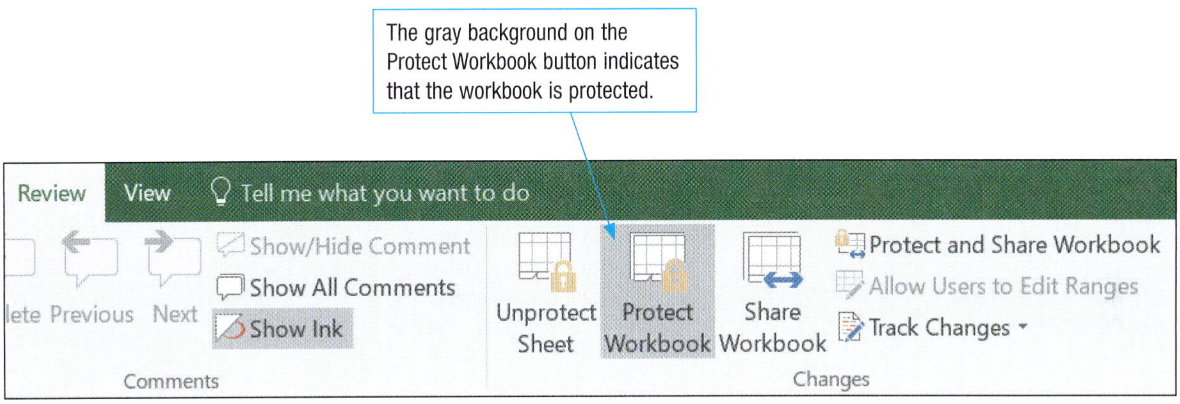

On the Job

Task 14.10 Protecting the Workbook Structure

Devon doesn't want users of the 14-Invoice workbook to be able to add or delete a worksheet unless they have a password. Protect the structure of the workbook and assign the workbook a password, and then verify that all the options for adding or deleting worksheets are grayed out (not available) at the sheet tab pop-up menu.

1. With the 14-Invoice workbook open, click the Protect Workbook button in the Changes group on the Review tab.

   The Protect Structure and Windows dialog box displays. The insertion point is in the *Password (optional)* text box. The *Structure* check box contains a check mark.

2. Type AExcel14.
3. Click the OK button.

   The Confirm Password dialog box displays with the insertion point in the *Reenter password to proceed* text box.

4. Type AExcel14.
5. Click the OK button.

   The dialog box closes.

6. Right-click the Invoice sheet tab and then verify that the worksheet structure cannot be modified.

   A pop-up menu displays (see Figure 14.32). All the options related to managing worksheets are grayed out, which means they are unavailable.

7. Click outside the pop-up menu, in the worksheet area.

   The pop-up menu closes.

8. Click the Save button on the Quick Access Toolbar and then close the workbook.

Figure 14.32 Sheet Tab Pop-Up Menu for a Protected Workbook

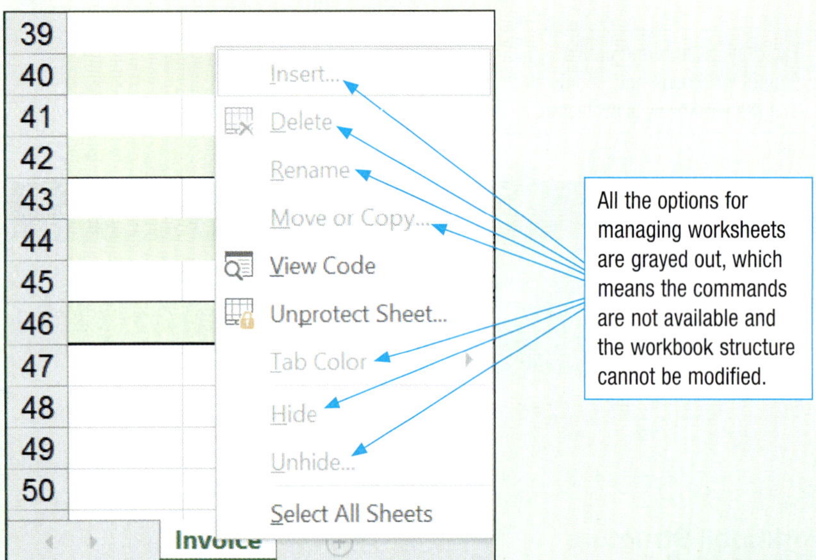

Model Answer

14.11 Protecting a Workbook with a Password

MOS Expert 1.2.6

Tutorial

Encrypting a Workbook with a Password

Workbook protection prevents unauthorized access to Excel data by requiring a password to open a workbook. The password to open a workbook is different from the passwords to protect a sheet and the workbook structure in that the password to open a workbook is encrypted. When you enter an **encrypted password**, the plain text you type is converted into a coded, or scrambled, format called **cipher text**. Cipher text can be read only by users who have the key to the code. **Encryption** prevents unauthorized users from retrieving the password.

▸ **Know This** about encrypting and unencrypting a workbook with a password

— To encrypt an open workbook with a password, click the File tab, click the Protect Workbook button at the Info backstage area, click the *Encrypt with Password* option, type the password in the *Password* text box at the Encrypt Document dialog box, click the OK button, type the password again in the *Reenter password* text box at the Confirm Password dialog box, click the OK button to close the dialog box, and then save the workbook.

— To remove encryption from an open workbook, click the File tab, click the Protect Workbook button in the middle panel at the Info backstage area, click the *Encrypt with Password* option, delete the password from the *Password* text box, click the OK button, and then save the workbook.

On the Job

Task 14.11 Encrypting a Workbook with a Password

Devon doesn't want anyone to make changes to the workbook containing the history of the changes that you created in Task 14.6. To protect the contents of the 14-Changes workbook, encrypt the workbook with a password.

1. Open the data file **14-Changes**, which you closed in Task 14.6.
2. Click the File tab.

   The Info backstage area displays. The *Protect Workbook* section displays with a yellow background because the History (2) worksheet is protected (see Figure 14.33).
3. Click the Protect Workbook button.

   A drop-down list displays.
4. Click the *Encrypt with Password* option.

   The Encrypt Document dialog box displays with the insertion point in the *Password* text box.
5. Type AExcel14 and then click the OK button.

   The Confirm Password dialog box displays with the insertion point in the *Reenter password* text box.
6. Type AExcel14 and then click the OK button.

   The dialog box closes. The text *A password is required to open this workbook* appears below the *Protect Workbook* section head.
7. Click the Back button.

   The Info backstage area closes.
8. Click the Save button on the Quick Access Toolbar and then close the workbook.
9. Reopen the data file **14-Changes**.

   The Password dialog box displays with the insertion point in the *Password* text box.
10. Type AExcel14 and then click the OK button.

    The dialog box closes. The 14-Changes workbook opens.
11. Close the 14-Changes workbook.

Figure 14.33 Info Backstage Area for a Protected Workbook

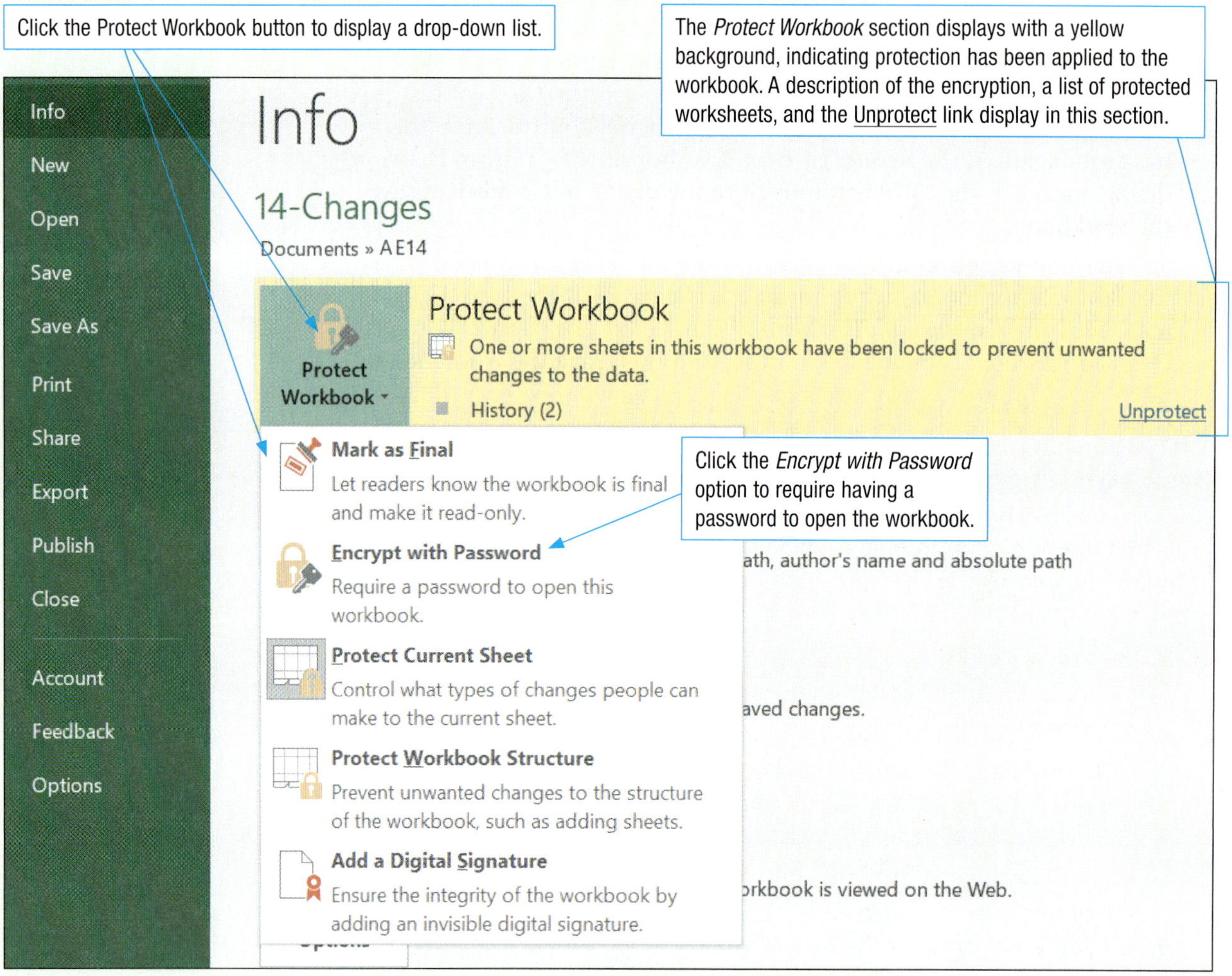

14.12 Applying International Number, Date, and Currency Formats

MOS Expert 2.4.1
MOS Expert 2.4.2

Tutorial

Applying International Number and Currency Formats

When distributing a workbook to clients or employees in other countries, you may need to change the formats for numbers, dates, and currencies. For example, countries differ in how they use commas, periods, and spaces as separators to designate number groups and decimal places. Table 14.1 illustrates how the same number is denoted in different countries.

Table 14.1 International Number Separator Formats

Example	Thousands Separator	Decimal Symbol	Countries
1,234,567.89	comma	period	Australia, China, English Canada, India, Japan, Ireland, Malaysia, New Zealand, Taiwan, Thailand, United Kingdom, United States
1 234 567,89	space	comma	Finland, France, French Canada, Norway, Sweden
1.234.567,89	period	comma	Austria, Brazil, Germany, Greece, Spain

▸ **Know This** about changing number, date, and currency formats for Microsoft applications on your computer

— The default number format used by all Microsoft Office applications, including Excel, is determined by the computer's operating system.

— To permanently change the formats of numbers, dates, and currencies for all the applications on your computer, use the *Region* section of the Windows Control Panel.

— To change how numbers display in only the Excel application on your computer, open Excel, click the File tab, click the *Options* option in the left panel at the Excel backstage area, click the *Advanced* option in the left panel at the Excel Options dialog box, click the *Use system separators* check box to remove the check mark in the *Editing options* section of the right panel, and then edit the symbols in the *Decimal separator* text box and the *Thousands separator* text box (see Figure 14.34).

Figure 14.34 Advanced Options at the Excel Options Dialog Box

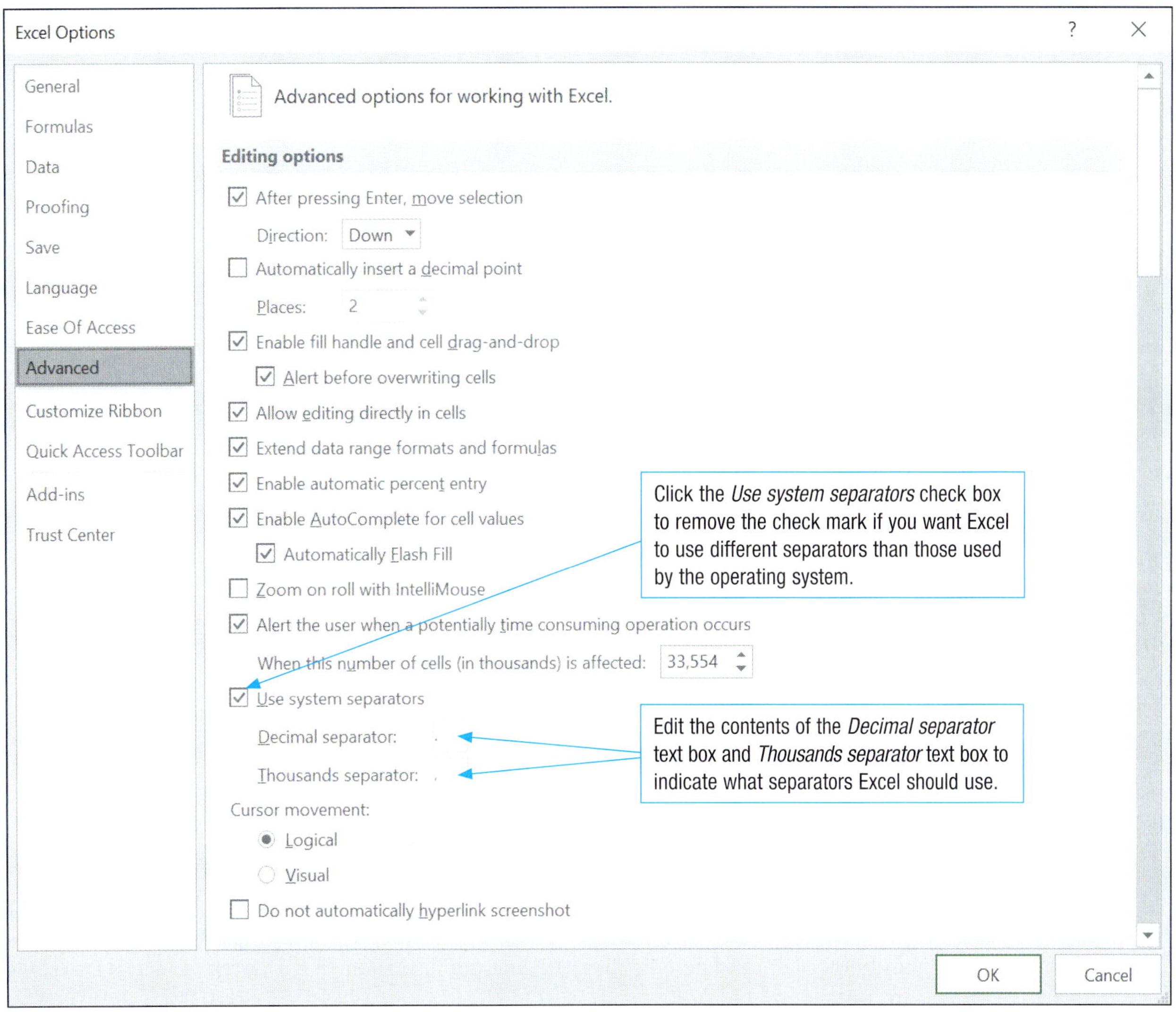

On the Job

Task 14.12 Applying International Number and Currency Formats

Devon attended an auto parts convention last week and met an investor who identified an untapped market for auto parts in Germany. Devon has decided to build a small sales force in Germany and target that market for sales beginning in January 2020. He's prepared a sales forecast for the first half of 2020 in the German market. Devon used the 2019 sales forecast for Florida sales as a template for the 2020 German sales forecast. In the 2020 German forecast, he's calculated the amounts in euros but left the US dollar symbol and separators. Devon asks you to change the currency symbol and reset Excel to use German number formatting, export the worksheet in a format that can be read by the investor and members of Devon's new sales team in Germany, and then reset Excel to use your operating system settings.

1. Open the data file **14-Forecast**.
2. Click the File tab and then click the *Options* option.

   The Excel Options dialog box displays.
3. Click the *Advanced* option.

   Advanced options for working with Excel display in the right panel.
4. Click the *Use system separators* check box in the *Editing options* section (see Figure 14.34 on page 715).

   The check box is empty.
5. Select the symbol in the *Decimal separator* text box and then type a comma (,).
6. Select the symbol in the *Thousands separator* text box and then type a period (.).
7. Click the OK button.

   The dialog box closes. The amounts in the range B5:G9 are formatted with a period as the thousands separator and a comma as the decimal symbol.
8. Select the range B5:G9 and then click the Number group dialog box launcher on the Home tab.

   The Format Cells dialog box displays with the Number tab active.
9. Click the Symbol option box arrow.
10. Scroll down the list and then click the *€ German (Germany)* option (see Figure 14.35).
11. Click the OK button.

    The euro symbol (€) displays after the amount in each cell.
12. Click the Save button on the Quick Access Toolbar.
13. Export the workbook as a PDF file.

    The PDF file will show the international number formatting you applied in Steps 1–12.
14. Save and then close the PDF file, if it opened when you published it.
15. With the Excel workbook open and active, click the File tab and then click the *Options* option.

    The Excel Options dialog box displays.

Reminder

To export the worksheet as a PDF, click the File tab, click the *Export* option in the left panel at the Excel backstage area, click the *Create PDF/XPS Document* option in the middle panel at the Export backstage area, click the Create PDF/XPS button in the right panel, and then click the Publish button at the Publish as PDF or XPS dialog box.

Figure 14.35 Format Cells Dialog Box

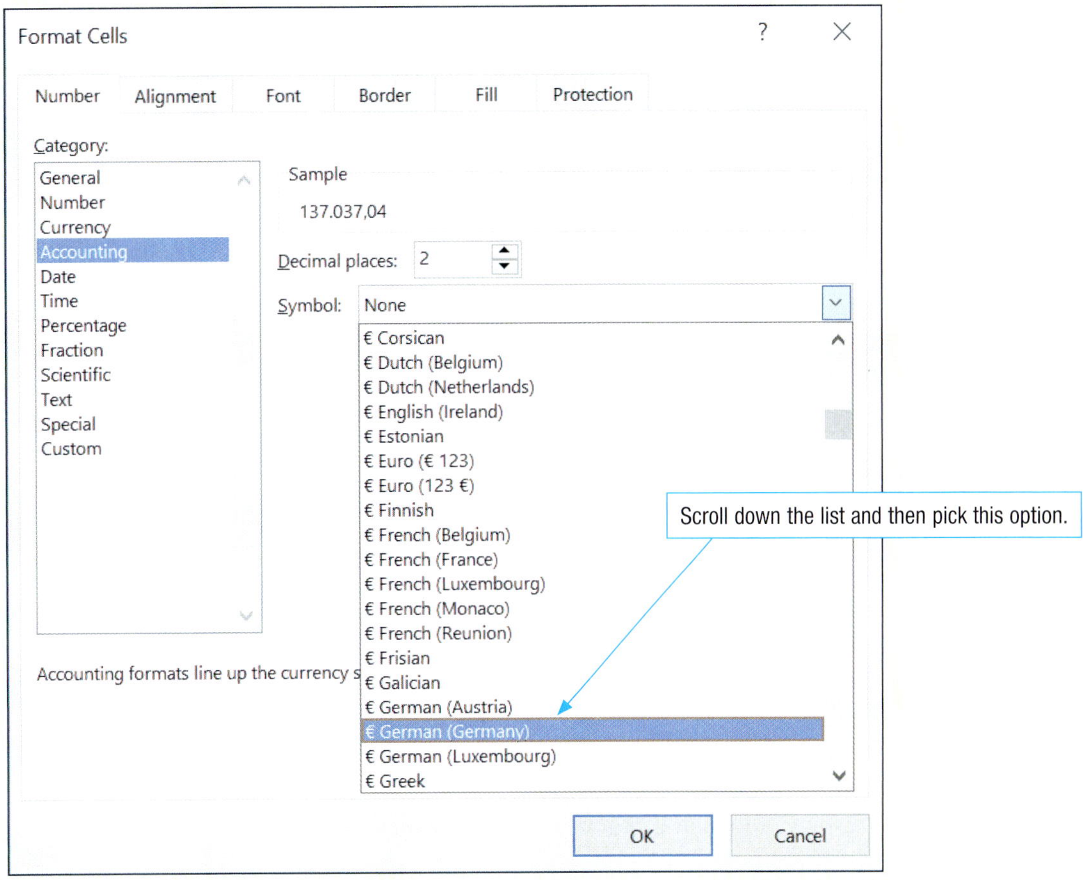

16. Click the *Advanced* option.

    Advanced options for working with Excel display.

17. Click the *Use system separators* check box.

    A check mark appears in the check box. Excel defaults back to using the operating system settings for number formatting, with a period as the decimal symbol and a comma as the thousands separator, after the OK button is clicked in the next step.

18. Click the OK button.

    The dialog box closes.

19. Click the Save button on the Quick Access Toolbar and then close the workbook.

Model Answer

14.13 Inspecting a Workbook for Properties

MOS 1.5.6

Tutorial

Inspecting a Workbook for Properties

Workbook properties include information tracked automatically by Excel, such as the names of individuals who have accessed and edited a workbook. By default, Excel displays property information at the Info backstage area and the workbook Properties dialog box. If you are sharing a workbook with others, you may not want them to see all the property information. For example, you may not want users to know the names of all the individuals who modified the file.

Before sharing a workbook, you can use the **Document Inspector** to scan the workbook for personal data and hidden information that others should not view, to list the results of the scan, and to remove sensitive and hidden items. You can also use the Document Inspector to reveal the presence of headers, footers, hidden items, and other invisible data in a workbook created by someone else.

▸ Know This about inspecting a workbook for properties and hidden items

— If any sensitive data or hidden information should remain confidential, remove it before sharing a workbook.

— Before inspecting a workbook and removing properties and hidden items, save a copy of the original workbook that retains all the content, using password protection or another security measure to limit access to the workbook.

— To inspect an open workbook for properties and hidden items, click the File tab, click the Check for Issues button in the middle panel at the Info backstage area, click the *Inspect Document* option at the drop-down list, click check boxes to remove check marks for items that are not to be scanned or removed at the Document Inspector dialog box, and then click the Inspect button.

— When the scan is completed, the results display in the *Review the inspection results* list box at the Document Inspector dialog box.

- A check mark displays for each category of data in which no sensitive or hidden items were found.
- A red exclamation mark displays for each category of data in which sensitive or hidden items were found.
- A Remove All button displays for each category of data you can remove from the workbook.

— A More Info button displays for each category of data you cannot remove. For example, hidden names cannot be removed by the Document Inspector. A **hidden name** is a name given by Excel to cells or ranges used in Solver scenarios. You would need to run a macro to remove hidden names.

— Review the results in each category, and then click the Remove All button to remove sensitive information and hidden items that you do not want other users to see.

— The *Inspect Workbook* section summarizes the information in the workbook you may want to remove before distributing it. The *Properties* section also lists information you may want to remove.

▸ Know This about allowing document properties and personal information to be saved in a workbook

— If the document properties and personal information are removed from a workbook, Excel automatically removes the *Author* and *Last Modified By* properties in the *Related People* section at the Info backstage area.

— To allow the *Author* and *Last Modified By* properties to be saved with the workbook, click the Allow this information to be saved in your file hyperlink in the *Inspect Workbook* section at the Info backstage area.

On the Job

Task 14.13 Inspecting a Workbook for Properties

Devon wants to finalize the 14-DVAutoPartsFinal workbook for his meeting next week. Before he does that, he wants you to inspect the workbook and remove any personal information and comments. Use the Document Inspector to identify and remove document properties, personal information, and any comments.

1. Open the data file **14-DVAutoPartsFinal**.
2. With the 14-DVAutoPartsFinal workbook open and any worksheet active, click the File tab.

   The Info backstage area displays (see Figure 14.36). The *Inspect Workbook* section summarizes the information in the workbook you may want to remove before distributing. The *Properties* section also lists information you may want to remove.

Figure 14.36 Property Information at the Info Backstage Area

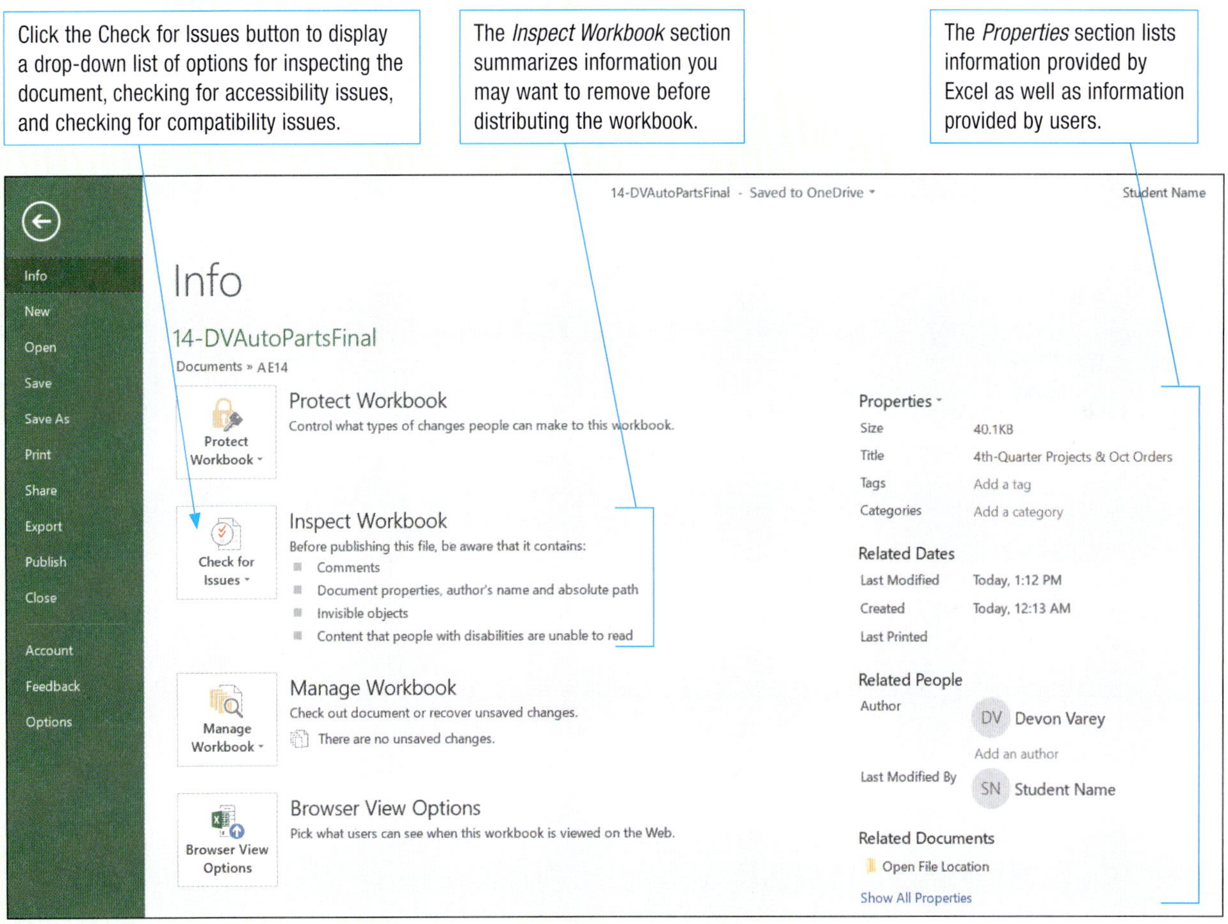

3. Click the Check for Issues button.

   A drop-down list displays.

4. Click the *Inspect Document* option.

   The Document Inspector dialog box displays.

5. Click the Inspect button.

   The inspection results display (see Figure 14.37).

Figure 14.37 Inspection Results at the Document Inspector Dialog Box

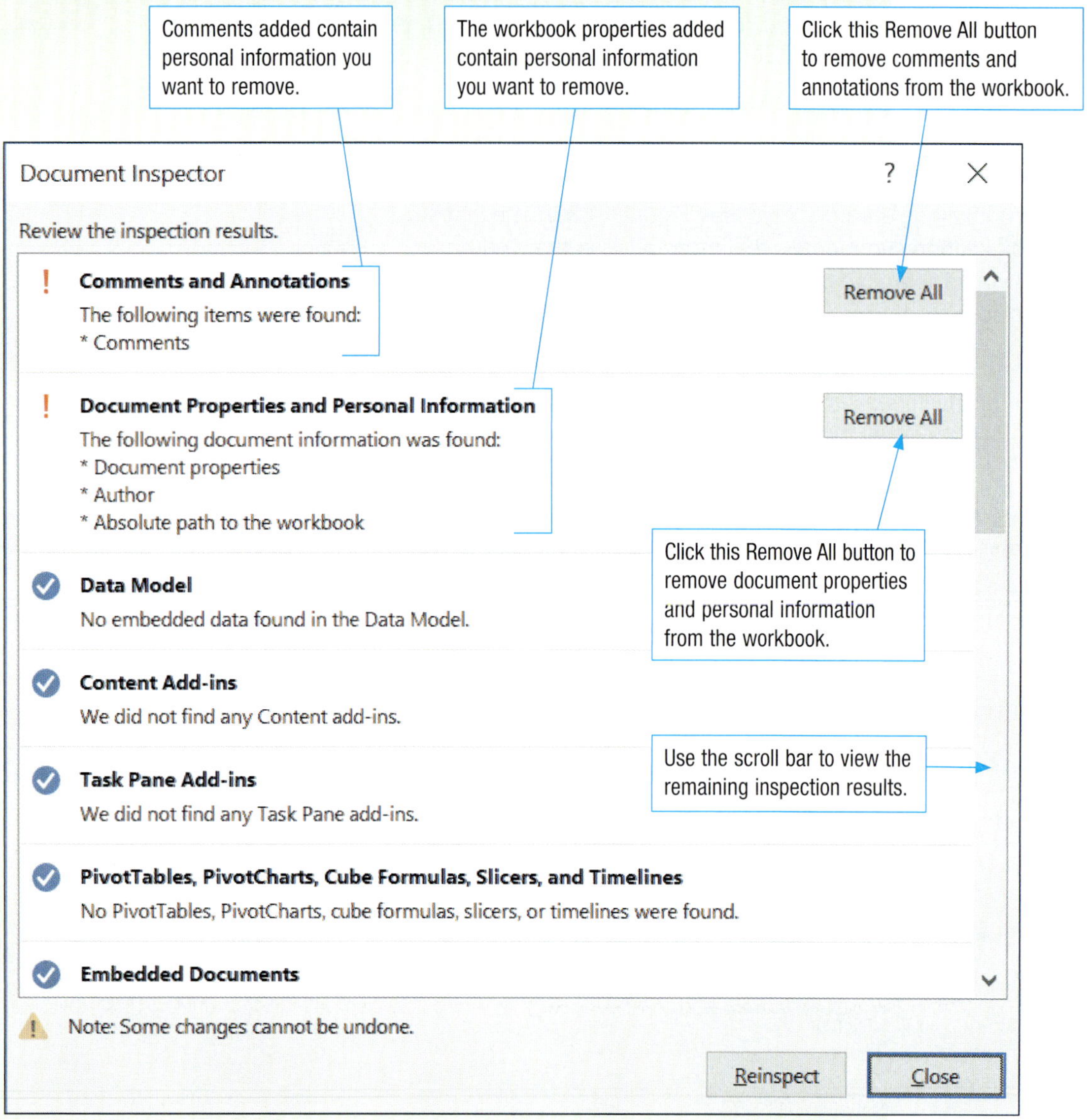

6. Click the Remove All button in the *Comments and Annotations* section.

   The *Comments and Annotations* section now displays with a check mark, indicating Excel has removed the comments.

7. Click the Remove All button in the *Document Properties and Personal Information* section.

   The *Document Properties and Personal Information* section now displays with a check mark, indicating Excel has removed this category of metadata.

8. Click the Close button.

   The Document Inspector dialog box closes. The Info backstage area continues to display.

9. Click the Allow this information to be saved in your file hyperlink (see Figure 14.38).

The hyperlink and the comment above it disappear. Any new metadata in the *Related People* section can now be saved with the workbook.

Figure 14.38 Allow this information to be saved in your file Hyperlink at the Info Backstage Area

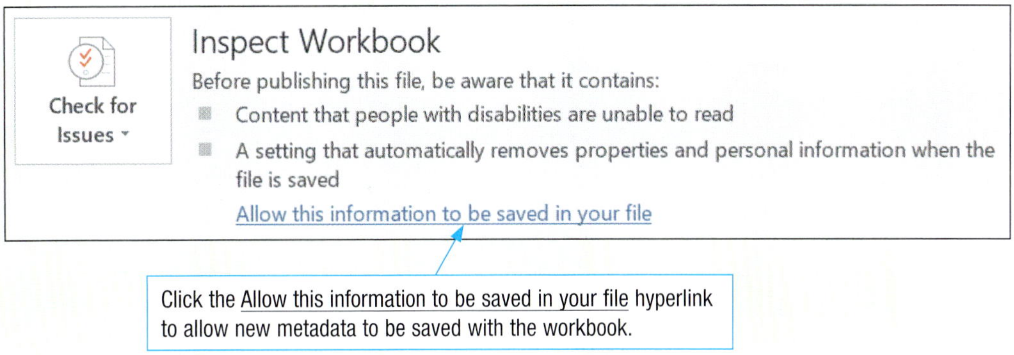

10. Click the Back button.

The Info backstage area closes and any worksheet is active.

11. Click the Save button on the Quick Access Toolbar.

14.14 Inspecting a Workbook for Accessibility Issues

MOS 1.5.7

Tutorial

Inspecting a Workbook for Accessibility Issues

Throughout the tasks in this textbook, you have inserted alternative text for objects such as tables, SmartArt graphics, and images. Alternative text is just one feature that may help users who take advantage of an assistive technology that provides an audio description of an Excel worksheet. You can use the **Accessibility Checker** in Excel to inspect a workbook for objects that do not have alternative text and for other types of content that is not readily visible to users.

▸ **Know This** about inspecting a workbook for accessibility issues

— Before distributing a workbook, identify and address any accessibility issues.

— To run the Accessibility Checker in an open workbook, click the File tab, click the Check for Issues button in the middle panel at the Info backstage area, and then click the *Check Accessibility* option at the drop-down list.

— When the accessibility check is completed, the results display in the *Inspection Results* section at the Accessibility Checker task pane.

— The *Inspection Results* list groups accessibility issues in three levels, using the headings *Errors*, *Warnings*, and *Tips*. A description explaining the impact of issues at each level and examples for each level are provided in Table 14.2.

▸ **Know More** ways to run the Accessibility Checker

– Click the Check Accessibility button in the Accessibility group on the Review tab.

— Under the heading for each level, Excel lists each object or cell that contains an accessibility issue, along with the name of the worksheet in which the object or cell is located.
— To learn more about an issue, click the name of the object or cell and then read the information in the *Why Fix?* section, which displays in the *Additional Information* section at the bottom of the Accessibility Checker task pane.
— To fix an issue, click the name of the object or cell and then follow the instructions in the *Steps To Fix* section, which displays at the bottom of the Accessibility Checker task pane.
— When you select an issue at the Accessibility Checker task pane, Excel displays the object or cell in the worksheet, if possible.
— When the problem has been corrected, it disappears from the *Inspection Results* list.
— Whenever possible, you should fix issues (especially errors) to ensure that the workbook is fully accessible to users. In some situations, a government body or other regulatory agency may require you to fix errors, but not require you to fix warnings and tips. Check with the agency that regulates your location, industry, or institution to find out the specific requirements for your situation.

▶ Know More ways to make your workbook more accessible

- Display the New backstage area, type *accessible* in the search text box, click the Start searching icon, click the *Accessible Template Sampler* option, and then click the Create button. Excel will download a workbook with various accessible templates organized into four categories (Calendars, Invoices, Budgets, and Calculators). The last tab, Learn More, provides a hyperlink to the Microsoft website, where you can learn more about making your workbooks accessible.
- These templates offer greater color contrast, a larger font, and input messages that can be used by assistive technology that provides an audio description of the content.
- The Make your Excel spreadsheets accessible web page also provides a hyperlink to the Microsoft Disability Answer Desk, where you can explore answers to questions regarding accessibility.

Table 14.2 Levels of Accessibility Issues

Level	Description	Examples
Errors	Workbook content that will be very difficult, if not impossible, for people with accessibility issues to understand	Objects (such as pictures, charts, tables, and shapes without labels) that do not have alternative text
Warnings	Workbook content that will be difficult for some people with accessibility issues to understand	Sheet tabs without unique names; split and merged cells
Tips	Workbook content that can be understood by people with accessibility issues but would be easier to understand if it were better organized	Audio and video without closed captioning

On the Job

Task 14.14 Inspecting a Workbook for Accessibility Issues

In preparing to distribute the 14-DVAutoPartsFinal workbook, Devon wants you to add a line chart depicting the fourth-quarter sales projections. He also wants you to change the data in the Orders worksheet to a table so he can take advantage of the flexibility of a table format. After you add the chart and the table, run the Accessibility Checker and fix issues that are listed as errors to ensure that users with accessibility issues will not find the workbook contents very difficult or impossible to understand. Fix only issues that are listed as errors, not issues listed as warnings and as tips.

1. With the 14-DVAutoPartsFinal workbook open and any tab active, click the File tab.

2. Click the Check for Issues button in the *Inspect Workbook* section at the Info backstage area and then click the *Check Accessibility* option.

   The Accessibility Checker runs and the inspection results display at the Accessibility Checker task pane (see Figure 14.39).

Figure 14.39 Inspection Results at the Accessibility Checker Task Pane

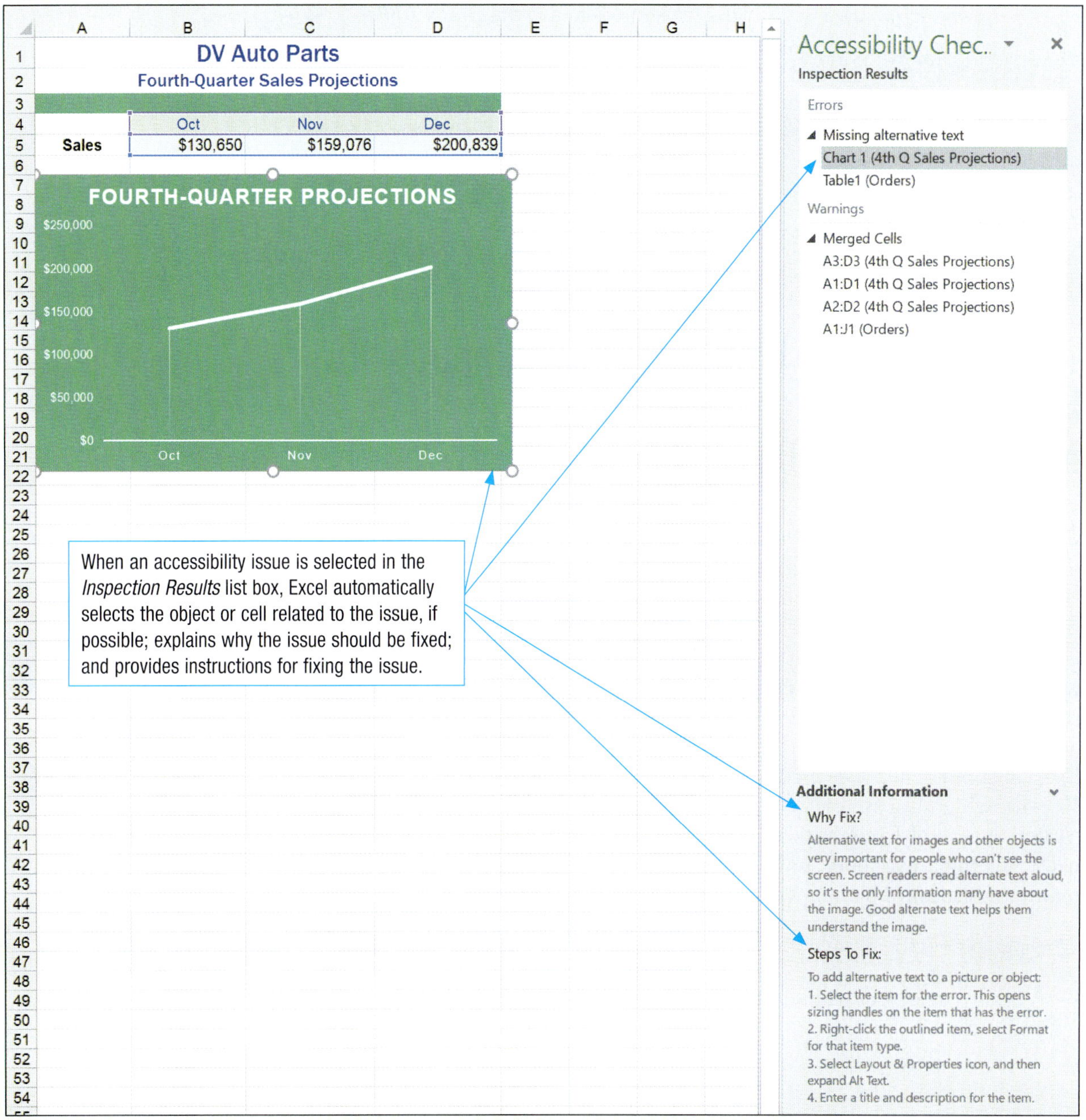

3. Click the *Chart 1 (4th Q Sales Projections)* accessibility issue in the *Inspection Results* list box and then add alternative text to the chart, typing Line Chart as the title and Chart depicting the fourth-quarter sales projections as the description.

   To add alternative text, follow the instructions in the *Steps To Fix* section at the Accessibility Checker task pane or the instructions in Chapter 6, Section 6.1 (see page 235). As soon as you start typing the title, the issue disappears from the *Inspection Results* list box. Continue typing until you have entered the complete title and description.

4. Click the *Table 1 (Orders)* accessibility issue in the *Inspection Results* list box and then add alternative text to the table, typing DV Auto Parts Orders as the title and October orders as the description.

   To add alternative text, follow the instructions in the *Steps To Fix* section at the Accessibility Checker task pane or the instructions in Chapter 7, Section 7.5 (see page 290). The *Table 1 (Orders)* issue disappears from the *Inspection Results* list box. The remaining issues in the list box are warnings about merged cells. You will not fix these issues.

5. Close the Accessibility Checker task pane.
6. Click the Save button on the Quick Access Toolbar.

Model Answer

14.15 Inspecting a Workbook for Compatibility Issues and Saving a Workbook in the Excel 97-2003 Format

MOS 1.5.8

Tutorial

Inspecting a Workbook for Compatibility Issues and Saving a Workbook in the Excel 97-2003 Format

When collaborating on an Excel workbook, you should run the **Compatibility Checker** to determine if someone using an earlier version of Excel will have problems viewing the workbook content. Newer features in Excel may not be **backward compatible**, meaning they cannot be viewed or are not fully functional in earlier versions of Excel. For example, if you run the Compatibility Checker on a workbook that contains the IFS function (see Chapter 9), which was new in Excel 2016, the checker will return the error code *#NAME?* in each cell containing the function.

When you save a file in the file format for an earlier version of Excel, Excel automatically does a compatibility check and provides a **Compatibility Report**, which is a summary about features that will lose functionality in the earlier version of Excel. Alternatively, you can run the Compatibility Checker before saving a workbook to identify areas that may need to be changed to maintain backward compatibility.

▸ Know This about compatibility issues

— A SmartArt object will be saved as an image in an Excel 97-2003 format and cannot be modified.

— Alternative text will not be saved with objects in a workbook saved in a version prior to Excel 2007.

▸ Know This about running the Compatibility Checker

— To run the Compatibility Checker in an open workbook, click the File tab, click the Check for Issues button in the middle panel at the Info backstage area, and then click the *Check Compatibility* option at the drop-down list to display the Compatibility Checker dialog box.

— The Compatibility Checker dialog box contains the *Summary* list box and the Find hyperlink.

- To locate a compatibility problem, click the Find hyperlink.
- To get more information about a loss of functionality, click the Help hyperlink.
- To copy the Compatibility Report to a new worksheet, click the Copy to New Sheet button.
- To select one or more versions of Excel to compare with the current file, click the Select versions to show button and then click one or more options at the drop-down list.

▸ **Know This** about saving a workbook in the Excel 97-2003 format and inspecting it for compatibility issues

- To save an open workbook in the Excel 97-2003 format and inspect it for compatibility issues: click the File tab; click the *Export* option; click the Change File Type button in the middle panel at the Export backstage area; click the *Excel 97-2003 Workbook (*.xls)* option in the *Workbook File Types* section of the right panel; click the Save As button; navigate to the storage location at the Save As dialog box; change the file name, if necessary; click the Save button; and then click the Continue button at the Microsoft Excel - Compatibility Checker dialog box.
- If you open a workbook with the Excel 97-2003 file extension, *.xls*, in Excel 2016, the text *[Compatibility Mode]* appears in the title bar after the file name and there is no loss of functionality.
- **Compatibility Mode** provides the workbook in a format that can be opened in earlier versions.
- To access current Excel features while working in Compatibility Mode, you can convert the workbook to the latest format as follows: click the File tab; click the Convert button; change the location and file name, if necessary; click the Save button; click the Yes button; close the workbook; and then reopen the workbook.

On the Job

Task 14.15 Inspecting a Workbook for Compatibility Issues and Saving a Workbook in the Excel 97-2003 Format

Devon will distribute the 14-DVAutoPartsFinal workbook to his sales associates before next week's meeting. He knows some of the sales associates are using older versions of Excel, and he needs to send them a copy of this workbook. He asks you to find out whether they will have any problems viewing the workbook content. Check for compatibility issues by running the Compatibility Checker, create a Compatibility Report, and then save a copy of the workbook with the Excel 97-2003 Workbook format and the name *14-DVAutoParts97*.

1. With the 14-DVAutoPartsFinal workbook open and any worksheet active, click the File tab.
2. Click the Check for Issues button in the *Inspect Workbook* section at the Info backstage area and then click the *Check Compatibility* option.

   The Compatibility Checker runs and the results display in the *Summary* list box at the Microsoft Excel - Compatibility Checker dialog box (see Figure 14.40).

3. Click the Copy to New Sheet button.

   The compatibility issues are copied to a new worksheet named *Compatibility Report*, which is placed at the end of the workbook, and the Compatibility Report worksheet is active. The report explains that some newer features (formatting and alternative text) will not be displayed when the workbook is saved as an Excel 97-2003 file.

Figure 14.40 Microsoft Excel - Compatibility Checker Dialog Box

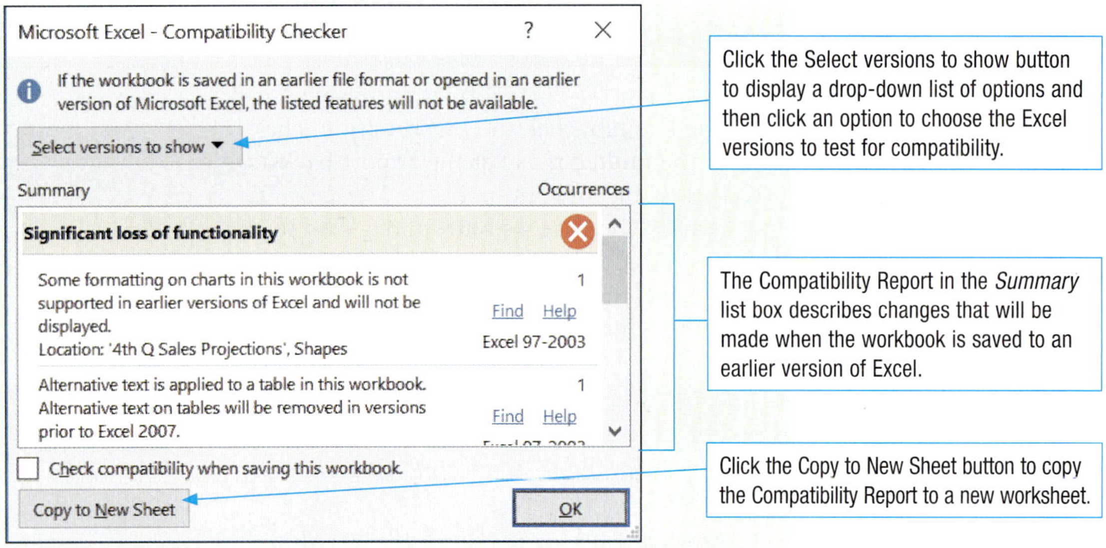

4. Click the Save button on the Quick Access Toolbar.

   The 14-DVAutoPartsFinal workbook is saved with the Compatibility Report.

5. If printing is required by your instructor, print the workbook.
6. Click the File tab, click the *Export* option, click the *Change File Type* option in the middle panel at the Export backstage area, click the *Excel 97-2003 Workbook (*.xls)* option in the *Workbook File Types* section of the right panel, and then click the Save As button.

   The Save As dialog box displays.

7. Select the text in the *File name* text box, type 14-DVAutoParts97, and then click the Save button.

   The Microsoft Excel - Compatibility Checker dialog box displays.

8. Click the Continue button.
9. Close the workbook.

Model Answer

14.16 Marking a Workbook as Final

Tutorial

Marking a Workbook as Final

You can mark a workbook that will be distributed to others as final to discourage users from making additions, deletions, and modifications. When a workbook is marked as final, it is changed to a read-only file and the *Status* property is set to final. In addition to protecting the workbook, **final status** also indicates to recipients that the content is considered complete.

▸ **Know This** about marking a workbook as final and removing the marking

— To mark an open workbook as final, click the File tab, click the Protect Workbook button in the middle panel at the Info backstage area, click the *Mark as Final* option at the drop-down list, click the OK button at the message box stating that the workbook will be marked as final and then saved, and then click the OK button at the message box stating that the workbook has been marked as final.

— The message box stating that the workbook will be marked as final will appear every time the workbook is opened unless a user clicks the *Don't show this message again* check box to insert a check mark at the message box.

— A workbook marked as final displays with the ribbon minimized, the text *[Read-Only]* at the end of the file name in the Title bar, and a message above the Formula bar informing the user that the author has marked the workbook as final to discourage editing.

— To remove the Mark as Final feature, redisplay the ribbon, allow changes to be made to the workbook, and then click the Edit Anyway button on the message bar.

— Marking a workbook as final is not as secure as using password-protected ranges because a user can click the Edit Anyway button and edit the file.

On the Job

Task 14.16 Marking a Workbook as Final

Devon is getting ready to distribute the 14-DVAutoPartsFinal workbook to the sales associates. He asks you to adjust the workbook settings so recipients will know the workbook is considered final and they should not add to, delete from, or modify it. Mark the workbook as final to meet Devon's requirement.

1. Open the data file **14-DVAutoPartsFinal**, click the 4th Q Sales Projections sheet tab, and then click the File tab.

   The Info backstage area displays.

2. Click the Protect Workbook button in the middle panel and then click the *Mark as Final* option at the drop-down list.

   A message box displays, stating the workbook will be marked as final and then saved.

3. Click the OK button.

   A second message box displays, stating that the workbook has been marked as final to indicate that editing is complete and this is the final version of the file.

4. Click the OK button.

   The message box closes. The Excel ribbon is minimized and a message above the Formula bar informs the user that the author has marked the workbook as final to discourage editing.

Model Answer

14.17 Sharing a Workbook in OneDrive

Microsoft OneDrive allows saving and sharing documents in a storage location on the Internet. If you save a workbook in OneDrive, you and others can access the file from any location using a computing device that has Internet access. Windows 10 automatically connects to your OneDrive account when you sign in to your account and will sync the contents of your OneDrive account with the OneDrive folder on your PC. **Syncing** is a process that updates the files saved in both locations so you are always working with the most up-to-date version.

When multiple people edit a shared workbook in OneDrive, they are all editing the same version of the file. There is no need to manage multiple versions of the same file, as would be necessary if the file were shared by email, for example.

Tutorial

Sharing a Workbook in OneDrive

▸ Know This about saving a workbook to OneDrive and sharing a workbook

— To save a workbook to OneDrive and share it: with any worksheet active, click the Share button in the Title bar; type a name in the *Invite people* text box; change the *Can edit* option, if necessary; type a message; click the Share button; and then click the OneDrive - Personal button. ***Note:*** *OneDrive is constantly changing, so the steps for saving and sharing a workbook in OneDrive may vary.*

▸ Know This about sharing a workbook saved to OneDrive

— After a workbook has been saved to OneDrive, you can invite people to share it.

— To share a workbook in OneDrive: with any worksheet active, click the Share button in the Title bar; enter email addresses in the *Invite people* text box at the Share task pane (see Figure 14.41); click the permission option box arrow and then click an option at the drop-down list, if necessary; type a message in the *Include a message (optional)* text box, if necessary; and then click the Share button.

— You can enter multiple names and email addresses in the *Invite people* box, inserting a semicolon after each name or email address.

— The names or email addresses of the workbook owner and of users who have been invited to share the workbook are listed at the Share task pane (see Figure 14.42 on page 730).

— To remove a user from a shared workbook or change the editing permission for a user, right-click the user's name or address at the Share task pane and then click either the *Remove User* option or the *Change permission to* option at the pop-up menu.

▸ Know This about editing a workbook shared in OneDrive

— To edit a workbook shared in OneDrive, users who are signed in to their Microsoft or Hotmail accounts may access the Excel Online application.

▸ Know More ways to save a workbook to OneDrive

- Click the File button; click the *Save* or *Save As* option; click the *OneDrive - Personal* option at the Save As backstage area; type a new file name in the file name text box, if necessary; and then click the Save button.

▸ Know More ways to invite people to share a workbook

- Type a name in the *Invite people* text box at the Share task pane and then click an email address at the drop-down results list.
- Click the address book button at the right of the *Invite people* text box and then choose people from your contacts list.
- Click the Get a sharing link hyperlink to create a link to share the workbook with others. Include this link in an email, a text, a Word document, or a PowerPoint presentation.

— A user who does not have a Microsoft or Hotmail account can sign up for a free account by going to login.live.com and then clicking the Sign up now button.

— Excel Online does not provide all the features that are available in the full version of Excel.

Figure 14.41 Share Task Pane

Enter the names or email addresses of people in the *Invite people* text box to invite them to share the workbook. Use semicolons to separate names or email addresses.

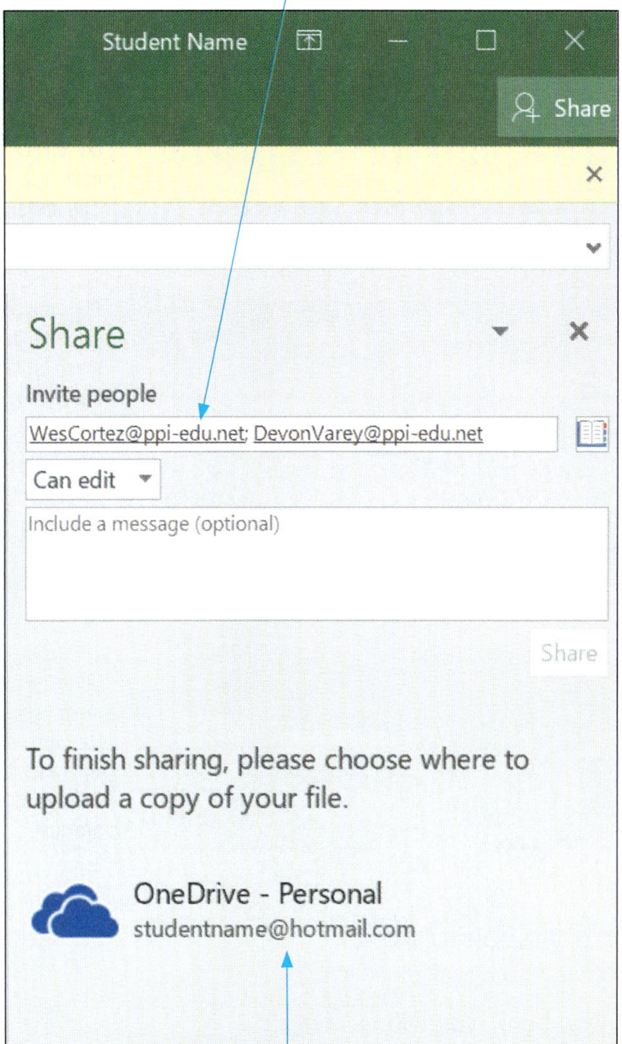

Click the OneDrive - Personal button to save the workbook to your OneDrive account if it has not already been saved to your OneDrive account.

▶ Know More about editing a workbook shared in OneDrive

- If you are using the latest version of Office 365, you can co-author a workbook with others. Co-authoring follows the same steps to share a workbook and is similar to sharing but offers a few more features.
- Ensure that AutoSave is on.
- When a co-author opens the workbook in OneDrive, his or her profile image will show in the upper right corner of the Excel window.
- To go to the worksheet location that is active for a co-author, click the co-author's profile image and then click the *Go to* option at the drop-down list.
- The cell or range you have selected will appear in green, and a cell or range selected by a co-author will appear in a different color. To display the name of the co-author, point to the selected cell or range.
- If you or a co-author are using an earlier version of Excel, a selected cell or range will not appear in a different color but the changes will display.
- If an Enable Editing button appears, click it before any changes are made.
- Any changes made to the document may take a few minutes to display.

Figure 14.42 Share Task Pane

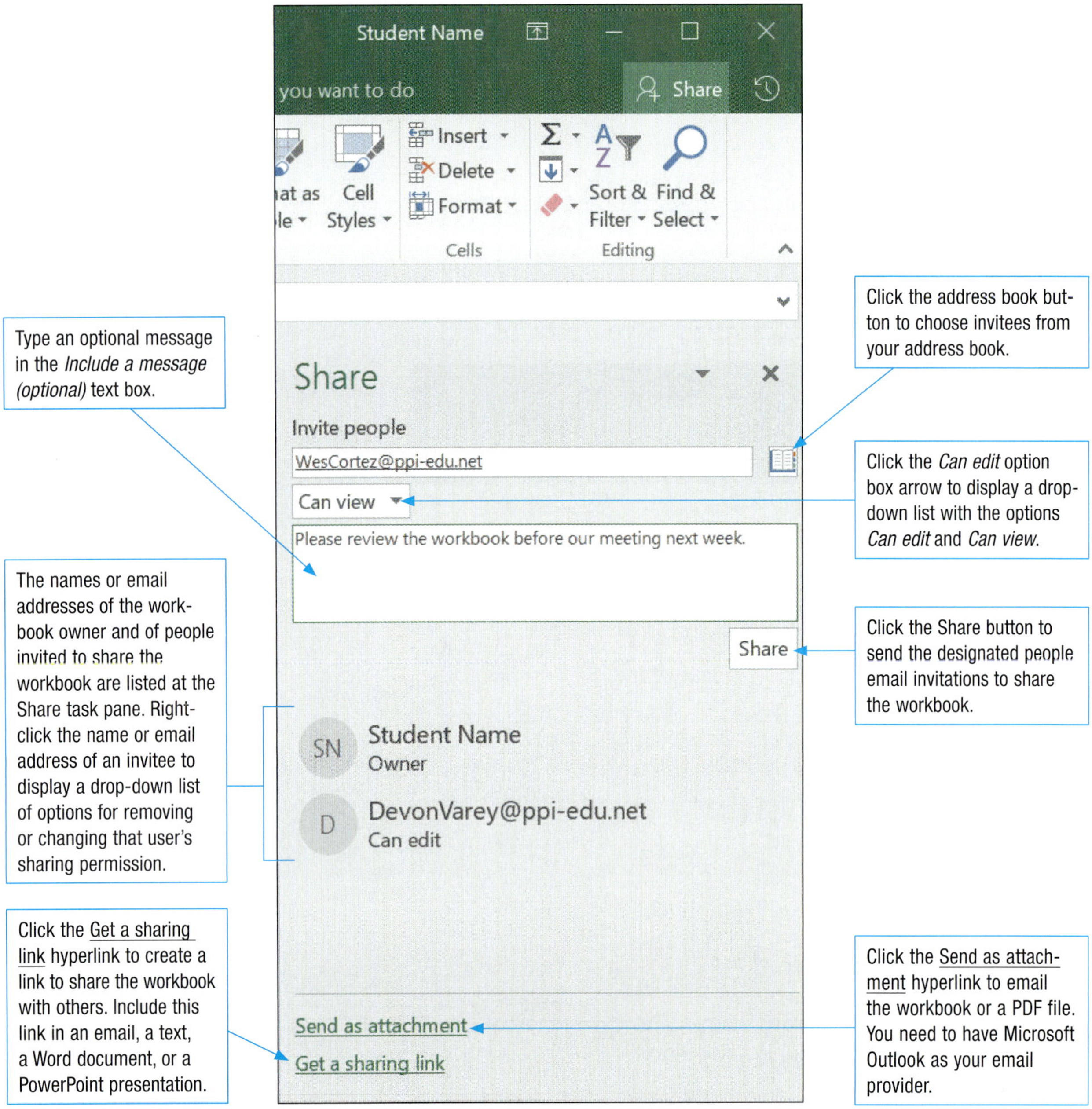

▸ **Know This** about accepting an invitation to work with a file saved in OneDrive

— When someone wants to co-author a workbook, you will receive an email with the subject *I shared "Workbook Name.xlsx" with you in OneDrive*.

— To open the shared file, click the View in OneDrive button under the filename in the body of the email. If necessary, sign in to your OneDrive account by clicking the Sign in button in the upper right corner of the screen.

— To edit the workbook, click the Edit Workbook button and then click either the *Edit in Excel* option or the *Edit in Browser* option.

- If you choose the *Edit in Browser* option, the workbook opens in Excel Online.
- If you have the latest version of Excel and you click the Edit in Excel button, Microsoft Excel will launch and you will be co-authoring with the other users of the workbook.
- If you do not sign in to your OneDrive account, click the Edit in Browser button and then click the Edit in Excel button, if necessary.
- If you have the latest version of Excel, click the *Shared with Me* option in the Open backstage area to display a list of workbooks that have been shared with you.

▸ **Know This** about sharing a workbook in SharePoint

- **Microsoft SharePoint** is a server application that allows you to share and collaborate on documents.
- Save your workbook to a SharePoint library for others to view and/or edit.

On the Job

Task 14.17 Sharing a Workbook in OneDrive

Devon wants to share the 14-DVAutoPartsFinal workbook with Wes Cortez so Wes can prepare his material for the meeting next week. Since this workbook has been marked final, Devon wants Wes to be able to view the workbook but not edit it. Save the workbook to OneDrive and then invite Wes to share it, giving him permission to view only. Also share the workbook with a classmate or your instructor, granting permission to view only, and then remove the classmate or instructor from the shared workbook.

1. With the 14-DVAutoPartsFinal workbook open and the 4th Q Sales Projections worksheet active, click the Share button in the upper right corner of the Title bar.

   The Share task pane displays and the insertion point is in the *Invite people* text box.

2. Type WesCortez@ppi-edu.net and then click in a blank area of the Share task pane.

   You may see a *searching* message in the Share task pane, indicating that Excel is looking for *Wes Cortez*.

3. Click the permission option box arrow and then click the *Can view* option at the drop-down list (see Figure 14.43).

   This setting ensures that Wes can view but not edit the workbook contents.

4. Click in the *Include a message (optional)* text box and then type Please review the workbook before our meeting next week.

   Include the period at the end of the sentence.

5. Click the Share button.

   If the workbook has been saved to OneDrive, an email is sent to Wes, inviting him to share the workbook, and his email address is listed at the Share task pane. If the workbook has not been saved to OneDrive, a message appears at the Share task pane with a button for uploading a copy of the workbook to your OneDrive account.

Figure 14.43 Share Task Pane with a Message and a Button for Saving the Active Workbook to OneDrive

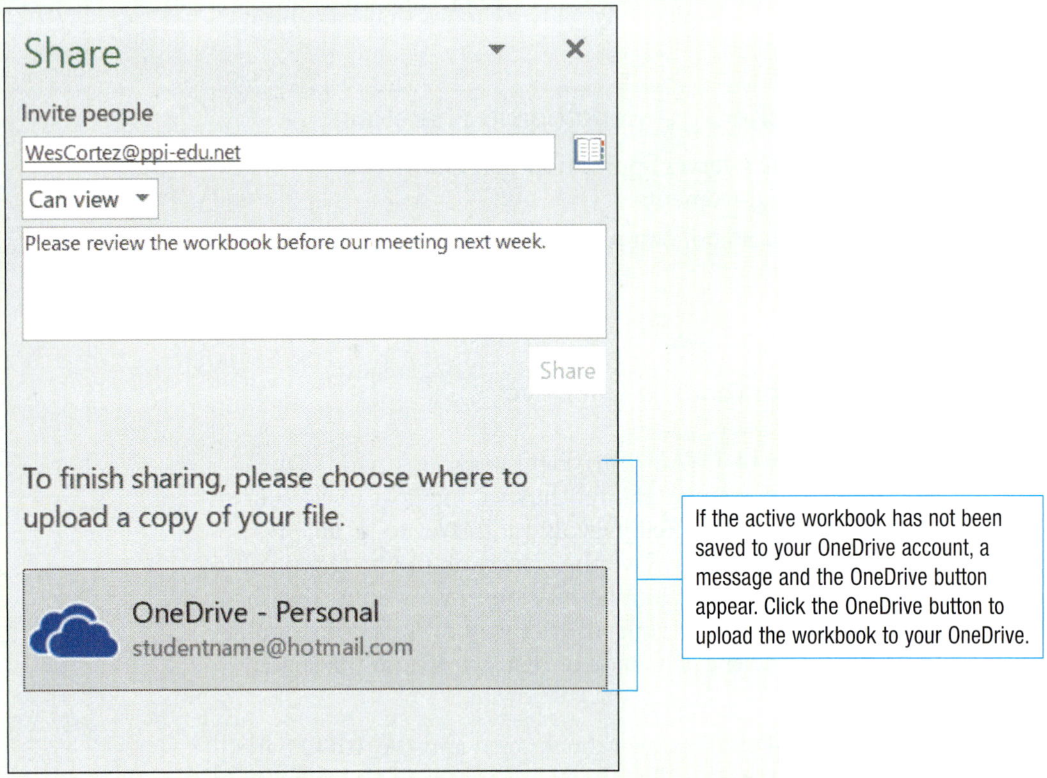

6. If the workbook has not been saved to OneDrive, click the OneDrive - Personal button at the Share task pane. ***Note:*** *If you have already saved the workbook to OneDrive, skip to Step 7.*
7. Invite your instructor or classmate to view the workbook. Type an appropriate message.
8. Check with your instructor or classmate to see if he or she received the email with the hyperlink to the workbook.
9. Right-click the name or email address of your instructor or classmate at the Share task pane and then click the *Remove User* option at the pop-up menu.

   The name or email address disappears from the task pane. The classmate or instructor no longer has permission to view the workbook.
10. Close the Share task pane and then save and close the workbook.

Model Answer

Chapter Summary

14.1 ▶ A workbook property provides descriptive information about the workbook data, such as the author's name, the title, the subject, the category to which the workbook is related, or a general comment about the workbook. Workbook properties are sometimes referred to as *metadata*.

▶ Excel automatically provides some information about workbook properties, including the size of the workbook, the date the workbook was last modified, the date the workbook was created, the date the workbook was last printed, and the name of the person who last saved the workbook. The user can add and modify information about other workbook properties, such as the workbook title, tags, categories, and authors.

14.2 ▶ A comment is a note that is attached to a cell and displays in a pop-up box. When a comment is attached to a cell, a colored triangle appears in the upper right corner of the cell. The comment box displays when a user points to the cell to which the comment is attached.

▶ All the comment boxes in a workbook can be displayed or hidden. Comment boxes can be resized using sizing handles, and comment text can be edited and formatted. Comments can also be copied and pasted, moved, printed, and deleted.

14.3 ▶ A shared workbook can be saved to a network folder that multiple users can access at the same time. Excel tracks each person's changes and displays a prompt if two or more people have the same workbook open at the same time and attempt to make changes to the same cell. By default, the changes made to a shared workbook are saved in a history log for 30 days.

14.4 ▶ When a workbook is shared, Excel automatically turns on the Track Changes feature. Track Changes records any changes made to a workbook and the names of the users who make the changes.

▶ By default, when a user opens more than one workbook at the same time, all the workbooks open in the same instance of Excel. Occasionally, it may be useful to open each workbook in a separate instance of Excel—for example, to view multiple dialog boxes at the same time.

14.5 ▶ If multiple users have copies of a shared workbook open and two or more users make a change to the same cell, a conflict will occur. The next time the workbook is saved, Excel will display a dialog box with a prompt asking the user to resolve the conflict by accepting either his or her change or the other user's change. If multiple conflicts occur in the same workbook, the user can review each change and choose which revision to accept, or accept all of his or her changes or all the other users' changes.

14.6 ▶ A history sheet (also called a *history list*) is a new worksheet that displays all the tracked changes that have been made to a shared workbook. The history sheet is automatically deleted from the original workbook when the workbook is saved. To refer to the history sheet later, the user must either print it or copy it to a new workbook.

14.7 ▶ It is good practice to review all the tracked changes in a workbook periodically and either accept or reject each change. The user can review the changes by highlighting all the changed cells and then navigating to each change and either accepting or rejecting it individually. Alternatively, the user can accept or reject all the tracked changes at once.

14.8 ▶ When the user is finished collaborating in a shared workbook, he or she can either stop sharing the workbook or turn off the Track Changes feature. If any changes made to a workbook have not yet been reviewed, the user should consider printing a copy of the history sheet before turning off Track Changes.

14.9 ▶ Worksheet protection prevents users from deleting or modifying cells that should not be changed in the worksheet. By default, in a protected worksheet, each cell is assigned the lock attribute—that is, every cell is locked. This means no one can insert, delete, or modify any of the worksheet contents. However, if some of the cells in the worksheet contain data the user wants others to be able to change, the user can clear the lock attribute on those cells. The user can also allow specific individuals to edit a protected worksheet by setting a password and giving the password only to those individuals.

▶ In a protected worksheet, cells containing formulas can be hidden so that when the user clicks in a cell with a formula, the formula does not display in the Formula bar. The cells containing the formulas must first be hidden and the worksheet must then be protected.

14.10 ▶ To prevent changes to the structure of a workbook—such as inserting a new sheet, deleting a sheet, and unhiding a hidden worksheet—the user can protect the structure of the workbook.

14.11 ▶ Unauthorized access to Excel data can be prevented by requiring a password to open a workbook. This type of password is encrypted, which means the plain text the user types is converted into a coded format called *cipher text*.

14.12 ▶ Distributing a workbook to clients or employees in other countries may require changing the formats for numbers, dates, and currencies. For example, countries differ in how they use commas, periods, and spaces as separators to designate number groups and decimal places. The default number format used by all Microsoft Office applications, including Excel, is determined by the computer's operating system.

14.13 ▶ The Document Inspector is used to scan the workbook for personal data and hidden information that others should not view, to list the results of the scan, and to remove sensitive and hidden items. The Document Inspector can also be used to reveal the presence of headers, footers, hidden items, and other invisible data in a workbook created by someone else. If any sensitive data or hidden information should remain confidential, it should be removed before the workbook is shared.

14.14 ▶ The Accessibility Checker is used to inspect a workbook for objects that do not have alternative text and for other types of content that is not readily visible to users. Accessibility issues are grouped in three levels: errors, warnings, and tips. Whenever possible, issues (especially errors) should be fixed to ensure that the workbook is fully accessible.

14.15 ▶ The Compatibility Checker is used to determine if someone with an earlier version of Excel will have problems viewing the workbook content. Newer features in Excel may not be backward compatible, which means they cannot be viewed or are not fully functional in earlier versions.

▶ When a file is saved in the file format for an earlier version of Excel, Excel automatically does a compatibility check and provides a Compatibility Report, which is a summary about features that will lose functionality in the earlier version. Alternatively, the Compatibility Checker can be run before a workbook is saved to identify areas that may need to be changed to maintain backward compatibility.

14.16 ▶ A workbook that will be distributed to others can be marked as final to discourage users from making additions, deletions, and modifications. When a workbook is marked as final, it is changed to a read-only file and the *Status* property is set to final. In addition to protecting the workbook, final status also indicates to recipients that the content is considered complete.

14.17 ▶ If a workbook is saved in OneDrive, the user and others can access the file from any location using a computing device that has Internet access. When multiple people edit a shared workbook in OneDrive, they are all editing the same version of the file.

Features Review

Feature	Ribbon Tab, Group	Button, Option	Keyboard Shortcut
accept or reject tracked changes	Review, Changes	, *Accept/Reject Change*	
change how numbers display in Excel	File	*Options*, *Advanced*	
change number of days changes are saved to history log	Review, Changes	, Advanced tab	
change user name associated with Excel	File	*Options*	
clear lock attribute in cells that can be modified	Home, Cells	, *Lock Cell* or *Format Cells*	
copy comment			Ctrl + C
delete comment	Review, Comments		
display all workbook changes in history sheet	Review, Changes	, *Highlight Changes*	
display or hide all comment boxes	Review, Comments		
display tracked changes	Review, Changes	, *Highlight Changes*	
edit comment	Review, Comments		
encrypt or remove encryption from open workbook	File	*Info*, Protect Workbook, *Encrypt with Password*	

...continues

Feature	Ribbon Tab, Group	Button, Option	Keyboard Shortcut
insert comment in active cell	Review, Comments		Shift + F2
format comment box	Home, Cells	, *Format Comment*	
format comment text	Home, Font		
give permission to edit protected cells in active worksheet	Review, Changes		
hide formulas in protected worksheet	Home, Cells	, *Format Cells*	
highlight tracked changes	Review, Changes	, *Highlight Changes*	
inspect open workbook for properties and hidden items	File	Check for Issues, *Inspect Document*	
mark workbook as final	File	*Info*, Protect Workbook, *Mark as Final*	
paste comment	Home, Clipboard	, *Paste Special*, insert bullet in *Comments* radio button	
print comments with worksheet	Page Layout, Page Setup		
protect active worksheet	Review, Changes or Home, Cells or File	, insert check mark in *Protect worksheet and contents of locked cells* check box or , *Protect Sheet* or *Info*, Protect workbook, *Protect Sheet*	
protect and unprotect structure of open workbook	Review, Changes or File	 or *Info*, Protect Workbook, *Protect Workbook Structure*	
remove shared access to workbook	Review, Changes	, remove check mark from *Allow changes by more than one user at the same time* check box	
run Accessibility Checker	File	*Info*, Check for Issues, *Check Accessibility*	
run Compatibility Checker	File	*Info*, Check for Issues, *Check Compatibility*	
save workbook in Excel 97-2003 format	File	*Export*, Change File Type, *Excel 97-2003 Workbook (*.xls)*	
save workbook to OneDrive and share it	File	*Save* or *Save As*, *OneDrive - Personal*	
share open workbook	Review, Changes	, insert check mark in *Allow changes by more than one user at the same time* check box	
turn Track Changes on or off	Review, Changes	, *Highlight Changes*	

...continues

Feature	Ribbon Tab, Group	Button, Option	Keyboard Shortcut
unprotect worksheet	Review, Changes or File	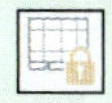 or *Info*, Unprotect	
view, add, modify workbook properties	File	*Info*, Properties	
view names of users who have shared workbook open	Review, Changes	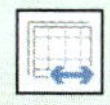	
view next comment	Review, Comments		
view previous comment	Review, Comments		

Recheck

Recheck your understanding of the concepts, features, and skills covered in this chapter by taking the Recheck quiz.

Workbook

Access the study tools, review exercises, assessments, and challenges for this chapter in the workbook available from this page in your ebook.

Automating Repetitive Tasks and Customizing Excel

Chapter 15

Chapter Goal

To improve productivity, accuracy, and efficiency by automating and customizing the Excel environment.

Learning Objectives

- **15.1** Pin and unpin workbooks in the *Recent* list
- **15.2** Customize the ribbon
- **15.3** Customize the Quick Access Toolbar
- **15.4** Hide and unhide ribbon tabs
- **15.5** Insert a screenshot or a screen clipping
- **15.6** Create, show, and delete custom views
- **15.7** Record a simple macro and save a macro-enabled workbook
- **15.8** Enable macros and assign macros to shortcut key combinations
- **15.9** Run a macro
- **15.10** Edit and rerecord a macro
- **15.11** Delete a macro
- **15.12** Manage macro security
- **15.13** Copy macros from workbook to workbook
- **15.14** Insert and configure form controls
- **15.15** Export and import XML data
- **15.16** Reset the ribbon and the Quick Access Toolbar

Precheck

Check your understanding of the concepts, features, and skills covered in this chapter by taking the Precheck quiz.

Data Files

Before beginning the chapter work, download the AE15 folder from this page in your ebook to your storage medium and then make AE15 the active folder.

Ebook Links

Access digital resources for this course from your ebook.

SNAP

If you are a SNAP user, go to your SNAP assignments page to complete the Precheck, Tutorials, and Recheck in this chapter.

Preview

On the Job

Scenario: DV Auto Parts

Devon Varey, owner of DV Auto Parts, has created a number of Excel workbooks for his business and finds that he spends a lot of time updating and managing the data he's collecting. He wants to increase his productivity by customizing the Excel ribbon and Quick Access Toolbar with commands that he uses frequently. He also wants to automate tasks he performs on a regular basis by creating macros and adding form controls to his workbooks. He asks you to help him make these changes.

Visual Reference: Automation and Customization Features in Excel

Figure 15.1 Worksheet with a Custom Toolbar and with Data Mapped for Exportation as an XML File

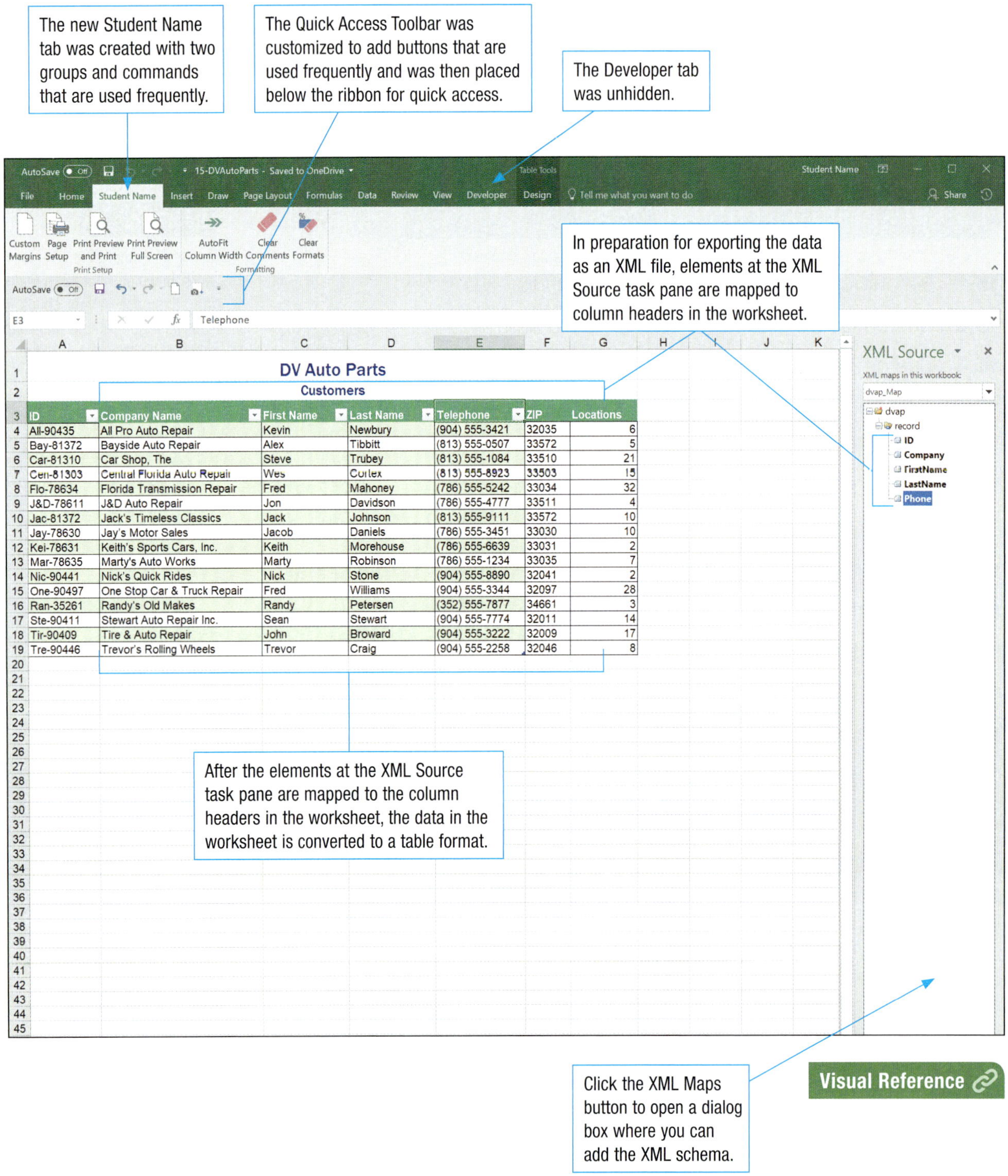

Figure 15.2 Worksheet with the Developer Tab Active and Form Controls Added

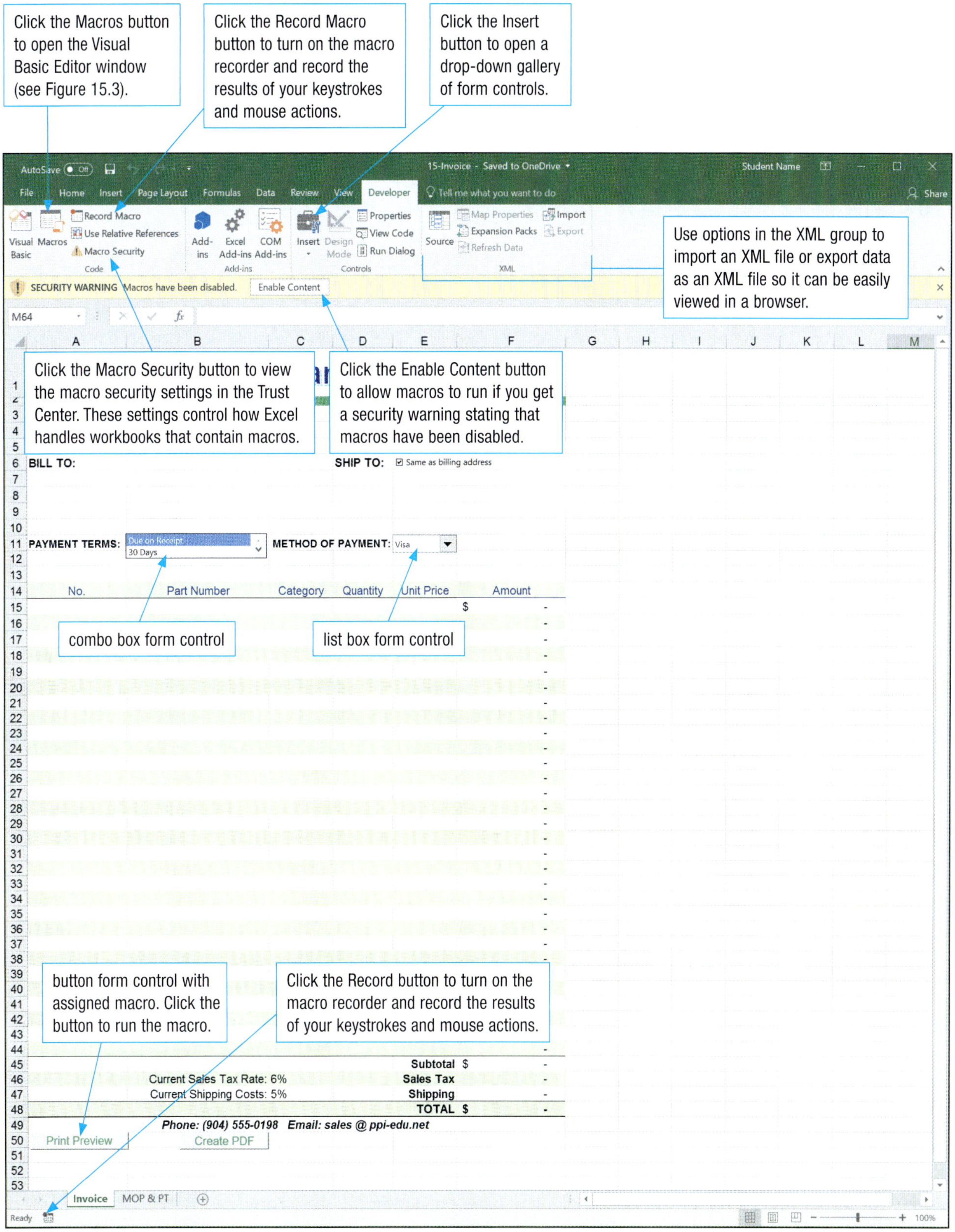

Visual Reference

Figure 15.3 Visual Basic Editor Window

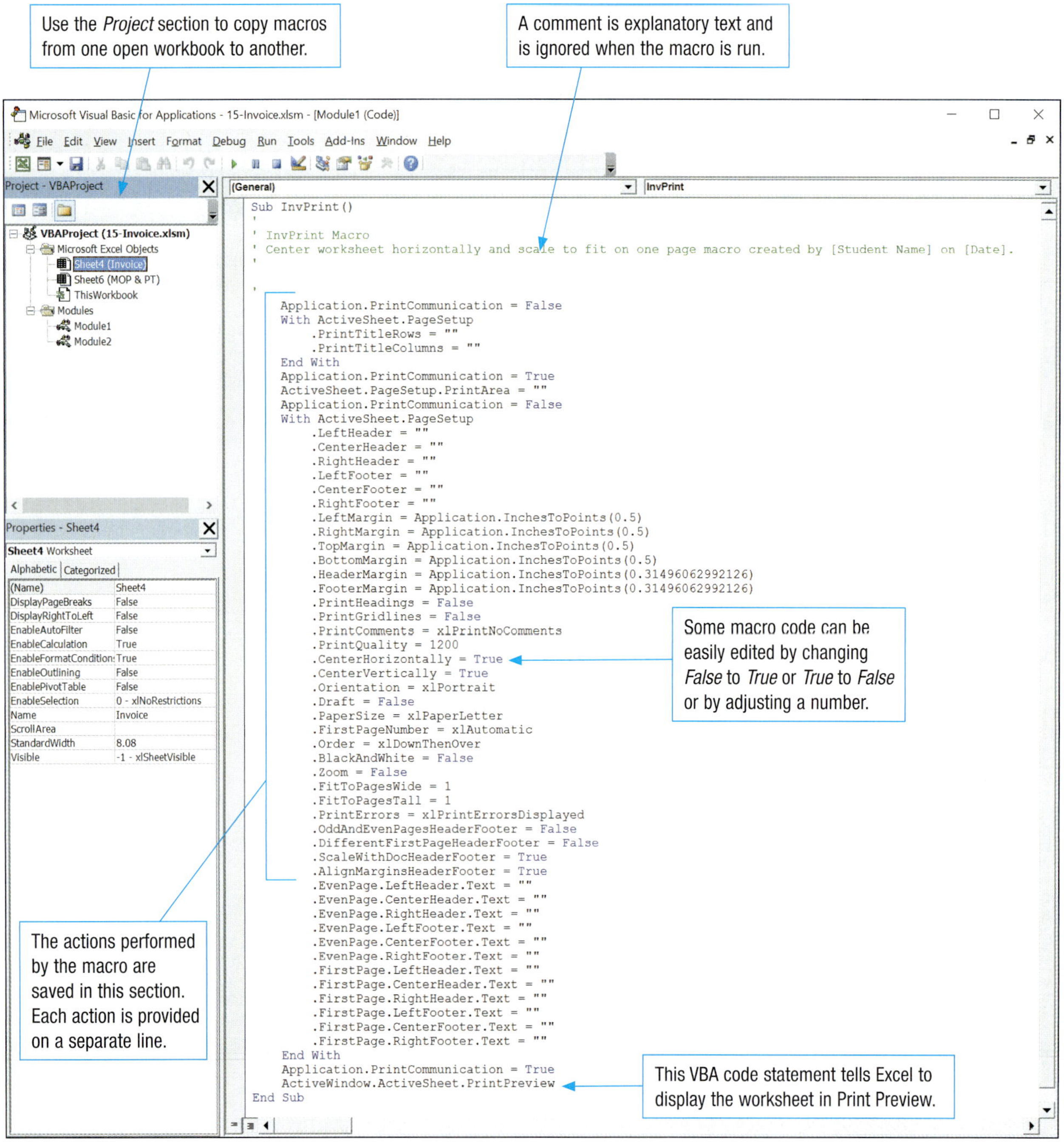

15.1 Pinning and Unpinning Workbooks in the *Recent* List

Visual Reference

Tutorial

Pinning a Workbook in the Recent List

In the ***Recent* list** at the Excel Start screen or at the Open backstage area, Excel automatically displays a list of the workbooks you have opened in order, starting with the one you opened most recently at the top. You can quickly reopen a workbook from this list by clicking the workbook name. If you **pin** a workbook in the *Recent* list, its name will always appear in the *Pinned* section at the top of the list, regardless of when you last opened the workbook. Consider pinning a frequently used workbook in the *Recent* list to save time navigating to the file.

▸ Know This about pinning and unpinning workbooks in the *Recent* list

— To pin a workbook in the *Recent* list, display the Excel Start screen or the Excel Open backstage area, point to the workbook name in the *Recent* list, and then click the left-pointing pushpin icon that appears at the right of the workbook name.

— A pinned workbook displays with a down-pointing pushpin icon in the *Pinned* section at the top of the *Recent* list.

— If you change the location or name of a pinned workbook, you can no longer open it from the *Pinned* category.

— More than one workbook can be pinned. Pinned workbooks are listed alphabetically.

— To unpin a workbook in the *Recent* list, click the down-pointing pushpin icon at the right of the workbook name.

▸ Know More ways to pin and unpin a workbook in the *Recent* list

- To pin a workbook in the *Recent* list, right-click the workbook name and then click the *Pin to list* option at the pop-up menu.
- To unpin a workbook in the *Recent* list, right-click the workbook name and then click the *Unpin from list* option at the pop-up menu.

On the Job

Task 15.1 Pinning a Workbook in the *Recent* List

Devon frequently works on the 15-DVAutoParts workbook. Pin the workbook so it will always appear at the top of the *Recent* list.

1. Open the data file **15-DVAutoParts**.
2. Click the File tab and then click the *Open* option.

   The Open backstage area displays with the *Recent* option selected in the middle panel.
3. Point to the workbook name *15-DVAutoParts* in the right panel.

   The workbook name is highlighted and a left-pointing pushpin icon appears at the right of the file name (see Figure 15.4).

Figure 15.4 Open Backstage Area with *Recent* List Displayed

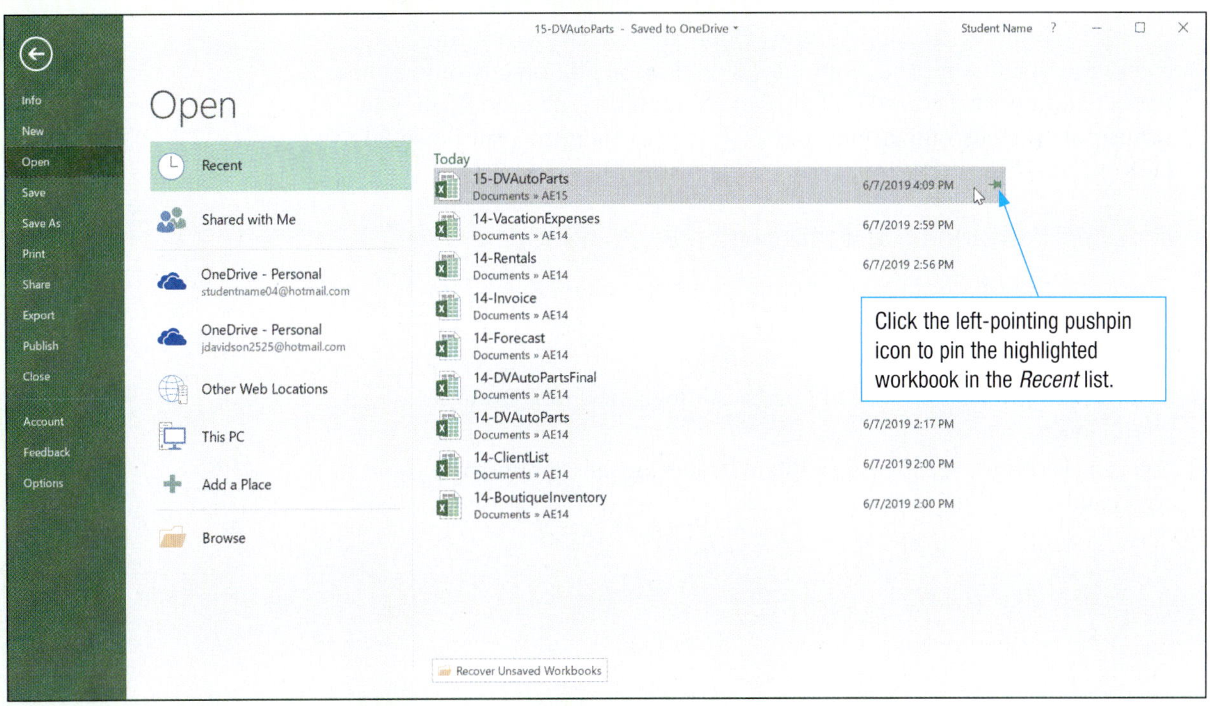

4. Click the pushpin.

   The workbook appears with a down-pointing pushpin icon in the *Pinned* section at the top of the *Recent* list.

5. Click the Back button.

15.2 Customizing the Ribbon

Tutorial

Exporting Customizations

Tabs and groups on the Excel ribbon make it easy to find and apply Excel features. You can customize the ribbon in your version of Excel by adding frequently used features to a custom group on an existing tab or by adding them to a custom group on a custom tab. You can copy these customizations to other computers—allowing you to make them available on all your devices and to share them with other users.

The Excel ribbon or Quick Access Toolbar may already have been customized on the computers in your institution's computer lab. (Customizing the Quick Access Toolbar is discussed in Section 15.3 of this chapter.) If that is the case, you will want to restore those customizations before you sign off a lab computer. You can save (export) ribbon and Quick Access Toolbar customizations and later reinstall (import) them. You will learn to export the settings in this section and how to import them in Section 15.16 of this chapter.

▸ **Know This** about exporting ribbon and Quick Access Toolbar customizations

— To save the current ribbon and Quick Access Toolbar settings in an export file, click the File tab, click the *Options* option, click the *Customize Ribbon* option in the left panel at the Excel Options dialog box, click the Import/Export button in the right panel, click the *Export all customizations* option at the drop-down list, and then click the Save button.

— Excel adds the file extension *.exportUI* to the export file name.

— Use the export file to import Excel ribbon and Quick Access Toolbar customizations to another computer. For example, if you customize the ribbon and Quick Access Toolbar on a computer in the school lab, you can export the customizations and then import them to your personal laptop or desktop.

▸ **Know This** about customizing the Excel ribbon

— The Excel ribbon displays commands in groups and displays groups on tabs (see Figure 15.5).

— Commands display as buttons or options.

— You can customize the Excel ribbon by adding a new tab, group, or command.

— You can also customize the Excel ribbon by moving tabs, groups, and commands.

Figure 15.5 Parts of a Ribbon

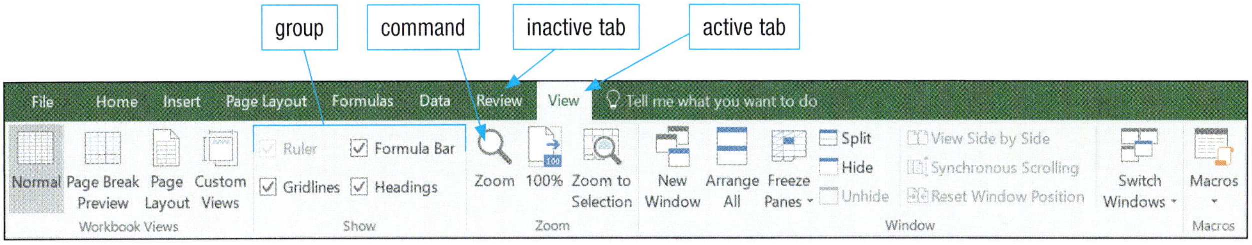

On the Job

Task 15.2a Exporting Customizations

Devon asks you to customize the Excel ribbon and Quick Access Toolbar to help him accomplish tasks more efficiently. Before you do that, you want to make a record of the existing settings, in case Devon wants to return to them at some point. Export the existing settings to a file called *15-ExcelCustomizations.exportUI*.

1. With the 15-DVAutoParts workbook open, click the File tab and then click the *Options* option in the left panel.

   The Excel Options dialog box displays (see Figure 15.6).

Figure 15.6 Excel Options Dialog Box with the *Customize Ribbon* Option Selected

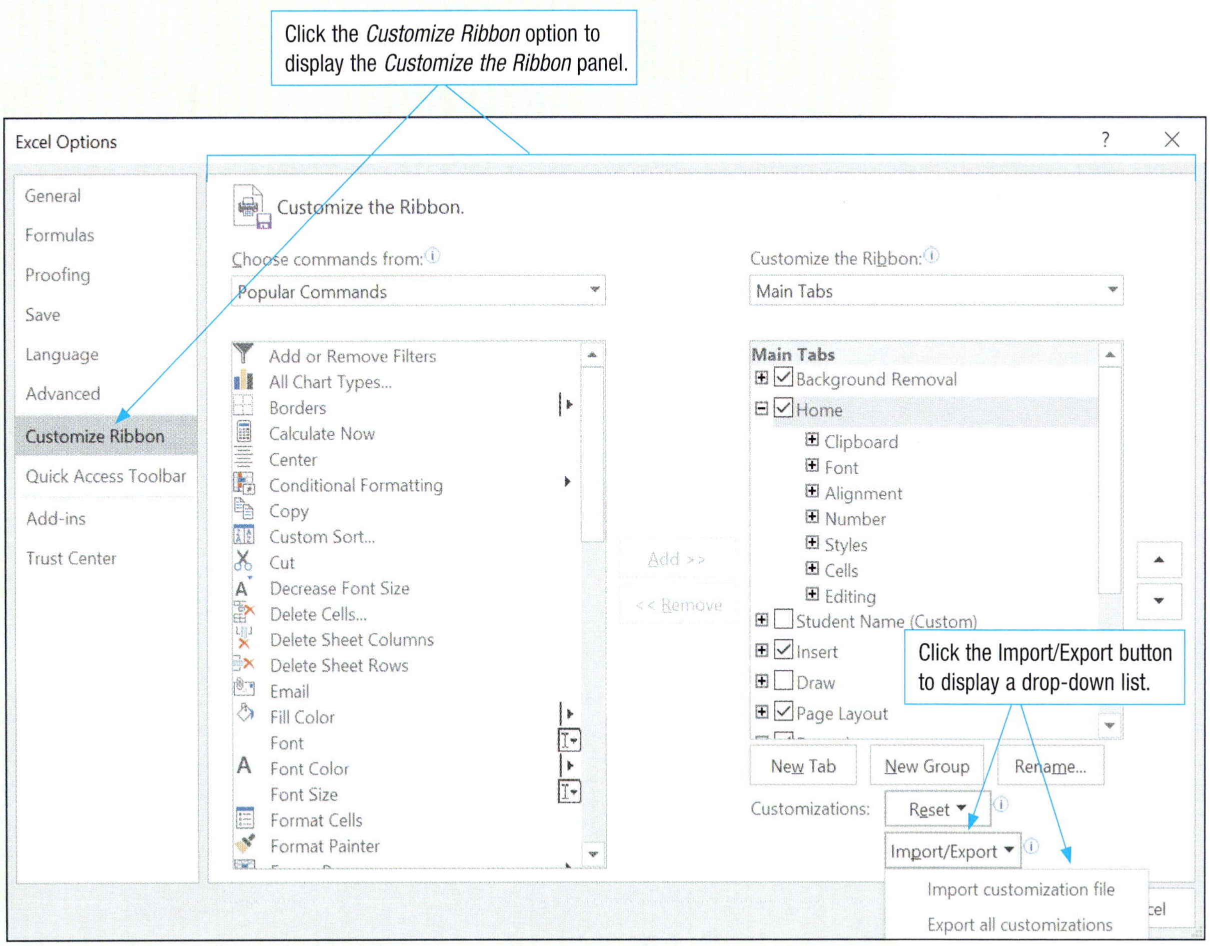

2. Click the *Customize Ribbon* option in the left panel.

   The *Customize the Ribbon* section displays in the right panel.
3. Click the Import/Export button.

   A drop-down list displays.
4. Click the *Export all customizations* option.

   The File Save dialog box displays.
5. Navigate to the AE15 folder on your storage medium.
6. Click in the *File name* text box, type 15-ExcelCustomizations, and then click the Save button.

   The File Save dialog box closes. The exported file is saved in the AE15 folder with the name *15-ExcelCustomizations.exportUI*. The Excel Options dialog box continues to display.
7. Click the OK button.

   The Excel Options dialog box closes. The 15-DVAutoParts workbook remains open.

▸ **Know This** about adding a custom tab and group

— You can add a custom tab and group to the right of an existing tab on the Excel ribbon.

— To add a custom tab and group to the Excel ribbon: click the File tab; click the *Options* option; click the *Customize Ribbon* option in the left panel at the Excel Options dialog box (see Figure 15.5 on page 745); click the *Customize the Ribbon* option box arrow in the right panel and then click an option at the drop-down list, if necessary; click the name of the existing tab that will be to the left of the custom tab in the *Customize the Ribbon* list box; and then click the New Tab button.

— The options available in the *Customize the Ribbon* list box depend on the option selected in the *Customize the Ribbon* option box. They may also vary depending on the version of Excel you are using.

— The options at the *Customize the Ribbon* option box drop-down list are *Main Tabs*, *All Tabs*, and *Tool Tabs* (see Figure 15.7). The *Main Tabs* option displays the tabs you see upon starting Excel. The *All Tabs* option adds the contextual tool tabs, such as the PivotTables Tools tab and the SmartArt Tools Design tab. The *Tool Tabs* option displays just the contextual tool tabs.

— When you add a custom tab, a custom group is added as well.

— The custom tab is positioned after the active tab.

▸ **Know This** about moving a tab or a group

— To move a tab or a group, click the name of the tab or group in the *Customize the Ribbon* list box and then click the Move Up button or Move Down button.

▸ **Know More** ways to add a custom tab and group

– Right-click a tab or group in the *Customize the Ribbon* list box in the *Customize the Ribbon* section at the Excel Options dialog box and then click the *Add New Tab* option or the *Add New Group* option at the pop-up menu.

▸ **Know More** ways to display the Excel Options dialog box with the *Customize the Ribbon* section active

– Right-click a tab on the Excel ribbon and then click the *Customize the Ribbon* option at the pop-up menu.

– Right-click the Quick Access Toolbar and then click the *Customize the Ribbon* option at the pop-up menu.

▸ **Know More** ways to move a tab or a group

– Right-click the name of the tab or group in the *Customize the Ribbon* list box and then click the *Move Up* option or *Move Down* option at the pop-up menu.

Figure 15.7 *Customize the Ribbon* Section at the Excel Options Dialog Box

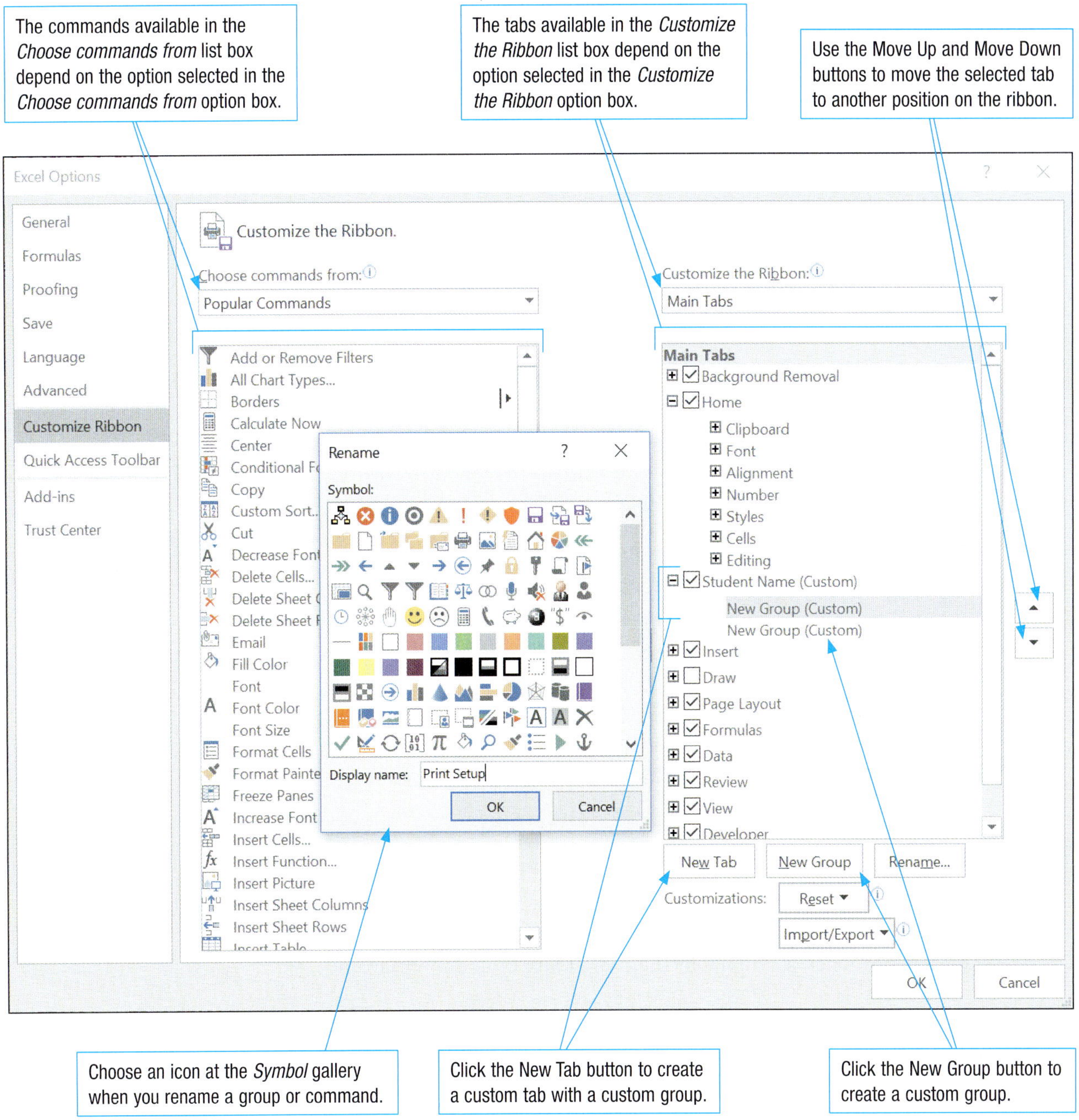

▸ Know This about adding a command

— You can add a command to a tab and group on the Excel ribbon.

— To add a command: click the File tab; click the *Options* option; click the *Customize Ribbon* option in the left panel at the Excel Options dialog box (see Figure 15.7); select the tab and group in the *Customize the Ribbon* list box in the right panel; click the *Choose commands from* option box arrow and then click an option at the drop-down list, if necessary; click the name of the command in the *Choose commands from* list box; and then click the Add button.

— The commands available in the *Choose commands from* list box depend on the selection in the *Choose commands from* option box.

- The options in the *Choose commands from* option box drop-down list are *Popular Commands*, *Commands Not in the Ribbon*, *All Commands*, *Macros*, *File Tab*, *All Tabs*, *Main Tabs*, *Tool Tabs*, and *Custom Tabs and Groups*.
- If a command is not available on any tab, click the *Commands Not in the Ribbon* option or *All Commands* option at the *Choose Commands from* option box drop-down list.
- The commands in the *Choose commands from* list box are organized in alphabetical order.

▶ **Know This** about renaming a tab, a group, or a command

- You can rename a tab or group in the original ribbon, but you cannot delete or modify the name or symbol associated with a command in the original ribbon.
- A command added to a custom or existing tab can be renamed.
- An optional symbol can be added to a tab or changed on a tab.
- To rename a tab, a group, or a command: display the Excel Options dialog box with the *Customize the Ribbon* section active; click the existing tab, group, or command name in the right panel; click the Rename button; type the new name to replace the highlighted name in the *Display name* text box at the Rename dialog box; select an icon at the *Symbol* gallery, if necessary; and then click the OK button.
- When you rename a tab, a group, or a command that already has a name, the Rename dialog box displays with a *Display name* text box.
- When you rename a custom group or a custom command, the Rename dialog box displays with the *Display name* text box and the *Symbol* gallery.
- An icon chosen at the *Symbol* gallery displays as a button on the ribbon, and the text entered at the *Display name* text box appears below the button icon.

▶ **Know More** ways to display the Rename dialog box

- Right-click the tab, group, or command name in the right panel at the Excel Options dialog box and then click the *Rename* option at the pop-up menu. If the *Rename* option does not appear in the pop-up menu, the command cannot be renamed.

▶ **Know This** about removing a tab, a group, or a command from the *Customize the Ribbon* list box

- To remove a tab, a group, or a command that you added to the *Customize the Ribbon* list box, click the name of the tab, group, or command in the list box and then click the Remove button.

▶ **Know More** ways to remove a custom tab, group, or command from the *Customize the Ribbon* list box

- Right-click the name of the tab, group, or command in the list box and then click the *Remove* option at the pop-up menu.

On the Job

Task 15.2b Customizing the Ribbon

Devon wants you to create a custom tab and add the Custom Margins, Page Setup, Print Preview and Print, and Print Preview Full Screen commands to a group named *Print Setup*. He also wants a second group called *Formatting* that contains the AutoFit Column Width, Clear Comments, and Clear Formats commands. He finds that he uses these commands frequently and wants quicker access to them. Customize the Excel ribbon by adding a custom tab and two custom groups and commands within the tab.

Note: *You will need the customizations applied in this task for the remaining tasks in the chapter. Customizations are applied to your current computer and may be removed from a shared computer (such as a lab computer) when you log off. If you need to change computers or log off a shared computer at any time during this* *chapter, follow the instructions in Task 15.2a to export the customized settings to a file called* AE15Cust.exportUI *and save the export file in the AE15 folder on your storage medium. Before continuing your Chapter 15 work on another computer, follow the instructions in Task 15.16 to import the AE15Cust.exportUI file into the other computer.*

1. With the 15-DVAutoParts workbook open and either worksheet active, click the Home tab, if necessary, click the File tab, and then click the *Options* option.

   The Excel Options dialog box displays (see Figure 15.7 on page 747).

2. Click the *Customize Ribbon* option in the left panel.

   The *Customize the Ribbon* section displays in the right panel. The *Home* option is selected in the *Customize the Ribbon* list box because the Home tab is active in the workbook.

3. Click the New Tab button in the right panel.

   The *New Tab (Custom)* option appears below the *Home* option in the *Customize the Ribbon* list box. The *New Group (Custom)* option appears below the new tab option and is selected. The new tab will display between the Home tab and the Insert tab on the ribbon.

4. Click the New Group button.

   A second *New Group (Custom)* option appears below the first one. The second new group will display on the same tab to the right of the first new group.

5. Click the *New Tab (Custom)* option in the *Customize the Ribbon* list box and then click the Rename button.

   The Rename dialog box displays with the *Display name* text box. The text *New Tab* is selected in the text box.

6. Type your first and last names and then click the OK button.

   The new tab option displays as *[Your Name] (Custom)* in the list box. The new tab will display with your name on the ribbon.

7. Click the first *New Group (Custom)* option and then click the Rename button.

   The Rename dialog box displays with the *Symbol* gallery and the *Display name* text box.

8. Type Print Setup and then click the OK button.

   The first custom group option displays as *Print Setup (Custom)* in the list box. The first new group will display with the name *Print Setup* on the ribbon. No symbol will be associated with the custom group.

9. Click the second *New Group (Custom)* option, click the Rename button, type Formatting, and then click the OK button.

   The second new group option displays as *Formatting (Custom)* in the list box. The second new group will display with the name *Formatting* on the ribbon.

10. Click the *Print Setup (Custom)* option in the *Customize the Ribbon* list box.

11. Click the *Choose commands from* option box arrow (displays as *Popular Commands*) and then click the *All Commands* option at the drop-down list (see Figure 15.8).

    All Excel commands appear in alphabetical order in the *Choose commands from* list box.

Figure 15.8 *Choose Commands from* Drop-Down List

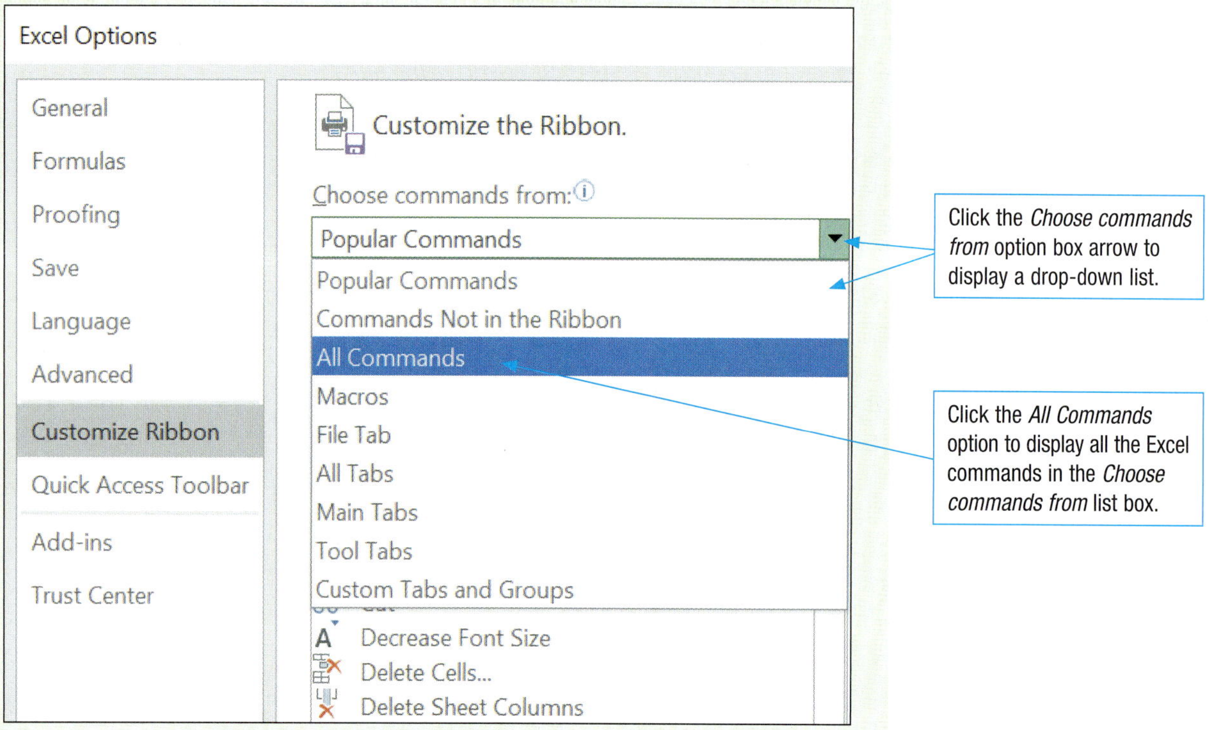

12. Scroll down the *Choose commands from* list box, click the *Custom Margins* option, and then click the Add button.

    The *Custom Margins* option appears under the *Print Setup (Custom)* option in the *Customize the Ribbon* list box, and the *Custom Margins* option is selected and has a blue circle icon. The Custom Margins button will appear as a blue circle in the Print Setup group on the tab with your name.

13. Click the Rename button, click the paper-with-a-folded-corner icon (second column, second row; see Figure 15.7), and then click the OK button.

    The icon for the Custom Margins command changes from a blue circle to a piece of paper with a folded corner.

14. Scroll down the *Choose commands from* list box, click the *Page Setup* option, and then click the Add button.
15. Repeat Step 14 to add the Print Preview and Print command and the Print Preview Full Screen command, in that order, to the Print Setup group.
16. Click the Formatting (Custom) option in the *Customize the Ribbon* list box and then repeat Step 14 to add the AutoFit Column Width, Clear Comments, and Clear Formats commands. ***Hint:*** *Scroll up the Choose commands from list box to find the AutoFit Column Width command.*
17. Add the green right-pointing double arrow icon (first column, third row at the *Symbol* gallery) to the AutoFit Column Width command, and add the eraser icon (sixth column, eleventh row) to the Clear Comments button. ***Hint:*** *Use the Rename button in the right panel of the* Customize the Ribbon *section at the Excel Options dialog box to add the icons. Scroll down to find the eraser icon.*

18. Click the OK button.

    The Excel Options dialog box closes.

19. Click the [Your Name] tab on the Excel ribbon.

    The new tab displays with the new groups and commands (see Figure 15.9).

20. If you need to leave the computer before starting the next task, export the customized settings to a file called *AE15Cust.exportUI* and save the export file in the AE15 folder on your storage medium. Before continuing your Chapter 15 work on another computer, follow the instructions in Task 15.16 to import the AE15Cust.exportUI file into the other computer.

Figure 15.9 New Tab with New Groups and Commands

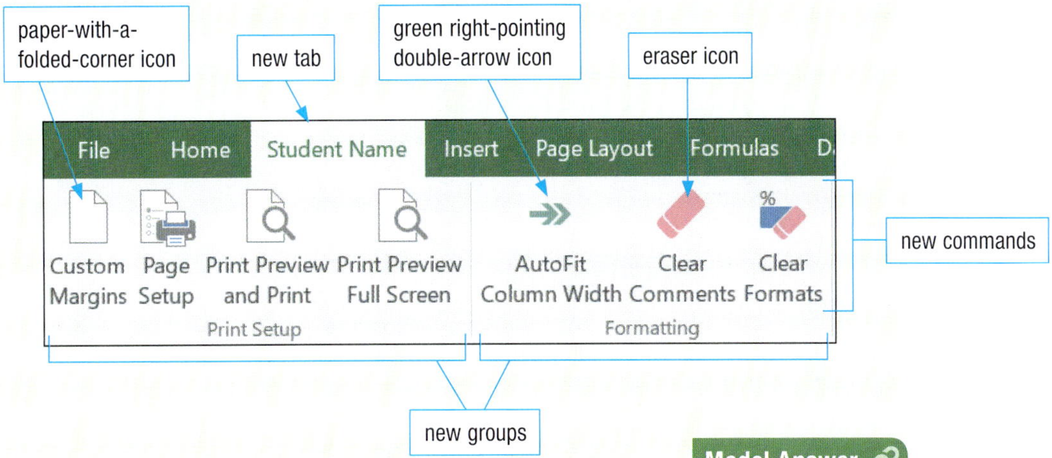

Model Answer

15.3 Customizing the Quick Access Toolbar

MOS 1.4.3

Tutorial

Customizing the Quick Access Toolbar

The Quick Access Toolbar contains a set of commands that are independent of the groupings on the active tab and display no matter what tab is active. This toolbar can be customized to display Excel commands that you use frequently so that you can access them quickly. By default, the Quick Access Toolbar displays above the Excel ribbon, but you can move it to display below the ribbon.

▸ **Know This** about adding a command to the Quick Access Toolbar

— To add a command to the Quick Access Toolbar, click the Customize Quick Access Toolbar button (see Figure 15.10 on page 753) and then click the command option at the drop-down list to display a check mark before the option.

— If the option for the command you want to add does not appear at the Customize Quick Access Toolbar button drop-down list: click the *More Options* option at the drop-down list; click the *Choose commands from* option box arrow in the *Customize the Quick Access Toolbar* section at the Excel Options dialog box and click an option at the drop-down list, if necessary; and then double-click the command option in the *Choose commands from* list box.

▸ **Know More** ways to display the Excel Options dialog box with the *Customize the Quick Access Toolbar* section active

- Right-click the Quick Access Toolbar and then click the *Customize the Quick Access Toolbar* option at the drop-down list.
- Right-click a tab on the Excel ribbon and then click the *Customize the Quick Access Toolbar* option at the drop-down menu.

— The options in the *Choose commands from* option box drop-down list and list box in the *Customize the Quick Access Toolbar* section are the same as in the *Customize the Ribbon* section (see Section 15.2).
— When you double-click a command option in the *Choose commands from* list box, the command option appears in the *Customize the Quick Access Toolbar* list box.
— The options available in the *Customize the Quick Access Toolbar* list box depend on the option selected in the *Customize* the *Quick Access Toolbar* option box.

▸ **Know More** ways to add a command to the *Customize the Quick Access Toolbar* list box
– Click the name of the command in the *Choose commands from* list box and then click the Add button.

▸ **Know This** about removing a command from the Quick Access Toolbar

— To remove a command from the Quick Access Toolbar, click the Customize Quick Access Toolbar button and then click the command option at the drop-down list to remove the check mark.
— If the command you want to remove does not appear at the Customize Quick Access Toolbar button drop-down list, click the *More Commands* option at the drop-down list and then click the command option to remove the check mark before it in the *Customize the Quick Access Toolbar* list box in the *Customize the Quick Access Toolbar* section at the Excel Options dialog box.

▸ **Know More** ways to remove a command from the *Customize the Quick Access Toolbar* list box
– Click the command option in the *Customize the Quick Access Toolbar* list box and then click the Remove button.
– Double-click the command option in the *Customize the Quick Access Toolbar* list box.

▸ **Know This** about rearranging commands on the Quick Access Toolbar

— To move a command on the Quick Access Toolbar, click the Customize Quick Access Toolbar button, click the *More Commands* option at the drop-down list, click the command in the *Customize the Quick Access Toolbar* list box in the *Customize the Quick Access Toolbar* section at the Excel Options dialog box, and then use the Move Up and Move Down buttons.

On the Job

Task 15.3 Customizing the Quick Access Toolbar

Devon asks you to help him customize his version of Excel so he can quickly create a new workbook. You suggest adding the New command and the Screen Clipping command to the Quick Access Toolbar, but Devon says he never uses the toolbar because it sits above the ribbon and he forgets it's there. Give Devon a good solution by adding the New command and the Screen Clipping command to the Quick Access Toolbar and then positioning the toolbar below the ribbon, where Devon is more likely to see it.

1. With the 15-DVAutoParts workbook open and either worksheet active, click the Customize Quick Access Toolbar button (see Figure 15.10).
   A drop-down list displays.
2. Click the *New* option at the drop-down list.
   The New button is added at the right end of the Quick Access Toolbar.
3. Click the Customize Quick Access Toolbar button and then click the *More Commands* option at the drop-down list.
   The Excel Options dialog box opens with the *Quick Access Toolbar* option selected in the left panel.

Figure 15.10 Customize Quick Access Toolbar Button Drop-Down List

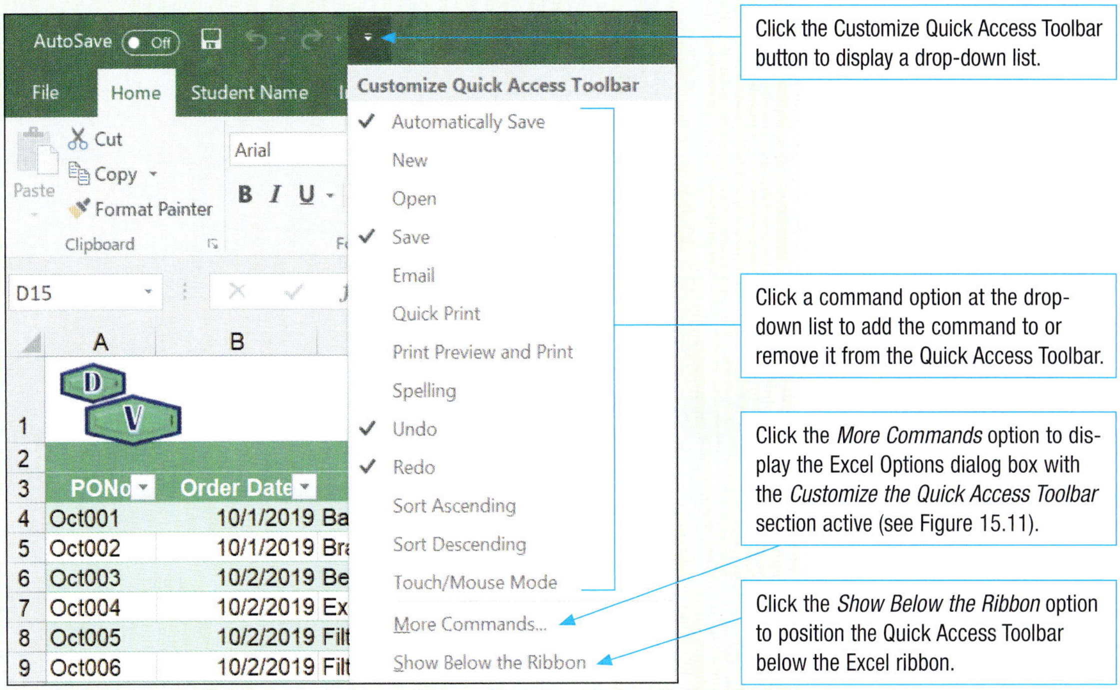

4. Click the *Choose commands from* option box arrow in the right panel and then click the *All Commands* option at the drop-down list.

   All Excel commands appear in alphabetical order in the *Choose commands from* list box.

5. Scroll down the *Choose commands from* list box and then double-click the *Screen Clipping* option (see Figure 15.11).

   The command option appears in the *Customize Quick Access Toolbar* list box.

Figure 15.11 *Customize the Quick Access Toolbar* Section at the Excel Options Dialog Box

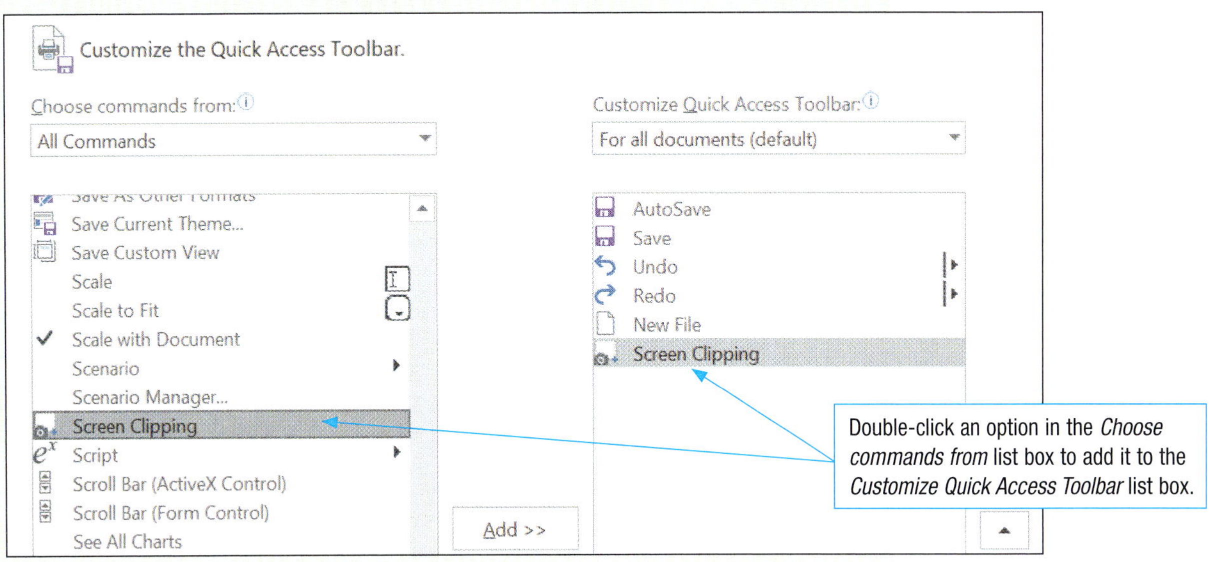

6. Click the OK button.

   The Excel Options dialog box closes and the Screen Clipping button appears at the right side of the Quick Access Toolbar.

7. Click the Customize Quick Access Toolbar button and then click the *Show Below the Ribbon* option.

   The Quick Access Toolbar displays below the ribbon (see Figure 15.12).

Figure 15.12 Custom Quick Access Toolbar Displayed Below the Ribbon

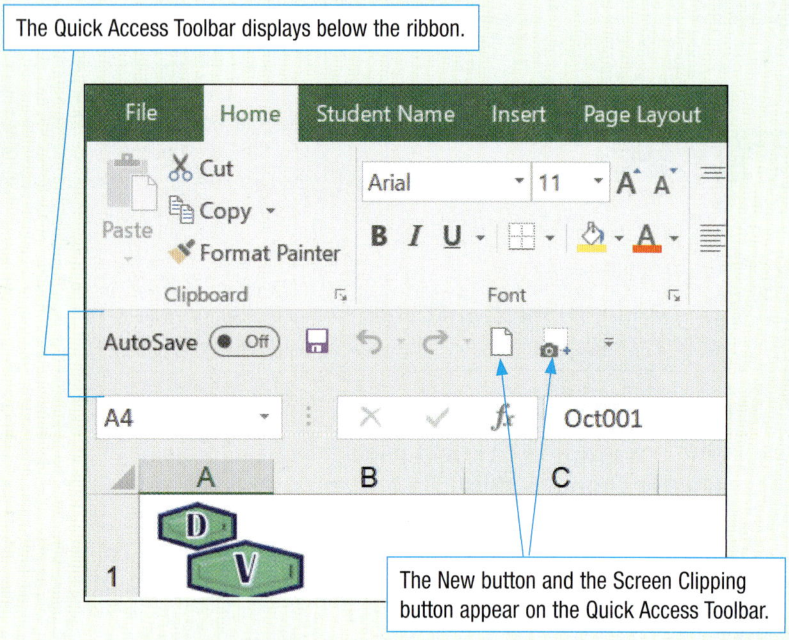

8. If you need to leave the computer before starting the next task, export the customized settings to a file called *AE15Cust.exportUI* and save the export file in the AE15 folder on your storage medium. Before continuing your Chapter 15 work on another computer, follow the instructions in Task 15.16 to import the AE15Cust.exportUI file into the other computer.

Model Answer

15.4 Hiding and Unhiding Ribbon Tabs

MOS Expert 1.1.6

Tutorial

Unhiding a Ribbon Tab

By default, Excel displays only the most commonly used tabs on the ribbon. The Draw tab and the Developer tab are hidden. You can unhide these tabs or hide any of the other tabs that you do not use.

The Draw tab contains commands you can use to choose different pens for writing on the active worksheet. It also offers a command you can use to open the Math Input Control dialog box, where you can write an equation using math symbols such as pi (π), which Excel converts into a typed equation (see Figure 15.13). The Developer tab contains commands used with macros and XML data (see Section 15.7 through Section 15.15).

Figure 15.13 Ribbon with the Draw Tab Active, the Developer Tab Available, and the Add-Ins Tab Hidden

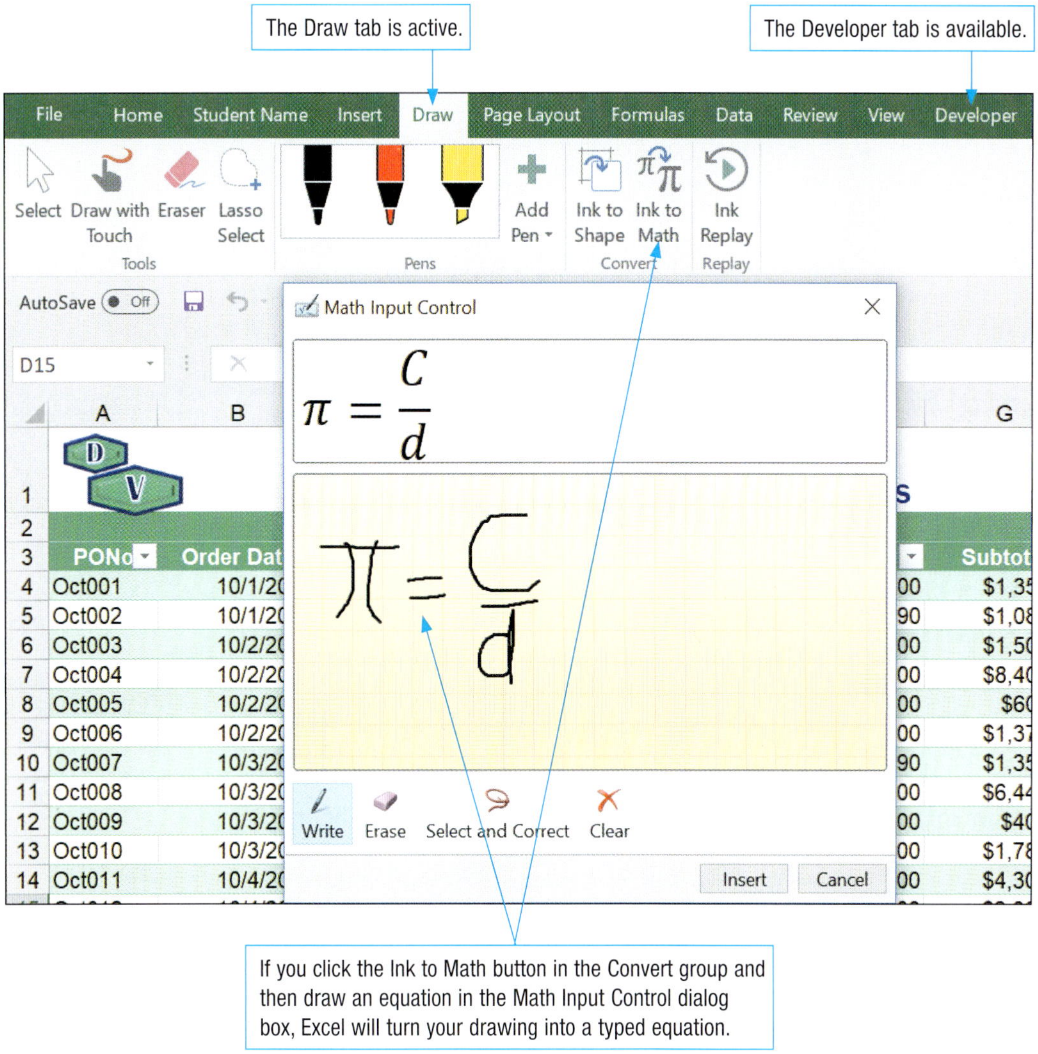

▸ **Know This** about hiding and unhiding ribbon tabs

— To unhide a ribbon tab, click the File tab, click the *Options* option, click the *Customize Ribbon* option in the left panel at the Excel Options dialog box, and then click the tab check box to insert a check mark in the *Customize the Ribbon* list box in the *Customize the Ribbon* section.

— To hide a ribbon tab, click the check box to remove the check mark in the *Customize the Ribbon* list box.

On the Job

Task 15.4 Unhiding a Ribbon Tab

Devon has mentioned that he always adjusts the layout in the 15-Invoice workbook to center the Invoice worksheet horizontally and scale it to fit on one page when printed. You decide to create a macro to help him with this. To work with macros, you will need the Developer tab, which is hidden by default. Unhide the Developer tab in your version of Excel.

1. With any workbook open click the File tab and then click the *Options* option.

   The Excel Options dialog box displays.

2. Click the *Customize Ribbon* option in the left panel.

   The *Customize the Ribbon* section displays in the right panel.

3. Click the *Developer* check box in the *Customize the Ribbon* list box.

   A check mark appears in the check box.

4. Click the OK button.

   The Excel Options dialog box closes and the Developer tab displays to the right of the View tab on the Excel ribbon.

5. If you need to leave the computer before starting the next task, export the customized settings to a file called *AE15Cust.exportUI* and save the export file in the AE15 folder on your storage medium. Before continuing your Chapter 15 work on another computer, follow the instructions in Task 15.16 to import the AE15Cust.exportUI file into the other computer.

15.5 Inserting a Screenshot or a Screen Clipping

Tutorial

Inserting a Screen Clipping in a New Workbook

Excel provides tools that allow you to quickly insert a screenshot or a screen clipping of an open window in a worksheet. A **screenshot** takes a picture of the entire screen, and a **screen clipping** captures part of a screen. Screenshots and screen clippings are useful for capturing an image of another open workbook, a Word document, or a browser window and inserting it into a workbook. For example, you could capture an image showing loan interest rate trends from a website and insert the image into a worksheet that contains data and formulas for calculating costs for financing the purchase of new equipment.

▸ Know This about inserting a screenshot of an open window

— A screenshot of a window shows the entire window.

— You can capture a screenshot of any open window.

— To insert a screenshot of an open window in an active worksheet, click the Screenshot button in the Illustrations group on the Insert tab and then click the thumbnail image of the open Excel window you want to capture at the *Available Windows* drop-down gallery.

— The *Available Windows* drop-down gallery displays all the windows you currently have open.

▸ Know This about inserting a screen clipping of an open window

— A screen clipping of a window shows just part of the window.

— You can capture a screen clipping of the last open window that was active.

— To insert a screen clipping of an open window in an active worksheet, make the window you want to capture active, make the worksheet active, click the Screenshot button in the Illustrations group on the Insert tab and then click the *Screen Clipping* option at the drop-down gallery, wait for the last active window to display with a white haze and the mouse pointer to turn into a black crosshairs, position the pointer at one corner of the part of the window to be captured, click and hold down the left mouse button, drag to select the part of the window, and then release the mouse button.

▸ Know This about editing a screenshot or a screen clipping

— To edit a screenshot or a screen clipping after inserting it, select the screenshot or screen clipping and then use tools on the Picture Tools Format tab.

On the Job

Task 15.5 Inserting a Screen Clipping in a New Workbook

Devon is a member of a group of small-business owners who meet monthly to share ideas for running a successful business. At the group's next meeting, Devon wants to show a screen clipping of the customizations you made to his Excel ribbon and Quick Access Toolbar. Insert a screen clipping of the customized ribbon and Quick Access Toolbar in a new workbook and then save the new workbook with a name that identifies its contents.

1. With the 15-DVAutoParts workbook open and the Orders worksheet active, click the [Your Name] tab.

   The [Your Name] tab is active.
2. Click the New button on the Quick Access Toolbar.

   A new Excel workbook opens.
3. Click the Screen Clipping button on the Quick Access Toolbar.

   The Customers worksheet in the 15-DVAutoParts workbook is active with a white haze over it in the Excel window, and the mouse pointer displays as a black crosshairs.
4. Position the crosshairs at the upper left corner of the Excel window, click and hold down the left mouse button, draw a box that captures the entire ribbon and the Quick Access Toolbar (see Figure 15.14), and then release the mouse button.

Reminder
The Screen Clipping button was added to the Quick Access Toolbar in Task 15.3.

Figure 15.14 Open Excel Window with the Screen-Clipped Area Drawn

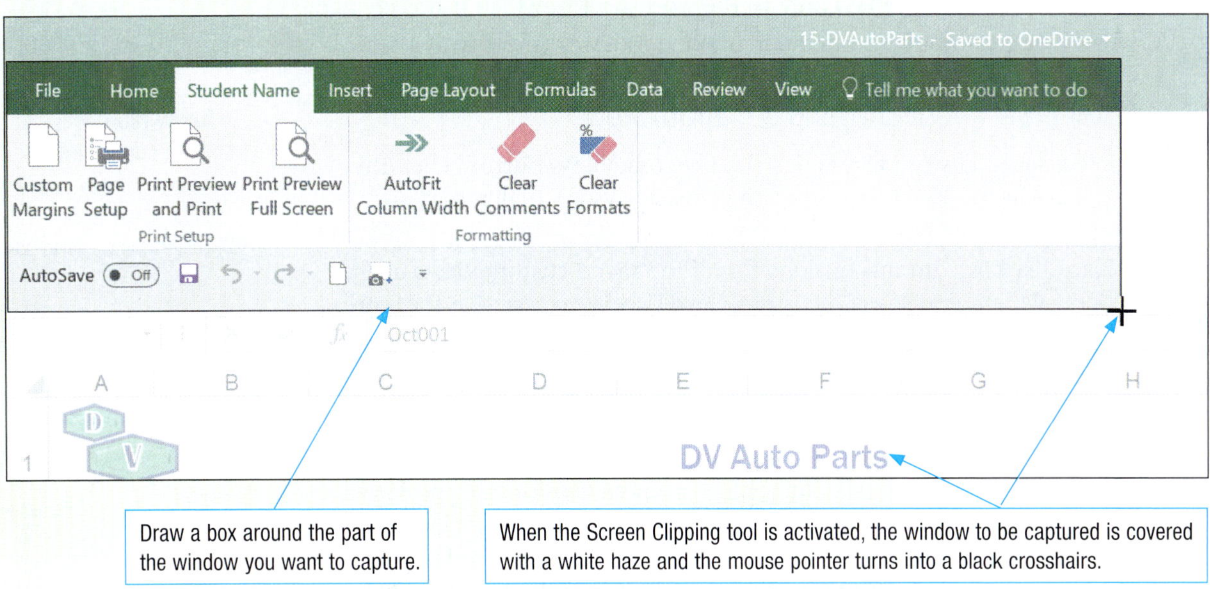

5. Click the Save button on the Quick Access Toolbar.
6. Navigate to the AE15 folder on your storage medium and then save the workbook, typing 15-RibbonQAT as the file name.
7. Close the 15-RibbonQAT workbook. Leave the 15-DVAutoParts workbook open for the next task.
8. If you need to leave the computer before starting the next task, export the customized settings to a file called *AE15Cust.exportUI* and save the export file in the AE15 folder on your storage medium. Before continuing your Chapter 15 work on another computer, follow the instructions in Task 15.16 to import the AE15Cust.exportUI file into the other computer.

Model Answer

15.6 Creating, Showing, and Deleting Custom Views

A **custom view** saves display and print settings for the active worksheet. These settings can involve column widths, row heights, hidden rows and/or columns, filter settings, cell selects, windows settings, page layout options, and print areas. For example, you might create and use a custom view to quickly display only the sales data for a particular week and hide the data for other weeks.

Tutorial

Creating and Deleting a Custom View

▸ Know This about creating custom views

— You can create multiple custom views for the same worksheet.

— To create a custom view for a worksheet, apply the required settings to the active worksheet, click the Custom Views button in the Workbook Views group on the View tab, click the Add button, type a name for the custom view in the *Name* text box at the Add View dialog box, and then click the OK button.

— After adjusting the worksheet to display the information to be included in the view, adjust the worksheet so the data you need is visible in the window. For example, press Ctrl + Home to make cell A1 active and show the top left portion of the worksheet.

— A custom view can be applied only to the worksheet in which it was created.

— A custom view cannot be created and applied to a worksheet with a table.

▸ Know This about showing a custom view

— To show a saved custom view, click the Custom Views button, click the view option in the *Views* list box at the Custom Views dialog box, and then click the Show button.

— The *Views* list box contains options for all the saved custom views in the workbook. When you select a custom view, Excel makes active the worksheet to which the view applies.

▸ Know More ways to show a custom view

- Double-click the view option in the *Views* list box at the Custom Views dialog box.

▸ Know This about deleting a custom view

— To delete a custom view, click the Custom Views button in the Workbook Views group on the View tab, click the custom view option in the *Views* list box at the Custom Views dialog box, and then click the Delete button, click the Yes button at the message box that asks whether you wish to delete the view, and then click the Close button at the dialog box.

On the Job

Task 15.6 Creating, Showing, and Deleting Custom Views

Devon periodically needs to display the orders for the first seven days in October as he prepares for upcoming meetings. He asks you to set up the 15-DVAutoParts workbook so he can do that easily and quickly. He also asks you to delete any previously created custom views. Use custom filters to create the custom view and then delete any previously created custom views.

1. With the 15-DVAutoParts workbook open and the Orders worksheet active, click the *Order Date* filter arrow in cell B3, point to the *Date Filters* option at the drop-down list, and then click the *Between* option at the second drop-down list.

   The Custom AutoFilter dialog box displays (see Figure 15.15). The text *is after or equal to* appears in the upper left option box, the *And* radio button contains a bullet, and the text *is before or equal to* appears in the lower left option box.

2. Click the upper right option box arrow and then click the *10/1/2019* option at the drop-down list.

   The date *10/1/2019* displays in the upper right option box.

Figure 15.15 Custom AutoFilter Dialog Box

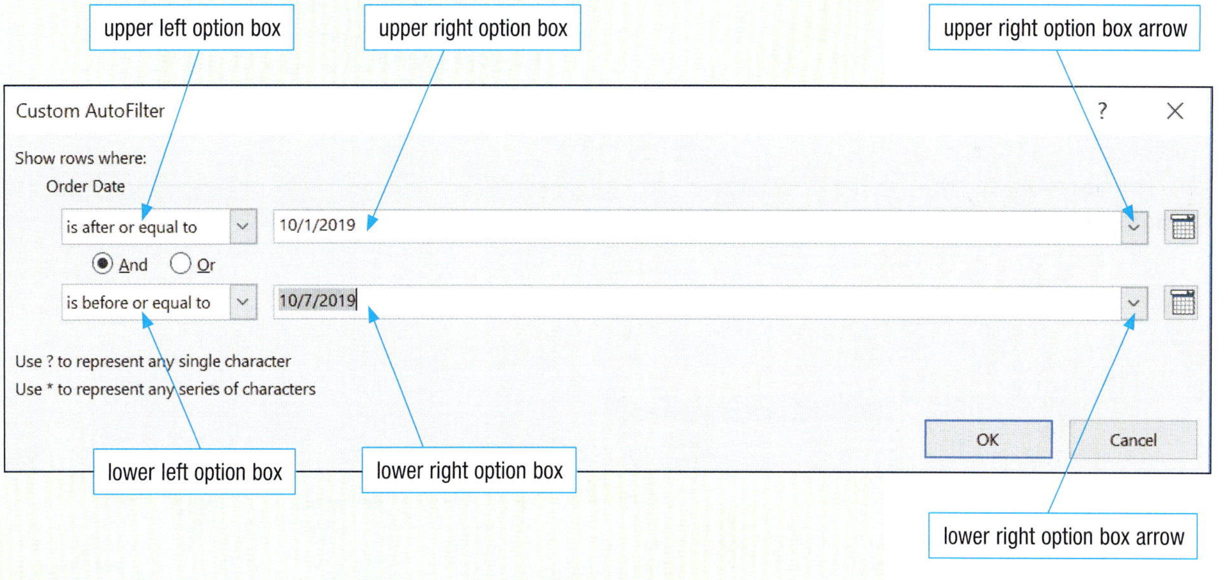

3. Click the lower right option box arrow, click the *10/7/2019* option at the drop-down list, and then click the OK button.

   The dialog box closes. The range A4:J36 in the worksheet filters to display the orders between October 1 and October 7, which is the range you selected for the FirstWeek custom view.

4. Press Ctrl + Home.

   Cell A1 is active.

5. Click the View tab, if necessary, and then click the Custom Views button in the Workbook Views group.

   The Custom Views dialog box displays.

6. Click the Add button.

   The Add View dialog box displays with the insertion point in the *Name* text box (see Figure 15.16).

Figure 15.16 Add View Dialog Box

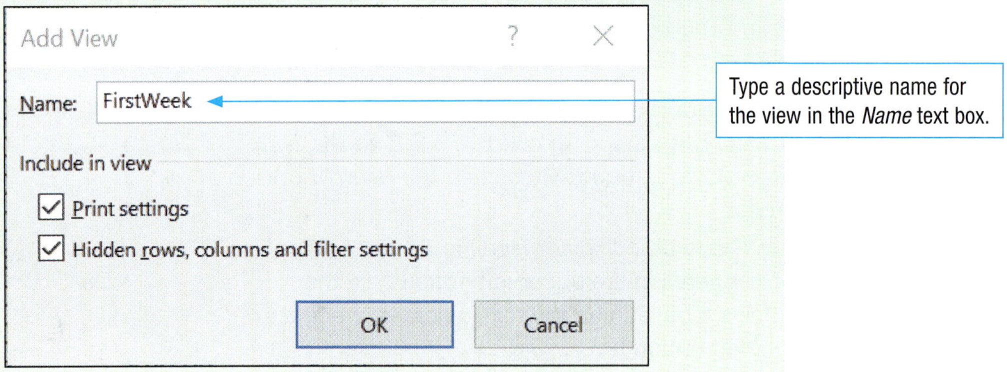

7. Type FirstWeek and then click the OK button.

   The dialog box closes.

8. Click the Custom Views button.

   The Custom Views dialog box displays with the *FirstWeek* option in the *Views* list box selected.

9. Click the *Wes Cortez - Personal View* option (see Figure 15.17) and then click the Show button.

   The Customers worksheet is active and the insertion point is in cell G5.

Figure 15.17 Custom Views Dialog Box

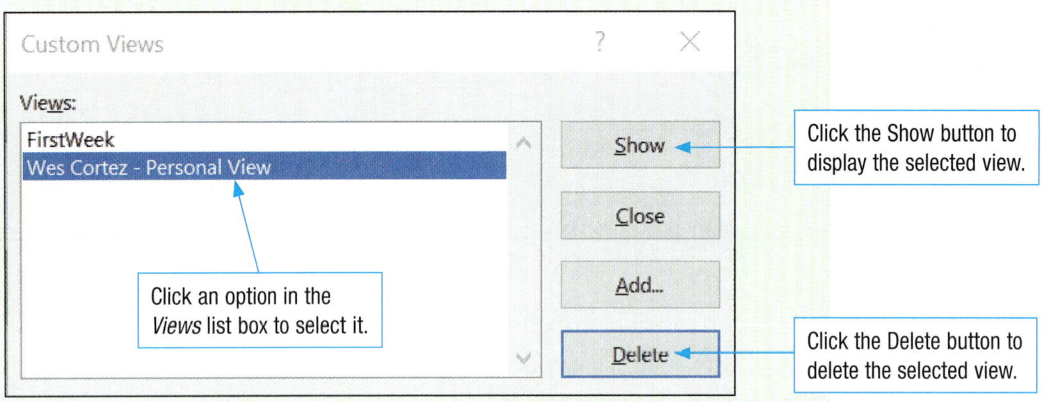

10. Click the Custom Views button and then click the *Wes Cortez - Personal View* option.

11. Click the Delete button.

    A message box displays, asking if you wish to delete the view.

12. Click the Yes button.

    The message box closes. The view is deleted from the *Views* list box. The *FirstWeek* view option is selected.

13. Click the Show button.

    The Orders worksheet is active and the *Order Date* column is filtered to show the first seven days of October.

14. Click the Save button on the Quick Access Toolbar and then close the workbook.
15. If you need to leave the computer before starting the next task, export the customized settings to a file called *AE15Cust.exportUI* and save the export file in the AE15 folder on your storage medium. Before continuing your Chapter 15 work on another computer, follow the instructions in Task 15.16 to import the AE15Cust.exportUI file into the other computer.

Model Answer

15.7 Recording a Simple Macro and Saving a Macro-Enabled Workbook

MOS Expert 2.3.4

Tutorial

Recording a Simple Macro and Saving the Workbook

A **macro** is a set of steps stored in sequence that can be run whenever the need arises. Create a macro to automate a task that is performed repeatedly without variation. For example, you might create a macro to change the page orientation to landscape and set custom left and right margins at 1.0 inch. Creating a macro not only saves time but also ensures that the steps will be performed consistently every time. Using macros can help prevent errors in data entry, formatting, and other worksheet tasks. A workbook that contains a macro is saved using the macro-enabled file format (with the file extension *.xlsm*).

▸ Know This about planning a macro

— Before creating a macro, plan the steps that are needed to perform a task.

— If the macro must start with a particular cell active, the first step of the macro should use a keyboard shortcut or the Go To command to move to that cell. For example, if the macro must start with cell A1 active, the first step of the macro should be pressing Ctrl + Home.

— Consider creating two macros instead of one macro if numerous steps need to be completed.

— Some actions cannot be performed in a macro. For example, you cannot end a macro in Print Preview view because the Stop Recording button does not display in that view.

▸ Know This about recording a macro

— **Recording a macro** involves turning on the recorder, completing the steps that are to be run whenever the task needs to be performed, and then stopping the recorder.

— To record a macro: click the Macros button in the Code group on the Developer tab (see Figure 15.18); enter a name, keyboard shortcut (demonstrated in Task 15.8), storage location, and description at the Record Macro dialog box (see Figure 15.19); click the OK button; complete the steps for the task; and then click the Stop Recording button on the Status bar (see Figure 15.20).

Reminder

The Developer tab is hidden by default. (See Section 15.4 for instructions on unhiding a tab.)

— When you record a macro, Excel saves each step you take. If you make a mistake, you can correct it without stopping the recording because Excel will save the steps you take to make the correction.

— After you record a macro in a workbook, the Start Recording button appears on the Status bar. You can use that button to record additional macros.

▶ **Know More** ways to record a macro

- Click the Macros button in the Macros group on the View tab and then click the *Record Macro* option at the drop-down list.
- Click the Start Recording button that appears on the Status bar after a macro has been recorded in the workbook.

Figure 15.18 Code Group on the Developer Tab

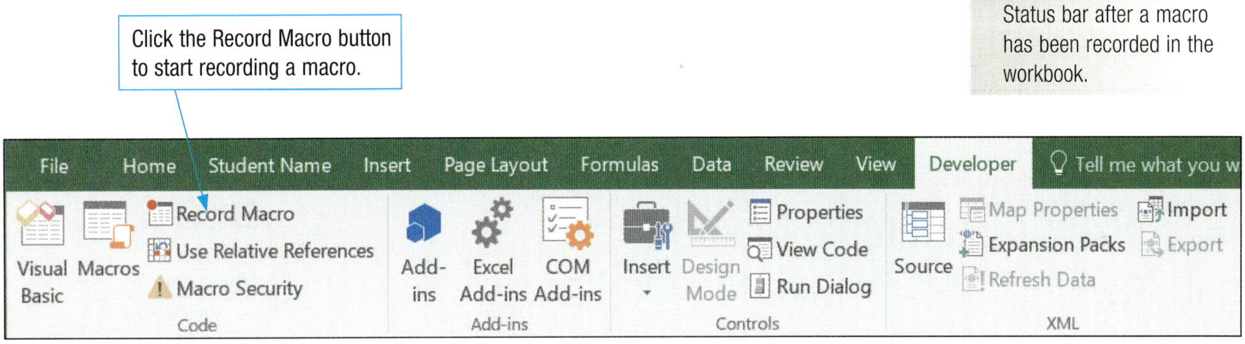

Figure 15.19 Record Macro Dialog Box

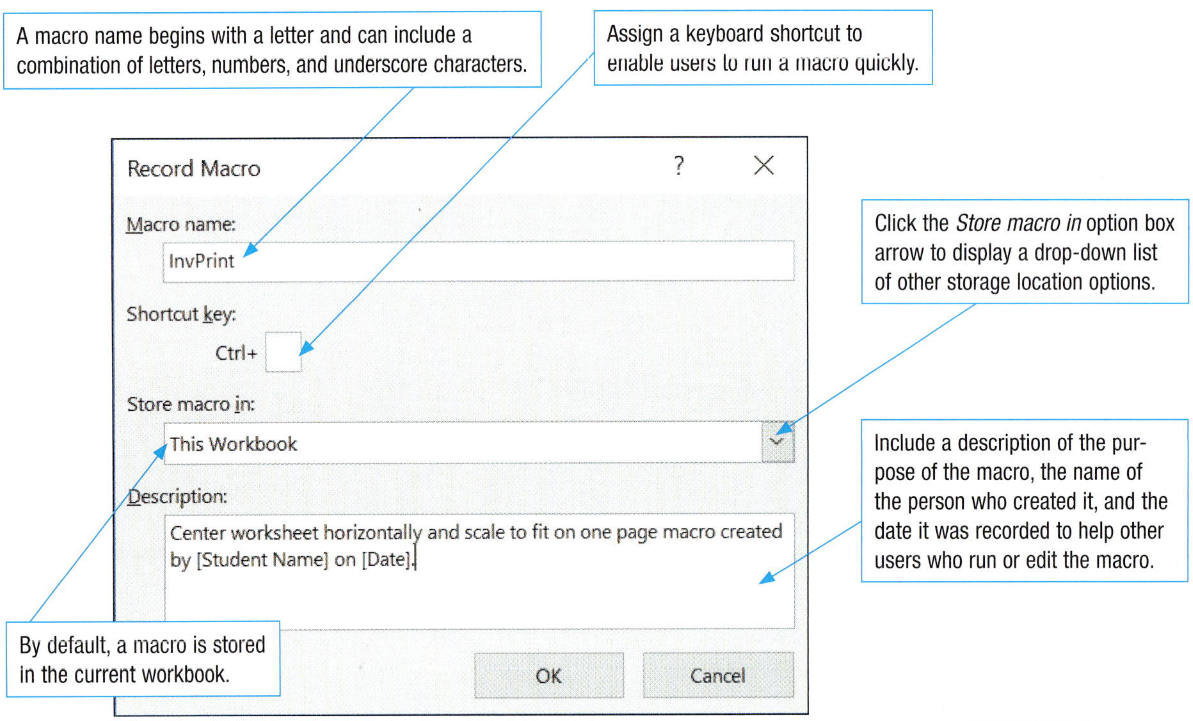

Figure 15.20 Stop Recording Button on the Status Bar

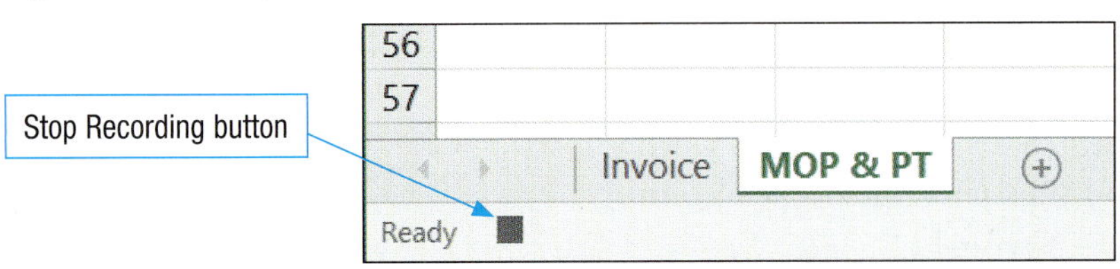

▶ **Know More** ways to stop recording a macro

- Click the Macros button in the Macros group on the View tab and then click the *Stop Recording* option at the drop-down list.
- Click the Stop Recording button in the Code group on the Developer tab.

▶ Know This about naming a macro

— A macro name must begin with a letter and can be a combination of letters, numbers, and underscore characters.
— A macro name cannot include spaces; use the underscore character to separate the words in a macro name.
— Each macro has to have a unique macro name.

▶ Know This about storing a macro

— By default, a macro is stored in the workbook in which it is created.
— You can store a macro in the default location, in a personal macro workbook, or in a new workbook.
— To change the location in which a macro is stored, click the *Store macro in* option box arrow at the Record Macro dialog box and then select an option at the drop-down list (see Figure 15.19 on page 762).
— If you select the *Personal Macro Workbook* option in the Store macro at the drop-down list, Excel will create a hidden workbook called *Personal* and save macros in it. This hidden workbook is called a **personal macro workbook**.
— Your personal macro workbook is saved in the location C:\Users\user name\AppData\Local\Microsoft\Excel\XLStart.
— Your personal macro workbook opens whenever Excel starts, and the macros stored in the personal workbook are available to any workbook.

▶ Know This about adding a macro description

— In a workbook that is being shared, the description should include the purpose of the macro, the name of the person who created it, and the date it was recorded in the *Description* text box at the Record Macro dialog box.

▶ Know This about macros and Microsoft Visual Basic for Applications

— When a macro is created in Excel, the commands are written and saved in the **Microsoft Visual Basic for Applications (VBA)** programming language.
— The default Excel file has the extension *.xlsx* and is an XML-based format that cannot store VBA code.
— To save the VBA code with the workbook, you need to save the workbook as a macro-enabled file, which has the extension *.xlsm*.
— VBA code can be viewed, edited, and debugged in the Visual Basic Editor, which can be opened from Excel.

▶ Know More about VBA

– VBA is available in all Office applications.

▶ Know This about saving a new workbook containing a macro

— To save a new workbook containing a macro, click the Save button on the Quick Access Toolbar, click the *Browse* option, navigate to the appropriate folder, type the file name, click the *Save as type* option box arrow, click the *Excel Macro-Enabled Workbook (*.xlsm)* option, and then click the Save button.

▶ Know This about saving an Excel workbook containing a macro

— To save an Excel workbook containing a macro, click the File tab, click the *Save As* option, click the *Browse* option in the middle panel at the Save As backstage area, click the save-as-type option box arrow in the right panel, click the *Excel Macro-Enabled Workbook (*.xlsm)* option at the drop-down list, and then click the Save button.

▶ Know More ways to save an Excel workbook containing a macro

- Click the Save button on the Quick Access Toolbar, click the No button, click the *Save as type* option box arrow, click the *Excel Macro-Enabled Workbook (*.xlsm)* option, and then click the Save button.
- Click the File tab, click the *Export* option, click the *Change File Type* option in the middle panel at the Export backstage area, and then click the *Macro-Enabled Workbook (*.xlsm)* option in the right panel.

On the Job

Task 15.7 Recording a Simple Macro and Saving the Workbook

Each time Devon prints the Invoice worksheet from the 15-Invoice workbook, he applies settings that center the worksheet horizontally on the page and scale the worksheet to fit on one page when printed. He asks if you can modify the workbook so he can apply those settings quickly, easily, and consistently. Create a simple macro to apply the settings and then save the Excel workbook as a macro-enabled workbook.

1. Open the data file **15-Invoice**.
2. With the Invoice worksheet active, click the Developer tab and then click the Record Macro button in the Code group (see Figure 15.18 on page 762).

   The Record Macro dialog box displays (see Figure 15.19 on page 762). The text *Macro1* is selected in the *Macro name* text box.
3. Type InvPrint.
4. Click in the *Description* text box, type Macro that centers a worksheet horizontally and scales it to fit on one page created by [Student Name] on [Date] and then click the OK button. ***Note:*** *Substitute your name for the placeholder text [Student Name] and the current date for the placeholder text* [Date]. ***Note:*** *Do not type a period at the end of the description text.*

   The dialog box closes. The macro recorder is on. The Stop Recording button displays on the Status bar (see Figure 15.20 on page 762).
5. Click the Page Layout tab and then click the Page Setup group dialog box launcher.

   The Page Setup dialog box displays with the Page tab active.
6. Click the *Fit to* radio button in the *Scaling* section.

   A bullet appears in the radio button. The worksheet will print on one page.
7. Click the Margins tab and then click the *Horizontally* check box in the *Center on page* section.

   A check mark appears in the check box.
8. Click the OK button.

   The dialog box closes. When printed, the worksheet will be centered horizontally on the page.
9. Click the Stop Recording button.

   The Record Macro button appears in place of the Stop Recording button on the Status bar.
10. Click the File tab and then click the *Save As* option.

    The Save As backstage area displays.

11. Navigate to the AE15 folder, if necessary.
12. Click the save-as-type option box arrow in the right panel (see Figure 15.21).
13. Click the *Excel Macro-Enabled Workbook (*.xlsm)* option at the drop-down list.

Figure 15.21 Save As Backstage Area

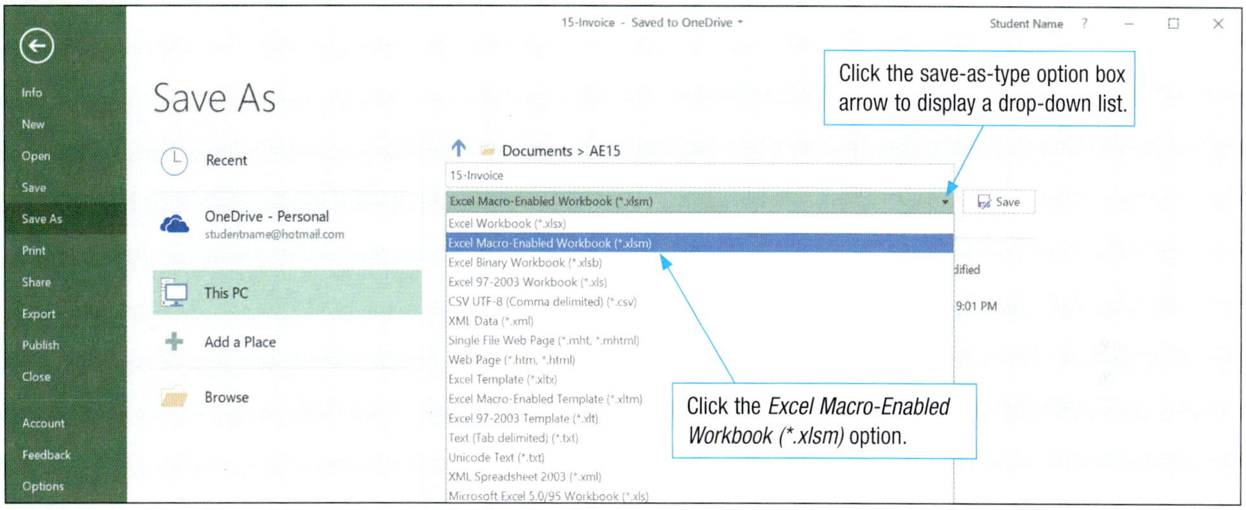

14. Click the Save button.

    The Save As backstage area closes. The file name appears with the file extension *.xlsm* in the title bar of the workbook if you have file extensions turned on.

15. Close the workbook.
16. If you need to leave the computer before starting the next task, export the customized settings to a file called *AE15Cust.exportUI* and save the export file in the AE15 folder on your storage medium. Before continuing your Chapter 15 work on another computer, follow the instructions in Task 15.16 to import the AE15Cust.exportUI file into the other computer.

Model Answer

15.8 Enabling Macros and Assigning Macros to Shortcut Key Combinations

MOS Expert 1.1.5

Tutorial

Enabling Macros, and Creating a Macro and Assigning It to a Shortcut Key Combination

When a workbook contains a macro, the default security setting is *Disable all macros with notification*. When the workbook is opened the first time, this setting causes a security warning to appear in a message bar between the ribbon and the Formula bar (see Figure 15.22), stating that macros have been disabled. Enable the macros in the workbook by clicking the Enable Content button. (See Section 15.12 in this chapter for more information about macro security.)

A macro can be assigned to a shortcut key combination. A keyboard shortcut allows the user to run the macro quickly by pressing the Ctrl key plus the chosen lowercase or uppercase letter.

Figure 15.22 Message Bar with a Security Warning and the Enable Content Button in a Macro-Enabled Workbook

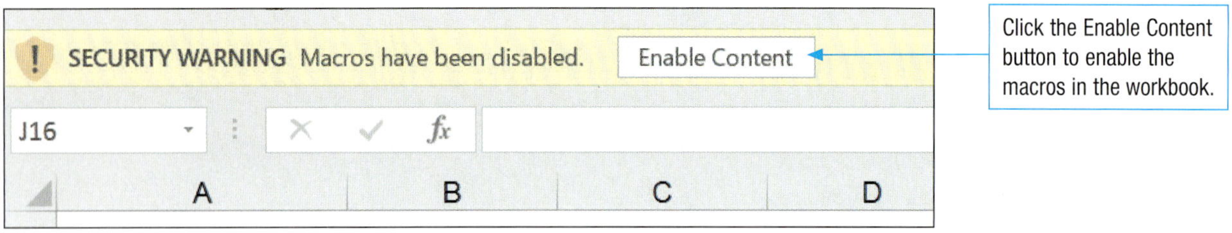

▸ Know This about enabling macros in a workbook

— To enable macros in a workbook, click the Enable Content button in the security warning message bar (see Figure 15.22).

— If you do not enable the content, the macros will remain disabled and cannot be used.

— When you enable macros in a workbook, the file name for the workbook is added to a list of trusted files. The security message will not appear the next time you open the workbook on the same computer.

▸ Know This about assigning macros to shortcut key combinations

— You can assign a macro to a shortcut key combination using the Ctrl key plus a letter key of your choice.

— Shortcuts are case sensitive. For example, if you choose the capital letter *R*, the shortcut will be Ctrl + Shift + R.

— Keyboard shortcuts are assigned at the Record Macro dialog box (see Figure 15.19 on page 762), which appears after you start recording a macro.

— If an Excel feature is already assigned to the chosen key combination, the macro assignment will override it. For example, by default, pressing Ctrl + p in Excel causes the Print backstage area to display. If a macro is assigned to Ctrl + p, using this keyboard shortcut will run the new macro instead of displaying the Print backstage area.

— Avoid overriding existing shortcut keys because such changes could confuse other users of the workbook.

— To view a list of Excel-assigned keyboard shortcuts: type *keyboard shortcuts* in the *Tell me* text box; click the *Get Help on "keyboard shortcuts"* option at the drop-down list; scroll down, if necessary; and then click the *Excel keyboard shortcuts and function keys for Windows* option at the results list.

On the Job

Task 15.8 Creating a Macro and Assigning It to a Shortcut Key Combination

Devon wants to be able to quickly save the macro-enabled 15-Forecast workbook as a PDF file, which he can easily send to colleagues who prefer to view documents as PDFs. Create a macro that performs the steps needed to accomplish this task and assign the macro to a keyboard shortcut.

1. Open the data file **15-Forecast** and then click the Enable Content button (see Figure 15.22 on page 766).
2. With the 2020 Sales Projections worksheet active, click the Developer tab and then click the Record Macro button in the Code group.

   The Record Macro dialog box displays with the text selected in the *Macro name* text box.
3. Type PDF.
4. Click in the *Shortcut key* text box, press and hold down the Shift key, type O, and then release the Shift key.

   The shortcut key will be Ctrl + Shift + O.
5. Click in the *Description* text box, type Macro that creates a PDF created by [Student Name] on [Date] and then click the OK button. ***Note:*** *Substitute your name for the placeholder text* [Student Name] *and the current date for the placeholder text* [Date]. ***Note:*** *Do not type a period at the end of the description text.*

   The dialog box closes. The macro recorder is on. The Stop Recording button displays on the Status bar.
6. Record the macro as follows:
   a. Click the File tab.
   b. Click the *Export* option in the left panel at the Excel backstage area.
   c. Click the *Create PDF/XPS Document* option in the middle panel at the Export backstage area, if necessary.
   d. Click the Create PDF/XPS button in the right panel.
   e. Navigate to the AE15 folder on your storage medium, if necessary; click the *Save as type* option box arrow at the Publish as PDF or XPS dialog box; and then click the *PDF (*.pdf)* option at the drop-down list, if necessary.
   f. Click the *Open file after publishing* check box to insert a check mark, if necessary.
   g. Click the Publish button.

   The dialog box closes and the PDF file opens.
7. Press Alt + Tab.

   The active window is now the Excel window.
8. Click the Stop Recording button.
9. Make the PDF active and then close it.

   The PDF is saved with the file name *15-Forecast.pdf* in the AE15 folder.
10. Click the Save button on the Quick Access Toolbar.
11. If you need to leave the computer before starting the next task, export the customized settings to a file called *AE15Cust.exportUI* and save the export file in the AE15 folder on your storage medium. Before continuing your Chapter 15 work on another computer, follow the instructions in Task 15.16 to import the AE15Cust.exportUI file into the other computer.

Model Answer

15.9 Running a Macro

Running a macro is sometimes referred to as *playing a macro*. Since a macro is a series of recorded steps, running a macro involves instructing Excel to play back the recorded steps. Think of a macro as a video. Each time the video is played, the same events occur.

Tutorial

Running a Macro

▸ Know This about running a macro

— To run a macro, click the Macros button in the Code group on the Developer tab, click the macro name in the list box at the Macro dialog box (see Figure 15.23), and then click the Run button.

— By default, the Macro dialog box displays all the macros in all open workbooks.

— If the macro has been assigned a shortcut key combination, you can use the shortcut key combination to run the macro.

— If the macro produces a file, it creates a new file each time it is run. The new file will have the same name as the old file and will override the old file. To save the new file without overriding the old file, save the new file with a different name.

▸ Know More ways to display the Macro dialog box

– Click the Macros button in the Code group on the Developer tab.

– Press Alt + F8.

▸ Know More ways to run a macro

– Double-click the name of the macro in the *Macro name* list box at the Macro dialog box.

Figure 15.23 Macro Dialog Box

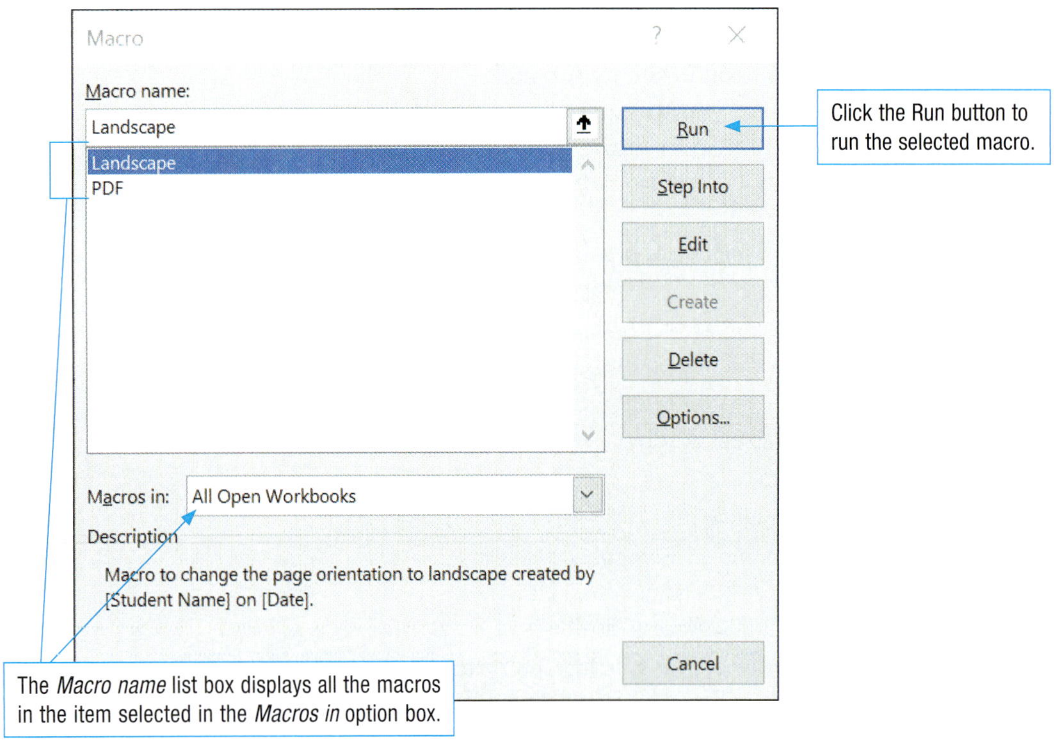

On the Job

Task 15.9 Running a Macro

Devon wants to be sure he can quickly run the macro you created for the 15-Forecast workbook in Task 15.8. Test the macro by running it with the shortcut key combination Ctrl + Shift + O.

Note: The PDF macro you created in Task 15.8 produced a PDF file called 15-Forecast.pdf. *The next time this macro is run, it will produce a new PDF file called* 15-Forecast.pdf *and the new PDF file will override the old one. If you need to keep a copy of each version, save the new PDF file with a new name—for example,* 15-Forecast-(15.9).pdf. *To save and rename a PDF file opened in Microsoft Edge, right-click anywhere in the open file, click the* Save As *option at the pop-up menu, type in a new file name, and then click the Save button.*

1. With the macro-enabled 15-Forecast workbook open, press Ctrl + Shift + O.

   The macro runs, and a PDF file is created and opens.
2. Close the PDF file.
3. Close the workbook.
4. If you need to leave the computer before starting the next task, export the customized settings to a file called *AE15Cust.exportUI* and save the export file in the AE15 folder on your storage medium. Before continuing your Chapter 15 work on another computer, follow the instructions in Task 15.16 to import the AE15Cust.exportUI file into the other computer.

15.10 Editing and Rerecording a Macro

Tutorial

Displaying the Visual Basic Editor Window and Editing a Macro

The actions performed while a macro is recorded are stored in VBA code. Each macro is saved as a separate module in a **VBA Project**, which is saved as part of the workbook file. A **module** can be described as a container for the steps in the macro.

You might want to edit a macro if you need to make a simple change and it is easy to decipher how to make the correction in the VBA code. For example, if the code uses conditional statements and you want to change a condition from *True* to *False*, you can easily edit the code (see Figure 15.24). You can also easily edit values such as margin and font size measurements. If several changes to a macro are required or you do not feel comfortable editing the VBA code, you can rerecord the macro.

▸ Know This about VBA code

— A comment is a line of text that appears in green and is preceded with an apostrophe in the VBA code. A **VBA comment** is explanatory text and is ignored when the macro is run.

— The word *Sub* and the name of the macro appear as the first line of a macro, and the words *End Sub* appear as the last line of a macro.

▸ Know This about using the Visual Basic Editor window to edit a macro

— To display the Visual Basic Editor window, click the Developer tab, click the Macros button in the Code group, click the macro at the Macro dialog box, and then click the Edit button.

— Edit a macro at the **Visual Basic Editor (VBE)** window (see Figure 15.24).

▸ **Know More** ways to display the Visual Basic Editor window

– Press Alt + F11.

— To save your edits, click the Save button in the Visual Basic Editor window.

— Use the Maximize button to expand the Visual Basic Editor window, and use the Restore Down button to make the window smaller.

▸ Know This about rerecording a macro

— When you record a new macro and save it with the same name as an existing macro, Excel prompts you to replace the existing macro.

— To open the last macro selected at the Macro dialog box, click the Visual Basic button in the Code group on the Developer tab.

Figure 15.24 Code Section at the Visual Basic Editor Window

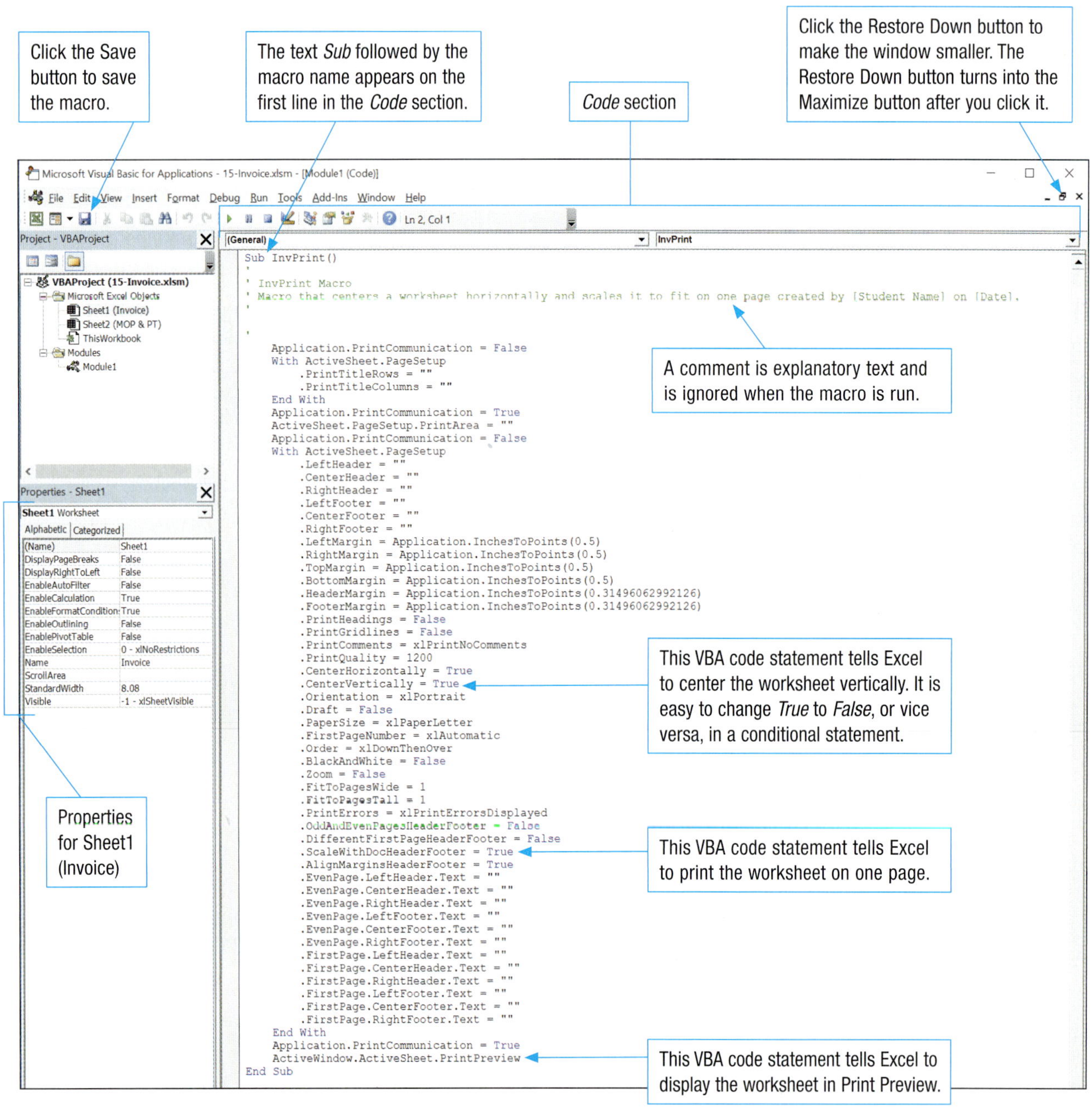

On the Job

Task 15.10 Editing a Macro

Devon likes to preview his work before he prints it, and he asks you to modify the InvPrint macro to display the Invoice worksheet in Print Preview. He's also decided that he wants the worksheet centered vertically as well as horizontally. Edit the macro to meet Devon's requests, using the code statement *ActiveWindow.ActiveSheet.PrintPreview* to tell Excel to display in Print Preview.

1. Open the data file **15-Invoice**, which you saved and closed at the end of Task 15.7, and then click the Enable Content button, if necessary.
2. With any worksheet active, click the Developer tab and then click the Macros button in the Code group.

   The Macro dialog box displays with the *InvPrint* option selected in the *Macro name* list box.
3. Click the Edit button.

   The Visual Basic Editor displays with the code for the InvPrint macro in the *Code* section (see Figure 15.25).
4. Scroll down to the bottom of the code and then place the insertion point at the end of the VBA code statement *Application.PrintCommunication = True*.
5. Press the Enter key and then type ActiveWindow.ActiveSheet.PrintPreview.

   Do not include a period after the word *PrintPreview*. If you do include a period, an error will occur.
6. Scroll up to the VBA code statement *Center Vertically = False*, select the word *False*, and then type True.
7. Click the Visual Basic Editor window Close button. ***Note:*** *Be sure to click the Close button for the Visual Basic Editor window, not the close button for the* Code *section of the window.*

   The VBA window closes. The Excel window remains open.

Figure 15.25 InvPrint Macro Code in the *Code* Section at the Visual Basic Editor

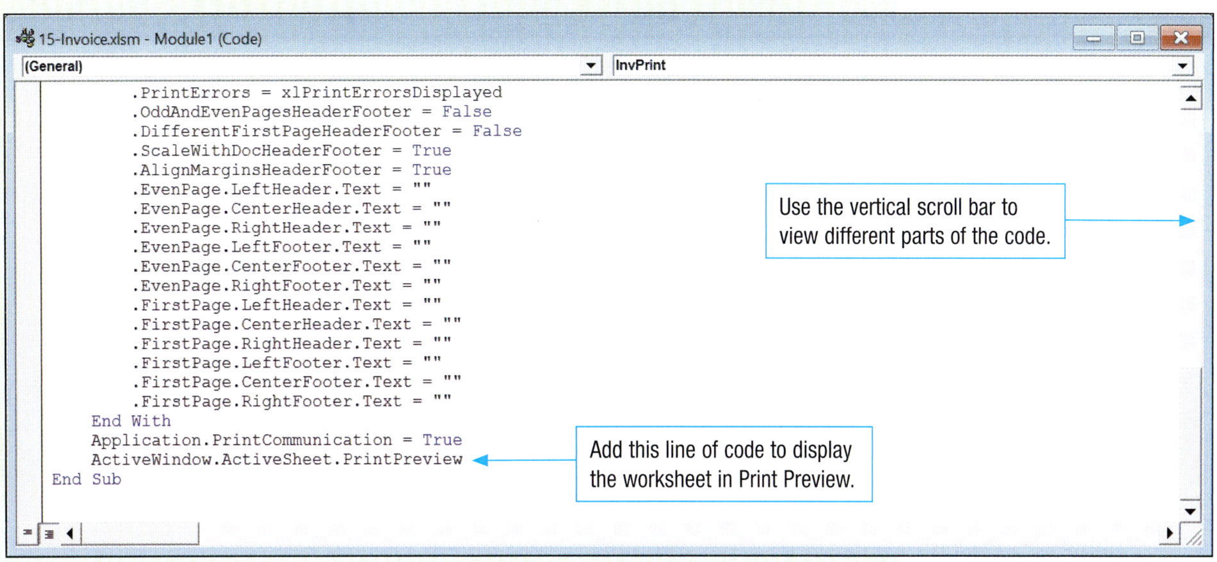

8. Click the Macros button in the Code group, verify that the *InvPrint* option is selected in the *Macro name* list box at the Macro dialog box, and then click the Run button.

   The dialog box closes. The worksheet displays in Print Preview centered both horizontally and vertically.

9. Click the Close Print Preview button in the Preview group on the Print Preview tab.

   The Print Preview closes. The workbook remains open.

10. Click the Save button on the Quick Access Toolbar and then close the workbook.

11. If you need to leave the computer before starting the next task, export the customized settings to a file called *AE15Cust.exportUI* and save the export file in the AE15 folder on your storage medium. Before continuing your Chapter 15 work on another computer, follow the instructions in Task 15.16 to import the AE15Cust.exportUI file into the other computer.

15.11 Deleting a Macro

If a macro is no longer needed, you can delete it. You may want to delete a macro that is no longer required to avoid accidentally running it and altering workbook data.

Tutorial

Deleting a Macro

▸ Know This about deleting macros

— To delete a macro, click the Macros button in the Code group on the Developer tab, click the macro name in the *Macro name* list box at the Macro dialog box, click the Delete button, and then click the Yes button at the message box asking if you want to delete the macro.

— When you delete a macro, the module still exists in the *Project* section at the Visual Basic Editor window.

On the Job

Task 15.11 Deleting a Macro

The 15-Forecast workbook contains a macro named *Landscape* that's never used. Clean up the workbook by deleting the unused macro.

1. Open the data file **15-Forecast**, which you closed at the end of Task 15.9, and then click the Enable Content button.

2. Click the Developer tab and then click the Macros button in the Code group.

   The Macro dialog box displays.

3. With the Landscape macro selected in the *Macro name* list box, click the Delete button.

   The dialog box closes and a message box displays, asking if you want to delete the Landscape macro.

4. Click the Yes button.

5. Click the Save button on the Quick Access Toolbar.

6. If you need to leave the computer before starting the next task, export the customized settings to a file called *AE15Cust.exportUI* and save the export file in the AE15 folder on your storage medium. Before continuing your Chapter 15 work on another computer, follow the instructions in Task 15.16 to import the AE15Cust.exportUI file into the other computer.

15.12 Managing Macro Security

Tutorial

Viewing Macro Security Settings

The Excel **Trust Center** is responsible for and blocks unsafe content when a workbook is opened. A workbook that contains a macro may contain a **virus**, which is an intrusive program that inserts copies of itself in computer files. The virus might cause unrecoverable malicious changes to the workbook when the macro is run.

You can control how Excel handles macros when a workbook is opened by adjusting the **macro security setting** in the Trust Center. The security warning that sometimes appears with the Enable Content button in the yellow message bar below the Excel ribbon when a workbook is opened is generated by the Trust Center. You can view and/or modify security settings that protect the computer from malicious content in the Trust Center.

▸ Know This about trusted locations

— The Trust Center maintains the **Trusted Locations list**, which is a list of places from which content can be considered trusted.

— After a location is added to the Trusted Locations list, Excel treats any file opened from that location as safe.

— Opening a workbook from a trusted location does not cause a security warning to display in the message bar, and Excel does not block any of the workbook content.

— Installing Excel creates a folder of templates provided by Microsoft. By default, Excel adds that folder to the Trusted Locations list. Additional folders may be added by a system administrator or network administrator.

▸ Know This about trusted publishers

— If a workbook contains macros, the Trust Center checks for a valid and current digital signature from an entity in the Trusted Publishers list before enabling the macros.

— A **digital signature** (also called a *digital ID* or a *digital certificate*) is a form of security that positively identifies the publisher of a workbook.

— A publisher is a person or company that has sent you a workbook. The **Trusted Publishers list** is a list of publishers that are considered safe.

— To add a digital signature, click the File tab, click the Protect Workbook button in the middle panel at the Info backstage area, click the *Add a Digital Signature* option at the drop-down list, click the Yes button at the message box asking whether you would like to get a digital ID from a Microsoft Partner now, select a service provider at the Microsoft support website, and then follow the steps to acquire a digital ID at the service provider's website.

— A digital signature becomes invalid if a workbook is edited. This prevents anyone from making changes to the workbook and then distributing the workbook with the same digital signature.
— The Trusted Publishers list is maintained by the user on the computer being used.
— To add a publisher to the list, enable content from that publisher and then click the option *Trust all content from this publisher.*

▸ **Know This** about macro security settings

— Depending on the active macro security setting, if the Trust Center cannot find the digital signature information with an entity in the Trusted Publishers list or the macro does not contain a digital signature, a security warning will display in the message bar.
— The macro security setting applies to all workbooks in Excel.
— The IT department will establish security settings for school or company computers.
— Table 15.1 describes the four available macro security settings.
— The default macro security setting is *Disable all macros with notification*.
— You can change the macro security setting in the Trust Center.

Table 15.1 Macro Security Settings for Workbooks Opened from Locations That Are Not Trusted

Macro Security Setting	Description
Disable all macros without notification	All macros are disabled and no security alerts appear.
Disable all macros with notification	All macros are disabled and security alerts appear with the option to enable content if the source of the file is trusted. This is the default setting.
Disable all macros except digitally signed macros	Macros that are not digitally signed are disabled and no security alerts appear for those macros. Macros that are digitally signed by publishers in the Trusted Publishers list are allowed to run and no security alerts appear for those macros. Macros that are digitally signed by publishers that are not in the Trusted Publishers list are disabled and security alerts appear for those macros.
Enable all macros (not recommended; potentially dangerous code can run)	All macros are allowed to run and no security alerts appear.

▸ **Know This** about changing the macro security setting

— To change the macro security setting, click the Macro Security button in the Code group on the Developer tab and then click the radio button to insert a bullet for the new setting option in the *Macro Settings* section in the right panel at the Trust Center dialog box (see Figure 15.26).
— Changing the macro security setting in Excel does not affect the macro security settings in other Microsoft programs, such as Word and Access.
— The security setting on the computer you are using may be different from the default option. Do not change the security setting on a computer that belongs to someone else without the owner's permission. If you are working on a school computer, check with your instructor before changing this setting.

▸ **Know More** ways to display the Trust Center dialog box

- Click the File tab, click the *Options* option, click the *Trust Center* option in the left panel at the Excel Options dialog box, and then click the Trust Center Settings button in the right panel.

Figure 15.26 Trust Center Dialog Box

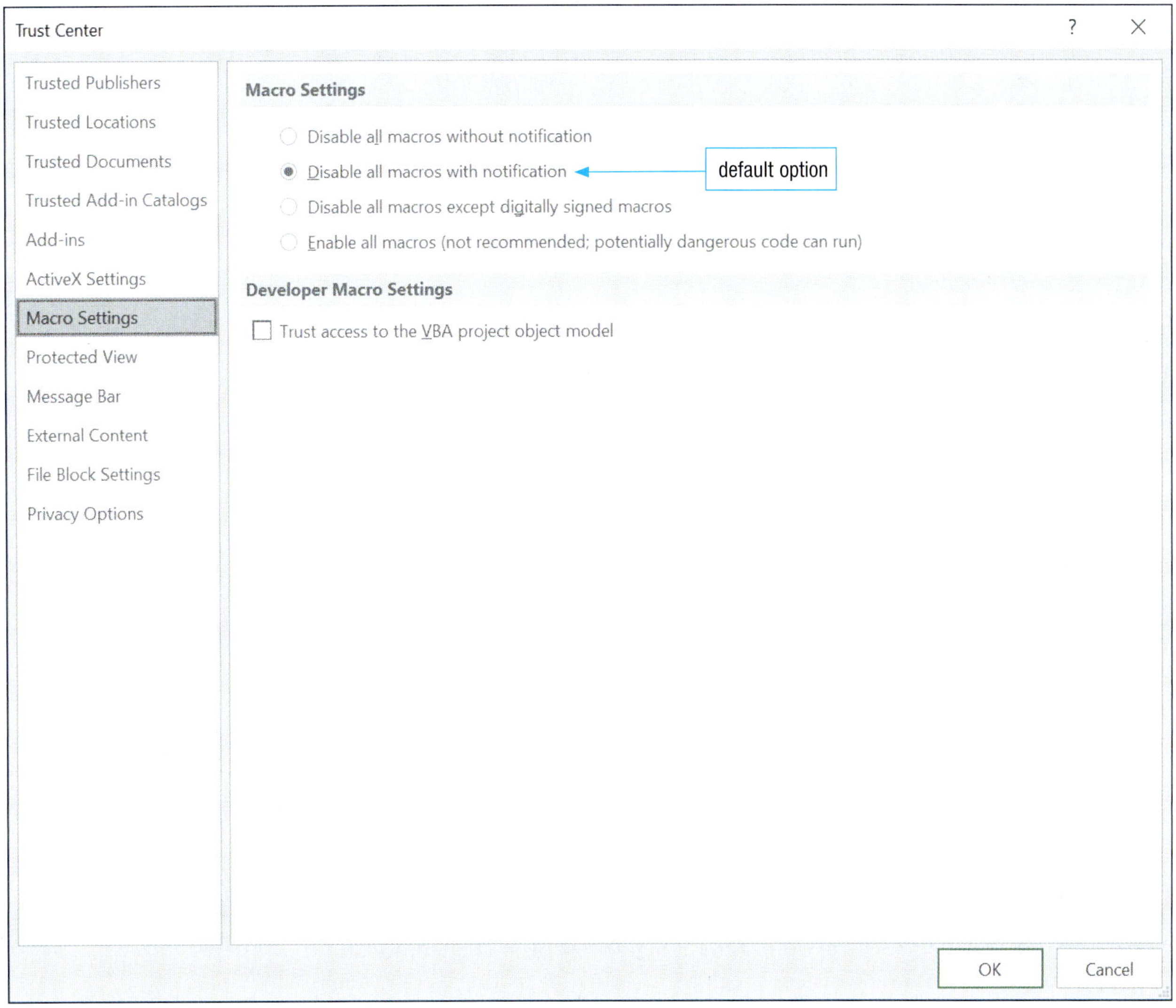

On the Job

Task 15.12 Viewing Macro Security Settings

You suggest to Devon that he use the default macro security setting on his computer to help ensure that no unsafe macros are run in his workbooks. You also decide that it's a good idea to check the macro settings on the computer you are using. After doing that, look at the list of trusted publishers and the list of trusted locations to become familiar with those parts of the Trust Center.

1. With the macro-enabled 15-Forecast workbook open, click the Macro Security button in the Code group on the Developer tab.

   The Trust Center dialog box displays with the *Macro Settings* option selected in the left panel (see Figure 15.26).

2. Review the options in the *Macro Settings* section in the right panel.

   Note which option is active on the computer you are using.

Note: The default setting is Disable all macros with notification. *The security setting on the computer you are using may be different from the default option. If you are working on a computer that does not belong to you, do not change the security setting without consulting the owner or administrator.*

3. Click the *Trusted Publishers* option in the left panel.

   If any publishers have been added to the list on the computer you are using, their names will appear in the *Trusted Publishers* list box in the right panel. If the list box is empty, no trusted publishers have been added.

4. Click the *Trusted Locations* option in the left panel.

   Review the paths and folder descriptions in the *Trusted Locations* list box in the right panel.

5. Click the OK button.

   The Trust Center dialog box closes.

6. If you need to leave the computer before starting the next task, export the customized settings to a file called *AE15Cust.exportUI* and save the export file in the AE15 folder on your storage medium. Before continuing your Chapter 15 work on another computer, follow the instructions in Task 15.16 to import the AE15Cust.exportUI file into the other computer.

15.13 Copying Macros from Workbook to Workbook

MOS Expert 1.1.2

Tutorial

Copying a Macro from Workbook to Workbook

By default, a macro is stored in the workbook that is active when it is recorded. Also by default, a macro in one workbook is available for use in other workbooks that are open at the same time. After a macro has been created, it can be copied to other workbooks where it can be modified to fit the specific needs of the workbook. For example, in the PDF macro, the name of the PDF can be changed.

▸ **Know This** about copying a macro from workbook to workbook

— To copy a macro from one workbook to another, open both workbooks, make the workbook containing the macro active, click the Visual Basic button in the Code group on the Developer tab, expand the contents of each workbook in the *Project* section in the left panel at the Visual Basic Editor window (see Figure 15.27), expand the contents of the modules in the *Project* section, drag the module to be copied from the originating workbook to the destination workbook, and then close the Visual Basic Editor window.

— You can scroll up and down in the *Project* section or adjust the size of the section, as necessary.

— To adjust the size of the *Project* section, hover the mouse pointer over the border between the *Project* section and the *Properties* section until the pointer turns into a two-headed arrow, click and hold down the left mouse button, drag the border down to the new size, and then release the mouse button.

Figure 15.27 *Project* Section at the Visual Basic Editor Window

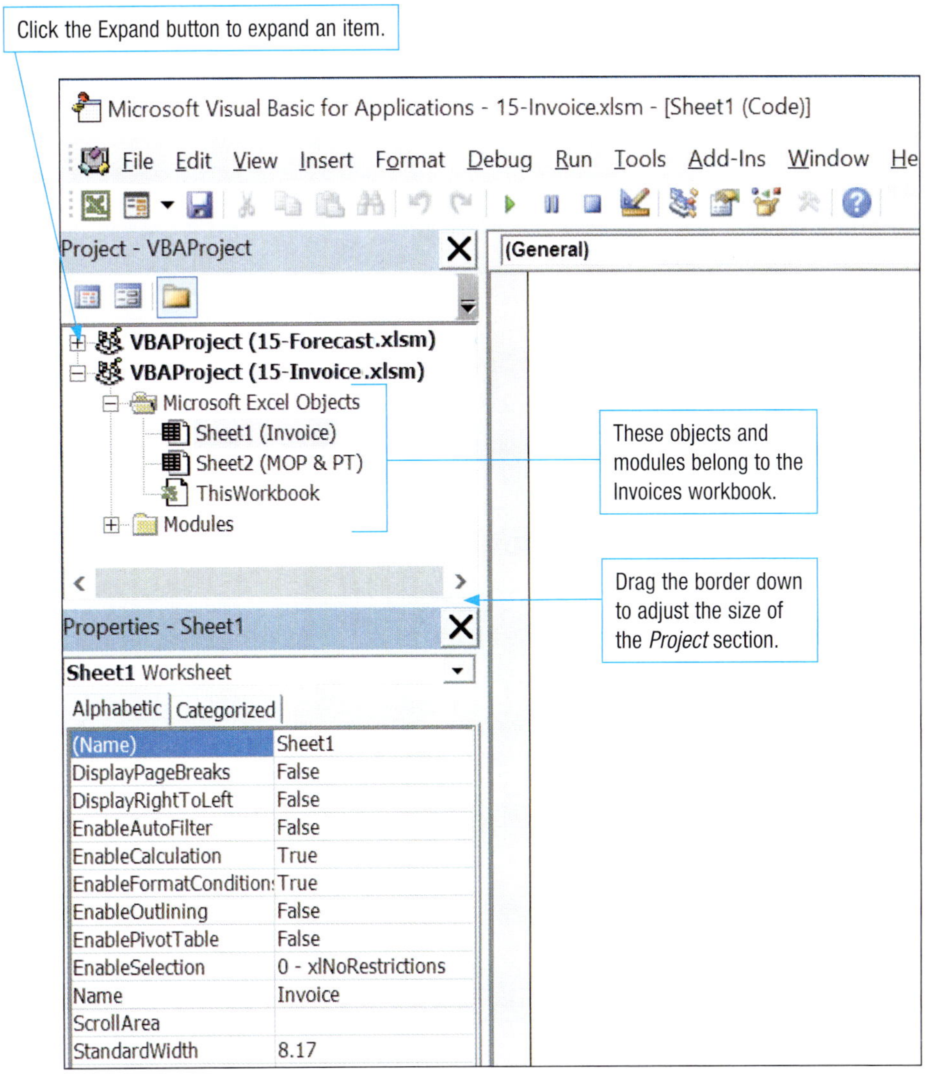

On the Job

Task 15.13 Copying a Macro from Workbook to Workbook

Devon wants to use the PDF macro you created in the 15-Forecast workbook in the 15-Invoice workbook. Copy the macro from one workbook to the other workbook and then modify it to save it as 15-Invoice.

1. With the macro-enabled 15-Forecast workbook open and active, open the data file **15-Invoice**, which you closed at the end of Task 15.10, and enable the content.

   The macro-enabled 15-Invoice workbook is active.

2. Click the Developer tab, if necessary, and then click the Visual Basic button in the Code group.

   The Visual Basic Editor window displays.

3. Click the Expand button for the *VBAProject (15-Forecast.xlsm)* list item in the *Project* section in the left panel, if necessary (see Figure 15.27).

   The VBA modules for the 15-Forecast project are displayed.

4. Click the Expand button for the Modules folder under the *VBAProject (15-Forecast.xlsm)* list item, if necessary.

   The Modules folder expands to display two VBA modules: Module1 and Module2. Module1 contains the Landscape macro you deleted in Task 15.11. Module2 contains the PDF macro you created in Task 15.8. To verify this, double-click the *Module1* module and then the *Module2* module in the *Project* section.

5. If you cannot see both workbooks and modules, hover the mouse pointer over the border between the *Project* section and the *Properties* section until the pointer turns into a two-headed arrow, click and hold down the left mouse button, drag the border down until all the items in the *Project* section display, and then release the mouse button.
6. Point to the *Module2* module for the 15-Forecast project, click and hold down the left mouse button, drag the *Module2* module to the Modules folder under the *VBAProject (15-Invoice.xlsm)* list item, and then release the mouse button.

   The Module2 module from the 15-Forecast project is copied to the Modules folder for the 15-Invoice project.

7. Click the Expand button for the Modules folder for the 15-Invoice project and then double-click the *Module2* module.

   Ensure that *Module2* displays in the Code section. The module name *Module2* is selected.

8. Type 15-Invoice.pdf to replace the selected module name and then click the Save button.

   When the macro is run, the file will be saved with the name *15-Invoice.pdf*.

9. Click the Visual Basic Editor window Close button.
10. Close the 15-Forecast workbook.
11. With the 15-Invoice workbook active, press Ctrl + Shift + O.

    The PDF macro that you copied from the 15-Forecast workbook to the 15-Invoice workbook runs. A PDF of the 15-Invoice workbook opens and is active. The name of the PDF is *15-Invoice*. Note that this is the same name as the PDF that resulted when you created the macro. Each time you run the macro, Excel creates a new PDF with the same file name. If you save the new PDF without changing the name, the new PDF will overwrite the previous PDF.

12. Save the PDF with a new name in the AE15 folder typing 15-InvoiceTest1 as the new name. ***Note:*** *Depending on which application opened the PDF, the steps for saving the PDF may vary.*
13. If printed work is required by your instructor, print the PDF.
14. Close the PDF file.

    The macro-enabled 15-Invoice workbook remains open.

15. Click the Save button on the Quick Access Toolbar.
16. If you need to leave the computer before starting the next task, export the customized settings to a file called *AE15Cust.exportUI* and save the export file in the AE15 folder on your storage medium. Before continuing your Chapter 15 work on another computer, follow the instructions in Task 15.16 to import the AE15Cust.exportUI file into the other computer.

Model Answer

MOS Expert 2.3.5

Tutorial

Inserting a Combo Box Form Control

15.14 Inserting and Configuring Form Controls

Insert a **form control** to allow users to enter information in a worksheet. For example, insert a combo box form control or a list box form control to allow users to select an option from a list, or insert a check box form control to allow users to select an option by inserting a check mark in a check box. After inserting a form control in a worksheet, you can configure the control to define how it will be used, resize the control, and align multiple controls.

▸ Know This about inserting form controls

— To insert a form control in an active worksheet, click the Insert button in the Controls group on the Developer tab, click a control form option in the *Form Controls* section at the drop-down list (see Figure 15.28), and then draw a box in the worksheet (see Figure 15.29).

Figure 15.28 Form Controls Insert Button Drop-Down List

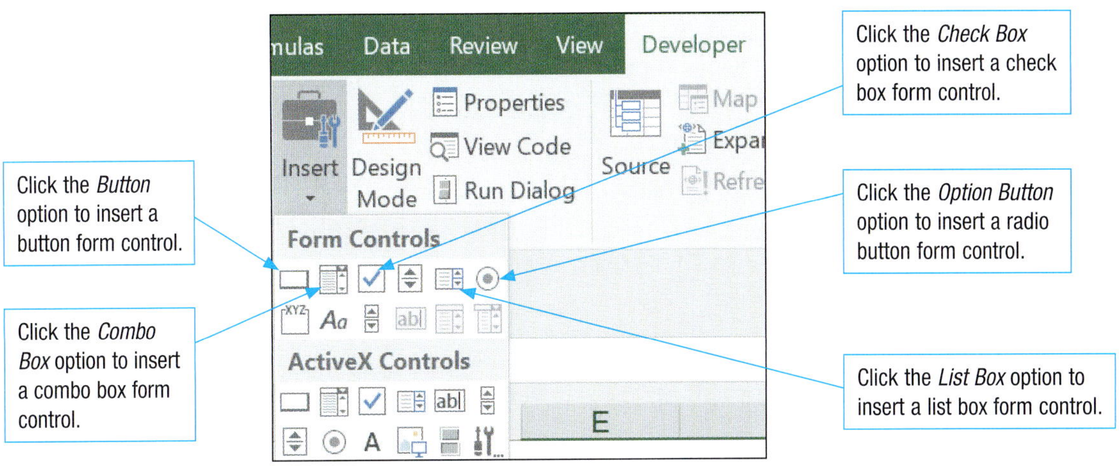

Figure 15.29 Combo Box Drawn in a Worksheet

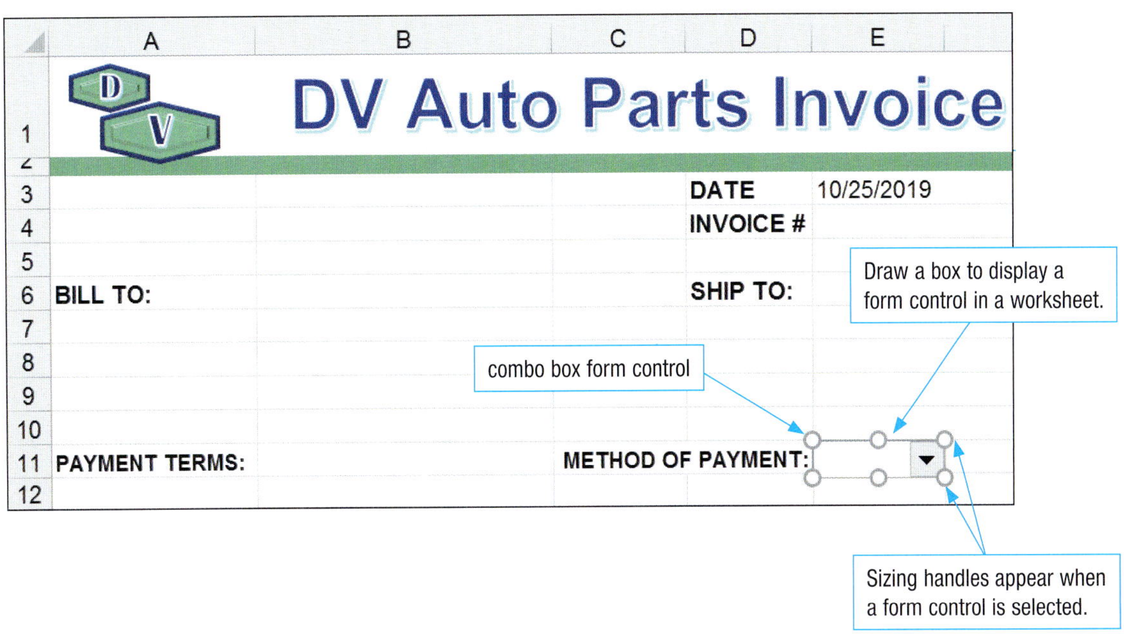

— The size of the form control box depends on the options of the control. For example, a form control that allows users to select from a drop-down list of two-letter state abbreviations (AL, AS, etc.) will be narrower than a form control that offers a drop-down list of city names (e.g., Abbeville, Aberdeen, etc.).
— A form control is added as an object in a worksheet.
— When you finish drawing a form control box, it is selected and sizing handles are visible on the border.
— To deselect a form control box, click in any worksheet cell outside the control.
— Refer to Table 15.2 for descriptions of selected types of form controls.

Table 15.2 Selected Types of Form Controls

Type of Form Control	Display	How to Use	Example
combo box form control	an option box with an arrow	Click the option box arrow to see a drop-down list of available options and then click an option at the drop-down list.	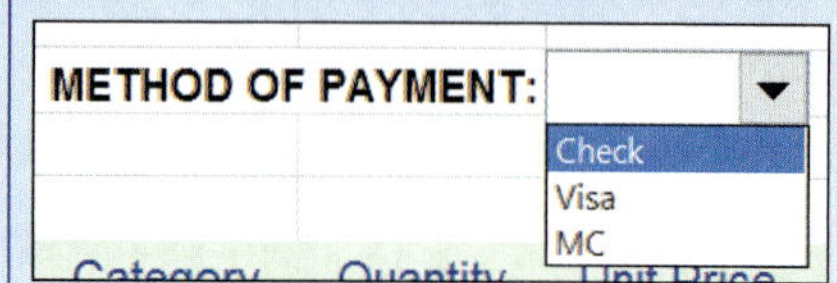
list box form control	a box containing all the available options—with scroll bars, if necessary	Click an option in the list box to select it. The control can be configured to allow the user to select more than one option.	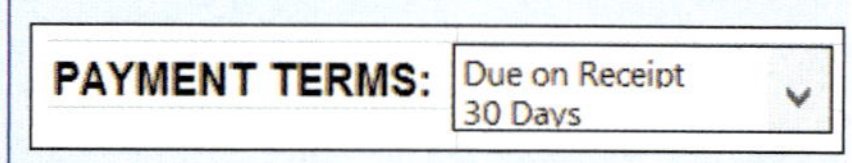
check box form control	a check box box with a text label	Click the check box to insert or remove a check mark.	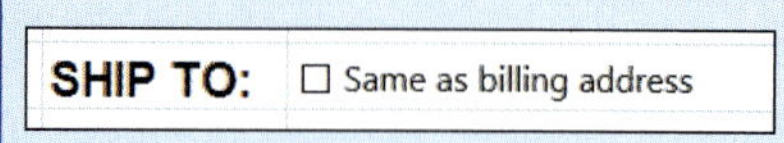
button form control	a button with a label and with a macro assigned to it	Click the button to run the macro.	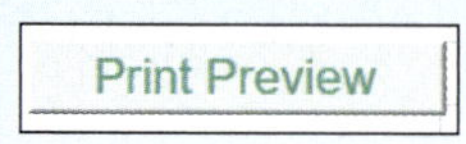
option button form control	a radio button with a label	Click the radio button to insert or remove a bullet.	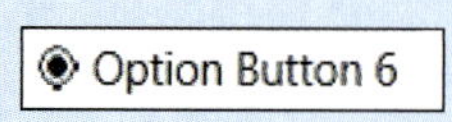

▸ **Know This** about configuring form controls

— To add options to a form control, right-click the control, click the *Format Control* option at the pop-up menu, and then enter information on the Control tab at the Format Control dialog box (see Figure 15.30).
— The information entered at the Format Control dialog box depends on the type of form control. For example, see the options available for a combo box in Figure 15.30.
— If the number entered in the *Drop down lines* text box is less than the number of items in the *Input range* text box, a scroll bar will appear at the drop-down list for the form control.

▶ **Know This** about the input range for combo box and list box form controls

— The input range is the worksheet range that contains the options available to users in the combo box drop-down list or the list box list. For example, *A2:A4* is the input range for a combo box drop-down list of the payment options shown in Figure 15.31.

— The first option in the input range is recorded as *1*, the second option is recorded as *2*, and so on. If you rearrange the input range, the first option in the list will still be recorded as *1*.

— If you put a cell reference in the *Cell link* text box at the Format Control dialog box, Excel will enter the corresponding number of the option chosen in that cell. For example, if *E11* is entered in the *Cell link* text box and the user chooses *Check* at the combo box drop-down list of options shown in Figure 15.32, a *1* will appear in cell E11; if the user chooses *Visa*, a *2* will appear in cell E11; and if the user chooses *MC*, a *3* will appear in cell E11.

— If the cell link is the same cell in which the control object is placed, the chosen option will appear in the form control box on top of the option number. For example, the option *Check* will appear in the combo box form control in cell E11, and the number *1* will appear in the same cell hidden underneath the form control. Figure 15.33 shows the control object moved to display *2* because *Visa* was chosen as the option.

Figure 15.30 Control Tab at the Format Control Dialog Box for a Combo Box Form Control

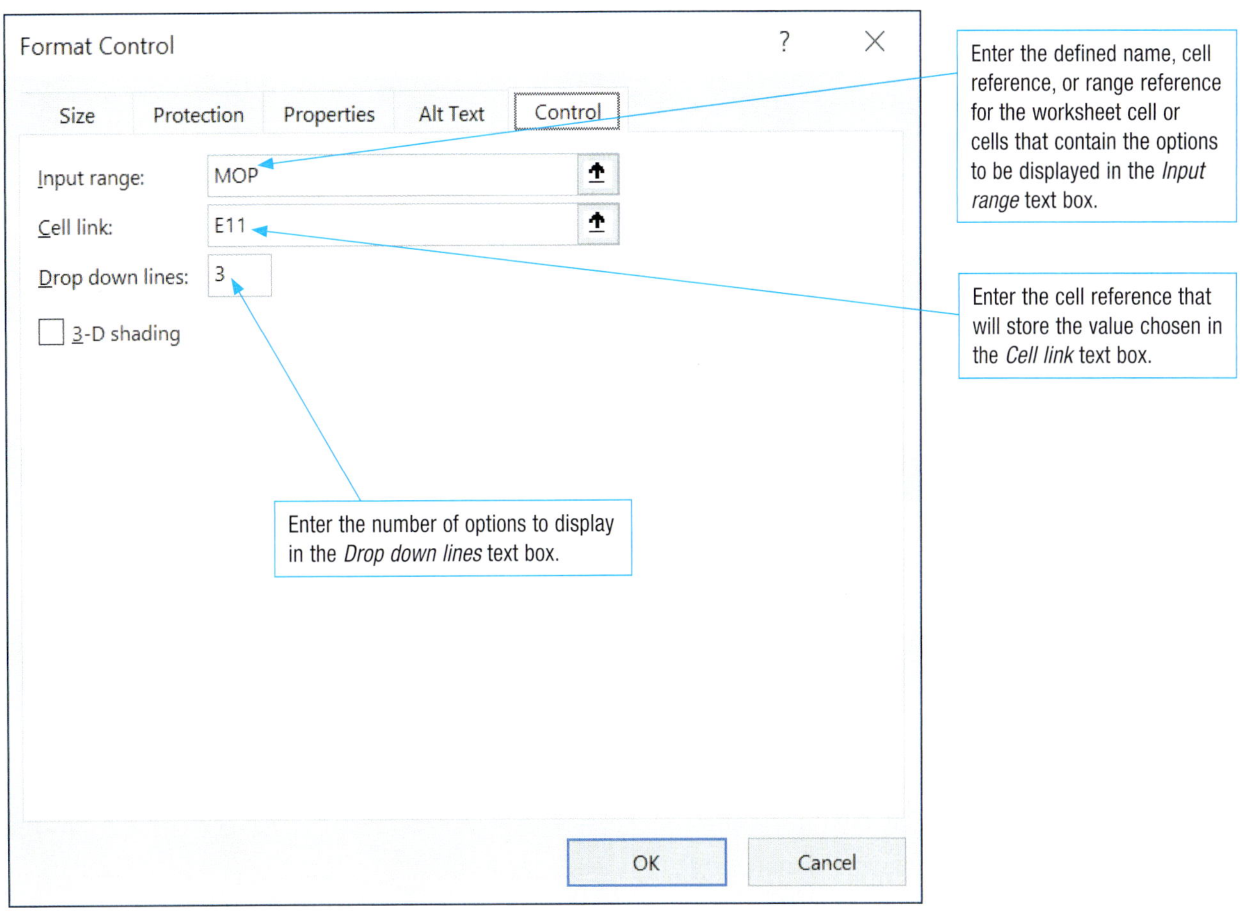

Figure 15.31 Method of Payment Options

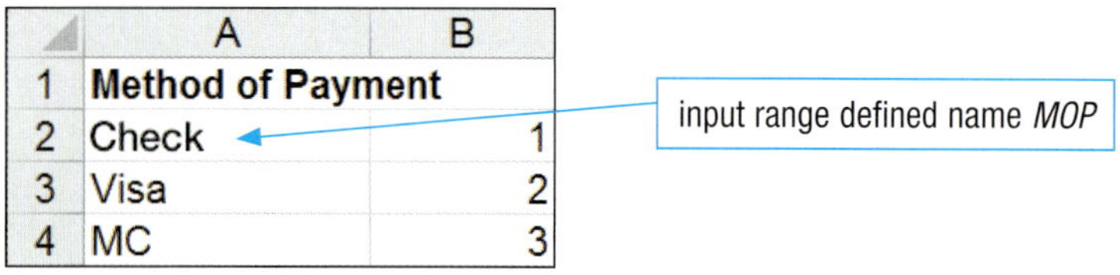

Figure 15.32 Combo Box Form Control Drop-Down List of Options

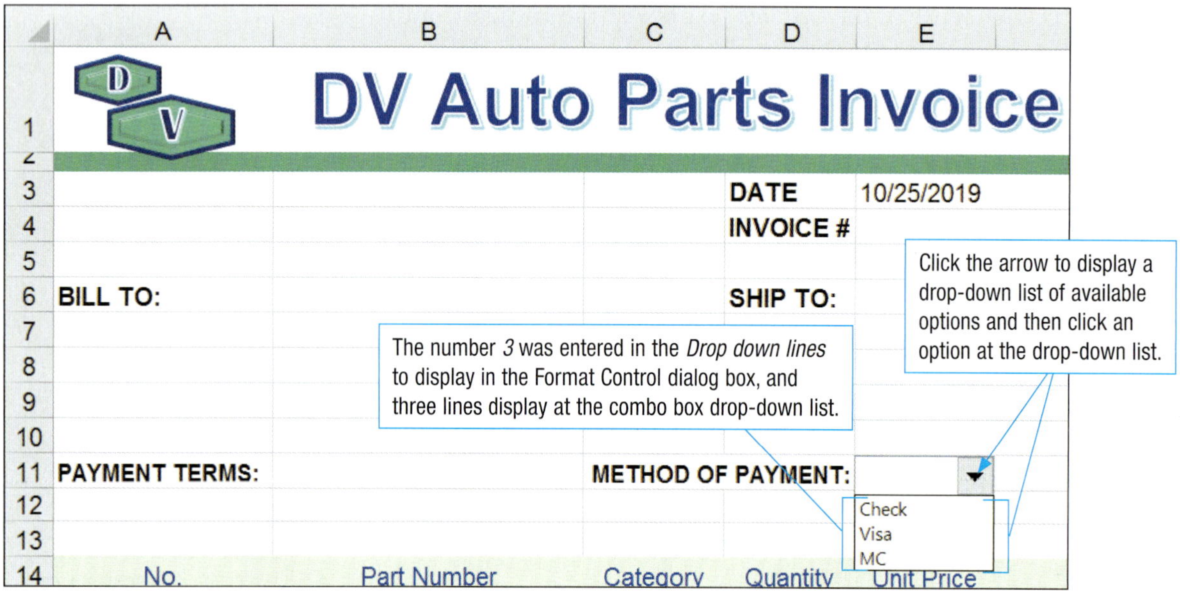

Figure 15.33 Combo Box Moved to Display the Contents of Cell E11

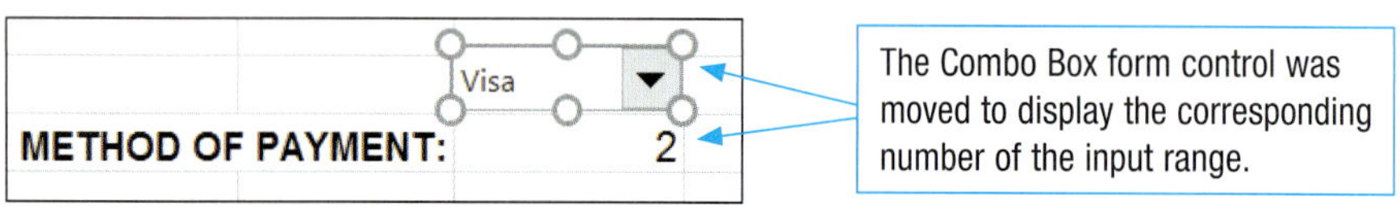

▸ Know This about creating a macro button form control

— Assigning a macro to a button form control allows the user to quickly run the macro without having to remember the shortcut key combination or ribbon commands.

— To create a button form control with a macro assigned to it, click the Insert button in the Controls group on the Developer tab, click the *Button (Form Control)* option, draw the button, click the macro name in the *Macro name* list box at the Assign Macro dialog box, and then click the OK button.

— Macro button form controls do not display in Print Preview and do not print. ***Note:*** *Other types of form controls do display in Print Preview and do print.*

▸ Know This about assigning a macro to a form control

— A macro can be assigned to any form control.

— To assign a macro to an existing form control, right-click the form control and then click the *Assign Macro* option at the drop-down list.

▸ Know This about renaming, formatting, and arranging button form controls

- By default, Excel names a new button control *Button X*, with the *X* replaced by the number of form controls in the workbook. For example, Button 4 is the fourth form control created in the workbook.
- The name of a button form control can be changed and should be intuitive. For example, if you create a button to print a worksheet, *Print* should appear as the text on the button.
- To change the name of a button control, select the control and then type the new name.
- To format a button form control, right-click the control, click the *Format Control* option at the drop-down list, and then use options at the Format Control dialog box. Most options on the Drawing Tools Format tab are grayed out.
- To organize multiple macro button form controls, select the controls and then use options in the Arrange group on the Drawing Tools Format tab. For example, click the *Align Top* option to line up the tops of the buttons across the page.

▸ Know This about selecting, moving, and resizing a form control

- To select a form control, press the Ctrl key and then click the control.
- To select multiple form controls, press and hold down the Ctrl key, click each control, and then release the Ctrl key.
- A selected form control displays with sizing handles.
- To move a form control, select the control and then drag it to the new location.
- To resize a form control, select the control and then use the sizing handles to change the size.

On the Job

Task 15.14a Inserting a Combo Box Form Control

Devon wants to have more control of the entries in some of the cells on the 15-Invoice workbook. He wants users of the Invoices worksheet in the 15-Invoices workbook to select a method of payment from a list of three options: Check, Visa, and MC. Devon has listed these options in the range A2:A4 in the MOP & PT worksheet and given the range the defined named *MOP*. Add a combo box form control to the worksheet, using the defined name *MOP* for the input range.

1. With the macro-enabled 15-Invoice workbook open, click the Invoice sheet tab, if necessary, to make the worksheet active.
2. Click the Developer tab, if necessary, and then click the Insert button in the Controls group.

   A drop-down list displays (see Figure 15.28 on page 777).
3. Click the *Combo Box (Form Control)* option (second column, first row in the *Form Controls* section).

4. Draw a box in cell E11 that is the same width as the cell (see Figure 15.29 on page 779).

   A combo box form control appears and is selected, and it has sizing handles around the border.

5. Right-click the border of the combo box and then click the *Format Control* option at the pop-up menu.

   The Format Control dialog box displays with the Control tab active (see Figure 15.30 on page 781).

6. Click in the *Input range* text box, type MOP, and then press the Tab key.

   The defined name *MOP* appears in the *Input range* text box and the insertion point is in the *Cell link* text box. The contents of the range A2:A4 in the MOP & PT worksheet will display as the three options at the combo box drop-down list.

7. Type E11 and then press the Tab key.

   The cell reference *E11* appears in the *Cell link* text box and the contents of the *Drop down lines* text box are selected. The option that a user selects at the combo box drop-down list will display in cell E11 in the worksheet.

8. Type 3. ***Note:*** *Do not type the period.*

   The number *3* appears in the *Drop down lines* text box. Three options will display on three lines at the combo box drop-down list.

9. Click the Alt Text tab, click in the *Alternative text* text box, type Method of payment combo box with the options Check, Visa, and MC, and then click the OK button. ***Note:*** *Do not type the comma after* MC.

   The dialog box closes.

10. Click the Save button on the Quick Access Toolbar.
11. If you need to leave the computer before starting the next task, export the customized settings to a file called *AE15Cust.exportUI* and save the export file in the AE15 folder on your storage medium. Before continuing your Chapter 15 work on another computer, follow the instructions in Task 15.16 to import the AE15Cust.exportUI file into the other computer.

Model Answer

On the Job

Task 15.14b Inserting a List Box Form Control

Devon wants users of the Invoice worksheet to select from a list of two payment terms: Due on Receipt and Due in 30 Days. Devon has listed these options in the range A7:A8 in the MOP & PT worksheet and given the range the defined named *PT*. Add a list box form control to the worksheet, using the defined name *PT* for the input range.

1. With the macro-enabled 15-Invoice workbook open and the Invoice worksheet active, click the Insert button in the Controls group on the Developer tab.

   A drop-down list displays.

2. Click the *List Box (Form Control)* option (fifth column, first row in the *Form Controls* section).

3. Draw a box in cell B11 that is the same width as the cell (see Figure 15.34).

   A list box form control appears and is selected.

Figure 15.34 List Box Drawn in the Invoice Worksheet

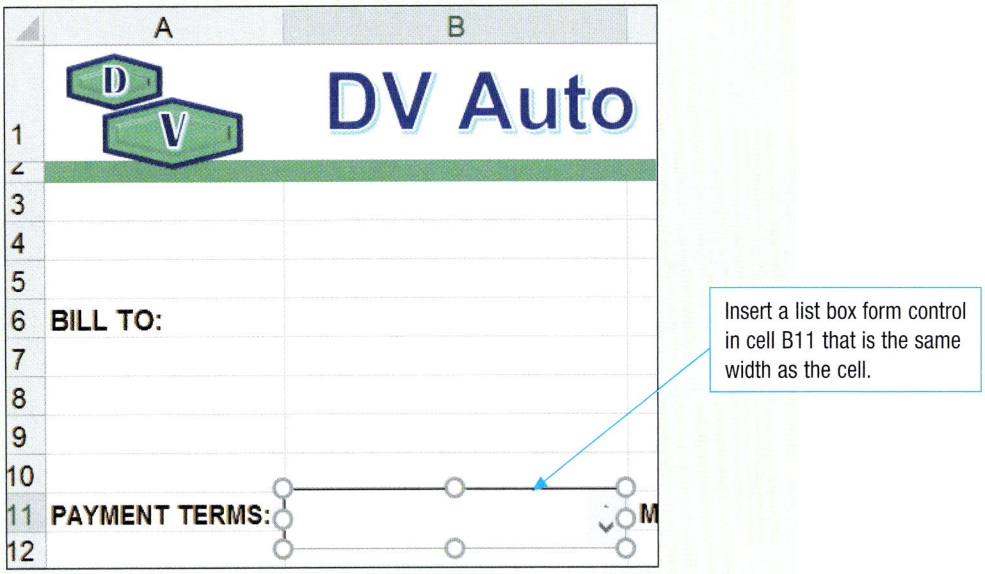

4. Right-click the border of the list box and then click the *Format Control* option at the pop-up menu.

   The Format Control dialog box displays with the Alt Text tab active.

5. Click the Control tab, click in the *Input range* text box, type PT, and then press the Tab key.

   The defined name *PT* appears in the *Input range* text box and the insertion point is in the *Cell link* text box. The contents of the range A7:A8 in the MOP & PT worksheet will display as the two options in the list box.

6. Type B11.

   The cell reference *B11* appears in the *Cell link* text box. The option that a user selects at the list box form control will display in cell B11 in the worksheet.

7. Click the Alt Text tab, click in the *Alternative text* text box, type Payment terms list box with the options Due on Receipt and 30 Days, and then click the OK button.

   The dialog box closes and the two options you entered in Step 7 appear in the list box form control.

8. Click the Save button on the Quick Access Toolbar.

9. If you need to leave the computer before starting the next task, export the customized settings to a file called *AE15Cust.exportUI* and save the export file in the AE15 folder on your storage medium. Before continuing your Chapter 15 work on another computer, follow the instructions in Task 15.16 to import the AE15Cust.exportUI file into the other computer.

Model Answer

On the Job

Task 15.14c Inserting a Check Box Form Control

Devon also wants users of the Invoice worksheet to be able to check a box to indicate that the shipping address is the same as the billing address. This will not only save users time but also could reduce data entry errors. Add a check box form control with the text *Same as billing address*.

1. With the macro-enabled 15-Invoice workbook open and the Invoice worksheet active, click the Insert button in the Controls group on the Developer tab.

   A drop-down list displays.

2. Click the *Check Box (Form Control)* option (third column, first row in the *Form Controls* section).
3. Draw a box in the merged cell E6 that is the same width as the cell (see Figure 15.35).

   A check box form control appears and is selected. The form control includes a check box followed by the text *Check Box 3*. The number *3* is the number of the control object inserted.

Figure 15.35 Check Box Form Control Inserted in the Invoice Worksheet

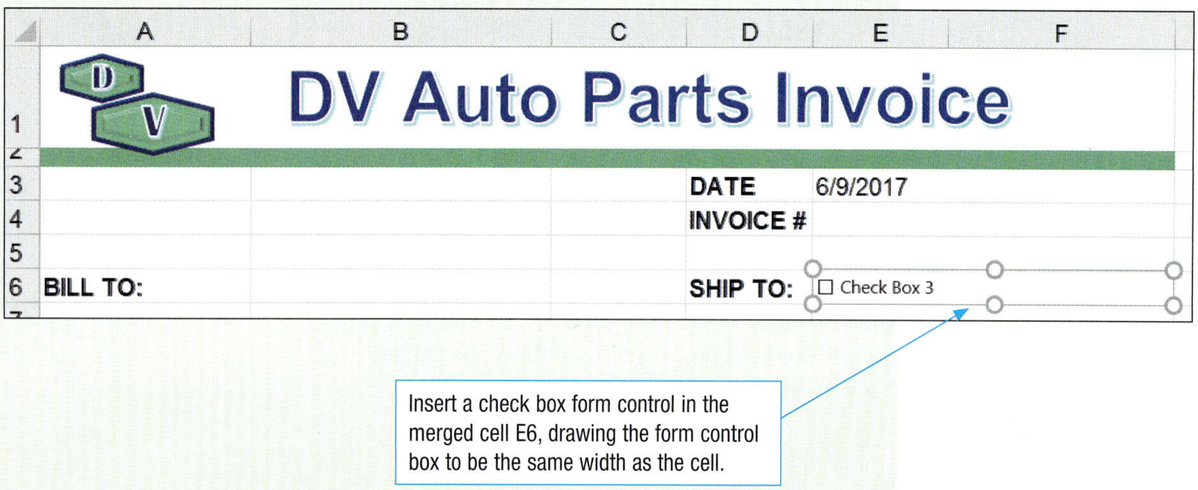

4. Click in the check box form control, select the text *Check Box 3*, press the Delete key, and then type Same as billing address.

   Excel automatically enters the control object text as the *Alternative text* text.

5. Click the Save button on the Quick Access Toolbar.
6. If you need to leave the computer before starting the next task, export the customized settings to a file called *AE15Cust.exportUI* and save the export file in the AE15 folder on your storage medium. Before continuing your Chapter 15 work on another computer, follow the instructions in Task 15.16 to import the AE15Cust.exportUI file into the other computer.

Model Answer

On the Job

Task 15.14d Inserting, Naming, Formatting, and Aligning Macro Button Form Controls

Devon wants users of the Invoice worksheet to be able to run the InvPrint macro and the PDF macro easily and quickly—without having to know the shortcut key combinations or how to use the Excel ribbon. Add two macro button form controls at the bottom of the worksheet, give each button a descriptive name, format the buttons to fit the appearance of the worksheet, and then align the buttons.

1. With the macro-enabled 15-Invoice workbook open and the Invoice worksheet active, scroll down until cell A50 is visible and then click the Insert button in the Controls group on the Developer tab.

   A drop-down list displays.

2. Click the *Button (Form Control)* option (first column, first row in the *Form Controls* section).
3. Draw a box in cell A50 that is the same size as the cell (see Figure 15.36).

   The Assign Macro dialog box displays.

4. Click the *InvPrint* option in the *Macro name* list box and then click the OK button.

   The Assign Macro dialog box closes. A button form control with the name *Button 4* appears in cell A50 and is selected.

5. Type Print Preview and then click in any worksheet cell outside the form control.

   The name *Print Preview* appears instead of the name *Button 4* and the form control is not selected.

6. Right-click the Print Preview button form control and then click the *Format Control* option at the pop-up menu.

   The Format Control dialog box displays.

7. Click the Font tab, if necessary; click the *Color* option box arrow; click the *Sea Green* option (fourth column, third row) at the drop-down palette; and then click the OK button.

   The dialog box closes. The font of the Print Preview button is green.

8. Click in any worksheet cell outside the Print Preview button form control.

   The control is not selected.

9. Click the Insert button in the Controls group and then click the *Button (Form Control)* option at the drop-down list.
10. Draw a box in cell B50 that is approximately two-thirds the width of the cell and aligned with the right border of the cell, as shown in Figure 15.36.

    The Assign Macro dialog box displays.

11. Click the *PDF* option in the *Macro name* list box and then click the OK button.

    The dialog box closes. A button form control with the name *Button 5* appears in cell B50 and is selected.

Figure 15.36 Button Control Forms in the Invoice Worksheet

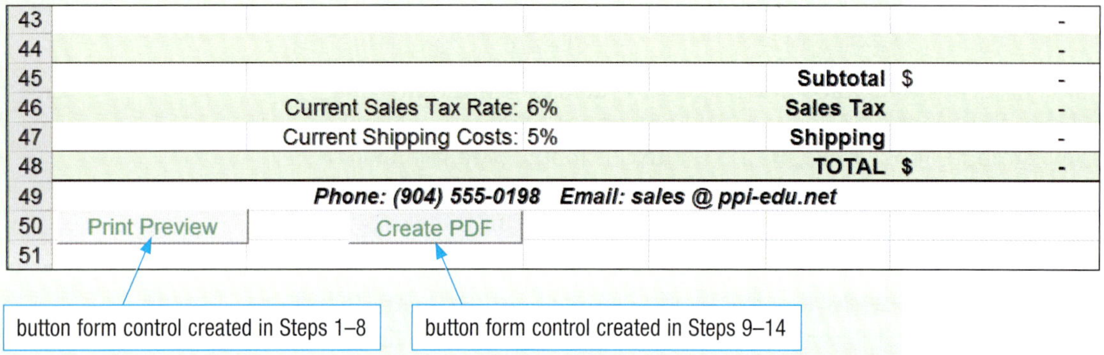

12. Type Create PDF and then click in any worksheet cell outside the form control.

    The name *Create PDF* appears instead of the name *Button 5* and the form control is not selected.

13. Right-click the Create PDF button form control and then click the *Format Control* option at the pop-up menu.

    The Format Control dialog box displays with the Font tab active.

14. Click the *Color* option box arrow, click the *Sea Green* option (fourth column, third row) at the drop-down palette, and then click the OK button.

    The dialog box closes. The font of the Create PDF button is green. Note that Excel automatically enters the button name as the alternative text.

15. Click in any worksheet cell outside the Create PDF form control.
16. If necessary, select the two button control forms and then use options on the Drawing Tools Format tab to align the controls so they appear as shown in Figure 15.36.
17. Click the Save button on the Quick Access Toolbar.
18. If you need to leave the computer before starting the next task, export the customized settings to a file called *AE15Cust.exportUI* and save the export file in the AE15 folder on your storage medium. Before continuing your Chapter 15 work on another computer, follow the instructions in Task 15.16 to import the AE15Cust.exportUI file into the other computer.

Model Answer

On the Job

Task 15.14e Testing Form Controls

Devon wants to be sure the form controls you added to the Invoice worksheet in Tasks 15.14a–15.14d work as intended. Test each form control, including the two macro button form controls.

1. With the macro-enabled 15-Invoice workbook open and the Invoice worksheet active, scroll up until cell B11 is visible and then click the *Due on Receipt* option in the list box form control in cell B11.

   The option *Due on Receipt* is selected (it has a blue fill with white text).

2. Click the combo box arrow in cell E11.

   Verify that the drop-down list displays the three options *Check*, *Visa*, and *MC*—each on its own line and in that order (see Figure 15.32 on page 782).

3. Click the *Visa* option.

   The payment method *Visa* appears in the combo box.

4. Click the check box in cell E6.

   A check mark appears in the check box, indicating that the shipping address is the same as the billing address.

5. Scroll down until cell A50 is visible and then click the Print Preview button form control.

   The InvPrint macro assigned to the Print Preview button form control runs and the Invoice worksheet displays in Print Preview, centered both vertically and horizontally on the page.

6. Click the Close Print Preview button in the Preview group on the Print Preview tab.

   The Print Preview closes. The Invoice worksheet remains active with cell A50 visible.

7. Click the Create PDF button.

   The PDF macro assigned to the Create PDF button form control runs and a PDF of the Invoice worksheet opens.

8. Save the PDF, typing 15-InvoiceTest2 as the name of the file, and then close the PDF.
9. Save and then close the macro-enabled 15-Invoice workbook.
10. If you need to leave the computer before starting the next task, export the customized settings to a file called *AE15Cust.exportUI* and save the export file in the AE15 folder on your storage medium. Before continuing your Chapter 15 work on another computer, follow the instructions in Task 15.16 to import the AE15Cust.exportUI file into the other computer.

Model Answer

15.15 Exporting and Importing XML Data

Tutorial

Exporting Worksheet Data as an XML File

Extensible Markup Language (XML) defines a set of rules that allows users to customize the markup language used to encode the data in a worksheet. XML code is easily understood and can be used to present workbook data in a browser. The **World Wide Web Consortium (W3C)** is an international organization that develops and maintains the standards of XML coding.

▸ Know This about XML schema

— To export an Excel worksheet as an XML file, you first need to create an XML schema for the worksheet.

— An **XML schema** is a document created in Notepad or another text editor that defines the XML file structure.

— Figure 15.37 displays the basic XML code used to create an XML schema, Figure 15.38 on page 791 is an example worksheet, and Figure 15.39 on page 791 is an example schema used to export the example worksheet data as an XML file.

▸ **Know This** about writing an XML schema

— The first two lines of code for an XML schema contain the **XML declaration**, which provides information on the XML version, the encoding being used to denote the characters, whether the document needs information from external sources, the file name, and where information about the standards can be found.

— XML code is written using tags. Each tag is enclosed in angle brackets (< and >), and tags must be used in pairs, with an **opening tag** and a **closing tag**. The closing tag includes a forward slash (/).

— Use the basic code in Figure 15.37 as a template for writing an XML schema.

— Replace the *<filename>* and *</filename>* tags with tags that provide the name of the file—for example, *<dvap>* and *</dvap>*.

— Replace the *<Tag>* and *</Tag>* tags with tags that provide the names of the worksheet columns—for example, *<CompanyName>* and *</CompanyName>*.

- The columns must be listed in the same order in the schema as they appear in the worksheet—with the left-most column in the worksheet appearing at the top of the list in the schema, and the right-most column in the worksheet appearing at the bottom of the list in the schema.
- The schema tag names do not have to be exactly the same as the worksheet column headers. For example, the worksheet column header *Company Name* can be changed to *CompanyName* in the schema.
- Do not use spaces in tag names.

— Provide the code for at least two records (see Figure 15.38 and Figure 15.39), with the opening tag *<record>* indicating the start of a record and the closing tag *</record>* indicating the end of a record. Excel will complete the schema based on the pattern established for those records.

Figure 15.37 Basic Schema Code

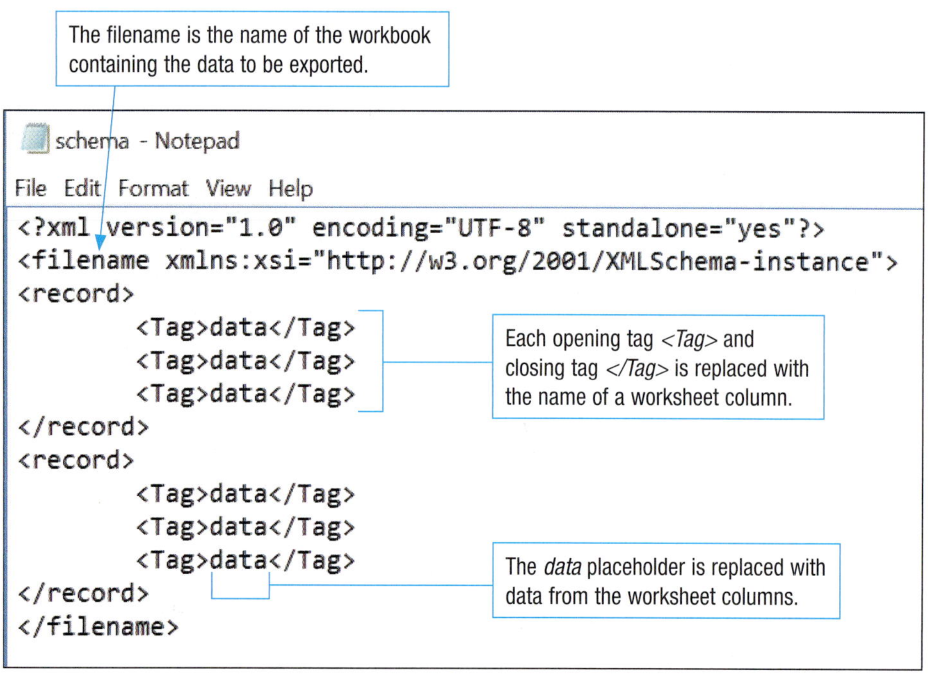

Figure 15.38 Example Worksheet

	A	B	C	D	E	F	G	H	I
1	**Company Name**	**First Name**	**Last Name**	**Phone Number**	**Category**	**Address**	**City**	**State**	**Zip**
2	Knudsen Elker Bogart LLP	Simona	VanBuuren	386-555-7319	Accounting Services	211 Lakeland Blvd.	Daytona	FL	32943
3	AutoMAX Inc.	Jayden	Hayward	734-555-8490	Auto Parts	2901 Commissioners Rd.	Wayne	MI	48073
4	Herd Inc.	Maurice	Buyze	210-555-4371	Auto Parts	4600 Council Court	San Antonio	TX	78941
5	Kartic International	Jasper	Martin	843-555-0730	Auto Parts	1107 Nobel Rd.	Ladson	SC	29381
6	Shine Janitorial Services	Lacey	Burova	407-555-6462	Cleaning Services	92 Marion Ave.	Lake Mary	FL	32940
7	QuickEats Vending Co.	David	Linh	352-555-7991	Confectionery/Food	55 Gorbe St.	Gainesville	FL	32860
8	Brunell Insurance Group	Alyssa	Skolar	646-555-0837	Insurance	910 Label St.	New York	NY	10089
9	Comtex IT Support	Talea	Obzen	925-555-8331	IT Services	45 Grant Ave.	Pleasanton	CA	94833
10	Grande Office Supplies	Parvez	Atkins	828-555-4304	Office Supplies	9412 Barder Lane	Hickory	NC	28072
11	Arpos Retail ERP	Griffin	Hill	612-555-3821	Software Provider	106 Highway Rd.	Chanhassen	MN	55037
12	Linexus Inc.	Priya	Kerden	352-555-8149	Telecommunication	782 South Crossing Rd.	Ocala	FL	34007

Figure 15.39 Example XML Schema

Provide at least two examples of records in the schema. When you export the data, Excel will fill in the rest.

supplierschema - Notepad

File Edit Format View Help

```
<?xml version="1.0" encoding="UTF-8" standalone="yes"?>
<dvsuppliers xmlns:xsi="http://w3.org/2001/XMLSchema-instance">
<record>
        <Company>Knudsen Elker Bogart LLP</Company>
        <FirstName>Simona</FirstName>
        <LastName>VanBuuren</LastName>
        <Phone>386-555-7319</Phone>
        <Category>Accounting Services</Category>
        <Address>211 Lakeland Blvd.</Address>
        <City>Daytona</City>
        <State>FL</State>
        <Zip>32943</Zip>
</record>
<record>
        <Company>AutoMAX Inc.</Company>
        <FirstName>Jayden</FirstName>
        <LastName>Hayward</LastName>
        <Phone>734-555-8490</Phone>
        <Category>Auto Parts</Category>
        <Address>2901 Commissioners Rd.</Address>
        <City>Wayne</City>
        <State>MI</State>
        <Zip>48073</Zip>
</record>
</dvsuppliers>
```

The columns must be listed in the same order in the schema as they are in the worksheet, but the column names do not have to be exactly the same.

▸ **Know This** about exporting a worksheet as an XML file

— To export data in an Excel worksheet as an XML file:

1. Click the Source button in the XML group on the Developer tab (see Figure 15.40).
2. Click the XML Maps button at the XML Source task pane (see Figure 15.41).
3. Click the Add button at the SML Maps dialog box (see Figure 15.42), navigate to the XML schema file at the Select XML Source dialog box, click the XML schema file in the file list pane, and then click the Open button.
4. Click the OK button at the message box that displays, stating that the specific XML source does not refer to a schema and that Excel will create a schema based on the XML source data. ***Note:*** *If an Error in XML message box displays, refer to the "Know This about errors when adding the schema file" feature on page 794, fix the errors in the schema file, and then try again to add the schema file.*
5. Click the OK button at the XML Maps dialog box.
6. Drag each element in the *XML maps in this workbook* list box at the XML Source task pane to its corresponding column header in the worksheet.
7. Click the Developer tab and then click the Export button in the XML group.
8. Type the file name in the *File name* text box and then click the Export button.

— When the schema file is added to workbook, each <*Tag*> tag in the XML code appears as an **XML element** in the *XML maps in this workbook* list box at the XML Source task pane.

— An **XML data map** connects the schema file to the worksheet. You create an XML data map by dragging each element from the list box at the XML Source task pane to its respective column header in the worksheet.

— When a worksheet column has been mapped to an XML element, it becomes an XML element and changes to a table format.

— The maximum number of rows (or records) that can be exported is 65,536.

— To redisplay the XML Source panel, click the Source button in the XML group.

Figure 15.40 XML Group on the Developer Tab

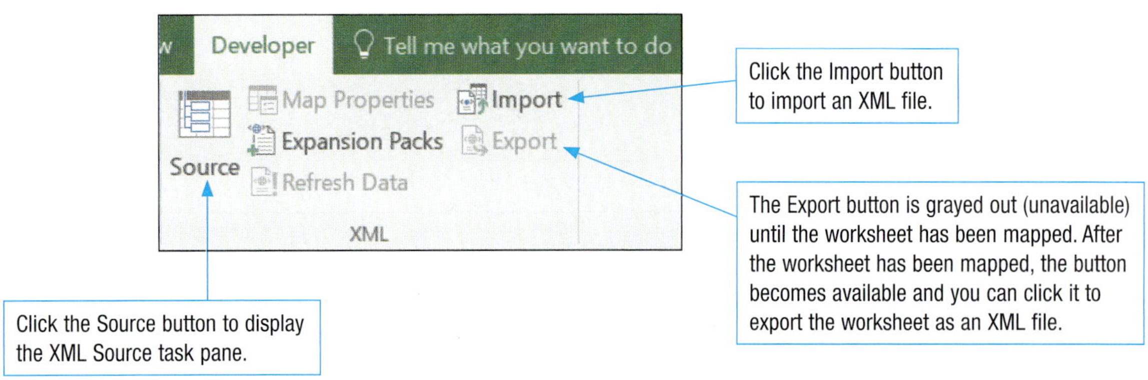

Figure 15.41 XML Source Task Pane

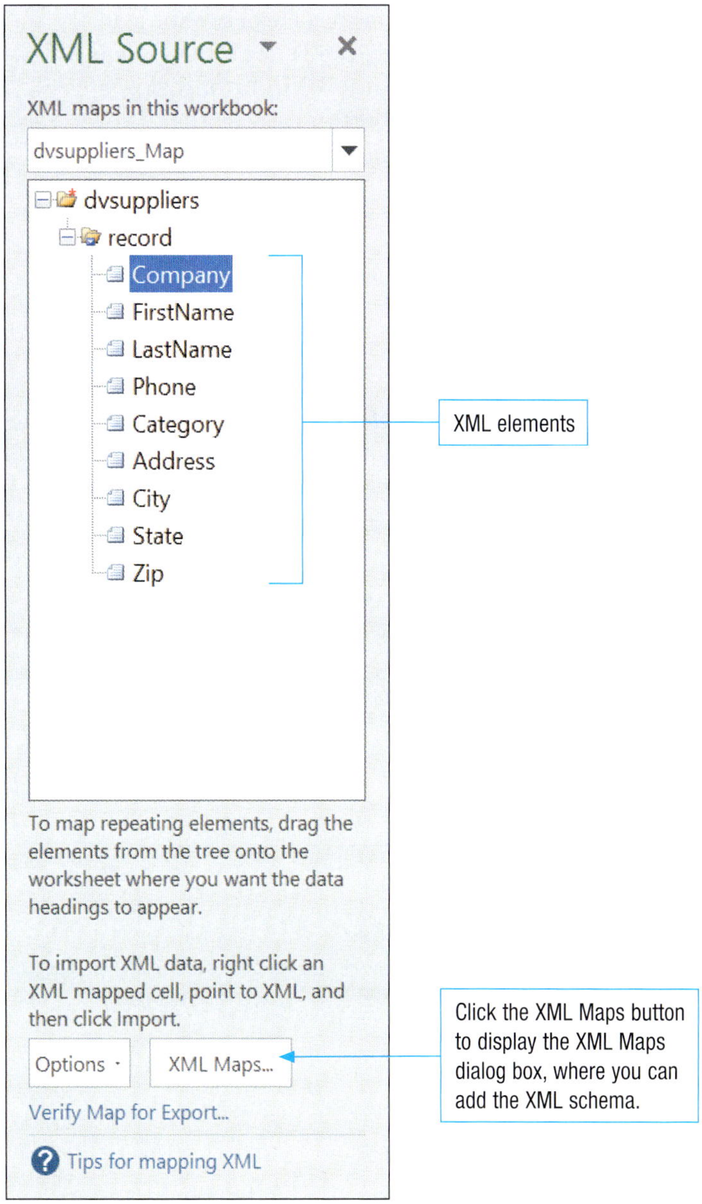

Figure 15.42 XML Maps Dialog Box

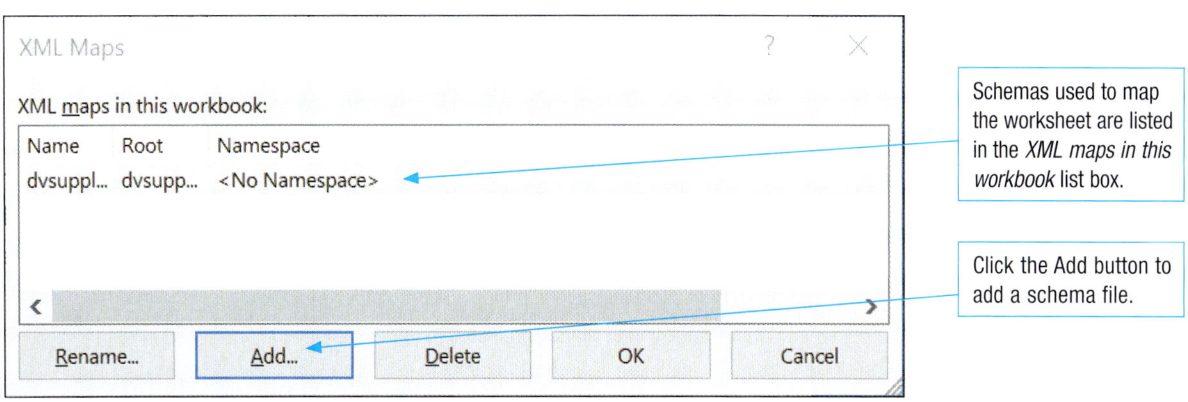

▸ **Know This** about errors when adding the schema file

— If an Error in XML message box displays, stating that Excel cannot load the specified XML or schema source (see Figure 15.43), click the Details button, read the information about the error at the XML Error dialog box (see Figure 15.44), and then click the OK button to close the dialog box or click the Details button for more information.

— Use the information at the XML Error dialog box to modify the schema and then try adding the schema again.

Figure 15.43 Error in XML Message Box

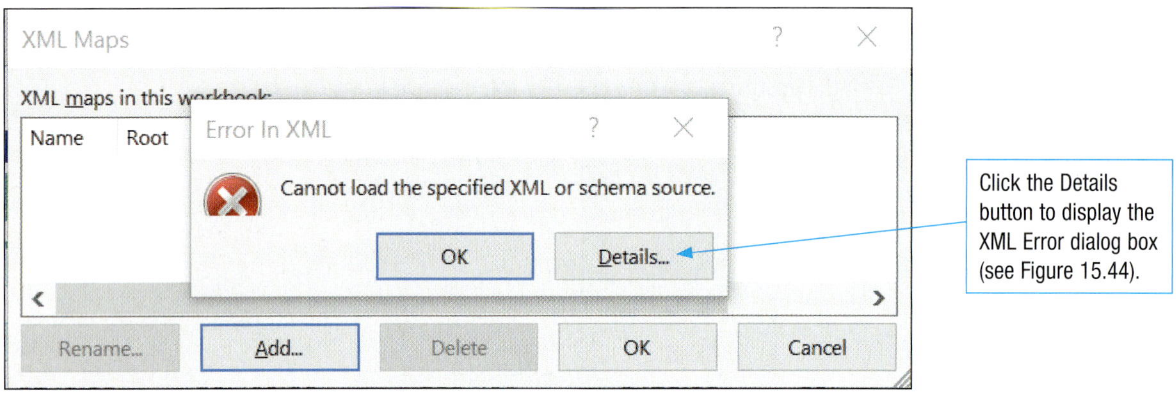

Figure 15.44 XML Error Dialog Box

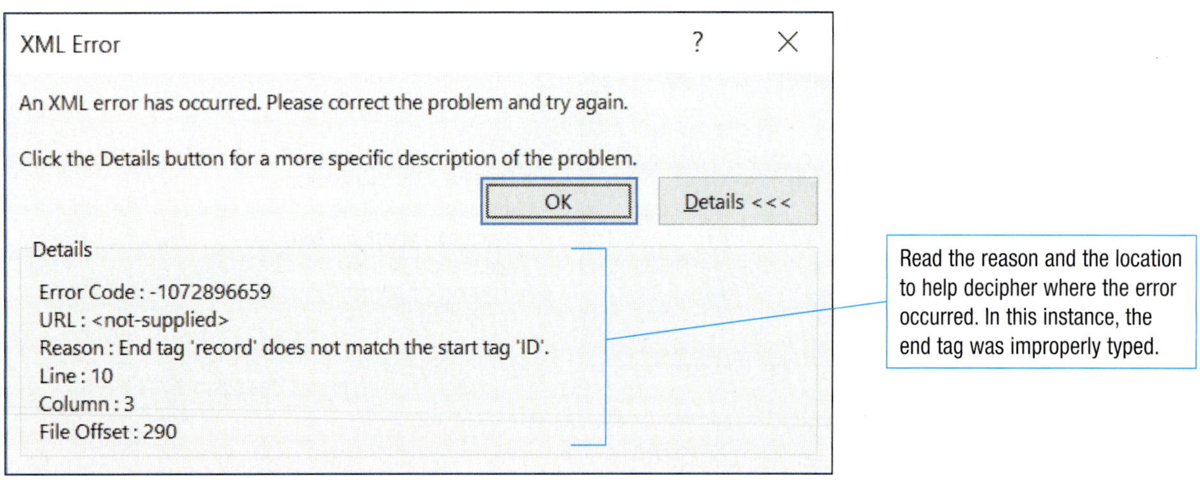

On the Job

Task 15.15a Creating an XML Schema and Exporting Worksheet Data as an XML File

Devon wants to convert the information in the Customers worksheet to an XML file that will later be viewed on the Internet. Create the schema and then convert the Customers worksheet to an XML file.

1. Open the data file **dvapschema** in Notepad.

   Open Notepad and then open the file. To see the XML file, you will need to select *All Files (*.)* at the *Document type* option box. The contents of the data file appear in a Notepad window.

2. Move the insertion point to the beginning of the first blank line (see Figure 15.45) and then type the following code, using the Tab key to indent the lines as shown

```
		<record>
		<ID>All-90435</ID>
		<Company>All Pro Auto Repair</Company>
		<FirstName>Kevin</FirstName>
		<LastName>Newbury</LastName>
		<Phone>(904) 555-3421</Phone>
	</record>
	<record>
		<ID>Bay81372</ID>
		<Company>Bayside Auto Repair</Company>
		<FirstName>Wes</FirstName>
		<LastName>Cortez</LastName>
		<Phone>(813) 555-0507</Phone>
	</record>
	</dvap>
```

   Proof your work carefully to ensure that the code in your file matches the code listed here exactly. Missing tags may cause Excel not to add the file as a map.

Figure 15.45 dvapschema File Displayed in Notepad

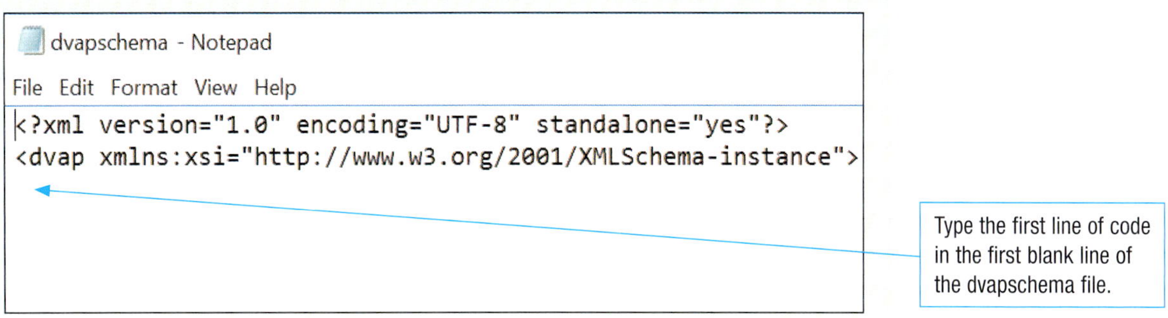

3. Save the file in the AE15 folder on your storage medium and then close Notepad.
4. Open the data file **15-DVAutoParts**, which you closed at the end of Task 15.6, and then click the Customers sheet tab.
5. Click the Developer tab and then click the Source button in the XML group (see Figure 15.40 on page 792).

   The XML Source task pane displays.

6. Click the XML Maps button (see Figure 15.41 on page 793).

   The XML Maps dialog box displays.

7. Click the Add button, navigate to the AE15 folder at the Select XML Source dialog box, click the *dvapschema* file in the file list pane, and then click the Open button.

   A message box displays, stating that the specific XML source does not refer to a schema and that Excel will create a schema based on the XML source data. ***Note:*** *If an Error in XML message box displays, refer to the "Know This about errors when adding the schema file" feature on page 794, fix the errors in the schema file, and then try again to the add the schema file. If you continue to have trouble, ask your instructor for help.*

8. Click the OK button.

   The message box closes and the XML file appears as an option in the *XML maps in this workbook* list box at the XML Maps dialog box.

9. Click the OK button.

   The dialog box closes. Each column name added in the schema file appears as an element in a hierarchy in the *XML maps in this workbook* list box at the XML Source task pane.

10. Drag the *ID* element in the list box at the XML Source task pane to cell A3 in the worksheet (see Figure 15.46).

    The *ID* column in the worksheet is converted to an XML element. The range A3:A19 in the worksheet is formatted as a table. The *ID* element in the list box at the XML Source task pane appears with bold formatting and is highlighted (it appears with a blue background and bold white text).

11. Drag the *Company* element in the list box at the XML Source task pane to cell B3 in the worksheet.

    The *Company Name* column in the worksheet is converted to an XML element. The range B3:B19 in the worksheet is formatted as a table. The *ID* element in the list box at the XML Source task pane appears with bold formatting. The *Company* element in the list box at the XML Source task pane appears with bold formatting and is highlighted.

Figure 15.46 Mapping of XML Source Elements to Worksheet Column Headers

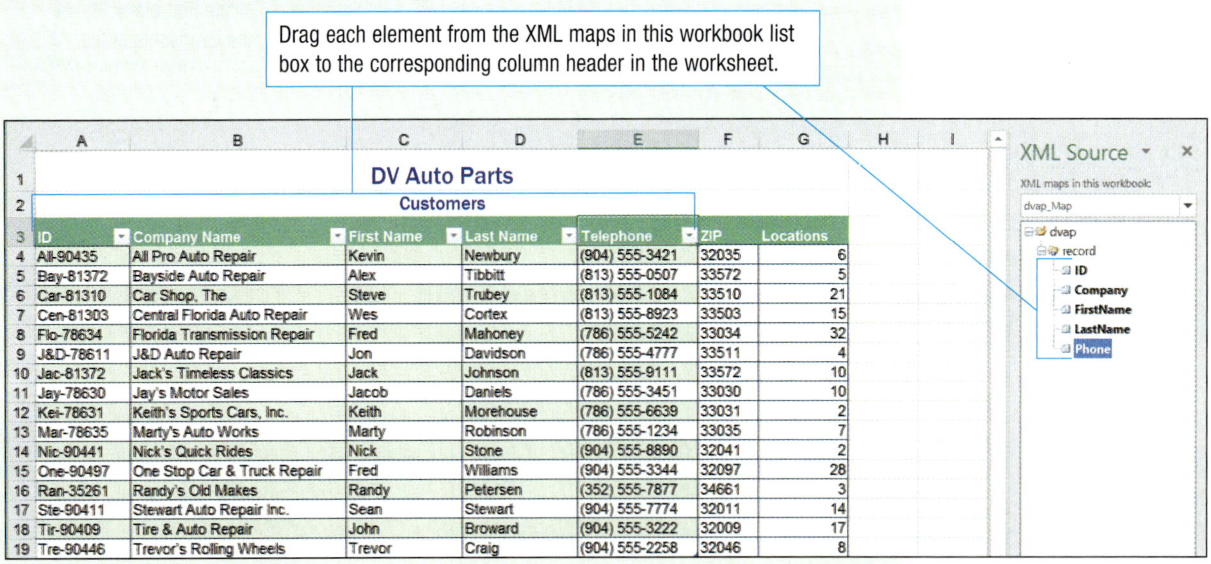

12. Repeat Step 11 to map the *FirstName*, *LastName*, and *Phone* elements in the list box at the XML Source task pane to the corresponding column headers in the worksheet.
13. Click the Developer tab, click the Export button, navigate to the AE15 folder, click in the *File name* text box, type Customers, and then click the Export button.
14. Open File Explorer, navigate to the AE15 folder, and then double-click the data file **Customers** in the file list pane. ***Hint:*** *To open File Explorer, right-click the folder icon at the task pane and then click the File Explorer option. After double-clicking the data file, if you are asked to choose the app to open the file with, choose a browser such as Microsoft Edge.*

    The Customers XML file opens.
15. Scroll through the file and notice that Excel added the rest of the customers from the worksheet.
16. Click the Close button on the Customers XML file and then click the Close button in the File Explorer window.
17. Click the Save button on the Quick Access Toolbar.
18. If you need to leave the computer before starting the next task, export the customized settings to a file called *AE15Cust.exportUI* and save the export file in the AE15 folder on your storage medium. Before continuing your Chapter 15 work on another computer, follow the instructions in Task 15.16 to import the AE15Cust.exportUI file into the other computer.

Model Answer

▸ Know This about importing an XML file into an Excel worksheet

— To import an XML file into an active Excel worksheet, click the Import button in the XML group on the Developer tab, navigate to the XML file at the Import XML dialog box, click the file in the file list pane, click the Import button, click the OK button at the message box stating that the specified XML source does not refer to a schema and that Excel will create a schema based on the XML source data, and then click the OK button at the Import XML dialog box.

— To import the data as an XML table into a new worksheet, click the Import button, navigate to the XML file, click the *XML table in new worksheet* radio button to insert a bullet, and then click the OK button.

▸ Know This about the data queries and connections

— When XML data is imported using the Import button in the XML group on the Developer tab, a connection is created.

— When XML data is imported using the Get Data button in the Get & Transform Data group on the Data tab, a query is created.

— For more information on queries and connections, see Chapter 13.

▸ Know More ways to import XML data

– To import an XML file into a new Excel worksheet, perform the following steps:

1. Click the Data tab in the Excel worksheet.
2. Click the Get Data button in the Get & Transform Data group.
3. Point to the *From File* option at the drop-down list and then click the *From XML* option at the second drop-down list.
4. Navigate to the folder containing the XML file at the Import Data dialog box and then double-click the file in the file list box.
5. Select the *record* option in the *Display Options* section at the Navigator dialog box.

continues…

On the Job

Task 15.15b Importing a Worksheet as an XML File

Devon has an XML file containing supplier information that he wants to have in the 15-DVAutoParts workbook. He asks you to import the information from the XML file into the Excel workbook.

1. With the 15-DVAutoParts workbook open, cell A1 in the Customers worksheet active, and the Developer tab active, click the Import button in the XML group.

   The Import XML dialog box displays.

2. Navigate to the AE15 folder on your storage medium, click the data file **supplier** in the file list pane, and then click the Import button.

   A message box displays, stating that the specified XML source does not refer to a schema and that Excel will create a schema based on the XML source data.

3. Click the OK button.

   The message box closes and the Import Data dialog box displays. The absolute cell reference *$A$1* appears in the *XML table in existing worksheet* text box. Excel will place the data starting in cell A1. ***Note:*** *your cell reference may vary depending on the active cell in the worksheet.*

4. Click the *XML table in new worksheet* radio button (see Figure 15.47).

   A bullet appears in the radio button.

Figure 15.47 Import Data Dialog Box

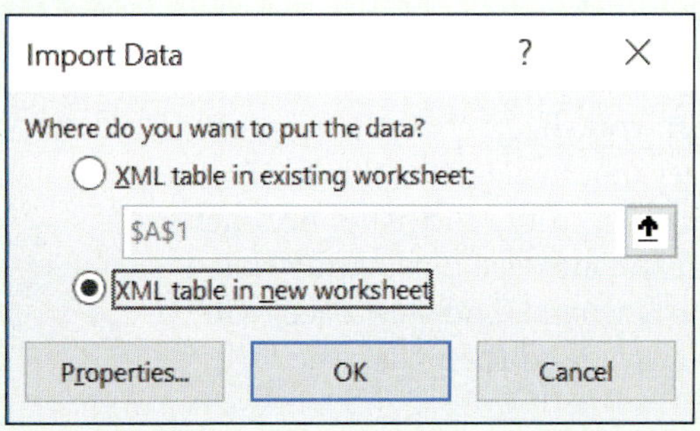

5. Click the OK button.

   The dialog box closes. The data appears in a new worksheet named *Sheet1*, to the left of the Customers worksheet.

6. Rename the Sheet1 sheet tab, typing Suppliers as the new name.
7. Click the Save button on the Quick Access Toolbar.
8. If you need to leave the computer before starting the next task, export the customized settings to a file called *AE15Cust.exportUI* and save the export file in the AE15 folder on your storage medium. Before continuing your Chapter 15 work on another computer, follow the instructions in Task 15.16 to import the AE15Cust.exportUI file into the other computer.

Model Answer

▶ **Know More** ways to import XML data

...continued

6. Perform one of the following actions:
   - To import the data without edits into a new worksheet without edits, click the Load button.
   - To import the data without edits into a different location, click the Load button arrow, click the *Load to* option at the drop-down list, and then choose options at the Import Data dialog box.
   - To edit the data (for example, to split the data or add or remove rows or columns), click the Edit button, make changes at the Query Editor window, and then click the Close & Load button.

15.16 Resetting the Ribbon and the Quick Access Toolbar

When custom tabs, the Developer tab (which is normally not displayed), or customizations of the Excel ribbon and the Quick Access Toolbar are no longer needed, you can restore the Excel ribbon and Quick Access Toolbar back to their original settings or import a customization file. You can also share custom ribbon and Quick Access Toolbar settings with others who may find them useful and time saving.

Tutorial

Importing Ribbon and Quick Access Toolbar Customizations

▸ **Know This** about resetting the ribbon and the Quick Access Toolbar

— To reset the original ribbon and the Quick Access Toolbar that came with Excel 2016, click the File tab, click the *Options* option, click the *Customize Ribbon* option in the left panel at the Excel Options dialog box, click the Reset button below the *Main Tabs* list box in the right panel, and then click the Reset button.

— Click the Reset button to display two options: *Reset only selected Ribbon tab* and *Reset all customizations*.

— Click *Reset all customizations* to restore the ribbon and the Quick Access Toolbar to their original settings and then click the Yes button at the message box that displays the question *Delete all Ribbon and Quick Access Toolbar customizations for this program?*

— The position of the Quick Access Toolbar (above or below the ribbon) does not change when the Quick Access Toolbar is reset.

▸ **Know This** about importing ribbon and Quick Access Toolbar customizations

— If you have exported ribbon and Quick Access Toolbar customizations (see Section 15.2), you can add those customizations to a workbook by importing the file.

— To import a file of ribbon and Quick Access Toolbar customizations, click the File tab, click the *Options* option, click the *Customize Ribbon* option in the left panel at the Excel Options dialog box, click the Import/Export button in the right panel, click the *Import customization file* option at the drop-down list, navigate to the saved customization file at the File Open dialog box, click the file name in the file list box, click the Open button, click the Yes button at the message box asking whether you want to replace all existing ribbon and Quick Access Toolbar customizations for this program, and then click the OK button to close the Excel Options dialog box.

— The position of the Quick Access Toolbar (above or below the ribbon) does not change when the Quick Access Toolbar is reset.

On the Job

Task 15.16 Importing Ribbon and Quick Access Toolbar Customizations

Devon no longer needs the customizations you created throughout this chapter. He now wants you to set the Excel ribbon and the Quick Access

Toolbar back to the way they appeared before you started making customizations in Task 15.2b. Recall that in Task 15.2a, you exported a file of the existing customizations and saved it to the AE15 folder on your storage medium. Use that file to restore the ribbon and toolbar settings as requested by Devon.

1. With the 15-DVAutoParts workbook open and any sheet tab active, click the File tab and then click the *Options* option.

   The Excel Options dialog box displays.

2. Click the *Customize Ribbon file* option in the left panel.

   The *Customize the Ribbon* section displays in the right panel.

3. Click the Import/Export button in the right panel.

   A drop-down list appears.

4. Click the *Import customizations file* option.

   The File Open dialog box displays.

5. Navigate to the AE15 folder.
6. Click the **15-ExcelCustomizations.exportUI** data file in the file list pane.
7. Click the Open button.

   A message box displays, asking if you want to replace all the existing ribbon and Quick Access Toolbar customizations for this program.

8. Click the Yes button.

   The message box closes. The Excel Options dialog box still displays.

9. Click the *Quick Access Toolbar* option in the left panel and then click the *Show Quick Access Toolbar* below the *Ribbon* check box below the *Choose Commands* from list box to to remove the check mark.

   The Quick Access Toolbar appears above the ribbon.

10. Click the OK button at the Excel Options dialog box.

    The dialog box closes. The Excel ribbon and the Quick Access Toolbar settings that you exported in Task 15.2a have replaced the ribbon and toolbar changes made in this chapter.

11. Close the workbook. Click the Don't Save button if prompted to save changes.

Model Answer

Chapter Summary

15.1 ▸ Pinning a workbook will ensure that its name always appears in the *Pinned* section at the top of the *Recent* list, regardless of when the workbook was last opened. More than one workbook can be pinned, and pinned workbooks are listed alphabetically.

15.2 ▸ The ribbon in a given version of Excel can be customized by adding frequently used features to a custom group on an existing tab or by adding them to a custom group on a custom tab. These customizations can be copied to other computers, making them available on multiple devices and allowing them to be shared with other users.

- The Excel ribbon can be customized by adding a new tab, group, or command and by moving tabs, groups, and commands. In addition, a tab or group on the original ribbon can be renamed, but the name or symbol associated with a command on the original ribbon cannot be deleted.

15.3 ▸ The Quick Access Toolbar can be customized to display Excel commands that are used frequently. Commands can be added to the Quick Access Toolbar and also removed and rearranged. By default, the Quick Access Toolbar displays above the Excel ribbon, but it can be moved to display below the ribbon.

15.4 ▸ By default, Excel displays only the most commonly used tabs on the ribbon. The user can unhide these tabs or hide any of the other tabs that he or she does not use.

- The Draw tab and the Developer tab are hidden. The Draw tab contains commands that allow using different pens for writing on the active worksheet. The Developer tab contains commands used with macros and XML data.

15.5 ▸ Excel provides tools that allow the user to quickly insert a screenshot or a screen clipping of an open window (for example, another open workbook, a Word document, or an Internet window) in a worksheet. A screenshot takes a picture of the entire screen, and a screen clipping captures part of a screen.

15.6 ▸ A custom view saves display and print settings for the active worksheet. A custom view can be applied only to the worksheet in which it was created, and multiple custom views can be created for the same worksheet.

15.7 ▸ A macro is a series of steps stored in a sequence that can be recalled and carried out whenever the need arises. Recording a macro involves turning on the recorder, completing the steps that are to be recalled and carried out, and then stopping the recorder.

- A workbook that contains a macro is saved using the macro-enabled file format (with the file extension *.xlsm*). By default, a macro is stored in the workbook in which it is created, but it can also be stored in a personal macro workbook or in a new workbook. A macro name must begin with a letter and can be a combination of letters, numbers, and underscore characters.
- When a macro is created in Excel, the commands are written and saved in Microsoft Visual Basic for Applications (VBA), which is a programming language. VBA code can be viewed, edited, and debugged in the Visual Basic Editor, which can be opened from Excel. To save the VBA code with the workbook requires saving the workbook as a macro-enabled file, which has the file extension *.xlsm*.

15.8 ▸ When a workbook that contains macros is opened the first time, the default security setting causes a warning to appear in the message bar, stating that macros have been disabled. The macros can be enabled by clicking the Enable Content button.

- A macro can be assigned to a shortcut key combination. A keyboard shortcut allows the user to run the macro quickly by pressing the Ctrl key plus the assigned lowercase or uppercase letter.

15.9 ▸ Running a macro involves instructing Excel to play back the recorded steps. Each time the macro is run, the same series of steps is performed.

15.10 ▶ The actions performed while a macro is being recorded are stored in VBA code. Each macro is saved as a separate module in a VBA Project for the workbook. The VBA code can be edited to make simple changes to a macro. In VBA code, a VBA comment is explanatory text and is ignored when the macro is run.

15.11 ▶ A macro that is no longer needed can be deleted. Deleting an unnecessary macro will help avoid accidentally running it and altering workbook data.

15.12 ▶ The Excel Trust Center is responsible for and blocks unsafe content when a workbook is opened. How Excel handles macros when a workbook is opened can be controlled by adjusting the macro security setting in the Trust Center. Security settings that protect the computer from malicious content can also be viewed and/or modified in the Trust Center.

- ▶ The Trust Center maintains the Trusted Locations list, which is a list of places from which content can be considered trusted. After a location is added to the Trusted Locations list, Excel treats any file opened from that location as safe.
- ▶ If a workbook contains macros, the Trust Center checks for a valid and current digital signature from an entity in the Trusted Publishers list before enabling the macros. A digital signature is a form of security that positively identifies the publisher of a workbook. The Trusted Publishers list is a list of publishers that are considered safe.

15.13 ▶ By default, a macro is stored in the workbook that is active when it is recorded. Also by default, a macro in one workbook is available for use in other workbooks that are open at the same time. After a macro has been created, it can be copied to other workbooks, where it can be modified to fit the specific needs of the users of these workbooks.

15.14 ▶ A form control can be inserted to allow users to enter information in a worksheet. For example, inserting a combo box form control or a list box form control will allow users to select an option from a list, and inserting a check box form control will allow users to select an option by inserting a check mark in a check box. After a form control has been inserted in a worksheet, it can be configured to define how it will be used; it can also be resized and aligned with other controls.

- ▶ Assigning a macro to a button form control allows the user to quickly run the macro without having to remember the shortcut key combination or ribbon command. The name of a button form control can be changed and should be intuitive.

15.15 ▶ Extensible Markup Language (XML) defines a set of rules that allows users to customize the markup language used to encode the data in a worksheet. XML code is easily understood and can be used to present workbook data on the Internet. The World Wide Web Consortium (W3C) is an international organization that develops and maintains the standards of XML coding.

- ▶ To export an Excel worksheet as an XML file, the user first needs to create an XML schema for the worksheet. An XML schema is a document created in Notepad that defines the XML file structure. XML code is written using tags. Each tag is enclosed in angle brackets (< and >), and tags must be used in pairs, with an opening tag and a closing tag. An XML data map connects the schema file to the worksheet.

15.16 ▶ When custom tabs, the Developer tab (which is normally not displayed), or customizations of the Excel ribbon and the Quick Access Toolbar are no longer needed, the Excel ribbon and Quick Access Toolbar can be restored back to their original settings. Custom ribbon and Quick Access Toolbar settings can also be shared with others.

Features Review

Feature	Ribbon Tab, Group	Button, Option	Keyboard Shortcut
add digital signature	File	*Info*, Protect Workbook, *Add a Digital Signature*	
add, remove, or rearrange command on Quick Access Toolbar			
add, rename, hide, unhide, move, or remove custom tab, group, or command on Excel ribbon	File	*Options*, *Customize Ribbon*	
arrange multiple form controls	Drawing Tools Format, Arrange		
assign macro to button form control	Developer, Controls	, *Button (Form Control)*	
change macro security setting	Developer, Code		
copy macro from one workbook to another	Developer, Code		
create, show, or delete custom view	View, Workbook Views		
display Macro dialog box	Developer, Code		Alt + F8
display Trust Center dialog box	File or Developer, Code	*Options*, *Trust Center*, Trust Center Settings	
display Visual Basic Editor window	Developer, Code		Alt + F11
delete or edit macro	Developer, Code		Alt + F11
edit screenshot or screen clipping	Picture Tools		
export or import Excel ribbon and Quick Access Toolbar settings	File	*Options*, *Customize Ribbon*, Import/Export	
export data in Excel worksheet as XML file	Developer, XML		
import XML file into Excel worksheet	Developer, XML		
insert form control	Developer, Controls		
insert screen clipping	Insert, Illustrations	, *Screen Clipping*	
insert screenshot	Insert, Illustrations		

continues...

Feature	Ribbon Tab, Group	Button, Option	Keyboard Shortcut
pin or unpin workbook in Recent list	File	*Open*, point to workbook name in *Recent* list, click pushpin icon	
record macro	Developer, Code or View, Macros	or , *Record Macro*	
reset original Excel ribbon and Quick Access Toolbar	File	*Options*, *Customize Ribbon*, Reset	
run macro	Developer, Code		Ctrl + assigned lowercase or uppercase letter
save workbook containing macro	File	*Save As*, *Browse*, save-as-type option box arrow, *Excel Macro-Enabled Workbook (*.xlsm)* or *Export*, *Change File Type*, *Macro-Enabled Workbook (*.xlsm)*	
stop recording macro	Developer, Code or View, Macros	, *Stop Recording*	
view list of Excel-assigned keyboard shortcuts		*Tell me* text box, *keyboard shortcuts* search term, *Get Help on "keyboard shortcuts"* option	

Recheck

Recheck your understanding of the concepts, features, and skills covered in this chapter by taking the Recheck quiz.

Workbook

Access the study tools, review exercises, assessments, and challenges for this chapter in the workbook available from this page in your ebook.

Index

B

C

D

E

F

G

H

I

K

L

M

N

O

Q

R

S

U

V

W

X

Z